W9-CXQ-158

World Wide Web Database

Developer's Guide
with Visual Basic® 5

Mark Swank
Drew Kittel
Mark Spenik
et al.

sams.net

201 West 103rd Street
Indianapolis, Indiana 46290

Copyright© 1997 by Sams.net Publishing

FIRST EDITION

All rights reserved. No part of this book shall be reproduced, stored in a retrieval system, or transmitted by any means, electronic, mechanical, photocopying, recording, or otherwise, without written permission from the publisher. No patent liability is assumed with respect to the use of the information contained herein. Although every precaution has been taken in the preparation of this book, the publisher and authors assume no responsibility for errors or omissions. Neither is any liability assumed for damages resulting from the use of the information contained herein. For information, address Sams.net Publishing, 201 W. 103rd St., Indianapolis, IN 46290.

International Standard Book Number: 1-57521-276-5

Library of Congress Catalog Card Number: 96-72072

2000   99   98   97   4   3   2   1

Interpretation of the printing code: the rightmost double-digit number is the year of the book's printing; the rightmost single-digit, the number of the book's printing. For example, a printing code of 97-1 shows that the first printing of the book occurred in 1997.

Composed in AGaramond and MCPdigital by Macmillan Computer Publishing

Printed in the United States of America

Trademarks

All terms mentioned in this book that are known to be trademarks or service marks have been appropriately capitalized. Sams.net Publishing cannot attest to the accuracy of this information. Use of a term in this book should not be regarded as affecting the validity of any trademark or service mark.

Visual Basic is a registered trademark of Microsoft Corporation.

Publisher and President	Richard K. Swadley
Publishing Manager	Rosemarie Graham
Director of Editorial Services	Cindy Morrow
Managing Editor	Jodi Jensen
Director of Marketing	Kelli S. Spencer
Product Marketing Manager	Wendy Gilbride
Assistant Marketing Manager	Rachel Wolfe

Acquisitions and Development Editor
Rosemarie Graham

Software Development Specialist
John Warriner

Copy Editors
Fran Blauw
Ryan Rader
Bart Reed

Indexer
Benjamin Slen

Technical Reviewer
Angela Murdock

Editorial Coordinator
Katie Wise

Technical Edit Coordinator
Lorraine E. Schaffer

Resource Coordinator
Deborah Frisby

Editorial Assistants
Carol Ackerman
Andi Richter
Rhonda Tinch-Mize

Cover and Book Designer
Alyssa Yesh

Copy Writer
David Reichwein

Production Team Supervisors
Brad Chinn
Charlotte Clapp

Production
Jenaffer Brandt
Jeanne Clark
Polly Lavrick
Anne Sipahimalani

Overview

Contents

III   Database Design and SQL

VI   Client-Side Development Using Visual Basic 5

VII Server-Side Database Applications Development

VIII   Web Database Examples and Applications

Appendixes

Dedications

To the next generation: John, Jessica, Sarah, David, Meredith, Alyssa, and Our New Edition.
—Mark Spenik

To my beautiful wife and best friend, Julie. I could not have asked for a better source of inspiration, support, and encouragement during the arduous ordeal of developing this book. You have been through this process before, yet you willingly accepted and shared in the sacrifices involved. Thanks for standing by my side with the love, patience, and support I needed to complete this undertaking. —Drew Kittel

To my son Tyler and his "little sister" Kayla. The times we spend together allow me to forget about everything else and focus on the much simpler and more important part of life—family. It's through the two of you that I receive all my energy and inspiration to drive forward in any adventure that I may embark upon. Thanks! —Mark Swank

Acknowledgments

As with each and every other book the three of us have had the opportunity to be a part of, we could never have completed such a task without an immense amount of help and support from others. It's through the great efforts of this "team" of individuals that an author is able to build and sculpt what will become the final product.

To the folks at O'Reilly & Associates Software, thanks for the copy of WebSite Professional Web Server used for many of the CGI examples in this book.

To all of our contributing authors, your timely and precise material has helped to make this book the comprehensive resource that it has become. We could never have completed this endeavor were it not for the great wealth of experience you have brought to the book.

And finally, to Rosemarie Graham, Jodi Jensen, John Warriner, and the rest of the Sams support team: Thanks once again for bringing it all together and molding our rough edges into what becomes the complete book.

—Mark Spenik, Drew Kittel, and Mark Swank

Special Acknowledgments from Mark Spenik

I want to thank my wife Lisa for her love and support! She was most understanding during those late nights and weekends of writing yet *another* book. To my family John, Denise, David, Kim, Adam, Chris, Gary, Debbie, Lisa, David, Bonnie, and all my nieces and nephews—thanks for the support! Thanks to the Meyers (Sam, Marge, and Jonathan) and the Rimes (Denise and Pat) families for all their encouragement. To my father, John, and to my late mother, Anna Jane—thanks for giving me the tools to succeed. To William Vaughan, president of Keiter, Stephens Computer Services, Inc., thanks for getting the company on the Internet fast-track. To the contributing authors who I have the pleasure to work with at KSCS and who really came through for us on this project, Troy Rackley and Anne Yagerline, thanks for 110 percent! And finally, to my coauthors, Mark Swank, a giant in this industry, and Drew Kittel, a true Webmaster, thanks for giving me the opportunity to work with you on this book.

—Mark Spenik

Special Acknowledgments from Drew Kittel

Once again I'd like to thank my family for their support and encouragement in this book effort and in all my other undertakings. And a special thanks to my parents for always being there and providing the support necessary to stick to the paths I've decided to follow. It has provided me the opportunity to be involved in some wonderful undertakings that would not have been possible otherwise.

To my coauthors: It's always nice to know when you take on a project like this that you can count on your partners—and you guys have come through time and again! A hearty thanks to Mark Spenik for agreeing to sign on to this project and then shouldering such a heavy load. Without a doubt, you brought an unparalleled expertise in VB to this project and helped to turn a good book into a great book. To Mark Swank—the fact that we've toiled through three books together and we're still on speaking terms speaks volumes! As with our past efforts, it has been a pleasure working with you. Thanks for the opportunities and for all your hard and dedicated work.

—Drew Kittel

Special Acknowledgments from Mark Swank

I'd like to thank my family and closest friends for understanding and encouraging me through this third book. If I had a penny for each time you cared enough to ask "How's the book coming?", I wouldn't have to write books. Thanks for all your support!

To Candy Burchell, you are always there to support me in anything that I do. Your confidence in me and encouragement has guided me through the completion of this book. Thanks for always being there!

And finally, to my two coauthors, Drew and Mark. Thanks for carrying the weight! It's funny how any one event can change the course of your life. Mark, were it not for you putting me in contact with Rosemarie, I wouldn't be writing this acknowledgment today. And Drew, had you not provided me the opportunities at the Department of Agriculture and agreed to partner with me on all our books, I most certainly would never have found the time to bring it all together and accomplish the things we have accomplished together. Thanks to both of you for everything.

—Mark Swank

About the Authors

Mark Spenik is the manager of Client/Server Technologies and Internet Development at Keiter, Stephens Computer Services, Inc., located in Richmond, Virginia. A graduate of George Mason University in Fairfax, Virginia, Mark entered the computer industry in 1985. He has designed and coded large scale C/S applications and has consulted with numerous firms in C/S development, implementation, and migration. He has a broad programming background, including HTML, assembly language, C, C++, and Visual Basic. Mark has hands-on experience with database implementation and administration. His specialty is Microsoft SQL Server, which he has used extensively since the early OS/2 days. Currently, Mark is busy helping clients in the Richmond area create active Web sites with Microsoft technologies. Mark is a Microsoft Certified Solution Developer. He is coauthor of *Microsoft SQL Server 6.5 DBA Survival Guide* (Sams Publishing) and *Visual Basic 5 Interactive Course* (Waite Group Press); he is a contributing author to *Microsoft SQL Server 6.5 Unleashed* (Sams Publishing). Mark can be reached via the Internet at mspenik@kscsinc.com.

Drew Kittel is a software developer and computer consultant in the Washington, D.C., area where he is currently working for Computer Science Corporation and NASA developing software to support the Landsat-7 Image Assessment System. Drew has over 13 years of software development and systems engineering experience. In the past, he has been involved in developing commercial Internet software, managing programs for technical services firms, managing a team of WWW application developers, and developing advanced satellite image processing and GIS applications for the U.S. Department of Agriculture. Drew is coauthor of *World Wide Web Database Developer's Guide* and *Designing and Implementing Microsoft Index Server,* both by Sams Publishing and written with Mark Swank.

Mark Swank is a Senior Systems Computer Consultant in the Washington, D.C., area. Mark is currently working as a consultant for Mindbank Consulting Group on a project with NASA Goddard Space Flight Center in Greenbelt, Maryland. Mark has served in several capacities related to Web-based Internet/Intranet development projects for organizations such as the U.S. Department of State, U.S. Department of Agriculture, and Ryland Mortgage Company. He has over 11 years of experience, having served as a C/UNIX developer, a UNIX systems administrator, an Oracle database administrator, a Web developer, and a Web administrator. Mark coauthored *World Wide Web Database Developer's Guide* and *Designing and Implementing Microsoft Index Server,* both by Sams Publishing and written with Drew Kittel.

Sanjaya Hettihewa is an accomplished Webmaster and a consultant specializing in integrating Windows NT–based information systems on the Internet. He has been living in the Washington, D.C., area for the past six years and has done extensive research in deploying Internet information systems utilizing various powerful and unique features of Windows NT. Sanjaya is the author of *Windows NT 4 Web Development and Windows NT Internet and Intranet Development,* and he has coauthored *Designing and Implementing Internet Information Server, Windows NT 3.51 Unleashed, FrontPage Unleashed, Internet Explorer Unleashed,* and *Internet Information Server Unleashed,* all by Sams and Sams.net Publishing. You can reach Sanjaya at `http://www.NetInnovation.com/` or, if you prefer the old-fashioned way, `sanjaya@NetInnovation.com`.

Troy D. Rackley is a consultant with Keiter, Stephens Computer Services, Inc. He began writing game programs on his Commodore VIC-20 and has continued to grow as technology has changed. Troy is currently certified as a Microsoft Certified Solution Developer (MCSD) and a Microsoft Product Specialist in Visual Basic (MCPS). He focuses on pushing the limits of object-oriented technologies, three-tiered client/server applications, and cutting-edge Internet Web designs. When he is not jacked into the local ISP, he enjoys becoming one with a totally different type of machine: his mountain bike. A perfectionist by nature, Troy also takes great enjoyment in disassembling things just to put them together again—somehow better. This applies to computers, software, Web sites, bicycles, and, recently, his house. He is currently trying to find time to build high-performance PCs to complete a multi-player game network at his Richmond home. Troy may be contacted at `trackley@erols.com`.

Orryn Sledge is a client/server consultant in the metropolitan Pittsburgh, Pennsylvania, area. He specializes in developing high-performance, mission-critical systems using Microsoft SQL Server, Sybase SQL Server, PowerBuilder, Visual Basic, and Access. He has been actively involved with SQL Server consulting since 1992. In addition to SQL Server consulting, he has trained several Fortune 500 companies on SQL Server administration and development. He is certified in SQL Server Administration, SQL Server Database Implementation, Windows NT Server and Workstation, Access, and Windows System Architecture I and II. Along with Mark Spenik, Orryn wrote *Microsoft SQL Server 6.5 DBA Survival Guide, Second Edition* and contributed to *Microsoft SQL Server 6.5 Unleashed, Second Edition,* both by Sams Publishing. Orryn can be reached on the Internet at `102254.2430@compuserve.com`.

Anne Yagerline is a project manager for client/server development at Keiter, Stephens Computer Services, Inc., in Richmond, Virginia. She develops Windows-based applications using Access, Visual Basic, VBA, and SQL Server for local, national, and international firms based in the Richmond area. She specializes in financial systems, stemming from her prior experience in the mortgage securities industry. Anne can be reached at `ahutchin@kscsinc.com`.

Tell Us What You Think!

As a reader, you are the most important critic and commentator of our books. We value your opinion and want to know what we're doing right, what we could do better, what areas you'd like to see us publish in, and any other words of wisdom you're willing to pass our way. You can help us make strong books that meet your needs and give you the computer guidance you require.

Do you have access to CompuServe or the World Wide Web? Then check out our CompuServe forum by typing **GO SAMS** at any prompt. If you prefer the World Wide Web, check out our site at `http://www.mcp.com`.

> **NOTE**
>
> If you have a technical question about this book, call the technical support line at 317-581-3833.

As the publishing manager of the group that created this book, I welcome your comments. You can fax, e-mail, or write me directly to let me know what you did or didn't like about this book—as well as what we can do to make our books stronger. Here's the information:

Fax: 317-581-4669

E-mail: `enterprise_mgr@sams.mcp.com`

Mail: Rosemarie Graham
         Sams.net Publishing
         201 W. 103rd Street
         Indianapolis, IN 46290

Introduction

As the number of available Web-based books continues to rise, finding the right book that covers the key topics for the subject material can be a daunting task. We've tried to make this book both a resource and a learning tool. For VB developers new to Web programming, the initial sections will help bring you up-to-date with Web technologies. If you are a Web developer eager to incorporate the functionality of Visual Basic, VBScript, and ActiveX technologies into your development platform, you will find the later chapters to be excitingly refreshing with real-world examples.

Be sure to check out the accompanying CD-ROM. It's jam-packed with software and all the source files from the book. If you're having problems with any of the examples, or if you have some comments or suggestions about the book, please let us know. We value your thoughts on this and any of the other books we've written.

Drew, Mark, and Mark
(Yes, we were once called "The Marks brothers" at work.)

dkittel@clark.net
mspenik@kscsinc.com
mswank@clark.net

I

The Essential Web Basics
for Visual Basic
Programmers

1

The Internet, World Wide Web, and Intranets

by Drew Kittel

The world of computers and information processing is growing rapidly. At the center of this amazing growth is the World Wide Web, also known as the *Web* and *WWW*. Just a few months ago, the Web was a medium for sharing documents among people and computers via the Internet. Today, it is fast becoming a distributed development environment capable of providing information and other application resources to millions of people around the world. In addition, corporations are implementing internal Webs and Web-based applications, known as *intranets*, to facilitate communications and sharing of information among employees. Intranets implement the same technologies as their Web counterparts and are springing up in organizations literally overnight—in many cases, changing the way business is conducted.

This chapter gives you the background necessary to understand what all the hoopla is about and what it can mean for you and your organization. It starts off with a presentation of some Internet background and history to set the stage for how the Web came into being. Then you'll learn what the Web is, what intranets are, and the meaning of Web databases. Later sections concentrate on the benefits that intranets hold for organizations and how you can use them to meet organizational information needs. You'll also discover the advantages of developing Web applications instead of developing traditional information systems, and you'll look at the benefits from both the user's and developer's perspective. Finally, you'll see some real-world cases of how some organizations and government agencies have used intranets to meet informational needs and to solve problems.

A Little Internet Background

The *Internet*, in its broadest sense, can be defined as a collection or interconnection of many different networks of computer hosts, clients, and servers that collectively provide and use information and connection services. This "network of computer networks" now includes a community that literally spans the globe and counts among its members nearly every country in the world.

Computers with access to the Internet come in all sorts of makes and models and run a variety of operating systems and applications. Strictly speaking, computers connected to the Internet are those that use the *Transport Control Protocol/Internet Protocol* (TCP/IP) suite, which is a common set of rules that allow a variety of systems to communicate. Computers on non-TCP/IP networks, however, can access the Internet through gateways that perform the necessary protocol translations and allow appropriate communications.

The Internet, also known as the *Net*, provides many standards, services, and protocols that allow individuals to access the huge number of resources available on the Net. This section provides a brief introduction and history of the Internet to give you a sense of the growth that has led to the phenomenon known as the World Wide Web.

Internet History

It might be hard to believe, but the Internet as we know it today owes its existence to the 1957 launch of a Soviet satellite called Sputnik. This event set off a chain of events that eventually resulted in the evolution of the Internet.

After the launch of Sputnik, President Dwight D. Eisenhower recognized the need for the United States to maintain technical superiority. As a result, the *Advanced Research Projects Agency* (ARPA) was founded with the charter of being the central research and development agency for the *Department of Defense* (DoD). ARPA's mission was to develop imaginative and innovative research ideas—often with high risk factors, but also with potentially significant positive technological impact.

In 1969, DoD tasked ARPA to perform research and experiments with the communications links between DoD and military contractors. A primary goal was to develop communications systems that could overcome disruptions caused by enemy attacks (remember that this was occurring during the Cold War). This marked the beginning of the ARPAnet. The initial system connected four sites:

■ Stanford Research Institute (SRI)
■ University of California at Santa Barbara (UCSB)
■ University of California at Los Angeles (UCLA)
■ University of Utah

In the early 1970s, Stanford University was tasked to research and experiment with multiple-packet switching technology—a mechanism that improved reliability of communications when some network connections were down or unreliable. Subsequent research and feasibility experiments led to the development of the TCP/IP suite. TCP/IP later became a communications standard in 1983 and was added to the University of California at Berkeley's BSD version of UNIX. BSD UNIX was a primary enabler in allowing numerous computers and computer networks to be added to the ARPAnet.

In 1985, The *National Science Foundation* (NSF) created the NSFnet program. NSF's interest in supercomputing applications led to the requirement for high-speed communications links to connect researchers to NSF supercomputer centers. Unable to use the ARPAnet for this purpose, NSF developed its own backbone with the assistance of MCI, IBM, and the University of Michigan. From this backbone, a number of regional networks were hung.

In 1989, ARPA, now renamed DARPA (the *D* standing for *Defense)*, pulled the plug on ARPAnet, and the NSFnet replaced ARPAnet as the backbone of the collection of local and regional TCP/IP networks that had become known as the Internet.

Internet and Web Milestones

Table 1.1 charts some of the significant events and milestones of Internet and Web history. Notice that the number and frequency of significant events pick up considerably as the timeline covers recent years.

Table 1.1. Internet and Web milestones.

Year	Events
1957	Sputnik is launched.
	ARPA is formed by DoD.
1967	Initial ARPAnet design paper is published.
1969	DoD commissions development of the ARPAnet.
1970	ARPAnet starts to use Network Control Protocol.
1972	*Internetworking Working Group* (INWG) is created to promote agreed-upon standards.
	The Telnet specification, RFC 318, is proposed.
1973	Ethernet idea is outlined in Bob Metcalfe's Ph.D. thesis (Harvard).
	The File Transfer specification, RFC 454, is proposed.
1974	Design of TCP/IP is detailed in "A Protocol for Packet Network Inter-communication," by Vint Cerf and Bob Kahn.
1976	UNIX-to-UNIX Copy (UUCP) is developed at Bell Labs.
1981	BITNET is established.
1982	TCP/IP is established as the protocol suite for ARPAnet, and DoD specifies TCP/IP as a standard.
1983	BSD UNIX 4.2 incorporates TCP/IP.
1984	Number of Internet hosts surpasses 1,000.
	The *Domain Name Service* (DNS) comes into existence.
1986	The NSFnet is created with a (then blazing) backbone speed of 56Kbps.
1987	The number of Internet hosts surpasses 10,000.
	UUNET is founded for the purpose of providing commercial Usenet and UUCP access.
1988	The infamous Internet worm makes its way across the Net, disabling or affecting more than 6,000 hosts.
	NSFnet upgrades its backbone speed to 1.544Mbps (T1).
1989	The number of Internet hosts surpasses 100,000.
	"Information Management: A Proposal" is written and circulated by Tim Berners-Lee of CERN (European Laboratory for Particle Physics).

Year	Events
1990	DoD pulls the plug on ARPAnet.
	Berners-Lee proposal is reformulated and the name *World Wide Web* (WWW) is coined.
	Initial WWW program, a WYSIWYG browser/editor, is developed.
1991	Brewster Kahle (Thinking Machines) invents the Wide Area Information Server.
	Paul Lindner and Mark McCahill (University of Minnesota) release Gopher.
	Phillip Zimmerman releases *Pretty Good Privacy* (PGP).
	CERN releases WWW library.
1992	Number of Internet hosts surpasses 1,000,000.
	The University of Nevada releases Veronica.
	Viola WWW GUI browser, by Pei Wei, is released and distributed with CERN's WWW.
1993	NSF creates InterNIC to provide specific Internet services, such as registration of domains.
	The first version of Mosaic for X, developed by Marc Andreesen, is released by NCSA.
	The White House goes online.
	The National Information Infrastructure Act is passed, and government agencies start getting serious about establishing a Web presence.
1994	Pizza Hut goes online with the first widely known commercial application.
	Spam takes on a new meaning as the law firm of Canter & Siegel send widespread e-mail to advertise "green card" lottery services.
	The first online cyberbank, First Virtual, is established.
1995	CompuServe, America Online, and Prodigy jump on the bandwagon and begin offering Internet connectivity.
	Marc Andreesen's upstart Netscape Communication Corporation goes public and wows the market with one of the highest (#3) initial public offering share prices in NASDAQ.
	The NSF no longer provides domain name registration for free. A $50-per-year fee is established.
1996	Sams.net publishes *The World Wide Web Database Developer's Guide*.

Internet and Web Growth

The number of users on the Internet is a subject of debate, primarily because what constitutes "a user" is in question. Is a user someone just browsing, someone seeking specific information, or someone taking advantage of applications made available by others? Should intranet users also be included in the tally? Although several estimates have been made, so far, no truly accurate way to determine the number of users exists; the number you get depends on who you're talking to and what his or her agenda happens to be. The only appropriate answer is: *A lot!* And everyone agrees that the number is growing exponentially.

Other more objective methods exist for gauging the growth of the Net. We do know that in 1969, the number of Internet hosts was a grand total of four. By mid 1995, that number had grown to more than 6.5 million hosts, and the number of domains was approximately 120,000. *Domains* are simply logical collections of Internet addresses that are part of a hierarchical addressing scheme known as the DNS. This growth is depicted in Figure 1.1.

FIGURE 1.1.

Internet growth.

Year	Hosts
1969	4
1984	1,024
1986	5,089
1987	28,174
1988	56,000
1989	159,000
1990	313,000
1991	617,000
1992	1,136,000
1993	2,056,000
1994	3,864,000
1995	6,642,000
1996	9,472,000

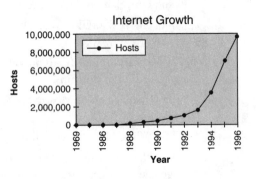

Year	Domains
1990	9,300
1991	18,000
1992	18,100
1993	28,000
1994	56,000
1995	120,000
1996	240,000

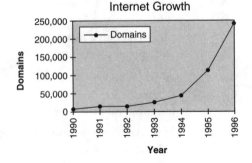

It's estimated that at the end of 1996, nearly 9.5 million hosts were connected to the Internet, with nearly 240,000 registered domains.

The growth of the Web is also phenomenal. One indicator of Web growth is sales of Web server products for Internet and intranet use. Unit sales of Web servers for Internet use are expected to grow from approximately 100,000 in 1995 to more than 300,000 by 1998. Intranet server sales are expected to make a gargantuan leap in sales during the same time from less than 25,000 to approximately 600,000. One can only guess how this translates to number of users. Once again, the answer is: A lot! Obviously, intranets offer a great many benefits; you'll see those benefits later in this chapter.

Key Technologies and Information Services

Internet users, Web surfers, and Internet-based applications take advantage of key technologies and information service applications, many of which were developed specifically for use on the Internet. Here is a brief overview of the more popular technologies:

- **TCP/IP:** The *Transmission Control Protocol/Internet Protocol* is the basic collection of protocols that computers, servers, and clients use to communicate over the Internet.

- **FTP:** The *File Transfer Protocol* is an Internet protocol and service that enables users to transfer files between computers on a network. FTP servers are among the most common information services on the Internet.

- **Telnet:** A client application for providing remote, character-based terminal access to a remote host (for example, VT 100 emulation).

- **Gopher:** A program for browsing files and directories of hosts (running Gopher servers) connected to the Internet. It's a simple menu-based system, but the items on the menu can be pointers to files or directories on other Gopher servers, FTP servers, Telnet services, and so on.

- **HTTP:** The *Hypertext Transport Protocol* is a TCP/IP-based protocol used by Web servers and browsers that defines the manner in which they communicate over the Web.

- **MIME:** The *Multipurpose Internet Mail Extensions* standard is a specification for enhancing the capabilities of Internet mail services and allowing new uses, such as multimedia messages.

- **Web servers:** A program that provides services to Web clients. These services generally are HTTP services that provide access to HTML document repositories or CGI applications. They also can be pass-through services such as FTP, Gopher, or Telnet.

- **Web browsers:** Programs such as Netscape Navigator, Mosaic, and Internet Explorer are among the dozens of available browsers (that is, Web clients) that allow easy navigation of Websites on the Internet and display documents written in HTML. Most of the popular commercial browsers are graphical-based, and many use extensions that allow inline images, as well as some audio and video capabilities, to be integrated.

■ **CGI:** The *common gateway interface* is a means by which Web servers can interface with other application programs and extend the services available from the Web server. You can provide access to your databases and applications via CGI programs, for example.

■ **HTML:** The *Hypertext Markup Language* is the primary language of documents served by Web servers. It provides a rich and growing set of tags that are embedded in documents to specify how the content should be formatted on a page. These tags also enable you to establish hypertext links from content in one document to content in other documents (which can be local or on a server anywhere in the world). HTML also provides mechanisms for invoking programs and services on Web servers.

What Is the World Wide Web?

First of all, I'd like to make it perfectly clear that the World Wide Web is not the Internet, and vice versa. They are closely related, though. The Internet is a network in every sense of the word; the Web, however, is not only a network, it is also a distributed set of communications applications and systems software with the following characteristics:

■ Typically resides on Internet hosts and clients (although, as you'll see shortly, autonomous intranets do exist)

■ Typically uses the TCP/IP network protocol

■ Understands HTML

■ Follows the client/server model of bidirectional data communications, information collection, and resource serving

■ Enables client programs to access servers using a variety of protocols, including HTTP, FTP, Telnet, and Gopher

■ Uses document and resource addressing via uniform resource locators (URLs)

■ Enables client programs to access information composed of a variety of media types, such as text, audio, and video

Although the Web is not restricted to using graphical-based client programs (browsers), these are by far the most popular in use on the Web today.

As a matter of historical reference, much of what constitutes the Web today owes its existence to concepts and ideas espoused by Tim Berners-Lee, a researcher at the CERN Particle Physics Lab in Geneva, Switzerland. In 1989, Berners-Lee developed and circulated for comment a proposal for a hypertext system with the following three components:

■ A consistent user interface that would remain the same across all platforms. The interface would provide access to a variety of different information sources on a variety of computers.

- Universal access to information. Any user on the network could access any information.

- The user interface would allow access to information and documents of a variety of types and protocols.

Subsequent research and development pursued as a result of this proposal led to the creation of Mosaic, the first graphical Web browser that helped spawn the great interest in the Web.

What Is a Web Database, and Why Use One?

Like any regular database management system, a Web database is a data store or information repository that can be accessed via a query language or programming API. Unlike conventional database systems, however, with Web databases, this access is not typically performed using instructions typed at a command line or issued through interfaces that are custom designed for use on a specific computer platform.

Web databases are accessed via other Web applications—specifically, forms that are developed using standardized HTML tags (and, in some cases, vendor-specific extensions), ActiveX controls, and client-side scripts using VBScript and JavaScript. Using facilities available in HTML, applications programs on the Web server are accessed through server-side programs via CGI, server-specific interfaces such as Microsoft's *Internet Information Server* (IIS) *application programming interface* (ISAPI) or server-side scripting environments such as IIS's Active Server pages (which use Visual Basic). HTML form interfaces enable you to create applications that integrate database functionality and provide access to organizational data repositories on behalf of Web clients (that is, a user and browser). You can design applications solely for the purpose of querying a database and returning specific information—for example, a profile of the top-selling salespeople in your organization during the previous quarter. The application also can use information pulled from a database to support more comprehensive applications. Sales statistics for a chain of stores could be pulled from a database, for example, and used to perform a statistical analysis of how various sales and promotions affected revenues during a given period of time.

This capability to integrate a database into applications that can be accessed by users utilizing a Web browser is what makes a database a Web database.

Most organizations maintain a variety of autonomous computer databases that support basic infrastructure needs (such as human resources) and classic information systems (such as corporate *management information systems* or MIS). In most Web-based applications, these databases serve as the basic building blocks for information services. Organizations might want to use these databases in their Web applications for several reasons:

- To better manage the serving of large, document-based information repositories to internal and/or external users of the information.

■ To better leverage and use legacy database systems, the information they contain, and existing applications.

■ To unlock the potential of unused information in organizational databases. Information from databases in various parts of an organization (for example, finance, human resources, project management, and so on) can be consolidated using Web-based applications and served to users as though it were from a single source. Databases do not have to be physically located with the user of the database application, either. Imagine an application that would poll the inventory databases of hundreds of specialty stores worldwide and build a custom online catalog of merchandise that meets a specific user's criteria.

■ To extend the functionality of your Web server so that you can make information you maintain available to the general public and internal users—a task currently undertaken by many organizations and government agencies whose primary product is information.

What Are Intranets?

Intranets are Web applications that are *internal to organizations.* These applications use Internet technologies such as Web servers; Web browsers; standard TCP/IP networks; and development tools such as HTML, ActiveX controls, client-side scripting (using VBScript, JScript, and JavaScript), server-specific APIs, and CGI programming. Like their Internet counterpart applications, intranet applications provide information and services to a number of users—in this case, the employees of the organization.

It's important to note that an intranet is not defined by any physical boundaries or geographical constraints. In fact, intranets are global in many cases. The intranet boundaries are defined by who has access to the information. This might be all employees of a company or only those members of a development team within a company. It all depends on the application and the requirements it fulfills.

Intranets have experienced an explosion in growth in recent months because they allow for fundamental changes in the way business processes are conducted. Intranet applications allow for more efficient, more effective, more accurate communications and dissemination of information, all of which contribute to greater productivity of employees.

Intranets Versus Groupware

In the past two years since Internet technologies have hit the big time, intranets have become an expanding application area for several organizations, agencies, corporations, and other businesses. Building upon Internet technologies, intranets have enabled these enterprises to quickly and fundamentally change the way in which many traditional business processes are conducted.

In doing so, intranets have diverted a large share of business away from common groupware vendors and applications, such as IBM Notes. (Notes is an information manager designed to allow a group of people or workgroups to share information across computer networks, even if those people are in different parts of the world.)

Cost is the primary reason why businesses choose to use an intranet. Here are some of the factors they consider when making this decision:

- Per-user installation cost typically is greater for groupware applications.

- Many groupware products, such as Notes, are based on proprietary networking architectures rather than the TCP/IP standard used by Internet and intranet applications. This makes the groupware applications more difficult to maintain and subsequently adds to their life-cycle cost.

- Learning curves for application developers using groupware products can be substantially higher. This factor negatively impacts both the cost and the speed with which these applications can be developed and deployed.

- Integrating intranet applications with existing legacy applications and databases generally is easier because the HTML/client-side scripting/CGI/Server API development models used by most current intranet applications is quite open and easily extended to integrate these other applications. The result is shorter, less costly development cycles. This is not always true of groupware products.

- User-training costs and time are reduced substantially with intranet applications. Users often are already familiar with the use of Web browsers and take quickly to new applications that use these browsers as interfaces.

- Although the functionality available through groupware products, such as automatic updating and version control of shared documents, exceeds that of typical intranet applications, this is likely to change dramatically in the future. Web servers, browsers, and development tools are offering an increasing array of capabilities.

Intranet Advantages

More and more, intranets are taking over and expanding some of the roles traditionally held by organizational information systems. In doing so, organizations are beginning to reap the benefits of this new technology and its applications. Intranets have enabled organizations to

- Centralize information
- Organize information
- Decrease costs and increase efficiency
- Improve the sharing of information
- Speed up development and distribution of applications
- Promote the creation of WWW pages

Centralized Information

Organizations are finding that intranets centralize information, which means that employees can go to a single source (their Web browser) to obtain information. This is true even in organizations with widely distributed sources of information and databases. Typically, this information is the most up-to-date and accurate organizational information available.

Web technologies enable employees to see and access distributed sources as if they are one large, virtual information base. A company might have manufacturing and production information at its facilities in Texas, for example, policy information at its corporate headquarters in Boston, and sales figures and marketing leads at each of its distributors' offices around the world. An employee at any regional office could have access to information from any of these sites via an organizational intranet. Employees do not need to be concerned with where information physically resides, because it appears as though it is from a common source.

Organized External Information Sources

Intranets not only help to organize and consolidate internal information, but they also serve as platforms for organizing and presenting information that exists outside the organization. Intranet applications can maintain WWW links to a variety of information sources of importance to an organization, such as the following:

■ Technical white papers made publicly available by competitors

■ Educational research papers

■ Online publications

■ Legislative information

■ Surveys

■ Competitors' publicly available product information

All these sources offer data and information that can improve the way an organization conducts its business or remains competitive. And with the advent of intelligent agents and automated Web-crawling informational robots, these technologies will be integrated into intranets so that employees can keep up with the latest developments affecting their organization.

Improved Cost and Time Efficiency

The use of intranets results in reductions in costs associated with creating and distributing traditional sources of internal information. Expenses associated with printing, copying, faxing, distributing, and mailing organizational publications, such as the following, are cut dramatically:

■ Newsletters

■ All-hands memoranda

- Meeting schedules, agendas, and minutes
- Project schedule status and updates
- Policy manuals

In large organizations, just the savings in paper costs often can offset the initial investment in the intranet itself. The time associated with creating and distributing this information also can be reduced dramatically, especially for publications for which the bulk of information could be drawn automatically from existing digital data sources.

Improved Information Sharing

Intranets greatly facilitate the sharing of internal information such as the following among all employees:

- Employee phone listings
- Training material and tutorials
- Product demonstrations
- Updated project schedules and timelines
- Technical product information

Faster Development Cycles

Internal information systems development often is plagued by long development cycles that result in some applications being outdated before they can be developed completely and delivered using many of today's standard development tools. Intranets are based on open-standard and Internet technologies and use development tools such as Web browsers, HTML, ActiveX controls, VBScript, Visual Basic 5, Web server APIs, and CGI programming. They also often seek to integrate with existing legacy applications and databases—a task they facilitate well. As a result, the development of intranet applications typically entails shorter development cycles, which in turn means that employees gain access to the applications faster, and the organization realizes gains in productivity from the development staff.

Promotion of WWW Page Creation

Introducing new technology to an organization often meets some resistance, especially when it results in a fundamentally new way of conducting some business processes. Intranets, however, seem to be having the opposite effect. Not only are employees embracing the technology and immediately understanding the positive impact of it, their experiences with intranets are encouraging them to develop and contribute information for internal use as well as for posting on organization's external Web pages. This results in cost reductions because others don't have to create this material. And employees begin to feel a greater sense of ownership and empowerment as they contribute.

Organizational Uses of Intranets

Intranets vary in their uses as much as the organizations themselves. Some organizations see intranet applications merely as a means to facilitate better communications and sharing of information, whereas others see intranets as an enabling technology that will result in entirely new ways of conducting internal business. This section presents some of the typical uses of intranets, including the following:

- Human resources functions
- Information dissemination and sharing
- Product and service information
- Employee training
- Project information

Human Resources

Human resource departments are developing intranet applications that give employees access to a variety of information traditionally handled by HR departments, including these:

- Corporate benefits information, including detailed insurance coverage information, educational benefits, leave accrual, and so on
- Up-to-date sick leave and vacation balances for individuals
- 401(k) balances/reallocations, fund profiles, and company contributions
- Profit sharing, retirement plans, and employee stock ownership cost and share values
- Employee policy and procedure manuals, complete with a hypertext-linked table of contents and text-search capabilities
- EEO information
- Employee orientation materials
- Skills and aptitude testing
- Internal job postings
- Employee surveys

Not only do such applications provide employees with up-to-date information, but they also reduce paper use, dissemination, and mailing costs. The HR staff also is less burdened by personnel requests for such information because employees now are able to immediately find the answers to many of their questions rather than waiting for an HR representative to find an answer for them.

Organizational Information Dissemination

Nearly everyone has worked in an organization where the flow of information was often non-existent, untimely, or inaccurate. Organizations that have historically depended on word-of-mouth, memoranda, newsletters, or e-mail are finding that intranets are a much better solution to disseminating information. Not only is the information controlled from a single source, but the process saves paper and publishing costs, and changes can be made and disseminated in real time (as opposed to the lengthy times involved with printing, copying, and mailing). Employees no longer need to be uninformed about organizational happenings. Not only are organizations using intranets to disseminate information, but smaller groups in the organization (even at the project level) are viewing it as a medium by which to share information. Typical uses for dissemination of information follow:

- Corporate newsletters
- Departmental and project group newsletters
- Updates and changes in organizational or corporate policies
- Corporate financial information, sales goals, and sales figures
- Recent hirings
- Reorganization updates
- Access to corporate databases, data repositories, and online technical libraries

Keep in mind that for large organizations, the cost and time savings that result from disseminating information from centralized sources using intranet applications can be substantial, especially for organizations that are widely distributed geographically.

Product/Service Information

Any organization that provides technical support services for products or uses an internal sales and marketing staff can potentially benefit from using an intranet. Several organizations now are making technical information about the products and services they offer available to employees handling customer service and trouble calls. Personnel can provide better service to customers when they have easy access to databases and internal information such as the following:

- Customer profiles
- Sales leads
- Marketing and promotional materials
- Product information
- Answers to frequently asked questions
- Pricing policies
- Warranties

And because the information is available internally to all employees, the result is a better educated and trained staff.

Employee Training

Most organizations consider training a necessity in maintaining a competitive edge and an appropriately educated staff. Yet, when it comes to funding training, many have a difficult time justifying the cost of sending employees to school or specialized courses. Intranet applications are starting to change this way of thinking. Online tutorials, seminars, briefings, and product demonstrations now can be provided to a wider number of employees at substantially lower per-employee costs than traditional classroom methods. And with the advances being made in Web-based audio, video, and multimedia technologies, as well as development tools such as Microsoft FrontPage 2.0, ActiveX controls, ActiveX documents, Active Server pages, VBScript, and Visual Basic 5, more comprehensive and functional intranet applications will begin to be implemented in the near future.

Some advantages of developing intranet training applications follow:

- Courses and seminars can be tailored to meet the specific needs of the organization and employees.
- Courses can be modularized for just-in-time training on a subject or subjects.
- Technical courses can be updated or added as technology changes and is made available to all employees immediately.
- Online availability encourages employees to pick up new skills they ordinarily might not attempt due to lack of funding for external classes.
- Online training promotes an active pursuit of professional development to the betterment of the employees and the organization.
- Employees can work through training materials at their own pace.

Project-Specific Information

As mentioned earlier, intranets are defined not by physical boundaries, but rather by who has access to information provided by the intranet. Organizational intranets are currently the most common form of intranet, but this is beginning to change. With the proliferation of low-cost personal Web servers that run on PCs, the concept of departmental and project intranets accessible only by employees in the department or project team are beginning to catch on. Some project intranets are even being viewed as temporary entities with a lifetime only as long as the project itself. Such intranets are providing project managers with secured information about budgets, labor costs, bid rates, and employees (including skills, education, resumes, work history, and salary). Intranets also provide project team members with current project-related information, such as

- Work breakdown structures
- Schedules and personnel assignments
- Gantt charts and PERT chart planning tools (graphical tools used for project planning and scheduling)
- Team meeting schedules
- Weekly and monthly goals
- Updates and project-related news
- Online requirements, specifications, and documents

Some of this information also can be "rolled up" and provided for use on organizational intranet pages.

Advantages of Web Application Development

Developing applications using Web-related technologies holds many advantages over developing traditional information systems and end-user applications. This is true whether the applications are being developed for internal users on an intranet or external users on the Web. This section explores some of the benefits of applications development using this technology from both the user's and developer's perspective.

The User's Perspective

End-users are the primary reason why applications are developed. Internal users want easy access to organizational information, and external users want to use databases and applications you provide access to. It's therefore critical that you develop applications that are easy and intuitive for your users—doing otherwise will ensure that users won't use them. Fortunately, Web applications provide many benefits to end-users that aren't as readily achievable by using traditional systems-development tools. Here are just a few of the benefits:

- Graphical user interfaces
- Abstraction of applications and query languages using forms
- Browser customization
- Quick and easy access to information, databases, and applications

Graphical User Interfaces

Remember when applications were text-based and command-line driven? Only recently have *graphical user interfaces* (GUIs) become the more common means of using an application. The GUI used by Web applications is the Web browser. These GUIs make life easier for end-users by enabling them to point and click to navigate applications. This makes selecting from lists, scrolling pages of information, viewing graphics, and entering inputs far easier than non-graphical systems. Standard HTML documents read by a variety of Web browsers are rendered in a common way regardless of the browser used. This enables people to use the same application regardless of the platform they are on. A person can use an application on a UNIX workstation using Netscape at work, for example, and he can use the same application later from a home PC using Microsoft's Internet Explorer. Users can concentrate on doing their work and applying the information they receive from these applications instead of worrying about the details of making the application run.

Abstraction of Applications and Query Languages

HTML forms and hypertext links provide mechanisms by which the details of an application can be abstracted for the user. Users no longer are required to have detailed knowledge of the application or its input parameters and valid values to use it. Instead, they're presented with forms complete with text-entry boxes, selection lists, scrollable menus, radio buttons, and checkboxes. These user-input objects guide the user to enter the information needed to execute an application or query a database. And users don't need to know the structure or table relations of the databases they access. In fact, they might be totally unaware that a database is integrated with the application. Form-input objects are used to collect the information necessary for a database query to be constructed by the application on behalf of users. Users just need to concentrate on how they can use the results of the application to their benefit.

Browser Customization

The current generation of graphical Web browsers enables users to customize many attributes to suit their tastes and preferences. Here are some of the attributes that are user-configurable:

- General appearance
- Font style
- Text, background, and link colors
- Image-rendering characteristics
- Plug-ins and helper applications definitions
- Language
- Newsgroup access

Quick and Easy Access to Information

Information has no value unless users can readily access it. Countless organizations have information in computer-based documents and databases, but how do users access this information without knowledge of its existence or how it can be accessed? Web applications are addressing this critical need by providing common interfaces to under-used corporate databases in many intranet applications. Additionally, agencies seeking to provide the public with access to the volumes of information they produce are finding that relatively simple Web interfaces provide users with access to a variety of information sources previously unavailable. Not only is the information being made available, but Web database applications are being developed that enable users to perform complex searches of the information by just clicking the mouse a few times.

The Developer's Perspective

Web technologies provide developers with a number of advantages over traditional development tools:

- Standard technologies
- Short learning curves
- Cross-platform compatibility
- Ease of integration
- Rapid GUI development

Standard Technologies

Web applications are built on standardized protocols such as TCP/IP and HTTP, and on technologies such as HTML and CGI.

Using a common network protocol (TCP/IP) as well as a browser/server communications protocol (HTTP) makes life easier for developers, because they don't need to worry about the implementation details. Web servers, browsers, and the computers on which they reside already have this built-in support. Developers can concentrate on the application instead of the communications details.

HTML is not a programming language in that it does not provide typical procedural language constructs for loops, conditions, calculations, storage, and so on. You can use it, however, to present applications, render images, and provide access to underlying programs (on the server) by using CGI and Web server APIs. HTML has the advantage that it is a (relatively) standard text-based markup language that requires no compiler. Additionally, client-side scripting (using VBScript, for example) and ActiveX controls provide the capability to greatly extend and improve the interactiveness of HTML forms. Applications can be developed using any simple text editor or word processor on any computer platform. The HTML code then can be installed on any Web server from which you want it to run.

CGI is the common interface that allows application programs to be written and executed by a Web server on behalf of a Web client. CGI programs can provide access to databases as well as existing applications or off-the-shelf software tools. Note that all major Web servers, such as Microsoft and Netscape, provide an API in addition to CGI. These APIs often provide additional functionality and performance benefits over CGI.

Short Learning Curves

Unlike traditional programming languages, HTML is relatively easy to master quickly. In fact, several development tools, such as Microsoft's FrontPage, provide even novice HTML developers with development tools that are as easy to use as most word processors. This means that non-programmers—even end users—can participate in developing GUI front ends to applications. This capability enables programmers to concentrate more on developing the underlying applications to be run on the server.

Cross-Platform Compatibility

Browsers are available for nearly any make or model of computer. Furthermore, by using standard HTML, you can develop applications interfaces that will run on most graphical browsers on almost any machine. Graphical user interfaces do not need to be specifically coded for the platform on which they will run.

Web applications also leverage benefits of the client/server model of computing. Because applications reside on the Web server host (or other computers it subsequently accesses), the application is developed for a single runtime environment. This means that any computer running a browser—whether it's a PC running Windows, a Macintosh, or a UNIX workstation—can access the same applications.

Ease of Integration

Because HTML provides the capability to easily invoke server-side programs via CGI or a Web server API, developers only need to know how to work within the CGI/server API environment in order to integrate CGI/API programs with new or existing applications such as databases or graphics-generation utilities. This is often no more than an extension of development environments with which developers are already familiar. Databases can be accessed in CGI programs using familiar database APIs, for example. CGI/server APIs are the glue that connects HTML GUIs on a Web browser to full-fledged applications on a Web server.

Rapid GUI Development

Anyone who has developed applications using a windowing system, such as X Windows System, will attest that the most time-consuming aspect actually is coding the user interfaces. All the work of the application is done in the callback routines invoked from the interfaces, however. Using HTML (as well as ActiveX controls and VBScript) as a GUI development environment reverses this situation. Often, browser-based interfaces can be developed in a matter of minutes or days rather than days or weeks, which enables developers to concentrate on the development of the underlying application. The result is shorter development cycles, allowing applications to reach end users more quickly. Also, modifications and enhancements to HTML and VBScript code typically are much faster than traditional development environments.

Real-World Examples: What Some Organizations Are Doing with Intranets

Organizations have turned to intranet technologies as a solution to some of their problems for various reasons. For some companies, the need to improve communications and disseminate important information within a geographically distributed organization prompted the use of the technology. In other organizations, such as government agencies, online access to information they produce was mandated; in still other organizations, technology was viewed as a means to consolidate, organize, and better share information while realizing cost savings at the same time. This section illustrates how some organizations have implemented and benefited from intranet technology.

RESOURCE

You can find additional information on how these and other organizations are using intranet and Web technologies at the following Web locations and by performing Internet searches using your favorite search engine (try keywords: `intranet`):

```
http://www.cio.com/WebMaster/wm_cases.html
http://home.netscape.com/comprod/at_work/white_paper/index.html
http://home.netscape.com/comprod/at_work/customer_profiles/index.html
http://home.netscape.com/comprod/at_work/press_clippings/index.html
```

McDonnell Douglas Commercial Aircraft Manufacturing

McDonnell Douglas (MDD), which recently signed an agreement to merge with Boeing, implements an intranet application that somewhat stretches the typical definition of an organizational intranet in that customers are viewed as part of the organization and are allowed access to the system.

MDD builds commercial airliners for more than 200 airlines worldwide. As part of its services, MDD provides aircraft service bulletins that contain critical information on how MDD aircraft should be modified and serviced. In the past, these bulletins, which averaged more than 25 pages, were printed and delivered to four or five customers per day, which resulted in more than four million pages of documentation being printed and mailed yearly. Obviously, this was a huge paper and mailing cost that MDD wanted to reduce. But that was only part of the problem. Because MDD services airlines around the world, bulletins often could take two or three weeks to arrive—an unacceptable period of time for the critical information in the bulletins.

MDD evaluated several alternative information-systems solutions to disseminate these bulletins worldwide and decided that an intranet solution was the best choice, because it was based on Commercial Off-The-Shelf (COTS) software and industry-standard network protocols. This ensured that MDD and their customers were not locked into a proprietary system costly to deploy and maintain. MDD provides access to the service bulletins via its home page. Customers simply access the home page via their browsers and view the bulletins, which are stored in Standard Generalized Markup Language (SGML) format on MDD's database. Additionally, MDD used Netscape's Secure Commerce Server to give customers access to some bulletins that contain airline proprietary information.

This intranet solution provided MDD and customers with many benefits, including the following:

- Costs were reduced. Intranet dissemination costs roughly half as much as the printing and mailing costs (while saving thousands of trees yearly).
- MDD improved customer support through the timely dissemination of bulletins via the intranet. Delivery is now in real-time for this critical information.
- Because the information is served from a database in SGML format, customers easily can integrate the files into their own documents. This improves the capability to archive the documents and perform future information searches electronically.

U.S. West's Global Village

U.S. West has implemented an intranet, dubbed the Global Village, that is accessible by more than 15,000 U.S. West employees. These are among the applications available to employees:

- Discussion forums that allow online meetings, discussion of projects, exchange of documents, and sharing of information
- An anonymous electronic suggestion box and "rumor mill" that allows corporate executives to address employee suggestions, public gripes, and rumors of the day

Functionality also is being added that will enable customer representatives to tap into the intranet to immediately service requests for call-waiting and other U.S. West services. The service representative will fill out online forms to enter the order and submit it to the phone-switching network applications. The result is that customer-service requests now are activated within minutes of entering the order instead of taking hours or a couple of days.

Among the benefits realized by U.S. West are improved communications, customer service and implementation, maintenance, and enhancement of some key applications by non-technical employees.

Turner Broadcasting

The intranet at Turner Broadcasting serves not only typical intranet objectives such as sharing corporate information, but it also serves as a laboratory and testing ground—a sort of internal test-marketing arena where employees preview and constructively criticize programs and materials to be released by Turner. Some of the services available on the Turner intranet follow:

- Access to ratings for Turner programs
- Receipt of customized daily newspapers (via e-mail) by simply filing out an online profile
- Viewing of sound bites and animated clips of Turner cartoons and programming, and feedback to the producers before programs are released for public consumption

Government Agencies

Government agencies, like other organizations, often have tremendous informational resources that would be of benefit to employees, but the sheer size of these agencies and the number of employees make dissemination of this information very inefficient and ineffective. Also, many agencies have employees who are distributed at various geographic locations, exacerbating the already difficult task of sharing information in a timely manner. Fortunately, Web technologies—especially the implementation of intranets—are beginning to help many agencies address these problems.

Sandia National Labs

Sandia National Labs' intranet gives employees access to a wide variety of information and applications. The goal of Sandia's intranet is to give employees a single virtual source of information. Some of the available information and functionality follow:

- Access to human-resource information such as policy manuals and vacation balances
- Project-management tools, such as database query tools for getting information on procurement expenditures, labor, inventory costs, and other information that historically required managers to obtain administrative support to acquire
- Conference room scheduling for the more than 50 available rooms on the Sandia campus
- Preservation of institutional knowledge through videotaping the departure of senior employees
- Dissemination of a newsletter, bulletins, and administrative information
- Access to engineering and manufacturing data, as well as scientific reports and journals
- Subscription services enabling employees to sign up to receive electronic services

Summary

This introductory chapter provided some fundamental information about the Internet and the World Wide Web in general. You learned what a Web database is and a bit about using intranets to benefit your organization. After learning the benefits that Web application development holds for both developers and users, you saw some examples of how other companies and organizations use Web and intranet technologies to meet their specific information-systems needs.

2

Doing Business on the Web

by Drew Kittel

Today's competitive business environment continually forces businesses to evaluate the means by which they conduct business and the ways in which they can quickly and effectively implement changes in response to competitive pressures and changes in the marketplace. Companies have long recognized that information technologies are effective and essential weapons for fighting these ongoing battles. With the introduction of Web-based technologies in recent months, businesses are dramatically rethinking the ways in which they use information technologies to address their problems.

A tremendous amount of hype and promise surrounds the business use of the Web. It is becoming clear that the Web is causing fundamental changes in the way many traditional business processes are conducted, although the Web is not a panacea or solution to all the problems of all businesses. The Web is a force to be reckoned with and a medium that most businesses need to consider using to some degree.

This chapter discusses many aspects of doing business on the Web and some of the advantages that may be realized. It takes a brief look at which market sectors have been successful in Web-based sales. This is followed by a look at the role databases may play in many Web business applications. Many different business activities can be conducted on the Web, and this chapter presents several possibilities, along with examples of what some businesses are doing today. The final section presents a number of points you should consider when doing business on the Web.

Today's Competitive Business Environment

Doing business in today's increasingly competitive marketplace requires companies to continually review their business processes. Unabated competition means that businesses must find ways to continually improve products and services, cut costs, provide more value to their customers, and effectively grow their customer base. Several competitive factors and pressures come into play for businesses operating in such an environment:

- Companies need to cut costs and improve the productivity of all employees—from clerical workers to highly educated "knowledge workers."
- Changes in organizational structure and the way companies operate are leading to new business models, such as collaborative product development and improved management of supply chains through integration with suppliers. Additionally, virtual stores, companies, and project teams increasingly are becoming commonplace on the Web.
- The rapidly changing marketplace requires that businesses not only respond to these changes effectively, but proactively change the way they do business, knowing that such change is part of today's business landscape. Mass marketing of many products and services may no longer be appropriate, however. Instead, niche marketing and targeting specific market segments often are more effective and efficient.

■ As markets continue to change rapidly, the life cycle of products and services shrinks in response. Astute businesspersons know that the speed at which a product or service gets to market has a direct impact on market share and bottom-line profits. With some products, advertising and introducing new products or services a few weeks before your competition can mean the difference between a gain or loss in profitability and market share.

■ The cost of products and services is no longer the only factor that many of today's customers consider. More of today's consumers are highly educated and demand responsive service, detailed information about your organization and the products and services you offer, and individualized support.

You can use Web-based applications to address many of these factors. Intranet applications such as those discussed in Chapter 1, for example, can provide internal productivity improvements and facilitate information sharing. External Web applications can address the remaining factors—especially those with some degree of interaction with customers and potential customers.

Why Should You Do Business on the Web?

Doing business on the Web is not restricted to the selling of products. As you will see throughout this chapter, doing business encompasses many activities and processes—from marketing surveys to direct sales to post-sales customer support. Bringing many of these business functions to the Internet can result in tremendous benefits to a company as well as to its customers and clients.

So why should your company consider doing business on the Web? The primary reason comes down to maintaining and improving the competitive posture of your business. Although Web technologies and business applications on the Web are still in relative infancy, maintaining a Website has become a service that is expected of businesses. In other words, *not* having a Website has become a determining factor for many customers.

The Web represents a marketplace embodying a number of unique elements that can help a business maintain or enhance its competitiveness and position its target markets:

■ Image enhancement
■ New channel for delivery of products
■ Improved customer services
■ Expansive reach
■ Qualified sales leads

Image Enhancement

Corporate image is an important element of any business's marketing strategy. Websites tailored to project a certain image to a certain clientele are becoming common. These sites may contain a wide spectrum of information related not only to the products and services they provide, but also to the unique qualities and capabilities that separate them from the competition. Some firms post additional information, such as social causes in which they are involved, or their corporate mission, goals, and philosophies. Still other firms choose to cite core capabilities and past performance. A small, high-technology firm may develop a Website that describes the variety of highly technical research and development contracts it has performed successfully, for example, complete with project abstracts that detail corporate capabilities.

Such use of the Web as a public-relations tool is important not only for maintaining a customer base but also for establishing new clientele and attracting top-quality talent to work for you.

New Channel for Delivery of Products

The Web quickly has moved from simply being a tool for public relations and enhancement of corporate image to a whole new means of delivering products and services. No longer are Websites used simply to tout products and to direct (potential) customers to traditional sales channels. Many sites now offer the capability to order products online directly. Some products are available for immediate delivery online as well. Many software vendors, for example, now enable customers to purchase and download registered software. Other companies, such as market-research firms, can provide copies of marketing studies and services online to paying customers.

Improved Customer Services

What do customers want? In addition to low prices, customers demand quality service. Web technologies allow businesses to provide improved "human-in-the-loop" and autonomous services much more effectively. No longer are laborious phone calls required to find technical product information or the answers to many common technical questions. Customers now can find much of this information directly on a vendor's Website—any time of day, any day of the year.

When a customer needs direct support, Web technologies such as e-mail, the Internet, and Intranet applications allow employees to handle and track far greater volumes of trouble and support calls than phone systems alone. Additionally, Web-based systems enable your company to record specific customer preferences and provide more individualized and personalized service.

Customers also want value-added services. Knowing what you have to offer is not enough; they want to know how it will benefit them or get suggestions on which products they can use to best solve their problems. To this end, many companies also provide customers with access to searchable knowledge bases, which include technical white papers, case studies, and suggestions on how particular products may be used.

Expansive Reach

What does *expansive reach* mean? Geography and time no longer are as relevant as they once were. The Web holds potential as a leveling technology and offers many advantages over traditional forms of advertising. Unlike many forms of print, radio, or television advertising, Web advertisements are not limited geographically. You have almost no boundaries on the audience you can reach. Even small companies, which historically had no way to attract business outside their immediate region, now can attract business outside their normal regions—even globally—in a cost-effective way. Whereas traditional forms of advertising are transient, require repetition, and are subject to being ignored by a large part of the target audience, Web advertisements are persistent, comprehensive in content, and have the advantage of many customers actively seeking out the advertisement.

Finally, because of standardization in the base capabilities of major Web browsers in use today, businesses easily can develop applications that customers can use on virtually any type of computer, running virtually any operating system. These applications can be developed without extensive customization or requiring customers to use expensive or proprietary systems.

Qualified Sales Leads

The Web offers a number of services, such as search engines, with which users can locate providers of products and services of interest. Someone interested in specialty products, such as hand-crafted Scandinavian wood furniture, easily can perform a Net search to find out whether and where any vendors of such products exist. What does this mean to a business? Visitors to your Website are coming there for a purpose: They are interested in what you have to offer. These visitors represent highly qualified sales leads and business opportunities. If even a small percentage of these leads results in direct sales, the cost of generating those sales is virtually nonexistent when compared to more traditional (and expensive) methods of sales, such as sending catalogs and direct mailings.

Advantages of Doing Business on the Web

The unique aspects of the Web marketplace translate to a number of advantages for businesses:

- ■ Reduced advertising and public relations costs and improved effectiveness in delivering your message to target audiences.
- ■ A wider audience, larger customer base, and potential for increased market share.

■ Improved customer satisfaction and loyalty through improved services and up-to-date information.

■ Improvements in employee productivity.

■ Reductions in costs because fewer customer support people are needed to handle traditional information publishing, dissemination, and mailings. Improved customer services also translate into a reduction in lost business—an often overlooked aspect of doing business that is difficult to quantify.

■ Reduced sales, advertising, and marketing costs.

■ The capability to measure and track what information and services are most used and valued by your customers. You can use this information as input to marketing strategies and future online services.

■ Reduced costs due to the automation of business processes, instantaneous delivery of information (and some products), and smaller staff requirements.

■ Reduced information processing, handling, and dissemination costs associated with paperwork, publishing, reproducing, mailing, personnel, and delivery times.

What's Hot in Sales on the Web

Several surveys of Web-based sales have come to the same conclusion: Mass market items are not the big sellers today. The current trend is toward purchases of upscale and specialty products and services. The order in which the various market sectors rank can be viewed in two ways. In terms of number of units sold, for example, market sectors can be ranked in roughly this order:

■ High-end computer software

■ Consumer electronics, stereo, and audio products

■ Computer hardware and accessories (especially for business use)

■ Travel-related services

■ Financial services

When viewed in terms of total dollar sales, however, the rankings change somewhat:

■ Real estate

■ Computer hardware and accessories (especially for business use)

■ High-end computer software

■ Travel-related services

■ Consumer electronics, stereo, and audio products

■ Financial services

These products and services reflect the demographics of the primary users on the Web today. It is estimated that affluent, young, professional, well-educated North American men make up roughly two-thirds of worldwide users of the Web today. North American women account for roughly another 20 percent.

Additionally, the amount of goods sold through the Web is projected to increase dramatically during the next few years. During 1995, it is estimated that more than $400 million in worldwide sales transactions occurred on the Web. That figure is projected to grow to more than $45 billion by 1998.

The Role of Databases in Web Business Applications

Web-based business applications enable companies to provide value-added services to their customers. Databases serve an integral role in many applications being developed for customer use and to improve the services provided to them. Some of the uses of databases in Web business applications follow:

- Personalized services can be provided by maintaining customer, supplier, and business partner profiles, needs, and preferences. Regular customers can query for account information, purchasing history, balance due, and so on, for example.

- Technical product information and knowledge bases enable customers to easily search for and obtain product specifications, pricing, suggested uses, and troubleshooting information. Customer support people and sales personnel can use these same informational databases to provide customer assistance.

- Intercompany agreements, transaction rules, accounting information, and purchasing and billing schedules allow automated ordering, purchasing, invoicing, and payment transactions to occur between businesses.

- Site access statistics; customer demographics; sales trends; and tracking by product, region, demography, and so on is possible.

- Inventory information can be used to automatically update offerings of online stores and can be integrated with internal inventory ordering and control systems. Inventory information also can be used to generate personalized online shopping catalogs and virtual stores offering goods that meet certain criteria specified by each shopper.

- Information brokers use databases that allow full content and context-based search capabilities of publications.

What Types of Business Activities Are Conducted?

This section presents a few ways in which businesses are using the Web.

RESOURCE

Numerous resources about Web-based business activities are available on the Internet. The following URLs provide excellent starting points. These sites offer information about Web-based business administration, investment, marketing, and sales, as well as links to additional sites with related information and examples of businesses conducting commerce activities via the Web:

```
http://www.commerce.net
http://www.yahoo.com/Business
http://www.einet.net/galaxy/Business-and-Commerce.html
http://www.oak-ridge.com/topibrp1.html
http://www.directory.net
```

NOTE

If you receive the following message when you try to access a URL, your browser is not configured to handle compressed files:

```
Unknown file type . . . You have started to download a file of type
application/x-compress. Click 'more info' to learn how to extend Navigator's
capabilities.
```

Online Shopping Malls

An increasing number of one-stop shopping Web sites are being developed. Many of these sites charge a fee to give retailers a link from the main Website pages to information specific to the offerings of each vendor. Other sites are more sophisticated and provide interfaces to product databases that allow comprehensive querying about products and the capability to seek out retailers with the lowest-cost items of interest. Figure 2.1 shows one example of an online mall.

Advertising

An increasing number of sites offers businesses (for a fee) the capability to advertise their products, services, giveaways, and special promotions. These electronic billboards are placed where they will be seen by a large number of Web users. This is especially true of the sites that provide Web search capabilities. Figure 2.2 shows advertising on the Open Text Index site. In this case, Internet banking services (another popular Web business) are advertised.

FIGURE 2.1.

An online shopping mall.

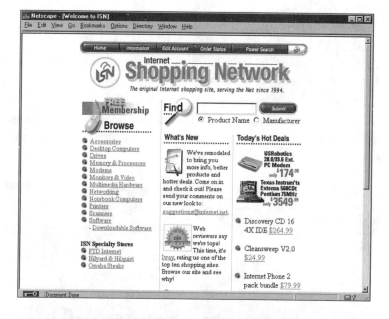

FIGURE 2.2.

Advertising on electronic billboards.

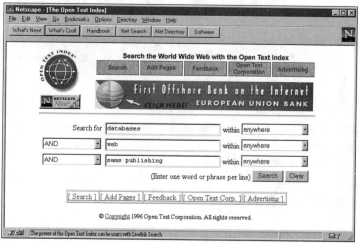

Although some people might view such advertisements as an annoyance, these billboards do serve the purpose of defraying the cost of providing many services, such as Internet search capabilities, at no cost to the user.

Securities Trading

Financial services firms were among the first to realize the potential of the Web. Some firms reported as many as 100,000 site visits in the opening months of operation. In many cases, these visits represented new, highly qualified customer prospects.

Nearly all large firms now have Websites that provide a full spectrum of information and services, from funds information to up-to-the-minute stock quotes, to investing strategies and applications that allow secure online securities trading. Figure 2.3 shows one example of such a site.

FIGURE 2.3.

e.schwab—The Charles Schwab Online Discount Brokerage Services site.

One particularly interesting aspect of the Schwab site is that it was able to leverage from previously developed custom applications and programming interfaces. These were integrated with Web applications to give the company an entirely new marketing channel while protecting its previous investments in custom software technology.

Customer Services

Many firms now provide varying forms of online customer services. Digital Equipment Corporation maintains an online bug-fix and software-patch knowledge base that its customers can tap, for example. This system was implemented at a low cost in a manner of weeks and offers customers a much-needed capability. Additionally, Microsoft Corporation maintains an extensive Website complete with late-breaking product information, free software downloads, white papers, search capabilities, and so on—all of which serve to improve customer satisfaction, build loyalty, and improve corporate image.

Federal Express provides an incredible example of how a very simple customer service application not only improved customer service but also saved the company a bundle of money. Figure 2.4 shows the online package-tracking service on the FedEx Airbill Tracking Website, and Figure 2.5 shows the results of an inquiry about a package.

FIGURE 2.4.

FedEx's package-tracking service.

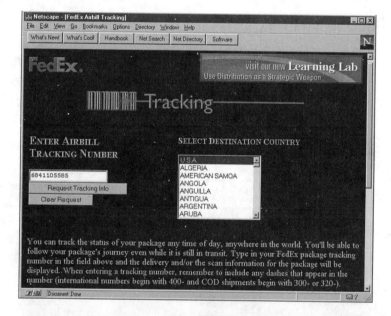

FIGURE 2.5.

The results of a package-tracking inquiry.

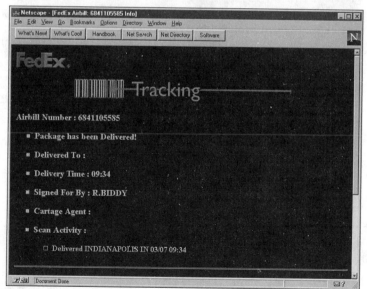

By implementing this service, FedEx improved response time to customer inquiries while decreasing the average cost per toll-free phone inquiry from about $7 to approximately 10 cents. Given the volume of packages FedEx handles yearly, this amounts to savings of hundreds of thousands of dollars with no reduction in service to their customers—a win-win situation.

Information Brokering

Information is a valuable commodity. More and more companies are recognizing this and providing information search-and-retrieval services. Unlike numerous Internet search services, these comprehensive information services are not fully underwritten by advertising and therefore require the user to pay a fee for the service. Figure 2.6 shows the Electric Library, which enables subscribers to comprehensively search hundreds of publications.

FIGURE 2.6.

Information brokering.

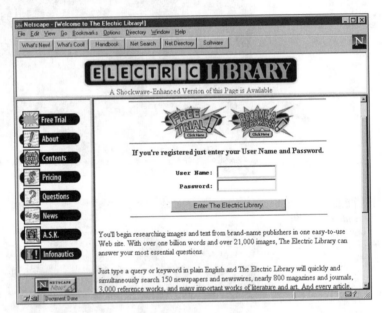

Such services give individuals and organizations near-instantaneous access to information of interest or importance.

Recruitment

Employment agencies abound on the Web today. Typically, these services are free of charge to job seekers and charge a fee to companies that want to post openings. Figure 2.7 shows one of the larger online recruitment services: the Online Career Center.

FIGURE 2.7.
The Online Career Center.

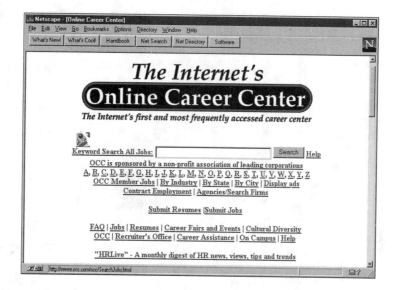

These services offer users comprehensive query capabilities so that they can search databases of regional, national, or international job listings that meet specific criteria such as location, salary, experience levels, educational background requirements, and job title. Many of these sites also give users information on salary surveys, resume writing and interviewing tips, and other information important to job seekers.

Specialized Product Sales

Specialty and niche market products represent some of the premier sales success stories on the Web. One company that has received much attention is Virtual Vineyards; its home page is shown in Figure 2.8.

This is a unique commercial application in several respects. First, it enables shoppers to order a variety of products online. Second, it gives customers a number of information sources and tips on wine selection, available products, and so on. Third, this is one of the first commerce sites developed from the ground up as a database-based application. Using new tools from Sybase (specifically, web.sql), the developers generated user interfaces, forms, and server-side applications to create page content displayed to shoppers and to handle and process customer orders and accounts. And, fourth, this is an instance where transaction security is implemented. Note the unbroken key symbol in the lower-left corner of the figure. This indicates that information passing between the server and the browser is securely encrypted.

FIGURE 2.8.

Virtual Vineyards:
Your Personal Food &
Wine Shop.

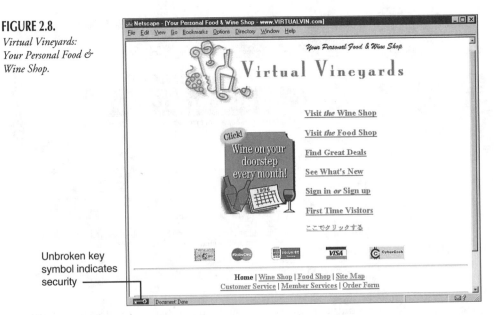

Unbroken key
symbol indicates
security

Real Estate

As stated earlier, surveys have indicated that real estate represents the largest market sector in terms of total dollar volume in sales on the Web. Real-estate listings seem to be a perfect match for the capabilities of the Web. Potential buyers can query property databases to obtain listings of properties in various cities, regions, and neighborhoods. They can limit their search to certain price ranges and requirements, such as number of bedrooms and types of amenities. They can even view a picture of the property—all without ever leaving home or dealing with an agent until they find something of interest. Imagine the amount of trouble this would save anyone faced with moving to another part of the country.

Figures 2.9 through 2.13 show screens from the search-and-listing service available at the Electronic Realty Agency (ERA) Website.

FIGURE 2.9.

Electronic Realty Agency's home page.

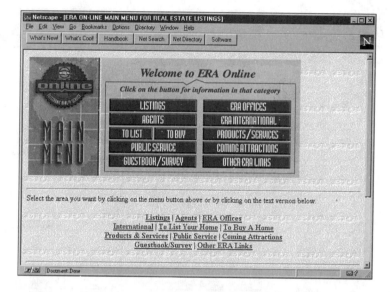

FIGURE 2.10.

Limiting your search to certain states.

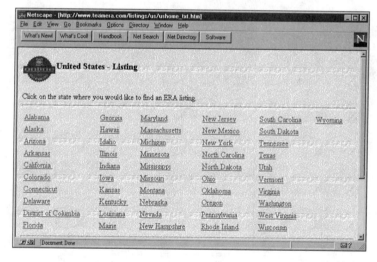

FIGURE 2.11.

Limiting your search to certain cities, property types, and price ranges.

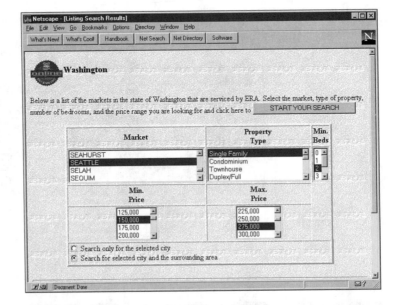

FIGURE 2.12.

A list of hypertext links for each property listing that meets the user's criteria.

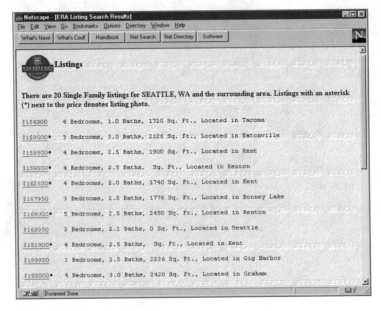

FIGURE 2.13.

The description of a property selected from the list of hypertext links.

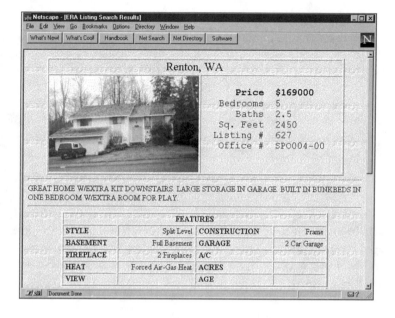

I included this full range of figures from this site to illustrate a couple of points. First, this is another application in which databases and database applications figure prominently in the service rendered to users. The sequence of figures illustrates and embodies many of the fundamental Web database development techniques and methods you will learn in this book. Second, this is an example of a site and application that is well-designed and laid out and is easy and intuitive for the user to operate. Third, the application, although simple to use, employs complex applications that offer the user much utility and value.

Getting Connected

A business can get connected to the Web and establish a Web presence in several ways.

With the rapidly decreasing cost of computer hardware and Web server software, many firms are choosing to host their own Website at their facilities. Doing so requires that your company purchase a leased line connection to the Internet through an *Internet service provider* (ISP).

> **NOTE**
>
> As Web-related hardware and software costs continue to fall, the relative cost of access to the Internet (especially "T1" lines, which are specialized connections that provide very high-speed access) is becoming the more significant cost issue. Depending on

geographical location, the number of Internet providers, telephone companies, and other access providers, such as regional cable companies, can vary greatly. Also, the array of services provided and their costs can vary greatly. The future promises to bring increased competition and reduced Internet access-service costs. But, for the meantime, it's wise to be an informed consumer. Research the various companies vying for your patronage, and carefully select one that provides the best value for the services you require today and may need in the future.

You can purchase hosting services from one of a number of companies that provide Internet connection Website management services. Purchasing these services frees you of the responsibility of maintaining the Web server hardware and software, as well as of security concerns that go along with connecting your facility to the Internet. But turning over your site to be managed by others also can limit the types of applications you can develop to run on their CPU and software (for example, do they have the software development and database management software you need?). This, in turn, limits the capabilities and services you may be able to offer your customers and users.

Considerations When Doing Business on the Web

Some important points for you to consider when doing business on the Web follow:

- Setting up a Website does not guarantee repeat visits or large numbers of sales. Your business must properly identify its target audience and provide information, services, and products that meet their needs. If your competitors have Websites, take a look at those to identify what they are doing well and poorly, and address these issues in your site design. If the site is to be geared toward the sale of products, take a strong look at the demographics of Web users and successful sales sites to see whether your products fall within market sectors with strong sales histories on the Web.

- Users of your site might be concerned with transaction security as well as the security of account information you collect. Your business should be concerned as well. You can take several precautions to protect your information, data, and facilities from prying eyes. Chapters 3, "Client/Server Computing," and 4, "HTTP Server and Browser Components," discuss data transactions, authentication, database integrity, and the implementation of firewalls in greater detail.

- Take a systematic view of potential life-cycle costs. The cost of a Website goes beyond the initial hardware and software purchase. You also must factor in cost of maintenance, programming, development of applications, management of data resources being served, personnel costs, and so on. Currently, cost/benefit trade-off analyses are somewhat controversial. Many industry analysts have been citing much higher than expected startup and operating costs, whereas many companies that have successfully deployed full-fledged Websites indicate average costs far below those put forth by industry analysts. Many companies also have cited a very rapid return on investment due to increased sales or reduced operating costs and higher productivity.

■ Strive to make your site easy to use, understand, and navigate. Page design, form design, data presentation, and navigation should be intuitive and as consistent as possible throughout your site.

■ Select an ISP carefully. Keep in mind that problems it has in keeping you connected reflect negatively on your business and can lead to complaints and lost business. Some factors you should consider when selecting an ISP are security, reliability, availability, performance, how long they have been in business, types of service and bandwidth available (and how they fit your Website needs), domain name services, and customer support. Get references when possible.

■ Provide a means for customer feedback—for example, e-mail addresses for key individuals or departments. Encourage customers to provide suggestions and requests for new and different information and services at your site.

■ Keep track of access to your site. Use page counters and check server access log files to better determine your user base.

■ Make the commitment to keep your site well-maintained and up to date. Solve problems with out-of-date or inaccurate information immediately.

Summary

The primary goal of this chapter was to give you a broad view of conducting business on the Web. You were introduced to issues and uses of technology that might be valuable to your business or organization. Subsequent chapters will discuss in much greater detail the methods and techniques required to develop Web-based business applications.

This chapter began with an overview of the competitive environment businesses face today, including the ever-present need to improve products and services while reducing costs. This was followed by a discussion on why doing business on the Web is such a good idea. Many potential benefits for businesses were discussed, including image enhancement, improved services, increased sales leads, and keeping a competitive edge. Next, you briefly looked at which market sectors have been successful in Web-based sales. Real estate and upscale and specialty goods and services are the big winners in Internet sales.

Databases play a significant role in Web business applications by providing the foundation for information services, customer account information, demographics statistics, product inventory levels, and product specifications. Finally, later sections presented examples of what some businesses are currently doing on the Web today and some important points a business should consider when conducting business on the Web.

Architectural Overview

3

Client/Server Computing

by Mark Swank

In its broadest sense, *client/server computing* can be described as the decentralization and redistribution of information technologies. The development of the client/server architecture was fueled by the introduction of *local area network* (LAN) technologies to the workplace. Research in the area of new LAN technologies originally was driven by the need to share resources, such as printers and magnetic storage, to reduce the relatively high cost of computer peripherals. As LAN technologies became more advanced, communications applications, such as electronic mail, extended the benefits of resource sharing on LANs to distributed, shared business applications and information.

Today, the client/server model of computing has given rise to business, scientific, and a variety of other applications that rely heavily on server-based processing. Individual users no longer require the massive computer technologies and processing power once needed to access huge data warehouses. The success and acceptance of the Web, intranets, and the Internet, for example, can be directly attributed to client/server technologies that enable both business and home users with desktop computers to access vast amounts of information.

Through the use of client/server technologies, corporate resources now can merge *online transaction processing* (OLTP), decision-support systems, intranet applications, and office automation tasks into a single environment. This mix of transactions results in a more complex information technology environment.

A Client/Server Overview

Client/server computing has been described as a logical extension of modular programming. The fundamental assumption of modular programming is that a large, complex piece of software can be separated into a set of constituent modules, each of which is designed to perform a limited set of functions very well. Each module then is invoked as part of a main program. Modular programming results in an environment where software development and maintainability is improved vastly. In a client/server computing model, all these modules do not need to be executed by the same program, and each part of the application doesn't need to execute on the same machine. Instead, an application can request that some processing occur by another process or program. In this kind of client/server computing environment, the process or program that requests a service is considered the *client*, whereas the process or program that provides a service is considered the *server*.

Taking this approach one step further, the client and server processes can be *distributed*. In other words, the processes can run on separate and dissimilar machines, each of which may run different software and operating systems. Many commercial and governmental organizations are using the client/server technologies to provide both intranet and Internet access to their vast amounts of information. A *relational database management system* (RDBMS) could be running on a UNIX server in California, while a Windows-based application that queries the database could be running on a user's desktop computer in Tokyo. The details of accessing a database system across the Pacific are abstracted to the user in Japan. The user might know that the database does not reside locally, but he doesn't need to worry about it; the client application takes care of the server communication details and obtains the requested data. This is part of the power of client/server computing. The method enables users to access computing and informational resources in a way not possible with conventional, non-distributed systems. An idea that began as a useful tool for local networks now works with global networks because of client/server computing.

The Client/Server Model

The client/server model is based on the concept that each application consists of two functional parts: one that initiates communication and another that responds to it. Generally, the process that initiates peer-to-peer communication is considered the *client*, whereas the process that responds to the initial request is considered the *server*. The server waits for incoming communications requests from a client, performs the requested actions for the client, and returns the result to the client. The client then retrieves data from the server.

Many conventional client/server application programs—such as FTP, Telnet, UseNet, *Internet Relay Chat* (IRC), and Mail—helped popularize the Internet and the Web. To perform file transfers, an FTP client process uses the File Transfer Protocol to communicate with an FTP server. To establish an interactive logon, a Telnet client uses the Telnet protocol to communicate with a Telnet server. News-reader programs use the *Network News Transfer Protocol* (NNTP) to communicate with UseNet news servers. IRC clients use the IRC protocol to send and receive messages from an IRC server. And, finally, Internet Mail client applications use the *Simple Mail Transfer Protocol* (SMTP) to communicate with a *Post Office Protocol* (POP) mail server. In each of these applications, the client initiates a connection with a server using the specified protocol, sends a request, and waits for a response. After receipt of the response, the client processes the information and continues its normal processing. Note that, in most cases, the client and server processes exist on separate computing platforms, but this does not always need to be the case. It certainly is possible to Telnet to the machine you currently are logged on to, for example. Although this capability might not be very practical, it does enable you to change the active user account without logging off the machine.

Web servers and browsers use the client/server architecture with the *Hypertext Transport Protocol* (HTTP). The client (browser) process requests a document from the server with a simple mouse click or keystroke, and the server returns the document for display by the browser. Behind the scenes, a client/server application handles all the transactions to request, receive, and process the document. By using event-driven architectures, preprocessing and post-processing can accomplish such tasks as building selection lists based on database queries, user input validation, and dynamic results presentation based on the returned content. The end-user is not required to know what is happening during the processing and most likely cares only that he gets the information requested. This ease of use has resulted in the phenomenal popularity of the WWW.

The Underlying Network

Client/server applications assume that an underlying network structure exists. The existence of this network structure is based on the need of multiple hosts to effectively communicate with each other. A user might access hundreds of Web servers during a single client session, for example. Consider what it would be like if communications on the Internet were not standardized or even reliable. With the number of machines now connected to the Web exceeding 30 million, it's extremely important to have an effective communications network.

Protocols enable client/server processes to communicate and exchange packets of data. Most protocols are based on some form of send-and-receive negotiation. A client might send a request to a server and expect the resulting information or an error message, for example. More advanced protocols include features such as packet identification and error-correction handlers.

The standard protocol used to guarantee reliable communications on the Web is TCP/IP. Before the Web became such a popular medium, TCP/IP was used primarily in UNIX-based networks. Almost all operating systems today support TCP/IP, however. All the latest versions of the Microsoft Windows 95 and NT operating systems include TCP/IP as part of the bundled software, for example. By using the *Serial Line Internet Protocol* (SLIP) and *Point-to-Point Protocol* (PPP), remote users also can use TCP/IP over dial-up phone lines. Most home-based Web users use dial-up communications methods such as SLIP and PPP to access the Web through local Internet service providers.

The TCP/IP protocol is divided into five conceptual layers, as Figure 3.1 shows.

FIGURE 3.1.
Conceptual TCP/IP protocol layers.

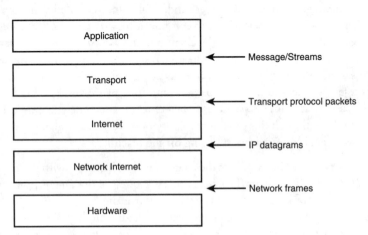

The Hardware Layer

The *hardware* (physical) layer is the lowest layer in the protocol stack. This layer is dependent on the actual physical implementation of the network. The most common hardware implementations usually are Ethernet (Thin Wire Ethernet, Thick Wire Ethernet, FDDI, 10BASE-T, and others) or Token Ring. For Ethernet implementations, the hardware layer uses an address (known as an *Ethernet address*) to uniquely identify each specific hardware component connected on the network. This layer is ultimately responsible for the delivery of network information packets.

The Network Interface Layer

The *network interface* layer is responsible for controlling the network hardware; it maps IP addresses to hardware addresses. Additionally, the network layer encapsulates and transmits outgoing data into standardized packets, and it accepts and de-multiplexes incoming data packets.

The Internet Protocol Layer

The *Internet protocol* (IP) layer sits above the physical layers (hardware and network interface) in the TCP/IP protocol layer stack. Internet *datagrams* are universal packets that resemble the frames of physical networks, and they enable hosts that use different technologies and different frame formats to communicate. The *User Datagram Protocol* (UDP) provides a datagram-oriented service. The IP layer accepts incoming datagrams and determines which module will process the datagram. If the datagram contains a *Transmission Control Protocol* (TCP) segment, for example, it must go to a TCP module for processing; if it contains a UDP segment, it must go to a UDP module for processing.

> **NOTE**
>
> It's important to note that the IP layer is independent of the network hardware. This independence enables the IP layer to encompass different types of networks regardless of how they are implemented physically. The IP layer uses an address (an IP address) to identify host computers and network-enabled peripherals connected to the network. Because the IP layer is not dependent on the underlying hardware layer, it can identify hosts on different physical networks.

The Transport Layer

The *transport* layer uses TCP and is independent of both the physical network and IP layers. After TCP receives a segment, it uses the TCP protocol port numbers to find the connection to which the segment belongs. If the segment contains data, TCP adds the data to a buffer associated with the connection and returns an acknowledgment to the sender. TCP uses this acknowledgment to guarantee reliable datagram delivery.

The Application Layer

At the top of the TCP/IP stack is the *application* layer, where an end user typically interacts. The protocols underlying the application layer are virtually transparent to the user. As a packet of information leaves the application layer, it enters the TCP layer, where a TCP header containing the destination and source port number is added. The packet then enters the IP layer, where an IP header containing a destination and source IP address is added. Next, the network frames are built, and the packet is passed to the hardware layer. Finally, the hardware layer adds its header and the appropriate address information and then sends the packet to its destination. When the packet reaches its destination, each layer removes and decodes its header information and then sends the remainder of the packet on until it reaches the destination application.

Architecture Diagrams

This section presents some architectural diagrams depicting sample intranet and WWW client/server applications.

Figure 3.2 shows an example of a typical intranet application. In this case, the departmental server may be a Web server, database server, or both. The local personal computer terminals in this figure may represent Telnet sessions, *Structured Query Language* (SQL) sessions, or even Web client sessions. Once connected to a server, users can execute protocol transactions supported by the specific server. A client database application can execute data queries, generate reports, and insert or update data in the database, for example.

FIGURE 3.2.

A simple intranet application.

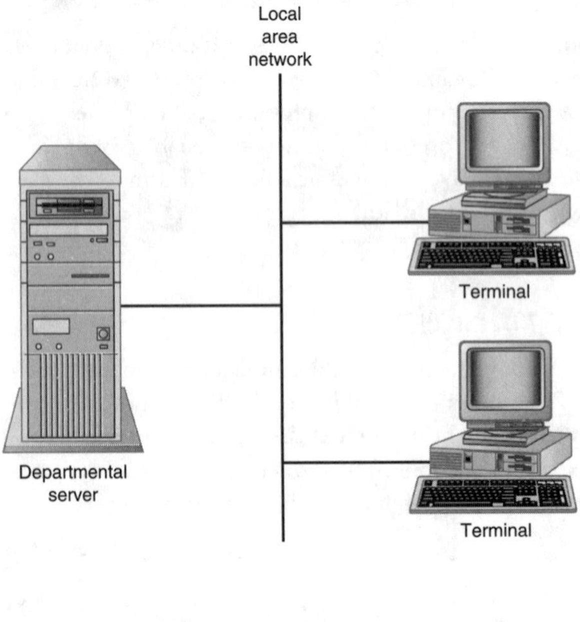

Local area network

Terminal

Terminal

Departmental server

Figure 3.3 takes the example in Figure 3.2 one step further by segmenting the LAN into three smaller LANs: the Administrative LAN, the Sales LAN, and the Technical Support LAN. The network hub (sometimes called a *bridge*) can be used to bridge and segment network traffic. This certainly would be the case in organizations that want to segment their intranet from the Internet. Many organizations today use hardware components that not only include the features available in bridges, but also can handle the routing of network traffic. These types of components sometimes are nicknamed *brouters* because of their capability to perform both the bridging and routing functions.

In this example, the Human Resources group, which probably resides on the Administrative LAN, can post internal job opportunities, healthcare information, and stock dividend data onto the Web Server for corporate employees to access.

FIGURE 3.3.

A corporate intranet application.

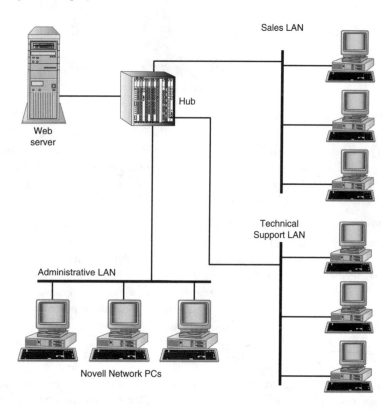

The term *intranet* does not mean that the network is physically internal to a location; it means that the network is internal to an organization and can be geographically distributed, as shown in Figure 3.4.

FIGURE 3.4.

*A corporate WAN
intranet application.*

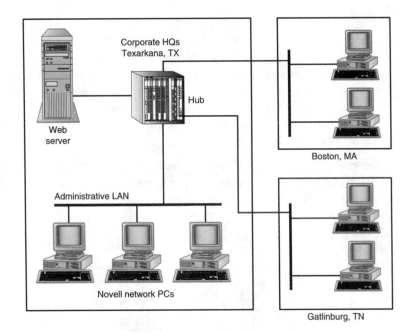

This figure depicts the same scenario as Figure 3.3, except that some branch offices are dispersed across the country and probably are connected with a high-speed connection line. In this example, a sales manager in Gatlinburg still can review corporate postings on the internal Web server just as simply as he can send e-mail to another sales manager in Boston.

Figure 3.5 incorporates Internet connectivity into an intranet LAN. This increases complexities by giving outside users access to the internal network. The figure illustrates the insertion of a security firewall when allowing Internet access. *Firewalls* manage and restrict access based on specified configuration parameters. A firewall can be configured to permit only specified protocol traffic access beyond the firewall point, for example. Firewalls generally are used to restrict the access of external users and to help safeguard the organizational data, resources, and information made available. This information can come in the form of simple marketing material, access to online technical support material, contact phone numbers, e-mail access to company personnel, or, in some cases, Telnet access to organizational computers.

Although enabling Internet access to your site introduces some complexities, it also provides benefits. Company employees who have an ISP can work from home, for example. More and more companies today are acting as internal ISPs for corporate employees by providing dial-up network access. Also, by providing access to online technical-support materials, a company requires fewer technical specialists to work support lines.

FIGURE 3.5.
A corporate WWW application.

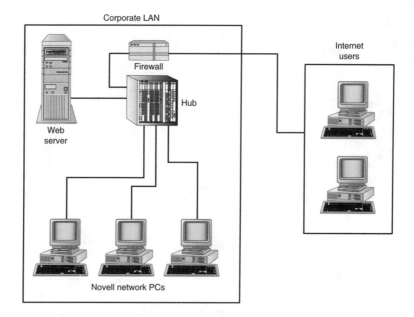

Figure 3.6 illustrates a case where access to the corporate database is provided. Note that no two functional components need to be on the same machine. The Web server can reside in Dallas, the product database in Washington, the sales group in Tokyo; the Internet users can be anywhere in the world. Several client/server applications actually are being used in this environment. The interaction between the Web server and the browser clients, as well as the communications between the Web server and the database server, are examples of client/server applications.

Security Issues

For many organizations, security might best be defined as the safeguarding of corporate resources. These resources can include such things as corporate secrets, computer data, or employee information. Many would argue that knowledge is absolute power. If a competitor knows your organization's weaknesses, it can use that knowledge to your disadvantage. When an organization provides Web access to its network resources, it also increases the potential for misguided intentions. This is why so much emphasis is placed on Web security.

RESOURCE

You can find the World Wide Web Security Frequently Asked Questions (FAQs) at
`http://www-genome.wi.mit.edu/WWW/faqs/www-security-faq.html`.

FIGURE 3.6.
A corporate WWW database application.

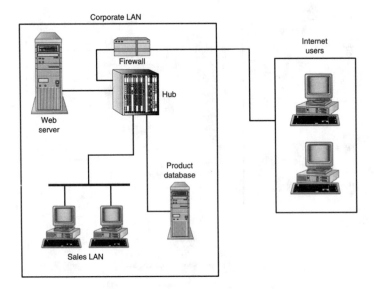

Many levels of security access controls are involved in the operation of a WWW database site. Each level has a specific relationship to the client/server applications that depend on its existence. This section discusses each type of security access control to provide a global view of the security measures that make up the WWW database site. This section is not the only source for security matters related to WWW database development. Hundreds of online resources provide details about security-related matters.

Web Server Security

This section is not intended to discuss the myriad Web server security nuances; entire books sometimes are devoted to the subject. Instead, this section informs you about the types of available security. For a more in-depth look at specific Web server security, check out the numerous online resources available for each of the major Web servers.

In basic HTTP authentication, passwords are passed over the network as uuencoded text. Although this is not human-readable text, anyone with a knowledge of network packets easily can trap and decipher a password. If you've ever attempted to download an HTML document and instead were prompted with a user ID/password dialog box, you've experienced basic HTTP authentication. This topic is covered more fully later in this chapter.

Web browsers, such as Netscape Navigator and Microsoft Internet Explorer, have options for notifying the user when the browser is about to transmit data that is not secure. By default, the dialog box appears every time your browser is about to transmit non-secure data. You can disable this warning by enabling the appropriate checkbox in the dialog box or by using an Options page entry. Figure 3.7 shows the Netscape Navigator Preferences dialog box used to set security options.

FIGURE 3.7.

Netscape Navigator security preferences.

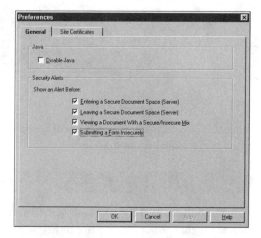

You can disable the use of the Java programming language in your Web browser by enabling the appropriate checkbox.

NOTE

Several security issues related to the use of Java currently are being addressed by Sun Microsystems.

Additional security notifications, such as entering a secure document space, leaving a secure document space, and viewing a document with a secure/nonsecure mix, can be configured in the Security Preferences dialog box.

Figure 3.8 shows the Security Information alert box that warns the user about non-secure data transmission.

Many additional security methods for controlling access to documents on your Web server exist. This section uses the *National Center for Supercomputing Applications* (NCSA) HTTP Web server as the basis for a brief discussion of security features available at the Web server level. The intent of this section is not to give exact details for configuration but to let you know that such security measures exist.

FIGURE 3.8.

*The Netscape
Navigator Security
Information alert box.*

Global Access

Hypertext Transport Protocol Daemon (httpd) global access security is maintained based on the directives contained in a global configuration file.

> **NOTE**
>
> Unless specified otherwise in the global configuration file, the default global access configuration file is `conf/srm.conf`, relative to the Web server root directory.

These directives determine host-level and user-level access to directories in the Web server directory tree. The global access configuration file is read-only when the Web server is started and therefore requires the Web server to be restarted after a modification is made to the configuration file.

Per-Directory Access

Per-directory access configuration enables users with write access permission to set up and configure access to documents they own. Users simply create a document in the directory tree to which they want to control access. This document maintains all the configuration information needed to authenticate hosts, users, and user passwords. This type of configuration does not require root access privileges on the system or write access to the server's primary configuration files. Unlike global-access security, per-directory configuration files are read and parsed for each access. Any modifications made to configuration files are enacted at runtime and are employed during the next file access.

> **CAUTION**
>
> Because per-directory configuration files are read and parsed by the server on each access, a degradation in file-access speeds can occur.

Host Filtering

Host filtering enables specified hosts to access a specified document tree. You can specify host filtering on a global or per-directory basis. Hosts with access are identified in the configuration file by a domain name or IP address.

Suppose that an organization has two separate and distinct environments. The first, a production environment, supports software that is currently in use. The second, a development environment, is used for the development of new software technologies. To control access to the development environment, the Web administrator can use host filtering so that only corporate hosts can access new developments. This configuration still permits corporate access to the secured environment, regardless of the geographic location of the hosts.

User Authentication

User authentication enables you to authenticate usernames and passwords before a user retrieves documents from the Web server. As Figure 3.9 shows, the Username and Password Required dialog box appears in Netscape Navigator when user authentication is specified for a directory structure on the Web server.

FIGURE 3.9.

The Netscape Navigator Username and Password Required dialog box.

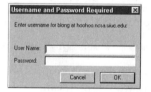

Securing Your Server

Previous sections focused on user security and how to control access to your documents. This section looks at Web server security from a different perspective—that of securing the Web server itself. Although the following examples are not the only possible security holes in your Web server configuration, they are some of the most common.

Control Your Document Domain

One of the nicest features of most Web servers is the capability to search directories. If your server is configured for automatic directory listings, any user has free access to view all documents in your Web document domain. Of course, this assumes that you aren't managing document access on a directory or user level. You might think that is why you have documents in your Web domain—so that users can access them. But what about documents that internal users place in the document root? Temporary files you forget to remove from your document domain can be another potential access risk, because they might contain information about your domain.

Web administrators should closely monitor and manage both domain access and document placement. One method of controlling the document domain is to enforce strict document security so that only the Web administrator can store and modify documents in the Web domain. This might sound a bit harsh, but, for some environments, it might be the only means for ensuring that your Website is safeguarded. Some sites maintain standard operating procedures for the placement of documents on the Web server for public consumption. In many government agencies, this is standard practice to ensure that classified material is not accidentally published. Every piece of information you leave available to hackers is just another piece of the puzzle to them.

Server-Side Includes

Server-Side Includes (SSIs) are specially formatted HTML commands that enable Web authors to accomplish tasks such as including standard document text in all their Web documents, executing CGI scripts (operating system programs that are executed and can return HTML-formatted data), executing operating system commands, and so on.

You can use SSIs to provide a means for reusing code, automatically generating document updates, and time-stamping your documents. Unfortunately, SSIs also have downsides. One is the use of the exec feature, which permits the execution of a program by the Web server.

Here's a sample exec SSI entry:

```
Visitor odometer: <em><!--#exec cgi="/cgi-bin/counter"--></em>
```

In this code, the CGI script /cgi-bin/counter is executed by the Web server, and any resulting text is displayed in place within the document. If /cgi-bin/counter accidentally is configured with world-write permissions (that is, anybody can edit and save the document), however, the file can be changed to execute a remove command that deletes the contents of any file or file system.

Good hackers (if there are such things) can find ways to penetrate your system. One hacker managed to modify a CGI script and have it mail him the password file for the system. Although this procedure is a cut above most hackers, the point is that the moment you connect to the outside world, your system is vulnerable to attack. Turning off the exec form of SSIs makes good sense.

Child Process Execution Privileges

If your Web server is configured to start child processes as the user root, you're more vulnerable than you realize. On such a system, any CGI script executed with root privileges is a major hole in your security, because any user effectively can execute the program with root privileges. Child processes, launched after the server accepts an incoming connection, can be configured to set the effective user ID (`setuid`) to another user. By default, most well-administered Web servers are configured to start child processes as user `nobody` or some other non-root user. Check your server configuration file to ensure that you're not executing child processes as `root`.

Secure Sockets

The *Secure Socket Layer* (SSL) protocol is a security protocol that grants client/server applications the capability to communicate with a secure session over the Internet. As illustrated in Figure 3.10, SSL sits between the transport and application protocol layers and prevents unauthorized eavesdropping, tampering, and message forgery.

FIGURE 3.10.
A Secure Sockets Layer diagram.

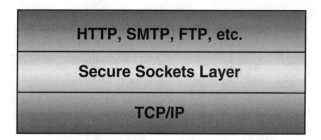

The SSL protocol is used to handle the transmission of secure information between the Web server and the Web client. This security can be in the form of server authentication, data encryption, and message integrity.

> **TIP**
>
> Netscape Navigator users can verify whether they are transmitting data using SSL by looking at the Key icon in the lower-left corner of the browser. If the key is not broken, SSL is being used.

CGI Execution Privileges

Similar to the `exec` feature of a server-side include, CGI scripts are executed by the server process supporting the client request for execution. This doesn't mean that CGI scripts are nonsecure, but that they are a vulnerability that must be monitored closely.

A good practice for Web administrators is to not allow any internal user or developer to generate CGI scripts without first approving them for use prior to implementation. Additionally, only the Web administrator should have write permission to any CGI-executable directory. By following this type of strict CGI execution privilege management, you can more readily circumvent potential problems before they occur.

Transaction Security

Transaction security over the Internet recently has become a hot commodity. Companies are vying intensely for a market share of Internet commerce. Many companies are looking to transaction security to guarantee that personal information (such as credit-card numbers, Social Security numbers, phone numbers, and so on) remains confidential.

One such company, CyberCash, has developed a Secure Internet Payment Service, which uses strong encryption to scramble charge and credit-card transaction information so that it can pass safely over the Internet. CyberCash provides the software free of charge as a service to its customers. Secure Internet Payment Service has been approved for global export by the United States government.

Secure servers are used to manage secure commerce transaction on the Internet. Most secure servers provide advanced security features, such as server authentication, data encryption, data integrity, and user authorization. Secure servers use WWW standards such as HTML, HTTP, HTTPS, CGI, and SSL to communicate with client browsers.

Database Access Control

Database access control is dependent on the *database management system* (DBMS) software in use. Standard database security is inherent to most database platforms. It is implemented with a user ID and password, which are maintained in database files. The user (or process) inputs a user ID and password combination and is provided access privileges granted to that user ID. These access privileges are granted to the user ID by database object owners.

You might wonder how this relates to Web database development. Because you can't possibly provide the entire WWW community with user ID access to your corporate database, you need to find a practical means to accurately and feasibly control database access.

You can use many mechanisms to provide access to your data repository. One of the simplest is the use of gateway software. Gateway software is available commercially for almost all databases. Additionally, some scripting languages (such as Perl) contain support for accessing a database through a defined set of database commands. The output of these commands then can be manipulated to present output in any desired format. Using gateway software, Web developers can maintain greater control over access to your data repository by specifying database accounts to use when accessing the database. A Web application that provides a read-only interface to a database query, for example, can use a database account with read-only privileges. This removes the possibility of accidentally deleting data by disallowing write access. Gateway software is discussed in greater detail in Chapter 6, "Database and Data Repository Access Methods," and Chapter 11, "Developing HTML Forms for Database Access and Application Interfaces."

Firewalls

Firewalls provide another means to secure your client/server environment. Firewall implementations can be in the form of hardware or software, and they easily can be configured so that only traffic that meets specified rules can pass through it. You could configure a firewall to enable all outgoing traffic but allow only incoming Internet e-mail traffic, for example. This doesn't mean that your network is invulnerable to e-mail attack, but it does reduce the chance of attack by limiting resource access from the outside world.

A Host-Based Firewall

A host-based firewall implementation is based on software running on a computer generally dedicated to security. This machine authenticates the transaction before passing it to the destination machine. Although host-based firewalls usually are designed to manage security at the application level, they can be configured to handle security at the network level as well.

A Router-Based Firewall

A router-based firewall implementation bases its security on a screening router hardware device. Screening routers use network data-packet filtering to manage security. This usually is accomplished with a set of rules configured in the router. A router-based firewall can be configured to enable outbound packets (those from the intranet to the Internet) to pass through the router, for example, while implementing filtering on inbound packets to determine whether access is allowed. Figure 3.11 depicts a router-based firewall implementation.

In this figure, the term *gateway* should not be confused with the term *database gateway*. A gateway can be either hardware or software and provides an interface between two or more entities. A database gateway allows a software program to access a database, just as a mail gateway allows external mail users to access internal mail users, for example. The IP provider backbone in Figure 3.11 is simply the organization's link to the remainder of the Internet.

Pretty Good Privacy Program

The *Pretty Good Privacy* (PGP) program, written by Phil Zimmerman, encrypts e-mail and data files. An additional feature of PGP is its capability to add a digital signature to a message without encrypting the signature. If the original message or signature is altered, PGP detects the modification.

PGP uses public key encryption, in which the encryption and decryption keys are different. Because it's impossible to derive one key from the other, the encryption key can be public knowledge. In order to send a PGP message, a user must encrypt the message with the destination user's encryption key. The decryption key itself is encrypted on your computer so that nobody can access your computer to decipher it.

FIGURE 3.11.

A router-based firewall network diagram.

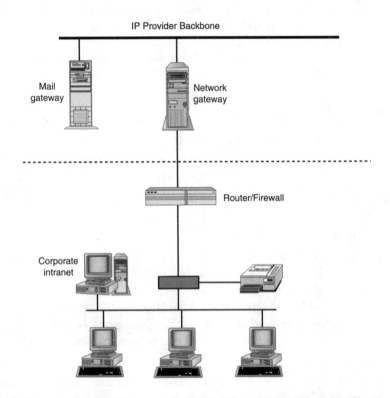

RESOURCE

Information on downloading and configuring PGP is available at
`http://netaccess.on.ca/ugali/crypt/`

Client/Server Benefits

If you ask a group of computer users how client/server computing has benefited them, you'll get a mixed bag of answers. Some will even tell you there are no advantages to client/server computing. After looking more closely at the true savings, though, you'll see that client/server computing has many advantages over mainframe technologies. This section presents a few examples of the benefits you can reap from a client/server environment.

Platform Independence

Platform independence is probably one of the greatest advantages that client/server applications offer. With a standard communications protocol suite, applications can communicate from around the world and from completely different hardware architectures. The capability of Web technologies to be platform independent is most evidenced in the fact that virtually all operating system platforms today include support for Web access. *Information technology* (IT) managers can seamlessly integrate existing hardware and software platforms into Web-based solutions without having to purchase compatible, homogeneous hardware platforms or single-vendor solutions. The client/server model provides a tremendous amount of flexibility and previously unavailable functionality. System designs now can be formulated by selecting the hardware, software, and networking components that best fill an organization's application requirements without having to worry about interoperability.

> **NOTE**
>
> System and network administrators might argue that client/server computing actually makes things worse. There is some truth to their viewpoint. Distributing applications and systems (sometimes across large distances) and using heterogeneous hardware and software platforms can result in a difficult administration task when compared to a centralized system.

Other Resources

As mentioned earlier in this chapter, a primary benefit of client/server computing is the capability to make use of others' computing resources and information. The Internet and WWW are built on the TCP/IP protocol and the huge suite of client/server applications (such as HTTP, FTP, SMTP, NNTP, and so on) that run in a TCP/IP environment. You could argue that it was the Internet that brought about many of the advances in client/server computing, subsequently spawning the WWW phenomenon.

Database applications fit naturally into the client/server model of computing. WWW database applications are a logical extension of the WWW client/server environment. Visual Basic is a well-suited development platform for bringing the WWW and database application development together. A user interacting with an embedded HTML form or Visual Basic application on a WWW browser (a database client) can launch a query to a database server at a location belonging to a different organization, for example. The server responds to the request by interacting with the database management system, formulates a response to the query, formats the response for display on the user's browser, and ships it back to the requesting client.

This book details how to bridge WWW client/server and database client/server environments in a Visual Basic development arena. Given a strong understanding of how these environments operate separately, you can begin to see how powerfully the three technologies complement each other.

Summary

This chapter first presented the client/server model and described the network architecture that underlies client/server computing. Architecture diagrams of intranet, Internet, WWW, and WWW database configurations illustrated the concepts.

The section on security issues focused on some of the key ways to manage security in a client/server database environment. The concept that security must be implemented at several places was introduced, followed by a brief description of security at the Web server level and Secure Socket Layer. You then looked at secure servers and how they aid in electronic commerce security with encrypted data transmissions. A brief explanation of firewalls and database access control followed.

Finally, you examined some of the benefits of client/server computing and learned about the complementary nature of client/server and database technologies.

The next chapter adds to your client/server understanding with a presentation of the WWW components that make up the WWW client/server computing environment. In doing so, it describes some of the application platforms available for both client and server WWW applications; it also covers the features that make up those platforms.

4

HTTP Server and Browser Components

by Mark Swank

The first three chapters of this book focused on using the Web and client/server technologies to access distributed data repositories. This chapter examines a few of the HTTP server and browser components that make up the Web and how they've brought about user-friendly GUI platforms for accessing data.

In the Beginning

Before the creation of the Web, users on the Internet came primarily from scientific and educational fields. Although the Internet was quite functional before GUIs came into being, it still was somewhat complex to use. Most interaction was text-based, but users could access other machines on the Internet in a variety of ways—through command-line programs such as Telnet, FTP, Gopher, WAIS, Veronica, and Mail. To the novice user, though, these interface programs seemed somewhat unfriendly.

When Tim Berners-Lee (credited with creating the WWW) first wrote his "Information Management Proposal" in 1989 and described his dream of a distributed hypertext system (later to become the WWW), this system was based on text-only ASCII files that appeared onscreen as 24 lines by 80 characters. This capability was deemed to be both sufficient and essential for the short term; the addition of graphics was an option. Today, full-fledged GUIs make accessing the vast wealth of data repositories a pleasure.

HTTP Servers

HTTP servers are based on the Hypertext Transport Protocol and provide access to distributed hypermedia documents, applications, and databases. HTTP is a stateless, object-oriented, application-level protocol that has existed since the early days of the WWW global information initiative. Why is HTTP considered a stateless protocol? Probably one of the major shortcomings of HTTP is its inability to maintain application information (sometimes called *state*) across multiple sessions. To overcome this limitation, you have to be creative with your HTML documents to pass state information between them.

HTTP servers operate under a request/response model in which a client establishes a connection with a server and submits a request. The server responds with a status line, including the message's protocol version and a success or error code, followed by a MIME-like message. This section presents a few of the major HTTP server applications available both commercially and as freeware products. (Other Web server resources are presented later in Table 4.1.)

NCSA httpd

NCSA httpd is an HTTP/1.0-compliant Web server credited with being one of the first HTTP servers available. NCSA httpd supports multiple schemes of authentication, including basic

HTTP authentication, MD5 authentication, and Kerberos version 4 and 5 authentication. NCSA httpd software is available in both binary and source form. Although the NCSA httpd software is copyrighted by The Board of Trustees of the University of Illinois, users are granted a license, at no fee, to use the httpd for academic, research, and internal business purposes only.

RESOURCE

The complete set of NCSA httpd documentation is available online in PostScript format at

`http://hoohoo.ncsa.uiuc.edu/docs/Postscript.html`

Additionally, NCSA has put together a pretty good tutorial about the setup and configuration of NCSA httpd. The topics in the tutorial include directory indexing, Server-Side Includes, security, CGI configuration, imagemaps, WAIS index searching, virtual hosting, and "How To" guides describing the latest features in NCSA httpd.

RESOURCE

You can access the NCSA httpd tutorial online at

`http://hoohoo.ncsa.uiuc.edu/docs/tutorials/`

If you're interested in learning about the features of a particular release, NCSA maintains an Upgrading NCSA httpd Web page at

`http://hoohoo.ncsa.uiuc.edu/docs/Upgrade.html`

Here is an NCSA list of precompiled executable platforms for httpd 1.5 (if your platform is not listed, you'll need to compile the source code):

AIX 3.2.5
HP-UX 9.05
IRIX 4.0.5
IRIX 5.3
Linux 1.2.13, libc 5.0.9 ELF
OSF/1 3.0
SunOS 4.1.3/Solaris 1.x
SunOS 5.3/Solaris 2.3 SPARC
SunOS 5.4/Solaris 2.4 x86
SunOS 5.4/Solaris 2.4 SPARC
Ultrix 4.0

RESOURCE

NCSA provides an online, step-by-step approach to compiling httpd source code at
`http://hoohoo.ncsa.uiuc.edu/docs/setup/Compilation.html`

RESOURCE

You can download the latest release and beta releases of the httpd software from the
NCSA httpd home page at
`http://hoohoo.ncsa.uiuc.edu/`

Apache HTTP Server

The Apache HTTP Server is maintained by The Apache Group and is derived from NCSA
httpd 1.3. The Apache software is available free of charge and can be redistributed freely. The
current release includes support for Database Method (DBM) authentication, customized
HTML/CGI responses to server errors, multiple `DirectoryIndex` directives, unlimited numbers of `Alias` and `Redirect` directives, content negotiation, and multihomed servers.

RESOURCE

You can get technical support for the Apache HTTP Server through the following
Usenet newsgroup:
`comp.infosystems.www.servers.unix`

Additionally, the Apache Group maintains a Majordomo List Server to keep users informed of
new bug fixes, security fixes, and general news and information about the Apache Server.

TIP

List servers provide automated e-mail mechanisms to keep subscribers up to date on
information pertinent to the specific list subject content. The mailing list `apache-`
`announce`, for example, contains information about new announcements related to the
Apache Web server.

You can subscribe to the `apache-announce` mailing list by sending an e-mail message to
`majordomo@apache.org` with the words `subscribe apache-announce` in the body of the message.

Here is a list of precompiled executable platforms for Apache Server:

A/UX 3.1
BSDI 1.1
BSDI 2.0
FreeBSD 2.1
HP/UX 9.07
IRIX 5.3
LINUX
NETBSD 1.1
SunOS 4.1.3
SunOS 5.4
Unixware 1.2

RESOURCE

You can download the latest release of the Apache Server software from the Apache HTTP Server Project at

`http://www.apache.org/`

Netscape Servers

Netscape Communications Corporation has designed several different Web servers and server components to support varying business and government needs. An entry-level server such as FastTrack Server is ideal for smaller businesses intending on simply publishing documents. For sites requiring more advanced features, such as security, dynamic web document generation through database queries, and document management, Netscape Enterprise Server is a better choice.

FastTrack Server 2.0

Netscape FastTrack Server 2.0 was designed for businesses that are just getting started on publishing intranet or Internet documents. FastTrack Server not only includes setup wizards, which make it easy to install, but it also includes the Netscape Navigator Gold client product to help you design and implement your Web documents directly on the Web server platform. Versions of FastTrack Server are available for the Windows 95, Windows NT (DEC Alpha only), DEC UNIX, and IBM AIX operating-system platforms. FastTrack Server easily can be upgraded to the more advanced Enterprise Server, making it an ideal stepping stone for any business that wants to get its feet wet in the Web publishing arena.

RESOURCE

For more information on the Netscape FastTrack Server, consult the FastTrack Server home page at

`http://www.netscape.com/comprod/server_central/product/fast_track/`

Enterprise Server

Enterprise Server is Netscape Communications Corporation's most advanced Web server product. Many companies and large government agencies use Enterprise Server because of its support for features such as *Secure Socket Layer* (SSL) 3.0, Java and JavaScript, *Simple Network Management Protocol* (SNMP), client-side certificate support, and document revision control.

RESOURCE

For more information on the Netscape Enterprise Server, consult its home page at

`http://www.netscape.com/comprod/server_central/product/enterprise/index.html`

SuiteSpot

SuiteSpot is Netscape's bundled suite of applications; it brings intranet development and deployment under a single product line. SuiteSpot includes these applications:

- *Catalog Server 1.0:* A search and indexing engine for intranets.
- *Enterprise Server 2.0:* Netscape's high-end Web server.
- *LiveWire Pro:* A Web database development platform for accessing both intranet and Internet databases. LiveWire Pro includes a fully functional version of Informix Online Workgroup SQL Database.
- *Mail Server 2.0:* An SMTP/IMAP/MIME-compliant e-mail server.
- *Netscape AppFoundry:* A source of freely available business applications and development tools.
- *News Server 2.0:* A discussion group server platform much like Usenet News.
- *Proxy Server 2.5:* A server used to replicate and filter the Web content of an intranet or the Internet. It cuts down on network traffic and provides faster response times.

Microsoft IIS 3.0

Microsoft *Internet Information Server* (IIS) 3.0 is a Windows NT-based WWW server that incorporates WWW services, Gopher and FTP services, an Internet Service Manager, an Internet

Database Connector, and the SSL. It also contains client browsers for Windows 3.11, Windows for Workgroups, Windows NT, and Windows 95.

IIS integrates well with the Microsoft BackOffice suite of products and includes the following features:

- Flexible, built-in logging
- Secure IIS administration
- High-performance database access
- Internet Database Connector

Using the Internet Database Connector, you can attach directly to Microsoft SQL Server, Microsoft Access, Oracle, Informix, Sybase, and other *open database connectivity* (ODBC) compliant databases. This built-in feature enables you to take advantage of elements such as stored procedures, triggers, and replication.

Other Web Server Resources

Additional HTTP servers have been ported to most major operating system platforms. Table 4.1 lists some of the Web servers and their platforms. If you're using a platform that isn't listed here, it doesn't mean that you can't run a Web server; it just means that you'll probably have to download the source code to a shareware HTTP server and compile it under your environment. Many shareware servers provide documentation about how to compile the source code.

Table 4.1. Web server resources.

Web Server	Platform	URL
Alibaba	NT 95	http://alibaba.austria.eu.net/
Basis WebServer	95	http://www.idi.oclc.org/html_files/products.htm
CL-HTTP	UNIX 3.1 MAC	http://www.ai.mit.edu/projects/iiip/doc/cl-http/home-page.html
CommerceBuilder	NT 95	http://www.aristosoft.com/ifact/prod1.htm
ConnectionServer	3.1	http://www.ics.raleigh.ibm.com/
EMWAC	NT	http://emwac.ed.ac.uk/html/internet_toolchest/https/CONTENTS.HTM
Fnord	NT 95	http://www.wpi.edu/~bmorin/fnord/

continues

Table 4.1. continued

Web Server	Platform	URL
FolkWebServer	NT 95	http://www.ilar.com/folkweb.htm
GN	UNIX	http://hopf.math.nwu.edu:70/
HP3000	HP	http://jazz.external.hp.com/
Hype-It	DOS	http://cykic.com/
JHTTPD	UNIX	http://cat.ncsa.uiuc.edu/~jwessel/ jhttpd/
MDMA	Solaris	http://sunsite.unc.edu/mdma-release/mdma.html
NaviServer	UNIX NT	http://naviserver.navisoft.com/index.htm
OracleWebServer	UNIX NT	http://www.oracle.com/products/websystem/webserver/ index.html
Plexus httpd	Perl	http://www.earth.com/server/doc/plexus.html
Purveyor	NT 95 VMS Netware	http://www.process.com/
SIAC Webserver	NT 95	http://wwwserver.itl.saic.com/
Spinner	UNIX	http://spinner.infovav.se/
W3C httpd	UNIX NT 95 MAC VMS	http://www.w3.org/hypertext/WWW/Daemon/
WebSite	NT 95	http://website.ora.com/
WN	UNIX	http://hopf.math.nwu.edu/
Zeus	UNIX	http://www.zeus.co.uk/products/server/

CGI and WinCGI

Through CGI scripts, the user (and the browser, for that matter) can interact with the Web server. *CGI scripts* are executable files (such as a DOS batch file, a UNIX shell script, a Perl language script, a C program, and so on) that allow dynamic communications between two applications.

WinCGI allows Windows-based Web servers and applications to communicate by means of INI-like files. The input request text of a WinCGI script is stored in a file by the Web server. The output response from a WinCGI script is stored in a file by the WinCGI script. Because the data stored in WinCGI scripts is INI-like, it can be retrieved with a Win32 API `GetPrivateProfileString` function call. The variables in the file are separated into the following seven sections:

- [Accept]
- [CGI]
- [Extra Headers]
- [Form External]
- [Form Huge]
- [Form Literal]
- [System]

Consider a database application interface to your Web server. As an end user of the application, you want to query and retrieve information as soon as it's available. Through CGI scripts, your Web server can query the database for information that you have requested and build the HTML code results on-the-fly for display on your Web browser.

There's no need to generate the HTML code whenever new documents or data is entered into the database. CGI scripts handle all that for you. You do have to write the CGI script, however. Once written, CGI scripts can provide end users with instant access to database updates. The next section discusses database-accessible CGI scripts more fully.

CGI has many benefits. One of them is that CGI enables existing applications to generate output (standard output, file output, and so on) that can be used as input to an HTML-generating CGI script. You don't need to rewrite existing code to generate HTML output; you simply have a CGI script execute your existing application, retrieve the output from that application, parse the output, and generate the HTML code. Talk about code reusability!

CGI scripts can provide output as simple as a list of users currently logged onto the Web server, or as complex as a system providing dynamically updated stock quotes. One good use of CGI scripts is to dynamically change the presentation of your Web documents each time they're accessed. Your CGI program could easily generate a random number used as an index into a database table of images, for example. Each time the CGI script is executed, a new image is displayed to the end user.

Database Gateway Software

Database gateway software is used to bridge the Web and database server environments. This does not mean that database gateway software uses the HTTP protocol to communicate with the Web server. Instead, it means that a Web server can use, as input for generating HTML-coded text, the output generated by existing database applications. Using gateways enables you to access rich document repositories to generate dynamic HTML output for display in the Web browser.

New Web database developers sometimes think that database gateway software is written in a new database language. This is not true at all. Remember that the Web server can use the output of one process as the input for another. This is also the case with most database gateway software. The output of the database gateway software can be used as input for generating the HTML code delivered to the user's Web browser. Because database gateway software exists in many formats and has existed since the first databases were developed, it's a perfect interface for bridging Web and database environments.

Web Browsers

As you probably already know, *Web browsers* are the end user's front-end interface to the Web. Web browsers communicate with HTTP servers for the transfer of hypermedia documents. This transfer can take place on the same machine (that is, both the Web server and client are co-located), within a *local area network* (LAN), across a *wide-area network* (WAN), and, most commonly, anywhere on the entire Internet.

The Web browser is responsible for receiving input from the end user, initiating document-transfer requests with Web servers, receiving the HTML-coded document from the server, and converting that same document into formatted output for display onscreen. Web browsers exist for virtually every operating system platform and are capable of communicating with all Web servers.

A Web browser's main function is to accept HTML input from a Web server and display the corresponding document based on the HTML tags included in the data. HTML 3.2 tags are discussed in more detail in Chapter 10, "An Overview of HTML 3.2."

HTML documents can contain hyperlinks. When clicked, *hyperlinks* cause the browser to contact the appropriate Web server for the document. Web browsers support predefined levels of HTML specifications. These specifications determine how the browser renders the HTML tags contained in the document. Because of the dynamically changing HTML environment, no two Web browsers support exactly the same levels of HTML conformance.

Just like Web servers, Web browsers come in many flavors and are supported on almost every hardware and software platform. Even though text-only browsers still are supported, most Web browsers provide a graphical front-end interface.

The following sections describe the three major Web browser applications, including some of the advanced features of each browser and features you will find most attractive. A final section presents a table of other Web browsers, the platforms to which they have been ported, and where you can access those products.

NCSA Mosaic

NCSA Mosaic is an Internet information browser and a WWW client developed at the University of Illinois at Urbana-Champaign. NCSA Mosaic was one of the first Web browsers, and it is responsible for the overwhelming support of the HTTP protocol in the WWW community.

NCSA Mosaic is supported on these software platforms:

■ Macintosh

■ Microsoft Windows 3.1, 95, and NT

■ X Window System

RESOURCE

You can download the latest release of NCSA Mosaic, release 2.1, and previous releases of NCSA Mosaic from the NCSA Mosaic FTP Server at
`ftp://ftp.ncsa.uiuc.edu/PC/Windows/Mosaic/`

This section reviews some of the major features available in Mosaic 2.0, as well as some of the features added in Mosaic 2.1.

Collaborative Sessions

NCSA Mosaic collaborative sessions enable a Mosaic client to chat with other Mosaic clients, to link Mosaic sessions with other Mosaic sessions, to send files, and to exchange data with other collaborators. Collaborative sessions work on the client/server principle. Each Mosaic client contains a collaborative client and server that enable communication between the sessions. Mosaic manages collaborative sessions with a Collaborative Session window. Figure 4.1 shows a sample collaborative session.

Advanced Hotlist Manager

Advanced Hotlist Manager provides greater control over an end users' predefined favorite URL entries. These entries, called *hotlists*, can be alphabetized automatically and checked for validity (see the next section, "AutoSurf"). Figure 4.2 shows the default Advanced Hotlist Manager window.

AutoSurf

The AutoSurf feature enables end-users to validate the links of all entries in their hotlist selections. By default, the AutoSurf feature checks the links of the currently loaded document. However, you can execute the AutoSurf feature from the Advanced Hotlist Manager and validate all your hotlist entries, or you can validate entries in a specified hotlist folder. Figure 4.3 shows the NCSA Mosaic AutoSurf Setup dialog box.

FIGURE 4.1.

A sample NCSA Mosaic collaborative session.

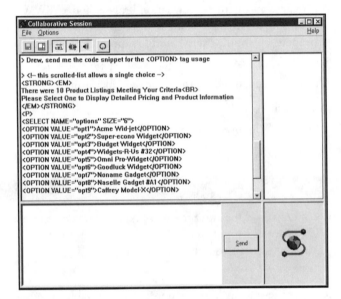

FIGURE 4.2.

The NCSA Mosaic Advanced Hotlist Manager window.

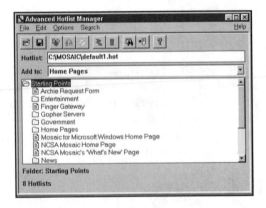

Network Time-Out

Network time-out enables the user to configure the amount of time the Web browser waits (in seconds) for a Web server to accept a connection. The default time-out value is 60 seconds.

Preferences

The Preferences dialog box gives users more flexibility in defining preferences for tasks such as document printing (see Figure 4.4). The Printing tab, for example, enables end users to specify options such as document title, document location, page counts, and date and time stamps that should be generated on the output document. Additional Preferences tabs are available for managing documents, news, directories, and windows preferences.

FIGURE 4.3.

The Mosaic AutoSurf Setup dialog box.

FIGURE 4.4.

The NCSA Mosaic for Windows Preferences dialog box.

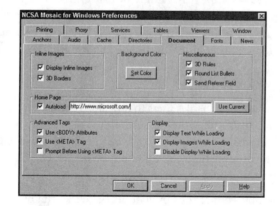

Netscape Navigator

Netscape Navigator is an Internet information browser that enables users to retrieve and view WWW multimedia documents. Netscape Navigator is compatible with NCSA Mosaic and contains additional features not yet available in other Web browsers; it comes in three flavors:

- ■ Netscape Navigator
- ■ Netscape Navigator Gold
- ■ Netscape Navigator Personal Edition

Navigator Gold includes document-editing and management capabilities. Navigator Personal Edition includes setup and configuration for automatic dial-up connections to most of the popular Internet service providers.

This section reviews a few of the major features available in Netscape Navigator 3.0.

RESOURCE

You can download a 90-day trial version of Netscape Navigator from the Netscape Communications home page at

`http://www.netscape.com/comprod/mirror/client_download.html`

Multimedia

Multimedia capabilities are included in Navigator 3.0 through Netscape's LiveAudio, LiveVideo, QuickTime Movie, and Live3D plug-ins. Users can embed standard sound formats such as AIFF, AU, MIDI, and WAV in HTML documents with LiveAudio. Through LiveVideo, Windows 3.1 and Windows 95 users can view embedded or linked AVI movies. The QuickTime plug-in enables Netscape Navigator to display QuickTime animation, music, audio, and video in a Web page while it's still downloading. Live3D provides Navigator 3.0 with 3D support for *Virtual Reality Modeling Language* (VRML) viewing. Interaction with text, images, animation, sound, music, and video are all possible with the Live3D plug-in.

Progressive Rendering

Progressive rendering enables users to download text and images simultaneously. The browser handles this by using multiple connections to the Web server. Each connection requests a different object (image or text). The real benefit of progressive rendering is that it appears to end users that the document is loading faster, because it enables them to see more of the objects and to access some links sooner.

Because multiple connections provide access to the data objects in parallel (rather than one at a time) in the order they appear in the document, however, they also increase the load on the Web server, ultimately slowing down the throughput on each of the multiple-connection sessions. Multiple connections, however, do not significantly affect download speed.

Continuous-Display Scrolling

By using the continuous-display scrolling feature, end-users can view the contents of a document before it fully loads. This capability enables end-users to make a more informed decision, based on whether to continue or terminate the loading process.

Secure Socket Layer

Using the SSL, Netscape Navigator provides security features that offer private communications with certified secure servers. The SSL provides data encryption, server authentication, message integrity, and optional client authentication for a TCP/IP session. Netscape Navigator supports the resource-access method https, which was created for specifying servers that support SSL.

Microsoft Internet Explorer

Internet Explorer is a WWW browser that integrates well with all Microsoft products. Even though Internet Explorer has been available for a shorter time than both Netscape Navigator and NCSA Mosaic, it has proven to be one of the best available Internet browsers. Internet Explorer 3.0 supports all HTML Level 3.2 tags as well as Netscape extensions tags, and even some of Microsoft's own extensions.

Internet Explorer is supported on all Microsoft Windows platforms and is available on the Macintosh platform.

RESOURCE

You can download the Internet Explorer browser from the Microsoft Internet Explorer home page at

`http://www.microsoft.com/ie/default.asp`

Here are a few of the major features available in Microsoft Internet Explorer 3.0:

- Cascading style sheets
- Improved support for plug-ins
- HTML layout control
- Java support with built-in JIT
- Improved JavaScript compatibility
- ActiveX Plug-and-Play controls
- Integrated media support with ActiveMovie
- Updated VRML control
- An improved ActiveX ControlPad
- Floating frames

Other Web Browser Resources

Additional Web browsers have been ported to most major operating system platforms. Table 4.2 lists some of the Web browsers and their platforms.

Table 4.2. Web browser resources.

Web Browser	Platform	URL
Albert	IBM VM/CMS	`ftp://ftp.nerdc.ufl.edu/pub/vm/www/`
Arena	X11	`http://www.w3.org/hypertext/WWW/Arena/`
Candle Web	X11 95	`http://www.candleweb.no/sw/sw.html`
Cello	Win3.1	`http://www.law.cornell.edu/cello/cellotop.html`
EnhancedMosaic	UNIX 95 MAC	`http://www.spyglass.com/products/`
Lynx	UNIX VMS	`http://www.wfbr.edu/dir/lynx/`
NetCruiser	Win3.1 95 NT	`http://www.netcom.com/faq/`
NewtScape	Newton	`http://www.netaxs.com/~weyer/newton/` `newtscape.html`
OmniWeb	Next	`http://www.omnigroup.com/Software/OmniWeb/`
WebExplorer	OS/2	`http://www.raleigh.ibm.com/WebExplorer/`
WebSurfer	Win3.1 95	`http://www.netmanage.com/netmanage/apps/` `websurfer.html`
WinWeb/MacWeb	Win3.1 95 MAC	`http://www.einet.net/tradewave/products/` `browsers.html`

Web Browser Interfaces to E-Mail

Mail support was one of the first neat features of Web browsers. You access Mail support through a dialog box to send e-mail messages to specified e-mail addresses. This address is specified in the HTML code with a hypertext link, identified as a Mailto resource (the Mailto resource is discussed in Chapter 10). After you click the hypertext Mailto link, the Mail dialog box appears. The Mailto resource is a very useful mechanism; end-users can interact directly with Web database developers on topics such as document design and layout suggestions, database-access questions, and general document-access issues.

E-mail interfaces became more advanced, enabling users of *Post Office Protocol* (POP) servers to access remote mail. With the addition of POP support in Web browsers, end users could retrieve e-mail from remote mail servers, organize e-mail documents through folder management from a common desktop environment, and control e-mail setup preferences.

Web Browser Interfaces to Usenet News

Another versatile feature of Web browsers is the integration of Usenet News support. Usenet News is a client/server application environment that uses the *Network News Transfer Protocol* (NNTP) to handle communications between Usenet servers and Usenet clients. Usenet News enables end users such as Web developers to subscribe to newsgroups that contain specific subject-related articles. Whenever a new article is posted to a newsgroup, all end users who subscribe to the newsgroup receive that article. Usenet News is a great way for Web database developers to stay informed about topics pertaining to their specific site requirements.

Previously, Usenet News *readers* (programs that access Usenet servers) consisted of standalone applications that managed Usenet groups and articles for the user. Today, most Web browsers have built-in support for Usenet News, enabling browser end users to access the full range of Usenet services. Support for Usenet News in Web browsers means that end users no longer need to have separate applications open to handle access to Usenet newsgroups.

> **CAUTION**
>
> Applications that support a Usenet News interface maintain a table or list of currently subscribed groups. They also maintain a list of previously read articles within each subscribed group. Because news-reader applications maintain their own tables and lists, the interoperability and management of groups and read articles is lost if different news-reader applications are used.

Netscape Navigator, NCSA Mosaic, and Microsoft Internet Explorer all have the capability to manage Usenet newsgroups and articles. Although the Usenet News interface windows of the three major Web browsers have subtle differences, they all provide the same support.

Table 4.3 lists Usenet newsgroups that offer information and support related to Web database development.

Table 4.3. WWW developer-related Usenet newsgroups.

Category	Newsgroup
Database	`comp.databases`
	`comp.databases.gupta`
	`comp.databases.ibm-db2`

continues

Table 4.3. continued

Category	*Newsgroup*
	comp.databases.informix
	comp.databases.ingres
	comp.databases.ms-access
	comp.databases.ms-sqlserver
	comp.databases.object
	comp.databases.olap
	comp.databases.oracle
	comp.databases.paradox
	comp.databases.pick
	comp.databases.progress
	comp.databases.rdb
	comp.databases.sybase
	comp.databases.theory
	comp.databases.xbase
	comp.databases.xbase.fox
	comp.databases.xbase.misc
WWW authoring	comp.infosystems.www.authoring.cgi
	comp.infosystems.www.authoring.html
	comp.infosystems.www.authoring.images
	comp.infosystems.www.authoring.misc
WWW browsers/servers	comp.infosystems.www.browsers.ms-windows
	comp.infosystems.www.servers.misc
	comp.infosystems.www.servers.ms-windows
	comp.infosystems.www.servers.unix
Programming language	comp.lang.basic.visual.database
	comp.lang.c
	comp.lang.c++
	comp.lang.java
	comp.lang.javascript
	comp.lang.perl.announce
	comp.lang.perl.misc
	comp.lang.perl.modules
	comp.lang.perl.tk
	comp.lang.tcl
Web security	comp.security
	comp.security.announce
	comp.security.firewalls
	comp.security.misc
	comp.security.unix

Bookmarks, Favorites, and Hotlists

Most Web browsers have one feature that enables you to save information on specific documents. In Internet Explorer, this feature is called *favorites*; in Netscape Navigator, it's called *bookmarks*; and, in NCSA Mosaic, it's called *hotlists*. This feature stores document lookup information that can save time when retrieving the document.

Bookmarks, favorites, and hotlists provide a shortcut retrieval mechanism for accessing Web documents. Most URL references in this book are set up by using Netscape bookmarks, for example. Having a readily available resource such as this makes tracking database updates, software updates, and new trends much simpler for Web database developers.

Summary

This chapter described the early specifications for Web browsers and how they eventually migrated into the Web browsers of today. Several of the major Web servers were presented, along with some of the other WWW components that interact with the Web server. You learned about the CGI interface—particularly its method of providing the Web server with a means of using the output from existing applications as the input to HTML generation.

You learned about database gateway software and how it bridges the gap between the WWW and data repositories. You examined some of the most common Web client applications in detail—especially some of the new features in each of those applications. Web browser interface tools that enhance the Web database development environment followed—specifically, the integration of e-mail and Usenet News as means for building a common Web environment.

Finally, you were introduced to bookmarks, hotlists, and favorites to facilitate quicker access to certain online documents.

III

Database Design and SQL

5

Database and Site Design

by Orryn Sledge

Developing a Website requires designing the visual component of the site and possibly a database component as well. For your Website to be successful, you need to have an understanding of these components. To help you further understand these components, this chapter focuses on the following topics:

■ Relational database design and development

■ Website design and development considerations

Relational Database Terminology

Knowing common relational database terminology is useful when designing a database yourself or conversing with your database administrator. The terminology discussed in the following section is common to most relational databases:

■ **Database**—A database is a centralized storage area for the collection and querying of data. Databases are typically organized into logical business components that contain one or more tables.

■ **Table**—A table is used to store data. It is organized in a row/column manner (see Figure 5.1). You can retrieve, modify, and remove data from a table by using the SQL language.

FIGURE 5.1.

An example of a table.

stor_id	stor_name	stor_address	city	state	zip	last_update
7066	Barnum's	567 Pasadena Ave.	Tustin	CA	92789	8/1/1995 4:25 PM
7067	News & Brews	577 First St.	Los Gatos	CA	96745	8/15/1995 3:00 PM
7131	Doc-U-Mat	24-A Avrogado Way	Remulade	WA	98014	3/11/1995 1:00 PM
8042	Bookbeat	679 Carson St.	Portland	CA	89076	4/25/1995 3:00 PM

■ **Row**—A row is a horizontal chunk of data within a table (see Figure 5.2). A row may also be called a *record*.

■ **Column**—A column is vertical chunk of data within a table (see Figure 5.2). A column may also be called a *field*.

FIGURE 5.2.

An example of a row and a column.

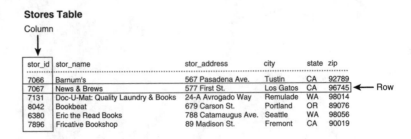

■ **Relationship**—A relationship is a link between tables (see Figure 5.3). Relationships allow flexibility of the presentation and manipulation of data. Data is structured using relationships among data items.

FIGURE 5.3.

Relationships among data items in a relational model.

Stores Table

stor_id	stor_name	stor_address	city	state	zip
7066	Barnum's	567 Pasadena Ave.	Tustin	CA	92789
7067	News & Brews	577 First St.	Los Gatos	CA	96745
7131	Doc-U-Mat: Quality Laundry & Books	24-A Avrogado Way	Remulade	WA	98014
8042	Bookbeat	679 Carson St.	Portland	OR	89076
6380	Eric the Read Books	788 Catamaugus Ave.	Seattle	WA	98056
7896	Fricative Bookshop	89 Madison St.	Fremont	CA	90019

Sales Table

stor_id	ord_num	date	qty	payterms	title_id
7066	QA7442.3	Sep 13 1985 12:00AM	75	On invoice	PS2091
7067	D4482	Sep 14 1985 12:00AM	10	Net 60	PS2091
7131	N914008	Sep 14 1985 12:00AM	20	Net 30	PS2091
7131	N914014	Sep 14 1985 12:00AM	25	Net 30	MC3021
8042	423LL922	Sep 14 1985 12:00AM	15	On invoice	MC3021
8042	423LL930	Sep 14 1985 12:00AM	10	On invoice	BU1032
6380	722a	Sep 13 1985 12:00AM	3	Net 60	PS2091
6380	6871	Sep 14 1985 12:00AM	5	Net 60	BU1032
8042	P723	Mar 11 1988 12:00AM	25	Net 30	BU1111
7896	X999	Feb 21 1988 12:00AM	35	On invoice	BU2075
7896	QQ2299	Oct 28 1987 12:00AM	15	Net 60	BU7832
7896	TQ456	Dec 12 1987 12:00AM	10	Net 60	MC2222
8042	QA879.1	May 22 1987 12:00AM	30	Net 30	PC1035
7066	A2976	May 24 1987 12:00AM	50	Net 30	PC8888
7131	P3087a	May 29 1987 12:00AM	20	Net 60	PS1372
7131	P3087a	May 29 1987 12:00AM	25	Net 60	PS2106
7131	P3087a	May 29 1987 12:00AM	15	Net 60	PS3333
7131	P3087a	May 29 1987 12:00AM	25	Net 60	PS7777
7067	P2121	Jun 15 1987 12:00AM	40	Net 30	TC3218
7067	P2121	Jun 15 1987 12:00AM	20	Net 30	TC4203
7067	P2121	Jun 15 1987 12:00AM	20	Net 30	TC7777

Discounts Table

stor_id	discount
7131	6.7
8042	5.0

■ **Index**—An index is a separate physical database structure created on a table that facilitates faster data retrieval when searching on an indexed column.

■ **Primary key**—A primary key is a single column or the combination of multiple columns that uniquely identifies the row in the table.

■ **Foreign key**—A foreign key is a single column or multiple columns that relate to the primary key in another table. This primary/foreign key relationship is how data is linked among multiple tables.

■ **Rule**—A rule is used to enforce a data constraint. Generally, rules are column-specific and are used to enforce simple business constraints. For example, if you have a business rule that states that all store IDs must be between 1 and 9999, you can create a database rule to enforce this business rule.

■ **Default**—A default is used to populate a column with a value when one is not supplied. For example, if you want the state code in a table to default to PA whenever a new record is added to the table, you can create a default that sets the state code to PA whenever the state code is not specified by the user.

■ **View**—A view is a virtual table that looks like a real table. Views limit the amount of data a user can see and modify. Views can be used to control user access to data and to simplify data presentation. (See Figure 5.4.)

FIGURE 5.4.

An example of a view.

stor_id	stor_name	stor_address	city	state	zip	last_update
7066	Barnum's	567 Pasadena Ave.	Tustin	CA	92789	8/1/1995 4:25 PM
7067	News & Brews	577 First St.	Los Gatos	CA	96745	8/15/1995 3:00 PM
7131	Doc-U-Mat	24-A Avrogado Way	Remulade	WA	98014	3/11/1995 1:00 PM
8042	Bookbeat	679 Carson St.	Portland	CA	89076	4/25/1995 3:00 PM
8100	Johnston	unknown	Fairfax	VA	23294	

Business Rule: End-users can only see the stor_name column

SQL Server Translation: CREATE VIEW end_user_view AS
SELECT stor_name
FROM stores

SELECT * FROM end_user_view

stor_name
Barnum's
News & Brews
Doc-U-Mat
Bookbeat
Johnston

Output from view

■ **Trigger**—A trigger is a user-defined collection of SQL that is automatically executed when an INSERT, DELETE, or UPDATE is executed against a table (see Figure 5.5). Triggers are flexible and powerful, which makes them useful for enforcing business rules, referential integrity, and data integrity. Triggers can be column-, row-, or table-specific.

FIGURE 5.5.

An example of a trigger.

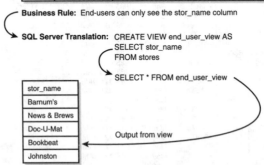

stor_id	stor_name	stor_address	city	state	zip	last_update
7066	Barnum's	567 Pasadena Ave.	Tustin	CA	92789	8/1/1995 4:25 PM
7067	News & Brews	577 First St.	Los Gatos	CA	96745	8/15/1995 3:00 PM
7131	Doc-U-Mat	24-A Avrogado Way	Remulade	WA	98014	3/11/1995 1:00 PM
8042	Bookbeat	679 Carson St.	Portland	CA	89076	4/25/1995 3:00 PM
8100	Johnston	unknown	Fairfax	VA	23294	8/1/1995 1:00 PM

Application Requirement: Every time a record is modified, update the last_update column to reflect the date and time of the modification.

SQL Server Translation:
```
CREATE TRIGGER stores_trigger ON dbo.stores
FOR INSERT, UPDATE
AS
UPDATE stores
SET last_update = GETDATE()
FROM stores, inserted
WHERE stores.stor_id = inserted.stor_id
```

This trigger automatically enters the date and the time of the last modification to the record.

stor_name
Barnum's
News & Brews
Doc-U-Mat
Bookbeat
Johnston

■ **Stored procedure**—A stored procedure is a compiled SQL program (see Figure 5.6). Within a stored procedure, you can embed conditional logic (if/else logic), declare variables, pass parameters, and perform other programming tasks.

FIGURE 5.6.

An example of a stored procedure.

stor_id	stor_name	stor_address	city	state	zip	last_update
7066	Barnum's	567 Pasadena Ave.	Tustin	CA	92789	8/1/1995 4:25 PM
7067	News & Brews	577 First St.	Los Gatos	CA	96745	8/15/1995 3:00 PM
7131	Doc-U-Mat	24-A Avrogado Way	Remulade	WA	98014	3/11/1995 1:00 PM
8042	Bookbeat	679 Carson St.	Portland	CA	89076	4/25/1995 3:00 PM
8100	Johnston	unknown	Fairfax	VA	23294	8/1/1995 1:00 PM

Application Requirement: Store name can be retrieved by passing a parameter to a stored procedure.

SQL Server Translation: CREATE PROCEDURE retrieve_store_name @stor_id integer AS
SELECT stor_name
FROM stores

execute retrieve_store_name 8100

Output from
stored procedure

stor_name
Johnston

Relational Database Design Guidelines

A properly designed database can increase data integrity and simplify data maintenance. To help you better understand how to design a database, the following concepts are discussed in this section:

- Why to normalize a database
- How to normalize a database
- Denormalization

Why Normalize a Database?

The following section briefly discusses why you should normalize a database. If your Website is primarily used to display data and not to modify data, you might not encounter some of the data modification problems discussed in this section.

- **Redundant data**—A normalized database reduces the amount of redundant data stored in a database. This reduces the amount of physical storage required to track data.

- **Inconsistent data**—Since redundant data is reduced in a normalized design, it can reduce the likelihood of inconsistent data. This leads to improved data integrity.

- **Data modification anomalies**—With a normalized design you reduce the risk of data modification anomalies. A data modification anomaly is when you must modify duplicate data in the system. Since you must modify the data more than once, you run the risk of the data not being properly modified throughout the system.

How to Normalize a Database Design

There are three standard normalization rules. After a design successfully passes a rule, it is said to be in # normal form (where the # represents 1st, 2nd, or 3rd). Rules are cumulative. For example, for a design to be in 3rd normal form, it must satisfy the requirements of the 3rd normal form as well as the requirements for 1st and 2nd normal forms.

Technically speaking, there are other types of normalization rules beyond 3rd normal form. However, for most database designs, the first three normal forms are sufficient. You seldom need to apply the other types of normalization. Therefore, this section concentrates only on the 1st, 2nd, and 3rd normal forms of database design.

- **1st normal form**   No repeating groups.
- **2nd normal form**   No nonkey attributes that depend on a portion of the primary key.
- **3rd normal form**   No attributes that depend on other nonkey attributes.

Now that you know the rules regarding normalization, let's apply them to a sample application.

For this application example, suppose that you are tracking training classes taken by each employee. Figure 5.7 contains the data elements tracked by this application. Each employee may have taken 0 or N (zero or many) training classes, and each employee will have 0 or 1 (zero or one) manager.

FIGURE 5.7.

Data elements for the sample design.

employee_id	char(5)
employee_name	char(35)
employee_address	char(35)
employee_city	char(35)
employee_state	char(2)
employee_zip	char(11)
manager_id	char(5)
manager_name	char(35)
training_id1	char(5)
training_description1	char(25)
training_date1	datetime
training_id2	char(5)
training_description2	char(25)
training_date2	datetime
training_id3	char(5)
training_description3	char(25)
training_date3	datetime

1st Normal Form

Look at the `training_id`, `training_description`, and `training_date` attributes in Figure 5.8. See how they are repeated? This violates the concept of 1st normal form: No repeating groups.

FIGURE 5.8.

Repeating groups.

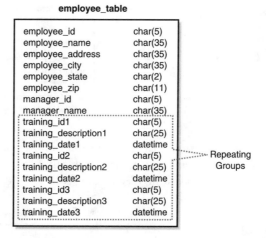

You can move the training information into a separate table called `employee_training` and create a relationship between the `employee` table and the `employee_training` table. Now the table design meets the requirements of 1st normal form. (See Figure 5.9.)

FIGURE 5.9.

Tables that meet the requirements of 1st normal form.

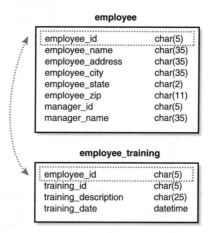

2nd Normal Form

In Figure 5.10, notice how the `training_description` attribute depends only on the `training_id` attribute and not on the `employee_id` attribute in the `employee_training` table. This violates 2nd normal form: No nonkey attributes can depend on a portion of the primary key (the primary key for this table is `employee_id` + `training_id`). This rule is applied only to entities that have compound primary keys (a primary key consisting of more than one attribute).

FIGURE 5.10.

A nonkey attribute depends on a portion of the primary key.

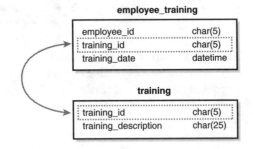

employee_training

employee_id	char(5)
training_id	char(5)
training_description	char(25)
training_date	datetime

training_description is dependent upon
training_id *not* employee_id

You can move the `training_description` attribute into a separate table called `training`. Relate the `training` table to the `employee_training` table through the `training_id` attribute. Now the design satisfies 2nd normal form. (See Figure 5.11.)

FIGURE 5.11.

Tables that meet the requirements of 2nd normal form.

employee_training

employee_id	char(5)
training_id	char(5)
training_date	datetime

training

| training_id | char(5) |
| training_description | char(25) |

3rd Normal Form

Look at the `manager_name` attribute for the `employee` table in Figure 5.12. The primary key for the `employee` table is the `employee_id` attribute. Does the `manager_name` attribute depend on the `employee_id` attribute? No! This violates 3rd normal form: No attributes can depend on other nonkey attributes.

FIGURE 5.12.

An attribute depends on a nonkey attribute.

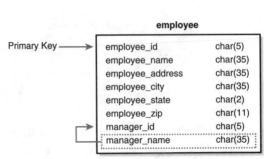

Primary Key ⟶

employee

employee_id	char(5)
employee_name	char(35)
employee_address	char(35)
employee_city	char(35)
employee_state	char(2)
employee_zip	char(11)
manager_id	char(5)
manager_name	char(35)

Manager_name is dependent upon
manager_id and NOT employee_id.

You can move the manager_name attribute into a separate table called manager. The manager table can be related to the employee table through the manager_id attribute. By making this change, the design meets the requirements of 3rd normal form. (See Figure 5.13.)

FIGURE 5.13.

Tables that meet the requirements of 3rd normal form.

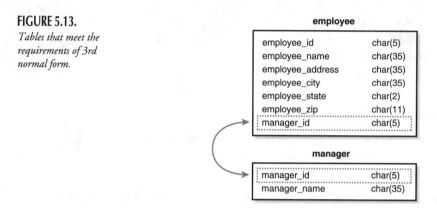

Now you have completed the normalization process (see Figure 5.14). This process helps isolate design flaws that can lead to an awkward and inefficient database design.

FIGURE 5.14.

A normalized database design.

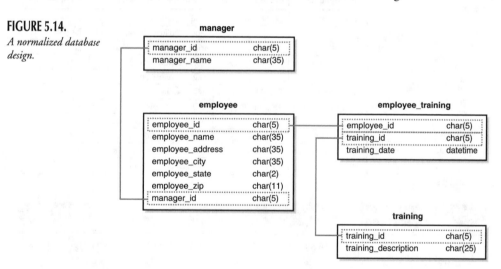

Denormalization

Denormalization means that you are purposely designing your database so that it is *not* in 3rd normal form. This is done to maximize performance or to simplify end-user reporting. Whenever you denormalize a database, you must be willing to forego the benefits gained from the 3rd normal form.

> **NOTE**
>
> I recommend that you start your initial database design in 3rd normal form. If you find that performance problems exist, selectively step back to 2nd or 1st normal form. Keep in mind that when you denormalize a database, you do so for a specific set of application requirements. Future requirements might not need or benefit from past denormalization decisions. In other words, only denormalize when you have to.

Performance

A database design in 3rd normal form may require more table joins to process a query than a design in 2nd or 1st normal form. These additional table joins can be expensive in terms of CPU and disk I/O.

Suppose that you need a report that lists the training classes taken by each employee. (See Figure 5.15.)

FIGURE 5.15.

A sample report.

employee name	manager name	training description	training date
Orryn Sledge	Bill Millen	SQL Server Admin	7/25/95
		PowerBuilder Development	8/25/95
		Introduction To COBOL	3/3/96
Victoria Breault	Chris Champ	Introduction To COBOL	1/1/96
		SQL Server Admin	7/1/96
Mike Sampres	Bill Millen	SQL Server Admin	6/1/96
Fred Humpress	Tina Smith	SQL Server Admin	8/1/96
		Introduction To COBOL	8/15/96
Stan Staples	Tina Smith	SQL Server Admin	8/1/96
		Introduction To COBOL	1/1/96
John Johnson	Tina Smith	SQL Server Admin	8/1/96

> **NOTE**
>
> The examples used in this section are overly simplistic; however, they *do* explain how multitable joins can complicate data processing.
>
> Also, if your Website is used to publish data and not to modify data, a denormalized design may provide better performance and simplify your queries.

To retrieve the data from your fully normalized database, you create the following query, which is a sample query for a fully normalized database:

```
SELECT a.employee_name, d.manager_name, c.training_description,b.training_date
FROM employee a, employee_training b, training c, manager d
WHERE a.emp_id = b.emp_id
 AND b.training_id = c. training_id
 AND a.manager_id = d.manager_id
```

As you can see, this simple report requires four tables to be joined. Assume that each table contains one million rows. Can you imagine the work involved to join four tables, each containing one million rows? You can be assured that performance will suffer.

To maximize performance, you sometimes have to step back to 2nd or 1st normal form. If you denormalized your data into a single table, you can use the following query, which is a sample query for a denormalized database:

```
SELECT employee_name, manager_name, training_description, training_date
FROM training_summary
```

Denormalization Techniques

Following is brief summary of the various techniques you can use to denormalize a database:

- **Duplicate data**—Duplicate data can reduce the number of joins required to process a query, thus reducing CPU and disk I/O usage.

- **Summary data**—Summary data can provide improved query performance by reducing or eliminating the steps required to summarize your data.

- **Horizontal partitioning**—Horizontal partitioning is the splitting of a table into two separate tables at the record level, thus reducing the number of rows per table. (See Figure 5.16.)

- **Vertical partitioning**—Vertical partitioning is the splitting of a table into two separate tables at the column level, thus reducing the number of columns per table. (See Figure 5.17.)

FIGURE 5.16.

Horizontal partitioning.

id	name	favorite_food	favorite_color	shoe_size
111-11-1111	Orryn Sledge	Pizza	Blue	9.5
222-22-2222	Victoria Breault	Ice Cream	Peach	6.0
333-33-3333	Mike Sampres	Pizza	Silver	9.0
444-44-4444	Fred Humpress	Fish	Red	10.0
555-55-5555	Stan Staples	Meat	Red	8.0
666-66-6666	John Johnson	Poultry	Black	9.0
777-77-7777	Mary Douglous	Pizza	White	6.0
888-88-8888	Jack Johnson	Pizza	Blue	10.0
999-99-9999	Jan Smithe	Pizza	Blue	10.0

With horizontal partitioning, a table is split into two tables at the row level. Usually, the split occurs at a predefined key value.

id	name	favorite_food	favorite_color	shoe_size
111-11-1111	Orryn Sledge	Pizza	Blue	9.5
222-22-2222	Victoria Breault	Ice Cream	Peach	6.0
333-33-3333	Mike Sampres	Pizza	Silver	9.0
444-44-4444	Fred Humpress	Fish	Red	10.0
555-55-5555	Stan Staples	Meat	Red	8.0

id	name	favorite_food	favorite_color	shoe_size
666-66-6666	John Johnson	Poultry	Black	9.0
777-77-7777	Mary Douglous	Pizza	White	6.0
888-88-8888	Jack Johnson	Pizza	Blue	10.0
999-99-9999	Jan Smithe	Pizza	Blue	10.0

FIGURE 5.17.

Vertical partitioning.

id	name	favorite_food	favorite_color	shoe size
111-11-1111	Orryn Sledge	Pizza	Blue	9.5
222-22-2222	Victoria Breault	Ice Cream	Peach	6.0
333-33-3333	Mike Sampres	Pizza	Silver	9.0
444-44-4444	Fred Humpress	Fish	Red	10.0
555-55-5555	Stan Staples	Meat	Red	8.0
666-66-6666	John Johnson	Poultry	Black	9.0
777-77-7777	Mary Douglous	Pizza	White	6.0
888-88-8888	Jack Johnson	Pizza	Blue	10.0
999-99-9999	Jan Smithe	Pizza	Blue	10.0

With vertical partitioning, a table is split into two separate tables and joined by a common key.

id	name
111-11-1111	Orryn Sledge
222-22-2222	Victoria Breault
333-33-3333	Mike Sampres
444-44-4444	Fred Humpress
555-55-5555	Stan Staples
666-66-6666	John Johnson
777-77-7777	Mary Douglous
888-88-8888	Jack Johnson
999-99-9999	Jan Smithe

id	favorite_food	favorite_color	shoe size
111-11-1111	Pizza	Blue	9.5
222-22-2222	Ice Cream	Peach	6.0
333-33-3333	Pizza	Silver	9.0
444-44-4444	Fish	Red	10.0
555-55-5555	Meat	Red	8.0
666-66-6666	Poultry	Black	9.0
777-77-7777	Pizza	White	6.0
888-88-8888	Pizza	Blue	10.0
999-99-9999	Pizza	Blue	10.0

Web-Specific Database Design Issues

Designing a Web-specific database is very similar to designing a database prior to the advent of the Internet. However, there are several issues that must be considered when designing Web-specific databases. The following is a brief list of issues relating to Web-specific databases:

- **Performance**—Internet users do not want to have to wait for their queries to process. Any queries that take more than a couple of seconds will probably frustrate the user and possibly cause him or her not to use your Web site. Therefore, you may need to use a denormalized design to achieve acceptable performance.

- **Backup**—The Internet is available 24 hours a day, 7 days a week. Your Website must be continuously available. This can complicate your backup strategy, which can impact your database design. If you choose to denormalize your design, you may increase the physical size of your database, and this can increase the time frame required to back up your database. The longer it takes to back up the system, the longer the database may be unavailable or unresponsive.

- **Replication**—Depending on the type of data your Website displays, you may choose to use replication to facilitate the transfer of information. For example, if you take orders through the Web and you report on your data using non-Web tools, you may want to replicate the information gathered from the Web to non-Web databases. Through replication, you can segment your databases, based on the use of the data.

- **Language**—The Internet is worldwide, which means that your Website may be viewed in foreign countries. Do you need to support multiple languages? If so, this can impact your database design because you need to track data in different languages.

Website Design and Development Considerations

When you design a Website, you are likely to encounter a myriad of problems, obstacles, and technical challenges. It is difficult to offer blanket solutions to these problems. Every site differs in its goals and objectives, the types and amounts of information it intends to serve, the number of users expected, and the composition of the development staff. To offer canned design solutions would be trying to impose a rigid structure on what is inherently a semi-structured activity. Fortunately, however, a variety of considerations and guidelines can aid you in the numerous decisions with which you will be faced.

In this chapter, we step back for a moment to present some issues related to site design. You will find that the material in this chapter does not offer many solutions but instead raises a number of questions—ones you should be asking yourself as you design a new Website or expand the capabilities of an existing site. Our intent is not to provide you with all the answers, but to invoke thought by raising some issues and providing you with the appropriate set of questions you need to answer in order to develop a successful Website.

What Is Design?

The term "design" may conjure up various meanings depending on whether you are an engineer, graphic artist, programmer, systems analyst, or database administrator. However, if you view design as a process, similarities emerge that span all disciplines.

Design entails planning and the conceiving of ideas that address certain needs. In many cases, especially with information systems design, it entails the confluence of many competing issues, the integration of efforts by personnel with multiple technical disciplines and backgrounds, and dealing with the ever-present problems of obtaining sufficient levels of resources to address the tasks at hand.

Looking at design from a system viewpoint requires an all-encompassing look at the system inputs, outputs, environment, processes, work flows, and transformation of inputs to outputs. It necessarily incorporates the contributions and effects of people ("the players") in the system, including end users, developers, managers, and technical staff. Additionally, system design looks at the existing problems (or opportunities), develops requirements and goals to address those problems and opportunities, proposes various alternative methods to implement solutions, and then examines the operational, technical, and economic feasibility of proposed alternative solutions. This entire process may be sequential, may overlap in stages to varying degrees, or may be iterative in nature. Every system design is different to varying degrees, but all incorporate aspects of the same processes.

The Players

Successful Website design and development requires a collective and cohesive effort as well as input from multiple disciplines, internal and external to the organization. Yet, too often, personnel with backgrounds that could contribute significantly to the system design are ignored or bypassed. Manufacturing companies often utilize integrated product development teams when developing a new product for market. These teams are comprised of members from all cognizant business functions and disciplines. The same concept can and should be employed when designing larger Websites. If you involve all persons with a stake in the system early on, the result is generally a better overall design.

This section takes a brief look at the roles played by various people involved in Website design. These roles vary to some degree depending on the size of the site under development and the amount of personnel resources assigned to undertake the development. In some cases, multiple roles may be undertaken by a single individual.

Webmaster

In earlier days, a Webmaster was seen to be the primary developer and maintainer of a Website. The Webmaster was someone with enough knowledge to establish and maintain a server, develop HTML pages, and perform some degree of system administration and handling of security issues. However, the Web is rapidly evolving from Websites that simply maintain static repositories of hypertext documents, to complex sites with extensive interactive services. These interactive services may range from serving documents, to incorporating database applications, to providing informational searches and numerous commercial activities. This has resulted in a division of labor, especially at larger sites.

Many sites now have established Web application teams with members who represent many technical disciplines. Increasingly, it is the role of the Webmaster to lead and manage the activities of the team members. Indeed, the Webmaster is becoming more of a system engineer in many respects and is the person responsible for making the final decisions on many site issues such as development schedules, design and content of documents, software and hardware to be employed, and the document style and programming standards. Of course, these decisions are not made in a vacuum, but rather with the input of the appropriate team members.

End Users and Audience

Your users are arguably the most important component of your Website. Presumably you would not be developing a site if you did not have an existing or potential user base to provide services and information to. In most cases, the users are the reason the Website exists, yet it is amazing how often end users are ignored during the design of systems because the design team feels that they already understand the users' needs.

It is very important to identify your audience and its informational needs. End-user involvement and feedback should be solicited during design (if possible) and after implementation to determine needs and requirements, as well as other issues such as time-sensitivity of information, available data formats, ease of use of applications at the site, and so on.

Web Page Developers

Web page developers are those persons responsible for the development of the more static portions of a Website (that is, HTML documents that are not generated on-the-fly). Although this may include some static forms, it typically entails documents translated from other sources and pages that establish links to other documents or applications.

In the not-too-distant past, coding HTML documents and Web pages required a fair amount of HTML knowledge and skill. With the advent of HTML and Web authoring tools, however, the technical skill level required of Web page developers has decreased dramatically, and nearly anyone with the ability to use a word processor can develop fully functional Web pages.

Programmers

Programmers are playing an increasingly important role in Website design and development. These folks are the ones responsible for extending the range of server-side services that can be provided by the Web server. This is done through the development of CGI programs and the use of gateway software, which allow the integration of other applications. These may include, among other things, the development of relational database applications that can be provided to users. Additionally, programmers are employing tools to improve the functionality of client-side applications. This includes extending the capabilities of Web browsers and applications through the use of Java, VBScript, and technologies such as Microsoft's ActiveX development environment. The ingenious use of these tools by Web programmers is likely to lead to the development of an entirely new generation of interactive Web applications in the very near future.

System Administrator

The system administrator is responsible for maintenance of the system hardware, troubleshooting network problems, backing up system and application data, and upgrading the system software. This person typically has in-depth knowledge of security, networking, and Internet issues as well as some working programming knowledge. Duties may overlap considerably with those of a conventional Webmaster, especially in the areas of Web server installation, configuration, upgrades, and maintenance.

Database Administrator

The database administrator (DBA) is the person responsible for the setup, maintenance, tuning, and backup of system databases. Ensuring the security and integrity of organizational data stores is the primary focus of this individual. Additionally, the DBA is generally consulted on issues regarding database design, performance, applications development, database security, and integration with Web site applications and their potential system impacts.

Site Content versus System Design

Content design deals with all the issues of presenting data and information to your user base. Content design deals with issues such as the following:

- Data types and formats, including text, images, graphics of various formats, and multimedia (such as audio and video)
- The informational content of pages and how pages are laid out
- Database report contents, design, and layout
- The use of colors, fonts, and backgrounds
- Consideration of the capabilities and shortcomings of the users' systems and Web browsers
- Meeting the stated site goals and objectives for providing information
- The design of forms to support interaction with users

Simply put, content design is concerned with *what* is delivered to users and *how* it is presented.

System design, on the other hand, is more concerned with the mechanics of delivering the information and the infrastructure required to make it all happen. It deals with issues such as the following:

- Server hardware and computing platform to be employed
- Web server software capabilities
- Operating systems
- CGI language(s), applications software, freeware tools, and gateway products to be used
- Roles and capabilities of the Website design and development staff
- Type of Internet connection employed
- Database system selected
- System performance goals (such as number of simultaneous users, service times, and so on)

In other words, system design is concerned with *how* information and services are provided.

Is there a relationship between what types of information and services you provide and the system hardware and software you select to provide it? You bet there is, and most of you know this intuitively. However, this relationship is often overlooked during design or upgrade cycles because these activities are not undertaken from a systematic point of view.

The content of pages and the types of services you provide can have a direct impact on the performance of your Web server hardware and software. Conversely, the capabilities of your Web server hardware and software can directly impact the types of services and information you can provide with reasonable levels of performance. As a result, these two facets of site design cannot be considered in isolation.

The remainder of this chapter presents considerations and raises issues that you should consider when designing your site. Although we present these broken down by content and system, we encourage you to continually question how these affect one another.

Site Structure

The structure of a Website depends on several factors. Depending on the types of documents the Web server will service, a site may be configured strictly as a document repository consisting of static HTML-coded documents. Under another scenario, it may be more appropriate to use a more advanced form of document control, such as a database or document-indexing product.

When choosing the type of site structure to use for your site, you also need to consider other areas such as document indexing, searching capabilities, administration, and document-updating capabilities. It would certainly not be feasible to service thousands of online static

HTML documents without having some form of search capability that end users can easily utilize to get direct access to specific document subject criteria. Also, the updating of static HTML documents can quickly become a Web administrator's worst nightmare. In short, you need to select a site structure that can be supported by current administrative resources, includes support for potential future expansion or migration to another site design, and still provides easy document access to your document audience.

System Design Considerations

This section presents numerous considerations and questions that you should ask when creating the system design. Notice that many of the questions flow down from the initial end-user requirements.

Many of the questions and considerations are easily addressable for intranet Websites and applications because these represent a more structured design environment with fewer intangibles about the user base. After all, it is substantially easier to determine the user requirements and to quantify the size of the user base for intranet applications. It is also easier to involve end users in the design process.

Designing a system for external use is a more difficult task. There are numerous unknowns about the desires, needs, and expectations of potential users. It is extremely difficult to quantify the size of the user base, expected usage and repeat frequency, peak periods, and how heavily the site will be used in the future. It also is virtually impossible to determine the amount of lost business or lost repeat visitors that result from a system that performs poorly or addresses inadequately many of the issues associated with page design and content. Still, educated attempts to answer the right set of design-related questions are better than blindly designing the system.

Get a firm idea of the goals and objectives of the system. Who are the end users? What are their informational requirements? What other services are to be provided? Will this require a document-based Website or database applications, or both?

How many end users are there, and is the number quantifiable? What is the expected frequency of site access (both in terms of static HTML documents and database access)? What amounts and types of data will be served? What CGI applications are required to support this, and what is the effect this may have on CPU, memory, and disk requirements? Will a single Internet connection provide the bandwidth necessary to service users during peak times?

Page Content and Layout Tips and Considerations

Hypertext documents differ from traditional print documents in that the relationship between pages and documents is blurred. Therefore, visual identity and navigational aids should be primary considerations. The following is a brief listing of basic page design considerations that you should think about when determining how information and services will be presented and provided to your users:

■ Remember that your site exists for the benefit of end users. Whenever possible, involve your end users to get their feedback regarding page layouts, form design, and page attributes such as color, fonts, and use of graphics. When developing intranet applications, end users may be personally involved, even to the extent of coding some of the HTML used to present pages. For external Web applications, it is not possible to directly involve end users; however, it is wise to give them some means of providing feedback (such as e-mail to the Webmaster) about the site. This allows you to address weaknesses (perceived or real) and to incorporate features desired by a large portion of your user base.

■ Always be cognizant of the effects that images and graphics (types, amounts, and formats) have on performance—both on your ability to serve data in a timely manner and on your users' ability to process the data on their system.

■ The data, information, and services you provide should be the primary focus. The software and hardware tools you employ should facilitate the communication of that information and enhance the way services are delivered.

■ Proper page design implies that data and information are presented with some forethought as to how a user will need to navigate the data returned. Provide navigational aids such as page identifications, button bars, and paging capabilities where appropriate.

■ Consider how certain types of information can be presented for best impact. Should you use a map or graphics generated on-the-fly, or will tabular data suffice?

■ Implement a consistent "look and feel" across all pages of a presentation. Be consistent in your use of layouts, formats, color, font sizes, and page backgrounds. Consider the use of storyboards to lay out the "flow" and structure of linked forms and documents.

■ If your page contains interactive form elements, maintain a logical ordering and grouping of input objects. Also, maintain consistent use of fonts, colors and backgrounds, placement of labels along input objects, and "tab order" of input objects.

Always remember that it is very easy for your message to get lost through misuse of the media. Poorly designed pages can serve to confuse your users and result in the under utilization or discontinued use of services you have to offer. The way a page is designed should enhance the use of the information presented, not obscure it.

Additional information on form design and data presentation is included in Chapter 8, "Using Classes and Objects in Visual Basic 5," and Chapter 9, "Visual Basic 5 Data Access Features," respectively.

> **RESOURCE**
>
> The Yale Center for Advanced Instructional Media (C/AIM) Web site contains a wealth of information on Web page design and data presentation. In particular, it contains the *Web Manual of Style* by Patrick J. Lynch. This manual is an excellent treatise that covers a range of topics including WWW interface design, Website structure, WWW page design, use of links and navigational aids, sample page templates, use of graphics (and effects on performance), and listings of additional resources for Web authoring, graphic interface design, and multimedia. The manual can be found at the following URL:
>
> `http://info.med.yale.edu/caim/manual`

Summary

Much thought must go into the process of designing and implementing a well-rounded Website. Unfortunately, many of the sites in existence today were created during the initial euphoria that resulted from every company and government agency wanting to create a Web presence as fast as possible. Many of these sites are now retrofitting their site configurations to handle expanded capabilities and to avoid exhausted resources and administrative nightmares. A well-planned Website can ease the downstream effects that both future expansion and new technologies will bring to the Web world.

6

Database and Data Repository Access Methods

by Mark Swank

Up to this point, this book has covered information about the technologies that laid the foundation for Web database development. This chapter and the following chapters build on that knowledge by introducing you to the components that provide the mechanism for integrating the Web with existing and new database platforms.

This chapter looks at the components that make up the database and database-access methods used in Web database development. Specifically, the focus is on databases, database-access methods, APIs, and publicly available search engines.

Before you get started, take a step back and look at the broader picture. As World Wide Web usage continues to grow at an astronomical rate, so does the desire to access existing data repositories. Many organizations have yet to realize the potential for using the WWW as an advertising vehicle, a means for providing information, and a communications medium. The drive to be competitive in the market will force businesses to look seriously at the Web and its offerings as solutions to existing needs, though.

The hype surrounding the Web is partly due to the fact that users can access data and information from anywhere in the world. Until recently, this data was almost all static in nature. Now, the capability to generate customized, dynamic data is becoming more commonplace and expected by users. Today, there is a greater need to provide Web access to the vast amounts of information in databases and data repositories. This need drives the ever-expanding realm of Web database access products. Not long ago, no built-in Web capabilities existed among the major database vendors. At that time, Web database developers had to use gateway programs with CGI scripts to integrate their data into Web documents. Today, each of the major database vendors has a new suite of Internet-access products available to bridge the Web database gap.

By looking at the whole picture, you can begin to see where the Web and database environments are moving—toward providing a common environment that guarantees ease of use, interoperability, secure transactions, and information access.

Large Database Systems

The demand for *online transaction processing* (OLTP) applications has grown incrementally over the past few years. From order-entry to real-time decision support, more and more organizations are using large database systems as a solution to the need to maintain and manage large volumes of data. Large database systems can be defined in many ways. This book refers to large database systems generally as being relational databases that are several gigabytes in size and operate in a multiuser environment.

The first thing that comes to mind when somebody mentions the term *large database systems* is a UNIX operating system with a relational database such as Oracle, Sybase, Informix, Ingres, and so on. This is often the case. Many relational databases also exist that operate in non-UNIX environments, however. With the introduction of Microsoft's Windows NT operating system, organizations now can bring large database systems into PC-based server environments. Additionally, many large database systems run under other operating systems such as VMS, AS400, and so on. The remainder of this book focuses primarily on large databases that operate in UNIX and desktop database systems operating under the Windows-NT environment: Oracle7 Universal Server, Sybase SQL Server 11, Microsoft SQL Server, Microsoft Access, and Borland Paradox 7.

Oracle7 Universal Server

Oracle Corporation's Oracle7 Universal Server provides a relational database environment that is both scaleable and reliable. Oracle7's scalability is demonstrated by its support for incrementally expanding networked database resources. Oracle7 Server has a built-in automatic and dynamic self-tuning capability, which can balance the processing workload evenly across your hardware and operating system resources.

Oracle7 Universal Server can be configured with up to six installed options: Context, Messaging, OLTP, Spatial Data, Video, and WebServer. This section briefly addresses some of the main features and options included in Oracle7 Universal Server. Although this is not an all-encompassing list of features, it does cover the features most large Oracle database installations use.

The Context Option

The Context option is a text indexing-and-retrieval system that enables normal text information to be leveraged as easily as normal structured database data. Context is very similar to more common text-indexing engines used on the Internet, and it supports the following features:

- Automatic text reduction
- Automatic classification
- Soundex/Fuzzy matches
- Proximity searches
- Boolean logic
- Multilingual stemming
- Relevance ranking
- Term weighting
- Thesaurus support
- Stop lists

The Context option ideally is suited to be used with the WebServer option for indexing large volumes of data, such as data managed on a Website.

The Messaging Option

The Messaging option is Oracle's groupware competing product built with the intent of leveraging the database technologies in most of the more common organizational tasks. These tasks include e-mail, document management, calendar planning, scheduling, and directory services.

Parallel Architecture

Oracle7's parallel architecture takes advantage of OLTP applications by distributing tasks across multiple processors or machines. For multinode configurations, the Oracle7 Parallel Server option provides a reliable, high-availability environment in which failure of any one node does not result in a loss of data.

The Oracle7 Parallel Query option provides a mechanism for scaling complex, ad hoc queries that run against large amounts of data. Parallel Query takes advantage of scalable architectures and parallel hardware configurations by dividing the query process into manageable subqueries and farming those subqueries out for processing. This allows multinode and multiprocessor environments to share the work load, which increases the speed at which the query can be executed.

Another use of Oracle's parallel architecture is for data and database recovery. Oracle7 can use multiple processes to recover the database or datafiles in parallel, speeding the online recovery. Rollback operations related to any uncommitted transactions are performed in parallel after startup, providing earlier system availability and improved performance.

Query Optimizer

Oracle7 Server has a built-in query optimizer for locating transactional data quickly and efficiently. This optimizer has two configurations: cost-based and rule-based. In the *cost-based* configuration, the optimizer dynamically selects the fastest available access path and satisfies query requests directly from indexes whenever possible. This process is accomplished by using fast, full-table scans, B-tree single-column and concatenated-index scans, clustered (prescanned) tables, and unique row identifiers. In the *rule-based* configuration, the optimizer uses specific rules defined by the developer to access the data. These rules can be in the form of hints to the optimizer. *Hints* enable the developer to help the optimizer determine the fastest access method to use. A hint can tell the optimizer to use a specific index or to perform a full table scan of the data, for example.

Indexing Schemes and Join Methods

Because large data repositories require high-performance access methods to reduce the time required to access vast amounts of data, Oracle7 includes integrated indexing schemes and join methods to deliver query responses quickly. Through the use of bitmapped indexes, Oracle7 Server can deliver dramatic performance benefits in large data repository access applications.

For ad hoc queries, Oracle7 Server can take advantage of hash joins to eliminate the need to perform sorts by using an in-memory hash table constructed at runtime.

High-Availability Features

Oracle7 Parallel Server uses a clustered computer environment to provide a mechanism for ensuring that your data is accessible in the event of a node failure. If a node in the cluster fails, users simply can resume processing by logging onto another operating node.

Oracle7 extends high availability by including an online backup facility, which allows administrators to perform backup activities while the database is running. This task can be accomplished without interrupting transaction processing. If a device fails, resulting in a loss of datafiles, the administrator can recover those lost datafiles to another device while continuing to process requests for data that has not been lost.

Another high-availability feature of Oracle7 is its symmetric replication. Symmetric replication can be used to replicate data from a primary system to one or more alternative systems. Each alternative site is fully accessible and can be used for query access (by using the Parallel Query option).

Read-Only Tablespaces

Oracle7 also supports read-only tablespaces, which save time by eliminating backup and recovery of static data. Organizations with static CD-ROM data archives can access that data as read-only tablespaces, thus reducing the size of their databases and associated database administration.

Sybase SQL Server 11

Sybase SQL Server 11 is much like Oracle7 Universal Server, because it is a client/server RDBMS built to meet the reliability and scalability demands of the most challenging business applications. SQL Server's support for disk mirroring and high-speed backup/restore minimizes the system impact of hardware failure. The Backup Server component of SQL Server assumes the task of handling all backup and restore functions, enabling the server to run ongoing applications.

SQL Server takes advantage of stored procedures and triggers to maintain integrity. When there is a chance for violation of data integrity, the Sybase trigger rolls back the transaction to preserve the integrity of your data. SQL Server meets C2 specifications for level of trust as defined by the National Computer Security Center.

This section briefly addresses some of the main features included in Sybase SQL Server 11. As noted in the "Oracle7 Universal Server" section, this is not an all-encompassing list of features; it is a list of the features that most large database installations use.

Web Access

Sybase's new SQL Server Professional for Windows NT is now Web-enabled with NetImpact Dynamo, which supports a JavaScript superset scripting language. NetImpact not only allows for Web-based database access, but it also provides the tools to create, manage, and maintain dynamic Web documents. NetImpact uses templates to access the database information. These templates are merely HTML documents with embedded SQL statements and/or embedded scripts. NetImpact Dynamo acts as a gateway between the Web server and the database engine by retrieving the requested HTML page; processing the embedded SQL statements against the specified database; and building the resulting HTML file, which the server then sends back to the Web browser.

Scalability

Sybase SQL Server scales easily from a small workgroup (usually fewer than 20 users) to a multiuser (thousands of users) solution. Because a SQL Server implementation is *linear* (the system load is determined by the number of users and the applications in use), organizations can better plan for changing hardware needs.

SQL Server is a multithreaded environment that implements a highly efficient thread manager to manage server sessions. This thread manager runs on top of the native operating system to deliver the highest performance possible. Because each SQL Server user connection requires only 48KB of system memory, system resources such as disk caching and application memory requirements can be extended to achieve maximum throughput.

Adaptable Workload Architecture

Sybase SQL Server efficiently manages both OLTP and decision-support applications through the use of multiple buffer caches, tunable block I/O sizes, and multiple levels of configuration tuning. Multiple buffer caches allow for the fine-tuning and optimization of multiple applications at the same time. Tunable block I/O sizes support bulk loading. Additionally, three levels of configuration tuning permit a high degree of system and application optimization.

Backup and Recovery Support

The Sybase SQL Server Backup Server component provides a mechanism for archiving large databases, while having little impact on overall system performance. Backup Server is optimized to run in environments as large as hundreds of gigabytes and can maintain backup speeds in excess of 50GB per hour.

Sybase SQL Server removes any potential single point of media failure by supporting database mirroring. Database mirroring supports the mirroring of database logs and the database itself. Through the use of Backup Server and database mirroring, Sybase databases of 100GB and larger can remain available and easy to manage.

Performance Features

SQL Server takes advantage of many performance-enhancing features to provide optimum throughput. Backup Server can off-load the dump from the server while supporting online backup, for example. This results in negligible performance impact on running applications. High-speed dump-and-load features enable you to rapidly back up very large databases. Through data partitioning, parallel loads and multiple concurrent inserts can occur simultaneously. Clustered indexes help speed up the update and retrieval of data rows almost as much in a large database as in a small database. Large databases (in excess of 2GB) are addressed in memory, resulting in extremely high performance returns.

Distributed Database Control

Through the programmatic use of *two-phase commit* (2PC), SQL Server ensures the data integrity of distributed applications. Programmatic 2PC provides a more detailed level of control over the transaction by allowing developers to manage errors individually for each transaction instead of leaving error-handling control to the system defaults.

Distributed Database Features

Because stored procedures insulate developers from implementation details, database administrators are given complete autonomy in configuring database objects. Through integrity control, SQL Server can execute transactions even when data is distributed among several servers. Sybase Replication Server enables organizations to use replication features to maintain consistency across a distributed database.

Database Management

Database administrators (DBAs) can define thresholds in the transaction log to initiate automatic log dumps. This feature ensures that the database does not lock up when the transaction log is full. Additionally, DBAs can configure audit trails to inform them of authorized activities. Central control of remote sites reduces manpower needs and gives DBAs greater control over their network environment for tasks such as backing up centrally managed remote databases. A feature of Sybase SQL Server Manager is the capability to manage multiple remote servers from a single location.

Desktop Database Systems

Desktop database systems are broadly defined as database platforms that operate in a user desktop environment such as Microsoft Windows 3.1, Windows 95, or Windows NT. These database systems generally are developed to support platforms for single users and workgroups and include databases such as Microsoft Access, Microsoft SQL Server, Microsoft FoxPro, Borland Paradox, and so on. This section covers Microsoft Access and Borland Paradox 7 desktop database systems.

Microsoft Access

Microsoft Access is a desktop database solution that integrates well with the entire suite of Microsoft Office products. Microsoft Access has many features geared toward the database developer. Some of these features include the use of wizards. *Wizards* are intelligent graphical tools that aid in the design of an application or process. This section examines a few of those wizards and discuss how they round out the Microsoft Access platform.

Database Wizard

The Database Wizard walks the developer through the process of building a new database graphically. To accomplish this, the Database Wizard uses a set of more than 20 standard template databases from which the developer can choose. The template set includes a database for asset tracking, a wine-list database, an order-entry database, and a video-collection database, to name just a few. Each of the standard databases has a default set of tables, which include standard indexing schemes to make the whole process as effortless as possible.

Form and Report Wizards

The Form and Report Wizards enable you to create your own forms and reports by selecting fields from any table in your database. Access even autoformats your form or report for you. You also can specify background pictures for your forms and reports.

Import/Export Wizards

You can use the Import/Export Wizards to help determine the types of data you are about to import or export. Additionally, these wizards help you select the correct field delimiters and data types in the source data. Access runs the Import Spreadsheet Wizard when you import or link text or spreadsheet data. Access runs the Text Export Wizard when you export data to an external file. You can import data from any of the following data sources:

- Microsoft Access
- Microsoft Excel spreadsheet
- Text files
- dBASE III, IV, V
- Microsoft FoxPro, FoxPro 3.0
- Other ODBC databases

Simple Query Wizard

You can use the Simple Query Wizard to create single-table or multiple-table queries based on user input. You also have the option of specifying query criteria such as the order in which the data is returned. One nice feature of Access query definitions is that they can be used as a data source for an application interface widget (similar to the way in which views are used in large database systems).

Table Analyzer Wizard

You can use the Table Analyzer Wizard to normalize your new database (or an existing database). By default, whenever you import text or spreadsheet data using one of the Import Wizards, Access asks whether you want to run the Table Analyzer Wizard against the newly imported data.

User-Level Security Wizard

You can use the User-Level Security Wizard to generate a completely new, secure database. This wizard exports copies of all the objects from the original database, secures the object types by revoking all permissions of the Users group for those objects in the new database, and then encrypts the new database. After running the wizard, you can grant permissions to users and/ or groups at your discretion.

Borland Paradox 7

The Borland Paradox 7 database is a desktop database system that integrates with client/server development environments to produce a scalable database product. With Paradox, you can connect to native high-performance SQL-linked databases such as Oracle, Sybase, Informix, and Microsoft SQL Server. Additionally, Paradox now has support for Microsoft Exchange/ MAPI, which provides an e-mail interface for the distribution of your information.

The Paradox Project Viewer organizes tables, reports, forms, scripts, and queries graphically. You quickly can generate forms and reports with Paradox's Form and Report style sheets.

Through enhanced OLE support, you easily can share information with Microsoft applications that use OLE Automation. Additionally, database developers now can create applications that use OLE custom controls (OCXs), such as the spell checker, spreadsheet controls, and graphic controls included in Paradox 7.

Shareware Database Engines

This section looks at two shareware databases (Postgres95 and Mini SQL) available for downloading on the Internet. Both these products have built-in capabilities for Web server access. In the case of Postgres95, Perl library routines can be used to access the database engine from within a CGI script. Mini SQL includes a w3-mSQL gateway product that handles the Web interface for you (w3-mSQL also is implemented as a CGI). Because functionality and capability vary between the products, this section does not go into too many specifics on either product.

Postgres95

Postgres95 is a relational database that implements an extended subset of ANSI SQL and maintains all the features of its original core product, Postgres 4.2. Postgres95 builds on the original research goals of the Postgres project; it can handle complex objects and rules, and it is highly extensible. Some of Postgres95's standard relational DBMS features follow:

- Concurrency control
- Declarative SQL queries
- Multiuser support
- Object-oriented inheritance
- Query optimization
- Transaction support
- User-defined operators, types, functions, and access methods

Postgres95 uses three separate processes to manage its client/server architecture. The *postmaster* is a daemon process that manages the communications between front-end and back-end processes. It is responsible for managing the allocation of the shared buffer pool and performing additional start-up initialization procedures. The Postgres *back-end database server process* executes client requests (queries, inserts, updates, deletes, and so on). Finally, the *front-end application process* requests a connection to a Postgres back-end through the postmaster. The postmaster starts a new Postgres back-end process for each new front-end client connection.

> **NOTE**
>
> The Postgres back-end process *must* run on the server machine. The front-end process can run on another machine or the same machine as the Postgres back-end process, however.

Postgres95 includes API library routines for C, Tcl, Perl, and Python. The C-library API set (`libpq`) includes routines that permit queries to be passed to the Postgres back-end process for execution. The Tcl API set (`libpgtcl`) includes routines used to create a new Tcl interpreter with commands for building Tcl-based clients. Use of the Perl API set (`pg95perl`) requires Perl 4.036. The Python API set (`PyGres95`) encapsulates its APIs through a Python object-oriented interface.

Mini SQL

Mini SQL (or mSQL) is a lightweight database engine designed with fast access and low memory requirements in mind. Mini SQL supports only a subset of SQL; it does not include features such as views, subqueries, and so on.

The complete Mini SQL package includes a database engine, a monitor program, a database administration program, a schema viewer, and a C-language API. Both the API and the database engine are designed to work in a client/server environment over a TCP/IP network.

The Mini SQL engine (msqld) is implemented as a UNIX daemon process that listens on a well-known port for client connections. Although the msqld process accepts multiple client connections, it is still a single-threaded process that manages client requests in a serialized manner.

Debugging capabilities are built into the Mini SQL engine to facilitate the monitoring of the client requests. Debug support is available through eight separate modules and can be enabled at runtime by an environment variable (MINERVA_DEBUG). You can set multiple levels of debug by separating them with a colon:

```
C-shell syntax       setenv MINERVA_DEBUG cache:key:mmap:query
Korn-shell syntax    MINERVA_DEBUG="cache:key:mmap:query";export MINERVA_DEBUG
```

Table 6.1 lists the eight available debug modules.

Table 6.1. Mini SQL debug modules.

Module	Displays
cache	Table-cache messages
error	Error messages
general	Messages not included in other modules
key	Key-based, data-lookup messages
malloc	Memory-allocation messages
mmap	Memory-mapped region messages
query	All queries before execution
trace	A call trace of all functions

To access Mini SQL databases from the Web, you can use the mSQL gateway w3-mSQL. See the "Database Gateways" section later in this chapter for a more detailed look at w3-mSQL.

Commercially Available Database/Web Products

Commercial built-in Web database interface products only recently have been announced. Developers can use these products to enter SQL commands directly into HTML files for the Web server to process. Usually, the Web server must be a by-product of the database, because no HTML standard allows for the insertion of SQL commands in structured HTML code. Because of the increasing focus on Web database products, though, it is my opinion that developers soon will see HTML standards for supporting ANSI SQL access through HTML tags.

This section discusses a few of the database Web products available today and the ways in which they integrate with the Web applications.

Oracle WebServer 2.1

Oracle WebServer 2.1 is a scalable Web server platform that provides the capability to build secure and dynamic Websites. A high-performance, advanced security and native database connectivity platform is built into WebServer 2.1, which enables Web database developers to create powerful Web database applications using industry-standard development tools. WebServer 2.1 takes standard HTTP servers one step further by integrating information server and management capabilities into a single environment. With WebServer 2.1, there is no need to bridge the Web and database environments with database gateway products.

Additional features of Oracle WebServer 2.1 include a high-performance and extensible architecture, end-to-end security, secure commerce, authentication and encryption capabilities, and Java capabilities on the server. Oracle has scheduled a new release of Oracle WebServer 3.0 for sometime during the 1st quarter of 1997.

This section covers some of the key components of Oracle WebServer 2.1 and how you can best use them in a Web database developer environment.

Web Server and Database Connectivity

A high-performance system called the Web Request Broker is built into Oracle WebServer 2.1. Web Request Broker links Oracle's WebServer to applications, databases, and even other HTTP listeners. Web Request Broker replaces the need for CGI scripts to access the database server as well as the need for CGI scripts, which tend to be resource-intensive processes. Through Web Request Broker, a high-performance native Oracle7 Server connection is established, which enables WebServer 2.1 to deliver relational, text, audio, video, and spatial data through standard Web browsers.

Security for Intranets and Internets

WebServer 2.1 supports the Secure Socket Layer 2.0 security standard for encrypting data between the browser and WebServer process. WebServer 2.1 also supports basic and digest authentication to prevent unauthorized access to Web server documents. By using SSL, WebServer 2.1 can securely pass encrypted data through industry-leading firewall products.

Standard database security features are common to all Oracle7 products and are built into the WebServer 2.1 Server through Oracle's Secure Network Services. These features provide a comprehensive security environment for the corporate network. Secure Network Services incorporates leading encryption capabilities and advanced systems for authenticating users and ensuring data integrity.

Open Web Development Architecture

The Web Request Broker ensures the interoperability of applications written in different languages and residing on different Web servers by providing an open API for building server objects. Web Request Broker supports development in Java, PL/SQL, C, and C++. An integrated Java runtime environment is built into Oracle WebServer 2.1; this environment includes extensions for Oracle7 that effectively enable developers to implement dynamic Web applications using native Java classes on the server.

PL/SQL Agent

In the previous release of Oracle WebServer, PL/SQL requests were handled by a process called the Oracle Web Agent. This enabled data-driven Web applications to be implemented by using PL/SQL—Oracle's procedural development environment. In WebServer 2.1, a new process called the PL/SQL Agent is used for translating and dispatching client PL/SQL requests directly to the Oracle7 Server. Listing 6.1 shows an example of a PL/SQL agent request.

Listing 6.1. A PL/SQL agent request.

```
create procedure emp_query as
cursor emp_cursor is select * from emp order by empno;
begin
   htp.htitle('Employee Update Form');
   htp.formOpen('/cgi-bin/ora/get_emp_info');
   htp.print('Select Employee');
   htp.formSelectOpen('emp_name');
   for emp in emp_cursor loop
      htp.formSelectOption(to_char(emp.fullname));
   end loop;
   htp.formSelectClose;
   htp.formSubmit('Query Database');
   htp.formClose;
end;
```

If it looks pretty intuitive, that's because it is.

LiveHTML Interpreter

WebServer 2.1 uses a LiveHTML Interpreter to enable developers to use *Server-Side Includes*, which are mechanisms that extend the capability of HTML pages by making callouts to applications and back-end servers.

WebServer System Manager

WebServer System Manager is a fully configurable tool for managing components of the Oracle WebServer 2.1 system. Web System Manager uses a collection of HTML forms and online, context-sensitive help facilities to quickly configure the Oracle WebServer.

Sybase Web.SQL

Web.SQL is a Sybase database interface product that creates transparent server-side extensions to HTML, allows both static and dynamic HTML to be mixed within a single HTML page, and allows for the creation of static templates that can be updated continuously with new content. Web.SQL supports inline SQL and Perl scripting calls and improves integration between Web servers and databases by decreasing the number of Web documents the Web server must manage.

Web.SQL includes support for native *Netscape Server API* (NSAPI) calls and offers scalability to support increasing Web traffic by maintaining open database connections to improve response time and lower system overhead.

RESOURCE

You can find additional information on Sybase's Web.SQL and other Web-based products at
`http://www.sybase.com/`

Data-Access Methods

You can integrate database access with the Web in numerous ways. The method you choose depends on several factors. One factor to consider is the database platform to which you want to provide access. Another factor is the type of access (database/Web server product, CGI scripting language, client APIs, database gateway, and so on) you want to use. Finally, you have to consider the cost of the access method.

Suppose that you want to integrate a Web server with your Oracle database. You might want to choose Oracle's WebServer solution. As mentioned earlier, this feature provides an all-in-one Web server database solution that takes advantage of the specific database-engine technologies to provide the fastest access to structured data. However, products such as these do not come free (unless you're talking about a Microsoft product such as IIS... just kidding, Bill!).

Major database vendors recognize the market for Web database integration and will continue to build on their core Internet technologies in the months to come. For users of large databases who have spent thousands of dollars on their database engine and supporting products, it might be more economical to choose such a solution. For organizations not willing to spend the big dollars on Web database-integration products, however, many gateway tools are available today. This section focuses on those types of access methods.

SQL and ODBC Access Products

Many products provide a Web server interface to *open database connectivity* (ODBC) compliant databases. This feature can be very advantageous, because ODBC drivers exist for all the major database vendors (Oracle, Sybase, Informix, Access, SQL Server, and so on).

Consider a situation in which a Web administrator has many database sources of information (for example, a Microsoft Access Products database, an Oracle Technical Support database, a Sybase Order-Entry database, and so on), but he wants to provide a WWW single-source database for access by a Web server. This easily could be implemented as a Microsoft Access WWW database that takes advantage of features such as external table imports (to import external data into a Microsoft Access table) and table linking (to access external database tables through ODBC) to provide a single-source view of the Web data.

This section looks at a few Web database interface products that provide SQL and ODBC database interfaces. Later chapters will give specific examples of using an ODBC-compliant database as a WWW, single-source database.

WebDBC 3.0

WebDBC 3.0 is a Web database interface application that enables Web servers to connect to existing SQL and ODBC-compliant databases. WebDBC has built-in support for Microsoft *Internet Server API* (ISAPI), *Netscape Server API* (NSAPI), and other Web server interface APIs.

You can invoke WebDBC by specifying a query URL in an HTML document. You can specify query URLs in one of three ways:

- Using a hypertext URL link
- Using a forms-based submitted URL
- Using a Query tag in a result file

In the case of a forms-based submitted URL, the contents of the form input widgets (textboxes, checkboxes, radio buttons, pop-up menus, and so on) are sent by the Web server to WebDBC for processing. A result file describes the layout of the data returned to the user. Additionally, a result file can generate another form containing a query URL constructed from information extracted from a previous database query. This capability provides a mechanism for constructing more refined database query results.

After the user selects a hypertext link or fills out an associated HTML form, WebDBC queries the specified database and incorporates the result file layout with the database query results to generate the HTML that is sent to the user's browser for rendering. HTML error files can be configured to return a predefined set of error messages that describe an error condition.

RESOURCE

You can find more information and an evaluation copy of WebDBC for Windows NT/95 at

http://www.ndev.com/

WebBase 4.0

WebBase 4.0 is a Web database server that provides access to existing databases and can operate in a standalone mode or with any standard Web server. One feature of WebBase is its capability to allow users to search a database as easily as hypertext is used in a document. WebBase is compatible with many database formats, including these:

- Microsoft SQL Server 4.2 and 6.0
- Microsoft Access 1.*x* and 2.0
- FoxPro database management system 2.0, 2.5, and 2.6
- Microsoft Excel 3.0, 4.0, and 5.0
- Btrieve
- dBASE III, IV
- Paradox 3.*x*, 4.0
- Oracle6, Oracle7
- Standard formatted text files

WebBase supports all features included in HTML Levels 1 and 2, as well as features included in the proposed HTML Level 3.2 specifications. WebBase permits SQL statements to be embedded anywhere in HTML documents and includes a full-featured macro language with standard control flow constructs such as if, case, forRow, forIndex, and so on. Additionally, WebBase includes many built-in functions for handling math, logic, comparisons, string manipulation, and dates. WebBase includes support for user-defined variables, session variables that hold state between pages, and system variables, such as %date%, %browserAddress%, %Netscape%, and so on.

RESOURCE

WebBase is available for Windows 3.1, Word for Windows 3.11 (with Win32s), Windows NT (Intel only), and Windows 95. You can download WebBase 4.0 and get additional information on the product from the product home page at

http://www.webbase.com/

Database Gateways

Database gateways are available for virtually all databases and have been ported to many operating system platforms. Many of these gateways use the interpreted language Perl. Perl is used for scanning arbitrary text files and extracting information from those text files.

> **RESOURCE**
>
> You can find additional information on Perl at
> `http://www.perl.com/perl/`

This section describes a few of the database gateway interfaces used for accessing the majority of the larger database platforms. Specifically, it covers Sybperl, Oraperl, Mini SQL, WDV, and GSQL. Sybperl and Oraperl are both Perl interfaces to the respective database products. WDV and GSQL are implemented through definition files that identify form layouts for queries. mSQL is implemented as a CGI that pre-parses HTML input files to convert `msql` directives into Mini SQL queries. The Mini SQL directive syntax is covered in detail, because it's simple when compared to that of the other gateway products. In a following section, "Other Database Gateway Products," you'll find a listing of additional database gateway interfaces and the platforms for which they have been ported.

Sybperl

Sybperl is a version of Perl that uses the Perl usersubs feature to allow access to Sybase databases. A subset of the Sybase DB-Library APIs has been mapped to Sybperl. In most cases, functions that have been mapped to Sybperl routines are the same as Sybase DB-Library routines unless otherwise noted. Additionally, Sybperl implements a subset of the newer Sybase Client Library API. Client Library is included with Sybase's `OpenClient` libraries as of the release of System 10.

> **RESOURCE**
>
> Sybperl support is available through a list-server mailing list. To subscribe to that list, send an e-mail message to this address:
> `SYBPERL-L@trln.lib.unc.edu`
> Include in the body of the message the text string `subscribe SYBPERL-L`.

Oraperl

Oraperl is a Perl-language interface to Oracle databases. Oraperl is implemented through patches to the Perl 4.*x* release and includes the use of *Oracle Call Interface* (OCI) calls. Although these calls are written specifically for Oracle V6, notes are available on building the Oracle7 version of Oraperl.

> **RESOURCE**
>
> You can find these notes on building the Oracle7 version of Oraperl, as well as the Oraperl distribution, at
> `ftp://ftp.demon.co.uk/pub/perl/db/perl4/oraperl/`

> **NOTE**
>
> The Oraperl community is not nearly as active as the Sybperl community. This is in part due to the fact that both the Sybperl and Oraperl user groups appear to be no longer supported by the parent database companies. This, as you can guess, is because both Oracle and Sybase now have their own Web database products available.

w3-mSQL

w3-mSQL is a World Wide Web database gateway used to access Mini SQL databases. w3-mSQL is implemented as a CGI script and provides full access to mSQL databases by HTML. w3-mSQL provides the capability to embed SQL queries within HTML documents so that data can be retrieved on-the-fly.

The w3-mSQL program is used as a CGI script to which w3-mSQL enhanced documents are passed as arguments. w3-mSQL interprets mSQL document directives in the following form to complete the processing of the document and return the HTML-formatted database data:

```
<! msql command args >
```

The `msql` directives include support for connecting to and disconnecting from Mini SQL databases, specifying query criteria, fetching query results, and formatting those results for display. Additional directives allow for the use of if-then-else constructs that can be used to determine how the resulting document will be formatted and displayed. Valid mSQL commands follow.

<! msql connect *[host]* >

The connect directive connects to an mSQL database engine that might reside anywhere on the network. A sample connect directive follows:

```
<! msql connect www.caffrey.com >
```

w3-mSQL supports only a single concurrent database connection from within a w3-mSQL HTML document. You can open a connection to another w3-mSQL database server from within the same HTML document, however, after you close out the previous connection. Additionally, you can access multiple databases from one database connection by using the database directive.

<! msql close >

The close directive closes the currently open mSQL database server connection.

TIP

A good practice is to close each database server connection within each HTML document immediately after completing all database transactions for that database server. This helps free up database resources for other processes.

<! msql database *DBName* >

The database directive enables you to select the mSQL database used to access your HTML document data. A sample database directive follows:

```
<! msql database mydb >
```

TIP

To access data from multiple mSQL databases that are managed by the same mSQL server, you can issue the database directive as many times as needed to access the specific database in which your data resides.

<! msql query "sql query text" *QueryHandle* >

The query directive submits a query to the database. The sql query text is submitted to the database, and returned data is stored in the *QueryHandle* for later processing. A sample query directive follows:

```
<! msql query "select last_name from employee" qh >
```

> **NOTE**
>
> The use of the term *query* in the query directive can be misleading. You actually can issue any SQL command, such as INSERT, UPDATE, DELETE, and so on. Note that, in cases other than SELECT, no data is returned in the QueryHandle.

After a query directive is processed by the w3-mSQL server, only the first row of data is returned to the query handle. As with a database cursor, the programmer must fetch the next and subsequent rows appropriately. w3-mSQL uses the fetch and seek directives to specify the current row data placed in the query handle.

When accessing multiple-column query-handle values, you use an @ for database variables, followed by the name of the query handle, followed by a period (.), followed by the numerical index of the desired field in the query handle row results. Suppose that you submitted this query directive:

```
<! msql query "select last_name,first_name, mi from employee" qh>
```

Your results would be stored as this:

- ■ @qh.0 would hold the last-name contents.
- ■ @qh.1 would hold the first-name contents.
- ■ @qh.2 would hold the middle-initial contents.

<! msql free *QueryHandle*>

The free directive releases the QueryHandle and frees any data associated with the query. A sample free directive follows:

```
<! msql free qh >
```

<! msql print "*format*" >

The print directive generates printed output of variable contents. Variables can be from the current row of a query handle, an environment variable, or from data passed to the document by a GET or POST request method.

The "*format*" string specifies the format (similar to a C printf()) of the string that is to be printed. Using the query directive as input for the variables, a sample print directive follows:

```
< ! msql print "Good morning @qh.1 @qh.2 @qh0, your path is $PATH" >
```

> **NOTE**
>
> When searching for variable-content holders, the w3-mSQL server first looks in internal w3-mSQL symbol tables and then looks for environment variables. This means that if both w3-mSQL symbols and environment variables have the same name, the w3-mSQL symbol value is used instead of the environment variable.

<! msql print_rows *QueryHandle* "*format*" >

The print_rows directive prints the entire contents of the query handle from the current cursor location to the end of the query handle. Using this directive speeds up HTML generation when used with tables, lists, and selection menus.

Take a look at a few examples. Don't worry about the HTML syntax just yet; Chapter 7 will cover that. For now, just focus on the use of w3-mSQL query results and how they are referenced.

You could create an HTML table with the following w3-mSQL syntax:

```
<! msql query "select title, author, isbn from publications" qh>
<TABLE>
<TR><TH>Title</TH><TH>Author</TH><TH>ISBN Number</TH></TR>
<! msql print_rows qh "<TR><TD>@qh.0</TD><TD>@qh.1</TD><TD>@qh.2</TD></TR>"
</TABLE>
```

<! msql if (*condition*) >
<! msql else >
<! msql fi >

w3-mSQL incorporates logic for an if-then-else construct. This is very useful for cases in which you do not want to parse the entire document. Take a look at a sample if-then-else w3-mSQL construct:

```
< ! msql if($author == "Swank") >
<P>Books by Mark Swank</P>
< ! msql else >
<P>Other Books</P>
<! Msql fi >
```

w3-mSQL uses standard C constructs such as ==, ¦¦, !=, >, <, and so on.

<! msql fetch *QueryHandle*>

The fetch directive fetches the next row of data from the query handle. A sample fetch directive follows:

```
<! msql fetch q1 >
```

```
<! msql seek QueryHandle Position>
```

The seek directive moves the position of the current data cursor in the specified query handle to the specified position.

> **NOTE**
>
> When a non-positive position number is specified, w3-mSQL replaces the value with a 0 and sets the cursor position to the first record in the query handle. When a position beyond the last record is specified, the cursor position is set to the last record in the query handle.

The following sample seek directive sets the current cursor record to record #33:

```
<! Msql seek qh 33 >
```

WDB

WDB is a WWW database gateway written in Perl and used as a CGI script for accessing SQL databases by a Web server. The current release of WDB supports interfaces to Sybase, Informix, and mSQL SQL databases. WDB has been ported to work with NCSA's HTTP server.

WDB uses a set of high-level, forms-definition files that describe a view of the database. Working template forms-definition files can be generated automatically based on database table structure information.

WDB is different from other Web database gateways, because it automatically creates HTML forms on-the-fly, based on query constraints defined by the end user. Another nice feature of WDB is its capability to convert data from the database into hypertext links, making it possible to access any database element directly through a WWW URL.

GSQL

GSQL is a WWW database gateway interface that provides an NCSA Mosaic forms interface to SQL databases. GSQL consists of two programs: gsql and sqlmain. gsql is a forms-creation program. sqlmain is the back-end process, which handles the processing of database queries. GSQL is a C program that is executed with a shell script by the HTTP server.

GSQL generates forms based on user input and commands found in SQL-specification procedure (proc) files. The proc files are used to map resulting fields of the SQL string execution to widgets (fields, buttons, pull-down menus, and so on) that are used for user input or selection. When the form is submitted, GSQL assembles the user input into a SQL query and forwards that query to the back-end database process (sqlmain) for processing.

Other Database Gateway Products

Many other database gateway products are available. Which one you choose to use certainly depends on the database you want to access. Table 6.2 lists a few database gateway products you might want to download and evaluate.

Table 6.2. Database gateway products.

Product	Database Support	URL
WebGenera	Sybase	`ftp://ftp.gdb.org/pub/letovsky/genera/genera.tar.Z`
Oraplex	Oracle	`http://moulon.inra.fr:80/oracle/wwworaperl_eng.html`
dbWeb	ODBC	`http://www.microsoft.com/intdev/dbweb/`
SoftwareEngine	Sybase	`http://www.engine.com/dbdoc/inst-get.html`
Sapphire	Sybase Oracle Informix	`http://www.bluestone.com/`
WebDatablade	ODBC	`http://www.informix.com/`
A-Xorion	ODBC	`http://www.clark.net/infouser/endidc.htm`

Client-Side APIs

Developers can design and implement their own API to provide Web access to their databases. In most cases, this is not necessary, because many products already are available to handle this function. As many developers know, however, something "right out of the box" seldom provides all the functionality needed in a particular situation, so you might need to develop your own interface to a database.

Almost all database platforms provide an API set of routines to enable developers to compile client programs using any one of several programming languages and compilers. In most cases, client applications are written in languages such as C and compiled using the appropriate database interface precompiler. Oracle database developers, for example, can write C programs (.pc extension) that include ProC SQL commands. The program then is precompiled using a ProC compiler, which translates ProC commands into Oracle APIs for accessing the database. The ProC compiler then generates C-compilable (.c extension) programs. Finally, the ProC-compiled (.c extensions) are compiled into a functional application or library routine by using a standard C compiler.

Publicly Available Search Engines

Have you ever used a search engine? Your answer probably is *yes*. Even if you didn't realize it, you probably have. Most Web servers today provide an input mechanism for users to search indexed documents.

Information is useless if it is not available for distribution. By using search engines, which provide an index into your document repositories, you greatly increase the availability of your information. Today, the problem is not finding information, because properly indexed information is easy to find. Instead, the task for data managers is managing the data and managing access to the data.

Before graphical Web browsers took the Web by storm, search engines provided a mechanism for searching text documents locally (and, in a few cases, globally). With the use of HTTP servers and graphical Web browsers came the need to integrate the indexing of HTML documents as well. In this context, Web search engines work quite well.

Search engines are available to serve many diverse applications. The most common use of search engines is to provide a manageable indexing capability for WWW documents. Another, more complex, use of search engines is to provide an Internet searching engine and indexing capability. The Harvest system, which is covered later in the section "Harvest 1.4," is an example of an information-retrieval system.

This section discusses a few of the available search engines used on intranets and the Internet.

Wide-Area Information Services (freeWAIS-sf)

First, WAIS is a protocol and not an application or server. Many people confuse the two by thinking that when they execute a WAIS search, their request is being serviced by a search engine called WAIS. This is not necessarily the case; instead, they are using a WAIS-compliant server (such as freeWAIS or freeWAIS-sf) to search a WAIS-specific indexed database of information. This section focuses specifically on the freeWAIS-sf distribution.

The WAIS protocol is based on the ANSI standard Z39.50 version 1 and uses only a subset of features of the Z39.50 specification. Specifically, requests that require the server to preserve state are not used. The WAIS protocol extends the basic features of the Z39.50 specification, however, by adding elements for relevance feedback.

Relevancy is used to identify documents that are more applicable to the query criteria. If a user specifies a search based on three different text strings (for example, `WWW`, `Database`, and `Developer`), the WAIS server returns relevancy rankings (usually between 1–1000) for documents that contain the text strings. These rankings are based on relevancy criteria such as the number of times a text string occurs in a document, the occurrence of multiple specified text strings (that is, if you specify three text strings and all three exist in the document), and so on.

FreeWAIS-sf now supports proximity search operators. Proximity searches enable the user to query based on the nearness of specific text strings in relation to some given criteria. A user can further refine a request for documents, for example, by specifying a proximity search of documents that contain the text string `"Bill"` within one word of the text string `"Gates"`. This type of search helps you avoid the "false hits" scenario you would experience in a non-proximity search when a document contains the two text strings `"bill"` and `"gates"` completely separated and with no relationship to each other.

NOTE

To activate proximity searches in your freeWAIS-sf distribution, you must specify them at compile time. Additionally, the standard string-search capability is not available when proximity searches are included.

The freeWAIS-sf documentation on proximity searches is very limited. A C-source file (`ir/query_1.1`) is included in the freeWAIS-sf source code, however, that is used to handle proximity searches. Feel free to look at the source code to identify the specification terms you can use with proximity searches. For those of you who do not want to hack into the code, you might consider not using proximity searches until further clarification of their usage is available.

RESOURCE

You can find information on downloading and configuring the freeWAIS-sf distribution at

`http://ls6-www.informatik.uni-dortmund.de/freeWAIS-sf/README-sf`

TIP

Support for freeWAIS-sf is available from the Usenet newsgroup `comp.infosystems.wais`. When posting articles to this group, make sure that you include the term `freeWAIS-sf` somewhere in the subject line and the specific version you are referring to somewhere in the body.

RESOURCE

For beta testers of freeWAIS-sf, a mailing list can be used to post and read art. To subscribe to this mailing list, send an e-mail message to

`majordomo@wsct.wsc.com`

Include the text string `subscribe wais` in the body. You can post messages to all subscribers of the mailing list by using this e-mail address:

`wais@wsct.wsc.com`

TIP

As is the case with most mailing lists, you can remove your e-mail address from the list by sending an e-mail to the same address to which you subscribed. Just use the body text `unsubscribe <mailing-list name>` instead of `subscribe <mailing-list>`. Some list servers use `enter` and `leave` rather than `subscribe` and `unsubscribe`.

RESOURCE

You also can link freeWAIS-sf with WWW clients, WWW servers, and Gopher servers. For more information on linking freeWAIS-sf to other servers, consult this URL:

`http://ls6-www.informatik.uni-dortmund.de/freeWAIS-sf/fwsf_6.html`

Glimpse 3.0

Glimpse (*global implicit search*) is an indexing and query system that enables you to search through files quickly and efficiently. You can use it to search small collections of documents as well as large data collections. Glimpse is the default search engine in Harvest.

Glimpse is a composition of several programs (glimpse, glimpseindex, agrep, glimpseserver, and so on) used to index documents as well as to search and manage glimpse indexes. To index an entire directory tree structure, for example, you would execute this command:

`glimpseindex <directory>`

The `glimpseindex` command then creates index files in the current working directory that will be used by the `glimpse` command for text searches.

Table 6.3 lists the command-line options that `glimpseindex` supports.

Table 6.3. `glimpseindex` command-line options.

Option	Function
-a	Adds the given file(s) and/or directories to an existing index
-b	Builds a medium-size index (20–30 percent of the size of all files), enabling a faster search

Option	Function
-B	Uses a hash table that is four times bigger (256KB entries instead of 64KB) to speed up indexing
-d `filenames`	Deletes the given file(s) from the index
-D `filenames`	Deletes the given file(s) from the list of filenames but not from the index
-E	Does not run a check on file types
-f	Incremental indexing
-F	`glimpseindex` receives the list of files to index from standard input
-H `directory`	Puts or updates the index and all other `.glimpse` files in `directory`
-i	Forces `.glimpse_include` to override `.glimpse_exclude`
-I	Provides a list of files to be indexed, but does not actually do the indexing
-M `x`	Uses *x*MB of memory for temporary tables
-n	Indexes numbers as well as text
-o	Builds a small index rather than a tiny one (7–9 percent of the sizes of all files), allowing a faster search
-s	Supports structured queries
-S `k`	*k* determines the size of the stop list
-w `k`	*k* determines the number of unique new words that will cause a file to be added to the indexing list
-z	Allows customizable filtering, using the file `.glimpse_filters` to perform the programs listed there for each match

CAUTION

When you specify the -M option, a large value of *x* may cause your system to run out of swap space.

To find all occurrences of the string texarkana in all files with cities somewhere in their name, for example, you would execute this glimpse command:

```
glimpse -F cities texarkana
```

To specify an AND search clause (one in which both text strings must occur in the search to return a value of true), use a semicolon to separate search strings, as in this example:

```
glimpse 'Military Intelligence;imagery'
```

Here, `glimpse` finds all lines that contain both `Military Intelligence` and `imagery`.

Glimpse supports three types of indexes: tiny, small, and medium. Tiny indexes usually are 2–3 percent of the size of all documents indexed. Small indexes are about 7–9 percent of the size of all documents indexed. Finally, medium-size indexes range from 20–30 percent of the size of all documents indexed. The larger the index, the faster the search. For most applications, though, the small index (`glimpseindex -o`) is sufficient.

Glimpse also can be executed by GlimpseHTTP (a Glimpse search engine to HTTP gateway). GlimpseHTTP provides tools that enable files to be searched through an HTTP interface.

Glimpse has been compiled and is known to work under the following operating systems:

AIX
FreeBSD
HP-mc68k
HPPA
Linux
NeXT
OSF/1 DEC Alpha
SGI
Sparc Solaris
Sparc Sun OS

RESOURCE

Information and downloading information for Glimpse and GlimpseHTTP is available at
`http://glimpse.cs.arizona.edu/ghttp/`

Htgrep

Htgrep is a Perl script used as a CGI interface to query any documents accessible by a Web server. Htgrep accepts a user-supplied query (normally, by HTML forms), converts it to a Perl regular expression, and applies it to a list of files or records. Records that match the query then are used as input to generate a valid HTML file.

Htgrep queries can be Boolean keyword searches or regular expressions. Htgrep supports the use of bulleted and numbered HTML lists. Additionally, plain text can be searched, with automatic recognition of URLs.

> **RESOURCE**
>
> You can access a FAQ that provides information on Htgrep at this URL:
> `http://iamwww.unibe.ch/~scg/Src/Doc/htgrep.html`
> A tarred version of Htgrep and other Perl utilities is available at this URL:
> `ftp://iamftp.unibe.ch/pub/scg/www/PerlLib.tar.gz`

SWISH

SWISH (*simple Web indexing system for humans*)—much like WAIS, Glimpse, and Htgrep—is used to index directories of files and to search the generated indexes. When indexing HTML files, SWISH can ignore data in tags and give higher relevance to information in header and title tags. Titles are extracted from HTML files and appear in the search results. SWISH can search an entire Website in a single pass, assuming that it's all within the same directory structure. When searching through HTML documents, SWISH can search for words that exist in HTML titles, comments, and emphasized tags.

Because SWISH indexes consist of only one file, they are easy to transport and maintain. Also, because SWISH is provided in full-source form, you can modify the code to support your own needs.

SWISH has been compiled and is known to work on these operating systems:

> BSDI 1.1
> IRIX 5.3/4
> OSF/1 2.0
> Solaris 2.4
> SunOS 4.1.3

Harvest 1.4

Harvest is a compilation of customizable tools for gathering information from diverse repositories, building topic-specific content indexes, flexibly searching the indexes, widely replicating them, and caching objects as they are retrieved across the Internet. Harvest can interoperate with WWW client/server applications such as HTTP, FTP, Gopher, and NetNews information resources. Harvest is built on a scalable architecture that, compared to other search engines, reduces network usage, server load, and disk space usage. Through this architecture, Harvest can reduce FTP, HTTP, and Gopher server load as well.

RESOURCE

You can find information on the Harvest Project at
`http://harvest.cs.colorado.edu/`

Harvest consists of several subsystems. The Gatherer subsystem retrieves information resources using a variety of standard access methods (FTP, Gopher, HTTP, NNTP, and local files) and then summarizes those resources in various type-specific ways to generate structured indexing information. A gatherer can retrieve a technical report from an FTP archive, for example, and then extract the author, title, and abstract from the paper to summarize the technical report. Harvest brokers or other search services then can retrieve the indexing information from the gatherer to use in a searchable index available through a WWW interface.

The Broker subsystem retrieves indexing information from one or more gatherers, suppresses duplicate information, incrementally indexes the collected information, and provides a WWW query interface to it.

The Replicator subsystem efficiently replicates brokers around the Internet. The Harvest replicator distributes copies of a broker's database to replicas running throughout the Internet. Replication distributes the server load on a broker, improving query performance and availability, and the replicator attempts to minimize network traffic and server workload when propagating updates.

The *Harvest Server Registry* (HSR) is a distinguished broker that holds information about each Harvest gatherer, broker, cache, and replicator on the Internet.

Summary

This chapter covered a great deal of information on databases and database repository access methods. It began with a discussion of large and desktop database systems, such as Oracle Universal Server, Sybase System 11, and Microsoft Access. It also reviewed shareware databases such as mSQL and Postgres95.

The chapter then identified Web database gateway products available both commercially and as shareware. You learned about using Microsoft ODBC and database gateways to provide access to Web database documents.

The chapter continued with a look at publicly available search engines. You learned what search engines are and the different types of search engines. Finally, you learned about the ways in which search engines can provide access to your documents as well as other indexed documents on the Internet.

7

SQL

by Anne Yagerline

You have learned the importance of creating a good design for your relational database. Now how do you manage the data that is stored there? This chapter covers SQL (Structured Query Language), which is the ANSI-standard relational database language used for managing objects, data, and security. You will learn about basic SQL statements and commands to allow you to access and manipulate your data.

Because the examples in this book involve either Microsoft SQL Server or Microsoft Access databases, both SQL contexts are covered, with highlights of the fundamental differences of each product's adaptation of SQL. In every case, you see an example for querying tables in the pubs database that comes with SQL Server. The Microsoft SQL Server statements are contrasted with the comparable Microsoft Access SQL statements only where the syntax differs. Figure 7.1 outlines the structure of the pubs tables authors, titleauthor, and titles used in the examples.

FIGURE 7.1.
Structure of the authors, titleauthor, and titles tables in the pubs *database.*

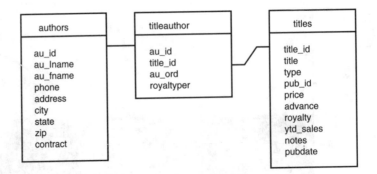

An Overview of Basic SQL Statements

The number of different types of SQL statements you can execute from your application is tremendous. Using SQL, you can perform any function from a simple table query, to creating tables and stored procedures, to assigning user rights. In this book, we want to stay in the realm of retrieving, updating, and reporting on data from Visual Basic. For this purpose, the most important SQL statements you need to know are SELECT, INSERT, UPDATE, DELETE, CREATE TABLE, and SELECT INTO. Brief descriptions of these commands are shown in Table 7.1.

Table 7.1. Important SQL statements.

Command	Description
SELECT	Retrieves columns and rows from a table or tables
INSERT	Adds rows to a table
UPDATE	Updates columns in existing rows in a table
DELETE	Deletes rows from a table

Command	Description
CREATE TABLE	Creates a new table based on the specified table schema
SELECT INTO	Creates a new table based on rows and columns output by a SELECT statement

These commands seem pretty simple, but they can be qualified to perform a number of complex functions, as you can see in the following examples.

SELECT

The SELECT statement is used to retrieve rows of data from your database into a recordset object. The SELECT statement specifies the columns of data you want to retrieve, where the columns are stored, what criteria the returned data must meet, and the sort order of the data. A SELECT statement can further group rows of data together and assign retrieval criteria at the group level. The components of the SELECT statement are described in Table 7.2.

Table 7.2. Components of a SQL SELECT statement.

Component	Description
SELECT	Specifies the columns of data to be retrieved
FROM	Specifies the tables from which to retrieve rows
WHERE	Specifies criteria that returned data must meet
GROUP BY	For aggregate queries, specifies the returned columns by which the data is to be grouped
HAVING	For aggregate queries, specifies criteria that the aggregate value returned must meet
ORDER BY	Specifies the sort order of the returned rows

So let us begin with a very simple SELECT statement. We will build on this statement as we move from one example to the next, adding complexity through the use of WHERE and ORDER BY clauses.

A Simple SELECT Statement

In the following example, you simply query several columns in the authors table:

```
SELECT au_id, au_lname, au_fname, state, zip, contract
FROM authors
```

The results of this simple query (shown in Figure 7.2) reveal that the data in the selected columns was returned for each row that exists in the authors table.

FIGURE 7.2.

The results of a simple
SELECT statement.

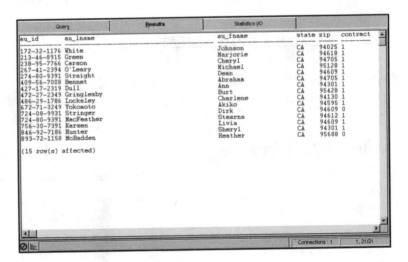

au_id	au_lname	au_fname	state	zip	contract
172-32-1176	White	Johnson	CA	94025	1
213-46-8915	Green	Marjorie	CA	94618	1
238-95-7766	Carson	Cheryl	CA	94705	1
267-41-2394	O'Leary	Michael	CA	95128	1
274-80-9391	Straight	Dean	CA	94609	1
341-22-1782	Smith	Meander	KS	66044	0
409-56-7008	Bennet	Abraham	CA	94705	1
427-17-2319	Dull	Ann	CA	94301	1
472-27-2349	Gringlesby	Burt	CA	95428	1
486-29-1786	Locksley	Charlene	CA	94130	1
527-72-3246	Greene	Morningstar	TN	37215	0
648-92-1872	Blotchet-Halls	Reginald	OR	97330	1
672-71-3249	Yokomoto	Akiko	CA	94595	1
712-45-1867	del Castillo	Innes	MI	48105	1
722-51-5454	DeFrance	Michel	IN	46403	1
724-08-9931	Stringer	Dirk	CA	94609	0
724-80-9391	MacFeather	Stearns	CA	94612	1
756-30-7391	Karsen	Livia	CA	94609	1
807-91-6654	Panteley	Sylvia	MD	20853	1
846-92-7186	Hunter	Sheryl	CA	94301	1
893-72-1158	McBadden	Heather	CA	95688	0
899-46-2035	Ringer	Anne	UT	84152	1
998-72-3567	Ringer	Albert	UT	84152	1

(23 row(s) affected)

Adding the WHERE Clause

Using the same basic SELECT statement, you can narrow down your results by adding a WHERE clause. Suppose that you only want to know the names of authors located in the state of California. In the following example, only those records whose state column has a value of 'CA' will be returned, as shown in Figure 7.3.

```
SELECT au_id, au_lname, au_fname, state, zip, contract
FROM authors
WHERE state = 'CA'
```

FIGURE 7.3.

The results of a simple
SELECT statement
demonstrating the
WHERE clause.

au_id	au_lname	au_fname	state	zip	contract
172-32-1176	White	Johnson	CA	94025	1
213-46-8915	Green	Marjorie	CA	94618	1
238-95-7766	Carson	Cheryl	CA	94705	1
267-41-2394	O'Leary	Michael	CA	95128	1
274-80-9391	Straight	Dean	CA	94609	1
409-56-7008	Bennet	Abraham	CA	94705	1
427-17-2319	Dull	Ann	CA	94301	1
472-27-2349	Gringlesby	Burt	CA	95428	1
486-29-1786	Locksley	Charlene	CA	94130	1
672-71-3249	Yokomoto	Akiko	CA	94595	1
724-08-9931	Stringer	Dirk	CA	94609	0
724-80-9391	MacFeather	Stearns	CA	94612	1
756-30-7391	Karsen	Livia	CA	94609	1
846-92-7186	Hunter	Sheryl	CA	94301	1
893-72-1158	McBadden	Heather	CA	95688	0

(15 row(s) affected)

Your WHERE clause can use several columns as criteria for row retrieval. If you additionally wanted only those rows whose contract value was zero, you would use a logical AND, as in the following:

```
SELECT au_id, au_lname, au_fname, state, zip, contract
FROM authors
WHERE state = 'CA' AND contract = 0
```

You can also have the query return rows for authors in any state except California. The way to indicate inequality in SQL is to combine a greater-than and a less-than sign (<>).

```
SELECT au_id, au_lname, au_fname, state, zip, contract
FROM authors
WHERE state <> 'CA'
```

> **NOTE**
>
> If you have ever created a query in Access using the Query By Example (QBE) grid and then viewed the SQL that it generated, you have noticed that a semicolon appears at the end of the statement. This is Access's way of terminating the SQL statement, although it is not necessary in order for the SQL statement to be executed. SQL Server has no such terminator and will treat a semicolon attached to the end of the statement as a syntactical error.

The WHERE clause can use a number of different comparison operators for checking field values. Table 7.3 lists and describes these operators.

Table 7.3. WHERE clause comparison operators.

Operator	Description
=	Is equal to.
>	Is greater than.
<	Is less than.
>=	Is greater than or equal to.
<=	Is less than or equal to.
< >	Is not equal to.
IN	Is in a specified list of values or in the results of a specified subquery.
BETWEEN..AND	Is between two values.
LIKE	Contains the same pattern as a specified string. The pattern being compared is a string that contains one or more wildcard characters. You should refer to Access and SQL Server help for a list of these operators.

In addition to a variety of comparison operators, the columns included in the WHERE clause can be checked using the AND and OR logical operators. If the AND operator is used, the conditions on both sides of the AND must be met for a row to be returned. The OR operator requires that at least one of the conditions must be met.

Adding the ORDER BY Clause

Now let's take your simple query one step further and sort the results by author last name (au_lname). To do this, you add an ORDER BY clause.

```
SELECT au_id, au_lname, au_fname, state, zip, contract
FROM authors
WHERE state = 'CA'
ORDER BY au_lname
```

The resulting rows are returned in ascending alphabetical order by the author's last name, as shown in Figure 7.4.

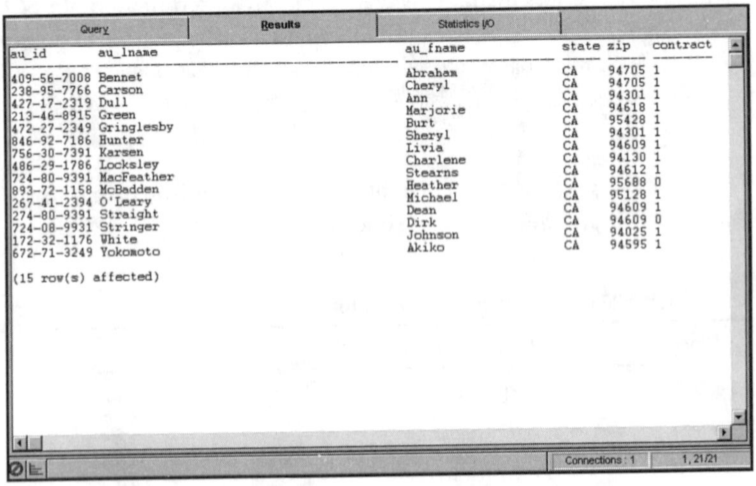

FIGURE 7.4.

The results of a simple SELECT *statement demonstrating the* ORDER BY *clause.*

au_id	au_lname	au_fname	state	zip	contract
409-56-7008	Bennet	Abraham	CA	94705	1
238-95-7766	Carson	Cheryl	CA	94705	1
427-17-2319	Dull	Ann	CA	94301	1
213-46-8915	Green	Marjorie	CA	94618	1
472-27-2349	Gringlesby	Burt	CA	95428	1
846-92-7186	Hunter	Sheryl	CA	94301	1
756-30-7391	Karsen	Livia	CA	94609	1
486-29-1786	Locksley	Charlene	CA	94130	1
724-80-9391	MacFeather	Stearns	CA	94612	1
893-72-1158	McBadden	Heather	CA	95688	0
267-41-2394	O'Leary	Michael	CA	95128	1
274-80-9391	Straight	Dean	CA	94609	1
724-08-9931	Stringer	Dirk	CA	94609	0
172-32-1176	White	Johnson	CA	94025	1
672-71-3249	Yokomoto	Akiko	CA	94595	1

(15 row(s) affected)

You can also sort the records in a field in descending order using the keyword DESC. Suppose you want to first sort the records in descending order by contract and then sort in ascending order by author last name. An example is shown in the following SQL statement:

```
SELECT au_id, au_lname, au_fname, state, zip, contract
FROM authors
WHERE state = 'CA'
ORDER BY contract DESC, au_lname
```

> **NOTE**
>
> Microsoft SQL Server offers several sort orders, with the default being dictionary order and case-insensitive. The sort order is defined during SQL Server installation and cannot be overridden, so you might want to consult your DBA to be sure how your results will be sorted. The default sort order for Access is ascending (A–Z, 0–9).

Using the WHERE Clause to Join Tables

You have seen several ways to use SQL SELECT statements to look at the data in the authors table by specifying columns to return, assigning retrieval criteria, and sorting the results. But in the real world, will you want to look at data from only a single table at a time? The answer is most likely "No." The data in the authors table has relationships with data in other tables in the pubs database. For instance, what if you want to know what titles were written by these authors? The author table alone won't tell you this. You must search the cross-reference table titleauthor, which links author to title by the columns au_id and title_id. Unfortunately, this isn't enough. Most of us don't recognize authors or titles by IDs or codes. We know them by names. Because the names of the authors are located in the table author, the titles are located in the table title, and the relationships between the two are located in titleauthor, you need a way to tie these three tables together in a single SELECT statement. You can do this using the WHERE clause.

```
SELECT authors.au_lname, authors.au_fname, titles.title
FROM authors, titleauthor, titles
WHERE
  authors.au_id = titleauthor.au_id AND
  titleauthor.title_id = titles.title_id
ORDER BY authors.au_lname, authors.au_fname, titles.title
```

The resulting list of authors and their titles is shown in Figure 7.5. Note the way you referenced the column names in this statement. When retrieving data from multiple tables in a single SQL statement, you must preface the column names that appear in more than one of the tables in the FROM clause with their associated table names in order to avoid an ambiguity error.

Using the JOIN Operator to Join Tables

Another way to join tables is by using the JOIN operator. This is the ANSI standard method for joining tables and uses the following syntax:

```
SELECT column1, column2, column3
FROM table1 JOIN table2
ON join criteria
```

FIGURE 7.5.

The results of a SELECT *statement demonstrating the use of the* WHERE *clause in joining tables.*

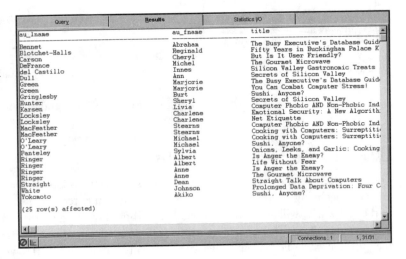

The JOIN operator indicates how rows should be returned from the joined tables. The ON clause acts like a WHERE clause, indicating which fields in the joined table should be compared for equality. Table 7.4 describes the different JOIN operators:

Table 7.4. Table JOIN operators.

JOIN *Operator*	*Description*
CROSS JOIN	Returns each row from the first table joined with each row from the second table, resulting in a returned number of rows equal to the product of the two tables' rowcounts.
INNER JOIN	Returns all rows from each table that meet the WHERE clause search criteria and where there is a match on the joined fields in the ON clause.
LEFT [OUTER] JOIN	Returns all rows from the table on the left side of the join that meet the WHERE clause search criteria and only those from the right side of the join where there is a match on the joined fields in the ON clause.
RIGHT [OUTER] JOIN	Returns all rows from the table on the right side of the join that meet the WHERE clause search criteria and only those from the left side of the join where there is a match on the joined fields in the ON clause.
FULL [OUTER] JOIN	Returns all rows from each table that meet the WHERE clause search criteria and where there is no match on the joined fields in the ON clause.

Using the JOIN operator, the SQL statement in the previous example would be written as follows:

```
SELECT authors.au_lname, authors.au_fname, titles.title
FROM (authors INNER JOIN titleauthor
    ON authors.au_id = titleauthor.au_id) INNER JOIN titles
    ON titleauthor.title_id = titles.title_id
ORDER BY authors.au_lname, authors.au_fname, titles.title
```

Access supports the following JOIN operators: INNER JOIN, LEFT JOIN, and RIGHT JOIN. SQL Server 6.5 supports all of the listed joins. Note that versions of SQL Server earlier than 6.5 do not use this syntax for joining tables. Instead, in those versions, the fields from two tables must be joined in the WHERE clause as shown in the previous example. To indicate a LEFT or RIGHT outer join in the WHERE clause, you would use the *= and =* operators, respectively, in place of the = operator. The following two left outer JOIN statements produce the same result and illustrate the two methods for joining tables:

```
SELECT column1, column2, column3
FROM table1 LEFT JOIN table2
ON table1.column1 = table2.column1

SELECT column1, column2, column3
FROM table1, table2
WHERE table1.column1 *= table2.column1
```

One use for an outer join would be to list all authors and, if they wrote a book, list the title_id of that book (through an outer join with titleauthor). If the author did not write a book, you would still be able to see the author's name listed, but the title_id would be returned as NULL.

Aggregate Functions in SQL Statements

Aggregate functions return summary values for specified columns or expressions in the form of sum totals, number of records, averages, and so on. The aggregate function might return a single value for all rows represented by the query. If a GROUP BY clause has been added to the SQL statement, such summary values will be calculated at each level of grouping. Table 7.5 lists the aggregate functions you can use. Note that the StDev and Var functions are not available in SQL Server.

Table 7.5. Aggregate functions.

Aggregate Function	*Description*
Avg	Returns the average of all values in the columns by taking their sum and dividing by the count.
Count	Returns the number of non-null values in the specified column or expression. If the expression is an asterisk (such as count(*)), the result will be the number of rows in the query.
Max	Returns the maximum value in the specified column or expression.

continues

Table 7.5. continued

Aggregate Function	Description
Min	Returns the minimum value in the specified column or expression.
StDev, StDevP	Return estimates of the standard deviation for a population or population sample (Access only).
Sum	Returns the sum of values in the specified column or expression.
Var, VarP	Return estimates of the variance for a population or a population sample (Access only).

The following statement illustrates the use of the count function on the entire titles table with no grouping:

```
SELECT count(title) 'titles'
FROM titles
```

The result is the total number of title records in the titles table, as shown in Figure 7.6.

FIGURE 7.6.

An example of the aggregate count function on the titles table.

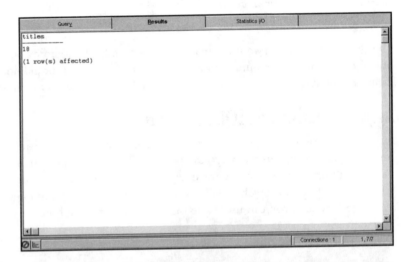

NOTE

You can use an alias to return a different name for a column or assign a name to a column that returns an expression (and, therefore, has no name). There are three ways to assign an alias to a column. (All three methods can be used in SQL Server. Only the first method can be used in Access.)

```
SELECT count(title) AS titles FROM titles
SELECT count(title) 'titles' FROM titles
SELECT 'titles' = count(title) FROM titles
```

Use of the GROUP BY Clause

The GROUP BY statement accepts a list of columns specifying how the results of a SELECT statement should be grouped. The SELECT statement returns one row for each set of distinct values in columns specified in the GROUP BY list. For example, Figure 7.5 shows a returned list of authors and the books that they wrote. Because some of the authors wrote more than one book, their names appear in more than one of the returned rows. By adding a GROUP BY clause we can group the returned rows by author last name and first name so that only one row will be returned for each distinct author name.

In the following example, we will apply the GROUP BY clause to the SELECT statement, the results of which are shown in Figure 7.5. Instead of returning the authors' titles, we will use the aggregate count function to determine the number of titles associated with each author. Because we have grouped the returned set of records by author last name and first name, each author will have its own title count, rather than the count being performed on an entire table, as in the previous example of the count function.

```
SELECT authors.au_lname, authors.au_fname, count(titles.title) 'titles'
FROM authors, titleauthor, titles
WHERE
   authors.au_id = titleauthor.au_id AND
   titleauthor.title_id = titles.title_id
GROUP BY authors.au_lname, authors.au_fname
```

With the results shown in Figure 7.7, you can determine how many books were written by each author.

FIGURE 7.7.

An example of a GROUP BY *query.*

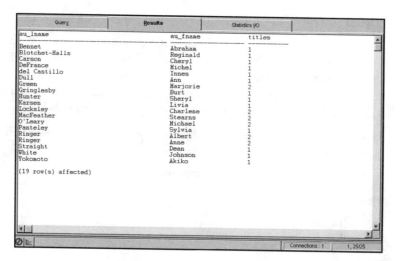

> **NOTE**
>
> At this point, you are familiar with the use of table names prefacing column names in order to avoid ambiguity in multitable queries. You also might have begun to notice that this can result in lengthy SQL statements. Using a table alias, you can shorten your SQL statement and make it easier to both read and type. Like the column alias shown earlier, the table alias is simply the use of a new name to represent the actual table name. They are often used to shorten the SQL statement and to enhance the readability of the WHERE clause, so the table names are usually replaced by an alias of a single character. Let's look at the preceding SQL example, replacing table names with aliases:
>
> ```
> SELECT a.au_lname, a.au_fname, count(c.title) 'titles'
> FROM authors a, titleauthor b, titles c
> WHERE
>    a.au_id = b.au_id and
>    b.title_id = c.title_id
> GROUP BY a.au_lname, a.au_fname
> ```
>
> The following SQL statements illustrate two ways to assign a table alias by assigning the simple alias a to the table author. Note that the syntax of the first example can be used in both Access and SQL Server, but only Access will support the second example.
>
> ```
> SELECT a.au_lname, a.au_fname FROM authors a
> SELECT a.au_lname, a.au_fname FROM authors AS a
> ```

Use of the HAVING Clause

Like the WHERE clause, the HAVING clause is used for specifying criteria for data to be returned in a query. The difference lies in the level at which the criteria is checked. The WHERE clause uses criteria to restrict rows of data returned by a query. The GROUP BY clause then forms the returned rows into groups and calculates any aggregate values. The criteria in the HAVING clause is then used to restrict groups of rows according to the group level data.

The following example shows how the HAVING clause is used to return only the names of authors who have written more than one book:

```
SELECT a.au_lname, a.au_fname, count(c.title) 'titles'
FROM authors a, titleauthor b, titles c
WHERE
   a.au_id = b.au_id and
   b.title_id = c.title_id
GROUP BY a.au_lname, a.au_fname
HAVING count(c.title) > 1
```

Figure 7.8 shows that only the authors with more than one book are returned by the query.

FIGURE 7.8.

The use of the HAVING *clause to determine which authors have written more than one book.*

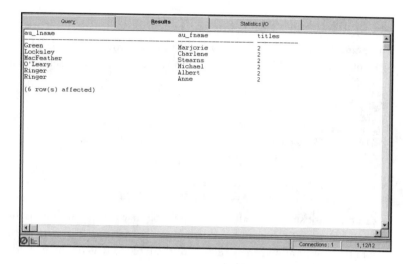

INSERT

The INSERT statement is used to add rows of data to a table. The INSERT statement specifies the table to which rows are to be added, the columns in which the data is to be stored, the source of the data being added, and the data itself. The components of the INSERT statement are described in Table 7.6.

Table 7.6. Components of a SQL INSERT statement.

Component	Description
INSERT INTO	Specifies the table to which rows are to be added.
column list	Specifies columns in which to add the data. It is necessary to provide a column list only when not all of the table's columns are to have data added. If left blank, the column list can be understood to be every column in the table, in the order in which they appear in the table structure.
VALUES (*value list*)	Specifies the values to be filled in the respective columns in the column list. (For example, the first value in the value list will be assigned to the first column in the column list, and so on.)
SELECT	The SELECT statement that will return rows to be added to the table.

Note that either a value list or a SELECT statement (not both) is used to provide the data to be added.

Use of the INSERT Statement with a Value List

This example shows the use of the value list to add a row to the title table, providing values for each column in the table. Note that with a value list, you can insert only a single row into the table.

```
INSERT INTO titles
VALUES
   ( 'SM1234', 'The Small Business Tax Guide', 'business', '1389', 15.99, 3000,
     10, 0, 'Tax guide for owners of small businesses', '1/1/1997')
```

You can also specify which columns to fill in the insert clause:

```
INSERT INTO titles (title_id, title)
VALUES ('SM5678', 'The Small Business Marketing Guide')
```

A reason for not specifying all values would be that you do not know those values and want any possible default values to be added. Note, however, that if there are no default values for the omitted columns and the structure of the table to which you are adding the row requires that an omitted column be filled, you will receive an error.

In the first example shown, you might have noticed that the list of columns in the insert clause was omitted. This is the equivalent of listing all columns in the table in the order in which they appear in the table structure. This saves you some typing time. However, it is usually better to include the column list so that, if fields are reordered or added to the table at a later date, the SQL statement does not need to be altered to reflect the structure change.

Use of the INSERT Statement with a SELECT Statement

This example shows the use of the SELECT statement to add one or more rows of data to the title table. Let's assume that the newtitles table is a temporary working table that holds new title information. From this table, you want to add all titles whose processing date is NULL.

```
INSERT INTO titles
( title_id, title, type, pub_id, price, advance, royalty, ytd_sales, notes,
  pubdate )
SELECT
  title_id, title, type, pub_id, price, advance, royalty, ytd_sales, notes,
  pubdate
FROM newtitles
WHERE procdate = NULL
```

> **NOTE**
>
> The INSERT INTO..SELECT statement can be interpreted as a two-part query. That is, the SELECT portion of the statement actually is performed by itself as "step one" of the statement. The resulting set of rows is then given to the INSERT INTO portion of the statement, which is "step two" of the statement. For this reason, there is no ambiguity

between the identical column lists in these two distinct portions of the SQL statement. Therefore, it is not necessary to preface the column names with the table names in order to distinguish those in the destination table from those in the source table.

UPDATE

The UPDATE statement is used to update column values in existing rows in a table. The UPDATE statement specifies the table to be updated, the columns to update, the new values to assign those columns, and criteria for the rows to be updated. Table 7.7 describes the components of an UPDATE statement.

Table 7.7. Components of a SQL UPDATE statement.

Component	Description
UPDATE	Specifies the table to be updated
SET	Specifies columns to update and the new values to assign to those columns
FROM	Specifies the tables to include in the UDPATE statement
WHERE	Specifies the criteria that determine which rows' columns are to be updated

Setting Columns to a Fixed Value with the UPDATE Statement

In some cases, you want to update columns in a table with a fixed value for every row in the table. For instance, assume that you want to update the processing date to January 1, 1997 for each row in the newtitles table (used in the previous example) that currently has a processing date of NULL:

```
UPDATE newtitles
SET procdate = '1/1/1997'
WHERE procdate = NULL
```

Setting a Column Value Based on Existing Column Values

Suppose you want to increase the price of each book in the title table by 10 percent of the current price. It would be difficult to update the table with fixed values (as in the previous example), because all books need to be updated to different prices. That could take all day. A better way to perform this update is to use the existing price as a base for the updated price.

Just as you can assign a fixed value to a column, you can also assign the results of an expression as shown in the following statement:

```
UPDATE titles
SET price = price * 1.10
```

Without knowing the value of any of the prices in the title table, you can successfully increase their values by 10 percent in one easy UPDATE statement.

Setting a Column Based on Values in a Joined Table

Now let's imagine that you want to update the publisher associated with all titles written by a specific author. The author information is nowhere to be found in the titles table. You can get that information only by joining the titles table with the titleauthor table. To do this, you add a FROM clause to the UPDATE statement. This FROM clause works the same way as the FROM clause in a SELECT statement. While the UPDATE clause indicates the table to be updated, the FROM clause indicates the source of the data with which to update that table. The following example updates the pub_id column to '1389' for all titles associated with au_id '998-72-3567':

```
UPDATE titles
SET pub_id = '1389'
FROM titles a, titleauthor b
WHERE
   a.title_id = b.title_id AND
   b.au_id = '998-72-3567'
```

DELETE

The DELETE statement allows you to remove rows from tables. This statement specifies the table from which rows are to be deleted and criteria for the rows to be deleted. Table 7.8 describes the components of a DELETE statement.

Table 7.8. Components of a SQL DELETE statement.

Component	Description
DELETE FROM	Specifies the table from which to delete rows
WHERE	Specifies the criteria that determine which rows are to be deleted

Using DELETE to Delete All Rows From a Table

To delete all rows from a table, you need only specify the name of the table from which to delete those rows. The following example shows how to delete all rows from the title table:

```
DELETE FROM titles
```

> **NOTE**
>
> SQL Server offers another method, called the TRUNCATE TABLE statement, for removing all rows from a table. It acts like a DELETE statement that has no WHERE clause, with a couple of important exceptions that should be noted. The DELETE statement deletes rows from a table one row at a time, logging each deletion as a transaction, and it can therefore be rolled back. The TRUNCATE TABLE statement, on the other hand, removes entries from a table pages at a time, and does not log individual row deletions. Rows removed from a table with a TRUNCATE TABLE statement cannot be recovered. The other important note is that delete triggers associated with a table will not be fired when that table is truncated. So why use a TRUNCATE TABLE statement? Speed. The TRUNCATE TABLE statement performs the task of removing all rows from a table much faster than a DELETE statement does. Just keep in mind that TRUNCATE TABLE always removes all the rows from a table and these rows are *not* recoverable.

But sometimes you don't want to wipe out all the rows in a table. Instead, assume that you want to delete only a specific title from the titles table.

Using DELETE to Delete Specific Rows from a Table

To delete specific rows from a table, you simply add the familiar WHERE clause. As you might expect, only the rows that meet the criteria of the WHERE clause will be deleted. Suppose you want to remove only the title 'Silicon Valley Gastronomic Treats', whose title_id is 'MC2222'. Here is how to do it:

```
DELETE FROM titles
WHERE title_id = 'MC2222'
```

This is a little bit more complex than the previous example, but it's still quite easy. Let's try one more.

Using DELETE to Delete Rows Based on a Joined Table

Imagine that the criteria for the delete are based on a value in another table. For example, what if you want to delete all titles written by the author whose au_id is '427-17-2319'? You must use the joined titleauthor table to determine which titles were written by each author. This is where Access and SQL Server handle the DELETE statement quite differently.

Access uses the following syntax to delete rows from one table based on data stored in one or more other tables:

```
DELETE titles.*
FROM titles, titleauthor
WHERE titles.title_id = titleauthor.title_id and titleauthor.au_id = '427-17-2319'
```

In SQL Server, you would perform the same function using the following syntax:

```
DELETE FROM titles
WHERE title_id IN
( SELECT title_id from titleauthor
  WHERE au_id = '427-17-2319' )
```

CREATE TABLE

The CREATE TABLE statement allows you to create a new table in the database. But the database should already be established by the DBA, you say, so why should you have to create a new table from Visual Basic? Sometimes you need to access the data in such a way that a SELECT statement would not effectively produce the desired results. For example, you might find that the set of data you need must be accessed and processed one row at a time through a cursor. Another example is a result set that would require table joins so complex that the query takes a very long time to run. In these cases, it is useful to have an empty table structured as you want the result set structured, so that you can fill in phases through either the use of a cursor or a combination of INSERT and UPDATE statements. Table 7.9 describes the components of a CREATE TABLE statement.

Table 7.9. Components of a CREATE TABLE statement.

Component	Description
CREATE TABLE	Specifies the table to be created
column list	Specifies the columns of the new table and their attributes

Using CREATE TABLE to Create the authors Table

To create a new table using the CREATE TABLE statement, you simply specify the table to create and the columns that will configure the table. The following statement creates the authors table as it is currently structured in the pubs database on SQL Server:

```
CREATE TABLE authors
( au_id id NOT NULL ,
  au_lname varchar (40) NOT NULL ,
  au_fname varchar (20) NOT NULL ,
  phone char (12) NOT NULL ,
  address varchar (40) NULL ,
  city varchar (20) NULL ,
  state char (2) NULL ,
  zip char (5) NULL ,
  contract bit NOT NULL )
```

As you might have guessed, although the statement structure is the same, the syntax used to create a table in an Access database is markedly different from that shown for SQL Server due to different data types and keywords in the two environments. Table 7.10 lists the valid SQL Server and Access data types, respectively.

Table 7.10. SQL Server and Access SQL data types.

Environment	Valid Data Types
SQL Server	`binary, varbinary, char, varchar, datetime, smalldatetime, decimal, numeric, float, real, int, smallint, tinyint, money, smallmoney, bit, timestamp, text, image`
Access	`binary, bit, byte, counter, datetime, single, double, short, long, longtext, longbinary, text`

SELECT..INTO

The SELECT..INTO statement is another way you can create a new table. This method differs from the CREATE TABLE method in that the structure of the table to create is not explicitly stated; rather, it is determined by the results of a SELECT statement. Table 7.11 lists the components of the SELECT..INTO statement.

Table 7.11. Components of a SELECT..INTO statement.

Component	Description
SELECT *column list*	Specifies the selected columns with which to build the new table
INTO	Specifies the name of the new table being created
FROM	Specifies the table or tables from which the column is being selected
WHERE	Specifies criteria that returned data must meet
GROUP BY	For aggregate queries, specifies the returned columns by which the data is to be grouped
HAVING	For aggregate queries, specifies criteria that the aggregate value returned must meet
ORDER BY	Specifies the sort order of the returned rows

Using SELECT..INTO to Create a New authortitles Table

Suppose that you want to store the results of a SELECT statement in a table for use later in your application or in a report. The SELECT..INTO statement allows you to do just that. You simply need to add the INTO clause to a standard SELECT statement. In this example, you use the SELECT statement from an earlier example, which displayed author names and the titles of books that the authors wrote, to create a new table called `authortitles`:

```
SELECT a.au_lname, a.au_fname, c.title
INTO authortitles
FROM authors a, titleauthor b, titles c
WHERE
  a.au_id = b.au_id and
  b.title_id = c.title_id
ORDER BY a.au_lname, a.au_fname, c.title
```

Now, if you select all rows from the `authortitles` table, you get the same results that you got in the `SELECT` statement, as shown in Figure 7.9.

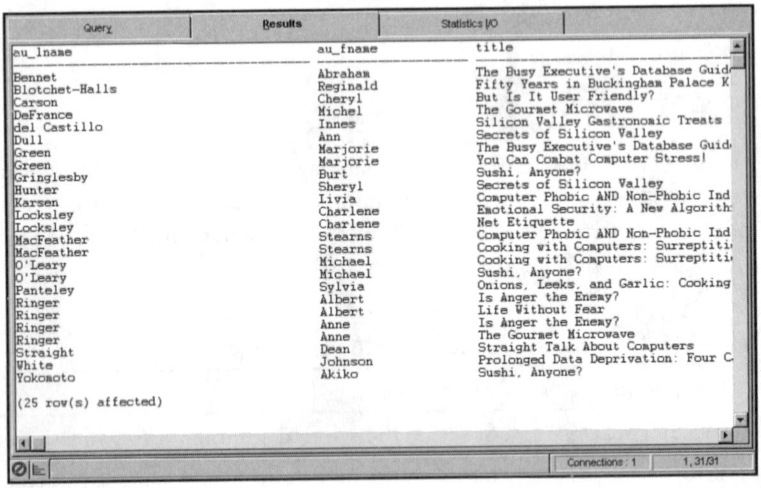

au_lname	au_fname	title
Bennet	Abraham	The Busy Executive's Database Guid
Blotchet-Halls	Reginald	Fifty Years in Buckingham Palace K
Carson	Cheryl	But Is It User Friendly?
DeFrance	Michel	The Gourmet Microwave
del Castillo	Innes	Silicon Valley Gastronomic Treats
Dull	Ann	Secrets of Silicon Valley
Green	Marjorie	The Busy Executive's Database Guid
Green	Marjorie	You Can Combat Computer Stress!
Gringlesby	Burt	Sushi, Anyone?
Hunter	Sheryl	Secrets of Silicon Valley
Karsen	Livia	Computer Phobic AND Non-Phobic Ind
Locksley	Charlene	Emotional Security: A New Algorith
Locksley	Charlene	Net Etiquette
MacFeather	Stearns	Computer Phobic AND Non-Phobic Ind
MacFeather	Stearns	Cooking with Computers: Surrepti
O'Leary	Michael	Cooking with Computers: Surrepti
O'Leary	Michael	Sushi, Anyone?
Panteley	Sylvia	Onions, Leeks, and Garlic: Cooking
Ringer	Albert	Is Anger the Enemy?
Ringer	Albert	Life Without Fear
Ringer	Anne	Is Anger the Enemy?
Ringer	Anne	The Gourmet Microwave
Straight	Dean	Straight Talk About Computers
White	Johnson	Prolonged Data Deprivation: Four C
Yokomoto	Akiko	Sushi, Anyone?

(25 row(s) affected)

FIGURE 7.9.
The results of using `SELECT..INTO` *to create the authortitles table.*

Summary

This chapter attempted to provide you with the basic tools for performing the most common SQL commands. You have learned how to retrieve rows in many different formats using the `SELECT` statement, as well as how to add, update, and delete rows in tables using the `INSERT`, `UPDATE`, and `DELETE` statements, respectively. You also learned how to create a new table using the `CREATE TABLE` or `SELECT..INTO` statements. All of these statements should get you pretty far, but you might find in your continued development that you require more functionality. You should take the time to try out the commands described here until you feel you have a good understanding of how they work. Then you should research and make use of some of the more advanced features described in SQL Server's Transact-SQL help file and the Microsoft Access help file. You should also become familiar with as many of those products' built-in functions as possible. Such functions will give you a much wider scope of options in the types of SQL statements you can create.

IV

Visual Basic Core Topics for Internet Developers

8

Using Classes and Objects in Visual Basic 5

by Mark Spenik

This chapter and the next chapter focus on topics that you must have a basic understanding of in order to develop Internet database applications. Chapter 9, "Visual Basic 5 Data Access Features," provides an overview of Visual Basic data access options. This chapter focuses on the foundation required to build ActiveX server components—classes and objects.

This chapter covers how to create a class in Visual Basic and add properties and methods to the class. If you are familiar with creating classes in Visual Basic, you should review this section because new class features added in Visual Basic 5, such as interfaces and friend methods, are discussed. This chapter also covers how Visual Basic classes and objects fit into the big picture of ActiveX technologies. Several code examples are given in this chapter, including an HTML table data presentation class and an example of using the Microsoft Internet Explorer 3.0 as an ActiveX component.

What Is ActiveX?

So what exactly is ActiveX? It turns out that ActiveX is not just a single thing. The textbook definition of ActiveX is a set of integrated technologies that enable software components in a networked environment to interoperate using any programming language. The ActiveX component strategy is shown in Figure 8.1.

FIGURE 8.1.
ActiveX component strategy.

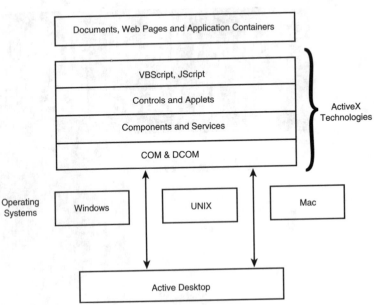

If you are a seasoned Visual Basic programmer, you might think this sounds familiar, similar to OLE (Object Linking and Embedding). OLE, which dealt with software component reuse, still exists, but much of OLE's functionality has been integrated into ActiveX, with some changes to increase component performance and limit size. ActiveX is designed to work in a network environment such as the Internet, and it is an open standard. The general goals of ActiveX are to provide packages of software that can be

- Created in any language
- Run on any operating system
- Used in applications
- Used within Internet/intranet applications with scripting languages

The bottom line is that ActiveX is a set of technologies that makes code reuse simple whether you are in a client/server environment or an Internet environment.

ActiveX is based on Microsoft's COM (Component Object Model) and DCOM (Distributed Component Object Model). COM and DCOM provide the underlying interfaces that allow ActiveX components to run anywhere. ActiveX components and controls are COM objects. Other elements of ActiveX are as follows:

- ActiveX controls
- ActiveX components
- ActiveX documents
- ActiveX scripting
- Java applets

ActiveX Controls

As a Visual Basic programmer, you need no introduction to ActiveX controls. After all, Visual Basic's flexibility relies heavily on using controls. So, how do ActiveX controls differ from the standard OLE (OCX) controls? For starters, ActiveX controls expose a simpler COM interface and are 50 percent to 75 percent smaller than their counterpart OLE controls. The smaller size of the control makes for faster download times in Internet-enabled applications. To further aid download time, ActiveX controls support asynchronous downloading. ActiveX controls automatically install and register themselves on a PC and are safe for scripting and execution. You will learn more about ActiveX controls, as well as how to write your own ActiveX controls, in Chapter 16, "Creating ActiveX Controls for the Web with VB 5."

ActiveX Components

An ActiveX component is an object or objects exposed by an application or component that can be controlled programmatically by other applications. ActiveX components are a shift in Visual Basic developer terminology. ActiveX components were referred to in previous versions of Visual Basic as OLE servers. So remember that an OLE server is now an ActiveX component. If you are not familiar with ActiveX components (OLE servers), pay close attention to this chapter, which shows you how to create classes—the foundation of exposed objects found in ActiveX components. You learn how to turn your classes into ActiveX components in Chapter 22, "Writing Server-Side Applications with VB 5 ActiveX Components."

ActiveX Documents

ActiveX documents are non-HTML documents that users can view and edit in a browser. ActiveX documents support features such as menu merging, toolbars, forms, and printing support. Visual Basic 5 applications and forms can be converted into ActiveX documents. You learn more about ActiveX documents, as well as creating an ActiveX database application in an intranet environment, in Chapter 15, "Creating ActiveX Documents for the Web with VB 5."

ActiveX Scripting

ActiveX scripting allows Web authors to build Web applications by piecing together ActiveX components. You can use scripting in Web applications to control objects or validate user input. Currently, ActiveX scripting includes Visual Basic scripting (VBScript) and JScript. VBScript is a subset of the full-blown version of Visual Basic. Many of the examples used throughout this book make use of VBScript. VBScript is covered in detail in Chapters 12 through 15. JScript is Microsoft's version of JavaScript, which was created by Netscape Communications.

Java Applets

Unless you have been on another planet for the last year or so, you have heard of Java. Java is the programming language, created by Sun Microsystems, that enables applications to execute on any platform, which makes it a great language for Internet applications. A Java applet is a Java code component created to provide additional capabilities in a Web page. ActiveX supports Java applets. As a matter of fact, ActiveX treats Java applets like ActiveX controls. By treating Java applets like ActiveX controls, Microsoft extends the capabilities of a Java applet, enabling Java applets to talk to other Java applets or other ActiveX controls. The Java Virtual Machine in ActiveX is also an ActiveX control, which means that Java applets could be used by other applications besides a browser.

ACTIVEX IS NOT A JAVA COMPETITOR

When Microsoft first released its vision of the Internet and ActiveX technologies, many people thought it was competing against Java, even though Java is a part of the ActiveX technologies. ActiveX does not compete directly with Java. ActiveX is not a programming language; Java is. ActiveX is not a platform; Java has the Virtual Machine, which is a platform. Sun has announced its intentions to make Java an operating system; ActiveX is not an operating system. ActiveX is an integration of technologies that enables and simplifies code reuse in an intranet/Internet environment.

An Overview of Visual Basic Classes and Objects

Prior to object-oriented programming, reusable code was implemented via cut-and-paste (which is not a great solution) and code libraries. Code libraries consisted of functions and procedures that programmers could use over and over without having to rewrite them. Code libraries work well in many cases, but the problems with code libraries become apparent as you begin to build and maintain several applications.

Suppose you are building an application to rate your favorite Websites. The application should have data elements defined, such as a variable called Default_Site. As you start to develop the application, you find that the code library does not contain all the functions you need. You are required to write your own functions to perform special validation on your data elements. Another problem arises when other developers begin to help you with your project. You have no way to restrict what they can and can't do with the data elements you have defined. (In other words, the data is not tied in any way to your validation routines.) Also, large code libraries can be difficult to use when poorly documented or extremely large.

To help remedy the problems associated with standard module programming practices, Visual Basic 4 introduced the class module. A class module is a template for Visual Basic objects. Class modules contain functions and procedures (*methods* in class terminology) and data elements (*properties* in class terminology) and provide encapsulation. Encapsulation is an object-oriented programming term to describe a unit that contains both data and code. Using encapsulation, you can control what values the data items accept or what actions can be performed on the data items. An object is an instance of the class (the actual representation used in code). In Visual Basic, objects are created from classes by obtaining a reference of the class. For example, you have a class called CFile. To use the class, you would create an object of the CFile class using the keyword New, shown in the following code snippet:

```
Dim oLogFile as CFile
Set oLogFile = New CFile
```

Visual Basic Objects, Classes, and Object-Oriented Programming

Object-oriented programming, referred to as *OOP*, is a programming practice that models the real world. Applications are designed around objects, and objects can consist of other objects. For instance, you can create an automobile object that consists of a tire object, an engine object, and so on. If you are not already familiar with OOP or would like to learn more, Macmillan Computer Publishing offers many fine books that go into great detail about OOP, such as *Visual Basic 5.0 Unleashed* by Sams Publishing, *VB 5.0 Interactive Course* by Waite Group Press, or *Doing Objects in Microsoft Visual Basic 5.0* by Ziff-Davis. The purpose here is to introduce OOP concepts found in Visual Basic.

Visual Basic has many object-oriented features, such as encapsulation and method overriding. Because you can create classes that support encapsulation using Visual Basic, you should use standard object-oriented design methodologies to create your applications. However, Visual Basic lacks the one truly object-oriented language feature—inheritance. *Inheritance* allows programmers to create new classes while inheriting all the methods and properties of other classes (including the code). Inheritance provides a very powerful method of code reuse. Visual Basic does not provide inheritance, but it does provide another model of code reuse—the ActiveX component model.

Using the ActiveX component object model (COM), you can create objects (components) that can be used by other applications. Programmers can build your component's functionality into their applications without having to rewrite the code. Although code inheritance works only with the language in which the class is created, the ActiveX component object model works with any programming language that supports ActiveX, such as Microsoft Access, Borland Delphi, or Powersoft's PowerBuilder. The ActiveX component model is a very powerful model for object reuse and has proven to be very popular and successful. After all, every custom control you use in a Visual Basic program is an example of the ActiveX component object model at work!

Why Use Classes and Objects?

For the programmer who is comfortable with procedural programming practices, or for the beginner who is wondering why he should use classes and objects in Visual Basic programming, the following sections give you a few reasons.

Reusability

Code reuse is much simpler when you use classes in Visual Basic applications—especially compared to passing around code libraries with instructions on how to use each function and the required setup code, as well as the old practice of cut and paste. With Visual Basic, you can write a class and document the class's features using the object browser (discussed later in this chapter). After the class is defined, coded, and tested, you can begin to use it in your applications as well as pass it around to colleagues. You will be surprised how easy it is to reuse classes. (I've used the same class for file I/O in three different books, all different applications!) After all, the setup code for using a class is always the same. You create an instance of the class, set properties, and invoke methods. To make your class reusable across multiple languages as well as add distributed computing functionality and Web distribution, you can turn the class into an ActiveX component (which is discussed in detail in Chapter 22). To a Visual Basic programmer, the code required to use an ActiveX component is the same as using a class.

Maintainability

Using classes and objects (ActiveX components) in your code eases program maintenance. If you need to change or modify the class or components, as long as you don't change the interface (by removing properties or methods), you don't have to worry about modifying all the code that uses the class or components. You make changes to the class, test the changes, and recompile the project. If you change an ActiveX component (object) without changing the interface, the code maintenance is much simpler. Test and recompile the component and replace the old component with the new one. All the applications that use the component do not need to be recompiled!

Simplifies Programming

How many times have you built an application to system requirement specs, only to have the users change the requirements at the last minute? This can be a daunting task when using procedural programming practices. What if your application has to keep track of several objects through various states? Have you ever tried tracking several objects using global variables, arrays, or databases? Across multiple forms? Applications can get complex very quickly! Classes simplify object tracking or use of multiple objects because each instance of the object contains the data (properties) for that particular instance of the object. You can create as many objects as you like and use collections to simplify multiple-object use.

Building a Visual Basic Class

Now that you know the textbook definition of a class and a few good reasons to use classes, let's walk through the steps required to create a Visual Basic class. Before getting started, you need to decide on the type of class you want to build. I recently had to build several different types of HTML tables with DAO (data-access objects) recordsets. I found that with the current toolset there was no easy way to test and tweak the VBScript and HTML used to generate the tables. That's about to change. In the following sections, you build a class called the DAOHTMLTable class. The class constructs HTML tables from DAO recordsets and predefined table formats.

NOTE

The DAOHTMLTable class uses objects and syntax that have not been discussed yet, such as HTML tables and DAO. The focus of this chapter is to create and use a Visual Basic class. As such, the code that deals with HTML table generation or DAO is not discussed in detail in this chapter. The code is well documented so that you can understand what is happening. If you are not familiar with HTML tables and want to learn more about them before continuing, see Chapter 11, "Developing HTML Forms for Database Access and Application Interfaces." DAO is discussed in detail in Chapter 9.

Before you can begin to create the class, you first must decide what attributes and actions the class has. Attributes become class properties, and actions become class methods. A high-level diagram of the DAOHTMLTable class is shown in Figure 8.2.

FIGURE 8.2.

The DAOHTMLTable *class.*

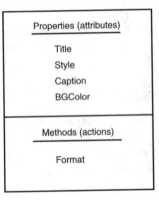

For the DAOHTMLTable class, shown in Figure 8.2, the following properties have been defined:

- ■ Title: Represents the title of the HTML page.
- ■ Style: The style of HTML table to generate.
- ■ Caption: Text to display directly above the HTML table.
- ■ BGColor: Background color of the table.

The DAOHTMLTable class has only a single method—Format. When the Format method is executed, an HTML table is dynamically generated using the DAO recordset passed to the method.

Building the DAOHTMLTable Class

In this section, you walk through the steps necessary to create a class using Visual Basic 5. You create the DAOHTMLTable class, shown in Figure 8.2, and an application to test the class. The test application creates an instance (object) of the DAOHTMLTable class and enables you to set the object properties such as the HTML table caption, the style of the HTML table, and the background color of the HTML table page. The test application uses the Access database—BIBLIO.mdb—that ships with Visual Basic. A DAO recordset based on the following SQL statement is created:

```
SELECT Titles.Title, Titles.ISBN, Authors.Author, Titles.[Year Published],
Publishers.[Company Name] FROM (([title author] INNER JOIN Titles
ON [title author].ISBN = Titles.ISBN) INNER JOIN Authors
ON [title author].Au_ID = Authors.Au_ID) INNER JOIN Publishers
ON Titles.PubID = Publishers.PubID Where Titles.[Year Published] >
1993 ORDER BY Titles.Title;
```

The Format method of the object generates the HTML used for the table. The HTML is saved to a file (using the CFile class) and then loaded into a browser control for viewing. The DAOHTMLTable class and the application to test the class can be found on the CD-ROM that accompanies this book. The project name is HTMLTest.VBP.

Using the Class Builder Utility

Start a new project called HTMLTest in Visual Basic. To add a class to the project, you can select Project from the Visual Basic menu and then select Add Class, or you can use a new graphical utility called the Class Builder Utility, which ships with Visual Basic 5. The Class Builder Utility is a Visual Basic add-in. (You must register the add-in before you can use it.)

> **NOTE**
>
> If you are unfamiliar with Visual Basic add-ins and how to register them, see Appendix A, "Features New to Visual Basic 5."

When you have registered the Visual Basic add-in, perform the following steps:

1. From the Visual Basic menu, select Add-Ins.
2. From the drop-down menu, select Class Builder Utility. The dialog box shown in Figure 8.3 appears.

To add a new class, click the Add New Class button, shown in Figure 8.3. The Class Module Builder dialog box appears, as shown in Figure 8.4.

FIGURE 8.3.
The Class Builder Utility dialog box.

Add New Propery to Current Class
Add New Method to Current Class

Add New Class ——

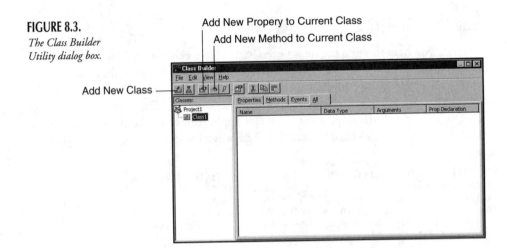

FIGURE 8.4.
The Class Module Builder dialog box.

Name the new class by entering the class name in the Name textbox, shown in Figure 8.4. For this example, type DAOHTMLTable. You will use this name to create objects (instances of the class). To add text comments about your class use the Description textbox found on the Attributes tab of the Class Module Builder dialog window, as shown in Figure 8.4.

Adding Properties

Properties are the attributes of the class. In the DAOHTMLTable example, the properties are as follows (in case you forgot):

- Title
- Style
- Caption
- BGColor

The simplest way to add a property is to declare a public variable in the class module declaration section, like this:

```
Public Style as Byte
```

This creates a class property Style with a Byte data type. The problem with creating a property using a public variable is that anyone can supply values to the property without the class validating whether or not the value supplied is valid. For instance, in the case of the Style property, the example only supports values from 0 to 2. What's to prevent a user from setting the value to 5? The idea of validating an object's data and not allowing the user to directly modify the object's data is a part of encapsulation called *data hiding*.

Visual Basic enables you to perform true data encapsulation and data hiding by using public property procedures and private variables. A property procedure is the attribute interface exposed to applications using your class. The actual data used by the class is stored in the class declaration module as private. By declaring the variables private, only functions and procedures within the class can directly modify these values. Applications using your class must use the property procedures to change the object's properties, allowing you to add validation code before setting the object's data values. Before discussing how to add a property procedure, let's look at how the property Style is implemented in the DAOHTMLTable class. The first step is to declare the private data member for the Style property in the class declaration section as follows:

```
Private mbytStyle As Byte        'Style of the HTML table to generate
```

To define the interface to the user's public property Style, the class property procedures Let (or Set) and Get are created.

> **NOTE**
>
> I often run into programmers who are confused by the property procedures Let, Get, and Set. The confusion stems primarily from when to use Let or Set. Use Let when the property represents non-objects such as strings, integers, and longs. Use Set when your property represents an object (another class, DAO, Excel, and so on). The Class Builder Utility helps clear up the confusion by automatically deciding whether to use Let or Set based on the data type for your property (demonstrated later in this chapter).

When the value of the Style property is changed, the Let procedure is invoked. The code for Let is as follows:

```
Public Property Let Style(ByVal bytNewStyle As Byte)
    If bytNewStyle > MAX_TABLE_VALUE Then
        mbytStyle = STANDARD_TABLE
```

```
    Else
        mbytStyle = bytNewStyle
    End If
End Property
```

Notice that the value passed in is defined as Byte. The property procedure also checks the value being passed in. If it exceeds a valid table style value (the constant MAX_TABLE_VALUE), the value passed in by the user is overridden and set to the default. Finally, the private (hidden) variable mbytStyle is set to the value passed in. To retrieve the property value, the Get procedure is called. The following code snippet is for the Get procedure for the property Style:

```
Public Property Get Style() As Byte
    Style = mbytStyle
End Property
```

The Get property procedure is very simple, setting the Style property to the value of the private variable mbytStyle.

> **TIP**
>
> To make a read-only property, remove the Let or Set property procedure.

To add a property procedure using the Class Builder Utility, shown in Figure 8.3, click the Add New Property to Current Class tool button. The Property Builder dialog box, shown in Figure 8.5, appears.

FIGURE 8.5.

The Property Builder dialog box.

Type the name of the property in the Name textbox (shown in Figure 8.5). Use the Data Type drop-down listbox to select a valid data type for your property. The proper Let or Set property procedure will be generated based on the data type selected. Using the Property Builder dialog box, select the type of property procedure you want to create. You've already learned about public property procedures and public variables. Friend property procedures are covered in detail in Chapter 22. Friend property procedures look like regular property procedures when used within a class in a Visual Basic project. However, if you use Friend property procedures in a reusable ActiveX component, the Friend property procedures are not visible to other applications (which means they are not part of the class's interface). New to Visual Basic 5 is the capability to designate a default property for your class. Like a default property on a custom control, if you set an object to a value without specifying a property, the default property is used. To add a text description about the property or associate a help file with the property, use the Attributes tab of the Property Builder dialog box. The code for the remaining DAOHTMLTable class properties is shown in Listing 8.1.

Listing 8.1. Property procedures and private variables for DAOHTMLTable.

```
'Class Private Variables
Private mstrTitle As String     'Title of HTML page
Private mbytStyle As Byte        'Style of the HTML table to generate
Private mstrCaption As String   'Caption of HTML page
Private mstrBGColor As String   'Color for the Table background

'Class Constants
'   HTML Table Styles Supported
Private Const STANDARD_TABLE As Byte = 0
Private Const LIST_TABLE As Byte = 1
Private Const TABLE_PER_ROW As Byte = 2
Private Const MAX_TABLE_VALUE As Byte = TABLE_PER_ROW

Public Property Get BGColor() As String
    BGColor = mstrBGColor
End Property

Public Property Let BGColor(ByVal strNewColor As String)
    mstrBGColor = strNewColor
End Property

Public Property Get Title() As String
    Title = mstrTitle
End Property

Public Property Let Title(ByVal strNewTitle As String)
    mstrTitle = strNewTitle
End Property

Public Property Get Caption() As String
    Caption = mstrCaption
End Property

Public Property Let Caption(ByVal strNewCaption As String)
    mstrCaption = strNewCaption
End Property
```

Adding Methods

Methods are the actions your object can perform. Class methods are no different from the functions and procedures you create in standard modules, except they are in a class module packaged with the data. You can add a class method by using the Visual Basic main menu. Select Tools and then Add Procedure from the drop-down list. To add a method using the Class Builder Utility, click the Add New Method to Current Class tool button (as you saw in Figure 8.3). The Method Builder dialog box appears, as shown in Figure 8.6.

FIGURE 8.6.

The Method Builder dialog box.

Enter the name of the method in the Name textbox. To add arguments, click the + sign, and the Add Argument dialog box appears, as shown in Figure 8.7.

FIGURE 8.7.

The Add Argument dialog box.

To add an argument, enter the argument name, select the data type, and click the OK button. Use the X sign to remove a selected argument, and use the arrow buttons to move an argument up or down.

To make the method a function (so that it returns a value), select the return data type in the Return Data Type combo box on the Method Builder dialog box (refer to Figure 8.6). The Declare as Friend? checkbox makes the method a Friend. Friend methods are similar to Friend property procedures in that they can be used within a Visual Basic project with the class but can't be used by other applications (because they are not part of the class interface). Checking the Default Method? checkbox makes the method the default for the class. To add a text description about the property or to associate a help file with the property, use the Attributes tab of the Property Builder dialog box. The code for the Format method is shown in Listing 8.2.

Listing 8.2. The Format method of DAOHTMLTable.

```
Public Function Format(recSource As Recordset) As String
Dim strHTMLReturn As String 'String to build HTML format
Dim intNumOfColumns As Integer 'Number of columns in the recordset
Dim fldRec As Field
Dim colFields As Fields
Dim intCount As Integer 'Generic Counter

    strHTMLReturn = ""
    'Set up our HTML String - Start with the basic HTML Document
    strHTMLReturn = "<HTML>" & vbCrLf
    If mstrTitle <> "" Then
        strHTMLReturn = strHTMLReturn & "<HEAD>" & vbCrLf & _
                        "<TITLE>" & mstrTitle & "</TITLE>" & _
                        vbCrLf & "</HEAD>"
    Else
        strHTMLReturn = strHTMLReturn & "<HEAD>" & vbCrLf & _
                        vbCrLf & "</HEAD>"
    End If

    strHTMLReturn = strHTMLReturn & "<BODY>" & vbCrLf
    strHTMLReturn = strHTMLReturn & _
                    "<H2>Example of using a VB class</H2>" & vbCrLf
    strHTMLReturn = strHTMLReturn & "<P>" & vbCrLf

    'Begin the Table format using the TAG Table
    If mbytStyle <> STANDARD_TABLE Then
        strHTMLReturn = strHTMLReturn & _
                        "<TABLE width=100% cellspacing=0 cellpadding=0 "
    Else
        strHTMLReturn = strHTMLReturn & _
                "<TABLE ALIGN=center FRAME=BOX BORDER=1 BORDERCOLOR=BLACK "
    End If

    'Add the table Background color
    strHTMLReturn = strHTMLReturn & "BGCOLOR = " & mstrBGColor & ">" & vbCrLf

    If mstrCaption <> "" Then
        strHTMLReturn = strHTMLReturn & "<CAPTION><B>" & mstrCaption & _
                        "</B></CAPTION>" & vbCrLf
    End If

    'Basic HTML string is setup - get the Number of Columns
    iNumOfColumns = recSource.Fields.Count - 1 'Make 0 based
    Set colFields = recSource.Fields

    'Generate Table based on the table Style selected
    Select Case mbytStyle
```

continues

Listing 8.2. continued

```
Case STANDARD_TABLE
    'Check for Column Headers First
    If mblnDisplayHeaders Then
        'Add column Headers
        For Each fldRec In colFields
            strHTMLReturn = strHTMLReturn & "<TH>" & fldRec.Name
        Next fldRec
        strHTMLReturn = strHTMLReturn & vbCrLf
    End If

    'Add The data rows
    While Not recSource.BOF And Not recSource.EOF
        strHTMLReturn = strHTMLReturn & "<TR>"
        For intCount = 0 To iNumOfColumns
            strHTMLReturn = strHTMLReturn & "<TD>" & _
                            recSource(intCount) & "</TD>" & vbCrLf

        Next intCount
        strHTMLReturn = strHTMLReturn & "</TR>"
        'Get the Next Record
        recSource.MoveNext

    Wend

Case LIST_TABLE
    'Add The data rows
    While Not recSource.BOF And Not recSource.EOF
        For intCount = 0 To iNumOfColumns
            strHTMLReturn = strHTMLReturn & "<TR> <TD align=center> " & _
                            colFields(intCount).Name & ":</td> <td> " & _
                            recSource(intCount) & "</TR>" & vbCrLf

        Next intCount

        'Add A Line
        strHTMLReturn = strHTMLReturn & "<HR>" & vbCrLf
        'Get the Next Record
        recSource.MoveNext
    Wend

Case Else
    'Add The data rows
    While Not recSource.BOF And Not recSource.EOF
        strHTMLReturn = strHTMLReturn & _
                    "<TABLE BORDER BORDERCOLOR=Black>" & vbCrLf

        For intCount = 0 To iNumOfColumns

            strHTMLReturn = strHTMLReturn & "<TR> <TD width=75> " & _
                            colFields(intCount).Name & ":</td> <td> " & _
                            recSource(intCount) & "</TR>" & vbCrLf
        Next intCount

        'Add A Line
        strHTMLReturn = strHTMLReturn & "</Table><HR>" & vbCrLf
        'Get the Next Record
        recSource.MoveNext
    Wend
```

```
      End Select

      'End HTML Doc
      strHTMLReturn = strHTMLReturn & "</TABLE>" & vbCrLf & _
                      "</BODY>" & vbCrLf & "</HTML>"
      'Return The string to the calling function
      Format = strHTMLReturn

End Function
```

Class Initialize and Terminate Events

Visual Basic classes have two predefined events—Initialize and Terminate.

> **NOTE**
>
> Besides properties and methods, Visual Basic 5 classes can have user-defined events that can be activated outside the class (just like ActiveX control events). Adding and using user-defined events is discussed in detail in Chapter 16.

The Initialize event occurs when an object (instance of the class) is created. Use the Initialize event to initialize property members and any other startup code required for the class. The Terminate event is fired when the object is destroyed by setting its object reference equal to the Visual Basic keyword Nothing. Use the Terminate event to destroy any objects used and reclaim any memory used by class variables. The Initialize and Terminate event code for the DAOHTMLTable is shown in Listing 8.3.

Listing 8.3. The DAOHTMLTable class Initialize and Terminate event code.

```
Private Sub Class_Initialize()
    'Initialize the object properties
    mstrTitle = ""
    mstrCaption = ""
    mstrBGColor = "White"
    mbytStyle = STANDARD_TABLE

End Sub

Private Sub Class_Terminate()
    'Clear strings used by the Object
    mstrTitle = ""
    mstrCaption = ""
End Sub
```

The DAOHTMLTable class is complete. Now let's create the form to test the completed class.

An Application to Test the Class DAOHTMLTable

To test the DAOHTMLTable class, add a single form to the project. The following form-level variables are used to test the class:

```
Public gdbBiblio As Database
Public gbnlBrowse As Boolean
```

The variable gdbBiblio is the Database object used for the Biblio.mdb database. The variable gbnlBrowse is used to determine whether the browser control should perform a navigate method or a refresh method. Because the application always writes the HTML string to the same file, after the file has been loaded, a refresh can be done instead of a navigate to reflect the changes made. The code shown in Listing 8.4 is responsible for loading the combo boxes used in the application and opening the database. The error-handling code in Listing 8.4 is quite interesting and worth a closer look. If the database used in the application, Biblio.mdb, is not located in the same directory as the test application, a dialog box is displayed to allow the user to locate and select the database.

Listing 8.4. The form frmMain load event code.

```
Private Sub Form_Load()
' Fill the combo list box with HTML table styles supported by
' the class DAOHTMLTable. Open the Access database that ships
' with Visual Basic Biblio.mdb. If the database is not found
' display a dialog box and allow the user to locate the database.
'
Dim strDBPath As String

    On Error GoTo Load_Error

    'Show the form
    frmMain.Show

    ' Set the global browser flag
    gbnlBrowse = False

    'Load the Style List box
    With cboStyle
        .AddItem "Standard"
        .AddItem "List"
        .AddItem "Table Each Row"
        .ListIndex = 0
    End With

    'Load the Background color List Box
    With cboColor
        .AddItem "White"
        .AddItem "Gray"
        .AddItem "Red"
        .AddItem "Blue"
        .AddItem "Yellow"
        .AddItem "Green"
        .ListIndex = 0
    End With
```

```
        strDBPath = App.Path & "\Biblio.mdb"

Try_Again:
        'Open the database
        Set gdbBiblio = OpenDatabase(strDBPath)

Load_Exit:
        'Check if the database was opened correctly
        If (gdbBiblio Is Nothing) Then
            'Database Not opened - Alert User and quit the application.
            MsgBox "Unable to open the database Biblio.mdb. Application exiting.", _
                    vbCritical, "Open Database Error"
            Unload frmMain
            Set frmMain = Nothing
            End
        End If

        Exit Sub


'Error handler - look for DAO error - database not found
Load_Error:

        'Look for File not found error
        If Err.Number = 3024 Then
            'Display the Common dialog box and allow the
            'user to locate Biblio.mdb
            dlgFile.ShowOpen
            If dlgFile.FileName <> "" Then
                strDBPath = dlgFile.FileName
                Resume Try_Again
            Else
                Resume Load_Exit
            End If
        End If

        'Display Error message
        MsgBox Err.Description, vbCritical, "Form Load Error"
        Resume Load_Exit

End Sub
```

The code that actually creates the DAOHTMLTable object is shown in Listing 8.5. The important aspects of the code are as follows: A DAO recordset is opened and an instance (object) of the DAOHTMLTable is created using the variable oHTMLPage and the keyword New. The properties for the object oHTMLPage are set based on the selection made on the form. The Format method of the object is used to format the recordset. The returned HTML string from the Format method is then written to a file. The file is created and saved using a simple Visual Basic class called CFile. CFile can be found on the CD-ROM that accompanies this book and is used to perform sequential file I/O. The file generated is called wwwdvtst.htm, located in the directory from which the test application is executed. The file is then loaded into the browser control using the navigate method. The application and an HTML table generated by the DAOHTMLTable class are shown in Figure 8.8.

FIGURE 8.8.

*The DAOHTMLTable
test application.*

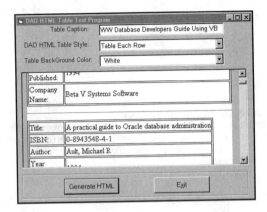

Listing 8.5. Generate HTML command button code.

```
Private Sub cmdFormat_Click()
Const SUCCESS = 1
Dim recTitles As Recordset
Dim oHTMLPage As DAOHTMLTable
Dim strHTML As String
Dim oHTMLFile As CFile
Dim strSQL As String

    Me.MousePointer = vbHourglass

    'Set up the SQL Statement to get all the titles published after 1993
    strSQL = "SELECT Titles.Title, Titles.ISBN, Authors.Author," & _
 "Titles.[Year Published], Publishers.[Company Name] " & _
            "FROM (([title author] INNER JOIN Titles ON " & _
 "[title author].ISBN = Titles.ISBN) INNER JOIN Authors ON " & _
            "[title author].Au_ID = Authors.Au_ID) INNER JOIN Publishers" & _
 " ON Titles.PubID = Publishers.PubID " & _
            "Where Titles.[Year Published] > 1993 " & _
            "ORDER BY Titles.Title;"

    'Open the Recordset
    Set recTitles = gdbBiblio.OpenRecordset(strSQL)

    'Create a DAOHTML Object
    Set oHTMLPage = New DAOHTMLTable

    'Set the Caption
    With oHTMLPage
        .Caption = txtCaption
        .Style = cboStyle.ListIndex
        .Title = "SAMS WWW DB Developers Guide Using Visual Basic"
        .BGColor = cboColor.Text
        strHTML = .Format(recTitles)
    End With

    'Create a file to save the HTML string to.
    Set oHTMLFile = New CFile
    With oHTMLFile
        .FileName = App.Path & "\wwwdvtst.htm"
```

```
            .IOMode = "Output"
            .IOType = "SEQUENTIAL"
            .OpenFile
            If .Status = SUCCESS Then
                .WriteAll (strHTML)
            End If
            .CloseFile
        End With
        Set oHTMLFile = Nothing

        'Display the File in the WebBrowser Object
        'If previously displayed then just refresh
        If gbnlBrowse Then
            WebBrowser.Refresh
        Else
            WebBrowser.Navigate App.Path & "\wwwdvtst.htm"
        End If

        'Make the Browser Visible
        WebBrowser.Visible = True

        'Close the recordset
        recTitles.Close
        Set recTitles = Nothing


End Sub
```

Test the application with different colors and table formats. Examine the code, especially the code segments that create and use objects based on Visual Basic classes. You can modify the Format method to add your own HTML table formats.

Interfaces

As mentioned earlier, Visual Basic does not allow you to reuse code by inheriting properties and methods from another class. (Of course, you can always cut and paste.) However, with Visual Basic 5, you can define a template for a class that describes methods and properties of the class without defining how the method or property is implemented (which means you use no code). You can then use these class templates to inherit the methods and properties of the template when creating other classes. After you have inherited the behavior of the class template, you then add the code to determine how the method and properties will be implemented. These reusable class templates are called interfaces. Besides describing methods and properties of a class, interfaces enable you to perform another object-oriented feature in Visual Basic called *polymorphism.* In OOP, polymorphism allows classes to have the same method or property, and the caller does not need to worry about the object type before calling the method. For example, a pencil object and a pen object, based on the SketchTool interface, both have a DrawLine method. Polymorphism is attained because you don't have to know which object (pen or pencil) of the derived `SketchTool` object is calling the `DrawLine` method. To create an interface, add a class module to a project and then define property procedures and methods without defining any code. Listing 8.6 shows an interface with a `DrawLine` method and a property called `Color`.

Listing 8.6. An example of a Visual Basic interface.

```
Public Sub DrawLine()

End Sub

Public Property Get Color() As Variant

End Property

Public Property Let Color(ByVal vNewValue As Variant)

End Property
```

To use an interface, declare a new class, and in the class module declarations section, add the Visual Basic keyword `Implements` with the name of the interface. For example, the following line of code uses the `SketchTool` interface:

```
Implements SketchTool
```

After you add the keyword `Implements`, you can add the implementation code for the properties and methods described by the interface. Interfaces are very powerful features that enable a programmer to define the behavior and members of a class without defining how they are implemented.

> **NOTE**
>
> When you base a new class on an interface, you must add implementation code for all methods and properties supplied by the interface.

Using Objects

This chapter has primarily concentrated on using Visual Basic 5 to create your own classes and use objects based on those classes. Besides using the classes you create, Visual Basic and the ActiveX environment contain a very rich environment of reusable objects. In this section, you create an application that uses objects exposed by the Microsoft Internet Explorer. (Yes, sometimes applications such as Microsoft Excel, Word, and Access supply objects.) The easiest way to view reusable components installed on your machine that you can use in your applications is to view the References dialog box, shown in Figure 8.9, which can be reached by selecting the Project menu selection on the Visual Basic main menu.

FIGURE 8.9.

The Visual Basic References dialog box.

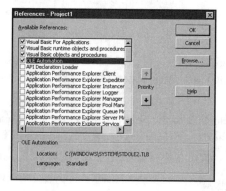

The References dialog box lists all the available ActiveX components (which were OLE servers in previous versions of Visual Basic) on your machine. To use a component in your Visual Basic program, you must first check the box by the component's name in the Visual Basic References dialog box. To view objects, methods, and properties of objects, forms, or classes in your Visual Basic project, use the Object Browser shown in Figure 8.10.

FIGURE 8.10.

The Visual Basic Object Browser dialog box.

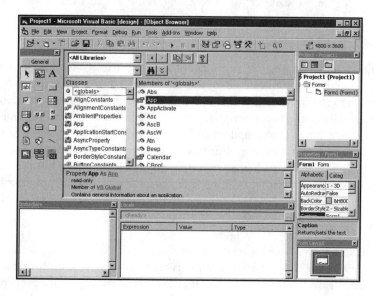

The Object Browser enables you to easily determine the available properties and methods of an object. The Object Browser also provides descriptions of the objects, properties, events, and methods.

> **NOTE**
>
> The Object Browser in Visual Basic 5 is a huge improvement over the Visual Basic 4 Object Browser. If you gave up on the VB 4 Object Browser, give the VB 5 Object Browser a try. I think you'll be impressed.

Using objects exposed by applications or ActiveX components is the same as creating and using objects with Visual Basic classes. The general steps to using an ActiveX component are as follows:

1. Add a reference to the object that you want to use in your Visual Basic project, using the Visual Basic References dialog box, shown in Figure 8.9.

2. Declare a variable to create an object reference.

3. Use the Visual Basic keyword `New` or the function `CreateObject` to create an instance of the object.

Early and Late Object Binding

When you have added a reference to the object you want to use, you can declare a variable to create the object. Whenever possible, you should declare the object variable using the actual object type of the object you are creating. For example, the following line of code declares an object variable of the type `InternetExplorer`:

```
Public moIE As InternetExplorer
```

Declaring a variable with the proper object type enables Visual Basic to determine the variable object type at compile time, not at runtime. Using the proper object type also enables Visual Basic to check the methods and properties used in your code with the object's exposed interface, valid methods, and properties at compile time instead of at runtime. Resolving the object type of a variable at compile time is called *early-binding*. As stated earlier, use early-binding whenever possible to take advantage of object validation and much better performance when creating objects. The alternative to early-binding is *late-binding*. Late-binding occurs when you declare a variable with the generic data type of `Object`. For example, the following code snippet defines a variable using the `Object` data type:

```
Public moIE As Object
```

Because the variable is declared using the generic `Object` data type, Visual Basic does not resolve the object type until the object is created, which is at runtime and not design-time. Because Visual Basic does not know the data type of the object, the properties and methods used in your code cannot be validated at compile time and could result in a runtime error if you use an invalid property or method. Remember to use early-binding whenever possible; resolving a variable's object type at runtime is costly! Use the generic Object tag only when you don't know the types of objects you will be creating.

Creating an Object from an ActiveX Component

Creating an instance of an ActiveX component (exposed object) is the same as creating an object of a Visual Basic class. Use the Visual Basic keyword New. The following example demonstrates using the keyword New to create an instance of the Internet Explorer object:

```
Public moIE As InternetExplorer
'Create an instance of the Internet Explorer.
    Set moIE = New InternetExplorer
```

You can also use the function CreateObject to create a new object (but the keyword New is the preferred method).

When you are finished using the object created by the ActiveX component, you need to destroy the object reference using the Visual Basic keyword Nothing, as in the following code snippet:

```
Set moIe = Nothing
```

Controlling the Internet Explorer

In this section, you examine a Visual Basic application that uses ActiveX components (objects). The application does the following:

■ Creates an object instance of the Microsoft Internet Explorer

■ Sets properties of the object

■ Controls Web Page Navigation

■ Shuts down the Microsoft Internet Explorer

The application project file is called cntrlie.vbp and is located on the accompanying CD-ROM. To run the application requires Internet Explorer 3.0 or greater and Visual Basic 5. To use the application, perform the following steps:

1. Open the Visual Basic project cntrlie.vbp.

2. From the Visual Basic main menu, select Run| Start.

3. Click the command button labeled Start. The Microsoft Internet Explorer starts and goes to your browser's home page, as shown in Figure 8.11.

4. Use the drop-down combo box, shown in Figure 8.11, to select a Website. When you select the site in the combo box, the Internet Explorer navigates to the selected page.

5. Click the Stop button to shut down the Internet Explorer.

FIGURE 8.11.

The application
cntrlie *controlling*
the Internet Explorer.

Before moving on to the next chapter, let's take a quick look at the code, shown in Listing 8.7.

Listing 8.7. Code for the Visual Basic project cntlrie**.**

```
Public moIE As InternetExplorer


Private Sub cboSite_Click()
Dim strURL As String

    'Combo box clicked

    If cboSite.Text <> "" Then
        strURL = cboSite.Text
        moIE.Navigate strURL
    End If
End Sub

Private Sub cmdStart_Click()
    'Create an instance of the Internet Explorer.
    Set moIE = New InternetExplorer

    'Make the Internet Explorer Visible
    moIE.Visible = True

    'Goto the home site

    'Enable the combo box
    cboSite.Enabled = True
    cmdStop.Enabled = True
    cmdStart.Enabled = False
```

```
End Sub

Private Sub cmdStop_Click()

    'Execute the Quit method
    moIE.Quit

    'Destroy our reference
    Set moIE = Nothing
    cmdStop.Enabled = False
    cmdStart.Enabled = True

End Sub

Private Sub Form_Load()
    'Load the combo box with some
    'important book and developers sites as
    'well as ActiveX examples.

    cboSite.AddItem "http://www.microsoft.com"
    cboSite.AddItem "http://www.mcp.com/mcp"
    cboSite.AddItem "http://www.kscsinc.com"
End Sub
```

An instance of the Microsoft Internet Explorer is created with the following lines of code:

```
'Create an instance of the Internet Explorer.
    Set moIE = New InternetExplorer
```

When you have an object instance of the Internet Explorer, you need to make the object visible using the Visible property. The following line of code makes the Internet Explorer visible:

```
moIE.Visible = True
```

After the Internet Explorer is visible, the application invokes the GoHome method to go to the designated home page of your Internet Explorer. The following code navigates to the selected Website:

```
If cboSite.Text <> "" Then
        strURL = cboSite.Text
        moIE.Navigate strURL
```

The following code snippet closes the Internet Explorer and cleans up the object reference:

```
'Execute the Quit method
    moIE.Quit

    ' Destroy our reference
    Set moIE = Nothing
```

Summary

In this chapter, you have seen an overview of ActiveX and the various technologies that make up ActiveX. You learn more about ActiveX and ActiveX scripting in Chapters 12 through 14. Chapters 16 and 17 cover creating ActiveX controls and ActiveX documents in great detail.

The most important bit of knowledge you could gain from this chapter is an understanding of how to create Visual Basic classes and how to use classes and components in code. This chapter serves as the foundation for creating and using ActiveX components, especially server components. Creating ActiveX components from Visual Basic classes is discussed in detail in Chapter 22.

The next chapter, "Visual Basic 5 Data Access Features," is the building block for understanding the different data access methods you will use in your database Web applications.

9

Visual Basic 5 Data Access Features

by Mark Spenik

Up to this point, you've covered an overview of database design and SQL, but very little information had to do specifically with Visual Basic. Well that's about to change. It's time to review the Visual Basic data access objects you will be using in an intranet and Internet environment.

The primary purpose of this chapter is to review the various Visual Basic data access objects used throughout this book. Code examples with lots of comments are provided to help refresh your Visual Basic data access skills. If you find you need more detail or do not understand the code examples, I suggest reading other Sams books that concentrate specifically on Visual Basic database development. If you're already an expert in Visual Basic data access objects, I suggest that you review this chapter. Several data access objects have been modified, such as the edition of RDO asynchronous events, and new objects have been added, such as ODBCDirect. This chapter also introduces a new and important data access object designed for Active Server Page Internet development—and maybe the future DAO and RDO replacement—called Active Data Objects.

> **TIP**
>
> If you are new to Visual Basic and want to learn more, check out *Teach Yourself Visual Basic 5 in 21 Days* by Sams Publishing or *Visual Basic 5 Interactive Course* by Waite Group Press.

An Overview of Visual Basic Data Access Features

When you discuss Visual Basic data access methods, it sounds like alphabet soup with acronyms such as DAO, RDO, ODBC, and ADO. Why are there so many different ways to access a database? The data access methods available to a Visual Basic programmer have evolved over time as Visual Basic has become a richer development environment for all types of database applications, from file-based database applications (such as dBASE and Access), to client/server database applications (such as Oracle, Sybase, Microsoft SQL Server, and Ingres), to the Internet. The following list shows the various data access methods available to a Visual Basic developer when developing intranet/Internet applications:

■ Native Database APIs
■ ODBC
■ DAO
■ RDO
■ ODBCDirect
■ OLE DB and ADO

Let's take a brief look at each of these data access methods and then make a determination of the proper times to use each method.

Native Database APIs

Native database APIs (Application Programming Interfaces) are typically used in a client/server environment in which a developer creates an application using a proprietary set of native database APIs. An example of a native database API is VBSQL for Microsoft SQL Server. Native database APIs enable a developer to write applications that use the full functionality of the database with no middleware and provide a high level of performance between the application and the database server. Building applications using the native database API typically requires writing more code than object-based solutions require. One drawback of using native database APIs is that when a Visual Basic application is written using a native database API, the application can't be easily ported to another database because the database APIs are propriety. (For example, you could not easily port a Visual Basic Oracle native API application to a Visual Basic Microsoft SQL Server application.)

ODBC

ODBC stands for *Open Database Connectivity*. ODBC is an open standard that provides a common set of API calls to manipulate databases. Application developers can write applications that make ODBC calls and will work with many databases, instead of writing programs specifically for a particular database (which is the case with native database APIs). Some advantages to the ODBC API over native database APIs are as follows:

■ A single API to any database with an ODBC driver. If a developer wants to use Oracle or Sybase, the API calls are the same when using ODBC. When using native database APIs, the developer would have to know the Oracle API and the Sybase API.

■ An open standard supported by many development tools. (It is not Visual Basic specific.)

■ Applications can be easily ported from one database to another.

■ Enables you to access data from more than one type of database from the same application.

Applications built with ODBC can take advantage of the majority of the functionality of the database and are as fast as applications developed using native database drivers.

> **NOTE**
>
> You might find people who, upon hearing about ODBC, automatically think *slow*. I have run many tests on my own, attended numerous technical conferences, and have

shown repeatedly that application processing speed using ODBC APIs versus native database APIs is about the same. I think ODBC got a bad name from poorly implemented version 1.0 drivers and Visual Basic applications using DAO and ODBC improperly.

ODBC applications can be ported easily by switching the ODBC driver instead of recoding the entire application. Using ODBC APIs requires a lot of coding, in some cases exceeding the amount of code required to write native database API applications. The architecture overview of an application accessing a remote database via ODBC is shown in Figure 9.1.

FIGURE 9.1.

An application accessing a remote database via ODBC.

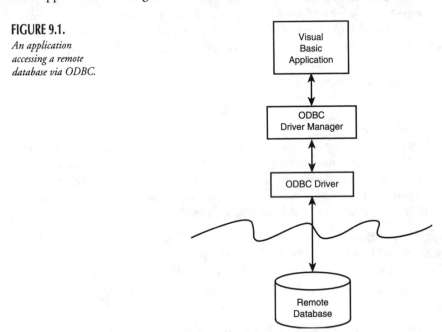

DAO

A DAO (data-access object) is probably the most familiar data access method available to Visual Basic programmers. DAO provides Visual Basic developers who have little or no SQL experience with a simple object model that can be used to create database applications. DAO was first introduced in Visual Basic 3 with Jet 1.1. Jet is the native database engine for the Microsoft Access database and is shared by Microsoft Visual Basic, Visual C++, Visual J++, and Access. DAO was enhanced to a 32-bit version, Jet 3.0, in Visual Basic 4 and has been further improved in Visual Basic 5 with Jet version 3.5. DAO consists of the Microsoft Jet engine and the data-access objects. The architecture overview of an application accessing an Access database and remote database via DAO is shown in Figure 9.2.

FIGURE 9.2.

An application accessing an Access database and a remote database via DAO.

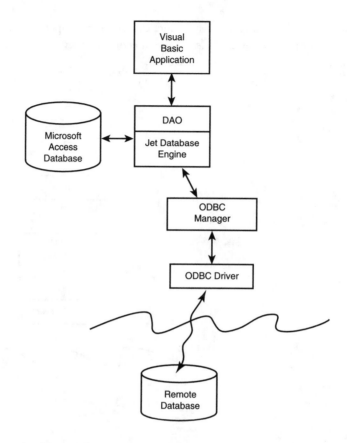

DAO can be used to create database applications with a lot less code than is required by either native database APIs or the ODBC APIs. The Jet engine is a very powerful feature-rich database engine. DAO can also be used against client/server databases using ODBC. However, accessing client/server databases via DAO adds overhead, less functionality, and, in many cases, poor performance when compared to the ODBC API or native database APIs. Microsoft addressed some of the performance problem in DAO 3.0. Later in this chapter, you learn how the performance problem has been addressed further in Visual Basic 5 with DAO and ODBCDirect.

RDO

To answer the cries for more performance and an object model designed specifically to handle ODBC client/server databases, Microsoft released RDO (Remote Data Objects) in the Visual Basic 4 Enterprise edition. RDO is a thin object model layered on top of the ODBC API designed to simplify and reduce the amount of code required to use the ODBC API. RDO enables you to use most of the functionality of the backend database, with higher performance than DAO and only a slight performance degradation compared to making direct ODBC API calls or using native database APIs. The architecture overview of an application accessing a remote database via RDO is shown in Figure 9.3.

FIGURE 9.3.

An application accessing a remote database via RDO.

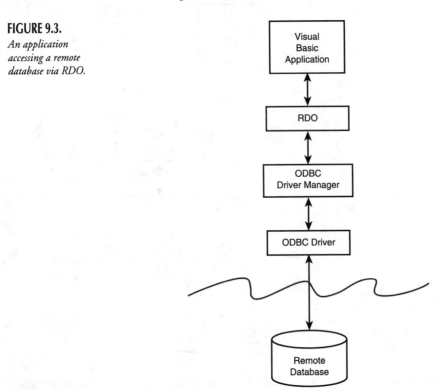

ODBCDirect

You bought Visual Basic 4 Enterprise edition and you were an experienced DAO programmer, but you needed to access remote ODBC databases as fast as possible, so you put in the extra work to learn a brand-new data-access object model—RDO. Welcome to Visual Basic 5 and another way to access client/server databases! This time it is that familiar object model DAO. Using ODBCDirect, you can now create applications that use the DAO object model, bypass the Jet engine, and access ODBC remote databases through RDO. That's right. ODBCDirect layers the DAO object model on top of RDO, as shown in Figure 9.4.

FIGURE 9.4.
An application accessing a remote database via ODBCDirect.

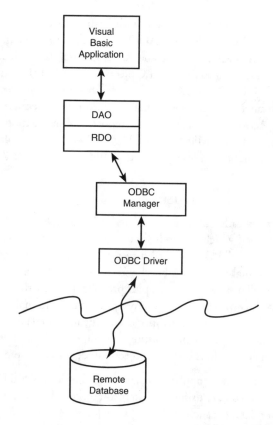

The advantage of ODBCDirect is that your application is immediately smaller because you don't load the Jet engine (which saves over 1MB), and you don't have to learn the RDO object model. Converting an existing Access database application to a remote ODBC database can now be accomplished with little or no code changes using ODBCDirect.

OLE DB and ADO

The data access methods discussed so far were created to handle client/server RDBMS and file-based database applications using Visual Basic. But with the increasing popularity of the Internet, expanding enterprise systems, and user demands to share and distribute data from many different data sources, a new object model designed for different data sources is required to handle various types of data such as RDBMS, spreadsheets, e-mail, groupware, and so on. Enter the OLE DB specification. OLE DB is a series of APIs based on COM that enables a C/C++ programmer to get at data from OLE DB providers. ADO (Active Data Objects) is a high-level object model that sits on top of OLE DB and gives Visual Basic developers a way to get at OLE

DB databases. ADO does not ship with Visual Basic 5. It is shipped as part of the Internet Information Server Version 3.0. ADO will be the primary data access object used when creating Active Server Pages. OLE DB and ADO are discussed in detail in Chapter 21, "Active Server Pages, OLE DB, and Active Data Objects." Several of this book's sample applications make use of ADO. OLE DB and ADO are mentioned now to let you know where they currently fit into the intranet/Internet development environment, because ADO will be all the rage when developing Active Server Pages. Recent reports and speculation, published at the time this book was written, state that Microsoft will begin to work on consolidating the RDO and DAO interface into a single data-access object. Could this be ADO? Possibly....

Which Object Do I Use?

With the many different data access methods available to a Visual Basic Internet/intranet database developer, which methods should you use? I will quickly rule out using native database APIs and calling the ODBC API directly. Both methods provide great performance, and in the days of Visual Basic 3, 16-bit clients, and client/server databases, they were much needed technologies that saved many complex projects. Both methods, however, require far too much low-level coding, providing too many opportunities to make mistakes in an ActiveX component. Also, the lack of an object model and the increased amount of code required reduces the overall productivity of the programmer. Finally, the direction Microsoft is taking with intranet and Internet applications is clearly object-based, whereas these two programming APIs are not.

For developing intranet applications, you can choose between DAO, RDO, and ODBCDirect. If the database you are using is a Microsoft Access database, use DAO. If you are accessing a client/server database such as Sybase, Oracle, or Microsoft SQL Server, use RDO. If you are porting an existing Access database application to a remote ODBC database, use ODBCDirect. Another factor in data access selection will be the edition of Visual Basic you have purchased. RDO is available only in the Enterprise Edition of Visual Basic.

For developing Internet server-side applications, ActiveX data-aware components, or OLEISAPI components, the data access choices are the same as for an intranet with the additional ADO option. Active Data Objects controlled via Active Server Pages and VBScript will be the primary method for database access from within an Internet server-side script because the ADO object model is supported by Active Server Pages.

DAO Refresher

In this section, you review commonly used DAO objects, properties, and methods, along with sample code. DAO is the object interface, provided to the Visual Basic programmer, that sits on top of the Jet engine. DAO's native database, accessed via Jet and DAO, is the Microsoft Access database. You can also access ODBC or ISAM databases using DAO and Jet. Let's get started by taking a look at the DAO object model shown in Figure 9.5.

FIGURE 9.5.
The DAO object model.

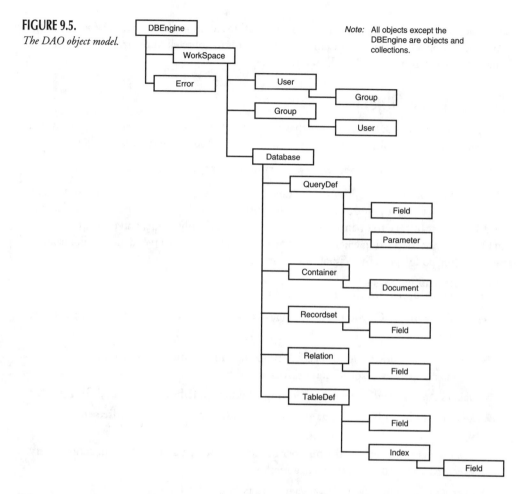

Note: All objects except the DBEngine are objects and collections.

The dbEngine **Object**

Looking at Figure 9.5, you can see that the dbEngine object is at the top of the object hierarchy. dbEngine contains all the other DAO objects and is responsible for overall engine options. You can find out the version of DAO using the Version property. You can also perform Access database maintenance functions, such as a database repair and compact, using the RepairDatabase and CompactDatabase methods of the dbEngine object.

The Workspace **Object**

A Workspace object provides you with a way to manage transactions and security by providing a session object for your application. You can create multiple Workspace objects or use the default Workspace object automatically created for you when you use DAO— dbEngine.*Workspaces*(0), where *Workspaces* is the collection of Workspace objects. You can use

`Workspace` objects to manage transactions or connections to multiple databases. When you begin a transaction on a `Workspace`, for example, the commit or rollback of the transaction affects all data modifications made within the `Workspace`.

The `Database` **Object**

An open database is a `Database` object that contains all the information about the open database, such as table definitions. The syntax for the `OpenDatabase` method is as follows:

```
Set db = workspace.OpenDatabase (name, options, read_only, connect)
```

In this syntax, `workspace` is optional (defaults to `workspaces(0)`), *name* is the name of the database you want to open, *options* are various options available when opening the database, `read_only` is set to `true` to open an Access database in read-only mode, and `connect` is used for an ODBC connection string when connecting to an ODBC client/server database. For example, the following code opens the Visual Basic sample Access database, `biblio.mdb`:

```
Dim dbBiblio as Database
Set dbBiblio = OpenDatabase("biblio.mdb")
```

When dealing with DAO, you use the `Database` object quite frequently, especially the following properties:

- `QueryTimeOut` allows you to specify a timeout value for queries. The value is in seconds; a value of `0` specifies no timeout.
- `Updatable` is a true/false value indicating whether a database can be modified.
- `Recordsets` is a collection that allows you to easily access open recordsets in the database.
- `RecordsAffected` returns the number of records affected as a result of an action query executed via the `Database Execute` method.
- `QueryDefs` is a collection of `querydef` objects in the database.
- `Name` is the name of the `Database` object.
- `Connection` is used when using DAO with an ODBC data source. Provides connection string information about the ODBC data source.

Important `Database` object methods are shown in Table 9.1.

Table 9.1. Important DAO `Database` object methods.

Method	*Description*
`Close`	Closes the open `Database` object.
`CreateProperty`	Enables you to create a custom property.
`CreateQueryDef`	Creates a new `querydef` object.

Method	Description
CreateTableDef	Creates a new table.
Execute	Executes a SQL string.
OpenRecordset	Opens a new Recordset object.

The Recordset Object

The Recordset object is the workhorse of DAO. You will use them all the time! A Recordset object represents the records returned in the underlying query or in a table. The syntax to create a Recordset is as follows:

```
Set rs = database.OpenRecordset (RecordSorce [, Recordtype[,
➦RecordOptions, [lockedits ]]])
```

In this syntax, RecordSource is the query string or table name to create the recordset. RecordOptions allows you to set options such as creating pass-through queries to client/server databases. lockedits enables programmers to specify various locking options. What about the Recordtype option? The Recordtype option enables you to pick the type of recordset you want. Let's take a closer look at the possible values for the Recordtype option.

dbOpenTable

The value of dbOpenTable creates a table type recordset. The table type recordset can be used only when working with an Access database and creates a recordset with all of the rows and columns in the table. You can add, update, or delete records in a table recordset.

dbOpenDynaset

dbOpenDynaset creates a dynaset recordset. A dynaset recordset is a dynamic recordset created by a query that can be used to add, update, or delete records in the underlying table or tables that make up the query. A keyset of all the records that make up the dynaset is generated when a dynaset is created. Records added or changed through the dynaset's AddNew and Edit methods will be reflected in the dynaset. Records added or deleted by other users after the dynaset's keyset has been created will not appear as members of the dynaset.

dbOpenSnapShot

dbOpenSnapshot creates a snapshot recordset. A snapshot is a static copy (picture) of the query at the time the snapshot was created. You cannot use a snapshot to add, update, or delete records in the table or tables in the query. When a snapshot is created, all the records (data) that make up the recordset are copied to the client machine and stored in memory or on the disk in the Windows temporary directory. So avoid creating snapshots that return a lot of records!

dbOpenForwardOnly

dbOpenForwardOnly is exactly the same as a snapshot recordset, except no cursor is created to manage the recordset, and you can walk only forward through the recordset. Performance is improved for single pass recordsets by not adding the overhead of creating a cursor or allowing backward scrolling. Remember that you can't add, update, or delete records when using a forward-only DAO recordset.

Recordset Navigation

Navigating through a recordset is quite simple. The following methods can be used to move through the recordset:

- MoveFirst moves to the first record of the recordset.
- Move moves a specified number of records in the recordset.
- MoveLast moves to the last record in the recordset.
- MoveNext moves forward to the next record in the recordset.
- MovePrevious moves backward to the previous record in the recordset.

To help determine whether you are at the end of the recordset or the start of the recordset, use the recordset properties BOF and EOF. The BOF and EOF properties return Boolean values (TRUE/FALSE), based on the current position of the recordset. BOF is TRUE if the current recordset is before the first record, and it is FALSE if it is on or past the first record. EOF is TRUE if the recordset is past the last record in the recordset, and it is FALSE if it is on or before the last record in the recordset. If both BOF and EOF are set to TRUE and the recordset RecordCount property is zero, no records are contained in the recordset. The code sample in Listing 9.1 shows an example of opening a recordset and walking through the recordset.

Listing 9.1. An example of navigating through a DAO recordset.

```
Private Sub Command1_Click()

'The following sample code demonstrates how to open and navigate through
'a recordset. This sample is based off of the sample
'Access database that ships with Visual Basic
'Biblio.mdb.

'Declare Variables
Dim dbBiblio As Database        'DAO Database Object
Dim recAuthors As Recordset     'DAO Recordset Object
Dim strSQL As String

'Set up generic error handler to trap any errors
On Error GoTo DB_Error
```

```
'Open the database
Set dbBiblio = OpenDatabase("Biblio.mdb")

'Set up the SQL string for the recordset
strSQL = "Select Author,Title from Authors a, [Title Author] b, Titles c " _
        & "Where a.Au_ID = b.Au_ID And b.ISBN = c.ISBN"

'Open a SnapShot Recordset
Set recAuthors = dbBiblio.OpenRecordset(strSQL, dbOpenSnapshot)

'Check for an empty Recordset
If Not recAuthors.EOF And Not recAuthors.BOF And recAuthors.RecordCount > 0 Then
    'The recordset is not empty
    'Navigate through the recordset
    With recAuthors
        .MoveLast    'Move to the last record using the MoveLast method
        .MoveFirst   'Move to the first record using the MoveFirst method
        While Not .BOF And Not .EOF   'Walk through each
                                      'record until we reach the end
            'Walk through the cursor set
            'displaying each column using
            'the debug object
            Debug.Print !Author      'Use the column name
            Debug.Print !Title
            .MoveNext                'Move to the next record

        Wend    'End While Loop
    End With
End If


Exit_Sample:
'Cleanup and Exit!
'Make sure the recordset and database were created
'then close them and release the objects.
If Not (recAuthors Is Nothing) Then
    recAuthors.Close
    Set recAuthors = Nothing
End If

If Not (dbBiblio Is Nothing) Then
    dbBiblio.Close
    Set dbBiblio = Nothing
End If

Exit Sub    'Exit the routine

'Generic Error Handler
DB_Error:
    'Display the error message and then exit
    MsgBox Err.Description
    Resume Exit_Sample

End Sub
```

Editing a Recordset

If you have created a recordset that can be modified (which would apply to everything but a snapshot or forward-only), you can use the AddNew method of the recordset to add a new record. The AddNew method has the following syntax:

```
Recordset.AddNew
```

When you have invoked the AddNew method, you have created a new placeholder in the recordset for the new row. You then populate each column in the recordset with the data and invoke the Update method to add the record. The following code snippet adds a new record to the Authors table in the biblio.mdb database:

```
With recAuthor
    .AddNew          'Time to add a new record
    !Au_ID = 200     'Set the author id
    !Author = "Spenik, Mark" 'The author name
    ![Year Born] = 1962     'The year born
    .Update    'Add the new record to the Authors table
End With
```

To modify an existing record, use the Edit method followed by the Update method, as shown in the following code snippet:

```
With recAuthor
    .Edit            'Modify the existing record
    !Author = "Spenik, Mark A." 'Change the author name - add the middle initial
    .Update    'Update the record
End With
```

To delete the current record in the recordset, use the Delete method, which has the following syntax:

```
Recordset.Delete
```

> **TIP**
>
> For maximum performance when using DAO and updating or deleting a large number of records, wrap the update and delete statements around a transaction and use SQL statements instead of walking through the records in the recordset using the Edit, Update, and Delete methods discussed earlier. The time savings is enormous and will increase as the number of records modified increases.

QueryDefs

A DAO QueryDef object is a stored query. The query can be a select statement consisting of one or more tables, or it can be an action query that adds, updates, or deletes records from one or more tables. QueryDefs offer a performance gain because a QueryDef is a precompiled SQL statement. *Precompiled* means that when a QueryDef is executed, the Jet engine does not have to compile the SQL statement. QueryDefs can accept parameters, and you can create temporary QueryDef objects (which are not saved to disk) at runtime. To create a QueryDef, you can use Microsoft Access or the Visual Basic Add-In Visual Data Manager, shown in Figure 9.6, and you can also create them using code.

FIGURE 9.6.

The Visual Data Manager Query Builder dialog box.

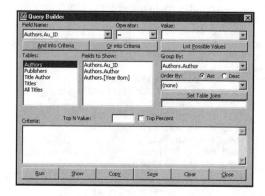

To run an action QueryDef, use the Execute method of the QueryDef object. To create a recordset, use the OpenRecordset method of the QueryDef. The code shown in Listing 9.2 is similar to the code in Listing 9.1, except the SQL statement is first saved as a temporary QueryDef object and is then used to create a recordset. After navigating through the recordset, the SQL statement is saved as a permanent QueryDef.

Listing 9.2. An example of creating and using QueryDefs.

```
Private Sub Command1_Click()

'The following sample code demonstrates how to create
'and use a QueryDef. This sample is based off of the sample
'Access database that ships with Visual Basic
'Biblio.mdb.

'Declare Variables
Dim dbBiblio As Database          'DAO datbase object
Dim recAuthors As Recordset       'DAO recordset object
Dim strSQL As String
Dim qdfAuthors As QueryDef        'DAO QueryDef object

'Set up a generic error handler to trap any errors
On Error GoTo DB_Error

'Open the database
Set dbBiblio = OpenDatabase("Biblio.mdb", False)

'Set up the SQL string for the recordset
strSQL = "Select Author,Title from Authors a, [Title Author] b, Titles c " _
      & "Where a.Au_ID = b.Au_ID And b.ISBN = c.ISBN"
```

continues

Listing 9.2. continued

```
'Create a temporary QueryDef using the CreateQueryDef method of
'the database object. Using "" instead of a name creates a temporary
'QueryDef.
Set qdfAuthors = dbBiblio.CreateQueryDef("", strSQL)

'Open a SnapShot Recordset using the querydef object OpenRecordset method.
Set recAuthors = qdfAuthors.OpenRecordset(dbOpenSnapshot)

'Check for an empty Recordset
If Not recAuthors.EOF And Not recAuthors.BOF And recAuthors.RecordCount > 0 Then
    'The recordset is not empty
    With recAuthors
        .MoveLast    'Move to the last record
        .MoveFirst   'Move to the first record
        While Not .BOF And Not .EOF
            'Walk through the cursor set
            'displaying each column using
            'the debug object
            Debug.Print !Author      'Use the column name
            'Debug.Print !Title
            .MoveNext                'Move to the next record

        Wend  'End While Loop

    End With
End If

'Create a permanent QueryDef named qryAuthorTitle
Set qdfAuthors = dbBiblio.CreateQueryDef("qryAuthorTitle", strSQL)

Exit_Sample:
'Cleanup and Exit!
'Make sure the recordset and database were created
'then close them and release the objects.
If Not (recAuthors Is Nothing) Then
    recAuthors.Close
    Set recAuthors = Nothing
End If

If Not (dbBiblio Is Nothing) Then
    dbBiblio.Close
    Set dbBiblio = Nothing
End If

Exit Sub    'Exit the routine

'Generic Error Handler
DB_Error:
    'Display the error message and then exit
    MsgBox Err.Description
    Resume Exit_Sample

End Sub
```

The Data Control

One advantage of using DAO is that you can create applications using the data control in a client/server or intranet environment. The data control enables you to create applications that can add, update, delete, and search for records by setting a few properties—and with little or no code. The data control enables you to bind columns in a recordset to other Visual Basic ActiveX controls such as the textbox control or the label control. The data control can be found on the Visual Basic toolbox, and it is shown in Figure 9.7.

FIGURE 9.7.

The data control on the Visual Basic toolbox.

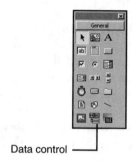

Data control ————

Further easing the creation of database applications is the Visual Basic add-in, the Data Form Wizard. You can use the Data Form Wizard to create fully functional forms similar to the one shown in Figure 9.8.

FIGURE 9.8.

A form generated by the Data Form Wizard.

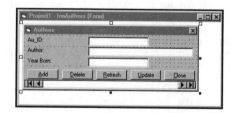

If you have not used the data control, review the Visual Basic documentation for more information and examples.

Using Attached Tables

Earlier I stated that ODBC was thought by many to be slow. Part of the performance problems had to do with early ODBC drivers. I think another part of the story is Visual Basic 3, DAO, and the data control using remote databases (client/server). When Visual Basic 3 first shipped, developers immediately started using DAO and the data control against remote databases such as Oracle, Sybase, and Microsoft SQL Server. As the number of data controls on the form increased and resultsets were returned to the form, it quickly became apparent that performance was an issue. The problem consisted of several factors—in some cases, poor performing ODBC drivers; the overhead of the Jet engine; and, at the time, an unpublished feature of the data control using remote data sources. It turned out that when using a data control to a remote database such as SQL Server, before the SQL statement was executed, Jet queried the backend database about the columns in the table, data types, and indexes. This caused a great deal of unknown overhead! Microsoft remedied the situation by publishing and documenting the feature in Visual Basic 4.

The proper way to use the data control or DAO with remote databases is to use Access attached tables. Attached tables store locally all the information about the remote database table required by Jet. Jet no longer has to query the remote data source about the table; therefore, overall performance is increased. I recommend using RDO or ODBCDirect when accessing a remote database. However, for those of you who are still in a 16-bit environment or who don't have RDO or ODBCDirect options available to you, Listing 9.3 shows an example of attaching remote ODBC tables to a Microsoft Access database. The example first deletes any attached tables found and then attaches tables whose names are in a local Access table called AttachedTables.

Listing 9.3. An example of attached tables.

```
Dim dbODBC As Database       'DAO database object
Dim tdTables As TableDef     'DAO table object
Dim rsAttach As Recordset    'DAO recordset object

    'Set up a generic error handler
    On Error GoTo ODBC_Error
    'Log on to the remote database. By only specifying ODBC in the connection
    'string parameter of the OpenDatabase method, you will be prompted
     'for a valid ODBC DSN,User Name and password.
    Set dbODBC = DBEngine.Workspaces(0).OpenDatabase("", 0, False, "ODBC;")
    'Check to make sure we are connected and an object created.
    If Not (dbODBC Is Nothing) Then

        'This section of code checks attributes of the
        'tableDefs in the access database and removes
        'all the attached tables found.
        '
        For Each tdTables In dbODBC.TableDefs
            'Check for attached table
            If (tdTables.Attributes And dbAttachedODBC) <> 0 Then
                'Remove the attached table
                dbODBC.TableDefs.Delete tdTables.Name
            End If
        Next tdTables
        'Open a recordset on a local Access database table that
        'contains the name of the remote table you wish to attach.
```

```
                    'The local Access table is called AttachedTables and
                    'contains a single column - TableName.
                    Set rsAttach = _
          dbODBC.OpenRecordset("Select TableName from AttachedTables;", dbOpenSnapshot)
                    Do Until rsAttach.EOF    ' Do until the end of the recordset is reached.
                        'Attach the table - Use the remote table name as the attached
                        'table name as well.
                        Set tdTables = dbODBC.CreateTableDef(rsAttach(0), 0, rsAttach(0), _
                                                    dbODBC.Connect)
                        tdTables.Attributes = dbAttachSavePWD
                        'Save the Table object
                        dbODBC.TableDefs.Append tdTables
                        'Release Object
                        Set tdTables = Nothing
                        'Get the next record
                        rsAttach.MoveNext    ' Move to next record.
                    Loop

        End If
ODBC_Exit:
    If Not (rsAttach Is Nothing) Then
        'Close the attached table reference
        rsAttach.Close
        Set rsAttach = Nothing
    End If
    'Close the ODBC database
    If Not (dbODBC Is Nothing) Then
        'Close the ODBC connection
        dbODBC.Close
        Set dbODBC = Nothing
    End If
    Exit Sub

'
' Error Handler
'
ODBC_Error:
    MsgBox Err.Description
    Resume ODBC_Exit
End Sub
```

RDO Refresher

This section is a review of commonly used RDO objects, properties, and methods. Even if you are familiar with RDO, read on. RDO has changed quite a bit!

RDO is the thin object interface over the ODBC APIs. RDO is designed to handle remote ODBC databases, including stored procedure calls, multiple resultsets, and asynchronous operations. The RDO object model is shown in Figure 9.9.

FIGURE 9.9.
The RDO object model.

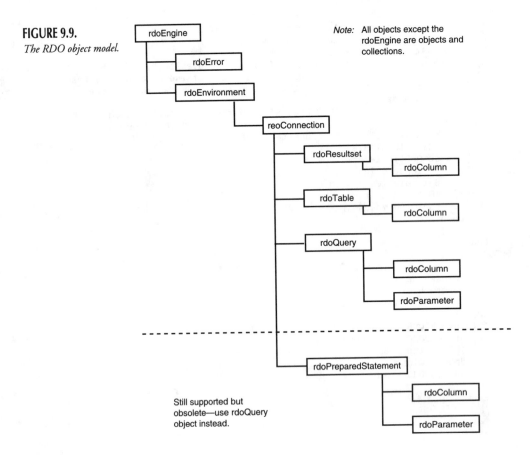

The rdoEngine Object

The rdoEngine is the top object in the RDO object hierarchy, shown in Figure 9.9. An application can have only a single instance of the rdoEngine, which contains all the other RDO objects and is responsible for overall engine options. The rdoEngine is created the first time you access an RDO object such as the default login timeout property (which is the number of seconds to wait before timing out during a login request). rdoEngine's equivalent DAO object is the dbEngine. Use the rdoEngine to set options such as the default cursor type library, used by resultsets. Speaking of default cursor types, the rdoEngine property rdoDefaultCursorDriver enables you to set the cursor library used by the ODBC manager. The available options are listed in Table 9.2.

Table 9.2. The `rdoDefaultCursorDriver` property settings.

Visual Basic Constant	*Cursor Description*
rdUseIfNeeded	Default property—can be server side or client side
rdUseODBC	Uses the ODBC cursor library
rdUseServer	Uses server-side cursor library
RdUseClientBatch	Uses RDO batch cursor library
rdUseNone	Does not create a cursor set

For more detail on the various cursor options, look through the Visual Basic Help files and documentation.

If you are executing stored procedures that use multiple Select statements or are executing multiple Select statements in one resultset, you must use the ODBC cursor library. For the best performance with a read-only forward-scrolling cursor, use the option rdUseNone, which eliminates the overhead required to create and manage a cursor.

> **NOTE**
>
> Not all remote ODBC databases support server-side cursors. For example, Microsoft SQL Server does, but Oracle 7.3 does not. If you want to use server-side cursors, check with your specific database manufacturer or related documentation for server-side cursor support.

The rdoEngine object also contains the InfoMessage event. The InfoMessage event fires when informational messages are sent back from a remote data source.

The rdoEnvironment **Object**

The rdoEnvironment object can be used to control transactions across multiple connections. The rdoEnvironment object contains methods for transaction management, such as BeginTrans, CommitTrans, and RollBackTrans. The rdoEnvironment object is equivalent to the DAO Workspace object. You automatically start with rdoEnvironments(0) when the RDO engine is created.

Transaction management events such as BeginTrans, CommitTrans, and RollBackTrans are also part of the rdoEnvironment.

The `rdoConnection` Object

The `rdoConnection` object represents an open or unopened connection to a remote ODBC database. Use the `rdoConnection` object to log on to the ODBC database. The equivalent DAO object is the `Database` object.

`rdoConnection` objects can now be free-standing objects and include events such as `QueryComplete`, `Connect`, and `Disconnect`, to name just a few. Let's look at a few code examples using the `rdoConnection` object. The following code snippet connects to SQL Server using the `OpenConnection` method of the `rdEnvironment` object:

```
Dim envSQLServer As rdoEnvironment
Dim cnnDBA As rdoConnection
Dim strConn As String
    strConn = "UID=sa;Database=pubs;DSN=local SQL Server;"
    Set En = rdoEnvironments(0)
    '            syntax for OpenConnection is
    '                Data Source Name, ODBC prompt,
    '                readonly, connection string, options
    Set cnnDBA = En.OpenConnection("", rdDriverPrompt, False, strSQL)
```

With Visual Basic 5, you can create a standalone `rdoConnection`. When you use a standalone connection object, the object does not automatically appear in the `rdoCollections` object, but it must be added. The following code snippet shows an example using a standalone `rdoConnection` object to make a connection to a remote ODBC database:

```
'Set some properties of the connection object
    'and then use the EstablishConnection method
    'to connect to the remote database.
    With cnnDBA
        .LoginTimeout = 10 'Set to 10 seconds
        .Connect = "UID=sa;DATABASE=pubs;" & _
                    "DSN=local SQL Server;"
        .EstablishConnection (rdDriverNoPrompt)
    End With
    'Add the connection to the collection
    rdoEnvironments(0).rdoConnections.Add cnnDBA
```

Other commonly used methods of the `rdoConnection` object are the `OpenResultset` method to create a resultset and the `Execute` method to execute a SQL statement or stored procedure that does not return any rows.

The `resultset` Object

The `resultset` object consists of the returned rows of a query or executed stored procedure. The DAO equivalent object is the `recordset` object; however, the `resultset` object supports many powerful features not found in a DAO recordset, such as the capability to support multiple result sets or asynchronous processing capabilities. A `resultset` object can be created using the `OpenResultset` method of the `rdoConnection` object and the `rdoQuery` object (discussed later). The syntax to create a resultset using the `rdoConnection` object is as follows:

```
Set rs =rdoConnection.OpenResultset (SQL_Name [,
                Cursortype [, LockFlag, [ResultOptions ]]])
```

In this syntax, `SQL_Name` is the query string or RDO object name used to create the recordset. `ResultOptions` enables you to set options such as asynchronous queries. The `LockFlag` enables programmers to specify various locking. The `CursorType` option enables you to pick the type of cursor you want for your resultset. Let's take a closer look at the possible values for the `CursorType` option.

rdOpenForwardOnly

`rdOpenForwardOnly` allows only forward scrolling and does not create a cursor keyset. Only a single row is retrieved at a time. You can add, delete, or update records using the forward-only resultset.

> **NOTE**
>
> This is a quick reminder that in DAO, you can't make modifications to a forward-only recordset. Also, in DAO, the records being returned in the query are referred to as a recordset. Records (rows) being returned in RDO are referred to as a resultset.

rdOpenKeyset

`rdOpenKeyset` is equivalent to the DAO dynaset. A keyset of all the records that make up the cursor is generated on the client or the server. The cursor generated is updatable so that you can add, delete, or modify records. On some ODBC sources, records added or changed through the resultset's `AddNew` and `Edit` methods will be reflected in the resultset. On other ODBC sources, records added using the `AddNew` and `Edit` methods will not appear as a member of the resultset until the resultset is refreshed.

rdOpenDynamic

`rdOpenDynamic` creates a cursor that is truly dynamic. The dynamic resultset contains an accurate resultset of all the current records, including those being added, updated, or deleted. The drawback to a dynamic resultset is that it has the highest cursor management overhead of all the cursor types (which equates to less than optimal performance).

rdOpenStatic

A static cursor is similar to the DAO snapshot, except that you can edit records in the resultset. A static cursor is a copy (picture) of the query data at the time the cursor was created. The cursor can reside on the client or the server. Changes made through the `AddNew`, `Update`, and `Delete` methods of the resultset object will appear as part of the resultset. Changes made using the `execute` method or made by other users will not appear until the resultset is refreshed.

Resultset Navigation

The following methods can be used to move through the resultset:

- ■ `MoveFirst` moves to the first row of the resultset.
- ■ `Move` moves a specified number of rows in the resultset.
- ■ `MoveLast` moves to the last row in the resultset.
- ■ `MoveNext` moves forward to the next row in the resultset.
- ■ `MovePrevious` moves backward to the previous row in the resultset.

You can also use the `AbsolutePosition` property to move to an absolute row position in the cursor.

To help determine whether you are at the end or start of the resultset, use the `BOF` and `EOF` properties of the resultset object. The `BOF` and `EOF` properties return Boolean values (`TRUE`/`FALSE`), based on the current position of the resultset. If `BOF` or `EOF` is `TRUE`, there is no current row, and any attempt to `Move` through the resultset will result in an error. When a resultset is open containing one or more rows, both `BOF` and `EOF` are `FALSE`. If both `BOF` and `EOF` are set to `TRUE` and the recordset `RowCount` property is zero, no records are contained in the resultset. The code sample in Listing 9.4 shows an example of opening and navigating through a resultset.

Listing 9.4. An example of navigating through an RDO resultset.

```
Private Sub Command1_Click()

'The following sample code demonstrates how to open and navigate through
'an RDO resultset. This sample is based off of the sample
'database that ships with Microsoft SQL Server pubs.


'Declare Variables
Dim envApp As rdoEnvironment
Dim conPubs As rdoConnection
Dim recAuthors As rdoResultset
Dim strSQL As String
Dim strMsg As String
Dim strConn As String
Dim errReport As rdoError


'Set up generic error handler to trap any errors
On Error GoTo DB_Error

'Set up the connection string. This string will vary from
'SQL Server to SQL Server.
'
strConn = "UID=sa;PWD=;Database=pubs;DSN=local SQL Server;"

'Obtain a reference to the default RDO Environment
Set envApp = rdoEnvironments(0)
```

```vb
    'Set default cursor type to use server side cursors
    rdoEngine.rdoDefaultCursorDriver = rdUseServer

    'Open a connection to SQL Server
    Set conPubs = envApp.OpenConnection("", rdDriverNoPrompt, False, strConn)

    'Set up the SQL string for the resultset
    strSQL = "Select au_id, au_lname, state from authors"


    'Open a static cursor
    Set recAuthors = conPubs.OpenResultset(strSQL, rdOpenKeyset)

    'Check for an empty Resultset
    If Not recAuthors.EOF And Not recAuthors.BOF And recAuthors.RowCount <> 0 Then
        'The recordset is not empty
        With recAuthors
            .MoveLast   'Move to the last record
            .MoveFirst  'Move to the first record
            While Not .BOF And Not .EOF
                'Walk through the cursor set
                'displaying each column using
                'the debug object
                Debug.Print !au_id & " " & !au_lname & " " & !state  'Use the
                                                                     'column name
                .MoveNext               'Move to the next row
        Wend  'End While Loop
            'Use the Absolute property to change the row position
            .AbsolutePosition = .RowCount - 3
            Debug.Print !state  'Display the value of the State column
        End With
    End If
Exit_Sample:
'Cleanup and Exit!
'Make sure the resultset and connection were created
'then close them and release the objects.
If Not (recAuthors Is Nothing) Then
    recAuthors.Close
    Set recAuthors = Nothing
End If

If Not (conPubs Is Nothing) Then
    conPubs.Close
    Set conPubs = Nothing
End If
Exit Sub     'Exit the routine

'Generic Error Handler
DB_Error:
    'Walk through the rdoErrors collection to
    'construct the error message string to display
    For Each errReport In rdoErrors
        strMsg = strMsg & errReport.Description & vbCrLf
    Next errReport
    'Display the error message and then exit
    MsgBox strMsg
    Resume Exit_Sample

End Sub
```

In the code sample shown in Listing 9.4, the generic error routine uses the RDO collections object `rdoErrors` to display all the error messages returned from the ODBC data source.

Editing a Resultset

If you have created a resultset that can be modified, you can use the `AddNew` method of the resultset, which has the following syntax:

```
Resultset.AddNew
```

When you have invoked the `AddNew` method, you have created a new placeholder in the resultset for the new row. You then populate each column in the resultset with the data and invoke the `Update` method to add the record. To modify an existing record, use the `Edit` method followed by the `Update` method. To delete the current record in the resultset, use the `Delete` method, which has the following syntax:

```
Resultset.Delete
```

When dealing with remote ODBC data sources, you can also make changes to the database using the `Execute` method with SQL statements or stored procedures.

Query Object

In RDO version 2.0, the `rdoPreparedStatement` objects are gone. (They are still supported for backward-compatibility, but they should no longer be used.) In their place is the new `rdoQuery` object. The `rdoQuery` object is similar to the DAO `QueryDef` object in that it functions as a set of compiled SQL statements. The `rdoQuery` object is designed to handle stored procedures with multiple input and output parameters, multiple resultsets, and SQL statements that use parameters. Parameters are managed via an `rdoParameter` collection associated with the `rdoQuery` object. An `rdoQuery` object can be created as a standalone object (like the `rdoConnection` object), or it can be created using the `CreateQuery` method of the `rdoConnection` object.

Let's look at an example that uses a `rdoQuery` object and the `rdoConnection` object `QueryComplete` event, which is fired when an asynchronous query completes. You might remember that in RDO version 1.0, your program had to poll to determine when an asynchronous query had completed. Now, with RDO 2.0, the asynchronous query process is event driven. Listing 9.5 shows an example of creating an `rdoQuery` object, executing an asynchronous query, and using the `QueryComplete` event to notify the user. The code to handle the asynchronous query is located in the procedure `conPubs_QueryComplete` in Listing 9.5. The example calls a SQL Server stored procedure that delays for 10 seconds. The stored procedure code is as follows:

```
create procedure usp_delay
as
/*
** Delay for 10 seconds and then return 0
*/
Waitfor Delay '00:00:10'
return 0
```

Listing 9.5. Executing an asynchronous query.

```
'Declare a standalone connection object.
'WithEvents allows us to code the query complete event for the
'object.
'
Private WithEvents conPubs As rdoConnection
Dim recAsync As rdoResultset
Dim qryStoredProc As rdoQuery

Private Sub Command1_Click()

'The following sample code demonstrates how to create
'an rdoQuery object and use asynchronous query events.
'
'Declare Variables
Dim strSQL As String
Dim strMsg As String
Dim strConn As String
Dim errReport As rdoError


'Set up generic error handler to trap any errors
On Error GoTo DB_Error

'Set up the connection string. This string will vary from
'SQL Server to SQL Server.
'
strConn = "UID=sa;PWD=;Database=pubs;DSN=local SQL Server;"

'Set up the query string
strSQL = "exec usp_delay"

rdoEngine.rdoDefaultCursorDriver = rdUseOdbc

Set conPubs = New rdoConnection
'Open a connection to SQL Server
With conPubs
    .QueryTimeout = 20  'Set to 20 seconds
    .Connect = strConn
    .EstablishConnection
    'Create a query object
    Set qryStoredProc = .CreateQuery("Delayed Query", strSQL)
End With
'Open the recordset asynchronously
Set recAsync = qryStoredProc.OpenResultset(rdOpenKeyset, _
                            rdConcurReadOnly, rdAsyncEnable)
Debug.Print "Waiting on query! But I'm not blocked!"
Exit_Sample:
Exit Sub    'Exit the routine

'Generic Error Handler
DB_Error:
    'Walk through the rdoErrors collection to
    'construct the error message string to display
    For Each errReport In rdoErrors
        strMsg = strMsg & errReport.Description & vbCrLf
```

continues

Listing 9.5. continued

```
     Next errReport
     'Display the error message and then exit
     MsgBox strMsg
     Resume Exit_Sample

End Sub


Private Sub conPubs_QueryComplete(ByVal Query As RDO.rdoQuery, _
                                ByVal ErrorOccurred As Boolean)
Dim strMsg As String

     strMsg = "Query: " & Query.Name & " completed."
     MsgBox strMsg

End Sub
```

RDO Data Control and the UserConnection ActiveX Designer

Like DAO, RDO has a data control that enables you to create applications that can add, update, delete, and search for records by setting a few properties and using little or no code. One new and exciting tool added in Visual Basic 5 is the ActiveX designer *UserConnection*. You can use the UserConnection designer to create rdoConnections and rdoQuery objects at design time. The designer provides an easy property page interface to set connection properties. You can also use the designer to create Query objects based on stored procedures or SQL statements. Microsoft Query integrates into the UserConnection designer so that you can create queries using drag and drop. An example of a UserConnection designer with several Query objects is shown in Figure 9.10.

FIGURE 9.10.

A UserConnection ActiveX designer.

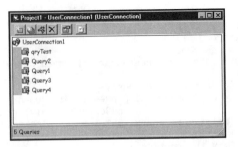

After you have used the designer to create a connection and associated queries, you can easily connect to the remote database and execute the queries as if they were methods of the Connection object. The following code snippet shows an example using a UserConnection designer called UserConnection1 to connect to a remote database, execute a stored procedure, and open a resultset:

```
Dim tstOne As New UserConnection1 'UserConnection Active X Designer
Dim myQuery As rdoQuery      'Rdo Query Object
Dim rsTest As rdoResultset
Dim myRet As String

'Establish the connection to the remote data source
tstOne.EstablishConnection
'Execute a stored procedure
myRet = tstOne.qryRollFinance
'Open a resultset
Set rsTest = tstOne.OpenResultset("Query4")
```

The UserConnection ActiveX designer cuts down on the lines of code you are required to write and makes remote database development a graphical experience.

ODBCDirect

As mentioned earlier, ODBCDirect allows you to continue to use the familiar DAO interface without using the Jet engine. Jet is replaced by RDO. The DAO objects are mapped to their equivalent RDO counterparts. Although not all RDO functionality is available, important features such as asynchronous queries and multiple resultsets are supported. ODBCDirect also supports the RDO dynamic resultset using the dbOpenDynamic option. Use ODBCDirect when you have an existing application using an Access database, and you want to move the application to a remote ODBC database such as Microsoft SQL Server or Oracle. If you are an experienced DAO programmer, you will like the performance benefit provided by ODBCDirect when using remote ODBC databases. However, with the changes to RDO and the addition of the UserConnection ActiveX designer, it's time to start learning RDO.

Using ODBCDirect requires creating an ODBCDirect workspace. This is accomplished using the CreateWorkspace method of the DAO dbEngine using the constant dbUseODBC, as shown in the following code snippet:

```
Dim wksODBC as Workspace
set wksODB = DBEngine.CreateWorkspace("ODBCDirectWKS","sa","book",dbUseODBC)
```

After you create an ODBCDirect workspace, the next step is to connect to the ODBC database. You can use the OpenDatabase method or the Connection object. The Connection object provides RDO features such as asynchronous connections and queries and the capability to create QueryDef objects on the remote database. You lose the additional RDO functionality when using the OpenDatabase method to connect to a remote ODBC database. When you have connected to the remote database, everything else is DAO!

To give you an example of porting existing DAO code to ODBCDirect, I have taken the DAO code used in Listing 9.1 and converted it to ODBCDirect. Instead of using the authors table from the biblio.mdb database, the following example uses the authors table found in the SQL Server database pubs. The ODBCDirect example is shown in Listing 9.6. Notice that the only major difference between Listing 9.1 and Listing 9.6 is the creation of the ODBC workspace (which is accomplished in the example by setting a DbEngine option instead of using the constant dbUseODBC in the CreateWorkspace method shown earlier) and the connection string option used in the OpenDatabase method.

Listing 9.6. Navigating through a recordset using ODBC Direct.

```
Private Sub Command1_Click()

'The following sample code demonstrates how to navigate through
'a recordset using ODBC Direct. This sample is based off of the sample
'database, Pubs that ships with Microsoft SQL Server.

'Declare Variables
Dim dbBiblio As Database
Dim wksODBC As Workspace
Dim recAuthors As Recordset
Dim strSQL As String
Dim strConn As String

'Set up generic error handler to trap any errors
On Error GoTo DB_Error

'Set the DAO engine default parameters
'to ODBC direct so that when a workspace is created
'it will use ODBC Direct
With DBEngine
    .DefaultType = dbUseODBC
    .DefaultUser = "sa"
    .DefaultPassword = ""
End With

'Create the ODBC Direct WorkSpace
Set wksODBC = DBEngine.Workspaces(0)

'The next step is to connect to the remote database.
'You can use the connection object to get RDO capabilities
'or for no code changes the database object. This sample uses the database
'object.
strConn = "ODBC;UID=sa;PWD=;Database=pubs;DSN=local SQL Server;"

'Open the database - which connects us to SQL Server
'
Set dbBiblio = OpenDatabase("Pubs", dbDriverNoPrompt, False, strConn)

'Set up the SQL string for the recordset
strSQL = "select * from authors"

'Open a SnapShot Recordset
Set recAuthors = dbBiblio.OpenRecordset(strSQL, dbOpenSnapshot)

'Check for an empty Recordset
If Not recAuthors.EOF And Not recAuthors.BOF And recAuthors.RecordCount > 0 Then
    'The recordset is not empty
    With recAuthors
        .MoveLast    'Move to the last record
        .MoveFirst   'Move to the first record
```

```
        While Not .BOF And Not .EOF
            'Walk through the cursor set
            'displaying each column using
            'the debug object
            Debug.Print !au_lname & " " & !state
            .MoveNext            'Move to the next record
        Wend   'End While Loop
    End With
End If
Exit_Sample:
'Cleanup and Exit!
'Make sure the recordset and database were created
'then close them and release the objects.
If Not (recAuthors Is Nothing) Then
    recAuthors.Close
    Set recAuthors = Nothing
End If

If Not (dbBiblio Is Nothing) Then
    dbBiblio.Close
    Set dbBiblio = Nothing
End If
Exit Sub    'Exit the routine

'Generic Error Handler
DB_Error:
    'Display the error message and then exit
    MsgBox Err.Description
    Resume Exit_Sample

End Sub
```

Summary

This chapter provided an overview of the many different methods and object models available to a Visual Basic Internet/intranet database developer. A quick overview and review of the important database objects and terms was provided, as well as sample code. The remaining chapters in this book use the various data access objects described in this chapter to build Internet/intranet applications and ActiveX components.

This chapter also provided some insight and suggestions on when to use each database object. Calling the ODBC API directly or using the native database drivers was ruled out because there are more flexible object models available that are easier to use and provide equivalent performance. Use DAO when dealing with an Access database. When working with remote ODBC databases, use RDO except in cases when you are porting existing DAO code to a remote ODBC database; in that case, use ODBCDirect.

This chapter also provided a very basic overview of the future of Microsoft data access technologies, OLE DB, and the Active Data Objects (ADO). You learn about these topics in great detail in Chapter 21. ADO is the data-access object of choice when writing server-side Visual Basic scripts (Active Server Pages). At the time this book was being written, Microsoft had begun to talk about eventually merging the DAO and RDO interface into a single data-access object interface. Microsoft has not committed to whether this single interface is ADO. So keep watching the Microsoft Website for the latest data-access object model to emerge; and in the meantime, continue to learn and use the data-access object models that are being shipped today with Visual Basic 5 and the Internet Information Server—DAO, RDO, ODBC Direct, and ADO.

V

Client-Side Development Using HTML, ActiveX, and Visual Basic Scripting

10

An Overview of HTML 3.2

by Mark Swank

Up to this point you've focused on some of the foundational building blocks that are required to implement a Web-based architecture database. This chapter expands on those concepts by describing how data is formatted and presented to users.

Creating your own Web documents using HTML is actually quite easy. Anyone with access to word processing software can design simple HTML pages almost immediately—as you can tell by the proliferation of home pages being posted by thousands of individuals and companies worldwide. This ease of use has helped make the World Wide Web the great phenomenon that it is today.

As HTML specifications become more refined, however, and as advances in Web technologies become more readily available, you'll find a rich and rapidly growing suite of tools at your fingertips for developing Web-based database applications and presenting data to the end user. To effectively present data, you'll need to take advantage of some of the more advanced features of HTML (that is, objects, tables, lists, and so on).

This chapter introduces you to HTML. First, it covers the HTML basics and conformance levels as well as reviews some of the HTML tags that make up Levels 0 and 1. Next, it explains the HTML/SGML relationship and talks a little about HTML authoring style guidelines, available HTML editors, and HTML conversion programs. Finally, it presents the HTML Level 2 specifications and the enhancements available in both HTML Level 3.2 and the Netscape extensions.

What Is HTML?

HTML, which stands for Hypertext Markup Language, is a simple yet powerful markup language used to generate platform-independent hypertext documents that are viewable by a Web browser. Markup languages use special document-formatting tags that are designed with a specific syntax for each tag. These tags are then included within other documents to specify the formatting and presentation of the document. HTML documents are based on Standard Generalized Markup Language (SGML) but with generic formatting tags that are appropriate for representing information from a wide range of domains.

HTML is used in many applications. Here are just a few of these applications:

- Hypertext news
- E-mail
- Documentation
- Hypermedia
- Database query results

The standardization of HTML was originally completed by the WWW consortium under Internet Engineering Task Force (IETF) Request for Comments (RFC) 1866. This standard, previously referred to as "HTML Version 2," has recently been superseded by the new specification HTML 3.2. Not all current browsers, however, implement the full set of features of HTML 3.2. A compliant browser is expected to ignore any element or attribute of the HTML 3.2 specification that it isn't designed to handle. In addition, some Web browsers define and handle their own extensions (such as Netscape Navigator and its Netscape extensions and Microsoft's Internet Explorer extensions).

HTML/SGML Relationship

SGML is an international standard for electronic document exchange. It is the basis of the HTML Internet standard that, together with URLs and HTTP, forms the foundation of the World Wide Web. HTML is an application of ISO Standard 8879:1986 Information Processing Text and Office Systems: Standard Generalized Markup Language (SGML).

Simply put, HTML documents are SGML documents with generic semantics that are designed for formatting and representing information. Each HTML document consists of data (actual contents of the document), a structure (headings, paragraphs, and so on) and a format (the final appearance of the document).

HTML Levels of Conformance

Five levels of conformance of HTML currently exist. These are referenced as Level 0 through Level 4:

Level 0   This is an implied level of conformance and isn't included as part of RFC 1866. This level includes HTML structure and comment elements, head-related and body-related elements such as headers, lists, and image support. Level 0 conformance is expected of all Web browsers.

Level 1   This conformance information is included as part of RFC 1866 and includes image-handling and character-formatting features such as emphasis and text highlighting. Level 1 conformance is supported by all graphical Web browsers.

Level 2   This conformance information is also included as part of RFC 1866. This level includes forms and character definitions. Along with Level 1 specifications, Level 2 makes up the majority of conformance that almost all graphical Web browsers support today.

Level 3.2   This conformance isn't included as part of RFC 1866 but has been proposed as extensions to RFC 1866. This level includes tables, figures, and graphical backdrops. Netscape Navigator and Microsoft Internet Explorer support proposed Level 3.2 HTML tags in addition to their own extensions.

Level 4   This conformance isn't included as part of RFC 1866 but is proposed to include mathematical formulae.

What Are URLs?

HTML uses URLs to identify the location of documents. These documents can exist on the same machine as the Web browser, on the same machine as the Web server, or on other Web servers. The structure of a URL includes the type of resource, the address of the Web server servicing the document, and the location of the document. The syntax is of the form

```
resource://host.domain[:port]/path/filename
```

where *resource* is one of the following values:

Value	Meaning
file	A file on your local system
ftp	A file on an anonymous FTP server
http	A file on a World Wide Web server
gopher	A file on a Gopher server
wais	A file on a WAIS server
news	A Usenet newsgroup
mailto	An SMTP mail interface
telnet	A connection to a Telnet-based service

Here is a sample URL:

```
http://www.mcp.com/sams
```

The port number can generally be omitted. If omitted, the default port of 80 (which is a reserved port and requires root execution privileges on UNIX-based machines) is assumed.

Figure 10.1 shows a sample Web page and URL in the Web browser.

FIGURE 10.1.
Web browser URL location.

What Are Tags?

HTML uses markup tags to tell the Web browser how to format and display the text. Additionally, tags are available for displaying inline images, invoking MPEG movie viewers, playing audio clips, specifying hypertext links, accepting user input, and invoking application programs via the Common Gateway Interface (CGI). The latter two topics are covered in detail in later chapters.

HTML tags are simply ASCII characters or character strings delimited by angle brackets (<>). Most tags are paired with an opening and closing tag. The opening tag tells the Web browser to begin special handling or formatting based on the specified tag. The closing tag signals the Web browser to stop special handling or formatting.

For example, to specify emphasized text, you would include it within the <EM> and </EM> tag pair. An example of <EM> tag use is as follows:

```
<EM>This would display as italicized (emphasized)</EM>
```

However, tags such as the line-break tag <BR> and the <INPUT> tag do not have closing tags.

> **TIP**
>
> Although the closing tag may be omitted for some HTML elements such as the paragraph `</P>`, the list item `</LI>`, the definition term `</DT>`, and the definition description `</DD>`, omitting closing tags decreases the readability of your source document.

Some tags have associated parameters, called attributes, such as color, background, width, and so on. Here is a sample tag attribute for specifying the width of a horizontal rule to be 80 percent of the page width:

```
<HR WIDTH=80%>
```

> **CAUTION**
>
> Keep in mind that not all tags and attributes are supported by all Web browsers. If not supported, the tag or attribute is simply ignored. This can cause an improperly formatted screen, as is the case with a Web browser that doesn't support the use of HTML tables. It is a good practice when authoring HTML documents to include only those HTML tags supported by the majority of browsers.

Markup Tags (Level 0)

The most basic set of tags needed to generate a HTML document is included in the Level 0 tag group. All Web browsers, both graphical and text-based, are expected to support Level 0. This section introduces some of the most common tags that make up Level 0.

`<HTML>` Tag

Every HTML document must include the `<HTML>` tag pair. This pair is the fundamental information required to allow a browser to interpret the enclosed context as an HTML document. The `<HTML>` tag serves to identify the beginning point, whereas the `</HTML>` tag identifies the ending point of the document. The `<HEAD>`, `<BODY>`, and associated sub-elements are included within the `<HTML>` tags. Here is an example of the `<HTML>` tag pair:

```
<HTML>
Other header and body tags
</HTML>
```

The Comment Tag

The comment tag is used to include useful information for the designer and reader. Properly documenting your documents is good HTML coding style. The syntax for the comment tag is as follows, where *string* is the comment:

```
<!-- string -- >
```

One common use for this tag is to identify revisions of the document. Here's an example:

```
<!-- Revisions: created 01/01/97 -- >
```

> **TIP**
>
> The comment tag can be used as a search mechanism for programs that update HTML documents automatically on-the-fly. For example, you can add the following comment to your HTML document:
>
> ```
> <!-- Load new documents here -- >
> ```
>
> You could then have a program search for that text string and insert new hypertext links just before or just after the comment.

<HEAD> Tag

The <HEAD> tag is used to identify prologue information, sometimes referred to as "header" information, for your document (this tag should not to be confused with header tags). Information contained within the <HEAD> and </HEAD> tag pair can be used by other programs, such as indexing engines.

The following example shows this tag pair added to the <HTML> tag example shown earlier:

```
<HTML>
<HEAD>
Other header tags
</HEAD>
Some body tags and data
</HTML>
```

As indicated in this example, the `<HEAD>` element can consist of other header tags or sub-elements such as `<TITLE>`, `<BASE>`, `<NEXTID>`, and `<ISINDEX>`, which are discussed in the following sections.

`<TITLE>` Tag

The `<TITLE>` tag is used to identify the content of the document and should be included in every HTML document. In some cases, the title is also used for document identification in other contexts. For instance, when used in conjunction with a Wide-Area Information Service (WAIS) search engine, the title is generally used as the document's hypertext link string. The title should succinctly identify the content of the document. In some Windows-based Web browsers, the title is used as the text for the title bar of the window.

Here's a sample `<TITLE>` tag that could be used to identify the outline for this book:

```
<TITLE>World Wide Web Database Developers Guide Using Visual Basic</TITLE>
```

> **TIP**
>
> Some search engines use the text contained with the title as a search index for the document. By properly crafting your titles, you can make your documents easier to search. For example, the title
>
> ```
> <TITLE>FY96 Sales Statistics</TITLE>
> ```
>
> is a more identifiable title than something like
>
> ```
> <TITLE>Stats</TITLE>
> ```

`<BODY>` Tag

The `<BODY>` tag is used to enclose the remaining portion of your document. The `<BODY>` tag enables you to control such attributes as the background color and an image to be tiled across the background. All other text and content tags are placed within the `<BODY>` and `</BODY>` tags. Here is a sample `<BODY>` tag that generates a yellow background, an image (`image.gif`) superimposed over the background, and a blue foreground for the text:

```
<BODY BGCOLOR="yellow" BACKGROUND="image.gif" TEXT="blue">
The actual text (included after HTML tags) of your document
</BODY>
```

Headings: The `<H#>` Tag

The `<H#>` tag is used for major and subtopic/subsection headings within HTML documents. The # symbol refers to the level of heading. HTML levels of headings are numbered 1 through 6, with 1 being the largest and 6 the smallest.

CAUTION

Successive spaces in an HTML document are replaced with a single space. Some exceptions to this rule are the paragraph and heading tags, where the spaces immediately following these tags are totally ignored.

Headings are displayed by browsers in larger and/or bolder fonts than normal body text. Heading 1 is the most prominent and is generally the first heading in a document. Subsequent headings (2–6) are displayed in gradually decreasing font sizes and are meant for use as subheadings within documents.

NOTE

Generally, headings are displayed in decreasing sizes beginning with <H1> as the first header, <H2> as the second header, and so on. However, it is perfectly valid to start with a smaller heading (larger number) in order to sustain better readability of your document.

The following example illustrates the heading levels and how they are used to display a document's hierarchy. Figure 10.2 displays the rendered text.

```
<HTML>
<HEAD>
<TITLE>WWW Database Developers Guide Using Visual Basic</TITLE>
</HEAD>
<BODY>

<H1>WWW DATABASE DEVELOPER'S GUIDE WITH VISUAL BASIC 5</H1>
<H2>Chapter 1. The Internet, World Wide Web and Intranets</H2>
<H3>A Little Internet Background</H3>
<H3>Internet History</H3>
<H3>Internet and Web Milestones</H3>
<H3>Internet and Web Growth</H3>
<H3>What is the World Wide Web</H3>
<H2>Chapter 2. Doing Business On The Web</H2>
<H3>Today's Competitive Business Environment</H3>
<H3>Why Do Business On The Web</H3>
<H3>What's Hot in Sales on the Web</H3>
<H3>The Role of Databases in Web Business Applications</H3>

</BODY>
</HTML>
```

FIGURE 10.2.

Sample title and heading as displayed on the Web browser.

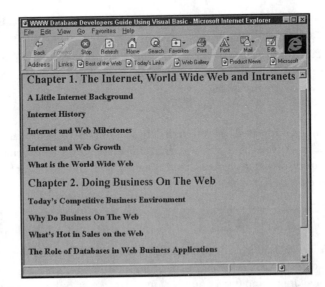

In some cases, the first heading used in the document and the title are identical. However, in multisectioned documents, the title tag should refer to the document as a whole, and the first-level header would be used to identify major topics. Within the document, subtopics could then be further identified with subsequent header levels.

> **TIP**
>
> Because graphical Web browsers display the header levels differently (that is, varying fonts, point sizes, colors, and so on), you may need to experiment with each heading to get the sizing you want for your document and to ensure that it will display as desired on the major graphical browsers in use. In text browsers, however, the point size remains unchanged by a heading.

Paragraphs: The <P> Tag

The <P> tag is used to separate paragraphs within the HTML document. Without the <P> tags in their proper locations, the displayed document becomes one large paragraph.

For example, consider text that is formatted as follows:

```
<HTML>
<HEAD>
<TITLE>WWW Database Developers Guide Using Visual Basic</TITLE>
</HEAD>

<H3>WWW DATABASE DEVELOPER'S GUIDE WITH VISUAL BASIC 5</H3>
```

```
<H4>A Guide To Developing Visual Basic Applications For Database
Access via the WWW</H3>

<P>This is paragraph #1.

This is paragraph #2.</P>

</BODY>
</HTML>
```

The Web browser would display the text as one continuous paragraph with word wrapping, as shown in Figure 10.3.

FIGURE 10.3.

Incorrect paragraph formatting.

A Web browser starts a new paragraph only when it reaches a new <P> tag in the source HTML document.

> **TIP**
>
> As a matter of style, and to preserve readability in HTML source files, headings should be placed on separate lines, and paragraphs should be separated by blank lines.

To repair the previous example, you would add <P> tags around each of the paragraphs to separate them appropriately, as shown here. Figure 10.4 shows the results.

```
<HTML>
<HEAD>
<TITLE>WWW Database Developers Guide Using Visual Basic</TITLE>
</HEAD>
```

```
<H3>WWW DATABASE DEVELOPER'S GUIDE WITH VISUAL BASIC 5</H3>

<H4>A Guide To Developing Visual Basic Applications For Database
Access via the WWW</H4>

<P>
This is paragraph #1.</P>

<P>
This is paragraph #2.</P>

</BODY>
</HTML>
```

FIGURE 10.4.

Correct paragraph formatting.

Web browsers ignore all indentations, extra white spaces, carriage returns, and blank lines in the source document because HTML relies almost entirely on the tags for formatting instructions.

> **CAUTION**
>
> Carriage returns in HTML files are insignificant to the Web browser. Word wrapping is handled automatically by the Web browser and can occur at any point in the source file.

Fortunately there are additional tags described subsequently that allow for special formatting such as indention and blank lines.

> **NOTE**
>
> The preformatted tag enables you to make formatted text display the same way in both the source document and the Web browser. See the <PRE> tag description later in this chapter.

Anchors: The <A> Tag

The <A> (anchor) tag is used to provide links from the current location in a document to other subsections within the same document as well as to other documents, images, audio, application programs, and so on, many of which may reside on other machines (local or remote). The Web browser highlights these links (usually with color and/or underlining) to indicate that they are hypertext links.

Linking to Another Document

The syntax for linking to a document on another machine is as follows:

```
<A HREF="resource://host.domain[:port]/path/filename"> Text to be hyperlinked</A>
```

Here is an actual hypertext link example from the United States Department of State's HEROES home page:

```
<P>
U.S. Government information regarding WANTED terrorists can be found at the
U.S. Department of State's <A HREF="http://www.heroes.net/pub/heroes/">
Counter-Terrorism Rewards Program</A> Homepage.</P>
```

In this example, the text `Counter-Terrorism Rewards Program` is enclosed within the anchor tag and would be displayed to the user as a hypertext link, highlighted in a different color, to identify it as a link to the referenced document. The user clicks the hypertext link, and the Web browser connects to the Web server (in this case `www.heroes.net`). After downloading the source HTML document, the Web browser reformats and presents the document to the reader.

> **CAUTION**
>
> Earlier releases of Web browsers allowed ill-formatted anchor hypertext reference lines (such as those with a missing end quote after the document name) to be interpreted and handled under the assumption that the close anchor identified the end of the document name. However, as Web browsers become more refined and as HTML standards become more defined, this won't be the case. For example, the current Netscape Navigator release 4.0 fails to interpret and display such ill-formatted tags.

Hypertext references can be in the form of either relative (relative to the document that references it) or absolute (full directory) pathnames. The general rule is that you should use relative links when possible because it simplifies Website administration by making it easier to move groups of documents to another physical storage location (for example, a different file system or directory) or Web server without requiring the links to be updated.

Here is an example of a relative hypertext reference:

```
<P>
<A HREF="filename.html">This is a relative link</A></P>
```

Notice that there is no reference to the *resource*, *host.domain*, *port*, or the *directory* in this example. The Web browser would know that the document is located in the same directory as the calling document.

Now, here's an example of an absolute reference:

```
<P>
<A HREF="/examples/filename.html">This is an absolute link</A></P>
```

You can see that the directory of the document, /examples/ is referenced in the hypertext link. The Web browser would know that the location of the document is absolute from the Web server's root directory.

NOTE

The Web server can be configured to support aliases (alternative, usually shorter, names that can be used in place of longer names) that enable the location of a file or directory to be moved without having to change the actual HTML documents that reference the moved files or directories.

Linking to a Specific Location Within the Same Document

Anchors can also be used to link to a specific location within a document. The syntax for linking to a specific location within the same document is as follows:

```
<A HREF="#named anchor">Text to be hyperlinked</A>
```

For example, suppose that you want to include a hypertext link at the top of your document that references material (say a subsection) further down in the document. To do this, you would set up your named anchor as in the following example:

```
<HTML>
<HEAD>
<TITLE>Named Anchor Example</TITLE>
<BODY>
<H1>WWW Database Developers Guide Using Visual Basic</H1>
<A HREF="#Chapter 1">
```

```
<H2>Chapter 1. The Internet, World Wide Web and Intranets</H2></A>
<H3>A Little Internet Background</H3>
<H3>Internet History</H3>
<H3>Internet and Web Milestones</H3>
<H3>Internet and Web Growth</H3>
<H3>What is the World Wide Web</H3>
<A HREF="#Chapter 2">
<H2>Chapter 2. Doing Business On The Web</H2></A>
<H3>Today's Competitive Business Environment</H3>
<H3>Why Do Business On The Web</H3>
<H3>What's Hot in Sales on the Web</H3>
<H3>The Role of Databases in Web Business Applications</H3>
```

The # used within the HREF attribute of the anchor tag identifies the text that follows it as a named anchor. Note that the anchor is placed inside double quotation marks.

The next step is to add the named anchors at the appropriate locations within your document, making certain you use the same anchor name you referenced in the HREF line. You do this using a slight variation of syntax: you use NAME instead of HREF to identify this position in the document as the place to "jump to" when the hypertext link referencing it is clicked. Here's an example:

```
<A NAME="Chapter 1"><H2>Chapter 1. The Internet, World Wide Web and Intranets</A>
</H2>
```

Here, a named anchor for Chapter 1 is created, called "Chapter 1".

> **NOTE**
>
> When specifying a named anchor, the closing </A> tag is not required because the anchor is not a hypertext link. It's just a location identifier within a document. However, it's good authoring practice to use the </A> closing anchor tag.

Linking to a Specific Location Within Another Document

Linking to a named anchor within another document simply requires adding the document name before the named anchor in the HREF attribute of the anchor tag establishing the link. Say you wanted to reference the actual text of Chapter 1 (which is assumed to be in another document called chap1.html) from within the book outline. To do this, you just modify the reference line with the named anchor as follows:

```
<A HREF="chap1.html#Chapter1">1. The Internet, World Wide Web, and Intranets</A>
```

When the reader clicks on the words *The Internet, World Wide Web, and Intranets* in the outline, the Web browser downloads the file chap1.html and takes the reader directly to the named anchor "Chapter1" in chap1.html.

Lists: The <LI> Tag

The <LI> (list item) tag is used to identify and group a list of items within a document. Lists will appear in the displayed document indented and with one list item per line. The <LI> tag is used in conjunction with the <OL> and <UL> tags described later.

> **NOTE**
>
> The <LI> tag is an example of an HTML tag that does not require an ending </LI> tag. The Web browser assumes that the next list item or closing list tag (</OL> or </UL>) identifies the end of any previous list item.

Ordered Lists: The <OL> Tag

The <OL> (ordered list) tag is used to identify those list items that should be automatically numbered by the Web browser when displayed. All list items within the start and end <OL> tags must begin with the <LI> tag.

The following code shows sample HTML code with <OL> and <LI> tags. Figure 10.5 shows how the formatted list looks onscreen.

```
<HTML>
<HEAD>
<TITLE>WWW Database Developers Guide With Visual Basic</TITLE>
</HEAD>

<H2>WWW DATABASE DEVELOPER'S GUIDE WITH VISUAL BASIC 5</H2>

<H3>A Guide To Developing Visual Basic Applications For Database
Access via the WWW</H3>

<P>
Chapters
<OL>
   <LI><A HREF="#Chapter1">The Internet, World Wide Web and Intranets</A></LI>
   <LI><A HREF="#Chapter2">Doing Business on the Web</A></LI>
   <LI><A HREF="#Chapter3">Client/Server Computing</A></LI>
</OL></P>
</BODY>
</HTML>
```

Notice that the Web browser automatically indented and numbered each of the list items.

FIGURE 10.5.
Ordered list example.

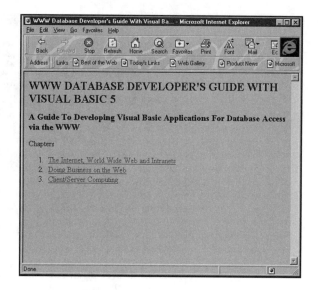

Unordered Lists: The <UL> Tag

The <UL> (unordered list) tag is used to identify list items that should be grouped together. Unlike <OL> list items, however, these list items are not numbered. All list items within the start and end <UL> tags must begin with the <LI> tag.

The following code shows how the <OL> tags example shown earlier would look using <UL> tags instead. Figure 10.6 shows how the formatted list looks onscreen.

```
<HTML>
<HEAD>
<TITLE>WWW Database Developers Guide With Visual Basic</TITLE>
</HEAD>

<H2>WWW DATABASE DEVELOPER'S GUIDE WITH VISUAL BASIC 5</H2>

<H3>A Guide To Developing Visual Basic Applications For Database
Access via the WWW</H3>

<P>
Chapters
<UL>
    <LI><A HREF="#Chapter1">The Internet, World Wide Web and Intranets</A></LI>
    <LI><A HREF="#Chapter2">Doing Business on the Web</A></LI>
    <LI><A HREF="#Chapter3">Client/Server Computing</A></LI>
</UL></P>
</BODY>
</HTML>
```

FIGURE 10.6.
Unordered list example.

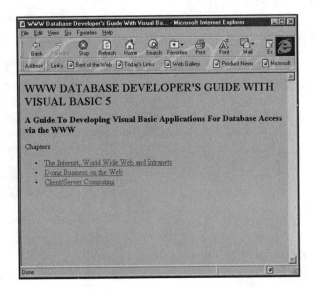

Notice that the Web browser used bullets instead of numbers.

Preformatting Text: The <PRE> Tag

The <PRE> (preformatted) tag allows the generation of source HTML documents that will maintain the same formatting when interpreted and displayed by the Web browser. All white spaces, carriage returns, and linefeeds in your document that are enclosed within the <PRE> and </PRE> tags will be retained by the Web browser.

> **CAUTION**
>
> When using preformatted text, be careful of the length of your document text because no word wrapping is forced by the browser. This could require the end user to scroll to the right to see all of the text.

Preformatted text is rendered in a monospaced font. You could, for instance, have your database output generated in table form and enclosed within <PRE> tags.

The following code shows a sample database query result using the <PRE> tag. Figure 10.7 shows how it is formatted onscreen.

```
<HTML>
<!-- PRE Tag Example -->
<!-- Author:  Mark Swank -->
<!-- Revision History:  1 January 1997 -->
<HEAD>
<TITLE>Swank Family</TITLE>
</HEAD>
```

```
<H2>Swank Family</H2>

<PRE>
First Name   MI   Last Name     Relationship
----------   --   ----------    ------------
Daniel       W.   Swank         Father
Helen        L.   Worthington   Mother
Charles      E.   Swank         Son
Jane         A.   Wendt         Daughter
June         A.   Laubach       Daughter
Robert       W.   Swank         Son
Roberta      J.   Davis         Daughter
Sherry       D.   Coonan        Daughter
</PRE>

</BODY>
</HTML>
```

FIGURE 10.7.

Preformatted text example.

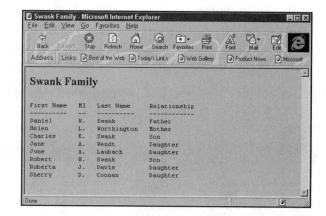

Line Breaks: The
 Tag

The
 (line break) tag has no closing tag. The <BR> tag is used to provide the HTML writer the ability to force a line break at a given point in the text. Text following the <BR> tag will be started at the left margin of the next line.

Horizontal Rules: The <HR> Tag

The <HR> (horizontal rule) tag is used simply to place a horizontal line on the document. Most Web authors use horizontal rules to separate specific sections of their documents. For example, the following code shows how to use the horizontal rule to break up the sections of a document:

```
<HTML>
<HEAD>
<TITLE>Example Horizontal Rule</TITLE>
```

```
<P>
<H3>Section Summary</H3>

<HR>

<P>
<H2>II. Architectural Overview</H2>
</BODY>
</HTML>
```

Markup Tags (Level 1)

Level 1 tags include those tags that support character formatting. These tags include support for text bolding, emphasis, monospace fonts, and so on:

Tag	Description
`<B>`	Delimits bold text.
`<EM>`	Places emphasis on text and is displayed as italic text.
`<I>`	Delimits italic text.
`<STRONG>`	Places strong emphasis on text and is displayed as bold text.
`<TT>`	Delimits teletype font text.

> **NOTE**
>
> The `<I>` and `<B>` tags are being replaced with the `<EM>` and `<STRONG>` tags, respectively. Although the `<I>` and `<B>` tags are still supported, it is recommended that you begin using the `<EM>` and `<STRONG>` tags.

Here is a combined example showing the different character formatting HTML tags discussed in this section. Figure 10.8 displays the rendered text.

```
<HTML>
<!-- Character Formatting HTML Tags Example -->
<!-- Author:  Mark Swank -->
<!-- Revision History:  1 January 1997 -->
<HEAD>
<TITLE>Character Formatting HTML Tags Example</TITLE>
</HEAD>
<BODY>

<H2>Character Formatting HTML Tags Example</H2>

<P>
Here is an example of how to break<BR>
text and force continuation on the next<BR>
line without wrapping.  This is accomplished<BR>
by adding the "break line" tag.</P>
```

```
<P>
<STRONG>Strong text looks like this.</STRONG></P>

<P>
<B>Bold text looks like this.</B></P>

<P>
<EM>Emphasized text looks like this.</EM></P>

<P>
<I>Italicized text looks like this.</I></P>

<P>
<TT>Teletype text looks like this.</TT></P>
</BODY>
</HTML>
```

FIGURE 10.8.

Example of character-formatting HTML tags.

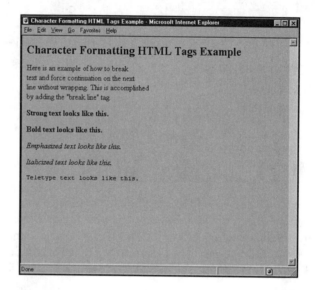

Inline Images: The `<IMG>` Tag

The image tag is used to display inline images. These inline images can serve many purposes—such as providing smaller (sometimes called *thumbnail*) images that are hypertext linked to a larger image, hypertext images that can appear as window selection buttons, and image maps that allow the browser to retrieve a specific document based on the location within the image that the end user selected.

> **NOTE**
>
> See the section titled "Handling Images" later in this chapter for a discussion on image sizing.

The image tag attribute ISMAP, when used with an image map file, enables the Web client to identify specific locations within an image that the user has clicked.

> **TIP**
>
> Image maps are a great front-end resource for point-and-click database access. A sample application is one in which a user clicks a specific state on a map of the United States and a database query for statistical information about that state is executed.

Image maps can be generated easily by map-editing software.

> **RESOURCE**
>
> Here are just a few programs available for editing image maps:
>
> | Program | Location |
> | --- | --- |
> | Mapedit | http://www.boutell.com/mapedit/ |
> | MapMaker | http://www.tns.lcs.mit.edu/cgi-bin/mapmaker |

HTML 2.0 Specifications

The basic introduction to HTML in this chapter covered those features of HTML found in Levels 0 and 1. With the proliferation of graphics-capable Web browsers such as Microsoft Internet Explorer, Netscape Navigator, and NCSA Mosaic, came the need to provide a means for interacting with the user. The main feature of the HTML Level 2.0 specification, and the method to support such interaction with the user, is the use of forms.

Forms are HTML documents that include user-input objects that provide an input method by which the user can interact with remote server and applications programs. Users can now use forms interfaces to communicate with remote services and applications such as online registration services, order-entry systems, user surveys, and so on. The number of uses for forms-based applications is endless.

This section introduces the <FORM> tag and its attributes. The next chapter covers it in greater depth and provides examples of each of the form attributes and form tag elements that enable the user to render input via form widgets, such as the following:

- Radio buttons
- Checkboxes
- Listboxes
- Text input

Forms: The <FORM> Tag

The <FORM> tag pair is used to identify an area within the HTML document that will include the user-input objects. The values of objects included within the <FORM> tag pair will be sent to the ACTION attribute for the form, as mentioned later. The syntax of the form tag is as follows (its attributes are described in the following sections):

```
<FORM METHOD="method" ACTION="action" ENCTYPE="enctype"></FORM>
```

METHOD Attribute

The <FORM> tag METHOD attribute is the method used to submit the form for processing. There are two valid choices for the METHOD attribute: GET and POST.

GET is the default method; it causes the form contents to be appended to the URL, as in the case of a normal query. POST causes the form contents to be sent to the processing server in a data body rather than as part of the URL.

ACTION Attribute

The <FORM> tag ACTION attribute is the URL of the processing server to which the form contents will be submitted.

Here is an example of the GET method's ACTION attribute:

```
<FORM METHOD="GET" ACTION="/cgi-bin/process_form?user=mark"></FORM>
```

Here is an example of the POST method's ACTION attribute:

```
<FORM METHOD="POST" ACTION="/cgi-bin/process_form"></FORM>
```

ENCTYPE Attribute

The <FORM> tag ENCTYPE attribute specifies the encoding to be used for the form contents. This attribute is generally omitted because it applies only if the METHOD is set to POST. Here is a FORM ENCTYPE attribute example:

```
<FORM METHOD="POST" ACTION="/cgi-bin/process_form"
  ENCTYPE="application/x-www-form-urlencoded"></FORM>
```

What's New in HTML 3.2

Many changes in the current 2.0 specification are implemented in the HTML 3.2 specification. One of the major proposed changes in the HTML specification under Level 3.2 is the addition of the <TABLE> tag. Database application developers will find this tag to be a great mechanism for formatting and presenting data in a familiar row-column approach.

Tables: The <TABLE> Tag

The <TABLE> tag is used to generate a row-cell matrix within the document. Cells may contain objects such as text, images, anchors, and so on. The table tag supports the following tag elements:

<TR>   Defines a new table row
<TH>   Defines a column header (caption)
<TD>   Defines the data (object) within a cell

The following sections describe the attributes for the <TABLE> tag.

BORDER

The BORDER attribute is used to indicate whether the table should be rendered with or without borders drawn around all table cells. If specified, the BORDER value specifies the border width as a number followed by an optional suffix. The standard units for widths are specified using the suffixes shown in Table 10.1.

Table 10.1. Standard units for widths.

Suffix	Unit
pt	Denotes points
pi	Denotes picas
in	Denotes inches
cm	Denotes centimeters
mm	Denotes millimeters
em	Denotes em units (equal to the height of the default font)
px	Denotes screen pixels

The default units are screen pixels. The number is an integer value or a real-valued number such as "2.5". The default is for no borders to be rendered. Here is a sample BORDER attribute specifying a border width of 2 centimeters:

```
<TABLE BORDER="2cm">
```

ALIGN

The ALIGN (horizontal alignment) attribute determines the appearance of objects based on the table tag element in which the ALIGN attribute appears. If used within the <CAPTION> element, the ALIGN attribute controls whether the caption is displayed above or below the table. If used within the <TR>, <TH>, or <TD> elements, it controls whether text inside the table cells will be left-justified, right-justified, or centered.

VALIGN

The VALIGN (vertical alignment) attribute is used within the <TR>, <TH>, and <TD> table tag elements and controls whether text inside the table cells will be aligned to the top of the cell, the bottom of the cell, or vertically centered within the cell. It also can specify that all the cells in the row should be vertically aligned to the same baseline.

NOWRAP

The NOWRAP attribute can be used to signify that lines within a cell cannot be wrapped to another line in order to fit the width of the cell.

> **CAUTION**
>
> The use of the NOWRAP attribute forces each line to its full width in order to fit the entire object within the cell. This may cause excessively wide cells.

COLSPAN

The COLSPAN attribute is used within the <TD> and <TH> elements; it is used to specify how many columns the cell should span. The default COLSPAN is 1.

ROWSPAN

The ROWSPAN attribute is used within the <TD> and <TH> elements; it is used to specify how many rows the cell should span. The default ROWSPAN is 1.

> **NOTE**
>
> If a row span causes the row to extend into rows that were never specified with a <TR> tag, the row will be truncated.

Table Example

Let's look at an example of a simple table. Don't be alarmed when you see tags in this example that haven't been covered yet. These new tags are important for illustrating the capabilities of a table. Some of the tags are Netscape extensions. The next section, "Netscape Extensions," provides the details for all table tags, and more information is provided in Chapter 11, "Developing HTML Forms for Database Access and Application Interfaces."

```
<HTML>
<!-- HTML Level 3 Table Example -->
<!-- Author:  Mark Swank -->
<!-- Date created:  1 January 1997 -->
<HEAD>
<TITLE>HTML Level 3.2 Table Example</TITLE>
</HEAD>
<BODY>

<CENTER>
<H1>HTML Level 3.2 Table Example</H1>

<TABLE BORDER="1" ALIGN="Center" CELLSPACING="5" COLS="4">
<CAPTION><STRONG>Product Sales</STRONG></CAPTION>
<TH ALIGN="CENTER">Product Line</TH>
<TH ALIGN="CENTER">Units Sold</TH>
<TH ALIGN="CENTER">Unit Price</TH>
<TH ALIGN="CENTER">Total Sales</TH>

<TR><TD>CDROM Drives</TD>
<TD>100</TD>
<TD>$295</TD>
<TD>$29,500</TD></TR>

<TR><TD>Hard Drives</TD>
<TD>200</TD>
<TD>$500</TD>
<TD>$50,000</TD></TR>

<TR><TD>Modems</TD>
<TD>50</TD>
<TD>$100</TD>
<TD>$5,000</TD></TR>

<TR><TD>Speakers</TD>
<TD>50</TD>
<TD>$50</TD>
<TD>$2,500</TD></TR>

</TABLE>
</CENTER>

<P>NCSA offers an online
<A HREF="http://www.ncsa.uiuc.edu/SDG/Software/Mosaic/Tables/tutorial.html">
table tutorial</A>.
<HR>

<ADDRESS>
<A HREF="http://www.clark.net/~mswank">Mark A. Swank</A><BR>
<A HREF="mailto:mswank@clark.net">mswank@clark.net</A>
</ADDRESS>

</BODY>
</HTML>
```

Figure 10.9 shows what the formatted table looks like onscreen.

FIGURE 10.9.
*HTML 3.2 table
example.*

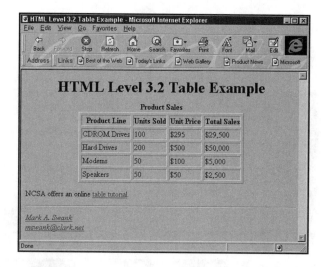

Netscape Extensions

Netscape Navigator supports many additional extensions to both the HTML 2.0 and 3.2 specifications. Other major browsers, such as Microsoft Internet Explorer, also support the majority of the Netscape extensions. To date, it has been Netscape's driving force that has led to many of the changes in both the 2.0 and 3.2 specifications. This section presents some of the major Netscape extensions, such as the use of color attributes, background images, and additional supported horizontal rule attributes.

The <BODY> Tag

The <BODY> tag is used to identify HTML elements that compose the body of the document. The <BODY> tag also includes several attributes that support formatting such as background images, background color, and text color. The following sections describe each of the <BODY> tag attributes.

Background Images

The HTML author has the option of adding a background image to the document. This image is visible by graphics-capable browsers only and is rendered by modifying the <BODY> tag as follows:

```
<BODY background="image_url">
```

Here, *image_url* points to a valid graphic image that will be tiled across the browser background.

Background Color

The background color attribute is specified as `bgcolor` and is used to specify a solid background color to be use for the document.

NOTE

Color attributes are referenced in hexadecimal (`#RRGGBB`) format. Red, green, and blue (RGB) values are used to identify the specific color combinations that produce the desired color.

For example, you could use the following tag, where `#FFFFFF` is a solid white background:

```
<BODY bcolor="#FFFFFF">
```

TIP

If you are a Microsoft Windows user, you can determine the RGB values for a color as follows:

Windows 3.1	Select Control Panel I Color I Define Custom Colors. Select a custom color from the Color Palette and the appropriate RGB values will be displayed for that color.
Windows 95	Select Control Panel I Display I Appearance I Color I Other. Select a custom color from the Color Palette and the appropriate RGB values will be displayed for that color.

Text Color

The text color attribute is specified as `text` and is used to specify a text color to be use for the document. The reference must be in hexadecimal (`#RRGGBB`) format, where `#FF0000` would generate red text:

```
<BODY text="#FF0000">
```

Link Color

The link color attribute is specified as `link` and is used to specify a color to be used for links within the document. The reference must be in hexadecimal (`#RRGGBB`) format, where `#FF0000` would generate red link text:

```
<BODY link="#FF0000">
```

Visited Link Color

The visited link color attribute is specified as vlink and is used to specify a color to be used for visited links within the document. The reference must be in hexadecimal (#RRGGBB) format, where #FF0000 would generate red link text:

```
<BODY vlink="#FF0000">
```

Active Link Color

The active link color attribute is specified as alink and is used to specify a color to be used for active links within the document. The reference must be in hexadecimal (#RRGGBB) format, where #FF0000 would generate red link text:

```
<BODY alink="#FF0000">
```

The <HR> Tag

The <HR> tag is used to specify placement of a horizontal rule. A horizontal rule is simply a horizontal line that can be of varying sizes and widths. The following sections describe each of the <HR> tag attributes.

size

The size attribute specifies the thickness to be used for the horizontal rule. The value of size is specified using the standard units of width, as noted in Table 10.1.

```
<HR size="3">
```

noshade

The noshade attribute is used to turn off horizontal rule shading. Shading is used to give the horizontal rule a three dimensional look.

```
<HR noshade>
```

width

The width attribute specifies the width of the horizontal rule. The value is specified using the standard units of width, as noted in Table 10.1. There is no range of values for the width of a horizontal rule. If specified using any unit other than percent (%), the horizontal rule can exceed and wrap around to the next document line. Here is a sample width attribute specifying the horizontal rule to consume 80 percent of the document width:

```
<HR width="80%">
```

align

The `align` attribute specifies the alignment of the horizontal rule. The values must be one of `left`, `right`, or `center`.

```
<HR align="left">
```

Horizontal Rule Example

As you can see, horizontal rules can be specified with many combined attributes to produce varying shapes and sizes. Here is a sample horizontal rule document that shows several ways to display horizontal rules. Figure 10.10 displays the rendered text.

```
<!-- HTML Horizontal Rule Example -->
<!-- Author:  Mark Swank -->
<!-- Revision History:  1 January 1997 -->
<HEAD>
<TITLE>Horizontal Rule Example</TITLE>
</HEAD>
<BODY>

<CENTER>
<H3>Horizontal Rule Example</H3>
</CENTER>

size=4
<HR size="4">

size=8
<HR size="8">

noshade
<HR noshade>

width=50%
<HR width="50%">

width=50% align=left
<HR width="50%" align="left">

</BODY>
</HTML>
<HTML>
```

The horizontal rule is not always visible when using colored backgrounds that blend with the same color scheme. Additionally, certain graphic backgrounds, such as those with lined images, can "hide" the rule from the naked eye.

FIGURE 10.10.
Horizontal rule example.

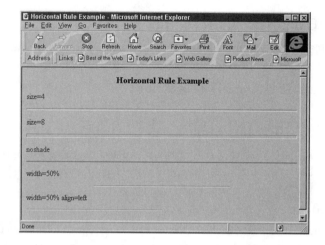

<BASEFONT> Tag

The <BASEFONT> tag is used to specify the base font size that the remainder of the document font attributes will use as a reference. There is currently only one attribute available for use with the <BASEFONT> tag: the size attribute.

size

The size attribute to the base font tag changes the current font size to a specified number. The number must be in the range of 1–7. Here is an example:

```
<BASEFONT size="1">
```

Blinking Text: The <BLINK> Tag

The <BLINK> tag generates blinking text for everything contained within the <BLINK> and </BLINK> tag pairs. There is no way to control the rate at which the blinking occurs:

```
<BLINK>This is blinking text</BLINK>
```

> **TIP**
>
> Most developers will agree that the <BLINK> tag can be somewhat obnoxious. However, there are occasions when the tag is useful. For example, you can enclose error-text strings within <BLINK> tags to make the text more identifiable.

Centering: The <CENTER> Tag

The <CENTER> tag causes all objects (text, images, and so on) contained between the <CENTER> and </CENTER> tag pairs to be centered:

```
<CENTER>This is centered text<CENTER>
```

Images: The <IMG> Tag

The <IMG> tag is used to specify attributes for an image that will be displayed within your document. The align attribute is the only <IMG> tag attribute.

align

The align attribute specifies the location of the image in relation to the object following it. The valid values for the align attribute are right, top, texttop, middle, absmiddle, baseline, bottom, and absbottom. Here is an example that would place the object following the image centered on the image:

```
<IMG align="center" src="image_source_url">
```

Tables: The <TABLE> Tag

Included in the Netscape extensions are three new table tag attributes. These attributes can be used to specify the width, cell spacing, and cell padding of the table. The following sections describe each of the <TABLE> tag attributes.

width

The width attribute specifies the width of the table border in standard unit widths:

```
<TABLE width="2cm">
```

cellspacing

The cellspacing attribute specifies the space around the table cells specified in standard unit widths:

```
<TABLE cellspacing="1">
```

cellpadding

The cellpadding attribute specifies the space (specified in standard unit widths) in the data cells:

```
<TABLE cellpadding="3pi">
```

HTML Style Guides

It must first be said that there are no defined standards of HTML authoring style. That's why these are called guides and not standards. Having said that, and after surfing the WWW quite a bit ourselves over the last few years, here are some of the notes we've taken pertaining to what the majority of Web authors consider to be good authoring practices.

Signing Your Documents

The general feeling is that all documents should be signed by their author so that the reader can formulate his or her own opinion as to the integrity of the document. Much like a signature block on a memo or the header of a document abstract, Web documents should identify the author.

HTML has a specific tag for specifying the author of a document. The <ADDRESS> tag is generally placed at the footer of the document (still before the </BODY> tag). A good practice is to add a Mailto anchor within your <ADDRESS> tag. The Mailto resource takes a Simple Mail Transfer Protocol (SMTP) mail address as its argument. When clicked, the anchor spawns an external mail application for the reader to generate an e-mail reply. Here is the signature block the author uses:

```
<ADDRESS>
<A HREF="http://www.clark.net/~swank">Mark A. Swank</A><BR>
<A HREF="mailto:mswank@clark.net">mswank@clark.net</A>
</ADDRESS>
</BODY>
</HTML>
```

Timestamp Your Documents

Another good authoring style is to timestamp all your documents. This identifies the date and time the document was last updated. Here is an example of a timestamp:

```
Last modified: <em>Wednesday, January 1, 1997 15:10p.m.</em>
```

TIP

You can automate the timestamp process by using a Server-Side Include command like this:

```
Last modified: <em><!--#echo var="LAST MODIFIED"-- ></em>
```

This will take the system timestamp of the last time the document was modified and return it to the Web browser for display.

Select a Good Title

Your title should refer to the document as a whole. Try to select a title that is short, yet addresses the content of your document. Remember, because indexing engines such as WAIS can use the title as the indexed value, a properly selected title is very important to both document identification and retrieval.

> **CAUTION**
>
> Because many applications will display document titles in window title bars and menus, the document title should ideally be fewer than 64 characters long.

Using Meaningful Links

Avoid at all costs the infamous "Click Here" link. Your hypertext links should relate to and possibly flow with the text content of your document. Generally, links that stand alone (those that are not included within the actual text of a sentence) should be short, succinct, and meaningful. Think of the text of your document as something you would want to be able to print and give to someone in paper form. You can't "click here" on paper.

Outline Your Documents When Possible

By using header tags, you can properly outline your document. The ultimate purpose of headers is not to provide a mechanism for changing the font or layout of your document, but rather to provide a standardized means for identifying components of your document.

Headings should follow the depth of your document, and you shouldn't skip heading levels as you go deeper into your document hierarchy. For example, your document should not contain an <H2> tag immediately followed by the <H5> tag for subsections.

Because Web browsers already place emphasis on headings using <H#> tags, you shouldn't use highlighting elements within a header. Such elements would include the <B> (bold) and <EM> (emphasize) tags.

Handling Images

Keep the size of your images to a minimum. Graphics Interchange Format (GIF) images have a maximum of 256 colors and therefore are not always best suited for high-resolution images. The Joint Photographic Experts Group (JPEG) format allows for much better image compression and can support more than 16 million colors.

Don't force readers to view an entire image if there's a good chance that they might not want to see it. Using much smaller thumbnail images is a very common practice for accessing larger images through hypertext links that can be expanded to full resolution when clicked. You may even choose to use simple hypertext links as a means for accessing images. By using this method, the end user isn't forced to download the image or thumbnail at all.

Use the ALT attribute when specifying images. This allows both text-only users and users with image-downloading turned off to get alternate text. Here's an example:

```
<IMG SRC="http://www.heroes.net/icons/next.gif" ALT="[Next Page]">
```

Text-only browsers would display [Next Page], whereas graphical browsers would display the actual image.

HTML Editors and Tools

HTML editors are programs that allow the user to create and edit HTML documents with little knowledge of the HTML specifications. The editor handles the validity of the tag in relation to its location within the document. HTML tools are programs that facilitate the conversion of documents to and from HTML format. Numerous HTML editors and tools are available today, and it would take several chapters to cover them all. For the sake of saving a tree, this section covers only a few of the products within each section: Internet assistants for Microsoft Office, shareware HTML editors, and commercial HTML editors.

> **RESOURCE**
>
> For an updated listing and review of available HTML editors and tools, see the HTML Editors Review home page:
>
> `http://www.techsmith.com/community/htmlrev/index.html`

Internet Assistants for Microsoft Office

Microsoft Corporation offers free add-ins to the Microsoft Office family of applications. These add-ins are designed to help individuals and businesses create and edit documents for the Web quickly and easily.

> **RESOURCE**
>
> All of these products are available for downloading from the Microsoft Download home page at
>
> `http://www.microsoft.com/msdownload/`

The following sections provide a quick review of the Microsoft products currently available.

Internet Assistant for Microsoft Word

Internet Assistant for Microsoft Word assists you in creating HTML documents from within Microsoft Word. The product automatically converts existing Word documents to HTML format, including text, graphics, and tables. It provides an interface to add special formatting such as Marquee text, Inline Video, and background sounds.

> **RESOURCE**
>
> You can download Internet Assistant for Microsoft Word from the following address:
> `http://www.microsoft.com/msword/internet/ia/`

Internet Assistant for Microsoft Excel

Internet Assistant for Microsoft Excel automatically converts an Excel spreadsheet to an HTML table, complete with background colors. Examples of converting Excel spreadsheets into HTML format are provided in Chapter 15, "Creating ActiveX Documents for the Web with VB 5."

> **RESOURCE**
>
> You can download Internet Assistant for Microsoft Excel from the following address:
> `http://www.microsoft.com/msoffice/msexcel/internet/ia/`

Internet Assistant for Microsoft PowerPoint

Internet Assistant for Microsoft PowerPoint converts existing PowerPoint slides into HTML-formatted pages. Additionally, this product automatically sets up hypertext links between your PowerPoint slides and generates image maps as needed.

> **RESOURCE**
>
> You can download Internet Assistant for Microsoft PowerPoint from the following address:
> `http://www.microsoft.com/msoffice/mspowerpoint/internet/ia/`

Shareware HTML Editors

Shareware editors are in abundance on the Internet. Many are very good and are well worth the minimal registration or usage fees associated with them. Most shareware products allow you to "try-on-the-fly" for a period of 30–90 days. The CD-ROM accompanying this book contains the current release (as of the printing of this book) of as many products mentioned as possible.

HoTMetaL PRO 3.0

HoTMetaL PRO was chosen the best HTML authoring tool for the World Wide Web by *PC Magazine*. HoTMetaL PRO 3.0 has a rich suite of editing tools with unique features designed especially for generating and testing HTML files. Version 3.0 includes an improved and more powerful import filter that enables you to import and convert documents created in other popular packages such as Microsoft Word, WordPerfect, and Lotus Ami Pro. Additional features, such as drag-and-drop editing, make designing Web pages even easier for all Web developers.

> **RESOURCE**
>
> An unsupported version of HoTMetaL PRO 3.0 can be downloaded from the following address:
>
> `http://www.sq.com/products/hotmetal/hmp-org.htm`

HTML Assistant

HTML Assistant is available both as shareware (HTML Assistant) and as a retail product (HTML Assistant Pro). This product was one of the first HTML editors on the market. It enables you to validate and test your work as well as organize and keep track of the Internet resources that you use.

> **RESOURCE**
>
> The shareware version is available from the following address:
>
> `http://www.brooknorth.com/welcome4.html`

WebEdit 2.0

WebEdit 2.0 is an easy-to-use HTML editing product. Its ease of use and rich editing features make it one of the best shareware interfaces available. Netscape extensions and HTML 3.2 support is included.

RESOURCE

WebEdit 2.0 can be downloaded from the following address:
`http://www.nesbitt.com/download.html`

WebElite

WebElite is a 32-bit Windows application that can create powerful forms and tables as well as color-coordinated pages. WebElite has a built-in HyperCritical syntax checker that does not allow the insertion of any unnecessary tags or information.

RESOURCE

You can download WebElite from the following address:
`http://www.safety.net/webelite/`

Commercial HTML Editors

Commercial HTML editors are quickly becoming widely available on all platforms. This section focuses on a few of the products that are in wide use and easily available for downloading and evaluation.

HTMLed Pro 1.1

HTMLed Pro is a very stable product that provides syntax highlighting (tags, text, and entities in different colors). It also offers table and forms editors, a customizable tool bar, the capability to open and save HTML documents from a remote server, and a suite of document templates. HTML 3.2 and Netscape extension support is included.

RESOURCE

You can download a time-limited demo of HTMLed Pro 1.1 from the following address:
`http://www.ist.ca/`

HotDog Pro 3.0

HotDog Pro is a fast, flexible, and user-friendly HTML editor with new enhancements such as previewing, table editing, and HTML checking.

> **RESOURCE**
>
> You can download a functional demonstration of HotDog Pro from the following address:
>
> `http://www.sausage.com.au/dogindex.htm`

Web Media Publisher Pro

Web Media Publisher Pro is a 32-bit Windows application that supports HTML 3.2, Netscape 2.0 extensions, and Microsoft Explorer features. Support for Java script editing is included. This package includes a Web timer for monitoring time spent authoring.

> **RESOURCE**
>
> You can download Web Media Publisher Pro for evaluation from the following address:
>
> `http://www.wbmedia.com/publisher/`

Microsoft FrontPage

Microsoft FrontPage is a commercially available client/server application that supports authoring, scripting, and Web-site management from a user's desktop, across a corporate LAN, or over the Internet. FrontPage includes an editor for creating and editing HTML pages, an add-in for graphically visualizing and managing complex Web sites, an add-in that includes text-search capabilities and discussion forums, an add-in for wizards and templates to help you create HTML pages, and finally an add-in for management and tasking to track the status of authoring tasks.

> **RESOURCE**
>
> For more information about FrontPage, visit the following address:
>
> `http://www.microsoft.com/msoffice/frontpage/`

HTML Translator/Conversion Programs

HTML conversion programs (filters) come in many different flavors, supporting a variety of formats. To review each one would be an enormous task, so this section lists only some of the shareware and commercially available filters, which are divided into the following categories:

- Word processor filters
- Plain-text filters
- Programming language filters
- Manual page filters
- Mail filters
- Frequently Asked Question filters

Word Processor Filters

Numerous filters are available for a variety of word processing formats. They are grouped into their respective formats for easy referencing in this section.

PostScript

PostScript filters can take a standard PostScript file and convert it into an HTML document. Here are URLs for two such filters:

Program	Program URL
ps2html	http://stasi.bradley.edu/ftp/pub/ps2html/ps2html-v2.html
PS2HTML	http://www.area.fi.cnr.it/area/ps2html.htm

Multiple Word Processor Formats

Many filters have been written that support multiple word processor formats. Filters such as these can convert multiple formats such as Microsoft Word, WordPerfect, and Rich Text Format documents into HTML files. Here's a list of URLs:

Program	Program URL
Cyberleaf	http://www.ileaf.com/cyberleafds.html
Html Transit	http://www.infoaccess.com/
Web Publisher	http://www.skisoft.com/
KEYview	http://www.ftp.com/
rtftohtml	http://www.sunpack.com/RTF/rtftohtml_overview.html
TagPerfect	http://www.jsp.fi/delta/deltatgp.htm
E-Publish	http://www.stattech.com.au/

Microsoft Word HTML Editors/Converters

Several programs are available that allow the editing or converting of documents formatted with Microsoft Word into HTML format via Word macros. The process is as simple as generating or importing the document into Word format, running the Word macro, and then saving the document in HTML format. Here's a list of a few programs available that provide this capability:

Program	Program URL
ANT_HTML	`http://www.w3.org/hypertext/WWW/Tools/Ant.html`
Easy Help/Web	`http://www.u-net.com/eon/easyhelp/easyhelp.htm`
rtftohtm	`http://www.w3.org/hypertext/WWW/Tools/RTFTOHTM.html`
CU_HTML.dot	`http://www.w3.org/hypertext/WWW/Tools/cu_html.html`
GT_HTML.dot	`http://www.gatech.edu/word_html/release.htm`
TagWizard	`http://www.jsp.fi/delta/deltatag.htm`
tbltohtml	`http://www.cadd.nps.usace.army.mil/tbl2html.htm`

WordPerfect Macros

Several programs are available that convert documents formatted with WordPerfect into HTML format via WordPerfect macros. Here are some examples:

Program	Program URL
WPMacros	`http://www.soton.ac.uk/~dja/wpmacros/`
wp2html	`http://www.res.bbsrc.ac.uk/wp2html/`

FrameMaker

Converters are available for translating FrameMaker files in FrameMaker document format or FrameMaker Interchange Format (MIF). Some of these programs also convert book files and tables as well as just text. Here are some examples:

Program	Program URL
WebMaker	`http://www.cern.ch/WebMaker/`
WebWorks	`http://www.quadralay.com/products/products.html`
FrameMaker5	`http://www.frame.com/`
mif.pl	`http://www.oac.uci.edu/indiv/ehood/mif.pl.doc.html`
edc2html	`http://www.oac.uci.edu/indiv/ehood/edc2html.doc.html`

LaTeX

LaTeX converters re-create the basic structure of LaTeX documents by generating navigation panels. Cross-references, citations, and footnotes are converted into hypertext links. Formatting information, such as mathematical equations and pictures, is converted into images that are automatically placed in the hypertext document. Here's a list of a few LaTeX translators:

Program	Program URL
latex2html	`http://cbl.leeds.ac.uk/nikos/tex2html/doc/`
	`latex2html/latex2html.html`
vulcanize	`http://www.plover.com/vulcanize/`
Tex2Rtf	`http://www.aiai.ed.ac.uk/~jacs/tex2rtf.html`
Jam	`http://www.w3.org/hypertext/WWW/Tools/JAM.html`
BetaFormat	`http://www.w3.org/hypertext/WWW/Tools/BETA.html`
Antex	`http://www.w3.org/hypertext/WWW/Tools/axtex.txt`

PageMaker

PageMaker translators are available that convert PageMaker stories into HTML files. Some include features such as automatic creation of a table of contents, story categorization, and image linking. Here are some PageMaker translators:

Program	Program URL
Dave	`http://www.bucknell.edu/bucknellian/dave/`
Pm2html	`http://www.w3.org/hypertext/WWW/Tools/PM2html.html`
PageMaker6	`http://w1000.mv.us.adobe.com/`

Plain-Text Filters

Plain-text filters take simple ASCII text files and convert them into HTML-formatted documents. In most cases, these filters simply provide paragraph formatting beyond the normal header information. Here are some plain-text filters:

Program	Program URL
text2html.sed	`http://www.w3.org/hypertext/WWW/Tools/bin/txt2html.sed`
txt2html.pl	`http://www.seas.upenn.edu/~mengwong/txt2html.html`
txt2html	`http://www.cs.wustl.edu/~seth/txt2html/`
WebIt	`http://futures.wharton.upenn.edu/~attau791/webit.html`
HtmlMarkup	`http://www.w3.org/hypertext/WWW/Tools/HTML-Markup.html`
Hyperize	`http://www.w3.org/hypertext/WWW/Tools/Hyperize.html`
findrefs	`http://www.w3.org/hypertext/WWW/Tools/findrefs.pl.html`

Programming Language Filters

Programming language source files can be converted into HTML markup. Most converters use HTML named anchors to identify references such as structures, functions, definitions, and so on. These types of converters are mainly for the purpose of reading source code. Here's a list of some programming language filters:

Program	*Language*	*Program URL*
src2html	C	`http://minnie.cs.adfa.oz.au/Src2html/index.html`
ctohtml	C	`http://www.w3.org/hypertext/WWW/Tools/ctohtml.txt`
src2www	C	`http://www.cs.purdue.edu/homes/young/software/src2www.html`
c++2html	C++	`http://www.atd.ucar.edu/jva/c++2html.html`
cxx2html	C++	`http://www.cv.nrao.edu/aips++/RELEASED/cxx2html/`
ObjectManual	C++	`http://www.w3.org/hypertext/WWW/Tools/ObjectManual.html`
ctoohtml	C++	`http://www.usc.edu/dept/robotics/personal/af0a/tools/ctoohtml/`
Root	C++	`http://root.cern.ch/`
src2www	ADA	`http://www.cs.purdue.edu/homes/young/software/src2www.html`
Floppy	FORTRAN	`http://vscrna.cern.ch/floppy/contents.html`
Light	FORTRAN	`http://www.cern.ch/Light/`
lisp2html	LISP	`http://www.w3.org/hypertext/WWW/Tools/Lisp2Html.html`

Manual Page Filters

Manual page filters convert standard UNIX manual pages into HTML-formatted documents. Some filters include features such as hypertext links to other manual page references, on-the-fly conversions to alleviate the need for preformatted pages, forms interfaces, and keyword searches. Here are some shareware/freeware manual page filters:

Program	*Program URL*
RosettaMan	`http://www.w3.org/hypertext/WWW/Tools/RosettaMan.html`
man2html	`http://www.w3.org/hypertext/WWW/Tools/cameron.txt`
man2html	`http://www.w3.org/hypertext/WWW/Tools/man2html.html`
man_html	`http://www.w3.org/hypertext/WWW/Tools/man_html.html`
man-cgi	`http://www.softlab.ntua.gr/~christia/man-cgi.html`
man2html	`http://www.w3.org/hypertext/WWW/Tools/nroff.txt`

Mail Filters

Mail filters provide facilities for converting SMTP mail into HTML documents. Some of the features of available mail filters include mail archiving, mail thread linking, and MIME support. Here are some shareware/freeware mail filters:

Program	Program URL
MHonArc	http://www.w3.org/hypertext/WWW/Tools/MHonArc.html
Hypermail	http://www.w3.org/hypertext/WWW/Tools/Hypermail.html
mlist2html	http://www.leo.org/~stumpf/src-dist/mlist2html/info.html
mail2html	http://www.w3.org/hypertext/WWW/Tools/georges-mail2html.html
CoCoBoard	http://jean-luc.ncsa.uiuc.edu/Codes/CoCoBoard/

Frequently Asked Questions Filters

Frequently Asked Questions (FAQ) filters can convert FAQ files that are in a standard format into HTML. Although some filters support the conversion of nonstandard FAQ format, most do not. A few of the major features supported by most FAQ filters include URL hypertext link recognition, e-mail addressee to Mailto links, character translations (such as converting the * character into a bullet), automatic generation of horizontal rules for section dividers, generation of a table of contents with hypertext links to subjects, and so on. Here are two FAQ filters:

Program	Program URL
faq2ms	http://iamwww.unibe.ch/~scg/Src/Scripts/
faq2html	http://www.w3.org/hypertext/WWW/Tools/faq2html.html

Benefits of HTML

Probably one of the greatest advantages of HTML, and the one most overlooked, is its capability to provide a rapid development platform. Any user can be generating HTML documents almost immediately with little training. This ease of use has been the catalyst for the proliferation of HTML and the WWW.

Another major advantage of HTML is its cross-platform compatibility. Web browsers and servers have been ported to virtually every computing platform. For high-end multiprocessor UNIX servers and desktop personal computers in the home, you can find HTML editors, desktop tools, authoring software packages, and even computer-based training software to make creating HTML documents easy.

Finally, HTML provides a mechanism for bringing text, sounds, images, and video to the desktop in a single application. With a multiplatform audience, HTML has become the universal language for document formatting on the Internet.

Summary

This chapter provided information on basic HTML levels, tags, and features. It briefly discussed both the HTML Level 2 FORM tag and the HTML Level 3.2 TABLE tag. Following that, you learned about Netscape extensions and saw examples of each. Finally, the chapter closed with a discussion of some of the benefits of HTML.

This chapter also identified commercial software, shareware, and freeware that you can use to enhance your Web database development skills and productivity. You now should have a good understanding of the basic HTML framework necessary for you to work through the subsequent chapters, which begin to look closely at interfacing Visual Basic with WWW databases.

11

Developing HTML Forms for Database Access and Application Interfaces

by Drew Kittel

This chapter expands on the discussion of HTML in Chapter 10, "An Overview of HTML 3.2," and explores a set of tags and attributes called *form elements*. These form elements enable you to do much more than just dress up a hypertext document; they bring a new and greatly needed functionality to HTML pages by enabling you to develop user interfaces. This is important, because forms extend HTML pages beyond the one-way presentation of a page to a reader to a two-way, interactive conversation between the page and the user of the form. In this chapter, you'll learn how to use forms to accept user input for several types of applications—most specifically, as a means to give users access to your database servers, databases, and other applications remotely distributed around the globe or resident on the same computer as the user's browser.

First, you'll see how forms are developed, and you'll see some examples of coding specific form elements. Next, you'll learn how to overcome some current limitations in HTML. Finally, you'll examine a few more comprehensive examples that use forms.

Developing HTML Forms

The *American Heritage Dictionary* defines a form as "a document with blanks for the insertion of details or information." Although this definition is accurate, forms in the context of an HTML page are much more functional. These forms provide an interface between a user and hidden applications, servers, or databases at some other (possibly very remote) locations. Forms enable a user to access information or provide input to some data repository. This access is provided via a number of server-side interface mechanisms such as CGI, server APIs (ISAPI and NSAPI, for example), the Internet Database Connector (IDC), Active Server pages, and server resident database gateway software. These mechanisms are covered in Part VII, "Server-Side Database Applications Development."

Forms Come in Many Forms

Forms come in many varieties, layouts, and levels of complexity. All forms are composed of a set of input objects that enable the user to enter data. Depending on the software tools available, forms can contain simple, text-based entry fields and graphical objects. Development environments such as the X Window System provide rich and functional sets of graphical objects that enable the user to do everything from entering text in a text-entry field to clicking the mouse on a variety of graphical objects. Other, less-capable systems, such as the now-dated VAX/VMS *Forms Management System* (FMS), represent the opposite end of the spectrum. User-input objects in these types of systems are not graphical, but instead are displayed onscreen using the ASCII character set. The functionality and user-friendliness (not to mention the attractiveness) of text-based forms are several steps below their graphical counterparts.

HTML forms provide a nice set of graphical input objects that you can use to build complex and functional forms and user interfaces. These objects include checklists, input fields, scrolled lists, radio buttons, and imagemaps. Figure 11.1 shows a typical online form you might use to order a pizza. In later sections, you'll see how to develop forms like this by using HTML.

FIGURE 11.1.

Using an online order form to get a pizza.

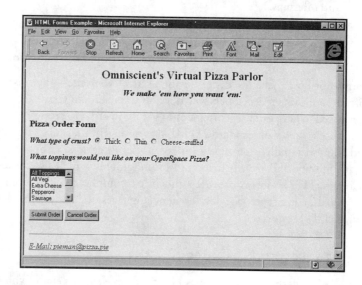

Forms: What Are They Good For?

I assume that, because you purchased this book, you have data, databases, information, and services you want to make available to the public, fellow employees, or potential customers. Making your services and information easily accessible is a key way to ensure that users keep returning to your Website.

Forms provide an ideal user interface to many applications. They enable virtually anyone who can use a mouse to access information, data, and services you provide. Because complex queries, questions, and operations can be executed by a user clicking a few buttons, answering a few questions, and submitting the form, you don't need to be concerned with complex query or programming languages. Instead, you can code the application to accept user inputs and formulate a query to a database or a request for some specialized processing of user data. Part VII describes the mechanisms by which user input on forms is passed to the Web server and how you can develop the applications that receive this input.

You can use forms such as these as interfaces to a variety of applications, including the following:

- Entry forms for users to order products from your online catalog.
- Entry forms for users to add information to your customer mailing lists, technical user group member lists, or guest lists.
- Forms to acquire input for surveys.

■ Forms to give users access to databases that enable them to acquire information about technical issues, special subjects of interest, and information about your product line and offerings.

■ Forms to provide technical or help-desk support for your products and services. With FAQs and database-access forms, this type of application can provide public users and in-house technical support representatives with the information they need.

Forms not only make life easier for the users of your site—they also simplify things for the software and system developers who develop and maintain your Website and applications. You don't need to have extensive programming skills in order to create HTML forms. Because these forms use a subset of standard HTML tags and attributes, they are relatively simple to code, and you can rapidly prototype a variety of user interfaces for applications. You typically can create, modify, and visually inspect forms in minutes, which also makes HTML forms easy to maintain. HTML forms provide a much less complicated development environment when compared to other interface development languages, such as UNIX shells, the X Window System, Tcl/Tk, and so on.

Forms Tags and Attributes

Considering all the powerful things HTML form elements enable you to do, you actually deal with surprisingly few tags and attributes. Table 11.1 presents the current HTML 3.2 form tags and their attributes. Valid attribute values are listed in brackets ([ ]) following each attribute name. The pipe (¦) symbol separating these values indicates that the possible selections are mutually exclusive.

Table 11.1. HTML 3.2 tags and attributes.

Tag	Attribute
`<FORM>`	`ACTION="url"`
`</FORM>`	`METHOD=[GET¦POST]`
`<INPUT>`	`TYPE=[TEXT¦CHECKBOX¦RADIO¦IMAGE¦PASSWORD¦SUBMIT¦`
	`RESET¦HIDDEN]`
	`NAME="name"`
	`VALUE="value"`
	`SIZE="nchars"`
	`MAXLENGTH="nchars"`
	`CHECKED`
`<OPTION>`	`SELECTED`
`</OPTION>`	`VALUE`
`<SELECT>`	`NAME="name"`
`</SELECT>`	`SIZE="number"`
	`MULTIPLE`

Tag	*Attribute*
`<TEXTAREA>`	`NAME="`*name*`"`
`</TEXTAREA>`	`ROWS="`*number*`"`
	`COLS="`*nchars*`"`

`<FORM>` Tag

You use the `<FORM></FORM>` tag pair to specify user-input objects. Inside this tag pair, you place sub-element tags that are to be interpreted and rendered by the browser. These form sub-element tags include the following:

`<INPUT>`	Renders user-input objects such as radio buttons, text fields, and checkboxes
`<OPTION>`	Specifies options in a selection list
`<SELECT>`	Creates selection lists
`<TEXTAREA>`	Creates freeform, text-input objects

These HTML form elements are what make HTML forms so powerful. Interactive user interfaces to your databases and applications can be developed very rapidly. These interfaces enable you to capture information from your users, formulate responses to their queries, run applications for them, and generate responses based on their input.

The `<FORM>` tag pair delimits the start and end of a form on an HTML page. Other form element tags must be placed within a `<FORM>` to be interpreted properly by the browser. The following general template of HTML code is used to render a form in the body of a page:

```
<!-- Declare start of form -->
<FORM METHOD="desired_method" ACTION="your_url_">
... form element (and other HTML) tags and attributes here ...

</FORM>
```

> **TIP**
>
> Unlike other HTML elements such as `<TABLE>` and `<LI>`, `<FORM>` tags cannot be nested. You can render more than one form on a single HTML page, however, simply by bracketing the contents of each form explicitly with the `<FORM>` tag pair. Additionally, other HTML elements—such as tables, lists, and style-markup tags—can be used within `<FORM>` to allow a great deal of flexibility in how forms are created and presented to the user. Finally, multipart or nested forms can be simulated by using `<A HREF>` links to named anchors within the same HTML document. You can use this technique to allow the user to jump between "subforms" within the main document.

Forms provide a tremendous amount of power, flexibility, and functionality to the user, but you may have noticed that only three attributes for the <FORM> tag exist:

```
ACTION
ENCTYPE
METHOD
```

How can only three attributes provide so much power? The answer lies in just what those three simple attributes can do.

These attributes are specified as follows and are described in this section:

```
<FORM METHOD="method_" ACTION="url_" ENCTYPE="form_content_encoding_">
```

ACTION Attribute

The ACTION attribute is where the action really starts. Presumably, you're interested in using forms so that you can acquire data from the user and do something useful with it. The value of the ACTION attribute specifies a URL to a CGI script, ISAPI program, IDC file, or Active Server page that will take some action on the user-supplied input after it is posted to the server. The action could be accessing a database based on a user query, generating a product-mailing request to your shipping department, running some other application programs, or simply mailing a message somewhere. The following code illustrates how an ACTION attribute is specified (don't worry about what the URL does at this point; that is covered in detail in Chapter 18, "The Common Gateway Interface (CGI)"):

```
<FORM ACTION="http://www.omniscient.com/cgi-bin/dosomething.exe">
```

ENCTYPE Attribute

The ENCTYPE attribute simply specifies the type of encoding to be used for the form contents (the input object field names and the values a user enters in these fields) when they are submitted to the server for processing. In most cases, this encoding is performed to ensure that information is passed to the server without values or characters being dropped, modified, translated, or otherwise misinterpreted. The default encoding for all forms follows:

```
<FORM ENCTYPE="application/x-www-form-urlencoded">
```

> **NOTE**
>
> ENCTYPE is typically not explicitly set; instead, it is allowed to default to the use of URL encoding because this is the encoding understood and implemented by most browsers, servers, and CGI/server API programs when performing HTML forms processing. URL encoding is discussed in detail in Chapter 18.

> **RESOURCE**
>
> Other encoding types do exist and can be specified explicitly. I've never witnessed such a case, though. For more information on encoding, see RFC1590 at the following URL:
>
> ```
> ftp://ftp.merit.edu/documents/rfc/rfc1590.txt
> ```

METHOD **Attribute**

The METHOD attribute can take one of two values: GET or POST. When a form submits data to the server, it can do so by using one of these two methods. The method specified determines how user input to a form is passed to an application, which then does some additional processing based on the values of that input. (The specifics of the GET and POST methods are covered in more detail in Chapter 18.)

You can specify the METHOD attribute (using POST, in this case) as this example shows:

```
<FORM METHOD="POST">
```

Note that the value for METHOD (GET or POST) is not case sensitive and can be specified in lower-case or uppercase.

> **TIP**
>
> For the simplest forms, such as those requiring only single-user input, GET is a sufficient method to use. Most forms, however, are designed to accept several inputs, and POST is the preferred method for these forms. The reason for using POST rather than GET is that the amount of data that can be passed to an application by using GET is limited; only a few noncomplex name/value pairs can be passed from a form. In contrast, POST allows for the passing of unlimited user-input data.

<INPUT> **Tag**

You use the <INPUT></INPUT> tag pair to render user-input objects for collecting data or information from the user for subsequent processing or action. Input objects include radio buttons, checkboxes, text-entry fields, images, and buttons. Input to these objects typically is passed to the server for some processing after a special form of user input, the Submit button, is clicked. The general minimal template of HTML code used to render a user-input object in a form follows:

```
<INPUT TYPE="type" NAME="name" VALUE="value" >
```

The `<INPUT>` tag has six attributes, which are described in this section:

```
CHECKED
NAME
SIZE
MAXLENGTH
TYPE
VALUE
```

CHECKED Attribute

You use the CHECKED attribute with radio buttons and checkboxes to specify that the initial state is displayed as being selected. The following code snippet displays two checkboxes on a single line:

```
<INPUT TYPE="checkbox" NAME="cb1" VALUE="selection1">
<INPUT TYPE="checkbox" NAME="cb2" VALUE="selection2" CHECKED>
```

The second checkbox will be rendered with a checkmark in the box, indicating that it is the initially selected value of the values presented.

NAME Attribute

The NAME attribute value identifies to the server from which user-input object a given input value originated. Additionally, common NAME values are used to group name/value pairs for sets of radio buttons when this information is passed to the server. To render a two-option radio button pair with the first selection set as the default, for example, you could use this general code:

```
<INPUT TYPE="radio" NAME="wid1" VALUE="selection1" CHECKED>
<INPUT TYPE="radio" NAME="wid2" VALUE="selection2">
```

SIZE and MAXLENGTH Attributes

The SIZE and MAXLENGTH attributes pertain only to TEXT (not TEXTAREA) type objects. You use MAXLENGTH to set the maximum length, in characters, of the text that can be input to the object. SIZE simply specifies the width, in characters, of the text object displayed on the form. The SIZE and MAXLENGTH attributes typically are used with a text-entry field, as in this example:

```
<INPUT TYPE="text" NAME="uname" SIZE="50" MAXLENGTH="80">
```

> **NOTE**
>
> Some codependence between these two attributes exists. If SIZE is assigned a value less than MAXLENGTH (which typically defaults to unlimited), the user input scrolls within the object until MAXLENGTH characters are entered. Also, if the value specified for SIZE

exceeds the width of the display area on the user's browser, the rendered field does not wrap to the next line; instead, it continues out past the browser's field of display, which forces the user to scroll horizontally to view the full field.

TYPE **Attribute**

The TYPE attribute value specifies the type of input object or field to render in the form. Table 11.2 lists these values.

Table 11.2. TYPE attribute values.

Attribute	Function
CHECKBOX	Specifies checkbox input objects that allow more than one option to be selected from those presented.
HIDDEN	Presets values in a form. No user input is rendered; therefore, no user input is possible.
IMAGE	Specifies an imagemap as an input field. The user provides input by clicking a location on the image. Using the IMAGE type performs the same function as clicking the Submit button. Names and user-supplied values for all user-input objects in the form are passed to the server, along with image x,y coordinates of the mouse-click location.
PASSWORD	Specifies a single-line, text-entry object that does not echo user input to the screen (typically, asterisks are displayed for each character typed).
RADIO	Specifies radio buttons that force a single choice from the set of mutually exclusive options presented.
RESET	Renders a button that clears any user input from the form objects and restores default values.
SUBMIT	Renders a button that submits the form for the processing specified by the ACTION attribute in the <FORM> tag. Name/value pairs for all user-input objects in the form are passed to the server.
TEXT	Specifies a single-line, text-entry object.

NOTE

In Table 11.2, valid attribute values are specified using all uppercase letters. This is not a requirement; you can use lowercase or uppercase letters.

VALUE **Attribute**

You use the VALUE attribute to preset the initial value of an object instance. If the user does not change the initial value, this is the value passed after he or she clicks the Submit button. For object types such as TEXT, which can have their values displayed, this is also the initial value displayed. To preset text that appears in a text-entry field, for example, you could use this code:

```
<INPUT TYPE="text" NAME="tid" VALUE="Your_Text_Here">
```

CAUTION

Because sets of radio buttons share a common name, one of the buttons for each set must have the VALUE attribute set; otherwise, the value passed to the server after the Submit button is clicked will be indeterminate.

SRC **and** ALIGN **Attributes**

Two additional attributes, SRC and ALIGN, are used solely with the IMAGE attribute. (Because these attributes are used only with the IMAGE attribute and are not strictly attributes for the <INPUT> tag, they were not listed in Table 11.2.)

SRC specifies a path to where the image file to be rendered resides. ALIGN aligns an image relative to text that accompanies it. Possible values are top, bottom, and center. You can use the IMAGE input type to perform a SUBMIT, which is similar to using the SUBMIT input type. You can use the following code to enable users to submit the form by clicking an image on the form:

```
... preceding form code ...
Submit the form by clicking on the bingo card image below and you
will be automatically registered in a drawing to win a free TV:<BR>
<INPUT TYPE="image"
Src="http://www.omniscient.com/images/bingo_card.gif"
Align="bottom">
... remainder of form code ...
```

You then can use the coordinates of the mouse click on the image to assign the user a random number for a promotional drawing—in this case, for a free TV.

<OPTION> **Tag**

You use an <OPTION></OPTION> tag pair to specify each selection in a selection list. You use this tag pair only within the <SELECT></SELECT> tag pair. The general HTML code required to place selections in a selection-list object follows:

```
<OPTION SELECTED NAME="name1"
VALUE="value1">Selection _  </OPTION>
<OPTION NAME="name2" VALUE="value2">Selection_2 </OPTION>
...
<OPTION NAME="nameN" VALUE="valueN">Selection N /OPTION>
```

There are two OPTION attributes:

```
SELECTED
VALUE
```

SELECTED Attribute

You use the SELECTED attribute to specify which option in the list of selections is selected initially. In the following code, the second option in the list is preselected when the list is rendered:

```
<OPTION SELECTED NAME="name1"
VALUE="value1">Selection1 </OPTION>
<OPTION NAME="name2" VALUE="value2" SELECTED>Selection 2 </OPTION>
...
<OPTION NAME="nameN" VALUE="valueN">Selection N </OPTION>
```

> **TIP**
>
> It's a good practice to use the SELECTED attribute to explicitly specify which <OPTION> is the default selection. Otherwise, the first selection in the list is the default value selected. This practice is useful in setting default values for applications. Doing so just means that users must take the time to change any values with which they don't agree.

VALUE Attribute

You use the VALUE attribute to set the value that will be passed to the server when an option in the list is selected. If no value is specified, the text following the <OPTION> tag is passed instead. In the following code, the value "value1" is sent to the server after the user clicks the Submit button:

```
<OPTION NAME="name1" VALUE="value1">Selection1 1</OPTION>
```

In the following code, the value "Selection1" is sent to the server after the user clicks the Submit button:

```
<OPTION NAME="name1">Selection 1 </OPTION>
```

<SELECT> Tag

You use the <SELECT></SELECT> tag pair to render user-input objects that enable the user to make one or more selections from a list of options presented. The SELECT input object is rendered as a pull-down menu or scrollable list, depending on how the attributes are set. User selections from these objects are passed to the server for processing after the Submit button is clicked. The <SELECT> tag is used with the <OPTION> tag. The general template of HTML code used to render a selection-list object in a form follows:

```
<SELECT NAME="desired name">
<OPTION VALUE="value1">Value1</OPTION>
<OPTION VALUE="value2">Value2</OPTION>
... other <OPTION> statements here ...
</SELECT>
```

There are two SELECT attributes:

```
NAME
SIZE
```

NAME **Attribute**

The NAME attribute value identifies to the server from which user-input object—in this case, a list of selections—a given selection value(s) originated. You can use the following code, for example, when rendering a selection list named dbase:

```
<SELECT NAME="dbase">
```

SIZE **Attribute**

You use the SIZE attribute value to specify the number of selections that are visible in the list when it is rendered on the form.

If the SIZE attribute is not specified or is given a value of 1, the selection-list object will be a pull-down menu. A pull-down menu always is initially rendered with a single selection visible, and it expands to show all selection options after the user clicks the pull-down menu button. For SIZE values greater than 1, the selection-list object is rendered as a scrollable list of options with SIZE number of options visible in the scrollable area.

By default, users are limited to single selections from a selection list. If you use the MULTIPLE attribute when creating a selection list, the user can select more than one option from the list. All options selected are passed to the server after the user clicks the Submit button.

Listing 11.1 shows the general template of HTML code used to render a pull-down menu and a scrollable selection-list object in a form.

Listing 11.1. An HTML template illustrating how to create pull-down menu and scrollable list objects.

```
<!-- create single-selection pull-down menu of selections -->
<SELECT NAME="desired name" SIZE="1">
<OPTION VALUE="value1">Value1</OPTION>
<OPTION VALUE="value2">Value2</OPTION>
... other <OPTION> statements here ...
</SELECT>

<!-- create multiple-selection scrollable list of selections -->
<SELECT NAME="desired name" MULTIPLE SIZE="#_of_visible_items">
```

```
<OPTION VALUE="value1">Value1</OPTION>
<OPTION VALUE="value2">Value2</OPTION>
... other <OPTION> statements here ...
</SELECT>
```

`<TEXTAREA>` Tag

You use the `<TEXTAREA></TEXTAREA>` tag pair to render a user-scrollable, text-input object that enables users to enter multiple lines of freeform text.

Three attributes are associated with the TEXTAREA tag:

> NAME
> ROWS
> COLS

NAME Attribute

The NAME attribute value identifies to the server in which user input object the text was written. You can use the following code, for example, to render a one-column by one-row freeform text field with the name "address":

```
<TEXTAREA NAME="address"></TEXTAREA>
```

ROWS and COLS Attributes

The ROWS and COLS attribute values specify the dimensions (in number of characters) of the text-display area. These values do not limit text entry, because the object is rendered with scrollbars that enable the user to easily traverse through text not displayed in the window area. The following code renders a freeform, text-input object with a display area of 4 rows by 40 columns:

```
<TEXTAREA NAME="address" ROWS="4" COLS="40"></TEXTAREA>
```

Lines of text longer than 40 characters still are accepted, but they do not wrap to the next line unless the user explicitly presses Enter.

> **NOTE**
>
> Any text between the `<TEXTAREA>` and `</TEXTAREA>` tags is used to prefill the text-input object displayed to the user. You can use these tags to present the user with text that requires some form of editing. Also, if the value specified for COLS exceeds the width of the display area on the user's browser, the rendered text field continues out past the browser's display, forcing the user to scroll the browser horizontally to view the full field.

Using Form Elements

As previously mentioned, HTML forms provide the means by which users can interact with applications and services—such as databases—that you intend to provide at your Website. It therefore is important that you gain a solid understanding of how to create these forms with user-input objects such as text fields, scrolling textboxes, radio buttons, checkboxes, and various selection lists and menus. This section presents a few code segments and figures to illustrate how to develop these form elements.

Specifying a Form on a Page

Consider the previous Pizza Parlor form (refer to Figure 11.1). Listing 11.2 shows an example.

Listing 11.2. An HTML template illustrating how a form is created on a page.

```
<!-- Declare start of form -->
<FORM METHOD="POST" ACTION="http://www.omniscient.com/cgi-bin/pizza.pl">

... form element (and other HTML) tags and attributes here ...

</FORM>
```

You can see that the form is rendered by using the POST method, as recommended for forms with multiple inputs. Additionally, the value of ACTION specifies the URL of a CGI script that presumably will process the customer's pizza order.

Creating Selection Lists and Pull-Down Menus

You can present selection lists in a form in two ways: by using scrolled lists and by using pull-down menus. Listing 11.3 demonstrates how each selection list is developed. Figure 11.2 shows the corresponding output for this program.

Listing 11.3. Two ways to create HTML selections lists.

```
<HTML>

<HEAD>
<TITLE>Creating a List Two Different Ways</TITLE>
</HEAD>
<BODY>

<CENTER>
<H2>Two Ways to Create a Selection List on a Form</H2>
</CENTER>
```

```
<HR>
<!-- Declare start of form (action does nothing) -->
<FORM METHOD="POST" ACTION="">

<!-- this scrolled-list allows multiple choices -->
<H3><EM>Multiple Selection Scrolled List</EM></H3>
<P>
<SELECT NAME="spectrum" MULTIPLE SIZE="8">
<OPTION VALUE="blk" SELECTED>Black
<OPTION VALUE="wht">White
<OPTION VALUE="red">Red
<OPTION VALUE="yel">Yellow
<OPTION VALUE="grn">Green
<OPTION VALUE="org">Orange
<OPTION VALUE="brn">Brown
<OPTION VALUE="pur">Purple
<OPTION VALUE="sil">Silver
<OPTION VALUE="au">Gold
</SELECT>
</P>

<P>
<!-- this pull-down menu allows one selection -->
<CENTER>
<H3><EM>Single Selection Pulldown</EM></H3>
<SELECT NAME="spectrum" SIZE="1">
<OPTION VALUE="blk">Black
<OPTION VALUE="wht">White
<OPTION VALUE="red">Red
<OPTION VALUE="yel">Yellow
<OPTION VALUE="grn" SELECTED>Green
<OPTION VALUE="org">Orange
<OPTION VALUE="brn">Brown
<OPTION VALUE="pur">Purple
<OPTION VALUE="sil">Silver
<OPTION VALUE="au">Gold
</SELECT>
</CENTER>
</P>

</FORM>

<HR>
<ADDRESS>
<A HREF="http://www.omniscient.com/ ">Omniscient Home Page</A>
<A HREF="mailto:dkittel@clark.net">E-Mail: dkittel@clark.net</A>
</ADDRESS>

</BODY>
</HTML>
```

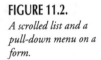

FIGURE 11.2.

A scrolled list and a pull-down menu on a form.

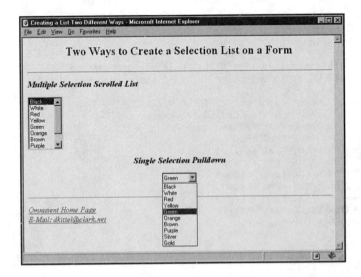

You should note a few things about the form in Figure 11.2. First, don't worry about the blank URL or lack of a Submit input button. These were omitted so that you can concentrate on the code for creating selection lists. Second, I generally set the VALUE attribute for each option entry explicitly. For example, I typically use the following code:

```
<OPTION VALUE="blk">Black
```

instead of this code:

```
<OPTION>Black
```

I've found that this practice provides a better level of control when coding server-side applications using CGI.

> **TIP**
>
> HTML does not explicitly provide good control over the horizontal and vertical placement of elements on a page. Form elements such as text-entry fields, lists, buttons, and boxes, however, may be better formatted and aligned on a page by putting these elements in an HTML table. Using a table results in a more professional look for your forms. See the section "Putting It All Together," later in this chapter, for examples that implement this technique.

Creating Radio Buttons and Checkboxes

Radio buttons and checkboxes are handy ways of acquiring user input when the user can select from only a few options. When the user is allowed to select more than one option, you should use a set of checkboxes. When the set of options is mutually exclusive and the user must choose one option, however, radio buttons force the user to make only a single selection.

Listing 11.4 demonstrates how radio buttons and checkboxes are developed as part of a form. Figure 11.3 shows the corresponding output for this program.

Listing 11.4. Using radio buttons and checkboxes in your form.

```
<HTML>

<HEAD>
<TITLE>Radio Button and Checkbox Example</TITLE>
</HEAD>

<BODY>


<h2 align="center">WHIT Radio's Drive Time Survey</h2>

</CENTER>

<HR>
<!-- Declare start of form -->
<FORM METHOD="POST" >

<P>
<EM><STRONG>What is your primary mode of transportation?</STRONG></EM>
<!-- Use radio buttons for mutually exclusive choices -->
</P>

<P>
<INPUT TYPE="radio" NAME="trans" VALUE="CAR" CHECKED> Car  <BR>
<INPUT TYPE="radio" NAME="trans" VALUE="BUS"> Bus <BR>
<INPUT TYPE="radio" NAME="trans" VALUE="SUB"> Subway <BR>
<INPUT TYPE="radio" NAME="trans" VALUE="FOOT"> Foot
</P>

<P>
<EM><STRONG>What are your favorite types of music?</STRONG></EM>
</P>

<P>
<!-- use checkboxes for multiple choices -->
<INPUT TYPE="checkbox" NAME="music1" VALUE="ROCK"> Rock  <BR>
<INPUT TYPE="checkbox" NAME="music2" VALUE="OLDIES"> Oldies  <BR>
<INPUT TYPE="checkbox" NAME="music3" VALUE="EASY"> Easy Listening  <BR>
</P>

</FORM>

<HR>
<ADDRESS>
<A HREF="http://www.omniscient.com">Omniscient Home Page</A><BR>
<A HREF="mailto:dkittel@clark.net">E-Mail: dkittel@clark.net</A>
</ADDRESS>

</BODY>
</HTML>
```

FIGURE 11.3.

Using radio buttons and checkboxes on a form.

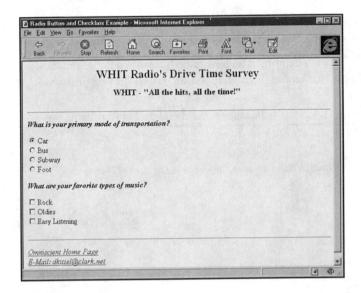

In this example, notice that the radio buttons were used to acquire user input from a set of options when just one response was desired. Additionally, as a brief note on form design, the "Car" option was preset as the default, because I assumed that this would be the primary selection for the multitude of respondents to this drive-time survey. This default setting saves the user only one mouse click, but it's a good idea to keep things as easy as possible for the user when presenting more complex forms. Also, notice how using checkboxes enables the user to submit more than one favorite type of music. Finally, you'll see that the form presented is not too useful, because no Submit input button is available, and no ACTION URL was specified in the HTML code.

Creating TEXT Input Fields

Using TEXT input fields and freeform TEXTAREA objects provides a great deal of flexibility when designing forms for acquiring input such as e-mail addresses, postal addresses, names, descriptive information, or common identifying numbers (such as telephone numbers, birth dates, Social Security numbers, or credit card numbers) from users. These and other types of user information critical to building comprehensive database queries, supporting electronic commerce applications and transactions, or providing online technical support cannot be appropriately acquired by using scroll lists, pull-down menus, radio buttons, and checkboxes. Just imagine having to develop an HTML form with radio buttons or a scrollable list of all possible e-mail addresses or Social Security numbers (and imagine how long it would take users to find and select their appropriate entries in that list!).

Listing 11.5 demonstrates how TEXT and TEXTAREA input elements are developed as part of a form. Figure 11.4 shows the corresponding output for this program.

Listing 11.5. Using TEXT and TEXTAREA input elements in your form.

```
<HTML>

<HEAD>
<TITLE>Using TEXT and TEXTAREA Form Elements</TITLE>
</HEAD>
<BODY>

<!-- Declare start of form -->
<FORM METHOD="POST" ACTION="">

<!-- Create a text area object -->
<P>
<STRONG>A prefilled, 4 Row x 40 Column TEXTAREA INPUT Element</STRONG><BR>
<TEXTAREA NAME="freeform" ROWS="4" COLS="50">
This is just a brief bit of initial, freeform text
put in to show the functionality of the TEXTAREA
element. Note the scrollability in
the horizontal and vertical directions.
</TEXTAREA>
</P>

<!-- Create various types of INPUT objects -->
<P>
<STRONG>Please enter your password (10 char maximum):</STRONG>
<INPUT TYPE="PASSWORD" NAME="passwd" SIZE="12" MAXLENGTH="10">
</P>

<P>
<STRONG>A few sample text-input objects
(note scrolling of first)</STRONG><BR>
<STRONG>User Input:</STRONG> <
INPUT TYPE="text" NAME="text1" SIZE="20" MAXLENGTH="80"><BR>
<STRONG>Larger User Input:</STRONG>
<INPUT TYPE="text" NAME="text2" SIZE="60" MAXLENGTH="80">
</P>

<!-- "multipart" text input -->
<P>
<STRONG>Enter the ISBN for your favorite book: </STRONG>
<INPUT TYPE="text" NAME="ccn1" SIZE="1" MAXLENGTH="1"> -
<INPUT TYPE="text" NAME="ccn2" SIZE="5" MAXLENGTH="3"> -
<INPUT TYPE="text" NAME="ccn3" SIZE="7" MAXLENGTH="5"> -
<INPUT TYPE="text" NAME="ccn4" SIZE="1" MAXLENGTH="1">
</P>

<P>
<INPUT TYPE="submit" VALUE="Send this info">
<INPUT TYPE="reset" VALUE="Clear Entries">
</P>
```

continues

Listing 11.5. continued

```
</FORM>

<HR>
<ADDRESS>
<A HREF="http://www.omniscient.com">Omniscient Home Page</A><br>
<A HREF="mailto:dkittel@clark.net">E-Mail: dkittel@clark.net</A>
</ADDRESS>

</BODY>
</HTML>
<HTML>
```

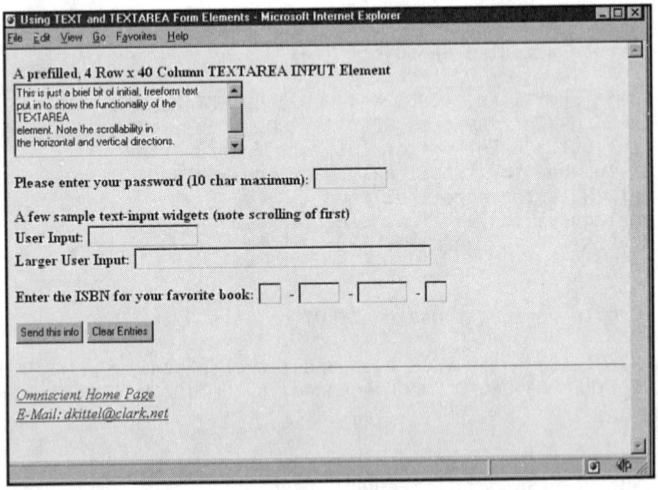

FIGURE 11.4.

Using TEXT *and*
TEXTAREA *elements on*
a form.

This example is much busier than the other examples so far in this chapter, and there is much to point out about it.

The TEXTAREA object demonstrates how you can initialize text for user validation or modification. Also, because the display window is somewhat small, scrollbars are included so that the user can enter or scroll through large text segments.

The code in Listing 11.5 includes an example of the PASSWORD input type to show that it does indeed mask the user's input. Using password fields is an obvious means of implementing an additional level of security, because passwords allow only privileged users to access your databases or applications.

> **CAUTION**
>
> Unless the Web browser and server explicitly support data encryption, passwords are transmitted as uuencoded text, and the network packets are susceptible to decoding.

The two TEXT input objects with different SIZE attribute values (but the same user input string of characters) demonstrate that the text will scroll until the MAXLENGTH value is reached.

> **TIP**
>
> The field names and the text-input boxes for these objects could have been better aligned by putting these elements in an HTML table. This technique is demonstrated in "Putting It All Together," later in this chapter.

You also can create logically grouped "sets" of TEXT input objects that can be used for accepting user input that consists of multiple parts—such as phone numbers, Social Security numbers, dates (for example, *mm-dd-yyyy* format), and so on.

Even though the form in Figure 11.4 doesn't do anything (note the blank ACTION URL), I included the SUBMIT and RESET INPUT types anyway just to show how they are rendered on the form. Clicking the Clear Entries button causes all user entries to be cleared. User modifications to the prefilled TEXTAREA are removed, and the area is returned to its initial state. Clicking the Send This Info button causes the browser to attempt to submit this information to the server, which results in an error message because no URL is found.

Overcoming the Limitations of Using HTML Forms

This section is really predicated on what is perceived as a limitation. I must warn you that the information presented in this section is somewhat biased. Developing a great deal of code in windowing environments, such as the X Window System, has led me to be somewhat spoiled by the functionality and level of control provided by these development environments. But, to be fair, I also realize that HTML is not and was not designed to be a true programming language. It has no concept of loops, conditional flow control, subroutines and libraries, data types, and all the other things that make a programming language a programming language. This is a mixed blessing, because it means that some neat functionality is lost. The gains in ease and rapidity of interface development, improved maintainability, debugging, and testing—not to mention how easy HTML is to learn—far outweigh what is lost, however.

This section presents what I perceive to be some limitations in developing user interfaces by using only HTML, as well as some ideas to circumvent these limitations. I don't provide examples of these solutions in this chapter, because they are presented in later chapters after some additional concepts and development methods are covered.

Controlling Placement of Input Objects

HTML lacks the capability to provide a fine level of control over placement of user-input objects on a form. Here are some methods you can use to address this drawback:

- Encapsulate user-input objects as data elements in <TABLE> elements to provide some control over alignment of the elements. Many HTML development tools—such as Microsoft FrontPage—provide *what you see is what you get* (WYSIWYG) development environments that provide point-and-click capabilities for creating HTML tables and fiddling with their row- and column-sizing attributes. You can use these tools to easily control alignment of input objects on your forms.

- Use the <IMG> tag, the HSPACE and VSPACE attributes, and a see-through pixel GIF image to provide some control over horizontal spacing between elements. (Remember that browsers chew up excess white space in an HTML document.)

- Use the <PRE> container tag to enforce formatting on some input objects.

This snippet of code, for example, creates a vertically aligned group of six checkboxes:

```
1<INPUT TYPE="checkbox" NAME="c1" VALUE="1">
2<INPUT TYPE="checkbox" NAME="c2" VALUE="2">
3<INPUT TYPE="checkbox" NAME="c3" VALUE="3">
4<INPUT TYPE="checkbox" NAME="c4" VALUE="4">
5<INPUT TYPE="checkbox" NAME="c5" VALUE="5">
6<INPUT TYPE="checkbox" NAME="c6" VALUE="6">
```

You can encapsulate these lines of code in a <PRE> container tag to enforce some formatting:

```
<PRE>
1<INPUT TYPE="checkbox" NAME="c1" VALUE="1">    2<INPUT TYPE="checkbox" NAME="c2" VALUE="2">
3<INPUT TYPE="checkbox" NAME="c3" VALUE="3">    4<INPUT TYPE="checkbox" NAME="c4" VALUE="4">

5<INPUT TYPE="checkbox" NAME="c5" VALUE="5">    6<INPUT TYPE="checkbox" NAME="c6" VALUE="6">
</PRE>
```

This code results in two columns of checkboxes, with each column separated by four spaces vertically. The last row of checkboxes has an additional space between it and the preceding row.

You can use this method to align and group sets of similar or dissimilar input objects while using most of the formatting and spacing you want. I encourage you to experiment with this technique to fine-tune the appearance of your forms.

NOTE

In Chapters 13, "ActiveX and ActiveX Controls," and 14, "Developing Advanced Forms for Database Access and Application Interfaces," you will be introduced to using ActiveX controls in HTML forms. You will see that you can use a special control called the *HTML Layout control* to have better placement control of HTML form objects displayed on ActiveX-compliant browsers, such as Microsoft's Internet Explorer.

Reacting to User Input

Unlike other user-interface environments, HTML provides no concept of a pop-up dialog box or the capability to dynamically react to user input without interacting with the server. You might want an OPTION list element to be populated with selections based on the user selecting a radio button, for example. You can emulate this functionality, but you must use multiple HTML forms, hidden variables, CGI or other server-side programming, saved state information, and new form generation to be presented to the user. Sometimes, you can emulate simple forms of this functionality by using links and references to named anchors in the same HTML document.

A much better solution to the problem of reacting to user input is to use client-side programs developed in VBScript or JavaScript. Chapters 12, "Introduction to Client-Side Web Application Development Using VBScript," 13, and 14 give you all the background necessary to extend the capabilities of your HTML forms by using VBScript and ActiveX controls.

Paging Versus Scrolling

Long forms require the user to scroll through many pages, which is not always desirable. Sometimes, you can handle this problem by using links and references to named anchors within the same HTML document. A simple implementation of this technique is demonstrated in the section "Forms That Support Electronic Commerce: The Malt Shop—An Online Store," later in this chapter.

For complex applications, the capability to jump among pages of forms while maintaining information about user input on previous pages requires multiple forms, hidden variables, CGI programming and interaction with the server, saved state information, and new forms generation to be presented to the user.

NOTE

Persistent HTTP *cookies* are mechanisms that enable server-side connections (for example, CGI scripts) to store and retrieve data and information on the client side. These cookies are a powerful means of saving the state of client-side inputs. Major browsers, such as Microsoft Internet Explorer and Netscape Navigator, support the use of cookies.

RESOURCE

You can find more information on persistent cookies at

```
http://home.netscape.com/newsref/std/cookie_spec.html
```

Using Server-Side Includes

HTML provides no concept of a subroutine. Through the judicious application of a technique called *Server-Side Includes* (SSIs), however, you can perform a certain degree of dynamic linking to HTML that is not in the current HTML document. In other words, the server includes HTML from a separate file in the current document at runtime. This capability could enable you to develop some standardized input-object sets that have a common look and feel as well as standard field names, object layouts, and so on. You then could reuse these includes in several applications. Here is the syntax:

```
<!--#include virtual="yourfilehere.txt" -->
```

The following code snippet, for example, creates a form with sets of user-input objects included by using SSIs:

```
<FORM METHOD="POST" ACTION="http://www.omniscient.com/cgi-bin/dosomething"
<!--#include virtual="/rss/satellite_boxes_vertical.txt" -->
... other form input objects and HTML ...
<!--#include virtual="/rss/name_text.txt" -->
<INPUT TYPE="SUBMIT" VALUE="Submit">
<INPUT TYPE="RESET" VALUE="Reset">
</FORM>
```

In this example, the server inserts the contents of the files `satellite_boxes_vertical.txt` and `name_text.txt` at the point they occur in the HTML document. These files contain HTML code that renders a set of checkboxes and a set of text-input objects in a standard onscreen format that facilitates reuse in many applications. For example, the following provides the contents of the `satellite_boxes_vertical.txt` file:

```
AVHRR<INPUT TYPE="checkbox" NAME="avhrr" VALUE="avhrr"><BR>
LANDSAT<INPUT TYPE="checkbox" NAME="landsat" VALUE="landsat"><BR>
IRS<INPUT TYPE="checkbox" NAME="irs" VALUE="irs"><BR>
SPOT<INPUT TYPE="checkbox" NAME="spot" VALUE="spot"><BR>
```

This file renders a standard set of checkboxes used to select a type of satellite(s) for queries in several applications I've developed.

> **NOTE**
>
> A performance penalty is incurred by the server because includes must be parsed at runtime. In most cases, however, the server performance is not noticeably degraded unless SSIs are used frequently or your server experiences very heavy use. It's also a relatively standard custom to name HTML files that use SSIs with an `.shtml` extension. When the server is properly configured, this extension serves as a hint to the server that these files require runtime parsing, whereas files with the regular `.html` extension do not.

Looking at Form Design Tips and Considerations

So far in this chapter, you've seen how to implement different form elements and how to use them as an interface to an application. This section presents some commonsense tips and considerations for designing the layout of your own forms:

■ When laying out input objects on your forms, try to logically order and group your input objects. Consider grouping objects by common function, theme, and so on. If you're designing an application to gather a lot of input and you need several pages of forms or subforms to do so, try to keep input that logically or functionally belongs together on the same page.

■ Try to maintain a consistent look and feel across all forms in an application. Keep these objectives in mind:

   ■ Use fonts, colors, and backgrounds consistently.

   ■ Consistently place labels on the same side of input objects, such as text fields, radio buttons, and checkboxes.

   ■ Consistently orient sets of checkboxes and radio buttons. Avoid mixing horizontal and vertical alignments. Align text-input fields (and their labels) vertically and horizontally to achieve a professional look.

   ■ Use and place navigational aides and button bars consistently.

■ When laying out text-input objects, consider the tab order of the fields—that is, the progression of the cursor when successive tabs are entered at the keyboard. You should lay out fields so that information is collected in a logical order. It makes sense, for example, to obtain customer mailing information in the order of name, street address, city, state, ZIP code, and perhaps phone and fax numbers. Often, existing printed forms can serve as a good model for an HTML equivalent.

■ When using text-input fields and TEXTAREA, freeform, text-entry boxes, keep in mind that your user's browser screen might not be the same size as your browser screen. Adjust the display size of text input and take advantage of the text-scrolling capabilities of these objects to save display space when it makes sense to do so.

■ Even though HTML does not provide a fine level of control over the placement of form elements, you often can use the <BR> tag or encapsulate elements within HTML tables to enforce the desired format. Also, judicious use of form elements encapsulated in <PRE> container tags often provides the desired results. I encourage you to fiddle with these techniques to fine-tune the look of your form (using an HTML development tool such as Microsoft's FrontPage Web authoring tool helps tremendously). Be aware of how browsers differ in their capabilities to display form elements and to provide support for HTML features such as tables.

■ When deciding which types of user-input objects to use for an application, carefully consider how the object will be used and what types of data it represents. Radio buttons, as well as scroll lists and pull-down menus with no MULTIPLE attribute specified, are appropriate when you're presenting a relatively small set of mutually exclusive selections. For lists that require savings in screen space, you can configure both pull-down menus and scroll lists to be compact and to provide users with single- or multiple-selection capabilities. If you are creating long lists of selections, be aware that radio buttons require too much room, and pull-down menus expand beyond the display size of most browsers; therefore, scroll lists are the best choice in these cases.

■ For applications such as database interfaces, the form-input objects presented should prompt users for the data required to formulate the query without requiring them to have any query-building experience or knowledge of the underlying data types, database structures, or table relationships.

■ Be cognizant of the CGI language in use when naming input objects on a form. Steer clear of names that correspond to keywords in the CGI language(s) in use. If you are using Visual Basic as the server-side development language, adherence to standard naming and coding conventions helps you avoid such problems. You can find coding and naming conventions for Visual Basic and VBScript in Appendixes B, "Visual Basic 5 Naming Conventions," and D, "Coding and Naming Conventions for VBScript Developers."

■ To the extent possible, pre-set default or common selections on buttons, checkboxes, and lists. Also, pre-fill text input fields when appropriate. This often makes things easier for users by requiring fewer explicit inputs.

■ When possible (for example, for intranet applications), involve your end users in the form-layout design. One of the strengths of HTML is rapid prototyping, and this enables developers and users to sit down together and quickly run through many iterations of form layouts until a desirable layout is achieved.

Putting It All Together

Now that you've seen some brief examples of how to create form elements using HTML, it's time to tie them all together to create forms that do something useful. This section presents more complex examples of developing forms. Here, you'll take a more comprehensive look at how to build user interfaces to applications and databases by using the HTML form elements presented in earlier sections. You'll look at three sample form applications:

▓ A magazine reader survey and subscription request form

▓ An online home brewing supply store (an electronic commerce application)

▓ A used-auto listing database search service (a Web database access application)

Take the time to review the code used to generate these application front-end forms. You'll find a great deal of useful, practical information that you can adapt to your own applications.

Forms for Online Reader Surveys and Subscriptions: Web.dB Journal

Web.dB is a fictitious trade journal geared toward the professional development and technical interests of Web database developers. The publishers of Web.dB are interested in maintaining (and hopefully increasing) their readership and market share, so they've decided to establish a Website with information about their publication, sample articles, and an online survey and subscription-application form. Not only does this Website enable the publishers to reach a wider audience at a lower cost than conventional advertising, but it also enables them to capture reader-profile information they can use to provide readers with better service and more appropriate articles and information. The publishers can also use this information to better target potential advertisers. Listing 11.6 illustrates the use of TEXTAREA, SELECT, OPTION, and INPUT (TEXT as well as RADIO, SUBMIT, and RESET buttons). Figures 11.5 and 11.6 show the results of this code.

Listing 11.6. Using TEXTAREA, SELECT, OPTION, and INPUT.

```
<HTML>

<HEAD>
<TITLE>Web.dB Journal - Reader Survey and Subscription Application</TITLE>
</HEAD>
<BODY>

<CENTER>
<H2><EM>Web.dB</EM> - Reader Survey and Subscription Application</H2>
</CENTER>
<HR>

<!-- Declare start of form -->
<!-- Action URL simply sends a string of name/value pairs -->
<!-- to be processed by the specified cgi program -->
```

continues

Listing 11.6. continued

```
<FORM METHOD="POST"  ACTION="http://www.omniscient.com/cgi-bin/elvin-magic.pl">

<!-- Create TEXT and TEXTAREA objects for name, e-mail, mail entry -->
<!-- Use TABLE to provide a bit of formatting control -->

<STRONG>Please provide the following personal information</STRONG>
<EM>(Please fill all fields)</EM>

<TABLE>
<TR>
<TD>Full Name: </TD>
<TD><INPUT TYPE="text" NAME="uname" SIZE="50"></TD><BR>
</TR>
<TR>
<TD>E-Mail: </TD>
<TD><INPUT TYPE="text" NAME="email" SIZE="50"></TD></BR>
</TR>
<TR>
<TD>Mailing<BR>Address: </TD>
<TD><TEXTAREA NAME="address" ROWS="5" COLS="50"></TEXTAREA></TD>
</TR>
</TABLE>

<P>
<STRONG>What is your company's main product/service</STRONG>
(choose the most applicable)</BR>

<!-- Use radio buttons to force mutually exclusive choices -->

DB-Software <INPUT TYPE="radio" NAME="bus" VALUE="sw" CHECKED>
Consulting <INPUT TYPE="radio" NAME="bus" VALUE="consult">
Engineering <INPUT TYPE="radio" NAME="bus" VALUE="engr">
Research <INPUT TYPE="radio" NAME="bus" VALUE="research">
ADP Services <INPUT TYPE="radio" NAME="bus" VALUE="adp">
</P>

<P>
<STRONG>What is your title?</STRONG> (choose the most applicable)</BR>

<!-- Use radio buttons to force mutually exclusive choices -->
President-CEO <INPUT TYPE="radio" NAME="title" VALUE="Pres" CHECKED>
Manager <INPUT TYPE="radio" NAME="title" VALUE="Manager">
Designer <INPUT TYPE="radio" NAME="title" VALUE="Designer">
Programmer <INPUT TYPE="radio" NAME="title" VALUE="Programmer">
Analyst <INPUT TYPE="radio" NAME="title" VALUE="Analyst">
</P>

<HR>

<!-- these scrolled-lists allow multiple choices -->
<!-- TABLE used to provide side-by-side formatting -->

<STRONG>Please tell us about your development environment</STRONG>
<EM>(Please select all that apply)</EM>

<P>
```

```
<TABLE NOBORDER>
<TR>
<TH>Languages</TH>
<TH>Data Bases</TH>
<TH>Describe Your Applications</TH>
</TR>
<TD>
<SELECT NAME="cgidev" MULTIPLE SIZE="8">
<OPTION VALUE="Perl5" SELECTED>Perl 5.0 </OPTION>
<OPTION VALUE="Magic">MAGIC </OPTION>
<OPTION VALUE="Sybperl">SybPerl </OPTION>
<OPTION VALUE="Oraperl">OraPerl</OPTION>
<OPTION VALUE="C">C </OPTION>
<OPTION VALUE="C++">C++</OPTION>
<OPTION VALUE="Unix Shells">Unix Shells</OPTION>
<OPTION VALUE="Python">Python</OPTION>
<OPTION VALUE="REXX">REXX</OPTION>
<OPTION VALUE="FORTRAN">FORTRAN</OPTION>
</SELECT>
</TD>
<TD>
<SELECT NAME="dbase" MULTIPLE SIZE="8">
<OPTION VALUE="Access" SELECTED>MS ACCESS</OPTION>
<OPTION VALUE="Sybase">Sybase</OPTION>
<OPTION VALUE="Oracle">Oracle</OPTION>
<OPTION VALUE="FoxPro">FoxPro</OPTION>
<OPTION VALUE="WDB">WDB</OPTION>
<OPTION VALUE="Web-Genera">Web-Genera</OPTION>
<OPTION VALUE="VAX DBMS">VAX DBMS</OPTION>
<OPTION VALUE="DB2">DB2</OPTION>
<OPTION VALUE="Informix">Informix</OPTION>
<OPTION VALUE="RdB">RdB</OPTION>
</SELECT>
</TD>
<TD>
<TEXTAREA NAME="description" ROWS="8" COLS="50"></TEXTAREA>
</TD>
</TR>
</TABLE>
</P>

<P>
<STRONG>
Do you currently develop/plan to develop Web-accessible databases?<
/STRONG><BR>

YES<INPUT TYPE="radio" NAME="dbyesno" VALUE="YES" CHECKED>
NO<INPUT TYPE="radio" NAME="dbyesno" VALUE="NO">
</P>

<P>
<STRONG>Do you want to receive/continue to receive a free subscription to
  <EM>Web.dB</EM>?</STRONG><BR>

<STRONG>YES!</STRONG><INPUT TYPE="radio" NAME="subscribe" VALUE="YES" CHECKED>
NO<INPUT TYPE="radio" NAME="subscribe" VALUE="NO">
</P>
```

continues

Listing 11.6. continued

```
<P>
<INPUT TYPE="submit" VALUE="Send My Subscription Now!">
<INPUT TYPE="reset" VALUE="Clear Form Entries">
</P>

</FORM>

<HR>

</BODY>
</HTML>
<HTML>
```

FIGURE 11.5.

Page 1 of the survey and subscription form.

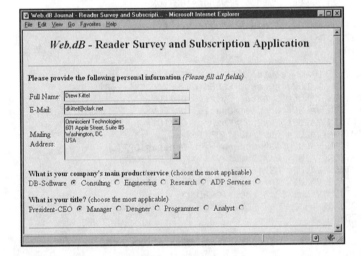

FIGURE 11.6.

Page 2 of the survey and subscription form.

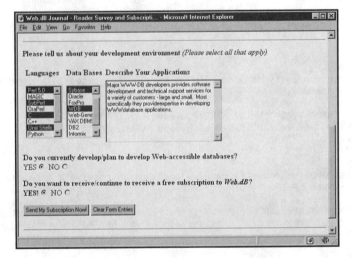

Requiring a user to scroll through lengthy forms might be perceived as a limitation of using HTML forms. In this case, however, the form has been laid out well, and the information it requests from the user is compact and succinct. Therefore, this form requires little scrolling by the user.

The ACTION attribute specifies a CGI routine that uses information collected from the form and passed to the routine. CGI is covered in detail in later chapters; I just want to point out that the data collected from users will be put to use.

The HTML TABLE element imposes a bit of formatting on the form TEXT and TEXTAREA elements. This provides a much better visual presentation by aligning the elements shown in Figure 11.5.

Finally, as a matter of good style, the informational request is laid out on the form in logical groups. The first part of the form requests personal information, and the remainder of the form focuses on technical information.

Forms That Support Electronic Commerce: The Malt Shop— An Online Store

Convenience and time savings are increasingly important to everyone in today's fast-paced world. Wouldn't you take advantage of the opportunity to log onto the Web and do some quick shopping if it were quick, easy, and enabled you to do the other things you'd rather be doing? Or what about trying to purchase specialty items? Maybe no conventional stores in your area carry the items you want. Like it or not, electronic commerce is coming of age and will address these and other issues in the not-too-distant future; Web technologies are there to lend a hand.

In this example, you'll see how easy it is to create an interface to an online store—in this case, The Malt Shop, which is a home-brewing supply store. Customers can enter information to be processed and used to ship their orders, query and build databases, check inventories (and automatically order items for restock), order special products, and so on.

This example illustrates the use of TEXTAREA and INPUT (TEXT as well as RADIO, SUBMIT, and RESET buttons). It also demonstrates using named anchors within an HTML document to facilitate paging and navigating a form that has multiple pages (subforms) while still maintaining a single point of form submission.

Listing 11.7 creates the forms interfaces shown in Figures 11.7 through 11.11.

Listing 11.7. Creating The Malt Shop form interfaces.

```
<HTML>

<HEAD>
<TITLE>The Malt Shop Online Ordering</TITLE>
```

continues

Listing 11.7. continued

```
</HEAD>
<BODY>

<!-- place a named anchor so we can always get back home -->
<A NAME="MaltShopMain">

<CENTER>
<H1>Welcome to <EM>The Malt Shop</EM></H1>
</CENTER>
<HR>

<!-- Declare start of form -->
<!-- Action URL simply sends a string of name/value pairs -->
<!-- to be processed by the specified cgi program -->

<FORM METHOD="POST" ACTION="http://www.omniscient.com/cgi-bin/brewing.pl">

<H2>
<EM>The Malt Shop</EM> stocks to widest variety of high quality
brewing ingredients and supplies.
</H2>

<!-- note use of references within this doc. -->
<!-- named anchors allow users to navigate the document more easily -->

<H3>Browse Our Catalog Input Forms and Select From the
Finest Quality Ingredients</H3>
<EM>When you have completed filling in your order on the following pages
you may submit your order by completing the information on page 4.</EM>
<P>
<STRONG>CATALOG TABLE OF CONTENTS</STRONG>
<UL>
   <LI><A HREF="#Malts"><STRONG>Page 1 - Malts and Kits
                             </STRONG></A></LI>
   <LI><A HREF="#Yeasts-Hops"><STRONG>Page 2 - Yeasts and Hops
                             </STRONG></A></LI>
   <LI><A HREF="#Supplies"><STRONG>Page 3 - Home Brewing Supplies
                             </STRONG></A></LI>
   <LI><A HREF="#Shipping"><STRONG>Page 4 - Fill Out Shipping
                          Information/Send Order</STRONG></A></LI>
</UL>
</P>

<P>
<STRONG>Other Miscellaneous Stuff</STRONG>
<UL>
<LI><A HREF="recipes-links.html"><STRONG>Links to Some of Our Favorite
   Home Brew Recipe Sites</STRONG></A></LI>
</UL>
</P>

<HR>
<A NAME="Malts"><H3>Dried Malts, Malt Extracts and Kits</H3>

<!-- TABLE provides good formatting -->
```

```
<TABLE BORDER="1">
<TR>
<TH>Malt Variety</TH>
<TH>Price per Unit</TH>
<TH>Quantity</TH>
</TR>
<TR>
<TD>MD Brand Light, 3 lb. bag, dried</TD>
<TD>$9.00</TD>
<TD><INPUT TYPE="text" NAME="mdlight1#" SIZE="4"></TD>
</TR>
<TR>
<TD>MD Brand Amber, 3 lb. bag, dried</TD>
<TD>$9.00</TD>
<TD><INPUT TYPE="text" NAME="mdamber1#" SIZE="4"></TD>
</TR>
<TR>
<TD>MD Brand Dark, 3 lb. bag, dried</TD>
<TD>$9.00</TD>
<TD><INPUT TYPE="text" NAME="mddark1#" SIZE="4"></TD>
</TR>
<TR>
<TD>EM Brand Light Extract, 3.3# lb. can</TD>
<TD>$10.75</TD>
<TD><INPUT TYPE="text" NAME="emdark1#" SIZE="4"></TD>
</TR>
<TR>
<TD>EM Brand Amber Extract, 3.3# lb. can</TD>
<TD>$10.75</TD>
<TD><INPUT TYPE="text" NAME="emdark1#" SIZE="4"></TD>
</TR>
<TR>
<TD>EM Brand Dark Extract, 3.3# lb. can</TD>
<TD>$10.75</TD>
<TD><INPUT TYPE="text" NAME="emdark1#" SIZE="4"></TD>
</TR>
<TR>
<TD>Kit of the Month, Premium Amber Bitters</TD>
<TD>$19.35</TD>
<TD><INPUT TYPE="text" NAME="kotm" SIZE="4"></TD>
</TR>
<TR>
<TD>Manager's Special, Cascades Bigfoot Ale Kit</TD>
<TD>$19.35</TD>
<TD><INPUT TYPE="text" NAME="mgrspec" SIZE="4"></TD>
</TR>
</TABLE>

<P>
<A HREF="#MaltShopMain">Back to Main Page</A><BR>
<A HREF="#Shipping">Submit Order</A>
</P>

<HR>
<A NAME="Yeasts-Hops"><H3>Yeasts and Hops</H3>
```

continues

Listing 11.7. continued

```html
<!-- TABLE provides good formatting -->

<TABLE BORDER="1">
<TR>
<TH>Hops and Yeast</TH>
<TH>Price per Unit</TH>
<TH>Quantity</TH>
</TR>
<TR>
<TD>Saaz Hops, 1 oz., pellets</TD>
<TD>$1.85</TD>
<TD><INPUT TYPE="text" NAME="Saaz1" SIZE="4"></TD>
</TR>
<TR>
<TD>Saaz Hops, 5 oz., leaf plugs</TD>
<TD>$8.90</TD>
<TD><INPUT TYPE="text" NAME="Saaz5" SIZE="4"></TD>
</TR>
<TR>
<TD>Hallertau Hops, 1 oz., pellets</TD>
<TD>$1.85</TD>
<TD><INPUT TYPE="text" NAME="haller1" SIZE="4"></TD>
</TR>
<TR>
<TD>Fuggles Hops, 1 oz., pellets</TD>
<TD>$1.45</TD>
<TD><INPUT TYPE="text" NAME="fuggle1" SIZE="4"></TD>
</TR>
<TR>
<TD>Goldings Hops, 1 oz., pellets</TD>
<TD>$1.45</TD>
<TD><INPUT TYPE="text" NAME="gold1" SIZE="4"></TD>
</TR>
<TR>
<TD>Sudz Bavarian Pilsner<BR>Liquid Yeast Culture</TD>
<TD>$4.25</TD>
<TD><INPUT TYPE="text" NAME="bavpil" SIZE="4"></TD>
</TR>
<TR>
<TD>Sudz Special London Ale<BR>Liquid Yeast Culture</TD>
<TD>$4.25</TD>
<TD><INPUT TYPE="text" NAME="splondon" SIZE="4"></TD>
</TR>
<TR>
<TD>Edme Ale Yeast, 5 gm dried</TD>
<TD>$1.00</TD>
<TD><INPUT TYPE="text" NAME="edale" SIZE="4"></TD>
</TR>
</TABLE>

<P>
<A HREF="#MaltShopMain">Back to Main Page</A><BR>
<A HREF="#Shipping">Submit Order</A>
</P>
```

```
<HR>
<A NAME="Supplies"><H3>Home Brewing Supplies</H3>

<!-- TABLE provides good formatting -->

<TABLE BORDER="1">
<TR>
<TH>Miscellaneous Brewing Supplies</TH>
<TH>Price per Unit</TH>
<TH>Quantity</TH>
</TR>
<TR>
<TD>6.7 gal. Plastic Fermenting Bucket</TD>
<TD>$11.85</TD>
<TD><INPUT TYPE="text" NAME="fbucket" SIZE="4"></TD>
</TR>
<TR>
<TD>5.6 gal. Plastic Bottling Bucket<BR>(w/spigot)</TD>
<TD>$11.85</TD>
<TD><INPUT TYPE="text" NAME="bbucket" SIZE="4"></TD>
</TR>
<TR>
<TD>Bottle Caps, 100 cnt.</TD>
<TD>$2.00</TD>
<TD><INPUT TYPE="text" NAME="caps" SIZE="4"></TD>
</TR>
<TR>
<TD>Airlocks</TD>
<TD>$2.00</TD>
<TD><INPUT TYPE="text" NAME="alock" SIZE="4"></TD>
</TR>
<TR>
<TD>Hydrometer, 10", triple scale</TD>
<TD>$5.25</TD>
<TD><INPUT TYPE="text" NAME="hydrom" SIZE="4"></TD>
</TR>

<TR>
<TD>Racking Tube, 6 ft. section</TD>
<TD>$2.00</TD>
<TD><INPUT TYPE="text" NAME="rtube" SIZE="4"></TD>
</TR>
<TR>
<TD>12, 16, 24, 32 oz. bottles</TD>
<TD>CALL!</TD>
<TD></TD>
</TR>
</TABLE>

<P>
<A HREF="#MaltShopMain">Back to Main Page</A><BR>
<A HREF="#Shipping">Submit Order</A>
</P>

<HR>
<A NAME="Shipping"><H3>Shipping Information</H3>
```

continues

Listing 11.7. continued

```
<STRONG>Please provide the following shipping information</STRONG>
<EM>(Please fill all fields)</EM>

<!-- Create TEXT and TEXTAREA objects for name, mail entry -->
<!-- Use TABLE to provide a bit of formatting control -->

<TABLE>
<TR>
<TD>Full Name: </TD>
<TD><INPUT TYPE="text" NAME="uname" SIZE="50"></TD><BR>
</TR>
<TR>
<TD>Mailing<BR>Address: </TD>
<TD><TEXTAREA NAME="address" ROWS="5" COLS="50"></TEXTAREA></TD>
</TR>
</TABLE>

<P>
<STRONG>Method of payment?</STRONG></BR>

<!-- Use radio buttons to force mutually exclusive choices -->

Credit Card <INPUT TYPE="radio" NAME="pymt" VALUE="cc" CHECKED>
Check/Money Order <INPUT TYPE="radio" NAME="pymt" VALUE="chmo">
<EM>Malt Shop</EM> Account<INPUT TYPE="radio" NAME="pymt" VALUE="msaccnt">
</P>

<P>
<STRONG>Method of shipment?</STRONG></BR>

<!-- Use radio buttons to force mutually exclusive choices -->

U.S Mail <INPUT TYPE="radio" NAME="shpmnt" VALUE="usmail" CHECKED>
Magic Overnight Delivery <INPUT TYPE="radio" NAME="shpmnt" VALUE="overnight">
Magic 2-Day Express <INPUT TYPE="radio" NAME="shpmnt" VALUE="twoday">
</P>

<P>
<STRONG>Do you want to be placed on our mailing list?</STRONG><BR>
<STRONG>YES!</STRONG><INPUT TYPE="radio" NAME="subscribe" VALUE="YES" CHECKED>
NO<INPUT TYPE="radio" NAME="subscribe" VALUE="NO">
</P>

<P>
<INPUT TYPE="submit" VALUE="I'm Gettin' Thirsty - Send My Order Now!">
<INPUT TYPE="reset" VALUE="Clear Form Entries">
</P>

</FORM>

<HR>

</BODY>
</HTML>
```

FIGURE 11.7.

The Malt Shop online store home page.

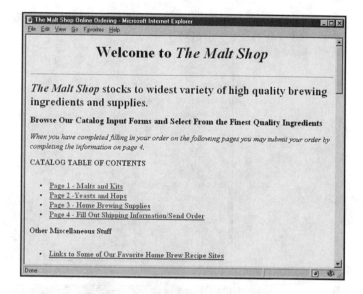

FIGURE 11.8.

Page 1 of The Malt Shop online order form.

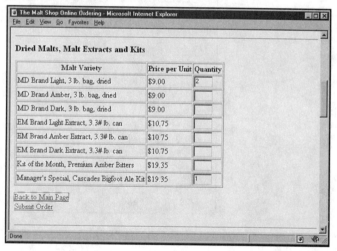

FIGURE 11.9.

Page 2 of The Malt Shop online order form.

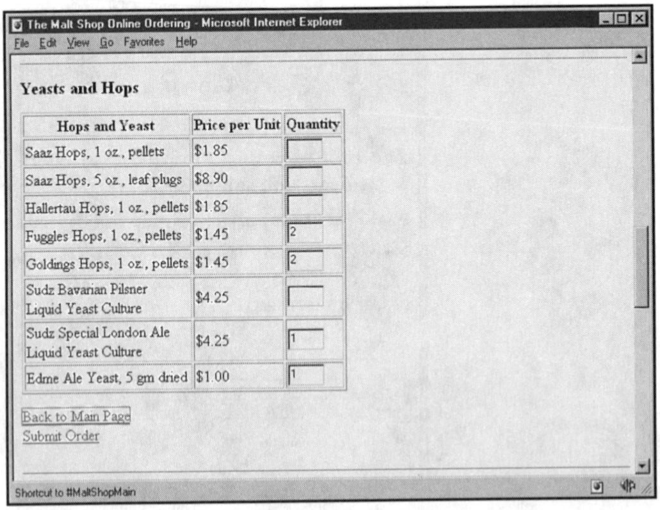

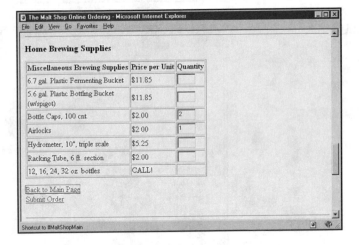

FIGURE 11.10.

Page 3 of The Malt Shop online order form.

FIGURE 11.11.
*Page 4 of The Malt
Shop online order form.*

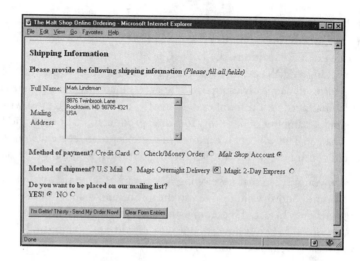

In the Web.dB example, you saw that scrolling through a short form isn't a great burden to the user. The Malt Shop example, by contrast, demonstrates a case where requiring the user to scroll through several pages would result in a form that was neither quick nor easy to use. In a full-fledged application (one with a few hundred pages of a catalog and/or items listing), scrolling clearly is not an option. To overcome this dilemma, I used links and references to named anchors within the HTML document to permit the user to "page to" certain locations within the form, and I required only one submission. Linking to external HTML documents or forcing the user to perform multiple submissions was not required. Additionally, I logically grouped contents presented on each page so that users easily can find what they want. You can extend these concepts to provide greater functionality in full-fledged applications.

The ACTION attribute specifies a CGI routine that uses the information collected from the form and passed to the routine. This routine may perform checks against an inventory database, generate shipping information to a warehouse, generate and return an invoice and total cost information for the user's approval before finalizing the sale, and so on. Using CGI routines is covered in great detail in Chapter 18 and Chapter 19.

I used the HTML TABLE element to impose a bit of formatting on the form TEXT elements used to present product information and order-quantity input fields, as shown in Figures 11.9 through 11.11. This element gives the order form a well-organized spreadsheet look and feel with which many users are accustomed.

Order forms of this type lend themselves well to automatic, on-the-fly generation techniques. In other words, instead of using static HTML forms that quickly can become outdated and require extensive revisions, the HTML used to render the form is created dynamically by the server using a database of product and price information to generate the page content. Generating forms dynamically using database-access methods and programs to generate HTML can substantially reduce the number of lines of HTML code you must write, and it also provides a tremendous amount of flexibility for when product lines, pricing, and other ordering information change. This concept is explored in more depth in later chapters, beginning with Chapter 18 and continuing with examples throughout the remainder of the book.

Finally, you can see that developing forms can become pretty involved for more substantial applications. I don't want to give you the impression that this development is difficult, though, because it isn't. In fact, this example illustrates just the opposite and points out one of the major benefits of HTML: just how good it is as a rapid prototyping and development tool. This example took less than one hour to code.

Forms That Support Web Database Access: Honest Abe's Used Auto Search

Finally, here is an example that addresses the meat of this book: giving people access to distributed data and information from databases they ordinarily would not be able to access. Thousands of people, companies, organizations, agencies, and institutions around the world want you to have easy access to their databases and repositories of information. Many of them, particularly government agencies, are developing Websites to provide that access at no cost. Some of these sites (intranets) are for use only by users internal to an organization, whereas other sites are for use by the public. Still other information and data providers seek to provide their information for a profit—by charging users for information accessed or by charging others a fee for posting the information.

Honest Abe's Used Auto Search (yet another fictitious company) falls into the latter category. Abe maintains a database of used vehicles and sellers for which he charges the seller a fee to be listed in the database. Abe then gives the used-auto buying public the capability to perform directed searches of the database. The form used by Abe's Website enables the user to structure a query and obtain information on vehicles that meet the buyer's preferences.

This example illustrates the use of TEXTAREA, SELECT, OPTION, and INPUT (text; checkboxes; and radio, submit, and reset buttons). Listing 11.8 creates the form interfaces shown in Figures 11.12 and 11.13. Figure 11.14 shows a sample of search results.

Listing 11.8. Honest Abe's Used Auto Search interface.

```
<HTML>

<HEAD>
<TITLE>Honest Abe's Used Auto Search Service</TITLE>
```

```
</HEAD>

<BODY>

<CENTER>
<H1>Honest Abe's Used Auto Search</H1>
</CENTER>
<p align="center"><em><strong>No Lemons, No Shysters, No Foolin'!</strong></em>
<img src="images/okhandjpg" align="middle" hspace="10" width="32"
height="51"></p>
<HR>

<!-- Declare start of form -->
<!-- Action URL simply sends a string of name/value pairs -->
<!-- to be processed by cgi program that queries a used car
<!-- database -->

<FORM METHOD="POST" ACTION="http://www.omniscient.com/cgi-bin/carquery.pl">

<P>
<H3>Fill out the following questionnaire and we will use the information
to search our extensive database of used car listings. <EM>If we
don't list it, it doesn't exist!</EM></H3>
</P>

<P>
<STRONG>What used vehicles are you interested in?</STRONG> <EM>(Select all
vehicles of interest from the following lists)</EM><BR>
<!-- These scrolled lists allow multiple choices -->
<!-- Table used to provide formatting -->
<CENTER>
<TABLE NOBORDER>
<TR>
<TH>Ford</TH>
<TH>Toyota</TH>
<TH>Specialty</TH>
</TR>
<TR>
<TD>
<SELECT NAME="ford" MULTIPLE SIZE="4">
<OPTION VALUE="escort" SELECTED>Escort</OPTION>
<OPTION VALUE="pinto">Pinto</OPTION>
<OPTION VALUE="mustang">Mustang</OPTION>
<OPTION VALUE="taurus">Taurus</OPTION>
<OPTION VALUE="bronco">Bronco</OPTION>
</SELECT>
</TD>
<TD>
<SELECT NAME="toyota" MULTIPLE SIZE="4">
<OPTION VALUE="mr2" SELECTED>MR2</OPTION>
<OPTION VALUE="camry">Camry</OPTION>
<OPTION VALUE="celica">Celica</OPTION>
<OPTION VALUE="forerunner">Forerunner</OPTION>
<OPTION VALUE="tercel">Tercel</OPTION>
</SELECT>
</TD>
<TD>
```

continues

Listing 11.8. continued

```
<SELECT NAME="special" MULTIPLE SIZE="4">
<OPTION VALUE="rolls" SELECTED>Rolls Royce</OPTION>
<OPTION VALUE="hv">HumVee</OPTION>
<OPTION VALUE="modelt">Model T</OPTION>
<OPTION VALUE="ferrari">Ferrari</OPTION>
<OPTION VALUE="dl">DeLorean</OPTION>
</SELECT>
</TD>
</TR>
</TABLE>
</CENTER>
</P>


<P>
<STRONG>Color preference(s)</STRONG> <EM>(check all that apply)</EM> <BR>
<INPUT TYPE="checkbox" NAME="c1" VALUE="wht">White<BR>
<INPUT TYPE="checkbox" NAME="c2" VALUE="blk">Black<BR>
<INPUT TYPE="checkbox" NAME="c3" VALUE="red">Red<BR>
<INPUT TYPE="checkbox" NAME="c4" VALUE="blue">Blue<BR>
<INPUT TYPE="checkbox" NAME="c4" VALUE="grn">Green
</P>


<P>
<STRONG>What is your price range?</STRONG><BR>
<!-- Use radio buttons to force mutually exclusive choices -->
&lt <STRONG>$</STRONG>1000<INPUT TYPE="radio" NAME="range" VALUE="range1">
<STRONG>$</STRONG>1000-$2000<INPUT TYPE="radio" NAME="range" VALUE="range2">
<STRONG>$</STRONG>2000-$3000<INPUT TYPE="radio" NAME="range" VALUE="range3">
<STRONG>$</STRONG>3000-$4000<INPUT TYPE="radio" NAME="range" VALUE="range4">
<STRONG>$</STRONG>4000-$5000<INPUT TYPE="radio" NAME="range" VALUE="range5">
<STRONG>$</STRONG>5000+<INPUT TYPE="radio" NAME="range" VALUE="range6">
</P>


<P>
<STRONG>Model year(s) of interest</STRONG> <EM>(check all that apply)</EM> <BR>
'88<INPUT TYPE="checkbox" NAME="yearc1" VALUE="88">
'89<INPUT TYPE="checkbox" NAME="yearc2" VALUE="89">
'90<INPUT TYPE="checkbox" NAME="yearc3" VALUE="90">
'91<INPUT TYPE="checkbox" NAME="yearc4" VALUE="91">
'92<INPUT TYPE="checkbox" NAME="yearc5" VALUE="92">
'93<INPUT TYPE="checkbox" NAME="yearc6" VALUE="93">
'94<INPUT TYPE="checkbox" NAME="yearc7" VALUE="94">
'95<INPUT TYPE="checkbox" NAME="yearc8" VALUE="95">
</P>


<P>
<STRONG>Please enter your Zip Code:</STRONG>
<INPUT TYPE="text" NAME="zip" SIZE="6" MAXLENGTH="5"><BR>
</P>


<P>
<STRONG>Find all matching vehicles in your</STRONG><BR>
<!-- Use radio buttons to force mutually exclusive choices -->
Local Area<INPUT TYPE="radio" NAME="location" VALUE="local">
State<INPUT TYPE="radio" NAME="location" VALUE="">
Region<INPUT TYPE="radio" NAME="location" VALUE="range2">
</P>
```

```
<P>
<STRONG>Order matches by</STRONG> <EM>(check all that apply)</EM><BR>
<INPUT TYPE="checkbox" NAME="orderbymake" VALUE="make">Make <BR>
<INPUT TYPE="checkbox" NAME="orderbymodel" VALUE="model">Model <BR>
<INPUT TYPE="checkbox" NAME="orderbyyear" VALUE="year">Year <BR>
<INPUT TYPE="checkbox" NAME="orderbyprice" VALUE="price">Price
</P>

<P>
<!-- this pull-down menu allows one selection -->
<STRONG>Maximum number of matches to return: </STRONG>
<SELECT NAME="maxhits" SIZE="1">
<OPTION VALUE="ten" SELECTED>10</OPTION>
<OPTION VALUE="twenty">20</OPTION>
<OPTION VALUE="fifty">50</OPTION>
<OPTION VALUE="hundred">100</OPTION>
</SELECT>
</P>

<P>
<INPUT TYPE="submit" VALUE="Submit Query">
<INPUT TYPE="reset" VALUE="Clear Form Entries">
</P>

</FORM>

<HR>

</BODY>
</HTML>
<HTML>
```

FIGURE 11.12.

*Page 1 of Honest Abe's
Used Auto Search form.*

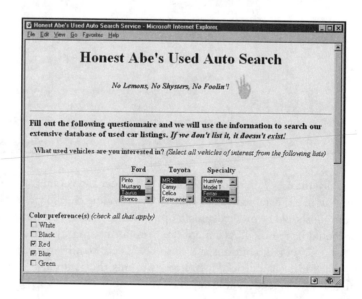

FIGURE 11.13.

Page 2 of Honest Abe's Used Auto Search form.

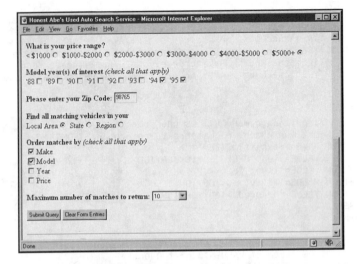

FIGURE 11.14.

Sample search results from Honest Abe's Used Auto Search.

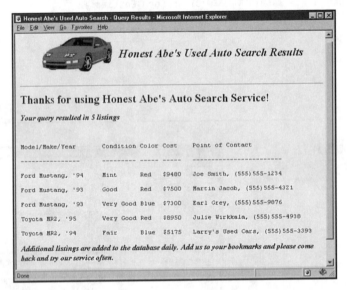

I provided the user with some control over the order and volume of information to be returned as a result of the database query. I did so by providing checkboxes for the user to specify how the output should be ordered and an option list to indicate the maximum number of matches that should be returned. As a matter of form formatting style, the form presentation often is cleaner if sets of radio buttons and checkboxes consistently are rendered vertically or horizontally when it is possible to do so. I chose to mix things up in this example just to show the different ways to render these objects.

A very simple HTML form is used to give a user easy access to information in Abe's database. Even though the form was simple to develop and is easy to use, it enables the user to construct powerful queries and directed searches for specific information with a few simple inputs. This is one of the primary reasons why Web database development is a rapidly growing discipline.

A nice addition you could make to this example is a link from the query results page back to the query page. This would enable users to reformulate or refine a query if they weren't satisfied with the results of the current query. An even nicer modification would be to pre-fill the form with input (state information) from the original query so that the user doesn't have to fill out all the entries again.

Summary

The goal of this chapter was to give you everything you need to know to immediately start developing HTML forms for database access and application user interfaces. Throughout, proper development techniques were emphasized, and notes and tips were provided on using form elements.

You began by learning what forms are, looking at the many varieties of forms, and using HTML to employ forms as a user interface to a variety of applications, such as information collection and electronic commerce. You learned how to use forms to give users controlled access to your databases, regardless of the level of their technical knowledge, computer literacy, or even where those databases physically exist relative to the users.

Next, you saw a detailed summary and reference of the HTML elements and attributes used to develop form interfaces, including a description and use of each element, as well as the proper syntax used to render each element.

Through a variety of code and figure samples, you saw how each type of form element is developed and how it looks when rendered by a Web browser. Examples included form elements such as TEXTAREA; SELECT; OPTION; and the INPUT types of radio buttons, checkboxes, passwords, and text. You also looked at using INPUT types of SUBMIT and RESET to send information collected from users to the server or to clear entries from the form.

The three comprehensive, practical examples near the end of this chapter illustrated how to use forms as interfaces to a variety of applications to perform tasks such as accessing controlled databases, gathering information, and participating in electronic commerce.

12

Introduction to Client-Side Web Application Development Using VBScript

by Sanjaya Hettihewa

VBScript has been designed to make it easier to develop client-side Web applications that run on the Web browser. A long time ago (which translates to about a year ago when talking about the Internet), people were discovering the virtues of providing dynamic information to users browsing a Web site. CGI applications were typically used to create Web pages that displayed dynamic information. Although this worked well in some cases, it did not work well for some people. The development of a CGI application typically meant learning a programming language such as C or C++, compiling the CGI application, transferring it to the CGI directory of a Web server, and testing the CGI application for bugs. Even the slightest change to the application meant recompiling the entire application and repeating the process of copying the application to a CGI directory and testing the application for bugs. To solve this problem, Web scripting languages such as JavaScript and VBScript were developed to aid in the development of client-side and server-side CGI applications.

Although Web scripting languages are widely used in the development of client-side CGI applications that run on the Web browser, Web scripting languages are also highly suitable for developing sophisticated server-side CGI applications. For example, Microsoft's latest server-side Web application development tool, Microsoft Visual InterDev, uses VBScript to interact with various objects on the Web server. Therefore, skills you learn in this chapter can be used not only to develop interactive client-side Web applications but also to develop server-side Web applications in the form of Active Server Pages. The purpose of this chapter is to introduce you to VBScript and discuss how various capabilities of VBScript can be used to develop interactive Web applications. See Appendixes C, "VBScript Language Reference," and D, "Coding and Naming Conventions for VBScript Developers," for information on VBScript coding conventions.

Where Do I Obtain VBScript?

You do not have to install VBScript per se. The VBScript engine is part of Internet Explorer and is installed on your system when you install Internet Explorer. If Internet Explorer 3.0 or later is not installed on your system, please install it before proceeding any further. Even if you have Internet Explorer 3.0 installed on your system, visit Microsoft's Internet Explorer Web page to find out the availability of a more recent version of Internet Explorer. (Internet Explorer 4.0 or later should be available for download by the time you read this.)

> **RESOURCE**
>
> Visit Microsoft's Internet Explorer Website at
> `http://www.microsoft.com/ie/default.asp`
> for the most up-to-date information about Internet Explorer.

Benefits of Using VBScript

There are many benefits to using VBScript. VBScript is a powerful, lightweight, easy-to-use, freely available, cross-platform, cross-language scripting language for the Internet. It is designed to leverage the skills and investments of millions of Visual Basic programmers to the Internet. This is great news for all the millions of Visual Basic programmers who want to leverage their Visual Basic skills to the Internet. If you are familiar with VBA or Visual Basic, you will feel right at home with VBScript. Before proceeding any further, let's quickly examine why VBScript is a powerful, lightweight, easy-to-use, freely available, cross-platform, and cross-language scripting language.

■ **VBScript is powerful.** Various capabilities of VBScript can be used to develop richly interactive Web pages that respond to user input in an intelligent manner. For example, when a user submits a form, a VBScript subroutine can be triggered to verify that the form is properly filled in with valid values. In the case of a server-side CGI application, VBScript can be used to process data submitted by users with the aid of ActiveX controls specially designed for Microsoft Active Server Pages.

■ **VBScript is lightweight.** VBScript code is lightweight, fast, and has been optimized to be transmitted via the Internet. Because VBScript code is lightweight, it can be quickly transmitted to users browsing a Website—even via relatively slow Plain Old Telephone Service (POTS) links to the Internet.

■ **VBScript is easy to use.** Compared to scripting languages such as JavaScript, VBScript is easier to use because it is based on the easy-to-learn BASIC (Beginner's All Purpose Symbolic Instruction Code) language.

■ **VBScript is freely available.** VBScript is a freely available scripting language. Microsoft has made VBScript freely available to software vendors so they can add scripting capabilities to their applications with the aid of VBScript.

■ **VBScript is cross platform.** By the time you read this, VBScript will be functioning on UNIX as well as Macintosh computers in addition to Windows 95 and Windows NT computers.

■ **VBScript is cross language.** VBScript supports any language (such as C++ and Java, for example) that enables objects to be compiled as ActiveX controls.

VBScript can be used to leverage the skills of millions of Visual basic programmers to the Internet. VBScript can be used to easily create active and intelligent Web pages. Because VBScript is supported by Microsoft, in the near future, you also will see a great deal of integration among VBScript and Internet Explorer/Active Desktop, Windows NT/95, Microsoft Office, and Microsoft BackOffice.

VBScript is a subset of Microsoft Visual Basic and is upwardly compatible with Visual Basic for Applications (VBA). VBA is shipped with Microsoft Office applications to make it easier for developers to build custom solutions using various components of Microsoft Office. The capability to provide scripting, automation, and customization capabilities for Web browsers and Web servers is a major feature of VBScript. If you are already familiar with Visual Basic, very shortly you will be able to leverage your skills to the Internet using VBScript. Be sure to visit Microsoft's VBScript home page for the most up-to-date information about VBScript. Microsoft's VBScript Web page contains in-depth information on VBScript data types, operators, flow control, event procedures, functions, and procedures. A VBScript language reference and tutorial also can be found at Microsoft's VBScript Website.

> **RESOURCE**
>
> Visit Microsoft's VBScript information Website for the most up-to-date information about VBScript at
> `http://www.microsoft.com/VBScript`

How VBScript Works

VBScript programs are defined between the two HTML tags `<SCRIPT LANGUAGE=VBS>` and `</SCRIPT>`. Browsers that support VBScript read the VBScript application contained between these two HTML tags and execute it after checking the code for any syntax errors. How VBScript works is shown in Figure 12.1.

FIGURE 12.1.
How VBScript works.

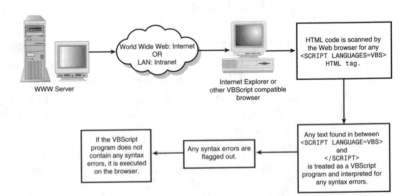

As you can see in Figure 12.1, a VBScript application is part of a regular HTML file and is enclosed between the two HTML tags `<SCRIPT LANGUAGE=VBS>` and `</SCRIPT>`. When a Web browser that supports VBScript encounters the `<SCRIPT LANGUAGE=VBS>` HTML tag, all text between that tag and `</SCRIPT>` is treated as a VBScript application and is checked for syntax errors. If the application does not contain any syntax errors, it is executed on the Web browser. If any syntax errors are detected, they are flagged by the VBScript interpreter, as shown in Figure 12.2.

FIGURE 12.2.

Syntax errors in VBScript programs are flagged by the VBScript interpreter.

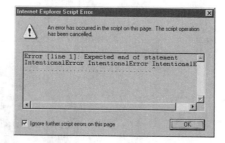

Dealing with Web Browsers that Do Not Support VBScript

The World Wide Web would be a better place for Web application developers if everyone used the same Web browser. Because this is not the case, you need to make sure your VBScript-enhanced Web pages are backwardly compatible with Web browsers that do not support VBScript. This is done by hiding the VBScript code from Web browsers that do not understand how to execute VBScript code. In order to hide VBScript code from "technologically challenged" Web browsers, VBScript code can be enclosed in two HTML comment tags, as shown in Listing 12.1. This prevents Web browsers that do not support VBScript from attempting to display the VBScript application as if it were part of the HTML code of the Web page.

Listing 12.1. Hiding VBScript code from Web browsers that do not support VBScript.

```
<SCRIPT LANGUAGE=VBS>
<!-- To hide VBScript code from technologically challenged
     Web browsers
... VBScript code ...
!-->
</SCRIPT>
```

Hello World!

Writing the classic Hello World! application with VBScript is very easy. For the purpose of this example, you will be shown how to create a Web page similar to the one shown in Figure 12.3. This Web page will have three buttons. The first button displays a message box with a greeting, the second button displays the current time, and the third button displays the current date. The Hello World! application uses HTML form controls for data entry. For an in-depth overview of HTML form controls and how they are used to interact with users, see Chapter 14, "Developing Advanced Forms for Database Access and Application Interfaces." Chapter 14 also covers advanced HTML form development with VBScript.

FIGURE 12.3.

The VBScript version of the classic Hello World! application.

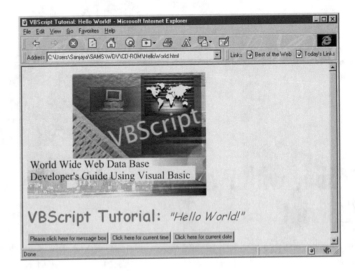

The Hello World! Dialog Box

The Hello World! dialog box, shown in Figure 12.4, is displayed each time a user clicks the "Please click here for message box" button in Figure 12.3. The Hello Word! application makes use of VBScript events. A VBScript event is generated each time a user interacts with a certain object on the Web browser. VBScript subroutines can "listen" and react to events. For example, when a user clicks a button, a VBScript subroutine can execute a series of VBScript statements. Visit Microsoft's VBScript information Web page (http://www.microsoft.com/VBScript/) for a comprehensive list of Web browser events supported by VBScript. If you look at the HTML page of the VBScript application (see lines 22 and 23 of Listing 12.5), you'll notice that the command button associated with the Hello World! dialog box is named BtnHello. As shown in line 1 of Listing 12.2, the OnClick event of the BtnHello command button is associated with the BtnHello_OnClick subroutine. Each time a user clicks the "Please click here for message box" button, the Web browser invokes the BtnHello_OnClick subroutine and any VBScript code defined in that subroutine is executed.

The BtnHello_OnClick subroutine is a very simple VBScript subroutine. The first three lines of code create strings that are displayed in the dialog box shown in Figure 12.4. Notice how the string concatenation operator (&) is used in line 4 to merge two strings and assign the result to a variable. The result then is displayed in the message box shown in Figure 12.4.

> **NOTE**
>
> Line numbers are not part of the VBScript code. Line numbers have been inserted to make it easier to refer to various lines of code. This applies to all subsequent code listings with line numbers.

Listing 12.2. The `BtnHello_OnClick` subroutine.

```
1: Sub BtnHello_OnClick
2:  titleString = "World Wide Web Data Base Developer's Guide Using Visual Basic"
3:  helloString = "Hello world! Welcome to the fun filled "
4:  helloString = helloString & "world of VBScript programming!"
5:  MsgBox helloString, 0, titleString
6: End Sub
```

FIGURE 12.4.

The Hello World! dialog box.

The Time Dialog Box

The `BtnTime_OnClick` subroutine is very similar to the `BtnHello_OnClick` subroutine. The only difference is that rather than concatenating two strings, it concatenates a string with the result of a function. The `time` function returns the current time. As shown in Figure 12.5, line 3 of Listing 12.3 displays the current time in a dialog box. The `BtnTime_OnClick` subroutine is associated with the `OnClick` event of the `BtnTime` command button.

Listing 12.3. The `BtnTime_OnClick` subroutine.

```
1: Sub BtnTime_OnClick
2:  timeString = "The time is " & time
3:  MsgBox  timeString , 0, "Time Dialog Box"
4: End Sub
```

FIGURE 12.5.

The Time dialog box.

The Date Dialog Box

The Date dialog box displays the current date, as shown in Figure 12.6. As you can see in line 2 of Listing 12.4, the result of one function (`date`) can be used as an argument (input) of another function (`DateValue`).

Listing 12.4. The `BtnDate_OnClick` subroutine.

```
1: Sub BtnDate_OnClick
2:  dateString = "Today's date is " & DateValue(date)
3:  MsgBox  dateString , 0, "Date Dialog Box"
4: End Sub
```

FIGURE 12.6.
The Date dialog box.

For your reference, the full source code of the Hello World! application is listed in Listing 12.5.

Listing 12.5. The Hello World! Web page.

```
 1: <!--
 2: © 1996 Sanjaya Hettihewa
 3: http://www.NetInnovation.com/sanjaya
 4: !-->
 5:
 6: <HTML>
 7: <HEAD>
 8: <TITLE>VBScript Tutorial: Hello World!</TITLE>
 9: </HEAD>
10:
11: <BODY BGCOLOR="#FFFFFF" TEXT="#0000FF"
12:       LINK="#B864FF" VLINK="#670000" ALINK="#FF0000">
13:
14: <IMG SRC="vbscript.jpg"><P>
15:
16: <B><FONT FACE="Comic Sans MS" SIZE=6 COLOR=RED>
17: VBScript Tutorial: <FONT></B>
18: <I><FONT FACE="Comic Sans MS" SIZE=5 COLOR=BLUE>
19:  "Hello World!" </I><P><FONT>
20:
21: <form>
22: <INPUT TYPE=BUTTON VALUE="Please click here for message box"
23:        NAME="BtnHello">
24: <INPUT TYPE=BUTTON VALUE="Click here for current time"
25:        NAME="BtnTime">
26: <INPUT TYPE=BUTTON VALUE="Click here for current date"
27:        NAME="BtnDate">
28: </form>
29:
30: <SCRIPT LANGUAGE="VBScript">
31: <!-- To hide VBScript code from technologically challenged browsers
32:
33: Sub BtnHello_OnClick
34:  titleString = "World Wide Web Data Base Developer's Guide Using Visual Basic"
35:  helloString = "Hello world! Welcome to the fun filled "
36:  helloString = helloString & "world of VBScript programming!"
37:  MsgBox helloString, 0, titleString
38: End Sub
39:
40: Sub BtnTime_OnClick
41:  timeString = "The time is " & time
42:  MsgBox  timeString , 0, "Time Dialog Box"
43: End Sub
44:
```

```
45: Sub BtnDate_OnClick
46:  dateString = "Today's date is " & DateValue(date)
47:  MsgBox  dateString , 0, "Date Dialog Box"
48: End Sub
49: !-->
50: </SCRIPT>
51:
52: </BODY>
53:
54: </HTML>
```

The Structure of a VBScript Application

Before developing VBScript applications, it is important that you understand their structure. A typical VBScript application is composed of the following components:

- HTML code
- VBScript code delimiters
- VBScript subroutines

The HTML code may contain any number of valid HTML statements. Listing 12.6 contains valid HTML statements in every line of code except lines 23–42.

VBScript code delimiters separate VBScript code from the HTML code of a Web page. Lines 23–24 and 41–42 of Listing 12.6 are examples of VBScript code delimiters. Notice how the HTML comment tags <!-- and --> are used to enclose the VBScript source code. These tags prevent VBScript-challenged Web browsers from interpreting the VBScript code as part of the text of the Web page and displaying it on the browser window.

A VBScript application is composed of one or more VBScript subroutines. VBScript subroutines are defined using the following syntax:

```
Sub <name of subroutine>
...VBScript statements...
End Sub
```

VBScript subroutines are contained between the two HTML tags <SCRIPT LANGUAGE="VBS"> and </SCRIPT>. Certain events associated with various objects of a Web page trigger VBScript subroutines to perform certain tasks. For example, when a user submits a form, before the data is sent to the Web server for processing, a VBScript subroutine can examine and validate the data entered by the user.

See lines 25–30, 32–35, and 37–40 in Listing 12.6 for examples of VBScript subroutines.

Listing 12.6. A typical VBScript application.

```
 1: <HTML>
 2: <HEAD>
 3: <TITLE>VBScript Tutorial: Hello World!</TITLE>
 4: </HEAD>
 5:
 6: <BODY BGCOLOR="#FFFFFF" TEXT="#0000FF"
 7:      LINK="#B864FF" VLINK="#670000" ALINK="#FF0000">
 8:
 9: <B><FONT FACE="Comic Sans MS" SIZE=6 COLOR=RED>
10: VBScript Tutorial: <FONT></B>
11: <I><FONT FACE="Comic Sans MS" SIZE=5 COLOR=BLUE>
12:   "Hello World!" </I><P><FONT>
13:
14: <FORM>
15: <INPUT TYPE=BUTTON VALUE="Please click here for message box"
16:      NAME="BtnHello">
17: <INPUT TYPE=BUTTON VALUE="What time is it?"
18:      NAME="BtnTime">
19: <INPUT TYPE=BUTTON VALUE="What date is it?"
20:      NAME="BtnDate">
21: </FORM>
22:
23: <SCRIPT LANGUAGE=VBS>
24: <!-- To hide VBScript code from technologically challenged browsers
25: Sub BtnHello_OnClick
26:   titleString = "World Wide Web Data Base Developer's Guide Using Visual Basic"
27:   helloString = "Hello world! Welcome to the fun filled "
28:   helloString = helloString & "world of VBScript programming!"
29:   MsgBox helloString, 0, titleString
30: End Sub
31:
32: Sub BtnTime_OnClick
33:   timeString = "The time is " & time
34:   MsgBox  timeString , 0, "Time Dialog Box"
35: End Sub
36:
37: Sub BtnDate_OnClick
38:   dateString = "Today's date is " & DateValue(date)
39:   MsgBox  dateString , 0, "Date Dialog Box"
40: End Sub
41: -->
42: </SCRIPT>
43:
44: </BODY>
45: </HTML>
```

The Role of VBScript in Web Page Development

Prior to client-side scripting languages such as VBScript, Web pages were mostly static entities. Interactivity in a Web page required the execution of a CGI application on the server and the display of the results of the CGI application on the Web browser. Although this worked well for some applications, it tied up valuable network and system resources. VBScript allows Web page developers to create multimedia-rich, interactive Web pages with great ease while conserving network bandwidth and Web-server system resources. The next sections discuss the role of VBScript in Web page development.

Automation of ActiveX Controls

ActiveX controls are powerful components that can be used to build sophisticated Web applications. By themselves, ActiveX controls are capable of performing limited tasks. For example, the Microsoft Forms 2.0 ComboBox ActiveX control is capable of displaying a list of items, and the Microsoft Forms 2.0 Image ActiveX control is capable of displaying a graphical image. Although, by themselves, these two components perform very limited tasks, VBScript can be used to glue together the two ActiveX controls and develop a VBScript application that automates these ActiveX controls. For example, a VBScript subroutine can enable a user to change the image displayed in the Microsoft Forms 2.0 Image ActiveX control when an image is selected using the Microsoft Forms 2.0 ComboBox ActiveX control.

Dynamic Web Applications

VBScript is ideal for developing dynamic Web applications that immediately respond to user interactions. The Mr. Potato Head application discussed next is an example of a Web application that is better implemented with a client-side scripting language such as VBScript as opposed to a server-side CGI application.

The application shown in Figure 12.7 is the CGI version of Mr. Potato Head. After a user selects various physical attributes of Mr. Potato Head, that information is transmitted to the Web server. A CGI application creates a graphic of Mr. Potato Head according to the physical attributes selected by the user and transmits the image to the Web browser, as shown in Figure 12.8. The CGI implementation of Mr. Potato Head is network intensive because data must be transferred between the Web browser and the Web server each time a user makes a selection. The CGI implementation is also processor intensive for the Web server because it must process a CGI request and create a Mr. Potato Head each time the user changes the appearance of Mr. Potato Head.

RESOURCE

Browse `http://winnie.acsu.buffalo.edu/cgi-bin/potatoe-cgi` to experiment with the CGI version of Mr. Potato Head.

FIGURE 12.7.

Selecting physical properties of Mr. Potato Head.

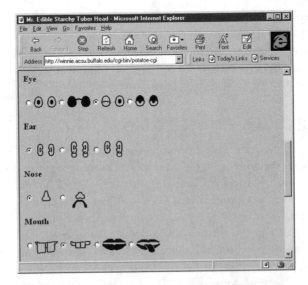

FIGURE 12.8.

Image of Mr. Potato Head created by a CGI application.

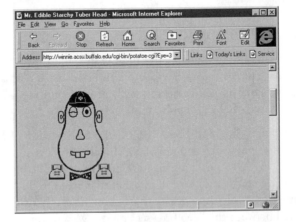

The ActiveX version of Mr. Potato Head (see Figure 12.9) addresses limitations of the CGI version of Mr. Potato Head. As you can see, the ActiveX version is more interactive and easier to use because it enables the user to change physical attributes of Mr. Potato Head on-the-fly without interacting with the Web server. Users can select physical attributes and drag-and-drop them on Mr. Potato Head. The ActiveX version of Mr. Potato Head is less processor intensive because it does not communicate with the Web server each time the user makes a change; it is less network intensive because all the processing is done locally.

RESOURCE

Browse the Web page at

`http://www.microsoft.com/ie/most/howto/layout/eggplant/begin.htm`

to experiment with the ActiveX version of Mr. Potato Head.

FIGURE 12.9.

The ActiveX version of Mr. Potato Head.

Error Checking

Error checking is a very important aspect of Web-application development. Lack of error checking usually results in flaky applications that are frustrating to use. Listed next are examples of how VBScript is used to perform error checking and to validate data entered by users.

■ A VBScript application can be used to ensure that all required data-entry fields of an HTML form are filled in.

■ A VBScript subroutine can be used to ensure that invalid data is not submitted for processing by a user. For example, a VBScript application can inform the user the date he entered (45/67/1996, for example) is invalid—without the expense of establishing an HTTP connection to a server-side CGI application.

■ VBScript can be used to verify that certain data is accurate before processing the data. For example, an online grocery-shopping application developed using VBScript can verify that the user really wants to order four eggs (because most people buy eggs by the dozen).

Manipulating Web Browser Objects

VBScript applications can modify Web-browser objects such as the background color of the current Web page. This feature is particularly useful when creating sophisticated Web applications. For example, a VBScript subroutine of a multiframe Web application can change the contents of several frames when a user selects a URL or presses a button.

VBScript Programming Tips

When developing applications using VBScript (or any other programming language), you should create source code that is easy to maintain and read. Messy source code often leads to buggy applications that are hard to maintain and debug. The following tips will help you develop VBScript applications that are easy to maintain.

Indent Source Code

While indentation does not affect the way a VBScript application is executed, the lack of indentation can make an application extremely difficult to debug and maintain. You should indent control structures of applications as shown in Listing 12.7—particularly if it is a complex or large VBScript application. Also, do not be afraid to add blank lines between VBScript code segments to enhance readability and clarity.

Listing 12.7. Indentation makes it easier to read VBScript source code.

```
Sub BtnEvaluate_OnClick
  IF (OperatorBox.Value = "?") THEN
     MsgBoxString = "A valid operator is required to carry out "
     MsgBoxString = MsgBoxString & "an evaluation."
     MsgBoxString = MsgBoxString & chr(10)
     MsgBoxString = MsgBoxString & "Valid operators are: +, -, *"
     MsgBox MsgBoxString , 48 , "Invalid operator!"
  ELSE
     IF (OperatorBox.Value = "+")  THEN
        answer = CDbl(Operand1Box.Value) + CDbl(Operand2Box.Value)
     ELSEIF (OperatorBox.Value = "-")  THEN
        answer = CDbl(Operand1Box.Value) - CDbl(Operand2Box.Value)
     ELSEIF (OperatorBox.Value = "*")  THEN
        answer = CDbl(Operand1Box.Value) * CDbl(Operand2Box.Value)
     End IF
     MsgBox answer , 64 , "Results of calculation"
     Operand1Box.Value = answer
     Operand2Box.Value = 0
  END IF
End Sub


Sub AddDigit ( digit )
  REM Just in case there are any preceeding zeros or spaces
```

```
Operand1Box.Value = CDbl (Operand1Box.Value)
IF ( OperatorBox.Value = "?") THEN
   IF ( Len ( Operand1Box.Value ) < 14 ) THEN
      Operand1Box.Value = Operand1Box.Value & digit
      Operand1Box.Value = CDbl (Operand1Box.Value)
   ELSE
      TooManyDigits
   END IF
ELSE
   IF ( Len ( Operand2Box.Value ) < 14 ) THEN
      Operand2Box.Value = Operand2Box.Value & digit
      Operand2Box.Value = CDbl (Operand2Box.Value)
   ELSE
      TooManyDigits
   END IF
END IF
End Sub
```

Code Continuation Character

The code continuation character is used to split relatively long VBScript statements. Generally, if a VBScript statement is over 80 characters long, you should use the code continuation character to break the VBScript statement into two or more lines. This makes it easier to indent the VBScript application for easy reading, as shown in Listing 12.8. The code continuation character is an underscore (_) placed at the end of the line to break a longer line, as demonstrated in lines 3–5 of Listing 12.8. Notice how the code continuation character makes the VBScript source code easier to read by preserving the indentation of the VBScript code.

Listing 12.8. VBScript code with the code continuation character.

```
 1: Sub OperatorBox_OnChange
 2:
 3:    IF (NOT((OperatorBox.Value = "+" ) OR _
 4:            (OperatorBox.Value = "-" ) OR _
 5:            (OperatorBox.Value = "*" ) OR _
 6:            (OperatorBox.Value = "?" ))) THEN
 7:       MsgString = "Do not type invalid characters "
 8:       MsgString = MsgString & "into the operator text box! "
 9:       MsgString = MsgString & chr(10)
10:       MsgString = MsgString & "The operator text box will now be reset."
11:       MsgString = MsgString & chr(10) & chr(10)
12:       MsgString = MsgString & "Valid input: +, -, *"
13:       MsgBox MsgString , 48 , "Invalid input detected!"
14:       OperatorBox.Value = "?"
15:    END IF
16:
17:  End Sub
```

Commenting Source Code

Commenting your source code can save hours or even days of application development time. In the software development industry, quite often, more time is spent maintaining existing applications than developing new applications. Commenting your source code makes it easier for you (or someone else) to understand your application and modify it without creating undue side effects. To insert a comment in a VBScript application, precede the comment with an apostrophe (') or the keyword Rem, like so:

```
' This is a comment
```

or

```
Rem This is a comment
```

> **TIP**
>
> When you are working on a complex application, use VBScript comments to document your code. Although you might understand how your application works when you are coding it, even after a few days, you might have a hard time determining how various algorithms in your application work.

Summary

VBScript is a powerful, light-weight scripting language for creating interactive, multimedia-rich, and ActiveX-enhanced Web applications. Before scripting languages such as VBScript, dynamic Web pages were created by server-side CGI applications. In some cases, the execution of server-side CGI applications is unnecessarily resource intensive. VBScript can be used in such cases to create dynamic content without any interaction with the Web server. If you are using Internet Information Server 3.0 or later, VBScript can also be used to develop server-side Web applications in the form of Active Server Web Pages.

13

ActiveX and ActiveX Controls

by Drew Kittel

The incorporation of <OBJECT>s in HTML 3.2 signaled the beginning of a new era in Web applications development. That might sound like a strong statement, but think about it for a moment. The <OBJECT> tag enables developers to incorporate virtually any object into a Web page. As a result, the possible ways to expand the functionality and interactiveness of your Web pages is becoming limited more by a developer's imagination than by technological barriers.

As you will begin to see in this chapter and later chapters, one of the easiest yet most powerful ways to extend the functionality of your Web applications is by using ActiveX technologies in general and ActiveX controls in particular. *ActiveX controls* are complex objects that can be inserted into your Web pages and manipulated and controlled by using VBScript. By using HTML <OBJECT>s and ActiveX controls with VBScript, developers quickly can incorporate components that suit their needs and build the type of powerful client-side applications that until just recently were simply not technologically possible.

What Is ActiveX?

ActiveX isn't any single thing; it is a set of new technologies unveiled by Microsoft in early 1996. Simply stated, ActiveX is a language-neutral set of integration technologies that enable software components to work together in a networked environment. This means that, regardless of the language used for development, the components still interoperate and communicate properly. ActiveX defines the packaging of software components and how those components should communicate. As a result, ActiveX components can be

■ Created in any language
■ Used with any application
■ Integrated with any scripting language
■ Run on any operating system

These qualities of ActiveX enable developers to easily create interactive applications and Websites using an open development framework.

The set of ActiveX technologies forms a framework for creating interactive Web content through the use of software components, scripts, and existing applications. Specifically, ActiveX technologies enable content providers and applications developers to easily create dynamic Web content and Web server extensions by using ActiveX controls, active scripting, and active document interfaces. You will learn more about these elements later in this chapter.

Why Use ActiveX?

Perhaps a better question would be, "Why wouldn't you use ActiveX?" This is a question for which we don't have a good answer. ActiveX simply enables developers to do too many good things to ignore. Consider these capabilities:

■ ActiveX controls and ActiveX scripting provide the infrastructure necessary to add language-neutral and tool-independent extensions to Web pages.

■ ActiveX controls enable developers to leverage existing OLE development tools and the investment they already have made in OLE.

■ ActiveX scripting enables you to drop any scripting engine into your application, enabling you to add behavior to Web pages in whatever scripting language you prefer.

■ ActiveX improves on the use of HTTP and FTP protocols from within applications through the use of IBind interfaces. These interfaces encapsulate a new protocol that supports binding to URLs dynamically from within your application. An application binds to a URL moniker, which then communicates through the appropriate protocol to activate the OLE object. This abstraction enables newly developed protocols to integrate neatly into your existing objects.

■ ActiveX descends from Win32, OLE, and OCX technologies and thus enables developers to build on their existing investments. Additionally, new development tools and environments such as Microsoft's ActiveX Control Pad and FrontPage provide native support for inserting ActiveX controls into your Web pages and then adding event handling routines using VBScript.

■ ActiveX enables you to leverage VB development investments by reusing existing controls and building new controls or modifying existing controls using VB 5 and VB 5 Control Creation Edition.

■ ActiveX enables Web applications developers to take advantage of the HTML 3.2 <OBJECT> tag by inserting ActiveX controls and manipulating them with VBScript. The result is extremely powerful client-side applications that were never before possible.

■ ActiveAnimation, ActiveMovie, and ActiveVRML provide a powerful foundation for highly interactive, animated, and multimedia-based content.

ActiveX Background and History

ActiveX is the result of a natural evolution and growth of existing Microsoft technologies. These technologies include the following controls:

■ *VBXs:* Visual Basic Controls, VBXs, are familiar to developers who have worked with earlier, 16-bit versions of Visual Basic.

■ *OCXs:* OLE Custom Controls, OCXs, are used by 32-bit versions of Visual Basic (4 and higher) as well as most other Windows programming languages. OCXs provide component integration based on OLE technology. (*OLE* is a set of standards dealing with communication between applications, registration, and storage issues.)

VBXs and OCXs enable you to quickly and easily expand the function of a program simply by inserting these components into your program to add needed functionality. As a result, the power of your programs can be expanded quickly, easily, and reliably by taking advantage of the communications, control, and functionality provided by these controls.

Because OCX technology is such a powerful programming model, it was only a matter of time before it was applied to Web applications development using rapidly maturing scripting languages such as VBScript. Technologically, however, an impediment still existed to fully applying this model to Web applications development. The steady evolution of controls in the Windows environment resulted in technologies that were somewhat bloated and platform specific:

■ OCXs carried considerable overhead involved in communicating according to the OLE protocols

■ OLE support was not available in many other environments

These problems were contrary to what was needed for controls that could be used on the Web:

■ Small, lightweight controls that are very functional, yet small and easily downloaded

■ Controls that can operate in a variety of operating environments

Microsoft addressed these needs by taking the best portions of OCX technologies and adding to them.

The resultant set of technologies was named ActiveX. Along the way, it was broadened significantly to incorporate not only ActiveX (formerly OCX) controls, but other technologies, such as active scripting and active documents central to Microsoft's Internet strategy.

ActiveX technologies are centered on the concept of treating applications, as well as traditional Web pages, as active documents that can be hosted in an all-encompassing shell. The idea is that the next generation Web browser will be capable of hosting nearly all interactions with the computer. In effect, the wide chasm that currently exists between operating system and browser will become much smaller as they are merged (at least in the Windows environment).

The Component Object Model (COM)

The *Component Object Model* (COM) is a client/server, object-based model that is the basic technical foundation cornerstone for ActiveX components. The model is designed to enable software components and applications to interact, even across networks, in a standard and uniform way. The COM standard is really partly a specification and partly an implementation:

■ The specification part defines the mechanisms for creating objects and for interobject communication. This specification part is language- and operating-system neutral, which means that as long as the standard is adhered to, development can take place in any language and on any operating system.

■ The COM library is the implementation part. The library provides a number of services that support the binary specification of COM.

Some characteristics of COM follow:

■ It is lightweight, fast, and supports versioning.

■ It is an open standard (language-neutral, development-tool neutral, and cross-platform capable). You easily can integrate COM objects for use in many languages, such as Java, Visual Basic, and C++.

■ ActiveX components are COM objects.

■ *Distributed COM* (DCOM) enables COM objects to interact across networks; it enables ActiveX components to run anywhere.

RESOURCE

You can find additional information, as well as complete COM and DCOM specifications, on Microsoft's OLE Development Website at

`http://www.microsoft.com/oledev/`

How COM Works

As stated previously, COM is a client/server-based model. When a client object wants to use the services provided by a server COM object, it uses one of the core services that are part of the COM library. The COM library is responsible for creating the server COM object and then establishing an initial connection between the client and server objects.

The connection is considered established when the server object returns a pointer to the client. This pointer points to an interface in the server object. The COM library now has completed its role in the process and leaves the objects to communicate directly with one another.

COM objects use interfaces to communicate with one another. An *interface* is a set of related functions that provide some sort of required services. Interfaces are language-independent. Any language capable of creating structures of pointers, as well as calling functions via pointers, can be used to implement COM interfaces.

COM objects can have multiple interfaces. After a client object obtains a pointer to a server object's interface, the client can invoke any of the functions or services provided by that interface. After an object finishes using services provided by the server object, the client simply informs the server that it is all done and terminates the connection between the two.

What Is a COM Interface?

COM interfaces are small sets of language-independent functions that are related in some way—logically or semantically. These interfaces provide the mechanism by which server objects make services available to client objects.

COM interfaces are given unique names by using *globally unique identifiers* (GUIDs). These identifiers are 128-bit numbers that are used to avoid name clashes that easily could occur by using human-readable names. GUIDs are guaranteed to be (nearly) unique by the COM specification. This specification indicates that 10 million GUIDs per second could be generated over the next 3,500 years (approximately) and that each of these GUIDs would be unique. This is unlikely to be the case with any human-readable form of naming.

COM server objects can supply more than one type of service; a separate interface is provided for each service. When a client object obtains a pointer from the server, it provides access only to the services provided by that specific interface. Clients can obtain pointers to other server interfaces through the IUnknown interface. IUnknown is a fundamental interface through which all other interfaces are derived, and it must be supported by all COM objects.

The IUnknown interface has a function called QueryInterface. Because all interfaces are derived from IUnknown, this function is present in all interfaces. QueryInterface has knowledge of all interfaces in the server object and therefore can provide a client with a pointer to any server interface to which it requires access.

COM Server Object Types

COM specifies three types of server objects:

■ *Remote servers:* Server objects that run on remote machines on a network. The server objects run in a different process space. These servers can be implemented as applications or as *dynamic link libraries* (DLLs).

■ *Local servers:* Server objects on the local machine. These objects run in a separate process space. This type of server is typically another application.

■ *In-process servers:* Server objects that are loaded into the client's process space. These are implemented via DLLs in Windows operating systems.

Regardless of where a server object is running (locally or remote), client objects always communicate with it in the same way. A client object accesses the services provided by a server object via a pointer to an interface on the server. For servers running in-process, the pointer can access the interface directly. For servers running locally or remotely, however, the pointer accesses a COM-supplied proxy server running in the same process space as the client. The proxy then generates a call to the local or remote server object on behalf of the client. COM server objects use a stub object supplied by COM. This stub receives calls from client objects and translates these to calls on the appropriate interface.

COM Foundation Components

COM primarily is concerned with the business of creating objects and facilitating standard communication between those objects. However, COM also provides a few other fundamental system-level objects:

- *Uniform data transfer:* COM defines standard interfaces and mechanisms by which clients and servers communicate and exchange information. Clients can use these interfaces to have the server inform it when data it receives has changed in some way. COM also defines data structures that are used to describe the data (and the medium through which it passes) passed between client and server.

- *Persistent storage objects:* COM defines a set of standard interfaces that enable other objects to save information about their state to a persistent storage device. This information is stored in hierarchically structured files that enable transactions and incremental access. Applications also can view the contents of this file and access named elements within it.

- *Persistent intelligent names (monikers):* COM defines a set of standard interfaces for the use of monikers. Instances of particular objects can be given names (monikers) so that clients can reconnect to the same instance of that object later. The exact same state is persistent across these connections. Operations also can be given names so that clients can repeatedly perform the operation by using the name only.

The ActiveX Object Model

The ActiveX Object Model consists of the following two pieces, both of which are in-process (DLL-based) COM types:

- The *Microsoft Hypertext Markup Language* (MSHTML) object
- The MSHTML Viewer component

All interfaces defined in the ActiveX Object Model are dual interfaces. In dual interfaces, the objects inherit and follow some simple rules. Therefore, they can be used by late-bind OLE Automation controllers (through the use of IDispatch::GetIdsOfNames and IDispatch::Invoke). They also can be used by early-bind controllers (for example, using a vtable).

The MSHTML Viewer Component

MSHTML is the HTML viewer part of the Microsoft Internet Explorer 3.0 (IE 3.0) browser. It can be hosted in both OLE document object containers and OLE control containers. It also can be used as a standalone OLE Automation component.

MSHTML implements the OLE Automation Object Model described by the HTML Scripting Object Model. With this object model, you can develop rich, interactive, multimedia HTML content. Client-side scripts (such as VBScript running in the browser), as well as externally running programs (such as VB 4 and VB 5), can use the object model.

The IExplorer Browser Object

The IExplorer Browser object is an in-process COM server. The IExplorer Browser is the core of what users see when using Internet Explorer 3.0. The Browser object also is a document object container. This container can host any document objects (such as Word, Excel, and even HTML) with the added benefit that it fully supports hyperlinks to any document type. Because it is a COM class object that implements all the interfaces needed to be used as an OLE control, the IExplorer Browser is itself an OLE control.

The IExplorer's `IShellExplorer` interface is the primary OLE Automation–compatible interface exposed by the IExplorer Browser OLE control. The `IInternetExplorer` interface is a superset of the `IShellExplorer` interface. It can be contained within any OLE control container, such as Internet Explorer 3.0, which raises some interesting possibilities. Imagine the added functionality you could give users by enabling them to embed and control a browser from within your Web applications (a browser-within-a-browser) as well as your VB applications.

ActiveX Controls

ActiveX controls are reusable software components developed by software vendors as well as VB developers like yourself. You easily can add these controls to Web pages by using the `<OBJECT>` tag. When used with VBScript, these controls can dramatically increase the interactiveness, functionality, and usefulness of your Website.

Straight COM objects combined with a few ActiveX interfaces can become Internet-enabled without modifying the existing object. You can create ActiveX controls from a variety of existing object types, such as the following:

- Objects that expose custom interfaces as well as the `IUnknown` interface
- OLE Automation servers that expose the `IDispatch`/dual interfaces
- Existing OLE controls (OCXs)
- OLE objects that use monikers

ActiveX controls provide a means of instantly adding new and dynamic functions to Web applications. These controls are the building blocks for client- or server-driven dynamic content. Controls exist that enable you to integrate virtually any media type (such as sound, video, animation, interactive input devices, and so on) into your Web applications. Later sections of this chapter and subsequent chapters present a variety of controls that you easily can obtain and implement rapidly. The use of these controls will be demonstrated in several examples.

ActiveX Scripting Services

ActiveX scripting defines a syntax- and language-independent architecture that enables you to add scripting and OLE Automation capabilities to programs. ActiveX scripting provides the necessary platform for developing script engines.

ActiveX scripting components can be grouped into two major categories:

■ *ActiveX scripting engines:* Scripting engines are OLE COM objects that support IOLEScript interfaces, with at least one of the IPersist interfaces and an optional IOleScriptParse interface. In simpler terms, the scripting engine is basically the language to be executed on the ActiveX scripting host. Of course, the most widely available scripting engine today is VBScript; other potential engines you are likely to see in the future include Perl, Lisp, and Delphi.

■ *ActiveX scripting hosts:* Hosts provide a platform on which to run ActiveX scripting engines. Currently, Internet Explorer 3.0 is the most common ActiveX scripting host. It provides an interpreter platform for VBScript. Other potential scripting hosts include other Web browsers (such as Netscape with the use of a plug-in), Web servers (server-based scripting such as that provided by Active Server Pages), and various Internet authoring tools.

ActiveX Documents

ActiveX documents are based on OLE document objects (DocObjects). The DocObjects technology is a set of extensions to OLE documents; it is the compound document technology provided by OLE. Documents that conform to the ActiveX standard can be opened within ActiveX document containers. In other words, they can be viewed within Internet Explorer 3.0. Documents that conform to the ActiveX standard follow:

■ Microsoft Office Binder
■ Microsoft Internet Explorer
■ Future Windows shells

Note that Binder is a sophisticated viewer capable of hosting a variety of documents so that you can create, edit, save, print, and view different kinds of information collectively. Internet browsers (such as IE 3) that adopt Binder technology not only facilitate the presentation of Internet-based information (such as HTML-based Web pages), but they also enable the browser to present documents from Microsoft Office and Microsoft Office–compatible applications. In the future, you will be able to view, navigate, and distribute virtually any document type (whether it is local or remote) by using browsers that adhere to ActiveX and DocObject container standards.

The ActiveX Server Framework

The ActiveX Server framework is based on the Microsoft *Internet Information Server* (IIS), which is an integrated component of Windows NT Server. The framework enables Web developers to take advantage of the powerful Microsoft BackOffice suite of products (which includes Microsoft SQL Server and Microsoft Exchange Server). The ActiveX Server framework consists of ActiveX Server scripting and ActiveX Server controls. ActiveX Server scripting can be written with any scripting language, including VBScript, Perl, C, or JavaScript. The CGI also is supported under the ActiveX Server framework. Through CGI, you can extend the functionality of your Web applications by giving clients access to services (such as databases) that they ordinarily would not be able to access.

Using ActiveX Controls in Your Applications

Remember that ActiveX controls enable you to rapidly improve the quality and functionality of your Web applications simply by embedding prepackaged objects in your Web pages. By adding VBScript programs to control these objects and handle various events, you can develop interactive and highly functional client-side applications that simply were not possible before. This section presents a few basics on using objects in your applications. Examples in later chapters discuss using ActiveX controls in greater detail.

Three primary sources exist for ActiveX controls. Microsoft provides many ActiveX controls with IE and a development tool called the ActiveX Control Pad. Table 13.1 summarizes these controls. Third-party vendors produce a dazzling number of ActiveX controls designed to perform specific tasks. Note that the control you need often already exists and can be cheaper to purchase than to write, debug, and maintain yourself. The third source for controls is you (and other benevolent developers who make their controls freely available on the Internet). Why would you write an ActiveX control? Sometimes you want to integrate some type of functionality into your program, but you cannot locate a control on the market that adequately meets your needs. In these cases, you have to do it yourself. Fortunately, VB 5 and VB 5 Control Creation Edition provide everything you need (including control-creation wizards) to develop your own controls.

> **RESOURCE**
>
> Although Microsoft has hinted that ActiveX will make its way into the UNIX world, ActiveX technologies currently are geared primarily toward the Microsoft environment. Internet Explorer 3.0 currently is the only Web browser that offers native support for ActiveX. NCompass Labs, however, has developed plug-ins for Netscape Navigator that provide the capability to use ActiveX controls, VBScript, and ActiveX documents with Navigator.

You can find more information on NCompass Labs and trial downloads at
`http://www.ncompasslabs.com/`

Controls Available with IE 3.0 and the ActiveX Control Pad

An increasing number of ActiveX controls are available for developers to use in their Web applications. Although a good number of these must be purchased from third-party vendors, Microsoft provides free a fair number of controls. Table 13.1 outlines those controls that ship with IE 3.0 and the ActiveX Control Pad.

Table 13.1. Standard ActiveX controls that ship with Internet Explorer and the ActiveX Control Pad.

Control	*Function*
The following controls ship with all installations (minimum, typical, and complete) of Internet Explorer.	
Web Browser	Provides a Web browser control (based on IE 3.0) that can display HTML pages, ActiveX controls, and ActiveX documents. It can be embedded within HTML documents to provide a browser within a browser.
Timer	Provides a timer control that can be programmed to execute actions/scripts at set time intervals.
Marquee	Provides a control built into Internet Explorer that scrolls any HTML file in a horizontal or vertical direction. The amount and delay of scrolling are configurable.
The following control ships with the complete installation of Internet Explorer.	
ActiveMovie	Displays streaming and non-streaming media (video, sound, and synchronized images with sound).

continues

Table 13.1. continued

Control	Function
The following controls ship with the complete installation of Internet Explorer as well as the ActiveX Control Pad.	
`HTML Layout`	Supports new HTML extensions published by the World Wide Web Consortium (W3C) that enable objects to be positioned exactly on a Web page. It displays 2D HTML regions inside IE 3.0 using new extensions to HTML.
`MS Forms 2.0 Label`	Creates basic text labels.
`MS Forms 2.0 Textbox`	Provides multiline text-entry and text-display windows.
`MS Forms 2.0 Combo Box`	Enables users to choose options from a drop-down list.
`MS Forms 2.0 List Box`	Enables users to choose options from a scrollable list.
`MS Forms 2.0 CheckBox`	Enables users to check an option.
`MS Forms 2.0 Option Button`	Enables users to choose between multiple options.
`MS Forms 2.0 Toggle Button`	Provides a two-state toggle button.
`MS Forms 2.0 Command Button`	Provides a basic pushbutton control.
`MS Forms 2.0 Tabstrip`	Enables users to select multiple pages via tabs. A nice real-estate-saving control.
`MS Forms 2.0 ScrollBar`	Provides basic horizontal and vertical scrollbars.
`MS Forms 2.0 Spin Button`	Provides a button that can be "pushed" up or down.
`MS ActiveX Image`	Progressively displays images in metafile, `.JPG`, `.GIF`, `.BMP`, or wavelet formats.
`MS ActiveX Hotspot`	Adds transparent hotspots to the HTML layout control.

Microsoft's ActiveX Control Component Gallery

In addition to the standard controls available with Internet Explorer and the ActiveX Control Pad, Microsoft makes several other controls available on its ActiveX Gallery Website. Table 13.2 lists the standard set of controls available. Note that this listing represents a minimal subset of the rapidly growing number of controls available from Microsoft and third-party vendors. This Website also provides links to several third-party controls available for downloading and evaluation.

Table 13.2. Standard Microsoft ActiveX controls available from the ActiveX Gallery Website (`http://www.microsoft.com/activex/gallery`).

Control	Function
Animated Button	Displays various frame sequences of an .AVI file, depending on the button state. It uses the Windows Animation common control. The .AVI file must be RLE compressed or 8-bit compressed.
Chart	Enables you to draw various types of charts with different styles. Great for providing graphical representations of data, such as that derived from database queries.
Gradient	Shades a given area with a range of colors (making the transition from a specified color to another specified color).
Label	Enables you to render and display text at any specified angle or along user-defined curves. The control supports Click, Change, MouseDown, MouseOver, and MouseUp events.
Menu	Enables developers to place menu buttons on the page that brings up a menu with the standard menu look and feel. Generates events that can be used in VBScripts.
Popup Menu	Displays a pop-up menu in response to the PopUp method being called. Generates an event after a menu item is clicked.
Popup Window	Displays a specified HTML document in a pop-up window. Can be used to provide tool tips or preview links.
Preloader	Downloads a file from a specified URL and puts it into the cache. Invisible at runtime and starts downloading when enabled. When the download finishes, the control fires a Complete event.
Stock Ticker	Displays continuously changing data by downloading the specified URL at regular intervals. The data can be in a text or .XRT format.

continues

Table 13.2. continued

Control	Function
View Tracker	Generates events whenever the control enters or leaves the viewing area. Developers can use this control to automatically modify properties or functionality on the page based on sectional input.

RESOURCE

The Microsoft ActiveX Component Gallery at

`http://www.microsoft.com/activex/gallery`

has numerous links to Microsoft and third-party controls available for downloading and evaluation.

Additionally, the site at

`http://www.browserwatch.com`

provides several links to controls developed by software vendors and other independent control developers.

Registering a Control

When ActiveX controls (OCX files) are installed on your system, they are registered with the operating system database known as the *Registry*. All ActiveX controls are referenced in Web pages by their unique class identifier (CLSID). Registering an OCX is a matter of placing this CLSID into the Registry. When you load the OCX file into an ActiveX Chart object, for example, the following CLSID is written into your system's Registry:

`FC25B780-75BE-11CF-8B01-444553540000`

This CLSID is called whenever a Web page needs to instantiate an instance of this Chart control.

Adding Controls to HTML Documents

Let me preface this section by stating that I don't really advocate adding controls to your HTML pages by hand. It is simply too easy to mistype something—especially CLSID strings. Additionally, a variety of tools exist that support easy insertion of controls into your documents; these tools include the Microsoft ActiveX Control Pad, Microsoft FrontPage, and SoftQuad's HotMeTaL product. I highly recommend that you at least download and learn how to use the

ActiveX Control Pad (available at the Microsoft site `http://www.microsoft.com/workshop/author/cpad/`). The ActiveX Control Pad not only enables you to easily insert controls, but it also provides a text editor for editing HTML; an object editor for easily inserting controls (and their hideously long CLSIDs); a page editor to create HTML layouts (you'll see more information on these layouts in later chapters); and a script wizard that provides easy access to a control's methods, properties, and events.

With those capabilities in mind, you still should understand how an ActiveX control is represented in your HTML. ActiveX controls are placed in HTML by using the <OBJECT> tag, which also includes the control's CLSID and other information (such as height and width) as tag attributes. You can set various property values for the control by including <param> tags within the <OBJECT>, </OBJECT> tag pair. ActiveX controls also have sets of properties and methods that can be set and reacted to by using VBScript. Listing 13.1 shows how you can place an ActiveX Label control on your page. The VBScript code shows how the Label's Click event is handled and used to display a simple dialog box.

Listing 13.1. Placing an ActiveX Label control on your page.

```
<OBJECT ID="lblCat"
  CLASSID="CLSID:978C9E23-D4B0-11CE-BF2D-00AA003F40D0"
  STYLE="TOP:104pt;LEFT:6pt;WIDTH:71pt;HEIGHT:17pt;ZINDEX:6;">
        <PARAM NAME="ForeColor" VALUE="16711680">
        <PARAM NAME="BackColor" VALUE="16777215">
        <PARAM NAME="Caption" VALUE="Categories:">
        <PARAM NAME="Size" VALUE="2505;600">
        <PARAM NAME="FontName" VALUE="Arial">
        <PARAM NAME="FontEffects" VALUE="1073741825">
        <PARAM NAME="FontHeight" VALUE="240">
        <PARAM NAME="FontCharSet" VALUE="0">
        <PARAM NAME="FontPitchAndFamily" VALUE="2">
        <PARAM NAME="FontWeight" VALUE="700">
</OBJECT>

Sub lblCat_Click()
   MsgBox "You clicked my label!"
End Sub
```

As you can see from this example, it is worth your while to learn how to use the ActiveX Control Pad or some other tool instead of typing all this for every control you decide to use.

Installing and Displaying Controls

In the scheme of things, not too many of the existing ActiveX controls are included with Internet Explorer or the ActiveX Control Pad. Instead, most controls are third-party controls or controls that you've developed. The upshot of this is that the controls don't initially exist on your users' machines, and in some way must exist for your users to get the controls and register them in their system's Registry.

Fortunately, ActiveX controls are designed so that if they don't already exist on the user's machine, they can be obtained from the source. This capability is supported by adding the CODEBASE attribute to the <OBJECT> tag when the control is added to your HTML. This attribute specifies the URL at which the control is located. When Internet Explorer encounters CODEBASE in an HTML page, for example, it checks the system Registry to see whether the control already is registered. If it isn't, the URL is used to download and register this control (subject to security settings on the user's system). After this one-time download, the control is maintained locally in an object cache on the user's machine.

The following code snippet illustrates how the CODEBASE tag is used to obtain a specific version of a control from Microsoft:

```
<OBJECT ID=iexr2 TYPE="application/x-oleobject"
CLSID="clsid:0CA4A620-8E3D-11CF-A3A9-00A0C9034920"
CODEBASE="http://activex.micorosoft.com/controls/iexplorer/
➥iestock.ocx#Version=4,70,0,1161">
```

Summary

This chapter gave you an overview of ActiveX and a glimpse at how this set of technologies gives you the opportunity to rapidly and easily improve the quality, interactiveness, and functionality of your Web applications. You now should understand the important role that ActiveX technologies will play in the future of Web applications development.

The chapter began with a brief overview of what ActiveX is and how it evolved from earlier Microsoft technologies, such as OLE and custom controls. You then looked at the Component Object Model (COM) and gained some insight into how ActiveX components actually are built on this client/server object model. Next, you examined the ActiveX Object Model. The main components of ActiveX technology were outlined: ActiveX controls, ActiveX scripting, ActiveX documents, and the ActiveX Server framework.

The remainder of the chapter was dedicated to ActiveX controls. You were introduced to a number of standard controls that are readily available from Microsoft. You also learned how these controls are registered on your system, added to Web pages, and distributed via the Web.

14

Developing Advanced Forms for Database Access and Application Interfaces

by Drew Kittel

Since mid-1996, technologies geared towards Internet and Web applications have been improving by leaps and bounds. With the introduction of the HTML 3.2 <OBJECT> tag, ActiveX controls, and client-side Visual Basic scripting within browsers such as Microsoft Internet Explorer 3.0, developers now have the tools to begin developing fully interactive Web applications. With the availability of these new technologies, the Web browser is rapidly becoming a full-fledged GUI development environment.

The goal of this chapter is to show you how you can leverage these technologies to develop HTML form interfaces for your Web database and other applications. You will be able to develop applications that are far more interactive and functional, as well as more aesthetically pleasing.

To start, you learn how VB scripts are attached to HTML documents and invoked by various events. Next, you discover how Microsoft's Internet Explorer browser is really composed of a hierarchical set of component objects (such as links, frames, scripts, forms, and object elements), each with its own set of events, properties, and methods that you can access through your VB scripts. You'll see just how powerful this object model for scripting is for developing dynamic user interfaces.

The final section is dedicated to applying the material you learned in earlier sections. In this section you learn more about how to format form objects and content using HTML tables as well as the HTML layout control—a nifty ActiveX control that provides fine placement of objects on a page. This is followed by two examples, a search engine query form and a database query form, which illustrate how VBScript, ActiveX, and HTML objects can be used to create application user interfaces, complete with interactive responses to user actions, input validation, and submission of forms via VBScript.

Using VBScript Within HTML

In Chapter 12, "Introduction to Client-Side Web Application Development Using VBScript," you were briefly introduced to the use of VBScript within HTML forms. However, the methods in which VB scripts are attached to your HTML documents and forms was only touched upon briefly. In this section, you learn about the three ways in which scripts are attached to and invoked from HTML documents:

- Using the <SCRIPT> tag
- Using attributes of HTML elements that support scripts
- Using custom URL types

Using the <SCRIPT> Tag

The <SCRIPT> tag is an element that is used for embedding scripts, such as VBScript or JScript, in an HTML document. Using the <SCRIPT> tag, the full source code for a script or scripts can be included within the body of the HTML document. Additionally, the SRC (that is, SRC=URL) attribute of the `<SCRIPT>` tag can be used to reference scripts outside of, or external to, the body of the document. This allows the use of URLs that point to a script from some other location.

The following simple script illustrates how a document's `write` method can be invoked to place a string into the current HTML document at the location of the script:

```
<HTML>
<BODY>
<SCRIPT language="VBScript">
<!--
   document.write("Welcome to Omniscient!")
-->
</SCRIPT>
 ... body of HTML document ...
 ... other <SCRIPT>s as required ...
</BODY>
</HTML>
```

Here are a few things to note about how `<SCRIPT>` is evaluated when a document is loaded:

- All code is executed at load time in the order in which it appears in the document. This means that if the script references an object, say an ActiveX control, any reference to that object must appear after the object has been defined. Therefore, it is often common to see scripts that reference objects in a document attached to the bottom of the document.

- The `write` method for a document can be used to insert text and objects, such as HTML intrinsic controls or ActiveX controls. In keeping with the preceding item in this list, these objects can be referenced only in script blocks which follow the script that defined them. You can refer to and copy references to objects that result from code downloads.

- Any method for an object can be invoked, but only after the object has been downloaded.

Scripts as Attributes of HTML Elements

Scripts can also be added to documents by using attributes of HTML elements (such as forms, buttons, and links) that support scripts. In other words, attributes are used to bind or associate specific scripts with specific events that can occur on the document. When an event occurs on the document (say, the user clicks a button on a form), the script that has been associated with the event is executed.

CAUTION

This method works for HTML elements such as links, buttons, and forms, but it does *not* work for items that were inserted using the `<OBJECT>` tag.

In the following example, a button's `onClick` event is associated with the script `btnPress`, by including `onClick=btnPress` as an attribute to the `<INPUT>` tag used to create the button. Similar syntax can be used to bind events with scripts in `<FORM>` and `<BODY>` tags as well. When the button is pressed, the script named `btnPress` is executed to display a `MsgBox` dialog to the user:

```
<FORM NAME="myForm">
   <INPUT TYPE="button" NAME="myButton" VALUE="pressed"
   onClick="btnPress" LANGUAGE="VBScript">
</FORM>

<SCRIPT LANGUAGE="VBScript">
sub btnPress
   MsgBox "You pressed my Button!"
end sub
</SCRIPT>
```

Note that the LANGUAGE attribute was specified with the input tag. If not explicitly stated, the language of the most recently encountered script block would be used; if none were encountered previously, JScript would be the default.

An alternative syntax can also be used to associate an event with a script. The general form of the syntax is

```
<SCRIPT FOR="object" EVENT="event" LANGAUAGE="language">
```

> **NOTE**
>
> Unlike the syntax used in the previous example, this method *can* be used for any named elements and any elements inserted using the `<OBJECT>` tag.

The following example illustrates the use of this alternative syntax:

```
<FORM NAME="myForm">
   <INPUT TYPE="button" NAME="myButton" VALUE="pressed">
   <SCRIPT FOR=myButton EVENT="onClick" LANGUAGE="VBScript">
      MsgBox "You pressed my Button!"
   </SCRIPT>
</FORM>
```

Using Custom URLs

It is also possible to invoke a script through the use of the anchor (`<A>`) tag combined with a custom URL type. This allows the execution of some script code when a hyperlink is clicked by a user. The general syntax used is

```
<A HREF="script-engine:script-code">link_content</A>
```

where `script-engine` represents the scripting engine to use and `script-code` is a string that evaluates to script code supported by the engine. The code is executed (in the context of the current page) at the time the URL is evaluated (that is, when the link is clicked).

The following example illustrates how JScript is used to display an Alert dialog when a link is pressed:

```
<A HREF="javascript:alert(document.title)">
Display title of current docuement</A>
```

> **CAUTION**
>
> Note that as of this writing, this syntax is *not* supported for VBScript in Microsoft Internet Explorer. In other words, the syntax does not support processing of VBScript in the URL itself. It is possible, however, to use the syntax to reference VBScript functions using the syntax
>
> ```
> <A HREF="javascript:VBScriptFunctionName()">link_content</A>.
> ```
>
> The following example illustrates how this syntax can be used to reference a VBScript function that displays a MsgBox dialog when the user clicks a link:
>
> ```
> <HTML>
> <!--
> <SCRIPT language="VBScript">
> SUB myVBFunction( )
>     MsgBox("You called a VBScript via JScript")
> END SUB
> -->
> </SCRIPT>
>
> <BODY>
>     This is a <A HREF="JavaScript:myVBFunction()">Display a VBScript MsgBox</A>
> </BODY>
> </HTML>
> ```

The Microsoft Internet Explorer Object Model for Scripting

In this section you learn about the structure of the scripting object model for Microsoft's Internet Explorer (IE) Web browser. The scripting object model provides a structured framework for manipulating component objects of the browser interface. It also provides the capability to embed applications developed using VBScript (note that the IE object model is also accessible from any scripting language, such as JScript, that is compatible with the ActiveX scripting framework).

So what does this mean to someone developing forms and user interfaces for database and other Web applications? Essentially, it means that you are no longer constrained by the limitations of HTML forms, interfaces, and server-side programs. Instead, Internet Explorer can now be viewed more as a graphical user interface development environment—not as sophisticated or rich in functionality as the X Window System for example, but an increasingly capable development environment nonetheless. You are now provided direct programmatic access to the objects, properties, and methods that make up Internet Explorer as well as the very elements, such as HTML form objects and ActiveX controls, used to create database query forms and application user interfaces.

It is now possible to develop user interfaces that integrate ActiveX controls, respond to user actions and events generated by form elements, implement client-side programs (for instance VBScript scripts run by an interpreter within the browser) to perform functions such as input validation, and even perform runtime changes to the characteristics of the interface itself. This type of user interface functionality is becoming increasingly commonplace, and days of using static HTML forms for Web applications are slipping quickly into history.

Figure 14.1 illustrates graphically the hierarchical nature of the scripting object model and depicts the objects to be presented in following sections. Note that the dotted lines following objects in this illustration indicate that multiple instances of that object type may exist. Here's a list of these objects:

- Window
- Document
- Link
- Anchor
- Form
- Element
- Script
- Frame
- History
- Navigator
- Location

FIGURE 14.1.

The Internet Explorer scripting object model and object hierarchy.

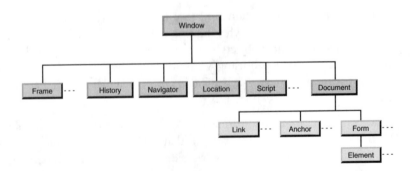

Table 14.1 summarizes the methods, events, and properties for the IE scripting object model components illustrated in Figure 14.1. These methods, events, and properties are all accessible to developers creating database forms and application user interfaces. They provide a rich set of functionality that can be tapped to created very complex and sophisticated interfaces for Web applications.

Table 14.1. A summary of the methods, events, and properties for each object in the Internet Explorer object scripting model.

IE Object	Methods/Event Handlers	Events	Properties
Window	alert, confirm, prompt, open, close, setTimeout, clearTimeout, navigate onLoad and onUnload event handlers	onLoad, onUnLoad	name, parent, opener, self, top, location, defaultStatus, status, frames, history, navigator, document
Document	write, writeLn, open, close, clear	N/A	linkColor, aLinkColor, vLinkColor, bgColor, fgColor, anchors, links, forms, location, lastModified, title, cookie, referrer
Link	onMouseMove, onMouseOver and onClick event handlers	onMouseMove, onMouseOver, onClick	href, protocol, host, hostname, port, pathname, search, hash, target
Anchor	N/A	N/A	name
Form	submit	onSubmit	action, encoding, method, target, elements
Element	click, focus, blur, select onClick, onFocus, onBlur, onChange and onSelect event handlers	onClick, onFocus, onBlur, onChange, onSelect	form, name, value, defaultValue, checked, defaultChecked, length, options, selectedIndex
History	back, forward, go	N/A	length
Navigator	N/A	N/A	appCodeName, appName, appVersion, userAgent
Location	N/A	N/A	href, protocol, host, hostname, port, pathname, search, hash

RESOURCE

An in-depth document on the IE object scripting model can be found at the Microsoft Website at

`http://www.microsoft.com/intdev/sdk`

In the `Programming Contents` frame, scroll down to the section for `ActiveX SDK docs` and click the `Scripting Obj Model` link. This will take you to a location where you can read the documentation online or download the full 70+ page document in `.zip` format. This document contains a wealth of information, including examples, on all the events, event handlers, methods, and properties summarized in Table 14.1.

The IE Window Object

As illustrated in Figure 14.1, the window object is the top-level object in the IE scripting object model and, as such, represents the IE window and its methods and properties. All windows contain the following component objects:

- Document—This is the document in the current window.
- Script—This is the scripting function. It is defined using the SCRIPT element in the window scope.
- Frame—An array of contained frame windows. Every frame is a window having its own properties (including a document).
- History—The history object for the current window. The history object is used to access the history list from the browser.
- Navigator—The navigator object for the current window. This object contains information regarding the browser application.
- Location—The location object for the current window. This object provides information regarding the location of the window's URL.

Naming a Window

Before a window can be accessed by name, it must first be given a name. This can be accomplished in a couple of ways. The following code creates a window with a name frame1 (with contents a.htm) by using the <FRAMESET> element:

```
<FRAMESET COLS = "200, *" FRAMEBORDER=0>
  <FRAME NAME= "frame1" SRC="a.htm">
  <FRAME NAME= "frame2" SRC="b.htm">
</FRAMESET>
```

The following snippet of code accomplishes the same thing by creating the window with a URL that uses the TARGET attribute:

```
<A HREF="a.htm" TARGET = "frame1" Click here to see a.htm in frame "frame1".</A>
```

One other method for giving a window a name is to use the window's open method, as follows, to create a window named foo (with contents a.htm):

```
<SCRIPT Language="VBScript">
window.open ("a.htm", "foo");
</SCRIPT>
```

> **CAUTION**
>
> As of Internet Explorer 3.0, the use of the open method is still not supported. It is expected to be supported in future versions of IE, however.

Referencing Window Object Properties and Methods

Window object properties and methods can be referenced directly by scripts while in the window scope. For example, it is possible to reference the window's name within a script using

```
winname = name
```

rather than using

```
winname = window.name
```

Similarly, the following script will obtain the name of the current page and display the name by invoking the window's alert method:

```
<SCRIPT LANGUAGE="VBScript">
    ...
    mystring = name
    alert mystring
    ...
</SCRIPT>
```

Finally, the properties of other window objects can be accessed without explicitly mentioning the window. The following code will obtain the name of the current window's parent:

```
<SCRIPT LANGUAGE="VBScript">
    ...
    mystring = parent.name
    ...
</SCRIPT>
```

Adding Scripts to a Window Event

Scripts can be added to window events by adding a script for either the onLoad or onUnLoad events in the <BODY> tag at the top of a page. Here's an example:

```
<HTML>
...
<BODY Language="VBScript" onLoad="MyProc">
...
```

```
<SCRIPT language="VBScript">
...
Sub MyProc
    MsgBox "This is sub MyProc"
End Sub
...
</SCRIPT>
....
</BODY>
</HTML>
```

Using this code results in the procedure `MyProc` being called when the page is loaded.

Calling Scripts from One Window to Another

It is possible to call scripts from one window object to another. For example,

```
top.my_script()
```

will execute the script `my_script()` in the topmost window.

The IE Document Object

As illustrated in Figure 14.1, the document object is the next level below the window object in the IE scripting object model. The document object reflects the current HTML document in the browser (as well as objects on the page such as links, forms, ActiveX controls, buttons, and so on.) All document objects contain the following component objects:

- ■ Link—An array of hyperlinks on the given document object
- ■ Anchor—An array of anchors on the given document object
- ■ Form—An array of forms on the given object

NOTE

Note that the existence of the forms array implies the capability to have multiple forms on a page; this is indeed possible. In fact, you could have scripts associated with one form that react to user actions and subsequently modify attributes of controls on another form. For example, several controls (such as checkboxes) have a property called `enabled`. It is conceivable that you may want to desensitize (that is, disable) such a control on one form due to a selection by the user on another form. This is easily implemented using code such as

```
Document.form(1).mycheckbox.enabled = False
```

within an event handler associated with the form represented by the array entry `Document.form(0)`. You could use similar methods to perform other runtime modifications to forms, such as adding or removing entries to a pull-down menu control.

Accessing Document Object Properties

A quick glance at Figure 14.1 reveals that scripts live within the window object, *not* the document object. Therefore, in order to access document properties, it is necessary that script developers use the syntax

`document.property`

to access the desired property. For example, a document's title can be obtained using the following script:

```
<SCRIPT LANGUAGE="VBScript">
   ...
   mystring = document.title
   ...
</SCRIPT>
```

Similarly, the background color of the HTML page could be set using the following script:

```
<SCRIPT LANGUAGE="VBScript">
   document.bgColor = "Blue"
</SCRIPT>
```

Accessing Forms Within a Document Object

There are two ways in which a form can be accessed in a document: reference by name or through the form array. The following example illustrates how a form (Form1) is addressed by name:

```
<FORM NAME="Form1">
    <INPUT TYPE="button" NAME="Button1" VALUE="Press" onClick="pressed">
</FORM>
```

For this case, a script could then access a button object (Button1) on the form by referring to form1 by name, as follows:

```
<SCRIPT LANGUAGE="VBScript">
sub pressed
   document.Form1.Button1.value = "Pressed"
end sub
</SCRIPT>
```

Alternatively, the button object (Button1) could be accessed by accessing form1 by index (that is, as the first element, or the element at Index 0, of the forms array for the document), as follows:

```
<SCRIPT LANGUAGE="VBScript">
sub pressed
   ...
   document.forms(0).Button1.value = "Pressed"
   arrayLen = document.forms.length    'get the length of forms array
   ...
end sub
</SCRIPT>
```

Notice in the preceding example that the length of the forms array was also obtained.

It is also possible to refer *directly* to contained elements that are *not* form types. For instance, suppose you have created an object, as follows:

```
<OBJECT Name="myObject">
</OBJECT>
```

It is then possible to directly reference this object (say, an ActiveX control) from within a script. For example, the following code could be used to set the object's color property:

```
<SCRIPT LANGUAGE="VBScript">
sub foo
     myObject.color = "purple"
end sub
</SCRIPT>
```

The IE Form Object

The form object is a level below the document object in the IE scripting object model. The form object represents a form in the HTML document. There can be multiple forms within a document object and all are kept as an array as well as by name. All form objects can contain elements, which are arrays of objects (such as HTML form intrinsic objects or ActiveX controls) contained within the form.

Accessing Elements Contained in a Form

Scripts can reside either within a form object *or* within a window object. In the previous section on document objects, you saw that scripts living outside the form need to access form elements (that is, HTML objects or ActiveX controls) by name (for example, `document.Form1.Button1.value = "Pressed"`) or via the form array (for example, `document.forms(0).Button1.value = "Pressed"`). However, there are cases where the script lies within the form itself:

```
<FORM NAME="thisForm">
<INPUT TYPE="button" NAME="Button1" VALUE="Press me">
<SCRIPT FOR="thisObject" EVENT="thisEvent" LANGUAGE="VBScript">
    ... your VBScript code here ...
</SCRIPT>
</FORM>
```

In this case, the elements on the form can be accessed *directly* as seen with `Button1` in the following example:

```
<FORM NAME="Form1">
<INPUT TYPE="button" NAME="Button1" VALUE="Press me">
<SCRIPT FOR="Button1" EVENT="onClick" LANGUAGE="VBScript">
    Button1.value="Click"       'direct access of this form element
</SCRIPT>
</FORM>
```

Accessing Methods for Elements Contained in a Form

Scripts can also access the methods of elements contained in a form. For example, say you had a form used to query a database, and that form contained text input fields such as the following:

```
<FORM name="myForm">
<input type="text" size="85" maxlength="100" name="author_name">
... other form elements ...
</FORM>
```

Suppose that a VBScript procedure performs validation of data input to this and other fields when the user submits the form. If the validation routine detected an error for a specific input, it would be nice to set the cursor back to this specific field so that the user can correct the input. This could be accomplished by invoking the focus method for the text input element where the error occurred. For example, the data validation routine could contain the following line of code to accomplish this:

```
call Document.myForm.author_name.Focus()
```

The IE Link Object

The link object is a level below the document object in the IE scripting object model. It is referenced as a read-only property array. Every link that appears in an HTML document has a corresponding link object constructed and an entry in the link array.

Links are defined in scripting as the anchor tag, <A>, containing an HREF attribute. Here's an example:

```
<A HREF="http://www.omniscient.com/">
```

All properties of link objects are read-only and are the same as the location object's properties. Link objects are only accessible via the indexed array. For example, the fourth link on an HTML page (if it exists) could be referenced using the following code to access the link object entry at Index 3 in the array (remember that arrays are 0-indexed):

```
<SCRIPT language="VBScript">
   ...
   thisLink = document.links(3).href
   ...
</SCRIPT>
```

In this example, thisLink is set to the value of the href property (that is, the complete URL for the link) for the fourth link on the page.

The IE Anchor Object

The anchor object is a level below the document object in the IE scripting object model. The object specifies an array of anchors for a given HTML document. Every anchor (that is, every <A> tag) that appears in an HTML document has a corresponding anchor object constructed and an entry in the array.

The anchor object is referenced as a read-only property array. For example, the fourth anchor on an HTML page (if it exists) could be referenced using the following code to access the anchor object entry at Index 3 in the array:

```
<SCRIPT language="VBScript">
    ...
    thisAnchor = document.anchors(3).name
    ...
</SCRIPT>
```

In this example, `thisAnchor` is set to the value of the `name` property for the fourth anchor on the page.

The IE Element Object

The element object is a level below the form object in the IE scripting object model. Element objects are commonly intrinsic HTML objects (such as radio buttons and text input boxes) that are placed on a form using `<INPUT>` tags. Additionally, the elements can be more complex objects, such as ActiveX controls, placed on a form with the `<OBJECT>` tag. Element objects can be referenced either by name or by array. In either case, the reference to the object must follow the identifier for the form on which it resides.

Element objects are of particular interest to Web application developers because elements on forms provide a primary means of interfacing with the user and collecting information (such as constraints and clauses for database queries) that will ultimately be used by the application at the Web server. Additionally, element objects on a form can be used for presenting data and information (for example, the results of a database query) to a user. This information might be presented graphically using an ActiveX charting control or may be used to construct secondary database query forms that use the result of the primary query to construct additional queries to support a drill-down analysis.

Intrinsic HTML Control Properties, Methods, and Events

Table 14.2 summarizes properties, events, and methods associated with HTML intrinsic controls.

Table 14.2. Intrinsic HTML control properties, methods, and events.

HTML Control	Properties	Methods	Events
button, reset, submit	form, name, value	click	onClick
checkbox	form, name, value, checked, defaultChecked	click, focus	onClick
radio	form, name, value, checked	click, focus	onClick

HTML Control	Properties	Methods	Events
password	form, name, value, defaultValue	focus, blur, select	N/A
text, textarea	form, name, value, defaultValue	focus, blur, select	onFocus, onBlur, onChange, onSelect
select	name, length, options, selectedIndex	focus, blur	onFocus, onBlur, onChange
hidden	name, value	N/A	N/A

Two Ways to Script Events from Objects

There are two primary ways to script events from objects. The first method uses the following syntax:

```
onEvent = "subroutine"
```

This method can be employed for all HTML intrinsic elements (that is, forms, buttons, links, and so on). For example, the following code uses this syntax to cause a MsgBox to be displayed when a button is clicked by the user:

```
<FORM name="myForm">
    <input type="button" name="myButton" value="Press Me Now!" onClick="pressed">
</FORM>

<SCRIPT language="VBScript">
sub pressed
   MsgBox "You really know how to press my buttons!"
end sub
</SCRIPT>
```

Note that this scripting method does *not* work for elements added to a form with the <OBJECT> tag.

The second method of scripting uses the following syntax:

```
FOR="object" EVENT="eventname"
```

This syntax is appropriate for use with any named element, including those added using the <OBJECT> tag. The following code uses this syntax to cause a MsgBox to be displayed when a button is clicked by the user:

```
<FORM name="myForm">
<input type="button" name="myButton" value="Press">
<SCRIPT FOR="Button1" EVENT="onClick" language="VBScript">
   MsgBox "You really know how to press my buttons!"
</SCRIPT>
</FORM>
```

The IE History Object

The history object is a level below the window object in the IE scripting object model. This object exposes methods (that is, forward, back, and go) for navigating through the current browser history list.

The IE Navigator Object

The navigator object is a level below the window object in the IE scripting object model. Navigator object properties (that is, appCodeName, appName, appVersion, and userAgent) provide script developers with information about the browser application.

The IE Location Object

The location object is a level below the window object in the IE scripting object model. The location object represents the current URL.

Setting any portion of the location object will cause the browser to automatically navigate to the newly constructed URL. For example, the following code can be used to cause the browser to navigate to the Omniscient Technologies site:

```
<SCRIPT language="VBScript">
   ...
   location.href="http://www.omniscient.com/"
</SCRIPT>
```

This technique could be employed to automatically route users to sites in response to a query posed by the user. Additionally, if an ActiveX browser control is used within an HTML document, this technique would be used to navigate the embedded browser to the site represented by the newly constructed URL.

Spicing Up Your Applications with ActiveX Controls and VBScript

Before the introduction of HTML 3.2 objects, ActiveX controls, and browsers (such as Internet Explorer) that support Visual Basic scripting, Web applications developers were shackled by the restrictions of intrinsic HTML 2.0 form objects and layout capabilities. These objects allowed virtually no client-side processing of user inputs or actions, such as a mouse click. Instead, all data validation, conditional logic, and forms input processing had to take place on the server. This took more time, consumed limited network bandwidth and server resources, and severely hampered the level of interactiveness a user could have with an application on a Web browser.

Using HTML 3.2 <OBJECT>s and a growing suite of available ActiveX controls, developers are now able to create highly interactive applications including

■ Customizable graphical controls such as dials, calendars, various forms of buttons, animations, movie loops, labels, slider bars, charts and graphs, tab strips and overlaid controls, and so on.

■ Non-graphical controls, such as timers, which can interact with and modify the behavior of other controls.

RESOURCE

The Microsoft ActiveX Control Pad is a Web authoring tool that enables developers to add ActiveX controls and ActiveX scripting (using VBScript or JavaScript) to HTML pages via an easy-to-use graphical interface. The Control Pad comes complete with several controls that can be added to your HTML to enliven your forms and create more functional, interactive applications. The ActiveX Control Pad is free and can be downloaded from

`http://www.microsoft.com/workshop/author/cpad`

This site also contains links to tutorials, white papers, FAQ samples, and a user discussion/support newsgroup.

You should also visit the ActiveX Gallery site at

`http://www.microsoft.com/activex/controls`

to check out many of the controls offered by third-party vendors.

What is so significant about these controls and objects? Well, two things really. First, most provide a rich set of modifiable parameters that allow developers to tailor how they are presented to the user. For example, size, relative placement, color, font styles, labeling and captions, and so on can be initialized and modified at runtime. Second, most of these objects and controls are dynamic in that they respond to events. These events can be time-related events (such as a specific date or time) or user events such as a mouse click on the object. The fact that these objects and controls respond to events enables developers to create response functions associated with specific events. These response functions are client-side VBScript or JavaScript programs that take some action based on the type of event and perhaps the state or value of some object's parameters. This functionality allows developers to break through the constraints of older HTML and browser technology to create applications that perform the following functions:

■ React immediately to user input
■ Validate user input and pop up warning message boxes when appropriate
■ Perform conditional processing

■ Change attributes of the presented form

■ Change values of parameters of other form objects

■ Automatically submit forms to the server for processing

All of this can be done strictly on the client side without communication with the server, until a form requires the application-specific processing the server provides (for example, database queries, interacting with a search engine such as Microsoft's Index Server, or other functionality provided by CGI and ISAPI programs).

RESOURCE

A wealth of information about Visual Basic scripting can be found at
`http://www.microsoft.com/vbscript`
This site includes links to VBScript examples that illustrate how VBScript can be incorporated along with HTML 3.2 form objects and ActiveX controls to jazz up your Web applications. There are also links to a VBScript FAQ and a downloadable tutorial and language reference.

Formatting Your Forms

An intuitive and aesthetically pleasing layout is part of a well-conceived and well-designed form. In the past, HTML has not been the best development environment when it came to satisfying the need for a form layout to be much more complex than a set of controls laid out in horizontal and vertical lines. However, three events have changed this situation dramatically:

■ The introduction of tables to HTML and widespread support by the most popular browsers.

■ The introduction of the HTML layout control.

■ The widespread availability of development tools, such as Microsoft's ActiveX Control Pad and FrontPage, which greatly simplify the use of tables and HTML layouts. Using these tools enables developers to format pages very easily using complex nestings of tables—something most HTML developers wouldn't want to try by hand. Additionally, HTML layout controls can be used to provide very granular placement of controls in a form in a manner very similar to building forms using Visual Basic.

Using HTML Tables

Figure 14.2 illustrates a form with several intrinsic HTML controls laid out using multiple nested HTML tables. Previously, developing such a form by hand would take a substantial amount of time. However, development tools now make developing such form layouts possible in a few minutes. Listing 14.1 provides the code for this form.

FIGURE 14.2.

A form layout that utilizes nested HTML tables.

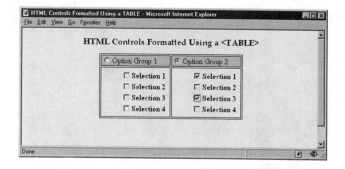

Listing 14.1. HTML code for the form illustrated in Figure 14.2.

```html
<html>
<head>
<title>HTML Controls Formatted Using a TABLE</title>
</head>

<body bgcolor="#FFFFFF">

<p align="center"><font size="4" face="Book Antiqua"><strong>HTML
Controls Formatted Using a &lt;TABLE&gt;</strong></font></p>
<div align="center"><center>

<form method="POST">
<table border="1" width="50%" bordercolor="#000000">
    <tr>
        <td width="50%" bgcolor="#98DCDA">
            <p><input type="radio" checked name="R1" value="V1">Option
            Group 1</p>
        </td>
        <td width="50%" bgcolor="#98DCDA"><input type="radio"
        name="R1" value="V2">Option Group 2</td>
    </tr>
    <tr>
        <td width="50%"><div align="center"><center>
        <table border="0" width="100%">
            <tr>
                <td width="25%"> </td>
                <td width="75%"><div align="center"><center>
                <table border="0">
                    <tr>
                        <td width="100%"><input type="checkbox"
                        name="R1C1" value="ON"></td>
                        <td><strong>Selection 1</strong></td>
                    </tr>
                    <tr>
                        <td width="100%"><input type="checkbox"
                        name="R1C2" value="ON"></td>
                        <td><strong>Selection 2</strong></td>
                    </tr>
                    <tr>
                        <td width="100%"><input type="checkbox"
                        name="R1C3" value="ON"></td>
```

continues

Listing 14.1. continued

```
                        <td><strong>Selection 3</strong></td>
                    </tr>
                    <tr>
                        <td><input type="checkbox" name="R1C4"
                        value="ON"></td>
                        <td><strong>Selection 4</strong></td>
                    </tr>
                </table>
                </center></div></td>
            </tr>
        </table>
        </center></div></td>
        <td width="50%"><div align="center"><center>
        <table border="0" width="100%">
            <tr>
                <td width="25%"> </td>
                <td width="75%"><div align="center"><center>
                <table border="0">
                    <tr>
                        <td width="100%"><input type="checkbox"
                        name="R2C1" value="ON"></td>
                        <td><strong>Selection 1</strong></td>
                    </tr>
                    <tr>
                        <td width="100%"><input type="checkbox"
                        name="R2C2" value="ON"></td>
                        <td><strong>Selection 2</strong></td>
                    </tr>
                    <tr>
                        <td width="100%"><input type="checkbox"
                        name="R2C3" value="ON"></td>
                        <td><strong>Selection 3</strong></td>
                    </tr>
                    <tr>
                        <td><input type="checkbox" name="R2C4"
                        value="ON"></td>
                        <td><strong>Selection 4</strong></td>
                    </tr>
                </table>
                </center></div></td>
            </tr>
        </table>
        </center></div></td>
    </tr>
</table>
 </form>
</center></div>

</body>
</html>
```

Using the HTML Layout Control

The HTML layout control was designed to give developers a fine level of control over the layout and placement of HTML-intrinsic controls, ActiveX controls, and other objects on an HTML page. Essentially, the layout control provides a container for several objects. This container is then inserted as an object within your HTML document. The following template illustrates how an HTML layout is inserted into an HTML document:

```
<html>
<head>
<title> </title>
</head>

... other HTML here ...

<!-- Insert HTML Layout Control here -->
<object id="object_id" classid="CLSID:class_id"
    align="baseline" border="0" style="LEFT:0;TOP:0">
    <param name="ALXPATH" valuetype="ref"
    value="file:drive:\fullpath\filename.alx">
</object>

... other HTML here ...

</body>
</html>
```

Tools such as the HTML Control Pad by Microsoft provide a visual tool for inserting objects onto a layout and fine-tuning the placement of these objects. The Control Pad enables the developer to drag and drop controls on a grid in a manner similar to developing forms in Visual Basic. The resulting layout is stored in an `.alx` file that is then referenced in an HTML document. All controls (as well as their methods and properties) can be referenced within VB scripts attached to the HTML document. An example of this is shown in the last section of this chapter.

Figure 14.3 shows a form that uses an HTML layout to emulate the formatting of the table shown in Figure 14.2. The code for this form is shown in Listings 14.2 and 14.3.

FIGURE 14.3.

A form constructed using the HTML layout control.

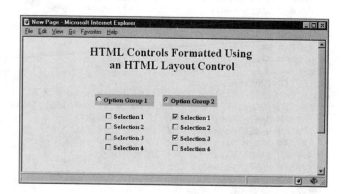

Listing 14.2. HTML code for the form illustrated in Figure 14.3.

```
<html>
<head>
<title>controls.htm</title>
</head>

<body bgcolor="#FFFFFF">

<p align="center"><font size="5">
<strong>HTML Controls Formatted Using <br>
an HTML Layout Control</strong></font></p>

<p>
<center>
<object id="controls_alx" classid="CLSID:812AE312-8B8E-11CF-93C8-00AA00C08FDF"
  align="baseline" border="0" style="LEFT:0;TOP:0">
  <param name="ALXPATH" valuetype="ref"
  value="file:D:\HTMLLayoutDir\controls.alx">
</object>
</center>
</p>
</body>
</html>
```

Listing 14.3. Code for the HTML layout control (`controls.alx`) referenced in Listing 14.2.

```
<DIV BACKGROUND="#ffffff" ID="Layout1"
 STYLE="LAYOUT:FIXED;WIDTH:329pt;HEIGHT:218pt;">
    <OBJECT ID="OptionButton1"
     CLASSID="CLSID:8BD21D50-EC42-11CE-9E0D-00AA006002F3"
     STYLE="TOP:25pt;LEFT:41pt;WIDTH:95pt;HEIGHT:18pt;TABINDEX:0;ZINDEX:0;">
        <PARAM NAME="BackColor" VALUE="14079914">
        <PARAM NAME="ForeColor" VALUE="2147483666">
        <PARAM NAME="DisplayStyle" VALUE="5">
        <PARAM NAME="Size" VALUE="3360;635">
        <PARAM NAME="Value" VALUE="0">
        <PARAM NAME="Caption" VALUE="Option Group 1">
        <PARAM NAME="GroupName" VALUE="R1">
        <PARAM NAME="FontName" VALUE="Book Antiqua">
        <PARAM NAME="FontEffects" VALUE="1073741825">
        <PARAM NAME="FontHeight" VALUE="200">
        <PARAM NAME="FontCharSet" VALUE="0">
        <PARAM NAME="FontPitchAndFamily" VALUE="2">
        <PARAM NAME="FontWeight" VALUE="700">
    </OBJECT>
    <OBJECT ID="OptionButton2"
     CLASSID="CLSID:8BD21D50-EC42-11CE-9E0D-00AA006002F3"
     STYLE="TOP:25pt;LEFT:149pt;WIDTH:89pt;HEIGHT:18pt;TABINDEX:1;ZINDEX:1;">
        <PARAM NAME="BackColor" VALUE="14079914">
        <PARAM NAME="ForeColor" VALUE="2147483666">
        <PARAM NAME="DisplayStyle" VALUE="5">
        <PARAM NAME="Size" VALUE="3122;635">
        <PARAM NAME="Value" VALUE="0">
        <PARAM NAME="Caption" VALUE="Option Group 2">
        <PARAM NAME="GroupName" VALUE="R1">
```

```
    <PARAM NAME="FontName" VALUE="Book Antiqua">
    <PARAM NAME="FontEffects" VALUE="1073741825">
    <PARAM NAME="FontHeight" VALUE="200">
    <PARAM NAME="FontCharSet" VALUE="0">
    <PARAM NAME="FontPitchAndFamily" VALUE="2">
    <PARAM NAME="FontWeight" VALUE="700">
</OBJECT>
<OBJECT ID="R1C2"
 CLASSID="CLSID:8BD21D40-EC42-11CE-9E0D-00AA006002F3"
 STYLE="TOP:66pt;LEFT:58pt;WIDTH:75pt;HEIGHT:18pt;TABINDEX:2;ZINDEX:2;">
    <PARAM NAME="BackColor" VALUE="16777215">
    <PARAM NAME="ForeColor" VALUE="2147483666">
    <PARAM NAME="DisplayStyle" VALUE="4">
    <PARAM NAME="Size" VALUE="2646;635">
    <PARAM NAME="Value" VALUE="0">
    <PARAM NAME="Caption" VALUE="Selection 2">
    <PARAM NAME="FontName" VALUE="Book Antiqua">
    <PARAM NAME="FontEffects" VALUE="1073741825">
    <PARAM NAME="FontHeight" VALUE="200">
    <PARAM NAME="FontCharSet" VALUE="0">
    <PARAM NAME="FontPitchAndFamily" VALUE="2">
    <PARAM NAME="FontWeight" VALUE="700">
</OBJECT>
<OBJECT ID="R1C4"
 CLASSID="CLSID:8BD21D40-EC42-11CE-9E0D-00AA006002F3"
 STYLE="TOP:99pt;LEFT:58pt;WIDTH:74pt;HEIGHT:18pt;TABINDEX:3;ZINDEX:3;">
    <PARAM NAME="BackColor" VALUE="16777215">
    <PARAM NAME="ForeColor" VALUE="2147483666">
    <PARAM NAME="DisplayStyle" VALUE="4">
    <PARAM NAME="Size" VALUE="2619;635">
    <PARAM NAME="Value" VALUE="0">
    <PARAM NAME="Caption" VALUE="Selection 4">
    <PARAM NAME="FontName" VALUE="Book Antiqua">
    <PARAM NAME="FontEffects" VALUE="1073741825">
    <PARAM NAME="FontHeight" VALUE="200">
    <PARAM NAME="FontCharSet" VALUE="0">
    <PARAM NAME="FontPitchAndFamily" VALUE="2">
    <PARAM NAME="FontWeight" VALUE="700">
</OBJECT>
<OBJECT ID="R1C3"
 CLASSID="CLSID:8BD21D40-EC42-11CE-9E0D-00AA006002F3"
 STYLE="TOP:83pt;LEFT:58pt;WIDTH:76pt;HEIGHT:18pt;TABINDEX:4;ZINDEX:4;">
    <PARAM NAME="BackColor" VALUE="16777215">
    <PARAM NAME="ForeColor" VALUE="2147483666">
    <PARAM NAME="DisplayStyle" VALUE="4">
    <PARAM NAME="Size" VALUE="2672;635">
    <PARAM NAME="Value" VALUE="0">
    <PARAM NAME="Caption" VALUE="Selection 3">
    <PARAM NAME="FontName" VALUE="Book Antiqua">
    <PARAM NAME="FontEffects" VALUE="1073741825">
    <PARAM NAME="FontHeight" VALUE="200">
    <PARAM NAME="FontCharSet" VALUE="0">
    <PARAM NAME="FontPitchAndFamily" VALUE="2">
    <PARAM NAME="FontWeight" VALUE="700">
</OBJECT>
<OBJECT ID="R1C1"
 CLASSID="CLSID:8BD21D40-EC42-11CE-9E0D-00AA006002F3"
 STYLE="TOP:50pt;LEFT:58pt;WIDTH:71pt;HEIGHT:18pt;TABINDEX:5;ZINDEX:5;">
```

continues

Listing 14.3. continued

```
        <PARAM NAME="BackColor" VALUE="16777215">
        <PARAM NAME="ForeColor" VALUE="2147483666">
        <PARAM NAME="DisplayStyle" VALUE="4">
        <PARAM NAME="Size" VALUE="2514;635">
        <PARAM NAME="Value" VALUE="0">
        <PARAM NAME="Caption" VALUE="Selection 1">
        <PARAM NAME="FontName" VALUE="Book Antiqua">
        <PARAM NAME="FontEffects" VALUE="1073741825">
        <PARAM NAME="FontHeight" VALUE="200">
        <PARAM NAME="FontCharSet" VALUE="0">
        <PARAM NAME="FontPitchAndFamily" VALUE="2">
        <PARAM NAME="FontWeight" VALUE="700">
    </OBJECT>
    <OBJECT ID="R2C4"
     CLASSID="CLSID:8BD21D40-EC42-11CE-9E0D-00AA006002F3"
     STYLE="TOP:99pt;LEFT:165pt;WIDTH:76pt;HEIGHT:18pt;TABINDEX:6;ZINDEX:6;">
        <PARAM NAME="BackColor" VALUE="16777215">
        <PARAM NAME="ForeColor" VALUE="2147483666">
        <PARAM NAME="DisplayStyle" VALUE="4">
        <PARAM NAME="Size" VALUE="2672;635">
        <PARAM NAME="Value" VALUE="0">
        <PARAM NAME="Caption" VALUE="Selection 4">
        <PARAM NAME="FontName" VALUE="Book Antiqua">
        <PARAM NAME="FontEffects" VALUE="1073741825">
        <PARAM NAME="FontHeight" VALUE="200">
        <PARAM NAME="FontCharSet" VALUE="0">
        <PARAM NAME="FontPitchAndFamily" VALUE="2">
        <PARAM NAME="FontWeight" VALUE="700">
    </OBJECT>
    <OBJECT ID="R2C3"
     CLASSID="CLSID:8BD21D40-EC42-11CE-9E0D-00AA006002F3"
     STYLE="TOP:83pt;LEFT:165pt;WIDTH:77pt;HEIGHT:18pt;TABINDEX:7;ZINDEX:7;">
        <PARAM NAME="BackColor" VALUE="16777215">
        <PARAM NAME="ForeColor" VALUE="2147483666">
        <PARAM NAME="DisplayStyle" VALUE="4">
        <PARAM NAME="Size" VALUE="2699;635">
        <PARAM NAME="Value" VALUE="0">
        <PARAM NAME="Caption" VALUE="Selection 3">
        <PARAM NAME="FontName" VALUE="Book Antiqua">
        <PARAM NAME="FontEffects" VALUE="1073741825">
        <PARAM NAME="FontHeight" VALUE="200">
        <PARAM NAME="FontCharSet" VALUE="0">
        <PARAM NAME="FontPitchAndFamily" VALUE="2">
        <PARAM NAME="FontWeight" VALUE="700">
    </OBJECT>
    <OBJECT ID="R2C2"
     CLASSID="CLSID:8BD21D40-EC42-11CE-9E0D-00AA006002F3"
     STYLE="TOP:66pt;LEFT:165pt;WIDTH:75pt;HEIGHT:18pt;TABINDEX:8;ZINDEX:8;">
        <PARAM NAME="BackColor" VALUE="16777215">
        <PARAM NAME="ForeColor" VALUE="2147483666">
        <PARAM NAME="DisplayStyle" VALUE="4">
        <PARAM NAME="Size" VALUE="2646;635">
        <PARAM NAME="Value" VALUE="0">
        <PARAM NAME="Caption" VALUE="Selection 2">
        <PARAM NAME="FontName" VALUE="Book Antiqua">
        <PARAM NAME="FontEffects" VALUE="1073741825">
        <PARAM NAME="FontHeight" VALUE="200">
```

```
            <PARAM NAME="FontCharSet" VALUE="0">
            <PARAM NAME="FontPitchAndFamily" VALUE="2">
            <PARAM NAME="FontWeight" VALUE="700">
    </OBJECT>
    <OBJECT ID="R2C1"
     CLASSID="CLSID:8BD21D40-EC42-11CE-9E0D-00AA006002F3"
     STYLE="TOP:50pt;LEFT:165pt;WIDTH:75pt;HEIGHT:18pt;TABINDEX:9;ZINDEX:9;">
            <PARAM NAME="BackColor" VALUE="16777215">
            <PARAM NAME="ForeColor" VALUE="2147483666">
            <PARAM NAME="DisplayStyle" VALUE="4">
            <PARAM NAME="Size" VALUE="2646;635">
            <PARAM NAME="Value" VALUE="0">
            <PARAM NAME="Caption" VALUE="Selection 1">
            <PARAM NAME="FontName" VALUE="Book Antiqua">
            <PARAM NAME="FontEffects" VALUE="1073741825">
            <PARAM NAME="FontHeight" VALUE="200">
            <PARAM NAME="FontCharSet" VALUE="0">
            <PARAM NAME="FontPitchAndFamily" VALUE="2">
            <PARAM NAME="FontWeight" VALUE="700">
    </OBJECT>
</DIV>
```

This example showed you how to emulate the formatting of the table shown in the previous example. Unlike tables, however, formatting provided by the HTML layout control is not limited to placing objects in rows and columns. You could just as easily lay out the controls in a circular pattern or any other format you want. You can even overlay controls on top of each other if you wish. This technique can be used in conjunction with the ActiveX shape controls to create visually appealing forms that use colored shapes as backdrops to controls placed on a page. This backdrop object can be a variety of shapes and, if used properly, can emphasize logical groupings of controls.

Implementing ActiveX Controls and VBScript: A Search Engine Query Form Example

In this section you get a glimpse of the greatly improved functionality and interactiveness that ActiveX controls and VBScript can bring to your applications. This example illustrates the construction of a form used to submit a query to Microsoft's Index Server (a content-indexing search engine tool for IIS). Several familiar HTML form objects are used along with the following ActiveX controls:

■ *Microsoft Forms 2.0 Label*. This control is used to display descriptive text such as titles, captions, or instructions. The default property is the Caption property and the default event is the Click event.

■ *Microsoft Forms 2.0 SpinButton*. This control is typically used for incrementing or decrementing numbers, scrolling through a range of values, or setting components of a date (such as the day, month, or year). Clicking the SpinButton only changes the value of the button, itself. However, code can be developed to use the button value to update another control. The default property is the Value property and the default event is the Change event.

■ *Microsoft Forms 2.0 TextBox.* This control is typically used to display information from a user. The font style and color can be preset as desired. The default property is the Value property and the default event is the Change event.

Figure 14.4 illustrates the Index Server query form created for this example.

FIGURE 14.4.
An Index Server Query form implementing ActiveX controls and VBScript subroutines to respond to user actions.

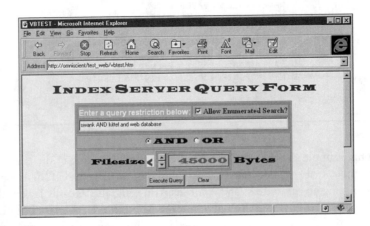

A few notes about this form:

■ The user can enter a query restriction in an HTML text input object.

■ The user can specify whether or not the Index Server will be allowed to perform an enumerated search. If the checkbox (named cbEnum) for using enumeration is selected, a VBScript subroutine (cbEnum_OnClick) is called to pop up a message box warning the user of the implications of such a search. This is illustrated in Figure 14.5.

FIGURE 14.5.
VBScript MsgBox used to warn users when they select a time-consuming search using the form shown in Figure 14.4.

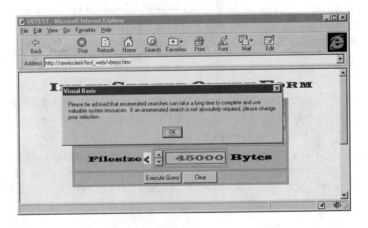

- The user can specify a relational operator to use for a file size restriction. An ActiveX label control (named lblInequal) is used to specify the direction (< or >) of the file size restriction relational operator. For this form, > is the initial value of the label caption. When the user clicks on the label, a VBScript subroutine (lblInequal_Click)is called to reverse the direction of relational operator from the currently displayed inequality.

- ActiveX SpinButton (named btnFSize) and TextBox (named txtFSize) controls are used to allow the user to specify a value for the file size restriction. When the user clicks the Up (Down) button, the SpinButton's internal value is incremented (decremented) by a preset amount. The increment value is preset to 10,000. Additionally, a TextBox control is created. VBScript code is used to initialize the display to the internal value of the SpinButton and the displayed value of the TextBox. When the user clicks the SpinButton, a VBScript is called to update the TextBox to display the internal value of the SpinButton. btnFSize_SpinUp is called for a click on the Up button; btnFSize_SpinDown for a click on the Down button. This allows the user to quickly increment or decrement the value to use for the file restriction. Of course, the user can also override this functionality and type in a specific file size if desired.

- A message box is used to immediately inform the user when a potentially time-consuming option (enumerated search) is selected. The capability to perform this function on the client side does away with the need to submit the form to the server, have the server check on the state of this checkbox, and then subsequently inform the user—a sequence of events that could result in two form submissions should the user choose to heed the warning.

- The user can specify a Boolean AND/OR operation. Selecting the AND radio button will cause a query restriction that results in a search for files meeting *both* the user-specified query restriction *and* the user-specified file size property restriction. Selecting OR causes a search for files meeting *either* the user query restriction *or* the file size restriction.

- The example illustrates the use of several font styles and colors as well as complex page formatting using several nested tables (note that formatting a form with the HTML layout control is demonstrated in a database query example at the end of this chapter). While not supported by all browsers, the use of various fonts, colors, and formatting should be considered because it provides a relatively easy means for dramatically dressing up your forms. We highly recommend the use of Web publishing tools, such as Microsoft's FrontPage, and forms development tools, such as the Microsoft ActiveX Control Pad. These tools greatly ease the burden of hand-coding complex HTML pages and forms by providing a point-and-click interface. They also provide significant support for insertion of ActiveX controls and development of VBScript and JavaScript programs.

RESOURCE

Additional information about FrontPage (including an occasional free beta version) can be found at the FrontPage site:

`http://www.microsoft.com/frontpage`

Listing 14.4 is a full listing for the HTML and VBScript code used to develop the form in Figure 14.4.

Listing 14.4. HTML and VBScript code for the Index Server Query form shown in Figure 14.4.

```
<html>

<head>
<meta http-equiv="Content-Type"
content="text/html; charset=iso-8859-1">
<meta name="GENERATOR" content="Microsoft FrontPage 2.0">
<title>Index Server Query Form</title>
</head>

<body bgcolor="#FFFFFF">

<p align="center"> <font color="#0000A8" size="5"
face="Wide Latin"><strong>I</strong></font><font color="#0000A8"
size="4" face="Wide Latin"><strong>NDEX </strong></font><font
color="#0000A8" size="5" face="Wide Latin"><strong>S</strong></font><font
color="#0000A8" size="4" face="Wide Latin"><strong>ERVER </strong></font><font
color="#0000A8" size="5" face="Wide Latin"><strong>Q</strong></font><font
color="#0000A8" size="4" face="Wide Latin"><strong>UERY </strong></font><font
color="#0000A8" size="5" face="Wide Latin"><strong>F</strong></font><font
color="#0000A8" size="4" face="Wide Latin"><strong>ORM</strong></font></p>

<form action="/scripts/vbtest.idq" method="GET" name="MainForm">
 <div align="center"><center>
 <table border="1" bgcolor="#A4B0BD" bordercolor="#008080"
   bordercolordark="#008080" bordercolorlight="#008080">
     <tr>
        <td align="center"><div align="center"><center>
        <table border="1" cellspacing="1" bgcolor="#A4B0BD"
        bordercolor="#008080" bordercolordark="#008080"
        bordercolorlight="#008080">
            <tr>
               <td align="center"><font color="#FFFFFF"
               size="3" face="Arial"><strong>Enter a query
               restriction below</strong></font><font
               color="#FFFFFF" size="4" face="Arial">:</font>
               </td>
               <td align="right">
               <input type="checkbox" name="cbEnum" value="ON">
               <strong>Allow Enumerated Search?</strong>
               </td>
            </tr>
```

```html
            <tr>
                <td colspan="2" width="80%">
                <input type="text" size="85" maxlength="100"
                 name="CiRestriction">
                </td>
            </tr>
        </table>
        </center></div></td>
    </tr>
    <tr>
        <td align="center"><div align="center"><center>
        <table border="0">
            <tr>
                <td align="center" width="50%">
                 <input type="radio" checked name="rbbool" value="AND">
                 <font face="Wide Latin"><strong>AND </strong></font>
                </td>
                <td align="center" width="50%">
                  <input type="radio" name="rbbool" value="OR"><font
                  face="Wide Latin"><strong>OR</strong></font>
                </td>
            </tr>
        </table>
        </center></div></td>
    </tr>
    <tr>
        <td align="center"><div align="center"><center>
        <table border="0">
            <tr>
                <td align="center" width="33%"><font size="3"
                  face="Wide Latin"><strong>Filesize</strong></font>
                </td>
                <td align="center" width="20%">
                  <object id="lblInequal" name="lblInequal"
                    classid="clsid:978C9E23-D4B0-11CE-BF2D-00AA003F40D0"
                    align="middle" border="0" width="16" height="24">
                    <param name="ForeColor" value="128">
                    <param name="BackColor" value="16777215">
                    <param name="Caption" value="&gt;">
                    <param name="Size" value="423;635">
                    <param name="FontName" value="Wide Latin">
                    <param name="FontEffects" value="1073741825">
                    <param name="FontHeight" value="360">
                    <param name="FontCharSet" value="0">
                    <param name="FontPitchAndFamily" value="2">
                    <param name="FontWeight" value="700">
                  </object>
                </td>
                <td align="center" width="34%"><div align="center"><center>
                <table border="1" bgcolor="#A4B0BD" bordercolor="#008080"
                 bordercolordark="#008080" bordercolorlight="#008080">
                    <tr>
                        <td align="center" width="8%">
                        <object id="btnFSize" name="btnFSize"
                         classid="clsid:79176FB0-B7F2-11CE-97EF-00AA006D2776"
                         align="baseline" border="0" width="16" height="31">
                         <param name="Size" value="418;781">
                         <param name="Min" value="5000">
```

continues

Listing 14.4. continued

```
                            <param name="Max" value="100000">
                            <param name="Position" value="5000">
                            <param name="SmallChange" value="10000">
                        </object>
                        </td>
                        <td align="center" width="20%">
                        <object id="txtFSize" name="txtFSize"
                         classid="clsid:8BD21D10-EC42-11CE-9E0D-00AA006002F3"
                         align="baseline" border="0" width="127" height="25">
                            <param name="VariousPropertyBits" value="746604571">
                            <param name="BackColor" value="13290186">
                            <param name="ForeColor" value="3084984">
                            <param name="BorderStyle" value="1">
                            <param name="Size" value="3329;670">
                            <param name="SpecialEffect" value="0">
                            <param name="FontName" value="Wide Latin">
                            <param name="FontEffects" value="1073741825">
                            <param name="FontHeight" value="240">
                            <param name="FontCharSet" value="0">
                            <param name="FontPitchAndFamily" value="2">
                            <param name="ParagraphAlign" value="2">
                            <param name="FontWeight" value="700">
                        </object>
                        </td>
                    </tr>
                </table>
                </center></div></td>
                <td><font size="4" face="Wide Latin">
                    <strong>Bytes</strong></font>
                </td>
            </tr>
        </table>
        </center></div></td>
    </tr>
    <tr>
        <td align="center"><input type="submit" value="Execute Query">
         <input type="reset" name="1" value="Clear">
        </td>
    </tr>
</table>
</center></div><p align="center"> </p>
<p align="center"> </p>
<p align="center"> </p>
<p align="center"> </p>
<p align="center"> </p>
<p align="center"> </p>
</form>

<script language="VBScript">
<!--

Dim F
```

```
Set F = Document.MainForm

btnMin = 5000
btnMax = 100000

F.btnFSize.value = btnMin
F.txtFSize.value = btnMin

sub btnFSize_SpinUp
   F.txtFSize.value = F.btnFSize.value
end sub

sub btnFSize_SpinDown
   F.txtFSize.value = F.btnFSize.value
end sub

sub lblInequal_Click
   if F.lblInequal.caption = ">" then
      F.lblInequal.caption = "<"
   else
      F.lblInequal.caption = ">"
   end if
end sub

sub cbEnum_OnClick
   if F.cbEnum.Checked then
      MsgBox "Please be advised that enumerated searches can take a long time
      ➥ to complete and use valuable system resources.  If an enumerated
      ➥ search is not absoultely required, please change your selection"
   end if
end sub
-->
</script>

</body>
</html>
```

Don't be fazed by the reference to an `.idq` file in the ACTION attribute for the form. This is simply a file used by Index Server to consolidate form content (passed to the server when the form is submitted) and then pose a query to the search engine.

RESOURCE

For additional information on Index Server, refer to *Designing and Implementing Microsoft Index Server* (Sams Publishing, ISBN: 1-57521-212-9). This book contains detailed information on what Index Server is, what functionality it provides, and how it can be integrated with your other Web applications (such as database queries).

Putting It All Together—Developing a Form for Database Access

In this section we pull together several of the concepts presented in earlier sections of this chapter to show you how to construct an interactive database query form using VBScript, ActiveX controls, and the HTML layout control. This example illustrates the construction of a form used to submit a query to the Microsoft SQL Server pubs database. The database query form can be seen in Figure 14.6.

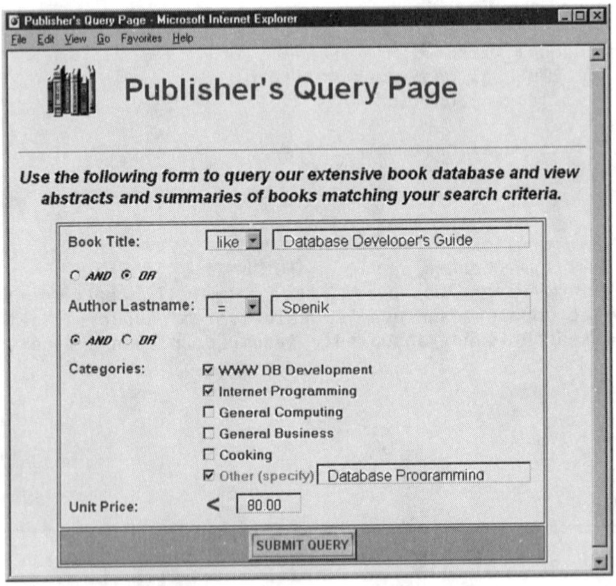

FIGURE 14.6.

The database query form used to query the MS SQL Server pubs database.

Creating the HTML Layout

An HTML layout control is used as a container for controls that will collect user input that is subsequently sent to the server and used to pose a query to the database. The following types of ActiveX controls are contained on the layout:

■ Microsoft Forms 2.0 Label provides labels for other controls on the layout, as well as provide an inequality (that is a "toggle-able" > or <) option associated with the price input textbox.

■ Microsoft Forms 2.0 TextBox collects user input regarding author names, book titles, and book prices.

■ Microsoft Forms 2.0 OptionButton provides the user with additional options (that is, AND and OR) on how the query will be constructed.

- ■ Microsoft Forms 2.0 ComboBox provides the user with options (that is, `like`, `in`, and =) on how input to the Book Title and Author Name textboxes should be used in a SQL `WHERE` clause.

- ■ Microsoft Forms 2.0 CheckBox enables the user to specify specific categories of books (in effect allowing more targeted queries).

These controls are used to enter information such as author names, book titles, book categories, and price information that will be read by VB scripts attached to the main HTML form and submitted to the server to formulate a query to the `pubs` database. This simple form provides great flexibility in the types of queries and clauses that can be constructed.

Figure 14.7 illustrates how the layout looks during construction using the HTML Control Pad.

FIGURE 14.7.

The construction of the HTML layout used in the database query form shown in Figure 14.6.

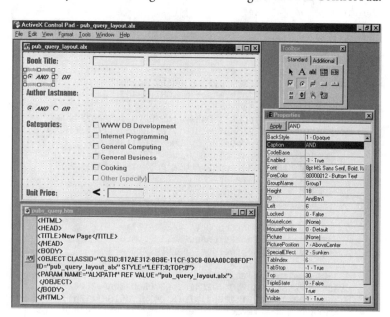

The code created by the HTML Control Pad is shown in Listing 14.5.

Listing 14.5. Code for the HTML layout (`pubs_query_layout.alx`) used by the pubs database query form shown in Figure 14.6.

```
<!--
  pub_query_layout.alx

  ALX HTML Layout and VBScript for Controls held within
  pubs_query.htm database query form

  created Feb 1997 - Drew Kittel
-->
```

continues

Listing 14.5. continued

```
<SCRIPT LANGUAGE="VBScript">
<!--

'Add menu items and set the default value displayed

Sub pub_query_layout_OnLoad()

call cboTitle.AddItem("like", 0)
call cboTitle.AddItem("in", 1)
call cboTitle.AddItem("=", 2)
cboTitle.value = "like"
call cboAuthor.AddItem("like", 0)
call cboAuthor.AddItem("in", 1)
call cboAuthor.AddItem("=", 2)
cboAuthor.value = "like"

end sub
-->
</SCRIPT>

<DIV BACKGROUND="#ffffff" ID="pub_query_layout"
 STYLE="LAYOUT:FIXED;WIDTH:386pt;HEIGHT:234pt;">
    <OBJECT ID="lblTitle"
      CLASSID="CLSID:978C9E23-D4B0-11CE-BF2D-00AA003F40D0"
      STYLE="TOP:5pt;LEFT:6pt;WIDTH:71pt;HEIGHT:17pt;ZINDEX:0;">
        <PARAM NAME="ForeColor" VALUE="16711680">
        <PARAM NAME="BackColor" VALUE="16777215">
        <PARAM NAME="Caption" VALUE="Book Title:">
        <PARAM NAME="Size" VALUE="2505;600">
        <PARAM NAME="FontName" VALUE="Arial">
        <PARAM NAME="FontEffects" VALUE="1073741825">
        <PARAM NAME="FontHeight" VALUE="240">
        <PARAM NAME="FontCharSet" VALUE="0">
        <PARAM NAME="FontPitchAndFamily" VALUE="2">
        <PARAM NAME="FontWeight" VALUE="700">
    </OBJECT>
    <OBJECT ID="txtTitle"
      CLASSID="CLSID:8BD21D10-EC42-11CE-9E0D-00AA006002F3"
      STYLE="TOP:3pt;LEFT:170pt;WIDTH:207pt;HEIGHT:17pt;TABINDEX:1;ZINDEX:1;">
        <PARAM NAME="VariousPropertyBits" VALUE="746604571">
        <PARAM NAME="Size" VALUE="7303;600">
        <PARAM NAME="FontName" VALUE="Arial">
        <PARAM NAME="FontHeight" VALUE="240">
        <PARAM NAME="FontCharSet" VALUE="0">
        <PARAM NAME="FontPitchAndFamily" VALUE="2">
    </OBJECT>
    <OBJECT ID="lblAuthor"
      CLASSID="CLSID:978C9E23-D4B0-11CE-BF2D-00AA003F40D0"
      STYLE="TOP:55pt;LEFT:6pt;WIDTH:110pt;HEIGHT:17pt;ZINDEX:2;">
        <PARAM NAME="ForeColor" VALUE="16711680">
        <PARAM NAME="BackColor" VALUE="16777215">
        <PARAM NAME="Caption" VALUE="Author Lastname:">
        <PARAM NAME="Size" VALUE="3881;600">
        <PARAM NAME="FontName" VALUE="Arial">
        <PARAM NAME="FontEffects" VALUE="1073741825">
        <PARAM NAME="FontHeight" VALUE="240">
        <PARAM NAME="FontCharSet" VALUE="0">
```

```
        <PARAM NAME="FontPitchAndFamily" VALUE="2">
        <PARAM NAME="FontWeight" VALUE="700">
</OBJECT>
<OBJECT ID="txtAuthor"
 CLASSID="CLSID:8BD21D10-EC42-11CE-9E0D-00AA006002F3"
 STYLE="TOP:55pt;LEFT:169pt;WIDTH:209pt;HEIGHT:17pt;TABINDEX:3;ZINDEX:3;">
        <PARAM NAME="VariousPropertyBits" VALUE="746604571">
        <PARAM NAME="Size" VALUE="7373;600">
        <PARAM NAME="FontName" VALUE="Arial">
        <PARAM NAME="FontHeight" VALUE="240">
        <PARAM NAME="FontCharSet" VALUE="0">
        <PARAM NAME="FontPitchAndFamily" VALUE="2">
</OBJECT>
<OBJECT ID="optAND1"
 CLASSID="CLSID:8BD21D50-EC42-11CE-9E0D-00AA006002F3"
 STYLE="TOP:30pt;LEFT:6pt;WIDTH:41pt;HEIGHT:18pt;TABINDEX:4;ZINDEX:4;">
        <PARAM NAME="BackColor" VALUE="16777215">
        <PARAM NAME="ForeColor" VALUE="2147483666">
        <PARAM NAME="DisplayStyle" VALUE="5">
        <PARAM NAME="Size" VALUE="1446;635">
        <PARAM NAME="Value" VALUE="1">
        <PARAM NAME="Caption" VALUE="AND">
        <PARAM NAME="GroupName" VALUE="Group1">
        <PARAM NAME="FontEffects" VALUE="1073741827">
        <PARAM NAME="FontCharSet" VALUE="0">
        <PARAM NAME="FontPitchAndFamily" VALUE="2">
        <PARAM NAME="FontWeight" VALUE="700">
</OBJECT>
<OBJECT ID="optOR1"
 CLASSID="CLSID:8BD21D50-EC42-11CE-9E0D-00AA006002F3"
 STYLE="TOP:30pt;LEFT:47pt;WIDTH:36pt;HEIGHT:18pt;TABINDEX:5;ZINDEX:5;">
        <PARAM NAME="BackColor" VALUE="16777215">
        <PARAM NAME="ForeColor" VALUE="2147483666">
        <PARAM NAME="DisplayStyle" VALUE="5">
        <PARAM NAME="Size" VALUE="1270;635">
        <PARAM NAME="Value" VALUE="0">
        <PARAM NAME="Caption" VALUE="OR">
        <PARAM NAME="GroupName" VALUE="Group1">
        <PARAM NAME="FontEffects" VALUE="1073741827">
        <PARAM NAME="FontCharSet" VALUE="0">
        <PARAM NAME="FontPitchAndFamily" VALUE="2">
        <PARAM NAME="FontWeight" VALUE="700">
</OBJECT>
<OBJECT ID="lblCat"
 CLASSID="CLSID:978C9E23-D4B0-11CE-BF2D-00AA003F40D0"
 STYLE="TOP:104pt;LEFT:6pt;WIDTH:71pt;HEIGHT:17pt;ZINDEX:6;">
        <PARAM NAME="ForeColor" VALUE="16711680">
        <PARAM NAME="BackColor" VALUE="16777215">
        <PARAM NAME="Caption" VALUE="Categories:">
        <PARAM NAME="Size" VALUE="2505;600">
        <PARAM NAME="FontName" VALUE="Arial">
        <PARAM NAME="FontEffects" VALUE="1073741825">
        <PARAM NAME="FontHeight" VALUE="240">
        <PARAM NAME="FontCharSet" VALUE="0">
        <PARAM NAME="FontPitchAndFamily" VALUE="2">
        <PARAM NAME="FontWeight" VALUE="700">
</OBJECT>
```

continues

Listing 14.5. continued

```
<OBJECT ID="chk1"
 CLASSID="CLSID:8BD21D40-EC42-11CE-9E0D-00AA006002F3"
 STYLE="TOP:104pt;LEFT:113pt;WIDTH:140pt;HEIGHT:18pt;TABINDEX:7;ZINDEX:7;">
    <PARAM NAME="BackColor" VALUE="16777215">
    <PARAM NAME="ForeColor" VALUE="16711680">
    <PARAM NAME="DisplayStyle" VALUE="4">
    <PARAM NAME="Size" VALUE="4939;635">
    <PARAM NAME="Value" VALUE="0">
    <PARAM NAME="Caption" VALUE="WWW DB Development">
    <PARAM NAME="FontEffects" VALUE="1073741825">
    <PARAM NAME="FontHeight" VALUE="200">
    <PARAM NAME="FontCharSet" VALUE="0">
    <PARAM NAME="FontPitchAndFamily" VALUE="2">
    <PARAM NAME="FontWeight" VALUE="700">
</OBJECT>
<OBJECT ID="chk2"
 CLASSID="CLSID:8BD21D40-EC42-11CE-9E0D-00AA006002F3"
 STYLE="TOP:121pt;LEFT:113pt;WIDTH:130pt;HEIGHT:18pt;TABINDEX:8;ZINDEX:8;">
    <PARAM NAME="BackColor" VALUE="16777215">
    <PARAM NAME="ForeColor" VALUE="16711680">
    <PARAM NAME="DisplayStyle" VALUE="4">
    <PARAM NAME="Size" VALUE="4586;635">
    <PARAM NAME="Value" VALUE="0">
    <PARAM NAME="Caption" VALUE="Internet Programming">
    <PARAM NAME="FontEffects" VALUE="1073741825">
    <PARAM NAME="FontHeight" VALUE="200">
    <PARAM NAME="FontCharSet" VALUE="0">
    <PARAM NAME="FontPitchAndFamily" VALUE="2">
    <PARAM NAME="FontWeight" VALUE="700">
</OBJECT>
<OBJECT ID="chk3"
 CLASSID="CLSID:8BD21D40-EC42-11CE-9E0D-00AA006002F3"
 STYLE="TOP:137pt;LEFT:113pt;WIDTH:116pt;HEIGHT:18pt;TABINDEX:9;ZINDEX:9;">
    <PARAM NAME="BackColor" VALUE="16777215">
    <PARAM NAME="ForeColor" VALUE="16711680">
    <PARAM NAME="DisplayStyle" VALUE="4">
    <PARAM NAME="Size" VALUE="4092;635">
    <PARAM NAME="Value" VALUE="0">
    <PARAM NAME="Caption" VALUE="General Computing">
    <PARAM NAME="FontEffects" VALUE="1073741825">
    <PARAM NAME="FontHeight" VALUE="200">
    <PARAM NAME="FontCharSet" VALUE="0">
    <PARAM NAME="FontPitchAndFamily" VALUE="2">
    <PARAM NAME="FontWeight" VALUE="700">
</OBJECT>
<OBJECT ID="chk4"
 CLASSID="CLSID:8BD21D40-EC42-11CE-9E0D-00AA006002F3"
 STYLE="TOP:154pt;LEFT:113pt;WIDTH:108pt;HEIGHT:18pt;TABINDEX:10;ZINDEX:10;">
    <PARAM NAME="BackColor" VALUE="16777215">
    <PARAM NAME="ForeColor" VALUE="16711680">
    <PARAM NAME="DisplayStyle" VALUE="4">
    <PARAM NAME="Size" VALUE="3810;635">
    <PARAM NAME="Value" VALUE="0">
    <PARAM NAME="Caption" VALUE="General Business">
```

```
        <PARAM NAME="FontEffects" VALUE="1073741825">
        <PARAM NAME="FontHeight" VALUE="200">
        <PARAM NAME="FontCharSet" VALUE="0">
        <PARAM NAME="FontPitchAndFamily" VALUE="2">
        <PARAM NAME="FontWeight" VALUE="700">
</OBJECT>
<OBJECT ID="chk5"
 CLASSID="CLSID:8BD21D40-EC42-11CE-9E0D-00AA006002F3"
 STYLE="TOP:170pt;LEFT:113pt;WIDTH:63pt;HEIGHT:18pt;TABINDEX:11;ZINDEX:11;">
        <PARAM NAME="BackColor" VALUE="16777215">
        <PARAM NAME="ForeColor" VALUE="16711680">
        <PARAM NAME="DisplayStyle" VALUE="4">
        <PARAM NAME="Size" VALUE="2223;635">
        <PARAM NAME="Value" VALUE="0">
        <PARAM NAME="Caption" VALUE="Cooking">
        <PARAM NAME="FontEffects" VALUE="1073741825">
        <PARAM NAME="FontHeight" VALUE="200">
        <PARAM NAME="FontCharSet" VALUE="0">
        <PARAM NAME="FontPitchAndFamily" VALUE="2">
        <PARAM NAME="FontWeight" VALUE="700">
</OBJECT>
<OBJECT ID="chk6"
 CLASSID="CLSID:8BD21D40-EC42-11CE-9E0D-00AA006002F3"
 STYLE="TOP:187pt;LEFT:113pt;WIDTH:99pt;HEIGHT:18pt;TABINDEX:12;ZINDEX:12;">
        <PARAM NAME="BackColor" VALUE="16777215">
        <PARAM NAME="ForeColor" VALUE="16292154">
        <PARAM NAME="DisplayStyle" VALUE="4">
        <PARAM NAME="Size" VALUE="3493;635">
        <PARAM NAME="Value" VALUE="0">
        <PARAM NAME="Caption" VALUE="Other (specify)">
        <PARAM NAME="FontEffects" VALUE="1073741825">
        <PARAM NAME="FontHeight" VALUE="200">
        <PARAM NAME="FontCharSet" VALUE="0">
        <PARAM NAME="FontPitchAndFamily" VALUE="2">
        <PARAM NAME="FontWeight" VALUE="700">
</OBJECT>
<OBJECT ID="txtOther"
 CLASSID="CLSID:8BD21D10-EC42-11CE-9E0D-00AA006002F3"
 STYLE="TOP:187pt;LEFT:204pt;WIDTH:173pt;HEIGHT:17pt;TABINDEX:13;ZINDEX:13;">
        <PARAM NAME="VariousPropertyBits" VALUE="746604571">
        <PARAM NAME="Size" VALUE="6103;600">
        <PARAM NAME="FontName" VALUE="Arial">
        <PARAM NAME="FontHeight" VALUE="240">
        <PARAM NAME="FontCharSet" VALUE="0">
        <PARAM NAME="FontPitchAndFamily" VALUE="2">
</OBJECT>
<OBJECT ID="optAND2"
 CLASSID="CLSID:8BD21D50-EC42-11CE-9E0D-00AA006002F3"
 STYLE="TOP:80pt;LEFT:6pt;WIDTH:41pt;HEIGHT:18pt;TABINDEX:14;ZINDEX:14;">
        <PARAM NAME="BackColor" VALUE="16777215">
        <PARAM NAME="ForeColor" VALUE="2147483666">
        <PARAM NAME="DisplayStyle" VALUE="5">
        <PARAM NAME="Size" VALUE="1446;635">
        <PARAM NAME="Value" VALUE="1">
        <PARAM NAME="Caption" VALUE="AND">
        <PARAM NAME="GroupName" VALUE="Group2">
```

continues

Listing 14.5. continued

```
            <PARAM NAME="FontEffects" VALUE="1073741827">
            <PARAM NAME="FontCharSet" VALUE="0">
            <PARAM NAME="FontPitchAndFamily" VALUE="2">
            <PARAM NAME="FontWeight" VALUE="700">
    </OBJECT>
    <OBJECT ID="optOR2"
     CLASSID="CLSID:8BD21D50-EC42-11CE-9E0D-00AA006002F3"
     STYLE="TOP:80pt;LEFT:47pt;WIDTH:36pt;HEIGHT:18pt;TABINDEX:15;ZINDEX:15;">
            <PARAM NAME="BackColor" VALUE="16777215">
            <PARAM NAME="ForeColor" VALUE="2147483666">
            <PARAM NAME="DisplayStyle" VALUE="5">
            <PARAM NAME="Size" VALUE="1270;635">
            <PARAM NAME="Value" VALUE="0">
            <PARAM NAME="Caption" VALUE="OR">
            <PARAM NAME="GroupName" VALUE="Group2">
            <PARAM NAME="FontEffects" VALUE="1073741827">
            <PARAM NAME="FontCharSet" VALUE="0">
            <PARAM NAME="FontPitchAndFamily" VALUE="2">
            <PARAM NAME="FontWeight" VALUE="700">
    </OBJECT>
    <OBJECT ID="lblPrice"
     CLASSID="CLSID:978C9E23-D4B0-11CE-BF2D-00AA003F40D0"
     STYLE="TOP:212pt;LEFT:6pt;WIDTH:73pt;HEIGHT:17pt;ZINDEX:16;">
            <PARAM NAME="ForeColor" VALUE="16711680">
            <PARAM NAME="BackColor" VALUE="16777215">
            <PARAM NAME="Caption" VALUE="Unit Price:">
            <PARAM NAME="Size" VALUE="2575;600">
            <PARAM NAME="FontName" VALUE="Arial">
            <PARAM NAME="FontEffects" VALUE="1073741825">
            <PARAM NAME="FontHeight" VALUE="240">
            <PARAM NAME="FontCharSet" VALUE="0">
            <PARAM NAME="FontPitchAndFamily" VALUE="2">
            <PARAM NAME="FontWeight" VALUE="700">
    </OBJECT>
    <OBJECT ID="lblInEqual"
     CLASSID="CLSID:978C9E23-D4B0-11CE-BF2D-00AA003F40D0"
    STYLE="TOP:206pt;LEFT:116pt;WIDTH:14pt;HEIGHT:22pt;ZINDEX:17;">
            <PARAM NAME="ForeColor" VALUE="16711680">
            <PARAM NAME="BackColor" VALUE="16777215">
            <PARAM NAME="Caption" VALUE="&lt;">
            <PARAM NAME="Size" VALUE="511;767">
            <PARAM NAME="FontName" VALUE="Arial">
            <PARAM NAME="FontEffects" VALUE="1073741825">
            <PARAM NAME="FontHeight" VALUE="400">
            <PARAM NAME="FontCharSet" VALUE="0">
            <PARAM NAME="FontPitchAndFamily" VALUE="2">
            <PARAM NAME="FontWeight" VALUE="700">
    </OBJECT>
    <OBJECT ID="cboTitle"
     CLASSID="CLSID:8BD21D30-EC42-11CE-9E0D-00AA006002F3"
     STYLE="TOP:3pt;LEFT:117pt;WIDTH:46pt;HEIGHT:17pt;TABINDEX:18;ZINDEX:18;">
            <PARAM NAME="VariousPropertyBits" VALUE="746604571">
            <PARAM NAME="DisplayStyle" VALUE="3">
```

```
                  <PARAM NAME="Size" VALUE="1623;600">
                  <PARAM NAME="MatchEntry" VALUE="1">
                  <PARAM NAME="ShowDropButtonWhen" VALUE="2">
                  <PARAM NAME="FontName" VALUE="Arial">
                  <PARAM NAME="FontHeight" VALUE="240">
                  <PARAM NAME="FontCharSet" VALUE="0">
                  <PARAM NAME="FontPitchAndFamily" VALUE="2">
          </OBJECT>
          <OBJECT ID="txtPrice"
           CLASSID="CLSID:8BD21D10-EC42-11CE-9E0D-00AA006002F3"
           STYLE="TOP:209pt;LEFT:140pt;WIDTH:53pt;HEIGHT:17pt;TABINDEX:19;ZINDEX:19;">
                  <PARAM NAME="VariousPropertyBits" VALUE="746604571">
                  <PARAM NAME="Size" VALUE="1870;600">
                  <PARAM NAME="Value" VALUE="50.00">
                  <PARAM NAME="FontName" VALUE="Arial">
                  <PARAM NAME="FontHeight" VALUE="240">
                  <PARAM NAME="FontCharSet" VALUE="0">
                  <PARAM NAME="FontPitchAndFamily" VALUE="2">
          </OBJECT>
          <OBJECT ID="cboAuthor"
           CLASSID="CLSID:8BD21D30-EC42-11CE-9E0D-00AA006002F3"
           STYLE="TOP:55pt;LEFT:117pt;WIDTH:45pt;HEIGHT:17pt;TABINDEX:20;ZINDEX:20;">
                  <PARAM NAME="VariousPropertyBits" VALUE="746604571">
                  <PARAM NAME="DisplayStyle" VALUE="3">
                  <PARAM NAME="Size" VALUE="1588;600">
                  <PARAM NAME="MatchEntry" VALUE="1">
                  <PARAM NAME="ShowDropButtonWhen" VALUE="2">
                  <PARAM NAME="FontName" VALUE="Arial">
                  <PARAM NAME="FontHeight" VALUE="240">
                  <PARAM NAME="FontCharSet" VALUE="0">
                  <PARAM NAME="FontPitchAndFamily" VALUE="2">
          </OBJECT>
  </DIV>

  <SCRIPT LANGUAGE="VBScript">
  <!--
  ' Change direction of inequality when clicked
  ' on by user
  sub lblInEqual_Click
     if lblInEqual.caption = ">" then
        lblInEqual.caption = "<"
     else
        lblInEqual.caption = ">"
     end if
  end sub
  -->
  </SCRIPT>
```

There is something very significant here that has not been explicitly pointed out previously. Not only is it possible to attach VB scripts to controls in your HTML files, it is also possible, as shown in the example, to attach scripts to the layout object itself and to objects within the layout. Listing 14.5 contains two such scripts. The script at the beginning of the file

(pub_query_layout_OnLoad()) is invoked by the layout control's OnLoad event and is responsible for loading options into the ComboBox control using the AddItem method. It also presets
the value property that is initially displayed. The script at the end of the file (lblInEqual_Click)
is used to toggle the displayed value of the inequality (<, >) label when the user clicks it.

Creating the HTML Form

A Microsoft Forms 2.0 CommandButton control is included in the HTML form that holds
the layout control. The event procedure (btnSubmit_Click()) associated with this button is used
to perform validation and checking of user entries to the fields on the form as well as invoke
the form's submit method in order to submit the form to the server for processing. Doing things
in this manner allows you to execute the code necessary to validate input and inhibit submission of the form should any problems be detected. This would not have been possible using an
intrinsic HTML SUBMIT button type.

The HTML and VBScript code for this form (refer to Figure 14.6) is shown in Listing 14.6.

Listing 14.6. HTML and VBScript code for the pubs database query form shown in Figure 14.6.

```
<!--
    pubs_query.htm - Database query form
    Contains HTML Layout, HTML controls and VBScript for Controls
    Created Feb 1997 - Drew Kittel
-->

<html>
<HEAD>
<title>Publisher's Query Page</title>
</HEAD>
<BODY bgcolor="#FFFFFF">

<DIV align="center">
<center>
<table border="0" width="100%">
    <tr>
        <td align="center" width="10%">
        <IMG src="books.gif"  width="64" height="64">
        </td>
        <td width="50%"><font color="#0000FF" size="6" face="Arial">
        <strong>Publisher's Query Page</strong></font>
        </td>
    </tr>
</table>
</center>
</DIV>
<hr>

<p align="center"><font size="4" face="Arial"><em><strong>
Use the following form to query our extensive book database
and view abstracts and summaries of books matching your search criteria.
</strong></em></font></p>
```

```
<FORM ACTION="http://dkittel.clark.net:8080/cgi-win/process_form_demo.exe"
      METHOD="POST"  NAME="QFORM">

<center>
<table border="1" width="80%" bordercolor="#0000FF">
    <tr>
        <td align="center">
        <OBJECT ID="qform_layout"
         CLASSID="CLSID:812AE312-8B8E-11CF-93C8-00AA00C08FDF">
            <PARAM NAME="ALXPATH" REF VALUE="pub_query_layout.alx">
        </OBJECT>
        </td>
    </tr>
    <TR>
        <TD ALIGN=CENTER bgcolor="#70BBF3">
        <OBJECT ID="btnSubmit" WIDTH=115 HEIGHT=32
         CLASSID="CLSID:D7053240-CE69-11CD-A777-00DD01143C57">
            <PARAM NAME="ForeColor" VALUE="16711680">
            <PARAM NAME="BackColor" VALUE="13750737">
            <PARAM NAME="Caption" VALUE="SUBMIT QUERY">
            <PARAM NAME="Size" VALUE="3037;846">
            <PARAM NAME="FontName" VALUE="Arial">
            <PARAM NAME="FontEffects" VALUE="1073741825">
            <PARAM NAME="FontHeight" VALUE="200">
            <PARAM NAME="FontCharSet" VALUE="0">
            <PARAM NAME="FontPitchAndFamily" VALUE="2">
            <PARAM NAME="ParagraphAlign" VALUE="3">
            <PARAM NAME="FontWeight" VALUE="700">
        </OBJECT>
        </TD>
    </TR>
</table>
</center>


<! -- preset hidden form variables used to send user input on Submit -->
        <INPUT TYPE=hidden NAME="TITLE" value=" ">
        <INPUT TYPE=hidden NAME="TITLEOP" value=" ">
        <INPUT TYPE=hidden NAME="TITLECLAUSE" value=" ">
        <INPUT TYPE=hidden NAME="AUTHOR" value = " ">
        <INPUT TYPE=hidden NAME="AUTHOROP" value = " ">
        <INPUT TYPE=hidden NAME="AUTHORCLAUSE" value=" ">
        <INPUT TYPE=hidden NAME="CAT1" value = "OFF">
        <INPUT TYPE=hidden NAME="CAT2" value = "OFF">
        <INPUT TYPE=hidden NAME="CAT3" value = "OFF">
        <INPUT TYPE=hidden NAME="CAT4" value = "OFF">
        <INPUT TYPE=hidden NAME="CAT5" value = "OFF">
        <INPUT TYPE=hidden NAME="CAT6" value = "OFF">
        <INPUT TYPE=hidden NAME="CATOTHER" value = "OFF">
        <INPUT TYPE=hidden NAME="INEQUALITY" value = " ">
        <INPUT TYPE=hidden NAME="PRICE" value = " ">

</FORM>
```

continues

Listing 14.6. continued

```vbscript
<SCRIPT LANGUAGE="VBScript">
<!--
''''''''''''''''''''''''''''''''''''''''''''''''
' Check if field has data or is empty
''''''''''''''''''''''''''''''''''''''''''''''''

Function ValidateTextField(formField, warnMessage)
    if Len(formField.Value) = 0 then
        alert warnMessage
        ValidateTextField = 0
        exit Function
    end if
    ValidateTextField = 1
End Function


''''''''''''''''''''''''''''''''''''''''''''''''''''''''
' This code is executed by a button click.
' Execution is prior to sending form contents
' via submit method
''''''''''''''''''''''''''''''''''''''''''''''''''''''''


Sub btnSubmit_Click()

    Dim F
    Set F = Document.QFORM

    ' Alert user that some field data may be missing (not
    ' that they are necessarily needed for the current query)

    dummy = ValidateTextField(F.qform_layout.txtTitle, "Title field is empty")
    dummy = ValidateTextField(F.qform_layout.txtAuthor, "Author field is empty")

    ' Don't allow submit if price is missing or < 0

    if ValidateTextField(F.qform_layout.txtPrice, "You must supply a Price
    ➥value!") = 0 then
        exit sub
    end if

    if F.qform_layout.txtPrice.Value < 0 then
        alert "Price value must be a positve number.  Re-enter a value and
        ➥re-submit the form"
        exit sub
    end if


    ' Obtain values of controls on HTML Layout Control
    ' and set hidden variables for submit to CGI program

    F.TITLE.value = F.qform_layout.txtTitle.Value
    F.TITLEOP.value = F.qform_layout.cboTitle.Value
    F.AUTHOR.value = F.qform_layout.txtAuthor.Value
    F.AUTHOROP.value = F.qform_layout.cboAuthor.Value
    F.INEQUALITY.value = F.qform_layout.lblInEqual.Caption
    F.PRICE.value = F.qform_layout.txtPrice.Value
```

```
' set boolean operators

if F.qform_layout.optAND1.value = 0 then
    F.TITLECLAUSE.value = "AND"
else
    F.TITLECLAUSE.value = "OR"
end if

if F.qform_layout.optAND2.value = 0 then
    F.AUTHORCLAUSE.value = "AND"
else
    F.AUTHORCLAUSE.value = "OR"
end if


' Create and echo a SQL-like query statement that illustrates to user
' what query will be used to query the database at the server.
' Ask user if this is correct and inhibit the submit if NO

sqlQuery = "SELECT  title,  price" + Chr(13) + "FROM  pubs..titles" +
➡Chr(13) + "WHERE" + Chr(13)

tClause = "     title" + " " + F.TITLEOP.value + " " + F.TITLE.value + " " +
➡F.TITLECLAUSE.value +Chr(13)
aClause = "     author" + " " + F.AUTHOROP.value + " " + F.AUTHOR.value +
➡ " " + F.AUTHORCLAUSE.value +Chr(13)
pClause = "     price" + " " + F.INEQUALITY.value + " " + F.PRICE.value +
➡ " " + Chr(13) + Chr(13)

' Determine what checkboxes are selected
' continue creation of SQL-like statement to echo

typeClause = "     type in ("

if F.qform_layout.chk1.value = True then
    F.CAT1.value = F.qform_layout.chk1.Caption
    typeClause = typeClause + F.qform_layout.chk1.Caption + ", "
end if
if F.qform_layout.chk2.value = True then
    F.CAT2.value = F.qform_layout.chk2.Caption
    typeClause = typeClause + F.qform_layout.chk2.Caption + ", "
end if
if F.qform_layout.chk3.value = True then
    F.CAT3.value = F.qform_layout.chk3.Caption
    typeClause = typeClause + F.qform_layout.chk3.Caption + ", "
end if
if F.qform_layout.chk4.value = True then
    F.CAT4.value = F.qform_layout.chk4.Caption
    typeClause = typeClause + F.qform_layout.chk4.Caption + ", "
end if
if F.qform_layout.chk5.value = True then
    F.CAT5.value = F.qform_layout.chk5.Caption
    typeClause = typeClause +  F.qform_layout.chk5.Caption + ", "
end if
if F.qform_layout.chk6.value = True then
    F.CATOTHER.value = F.qform_layout.txtOther.Value
    typeClause = typeClause + F.qform_layout.txtOther.Value + ", "
end if
```

continues

Listing 14.6. continued

```
    typeClause = typeClause + " )" + Chr(13)


    ' Finish formulating query and prompt user to validate it
    ' if user clicks on No button, exit the sub without submit
    ' of form.  Otherwise submi the form.

    sqlQuery = sqlQuery + tClause + aClause + typeClause + pClause
    sqlMessage = "Your are about to send the following query" + Chr(13) +
Chr(13)
    sqlMessage = sqlMessage + sqlQuery + "Is this correct?"

    if MsgBox(sqlMessage, vbYesNo, "Validate Query") = vbNo then
        exit sub
    end if

    ' SUBMIT

    call Document.QFORM.Submit()

end sub

-->
</SCRIPT>

</BODY>
</html>
```

Here are a few things to note about this example:

- The event procedure btnSubmit_Click() performs most of the work of collecting values of form fields from input objects on the layout control. It does so by using full references to the objects and the property of interest (for example, F.qform_layout.txtOther.Value was used to obtain the input to the textbox if the user selected Other as a book category). The procedure also performs a series of validations and checking of input by the user.

- The function ValidateTextField is called by btnSubmit_Click to determine if certain text input objects have any content entered by the user. If the return value from this function indicates that a field is empty, the user is warned via an Alert dialog. In the case of the price field, the btnSubmit_Click procedure is exited before the form is submitted, thereby forcing the user to enter an appropriate input before the form is submitted to the user.

- As btnSubmit_Click is processing the user's inputs to the form, it also uses those values to construct a SQL-like statement that the user is asked to validate. This statement is displayed using a message box with Yes and No buttons (an example of which can be seen in Figure 14.8). If the user is not satisfied that the query to be submitted is appropriate, he can click No, in which case the procedure is exited and the user is allowed to modify input to the form. If the user selects Yes, the form is submitted (that is, its `submit` method is invoked).

FIGURE 14.8.

This message box asks the user to validate that the SQL query constructed is what the user intended.

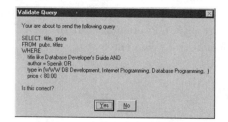

■ `btnSubmit_Click` uses values obtained from objects on the ALX layout to set values for `HIDDEN` form elements. It is the name and value pairs of these form elements that are sent to the server when the form is submitted.

■ If all validations and user responses indicate that the form content and query formulation are okay, then `btnSubmit_Click` invokes the form's submit method to submit the form and its contents to the server for processing. In this example, the `ACTION` attribute associated with the form specifies that the CGI program `process_form_demo.exe` will be used to process the form data. Don't worry about what this program does or how it is created right now—Chapter 18, "The Common Gateway Interface (CGI)," will show you all about CGI, developing Windows CGI programs using Visual Basic, and how this program is created. For now it is enough to know that this program echoes back an HTML representation of the input supplied by the user. The results of this for the form shown in Figure 14.6 are illustrated in Figure 14.9.

FIGURE 14.9.

The form content (that is, field name and value pairs) received at the server when the form shown in Figure 14.6 is submitted.

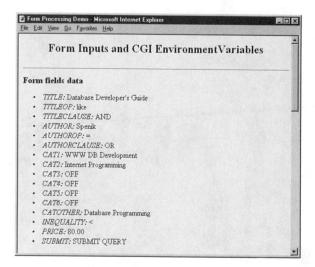

■ Using client-side scripts to perform validations and checks on user input, as well as immediately alerting the user to possible problems has distinct advantages to performing these checks at the server. First, the user is provided immediate feedback and is afforded the opportunity to correct mistakes without having to wait for the form to be validated at the server and an error response returned. Second, network traffic is reduced and server CPU resources are conserved by not submitting and responding to forms containing invalid content.

Summary

The goal of this chapter was to show you how to employ HTML 3.2 objects, ActiveX controls, and VBScript to develop form interfaces for your Web database and other applications and to make them far more interactive and functional than those created with HTML 2.0 alone.

We started the chapter by showing you how VB scripts are attached to HTML documents, associated with certain events, and then executed when those events occur. Next, we presented an overview of the Internet Explorer object model for scripting and showed numerous examples of how component objects, events, methods, and procedures can be accessed by your VB scripts.

The final section of the chapter was dedicated to applying the material you learned in earlier sections. We demonstrated how to format form objects and content using HTML tables as well as the HTML layout control. We also presented two in-depth examples, a search engine query form and a database query form, which illustrated how tables and the HTML layout control can be used to create nice form layouts. We also demonstrated the power of combining VBScript, ActiveX, and HTML objects to create application user interfaces, complete with interactive responses to user actions, input validation, and submission of forms via VBScript.

VI

Client-Side Development Using Visual Basic 5

15

Creating ActiveX Documents for the Web with VB 5

by Mark Spenik

In this chapter, you will learn about an exciting new Visual Basic 5 intranet/Internet technology called ActiveX documents. This chapter will show you how to create ActiveX documents and suggest how, when, and where to use ActiveX documents.

ActiveX Document Overview

ActiveX documents enable you to develop Visual Basic 5 applications that can be used in container applications, such as Microsoft Internet Explorer or Microsoft Outlook. An ActiveX document is not a traditional standard word processing document, such as a Microsoft Word document or a Lotus Word Pro document. Instead, think of an ActiveX document as a Visual Basic Internet application. ActiveX documents are designed and created in the Visual Basic 5 development environment and can use ActiveX controls and forms.

You might be confused by the word *document* in *ActiveX document* instead of *application.* Step back for a moment and think about a Microsoft Excel spreadsheet used to compute a tax return. The spreadsheet contains the formulas and data required to generate a tax return. The spreadsheet offers application-like functionality because it can be used to perform tasks such as computing tax returns. The spreadsheet alone is not an application, however; it requires the application Microsoft Excel to create and use the spreadsheet. You can give your friends a copy of the tax return spreadsheet, and they can do their taxes as long as they have Microsoft Excel. One other point: The Excel spreadsheet also can be viewed in other applications that act as containers—for example, a Visual Basic application using the OLE2 custom control. An ActiveX document created in Visual Basic 5 is similar to the Excel spreadsheet. By itself, the ActiveX document is not an application. With a valid container application and ActiveX component, the ActiveX document performs like an application.

To help you nail down the full concept of an ActiveX document, look at the example shown in Figure 15.1.

FIGURE 15.1.

Visual Basic ActiveX document architecture.

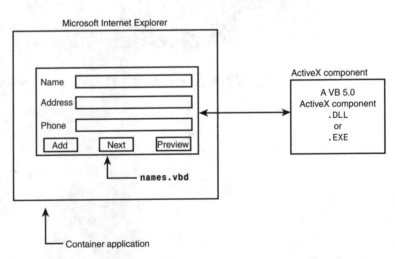

Figure 15.1 shows the Microsoft Internet Explorer acting as a container application for an ActiveX document. The file `names.vbd` is the ActiveX document. The ActiveX document contains textboxes and buttons that enable users to update a database with personal address information. In order for an ActiveX document to execute, an ActiveX component, in addition to a container application and an ActiveX document, is required (such as an Excel spreadsheet requiring Microsoft Excel). When you create an ActiveX document with Visual Basic 5, a document file (`.vbd` extension) and an ActiveX component are generated (in-process, such as DLL, or out-of-process, such as EXE).

How an ActiveX Document Works in a Web Environment

When using an ActiveX document in a Web application, the ActiveX document is not placed on a Web page; instead, the ActiveX document *replaces* the Web page. When a user accesses a URL with an ActiveX document, the ActiveX document and any required ActiveX controls are loaded to the client machine along with the ActiveX component required to execute the ActiveX document. The downloaded ActiveX controls and the ActiveX component are registered on the client machine. The HTML page that loads the ActiveX document uses script to invoke the ActiveX document via the `OnLoad` event. The HTML page is replaced by the ActiveX document, and the ActiveX document executes in the container application on the client machine. ActiveX documents cannot execute without a container application.

> **NOTE**
>
> Several applications can host ActiveX documents, such as Microsoft Outlook, Visual Basic 5, and Microsoft Internet Explorer. The focus of this book is Web database development. As such, this chapter focuses on using ActiveX documents in a Web browser (for example, Microsoft Internet Explorer).

When and Why to Use ActiveX Documents

ActiveX documents are a really cool Visual Basic 5 feature, but those of you who program for a living and want to try out this new technology will ultimately face the manager afraid of technology or the internal software police who must study every technology to death (until it's old technology) and officially approve it before anyone is allowed to use it. How do you justify using ActiveX documents? I believe that the strength of ActiveX documents will prove to be in an intranet environment as opposed to an Internet environment. In an intranet environment, ActiveX documents enable you to perform these tasks:

- Viewing and modifying corporate databases using ODBC, DAO, RDO, and data-bound ActiveX controls
- Providing the user interface tier in a three-tier architecture application

If you are thinking that these tasks are identical to the tasks you currently use Visual Basic and other development tools to perform, you are correct. But the advantage that ActiveX documents offer over current development tools is the buzzword of the late 1990s: *lower-cost ownership.* ActiveX documents are easier to install and maintain than existing client/server applications, which results in a lower cost of ownership. ActiveX documents install themselves from a central code base, for example. No information system personnel must go from PC to PC (or use software such as Microsoft SMS) to perform software installations. When a new employee starts work, instead of ensuring that he has all the proper applications, you can have them access a URL, and the application installs itself. When the ActiveX document requires a revision, you just have to change the software in one location. No need to worry about upgrading a user to a newer version or that a user is working with an older version. When a user accesses the revision via a Web browser, the ActiveX document automatically upgrades itself.

The ease of software distribution via ActiveX documents makes ActiveX documents very attractive in an intranet environment. If your company executes all your applications from a central directory on a LAN instead of installing them on users' PCs, you probably are thinking that ActiveX documents will not cut your cost of ownership because your applications are installed in only one location anyway. In this type of environment, ActiveX documents offer better performance because running applications from a LAN is always slower than executing them from a client PC. Also, you have the added benefit of no software distribution requirements. And even though you might have all your applications installed on a LAN, IS personnel are often required to run minimum setup and installation procedures on client machines when giving them access to new applications.

ActiveX documents are not restricted to the intranet and can be used as well on the Internet. You might want to use an ActiveX document when you find HTML and VBScript lacking in functionality for a complex client form. You might prefer to use ActiveX documents instead of a standard HTML page because of the powerful features of Visual Basic 5's design environment and integrated debugger compared to the current HTML and scripting environment.

> **NOTE**
>
> You cannot use ActiveX documents over the Internet to interact with corporate databases using standard Visual Basic 5 controls and ODBC (which can be performed in an intranet). Microsoft has introduced a technology called *Advanced Data Connector* (ADC), which enables you to use bound data connections to a corporate database via the Internet (HTTP). ADC is covered in Chapter 23, "MS SQL Server Internet Capabilities."

Creating an ActiveX Document

ActiveX documents are easy to build and test. This section will give you a detailed walkthrough of the steps required to create an ActiveX document. You will learn about the primary object that makes up an ActiveX document: the UserDocument object.

> **TIP**
>
> You will get the most out of the next section if you follow along and perform each step in Visual Basic 5. The database application created in this section is not included on the CD-ROM that accompanies this book.

The UserDocument

Before going over the steps required to create an ActiveX document, you should understand the primary object used to create ActiveX documents: the UserDocument. The UserDocument is the equivalent of a Visual Basic form in a standard client/server project. Like a standard Visual Basic form, the UserDocument object has events, properties, methods, and ActiveX controls (except the OLE2 control) that can be placed on the UserDocument object.

Steps to Create an ActiveX Document

To create an ActiveX document, follow these steps:

1. Create a new Visual Basic project by selecting File|New Project from the Visual Basic menu. The Visual Basic New Project dialog box, shown in Figure 15.2, appears. Double-click the ActiveX Document DLL icon in the New Project dialog box.

FIGURE 15.2.
The Visual Basic New Project dialog box.

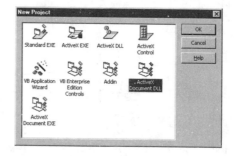

> **NOTE**
>
> An ActiveX document's associated ActiveX components can be created as DLLs or EXEs. You will learn more about the differences between an ActiveX DLL and EXE in Chapter 22, "Writing Server-Side Applications with VB 5 ActiveX Components." When developing ActiveX documents, it is important for you to know that the ActiveX DLL will provide you with the best performance. One drawback of an ActiveX DLL is that when you use Internet Explorer as the ActiveX document container, the ActiveX document using an ActiveX DLL cannot display any modeless forms (all forms must be modal). An ActiveX document using an EXE component can display modeless forms in Internet Explorer.

The new project contains a single UserDocument object called UserDocument1.

2. Double-click UserDocument1 in the Visual Basic Project box. UserDocument1 appears, as shown in Figure 15.3. Notice that the UserDocument object resembles a standard Visual Basic form. Like a standard Visual Basic form, you can set UserDocument properties by using the standard Properties dialog box.

FIGURE 15.3.

The UserDocument *object in a Visual Basic project.*

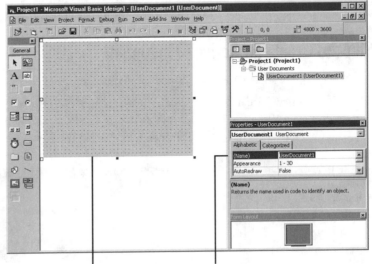

UserDocument1 object   Properties dialog box

3. Add the following ActiveX controls to UserDocument1: a data control and three textboxes. UserDocument1 should look similar to Figure 15.4.

4. Set the data control's DatabaseName property to the Microsoft Access database that comes with Visual Basic 5, Biblio.mdb. Biblio.mdb is located in the directory in which Visual Basic 5 is installed.

FIGURE 15.4.

The UserDocument *object with ActiveX controls.*

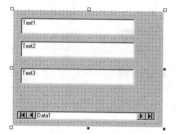

5. Set the data control's RecordSource property to Authors (the Authors table in the Biblio.mdb database).

6. Set the DataSource property on all three textbox controls to Data1.

7. Set the textbox control's DataField property to Au_Id for text1, Author for text2, and Year Born for text3.

You now have constructed an ActiveX document.

Testing and Debugging the ActiveX Document

You now are ready to test the ActiveX document you created. To test the ActiveX document, run the project from Visual Basic by choosing Run | Start. Open Microsoft Internet Explorer. From Microsoft Internet Explorer, open the User1Document.vbd file. The file is located in your Visual Basic directory, because the project was not saved. The ActiveX document loads into Internet Explorer, as shown in Figure 15.5.

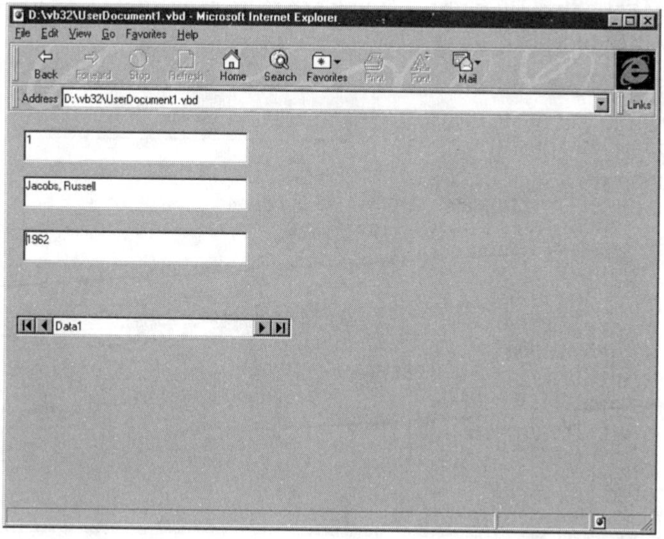

FIGURE 15.5.

Microsoft Internet Explorer displaying an ActiveX document for database manipulation.

Click the data control. Notice the way in which you move through each record. Try to update a record. Your ActiveX document is manipulating the Authors table as if you had generated a standard Visual Basic project, except that you are doing it from within a browser.

You can debug ActiveX documents by using the same techniques you normally use when debugging Visual Basic projects, such as setting breakpoints and stepping through code. Remember that your ActiveX document uses a container application such as Microsoft Internet Explorer, however, and stopping the ActiveX document could cause errors to occur in the container application. Breaking into a running ActiveX document project by using a breakpoint or pressing Ctrl+Break does not cause errors in Internet Explorer. Also, single-stepping through code does not cause errors to occur in Internet Explorer. Stopping the application or changing code that requires resetting the project and starting a new session without shutting down Internet Explorer first causes errors in Internet Explorer. So before stopping your ActiveX document when debugging, it's a good practice to first quit the container application (Internet Explorer) and then stop your ActiveX document.

Using ActiveX Documents from the Web

When you create an executable for an ActiveX document using Visual Basic 5, two files are generated: the ActiveX document that has the file extension .vbd and the ActiveX component required by the ActiveX component (a DLL or EXE). To access your ActiveX document from the Web, you first need to reference the document in HTML. Because the ActiveX document will replace the existing HTML page, you should create a special HTML page that references your ActiveX document by using the <OBJECT> tag, as well as invoking the ActiveX document event Window_OnLoad. You then can jump to the ActiveX document HTML page from another HTML page by using an anchor link or a redirect. Listing 15.1 shows an example of an HTML page used to load an ActiveX document called UserDocument1.

Listing 15.1. An HTML page to load an ActiveX document.

```
<HTML>
<OBJECT ID="UserDocument1"
CLASSID="CLSID:9D456E21-883D-11D0-9CE8-444553540000"
CODEBASE="Project1.CAB#version=1,0,0,0">
</OBJECT>

<SCRIPT LANGUAGE="VBScript">
Sub Window_OnLoad
    Document.Open
    Document.Write "<FRAMESET>"
    Document.Write "<FRAME SRC=""UserDocument1.VBD"">"
    Document.Write "</FRAMESET>"
    Document.Close
End Sub
</SCRIPT>
</HTML>
```

The HTML and script in Listing 15.1 will load the `UserDocument` object and the ActiveX component from a Website, install and register them on a client machine, and activate the ActiveX document. The ActiveX document and ActiveX component are compressed together in a special download file called a *cabinet file*. Cabinet files and Internet/intranet distribution are covered in detail in Chapter 17, "Distributing ActiveX Documents and Controls via the Web Using VB 5."

> **TIP**
>
> Visual Basic 5's Application Setup Wizard can generate Internet/intranet distribution packages. For an ActiveX document, the Setup Wizard creates the required cabinet files as well as the HTML required to invoke the ActiveX document. The Application Setup Wizard is covered in Chapter 17.

Adding Forms and Additional `UserDocuments`

Earlier in this chapter, I told you to think of an ActiveX document as an Internet version of a Visual Basic application, and the `UserDocument` object as a Visual Basic form. And these are good analogies. However, when creating an ActiveX document project, you can add standard Visual Basic forms to your project. The forms are Visual Basic forms rather than ActiveX documents. A form must be called initially by an ActiveX document, which means that a user cannot access that form without first accessing an ActiveX document. After a form is loaded, it can load other forms. The one restriction when using forms is that if your ActiveX component is a DLL (in-process), forms can be loaded only as modal. Figure 15.6 shows a database application that uses a form to display a secondary table in a grid.

FIGURE 15.6.

An ActiveX document and form displaying database information.

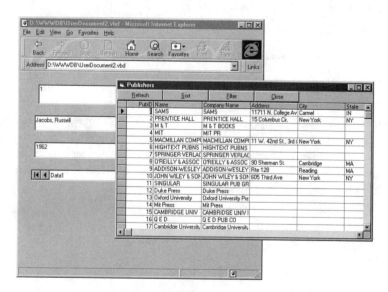

Notice how the form in Figure 15.6 looks exactly like a standard Visual Basic form (after all, it *is* a standard Visual Basic form). The form was created by selecting Database Grid Form from the Form Wizard. Both the form and the ActiveX document in this figure use ActiveX data controls and DAO. The database used is the Microsoft Access database `Biblio.mdb`.

In addition to adding forms to an ActiveX document project, you can add additional `UserDocuments` in much the same way that you add an additional form. You can add additional forms and `UserDocuments` to a project by choosing Project | Add Form or Add UserDocument. Each `UserDocument` object you add to a project generates an ActiveX document (a file with a `vbd` extension). A single ActiveX component is generated and shared by all the ActiveX documents in the project.

When to Use Forms or `UserDocuments`

So what are the guidelines for using forms or `UserDocuments` when building screens in an ActiveX document application? If you want the user screen to be contained within the browser, you should use ActiveX documents. If you want to navigate directly to the user screen, you should use a `UserDocument` because forms can be called only from ActiveX documents. Use forms when the screen you are displaying to the user is a secondary screen that requires a user to start from the ActiveX document.

Navigating Between Forms and Other ActiveX Documents from an ActiveX Document

The same syntax is used to display a form from an ActiveX document as a standard Visual Basic application. The following line of code called from an ActiveX document, for example, displays a modeless form named `frmTest`:

```
frmTest.Show
```

This line of code called from an ActiveX document shows a modal form:

```
frmTest.Show vbModal
```

Remember that when you use Internet Explorer as a container application, ActiveX documents that use in-process components (DLLs) can show only modal forms. To help determine whether a container can display a modal form, you can use an `App` object property new to Visual Basic 5: `NonModalAllowed`. If `NonModalAllowed` is `True`, the container can show modal forms. The following code checks the `App` object property `NonModalAllowed` and displays a modal or non-modal form based on the property value.

```
If App.NonModalAllowed Then
    frmTest.Show
Else
    frmTest.Show vbModal
End If
```

Navigating between ActiveX documents requires a different technique. To navigate from one user document to another requires using the Visual Basic 5 `Hyperlink` object and the `UserDocument` object. The `Hyperlink` object enables you to jump to a URL in a Web environment. The `Hyperlink` object has the following methods:

- ■ `NavigateTo`: Goes to a specific URL
- ■ `GoBack`: Navigates back to the URL in the History list
- ■ `GoForward`: Navigates forward to a URL in the History list

Use the base ActiveX document object, `UserDocument`, to navigate between ActiveX documents. To navigate to another ActiveX document, for example, use the `UserDocument` property `Hyperlink`, which obtains a reference to the `Hyperlink` object. The following code is in the `click` event of an ActiveX document called `UserDocument1` and navigates the Web browser to a second ActiveX document located in the same directory called `UserDocument2`:

```
Private Sub Command1_Click()
    UserDocument.Hyperlink.NavigateTo _
        App.Path & "\" & "UserDocument2.vbd"
End Sub
```

Communicating Between ActiveX Documents

When creating a standard Visual Basic application, you can control the order in which clients view your forms. For example, `Form2` is loaded from a button on the startup form (for example, `Form1`). The user can't get to `Form2` without first starting at `Form1`. ActiveX documents don't offer you the same luxury and control over your user; because ActiveX documents are standalone objects, users can access them directly by entering the URL. You also may have ActiveX documents that need to share information. Sharing information or tracking document order requires the use of global variables. To add global variables to an ActiveX document application, add a standard Visual Basic module to the project. Declare the global variables shared by the ActiveX documents in the module. This example declares a global string variable called `strDoc`:

```
Public strDoc as String
```

To share information, set the variables in one ActiveX document and read them from another or modify them. You also can declare global references to objects such as a `UserDocument` object. You can use global variables of object references or other data types to track document order. When using an object, use the function `Is Nothing` to determine whether the object is set. If the object or global variable has been set properly, you know the correct document order has been followed. If the variable is not set properly, you can use the `Hyperlink` object to force the user to the proper starting ActiveX document. If you use global object variables, make sure that you set them to `Nothing` when you are finished to properly release the object reference.

Other ActiveX Document Features

ActiveX documents have some very unique features that make them very easy to use in an intranet/Internet environment, such as the capability to persist data and asynchronous downloading capabilities. This section takes a closer look at some additional ActiveX document features.

Menu Integration

If an ActiveX document has a menu, the menu is merged with the menu of the container application. You add menus to ActiveX documents in the same way that you add menus to a Visual Basic form, by using the Visual Basic Menu Editor. Figure 15.7 shows an example of an ActiveX document's menu merged with Microsoft Internet Explorer's menu.

FIGURE 15.7.

An ActiveX document menu merged with Microsoft Internet Explorer.

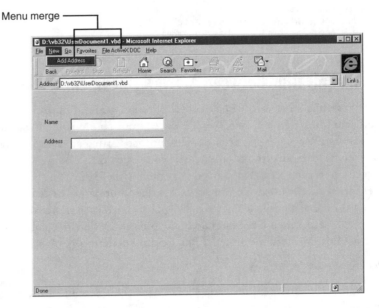

The `PropertyBag`

When using Microsoft Internet Explorer as a container application for an ActiveX document, you can use an object called `PropertyBag` to save and store data for the ActiveX document. After data is saved, the next time the ActiveX document is loaded, the saved properties can be retrieved and placed in the ActiveX document. When using Microsoft Internet Explorer, the values you save are written to the ActiveX document vbd file. The `PropertyBag` object has two methods: `ReadProperty` and `WriteProperty`. `ReadProperty` is used to read property values from the property bag, and WriteProperty is used to write values to the property bag. To write properties to the property bag when a value on the ActiveX form has changed, execute the PropertyChanged method, which notifies Internet Explorer that a property has changed. When Internet Explorer is terminated or moves to another page, the UserDocument WriteProperties event is fired. When the event fires, save any UserDocument variables by using the PropertyBag object's WriteProperty method. The variable name used to save the value does not have to match the name of the ActiveX control (label and textbox, for example) on the ActiveX document. The following example saves an ActiveX textbox named MyText to a file by using the PropertyBag object:

```
Private Sub UserDocument_WriteProperties(PropBag As PropertyBag)
    PropBag.WriteProperty "MyText", MyText.Text
End Sub
```

The syntax for the PropertyBag object's WriteProperty method follows:

```
PropBag.WriteProperty Variable, Value_to_Store, Default_Value
```

(Note: The Default_Value is optional.) When the ActiveX document is read, the ReadProperties event of the UserDocument object fires. When the event fires, use the PropertyBag object's ReadProperty method to retrieve values and place them in the ActiveX document. The following example reads the variable MyText stored in the WriteProperties event and sets the value of the ActiveX control MyText on the ActiveX document:

```
Private Sub UserDocument_ReadProperties(PropBag As PropertyBag)
 MyText.Text = PropBag.ReadProperty("MyText")
End Sub
```

The syntax for the PropertyBag object's ReadProperty method follows:

```
PropBag.ReadProperty(Value_to_Retrieve,Default)
```

(Note: The Default_Value is optional.) You also can save and read binary data types, such as pictures, by using the PropertyBag object's methods.

ViewPort

ActiveX documents can be displayed only in a container application such as Microsoft Internet Explorer. The viewing area of the container application in which the ActiveX document is displayed is called the *ViewPort*. Because an ActiveX document is designed to run in a container application, you can never be sure of the viewing area provided by the container application. If the container application viewing area is not large enough to display your ActiveX document, scrollbars appear so that the ActiveX document can be viewed. The UserDocument properties MinHeight and MinWidth set the minimum amount of viewing area required before scrollbars appear. Figure 15.8 shows an ActiveX document with scrollbars as a result of using a ViewPort that is too small.

FIGURE 15.8.
An ActiveX document with scrollbars.

Asynchronous Downloading

ActiveX documents support asynchronous downloads. Using asynchronous downloading, an ActiveX document can load large objects such as pictures or bitmaps in the background, which enables the ActiveX document to display before all the graphics arrive. To use asynchronous downloading, use the `AsyncRead` method of the `UserDocument` object. `AsyncRead` initiates the downloading process. When the download completes, the `AsynchReadComplete` event is fired.

Converting Existing Database Applications into ActiveX Documents

ActiveX documents sound great, but it sure would be nice to try them out with existing applications to check out the benefits of an ActiveX document database application in an intranet environment. No problem! Visual Basic 5 comes with an ActiveX Document Migration Wizard that migrates existing applications to ActiveX documents. This section walks you through the conversion of an existing Visual Basic database application into an ActiveX document database application. Figure 15.9 shows the Visual Basic application you'll migrate in this section.

FIGURE 15.9.
A Visual Basic database application.

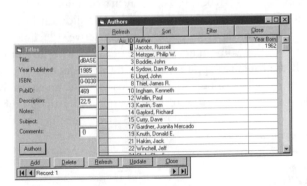

The database application in Figure 15.9 uses a Microsoft Access database that is located on a shared drive on a LAN. The database is used by 15 to 20 users. The application uses DAO to access the database. Whenever the application is modified, the new executable must be installed on all the user machines that use the application. Now take a look at the steps required to upgrade the application to ActiveX documents. The ActiveX Document Migration Wizard is a Visual Basic add-in.

To modify an existing Visual Basic project to an ActiveX document, follow these steps:

1. Open the project you want to migrate and then start the ActiveX Document Migration Wizard by selecting the ActiveX Document Migration Wizard from the Visual Basic Add-In menu. The ActiveX Document Migration Wizard-Form Selection dialog box appears, as shown in Figure 15.10.

FIGURE 15.10.

The ActiveX Document Migration Wizard-Form Selection dialog box.

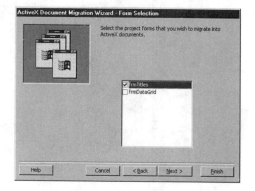

2. The Form Selection dialog box displays all the forms in the project. Enable the checkboxes beside the forms you want to convert to ActiveX documents. Click Next, and the ActiveX Document Migration Wizard-Options dialog box appears, as shown in Figure 15.11.

FIGURE 15.11.

The ActiveX Document Migration Wizard-Options dialog box.

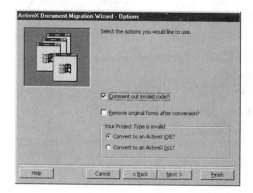

3. The Options dialog box enables you to select different options offered by the migration utility. Enable the Comment out invalid code? checkbox to have the wizard comment out invalid code. To remove the selected forms from the project and replace them with ActiveX documents, enable the Remove original forms after conversion? checkbox. Because the project being converted is not an ActiveX document project, you must select the type of ActiveX document to generate (DLL or EXE) by selecting the proper radio button. The default value is EXE. After you select the proper options, click Next. The Finished dialog box appears, as shown in Figure 15.12.

FIGURE 15.12.

The ActiveX Document Migration Wizard-Finished dialog box.

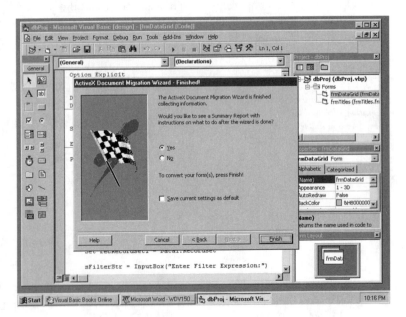

4. The wizard, by default, generates a summary report that tells you what to do after the migration is finished. To complete the migration, click Finish. The wizard migrates the selected forms to ActiveX documents. Invalid code or unsupported event procedures are commented out. Figure 15.13 shows the migrated application.

Keep in mind that when you migrate database applications to an intranet environment using ActiveX documents, the client PCs still must have the proper ODBC drivers installed on their machines when accessing an ODBC database. When using file databases, such as Microsoft Access, it is a good idea to use the full network UNC name for the location of the database file (for example, \\SERVER\SHARE\Directory path\FILE) instead of just using a shared drive letter. Using the full network name removes the possibility of your application not finding the database because of different drive mappings on a client PC.

FIGURE 15.13.

Migrating Visual Basic applications to ActiveX documents.

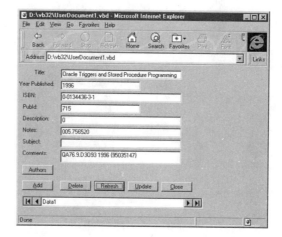

Summary

ActiveX documents enable you to bring your current Visual Basic database skills to the intranet. You can easily create new Web-based database applications that use current Visual Basic database object models, such as DAO and RDO. You also can use the Migration Wizard to transform existing Visual Basic applications into ActiveX documents. The major benefit of ActiveX document database applications is the capability to automatically distribute the software and any modifications via the Web. ActiveX documents are not restricted to the intranet. You can use ActiveX documents to replace existing HTML pages or in cases when performing a client-side task is too difficult to perform with HTML and script on the Internet.

16

Creating ActiveX Controls for the Web with VB 5

By Troy Rackley

Perhaps the most interesting feature of Visual Basic 5 is the capability to create ActiveX controls. What was once reserved for C++ programmers with a master's degree in Microsoft's Component Object Model now is available to Visual Basic programmers. ActiveX controls are presented in a simplified, object-oriented form with which VB programmers have become familiar. The simplification, however, does not hinder the possibilities available; you can create robust, distributable controls with ease.

This chapter presents a background on the creation of ActiveX controls and starts you on your way to creating custom controls. You will build some simple controls in this chapter that introduce you to the facilities available as a VB programmer.

An Overview and Introduction to the Terminology

Why build ActiveX controls? You might think that there are plenty of control vendors out there. "Why should I build controls when I need to get business-critical work done?" Or, "Hasn't XYZ company already built and tested the do-everything widget?" The answer is *no*. All programmers have controls they know and love, and they continue to write the same code over and over to get a familiar behavior out of that control. By creating reusable components, you might spend less time implementing common code required to use tools created by others. Creating ActiveX controls is a convenient way to encapsulate common functionality.

Programmers also have controls that can do almost everything they need. Sometimes they sacrifice functionality in an application because their current controls don't provide it. At times, programmers must write ugly looking code to accomplish a task their controls do not provide. Now Visual Basic provides a way for programmers familiar with its object model to access the desired functionality without having to build the entire control from scratch.

Visual Basic 5's new control-creation capabilities are based on the *Component Object Model* (COM). This component standard enables the controls you create to be fully functional in environments that support COM. You can use ActiveX components in Visual Basic, C++, Delphi, PowerBuilder, ActiveX-capable Internet browsers, and the Microsoft Office suite of applications.

Using ActiveX controls on the Internet/intranet can provide a dynamic diversion from static HTML. You can place ActiveX controls on Web pages to present a more exciting environment.

Variations of ActiveX Components in VB 5

New terminology has come along with Visual Basic's new look and feel. What were once called *OLE servers* have become *ActiveX components*. Although the names have changed, the underlying idea is still the same; the notion of the client using some functionality provided by the server still exists. The new terminology allows for further classification of the types of servers (or components) that might be created.

When you start a new project in VB 5, you are presented with the types of projects you can create. Of the component types, you can create code components or interactive components. *Code components* provide an easy way to package libraries of code for reuse. ActiveX executables and ActiveX DLLs are types of code components. These component types are different in the way in which they are executed. *ActiveX executables* are *out-of-process* components; they run in their own address space. You must start an ActiveX executable manually. *ActiveX DLLs* (formerly known as *OLE DLLs*) are *in-process* types of code components; they run in the address space on another application. DLL components cannot operate on their own; other applications or components must initiate the DLLs. An ActiveX control is an example of an interactive component. Like ActiveX DLLs, ActiveX controls run in-process, but they are more suited for interacting with the user or developer. These controls can provide both design-time and runtime behaviors. ActiveX controls (formerly known as *OLE controls*) compile into .ocx files and work in all environments that support OCXs. This process is called *component-based software development*. This development can cut production cycles and enable you to assemble robust applications from tested standard objects.

VB 5 Control-Creation Features

Visual Basic has many features dedicated to the authoring of ActiveX controls. This section lists the enhancements to the design environment and the language in the ActiveX author's bag of tricks.

IDE Features

The Visual Basic design environment provides the features listed in Table 16.1 to help you develop custom ActiveX controls.

Table 16.1. VB 5 IDE features.

Feature	Function
ActiveX Interface Wizard	Walks you through adding properties, methods, and events to your control.
Control Designer	Works much like the Form Designer; you use it to build the appearance of your control.
Project groups	Enables you to open related projects in IDE at one time. Great for testing controls.
Property Page Wizard	Walks you through designing and implementing Property pages for your controls.
Setup Wizard	Packages your components specifically for deployment on the Web.

Language Features

The Visual Basic language has been enhanced to facilitate the construction of ActiveX controls. Some of the language enhancements that may help the control developer are listed in Table 16.2.

Table 16.2. VB 5 language features.

Feature	Function
Ambient object	Provides hints to your control about how to best display itself in the container
Asynchronous downloading	Speeds the downloading of a control's properties over the Internet
Enumerations	Add enumerated constants to your control just like Visual Basic's built-in constants
Events	Enable you to declare, raise, and handle any existing or new events
Extender object	Specifies properties or methods provided by the container of your control
Hyperlink	Enables your control to specify a URL for an Internet-aware container
Implements statement	Offers polymorphism features by enabling your control to provide multiple interfaces
PropertyBag object	Holds persistent information to be stored across invocations of your control
PropertyPage object	Adds robust dialog boxes for users of your control to adjust its behavior
UserControl object	Provides a base on which you can build your control

An Overview of ActiveX Control Development

Normal application development follows a familiar cycle. Here is a simplified version of this cycle:

1. Design the physical interface in Design mode.
2. Modify some properties and add some code.
3. Run the project and test the functionality.
4. Create an executable that runs on its own.

To build ActiveX controls, you must follow a more complex procedure. The process you follow to design and implement the appearance of your control is similar to the one you use to create a standard program. You cannot execute controls directly, however. This requires that you, the control author, also produce an application that tests the features and properly debugs the control.

> **NOTE**
>
> Remember that the idea behind building ActiveX controls is that you will encapsulate some common functionality to be used by other applications. You might need to put some more thought into making your control generic enough to be used by many types of environments. If you properly debug your control, it may be more functional in those environments.

The standard procedure for building most ActiveX controls follows:

1. Determine the look and feel of your control.
2. Decide what type of functionality you want to provide with your control.
3. Design the appearance of your control.
4. Design the public interface (properties, methods, and events).
5. Create the project group with your control project and a test application project.
6. Implement the appearance of your control.
7. Implement the interface of your control.
8. Test each interface or appearance modification.
9. Design and implement your Property pages.
10. Compile your control and test it with all potential target environments.

Examining Methods of Control Creation

You can build an ActiveX control in three ways. You can subclass an existing control, assemble a new control composite from several existing controls, or write your own control from scratch. The method you select depends on the appearance or behavior you want your control to provide and whether existing controls can provide some of that behavior for you. This section examines the methods and looks at some examples that use each method.

Subclassing an Existing Control

Control subclassing is perhaps the easiest method to use when creating an ActiveX control. First, you select and draw the control you want to subclass. You begin with a completely tested control, such as a textbox. Then you decide whether to inherit all its current features or some subset of those features. Next, you add some behavior (property or method) that the existing control does not have. You can even change the default behavior of the events or methods of the subclassed control.

All physical painting behavior of your control on the form is handled internally by Windows and the subclassed object. All you have to worry about is the location of the subclassed control on your ActiveX.

> **NOTE**
>
> You should consider some licensing issues when using other authors' controls. You must have purchased a valid copy of a control in order to use it in controls you create. Just keep in mind that if you use Visual Basic's intrinsic control (built into VB), no additional `.ocx` files need to be distributed.

Examples of a subclassed control follow:

- A `PictureBox` control that enables you to specify a transparent color
- A `TextBox` control that accepts only phone numbers
- A button that provides an audible signal when clicked

Assembling a New Control Composite

Another method of creating an ActiveX control is to combine several existing controls into one logical unit. This sort of encapsulation allows for speedy development cycles when common user interface (UI) features are used throughout an application. How many times have you used separate controls for name, address, city, state, and ZIP code in a customer screen, or the user ID/password combination for a logon screen? You can create these types of objects easily as a composite control. Each interface element has been previously tested and debugged. You then are free to concentrate on the functions you want to provide. You are limited only by the huge array of available controls from which to build. You can choose to expose certain properties to the constituent controls, gathering the strengths from each control and masking any of the complexities.

Like the subclassing method, the composite control method is dependent on its constituents. All runtime painting behavior is controlled by the contained controls.

Any properties or methods your composite exposes can map directly to the default behavior of the constituents. Suppose that a user changes the State listbox on your Address control. In the code for the clicked event of the listbox, you can fire off a `Changed` event in your control.

Examples of a composite control follow:

- A splitter control that offers multiple sizable containers, such as HTML frames
- A tree control that can show columnar data at each node
- A set of two lists, which enables you to move items easily back and forth

Building a Control from Scratch

Building a control from scratch offers the most flexibility of all the methods. You must write all the code that handles the appearance of your control. No constituent controls or confines are placed on your control's painting behavior. All drawing must be done by graphics methods or Windows API calls in your control's Paint event. You have ultimate control over the interface (properties, methods, and events) that you provide. This method is recommended if your ActiveX control needs complete authority over its runtime or design-time appearance.

One advantage of building a control from scratch is that it has no dependencies on other controls. You can distribute this control without any licensing issues or added weight of constituent .ocx files.

Examples of controls that are built from scratch follow:

- A listbox that contains checkbox-like items
- A stock ticker window that displays updated stock information
- A multistate button that offers more than just an up or down setting, such as a stereo's volume control

Understanding the UserControl Object

Any ActiveX control you build is based on a UserControl object. Like a form in a standard executable file, a UserControl object is composed of code elements and visual elements. Each object has its own Code window and Visual Design window. You place controls on a UserControl object just as you would any Visual Basic form. The UserControl object is maintained as a plain text file with a .ctl extension. Visual elements that cannot be represented textually are stored in a binary .ctx file.

A project can contain more than one UserControl object. You can package a set of common controls in this manner. After the controls are compiled, they are placed in a single .ocx file. If these controls are made public, they may be used to develop other applications.

Remember that a UserControl cannot execute by itself; it must be placed on a form in order to operate. The form it is placed on is referred to as the *container* (or *parent*) of the UserControl. You also can have the control itself serve as a container by placing controls directly on its surface during UserControl authoring or by allowing others to place controls on it during application development.

The interface (properties, methods, and events) exposed by the control is entirely up to you, the author. If the UserControl contains other controls, you can present properties of those constituents to look like properties of the UserControl. You accomplish this task by using delegation. You can delegate a particular interface from one control to the UserControl object itself. You might want an occurrence of a Changed event in a contained textbox to fire the Changed event of the UserControl, for example. To the user, typing in the textbox simply appears to fire the UserControl's Changed event directly. You will see examples of delegation when we map events in "Using the ActiveX Control Interface Wizard," later in this chapter.

Key UserControl Properties

The control author interacts with UserControl properties exactly as if he or she were manipulating form properties. Table 16.3 lists some properties useful in control creation.

Table 16.3. UserControl properties.

Property	Function
Alignable	Specifies whether a control can be aligned to the top, bottom, left, or right of its containing object. If so, it can use the extender Align property.
Ambient	Returns the AmbientProperties object of the control. This is where the UserControl can access some current properties of the containing object. (See "Working with the Parent Container," later in this chapter.)
CanGetFocus	Specifies whether the UserControl can receive the focus.
ContainedControls	Returns the collection of controls in the UserControl.
ControlContainer	Specifies whether the UserControl can act as a container for other controls.
DefaultCancel	Specifies whether the UserControl can act as a default or Cancel button for the form. If so, the extender properties Default and Cancel are available.
EditAtDesignTime	Specifies whether a control can become active during the developer's design-time.
EventsFrozen	Specifies whether the container currently is ignoring events raised by the control.
Extender	Returns the Extender object of the control. The Extender object holds properties of the control that actually are managed by the container of the control instead of by the control itself. (See "Working with the Parent Container," later in this chapter.)

Property	Function
Hyperlink	Returns the Hyperlink object of the control. By using the properties and methods of the Hyperlink object, your ActiveX control can request a hyperlink-aware container, such as Microsoft Internet Explorer, to jump to a given URL.
InvisibleAtRuntime	Specifies whether the control has a visible representation during runtime.
ParentControls	Returns a collection of controls owned by the parent of the UserControl.
PropertyPages	Specifies a string array containing the names of the Property pages in the project associated with this control.
Public	Determines whether the UserControl control can be shared with other applications.
ToolBoxBitmap	Specifies the image that will represent the UserControl in the Visual Basic toolbox during design-time. The size of the bitmap should be 16×15 pixels, but the bitmap specified by this property is scaled to these dimensions if necessary.

Key UserControl Methods

Table 16.4 lists some key UserControl methods available to the control author at design-time.

Table 16.4. UserControl methods.

Method	Function
AsyncRead	Begins the background process of reading a property value of the UserControl from a file or URL.
CancelAsyncRead	Stops a background-download process of a UserControl property value.
CanPropertyChange	Asks the container whether a UserControl property bound to a data source can have its value modified.
PropertyChanged	Indicates that a UserControl property has been modified. This is required to determine whether a control needs to save its properties (in the WriteProperties event) to the containing form file.

Key UserControl Events

Whenever you add a UserControl object that you have authored to a form, a design-time instance is created. At this point, the control is in Run mode. Any behavior that you have put in the UserControl now is active. When you run the form, the design-time instance is destroyed, and a runtime instance is created. As properties are changed at design-time, they are saved to a copy of the form (.frm). Table 16.5 lists the key events in a UserControl's lifetime.

Table 16.5. UserControl events.

Event	Description
AmbientChanged	Occurs after one of the Ambient property values is changed in the container.
AsyncReadComplete	Occurs when a specific property finishes downloading.
Initialize	Occurs when an instance of the control is created.
InitProperties	Occurs once when an instance of a control is added to a form. This is where you can supply default values for a control's properties.
Paint	Fires whenever the container instructs the control to paint itself.
ReadProperties	Occurs after the control is initialized. This is where persistent property values are set from the containing form file (.frm).
Resize	Occurs after the control is initialized and every time it is resized—whether in Design mode or at runtime.
Show	Called before the container begins to display itself.
Terminate	Occurs after the control is destroyed.
WriteProperties	Occurs when a design-time instance of the control is being destroyed and at least one property has changed. The properties are written to the containing form file.

Working with the Parent Container

This section explores how the UserControl object can communicate with its environment—most often, the form on which it is sitting. As a control author, you can access the containing object through the read-only Parent and ParentControls properties. The ParentControls property is a collection that is useful when performing some actions on the controls on the form. This property allows iteration through these controls.

> **NOTE**
>
> Remember that the control's container is not always a form. Many other types of containers exist, such as tabs, picture boxes, and frames. Do not count on the container object having all the properties or methods of a standard form when accessing the Parent properties.

In addition to the Parent properties, the Extender object and AmbientProperties objects enable you to interact with the container.

Extender **Object**

The containing object best handles some of a control's interface. The Top and Left properties, for example, determine where on the form your control is placed. This type of container-specific information is supplied to the ActiveX author by means of the Extender object. This object supplies properties, methods, and events that do not need to be implemented by your UserControl.

> **NOTE**
>
> The Extender object is not available when the Initialize event is raised, but it is available when the InitProperties event or ReadProperties event is raised. These properties are said to be *late bound*.

Table 16.6 lists the set of Extender properties implemented by all containers.

Table 16.6. Extender properties.

Property	Function
Default, Cancel	Determines whether the control behaves as a default or Cancel button on the form
Name	Specifies the user-defined name of the control
Enabled	Specifies whether the control has been enabled
HelpContextID	Specifies a numeric reference used for Help lookups
Index	Keeps track of control-array instances
Left, Top, Width, Height	Determines the location on the Parent container
Parent	Specifies an object that represents the container of the control, such as a form

continues

Table 16.6. continued

Property	Function
Visible	Determines whether the control is visible at runtime
ToolTipText	Optional text pop-up hints

One example of a common use of an Extender property is to help supply default text for a contained TextBox control. Suppose that your control is called TextWidget. When an instance of this control is added to a form, it has a default name supplied for it, such as TextWidget1. This widget may have a subclassed textbox contained in it. One common behavior is to make the default Text property of a textbox the same as the name of the control. You can accomplish this easily by using the Extender.Name property in the InitProperties event, as this example shows:

```
Private Sub UserControl_InitProperties()
    Text = Extender.Name
End Sub

Public Property Text(Byval sNewVal As String)
    txtBase.Text = sNewVal
End Sub
```

When a TextWidget control is added to a form, its Text property is set to its name—for example, TextWidget1 and TextWidget2.

> **NOTE**
>
> Remember that the InitProperties event is fired only once for each control. It occurs after the control instance is added to the form. So when you change the name of the control, the Text property in the TextWidget example is not altered.

AmbientProperties **Object**

Containers provide hints to your UserControl about how they should best display themselves. These hints enable the UserControl to provide an appearance and behavior that is consistent with the container. An example is the Ambient Font property. Ambient.Font references the font that the containing form is using. For your control to appear similar to the form, you should use the same font.

Like the Extender properties, the Ambient properties also are specific for each container object. Several standard properties should be implemented by all containers. Table 16.7 lists some of the key Ambient properties.

Table 16.7. `Ambient` properties.

Property	Function
DisplayName	Specifies the user-defined name of the control. This property is identical to the `Extender.Name` property.
Font, TextAlign	Specifies the current font settings for the container.
ForeColor, BackColor, Palette	Specifies the colors your control can use to keep it consistent with the container.
UserMode	Determines when the instance of the control is executing; `UserMode` is false during design-time and true during runtime.

WARNING

A control can access `Ambient` properties that are specific to a particular container, but this limits its use to containers that have that property. When the control is compiled, it has no way of knowing in what type of container it may be placed. Be aware that, in order to use non-standard properties, the control should handle any errors in cases where the `Ambient` property does not exist.

Perhaps the most useful `Ambient` property is the `UserMode` property. `UserMode` offers a higher level of control over the design-time and runtime behaviors your control provides. Suppose that you want to change the way your control handles `Resize` events during design-time. Examine the following code:

```
Private Sub UserControl_Resize()

    '-Do not allow sizing of the control design time
    '  Keep the control the size of the contained TextBox
    If Not Ambient.UserMode Then
        Height = txtBase.Height
        Width =  txtBase.Width

    End if

End Sub
```

The `Resize` event of a `UserControl` can fire at design-time or runtime. This code allows dynamic runtime changes to the control's appearance, but it restricts the size to the constituent `TextBox` dimensions at design-time.

Building an ActiveX Control

Now you'll start to build a simple control. What should you build? They say that necessity is the mother of invention, and ActiveX development is a perfect example of this. In the last application I worked on, it was proclaimed that all textual input from the user was to be upper-case. Simple enough, right? Did I mention that all 20 or so previously built forms needed this new behavior? That meant that whenever a KeyPress event occurred in any of the forms, I had to convert that key to an uppercase character. Each form's KeyPreview property was turned on, a piece of common code was checked if the active control was a TextBox, and then the key press was converted. Accommodating, but repetitive and very ugly! If the TextBox control only had a Case property, I could set this at design-time and leave it up to the control to specify lower-case, uppercase, or whatever.

Never fear—ActiveX control creation is here. I simply could subclass the TextBox control and add the Case property to it. This is the background for the NewText control that follows. You will use only one control to build it (a TextBox), and you will implement the features described so far in this chapter.

Creating a New Control Project

Before you can begin work on a new control, you must set up the required project files. Follow these steps:

1. Choose File | New Project. In the New Project dialog box that appears, double-click the ActiveX control icon to create a new project. The ActiveX Control Designer and default project are created for you, as Figure 16.1 shows.

2. Rename Project1 by right-clicking it in the Project window and choosing Properties. In the Properties dialog box that appears, change Project1 to NewTextControl and click OK.

3. Double-click UserControl1 in the Project window and edit its Name property in the Properties window. Change it to NewText.

WARNING

Make sure that you name your control appropriately. Each time someone adds your control to his form, a unique name is generated. An incremental number is appended to the name by default. An ActiveX control with the name UserControl1 at design-time, for example, becomes UserControl11 when added to a form.

FIGURE 16.1.

Newly created
`UserControl1` *and*
`Project1`.

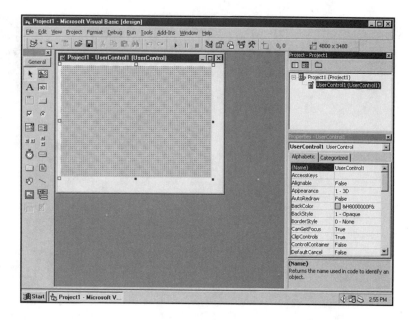

4. Add a test project to the group. Choose File | Add Project. Select Standard Exe from the list of available project types and press OK. A `Form1` is added to this project.

5. Rename `Form1` to `frmTest` and `Project1` to `NewTextTester`.

6. Save all files by using Table 16.8 as a guide.

Table 16.8. Objects and their associated filenames.

Object	Filename
`NewTextControl` project	`NewTextControl.vbp`
`NewText` control	`NewText.ctl`
`NewTextTester` project	`NewTextTester.vbp`
`FrmTest` form	`Test.frm`
`NewText` project group	`NewText.vbg`

The project group and associated project files now are all set and should look similar to those in Figure 16.2.

FIGURE 16.2.

The NewText *project group.*

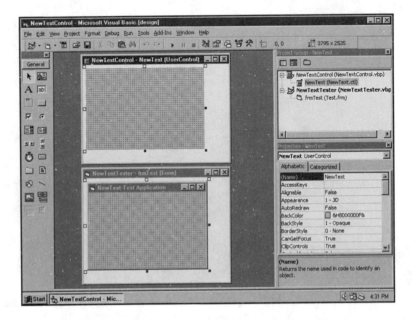

Adding a UserControl to the Test Application

As you develop features in your UserControl, it helps to see the immediate results. Visual Basic programmers have become used to this familiar code-run-debug cycle. The UserControl code begins to run as soon as you place an instance on the test form. You can step through the Initialize or InitProperties just as you would the Load event of a standard form.

To add the current NewText control to the test form, follow these steps:

1. Double-click the area of UserControl to display the Code window. Add the following code to the UserControl_Initialize and UserControl_InitProperties events:

```
Private Sub UserControl_Initialize()
    Debug.Print "A NewText control was Initialized, but I do not know its
    ➡name"
End Sub

Private Sub UserControl_InitProperties()
    Debug.Print "A NewText control called "& Ambient.DisplayName & "has been
    ➡added"
End Sub
```

2. Close the Code window for the NewText control and close the NewText Design window (if it is open). The default icon for a user control appears in the toolbox.

3. Double-click frmTest in the Project window. The Form Designer appears.

4. Click the NewText icon in the toolbox. A set of cross hairs appears when the mouse cursor is over the test form.

5. Click-and-drag on the test form to create a copy of the NewText control on the form. This control appears as a flat, transparent rectangle with sizing handles.

NOTE

If you look at the Properties window, you will see the default set of properties with which each UserControl begins. The Extender object of the control provides these properties. These properties appear to the user to be seamlessly integrated.

---

6. Double-click the NewText UserControl object in the Project window to bring the NewText Designer to the front. Notice that the instance of NewText1 on the test form has been filled with hatch marks to indicate that it is inactive, as Figure 16.3 shows. You can resize the UserControl on the test form; however, when it is inactive, no UserControl events will occur.

FIGURE 16.3.

The NewText *instance is deactivated during design-time.*

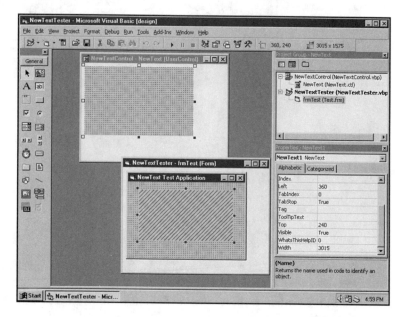

> **NOTE**
>
> Opening any object (a Code window or a Control Designer) in a control project deactivates all running instances of the control. When switching from different projects in a grouped project such as this, you are prompted to close Control Designers and Code windows that are open.

Adding Constituent Controls

Your control still does not have a function, so now you'll add a constituent control using the Designer Form. Follow these steps:

1. Double-click the icon for the TextBox control in the toolbox to add a TextBox to the UserControl. The UserControl now looks similar to Figure 16.4.

FIGURE 16.4.

Adding a textbox to the NewText control.

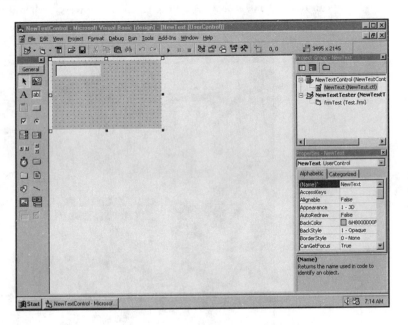

2. Name the textbox txtBase. This is the control on which you will base all your subclassing.

3. Double-click any blank area on UserControl to bring up the Code window. Add the following lines to the UserControl_Resize event to ensure that the TextBox control always is resized to fill the entire UserControl area:

```
Private Sub UserControl_Resize()
    '-Force the TextBox control to fill the NewText's
    '  visible surface area
    txtBase.Move 0, 0, ScaleWidth, ScaleHeight
End Sub
```

4. Add the following lines to the `InitProperties` event:

   ```
   '--Default the TextBox to show the name
   '  of the control
   txtBase.Text = Extender.Name
   ```

5. Close the `NewText` Code window and the Designer to put the control into Run mode. Bring `frmTest` to the front by double-clicking it in the Project window.

6. The `NewText` control now appears as a `TextBox` on the form. Test the `Resize` event code by resizing the control at design-time. Add new controls to test the `InitProperties` code you changed, as shown in Figure 16.5.

FIGURE 16.5.

Effects of the `InitProperties` *event.*

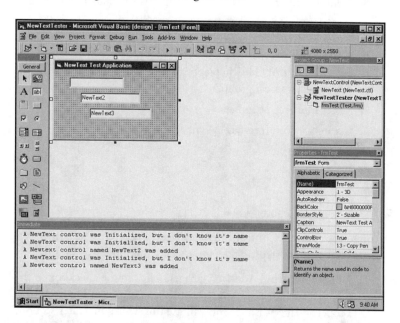

NOTE

The `NewText` control originally added to your test form does not show its name, because the `InitProperties` event for that control fired before you added that code. `InitProperties` is executed only once when the control is added to the container. Also, you have yet to tell your control how to save property values from one design invocation to the next. The next time you open the test form, the `InitProperties` event does not fire and your `NewText` boxes are empty.

Using the ActiveX Control Interface Wizard

Now that you have placed the required appearance elements on your NewText control, you need to define the public interface it exposes to the developer using it. To do this, you use an add-in that ships with Visual Basic called the *ActiveX Control Interface Wizard*. This wizard simplifies the building of subclassed or composite type controls by enabling you to use interface elements (also called *members*) from the constituent objects used to build your control. The members that you decide to expose make up your new control's interface.

You can use the ActiveX Control Interface Wizard to perform these tasks:

- Add standard property, method, and event names for your user control
- Add new custom property, method, and event names for your user control
- Define attributes for the public property, method, and event names

The ActiveX Control Interface Wizard presents the following sections:

- Introduction
- Select a Control (This step appears only when you have more than one UserControl in the current project group.)
- Select Interface Members
- Create Custom Interface Members
- Set Mapping
- Set Attributes
- Finished
- Summary Report

To use the ActiveX Control Interface Wizard, you must add it to the development environment. Follow these steps to add and execute the Interface Wizard:

1. Choose Add-Ins | Add-In Manager. Click in the checkbox to the left of VB ActiveX Control Interface Wizard to enable it, as shown in Figure 16.6. Also enable VB Property Page Wizard. You will use this wizard in a later section, "Adding Property Pages," to design Property pages for your control. Click OK to close the Add-In Manager.

FIGURE 16.6.

The Visual Basic Add-In Manager.

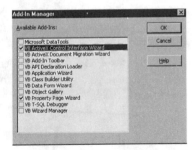

2. The VB ActiveX Control Interface Wizard option now is visible at the bottom of the Add-Ins menu. Click that option to launch the wizard.

   The wizard introduction screen appears, giving you a quick overview of the process to follow. It then notes that you already should have added all the design elements (UI objects) to your control prior to running the wizard. The wizard inspects those controls and provides their properties, methods, and events for you to pick from in the next step.

3. Enable the Skip this screen in the future checkbox to bypass the introduction screen on successive uses of the wizard; then click Next to move to the next step.

   The Select Interface Members screen appears, as shown in Figure 16.7. The wizard has inspected the public interface of all the objects in your UserControl. A list of all these available interface members appears in the Available names box. A list of the selected members your control is to expose appears in the Selected names box. The wizard preselects the set of properties, methods, and events common to most controls.

FIGURE 16.7.

The Select Interface Members step.

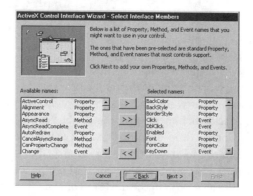

4. Add the following interface members for the Change event and the Text property to the Selected names list. Remove the BackStyle property from the list, because your TextBox will fill the entire UserControl. Click Next to advance to the next step of the wizard.

NOTE

In order for your control to provide all the functionality of a common TextBox control, you would have needed to select additional interface members. Properties like PasswordChar and MultiLine would give your control the look and feel consistent with the built-in TextBox.

5. The Create Custom Interface Members screen appears next. Here, you add any additional properties, methods, or events to the control. You will add a property called TextCase to this control. Click New to add a new member. You are then presented with the Add Custom Member dialog box. Type TextCase in the Name field and click OK. The wizard then shows this new member in the My Custom Members list, as Figure 16.8 shows. Click Next to continue.

FIGURE 16.8.

Adding a custom interface member.

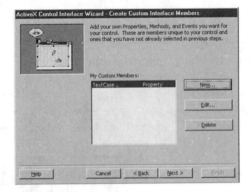

6. The Set Mapping screen appears next, as shown in Figure 16.9. This step enables you to map the functionality of the public property, method, and event names to underlying private property, method, and event names on the user control and constituent controls. Select each member in the Public Name list and then choose a control in the Maps to Control drop-down listbox. If a member of the same name exists, it is filled in the Maps to Member drop-down listbox. After you map the public KeyDown event to the KeyDown in your base TextBox, for example, any occurrence of a KeyDown in the TextBox fires a KeyDown in the NewText control. You do not need to map custom functions because you will be implementing those yourself.

TIP

You can map multiple public members to one control at a time. To do this, click the public names you want while pressing Ctrl. Then choose the control you want.

7. Map all public names to the TextBox control with the exception of your new TextCase property. Then click Next.

FIGURE 16.9.

*The Set Mapping
wizard step.*

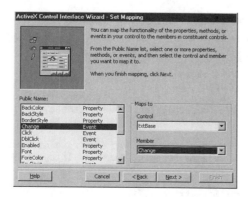

8. Now you need to set the attributes of the new `TextCase` property. The Set Attributes screen shown in Figure 16.10 enables you to set the attributes for any property, method, and event names that you did not map in step 7. Here, you can select the data type, default value, and behavior of the control at runtime or design-time. You will add an `Enumerated` type to use with this property, so you can accept the default settings and exit this screen. Fill in the `Description` field to show a description in the Property window. Then click Next.

FIGURE 16.10.

*The Set Attributes
wizard step.*

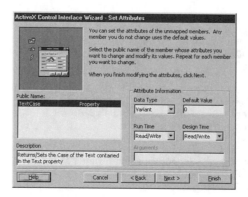

9. The Finish screen appears, explaining that it has gathered all the required information to create your control's interface. It also enables you to view a summary report. The summary is simply a to-do list you can follow to complete modifications to your control. You can save this report to a text file for later inspection.

When the wizard is finished, it generates all the code required to implement the selections you made. Listing 16.1 displays the code generated from these steps. Various comments are added with warning messages. These comments help the wizard remember the choices you made in previous visits.

Listing 16.1. Code created by the Interface Wizard.

```
'Default Property Values:
Const m_def_TextCase = 0
'Property Variables:
Dim m_TextCase As Variant
'Event Declarations:
Event Click() 'MappingInfo=txtBase,txtBase,-1,Click
Event DblClick() 'MappingInfo=txtBase,txtBase,-1,DblClick
Event KeyDown(KeyCode As Integer, Shift As Integer) 'MappingInfo=txtBase,txtBase,
➥-1,KeyDown
Event KeyPress(KeyAscii As Integer) 'MappingInfo=txtBase,txtBase,-1,KeyPress
Event KeyUp(KeyCode As Integer, Shift As Integer) 'MappingInfo=txtBase,txtBase,
➥-1,KeyUp
Event MouseDown(Button As Integer, Shift As Integer, X As Single, Y As Single)
'MappingInfo=txtBase,txtBase,-1,MouseDown
Event MouseMove(Button As Integer, Shift As Integer, X As Single, Y As Single)
'MappingInfo=txtBase,txtBase,-1,MouseMove
Event MouseUp(Button As Integer, Shift As Integer, X As Single, Y As Single)
'MappingInfo=txtBase,txtBase,-1,MouseUp
Event Change() 'MappingInfo=txtBase,txtBase,-1,Change


'WARNING! DO NOT REMOVE OR MODIFY THE FOLLOWING COMMENTED LINES!
'MappingInfo=txtBase,txtBase,-1,BackColor
Public Property Get BackColor() As OLE_COLOR
    BackColor = txtBase.BackColor
End Property

Public Property Let BackColor(ByVal New_BackColor As OLE_COLOR)
    txtBase.BackColor() = New_BackColor
    PropertyChanged "BackColor"
End Property

'WARNING! DO NOT REMOVE OR MODIFY THE FOLLOWING COMMENTED LINES!
'MappingInfo=txtBase,txtBase,-1,ForeColor
Public Property Get ForeColor() As OLE_COLOR
    ForeColor = txtBase.ForeColor
End Property

Public Property Let ForeColor(ByVal New_ForeColor As OLE_COLOR)
    txtBase.ForeColor() = New_ForeColor
    PropertyChanged "ForeColor"
End Property

'WARNING! DO NOT REMOVE OR MODIFY THE FOLLOWING COMMENTED LINES!
'MappingInfo=txtBase,txtBase,-1,Enabled
Public Property Get Enabled() As Boolean
    Enabled = txtBase.Enabled
End Property

Public Property Let Enabled(ByVal New_Enabled As Boolean)
    txtBase.Enabled() = New_Enabled
    PropertyChanged "Enabled"
End Property
```

```
'WARNING! DO NOT REMOVE OR MODIFY THE FOLLOWING COMMENTED LINES!
'MappingInfo=txtBase,txtBase,-1,Font
Public Property Get Font() As Font
    Set Font = txtBase.Font
End Property

Public Property Set Font(ByVal New_Font As Font)
    Set txtBase.Font = New_Font
    PropertyChanged "Font"
End Property

'WARNING! DO NOT REMOVE OR MODIFY THE FOLLOWING COMMENTED LINES!
'MappingInfo=txtBase,txtBase,-1,Refresh
Public Sub Refresh()
    txtBase.Refresh
End Sub

Private Sub txtBase_Click()
    RaiseEvent Click
End Sub

Private Sub txtBase_DblClick()
    RaiseEvent DblClick
End Sub

Private Sub txtBase_KeyDown(KeyCode As Integer, Shift As Integer)
    RaiseEvent KeyDown(KeyCode, Shift)
End Sub

Private Sub txtBase_KeyPress(KeyAscii As Integer)
    RaiseEvent KeyPress(KeyAscii)
End Sub

Private Sub txtBase_KeyUp(KeyCode As Integer, Shift As Integer)
    RaiseEvent KeyUp(KeyCode, Shift)
End Sub

Private Sub txtBase_MouseDown(Button As Integer, Shift As Integer, X As Single,
➥Y As Single)
    RaiseEvent MouseDown(Button, Shift, X, Y)
End Sub

Private Sub txtBase_MouseMove(Button As Integer, Shift As Integer, X As Single,
➥Y As Single)
    RaiseEvent MouseMove(Button, Shift, X, Y)
End Sub

Private Sub txtBase_MouseUp(Button As Integer, Shift As Integer, X As Single,
➥Y As Single)
    RaiseEvent MouseUp(Button, Shift, X, Y)
End Sub

Private Sub txtBase_Change()
    RaiseEvent Change
End Sub
```

continues

Listing 16.1. continued

```
'WARNING! DO NOT REMOVE OR MODIFY THE FOLLOWING COMMENTED LINES!
'MappingInfo=txtBase,txtBase,-1,Text
Public Property Get Text() As String
    Text = txtBase.Text
End Property

Public Property Let Text(ByVal New_Text As String)
    txtBase.Text() = New_Text
    PropertyChanged "Text"
End Property

Public Property Get TextCase() As Variant
    TextCase = m_TextCase
End Property

Public Property Let TextCase(ByVal New_TextCase As Variant)
    m_TextCase = New_TextCase
    PropertyChanged "TextCase"
End Property

'Initialize Properties for User Control
Private Sub UserControl_InitProperties()
    m_TextCase = m_def_TextCase
End Sub

'Load property values from storage
Private Sub UserControl_ReadProperties(PropBag As PropertyBag)

    txtBase.BackColor = PropBag.ReadProperty("BackColor", &H80000005)
    txtBase.ForeColor = PropBag.ReadProperty("ForeColor", &H80000008)
    txtBase.Enabled = PropBag.ReadProperty("Enabled", True)
    Set Font = PropBag.ReadProperty("Font", Ambient.Font)
    txtBase.Text = PropBag.ReadProperty("Text", "")
    m_TextCase = PropBag.ReadProperty("TextCase", m_def_TextCase)
End Sub

'Write property values to storage
Private Sub UserControl_WriteProperties(PropBag As PropertyBag)

    Call PropBag.WriteProperty("BackColor", txtBase.BackColor, &H80000005)
    Call PropBag.WriteProperty("ForeColor", txtBase.ForeColor, &H80000008)
    Call PropBag.WriteProperty("Enabled", txtBase.Enabled, True)
    Call PropBag.WriteProperty("Font", Font, Ambient.Font)
    Call PropBag.WriteProperty("Text", txtBase.Text, "")
    Call PropBag.WriteProperty("TextCase", m_TextCase, m_def_TextCase)
End Sub
```

Examine the code generated by the Interface Wizard. Notice that each event is declared near the beginning. These events and the events provided by the Extender object are available to the user of this control at design-time. Following the events is a set of Let and Get procedures for each added property. Also notice the delegation of events from the TextBox control to the UserControl's events declared earlier. This is accomplished by the RaiseEvent function. Finally, note the `ReadProperty` and `WriteProperty` events. Here, you can see the procedure for saving and reading persistent property values. You should use the code generated by the wizard as a model if you create controls from scratch or add any interface members to a control.

Modifying the Control's Code

Your `NewText` control still requires a little work to be functional. The first item on your list is to set up the types of cases (uppercase, mixed case, and so on) your `NewText` control will handle. You need the `NewText` control to handle normal upper- and lowercase as well as mixed-case letters if you want to leave the case as the user enters it. You will make mixed case (or no case distinction) the default for this property. One last case would be useful—one that capitalizes the first character of each word; this type of case commonly is called *initial caps*.

To save the user of your control from having to remember any codes for these types, you will create an enumeration. The enumeration will hold all the possible `TextCase` values. Your `Enum` statement for those cases looks like this:

```
'-- Define an enumerated type for the
'   new TextCase property
Public Enum Cases
    MixedCase = 0
    UpperCase = 1
    LowerCase = 2
    InitialCaps = 3
End Enum
```

You then can replace the private member variables and the default values generated by the wizard from this:

```
'Default Property Values:
Const m_def_TextCase = 0
'Property Variables:
Dim m_TextCase As Variant
```

to this:

```
'Default Property Values:
Const m_def_TextCase = MixedCase

'Property Variables:
Dim m_TextCase As Cases
```

You then can replace the standard property `Let` and `Get` procedure stubs that were generated by the wizard with the two functions in Listing 16.2.

Listing 16.2. Modified property `Let` and `Get` procedures for `TextCase`.

```
Public Property Get TextCase() As Cases
    TextCase = m_TextCase
End Property
```

continues

Listing 16.2. continued

```
Public Property Let TextCase(ByVal New_TextCase As Cases)

    Select Case New_TextCase
        Case MixedCase
        Case UpperCase
            Text = UCase$(Text)
        Case LowerCase
            Text = LCase$(Text)
        Case InitialCaps
            Text = InitialUCase(Text)
        Case Else
            MsgBox "Invalid Property Value: " & New_TextCase
            Exit Property
    End Select
    m_TextCase = New_TextCase
    PropertyChanged "TextCase"

End Property
```

As you can see, the TextCase Let procedure now accepts a parameter of type Cases, which you defined with your Enum statement. For mixed case, you do not care what the case is in the Text field, so no code is needed. For uppercase and lowercase, you can use the appropriate Visual Basic functions. Next, you must add a function for handling your initial caps type of case. Listing 16.3 shows the code you need to convert any string to initial caps.

Listing 16.3. Converting strings to initial caps.

```
Private Function InitialUCase(ByVal sInText As String) As String
'-- convert the incoming string to initial caps
Dim sOutText As String
Dim i As Integer
Dim sCurrChar As String
Dim sLastChar As String

    '-- Loop through the input string and add each
    '  character to the output string
    For i = 1 To Len(sInText)

        '-- get the current character
        sCurrChar = Mid$(sInText, i, 1)

        If sLastChar = " " Or sLastChar = "" Then
            '-- Force uppercase if it is a new word
sOutText = sOutText & UCase$(sCurrChar)
        Else
            sOutText = sOutText & LCase$(sCurrChar)
        End If

        '-- save the last character
        sLastChar = sCurrChar
```

```
Next
'-- return the result
InitialUCase = sOutText

End Function
```

The last enhancement you need to make before you begin to test your control is to change the way you set your default `Text` property. In the section "Adding Constituent Controls," you added code to set the `Text` property of the `txtBase` control to default to the name of the control. You did this in the `InitProperties` event. Now, through delegation, you are directing the contents of your `txtBase` control to the public `Text` property of `NewText`. Your line in the `InitProperties` event now should look like this:

```
Text = Extender.Name
```

Text in this line references the `NewText.Text` property.

You also should make sure that your properties are being written to the form file correctly. Between coding and debugging sessions, you need to make sure that properties in your control are saved to the plain text file of the containing form. The events that handle property persistence across sessions are `WriteProperties` and `ReadProperties`. These events both manipulate an object called the `PropertyBag`. The `PropertyBag` stores the control's property values in the containing form's file. When the form is read into memory, those data values also are read. When the developer changes properties, a flag is set to alert the `WriteProperties` event procedure to fire, thereby writing those changes.

> **NOTE**
>
> It is the responsibility of the control author to ensure that all properties enable procedures to signal that a modification has been made. The `PropertyChange` method alerts the system that it needs to save a particular property value.

Modify the `ReadProperties` event so that the `Text` property defaults to the control's name:

```
txtBase.Text = PropBag.ReadProperty("Text", Extender.Name)
```

Set the same default value when the `PropertyBag` is written to the file in the `WriteProperties` event:

```
Call PropBag.WriteProperty("Text", txtBase.Text, Extender.Name)
```

Now your default text value should work and be persistent across development sessions. You now should test the functionality you added.

Testing the Control

To test the functionality of your control, you need to revisit your test project and update it to use the new features of NewText. Follow these steps to enhance the test form:

1. Close the Design window and the Code window for the NewText control. Double-click frmTest in the Project window to bring it to the front.

2. Remove all instances of your NewText control so that it is a blank form. Double-click the NewText control in the toolbox. This adds a new instance of NewText to your form. The name of the control should appear in the NewText box. Resize the control to the appropriate size to hold one line of text.

3. Examine the Property window. A new property should be listed for TextCase. The default value (MixedCase) is visible. Notice that a description should be listed below the Property window stating the purpose of the TextCase property. Click the upper-case type from the combo box. If all is well, expect to see the text in NewText1 in all uppercase.

4. Close the form and reopen it. ReadProperties and WriteProperties should have ensured that the changes to any property values persisted.

You now have tested the behavior of the control at design-time. In order to test the behavior at runtime, you must add additional support on your test form. Follow these steps:

1. Add a control array of four option buttons called optCase to the form. Set the following properties:

Object	Property	Value
optCase(0)	Caption	Mixed case (default)
	Value	True
optCase(1)	Caption	Uppercase
optCase(2)	Caption	Lowercase
optCase(3)	Caption	Initial caps

2. Double-click one of the buttons. This brings up the Code window. Add the following code to the optBase_Click event:

```
Private Sub optCase_Click(Index As Integer)

    Select Case Index
        Case 0
            NewText1.TextCase = MixedCase
        Case 1
            NewText1.TextCase = UpperCase
        Case 2
            NewText1.TextCase = LowerCase
        Case 3
            NewText1.TextCase = InitialCaps
    End Select

End Sub
```

3. Add the following code to the `KeyPress` event of the textbox so that text entered into the `NewText` control at runtime follows the case guidelines you have set:

```
Private Sub txtBase_KeyPress(KeyAscii As Integer)

Dim nLoc As Integer

    '-- Check to see whether a letter was pressed
    If UCase(Chr$(KeyAscii)) <= "Z" And UCase$(Chr$(KeyAscii)) <= "Z" Then
        Select Case TextCase
            '-- Mixed case allows any combination of cases
            Case MixedCase

            '-- force the character to uppercase
            Case UpperCase
                KeyAscii = Asc(UCase$(Chr$(KeyAscii)))

            '-- force the character to lowercase
            Case LowerCase
                KeyAscii = Asc(LCase$(Chr$(KeyAscii)))

            '-- force the character to upper or lower
            '   based on what the previous character was
            Case InitialCaps
                '-- Sel start tells us where the caret is
                nLoc = txtBase.SelStart

                '-- if we are at the beginning of a word
                '   force this character UP
                If nLoc = 0 Or Trim$(txtBase.Text) = "" Then
                    KeyAscii = Asc(UCase$(Chr$(KeyAscii)))
                Else
                    '-- if the last character was a space
                    '   force it UP
                    If Mid$(txtBase.Text, nLoc, 1) = " " Then
                        KeyAscii = Asc(UCase$(Chr$(KeyAscii)))

                    Else '-- force it down
                        KeyAscii = Asc(LCase$(Chr$(KeyAscii)))
                    End If

                End If
        End Select

    End If

    'Send the Keypress event on to the NewText control
    RaiseEvent KeyPress(KeyAscii)
End Sub
```

4. Run the project by clicking the Start button or by choosing Run | Start. The test form should look similar to Figure 16.11.

FIGURE 16.11.

The NewText *test application in action.*

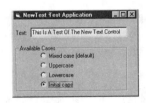

Adding Property Pages

After you complete all the properties you want for your control, you can choose to implement Property pages. *Property pages* enable you to represent more complex data and property data types that are not easily modified in Visual Basic's Property window. Although your NewText control is small, you will build a simple Property page to see how easy it is. To get started designing Property pages for your control, you will run the Property Page Wizard. This wizard offers a simple approach to Property pages and introduces you to the procedure.

To add a Property page, follow these steps:

1. Start the Property Page Wizard by clicking the appropriate option on the Add-Ins menu (you added this option to the Add-Ins menu while you were adding the ActiveX Interface Wizard). The introductory screen appears first. Enable the Skip this screen in the future checkbox and click Next to continue to the next step.

2. The next screen that appears is Select the Property Pages. If your user control exposes properties of type OLE_COLOR, Font, or Picture, default Property pages are available. Click Add, and a Property page called ppgGeneral appears. By clicking in each box, enable the checkboxes next to the default pages that you want to be available. Arrange the pages by clicking the up- and down-arrows to move the selected pages. The wizard then should look similar to Figure 16.12. Click Next.

FIGURE 16.12.

Selecting the Property pages.

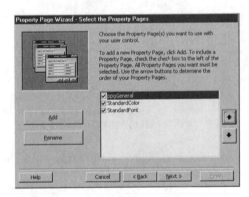

3. The wizard next presents the Add Properties screen, shown in Figure 16.13. Here you select the properties that you want to display on each page. The Available Properties box is filled with properties the wizard knows how to implement. You cannot modify the default pages for color and font. Drag each property in the Available Properties box to the ppgGeneral page tab. Then click Next.

FIGURE 16.13.
The Add Properties screen.

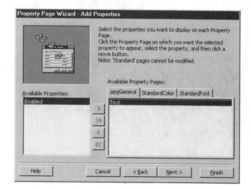

4. The Finish screen appears. The Property Page Wizard has added one Property page file to your project. Click Finish to exit the wizard. The newly created Property page now is visible.

NOTE

When designing Property pages, you do not have to provide tabs or an OK, Cancel, or Apply button. These are provided for your Property Page dialog box. You must, however, provide the name of each tab for non-standard pages.

5. Select the Caption property in the page's Property window. Change the caption to General. Add the same option buttons that you added to the test application and reposition the other controls so that the Property page looks similar to Figure 16.14.

FIGURE 16.14.
The General Property page.

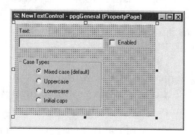

Now that your Property page design elements are placed, you must integrate them with your control. The `SelectedControls` collection of the `PropertyPage` object enables you to interact with the control. When a Property page is opened during design-time, at least one control must have been selected. You will use the `SelectedControls(0)` element to reference the first control selected. The `Changed` property of the `PropertyPage` object signals the availability of the Apply button contained in the `PropertyPage` dialog box.

The key events of a Property page object are the `SelectionChanged` and `ApplyChanges` events. When a developer selects different controls, you should update the values in your Property pages. Place code in the `SelectionChanged` event to examine the selected controls collection. When changes are made on the Property pages, you must enable the Apply button by setting `Changed` to `True`. After the Apply button is clicked, the `ApplyChanges` event is fired. Place code here to update all the selected controls with the correct values from the Property page controls.

You need to make the following modifications to your General Property page:

1. Add the following code to enable the Apply button after one of your `optCase` buttons is clicked:

```
Private m_nTextCase As Integer

Private Sub optCase_Click(Index As Integer)
    m_nTextCase = Index
    Changed = True
End Sub
```

2. Add the following line to the `SelectionChanged` event. When the user selects a different `NewText` control, the properties of that control are displayed on the General tab.

```
optCase(SelectedControls(0).TextCase).Value = true
```

3. Add the next line to the `ApplyChanges` event. This ensures that after the user clicks the Apply button, the values in the `Case` option are updated.

```
optCases(SelectedControls(0).TextCase).Value = true
```

> **NOTE**
>
> This example only saves changes to the first control selected (`SelectedControls(0)`). You must loop through the selected controls collection if you want to apply the same property value to multiple controls.

4. Close the Designers and Code windows on the Property page. Access the test application by double-clicking `frmTest` in the Project window. Right-click a `NewText` control in the test form to show the context menu, and choose Properties.

5. Test the functionality of the Property page you created. Figure 16.15 shows the completed Property pages in action.

FIGURE 16.15.
NewText *Property pages.*

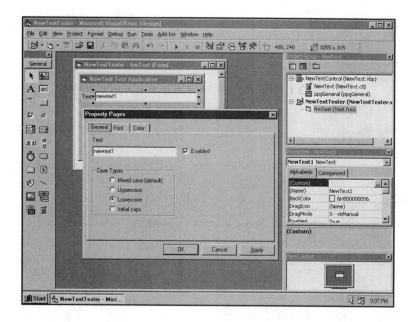

Using Compile Options

You can compile an ActiveX control separately or include it in a project. You can use public controls outside of Visual Basic in environments that support .ocx files. Private controls are stored in .ctl files and must be added to and compiled into the respective projects.

The Project Properties dialog box offers several compile options for creating a public component.

Require License Key

If you are compiling a component that you want to distribute to other developers or Web servers, choose the Require License Key option. When the project is built, Visual Basic creates a license file (.vbl). For a developer or Website to use your control, the .vbl file must be registered on that machine. The Setup Wizard helps you build the proper setup program to accomplish this registration. If you require the license key and someone uses your control without the authorized setup program, he will not be able to use your control for development.

P-Code Versus Native Code

Another option available when compiling your component is whether to compile using p-code (interpreted) or native code. For controls designed for Web page development, you probably will want to compile using p-code. This method usually produces a smaller .ocx than using native code. Compiling the NewText control with p-code, for example, creates a 26KB .ocx file.

Compiling the same control using native code using the Optimize for Small Code option results in a 33KB .ocx file. Web developers usually prefer the speed of downloading instead of an unnoticeable degree of speed efficiency with native code. Which option you decide to use depends on your particular situation.

Versioning

The Component tab of the Project Properties dialog box also offers options for version compatibility. This enables you to control the compatibility of your component with earlier versions and applications that use those versions. The compatibility options for a control project follow:

- ■ *No Compatibility:* Use this option for a new control filename or when you are making a clean break from previous versions. The user of your controls must upgrade to the newest version.
- ■ *Project Compatibility:* Use this option for new development. The location box specifies the .ocx file with which this control will be compatible.
- ■ *Binary Compatibility:* This option ensures compatibility with applications currently compiled with your control.

To compile your NewText control, choose File | Make NewText.ocx. Click the Options button in the Make Project dialog box to display the Project Property pages. Here, you may increment the version number of the control or set it to increment automatically on each compile. Other options include setting the company name, project name, copyright, and trademark information that will be visible when a user is viewing your control from within Windows Explorer.

You now are ready to start building a real application with your control.

Looking at Internet Features

Most often, ActiveX controls are placed on forms to capture some information from the user or to offer some dazzling effect. The same is true on Internet or intranet Web pages. ActiveX controls created in VB 5 are lightweight and can be used to spruce up any static Web page. The client, however, must have a ActiveX-capable browser or an appropriate plug-in to view and interact with the ActiveX controls. When placed on a Web page, an ActiveX control should offer the same behavior as it does on a form.

Internet features are available when the controls are placed in an Internet-aware container, such as Microsoft's Internet Explorer.

Asynchronous Downloading

Your control can contain images or other large amounts of data. If so, you might choose to download this information in the background. To see an example of this process, look at most Web pages developed today. When a browser begins loading a page for view and encounters an HTML image tag, it spawns a background process to load the image and then continues to read the rest of the inline text.

Controls built in Visual Basic can download large property values (such as images) asynchronously. The control can begin a background loading process by calling its own `AsyncRead` method. The `AsyncRead` method has the following syntax:

```
AsyncRead Location, Type, Property
```

The `Location` argument is a string that determines the path or address of the data or picture. This can be any valid URL, such as this:

```
file://c:\Multimedia files\logo.gif
```

or this:

```
http://www.kscsinc.com/CardShop/images/activex.gif
```

The `Type` argument specifies one of three types of data that can be downloaded:

- *VbAsyncTypeByteArray*: The data requested is received in a byte array. It is the responsibility of the control author to know how to handle this data format.

- *vbAsyncTypeFile*: The data requested is received in a temporary file created by Visual Basic. The temporary filename is available when the download is complete.

- *vbAsyncTypePicture*: The data requested is received in a `Picture` object.

The `Property` argument is a string that specifies the name of the property that will receive this data. An example using the `AsyncRead` method follows:

```
Private Sub cmdGetPic_click()
    '--Download the picture from the URL specified
    '  by txtURL
    cmdCancel.Enabled = True
    AsyncRead txtURL.Text, vbAsyncPicture, "Picture"
End Sub
```

Downloading the control might call `AsyncCancelRead` at any time to stop the process, though. It takes a property name string as an argument and only stops the download for that particular property. The following code illustrates how to use a Cancel button to stop a transfer:

```
Private Sub cmdCancel_click()
    CancelAsyncRead "Picture"
End Sub
```

When each property download is complete, the `AsyncReadComplete` event is fired. In the event, an `AsyncProperty` object is specified. This object contains the following properties:

- *AsyncType*: The picture, file, or byte array type.
- *PropertyName*: The name of the property that has finished loading.
- *Value*: In the case of the picture or byte array types, this property holds the data received. If the type is a file, the value is a string containing the temporary filename that Visual Basic created.

The following code fragment provides an example of how you might use a property after a download has been completed:

```
Private Sub UserControl_AsyncReadComplete(AsyncProp As VB.AsyncProperty)
On Error goto err_AsynComplete

    Select Case AsyncProp.PropertyName
        Case "Picture"
            Set Picture = AsyncProp.Value
    End Select

err_AsyncComplete:
    MsgBox Err.Number & ": " & Err.Description & " occurred in " &
Ambient.DisplayName & ".AsyncReadComplete."
End Sub
```

> **NOTE**
>
> Be aware that some type of error might occur during transmission of the property data, thus stopping the download. If so, that error is raised when the `Value` property of the `AsyncProperty` object is accessed. Proper error-handling code is required to address this issue.

The `Hyperlink` Object

By using the `Hyperlink` object, a control can take over a hyperlink-aware container. The control can then force the container to jump to a specific URL or navigate backward or forward through its history list. The `Hyperlink` object contains these three methods:

- *GoBack*: Moves backward through the history list.
- *GoForward*: Moves forward through the history list.
- *NavigateTo*: Jumps the Internet-aware container to a specified URL in the target string. You optionally can specify a document location as the following code fragment:

  ```
  Private Sub UserControl_Click()
      '-Go to the Virginia's weather page
      Hyperlink.NavigateTo "http://www.weather.com", "va.htm"
  End Sub
  ```

If the container is not hyperlink-aware, the application registered on the client machine, such as a browser, is launched. Errors are raised if no entries are in the history list or the specified URL or document is not available.

Internet Component Download Features

In order for controls to be used with Web pages, they first must be downloaded to the client machine. It is the browser's responsibility to copy the required files and install the components only if they do not currently exist. Several Internet component download features follow:

- ■ *Cab files.* Using the Setup Wizard, the control developer can place the control and any of the required dependent files into one cabinet (.cab) file. This .cab file then is compressed to facilitate faster downloads. After the browser processes an HTML document and encounters an <OBJECT> tag, it checks to see whether it needs to download the object. The code-base parameter in the <OBJECT> tag specifies the location from which to download the .cab files.

- ■ *MSVBVM50.DLL:* The runtime library required for all controls created with Visual Basic. If this file is not located on the client machine, the setup process specifies where it should be downloaded.

- ■ *Digital signatures.* Code-signing ensures the user of the control that a path to the author is available in case the control causes any harm to the client machine. Authors use an authorizing company to certify that the control is safe. Controls also can be marked as *safe for scripting* or *safe for initializing,* which backs up the claims of the control's reliability in those respects.

- ■ *Licensing support.* Helps protect control authors from others using unauthorized versions of their controls to develop and distribute new controls. License keys can be compiled into the control and provided along with the setup of the control. These keys are required for the control to be instantiated in development environments or on Web pages.

- ■ *Interface versioning.* Ensures that the client machine has at least the same version of the control required for the HTML page. Lower versions of controls prompt an immediate download of the newer version.

You can find more detailed information on the Internet component download facilities in Chapter 17, "Distributing Active X Documents and Controls via the Web Using VB 5."

Introducing the `DatePicker` Control

Now that you see how easy it is to add functionality to a TextBox control, you probably have plenty of ideas about the types of controls you want to build. Because this new frontier for Visual Basic is so broad, this section provides another example of a type of control you can create. It is a composite control that contains features of a date selection box. You can use it simply to enter a date into its constituent textbox, or you can click the drop-down arrow and select from a scrollable calendar, as the test application in Figure 16.16 shows.

FIGURE 16.16.

The DatePicker
control example in
action.

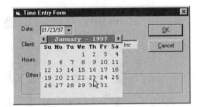

The DatePicker control is a slim 35KB (a download screamer). It was built using only a TextBox control and a handful of PictureBox controls. The calendar display was performed simply by using Print statements directly to one of the PictureBox controls. It is simplistic by design, yet functional. Examining the source code for the DatePicker control may help you learn more of the options now available to a Visual Basic ActiveX control designer.

Summary

This concludes the discussion of building ActiveX controls in Visual Basic 5. Although we have covered only a portion of the features and capabilities available in control development with VB 5, you should now have a basic understanding of the concepts involved. A more detailed discussion of ActiveX development could have filled an entire book this size.

The simple controls created in this chapter make use of wizard shortcuts provided by the developers at Microsoft. These wizards offer a fast way to build ActiveX components and at the same time provide the flexibility required to accomplish otherwise difficult tasks. If you can understand and learn from the process in which these wizards help you to build controls, you should be ready to create some more complex components on your own. Because control creation in Visual Basic is as simple as creating standard applications, it should soon become the method of choice for the multitude of programmers with VB skills.

There are an infinite number of possibilities available for the use of ActiveX controls in Internet/ intranet environments. They may range from the interface objects that we have created for simple Web page design to the integrated client/server controls that communicate to stores of enterprise data. Whatever the function, the fact remains that VB programmers now have another trick up their sleeves and the Web of the future promises to be teeming with their active creations.

17

Distributing ActiveX Documents and Controls via the Web Using VB 5

by Mark Spenik

One of the most promising features of an Internet/intranet environment is the software distribution model. In an Internet/intranet environment, the client browser is responsible for downloading Web pages, ActiveX controls, Java applets, images, and any other files required to display the page. The browser also is responsible for determining whether the file already exists on the machine or needs to be downloaded on the machine.

Before getting further into Web downloads, take a minute to look at the process of software distribution in a typical client/server environment where you create an application and a setup program for the application. The setup program contains all the files required to run your application as well as a program responsible for copying the file to the proper location on a user's machine. Someone then has to go to the user's machine, ask the user to quit what he is doing, and run the setup program to install the application. In large organizations, you can speed up this process by using software programs that specialize in software distribution and maintenance—for example, Microsoft SMS.

What happens when you are ready to release another version of the application? You have to update each user's machine with any files that have been modified or upgraded. Further complicating this environment are the installations of other custom or off-the-shelf applications. How often have you had a user call about an application you wrote that worked fine for more than a year but then suddenly stopped working, only to find that another application recently was installed that improperly replaced a DLL used by your application? Software distribution and maintenance definitely can become a headache.

Now, contrast client/server software distribution to the Internet/intranet environment. In this environment, Web applications are distributed to users without any physical intervention by the application author or any other Information Systems (IS) staff member. If a new user needs the application, you can tell him the URL of the application, and you're done (assuming that he has the proper permissions to use the URL). If you upgrade or make changes to the application, no problem. Change the pages and components on the Website, and you're done! As users access the URL, the browser determines which files have changed and downloads the changes to the user's PC. Other Web applications are installed in a similar fashion, so you don't have to worry about poorly written setup programs overwriting files with older versions. From an administrative point of view, the Internet/intranet environment is much simpler. From a maintenance point of view, the intranet environment again simplifies problems by enabling an administrator to set up directories with the latest components, applets, and applications available for use by anyone with a browser.

So what are the drawbacks? One issue in an Internet environment is security against rogue components or applications. When a component is being downloaded to your PC, you might be concerned that it may damage your machine. After all, it's not like going to the local software store or consulting firm and purchasing a shrink-wrapped software package. Security from rogue applications in a secure company intranet is less of an issue. In an intranet environment, network bandwidth and the overall performance of application download times are major concerns. Despite the concerns, distributing applications via the Web has great potential for companies and organizations to reduce the cost of software ownership and maintenance.

This chapter describes using Visual Basic 5 to create installation packages that enable your ActiveX controls and ActiveX documents to be downloaded and installed via an Internet/intranet environment.

Examining Files Used in the Download Process

In this section we take a close look at how software is loaded and installed from the Web to the client PC. Before taking a closer look at a Web software installation, you should review some of the important files used in the download process. These files make the distribution of software via the Web possible. The two files used in Web software distribution are

> Cab Files
> INF File

Cab Files

Cabinet files (referred to as *cab* files) are compressed files that contain all the files required to load and install an ActiveX control or ActiveX document on a client machine. Cab files have a file extension of .cab. Typical cab files are the ActiveX control (ocx), the INF file, and any other files or DLLs required by the ActiveX control that are not part of a secondary cab file.

The INF File

The INF file is compressed into the cab file and is the initialization file for the installation process. The INF file contains all the information on how to download and install the component, including the location for any required secondary cab files. The cab file for the runtime Visual Basic DLL or for DAO is a secondary cab file. The INF file has a file extension of .inf. You can view the .inf file using any text editor—for example, Notepad.

The Download Process

Figure 17.1 shows the download process of ActiveX components or controls via the Web. Take a look at Figure 17.1 to get a clear understanding of the application download process via the Web. The Web page MyHTML is on the Web server MyServer. MyHTML contains a single ActiveX control on the page called MyActiveX.ocx. A person on the user machine goes to the URL of the Web page MyHTML.

FIGURE 17.1.

The Web application download process.

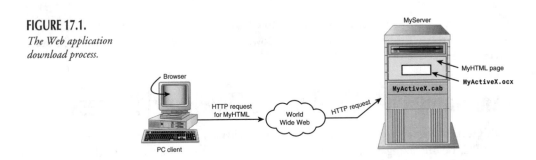

The following steps outline the download process:

1. The Web page is downloaded. The browser encounters the <OBJECT> tag for the ActiveX control and uses the tag CLASSID to check the system Registry for the CLASSID. If the CLASSID is found on the user's machine, go to step 8; otherwise, go to step 2.

2. The CLASSID for the MyActiveX control is not found on the user's machine, so the browser uses the tag CODEBASE to download the cab file MyActiveX.cab.

3. The cab file is loaded on the user's machine.

4. The INF file found in the cab file is processed. The browser (Internet Explorer) uses the cab file to set up Registry settings for the control, such as Safe for Scripting.

5. The INF file references the Visual Basic runtime DLL Vbrun500.dll. The browser checks the Registry to see whether Vbrun500.dll is on the local machine. If Vbrun500.dll is found, go to step 7; otherwise, go to step 6.

6. The INF file tells the browser to retrieve the Vbrun500.dll cab file from the Microsoft Website. The browser retrieves the Vbrun500.dll cab file and uncompresses the cab file installing Vbrun500.dll.

7. The MyActiveX control is installed and registered on the local machine.

8. The MyActiveX control is instantiated on the Web page MyHTML.

Providing Component and Control Security

One of the prevalent fears of downloading software from the Web is the fear of destructive and harmful controls or components that may damage the client machine. Microsoft has provided several security mechanisms to help prevent harmful software from making it to a user's machine. The security mechanisms with ActiveX controls and ActiveX components follow:

- Digital signatures
- Safe for scripting
- Safe for initialization

Digital Signatures

Digital signatures are obtained from a certificate authority. A digital signature enables the Web browser user to determine the author of the control (who may be liable). After the source of the control is identified, the user can decide whether to download the control.

Safe for Scripting

When an ActiveX component or ActiveX control is marked as *safe for scripting*, the creator of the component or control is making a guarantee that, regardless of how the component or control is used in a script (VBScript or JavaScript), it cannot harm the user's PC in any way. A control or component that tries to obtain information about a user is *never* safe for scripting. A control that performs any of the following actions as a result of scripting may not be safe for scripting:

- Inserting information into INI files or the Registry
- Creating a file with a name provided from a script
- Getting information from the Registry or INI file
- Providing a filename from a script and then reading the file on a hard drive

> **NOTE**
>
> Trying to determine which actions are safe and unsafe can be difficult, and a full discussion of this topic is beyond the scope of this book. Microsoft's own documentation states that the process is not easy. Check the Microsoft Website at www.microsoft.com/devonly/ and Visual Basic 5 documentation on "Building Internet Applications" for more detailed guidelines to determine what is safe and unsafe.

Safe for Initialization

When an ActiveX component or ActiveX control is marked as *safe for initialization,* the creator of the component or control is guaranteeing that, regardless of how it is initialized, it cannot harm the user's PC. Safe for initialization is not as strict a standard as safe for scripting, because safe for initialization is concerned only with how the control is initialized instead of the methods and properties of the control.

> **NOTE**
>
> The default security setting for Microsoft Internet Explorer prevents any non-digitally signed ActiveX controls or ActiveX components from loading on a client machine. The default setting also prevents any ActiveX controls or ActiveX components from being instantiated if they are not marked as safe for scripting and safe for initialization.

Creating an Internet Downloadable Installation Package

Visual Basic 5 includes a utility called the Application Setup Wizard that walks you through the steps required to create a downloadable Web installation package that can be installed on a Windows platform. To create a Web installation package using the Setup Wizard, perform these steps:

1. From the Windows 95 or NT 4.0 task bar under Visual Basic 5 (or from the Visual Basic program group in NT 3.51), select the Application Setup Wizard. The introductory screen appears. (If you do not want this screen to appear the next time you start the wizard, enable the Skip this Screen in the future checkbox.) Click Next. The Select Projects and Options dialog box appears, as shown in Figure 17.2.

FIGURE 17.2.
The Select Project and Options dialog box.

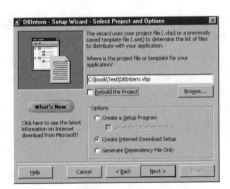

2. Select the Visual Basic project and the type of setup program you want to create. Click the Browse button to locate the project. If you want to rebuild (compile) the project before creating the setup files, leave the Rebuild the Project checkbox enabled. Because you want to generate setup files for Web downloads, enable the Create Internet Download Setup checkbox and then click Next. The Internet Distribution Location dialog box appears, as shown in Figure 17.3.

FIGURE 17.3.

The Internet Distribution Location dialog box.

3. Select the drive and directory where you want to generate the files for the Internet download package (cabinet files, HTML files, support files, and so on). Then click Next. The Internet Package dialog box appears, as shown in Figure 17.4.

FIGURE 17.4.

The Internet Package dialog box.

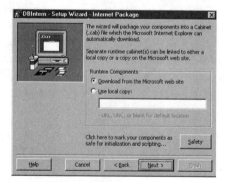

4. Here, you can create a primary cab file for downloading your application. The primary download file includes the components of the project (ActiveX controls, ActiveX DLLs, and ActiveX executables, for example) as well as the INF file, links to other cab files, and any additional files not located in any of the linked cab files. You also can specify where additional cab files are located. The default setting goes to the Microsoft Website for digitally signed secondary components, such as the Visual Basic runtime or DAO. This is a great way to get the latest component upgrades. Even better, you don't have to maintain a site with the Microsoft digitally signed components.

For a secure and fast intranet site, you might want to select the Use local copy radio button so that you can retrieve secondary cab files on your local network instead of the World Wide Web. To mark safety options for your components, click Safety to display the Safety dialog box shown in Figure 17.5.

FIGURE 17.5.

The Safety dialog box.

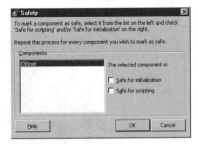

Select components in the Components listbox and enable the Safe for initialization or Safe for scripting checkbox for each component as appropriate.

CAUTION

Refer to the section "Providing Component and Control Security" earlier in this chapter and read the Microsoft Visual Basic 5 documentation on what it means to be safe for initialization and safe for scripting in the section "Packaging ActiveX Components for the Web." Saying that your component is safe for initialization and scripting guarantees users of your control that it will *never* corrupt or damage their systems. To quote the Setup Wizard Help file associated with the Safety dialog box, "Marking a component as either safe for scripting or safe for initialization may imply that you are accepting liability for this guarantee."

After you mark your components with the proper safety options, click OK. In the Internet Package dialog box, click Next. The ActiveX Components dialog box appears, as shown in Figure 17.6.

FIGURE 17.6.

The ActiveX Components dialog box.

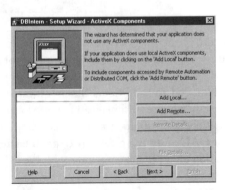

5. Here, you can add additional ActiveX components to include in the cab file. To add a component stored locally, click Add Local. For remote components, click Add Remote. After you add any additional components, click Next. The wizard then begins to process your previous selections and displays the File Summary dialog box shown in Figure 17.7.

FIGURE 17.7.

The File Summary dialog box.

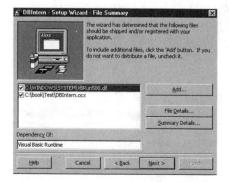

6. In the File Summary dialog box, you list all the files that are part of your application and will be distributed with your application. If you want to prevent a file from being distributed, disable the checkbox to the left of the filename. You can add additional files by clicking Add. To check file details such as size and version, click File Details. For a summary of the total number of files in the application and the uncompressed size of the setup and application files, click Summary Details. To continue the setup process, click Next. The Finished dialog box shown in Figure 17.8 appears.

FIGURE 17.8.

The Finished dialog box.

7. To complete the installation, click Finish. The Setup Wizard creates the Internet download package in the selected directories. After the package has been created, a Completion dialog box appears. To save the answers to each of the Setup Wizard steps for later use, click the Save Template button shown in Figure 17.8. You can then use the saved template to create setup and distribution files without walking through the Setup Wizard.

The files created for the setup are placed in the directory you selected in step 3. A subdirectory called Support is created off the selected directory.

Web Installation Example

I created a Web installation for a simple custom control I developed called Proocx1.ocx. I selected the option to retrieve secondary cab files from the Microsoft Website. On the local directory, I chose to build the Web installation package. The Application Setup Wizard built two files: a cab file called Proocx1.cab and an HTML file to use as an example for using my control called Proocx1.HTM. Listing 17.1 shows this HTML file.

Listing 17.1. An HTML file generated by the Application Setup Wizard.

```
<HTML>
<!--    If any of the controls on this page require licensing,
you must create a license package file.
Run LPK_TOOL.EXE in the tools directory to create the required LPK file.

<OBJECT CLASSID="clsid:5220cb21-c88d-11cf-b347-00aa00a28331">
    <PARAM NAME="LPKPath" VALUE="LPKfilename.LPK">
</OBJECT>
-->

<OBJECT
    classid="clsid:E097C06E-5B61-11D0-95E3-8FAF3182360A"
    id=UserControl1
    codebase="Proocx1.CAB#version=1,0,0,0">
</OBJECT>
</HTML>
```

The Application Setup Wizard placed the following files used to create the cab file in the Support subdirectory:

- *Proocx1.DDF*: Contains the DDF files to be used by the compression program
- *Proocx1.OCX*: Contains the custom control to install and register
- *Proocx1.INF*: Contains all the file dependencies, setup, version, and safety information for Proocx1.ocx

You can modify the INF file in the Support directory and regenerate the cab file with your modifications.

Summary

In this chapter, you learned how to create a package for Web installations using the Application Setup Wizard in Visual Basic 5. You examined the steps and files involved in the Web download process. Generate Web installations for your custom controls and try them out. If your company has an intranet, you might find Web installation an easy way to cut the cost of software installation and maintenance.

VII

Server-Side Database Applications Development

18

The Common Gateway Interface (CGI)

by Drew Kittel

This chapter discusses the *Common Gateway Interface* (CGI) and the role it plays in linking client-side actions (such as database access requests) to server-side reactions (such as database access and queries, as well as the subsequent dynamic generation of HTML for data presentation). You've already looked at using HTML user interfaces (enhanced with ActiveX and VBScript) to support database access on the client side. Now it's time to start looking at one of the most popular methods for handling information submitted from these forms to a Web server—this is the world of CGI. This chapter demystifies CGI and shows you that it really is no more than another component of a distributed applications development environment.

This chapter begins with an introduction to just what CGI is and some of the tasks it can help you accomplish. A discussion on CGI input and output processing follows, including some specifics on environment variables and their uses, as well as the methods used by the client to make a request to the server when an HTML form is submitted.

Next you will discover how the Windows CGI interface provides an easy means for developing CGI applications in a Windows development environment. Additionally, you will see how the enterprising work of some sharp Visual Basic developers has resulted in a publicly available module of VB code that greatly simplifies development of Web applications using Windows CGI and Visual Basic.

Finally, the remainder of the chapter takes a look at using the DB-Library VB API that comes with Microsoft SQL Server to create sophisticated Web database applications.

What Is CGI?

CGI is most simply described as a means by which a Web server can communicate with applications external to the server software and have those applications perform some processing on its behalf. In essence, CGI is a server-side process that serves as a go-between for the Web server and other applications programs, information resources, and databases. These information resources and databases can reside on the same physical machine as the Web server or on a machine at some other geographical location.

CGI provides a standard interface between the Web server and external applications. These applications commonly are referred to as *gateway programs, CGI programs,* or simply *CGI scripts*. This interface abstracts the details of communications between the Web server and the CGI program to the point where the only detail that application developers really need to know about the interface is how to input data into and retrieve data from their application. You therefore need no fundamental knowledge of the process of communicating directly with HTTP servers to use programs such as database query programs. You just need to understand how to handle the data that the server passes to the program and return the data generated by the program.

CGI programs extend the basic functionality of the Web server and give it the capability to service a variety of Web client requests that the server alone ordinarily would not be able to accommodate. CGI provides the mechanism for giving Web clients (your users) access to any application or resource to which you want to provide access.

> **RESOURCE**
>
> The *National Center for Supercomputing Applications* (NCSA) Website has some tremendous information on CGI, the CGI specification, CGI environment variables, and a number of other Web-related topics. The URL for this site is
> `http://hoohoo.ncsa.uiuc.edu`

Gateway Program, CGI Program, or CGI Script?

Gateway program, *CGI program*, and *CGI script* are essentially three names for the same thing; the remainder of this chapter uses the term *CGI program*. CGI programs contain the code that accepts data from the Web server (most often passed on from its Web clients) and does something with that data. Tasks can range from various forms of processing, accessing information resources, creating output, or all of these. CGI programs can be developed in virtually any language supported on the Web server host machine, including compiled and interpreted languages such as C, C++, Java, JavaScript, Visual Basic, FORTRAN, Perl, Awk, Expect, and Tcl, as well as some of the newer Perl extensions for client/server database access—for example, Sybperl and Oraperl.

What Can CGI Programs Do?

A CGI program enables you to develop applications that greatly extend the functionality and capabilities of your Web server. In doing so, you can integrate other system resources, such as databases, document repositories, statistical applications, specialty processing, and so on with your Web server. These resources do not need to be local to the server host machine; they can be geographically distributed databases and applications that the CGI program can access. In other words, a CGI program running on a machine in Washington, D.C., can be designed to access databases on machines in Los Angeles, California, or any other location around the globe.

By providing a means to access resources external to your Web server, CGI programs extend the availability of these resources to your Web clients. What does this mean? Suppose that your organization has a database of information that it wants the public or users internal to the organization to be able to access. You now can develop CGI programs that accept user input from an HTML forms interface and use that input to perform complex searches and queries against the database. Other applications can be processing HTML order forms for your online store. This order processing also can be integrated with applications that perform inventory and warehouse management, accounting, and so on.

One of the most powerful aspects of CGI programming is that it gives you a means of generating HTML documents on-the-fly. No longer does your Website have to be a repository of static documents and data. Using CGI, you can develop applications that enable users to create dynamic, customized HTML documents and data presentations by specifying their unique content.

The CGI Data-Flow Process

The typical steps in the CGI data-flow process follow, as shown in Figure 18.1:

1. A Web client (for example, a browser) makes a connection to a Web server at the server's address (and port number, if indicated) in the URL.

2. The Web client sends a request. This request generally is made by using one of two methods: GET or POST.

3. Data from the requesting client (such as user input on an HTML form) is passed from the server to the CGI program referenced in the initial URL.

4. The CGI program reads in the requesting client's data that it received from the Web server and performs some processing on the client's behalf.

5. The CGI program generates a response to the client. Typically, this response is an HTML document, but it can be some other type of document. This response is passed to the client via the server.

6. After passing the server response to the requesting client, the server closes the connection to the client. An exception to this is when the CGI program continues to push data to the client in a technique called *server push*. In this case, the connection is maintained.

FIGURE 18.1.

The CGI data-flow process.

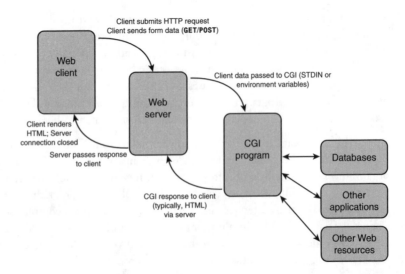

CGI Input and Output Processing

A Web server and a CGI program can communicate and pass data to one another in four ways:

- *Environment variables.* Values inherited by a program from the runtime environment on the system that invoked the program. In the case of CGI, the variables are set by the Web server and inherited by the CGI program it executes.

- *Standard input.* The system's standard input file descriptor. On most UNIX systems, for example, standard input is where a command or program takes its inputs. This can be a terminal device or the output from another program.

- *Standard output.* The system's standard output file descriptor. On most UNIX systems, for example, standard output is where a command or program writes its output. This can be a terminal device or the input to another program.

- *Command line.* A method by which data is split up and passed to a program as if it were placed on a command line. The UNIX convention of passing this data to the program is used. An array of pointers to strings that make up the input, argv, and a value signifying the number of entries in the argv array, argc, are passed to the CGI program. This method is used only for ISINDEX queries, which are discussed later in this chapter.

Actually, CGI programs and a Web server can communicate through one additional method: by using a Windows .INI file. This method is specific to a specialized form of CGI known as Windows CGI. Because the Windows CGI specification is of particular interest to CGI developers in the Windows operating system environment, the latter half of this chapter (beginning with the section entitled "What is Windows CGI?") is dedicated to covering it in detail.

What Is CGI Data Input?

CGI input data is data submitted by the requesting client to the server, which the CGI program uses to perform some action, such as a database query. Depending on the way in which the client request is made (for example, the forms request METHOD=POST), this input data may be encoded before being passed by the server to the CGI program by environment variables or by standard input. When standard input is used, the length of the input string still is passed through an environment variable.

In addition to the actual data, the server also may pass information to the CGI program detailing the type of data that was passed. This is the case when the data is passed to the program by standard input. Standard input gives the CGI program a means of determining how it is supposed to handle or process the input data. This data type information also is passed through an environment variable.

NOTE

Because input data may be encoded or passed by more than one method, CGI programs need to be designed to determine the method of data passing used, as well as the amount of data passed, so that the entire input can be read into the program in an appropriate manner.

What Is CGI Data Output?

A CGI program can generate a variety of types of output. This output can consist of instructions to the server to perform some task, such as calling another program or perhaps redirecting the client to obtain resources at another URL. More often, though, this output consists of HTML, ActiveX controls, and VBScript generated to present the results of some action performed for a requesting client. These results could be the results of a database query, for example.

CGI output always is returned by standard output. Even in cases when the CGI program has no data to return, it must generate a response indicating this. Two methods of return are possible: parsed-header output and non-parsed headers. With *parsed-header output*, CGI scripts produce output that is interpreted by the server and sent to the client. The script is not required to send an HTTP header, because this function is handled by the server when it parses the script output before passing it on to the Web client. Parsing incurs some overhead in processing by the server. Sometimes, you may want to avoid the overhead of this additional processing. To do so, CGI scripts can generate an HTTP header directly to avoid parsing by the server. These scripts must be prefixed by `nph-` to tell the server that output is to be passed directly to the client without parsing. Parsed header output is the only concern here, because this is the form that servers are required to support.

When the CGI program has data to return to the client, the data must be sent in a specific format:

```
Data Header (of a type understood by the server)
     . . .a blank line . . .
the body of the response (i.e. optional output data to the requesting client)
```

As noted, the response data is optional, but if it is included, it must be prefaced by a MIME `Content-type` data header as seen in the following line of code:

```
Content-type: text/html
```

NOTE

Multipurpose Internet Mail Extensions (MIME) is the latest standard for Internet mail and transfer of a variety of media types, including text, images, audio, and video. For more information about MIME, refer to Appendix G, "An Overview of MIME."

If the output data is not included, the data header must be a Location type (a URL), such as this:

```
Location: http://www.north.pole/santas_list.html
```

or a Status type (a message string), such as this:

```
Status: msg# msg_text
```

The server reads the CGI output and takes action depending on the header it finds. If the header is a Content-type header, the output is returned to the client. If the header is a Location type, the server ignores anything following the Location header and instead directs the client to access data or resources at the URL specified. If the header is a Status type, *msg#* and *text* enable the server to override the defaults it normally would return to the client.

CGI Environment Variables

Whenever you are working on a computer, running a program, or simply logging on, background variables are part of your working environment. These background variables are known as *environment variables* and typically are set automatically when you log on, established by a program at runtime, or even defined and set explicitly by you. Typically, environment variables persist for the life of a parent process and are passed to or inherited by child processes and applications of the parent.

Several standard CGI environment variables are defined when a server executes a CGI program. These can be used to pass data between the server and the CGI program. These variables come in two basic types. The first type of variable is the variable set during all client requests; this is a *not request-specific* variable. The second type of variable is a variable specific to the client request the CGI program is fulfilling; this is a *client-specific* or, more commonly, *request-specific* variable.

> **NOTE**
>
> Although a standard set of environment variables common to all Web browsers exist, most vendors also define additional HTTP_ environment variables. Netscape browsers also define HTTP_REFERER and HTTP_CONNECTION, for example, which indicate the referring HTML document and the connection type, respectively. Examples of these values follow:
> ```
> HTTP_REFERER=file:///C¦/My Documents/SAMS/WebDev/echoenv.html
> HTTP_CONNECTION=Keep-Alive
> ```

Environment variable values are used by CGI programs primarily as a means of attending to client requests for processing, database accesses, and so on. Sometimes, however, the variables are used to determine the client's type of Web browser. In other cases, the variables may be used to maintain and pass state information between the client and the CGI program between independent requests for service from the client. This need for state information occurs because HTTP is a stateless protocol. Therefore, after a client/server connection is dropped, your CGI program has no knowledge or memory of preceding connections unless you explicitly build in a mechanism for maintaining this information. You can maintain the state of user input to a form, for example, by designing CGI applications that embed these values as hidden fields in subsequent HTML documents that it generates for the client.

A list of 19 standard CGI environment variables follows (variables that are not request-specific are so indicated):

```
AUTH_TYPE
CONTENT_LENGTH
CONTENT_TYPE
GATEWAY_INTERFACE (not request-specific)
HTTP_ACCEPT
HTTP_USER_AGENT
PATH_INFO
PATH_TRANSLATED
QUERY_STRING
REMOTE_ADDR
REMOTE_HOST
REMOTE_IDENT
REMOTE_USER
REQUEST_METHOD
SCRIPT_NAME
SERVER_NAME  (not request-specific)
SERVER_PORT
SERVER_PROTOCOL
SERVER_SOFTWARE (not request-specific)
```

The following sections briefly describe each of the CGI environment variables.

AUTH_TYPE

For servers that support user authentication and run protected CGI programs, the value of the AUTH_TYPE variable details the method used to validate users. The authentication method is protocol-specific. For example, this code indicates the most common value used:

```
AUTH_TYPE = Basic
```

In this case, a basic authentication scheme requires that a client provide a password and user identification in order to authenticate itself.

CONTENT_LENGTH

The CONTENT_LENGTH variable represents the length (in characters) of the data buffer sent by the client to the server during a request. For example, a test request for forms processing on the server reported this:

```
CONTENT_LENGTH=105
```

CONTENT_TYPE

The value of the CONTENT_TYPE variable represents the MIME type of the data sent from the client to the server as the result of a METHOD=POST request from the client. This method commonly is used in HTML forms processing. If no data is sent, the value is set to NULL. For example, a test request for forms (using POST) processing on the server reported this:

```
CONTENT_TYPE=application/x-www-form-urlencoded
```

This is the default encoding for forms.

GATEWAY_INTERFACE

The GATEWAY_INTERFACE variable simply contains the version of the CGI specification to which the server complies. This environment variable is not request-specific. The server reports this value as the following, which indicates CGI 1.1:

```
GATEWAY_INTERFACE=CGI/1.1
```

HTTP_ACCEPT

The value of the HTTP_ACCEPT variable is a comma delimited list of all the MIME data types the requesting client will accept. MIME is covered in more detail in Appendix G, but basically seven MIME types are used by HTTP. These include application, text, multipart, message, image, audio, and video. All these types also have subtypes associated with them. For example, GIF is a subtype of image. My server reported that a Microsoft Internet Explorer Web client accepts the following image types:

```
HTTP_ACCEPT=image/gif, image/x-xbitmap, image/jpeg, */*
```

Note that the value of HTTP_ACCEPT is a list of accepted MIME types and is formatted as *type/subtype*, *type/subtype*, and so on.

HTTP_USER_AGENT

The HTTP_USER_AGENT variable contains the Web browser the client used to send a request. It provides a nice way for CGI programs to format output to take advantage of extensions used by certain browsers or to accommodate shortcomings of some browsers. The server reported the following for a Microsoft Internet Explorer Web client, for example:

```
HTTP_USER_AGENT=Mozilla/1.22 (compatible; MSIE 2.0; Windows 95)
```

In this case, the value of the environment variable indicates that the client Web browser is *Microsoft Internet Explorer* (MSIE) 2.0 running under Windows 95 and that it is compatible with Netscape (Mozilla) 1.22.

PATH_INFO

The value of the PATH_INFO variable represents extra path information supplied by the client. Servers can decode this information from URLs before executing the CGI script. Notice the following URL in an HTML forms interface document:

```
<FORM METHOD="POST" ACTION="http://jupiter.omniscient.com/cgi-bin/test-env/
extrastuff">
```

This URL points to a CGI program called test-env and is appended with additional information (extrastuff). This resulted in the server reporting the following:

```
PATH_INFO=/extrastuff
```

CGI applications typically do not have any knowledge of the method by which this value was set. It is up to the developer to know the context in which this value may be used. This variable gives the developer another method of passing information from an HTML document to a CGI program. Suppose that an anchor with the following URL is in the document:

```
<A HREF="http://jupiter.omniscient.com/cgi-bin/myVBGateway.exe/
param1=val1+param2=val2
```

This results in the following PATH_INFO variable value:

```
PATH_INFO=/param1=val1+param2=val2
```

This variable provides a method by which two additional parameters might be passed to the CGI program myVBGateway.exe, which then could obtain these values from the PATH_INFO environment variable.

PATH_TRANSLATED

The value of the PATH_TRANSLATED variable is a virtual-to-physical PATH_INFO mapping provided by the server. In other words, it represents the server's attempt to provide a full operating system absolute path to the data indicated in PATH_INFO. For the URL specified in the FORM ACTION attribute in the previous example, that is

```
="http://jupiter.omniscient.com/cgi-bin/test-env/extrastuff"
```

the server uses the server's DocumentRoot value of /usr/local/etc/httpd/htdocs to translate the full path to this:

```
PATH_TRANSLATED=/usr/local/etc/httpd/htdocs/extrastuff
```

QUERY_STRING

The value of the QUERY_STRING variable is a URL-encoded string that is appended after a question-mark (?) character at the end of the URL referencing the CGI routine being executed. *URL-encoding* is a method of translating some data values to be transferred between the client and server to ensure that the data sent is received intact. URL-encoding and using the METHOD=GET form request method to set this variable are discussed in the sections "Getting Client Data to a CGI Program" and "Query Strings" a bit later in this chapter.

For a METHOD=GET test, the following URL-encoded data string was sent to the server by the client:

```
http://jupiter.omniscient.com/cgi-bin/test-env?uname=&email=&address=&bus=sw
➡&title=Pres&cgidev=Perl5&dbase=Access&description=&dbyesno=YES&subscribe=YES
```

The server reported the value of the QUERY_STRING variable as this:

```
QUERY_STRING=uname=&email=&address=&bus=sw&title=Pres&cgidev=Perl5
➡&dbase=Access&description=&dbyesno=YES&subscribe=YES
```

REMOTE_ADDR

The REMOTE_ADDR variable contains the value of the *Internet provider* (IP) address for the requesting client or agent (which actually may be a host of the requesting client). For the previous test examples, the server reported the following:

```
REMOTE_ADDR=168.143.1.44
```

REMOTE_HOST

The REMOTE_HOST variable contains the full DNS hostname for the requesting client or agent if the server is able to obtain this information. Otherwise, the value is NULL. For the previous test examples, the server reported the following:

```
REMOTE_HOST=dkittel.clark.net
```

REMOTE_IDENT

The REMOTE_IDENT variable contains the name of the remote user as retrieved from the server if the HTTP server supports RFC 931 identification. The RFC 931 Authentication Server documentation states that HTTP servers supporting this feature should make an effort to identify the requesting client or agent. This is not considered a valid means of authenticating users. Enabling this feature also can result in performance degradation because extra work is imposed on the server to attempt identification. An example of this variable follows:

```
REMOTE_IDENT=kittel.omniscient.com
```

REMOTE_USER

The REMOTE_USER variable contains the authenticated user's name if the server supports user authentication and the CGI application program is protected from unauthorized use. If the AUTH_TYPE variable is set to basic, for example, the REMOTE_USER variable can be set by using the user's identification as sent by the client. An example of this process follows:

```
REMOTE_USER=julie_wirkkala
```

REQUEST_METHOD

The REQUEST_METHOD variable contains the client request method. The GET and POST methods are by far the most popular and widely used methods.

In the previous test example of a request for forms processing, METHOD=POST was specified. The server subsequently reported the following:

```
REQUEST_METHOD=POST
```

> **RESOURCE**
>
> HTTP servers can service other request types, although POST and GET are by far the most widely used. For information on other methods in the HTTP specification, visit these URLs:
>
> ```
> http://www.w3.org/hypertext/WWW/Protocols/HTTP/Request.html
> http://www.w3.org/hypertext/WWW/Protocols/HTTP/Methods.html
> ```

SCRIPT_NAME

The SCRIPT_NAME variable contains a virtual path to the CGI program being executed by the server. For the previous text example, the server reported this:

```
SCRIPT_NAME=/cgi-bin/test-env
```

SERVER_NAME

The SERVER_NAME variable contains the Web server hostname, DNS alias, or IP address. This environment variable is not request-specific. The server reports this value as the following:

```
SERVER_NAME=jupiter.omniscient.com
```

In this case, the Web server hostname, `jupiter.omniscient.com`, was set. In other cases, the following DNS alias might be returned:

```
SERVER_NAME=jupiter
```

Or an IP address can be returned, such as this:

```
SERVER_NAME=555.555.0.19
```

SERVER_PORT

The SERVER_PORT variable contains the port to which the client request was sent. *Ports* are communications sockets used by TCP/IP applications. Most TCP/IP applications use a well-known port identifier. Such is the case with HTTP, which uses port number 80 as a default. It is possible, however, for the port number to be explicitly called out in the URL. A server may use a port number such as 8080 as the designated port for the HTTP server. In this case, URLs need to explicitly reference the port, as this example shows:

```
http://jupiter.omniscient.com:8080/cgi-bin/test-env
```

The server reported the following:

```
SERVER_PORT=8080
```

Using different port numbers enables multiple servers to be run from the same machine. This can be beneficial for establishing servers for CGI testing as well as separate intranets.

SERVER_PROTOCOL

The SERVER_PROTOCOL variable contains information about the protocol used by the requesting client. This variable includes both the name and revision number. For the earlier test example, the server reported this:

```
SERVER_PROTOCOL=HTTP/"1.0
```

SERVER_SOFTWARE

The SERVER_SOFTWARE variable contains the name and version number of the Web server that is tending to Web client requests and running the CGI. This environment variable is not client-request-specific. The server reports this value as the following:

```
SERVER_SOFTWARE=NCSA/1.5
```

In this case, the server software is the NCSA Web server, Version 1.5.

Getting Client Data to a CGI Program

A server can pass client data to a CGI program by using several methods. Two methods are by far the most functional and widely used: GET and POST. This section contains references to query strings and URL-encoding. This material is covered in the sections "Query Strings" and "URL-Encoding" presented a bit later. Feel free to flip forward for a look at this material if you get curious during the discussion of GET and POST.

Using the GET Method for <FORM> Input

The GET method is used to pass user input to an HTML form to a CGI program for processing. Although GET is the default value for the METHOD attribute, it is considered to be the less-preferred method for forms-input handling because of limitations on the amount of data that can be passed using GET (a limitation not incurred by using the POST method). Because writing CGI programs that obtain their input from the QUERY-STRING environment variable is very straightforward, GET still is useful for simpler forms with only a few input objects. A fair number of older HTML and CGI programs still exist that use GET.

After a user clicks the Submit button on a form, the client browser URL-encodes and assembles user-input data into a query string that is appended to the Action URL specified in the <FORM> tag in the HTML document. A particular request to the server may look like this:

```
GET /cgi-bin/dosomething.exe?name=myname&title=developer HTTP/1.0
```

The server then passes the URL-encoded user-input query string to the CGI program through the QUERY_STRING environment variable.

> **NOTE**
>
> If the user fails to enter anything in text and password-entry fields, the field value is empty, but the field name still is appended to the URL query string as "fieldname=". Also note that disabled checkboxes are ignored entirely and are not appended as part of the query string.

> **CAUTION**
>
> As mentioned previously, GET is useful for very simple forms. However, GET has serious limitations on the amount of user-input data that can be transmitted from the browser to the server and subsequently to the CGI program. The amount of data that can be transferred typically is limited to 256 characters. This limitation can be especially constrictive for forms with multiple fields and forms with TEXTAREA input objects. The amount of data, along with URL encoding, easily can surpass the limitations of GET, resulting in data being truncated while being passed. For this reason, POST is the preferred method for forms processing.

Using the POST Method for <FORM> Input

After a user clicks the Submit button on a form, the client browser URL-encodes user input in the same manner it does for GET; however, the data is *not* appended to the specified Action URL. Instead, the data is sent in a data block to the server as part of the POST operation. (A *data block* is simply a stream of data, of arbitrary length, passed to the CGI program.) In this case, the Action URL is the URL to which the data block is POSTed. A particular request to the server might look like this:

```
POST /cgi-bin/dosomething.exe HTTP/1.0

Accept: text/plain
Accept: text/html
Accept: */*
Content-type: application/x-www-form-urlencoded
Content-length: 36
ford=escort&toyota=mr2&special=rolls
```

The server now passes the encoded user data to the CGI program by standard input. Additionally, the CONTENT_LENGTH and CONTENT_TYPE environment variables are set for use by the CGI program.

> **CAUTION**
>
> Developers of CGI programs should be aware that when sending data to the CGI program using POST, the server is not required to send an *End-of-File* (EOF) character at the end of the data. You should use the environment variable CONTENT_LENGTH to determine how much data your CGI program needs to read from the standard input file descriptor.

Query Strings

Earlier, you learned that the value of the QUERY_STRING environment variable is obtained from a URL-encoded string that is appended after a ? character at the end of the URL that references the CGI routine being executed. But how is the information added to the end of the URL in the first place? This can occur in two ways.

In the first method, the query information is added manually to an anchor's HREF URL in an HTML document. The URL in the following anchor, for example, references a program that prints a list of all employees due for a promotion this year:

```
<A HREF http://www.north.pole/print-promotion-list.exe>List Promotions</A>
```

However, the URL may be manually appended with query string information to cause the CGI program to print a list only if a certain specified name or names are on the list:

```
<A HREF http://www.north.pole/print-promotion-list.exe?Mark+Drew>
➡Display Promotions List</A>
```

In the second method, HTML forms using the GET method cause encoded user form input to be appended to the URL.

URL-Encoding

URL-encoding is a method by which requesting client data is changed or remapped to encoded characters before the server passes that data to a CGI program. URL-encoding causes the following things to occur:

- Spaces are mapped to the plus-sign (+) character.
- Certain keyboard characters are mapped to a percent (%) character appended with their hexadecimal equivalents.
- Field data passed from HTML forms is concatenated with the ampersand (&) character.
- For each field from a form, an equal-sign (=) character is used as a separator between the field name and the value the user inputs to the field.

Suppose that you have a form using the POST method. This form has three user-input fields for the user's name, e-mail address, and some free-form text. The user fills the fields as follows:

```
User name field (uname) is set to Drew Kittel
E-mail field (email) is set to kittel@lnk.com
Freeform text (description) is set to ~!@#$%^&*()-=+¦\/~
```

When the form is submitted, the requesting client's data is URL-encoded according to the previously described specifications, and the server then passes this data to the CGI program. In this case, the URL-encoded data sent to the CGI program via standard input follows:

```
uname=Drew+Kittel&email=kittel@lnk.com
➥&description=%7E%21@%23%24%25%5E%26*%28%29-%3D%2B%7C%5C%2F%7E
```

Note that the form name/value pairs are separated by & characters and that the actual field names and their respective values are separated by = characters. Finally, note how some of the characters in the free-form text are mapped to %hex-equivalent. For example, the = character in the free-form text was encoded as %3D. This differentiates it from the = character the server uses as a separator for field names and values.

> **NOTE**
>
> According to the HTTP specification, certain characters do not need to be encoded as hexadecimal. In the preceding example, you can see that the at sign (@), period (.), minus sign (-), and asterisk (*) characters were *not encoded* before the data was passed to the CGI program.

Data provided by a requesting client using forms with GET and POST methods always is URL-encoded before being passed to the CGI program.

What Is Windows CGI?

As stated in earlier sections, CGI specifies that data passed to back-end programs, such as a database program, be passed by environment variables or standard input. This specification is very specific to UNIX-type environments and does not suit the Windows development environment particularly well.

The Windows CGI specification was developed to provide a framework for how Web servers should implement CGI interfaces that support the development of CGI applications in a Windows environment. Unlike its UNIX counterparts (or any other known CGI interfaces), the Windows CGI interface does the work of decoding and parsing URL-encoded data passed to the server from the browser client. This decoded data is provided to back-end CGI programs via a formatted profile file (and, in some instances, a raw content file). The profile file is simply a version of the very familiar Windows .INI file.

The Windows CGI interface is the only known CGI interface that performs the work of decoding and parsing form data for you. Doing things in this manner greatly improves the capability to develop Web applications using common Windows development tools, such as Visual Basic and Visual Basic for Applications. This process also enables developers to focus on developing the application instead of worrying about the details of how data is passed from the client to the server and to CGI programs.

> **RESOURCE**
>
> Not all Windows Web servers provide support for the Windows CGI specification and Windows CGI applications. Currently, O'Reilly WebSite servers and Netscape FastTrack and Enterprise servers *do* provide this support. You can download evaluation versions of O'Reilly's WebSite server from
>
> `http://www.ora.com/`
>
> Evaluation versions of Netscape's servers are available for downloading at
>
> `http://www.netscape.com/`
>
> Additionally, you can get the full Windows CGI 1.3a Interface specification at the O'Reilly WebSite central site at
>
> `http://website.ora.com/wsdocs/32demo/windows-cgi.html`

How Windows CGI Works

In the following sections, you'll examine a few fundamental concepts about the workings of Windows CGI. In particular, you'll learn about these topics:

- The Windows CGI data-flow process
- Windows CGI I/O spooling
- Data decoding performed by the server
- The server launching a Windows CGI program
- The .INI file and its components

The Windows CGI Data-Flow Process

Figure 18.2 illustrates the data flow and processing performed during the request-response cycle. Windows CGI responds to and services requests from client browsers by following these steps:

1. The client browser submits a request to the server. Typically, the request includes data from an HTML form to be processed by a CGI program.

2. The server receives the request and scans the URL to determine the CGI program to be executed.

3. The server splits the request into headers and content. Any raw content is spooled into the temporary input file.

4. The server converts header data into named variables in the server, combines these variables with other server variables, and writes this information to the temporary .INI file.

5. The server decodes and parses any form content accompanying the request. It creates a named variable for every form field and adds this information to the .INI file.

FIGURE 18.2.

The Windows CGI data-flow process.

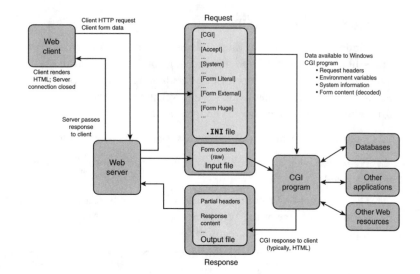

6. The server creates a temporary output spool filename and adds the input and output spool filenames to the `.INI` file. At this point, the request package (`.INI` file and raw-content input file) created by the server contains everything the CGI program needs to process the client request and generate a response.

7. The server then launches the specified CGI program by executing the `CreateProcess()` service. It provides the full path to the `.INI` file so that the CGI program knows where to find the data it needs to perform its function.

8. The CGI program locates the `.INI` file and extracts its contents by using the `GetPrivateProfileString()` Windows system call.

9. The CGI program now can use the data extracted from the `.INI` file to perform its tasks. This might include formulating a query to a SQL database, using VBA to interact with an Excel spreadsheet or an Access database, or performing any number of other operations on behalf of the client.

10. After performing its tasks, the CGI program typically generates a response to the client browser. In constructing the response, the CGI program creates an output spool file using the filename specified by the server in the `.INI` file. It then writes response data (which consists of two sections: a `Content-type` header and the actual response content) into this spool file. This response content can be anything, such as plain text or images, but it typically is composed of HTML. Note that more sophisticated applications may embed ActiveX controls and VBScript into the returned HTML as well. After writing the response data, the CGI program exits.

11. When the server determines that the CGI program has finished running, it reads data from the output spool file, generates a complete HTTP-compliant response, and forwards the response content to the requesting browser.

Windows CGI I/O Spooling

The Windows CGI specification stipulates that servers implementing the Windows CGI interface should provide for a spooled exchange of data between the Web server and CGI programs. In order to ensure efficient transfers of data between spool files and the network, the specification also recommends that the server use memory-mapping techniques while minimizing the number of network I/O requests used.

I/O spooling is performed by Windows CGI-compliant servers for a number of reasons:

■ Network socket I/O capabilities are not native to most rapid application development packages.

■ Use of socket I/O techniques in the Windows environment is complex and requires a strong knowledge of the Win32 network interface. Additionally, complex buffering of input and output data is required for network efficiency.

■ Spooled input (content submitted via the POST method) is memory-mappable, which supports more efficient processing than stream techniques.

■ Sockets cannot be inherited by 16-bit programs.

■ Reference spool files can be used for testing and debugging CGI applications.

Data Decoding Performed by the Server

A browser can send form data to a server in one of two ways:

■ *URL-encoded data:* This is a method by which data passed from a client browser is mapped so that some characters are encoded as different values. See the previous sections "Query Strings" and "URL-Encoding" for detailed information on URL-encoding.

■ *Multipart form data:* A data format that permits efficient uploading of files via forms. The browser indicates this method of sending data with a Content-type header of multipart/form-data.

Windows CGI-compliant servers are required to support both of these form data types.

> **NOTE**
>
> The Windows CGI specification requires that compliant Web servers decode HTML data when it is submitted via the POST method. However, the specification does *not* require decoding of form data that appears in the query string portion of a request URL (such as that submitted via the GET method). Note that the query string data still is available via the CGI environment variable CGI_QueryString provided by the CGI32.BAS framework (which is covered in a later section of this chapter entitled "CGI32.BAS: A Framework for Developing Windows CGI Applications Using Visual Basic"), but it then is up to the developer to decode and parse the data in this string.

How the Server Launches Windows CGI Programs

The Windows CGI specification states that compliant servers must launch a CGI program by using the `CreateProcess()` service with the following command line:

```
win-cgi-exe cgi-data-file
```

Here, `win-cgi-exe` is the complete path to the CGI program executable, and `cgi-data-file` is the complete path to the CGI data file.

NOTE

The CGI program executable does not actually need to be an executable file. It can be a document file if the appropriate association to a corresponding application program already has been established. Compliant servers will attempt to find the associated application and launch it to process the document.

The Windows CGI Profile (`.INI`) File

As previously stated, Windows CGI-compliant Web servers pass data to CGI programs via a private profile (`.INI`) file. The data in this file is maintained in key-value format so that CGI programs can use standard Windows API calls for extracting key-value pairs from the file. The profile file consists of eight sections per the following template:

```
[CGI]

[Accept]

[System]

[Extra Headers]

[Form Literal]

[Form External]

[Form File]

[Form Huge]
```

- ▪ `[CGI]`: This section contains most of the standard CGI environment variables, each provided as a string value. If the value is an empty string, the keyword is omitted from this section.

- ▪ `[Accept]`: This section contains a listing of the MIME data types that are accepted by the client that sent the request. Entries in this section are in one of two formats:
  ```
  Accept: type/subtype {parameters}
  ```

Or, if no parameters are present,

`Accept: type/subtype=Yes`

You can find additional information on MIME in Appendix G.

NOTE

CGI programs using the `CGI32.BAS` framework (covered later in this chapter) can use the `GetPrivateProfileString()` function using `NULL` for the key name to return all the keys (that is, `Accept` types) listed in this section. Keys are returned as a null-delimited string with a double-null terminator.

- `[System]`: This section contains information specific to Windows CGI. The following keys are used: `GMT Offset`, `Debug Mode`, `Output File`, and `Content File`.

- `[Extra Headers]`: This section contains extra headers included with the request. For example, it is common to see the browser type listed with the `User-agent` key. The information is in `key=value` format.

NOTE

CGI programs using the `CGI32.BAS` framework can use the `GetPrivateProfileString()` function using `NULL` for the key name to return all the keys (extra headers) listed in this section. Keys are returned as a null-delimited string with a double-null terminator.

- `[Form Literal]`: This section contains form data that already has been decoded by the server (if the request was sent using the `POST` method and a `Content-type` of `application/x-www-form-urlencoded` or `multipart/form-data`). Information in this section is stored in `key=value` format, where *key* is the form field name and *value* is the corresponding form field value.

NOTE

When HTML forms contain `SELECT MULTIPLE` form objects, there will be multiple occurrences of the key (form field name). Windows CGI-compliant servers handle this case by generating a `key=value` pair for the initial occurrence and then appending a sequence number to each subsequent occurrence. You can see an example of this in the output generated by the `process_form_data.exe` program in Figures 18.5 through 18.7. *It is necessary for the CGI program to detect and properly handle these tagged keys.*

■ [Form External]: When a decoded string exceeds 254 characters, or if it contains control characters or quotation marks, the string is written to an external file. The entry in this section is of the form

key=pathname length

where *pathname* is a path to the temporary file that contains the decoded string and *length* is the length of the string in bytes.

NOTE

You must open the temporary file listed in this section in binary mode unless you are certain that the data is all text.

■ [Form Huge]: When raw value strings exceed 65,536 bytes, *no decoding is performed by the server.* The field contained in this section is listed as

key=offset length

where *offset* is the number of bytes from the beginning of the content file to the start of the raw value string for this *key*, and *length* is the length of the string in bytes.

NOTE

You can use *offset* to perform a seek to the start of the raw value string, and then you can use *length* to read the appropriate amount of data. The file should be opened in binary mode unless you are certain that its contents are all text.

■ [Form File]: When requests are in the format multipart/form-data, file uploads may be included. If this is the case, each file is uploaded and placed into external temporary files. Every uploaded file is listed in this section as the following:

key=[pathname] length type xfer [filename]

where *pathname* is the path to an external file that contains an uploaded file, *length* is the length (in bytes) of the uploaded file, *xfer* is the content-transfer encoding used during the upload, and *filename* is the name of the original file uploaded. Note that the brackets shown in this statement are required.

CGI32.BAS: A Framework for Developing Windows CGI Applications Using Visual Basic

In the previous section, you discovered in great detail how the Windows CGI interface works. In particular, you saw how the interface takes care of many details, such as I/O spooling and the tedious task of decoding URL-encoded form data. Your CGI program still must do a bit of work, though, before it can complete the specific tasks it was designed to perform. Consider how you would perform these tasks:

■ Getting form data out of the .INI and inputting files in the request package created by the server

■ Accessing and using CGI environment variables

■ Handling error conditions

■ Sending response data back to the requesting client

Because these are functions that should be performed by any well-conceived CGI program, wouldn't it be nice if some proven development tools existed that took care of many of these details for you and enabled you to focus on the application?

Thankfully for VB developers, such a set of proven tools does exist in the form of the Windows CGI framework for Visual Basic. This framework is a 32-bit Visual Basic module (CGI32.BAS) that can be added to your VB projects to provide the following functionality:

■ Defining several variables that can be used in your program (see Table 18.1 for a summary of these variables).

■ Providing a number of functions that simplify retrieving form data from the .INI file.

■ Providing functions for gracefully trapping errors in your CGI programs (see Table 18.2 for a summary of these functions).

■ Defining a Sub Main() routine for your CGI program.

■ Providing utility functions for sending response data to the output spool file (see Table 18.2 for a summary of these functions).

RESOURCE

The CGI32.BAS framework module for Visual Basic is the result of some exceptionally fine work by Robert Denny. Anyone who has developed CGI applications in a language such as Perl or C will appreciate the degree to which this framework simplifies the task of using data submitted by HTML forms as well as sending data back to the client browser. This simplicity avoids the need to reinvent the wheel and enables developers to focus on the most important task at hand: developing CGI programs that provide value to their users. The CGI32.BAS framework actually was developed for Visual Basic 4, but development and testing of applications during the writing of this book found that it worked without a hitch in Visual Basic 5 as well. The framework module is available as a zipped file (CGI32.ZIP), and you can download it free of charge from the O'Reilly Software Library at

http://software.ora.com/techsupport/software/extras.html

Using the CGI32.BAS Framework in Your Applications

Using the CGI32.BAS framework in your applications requires that you structure your applications in a specific way and keep a few additional considerations in mind:

- Because the CGI32.BAS framework provides a Sub Main(), VB projects that use the framework should be set to start in Sub Main instead of in a form.

- When the CGI program runs, the Main routine provided by the framework extracts all form data, request headers, and environment variables and stores them in global variables where they are accessible directly or via utility routines (see Tables 18.1 and 18.2 for more information).

- The Main routine provided by the framework establishes a global exception handler that traps runtime errors and produces some response before the CGI program is allowed to exit.

- After the setup of the CGI environment is complete, the framework calls the CGI_Main() routine. This is a routine that you must write. In other words, this is where the work your CGI application performs is actually done.

- It is important that you never abort or perform an exit within a CGI program that uses the framework. Doing this can cause the program to hang or exhibit undesirable results.

- All CGI programs that use the framework must include a simple routine called Inter_Main(). In most cases, this routine is coded to simply display a MsgBox if the CGI executable is invoked by double-clicking it.

- Typically, when new VB projects are created, a .frm form file is automatically included, along with a few .ocx custom control files. In most instances, you will not need the form and can discard it (the VB SQL Server API example at the end of this chapter demonstrates a case where the form is required). Additionally, you should attempt to remove as many controls and references to OLE libraries as possible. You can accomplish this by trying to disable checked entries on the Components and References submenus from the Project menu on the VB 5 main menu bar (you use the Custom Controls and References submenus from the Tools menu on the VB 4 main menu bar).

- To include the CGI32.BAS framework in your VB 5 project, simply choose Project | Add File. In the Add File dialog box, locate and select CGI32.BAS on your system (if you are using VB 4, you'll choose File | Add File).

- In most cases, you simply can compile your program as a standard .EXE executable and place it in the appropriate path used for Windows CGI applications on your system. On the WebSite server, for example, Windows CGI programs are placed in the \WebSite\cgi-win directory.

A Sample `CGI_Main()` Program

As previously mentioned, `CGI_Main()` is a program you write to perform the primary functions of your CGI program—it is where the meat of your application resides. This program is called from the `Main()` program in the `CGI32.BAS` framework. Listing 18.1 shows a simple `CGI_Main()` program that uses the `WebDate()` and `Send()` functions supplied by the framework and returns the date and time at the Web server.

Listing 18.1. A simple `CGI_Main()` program.

```
Sub CGI_Main()
    Send("Content-type: text\html")
    Send( " ")
    Send("<HTML><HEAD><TITLE>Web Server Date/Time</TITLE></HEAD>")
    Send("<BODY>")
    Send("The Web Server Date/Time is: " & WebDate())
    Send("</BODY></HTML>")
End Sub
```

A Sample `Inter_Main()` Program

The `Inter_Main()` program is called from the `Main()` program in the `CGI32.BAS` framework if the CGI program is executed from Windows (if a user double-clicks the `.exe` filename). For most CGI applications, it is sufficient to have the program display a message box stating that this program is a CGI program. The following example illustrates how this is done:

```
Sub Inter_Main()
MsgBox "This is a Windows CGI Program"
End Sub
```

Windows CGI Global Variables

Table 18.1 provides a listing and description of global CGI variables provided by the Windows CGI Visual Basic framework. The use of many of these variables is demonstrated in Listing 18.2 and Figures 18.5 through 18.7. Data types in this table are specified as the following:

HT	HugeTuple
I	Integer
S	String
T	Tuple
V	Variant

Table 18.1. Global CGI variables provided by the Windows CGI Visual Basic framework.

Variable	Description	Data Type
The following variables hold server information		
CGI_GMTOffset	Number of seconds from Greenwich Mean Time (GMT).	V
CGI_ServerAdmin	Server administrator's e-mail address.	S
CGI_ServerSoftware	Name and version of Web server software (for example, WebSite/1.1f).	S
CGI_Version	CGI version this server complies with (for example, CGI/1.2).	S
The following variables hold browser and user information		
CGI_AcceptTypes	MIME data types accepted by the browser.	T
CGI_From	E-mail address of the user. This rarely is supplied by the user's browser.	S
CGI_NumAcceptTypes	Number of MIME data types accepted by the browser.	I
CGI_Referer	URL that referred to the CGI program.	S
CGI_RemoteAddr	IP address for the remote host running the browser.	S
CGI_RemoteHost	Hostname for the remote host running the browser.	S
CGI_RequestProtocol	Name and revision of protocol used (for example, HTTP/1.0).	S
The following variables hold information about executable, logical, and physical paths		
CGI_ContentFile	Full path to a file that contains any attached data (for example, POST data).	S
CGI_ContentLength	Length (in bytes) of attached ContentFile data.	L
CGI_ContentType	MIME content types of request with attached data (for example, POST data).	S
CGI_ExecutablePath	Path to the CGI program being run.	S
CGI_FormTuples	*name=value* pairs sent by the form (if any).	T

continues

Table 18.1. continued

Variable	Description	Data Type
The following variables hold information about executable, logical, and physical paths		
CGI_HugeTuples	Large *name=value* pairs.	HT
CGI_LogicalPath	Logical or extra path information.	S
CGI_NumFormTuples	Number of *name=value* pairs sent by the form (if any).	I
CGI_NumHugeTuples	Number of large *name=value* pairs.	I
CGI_PhysicalPath	Physical path—the translated version of the logical path in CGI_LogicalPath.	S
CGI_QueryString	Encoded portion of the URL appended after the ? character. This contains GET data or the query string (if it exists).	S
CGI_RequestMethod	Request method (for example, GET or POST).	S
CGI_ServerName	Server hostname for the request (this can vary in multihomed configurations).	S
CGI_ServerPort	Port number associated with the request.	I
The following variables hold information about security		
CGI_AuthPass	Authorized user's password (only if enabled).	S
CGI_AuthRealm	Authorized user's realm.	S
CGI_AuthType	Authorization method.	S
CGI_AuthUser	Authorized user's name.	S
The following variables hold other miscellaneous information		
CGI_DebugMode	CGI tracing flag from the server.	I
CGI_ExtraHeaders	Extra header information supplied by the browser.	T
CGI_NumExtraHeaders	Number of extra headers supplied.	I
CGI_OutputFile	Full path to the file in which the Web server expects the CGI program's response.	S

Windows CGI Utility Functions

Table 18.2 provides a listing and description of utility functions provided by the Windows CGI Visual Basic framework. The use of many of these functions is demonstrated in Listing 18.2 and Figures 18.5 through 18.7. Return value types in this table are specified as the following:

N/A	Not applicable
T/F	True or False
S	String

Table 18.2. Utility functions provided by the Windows CGI Visual Basic framework.

Function	Description	Return Type
ErrorHandler()	Global exception handler.	N/A
FieldPresent()	Tests for the presence of a form field (especially useful to determine whether checkboxes on a form were checked).	T/F
GetSmallField()	Retrieves the contents (for example, a value from a *name=value* pair) of a named form field.	S
PlusToSpace()	Removes plus sign (+) delimiting characters from a string. The + signs are converted to spaces.	N/A
Send()	Writes a string into the output spool file. This function is used heavily for formatting HTML output to the client.	N/A
SendNoOp()	Sends a complete response that causes the browser to do nothing and to stay on its current page.	N/A
Unescape()	Removes URL-escaping from a string; returns a modified string.	S
WebDate()	Returns a Web-compliant date and time string (in GMT).	S

Getting Something Useful Out of a Windows CGI Program

You may remember that one of the benefits of using CGI applications is the capability to generate HTML on-the-fly. This capability to generate HTML documents and data presentations dynamically is not just a nice feature—it is an essential feature when providing access to database, customer service, and electronic commerce applications. These types of applications are interactive by nature and require the capability to formulate responses and outputs at runtime. Prepackaged HTML and static documents may be served up, but more often, responses need to be customized according to the user's input. Besides, it just isn't practical or desirable to have canned output for every permutation of database query a user's form inputs might generate.

Generating HTML on-the-fly might sound complicated, but by using Windows CGI and the CGI32.BAS framework utility functions, it's actually remarkably easy if you remember the following two points. First, a specific format is required if the CGI program is returning data to the requesting client. The format requires a data header, followed by a blank line, followed by the data to be returned. The required format follows:

```
Content_type: text/html

start of HTML document
    ...body of document...
end of HTML document
```

Note that the blank line after the data header is absolutely required. This action is something that is required time and again, and it easily can be implemented as the subprocedure (see the SendHTMLStart procedure in Listing 18.2).

Second, CGI programs that use the framework should never abort or perform an exit within the CGI program. This can cause the program to hang or exhibit undesirable results.

Generating dynamic HTML that uses the CGI32.BAS framework module and its Send() utility function is demonstrated in the next section.

A Sample Windows CGI Visual Basic Program

Up to this point, you've been introduced to how Windows CGI interface passes form data to a Windows CGI program and is used to return data to a client. Additionally, you saw an overview of the CGI32.BAS framework and the functionality it provides. Now it's time to look at how the CGI32.BAS Visual Basic framework actually can be used by a CGI program to access the form data and then dynamically generate a response back to the client browser.

Listing 18.2 presents the Windows CGI Visual Basic program process_form_demo.exe. This program uses several CGI32.Bas utility functions and global variables to obtain information about HTML form input and CGI environment variables from the CGI request package created by the server. It then uses the CGI32.BAS Send() function to echo this information back to the client browser in the form of an HTML document. This program can be used with any HTML form and provides a nice way to test HTML forms in your applications.

In this sample Windows CGI Visual Basic program, a user is presented with the HTML form shown in Figures 18.3 and 18.4.

FIGURE 18.3.

An online reader survey and subscription application form used to invoke the CGI program shown in Listing 18.1.

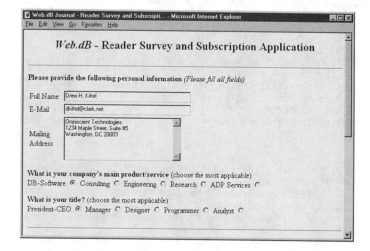

FIGURE 18.4.

A continuation of the online reader survey and subscription application form shown in Listing 18.1.

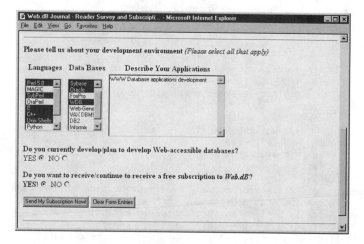

This form, an online reader survey and subscription application for a trade magazine, asks the user to input demographic information and then submit it to qualify for a subscription. Listing 18.2 shows the HTML code for this form.

Listing 18.2. Code listing for `dBWeb_form.htm`, an online reader survey and subscription application.

```
<!DOCTYPE HTML PUBLIC "-//IETF//DTD HTML//EN">
<html>

<head>
<meta http-equiv="Content-Type" content="text/html; charset=iso-8859-1">
<meta name="GENERATOR" content="Microsoft FrontPage 2.0">
<title>Web.dB Journal - Reader Survey and Subscription Application</title>
</head>

<body bgcolor="#FFFFFF">
<!-- Example: Magazine Reader Survey and Subscription Form -->
<!-- Author:  Drew Kittel -->
<!-- HTML Specifications: HTML Level 2.0 Compliant (w/TABLE) -->
<!-- Revision History: created 10 Mar 1996 -->
<h2 align="center">
<em>Web.dB</em> - Reader Survey and Subscription Application</h2>

<hr>

<form action="http://dkittel.clark.net:8080/cgi-win/process_form_demo.exe"
method="POST">
<!-- Create TEXT and TEXTAREA widgets for name, e-mail, mail entry -->
<!-- Use TABLE to provide a bit of formatting control -->
<p><strong>Please provide the following personal information</strong> <em>
(Please fill all fields)</em> </p>
    <table border="0">
        <tr>
            <td>Full Name: </td>
            <td><input type="text" size="50" name="uname"></td>
            <td><br>
            </td>
        </tr>
        <tr>
            <td>E-Mail: </td>
            <td><input type="text" size="50" name="email"></td>
        </tr>
        <tr>
            <td>Mailing<br>
            Address: </td>
            <td><textarea name="address" rows="5" cols="50"></textarea></td>
        </tr>
    </table>
<p><strong>What is your company's main product/service</strong>
    (choose the most applicable) <br>
<!-- Use radio buttons to force mutually-exclusive choices -->
DB-Software <input type="radio" checked name="bus" value="sw">
Consulting <input type="radio" name="bus" value="consult">
Engineering <input type="radio" name="bus" value="engr">
Research <input type="radio" name="bus" value="research">
ADP Services <input type="radio" name="bus" value="adp"> </p>
<p><strong>What is your title?</strong> (choose the most applicable) <br>
<!-- Use radio buttons to force mutually-exclusive choices -->
President-CEO <input type="radio" checked name="title" value="Pres">
Manager <input type="radio" name="title" value="Manager">
Designer <input type="radio" name="title" value="Designer">
Programmer <input type="radio" name="title" value="Programmer">
```

```
Analyst <input type="radio" name="title" value="Analyst"> </p>
    <hr>
<!-- These scrolled lists allow multiple choices -->
<!-- TABLE used to provide side-by-side formatting -->
<p><strong>Please tell us about your development environment</strong>
<em>(Please select all that apply)</em> </p>
    <table border="0" noborder>
        <tr>
            <th>Languages</th>
            <th>Data Bases</th>
            <th width="20%">Describe Your Applications</th>
        </tr>
        <tr>
            <td><select name="cgidev" multiple size="8">
                <option selected value="Perl5">Perl 5.0 </option>
                <option value="Magic">MAGIC </option>
                <option value="Sybperl">SybPerl </option>
                <option value="Oraperl">OraPerl</option>
                <option value="C">C </option>
                <option value="C++">C++</option>
                <option value="Unix Shells">Unix Shells</option>
                <option value="Python">Python</option>
                <option value="REXX">REXX</option>
                <option value="FORTRAN">FORTRAN</option>
            </select> </td>
            <td><select name="dbase" multiple size="8">
                <option selected value="Access">MS ACCESS</option>
                <option value="Sybase">Sybase</option>
                <option value="Oracle">Oracle</option>
                <option value="FoxPro">FoxPro</option>
                <option value="WDB">WDB</option>
                <option value="Web-Genera">Web-Genera</option>
                <option value="VAX DBMS">VAX DBMS</option>
                <option value="DB2">DB2</option>
                <option value="Informix">Informix</option>
                <option value="RdB">RdB</option>
            </select> </td>
            <td><textarea name="description" rows="8" cols="50"></textarea>
            </td>
        </tr>
    </table>
<p><strong>Do you currently develop/plan to develop
Web-accessible databases?</strong><br>
YES<input type="radio" checked name="dbyesno" value="YES">
NO<input type="radio" name="dbyesno" value="NO"> </p>
<p><strong>Do you want to receive/continue to receive a free subscription
to </strong><em><strong>Web.dB</strong></em><strong>?</strong><br>
<strong>YES!</strong><input type="radio" checked name="subscribe" value="YES">
NO<input type="radio" name="subscribe" value="NO"> </p>
<p><input type="submit" value="Send My Subscription Now!">
<input type="reset" value="Clear Form Entries"> </p>
</form>

<hr>

<p> </p>
</body>
</html>
```

When the survey form is submitted, this Action URL is invoked:

```
action="http://dkittel.clark.net:8080/cgi-win/process_form_demo.exe"
➥method="POST"
```

Form data is passed to the server, and the CGI program `process_form_demo.exe` is launched.

Figures 18.5 through 18.7 illustrate the dynamic HTML generated by the program and returned to the client.

FIGURES 18.5.

Dynamic HTML generated by the program and returned to the user. (Remainder of this form is shown in Figures 18.6 and 18.7.)

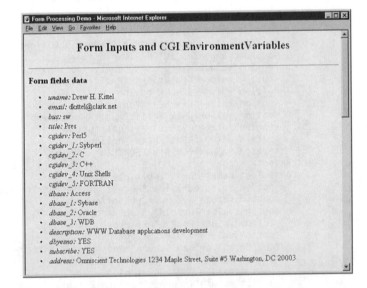

FIGURE 18.6.

Figure 18.5 continued.

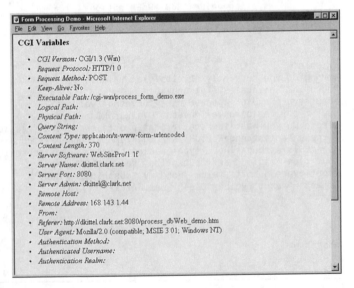

FIGURE 18.7.
Figures 18.5 and 18.6 continued.

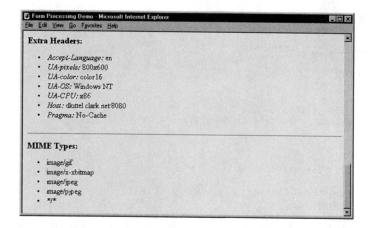

Listing 18.3 shows the VB code for `CGI_Main()`, `Inter_Main()`, and a few subroutines used to create the executable.

Listing 18.3. Code listings for modules used to create the `process_form_demo.exe` CGI program.

```
Attribute VB_Name = "Process_Form_Demo"
Option Explicit

Sub CGI_Main()

    Dim i As Integer

    SendHTMLStart

    Send ("<HTML><HEAD><TITLE>Form Processing Demo</TITLE></HEAD>")
    Send ("<body bgcolor=#FFFFFF>")
    Send ("<CENTER>")
    Send ("<H2>Form Inputs and CGI EnvironmentVariables</H2>")
    Send ("</CENTER>")
    Send ("<HR>")

    SendFormTuples

    Send ("<HR>")

    SendCGIVariables

    Send ("<HR>")

    SendExtraHeaders

    Send ("<HR>")

    SendMIMETypes

    ' Now return to complete HTTP.
```

continues

Listing 18.3. continued

```
    Send ("</BODY></HTML>")

End Sub


Sub Inter_Main()
    MsgBox "This is a Windows CGI program"
End Sub


Sub SendCGIVariables()

    Send ("<H3>CGI Variables</H3>")
    Send ("<UL>")
    Send ("<LI><I>CGI Version: </I>" & CGI_Version)
    Send ("<LI><I>Request Protocol: </I>" & CGI_RequestProtocol)
    Send ("<LI><I>Request Method: </I>" & CGI_RequestMethod)
    If CGI_RequestKeepAlive Then
        Send ("<LI><I>Keep-Alive: </I>  Yes")
    Else
        Send ("<LI><I>Keep-Alive: </I>  No")
    End If
    Send ("<LI><I>Executable Path: </I>" & CGI_ExecutablePath)
    Send ("<LI><I>Logical Path: </I>" & CGI_LogicalPath)
    Send ("<LI><I>Physical Path: </I>" & CGI_PhysicalPath)
    Send ("<LI><I>Query String: </I>" & CGI_QueryString)
    Send ("<LI><I>Content Type: </I>" & CGI_ContentType)
    Send ("<LI><I>Content Length: </I>" & CGI_ContentLength)
    Send ("<LI><I>Server Software: </I>" & CGI_ServerSoftware)
    Send ("<LI><I>Server Name: </I>" & CGI_ServerName)
    Send ("<LI><I>Server Port: </I>" & CGI_ServerPort)
    Send ("<LI><I>Server Admin: </I>" & CGI_ServerAdmin)
    Send ("<LI><I>Remote Host: </I>" & CGI_RemoteHost)
    Send ("<LI><I>Remote Address: </I>" & CGI_RemoteAddr)
    Send ("<LI><I>From: </I>" & CGI_From)
    Send ("<LI><I>Referer: </I>" & CGI_Referer)
    Send ("<LI><I>User Agent: </I>" & CGI_UserAgent)
    Send ("<LI><I>Authentication Method: </I>" & CGI_AuthType)
    Send ("<LI><I>Authenticated Username: </I>" & CGI_AuthUser)
    Send ("<LI><I>Authentication Realm: </I>" & CGI_AuthRealm)
    Send ("</UL>")

End Sub

Sub SendExtraHeaders()

    Dim i As Integer

    If CGI_NumExtraHeaders > 0 Then
        Send ("<H3>Extra Headers:</H3>")
        Send ("<UL>")
```

```
        For i = 0 To CGI_NumExtraHeaders - 1
            Send ("<LI><I>" & CGI_ExtraHeaders(i).key & ": </I>" &
                ➥CGI_ExtraHeaders(i).value)
        Next i
        Send ("</UL>")
    End If

End Sub

Sub SendFormTuples()

    Dim i As Integer

    Send ("<H3>Form fields data</H3>")
    If CGI_NumFormTuples > 0 Then
        Send ("<UL>")
        For i = 0 To CGI_NumFormTuples - 1
            Send ("<LI><I>" & CGI_FormTuples(i).key & ": </I>" &
                ➥CGI_FormTuples(i).value)
        Next i
        Send ("</UL>")
    Else
        Send ("(none)")
    End If

End Sub

Sub SendHTMLStart()
    Send ("Content-type: text/html")
    Send ("")
End Sub


Sub SendMIMETypes()

    Dim i As Integer

    Send ("<H3>MIME Types:</H3>")
    If CGI_NumAcceptTypes > 0 Then
        Send ("<UL>")
        For i = 0 To CGI_NumAcceptTypes - 1
            If CGI_AcceptTypes(i).value = "Yes" Then
                Send ("<LI>" & CGI_AcceptTypes(i).key)
            Else
                Send ("<LI>" & CGI_AcceptTypes(i).key & " (" &
                    ➥CGI_AcceptTypes(i).value & ")")
            End If
        Next i
        Send ("</UL>")
    Else
        Send ("(none)")
    End If

End Sub
```

Most of this program is very straightforward and can be easily understood by briefly studying the variables and functions summarized in Tables 18.1 and 18.2. You should note a few things about this example:

■ The values of environment variables and form field values supplied by the user (which are not known to the CGI program until runtime) are made part of the HTML document returned to the client.

■ The HTML response to the client truly is generated on-the-fly.

■ The <HTML> tags sent in the response are not strictly necessary because the Content-type header identifies this data as HTML to the client.

■ CGI_Main and Inter_Main programs are both supplied as required by the framework. The CGI_Main program calls a number of subprocedures responsible for processing form data sent when a form is submitted, as well as for reading the values of global CGI variables created by the CGI32.BAS framework. The SendFormTuples subprocedure, for example, loops through all form data (decoded key=value pairs) in the [Form Literal] section of the profile file and returns this information to the client in the form of an HTML list. The SendCGIVariables subprocedure, on the other hand, sends back the value of CGI variables in the form of an HTML list.

As you can see, dynamic HTML generation in a CGI program is very straightforward. Of course, this is a simple example that simply uses HTML tags for creating lists. But the example does demonstrate how powerful this method can be when your CGI integrates other processing, database accesses, and subroutines designed to streamline the generation of the HTML tags and data returned. It also is possible to generate very complex responses to the requesting client. Data retrieved from a database, for example, could be formatted in very elaborate HTML tables using a variety of header fields, different font sizes and styles, as well as different font colors and table cell background colors for emphasis and to create visually appealing presentations of data. Additionally, dynamic generation of responses to the client could be used to generate graphical charts using specialized ActiveX controls. VBScript also could be included to enable the user to manipulate attributes of the displayed chart, such as color, title, graph style, and so on. These techniques are explored in greater detail in Chapter 19, "Database Results Presentation Using HTML and CGI."

Accessing Web Databases Using CGI

Now it's time to explore how a Web server can use the power of CGI programs to access databases and submit queries on behalf of a Web client. This is an exciting time to be involved in Web database development. The world is just now realizing the potential of Web-based database applications. Individuals, organizations, and agencies are rushing to exploit the technology and implement these systems. This section provides you with some of the tools required to get involved right away.

In this section, you'll briefly examine some of the common methods used to access Web databases. You'll look at the reasons for my opinion that customized CGI programs offer one of the most flexible means of providing that access. You'll also see that all useful CGI database applications must accomplish a series of basic steps. Finally, you'll be presented with an example that illustrates how Windows CGI and the Visual Basic API for Microsoft's SQL Server can be used to develop Web database applications.

A Brief Summary of Common Web Database Access Methods

Currently, a few fundamental methods exist by which Web servers can access database systems on behalf of a Web client. Most of these methods use extensions to or are some variant of CGI programs. Note that each method has its inherent strengths and weaknesses, and some have implementations specific to the database system and Web server being used. The following sections briefly explore these common methods:

■ HTML-embedded SQL extensions

■ Codeless interfaces

■ Web server API programs

■ Custom CGI programs

HTML Embedded SQL Extensions

Many database systems provide a mechanism for embedding SQL statements directly within HTML files passed to the Web client by the Web server. When a user submits a query, the HTML file is passed to a CGI program, which parses the SQL statements and passes these on to the database system. Results of the SQL query subsequently are retrieved by the CGI program, reformatted to HTML, and returned to the requesting client. This mechanism is typical of many shareware databases and gateways. Additionally, the developer often is limited in his capability to modify the CGI program performing the actual database access and formatting of results. Chapter 24, "The Development of a PC-Based WWW Database System," demonstrates the use of *DBGateway*—a gateway application (developed using Windows CGI and Visual Basic) that uses HTML-embedded SQL.

Codeless Interfaces

Essentially, codeless types of access methods consist of software toolsets (often Perl scripts) that work with developer-defined template files. These template files specify various views into the database and the way in which extracted data should be manipulated and formatted when returned to the requesting client. Programs within the software toolset use these template files to automatically generate HTML forms. These forms, when submitted by the user, are then processed by CGI programs, which query the database and format the results in accordance with the predefined templates.

Most of the toolsets available today are somewhat manual in nature. In the near future, however, visual programming tools that implement drag-and-drop technology for building forms interfaces, specifying database queries, and detailing the format of results sent to the user should become more prevalent.

Custom CGI Programs

Customized CGI programs are gateway programs specifically written to accept and process Web client requests for a service provided by the Web server. Typically, these requests are submitted by users in the form of input they have entered in an HTML form. CGI programs designed for database access parse this user input, formulate queries based on the input, connect to the database and submit the query, and accumulate results. They also can manipulate these results or perform some other specialized processing and dynamically create HTML documents, which subsequently are sent back to the Web client.

Web Server API Programs

The use of Web Server APIs is becoming increasingly more popular. Most major Web servers now have an API available to applications developers. Microsoft has ISAPI for Internet Information Server (IIS), Netscape has NSAPI for its line of servers, and O'Reilly has WSAPI for its WebSite servers.

Server API programs provide many of the same benefits of CGI because they are very flexible and enable developers to greatly extend the functionality of the server. Most server APIs do not allow developers to choose the language in which they would like to develop their applications, however. In other words, the server API is language-specific. Additionally, although many server API programs realize a significant performance advantage over their CGI counterparts, this advantage often is realized because the application shares process space with the server itself. This can be dangerous; if a bug causes an application to die, for example, the server may crash as a result.

Why Use Customized CGI Programs for Database Access?

Currently, customized CGI programs are by far the most common method for accessing Web databases. CGI programs give developers a tremendous amount of power and flexibility in extending Web server functionality. Without question, other methods, such as those described earlier, have their place and provide advantages when dealing with well-defined and structured systems. As most experienced software developers have discovered, though, there invariably comes a time when development tools don't provide the functionality, flexibility, or power to do what is necessary to get the job done. Custom CGI programs provide this functionality, flexibility, and power by enabling developers to design the application to best suit the problem at hand.

A custom CGI program allows for development of applications that access databases in a variety of ways, including these:

- SQL queries, which typically are used to access relational database systems
- Non-SQL queries, which typically are used to access nonrelational database systems, such as network, hierarchical, and CODASYL model databases (some very large legacy systems still use this type of database)
- Stored procedures, which typically are database-resident SQL "programs" or batches of commands
- Database-specific APIs
- Open Database Connectivity (ODBC) API

Additionally, custom CGI programs provide distinct advantages over other methods, including these:

- Developers maintain complete control over the application being developed and the mechanisms by which user input is validated and the database is accessed.
- The learning curve for CGI developers is often significantly shorter than for gateway products or server APIs.
- Developers can more fully exploit advanced methods such as vendor-specific SQL extensions and functionality including the use of triggers, database client-side cursors, and server-side cursors.
- Developers often have a choice of the language in which they want to develop the CGI program. In fact, mixed-language development is readily accommodated if it is necessary.
- Other access methods often are specific to a single database or Web server, whereas custom CGI programs provide the flexibility to access multiple types of databases on a variety of Web servers through a number of programming interfaces. Additionally, custom CGI programs enable developers to write programs that can access multiple, heterogeneous, geographically distributed database servers.
- Complex applications can be developed. These can include preprocessing of user input, interaction with several database servers and information repositories, additional manipulation and processing of database results, integration with other custom or commercial applications, use of multiple APIs, and generation of complex, dynamically created HTML data presentations.

The Flow of a Basic CGI Database Program

Figure 18.8 illustrates the basic steps required in all useful CGI database access programs. The basic steps apply to most programs, but the sequence may vary somewhat from application to application. All useful programs perform the following tasks, however:

- Reading, parsing, and decoding data passed from an HTML form (in the case of Windows CGI, this is handled for you)
- Creating a database query or command
- Connecting to the database server and sending the query/command
- Fetching results of the query/command from the server
- Formulating and sending a response (typically, HTML and possible ActiveX controls and VBScript) to the Web client through the Web server
- Putting a stop to the sending of output and returning to the server

FIGURE 18.8.

The fundamental steps that make up basic CGI database programs.

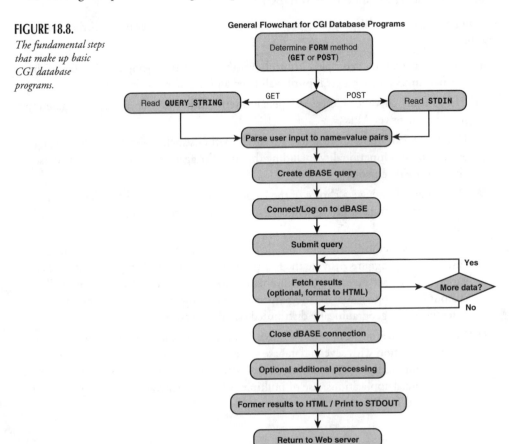

Developing Web Database Applications Using MS SQL Server and the Visual Basic DB-Library API

In this section, you will explore a method of developing Web database Windows CGI applications using Visual Basic. Specifically, you will examine all the fundamentals required to begin developing Web database applications that use Microsoft's SQL Server 6.5 database. In doing so, you will be introduced to the Microsoft DB-Library Visual Basic API for SQL Server.

RESOURCE

You can download a 120-day free evaluation copy of SQL Server from the free software link on the main page at the Microsoft Website at

`http://www.microsoft.com/`

This evaluation version is a full copy of the SQL Server 6.5 product and includes the DB-Library API for developing VB applications. Note that the main setup program included with the downloadable version does *not* perform a full installation of all components of the product. You must manually execute the setup programs under the following directories to install ODBC, *Programmer's Toolkit* (PTK) and other VBSQL sample and help components, respectively. These directory paths are all relative from the temporary installation directory created by the main setup program:

`/I386/ODBC/Setup.exe`

`/PTK/I386/Setup.exe`

`/PTK/Vbsql/Setup.exe`

When installing the PTK components, make certain that if you are running IIS on your system you first shut down the server before running the setup program. Otherwise, the PTK installation will hang occasionally.

NOTE

Examples and code snippets for this chapter were developed using VB 5 and SQL Server 6.5; however, the API is designed to work with SQL Server 6.0 and VB 4 as well. Some minor differences in programmatic syntax need to be accounted for. See "SQL Server Books Online," the online reference documentation that comes with SQL Server, for details on developing VB applications for Version 6.0.

What Is the Microsoft DB-Library Visual API?

Microsoft DB-Library is a library of functions that enables very sophisticated client/server applications to be developed for SQL Server. The VB API is a set of Visual Basic functions and routines that lets your application (in this case, your CGI program) interact directly with Microsoft SQL Server. Functionality in the VB API represents a subset of the functionality available in the C language API.

As you will see in subsequent sections of this chapter, this API enables you to develop CGI programs that act as clients to SQL Server databases. The DB-Library API provides these database client programs with the capability to make multiple connections to SQL Server databases, send very complex Transact-SQL queries to the databases, and retrieve results of those queries. The interface also provides the mechanisms necessary to use more sophisticated SQL Server capabilities, such as stored procedures, triggers, and cursors.

By using the VB API, SQL Server now becomes an integral part of your Visual Basic CGI programs and enables you to perform virtually any database operation supported by SQL Server on behalf of Web clients submitting requests from their browsers. CGI database applications can include standard database operations such as these:

- Retrieving and updating values from a database directly
- Manipulating database values from database tables
- Inserting program values into a database
- Moving data between SQL Server and an operating-system file

CGI database applications also can perform more complex operations, such as these:

- Connecting to multiple, geographically distributed SQL Server databases
- Creating new databases
- Adding and populating tables
- Working with images
- Performing *bulk copy* (BCP) tasks
- Administering SQL Server remotely via a Web browser interface

DB-Library Files Required for Visual Basic Applications

Several files are necessary for developing applications using the VB API; these are summarized in Table 18.3. Note that many of these files are *not* included with DB-Library for Visual Basic; therefore, you need to make certain that they already exist on your system.

Table 18.3. Files required for developing Visual Basic DB-Library applications.

Filename	Description	*Included with DB-Library?*
VBSQL.OCX	OLE custom control for DB-Library for Visual Basic. Contains all library functions required to develop client applications. Located in the \PTK\I386 directory under the temporary installation directory used by the main setup program when SQL Server was installed.	Yes
VBSQL.BAS	An include file that contains all DB-Library Visual Basic function and routine declarations. Located in the \MSSQL\DBLIB\INCLUDE directory of the SQL Server installation on your system.	Yes
MFC40.DLL	A current version of the *Microsoft Foundation Class* (MFC).	Yes
NTWDBLIB.DLL	The DB-Library for Win32 (Windows 95 and Windows NT).	No, but included with SQL Server
MFCANS32.DLL	The MFC ANSI to Unicode Translation layer.	No
MSVCRT40.DLL	The Microsoft Visual C Runtime Library.	No, but included with SQL Server

Creating a VB 5 Project Using DB-Library

To create a VB 5 project that uses the DB-Library Visual Basic API, you should follow these five basic steps:

1. Create a new Visual Basic project.
2. Add the DB-Library for the Visual Basic header file to your project.

3. Add the DB-Library for Visual Basic OLE custom control to your toolbox.

4. Add the DB-Library for Visual Basic OLE custom control to a form in your project.

5. Add code to the error-handling and message-handling event procedures.

Adding the VBSQL.BAS DB-Library Header File to the Project

To add the VBSQL.BAS DB-Library OLE header file to the project, perform these steps:

1. Choose Project | Add File. The Add File dialog box appears.

2. Select the VBSQL.BAS file. This file is located in the \MSSQL\DBLIB\INCLUDE directory of the SQL Server installation on your system.

3. Click OK. The Project window now includes the VBSQL.BAS module. Visual Basic automatically generates a unique name for this module. For new projects, the default name for this module is Module1. It is recommended that you *not* make changes to the VBSQL.BAS header file.

Adding the VBSQL.OCX DB-Library OLE Custom Control to the Toolbox

To add the VBSQL.OCX DB-Library OLE custom control to the project toolbox, follow these steps:

1. Choose Project | Components. The Components dialog box appears, as shown in Figure 18.9.

FIGURE 18.9.

The components dialog box.

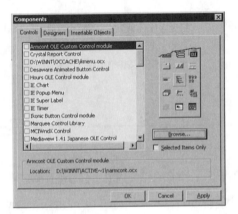

2. Click Browse. The Add ActiveX Control dialog box appears, as shown in Figure 18.10.

FIGURE 18.10.
The Add ActiveX Control dialog box.

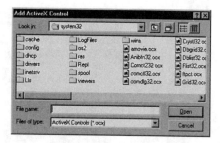

3. Search for and select the VBSQL.OCX file. The evaluation copy of SQL Server 6.5 is located in the \PTK\I386 directory under the temporary installation directory used by the main setup program when SQL Server was installed.

4. Click Open. The Available Controls list now includes the Vbsql OLE Custom Control module, as shown in Figure 18.11.

5. Select the control and click OK. The DB-Library for Visual Basic OLE custom control now is included in the toolbox. Its associated tool tip is Vbsql, as shown in Figure 18.12.

FIGURE 18.11.
Adding the VBSQL.OCX *custom control to the project toolbox.*

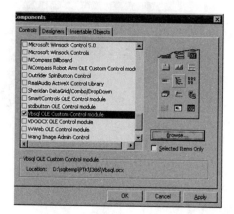

Adding the VBSQL.OCX DB-Library OLE Custom Control to a Form in the Project

To add the VBSQL.OCX DB-Library OLE custom control to a form in the project, perform the following steps. *Do not add a control to more than one form.*

1. From the toolbox, select the DB-Library for Visual Basic OLE custom control, as shown in Figure 18.13.

FIGURE 18.12.

The VBSQL.OCX *control has been added to the project toolbox.*

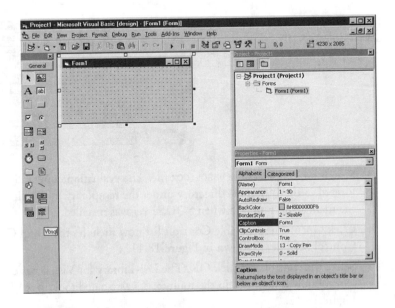

FIGURE 18.13.

Selecting the VBSQL.OCX *control.*

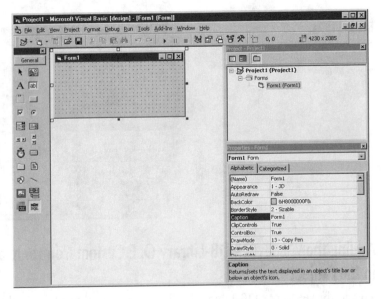

2. Move the pointer onto a form in the project. At this point, the cursor becomes a cross-hair.

3. Drag the crosshair cursor to place the control on the form, as shown in Figure 18.14. The control will be called Vbsql1 by default.

4. Set the Visible property of the control to False, as shown in Figure 18.14.

FIGURE 18.14.

Adding the VBSQL.OCX
control to a form in the
project.

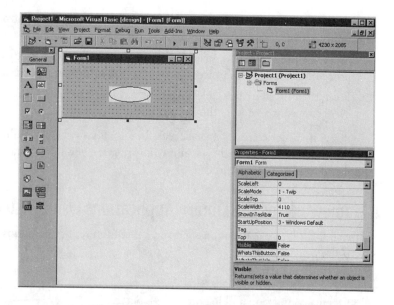

NOTE

It is only necessary to add a single VBSQL.OCX control to a single form in the project. This form always should be loaded using the LOAD method (typically, as an initial operation in your application) so that the DB-Library functions are available. Do not use the UNLOAD method to unload the form containing the control until all operations within the program requiring SQL Server have been fully completed and the connections to the databases in use are closed. Also note that it is not necessary to invoke the SHOW method for the form containing the VBSQL.OCX control because it never needs to be displayed visually.

Adding Error-Handling and Message-Handling Event Procedures

The VBSQL.OCX custom control has two event procedures that can be used within your applications:

■ Sub Vbsql1_Error: Used when DB-Library error events occur.

■ Sub Vbsql1_Message: Used when SQL Server messages are received.

Use of these handlers is not required, but it is recommended that any complex database program include at least some nominal form of these error and message handlers.

To edit these error-handling and message-handling event procedures in your project, perform these steps:

1. Double-click the DB-Library for Visual Basic OLE custom control on the form in the project. The Visual Basic code appears.

2. From the Procedure box, select Error to bring up the DB-Library error-handler event procedure. Modify this procedure as appropriate for your application.

3. From the Procedure box, select Message to bring up the SQL Server message-handler event procedure. Modify this procedure as appropriate for your application.

Note that Visual Basic creates a `VBSQL.OCA` file (usually in the same directory as `VBSQL.OCX`). This file is used to store cached-type library information and other data specific to the custom control and to re-create it as needed.

A Framework for DB-Library Applications Using Visual Basic

Nearly all DB-Library applications perform a common set of operations or steps:

1. Provide an error handler.
2. Initialize DB-Library for Visual Basic.
3. Open a connection and log on to SQL Server.
4. Send Transact-SQL statements to SQL Server.
5. Process the results of SQL statements sent to SQL Server.
6. Close the connection(s) to SQL Server and exit the application.

The following sections briefly describe each of these steps.

> **NOTE**
>
> A complete reference and descriptions of all DB-Library functions (including those referenced in subsequent sections of this chapter) are available in "SQL Server Books Online," the online reference documentation delivered with SQL Server.

Providing Error Handlers

As previously mentioned, the `VBSQL.OCX` control provides the error-handling interface for your application. When added to the primary form in an application, it installs two error-handler event procedures, assigns them the default names `VBSQL1_Error` and `VBSQL1_Message`, and supplies the appropriate parameter list as part of each procedure name. Note that only one error handler control can be placed in an application.

After error handlers are added to a form, implementing them is as easy as adding the required code to perform whatever specialized error handling is appropriate for your application.

Initializing DB-Library

Before calling any DB-Library functions or performing any operations with SQL Server, your application must initialize the DB-Library for use. A special function, SqlInit, is provided for this task. SqlInit takes no parameters and returns the DB-Library version number as a string. Note that the program's error handlers should be available before SqlInit is called. The following code snippet demonstrates the use of this function:

```
IF SqlInit() = "" THEN
    PRINT "DB-Lib was not properly initialized"
    ... other error-handling code ...
END IF
```

Connecting and Logging On to SQL Server

After the application has been initialized, it interacts with SQL Server by opening one or more SQL Server connections (using appropriate user logon information). Client applications use connections to send SQL queries and other statements to SQL Server. The connection also serves as a means for receiving the results of statements sent to SQL Server.

Opening a connection to SQL Server requires using the SqlLogin, SqlSetLUser, SqlSetLPwd, SqlSetLApp, and SqlOpen functions provided by DB-Library. SqlLogin allocates a SQL Server logon record and returns an identifier for that logon record initially filled with attributes assigned default values. The logon record is made up of a set of attributes that are initially assigned default values. SqlSetLUser and SqlSetLPwd set the username and password logon record attributes that will be used to log onto SQL Server. SqlSetLApp sets the application name that appears in the SQL Server sysprocesses system table. Finally, SqlOpen logs onto SQL Server using the SqlLogin logon record, establishes a connection, and returns a connection identifier that remains associated with the connection for as long as the connection remains open. SqlOpen can be used to open multiple connections to SQL Server, thus providing the potential to develop very complex applications. The following snippet of code demonstrates the use of these functions:

```
Login = SqlLogin()
Result = SqlSetLUser(Login, "Guest")
Result = SqlSetLPwd(Login, "c0rnd0gs")
Result = SqlSetLApp(Login, "webguest_pubs")
SqlConn = SqlOpen(Login, "OMNISCIENT")
```

As an alternative, DB-Library also provides a convenience function called SqlOpenConnection, which combines the work of several lower-level functions into a single function. This function provides a more convenient method for logging on to SQL Server and opening a connection in one step, thus reducing the amount of code needed to log on as a user and open a connection.

Sending SQL Statements to SQL Server

After an application successfully establishes a connection to SQL Server, it can begin the task of doing some real work. DB-Library provides two functions—SqlCmd and SqlExec—

for sending Transact-SQL statements to SQL Server for execution. SqlCmd is used to buffer commands to be sent to SQL Server. It can be called several times in succession to append commands to contents already in the buffer (just be certain that blank spaces are provided where appropriate). Additionally, several SQL statements may be buffered to be sent all at once.

After the command buffer is filled with SQL statements to send, SqlExec actually sends the buffer contents to SQL Server. The following snippet of code demonstrates how these functions can be used to obtain two columns of data from the pubs demonstration database delivered with SQL Server. Note the use of the SqlConn data structure returned from a previous call to SqlOpen:

```
Result = SqlCmd(SqlConn, "SELECT au_lname, city")
Result = SqlCmd(SqlConn, " FROM pubs..authors")
Result = SqlCmd(SqlConn, " WHERE state = 'MD'")
Result = SqlExec(SqlConn)
```

As an alternative, DB-Library also provides the functions SqlSend and SqlOk, which can be used in place of SqlExec.

Processing SQL Server Results

After SQL statements are sent to SQL Server for execution, it is necessary to retrieve the results of those statements (and optionally perform some application-specific processing on the data). DB-Library provides two functions—SqlResults and SqlNextRow—for retrieving the results of Transact-SQL statements.

SqlResults sets up the results of a SQL statement for processing. It is called once for *each* SQL statement that was previously sent in the command buffer and should return the value SUC-CEED. Additionally, it is called a final time to return the NOMORERESULTS indicator (which signifies that there are no more results for the current SQL statement being processed).

After SqlResults returns SUCCEED (when results of the current SQL statement being processed become available), SqlNextRow is called in succession (until it returns NOMOREROWS) to retrieve rows of data returned. Note that, unless row buffering has been enabled, the processing of each row returned must be performed after SqlNextRow returns SUCCEED and before the next call to SqlNextRow. The following snippet of code demonstrates the use of these functions:

```
Result = SqlResults(Sqlconn)

IF Result = SUCCEED THEN

DO UNTIL SqlNextRow(Sqlconn) = NOMOREROWS
    Name = SqlData(Sqlconn, 1)
    City = SqlData(Sqlconn, 2)
    ... perform additional application-specific processing here ...
LOOP

END IF
```

> **NOTE**
>
> Transact-SQL statements return two types of result rows: regular rows and compute rows. *Regular rows* are generated from columns in a Transact-SQL SELECT statement, whereas *compute rows* are generated from columns in a COMPUTE clause. These two types of rows contain very different data; therefore, applications must process them separately. DB-Library provides the functions SqlData and SqlAData for processing regular and compute column results, respectively. For more details, see "SQL Server Books Online," the online documentation that comes with SQL Server.

Closing SQL Server Connections and Exiting the Application

After the SQL Server client application performs its work, it must close any open connections to SQL Server, free memory resources, and exit in a clean manner. DB-Library provides the SqlExit and SqlWinExit functions to perform these tasks. SqlExit closes *all* SQL Server connections opened by an application and also frees system memory associated with each connection. (Note that single, specific connections can be closed by using the SqlClose function.) SqlWinExit is used to free all memory allocated to a Windows application by DB-Library. The following snippet of code illustrates how these functions are used in response to a user clicking a button on a form in an application:

```
SUB AppQuit_Click()
    SqlExit
    SqlWinExit
END SUB
```

Developing a VB CGI Application Using DB-Library and the CGI32.BAS Framework

This section ties together much of the material of previous sections on Windows CGI and the SQL Server DB-Library API for Visual Basic. It presents a basic template for CGI applications that integrates these tools, provides a few rules, and finally presents a simple Windows CGI application that demonstrates how all these are tied together.

> **TIP**
>
> Before implementing any Web database applications, consult your DBA and Webmaster about system and database access privileges of guest accounts set up for Web database applications. This step is important to ensure that the integrity of your database is maintained and that users are accorded the appropriate select, add, modify,

and delete privileges consistent with your site's policies. Additionally, strongly consider the use of client-side VB scripts as well as subroutines in your CGI programs to validate user input and ensure that sensible SQL queries will be formulated, especially in those cases where users are allowed to insert or modify data in the database.

CGI_Main **and the DB-Library**

Earlier in this chapter, you learned that the CGI32.BAS framework for Visual Basic requires a CGI_Main() procedure, and that it is within this procedure that most of the work of your CGI application is done. Therefore, it stands to reason that any database work using the DB-Library API also must be performed from within this procedure. The following code shows a generalized template of a CGI_Main() procedure that uses the DB-Library to perform some database processing on behalf of a Web client. Notice the close correspondence with the general flowchart for CGI database programs in Figure 18.8.

```
Sub CGI_Main()
        Load the form containing the VBSQL.OCX control
        Initialize DB-Library using SqlInit
        Use CGI32.BAS functions to obtain form data submitted with the request
        Open a Connection and login using SqlSetLUser, SqlSetLPwd, SqlSetLApp,
        ➡SqlOpen
        Formulate SQL statements using form data submitted with the request
        Add SQL statements to the command buffer using SqlCmd
        Send the command buffer using SqlExec
        Retrieve and process returned results using SqlResults, SqlNextRow and
        ➡SqlData
        Perform any (optional) application-specific processing of results data
        ➡(using your own code, third-party software libraries, stats packages, etc.)
        Format results for presentation to the client using Send (output can include
        ➡HTML, ActiveX content as well as VBScript)
        Clean up connections and memory resources using SqlExit and SqlWinExit
        Unload the form containing the VBSQL.OCX control
        Return to CGI32.BAS Sub Main()
End Sub
```

In addition to previously presented guidelines for developing applications using CGI32.BAS, the following general rules apply to Windows CGI applications using DB-Library:

- Load the form containing the VBSQL.OCX control, but do not Show it. The form only serves as a container for the control, and loading it enables the rest of the application to access the DB-Library functions.

- Perform SqlExit and SqlWinExit before unloading the form.

- Be sure to Unload the form containing the VBSQL.OCX control from within the CGI_Main() routine before the control is returned to the CGI32.BAS framework. Failure to do so will cause your CGI application to hang.

- Do not call the End statement. Unload is the preferred (and safe) method for closing the main form.

Putting It All Together: A Sample Windows CGI Database Application

This section presents a simple Web database query example that ties together many of the concepts presented in this chapter. This example illustrates how user input to an HTML form can be used by a Windows CGI Visual Basic 5.0 program to formulate a query, send the query to a Microsoft SQL Server database, fetch results of the query, and very simply present the results to the user (Web client). The example uses the `CGI32.BAS` framework, the SQL Server DB-Library API for Visual Basic, and the sample pubs database that comes with SQL Server.

The pubs Simple Query Form

The HTML form shown in Figure 18.15 is used to accept user input for simple queries against the SQL Server pubs database. Listing 18.4 shows the HTML code for this form.

FIGURE 18.15.

A form for the simple SQL Server pubs database query.

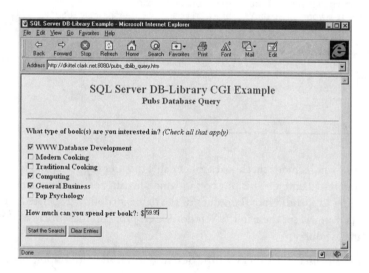

Listing 18.4. HTML code for the pubs database query form shown in Figure 18.15.

```
<html>
<head>
<meta name="GENERATOR" content="Microsoft FrontPage 2.0">
<title>SQL Server DB-Library Example</title>
<!-- pubs database query form -->
<!-- Author:  Drew Kittel -->
</head>

<body bgcolor="#FFFFFF">

<h2 align="center"><font color="#0000FF">SQL Server DB-Library
CGI Example<br>
```

continues

Listing 18.4. continued

```
</font><font color="#0000FF" size="4">Pubs Database Query </font></h2>

<hr>

<form action="http://dkittel.clark.net:8080/cgi-win/pubs_dblib_query.exe"
➥method="POST">
<p><b>What type of book(s) are you interested in?</b>
<em>(Check all that apply)</em> </p>
<p><input type="checkbox" name="btype0" value="wwwdbdev">
   <strong>WWW Database Development </strong><br>
<input type="checkbox" name="btype1" value="mod_cook">
   <strong>Modern Cooking</strong> <br>
<input type="checkbox" name="btype2" value="trad_cook">
   <strong>Traditional Cooking</strong> <br>
<input type="checkbox" name="btype3" value="popular_comp">
   <strong>Computing</strong> <br>
<input type="checkbox" name="btype4" value="business">
   <strong>General Business</strong> <br>
<input type="checkbox" name="btype5" value="psychology">
   <strong>Pop Psychology</strong> <br>
</p>
<p><b>How much can you spend per book?:</b>
  $<input type="text" size="6" name="uprice"> </p>
<p><input type="submit" value="Start the Search">
   <input type="reset" value="Clear Entries"> </p>
</form>
</body>
</html>
```

This form includes checkboxes that enable the user to specify the type of book(s) in which he is interested and a text input box in which he can enter the maximum price (per book) he is willing to spend. Note the values of the name attributes associated with these user-input objects; you will see these in the Windows CGI program that processes this form and handles the database query.

After the user clicks the Start the Search button, the form inputs are submitted to the server. The METHOD and ACTION attributes assigned to this form specify the CGI program to be used by the server and the method by which user input is passed. In this case, the CGI program that will process the user input is called pubs_dblib_query.exe, and the POST method is used. This means that the CGI program will need to read decoded form data (in *key=value* format) from the [Form Literal] section of the profile (.INI) file.

The pubs Query CGI Database Program

The program used to handle the simple pubs database query is a VB 5 program that uses the DB-Library VB API and the CGI32.BAS framework, both of which were covered in detail earlier in this chapter. Because the CGI32.BAS framework does all the work of decoding form data submitted using the POST method, the only thing the CGI developer needs to know at this point is the names of the form-input objects (the checkboxes and text-input field). The values associated with these input widgets now can be obtained directly from the profile file using the GetSmallField() and FieldPresent() functions provided by the CGI32.BAS framework.

Listing 18.5 shows the code for the entire CGI program. As you look through the code and explanations that follow it, note how each of the steps specified in the flowchart in Figure 18.8 is implemented.

Listing 18.5. VB code for the `pubs_dblib_query.exe` Windows CGI program used to process input to the form shown in Figure 18.15.

```
Attribute VB_Name = "PUBS_DBLIB_QUERY"

Option Explicit
    Dim Login
    Dim Result
    Dim SqlConn
    Dim Title
    Dim Price

    Dim Clauses As String

    'Form field name variables
    Dim btype0 As String
    Dim btype1 As String
    Dim btype2 As String
    Dim btype3 As String
    Dim btype4 As String
    Dim btype5 As String
    Dim uprice


Sub CGI_Main()

    'Load (but don't show) the form containing the
    'VBSQL.OCX control

    Load Form1

    SendHTMLStart

    Send ("<HTML>")
    Send ("<HEAD><TITLE>SQL Server Query Results</TITLE></HEAD>")

    Send ("<body bgcolor=#FFFFFF>")
    Send ("<CENTER>")
    Send ("<H2><font color=#0000FF>SQL SERVER Query Results</font></H2>")
    Send ("</CENTER>")
    Send ("<HR>")

    'Process form inputs and format the clauses portion
    'of SQL query
```

continues

Listing 18.5. continued

```
Clauses = "type in ("

If FieldPresent("btype0") Then
    Clauses = Clauses & Chr(34) & GetSmallField("btype0") & Chr(34) & ", "
End If
If FieldPresent("btype1") Then
    Clauses = Clauses & Chr(34) & GetSmallField("btype1") & Chr(34) & ", "
End If
If FieldPresent("btype2") Then
    Clauses = Clauses & Chr(34) & GetSmallField("btype2") & Chr(34) & ", "
End If
If FieldPresent("btype3") Then
    Clauses = Clauses & Chr(34) & GetSmallField("btype3") & Chr(34) & ", "
End If
If FieldPresent("btype4") Then
    Clauses = Clauses & Chr(34) & GetSmallField("btype4") & Chr(34) & ", "
End If
If FieldPresent("btype5") Then
    Clauses = Clauses & Chr(34) & GetSmallField("btype5") & Chr(34) & ", "
End If

Clauses = Clauses & Chr(34) & Chr(34) & ") AND price < " &
➥GetSmallField("uprice")


'Initialize DB-Library
If SqlInit() = "" Then
  Send ("<EM><B>The program encountered an error</B></EM><BR>")
  Send ("<EM><B>DB-Library was not properly initialized</B></EM>")
Else
'Get a Login record and set login attributes.
    Login = SqlLogin()
    Result = SqlSetLUser(Login, "Guest")
    Result = SqlSetLPwd(Login, "c0rnd0gs")
    Result = SqlSetLApp(Login, "webguest_pubs")

'Get a connection for communicating with SQL Server.
    SqlConn = SqlOpen(Login, "OMNISCIENT")

'Put the command into the command buffer.
    Result = SqlCmd(SqlConn, "SELECT title, price")
    Result = SqlCmd(SqlConn, " FROM pubs..titles")
    Result = SqlCmd(SqlConn, " WHERE " & Clauses)

'Send the command to SQL Server and start execution.
    Result = SqlExec(SqlConn)

'Process the command.
'Retrieve result rows, format lightly and send to client.

    Result = SqlResults(SqlConn)
    If Result = SUCCEED Then
        Send ("<PRE>")
```

```
        Do Until SqlNextRow(SqlConn) = NOMOREROWS
            Title = SqlData(SqlConn, 1)
            Price = SqlData(SqlConn, 2)

        ' ... other application-specific processing here ...

            Send ("<EM>" & Title & "   " & Price & "</EM>")
        Loop
        Send ("</PRE>")

    End If

'Close connection and exit program.
    SqlExit
    SqlWinExit

    End If

    'Unload the  form containing VBSQL.OCX control

    Unload Form1

    'Now return to complete HTTP
    Send ("</BODY></HTML>")

End Sub

Sub Inter_Main()
    MsgBox "This is a Windows CGI program"
End Sub

Sub SendHTMLStart()
    Send ("Content-type: text/html")
    Send ("")
End Sub
```

The output generated by the program in response to the query shown in Figure 18.15 is shown in Figure 18.16.

FIGURE 18.16.

Results of the simple query shown in Figure 18.15.

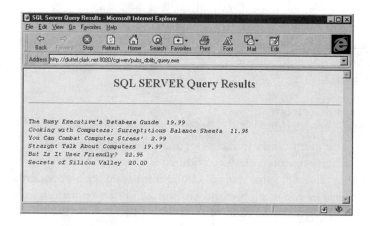

The program begins with a few variable declarations followed by a call to the `SendHTMLStart` procedure. This procedure simply sends an HTML `Content-type` header to the server for inclusion in the response package to be sent to the client. Following this, the standard `<HTML>`, `<BODY>`, `<TITLE>`, and `<HEAD>` tags used to begin an HTML document are sent using the `CGI32.BAS` `Send()` function. Note that the page also is made a bit more aesthetically pleasing by setting the background color and the color of the font used for heading text.

When the form in Figure 18.15 is submitted (using the `POST` method, in this case), the Web server decodes the form data and creates the request package, as described earlier in this chapter. At this point, the data is readily available to the program by using the `CGI32.BAS` functions `FieldPresent()` (to first check whether data for each specific checkbox in the field was sent) and then `GetSmallField()` (which retrieves the value associated with the key—the name of the form field). For example, this code first checks to see whether data for the WWW Database Development checkbox in Figure 18.15 exists (that is, whether the user enabled the checkbox):

```
If FieldPresent("btype0") Then
        Clauses = Clauses & Chr(34) & GetSmallField("btype0") & Chr(34) & ", "
End If
```

If this data does exist, the `Clauses` string is appended with the current content of the string, a quotation mark (`"`) (using the `Chr(34)` function, the value of the field as retrieved by the `GetSmallField` function), another quotation mark (`"`), and, finally, a comma (`,`) character. This sequence is repeated for each checkbox in the form to determine whether it was selected. The value of the price input field also is determined in this manner and is used to append the `Clauses` string with a `< price` condition. For the user input shown in Figure 18.15, the result of these operations is a `Clauses` string of

```
type in ("wwwdbdev", "popular_comp", "business", "") AND price < 59.95
```

Now that the user's form input has been processed, the program sets about the work of initializing the DB-Library, getting a connection, and logging on. Note that a `Guest` account has been established on the SQL Server. This account has limited privileges (essentially, read-only) to the `pubs` database that is to be queried. After a connection is successfully established, three calls to the `SqlCmd` function formulate a SQL statement to send to the `pubs` database. Note that, although the bulk of the query could be hard-coded, you still can support ad-hoc user queries by appending the `Clauses` string that was formulated by using form data from the user. For example, the SQL statement created and sent to the server as a result of input in Figure 18.15 follows:

```
SELECT title, price
FROM pubs..titles
WHERE type in ("wwwdbdev", "popular_comp", "business", "") AND price < 59.95
```

After the query is sent to the server and executed, the `SqlResults`, `SqlNextRow`, and `SqlData` DB-Library functions are used within a loop to retrieve each row returned from the server. Within this loop, a minimal amount of formatting is performed by using the HTML `<PRE>` tag. This enables you to simply send each record of data returned from the query back to the requesting client in the form of preformatted text. Note that, with a little more work and imagination, the output generated dynamically at this stage of the program could include tables complete with headers, various background colors, and fonts. You could even develop your own set of VB functions that use the Send() function and <TABLE> tags to support creation and population of various types of HTML tables to be returned to the client.

After all data from the server is processed, formatted, and sent to the server for inclusion in the response package, the SqlExit and SqlWinExit calls are made to clean up before finally unloading the form that contains the VBSQL.OCX control. The program then sends the closing </BODY> and </HTML> tags before returning to the Sub Main program in the CGI32.BAS framework.

> **RESOURCE**
>
> As you have seen in this chapter, Windows CGI provides a very powerful method for developing Web database applications. In addition to providing an interface to SQL Server databases via the DB-Library API, Windows CGI can be used to interact with ODBC databases using Visual Basic data-access objects (DAOs). The following site presents a chapter from *Using CGI, Special Edition,* published by Que Corporation, that illustrates in great detail how you can accomplish this task:
>
> http://www.mcp.com/37064500504674/que/et/se_cgi/Cgi21fi.htm

Summary

This chapter presented an in-depth overview of CGI and what it enables Web application developers to do. It emphasized that the primary strength of CGI is that you can use it to expand the functionality of the Web server and then make that functionality accessible to Web clients. You saw that CGI programs invoked via HTML forms give users access to databases, resources, and applications that previously were not accessible.

You then took a brief look at the CGI data-flow process and how data moves from a Web client to the server and then to the CGI program. You learned how results from a CGI program follow this path back to the requesting client. You then delved into CGI input and output, examining the various methods to move client data to the server and on to the CGI program. CGI environment variables were introduced, the differences between GET and POST methods were outlined, and URL encoding was explained in depth.

The remainder of this chapter focused on using CGI in a Windows development environment. You explored using the Windows CGI and took a long look at how CGI32.BAS simplifies the task of developing Windows CGI Visual Basic. Next, you discovered how you can use Windows CGI with the Microsoft SQL Server DB-Library VB API to create Web database applications to perform a variety of complex operations on behalf of Web clients. Finally, the chapter pulled these concepts together by presenting an example showing how to put these concepts into practice.

19

Database Results Presentation Using HTML and CGI

by Drew Kittel

This chapter focuses on the presentation of database information. Assume that users have submitted requests to your server, and your server and CGI programs now must respond to the user requests for information by executing programs that access your database and applications and obtain results. After the CGI programs obtain these results, they must be returned to the users in a format in which they can be used effectively. HTML 3.2 provides a number of methods that enable Web browsers to effectively present information and output from a variety of applications—in ways that are not only meaningful to the user but visually appealing as well. But as you'll see, by throwing in a few ActiveX controls and VBScript, you can create some truly outstanding presentations without a great deal of work.

This chapter briefly discusses issues of style, and then it more fully explores how you can use preformatted text, HTML-formatted text, graphics, and some forms elements to effectively and efficiently display the results of a user request. You'll also see how to use HTML 3.2 elements—specifically, tables, colors, and fonts—to enhance the readability, layout, and visual quality of the presentation. Along the way, you'll see several examples illustrating these techniques.

This chapter also explores techniques that use CGI programs to render database output in a variety of ways. You'll see how to use CGI programs to create tables of database output and lists of hypertext links based on results of a database query, as well as how to dynamically create other HTML forms complete with input objects such as checkboxes, radio buttons, and selection lists. These forms will be created dynamically by using the results of an initial database query.

The final section of this chapter is dedicated to an example that ties together all the concepts presented in this chapter. This example will show you how to present database information graphically to enhance the readability and interpretation of datasets returned in response to users' queries. In particular, you'll see how you can create various controls (such as Charts and ComboBoxes) and VBScripts *dynamically* with CGI programs and use them to create interactive charts that graphically summarize query results for your users.

What Are Data and Information?

Data often is described as a collection of raw, unprocessed, singular entities of information, whereas *information* is described as processed data. Processed data implies that the original data has undergone some value-added processing in order to become information. From a systems point of view, data is what is put into the system and then undergoes processing within the system. Information is what the system outputs.

This is certainly the case with all the nuggets of data put into a database. After processing a user query, sets of data are selected from the database, manipulated in various ways, and output as information—presumably with some relevance or importance to the user performing the query.

Because one person's information often can be another person's data, this chapter doesn't strictly differentiate between data and information; instead, the two terms are used interchangeably. This chapter also adopts the convention that information is virtually anything of importance to users, whether it is needed to make important business decisions, develop an environmental impact statement, fuel a decision-support system, provide input and feedback for intelligent tutoring systems, determine whether a vendor has a product in the color you want, ascertain which of your employees has the appropriate skills and background to work on that next big proposal, or just something that satisfies the personal curiosity of a user. The list is virtually endless.

What Is Information Presentation?

Raw data is queried and filtered to generate a data set that provides specific information. *Presentation* is the display of this data that has been designated as meaningful to the user.

It certainly is possible (and easy) to respond to a user query for information by filling the screen with several lines of unformatted, incomprehensible text, garish colors, and a jumble of pictures. But information presentation implies more than that. It implies that the information is presented in a way that makes sense for the data types being displayed and that the output is formatted so that the user immediately can do something useful with it, regardless of whether that something is reading a book excerpt or review, evaluating the technical specifications of some vendor's piece of hardware, learning about the potentially devastating effects of the next volcanic eruption in the Pacific northwest (complete with maps predicting areas of damage), or performing a detailed analysis of financial information in tabular form and accompanying pie-chart graphics.

Information presentation also implies that the information is presented with some forethought about how a user will navigate through it. Returning 100 pages of financial data tables and graphs as a single, scrollable document wouldn't make sense when the data could be presented with an index and paging capabilities. It's easy for the message to get lost through misuse of the media. The way data is presented should enhance its use rather than obscure it.

Data Types and Formats

A staggering number of data types is associated with database systems and other development environments on the market: CHAR, DATE, LONG, RAW, *binary large objects* (BLOBs), NUMBER, VARCHAR, MONEY, VARBINARY, INT, BIT, FLOAT, REAL, and so on. For the purposes of data presentation, though, most of these boil down to the following handful of constituent data types:

■ Character strings generally consisting of up to 255 characters

■ Variable-length alphanumeric text (which generally is limited only by the constraints of a particular system)

- Graphics images in a variety of formats
- Audio snippets
- Video clips

The remainder of this chapter focuses on the presentation of information that is essentially textual and graphical.

Textual Data

Textual data is used to present varying combinations of alphabetic characters, punctuation, words, numbers, and symbols (such as those used in mathematical formulas). Textual data can be presented in several forms: free-form, preformatted, tabular, or all of these forms.

Graphical Data

Graphical information is data displayed as a pictorial presentation. Common types of graphical data include pictures, photographs, images, figures, graphs, graphics, drawings, and maps.

Graphical information can be presented in black-and-white or color choices ranging from 256 colors for 8-bit color; 65,536 (64KB) colors for 16-bit color; and up to 16 million colors with 24-bit color graphics.

Numerous graphics formats and methods are used to store and render graphical information. Many of these are open formats, although some are proprietary. Others implement *lossy* compression methods, in which some data is deliberately discarded to reduce the size of the compressed file or to store data at a reduced resolution to decrease the use of disk space and to speed rendering times. Many graphics are uncompressed and at full resolution.

For your purposes, the most useful of these formats are those the majority of graphical Web browsers understand, interpret, and render for the user. These formats and their file extensions follow:

- *Graphics Interchange Format* (.gif): A bitmap file format and the primary Internet format for 1-bit to 8-bit color graphics and images.
- *Joint Photographic Experts Group* (.jpeg and .jpg): A bitmap file format and the primary Internet format for 24-bit color graphics and images.
- *Tag Image File Format* (.tif and .tiff): A bitmap file format used for 1-bit to 24-bit graphics and images.
- *PostScript* (.ps)/*Encapsulated PostScript* (.eps): A page-definition language used to define how graphics are rendered to the screen. Image and bitmap data can be encapsulated within the PostScript file.
- *X Bitmap* (.xbm): The primary Internet format for monochromatic bitmap images.

In addition to these formats, several other graphics file formats are in widespread use and understood by several of the major Web browsers. Also, helper applications and plug-ins can be invoked to render formats that the browser itself cannot handle.

Anchor Elements

Anchor elements aren't so much a type of data as they are a pathway to other data. They're covered in this chapter because they commonly are used in information presentations, enabling users to access other information with a simple click of a mouse. Anchor elements, along with the HREF attribute, enable you to specify URLs to data, information, services, and applications. Generating these links to information as a result of a database query is a common practice.

One example of such an application is a user-interface form enabling the user to query for all corporate monthly financial reports in which sales for a specific suite of products rose a certain percentage during a specified time. The result generated by the server might be a list of anchors to specific reports—perhaps with a brief synopsis of the reports' contents. Clicking the URL would cause the full reports' contents, complete with any associated graphics, to be rendered for the user. In this example, the URLs might be links to static HTML documents or links to server programs that read the report data from a database and generate the HTML on the fly.

Static Data

Static data is data presented to the user that does not change during the time it is in use. Textual data, reports, static graphics, URLs, and tables of these types of data typically are not updated while in use by the user.

Dynamic Data

Dynamic data, on the other hand, is data presented to the user that is in motion—changing periodically or in response to some user action. ActiveX controls provide many exciting possibilities for enabling users to dynamically tailor presentations (such as the style and attributes of charts and graphics derived from database query results) in response to actions taken on the client browser.

Animating graphics components of the information presentation is an obvious example. Many methods exist for dynamically creating information presentations. These techniques include server push (currently only supported by Netscape browsers), ActiveX controls, animated GIF images, helper applications for rendering video clips and audio snippets, and plug-in applications supported by browsers (such as Netscape and Java programs).

Data Presentation Using HTML 2.0

HTML 2.0 provides several elements that enable you to present various data types in meaningful and visually appealing ways. The following sections explore some of the most common elements.

Using <PRE>

The <PRE> tag is handy when you need to retain the original formatting of the source document used to create an HTML document. Using <PRE> causes text to be displayed in a fixed-width font. Using the <PRE> tag also causes original whitespace, carriage returns, and line feeds in the source document to be retained.

> **TIP**
>
> Because the fixed-width font varies between types of browsers, it's a good practice to test the document on different types of browsers to verify that the text will format correctly.

Often it is desirable to maintain the original document formatting because you might want to make documents in different formats available to users via Web browsers without having to convert the document contents to HTML. You also might want to quickly present the results of a database query without reformatting the results in HTML. Suppose that you maintain a database of products for your online store. A user can fill out an online form to obtain pricing information about your econo-widget products. When submitted, the form sends a SQL query like the following to your database server:

```
select name, id, price
    from widget_table
    where type="econo_widget" and price < $250.00
    order by price desc
```

The result of this query might be the following:

```
name                id        price
- - - - - - - - - - - - - - - - -   - - - - - - -   - - - - - -
Super-econo Widget  12345     $199.99
Budget Widget       98765     $189.45
Goodluck Widget     47586     $103.27

(3 rows affected)
```

For a browser to present the database results formatted exactly as shown here, you must surround the results with the <PRE> tag pair. Listing 19.1 shows how you can use <PRE> to retain the formatting of the original database results.

Listing 19.1. Using <PRE> to retain the formatting of the original database results.

```
<HTML>

<HEAD>
<TITLE>PRE Tag to Maintain Database Results Formatting</TITLE>
</HEAD>

<BODY>

<CENTER>
<H1>Product Query Search Results</H1>
</CENTER>
<HR>

<P>
<STRONG>Using &ltPRE&gt to Maintain Formatting</STRONG><BR>
<PRE>
<!-- these are the actual results from the query -->
name             id      price
----------------  -------  ------
Super-econo Widget 12345   $199.99
Budget Widget      98765   $189.45
Goodluck Widget    47586   $103.27

(3 rows affected)

</PRE>
</P>

<P>
<STRONG>Without &ltPRE/&gt</STRONG><BR>
<!-- lack of PRE tag allows browser to "format" the results -->
name             id      price
----------------  -------  ------
Super-econo Widget 12345   $199.99
Budget Widget      98765   $189.45
Goodluck Widget    47586   $103.27

(3 rows affected)

</P>


</BODY>
</HTML>
```

Figure 19.1 shows the results of using the HTML <PRE> tag to retain the original format of the source data.

FIGURE 19.1.

*Using the HTML
<PRE> tag to retain
formatting.*

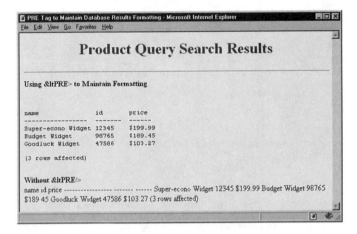

The advantages of using the <PRE> tag instead of letting the browser strip whitespace and impose formatting is obvious in this example. Even with the use of <PRE>, though, the presentation leaves much to be desired. Some of the methods for dressing up this output are discussed later in this chapter.

HTML-Formatted Text

In many cases, you'll simply want to present the user with a body of text in which formatting data fields is not a great concern. In these cases, the browser strips excessive whitespace, ignores carriage returns, and performs automatic word wraps (all of which were shown in Figure 19.1). To enforce some degree of formatting on the rendered document, you can use HTML elements such as <P> and <BR>.

Inline Graphics Using <IMG>

Using graphics in your presentations can serve two important purposes. Obviously, they can make your presentations more attractive. They often can communicate complicated concepts more easily and clearly than a textual explanation. A single graph or chart can help make sense of a table full of numbers, for example. In other cases, a well-designed graphic can make the same point as several lines of text. Think of all the times somebody tried to explain something to you in words but just couldn't sufficiently communicate his point. Then he drew you a picture, and you immediately understood what he was attempting to communicate. That is the power of graphics.

Many Web-based applications, such as database-access and electronic-commerce applications, are perfectly suited for handling graphical data. Imagine a database application that enables the user to obtain the high and low temperatures for various United States cities during a specified date range. This is an application that conceivably could return many numbers the user would need to analyze. If the data also was returned in graphical form as a time-series graph, however, the user could rapidly glean much of the desired information simply by looking at the graph.

How often are you willing to spend your money based solely on a vendor's description of a product? Now imagine an online store that enables you to leaf through the pages of an electronic catalog. Graphics and images, along with the descriptive text, enable potential customers to see what they're getting and increase the likelihood of a sale. Anchors that provide hypertext links to additional product specifications easily could be included as well.

The <IMG> Tag

Using the HTML <IMG> tag enables you to insert graphics inline on the page. The general syntax follows:

```
... other HTML ...
<IMG SRC="url to your image" ALIGN="your desired alignment"
ALT="alternate text to display">
... other HTML ...
```

You can insert an image virtually anywhere you can insert text in an HTML document. The image is inserted inline in the body of the HTML page as if it were a single character of text (except it's the size of your image). In the following code, for example, the image is rendered on the page directly next to the emphasized text:

```
<EM>Text aligned</EM> <IMG SRC="omniscient.gif">
```

Note that images cannot be registered to a specific location on the page; in other words, there are no attributes that enable you to specify a coordinate location at which to render the image.

SRC

The SRC attribute value is the image that is to be placed inline in your presentation. As shown in the general syntax for <IMG>, the value of this attribute is a URL that points to the image file location. The SRC attribute must be specified. Note that various browsers support inline rendering of different image formats. The major browsers such as Microsoft Internet Explorer, Netscape Navigator, and Mosaic, all support the most common types—specifically, GIF and JPEG. A JPEG image might be specified as the following:

```
<IMG SRC="caffrey_technologies.jpg">
```

ALT

The ALT attribute specifies a string of text to be displayed by browsers incapable of displaying the specified SRC image. Some browsers such as Microsoft's Internet Explorer use the ALT text immediately and replace it with the actual image after the image is loaded. If you use the following HTML code, for example, the browser immediately renders the text WWidgets-Logo and then replaces it with the image specified by IMG SRC after it is loaded:

```
<IMG SRC="wirkkala_widgets.gif" ALT="WWidgets-Logo">
```

ALIGN

The ALIGN attribute specifies how text adjacent to the inline image should be aligned with the image. The values of this attribute are limited to top, bottom, and middle. The following code shows how an image is rendered on the left-hand side of the text and aligned so that the top of the image is on the same line as the text string:

```
<B>Here's our corporate logo</B><IMG SRC="omniscient.gif"
ALT="OMNISCIENT" ALIGN=top>
```

Rendering an Inline Image

Listing 19.2 shows how you can use <IMG> and the ALIGN attribute to display graphics inline with other text. Figure 19.2 shows the corresponding output. This code renders the same GIF image in three ways. The first case shows how the top edge of an image is aligned with preceding text. The second case illustrates how the vertical center line of an image is aligned with text that precedes and follows the inline image. The third case demonstrates aligning the bottom edge of an image with text.

Listing 19.2. Using <IMG> and ALIGN to display graphics inline with other text.

```
<html>

<head>
<title>Use of IMG Tag for Inline Graphics/Images</title>
<!-- Example: Use of IMG Tag for Inline Graphics/Images -->
</head>

<body bgcolor="#FFFFFF">

<h2 align="center">
<font color="#0000FF">
Examples of In-line
Graphics/Images
</font></h2>

<hr>

<p><b>Text aligned with top of image</b><img src="omni.gif"
alt="OMNI" align="top" width="173" height="71"> </p>

<p><b>Text aligned</b> <img src="omni.gif" alt="OMNI"
align="middle" width="173" height="71"> <b>with the middle of
image</b> </p>
```

```
<p><b>Text aligned with bottom of image</b> <img src="omni.gif"
alt="OMNI" width="173" height="71"> </p>
</body>
</html>
```

FIGURE 19.2.

Using the <IMG> *tag to embed inline graphics and images.*

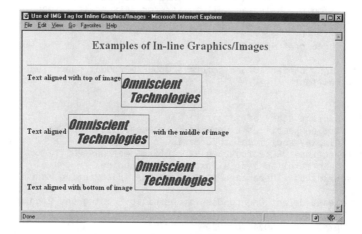

The ALT attribute specifies that the text string "OMNI" should be displayed if the browser is unable to load the image specified in the SRC URL. Notice in Figure 19.2 that there is a character of whitespace between the image and adjacent text in the bottom two images. This keeps the browser from placing the image directly adjacent to the text, as it does in the first image. You may have surmised that the <IMG> tag's attributes limit your capability to neatly flow text around inline images. Later sections in this chapter present some extensions to <IMG> attributes.

Presentations Using <SELECT> and <OPTION>

Historically, the <SELECT> element and <OPTION> subelement have not seen a great deal of use for presentations of information, such as the results of a database query. After all, they're form elements and were designed for acquiring user input. These lists, however, can function as both presentation devices and input elements.

An earlier example in this chapter used <PRE> to retain the original formatting of results from a simple database SQL query. Suppose that the result of a user's initial query is a list of 20 products, and you want the user to be able to obtain more detailed information on one or more of the products. It would be nice to save some screen space by displaying the initial query results in a scrollable option list and to provide a second round of user input that would enable the user to obtain details on select products. The code in Listing 19.3 shows how you could accomplish this, and Figure 19.3 illustrates the form.

Listing 19.3. Using OPTION lists for presenting data.

```html
<html>

<head>
<title>Using an OPTION list for data presentation</title>
<!-- Example - Using an OPTION list for data presentation
</head>

<body bgcolor="#FFFFFF">

<h1 align="center"><font color="#0000FF">Product Query Search
Results</font></h1>

<hr>
<!-- Declare start of form   -->
<!-- action specifies a routine to process listinput and -->
<!-- display additional information on the product -->
<form action="URL%20for%20cgi%20routine" method="POST">
<!-- this scrolled-list allows a single choice -->
<p><em><strong>There were 10 Product Listings Meeting Your Criteria<br>

    Please Select One to Display Detailed Pricing and Product
    Information </strong></em></p>
    <p><select name="options" size="6">
        <option value="opt1">Acme Wid-jet</option>
        <option value="opt2">Super-econo Widget</option>
        <option value="opt3">Budget Widget</option>
        <option value="opt4">Widgets-R-Us #32</option>
        <option value="opt5">Omni Pro-Widget</option>
        <option value="opt6">Goodluck Widget</option>
        <option value="opt7">Noname Gadget</option>
        <option value="opt8">Naselle Gadget #A1</option>
        <option value="opt9">Caffrey Model-X</option>
        <option value="opt10">Widget Solutions</option>
    </select><!-- other options here --> </p>
    <p><input type="submit" value="Display Product Information"> </p>
</form>
</body>
</html>
```

Listing 19.3 illustrates a manually intensive way of making a presentation. The HTML for this example was all hand-coded. Presenting the results of a database query in lists (or any other form element, for that matter) can easily be accomplished by using programs that generate the required HTML automatically. Later sections of this chapter explore methods for developing these programs.

FIGURE 19.3.

Using a list for data presentation.

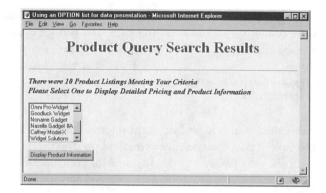

Presentations Using HTML 3.2 and Netscape Extensions

Although HTML 2.0 enables you to do many things, it has definite limitations. Fortunately, the major browser manufacturers and HTML standards folks realized this and have been adding functionality to their browsers and trying to agree on the content of the HTML 3.2 standard. Additionally, each browser manufacturer continues to add non-standard features in a continuing effort to stay ahead of the other guys. Changes are occurring at a staggering pace. Just keeping up with the latest browser functionality can be a full-time endeavor. This situation is complicated further by each vendor's desire to incorporate functions that its competitors have not yet implemented or are implementing in a different manner. The following sections introduce several features of HTML 3.2 and some common extensions.

RESOURCE

The following site maintains a current listing of browser functionality, as well as sample programs and a variety of interesting links to other sites:

`http://www.browserwatch.com/`

Presentations Using <TABLE> Elements

<TABLE> elements also are well-suited to information presentations. This is true especially for presenting information extracted from a database. Information stored in a relational database is by nature organized in row/column formats. Therefore, results of SQL queries are suited perfectly to the use of tables to nicely format and present this information to the user. This section illustrates how you can accomplish this task.

The following code uses <TABLE> elements to format the query results. This code creates a table that is three columns wide and uses three table data tags for each row of database results presented in the table:

```
<TR>
<TD>data_field1</TD><TD>data_field2</TD>
<TD>data_field3</TD>
</TR>
```

This code enables you to logically present information about each data record in a separate row in the table. Again, this code demonstrates how data that is essentially row/column (database record/fields) by nature is perfectly suited for presentation in a table format.

In the resulting presentation, notice that the BORDER and CELLPADDING attributes provide a nice delineation between cells and cell contents and ensure that cell contents don't touch the borders (see Listing 19.4). Using <TABLE> also enables you to provide a descriptive heading for each column. The ALIGN attribute enables you to horizontally align cell contents, much as you would in a spreadsheet. Finally, the presentation of the database results in this format is by far the most logical, intuitive, and easy to read of all examples presented so far. Figure 19.4 shows the results of the code in Listing 19.4.

Listing 19.4. Using the <TABLE> feature for presenting data.

```
<HTML>

<HEAD>
<TITLE>TABLE for Database Results Formatting</TITLE>
</HEAD>

<BODY>

<CENTER>
<H2>Product Query Search Results</H2>
</CENTER>
<HR>

<P>
<STRONG><EM>
There Were 10 Product Listings Meeting Your Criteria
</EM></STRONG>
</P>

<P>
<!-- TABLE used to format query results.  Note use of More -->
<!-- descriptive headings -->
<TABLE BORDER="1" CELLPADDING="4">
<TR>
<TH>Product Name</TH>
<TH>Product ID</TH>
<TH>Unit Price</TH>
</TR>
<TR>
```

```
<TD>Acme Wid-jet</TD><TD ALIGN="right">92234</TD><TD ALIGN="right">$244.95</TD>
</TR>
<TR>
<TD>Super-econo Widget</TD><TD ALIGN="right">12345</TD>
<TD ALIGN="right">$199.99</TD>
</TR>
<TR>
<TD>Budget Widget</TD><TD ALIGN="right">98765</TD>
<TD ALIGN="right">$189.45</TD>
</TR>
<TR>
<TD>Widgets-R-Us #32</TD><TD ALIGN="right">BA642</TD>
<TD ALIGN="right">$177.33</TD>
</TR>
<TR>
<TD>Omni Pro-Widget</TD><TD ALIGN="right">33-12</TD>
<TD ALIGN="right">$137.89</TD>
</TR>
<TR>
<TD>Goodluck Widget</TD><TD ALIGN="right">47586</TD>
<TD ALIGN="right">$103.27</TD>
</TR>
<TR>
<TD>Noname Gadget</TD><TD ALIGN="right">QR722</TD>
<TD ALIGN="right">$99.17</TD>
</TR>
<TR>
<TD>Naselle Gadget #A1</TD><TD ALIGN="right">33987</TD>
<TD ALIGN="right">$88.25</TD>
</TR>
<TR>
<TD>Caffrey Model-X</TD><TD ALIGN="right">X3379</TD>
<TD ALIGN="right">$79.75</TD>
</TR>
<TR>
<TD>Widget Solutions</TD><TD ALIGN="right">T-129</TD>
<TD ALIGN="right">$74.32</TD>
</TR>
</TABLE>
</P>

</BODY>
</HTML>
```

NOTE

Using <TABLE> elements to format data has barely been touched on here. You can do many fancy things, including nesting tables within tables, using graphics and images in table cells, and using anchors with HREF URL links to other documents and programs. You can even use <TABLE> elements to impose page-layout designs that include text and graphics. You should experiment with this powerful data-presentation tool.

FIGURE 19.4.

Using <TABLE> elements to format database query results.

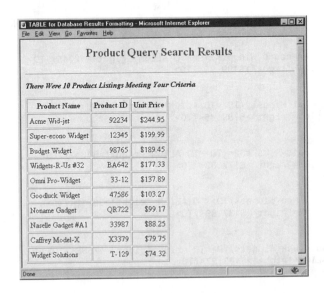

Using Popular Netscape Extensions

The HTML specification has some serious limitations when it comes to dressing presentations of information for your users. Often, the appropriate use of color, font styles, or page backgrounds can enhance your overall presentation and emphasize key components of the information provided to your users. Fortunately, Netscape introduced extensions to the HTML 2.0 standard that enable you to better control the overall look of the information on your pages. This functionality is provided by the <FONT> tag and the COLOR attribute, as well as the BACKGROUND attribute used with the <BODY> tag. Most of the major vendors have incorporated these extensions into the latest versions of their products. Additionally, vendors such as Microsoft continue to provide additional capabilities for using a variety of fonts, table cell background, border colors, and so on.

Font Size and Color

Netscape introduced the capability to specify font size and color changes for specific sections of text within an HTML document. Other browsers, such as Microsoft Internet Explorer and Mosaic, also support these features and have added their own extensions as well. Judicious use of fonts and colors can make a data presentation not only more attractive, but it can help outline and format a page to make the overall presentation more effective. The following code shows how you can display various font sizes, styles (in this case, those supported by Internet Explorer), and colors using this general syntax:

```
<FONT SIZE="desired_size" COLOR="#hex_value_for desired_color"
face="desired_style">your_text</FONT><BR>
```

In this case, FONT SIZE takes on an integer value from 1 to 8. COLOR takes on a hexadecimal value of the format #RRGGBB, which specifies the red, green, and blue components of the desired color. For example, #FF0000 specifies red text. face specifies the font style (such as Braggadocio) to use. Listing 19.5 shows how several font styles and colors can be added to a Web page and Figure 19.5 shows the results of this code.

Listing 19.5. Adding font styles and colors to a Web page.

```
<html>

<head>
<title>Colors and Fonts</title>
<!-- Example: Use of Font sizes Styles and Color-->
</head>

<body bgcolor="#FFFFFF">

<h1 align="center">Various Font Sizes, Styles and Colors</h1>

<hr>

<p>
<font color="#FF0000" size="1" face="Optimum">
This text is font size 1 and color red.</font><br>
<font color="#00FF00" size="2">
This text is font size 2 and color green.</font><br>
<font color="#0000FF" size="3" face="Modern">
This text is font size 3 and color blue.</font><br>
<font color="#FF8040" size="4" face="Impact">
This text is font size 4 and color orange.</font><br>
<font color="#0000FF" size="5" face="Braggadocio">
This text is font size 5 and color blue.</font><br>
<font color="#FF0000" size="6" face="Matisse ITC">
This text is font size 6 and color red.</font><br>
<font color="#00FF00" size="7" face="Britannic Bold">
Font size 7 and color green.</font><br>
<font color="#808080" size="7" face="Comic Sans MS">
Font size 8 and color grey.</font><br>
</p>
</body>
</html>
```

Page Backgrounds

The BACKGROUND attribute extension enables you to fill in page backgrounds by tiling a specified image—most commonly, a GIF or JPEG image. Browsers can do this efficiently by loading the image a single time from the server and then pulling it out of the local cache as necessary for the tiling process.

FIGURE 19.5.

Using different font sizes, styles, and colors.

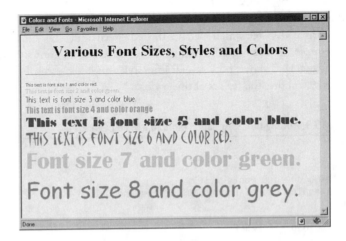

You can specify a page for your HTML document by adding the BACKGROUND attribute to the <BODY> tag and specifying a URL that references the image file you want to tile as the background. The following code shows how to do this, and Figure 19.6 shows the results:

```
<BODY BACKGROUND="omni.gif">
```

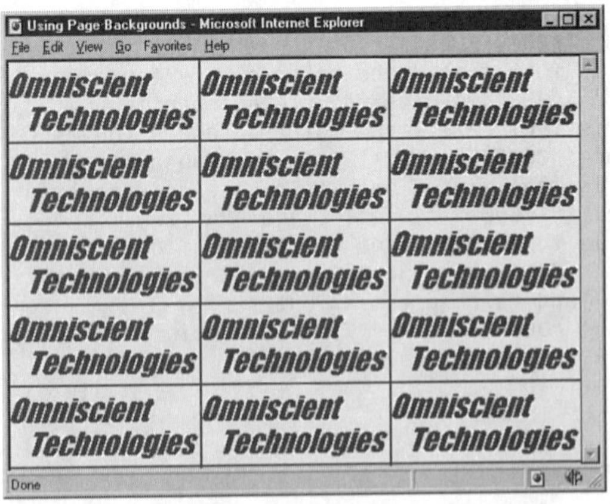

FIGURE 19.6.

Creating a background of tiled images.

CAUTION

Use page backgrounds with caution and forethought as to the content and color of data and other text presented on the page. It's too easy to choose a background image that makes the information difficult to read.

Making Text Flow Around Inline Images

The following attribute extensions to `<IMG>` enable you to flow text around inline images:

```
HSPACE and VSPACE
BORDER
HEIGHT and WIDTH
ALIGN
CLEAR
```

These attribute extensions have been broadly accepted by most of the major browser vendors, such as Microsoft Internet Explorer and Mosaic.

HSPACE and VSPACE

These attributes enable you to specify the amount of space that should exist between an image and the text that flows around it. Both values are specified in pixels. For example, the following code specifies that a horizontal separation of 8 pixels should exist between the right side of the image and the specified text:

```
<IMG SRC="omni.gif" ALT="OMNI" ALIGN=left HSPACE=8 VSPACE=2>
<FONT SIZE=5>Since 1991
```

Additionally, the text will be vertically aligned 2 pixels below the top edge of the image.

BORDER

The `BORDER` attribute enables you to embed the `<IMG>` tag in an anchor so that it responds as a hypertext link after you click it. The `BORDER` attribute controls the width of the border drawn around an image to indicate it is a hypertext link. The value is specified in pixels; a value of 0 suppresses the border from being rendered. The following code specifies an image as a hypertext link with a border 2 pixels wide:

```
<A HREF="your_url_here"><IMG SRC="your_image_here" BORDER=2></A>
```

TIP

This technique enables you to use images as buttons to link to other documents or to invoke routines specified by the `HREF` URL in your anchor. Several publicly available images resembling buttons exist, and you can specify them in `<IMG>` so that you can add button bars to your presentations.

HEIGHT and WIDTH

Use the `HEIGHT` and `WIDTH` attributes to specify the height and width of the image or graphic to be displayed. If the specified height and width do not match the source image dimensions, the browser attempts to scale the image to fit the specified sizes. These attribute values are specified in pixels. The following code, for example, specifies that the image should be rendered at a size of 250 pixels high by 350 pixels wide:

```
<IMG SRC="omin.gif" HEIGHT=250 WIDTH=350>
```

But what if the source image file were only 150×200 pixels? In that case, the browser would rescale the source image data to fit the specified height and width.

CAUTION

Scaling the specified image can result in a degradation of quality in the rendered image. This process may result in blockiness, poor spatial resolution (reduced detail), and changes in the aspect ratio. In some cases, rescaling the image may result in slower image-rendering speeds. Often it's better to just specify an image of the desired dimensions.

ALIGN Extensions

You might remember that in HTML, the ALIGN attribute can take on the values of top, middle, or bottom. In these cases, the value specifies how the inline image should be aligned with the baseline of contiguous text. In effect, the image acted as though it were a character of text and was subject to word wrapping along with the rest of the text. Extensions to the ALIGN attribute modify this behavior. The extended ALIGN attribute now can take values of left or right, which means that the image is rendered to the left or right side of the text and acts as a container for that text instead of wrapping with the text. In effect, the image boundary now determines where lines of text will wrap to the next line. This enables you to create pages of text with inline images where the text flows around the boundaries of the image. The following code specifies a left-aligned image (the image appears to the left of the text), for example:

```
<IMG SRC="your_image" ALIGN="left">your_text
```

Text is bounded by the right side of this image until the left-hand margin is clear to the edge of the browser window, at which point it is bound by the browser and not the right side of the image. This gives the appearance that the text has wrapped around the right side of the image and along the bottom of the image. You can see the results of this technique in Figure 19.7, in the section "Using HTML Extensions: An Example."

CLEAR

Use the CLEAR attribute to specify the end of the <IMG> container (note that there is no </IMG> tag). Using CLEAR in an HTML element stops the flow of text around an image. The following code illustrates use of the CLEAR attribute:

```
<IMG SRC="your_image"
ALIGN="left">your_text<BR CLEAR=LEFT>
```

Note that, if the supplied text was not long enough to reach the bottom of the image, <BR CLEAR=LEFT> indicates that the browser should page down until it finds a clear left margin (beyond the bottom of the image) before rendering any subsequent HTML.

Using HTML Extensions: An Example

The code in Listing 19.6 illustrates how you can use the HTML extensions previously presented to format a page. In this example, a left-aligned image is rendered to show you how to make text flow around the image, in effect making the image a container for that text. Additionally, this listing demonstrates how you can use an <IMG> tag in an <A HREF> anchor to allow an image to be used as a hypertext link.

Listing 19.6. Formatting a page by using the <IMG> HTML extension.

```
<html>

<head>
<title>Using IMG Extensions</title>
</head>

<body bgcolor="#FFFFFF">

<h1 align="center"><em>Welcome to Omniscient Technologies</em></h1>

<hr>

<p><img src="omni.gif" alt="omni" align="left" clear="left" hspace="8"
vspace="2" width="173" height="71"><font size="5"><em>Since 1991,
Omniscient Technologies has been actively involved in image and
signal processing, expert systems, fuzzy logic, and neural</em></font><em>
</em><font size="5"><em>networks routinely used in development of
solutions to image and signal processing problems. Omniscient
provides customers with advanced solutions to technically
challenging problems in Remote Sensing, GIS, Simulation Systems
and imaging technologies such as Feature Extraction, Sensor
Fusion and Automatic Target Recognition. Omniscient is also
actively involved in the WWW phenomenon and is currently heavily
involved in the development of WWW Database Applications for our
clients.</em> </font></p>

<hr>
```

continues

Listing 19.6. continued

```
<address>
    <a href="http://www.omniscient.com"><img src="omni.gif"
    alt="OMNI" width="80" height="40"></a> <a
    href="mailto:kittel@omniscient.com">E-Mail:
    kittel@omniscient.com</a>
</address>
</body>
</html>
```

The ALIGN=left extension specifies that the omni.gif source image should be placed to the left of the text. The CLEAR attribute within the <BR> tag ends the wrapping of text at the right image boundary and continues the next line of text at full-screen width. The HSPACE and VSPACE attribute extensions provide fine control over how close the text appears next to the image. They give the page a polished, formatted, newsletter quality—a nice touch when presenting information such as company financial reports.

The ADDRESS portion of the code also illustrates several of the Netscape extensions. The original omni.gif image is scaled down considerably using the HEIGHT and WIDTH attribute extensions. Also, the scaled image is embedded in an anchor, with an HREF URL pointing to the corporate home page address. The BORDER attribute gives a slightly bolder border to identify this explicitly as a pushbutton link.

Figure 19.7 shows the result of Listing 19.6.

FIGURE 19.7.

Using <IMG> attribute extensions.

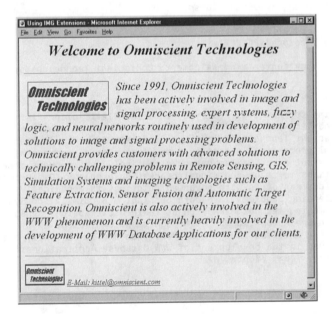

Information Presentation Style Guidelines

A simple credo applies to developing Web-based applications: *If you build it, they will come. But if you build it well, they will come in large numbers, again and again.* The data and information you present should take center stage, and the tools you use to present it should facilitate the communication of that information.

HTML and vendor extensions provide a rich set of tools, techniques, and tricks for presenting information to your users. There can be a downside to all this functionality, though: It's easy to get caught up in the available "gee whiz" features. By adding too many bells and whistles, you detract from the very thing that brought users to your site in the first place—the information and services they want.

Here are some simple HTML style guidelines for presenting information to your users:

■ Fancy features might catch user attention, but the novelty eventually wears off. Thoughtful design and ease of use will result in repeat visits (critical for commerce applications). Use novelty features only when they add something to the presentation.

■ Nothing is more frustrating to users than knowing that information is available, but having trouble finding or accessing it. Make your presentations clear and intuitive. Provide navigational aides such as page identifications: Next Page, Prior Page, and Home buttons, or button bars where appropriate.

■ Keep pages short so that users don't have to do too much scrolling. When possible, use graphics that fit within the default horizontal bounds of most browsers. Excessive scrolling detracts from the information being presented.

■ Implement a consistent look and feel across all pages of a presentation. Use logical, intuitive layouts and formats, and use colors, font sizes, and page backgrounds consistently throughout your presentation.

■ Use text wrapping with <IMG> or <FIG> when appropriate.

■ Take advantage of the formatting provided by <TABLE>. Editing tools, such as Microsoft's FrontPage, now make creation of complex and tightly formatted tables as easy as using a word processor.

■ Explore the functionality provided by the growing legions of ActiveX controls (such as charting and graphing controls) now available. In fact, it's now very easy using Visual Basic 5 and Visual Basic Control Creation Edition to make your own controls. These controls often provide the best of all worlds: a polished, highly interactive look and feel without detracting from the information being presented.

When using graphics and images, the following guidelines apply:

- Graphics and images should be an integral part of the presentation—not just a gimmick to make the page pretty.
- Be courteous to users with non-graphical browsers by using the ALT attribute within <IMG>.
- When possible and appropriate to the application, display thumbnail images with links to the full-size versions. This is important especially in graphics-intensive presentations where rendering time may be a factor.
- Use a GIF format rather than JPEG when possible and appropriate to the type of image data being presented. Most graphics and images can be displayed very well with the 8-bit resolution of GIF. Users will appreciate the quick rendering time that results from smaller image files.
- Use an interlaced GIF format when possible. It gives the user the impression that the image is loading more quickly by first loading a low-resolution version and then filling in detail later. This method also gives users quicker access to links included in the presentation.
- Use transparent background images when possible. Transparency blends the image background color to match the background of the underlying document. This makes the image look like a functional piece of the document instead of something pasted on top of the document.

Presenting Database Output Dynamically Using CGI

Chapter 18, "The Common Gateway Interface (CGI)," presents an example that uses the <PRE> tag to perform on-the-fly formatting of query results fetched from a database. Although you can use the <PRE> tag to adequately format results from very simple queries, the resulting presentations might be visually unappealing. <PRE> also is very limiting when you want to present more than just simple textual data. What if you also want to provide nicely formatted tables, generate form input objects based on initial query results, add graphics, or provide links to other data types such as graphics, audio, or video? This section presents a number of methods for accomplishing all these things.

The Simple pubs Database Query Revisited

Chapter 18 presents an example illustrating how form input can be used by a Windows CGI program to perform simple queries against the Microsoft SQL Server pubs database. The next few examples here revisit and build on the CGI program presented in that example. These examples show methods for presenting the query results in a variety of ways by generating the necessary HTML on-the-fly. To refresh your memory, Figure 19.8 shows the pubs simple query form, along with the actual input used for the following examples. You'll learn how to perform the following tasks:

- Format query results on-the-fly by using the HTML <TABLE> tag.
- Use query results as options in a <FORM> selection list.
- Generate lists of hypertext links by using query results.
- Use query results to create sets of <FORM> checkbox objects.

FIGURE 19.8.

The pubs *database query form showing input used for examples.*

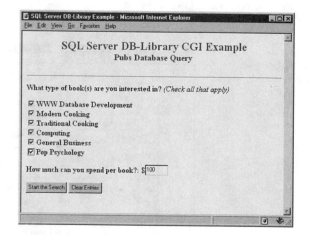

For the examples in the following sections, you'll concentrate on the portion of the CGI program associated with generating the HTML to present results to the user.

TIP

When reviewing the following examples, keep in mind that although they are presented independently, you can combine these techniques to produce comprehensive, visually appealing, and effective presentations. Remember that virtually anything you can code by hand using HTML can be implemented in a CGI program. Additionally, CGI programs enable you to integrate external applications to process database results and incorporate some very interesting presentations. Integrating ActiveX controls designed for graphing and charting data is an especially effective way to enhance your presentations.

Generating Database Output Formatted with an HTML <TABLE>

Relational databases are composed of tables of data conceptually laid out in rows and columns. This format provides a logical way of dealing with the data. You're probably familiar with database reports full of rows and columns of text and numbers. Wouldn't it be nice if there were an easy way to improve the appearance and readability of these reports? Well, HTML provides that capability quite nicely. Figure 19.9 illustrates how database results from the simple pubs query can be formatted on-the-fly and presented to the user in table format. This output is generated by the following ACTION attribute that was specified in the form:

```
<form
 action="http://dkittel.clark.net:8080/cgi-win/pubs_tables.exe"
 method="POST">
```

FIGURE 19.9.

The pubs *database query results formatted by using* <TABLE>.

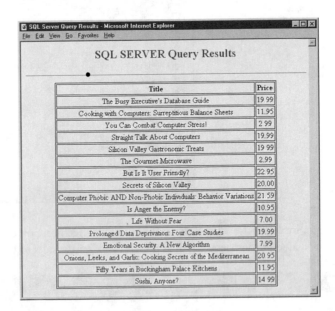

The formatting in Figure 19.9 was accomplished by using the HTML <TABLE> container tag and <TABLE> elements within the portion of the CGI program that renders HTML output. Listing 19.7 shows the portion of the pubs_tables.exe CGI routine responsible for generating this output.

Listing 19.7. VB code used to generate the table output shown in Figure 19.9.

```
Result = SqlResults(SqlConn)
        If Result = SUCCEED Then
            Send ("<center>")
            Call HTMLTableStart("80", "1", "#00000F", "")
            h_array(0) = "Title"
            h_array(1) = "Price"
```

```
        Call HTMLTableHeaders("center", 2, h_array)
        Do Until SqlNextRow(SqlConn) = NOMOREROWS
            d_array(0) = SqlData(SqlConn, 1)
            d_array(1) = SqlData(SqlConn, 2)
            Call HTMLTableDataRow("center", 2, d_array)
        Loop
        Call HTMLTableEnd

        Send ("</center>")
    End If
```

This code spools to the results package the HTML code required to create a table and specify the table headers. It then enters a loop that does the following:

■ Fetches a record of results data from the database

■ Puts the data into an array

■ Calls HTMLTableDataRow to spool the necessary HTML tags specifying a table row, table data, and the actual data to be put into the table

This looping continues until database results are exhausted, at which time the closing HTML tags necessary to end the table and the HTML document are printed. Note that this code relies on a set of simple HTML subprocedures developed to help make the program more modular and readable. These procedures simplify the process of creating HTML by enabling you to call routines that accept input for table attributes (such as width and colors) and arrays of data used to populate table header and data cells. These procedures in turn use the CGI32.BAS framework procedure Send() to spool results to the results package. The code for these subroutines is in the HTML.BAS module on the CD-ROM that accompanies this book; it also is shown in Listing 19.8.

Listing 19.8. HTML.BAS subprocedures used to format database output into HTML tables.

```
Sub HTMLTableStart(width, border, bordercolor, bgcolor)
    Send ("<table width=" + width + "%" + " border=" + border + " bordercolor="
    ➥ + bordercolor + " bgcolor=" + bgcolor + ">")
End Sub

Sub HTMLTableHeaders(alignment, nelements, header_array)
    ndx = 0
    Send ("<TR>")
    For ndx = 0 To (nelements - 1) Step 1
        Send ("<TH align=" + alignment + ">" + header_array(ndx) + "</TH>")
    Next
    Send ("</TR>")
End Sub

Sub HTMLTableDataRow(alignment, nelements, data_array)
    ndx = 0
    Send ("<TR>")
```

continues

Listing 19.8. continued

```
    For ndx = 0 To (nelements - 1) Step 1
        Send ("<TD align=" + alignment + ">" + data_array(ndx) + "</TD>")
    Next
    Send ("</TR>")
End Sub

Sub HTMLTableEnd()
    Send ("</table>")
End Sub
```

Even though this is a simple example, you can extend it easily to produce fancier, more comprehensive formatted output. Assuming that you, as a CGI developer, have a fundamental understanding of the types of results returned from queries posed to the database, you can modify the loop in this program to allow results of more complex queries with order by, group by, and compute by clauses to be appropriately formatted in a table (or tables) to be rendered on your users' browsers. Additionally, you can enhance the supplied routines to create nested tables and set additional table and cell properties.

Generating Database Output Formatted as a <FORM> Selection List

Sometimes, the results of a database query can be quite lengthy. Inserting all this data as rows in a table might force the user to scroll through numerous pages to view the results. Alternatively, you could code more complex mechanisms to enable users to page back and forth between pages of tables. This might be warranted for some applications; however, for simple applications, it's often sufficient to display the results in a scrollable selection list. Figure 19.10 illustrates how nicely you can format database results from the simple pubs query on-the-fly and present it to the user in scrollable list format. This output is generated by the following ACTION attribute that was specified in the form:

```
<form
 action="http://dkittel.clark.net:8080/cgi-win/pubs_optlist.exe"
 method="POST">
```

The formatting in Figure 19.10 was accomplished by using the HTML <SELECT> container tag and elements within the portion of the CGI program that renders HTML output. Listing 19.9 shows the portion of the pubs_optlist.exe CGI routine responsible for generating this output.

FIGURE 19.10.

The pubs *database query results formatted as a selection list.*

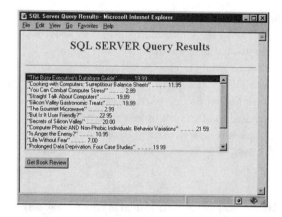

Listing 19.9. VB code used to generate the selection list shown in Figure 19.10.

```
Call HTMLFormStart("myForm", "POST",
➥"http://www.omniscient.com/cgi-win/book_review.exe")
        Call HTMLSelectStart("mySelectList", 12)
        Result = SqlResults(SqlConn)
        If Result = SUCCEED Then
            Do Until SqlNextRow(SqlConn) = NOMOREROWS
                title = SqlData(SqlConn, 1)
                title_id = SqlData(SqlConn, 2)
                price = SqlData(SqlConn, 3)
                Call HTMLSelectOption(title_id, Chr(34) + title + Chr(34) +
                ➥ " .......... " + price)
            Loop
            Call HTMLSelectEnd
            Send ("<P>")
            Call HTMLButton("SUBMIT", "Get Book Review", "htmBtn")
            Call HTMLFormEnd
        End If
```

This code spools to the results package the HTML code required to create a scrollable selection list. It then enters a loop that does the following:

■ Fetches a record of results data from the database.

■ Puts the data into an array.

■ Calls HTMLSelectOption to spool the necessary HTML tags specifying a list option and the option value. Notice that title IDs are used to supply values for the VALUE attribute of each entry in the list.

This looping continues until database results are exhausted, at which time the closing HTML tags necessary to end the selection list and the HTML document are printed. Notice that the CGI program was required to supply <FORM> container tags bracketing the portion of the generated HTML that would render the selection-list object. This code also relies on a set of simple HTML subprocedures developed to help make the program more modular and readable. These procedures simplify the process of creating HTML by enabling you to call routines that accept arrays of data used to create list option entries. These procedures, in turn, use the CGI32.BAS framework procedure Send() to spool results to the results package. The code for these subroutines is in the HTML.BAS module on the CD-ROM that accompanies this book; it also is shown in Listing 19.10.

Listing 19.10. HTML.BAS **subprocedures used to format database output into HTML scrollable selection lists.**

```
Sub HTMLFormStart(fname, method, action)
    Send ("<FORM name=" + fname + " method=" + method + " action=" +
    ➥Chr(34) + action + Chr(34) + ">")
End Sub

Sub HTMLFormEnd()
    Send ("</FORM>")
End Sub

Sub HTMLSelectStart(sname, Size)
    Send ("<SELECT name=" + sname + " size=" + CStr(Size) + ">")
End Sub

Sub HTMLSelectOption(Value, optiontext)
    Send ("<OPTION value=" + Value + ">" + optiontext + "</OPTION>")
End Sub

Sub HTMLSelectEnd()
    Send ("</SELECT>")
End Sub
```

Once again, this is a simple example, but it illustrates some key points. You can save screen real estate by presenting results in a selection list. You can save users some effort by not requiring them to scroll several pages. Additionally, you might save yourself work by not having to code paging applications. You can develop CGI routines that can be used to dynamically create secondary forms based on the results of your users' queries. This yields a type of dynamism to your applications that is impossible to achieve with hard-coded static forms. You easily can modify this example to perform additional manipulation of the results data, to create pop-up menus or multiple selection-list objects, and so on.

Generating Database Output Formatted as Lists of Hypertext Links

Sometimes it's only necessary to provide a minimal response to an initial database query with the idea that the user will narrow her search for information based on the results of that initial query. In this case, it might be sufficient to display database results as a list of hypertext links that the user can click to obtain more information about the subject listed. These links can be references to other HTML documents, data of a variety of MIME types, or a CGI routine that performs some desired action.

Figure 19.11 illustrates how you can format database results from the simple pubs query on-the-fly and present it to the user as a list of hypertext links. In this example, the user can click a link to obtain additional information about the book title of interest. This output is generated by the following ACTION attribute that was specified in the form:

```
<form
 action="http://dkittel.clark.net:8080/cgi-win/pubs_links.exe"
 method="POST">
```

FIGURE 19.11.

The pubs *database query results formatted as a list of hypertext links.*

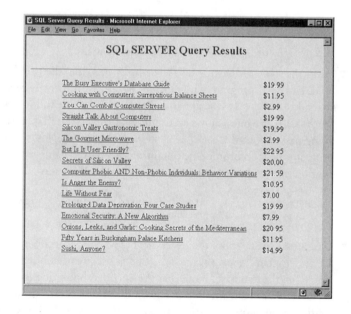

The formatting in Figure 19.11 was accomplished by using the HTML `<A HREF>` anchor container tag within the portion of the CGI program that renders HTML output. Listing 19.11 shows the portion of the `pubs_links.exe` CGI routine responsible for generating this output.

Listing 19.11. VB code used to generate the formatted list of hypertext links seen in Figure 19.11.

```
Result = SqlResults(SqlConn)
        If Result = SUCCEED Then
            Send ("<center>")
            Call HTMLTableStart("80", "0", "", "")
            h_array(0) = "Title"
            h_array(1) = "Price"
            Do Until SqlNextRow(SqlConn) = NOMOREROWS
                title = SqlData(SqlConn, 1)
                title_id = SqlData(SqlConn, 2)
                price = "$" + SqlData(SqlConn, 3)
                d_array(0) = HTMLLink(base_url + book_review_cgi +
                ➥title_id, title)
                d_array(1) = price
                Call HTMLTableDataRow("left", 2, d_array)
            Loop
            Call HTMLTableEnd
            Send ("</center>")
        End If
```

In this example, a loop is entered that does the following:

■ Fetches a record of results data from the database.

■ Performs some formatting on the data. In this case, the title ID is used with a base URL and CGI program name (`book_review.exe`) to create text for a hypertext link that adds a QUERY_STRING appended to the URL. The following code snippet generated by the CGI program shows an example of this. Note that, because information is being passed with the QUERY_STRING instead of by the POST method, the win-cgi CGI program must accommodate obtaining this passed value by reading the appropriate portion of the profile (.INI) file created by the Web server.

```
<TD align=left>
<A HREF="http://www.omniscient.com/cgi-win/book_review.exe?BU1032">
 The Busy Executive's Database Guide</A></TD>
<TD align=left>$19.99</TD>
```

■ Calls HTMLLink to spool the necessary HTML tags specifying an <A HREF> reference to a CGI program (book_review.exe) that subsequently obtains and returns this information from the database. Note that the encoded book title is appended to the URL and is passed via the GET method to the CGI routine. Note also that the HTML table routines from a previous example were used so that the links could be displayed in a nicely formatted style.

This looping continues until database results are exhausted, at which time the closing HTML tags necessary to end the selection list and the HTML document are supplied. This code also relies on a simple HTML subprocedure developed to help make the program more modular and readable. This procedure simplifies the process of creating HTML by enabling you to call a routine that accepts data used to create hyperlinks. This procedure, in turn, uses the CGI32.BAS framework procedure Send() to spool results to the results package. The code for this subroutine is in the HTML.BAS module on the CD-ROM that accompanies this book and is shown in the following snippet:

```
Function HTMLLink(href, linktext)
  HTMLLink = "<A HREF=" + Chr(34) + href + Chr(34) + "> " + linktext + "</A>"
End Function
```

Generating Database Output Formatted as a Set of <FORM> Checkboxes

Figure 19.12 illustrates how you can format database results from the simple pubs query on-the-fly and present it to the user as a form with a set of form checkbox objects. In this example, the user can click a box or boxes and then click the Submit button to see book reviews about the book titles of interest. This output is generated by the following ACTION attribute that was specified in the form:

```
<form
 action="http://dkittel.clark.net:8080/cgi-win/pubs_cbox.exe"
 method="POST">
```

FIGURE 19.12.

The pubs *database query results formatted as a set of checkboxes.*

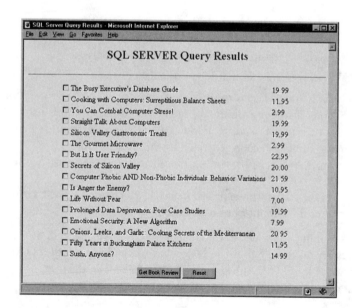

The formatting in Figure 19.12 was accomplished by using the HTML <INPUT> tag within the portion of the CGI program that renders HTML output. Listing 19.12 shows the portion of the pubs_cbox.exe CGI routine responsible for generating this output.

Listing 19.12. VB code used to generate the formatted set of checkboxes shown in Figure 19.12.

```
Call HTMLFormStart("myForm", "POST",
➥"http://www.omniscient.com/cgi-win/book_review.exe")
        Result = SqlResults(SqlConn)
        If Result = SUCCEED Then
            Send ("<center>")
            Call HTMLTableStart("80", "0", "", "")
            Do Until SqlNextRow(SqlConn) = NOMOREROWS
                title = SqlData(SqlConn, 1)
                title_id = SqlData(SqlConn, 2)
                price = SqlData(SqlConn, 3)
                d_array(0) = HTMLCheckBox("cb" + title_id, title_id,
                ➥title, " ")
                d_array(1) = price
                Call HTMLTableDataRow("left", 2, d_array)
            Loop
            Call HTMLTableEnd
            Send ("<P>")
            Call HTMLButton("SUBMIT", "Get Book Review", "htmSubmitBtn")
            Call HTMLButton("RESET", "Reset", "htmResetBtn")
            Send ("</center>")
        End If
```

In this example, a loop is entered that does the following:

■ Fetches a record of results data from the database.

■ Performs some formatting on the data.

■ Calls HTMLCheckBox to spool the necessary HTML tags specifying an <INPUT> tag with a TYPE=checkbox attribute for each title returned. Notice also that the title and price are concatenated to create unique NAME and VALUE attribute values as shown in the following snippet of code generated by the CGI routine:

```
<TD align=left><INPUT type=checkbox name=cbBU1032 value=BU1032> The Busy
➥ Executive's Database Guide</TD>
```

These values will be passed in *name=value* pairs (to the CGI routine book_review.exe) after the Submit button is clicked.

This looping continues until database results are exhausted, at which time the HTML tags necessary to render Submit and Reset buttons and to close the HTML document are supplied. The code for HTML subroutines used is available in the HTML.BAS module on the CD-ROM that accompanies this book.

Creating Graphical Database Output Presentations Dynamically

In this chapter, you have seen some fairly powerful methods for dynamically creating presentations of database results. Many times, however, simply giving users access to raw database information, no matter how nicely formatted, does not ensure that the reader will make sense of the overall content. Providing a graphical representation of that same data, however, certainly can make understanding it far easier for the reader. In addition, a visual representation of the information tends to hold the reader's interest far longer than plain text.

The old adage *A picture is worth a thousand words* holds true in many cases when trying to make sense of large, often complex, datasets. Consider the daily stock information in your local newspaper. Staring at that jumble of stock prices and trending information can cause the most steadfast individual to become disinterested in the data content. When you present that same data in a graphical form, such as a bar graph or a pie chart, however, the reader instantly gains a better understanding of the meaning of the data. This is the power of data visualization, and it's not difficult for you to tap into this power. In the remainder of this chapter, you'll explore a comprehensive example that illustrates how to significantly improve your presentations by adding ActiveX controls (in particular, the Chart and ComboBox controls) and VBScripts that use many of the same CGI techniques you've learned so far. Figure 19.13 shows a bar chart (one of the many styles possible) generated by using the Microsoft Chart control.

FIGURE 19.13.

A simple bar chart generated by using the Microsoft ActiveX Chart *control.*

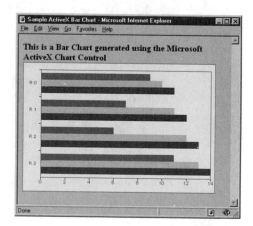

The Microsoft Chart Control

The Microsoft ActiveX Chart control enables you to present data in graphical formats such as pie charts, bar charts, area charts, and line graphs. You can add this control to your Web applications in the same manner as any other ActiveX control. The Microsoft Chart control enables you to present data by using the following chart styles:

- Pie
- Point
- Line
- Area
- Bar

■ Column

■ Stocks

Unlike many ActiveX controls, the Chart control has no events and only two methods. These methods follow:

■ AboutBox: Displays the About dialog box for the chart.

■ Reload: Forces the data specified in the URL property to be downloaded and read again (see Table 19.1).

Even though it has no events and only two methods, the Chart control has many properties that enable developers to control the chart's appearance onscreen. Table 19.1 summarizes the many properties you can set explicitly by using OBJECT parameters or VBScript code.

Table 19.1. Microsoft Chart control properties.

Property	Function
BackStyle	Sets the background according to the following values: Transparent: 0 Opaque: 1
ChartType	Specifies the type of chart you want. The supported chart styles and their corresponding property values follow: Simple pie: 0 Pie with wedge out: 1 Simple point chart: 2 Stacked point chart: 3 Full point chart: 4 Simple line chart: 5 Stacked line chart: 6 Full line chart: 7 Simple area chart: 8 Stacked area chart: 9 Full area chart: 10 Simple column chart: 11 Stacked column chart: 12 Full column chart: 13 Simple bar chart: 14 Stacked bar chart: 15 Full bar chart: 16 HLC stock chart: 17 HLC stock chart WSJ: 18 OHLC stock chart: 19 OHLC stock chart WSJ: 20

Property	Function
ColorScheme	Specifies which set of five predefined colors (used to fill regions) you want to use. Possible values are 0, 1, 2, 3, and 4.
Columns	Specifies the number of columns in the data series.
DataItem	Specifies data values identified by the RowIndex and ColumnIndex properties. To set data values, the RowIndex and ColumnIndex properties first must be set to reference the data point. To specify a value of 7 for row 3, column 2, for example, set the RowIndex property to 3; the ColumnIndex property to 2; and the DataItem property value to 7.
DisplayLegend	Determines whether a legend is displayed by specifying one of these values: Hide legend: 0 Show legend: 1
GridPlacement	Determines how grids are drawn according to these settings: Gridlines in the background (under chart): 0 Gridlines in the foreground (over chart): 1
HorizontalGrid, VerticalGrid	Specifies horizontal and vertical grids.

PARAM tags	Specifies the data values for the chart. For example,
	`<PARAM NAME="Data[0][0]" VALUE="9">`
	`<PARAM NAME="Data[0][1]" VALUE="10">`
	`<PARAM NAME="Data[0][2]" VALUE="11">`
	`<PARAM NAME="Data[1][0]" VALUE="7">`
	`<PARAM NAME="Data[1][1]" VALUE="11">`
	`<PARAM NAME="Data[1][2]" VALUE="12">`

RowIndex, ColumnIndex	Specifies the row and column indexes; used with the DataItem property.
RowName, ColumnName	Used with the RowIndex and ColumnIndex properties to specify a name for the row and column. These names are used in legends and labels.
Rows	Specifies the number of rows in the data series.
Scale	Determines the percentage scaling factor. The default is 100 percent scaling. Valid values are in the range of 1 to 100.
URL	Specifies a URL to a data file used to populate the chart.

The use of most of these control properties is demonstrated in the example in later sections of this chapter, with the exception of reading data from a file by using the URL property. Additional information on this and other properties is available from the online developer's reference that accompanies VB 5.

You can place the Chart control into your HTML or HTML layouts simply by using the OBJECT tag. The example in Listing 19.13, generated by using the ActiveX Control Pad, illustrates how a control for a bar chart might look in your HTML code. You saw the results of this code in Figure 19.13.

Listing 19.13. Creating a bar chart.

```
<OBJECT ID="iechart1" WIDTH=412 HEIGHT=269
 CLASSID="CLSID:FC25B780-75BE-11CF-8B01-444553540000">
    <PARAM NAME="_ExtentX" VALUE="10901">
    <PARAM NAME="_ExtentY" VALUE="7117">
    <PARAM NAME="Rows" VALUE="4">
    <PARAM NAME="Columns" VALUE="3">
    <PARAM NAME="ChartType" VALUE="14">
    <PARAM NAME="Data[0][0]" VALUE="9">
    <PARAM NAME="Data[0][1]" VALUE="10">
    <PARAM NAME="Data[0][2]" VALUE="11">
    <PARAM NAME="Data[1][0]" VALUE="7">
    <PARAM NAME="Data[1][1]" VALUE="11">
    <PARAM NAME="Data[1][2]" VALUE="12">
    <PARAM NAME="Data[2][0]" VALUE="6">
    <PARAM NAME="Data[2][1]" VALUE="12">
    <PARAM NAME="Data[2][2]" VALUE="13">
    <PARAM NAME="Data[3][0]" VALUE="11">
    <PARAM NAME="Data[3][1]" VALUE="13">
    <PARAM NAME="Data[3][2]" VALUE="14">
    <PARAM NAME="HorizontalAxis" VALUE="0">
    <PARAM NAME="VerticalAxis" VALUE="0">
    <PARAM NAME="hgridStyle" VALUE="0">
    <PARAM NAME="vgridStyle" VALUE="0">
    <PARAM NAME="ColorScheme" VALUE="0">
    <PARAM NAME="BackStyle" VALUE="1">
    <PARAM NAME="Scale" VALUE="100">
    <PARAM NAME="DisplayLegend" VALUE="0">
    <PARAM NAME="BackColor" VALUE="16777215">
    <PARAM NAME="ForeColor" VALUE="32768">
</OBJECT>
```

RESOURCE

Several third-party charting, graphing, and data-visualization controls are available (although most charge a fee). Several of these charts provide capabilities well beyond the relatively simple functions provided by the Microsoft Chart control. Many of these controls provide methods for reading data from a number of popular file formats, for example, and others provide additional chart styles and control over chart attributes such as size, colors, fonts, and labeling. Finally, data-visualization controls such as mapping controls and flowcharting controls, as well as data-processing controls for manipulating your data prior to presentation, can be obtained. The following Website provides an excellent starting point to find information on a variety of control types; it also enables you to download some trial versions:

`http://www.activeX.com/index.html`

The Publishers Sales Information Database Application

In the remaining sections of this chapter, you will explore a VB/CGI application that enables users to perform queries of sales information against the pubs database supplied with Microsoft SQL Server. This application enables the user to perform the following types of queries:

- Get sales information by author last names
- Get sales information by book titles
- Get sales information by publishers
- Get sales information by stores

So far, you probably are familiar with this type of functionality. In fact, the basics of this functionality were covered in detail in Chapter 18. What is new about this example is the way in which results are presented after they are fetched from the database. This application enables users to view information retrieved in two ways:

- By number of books sold
- By total dollar sales

This information is presented in graphical format using the Microsoft Chart object presented in the previous section. This is accomplished by extending the techniques used to dynamically create HTML intrinsic objects to ActiveX controls. But that isn't all the functionality provided to the user! After the chart is presented to users, they can change the style of chart used to display the database query results, the type of grid, and the color scheme. This functionality is provided through the use of ActiveX ComboBox controls and VBScript, both of which are created dynamically and added to the HTML document returned to the user. You'll see the following tasks demonstrated in this example:

- Using the Microsoft Chart control to graphically present data returned from a user's database query.
- Using CGI to dynamically create ActiveX controls.

■ Using CGI to dynamically create VBScripts used to set the displayed chart's `RowNames`.

■ Using CGI to read VBScripts from a file and add them to the HTML document sent to the user. These scripts set the available options on `ComboBox` controls and handle events when users modify the chart's display attributes.

The `pubs_sales_info` Query Form

Figure 19.14 shows the `pubs_sales_info.htm` query form that enables users to retrieve various types of sales information from the `pubs` database. Listing 19.14 shows the code for this form, and Figure 19.15 shows the results of the query.

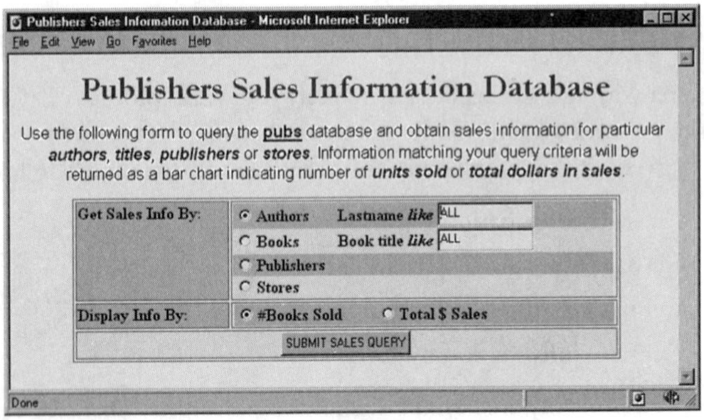

FIGURE 19.14.

The Publishers Sales Information Database query form.

Listing 19.14. Using `pubs_sales_info.htm` to create the database query form shown in Figure 19.14.

```
<html>
<head>
<title>Publishers Sales Information Database</title>
</head>

<body bgcolor="#FFFFFF">

<p align="center">
<font color="#0000FF" size="6" face="Garamond"><strong>
PublishersSales Information Database</strong></font></p>

<p align="center">
<font color="#000000" size="3" face="Arial">
Use the following form to query the <strong><u>pubs</u></strong>
database and obtain sales information for
➥ particular<em><strong>authors</strong></em>,
<em><strong>titles</strong></em>, <em><strong>publishers</strong></em>
or<em><strong>stores</strong></em>. Information matching your query criteria
➥ will be returned as a bar chart indicating number of <em><strong>units
➥ sold</strong></em> or <em><strong>total dollars in
➥ sales</strong></em>.</font></p>
```

```
<form action="http://dkittel.clark.net:8080/cgi-win/pubs_sales_info.exe"
method="POST" name="SALESINFO">
    <div align="center"><center><table border="1" width="85%"
    bordercolor="#808080">
        <tr>
            <td valign="top" width="20%" bgcolor="#CDCDCD">
            <strong>Get Sales Info By:</strong></td>
            <td width="50%"><div align="left"><table border="0"
             cellspacing="0" width="100%">
                <tr>
                    <td width="15%" bgcolor="#CDCDCD">
                    <input type="radio" checked name="QUERYBY"
                    value="AUTHOR"><strong>Authors </strong></td>
                    <td width="50%" bgcolor="#CDCDCD"><strong>Lastname</strong>
                    <em><strong>like </strong></em><input
                    type="text" size="15" name="LNAME"
                    value="ALL"></td>
                </tr>
                <tr>
                    <td width="15%" bgcolor="#EFEFEF">
                    <input type="radio" name="QUERYBY"
                     value="TITLE"><strong>Books</strong></td>
                    <td width="50%" bgcolor="#EFEFEF"><strong>Book
                    title</strong><em><strong> like</strong></em>
                    <input type="text" size="15" name="TITLE"
                    value="ALL"></td>
                </tr>
                <tr>
                    <td width="15%" bgcolor="#CDCDCD">
                    <input type="radio" name="QUERYBY"
                     value="PUBLISHER"><strong>Publishers</strong></td>
                    <td width="50%" bgcolor="#CDCDCD"> </td>
                </tr>
                <tr>
                    <td width="15%" bgcolor="#EFEFEF">
                    <input type="radio" name="QUERYBY"
                     value="STORE"><strong>Stores</strong></td>
                    <td width="50%" bgcolor="#EFEFEF"> </td>
                </tr>
            </table>
            </div></td>
        </tr>
        <tr>
            <td valign="top" width="20%" bgcolor="#CDCDCD">
             <strong>Display  Info By:</strong></td>
            <td><div align="center"><center><table border="0"
            cellspacing="0" width="100%">
                <tr>
                    <td width="30%" bgcolor="#CDCDCD">
                    <input type="radio" checked name="INFOBY"
                    value="QTY"><strong>#Books Sold</strong></td>
                    <td valign="top" width="50%" bgcolor="#CDCDCD">
                    <input type="radio" name="INFOBY" value="SALES">
                    <strong>Total $Sales</strong></td>
```

continues

Listing 19.14. continued

```
                    </tr>
                </table>
                </center></div></td>
        </tr>
        <tr>
            <td align="center" colspan="2" bgcolor="#EFEFEF">
            <input type="submit" name="SUBMIT"
            value="SUBMIT SALES QUERY"></td>
        </tr>
    </table>
    </center></div>
</form>
</body>
</html>
```

After a user submits a query using this form, the ACTION attribute specifies that the CGI program pubs_sales_info.exe be executed to perform the query and generate results. Figure 19.15 shows a sample of the results generated.

FIGURE 19.15.
Results of the database query shown in Figure 19.14.

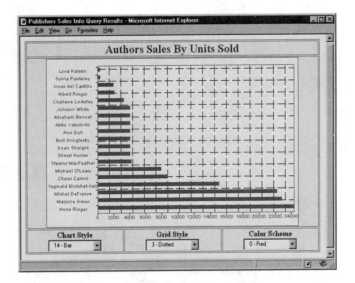

The pubs_sales_info CGI Program

The pubs_sales_info Windows CGI program is invoked after the user submits the pubs_sales_info query form discussed in the previous section. It is responsible for interfacing with the pubs database on behalf of a Web client, posting a query, and presenting the results of that query back to the user. This program uses functions from CGI32.BAS Visual Basic framework (presented in Chapter 18) to obtain form input and send information to the results package that the Web server sent to the user. The program also relies on the VB API to SQL Server (presented in Chapter 18). HTML convenience functions developed for examples earlier in this chapter also were used.

The pub_sales_info program was developed using VB 5 (although all code should work with VB 4 as well); it consists of a single form (Form1.frm) and several modules:

- ■ AxChart (AxChart.bas): Contains a function to create an ActiveX Chart control and code to create the VBScript procedures to add RowNames to the chart.
- ■ AxComboBox (AxComboBox.bas): Contains code to create an ActiveX ComboBox control.
- ■ CGI_Framework (CGI32.BAS): Contains all the functions necessary to handle form input and send HTML responses when developing Windows CGI-compliant programs.
- ■ cgi_pubs_chart (cgi_chart.bas): The main subprocedures (CGI_Main and Inter_Main) for creating pub_sales_info.exe.
- ■ htmlstuff (html.bas): Contains procedures and functions for creating HTML tables, forms, buttons, selection lists, and checkboxes. Also contains code for the SendVBScript procedure used to embed VB scripts in HTML documents sent to the user.
- ■ VBSQL (vbsql.bas): The SQL Server VB API package.

Listing 19.15 shows the code for the main module cgi_chart.bas—the CGI_Main() procedure required by Windows CGI and the CGI32.BAS framework.

Listing 19.15. cgi_chart.bas—the main module used to create the pubs_sales_info.exe Windows CGI program.

```
Option Explicit

    Dim Login
    Dim Result
    Dim SqlConn

Sub CGI_Main()

    Dim chartTitle

    Dim d_array(100) As String
    Dim h_array(100) As String
    Dim params(100, 2)
    Dim rownames(100)

    Dim ndx
    Dim numParams
    Dim numNames
```

continues

Listing 19.15. continued

```
' variables for forming query
Dim sqlDB As String
Dim sqlSelect As String
Dim sqlFrom As String
Dim sqlWhere As String
Dim sqlGroupBy As String
Dim sqlHaving As String
Dim sqlOrderBy As String
Dim sqlCmdString As String

' variables for handling form data
Dim bookTitle As String
Dim authorLName As String
Dim queryType As String
Dim InfoType As String

' variables for handling db results
Dim firstName
Dim lastName
Dim storeName
Dim storeID
Dim numSold
Dim title
Dim publisher

'Load (but don't show) the form containing the
'VBSQL.OCX control

Load Form1

SendHTMLStart

Send ("<HTML>")
Send ("<HEAD><TITLE>Publishers Sales Info Query Results</TITLE></HEAD>")

Send ("<body bgcolor=#FFFFFF>")

'Process form inputs and format the
'appropriate SQL query

queryType = GetSmallField("QUERYBY")
InfoType = GetSmallField("INFOBY")

Select Case queryType
    Case "AUTHOR"
        If InfoType = "QTY" Then
            sqlSelect = "SELECT authors.au_fname, authors.au_lname,
            ➥ Sum(titles.ytd_sales) "
            sqlOrderBy = " ORDER BY Sum(titles.ytd_sales)"
            chartTitle = "<H2 align=center><font color=#0000FF>Authors
            ➥ Sales By Units Sold</font></H2>"
        Else
            sqlSelect = "SELECT authors.au_fname, authors.au_lname,
            ➥ Sum(titles.ytd_sales*titles.price) "
```

```
            sqlOrderBy = " ORDER BY Sum(titles.ytd_sales*titles.price)"
            chartTitle = "<H2 align=center><font color=#0000FF>Authors
            ➥ Sales By Total Dollars (Thousands)</font></H2>"
        End If

        sqlFrom = " FROM authors, titleauthor, titles "
        sqlWhere = " WHERE titleauthor.au_id = authors.au_id AND
        ➥ titles.title_id = titleauthor.title_id "
        sqlGroupBy = " GROUP BY authors.au_fname, authors.au_lname"
        authorLName = GetSmallField("LNAME")

        If authorLName = "ALL" Then
            sqlHaving = " HAVING (authors.au_lname Like '%') "
        Else
            sqlHaving = " HAVING (authors.au_lname Like '%" +
            ➥ authorLName + "%') "
        End If

Case "TITLE"
    If InfoType = "QTY" Then
        sqlSelect = "SELECT titles.title, Sum(titles.ytd_sales) "
        sqlOrderBy = " ORDER BY Sum(titles.ytd_sales)"
        chartTitle = "<H2 align=center><font color=#0000FF>Book Sales
        ➥ By Units Sold</font></H2>"
    Else
        sqlSelect = "SELECT titles.title, Sum(titles.ytd_sales*price) "
        sqlOrderBy = " ORDER BY Sum(titles.ytd_sales*price) "
        chartTitle = "<H2 align=center><font color=#0000FF>Book Sales
        ➥ By Total Dollars (Thousands)</font></H2>"
    End If
    sqlFrom = " FROM titles "
    sqlWhere = " WHERE titles.price Is Not Null "
    sqlGroupBy = " GROUP BY titles.title "
    bookTitle = GetSmallField("TITLE")

    If bookTitle = "ALL" Then
        sqlHaving = " HAVING (titles.title Like '%') "
    Else
        sqlHaving = " HAVING (titles.title Like '%" + bookTitle + "%') "
    End If
Case "PUBLISHER"
    If InfoType = "QTY" Then
        sqlSelect = "SELECT publishers.pub_name, Sum(titles.ytd_sales) "
        sqlOrderBy = " "
        chartTitle = "<H2 align=center><font color=#0000FF>Publisher
        ➥ Sales By Units Sold (Thousands)</font></H2>"
    Else
        sqlSelect = "SELECT publishers.pub_name,
        ➥ Sum(titles.ytd_sales*price) "
        sqlOrderBy = " "
        chartTitle = "<H2 align=center><font color=#0000FF>Publisher
        ➥ Sales By Total Dollars (Thousands)</font></H2>"
```

continues

Listing 19.15. continued

```
                End If
                sqlFrom = " FROM publishers, titles "
                sqlWhere = " WHERE  titles.pub_id = publishers.pub_id AND
                ➥ ((titles.ytd_sales Is Not Null)) "
                sqlGroupBy = " GROUP BY publishers.pub_name "
                sqlHaving = " "
        Case "STORE"
            If InfoType = "QTY" Then
                sqlSelect = "SELECT stores.stor_name, stores.stor_id,
                ➥ Sum(sales.qty)"
                sqlOrderBy = " ORDER BY Sum(sales.qty)"
                chartTitle = "<H2 align=center><font color=#0000FF>Stores
                ➥ Sales By Units Sold</font></H2>"
            Else
                sqlSelect = "SELECT stores.stor_name, stores.stor_id,
                ➥ Sum(sales.qty*titles.price)"
                sqlOrderBy = " ORDER BY Sum(sales.qty*titles.price)"
                chartTitle = "<H2 align=center><font color=#0000FF>Stores
                ➥ Sales By Total Dollars</font></H2>"
            End If
            sqlFrom = " FROM sales, stores, titles "
            sqlWhere = " WHERE sales.stor_id = stores.stor_id AND
            ➥ titles.title_id = sales.title_id "
            sqlGroupBy = " GROUP BY stores.stor_name, stores.stor_id "
            sqlHaving = " "

    End Select

    sqlCmdString = sqlSelect + sqlFrom + sqlWhere + sqlGroupBy +
    ➥ sqlHaving + sqlOrderBy

    'Initialize DB-Library
    If SqlInit() = "" Then
        Send ("<EM><B>The program encountered an error</B></EM><BR>")
        Send ("<EM><B>DB-Library was not properly initialized</B></EM>")
    Else
        'Get a Login record and set guest login attributes.
        Login = SqlLogin()
        Result = SqlSetLUser(Login, "Guest")
        Result = SqlSetLPwd(Login, "c0rnd0gs")
        Result = SqlSetLApp(Login, "webguest_pubs")

        'Get a connection for communicating with SQL Server.
        SqlConn = SqlOpen(Login, "OMNISCIENT")

        'Put the command into the command buffer.
        Result = SqlCmd(SqlConn, sqlCmdString)

        'Send the command to SQL Server and start execution.
        Result = SqlExec(SqlConn)
        Result = SqlResults(SqlConn)

        If Result = SUCCEED Then
            numParams = 0
            Call HTMLTableStart("100", "1", "#808080", "#EFEFEF")
            Do Until SqlNextRow(SqlConn) = NOMOREROWS
```

```
    Select Case queryType
        Case "AUTHOR"
            firstName = SqlData(SqlConn, 1)
            lastName = SqlData(SqlConn, 2)
            numSold = SqlData(SqlConn, 3)
            rownames(numParams) = firstName + " " + lastName
            params(numParams, 0) = "data[" + CStr(numParams) +
            ➥ "][0]"
            If InfoType = "QTY" Then
                params(numParams, 1) = CStr(CInt(numSold))
            Else
                params(numParams, 1) = CStr(CInt(numSold / 1000))
            End If
        Case "TITLE"
            title = SqlData(SqlConn, 1)
            numSold = SqlData(SqlConn, 2)
            rownames(numParams) = Left(title, 10) + "..."
            params(numParams, 0) = "data[" + CStr(numParams) +
            ➥ "][0]"
            If InfoType = "QTY" Then
                params(numParams, 1) = CStr(CInt(numSold))
            Else
                params(numParams, 1) = CStr(CInt(numSold / 1000))
            End If
        Case "PUBLISHER"
            publisher = SqlData(SqlConn, 1)
            numSold = SqlData(SqlConn, 2)
            rownames(numParams) = Left(publisher, 8) + "..."
            params(numParams, 0) = "data[" + CStr(numParams) +
            ➥ "][0]"
            params(numParams, 1) = CStr(CInt(numSold / 1000))
        Case "STORE"
            storeName = SqlData(SqlConn, 1)
            storeID = SqlData(SqlConn, 2)
            numSold = SqlData(SqlConn, 3)
            rownames(numParams) = Left(storeName, 15) + "..."
            params(numParams, 0) = "data[" + CStr(numParams) +
            ➥ "][0]"
            params(numParams, 1) = CStr(numSold)
    End Select

    numParams = numParams + 1

Loop

numNames = numParams
params(numParams, 0) = "Rows"
params(numParams, 1) = CStr(numParams)
numParams = numParams + 1
params(numParams, 0) = "Columns"
params(numParams, 1) = "1"
numParams = numParams + 1

Send ("<TR><TH COLSPAN=3>" + chartTitle + "</TH></TR>")
Send ("<TR><TD align=center COLSPAN=3>" +
➥ MakeAxChart("pubsSalesChart", numParams, params, "AxChartLoad",
➥ numNames, rownames) + "</TD></TR>")
```

continues

Listing 19.15. continued

```
          Send ("<TR><TD align=center><B>Chart Style</B><BR>" +
          ➥ MakeAxComboBox("styleCBox") + "</TD>")
          Send ("<TD align=center><B>Grid Style</B><BR>" +
          ➥ MakeAxComboBox("gridCBox") + "</TD>")
          Send ("<TD align=center><B>Color Scheme</B><BR>" +
          ➥ MakeAxComboBox("colorCBox") + "</TD></TR>")

          Call HTMLTableEnd

      End If

  'Close connection and exit program.
      SqlExit
      SqlWinExit

  End If

  'Unload the form containing VBSQL.OCX control

  Unload Form1

  ' add scripts to handle user interactions with
  ' combo box controls
  SendVBScript ("D:\WebSite\htdocs\pubs_sales_scripts.txt")

  'Now return to complete HTTP
  Send ("</BODY></HTML>")

End Sub

Sub Inter_Main()
    MsgBox "This is a Windows CGI program"
End Sub
```

The `pub_sales_info` Windows CGI program does the following:

■ Extracts user input (using `GetSmallField`) to the form from the contents sent to the server and stored in the profile file.

■ Determines the type of query (by author, by title, by publisher, or by store) as well as the type of results to display (by number of books sold or by total dollars sales).

■ Determines whether the default (ALL) for author last name or book title was replaced with a user-specified value.

■ Formulates a SQL query string (based on user input of query type, query restrictions, and type of results to be displayed) to send to SQL Server. For the query settings in the form in Figure 19.14, for example, the following SQL command string is created:

```
SELECT authors.au_fname, authors.au_lname, Sum(titles.ytd_sales)
FROM authors, titleauthor, titles
WHERE titleauthor.au_id = authors.au_id AND
      titles.title_id = titleauthor.title_id
GROUP BY authors.au_fname, authors.au_lname
HAVING (authors.au_lname Like '%')
ORDER BY Sum(titles.ytd_sales)
```

■ Formulates a title string for the displayed results.

■ Uses VB API functions to obtain a connection (as guest) to the pubs database and submit the previously constructed query string for execution.

■ Starts an HTML table (using functions from the previously presented HTML.BAS module) in which an ActiveX Chart object and ComboBox controls will be added as data items.

■ Enters a loop that uses VB API functions to fetch query results until no more rows are available. As each row of results is retrieved, the results are formatted in a manner dependent on the type of query posed and the type of results (that is by quantity or dollar sales) specified. Formatted results are added to two arrays that are passed to the MakeAxChart function after the loop finishes. One array holds data used to populate the chart, and the other is a list of RowNames used to add labels to the chart.

■ Calls the MakeAxChart and MakeAxComboBox functions to create the chart to display the data retrieved and to create the ComboBox controls that enable the user to modify the chart's display attributes. These objects are created as table data elements to present a nicely formatted page (like those in Figures 19.16 through 19.19).

■ Closes the connection to the database and unloads the form that contains the VB API OCX control.

■ Calls the SendVBScript procedure to send "canned" VBScripts for this chart display to the results package that will be sent by the server to the Web client.

Figures 19.16 through 19.19 illustrate the results from various user queries with different chart-style modifications selected by the user after the results are displayed. These figures demonstrate the range of output that can be generated dynamically by pubs_sales_info.exe, as well as many of the types of user selectable settings that can be applied after the results are returned. Once again, ActiveX controls and VBScript have provided a powerful mechanism for dynamically creating interactive page content—in this case, from user-specific database query results.

FIGURE 19.16.

Results of the database query requesting sales information by book (with the word computer *in the title).*

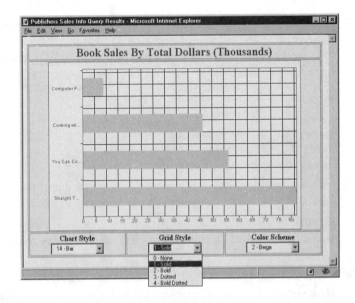

FIGURE 19.17.

Results of the database query requesting sales information by publisher and presented by number of units sold.

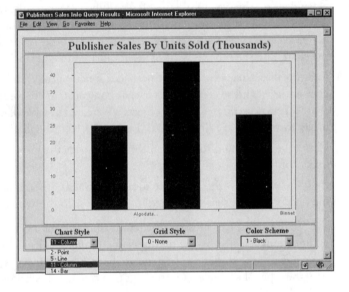

FIGURE 19.18.

Results of the database query requesting sales information by store and presented by number of units sold.

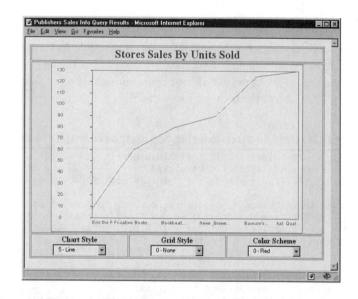

FIGURE 19.19.

Results of the database query requesting sales information by all book titles and presented by number of units sold.

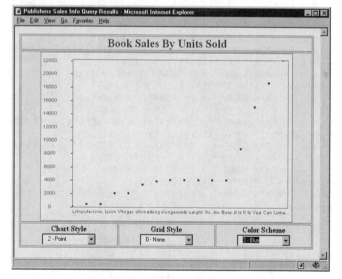

The MakeAxChart, MakeAxComboBox, and SendVBScript Routines

This section presents a few details about pertinent routines in the AxChart, AxComboBox, and htmlstuff modules. Material covered in earlier sections is not repeated here (such as HTML convenience routines for creating tables and HTML intrinsic controls).

The MakeAxChart Function

The MakeAxChart function is part of the AxChart module and is used to create an instance of a bar chart object with some attributes hard-coded, such as the size. Notice that you could modify this function to avoid the use of hard codes and enable most properties to be set at runtime. Listing 19.16 shows the code for MakeAxChart.

Listing 19.16. Using the MakeAxChart function to create an instance of an ActiveX Chart control.

```
' Basic chart object attributes/values were
' generated using ActiveX Control Pad
' chart type 14 is a simple bar chart (n rows x 1 col per row)

Function MakeAxChart(id, nelements, params, subname, nnames, rownames)
    s = "<OBJECT id=" + Chr(34) + id + Chr(34) + "WIDTH=539 HEIGHT=352" + Chr(13)
    s = s + "CLASSID=" + Chr(34) + "CLSID:FC25B780-75BE-11CF-8B01-444553540000"
➥ + Chr(34) + ">" + Chr(13)
    s = s + "<PARAM NAME=" + Chr(34) + "_ExtentX" + Chr(34) + "VALUE=" + Chr(34)
➥ + "14261" + Chr(34) + ">" + Chr(13)
    s = s + "<PARAM NAME=" + Chr(34) + "_ExtentY" + Chr(34) + "VALUE=" + Chr(34)
➥ + "9313" + Chr(34) + ">" + Chr(13)
    s = s + "<PARAM NAME=" + Chr(34) + "ChartType" + Chr(34) + "VALUE=" +
➥ Chr(34) + "14" + Chr(34) + ">" + Chr(13)
    s = s + "<PARAM NAME=" + Chr(34) + "HorizontalAxis" + Chr(34) + "VALUE=" +
➥ Chr(34) + "0" + Chr(34) + ">" + Chr(13)
    s = s + "<PARAM NAME=" + Chr(34) + "VerticalAxis" + Chr(34) + "VALUE=" +
➥ Chr(34) + "0" + Chr(34) + ">" + Chr(13)
    s = s + "<PARAM NAME=" + Chr(34) + "hgridStyle" + Chr(34) + "VALUE=" +
➥ Chr(34) + "3" + Chr(34) + ">" + Chr(13)
    s = s + "<PARAM NAME=" + Chr(34) + "vgridStyle" + Chr(34) + "VALUE=" +
➥ Chr(34) + "3" + Chr(34) + ">" + Chr(13)
    s = s + "<PARAM NAME=" + Chr(34) + "ColorScheme" + Chr(34) + "VALUE=" +
➥ Chr(34) + "0" + Chr(34) + ">" + Chr(13)
    s = s + "<PARAM NAME=" + Chr(34) + "BackStyle" + Chr(34) + "VALUE=" +
➥ Chr(34) + "1" + Chr(34) + ">" + Chr(13)
    s = s + "<PARAM NAME=" + Chr(34) + "Scale" + Chr(34) + "VALUE=" + Chr(34) +
➥ "100" + Chr(34) + ">" + Chr(13)
    s = s + "<PARAM NAME=" + Chr(34) + "DisplayLegend" + Chr(34) + "VALUE=" +
➥ Chr(34) + "1" + Chr(34) + ">" + Chr(13)
    s = s + "<PARAM NAME=" + Chr(34) + "BackColor" + Chr(34) + "VALUE=" +
➥ Chr(34) + "16777215" + Chr(34) + ">" + Chr(13)
    s = s + "<PARAM NAME=" + Chr(34) + "ForeColor" + Chr(34) + "VALUE=" +
➥ Chr(34) + "32768" + Chr(34) + ">" + Chr(13)

    ' build rest of params using input array here

    ndx = 0
    For ndx = 0 To (nelements - 1) Step 1
        s = s + "<param name=" + Chr(34) + params(ndx, 0) + Chr(34)
        s = s + " value=" + Chr(34) + params(ndx, 1) + Chr(34) + ">" + Chr(13)
    Next
    s = s + "</OBJECT>" + Chr(13) + Chr(13)

    ' Build script that sets row names on graph when window loads
    ' (this assumes n rows x 1 col per)
```

```
    vbs = "<SCRIPT Language=" + Chr(34) + "VBScript" + Chr(34) + ">" + Chr(13)
    vbs = vbs + "Sub " + subname + Chr(13)

    vbs = vbs + id + ".ColumnIndex=0" + Chr(13)

    ndx = 0
    For ndx = 0 To (nnames - 1) Step 1
        vbs = vbs + id + ".RowIndex=" + Chr(34) + CStr(ndx) + Chr(34) + Chr(13)
        vbs = vbs + id + ".RowName=" + Chr(34) + rownames(ndx) + Chr(34) + Chr(13)
    Next
    vbs = vbs + "End Sub" + Chr(13)
    vbs = vbs + "</SCRIPT>" + Chr(13) + Chr(13)

    MakeAxChart = s + vbs

End Function
```

MakeAxChart takes a 2D array of param names and values used to further specify the data to be displayed by the chart. Additionally, the function takes a 1D array of row names used to dynamically create an inline VBScript at runtime (the name of the script also is specified by a passed-in parameter). This script is used to set the RowName labels displayed on the chart. As you will see shortly, this script is called from a window_onLoad() procedure when the window initially is loaded in the client's browser. MakeAxChart returns a string that fully specifies a chart object that can be embedded into an HTML document. The base chart object used in this function first was created by using the ActiveX Control Pad. Code generated by this tool then was cut and pasted into this VB function.

The MakeAxComboBox Function

The MakeAxChart function is part of the AxComboBox module and is used to create an instance of a ComboBox object with some attributes hard-coded (such as the size). You can modify this function to avoid the use of hard codes and enable most properties to be set at runtime. Listing 19.17 shows the code for MakeAxComboBox.

Listing 19.17. Using the MakeAxComboBox function to create an instance of an ActiveX ComboBox control.

```
Function MakeAxComboBox(id)
    s = "<OBJECT id=" + Chr(34) + id + Chr(34) + "WIDTH=115 HEIGHT=24" + Chr(13)
    s = s + "CLASSID=" + Chr(34) + "CLSID:8BD21D30-EC42-11CE-9E0D-00AA006002F3"
    ➥ + Chr(34) + ">" + Chr(13)
    s = s + "<PARAM NAME=" + Chr(34) + "VariousPropertyBits" + Chr(34) +
    ➥ "VALUE=" + Chr(34) + "746604571" + Chr(34) + ">" + Chr(13)
    s = s + "<PARAM NAME=" + Chr(34) + "DisplayStyle" + Chr(34) + "VALUE=" +
    ➥ Chr(34) + "3" + Chr(34) + ">" + Chr(13)
    s = s + "<PARAM NAME=" + Chr(34) + "Size" + Chr(34) + "VALUE=" + Chr(34) +
```

continues

Listing 19.17. continued

```
➡ "3037;635" + Chr(34) + ">" + Chr(13)
s = s + "<PARAM NAME=" + Chr(34) + "MatchEntry" + Chr(34) + "VALUE=" +
➡ Chr(34) + "1" + Chr(34) + ">" + Chr(13)
s = s + "<PARAM NAME=" + Chr(34) + "ShowDropButtonWhen" + Chr(34) + "VALUE="
➡ + Chr(34) + "2" + Chr(34) + ">" + Chr(13)
s = s + "<PARAM NAME=" + Chr(34) + "FontCharSet" + Chr(34) + "VALUE=" +
➡ Chr(34) + "0" + Chr(34) + ">" + Chr(13)
s = s + "<PARAM NAME=" + Chr(34) + "FontPitchAndFamily" + Chr(34) + "VALUE="
➡ + Chr(34) + "2" + Chr(34) + ">" + Chr(13)
s = s + "</OBJECT>" + Chr(13) + Chr(13)

    MakeAxComboBox = s

End Function
```

MakeAxComboBox takes a single parameter that is used to set the object's ID. Note that no other properties associated with the object are set at this time. Instead, CGI_Main calls the SendVBScript procedure to embed VBScript that is invoked when the document is loaded. It is here that options and the initial settings of the ComboBox objects are set. MakeAxComboBox returns a string that fully specifies a ComboBox object that can be embedded into an HTML document. The base ComboBox object used in this function first was created by using the ActiveX Control Pad. Code generated by this tool then was cut and pasted into this VB function.

The SendVBScript Procedure

SendVBScript simply reads a text file that contains VBScript code that needs to be embedded into an HTML document. It then uses the CGI32.BAS Send() function to forward this to the response package that is returned to the Web client browser. Listing 19.18 shows the code for SendVBScript.

Listing 19.18. Using the SendVBScript procedure to read a file containing VBScript code and embedding the script into an HTML document.

```
Sub SendVBScript(filepath)
    Open filepath For Input As #11
    Do While Not EOF(11)              ' loop while not end-of-file
        Line Input #11, LineOfText    ' read line into variable
        Send (LineOfText)             ' send string to results package
    Loop
    Close #11
End Sub
```

The pubs_sales_info.exe CGI program uses this procedure to read the pubs_sales_script.txt file and send its contents to the response package. Listing 19.19 shows the contents of pubs_sales_script.txt.

Listing 19.19. Using the `pubs_sales_script.txt` file, which contains VBScript code to be embedded in the HTML document returned to a user.

```
<SCRIPT LANGUAGE="VBSCRIPT">
<!--

Sub window_onLoad()

    styleCBox.AddItem "2 - Point"
    styleCBox.AddItem "5 - Line"
    styleCBox.AddItem "11 - Column"
    styleCBox.AddItem "14 - Bar"
    styleCBox.Text="14 - Bar"

    gridCBox.AddItem "0 - None"
    gridCBox.AddItem "1 - Solid"
    gridCBox.AddItem "2 - Bold"
    gridCBox.AddItem "3 - Dotted"
    gridCBox.AddItem "4 - Bold Dotted"
    gridCBox.Text = "3 - Dotted"

    colorCBox.AddItem "0 - Red"
    colorCBox.AddItem "1 - Black"
    colorCBox.AddItem "2 - Beige"
    colorCBox.AddItem "3 - Blue"
    colorCBox.AddItem "4 - Green"
    colorCBox.Text = "0 - Red"

    ' call the vbscript that was dynamically added to the
    ' chart object used to plot pubs sales data

    call AxChartLoad

End Sub


Sub colorCBox_Change()
    pubsSalesChart.ColorScheme = CInt(Left(colorCBox.Text, 1))
End Sub

Sub gridCBox_Change()
    pubsSalesChart.hgridStyle = CInt(Left(gridCBox.Text, 1))
    pubsSalesChart.vgridStyle = CInt(Left(gridCBox.Text, 1))
End Sub

Sub styleCBox_Change()
    pubsSalesChart.ChartType = CInt(Left(styleCBox.Text, 2))
End Sub

-->
</SCRIPT>
```

Once embedded into the HTML document, this code is invoked by the windows `onLoad` event. Therefore, when the document is loaded by the client browser, this code is executed and is used to set options in the `ComboBoxes` that were created to enable users to modify the attributes of the chart that display results of the users' database queries. Additionally, the code defines other VBScript procedures used to handle interactions with the ComboBoxes. A change in setting on the styleCBox ComboBox, for example, results in the chart style being changed onscreen. Finally, note the call to AxChartLoad. This is the VBScript procedure name passed to MakeAxChart and used to generate an inline script for setting the row names displayed on the charts. Including it here ensures that the row names are set when the document is loaded by the client browser.

A Few Closing Comments about This Example

Here are a few closing comments about this application:

■ The ActiveX Control Pad and FrontPage tools were used heavily to prototype controls used in this application. This saves a tremendous amount of typing and ensures that the code used to create ActiveX controls is correct.

■ A true application should include form validation on the client side. After all, that is one of the strengths of VBScript. Additionally, the VB CGI procedures should include more error handling. In both cases, these were left out to accentuate the actual working of the program.

■ You can easily modify all modules, functions, and procedures shown to add functionality required for your specific applications. Feel free to use this code as the basis for libraries that you build.

■ This application demonstrated the simple cases of querying information from a database. There is no reason why you can't apply the same techniques to applications that add information to your databases, however, to modify existing information or use advanced features such as stored procedures and triggers. You are strongly encouraged to study the functionality provided by the SQL Server VB API to learn more about what this interface enables you to do.

■ The techniques demonstrated in this chapter are in no way limited to charts and combo boxes. Using CGI, you can create dynamically anything that you can code by hand using objects. This means that you can take advantage of third-party controls, HTML layouts, and ActiveX controls you develop on your own to provide your users with incredibly dynamic and interactive interfaces to your databases and other applications.

Summary

After defining data, information, and an information presentation, this chapter provided an overview of the data types and formats you're likely to encounter. You next looked at using HTML 2.0 elements for data presentations. You examined information on using preformatted text, HTML-formatted text, inline graphics, and the <IMG> element and its attributes. Finally, using the <SELECT> list as a user-input form element and a data-presentation tool was explained.

Examples of HTML 3.2 data-presentation techniques were introduced. Using the <TABLE> element as a formatting tool was discussed in great detail. Extensions such as color, font size, and page backgrounds were discussed, with a focus on using them to enhance presentations. Extensions to the <IMG> element attributes also were presented. Examples showed how these extensions enable you to develop data presentations in which text wraps around inline graphics and images. This section closed with a brief mention of the new HTML 3.2 <FIG> container element.

After a brief summary of style guidelines for developing effective presentations, you jumped right into examples of how you can use CGI programs to dynamically create presentations of data fetched from your databases. These examples included generating HTML tables, hypertext links, and <FORM> elements such as selection lists and checkboxes. You learned that not only can you combine these techniques to produce nicely formatted data presentations, but that you also can use them to dynamically generate additional forms based on the results of a user's query.

The final section presented a sample application that illustrated how you can develop graphical, interactive presentations by using CGI programs to create ActiveX controls and VBScript on-the-fly. The techniques in this example included a number of VB modules that provide a powerful foundation you can use and expand on for developing your own applications.

20

The IIS Internet Database Connector (IDC)

by Mark Swank

The IIS Internet Database Connector is an ISAPI DLL that can provide a Web application access to database information through an associated ODBC driver. This chapter expands on the knowledge you gained in previous chapters and provides the fundamental information needed to begin building Web-based applications for accessing ODBC databases.

Using the Internet Database Connector

The IDC is an *Internet Server API* (ISAPI) DLL used to retrieve information from ODBC databases. The IDC translates queries into SQL statements by replacing SQL statement variables with user-input data, which is then passed to the respective database driver for processing, as shown in Figure 20.1.

> **NOTE**
>
> The associated file that provides the IDC ODBC access is HTTPODBC.DLL and is automatically installed with IIS.

FIGURE 20.1.
IDC access through HTTPODBC.

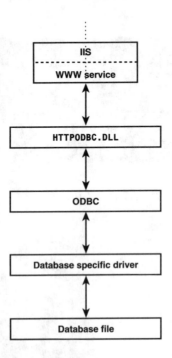

IDC uses simple ASCII text files with an .idc extension that contain such information as the data source, HTML extension files (.htx), SQL statements, and so on.

> **TIP**
>
> The latest release of Microsoft FrontPage 97 includes a wizard for generating the code required to build IDC result documents.

This section focuses on how to set up the proper IDC files and HTML extension files required to integrate database access into a WWW application.

Required IDC Data File Fields

All IDC (`.idc`) files must have three required fields in order to properly handle the retrieval and formatting of database information: `Datasource`, `SQLStatement`, and `Template`. Each of these fields is explained in this section.

Datasource

The `Datasource` field is the ODBC data source that identifies the database connection information specific to your application.

> **NOTE**
>
> The `Datasource` field used with the IDC requires that the ODBC resource be set up as a system DSN. System DSN capabilities were introduced under ODBC 2.5, which is included with Microsoft IIS.

If the DSN resource for a specific database is named `mydatabase`, for example, the IDC `Datasource` entry looks like this:

```
Datasource: mydatabase
```

SQLStatement

The `SQLStatement` field identifies the actual SQL query that will be executed by the IDC. Parameter values can be contained in `SQLStatement`. If used, parameter values must be enclosed in percent (%) characters. If a `SQLStatement` entry will span multiple lines, subsequent lines must begin with a plus (+) sign. Here's a sample `SQLStatement` field:

```
SQLStatement:
+ SELECT FirstName, LastName
+ FROM Employees, Orders
+ WHERE Employees.EmployeeId = Orders.EmployeeId
+ AND OrderId = '%orderid%'
```

Template

The `Template` field is the name of the HTML extension file that contains the normal HTML code with the extended database-definition information. The main Web page for an application might use the template filename `main.htx`, for example. The entry in the corresponding `.idc` file looks like this:

```
Template: main.htx
```

> **NOTE**
>
> By convention, template files use the filename extension `.htx` and generally use the same prefix as the corresponding `.idc` file (`main.idc` and `main.htx`, for example).

Optional IDC Data File Fields

Additional fields are available for inclusion in the IDC file. These fields contain information such as default parameters, caching expiration settings, maximum field sizes, maximum number of rows returned, username, password, required parameters, and content type. This section explains each of the optional fields.

Content Type

The `Content Type` field specifies the Multipurpose Internet Mail Extensions (MIME) type that the query will return. By default, the standard `text/html` MIME type is returned. The following code specifies the MIME type for a GIF image, for example:

```
Content Type: image/gif
```

DefaultParameters

The `DefaultParameters` field specifies default values for designated entries. You can use this field to specify column default values for table columns that are configured as `NOT NULL`, for example. A sample `DefaultParameters` field looks like this:

```
DefaultParameters: payment=creditcard
```

Expires

The `Expires` field specifies the number of seconds the IDC waits before refreshing a cached output page. For scenarios in which multiple identical queries are executed, the IDC can return the cached values without having to access the database.

> **NOTE**
>
> By default, the IDC does not cache output pages. It does so *only* when an Expires field is specified.

To have a document cached for one hour, for example, you can specify the following Expires field in the .idc file:

```
Expires: 3600
```

MaxFieldSize

The MaxFieldSize field specifies the maximum number of bytes allocated by the IDC for each field in the .idc file.

> **NOTE**
>
> The default field size is 8,192 bytes. If a query results in more bytes than allocated by the IDC MaxFieldSize field, subsequent data is truncated.

To specify a MaxFieldSize of 64,000 bytes, use the following syntax in the MaxFieldSize field entry:

```
MaxFieldSize: 64000
```

MaxRecords

The MaxRecords field specifies the maximum number of records the IDC returns for each user query.

> **CAUTION**
>
> The MaxRecords field has no default value. If the value is left unspecified, a single query could return as many as 4 billion records.

Take a look at a sample MaxRecords field entry that returns no more than 500 records:

```
MaxRecords: 500
```

ODBCOptions

The ODBCOptions field specifies any advanced options to be passed to the database-specific ODBC driver. When multiple options are specified, they are separated by a comma. Table 20.1 lists the advanced ODBC options available. A sample ODBCOptions entry looks like this:

```
ODBCOptions: SQL_ACCESS_MODE=1, SQL_MAX_ROWS=100, SQL_QUERY_TIMEOUT=60
```

Table 20.1. Advanced ODBC options.

Option	Value(s)	Description
SQL_ACCESS_MODE	0=read/write 1=read only	Determines whether updates to the database are allowed. Default=0
SQL_LOGIN_TIMEOUT	Integer	Specifies the number of seconds to wait for a response before returning an error message. If set to 0, HTTPODBC waits indefinitely. When the ODBC data source also has a specified time-out, the lesser value is used. Default=0
SQL_MAX_LENGTH	Integer	Specifies the maximum number of bytes returned from a binary or character column. Note that this option is available only with drivers that support it.
SQL_MAX_ROWS	Integer	Specifies the maximum number of rows returned from a single SQL query. A value of 0 returns all rows. Default=0
SQL_NOSCAN	0=search for and convert escape clauses in the SQL string 1=do not search for and convert escape clauses in the SQL string	Specifies whether escape clauses in the SQL string are searched for and converted. Escape clauses are enclosed in curly braces ({}). Searching for escape clauses can degrade query performance. Default=0
SQL_OPT_TRACE	0=trace off 1=trace on	Specifies whether ODBC function calls are written to a trace file. A value of 1 causes all ODBC function calls to be written to a trace file. A value of 0 specifies that no calls should be written to a trace file. Default=0

Option	Value(s)	Description
SQL_OPT_TRACEFILE	Filename	Specifies the filename in which trace information should be written. Used with the SQL_OPT_TRACE option. Default=SQL.LOG
SQL_PACKET_SIZE	Integer	Specifies the number of bytes of the network packet size in which the database driver and IIS will communicate.
SQL_QUERY_TIMEOUT	Integer	Specifies the number of seconds to wait for the SQL statement to execute and return results. If the SQL_QUERY_TIMEOUT number of seconds is reached, an error message is returned. A value of 0 results in no time-out.
SQL_TRANSLATE_DLL	Filename	Specifies the name of the DLL file that contains the SQLDriverToDataSource and SQLDataSourceToDriver functions, which are used by the database driver to complete tasks such as character translation.
SQL_TRANSLATE_OPTION	Integer	Used with the SQL_TRANSLATE_DLL option. Consult the specific translator documentation for option values.
SQL_TXN_ISOLATION	1=read uncommitted 2=read committed 4=repeatable read 8=serializable 16=versioning	Specifies the transaction isolation level. For more information on this option, see the SQL documentation.
Integer	Driver-specific	Enables you to specify special options supported by some drivers. You can specify these by using the option number, as in *number=value*.

Password

The Password field specifies the password to be used with the Username field. If the password for the specified username is null, this field is not required. The syntax for the Password field follows:

```
Password: webpassword
```

RequiredParameters

The `RequiredParameters` field specifies those parameters that *must* contain data when returned from the client browser. If a required parameter is not returned, the IDC returns an error to the client browser. A sample `RequiredParameters` field looks like this:

```
RequiredParameters:  logon, password
```

Username

The `Username` field specifies the user account name to use when connecting to the ODBC resource.

NOTE

If you specified the Integrated Security option when using Microsoft SQL Server, the username and password fields in the `.idc` file are ignored.

A sample `Username` field entry specifying the logon `webaccess` looks like this:

```
Username:  webaccess
```

Using HTML Extension (.htx) Files

Hypertext extension files are used by Microsoft IIS to identify specially formatted HTML documents, including the special tags used to handle such items as looping constructs for multidocument result sets and `if-then-else` control blocks.

.htx File Tags

In addition to standard HTML tags and data, `.htx` files can consist of special HTML-like tags that permit the result-set documents to be processed and output to be generated based on the conditions that the tags validate. In this section, you learn how to use these tags to identify the block of HTML code that will be processed for each result-set document, to perform `if-then-else` test conditions, and to identify special formatting of output.

<%begindetail%> and <%enddetail%> Tags

The `<%begindetail%>` and `<%enddetail%>` tags surround the portion of the HTML extension file in which the query result-set documents will be merged. Each record returned in the result set is processed against the HTML code contained in the Detail section. From a programmer's point of view, the `<%begindetail%>` and `<%enddetail%>` tags act much like a `for each` looping construct because, if no records are returned, the Detail section is ignored. You reference column names (results data) in the Detail section by enclosing them between `<%` and `%>` symbols.

> **NOTE**
>
> An HTML extension file can contain only one set of `<%begindetail%>` and `<%enddetail%>` tags.

Suppose that the following `SQLStatement` is specified in the associated `.idc` file:

```
SQLStatement:
+ SELECT FirstName, LastName, Address, City, State, ZipCode
+ FROM Employees
+ ORDER BY LastName ASC
```

The following `.htx` file code shows how the `<%begindetail%>` and `<%enddetail%>` tags are used, as well as how column results are referenced in the Detail section:

```
<!--
    Process returned record set data and display the abstract and
    other associated record data.
-->
<%begindetail%>
<p><b>
<i>Record #:</i> <%CurrentRecord%><br>.
<i>Name:</i> <%FirstName%> <%LastName%><br>
<i>Address:</i><%Address%><br>
<i>City:</i> <%City%><br>
<i>State:</i> <%State%><br>
<i>Zip Code:</i> <%ZipCode%><br>
</b>
<%enddetail%>
```

`<%if%>`, `<%else%>`, and `<%endif%>` Tags

The `<%if%>`, `<%else%>`, and `<%endif%>` tags form a conditional logic control flow that can be used to determine how records are processed. The most common use of the `if-then-else` statement is to determine whether any records were returned by the query. If no records are returned, a standard reply can be generated, such as `No records found to match query. Please try again.`

The `.htx` file code that uses the built-in variable `CurrentRecord` to determine whether no records were returned from the query follows:

```
<!--
    Example htx file code to check the status of the built-in
    variable CurrentRecord to verify when no records were
    returned from the query.
-->
<%begindetail%>
<%if CurrentRecord EQ 0%>
```

```
    Query results:
<%endif%>
<p><b>
<i>Record #:</i> <%CurrentRecord%><br>.
<i>Name:</i> <%FirstName%> <%LastName%><br>
<i>Address:</i><%Address%><br>
<i>City:</i> <%City%><br>
<i>State:</i> <%State%><br>
<i>Zip Code:</i> <%ZipCode%><br>
</b>
<%enddetail%>

<P>
<%if CurrentRecord EQ 0%>
    <I><B> No records found to match query.  Please try again.</B></I>
    <P>
<%endif%>
```

The syntax for using the `<%if%>`, `<%else%>`, and `<%endif%>` tags follows:

```
<%if condition%>
    HTML code
<%else%>
    HTML code
<%endif%>
```

where `condition` has the following form:

```
valueX operator valueY
```

Table 20.2 displays the list of valid `condition` operators.

Table 20.2. Valid condition operators.

Operator	Condition (True If)
EQ	*valueX* is equal to *valueY*
LT	*valueX* is less than *valueY*
GT	*valueX* is greater than *valueY*
CONTAINS	Any part of *valueX* contains the string *valueY*

x and y may be in the form of built-in variables, column names, an HTTP environment variable name (see the next section for a complete listing of HTTP variables), or a constant.

Integrating IDC with Other Applications

A very interesting and powerful aspect of IDC is its capability and flexibility to be integrated with other applications. Microsoft Index Server is just such an application.

RESOURCE

A good resource for information and examples on how to use Microsoft Index Server can be found in *Designing and Implementing Microsoft Index Server*, Swank & Kittel, Sams Publishing.

For example, consider an application in which you want your IDC query results to be used to create customized, dynamic, on-the-fly HTML query forms and query restrictions for an Index Server application. Likewise, results from Index Server queries can be manipulated to create dynamic forms for other applications as well. For example, results from an Index Server query could be used to dynamically create SQL statements used to extract information from a database. The possibilities are endless. With some imagination and creativity, you can easily develop applications that integrate Index Server with legacy databases, spreadsheets, statistical packages, and so on.

Integrating IDC and Index Server—A Simple Example

This section presents a simple example of how an IDC application can be used to dynamically create query forms for subsequent use with Index Server. This example uses the IIS Internet Database Connector to extract names of authors of specific types of books from a publisher's database. These names are then used to create a query form that allows users to select an author and provide additional query restrictions. This form is submitted to Index Server, which searches the corpus for documents referencing the author and matching other restrictions entered by the user.

RESOURCE

Additional detailed information about IDC can be found in Chapter 8, "Publishing Information and Applications," in the online documentation included with IIS.

Microsoft provides a free GUI-based publishing utility called dbWeb, which is used to quickly publish open database connectivity (ODBC) databases via IIS and IDC on the Web. dbWeb utilizes IDC but does not require extensive knowledge of SQL, HTML, or other programming methodologies. As such, it provides a powerful mechanism for the creation of `.idc` and `.htx` files (in addition to the many other database creation and management functions it provides) that can be integrated with your Index Server applications.

dbWeb is free and can be downloaded from

`http://www.microsoft.com/intdev/dbweb/dbweb.htm`

Invoking the .idc File

.idc files can be invoked by specifying the path to an .idc file in the action URL for an HTML form or in an href anchor for an HTML hyperlink. For this example, we have created a link in the frames-based utility illustrated in Figure 20.2. The following code creates the link to the Database Integration example.

```
<a href="/scripts/test_web/idcexample.idc?">
```

FIGURE 20.2.

A frames-based query tool that provides links to a variety of query examples developed for this book, including an example of an IDC-Index Server integration.

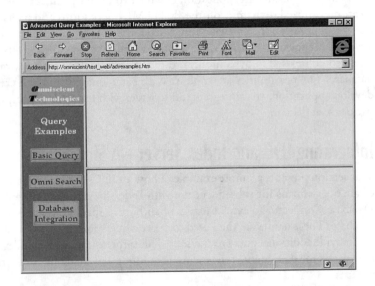

Clicking the Database Integration link invokes the idcexample.idc file, which is used by IIS to perform a query against a database. Notice that no parameters were appended to the URL in this case. However, like .idq files, IDC files can accept and perform substitutions of parameters passed as appended query strings or from HTML forms.

Contents of the .idc File

The .idc file is used to specify a SQL Statement or statements to be used for querying a database. There are also several optional parameters and ODBC fields that can be set in .idc files, but Listing 20.1 illustrates the use of the three required fields (Datasource, Template, and SQLStatement).

Listing 20.1. Contents of the idcexample.idc file.

```
Datasource: Web SQL
Username: sa
Template: idcexample.htx
SQLStatement:
```

```
+SELECT au_lname, au_fname, type, title
+FROM pubs.dbo.authors a,  pubs.dbo.titleauthor ta, pubs.dbo.titles t
+WHERE    a.au_id = ta.au_id and ta.title_id = t.title_id and
➡(t.type like '%%comp%%' or t.type like '%%bus%%' or t.title like '%%comp%%')
+ORDER BY au_lname
```

Datasource refers to the System DSN specified using ODBC application under Control Panel. In this case, we associated Web SQL with the local Microsoft SQL Server database on our server.

Template refers to the .htx file used to format the results from the database query.

SQLStatement refers to the SQL query submitted to the database. The + signs simply indicate a continuation to the next line in the file. In this example, the SQL statement queries the publisher's database for all authors of all computer and business books as well as all books that have a word like *computer* in the title.

Contents of the .htx File

.htx files used with IDC applications are very similar to those used for Index Server applications. Basically, they specify how database results are to be formatted as HTML and displayed to the user. Because they specify HTML output, they can also be used to dynamically create HTML forms based on the results of the database query. This means that static query forms are a thing of the past. Instead, forms can be dynamically created and tailored to a user's functional and informational requirements. Figure 20.3 illustrates the results of the database query, which were formatted to create a secondary HTML form used to make an Index Server query.

FIGURE 20.3.

Results of a database query can be formatted in an .htx file to dynamically create an HTML form for use with Index Server.

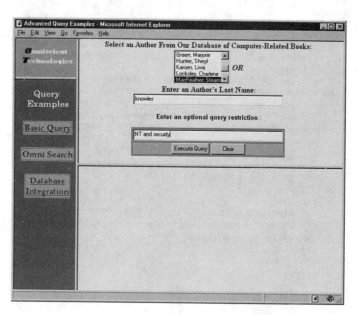

Listing 20.2 provides the content of the .htx file used to format the results of the database query performed by the .idc file in the previous section. This listing demonstrates how results of an IDC query can be formatted for use as another HTML form that is in turn used to make queries to Index Server.

Listing 20.2. Contents of the `idcexample.htx` file.

```
<!DOCTYPE HTML PUBLIC "-//IETF//DTD HTML//EN">
<html>
<head>
<meta http-equiv="Content-Type"
content="text/html; charset=iso-8859-1">
<meta name="GENERATOR" content="Microsoft FrontPage 2.0">
<title>Authors</title>
</head>
<body bgcolor="#E8E8E8">
<form action="/scripts/test_web/author_queryhit.idq" method="GET">

<center>
<strong>Select an Author From Our Database of Computer-Related Books:</strong>
<BR>
<select name="UserAuthor" size="5">
<%begindetail%>
<option value="<%au_lname%>"><%au_lname%>, <%au_fname%> </option>
<%enddetail%>
</select> <B><EM>OR</EM></B>
</center>
<center>
<strong>Enter an Author's Last Name:</strong><BR>
<input type="text" size="60" maxlength="100" name="UserAuthor2">
<P>
<input type="hidden" name="CiMaxRecordsPerPage" value="10">
<input type="hidden" name="CiScope" value="/">
<input type="hidden" name="TemplateName" value="basic_queryhit">
<input type="hidden" name="CiSort" value="rank[d]">
<p align="center">
    <font size="2" face="Arial"><strong>Enter an optional query restriction
    </strong></font>:</p>
    <div align="center"><center><table border="1" cellspacing="1"
    width="50%" bgcolor="#A4B0BD" bordercolor="#008080"
    bordercolordark="#008080" bordercolorlight="#008080">
        <tr>
            <td align="center" colspan="2" width="80%"><input
            type="text" size="60" maxlength="100"
            name="CiRestriction"></td>
        </tr>
        <tr>
            <td align="center"><input type="submit"
            value="Execute Query"> <input type="reset" name="1"
            value="Clear"></td>
        </tr>
    </table>
    </center></div>
</form>
</body>
</html>
```

A few notes about this file are as follows:

- The `.htx` file creates a form with an action URL that invokes an Index Server `.idq` file (`author_queryhit.idq`) when the form is submitted.

- The detail section is used to add options to a pull-down menu form object. Author names returned from the database are substituted for the displayed option as well as the option value attribute. This way, the name and value of a selected option can be passed to the `.idq` file referenced when the form is submitted.

- Additional form input objects, including hidden parameters, are created in a manner that enables the user to override the list of authors pulled from the database and supply his or her own ad-hoc entry. Additionally, the user can augment the Index Server query by providing additional query restrictions.

When the user submits the form, parameters are substituted in the `.idq` file referenced, Index Server performs the query, and an `.htx` report template file is used to format the results. Figure 20.4 illustrates the output for such a query.

FIGURE 20.4.

The final results of a two-stage query IDC-Index Server application. The first stage pulled author information from a database and created a form. The second stage used inputs to the form to perform an Index Server query.

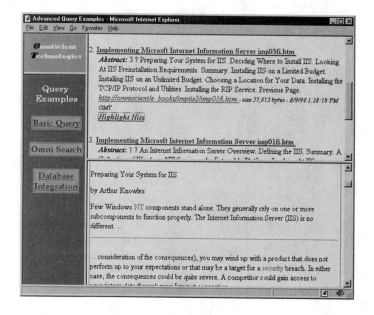

Summary

The IIS Internet Database Connector provides a standardized solution through the use of ODBC connectivity for accessing databases via Web-based applications. IDC files (`.idc`) work with HTML extension files (`.htx`) to identify the key components required by IIS to access a database and format query results based on special tags inserted into the `.htx` file.

21

Active Server Pages, OLE DB, and Active Data Objects

by Mark Spenik

In this chapter, you will learn about one of the most powerful Web development environments available to WWW database developers using Visual Basic: Active Server Pages (ASPs). By using ASPs, you can write powerful Web pages that enable you to generate dynamic HTML and perform state management without using CGI or ISAPI programs. You also will learn about the newest database object model called Active Data Objects (ADOs). Of course, the best way to learn about Active Server Pages is to create a few ASP applications. In this chapter, you will learn how to use ASPs to create a site counter, advertising pages, and a timesheet application. You will use the ASP environment (ActiveX Server framework) to generate more complex applications in Chapters 22, "Writing Server-Side Applications with VB 5 ActiveX Components."

An Overview of the Microsoft ActiveX Server Framework (Denali)

Denali was the code name for Microsoft's server-side scripting framework now called the *ActiveX Server framework*. The ActiveX Server framework is part of Microsoft IIS 3.0 running on Windows NT 4.0. Figure 21.1 shows the architecture of the ActiveX Server framework.

FIGURE 21.1.

The ActiveX Server framework architecture.

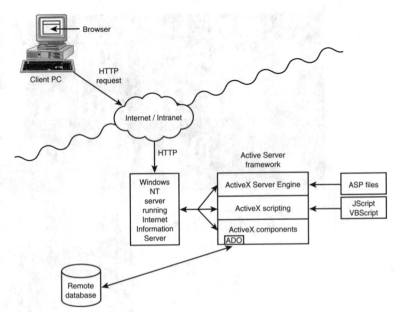

As shown in Figure 21.1, the ActiveX Server framework consists of a server-side scripting engine with a default script language of VBScript. As well as providing server-side scripting, the framework provides advanced features required to write complex Web applications, such as intrinsic objects, and ActiveX components, such as ADO. Active Server Pages (ASPs) are the building blocks of the ActiveX Server framework. ASP scripts can use ActiveX components, manage state, retrieve information from databases, store information, and generate HTML on-the-fly to send back to the browser.

Now refer to Figure 21.1 to see how the Active Server framework actually works. A client using a Web browser requests an ASP from the Website. The IIS receives the client HTTP request and passes it to the Active Server framework runtime—an ISAPI application. The ASP file is parsed. HTML found in the file is sent back to the browser. Scripts found in the file are processed on the server instead of the client. The ASP script's output (which can be static or dynamic HTML) is sent back to the client browser. Because the scripts execute on the Web server, you can take advantage of any databases or components to which the server has access. Because ASP can send back only HTML, you don't have to worry about the scripting capabilities of the client browser unless you are using client-side scripts.

Creating an ASP requires only standard knowledge of HTML. As a matter of fact, you can create an Active Server page by taking a standard HTML file and changing the file extension to asp, which is the extension of an ASP. One powerful feature of ASP is the capability to mix inline HTML and script. The script is processed on the server, and the static and dynamic HTML is sent to the client browser. If the browser user decides to view the source of the Web page, he sees only the HTML—not the script used to generate the dynamic parts of the HTML. Figure 21.2 shows a simple Web page created by using ASP.

FIGURE 21.2.

A sample Web page generated by an Active Server Page.

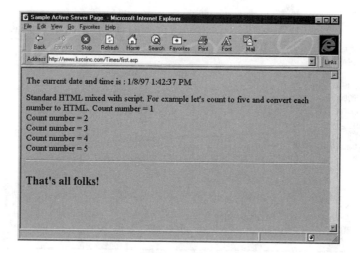

Listing 21.1 shows the HTML sent back to the browser.

Listing 21.1. HTML sent back to a browser from an ASP.

```
<HTML>
<HEAD>
<Title> Sample Active Server Page </TITLE>
</HEAD>
<BODY>
<Font size="4">
The current date and time is : 1/8/97 1:42:37 PM
<P>
Standard HTML mixed with script. For example
let's count to five and convert each number to HTML.

Count number = 1 <BR>

Count number = 2 <BR>

Count number = 3 <BR>

Count number = 4 <BR>

Count number = 5 <BR>

<HR>
<H2>That's all folks!</H2>
</BODY>
</HTML>
```

Listing 21.2 shows the ASP used to generate the sample page.

Listing 21.2. The Active Server Page used to generate a simple HTML page.

```
<HTML>
<HEAD>
<Title> Sample Active Server Page </TITLE>
</HEAD>
<BODY>
<Font size="4">
The current date and time is : <%=Now%>
<P>
Standard HTML mixed with script. For example
let's count to five and convert each number to HTML.
<% For x=1 to 5 %>
Count number = <% =x %> <BR>
<% Next x %>
<HR>
<H2>That's all folks!</H2>
</BODY>
</HTML>
```

Notice the differences between the HTML page sent back to the Web browser in Listing 21.1 and the HTML and script used to create the Web page shown in Listing 21.2.

> **NOTE**
>
> While browsing the Microsoft Website (`http:\\www.microsoft.com\`), pay attention to the various Web page file extensions you see as you go from page to page. What do you see? What else—asp extensions! Microsoft's own Website makes heavy use of ASPs.

ASPs give Web page developers the following advantages over standard Web application development:

- ASPs combine HTML with script in the same file for better application flow.
- Because the scripts are processed on the server, you don't have to worry about the browser's script capabilities.
- ASPs support VBScript and JScript.
- ASPs operate on the Advanced Intrinsic Object Model.
- ASPs provide state management.
- ASPs enable Visual Basic developers to perform functions that previously required CGI or ISAPI programming.
- ASPs provide easy access to databases via ADO.
- ASPs integrate ActiveX server components.

So what are the drawbacks of using ASPs? Well, I haven't encountered many. Debugging can be tricky. The error messages returned by ASPs are much better than some of the error messages encountered while writing VBScript client applications, but debugging still can be difficult. Also, if you want to save information about a user from session to session, you still need to use cookies.

Before going further into ASP, it is important to understand what makes up an ASP application. An ASP application consists of a virtual directory on a Web server and all the files and directories that exist in the virtual directory. Each ASP application can contain a single file named `Global.asa`, which must be stored in the application root directory. The `Global.asa` file contains several object events (discussed later in this chapter in the section "`Application Object`") that can be used to initialize the application or user sessions. The application's virtual directory must have read and execute privileges on the IIS.

Active Server Page Syntax

Active Server Pages consist of the following elements:

- HTML tags
- Script
- Text

The Active Server Page environment is very familiar to an HTML or Visual Basic developer, because it combines HTML and VBScript to create Web applications. As you learned earlier, the default scripting language for the ActiveX Server framework is VBScript. You can change the default scripting language to be JScript by modifying a Registry key on the NT server. You also can write pages that use both VBScript and JScript.

> **NOTE**
>
> In case you were wondering, JavaScript and JScript are one and the same. JScript is the name Microsoft gives to its version of JavaScript.

Delimiters and Expressions

Regardless of the script you use, the delimiters <% and %> denote script commands from HTML syntax in ASP. HTML tags and features remain unchanged in an Active Server Page. For example, the line

```
<% For x=1 to 5 %>
```

is the start of a VBScript For Next loop. The delimiters <% and %> indicate to IIS that the line is script and not HTML. This example shows a mix of HTML syntax with script:

```
<BODY>
<Font size="4">
The current date and time is: <%=Now%>
<P>
```

The tags <BODY>, <FONT>, and <P> are sent back to the browser along with the text The current date and time is:. The text <%=Now%> is not sent back to the browser, because it is enclosed in the script delimiters <% and %>. The equal sign (=) specifies that the output should be sent to the browser. In this case, the VBScript function Now, which retrieves the current date and time, sends the current date and time back to the browser.

NOTE

The script used between the delimiters <% and %> must be the default script. To use script other then the default script, you must use the SCRIPT tag discussed in the next section.

You also can mix script and HTML within loops and conditional statements, as shown in this example:

```
<% If iNum > 10 Then %>
<H2>Welcome to the Old Timers Club</H2>
<%Else%>
<H2>Welcome to the New Timers Club </H2>
<%End%>
```

Script can span lines, as this example shows:

```
<%
If iNum > 10 Then
    strMsg = "Welcome to the Old Timers Club"
Else
    StrMsg = "Welcome to the New Timers Club"
End
=StrMsg     'Send to the Browser
%>
```

The <SCRIPT> Tag, Include Files, and Comments

You can use the <SCRIPT> tag in statements, procedures, or commands to use any valid scripting language. For example, the following syntax declares a JScript code block:

```
<SCRIPT LANGUAGE=JSCRIPT>
//Do something in Script
</SCRIPT>
```

You can add to the <SCRIPT> tag an additional attribute called RUNAT, which tells the Active Server framework where to execute the script. Currently, the only valid value for the RUNAT attribute is SERVER. By using the RUNAT=SERVER attribute when creating procedures and functions, you can call from within an ASP page or from other ASP pages; otherwise, you get syntax errors when calling the procedure.

ASP supports Server-Side Include files so that you can include information before an ASP page is processed. The syntax for relative paths follows:

```
<!--#INCLUDE FILE="path/myinclude.inc"-->
```

To use an IIS virtual directory, use this syntax:

```
<!--#INCLUDE VIRTUAL="/includes/myinclude.inc"-->
```

You can use other ASP files as include files.

As always, you should use many comments when developing ASP pages. When commenting HTML sections, you need to use the HTML comment delimiters `<!--` and `-->`. Comments in script sections use the standard comment syntax of the scripting language: a single quotation mark (`'`) for VBScript and two forward slashes (`//`) for JScript. When writing scripts, include many comments; the comments are not sent back to the browser, because the scripts are executed on the server.

Sending Scripts Back to the Client

ASP scripts execute on the server and are not sent to the browser. You might be asking yourself, "How do I generate Web pages with client-side validation?" Simple: Use the `<SCRIPT>` tag and then enclose the client-side scripts within the HTML comment delimiters `<!--` and `-->`. The following example sends back a client-side script to display a message box when the procedure `cmdSend_OnClick` is invoked:

```
<SCRIPT LANGUAGE="VBSCRIPT">
<--
Sub cmdSend_OnClick
'Client side script
    MsgBox "Hello World!"
End Sub
-->
</SCRIPT>
```

Variable and Object Scope

ASP variables and objects can have application, session, or page scope. *Application scope* enables the variable or object to be shared by all users. *Session scope* enables any page in a user session to share the object or variable. *Page scope*, the default, is available only while the page is processing. You will learn in the next section how to create application- and session-level variables. When using ActiveX components, an *application scope component* is a single instance of the component shared by all users that is destroyed when the application ends. A *session scope component* is a single instance of the component per user session and is destroyed when the session ends. A *page scope object* is created while processing the page and is destroyed when the page processing completes.

Active Server Pages' Intrinsic Objects

Active Server Pages provide several objects that do not need to be instantiated (created) before using them in scripts. These intrinsic (built-in) objects enable you to perform many tasks that previously would have required ISAPI or CGI programs. The built-in objects follow:

■ Application

■ Session

■ Server

■ Request

■ Response

This section takes a closer look at each object.

Application **Object**

Properties: None

Methods: Lock, Unlock

Events: Application_OnStart, Application_OnEnd

Collections: None

You can use the Application object to store variables with application scope that can be shared by multiple users. You can add application scope variables by referencing the variable and setting a value. For example, the following code sets the value of the application scope variable Start to "Step1":

```
Application("Start") = "Step1"
```

You can use the Lock and Unlock methods to prevent multiple users from simultaneously modifying the same application variable. The Application object has no properties, but it does have two events—Application_OnStart and Application_OnEnd—that exist in the Global.asa file. The Application_OnStart event is fired once when the first user accesses the application. After the Application_OnStart event is fired, it will not run again until an Application_OnEnd event occurs. The Application_OnEnd event occurs when the IIS is shut down.

> **WARNING**
>
> While writing this chapter, I noticed that a few well-known Visual Basic publications incorrectly stated that application variables provide static variable storage even when the IIS or the Windows NT Server is shut down. WRONG!! Application variables exist during the lifetime of the application session. Shutting down your Web server resets all your application-level variables. For persistent data storage, you need to use a database or files.

Session **Object**

Properties: SessionId, Timeout

Methods: Abandon

Events: Session_OnStart, Session_OnEnd

Collections: None

Whereas the `Application` object shares information about an entire application, the `Session` object stores information required for a user session. Variables or objects stored in the `Session` object can be used throughout the entire user's session. Using session scope variables enables you to easily perform state management in a multiuser environment. The following line adds a session-scope variable named `employee`:

```
Session("employee") = "Mark Spenik"
```

You also can create a session-scope object by using this code:

```
Set Session("object name") = Server.CreateObject("Object to Create")
```

You can invoke a `Session` object's methods by using this syntax:

```
Session("object name").Method
```

Or, you can obtain a reference by using the set command.

Using the `<OBJECT>` Tag for Application and Session Scope

You can use the `<OBJECT>` tag in the `Global.asa` file to declare components with application or session scope. Using the `<Object>` tag is much faster for creating application-and session-scope objects than using the `CreateObject` method of the `Server` object, because ASP does not instantiate components declared in `<Object>` tags until they are referenced by script. Another advantage of using the `<OBJECT>` tag is that the component automatically goes into the application or session name space, which means that you can refer to the component without referencing the `Application` or `Session` object. This technique will be demonstrated shortly in the first ASP example.

Server Object

Properties: `ScriptTimeout`

Methods: `CreateObject`, `HTMLEncode`, `MapPath`, `URLEncode`

Events: None

Collections: None

The `Server` object enables you to access utility functions. You can use the `ScriptTimeout` property to set the amount of time a script can execute before timing out. The method you will use quite frequently is `CreateObject`. The `CreateObject` method creates an instance of the ActiveX server component (just like VB5.0's `CreateObject` function). After you create the component, you can use the component's methods and properties. The following example uses `CreateObject` to create an ADO connection:

```
<%Set oDBTime = Server.CreateObject("ADODB.Connection")%>
```

Request **Object**

Properties: None

Methods: None

Events: None

Collections: `ClientCertificate, Cookies, Form, QueryString, ServerVariables`

The `Request` object is one of the most powerful intrinsic objects and certainly the most popular object for people who have struggled with CGI programs and parsing HTTP requests. The `Request` object enables ASP developers to easily retrieve values during an HTTP request from a client browser to a server. The capability to easily retrieve client browser values is made possible by using the `Request` object's various collections. You can use the `Request` object collections to retrieve cookies, values from forms, query string values, and environment variables. To access variables contained in the `Request` object collection, use this syntax:

```
Request.CollectionName("variable")
```

Now take a look at the `Form` collection. Processing form values can become tedious when using regular HTML and CGI; however, by using the `Form` collection, you easily can retrieve values entered in a form and submitted to the Web server. There's no need to parse and interrupt the string sent to the server; ASP does it all for you. Suppose that you have a textbox on a form called `UserName`. To get text entered in the textbox, you use the `Form` collection:

```
<%=Request.Form("UserName")%>
```

Processing a query string is just as easy. Suppose that the following URL request is sent to the server:

```
<A HREF="addtime.asp?EmpName=Mark+Spenik&Client=SAMS">
```

The following code retrieves the values and stores them in a local variable:

```
<% strName = Request.QueryString("EmpName")
 strClient = Request.QueryString("Client") %>
```

The variable `strName` contains the string `Mark Spenik`. As stated earlier, ASP parses out the form's query string format delimiters for you. If multiple `EmpNames` are sent, the `QueryString` object creates a collection named `EmpName` that contains the multiple names, which can be accessed with this code:

```
Request.QueryString("EmpName")(1)
Request.QueryString("EmpName")(N)
```

If multiple `EmpNames` are sent to the server and you access the variable without an index value, all the values are returned in a comma-delimited string.

Response **Object**

Properties: `Buffer, ContentType, Expires, ExpiresAbsolute, Status`

Methods: `AddHeader, AppendToLog, BinaryWrite, Clear, End, Flush, Redirect, Write`

Events: None

Collections: Cookies

You use the `Response` object to send information back to the client browser by using the various methods of the `Response` object. You use the `Redirect` method to direct a user to a URL. You use the `Write` method to send string information back to the current HTTP session, and you use the `Cookies` collection to set a cookie value. The following example redirects a user to the Microsoft Website:

```
<%Response.Redirect "http://www.microsoft.com"%>
```

This example sends HTML back to the client browser:

```
<%Response.Write "<H2>Thanks for the visit, come again!</H2>"%>
```

Active Server Components

By using ASP, you can use ActiveX components to enhance your Web-based applications. You can use ActiveX components that you write yourself using Visual Basic 5.0 (this is discussed in the next chapter) or the ActiveX components included with ASP. The ActiveX components included with ASP follow:

- *Ad-rotator component:* Enables you to randomly display advertisements on your Web page. The advertisements are stored in a text file used by the Ad-rotator component to make adding or removing advertisements easy.

- *Browser-capabilities component:* Enables you to determine the capabilities of a browser—for example, whether the browser supports VBScript.

- *File-access component:* Enables you to use the `TextStream` and `FilesStream` object to create, read, or write files on the server.

- *Content-linking component:* Enables you to create applications that logically navigate through ASP pages without using URLs.

- *Database-access component: Active Data Objects* (ADO) is included with ASP, which is covered later in this chapter in the "Active Data Objects" section.

You will become familiar with some of the other ActiveX components in the examples in this chapter, as well as the examples presented in Chapter 22.

An Active Server Home Page with Advertising

Before moving on to ADO and OLE DB, take a look at how you can use ASP and some of the intrinsic objects and ActiveX components discussed so far to create a home page. In this example, the home page will keep track of the number of site visitors and use the Ad-rotator component to display a few advertisements. The visitor counter will be stored in a text file so that, after the Web server is shut down and restarted, the counter will reflect the accurate number of visitors. If the user clicks on one of the advertisements displayed, the application will redirect them to the Macmillan Publishing Website and store the number of redirects performed in a text file. Figure 21.3 shows the completed ASP application.

FIGURE 21.3.

An active server home page with an advertisement example.

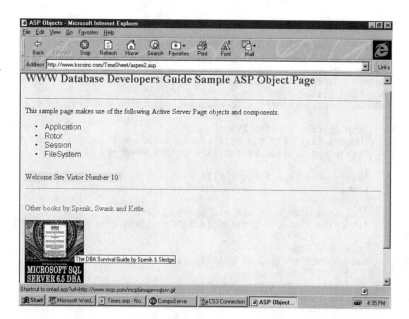

> **NOTE**
>
> You can find the following ASP files on the CD-ROM that accompanies this book. The main application file is `aspex2.asp`. I used a virtual directory named `TimeSheet` and included all the files used in the application root directory.

The application uses the following intrinsic objects:

■ `Application`

■ `Session`

■ Server

■ Response

The following ActiveX components are used:

■ AdRotator

■ FileSystemObject

Now you'll examine how the application was put together. First, look at the contents of the file Global.asa, which contains the events for the Application and Session objects. Listing 21.3 shows the Application object Application_OnStart event.

Listing 21.3. The Application_OnStart event.

```
<SCRIPT LANGUAGE=VBScript RUNAT=Server>
SUB Application_OnStart
'Active Server Page Example
'Author: Mark Spenik
'Revision History: Jan. 6, 1997
' Global application file. Contains application and session startup and end events
'
    'Application Startup Event
    'Open a file with the site count. We are writing the count to a file
    'since Application variables are lost when the IIS server is shut down.

    'Set up the path for the file with the site count.
    strVisitCountFile = Server.MapPath ("/TimeSheet") + "\visitc.txt"

    'Get an instance of the FileSystemObject
    Set oFile = Server.CreateObject("Scripting.FileSystemObject")

    'Open the File
    Set oCount= oFile.OpenTextFile (strVisitCountFile, 1, FALSE, FALSE)

    'Initialize the Vistor Counter
    Application("NumVisitors") = oCount.ReadLine
    oCount.Close

END SUB
</SCRIPT>
```

In the Application_OnStart event, the file visitc.txt is read and stored in the Application variable NumVisitors. The file is opened by creating an instance of the Scripting.FileSystemObject using the CreateObject method of the intrinsic Server object.

After the Application_OnStart event fires, the Session_OnStart event shown in Listing 21.4 is executed.

Listing 21.4. The `Session_OnStart` event.

```vbscript
<SCRIPT LANGUAGE=VBSCRIPT RUNAT=Server>
Sub Session_OnStart
    'Let's use the Application Object to keep track of the number
    'of visitors for this page.


    'Set up the path for the file with the site count.
    strVisitCountFile = Server.MapPath ("/TimeSheet") + "\visitc.txt"

    'Get an instance of the FileSystemObject
    Set oFile = Server.CreateObject("Scripting.FileSystemObject")

    'Open the File
    Set oCount= oFile.CreateTextFile (strVisitCountFile, TRUE, FALSE)

    Application.Lock 'Prevent another user from updating
                     'The counter while we update it.

    Application("NumVisitors") = Application("NumVisitors") + 1

    'Write out to the file
    oCount.WriteLine(Application("NumVisitors"))

    Application.UnLock 'Unlock for other users

    'Change the timeout for the session object.
    Session.Timeout = 5    'Time the session out in 5 Minutes

    oCount.Close
End Sub

Sub Session_OnEnd

End Sub

</SCRIPT>
```

In the `Session` object `OnStart` event, the number-of-visitors counter, `NumVisitors`, is incremented and written back to the file `visitc.txt`. The `Application` object methods `Lock` and `Unlock` are used to make sure that the global variable is not being incremented by another session. The application writes the number-of-visitors counter to the file for every session. In a heavily used Website, you might want to write the counter to the file only every 50 to 100 sessions. The `Session.Timeout` value that defaults to 20 minutes is set to 5 minutes. The application does not contain an `Application_OnEnd` or `Session_OnEnd` event. The last item in the `Global.asa` file is the creation of the application-level Ad-rotator object called `oAd`, shown here:

```
<OBJECT RUNAT=Server SCOPE=Session ID=oAd PROGID="MSWC.Adrotator">
</OBJECT>
```

The `<OBJECT>` tag is used instead of the `CreateObject` method for the performance and name-referencing benefits described earlier in this chapter. The file `aspex2.asp` is the starting page for the application and is shown in Listing 21.5.

Listing 21.5. The Active Server Page aspex2.asp.

```
<HTML>
<!-- Active Server Page Example Using Objects and Componets-->
<!-- Author: Mark Spenik -->
<!-- Revision History: Jan. 6, 1997 -->
<!--                                 -->
<!-- This example uses several Active Server components and -->
<!-- intrinsic objects to display various advertisements.   -->
<!-- This sample also includes a working page counter and   -->
<!-- redirection to the advertiser's site. A counter is also -->
<!-- kept for each time a user uses this page to get to the  -->
<!-- advertiser's site.                                      -->
<!--                                 -->
<HEAD><TITLE>ASP Objects</TITLE></HEAD>
<STYLE>
H2 { color:Blue }
P { font-size: 12pt;color:Purple}
SPAN { background:yellow }
UL {font-family:arial;font-size 12pt;}
</STYLE>

<BODY BGCOLOR="ghostwhite">
<H2>WWW Database Developers Guide Sample ASP Object Page</H2>
<HR>
This sample page makes use of the following Active Server Page
objects and components:
<UL>
<LI>Application
<LI>AdRotor
<LI>Session
<LI>FileSystem
</UL>
<BR>
<SPAN>
Welcome Site Vistor Number <%=Application("NumVisitors")%>.
</SPAN>
<HR Size=2>
<P>
Other books by Spenik, Swank and Kittel...
<P>
<%= oAd.GetAdvertisement("adsams.txt") %>
<p>
<FORM METHOD="POST" ACTION="aspex2.asp">
<INPUT TYPE=SUBMIT Value="View Next Ad">
</FORM>
</BODY>
</HTML>
```

The file aspex2.asp consists almost entirely of standard HTML and only a few lines of script.
The following line, for example, uses the Adrotator object to retrieve an advertisement using
the rotator-schedule file shown in Listing 21.6:

```
<%= oAd.GetAdvertisement("adsams.txt") %>
```

The Ad-rotator component's schedule file has the following optional parameters:

```
Redirect URL
Width
Height
Border
```

The Redirect parameter is the file or DLL to implement redirection. Height and Width specify the number of pixels to use for the advertisement, and Border specifies the border thickness of the hyperlink border around the advertisement. After the optional parameters come the parameters for each advertisement, which have the following format:

```
advertismentURL
advertismentHomePageURL
AdText
AdImpressions
```

Here, advertismentURL is the URL to the advertisement's image file. advertismentHomePageURL is the address to the advertiser's home page. AdText is displayed if the browser does not support graphics and is displayed as a Tooltip in Internet Explorer 3.0. AdImpressions is a number between 0 and 4,294,967,295 that determines the frequency at which the advertisement is displayed on the page. For this example, AdImpressions was set to 35, 35, and 30. This translates to 35 percent, 35 percent, and 30 percent.

Notice that, because the <OBJECT> tag in the file Global.asa was used to create the application-scope object, you do not need to reference the Application object to use the Adrotator object oAd.

The last file used in the application is the redirect file defined in the Ad-rotator schedule file in Listing 21.6. When a user clicks on one of the advertisements displayed, the redirect file is executed. Listing 21.7 shows the redirect file cntad.asp.

Listing 21.6. The Ad-rotator schedule file: adsams.txt.

```
redirect cntad.asp
width 125
height 155
border 1
*
sqlsrv.gif
http://www.mcp.com/mcp
The DBA Survival Guide by Spenik & Sledge
35

wwdb.gif
http://www.mcp.com/mcp/
The World Wide Web Database Developer's Guide by Swank & Kittel
35

index.gif
http://www.mcp.com/mcp/
The Microsoft Index Server Guide by Swank & Kittel
30
```

Listing 21.7. The redirect ASP file: `cntad.asp`.

```
<SCRIPT LANGUAGE=VBScript RUNAT=Server>
SUB UpdateCounter
 ' This script executes when the user clicks an Ad and redirects
   ' to the Macmillan Publishing site.

    'Set up the file name
    RedirectCountFilename = Server.MapPath ("/TimeSheet") + "\redirect.txt"

    'Create the File System Object
    Set oFileObject = Server.CreateObject("Scripting.FileSystemObject")

    'Open The File
    Set oFile= oFileObject.OpenTextFile (RedirectCountFilename, 1, FALSE, FALSE)
    Application("iNumRedirects") = oFile.ReadLine
    oFile.Close

    Set oFile= oFileObject.CreateTextFile (RedirectCountFilename, True, FALSE)

    'Lock the file so we have can update the counter value.
    Application.lock

    'Increment and write the value back to the file
    Application("iNumRedirects") =  Application("iNumRedirects") + 1
    oFile.WriteLine(Application("iNumRedirects"))

    'Unlock the application
    Application.unlock

    'Close the file
    oFile.Close

END SUB
</SCRIPT>
<%Call UpdateCounter
'Now Redirect the browser to the Macmillan Publishing site.
Response.Redirect "http://www.mcp.com/mcp"
%>
```

The script used to update the number-of-redirects counter is similar to the script used to update the number-of-visitors counter. The following script uses the intrinsic object `Response` to redirect the browser to the Macmillan Publishing Website:

```
Response.Redirect "http://www.mcp.com/mcp"
```

Active Data Objects

The ADO component installed with Active Server Pages provides a simplified, high-powered data object model that enables you to access databases using an OLE DB provider, including the Microsoft ODBC provider. *OLE DB* is Microsoft's next-generation specification for data access. The general idea of OLE DB is for data consumers (applications) to access a wide variety of data through service providers. OLE DB is based on the need to access and manipulate other forms of data besides relational databases using a native dialect (not necessarily SQL). If you want to retrieve spreadsheet cells from an Excel spreadsheet, you would use the service provider for Excel spreadsheets; for ODBC databases, you would use the ODBC database service provider. OLE DB is an API set that enables C++ developers to create data providers, service providers, and data consumers. ADO enables Visual Basic developers to use the OLE DB ODBC service provider to access and manipulate database. ADO resembles RDO and ODBC Direct in some ways, but it has a much simpler object model, as Figure 21.4 shows.

FIGURE 21.4.
The ADO model.

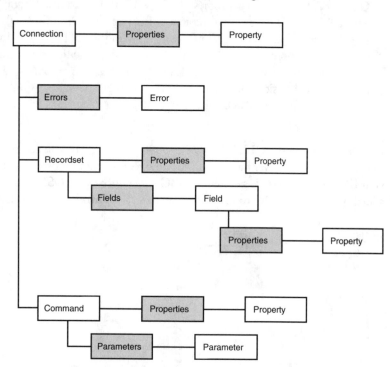

Note: Shading indicates a collection

To simplify scripting and programming, many of the ADO objects can be created independent of other objects. The Recordset object, for example, does not require the programmer to create a Connection object first (a loose object hierarchy). Using independent objects might seem a bit strange to an experienced DAO programmer, but once you get used to the ADO model, you will find it simple to use. By using ADO, you can create fully scrollable recordsets that can be updated. ADO supports the following features:

■ Batch updates

■ Stored procedures (including multiple recordsets)

■ Free-threaded objects (see Chapter 23 for threading models)

■ Various cursor types

■ Recordset cache management

For a Visual Basic database Web developer, ADO provides one of the simplest methods to use database information across the World Wide Web.

TIP

One of the best ways to get more familiar with ADO is to install it on your PC so that you can use ADO from Visual Basic 5.0. Because ADO uses OLE DB, you must install OLE DB as well. For Windows 95 or Windows NT, you can install OLE DB and ADO by installing the OLE DB SDK or installing Microsoft Visual Interdev, which includes Active Server Pages for the Windows 95 personal Web server. If you develop Visual Basic applications on a Windows NT Server or Workstation, installing IIS 3.0 also installs ASP and OLE DB.

Because ADO uses the OLE DB ODBC service provider, you can access any ODBC database to which your Web server has access. The only requirement for using a database with ADO on your IIS 3.0 Web server is a system ODBC *data source name* (DSN). After the system DSN is added, you can use ADO to access the database, as shown in Figure 21.5.

FIGURE 21.5.

Accessing a database via the Web using ADO.

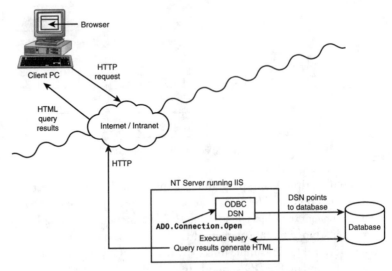

Before using ADO in an Active Server Page, take a quick look at the ADO `Connection` object and `Recordset` object.

Connection **Object**

Use the `Connection` object to establish a session with an OLE DB data source. You can use the `Connection` object to close the connection to the data source, control transactions, create recordsets, or execute commands. The following example creates a `Connection` object to a Microsoft database using a DSN called `TimeSheet`:

```
<%  'Create an instance of the ADO object
    Set oDBTime = Server.CreateObject("ADODB.Connection")

    'Open the database
    oDBTime.Open "TimeSheet" %>
```

Recordset **Object**

The `Recordset` object consists of the returned rows of a query or executed stored procedure. The `Recordset` object can be created independent of any other objects and supports many powerful features, such as the capability to support multiple query result sets. `Recordset` objects can be created by using the `Execute` method of the `Connection` object and the `Command` object or the `Open` method of the `Recordset` object (discussed later). The following code shows an example of creating an independent `Recordset` object:

```
'Create an ADO recordset to add a new record
    set rsTimeSheet = CreateObject("ADODB.Recordset")

    'Set the Recordset Properties
    rsTimeSheet.CursorType = adOpenKeyset
    rsTimeSheet.Source = "Select * From EmpTime"
    rsTimeSheet.Open
```

The idea of creating a `Recordset` object without first defining a query or table will seem unusual to DAO programmers. When you create an independent `Recordset` object, a `Connection` object still is created, but it is not assigned to an object variable. You can assign an existing `Connection` object to a `Recordset` object before you open the `Recordset` object by using the `ActiveConnection` property or using the `ActiveConnection` argument in the `Recordset` `Open` method. The `Recordset` object can have one of the following cursor types:

- Forward-Only
- Keyset
- Dynamic
- Static

Forward-Only

Forward-Only creates a static cursor that provides forward scrolling only, which improves performance. Use a Forward-Only cursor when you need to make only a single pass through the data—for example, when you are filling a combo box on a Web page. Forward-Only is the default cursor used by ADO. You can make modifications to a Forward-Only cursor; however, changes made by other users are not visible.

Keyset

A Keyset cursor allows forward and backward movement, as well as bookmarks, through the recordset. The Keyset cursor is updatable, so you can add, delete, or modify records. Records added or deleted by other users are not visible; however, updates made by other users are visible.

Dynamic

The Dynamic cursor contains an accurate recordset of all the current records, including those being added, updated, or deleted by other users. All types of recordset cursor movement are provided, except for bookmarks, which are supported only if the provider supports them.

Static

A Static cursor is a copy (picture) of the query data at the time the cursor was created. A Static cursor provides all directions of movement as well as a cursor that can be updated. Changes made by other users do not appear until the recordset is refreshed.

Recordset Navigation

You can use the following methods to move through the recordset:

- ■ *MoveFirst*: Moves to the first row of the recordset
- ■ *Move*: Moves the recordset a specified number of rows
- ■ *MoveLast*: Moves the recordset to the last row
- ■ *MoveNext*: Moves forward to the next row in the recordset
- ■ *MovePrevious*: Moves backward to the preceding row in the recordset

You also can use the AbsolutePosition property to move to an absolute row position in the cursor.

To help determine whether you are at the end or start of the recordset, use the BOF and EOF properties of the Recordset object. The BOF and EOF properties return Boolean values (TRUE/FALSE) based on the current position of the recordset. If BOF or EOF is TRUE, there is no current row, and any attempt to move through the recordset results in an error. When a recordset is open and contains one or more rows, both BOF and EOF are FALSE. If both BOF and EOF are set to TRUE and the Recordset RowCount property is 0, no records are contained in the recordset.

Editing a Recordset

If you have created a recordset that can be modified, you can use the AddNew method of the recordset, which has the following syntax:

```
Recordset.AddNew
```

The AddNew method creates a placeholder in the recordset for the new row. You then populate each column in the recordset with data and invoke the Update method to add the record. To modify an existing record, modify the fields you want to change and use the Update method.

> **NOTE**
>
> Both the AddNew method and the Update method have optional parameters called Fields and Values that enable you to provide argument lists.

To delete the current record in the recordset, use the Delete method, which has the following syntax:

```
Recordset.Delete AffectRecords
```

The parameter AffectRecords is an optional parameter that determines how many records are deleted. The default is to delete only the current record. The value adAffectGroup deletes all records that satisfy the Filter property of the recordset.

> **TIP**
>
> When creating a Recordset object to update records, make sure that you pass all the parameters required in the Recordset Open method or set the Recordset properties for CursorType, LockType, and Source prior to opening a Recordset object. While working on one of the examples, I wanted to use the AddNew and Update methods to add a new record to a Microsoft database. I selected the proper cursor type, and I took the default for the lock type (I did not set the LockType property). However, the ADO default for lock type always creates a read-only cursor regardless of the cursor type selected. So, when creating a recordset for record modifications, don't use the defaults. Remember that you also can use standard SQL to add or update records. Most of the examples shipped with ASP use the SQL approach.

An Active Server Page Using ADO: A Timesheet Application

In this section, you'll try some ADO examples by creating an application that retrieves and adds records to a database using ASP and ADO. The sample application shown in Figure 21.6 is a timesheet application.

FIGURE 21.6.

An ASP timesheet application.

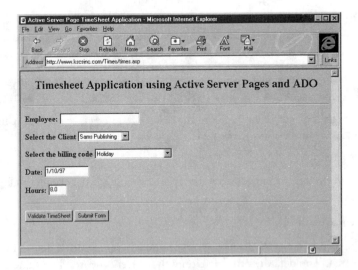

I have worked for several computer consulting companies, and one thing always remains the same: *you gotta do your timesheet daily*! So this timesheet application enables you to enter your timesheet over the World Wide Web. After you fill out the timesheet and submit the form, the timesheet entry is saved on an Access database on the Web server.

> **NOTE**
>
> The Microsoft Access database `Times.mdb` and the ASP files `times.asp` and `addtime.asp` make up the timesheet application and are included on the CD-ROM that accompanies this book.

Some important application features follow:

■ Populating an HTML selection using ADO

■ Using dependent and independent `Recordset` objects

■ State management

■ Saving a record using ADO

■ Form processing using the ASP `Request` object

■ Sending client-side validation scripts back to the client

The timesheet application does not have a `Global.asa` file, so there are no application or session events. The main ASP file is `times.asp`. Listing 21.8 shows the ASP HTML and script for `times.asp`.

Listing 21.8. ASP HTML and script for the file `times.asp`.

```
<HTML>
<!-- Active Server Page Example Using Active Data Objects -->
<!-- Author: Mark Spenik -->
<!-- Revision History: Jan. 6, 1997 -->
<!-- This example uses Active Data Objects to fill a combo box -->
<!-- and to store the data entered in the timesheet.          -->
<!-- This example also uses Active Server Pages to execute client and server -->
<!-- side scripts.       -->
<!--                                                                  -->
<HEAD>
<Title>Active Server Page TimeSheet Application</TITLE>
</HEAD>
<BODY BGCOLOR="Tan">
<CENTER>
<H2>Timesheet Application using Active Server Pages and ADO</H2>
</CENTER>
<HR SIZE=2>
<!-- Declare the start of the form. -->
<FORM NAME="TimeSheet" METHOD="POST" ACTION="http://www.kscsinc.com/
   Times/addtime.asp">
<B>Employee:</B> <INPUT TYPE="text" NAME="txtEmployee" Size=30 Value="">
<p>
<B>Select the Client</B>
<%  'Create an instance of the ADO Recordset object

    set rsClients = CreateObject("ADODB.Recordset")

    'Open a resultset based on the SQL Statement
    rsClients.Open "SELECT ClientName FROM Clients","DSN=TimeSheet"
%>
<!-- Notice in the following section the mixture of HTML with server side script -->
<SELECT NAME="cmbClient">
<% Do While Not rsClients.EOF %>
<OPTION><%=rsClients("ClientName")%>
<%
        rsClients.MoveNext
   Loop
   rsClients.Close
   Set rsClients = Nothing
%>
</SELECT>
<p>
<B>Select the billing code</B>
<SELECT ALIGN=CENTER Name="cmbCode">
<OPTION>Holiday
<OPTION>Vacation
<OPTION>Sick
<OPTION>Client Server Consulting
<OPTION>Work Group Consulting
<OPTION>Internet Consulting Services
</Select>
<p>
<B>Date:</B> <INPUT TYPE="text" NAME="txtWorkDate" Size=15 Value=<% =Date %>>
<p>
<B>Hours:</B> <INPUT TYPE="text" Name="txtHours" Size=4 Value="8.0">
```

continues

Listing 21.8. continued

```
<BR>
<HR>
<INPUT TYPE="Button" Name="cmdAdd" Value="Validate TimeSheet">
<INPUT TYPE=SUBMIT VALUE="Submit Form">
<SCRIPT LANGUAGE="VBScript">
<!--
Sub window_onLoad()
Dim CurrentForm

    'Set the focus to the text box
    Set CurrentForm = Document.TimeSheet

    CurrentForm.txtEmployee.Focus
    Set CurrentForm = Nothing
end sub

Sub cmdAdd_OnClick
Dim vTemp
Dim CurrentForm

    'Set the focus to the text box
    Set CurrentForm = Document.TimeSheet

    'Perform client side validation before sending the
    'results to the server.
    vTemp = CurrentForm.txtEmployee.Value
    If VTemp = "" Then
        MsgBox "You must enter an Employee Name.",48, "Blank Name"
        Exit Sub
    End If

    'Make sure the date is valid.
    vTemp = CurrentForm.txtWorkDate.Value
    If NOT IsDate(vTemp) Then
MsgBox "You must enter a valid date in the date field.",48, "Invalid Date"
        Exit Sub
    End If

    'Make sure they at least worked 8 hours
    vTemp = CurrentForm.txtHours.Value
    If vTemp < 8.0 Then
        MsgBox "You must enter at least 8 hours in the hours field.",
        ➥48, "Incorrect Number of Hours"
        Exit Sub
    End If
    'If you wanted to submit the form from the client validation routine, you
    'would have to parse the form and build the query string to send back.
    'The following line is an example of what is required. Note only the
    'first variable txtEmployee is shown. You would have to include all
    'of the fields in the query string.
    'Window.Location.HREF = "http://www.kscsinc.com/Times/
    'addtime.asp?txtEmployee=Mark"

End Sub

-->
```

```
</SCRIPT>
</BODY>
</HTML>
```

Now look at some of the HTML and script used in the ASP file. First examine how an HTML selection list is populated using an ADO recordset. The script and HTML used to populate the selection list is a good example of combining ASP, ADO, and HTML to produce Web pages using database information. I think you will find from a developer perspective the improvement of ADO over htx and idc files. The selection list population script follows:

```
'Open a resultset based on the SQL Statement
    Set rsClients = oDBTime.Execute(SQLQuery) %>
<!-- Notice in the following section the mixture of HTML with server side script -->
<SELECT NAME="cmbClient">
<% Do While Not rsClients.EOF %>
<OPTION><%=rsClients("ClientName")%>
<%
    rsClients.MoveNext
    Loop
%>
</SELECT>
```

This example shows you how to use ASP to send client-side validation scripts back to the client. The form validation could have been done on the server after the client had submitted the form.

Test the client-side validation by leaving the Employee Name field empty and click the Validate TimeSheet button (see Figure 21.6). A message box appears, notifying you that you must enter an employee name. For the sake of showing many different ASP features in a single form, the timesheet application has two buttons instead of one. Normally, the Validate TimeSheet button would validate and submit the form. To do this, you must set the IE Window.Location.HRef property to the proper ASP file with a parsed query string. I did not write the function to scan the form and build the proper query string. Instead, I added a Submit button to the page to show how you can use the Active Server Page Request object to parse a form. Listing 21.8 shows the client-validation script in the <SCRIPT> tag section between the HTML comment delimiters <!-- and -->.

The Submit button on the form calls the URL addtimes.asp, which is shown in Listing 21.9.

Listing 21.9. ASP addtimes.asp code.

```
<%
    'Make sure user started at the proper pages and
    'filled in the form values
    If Request.Form("txtEmployee") = "" OR Request.Form("txtHours") = "" Then
        Response.Redirect("Times.asp")

    End If
```

continues

Listing 21.9. continued

```
%>
<HTML>
<HEAD>
<Title> TimeSheet Response </TITLE>
</HEAD>
<BODY>
<%
    'Create an instance of the ADO object
    Set oDBTime = Server.CreateObject("ADODB.Connection")

    'Open the database
    oDBTime.Open "TimeSheet"

    'Create an ADO recordset to add a new record
    set rsTimeSheet = CreateObject("ADODB.Recordset")

    'Set the Recordset Properties
    rsTimeSheet.CursorType = adOpenKeyset
    rsTimeSheet.LockType = adLockOptimistic
    rsTimeSheet.ActiveConnection = oDBTime
    rsTimeSheet.Source = "Select * From EmpTime"
    rsTimeSheet.Open

    'Check to make sure Updates are supported
    sResponse = "<H2>Sorry your timesheet was not added. Invalid server
    ➡cursor.</H2>"
    If rsTimeSheet.Supports(adUpdate) Then
    ' rsTimeSheet.Open "SELECT * FROM EmpTime", oDBTime,
    ➡adOpenKeyset, adLockBatchOptimistic

        'Add a new record
        rsTimeSheet.AddNew
        'Set the data values
        rsTimeSheet("Employee") = Request.Form("txtEmployee")
        rsTimeSheet("WorkDate") = Request.Form("txtWorkDate")
        rsTimeSheet("ClientName") = Request.Form("cmbClient")
        rsTimeSheet("BillCode") = Request.Form("cmbCode")
        rsTimeSheet("Hours") = Request.Form("txtHours")
        'Add the record
        rsTimeSheet.Update

        'Check for Errors
        If oDBTime.Errors.Count > 0 Then
            Set oError = oDBTime.Errors(0)
            If oError.Number <> 0 Then
                sResponse = "<H3>Timesheet Error </H3><BR><P>"
                sResponse = sResponse & "Error adding your timesheet
                ➡to the database."
                sResponse = sResponse & "Error: " & oError.Description
            End If
        Else
            sResponse = "<H2>Timesheet Added.</H2><BR><H3>Thanks!</H3><BR><P>"
        End If
    End If
    Response.Write sResponse
    rsTimeSheet.Close
```

```
    oDBTime.Close
%>
</BODY>
<!--#include virtual="/ASPSamp/Samples/adovbs.inc"-->
</HTML>
```

The `addtimes.asp` script uses an example of state management and minimum validation to determine whether you have assessed the page without coming from the `times.asp` page or whether you have left some fields empty. If the fields are empty, the script redirects the user's browser to the starting ASP page, `times.asp`. The script to perform this feature follows:

```
<%
    'Make sure user started at the proper pages and
    'filled in the form values
    If Request.Form("txtEmployee") = "" OR Request.Form("txtHours") = "" Then
        Response.Redirect("Times.asp")

    End If
%>
```

A `Recordset` object is created independently and then assigned to the existing connection. The `Recordset` object properties are set to create an updatable recordset, and the `Recordset` object is created using the `Open` method, as shown in this code:

```
'Create an ADO recordset to add a new record
    set rsTimeSheet = CreateObject("ADODB.Recordset")

    'Set the Recordset Properties
    rsTimeSheet.CursorType = adOpenKeyset
    rsTimeSheet.LockType = adLockOptimistic
    rsTimeSheet.ActiveConnection = oDBTime
    rsTimeSheet.Source = "Select * From EmpTime"
    rsTimeSheet.Open
```

You can check the capabilities of a `Recordset` object by using the `Supports` method. The following line of script queries to check whether the `Recordset` object created can be updated:

```
If rsTimeSheet.Supports(adUpdate) Then
```

The code to add the new record and populate the new row will look very familiar to Visual Basic database developers. Notice how the data is retrieved from the form using the ASP `Request` object. The script follows:

```
'Add a new record
        rsTimeSheet.AddNew
        'Set the data values
        rsTimeSheet("Employee") = Request.Form("txtEmployee")
        rsTimeSheet("WorkDate") = Request.Form("txtWorkDate")
        rsTimeSheet("ClientName") = Request.Form("cmbClient")
        rsTimeSheet("BillCode") = Request.Form("cmbCode")
        rsTimeSheet("Hours") = Request.Form("txtHours")
        'Add the record
        rsTimeSheet.Update
```

If an error occurs, an `Error` object is added to the `Connection` object's `Errors` collection. You can check to see whether an error has occurred by checking the number of `Error` objects in the collection, as this code shows:

```
If oDBTime.Errors.Count > 0 Then
```

If the record is saved successfully, a success string is sent back to the browser, as shown in Figure 21.7.

FIGURE 21.7.

The ASP timesheet application successful entry screen.

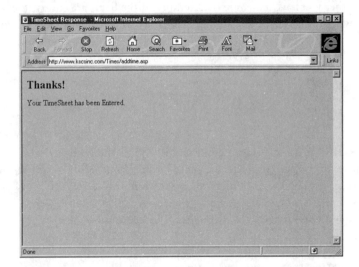

The string is built and sent back to the client browser by using the `Response` object:

```
Response.Write sResponse
```

Finally, to use the constants for ADO in the script file, you must include the ADO include file `adovbs.inc`, which is installed with ASP with this code:

```
<!--#include virtual="/ASPSamp/Samples/adovbs.inc"-->
```

Summary

This chapter introduced you to the Microsoft ActiveX Server framework and Active Server Pages. You should be familiar with the available intrinsic objects and components supplied with ASP, as well as the general syntax used to create Active Server Pages. Active Server Pages provide Web developers with a very powerful toolset for generating dynamic and interactive Web pages. You also were introduced to a database model that uses OLE DB called *Active Data Objects* (ADO).

In the next chapter, you will look at creating your own ActiveX Server components and using them from ASP.

22

Writing Server-Side Applications with VB 5 ActiveX Components

by Mark Spenik

In this chapter, you will learn how to use Visual Basic 5 to write ActiveX components that you can use in server-side applications. You will look at creating business components and components to be used specifically in an Active Server Page environment. You will learn about the thread model supported by Visual Basic 5 components, and you will take an existing Visual Basic class and turn it into an ActiveX component. Creating OLEISAPI components is covered as well.

Overview of VB 5 ActiveX Component's for the World Wide Web

Visual Basic 5 enables you to easily generate ActiveX components (called *OLE servers* in Visual Basic 4). The ActiveX components you create can be used by other applications or development environments, such as Microsoft Excel or Powersoft's PowerBuilder. You can use ActiveX components in a client/server environment, desktop environment, distributed computing environment, or Internet/intranet environment. This chapter focuses on creating ActiveX components to be used in an Internet/intranet environment—more specifically, the Internet/intranet server environment. You can use ActiveX components in a Web-based client much in the way you use ActiveX controls. Instead of an ActiveX control loading to the user's PC, the ActiveX component loads to a user's PC and is used via VBScript. This chapter focuses on building ActiveX server components. You will look at the following types of server components:

- Standard ActiveX components
- ActiveX components designed for ASP
- OLEISAPI

Active Server Pages provide the perfect environment for using ActiveX server components. Most of your Web-based server applications probably will be written using ASP, so this chapter concentrates on using ActiveX components in an ASP environment. The standard, non-ASP environment will be covered as well, via OLEISAPI.

> **NOTE**
>
> Throughout this chapter, when you see a reference to an ActiveX component, the reference is to an ActiveX component created with Visual Basic 5 unless otherwise noted.

Standard ActiveX Components

What this chapter refers to as *standard ActiveX components* are those components in your organization that can be used by any tool or application that supports ActiveX components. Standard components can be the business rules created by your company and used by other applications for validation and computations. The important point about a standard ActiveX component is that you do not have to modify it in any shape or fashion to use the component in any ActiveX-compliant tool or application, such as ASP, Visual Basic, or Microsoft Access.

ActiveX Components Designed for ASP

ActiveX components designed for ASP are components that take advantage of Active Server Page intrinsic objects or components. You build the component to use objects provided in the ASP environment. Because the components rely on ASP objects, they will not work outside of the ASP environment. These components could be business rules, utility functions, or other operations that are difficult to perform with standard Web-based tools.

OLEISAPI

When the Microsoft Internet Information Server (IIS) first shipped, ISAPI was (and still is) the API set provided to C and C++ programmers to extend the capabilities of the Web server. Visual Basic programmers were left out of the loop until Microsoft developed the OLEISAPI DLL (OLE2ISAPI.DLL) that enables Visual Basic programmers to use ActiveX components in standard HTML. This chapter will briefly cover OLEISAPI; however, I would no longer use OLEISAPI now that Microsoft Active Server Pages and the ActiveX Server framework are available. The ActiveX Server framework is a much better environment for using ActiveX components than OLEISAPI. I'll go into more detail about why I think OLEISAPI is outdated when the topic is covered in detail later in this chapter in the section "Using OLEISAPI."

Generating and Registering an ActiveX Server Component

ActiveX server components are simple to generate using Visual Basic 5. You can create components that are out-of-process (*.exe) or in-process (DLLs). Using out-of-process versus in-process is discussed later in this chapter in the section "Selecting the Proper Component Type (DLL or EXE) and Thread Model."

CAUTION

When creating server-side components, do not display any forms, dialog boxes, or message boxes. Server-side components do not have a user interface.

This section walks you through an example of creating an ActiveX DLL that you can use on a Microsoft IIS Web server. For this example, you will use the class DAOHTML, which was developed in Chapter 8, "Using Classes and Objects in Visual Basic 5."

Start a new Visual Basic ActiveX DLL project. Copy the file `DaoHTML.cls` from the CD-ROM at the back of this book to a working directory on your PC. Perform the following steps:

1. Add the class `DAOHTML` to the new project. Choose Project | Add Class Module to display the Add Class Module dialog box shown in Figure 22.1.

FIGURE 22.1.

The Add Class Module dialog box.

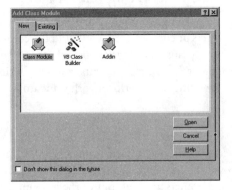

2. Select the Existing tab. Then locate the file `DaoHTML.cls` copied from the book's CD-ROM. Select `DaoHTML.cls` and click Open. The class module `DAOHTML` is added to the project.

3. Select the default class in the project `Class1`. Remove the class by choosing Project | Remove class1. The project now contains only the class module `DAOHTML`. In Visual Basic 4, an entry point was required when creating an ActiveX component. Typically, a module with a dummy procedure called `main` was added as the entry point. Visual Basic 5 no longer requires you to create a dummy entry point for ActiveX components. When generating DLLs, the startup object should be `none`, unless you want to initialize the DLL. To learn how to create an entry point for a DLL, proceed to the next step; otherwise, skip to step 6.

4. Choose Project | Add Module to display the Add Module dialog box shown in Figure 22.2.

FIGURE 22.2.

The Add Module dialog box.

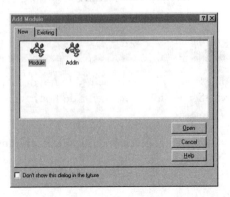

5. Click Open and enter the following line of code in the Module window:

```
Sub Main
```

Press Enter. The line `End Sub` is added automatically. To add the entry point `Main` to your ActiveX component, you would select `Sub Main` in step 8 from the Project Properties dialog box. The entry point is called when your component is created using the `CreateObject` method or the keyword `New`. You then would add code required to initialize your component; dummy entry points are not required in Visual Basic 5. You should create entry points only when you want to initialize variables for the component. Remember that when a Visual Basic class is used to create an object, the class initialize event is invoked. The `DAOHTML` class uses DAO, so you must add a DAO reference to the project to create the object.

6. To add the DAO reference, choose Project | References. The References dialog box appears. Enable the Microsoft DAO 3.5 Object Library checkbox and click OK (see Figure 22.3).

FIGURE 22.3.

The References dialog box.

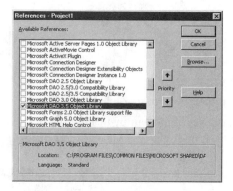

7. Choose Project | *ProjectName* Properties, where *ProjectName* is the name of your project, to display the Project Properties dialog box shown in Figure 22.4.

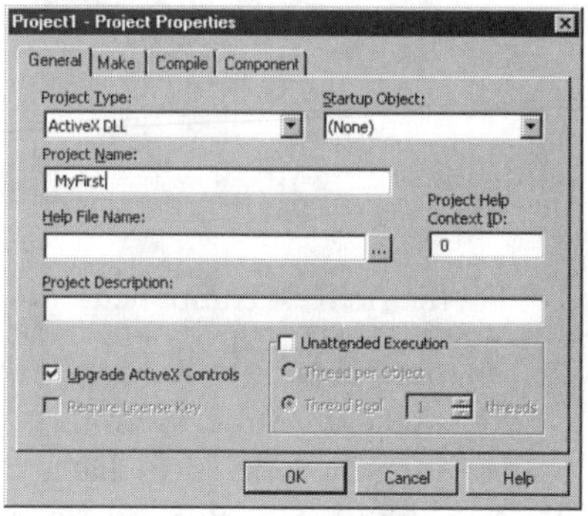

FIGURE 22.4.

The Project Properties dialog box.

8. Use the Project Properties dialog box to name the project. The project name is important when creating an ActiveX component, because the project name will be part of the string used to reference and create the ActiveX component. Enter the name **MyFirst** in the Project Name textbox.

   Notice that the Project Type drop-down combo box displays ActiveX DLL. The Project Type property tells Visual Basic what type of component to create. The Startup Object combo box defaults to None. For most ActiveX DLLs, you should use the default. If your component requires startup code, select Sub Main in the combo box (and complete steps 4 and 5). Then click OK.

9. Click the class module DAOHTML. In the Visual Basic Properties dialog box for the class, set the Instancing property to 5-MultiUse (see Figure 22.5).

FIGURE 22.5.

The Properties dialog box.

10. Save the project by choosing File | Save.

11. Now create the component by making the ActiveX DLL. Choose File | Make MyFirst.DLL to display the Make Project dialog box shown in Figure 22.6.

FIGURE 22.6.

The Make Project dialog box.

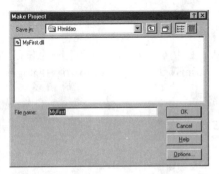

12. Click OK to create the ActiveX component.

You now have created an in-process ActiveX component. You can use the ActiveX component you created just like you would any other ActiveX component. First, you add a component reference to your project using the References dialog box. Then, you create a new instance of the component using Visual Basic 5, as this code shows:

```
Dim oTest As New MyFirst.DAOHTMLTable
```

The following example creates a new instance of MyFirst in an Active Server Page:

```
<% set oTest = Server.CreateObject("MyFirst.DAOHTMLTable")%>
```

Notice the string name used to reference an ActiveX component in ASP. The first part of the string is the name of the Visual Basic project used to create the component. The second part of the string is the module class name exposing the properties and methods you wish to use.

Registering the ActiveX Component on the Server

Before you can use your ActiveX component, you must register the component on your Windows NT Web server. Registering a component writes information about your component to the server's system Registry. You can automatically register an out-of-process ActiveX component (*.exe) by running the component on the server. To register an in-process ActiveX component requires the utility regsrv32.exe. This utility is located on the Visual Basic Professional and Enterprise CD-ROMs. If you installed Active Server Pages on your Windows NT Server and used the standard defaults, you can find the regsrv32 utility in the directory *<drive letter>*:\winnt\system32\inetsrv\asp\cmpnts.

To register your ActiveX in-process component, perform these steps:

1. On the server or machine on which you want to register the component, open a DOS command prompt window.

2. Go to the directory where the regsrv32 utility exists.

3. At the command prompt, enter the following code and then press Enter:

```
regsrv32 full path of the ActiveX component/component file name
```

A message box appears, telling you that your component has been registered successfully. To register the ActiveX component created in the preceding example (assuming that the component is stored in a directory called c:\components), you would enter the following at the command prompt:

```
regsrv32 c:\component\MyFirst.dll
```

Selecting the Proper Component Type (DLL or EXE) and Thread Model

Visual Basic 5 enables you to create ActiveX code components that are in-process (DLLs) or out-of-process (EXEs). Further complicating the type of component to create is the thread model to select. Visual Basic 5 enables you to mark components as thread safe and to generate components that support multiple threads or single threads. Because the focus of this chapter is on creating server-side ActiveX components that will be used in the Microsoft ActiveX Server framework, the type of component to generate is simplified, as well as the proper thread model. For ActiveX server-side components, should you create an in-process (DLL) or out-of-process (EXE) component? For the answer, read the following tip.

TIP

When creating Web-based server ActiveX components, create the component as an in-process component (an ActiveX DLL). Generating an ActiveX DLL provides better performance than out-of-process components, because the in-process component runs in the same process space as the application that uses the component (IIS). The application therefore can reference the component's properties and methods without making the costly cross-process calls required for out-of-process components. Out-of-process components do have some positive features not available to in-process components that can be used in a distributed computing or client/server environment, such as asynchronous callbacks or asynchronous notification events. In a Web-based environment, stick to using ActiveX DLLs.

The Visual Basic 5 ActiveX Component Thread Model

Before examining the thread model used by Visual Basic 5 when creating ActiveX components, take a quick look at the definition of a thread.

A *thread* is executing code. Every application in a Windows environment has at least a single thread of execution. An application or component is *multithreaded* if the application can create more than one thread of execution. Suppose that you have a financial database application and you have a computation that executes for a long time. If your application is multithreaded, you can start your computation by creating a thread to perform the computation. Then, while the computation thread is executing, you can begin to edit a database table using another thread. Multitasking preemptive operating systems, such as Windows NT and Windows 95, allocate separate time slices for each thread to execute (the computation thread and the edit table thread, for example), which gives the appearance of performing both tasks simultaneously. A thread model describes the environment in which a single or multiple thread executes and interacts with other threads. The Active Server framework supports several thread models. As a Visual Basic developer, however, you will be concerned only with the thread model used by *all* Visual Basic components (in-process and out-of-process), which is the Apartment Thread model shown in Figure 22.7.

In the Apartment Thread model, each thread contains its own container, or *apartment*, where all the objects created and used by the thread reside. The objects created in the apartment are unaware of other objects residing in other apartment threads. Each apartment has its own copy of global variables, which eliminates the possibility of multiple threads overwriting global data variables and makes the Apartment Thread model safe for use in multithreaded clients.

Objects in the same apartment can share information via global variables without any performance penalty. Objects residing in other apartments can share information with each other by using object references. When objects communicate across apartments, a mechanism called *cross-threaded marshaling* is used. The performance of cross-threaded marshaling is slow and is comparable to the performance of cross-process marshaling used to communicate with out-of-process ActiveX components.

FIGURE 22.7.
The Apartment Thread model.

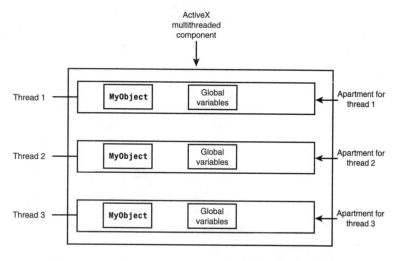

The Instancing Property and Single or Multithreaded ActiveX Components

Every class you create with Visual Basic has an Instancing property, which determines how the class or object is created (see Figure 22.8). When developing ActiveX server components, you should create your ActiveX server components as DLLs (in-process components) most of the time to simplify the values of the Class Instancing property.

FIGURE 22.8
The Class
Instancing
property.

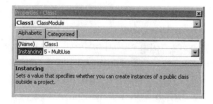

The default value of the Instancing property for an ActiveX DLL is MultiUse (an integer value of 5) and single threaded. For an ActiveX server-side component, always set the Instancing property to MultiUse. When a DLL is created using the MultiUse property and a single thread, a single copy of the object is loaded into the address space of the client. What happens when multiple users want to use the same object? To understand the behavior of a MultiUse component with multiple users, take a look at the example in Figure 22.9.

FIGURE 22.9.

A MultiUse, *single-threaded ActiveX component with multiple users.*

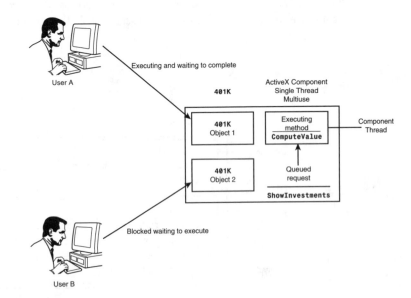

The 401K object is used to manage an employee's 401(k) investment plan and has two methods: ComputeValue and ShowInvestments. The ComputeValue method takes several minutes to perform, and the ShowInvestments method occurs simultaneously. User A accesses a Web page that creates an instance of the 401K object, which is an ActiveX single-threaded DLL created with Visual Basic 5. User A begins to execute the ComputeValue method. User B accesses the same Web page and shares the same DLL for the 401K object being used by User A. User B executes the ShowInvestments method; however, the results are not returned immediately. Instead, User B finds herself blocked waiting for User A's ComputeValue method to complete execution. So what's going on? When the Instancing property of a component is set to MultiUse, a single instance of the DLL can be shared by multiple users simultaneously to create objects. What if users overwrite each other's data? No problem: To prevent user requests from overlapping and possibly overwriting global or local variables, the ActiveX component uses serialization. *Serialization* ensures that the component will execute only one user request at a time from start to completion. Pending requests are queued up and executed in turn. Using the example in Figure 22.9, User B is blocked waiting for User A's request to complete. Blocking quickly can become a big problem in an Internet/intranet environment. Fortunately, Visual Basic 5 enables you to create multithreaded ActiveX DLLs.

NOTE

You cannot spawn (create) a new thread by using a Visual Basic application or component. Multithreaded clients such as IIS, however, can take advantage of multithreaded ActiveX components and create multiple threads using a multithreaded Visual Basic component. When IIS creates an object from a multithreaded component, IIS creates a new thread for the object. If the Visual Basic component is marked as single threaded, IIS cannot create a new thread.

With Visual Basic 5, you can create multithreaded ActiveX DLLs. Use the example with the 401K object but, this time, assume that the DLL is created to be multithreaded. Examine Figure 22.10 to walk through the multiuser example and see how you can avoid blocking.

FIGURE 22.10.

A MultiUse, *multithreaded ActiveX component with multiple users.*

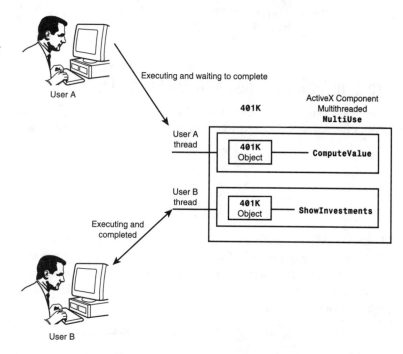

User A accesses a Web page that creates an instance of the 401K object, which is an ActiveX multithreaded DLL created with Visual Basic 5. User A begins to execute the ComputeValue method. User B accesses the same Web page and shares the same DLL for the 401K object being used by User A. User B executes the ShowInvestments method, and the results are returned immediately. User B is not blocked waiting for User A's request to complete. Instead, in a multithreaded ActiveX component, when User B creates a 401K object, User B's 401K object creates a separate thread and apartment in which User B's objects can reside. Any object that User B creates will live inside User B's apartment thread, as shown in Figure 22.10. Objects in User B's apartment can communicate with each other, because they are in the same address space. Objects also can communicate with objects in other threads using cross-process marshaling. The cross-process call is serialized in the thread you are calling, and the calling thread is blocked until the request can be completed.

> **TIP**
>
> When creating ActiveX server components, you should create multithreaded DLLs. This provides you with the best ActiveX component performance and eliminates possible multiuser blocking during execution of lengthy methods. There is one drawback of a multithreaded ActiveX DLL created with Visual Basic: If a fatal error occurs in one apartment and terminates the thread, any other threads using the component also are terminated.

Creating Multithreaded ActiveX Server DLLs

When you create a multithreaded ActiveX server DLL, the component cannot require any user interaction. ActiveX DLLs that use any of the following cannot be multithreaded:

■ Controls

■ Forms

■ ActiveX documents

■ Classes created with ActiveX designers

Message boxes and system-error messages are suppressed and can be written to the Windows NT Event log by setting the Visual Basic App object's LogMode property. To set the LogMode property, use the App object's StartLogging method. ActiveX DLLs that require user interaction or that contain controls, forms, ActiveX documents, or classes generated by ActiveX designers are only single threaded.

To create a multithreaded ActiveX DLL, perform these steps:

1. Make sure that the project does not contain any controls, forms, ActiveX documents, or classes created by using an ActiveX designer. If the project contains any of these elements, remove them. Otherwise, you will be unable to create a multithreaded DLL.

2. From the Visual Basic main menu, choose Project | Properties. The Project Properties dialog box appears, as shown in Figure 22.11.

3. In the General tab, enable the Unattended Execution checkbox.

4. Click OK to save the change.

FIGURE 22.11.
The Project Properties dialog box.

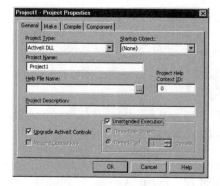

When the ActiveX DLL is compiled with the Unattended Execution checkbox enabled, a DLL that supports multithreading is generated. When creating multithreaded ActiveX components, keep in mind that Visual Basic DLLs use Apartment model threading and that ActiveX component automation uses serialization of requests to prevent multiple threads from executing a new operation before previous operations have completed. Keeping component serialization intact is important, because Visual Basic ActiveX components are not re-entrant. *Re-entrancy* is the capability of code to be executed by a thread, and, before the thread completes, the thread yields control of the processor to another thread to process the same code. When the second thread yields processor control, the variables and stack pointer are restored to the exact state prior to the processor yielding control to another thread. Visual Basic ActiveX components are *not re-entrant,* so when creating ActiveX components, *do not* do any of the following in your component, because it might cause the processor to yield to another thread before completing the current operation:

■ Call DoEvents

■ Raise an event handled by an object on another thread or process

■ Invoke a method or property of an object in another thread or process

Now that you have learned that you should create ActiveX components that are multithreaded DLLs, start to think of all the different server-side ActiveX components you can use to energize your Web pages and how your Visual Basic skills can continue to aid you in the Web development environment.

Using OLEISAPI

When Microsoft released IIS, the ISAPI API was released to enable C programmers to write ISAPI programs and filters to extend the services provided by IIS. Well, what about the Visual Basic programmers? OLEISAPI was Microsoft's answer. OLEISAPI is a DLL provided by Microsoft that enables Visual Basic developers to use ActiveX components in Web pages with IIS. OLEISAPI was okay when it was the only way for a Visual Basic programmer to use ActiveX components with Microsoft's IIS. But with the release of IIS 3.0 and the ActiveX Server framework, I strongly urge you *not* to use OLEISAPI unless you are using an older version of Microsoft IIS that does not support Active Server Pages.

Here are a few reasons why using ActiveX components with Active Server Pages is preferred over OLEISAPI:

■ OLEISAPI does not enable you to use your ActiveX components without using a template. The template has the required HTML Action methods, such as DoPost and DoGet. Active Server Pages enable you to use the ActiveX components without any special methods. The ActiveX component you use with Microsoft Access, for example, also can be used on your Web server without any modifications.

■ OLEISAPI requires a special DLL, oleisapi.dll, that can be obtained from Microsoft's Website as well as various product CD-ROMs. Active Server Pages is part of IIS 3.0.

■ You must write the code to parse the incoming HTML string and, based on the string passed in, determine which method of your ActiveX component you want to call. Active Server Pages parse out special HTML characters embedded in strings sent to the server for you so you do not have to know that a plus sign (+) equals a space. Also, Active Server Pages enable you to directly invoke methods of your ActiveX component.

■ You must write the code to generate the HTML to return to the browser in your component. If you decide to experiment or change the format of the HTML returned, you have to recompile and reinstall the DLL to test out the changes. Reinstalling your DLL requires shutting down IIS, because the DLL is loaded into IIS's memory.

The bottom line is that, if you currently are using OLEISAPI and you can switch to Active Server Pages, do so! If you do not have Active Server Pages installed on your IIS, what are you waiting for? Time to upgrade!

If you still want to experiment with OLEISAPI, Microsoft includes OLEISAPI examples on the VB 5 CD as well as on its Website. You also must make sure that oleisapi.dll is in a directory with execute permission. When creating an OLEISAPI component, you must add the method you will use to invoke the component. If you want to submit a form for a guest registration database using the HTML form action Post, for example, you would add the following method to your class:

```
Sub DoGet(strHTMLrequest As String, strHTMLResponse As String)

    'Add code to parse the HTML string sent from the Server
    'Add code to determine the proper Method you wish to invoke for your component
        'For instance, if you were adding an entry to a Guest Registration Database
        ➥you
        'could call a function or procedure called AddGuest
    'Add code to properly format an HTML response and then set the string
        'strHTMLResponse to the HTML string you want to send back to the browser.

End Sub
```

The following HTML shows how to call a component from a Web page using OLEISAPI:

```
<FORM ACTION="/oleisapi/oleisapi.dll/GuestAdd.WebOLE.DoPost" METHOD="Post">
```

In the HTML line using OLEISAPI, `GuestAdd` is the component, `WebOLE` is the Visual Basic class and `DoPost` is the method. One last comment on OLEISAPI: In the next two sections, you will see how much simpler it is to use existing and new ActiveX components in your Web pages, because they require fewer restrictions and programming than OLEISAPI.

Using Standard ActiveX Components

By using Active Server Pages, you can use existing ActiveX components in your Web pages that also can be used in any application or development tool that supports ActiveX components, such as Microsoft Excel, Powersoft's PowerBuilder, Borland's Delphi, or Microsoft's Visual Basic. Unlike OLEISAPI, ASP enables you to use existing ActiveX components in your Web pages without any component modifications required.

What kind of coding routines make good ActiveX components? The typical scenario given for generating standard ActiveX components is the three-tier architecture for software systems. The typical three-tier system consists of the upper tier, called *user services*, which provides user interaction services; a middle tier, called *business services*; and the bottom tier, which provides *data services*. In a three-tier architecture, ActiveX components are the perfect solution for the middle-tier business rules. ActiveX component reuse enables you to create the business rule one time and to use the rule-based component in other applications, including Web-based applications.

For this book, instead of creating a fictitious ActiveX business-rule component to use in an Active Server Page, you'll generate a component that enables you to use one of my favorite missing functions from VBScript in a Web page: the Visual Basic `Format` function. The `Format` function enables you to take a numeric or date expression and format the expression based on a specific format mask you provide. VBScript does not support the `Format` function, so to display a date in the format `Tuesday, January 28, 1997` requires some work using VBScript, not to mention that changing the date format to `19970128` requires more VBScript work. The syntax for the `Format` function follows:

```
Format(express [, format[, firstdayofweek[, firstweekofyear]]])
```

where `express` is the numeric or date expression to evaluate, and `format` is the mask to use to properly format the expression. `firstdayofweek` and `firstweekofyear` are Visual Basic constants and optional parameters that will not be used in your ActiveX component. The ActiveX component will be a simple component that wraps a few lines of code around the `Format` function and exposes methods and properties that permit you to use the `Format` function in an Active Server Page. The ActiveX component is called `FormatVB.DLL`. The component will be generated as an in-process (DLL), multithreaded ActiveX component.

> **NOTE**
>
> The following code for the ActiveX component FormatVB.DLL is located on the CD-ROM that accompanies this book. The Visual Basic project name is FormatVB.vbp. The Active Server Page used to demonstrate the component also is on the CD-ROM and is called Format.asp.

The FormatVB component is based on the NumDate class, which has the following properties:

- Expression
- FormatMask
- FType
- ErrorMessage

The Expression property is a variant data type and holds the number or date to format. The FormatMask property is a string that holds the mask to use to format the expression. The ErrorMessage property helps you debug the component. If an error occurs while formatting an expression, the ErrorMessage property contains the Visual Basic error message generated; otherwise, for successful operations, it is empty. The property FType determines whether the expression is a date or numeric value. FType is not really required for this component, because the Format function takes a variant data parameter for the expression. I included it, however, to show you how to use Visual Basic 5 enumerations. *Enumerations* enable you to define groups of constants. Even more important, when properly defined, enumerations show up in the Object Browser for your ActiveX component as well as in the Auto-Code feature of the Visual Basic Editor when setting your components properties that have enumerations.

The following enumeration, for example, declares two constants that will be assigned the values 0 and 1:

```
'Valid Property Values for the Type property
Public Enum FTypeValue
    ftDate
    ftNumeric
End Enum
```

Now, to tie the enumeration to a property to take advantage of the Auto-Code feature of the Visual Basic Editor and Object Browser, assign the enumeration type as the return or input data type of the property. For example, the FType Get property procedure follows:

```
Public Property Get FType() As FTypeValue
'used when retrieving value of a property, on the right side of an
'assignment.  Syntax: Debug.Print X.Type
    FType = mvarType
End Property
```

The FormatVB object contains a single method called DoFormat that returns a variant with the properly formatted date or numeric. The DoFormat method checks to see whether the

Expression property contains a valid numeric or date. If the expression is a valid numeric or date, the DoFormat property executes the Visual Basic Format function and returns the formatted output. Listing 22.1 shows the entire code for the NumDate class.

Listing 22.1. The NumDate class.

```
'local variable(s) to hold property value(s)
Private mvarExpression As Variant 'local copy
Private mvarFormatMask As String 'local copy
Private mvarErrorMessage As String 'local copy
Private mvarType As Integer 'local copy
'
'Valid Property Values for the Type property
Public Enum FTypeValue
    ftDate
    ftNumeric
End Enum
Public Property Let FType(ByVal vData As FTypeValue)
'used when assigning a value to the property, on the left side of an
'assignment.  Syntax: X.Type = 5
    mvarType = vData
End Property

Public Property Get FType() As FTypeValue
'used when retrieving value of a property, on the right side of an
'assignment.  Syntax: Debug.Print X.Type
    FType = mvarType
End Property

Public Property Let ErrorMessage(ByVal vData As String)
'used when assigning a value to the property, on the left side of an
'assignment.  Syntax: X.ErrorMessage = 5
    mvarErrorMessage = vData
End Property
Public Property Get ErrorMessage() As String
'used when retrieving value of a property, on the right side of an
'assignment.  Syntax: Debug.Print X.ErrorMessage
    ErrorMessage = mvarErrorMessage
End Property

Public Function DoFormat() As Variant
Dim vReturnValue As Variant

    'Set up an Error Handler
    On Error GoTo DoFormat_Error
    'Initialize the return values
    vReturnValue = ""
    mvarErrorMessage = ""

    'Check to make sure the expression to format is
    'valid for the type selected
    If mvarType = ftDate Then
        If Not IsDate(mvarExpression) Then
            mvarErrorMessage = "The value in the Expression " & _
                            "property is not a valid date."
        End If
```

continues

Listing 22.1. continued

```
    Else
        'Check for valid Numeric Value
        If Not IsNumeric(mvarExpression) Then
            mvarErrorMessage = "The value in the Expression " & _
                                "property is not a valid numeric."
        End If
    End If

    'If the expression is a valid date or numeric
    'perform the Format function.
    If mvarErrorMessage = "" Then
        vReturnValue = Format(mvarExpression, mvarFormatMask)
    End If

'Standard Exit
DoFormat_Exit:

    'Return the Formatted value
    DoFormat = vReturnValue
    Exit Function

'Standard Error Handler
'
DoFormat_Error:
    mvarErrorMessage = "Error Formatting expression. " & Err.Description
    vReturnValue = ""
    Resume DoFormat_Exit
End Function

Public Property Let FormatMask(ByVal vData As String)
'used when assigning a value to the property, on the left side of an
'assignment.  Syntax: X.FormatMask = 5
    mvarFormatMask = vData
End Property
Public Property Get FormatMask() As String
'used when retrieving value of a property, on the right side of an
'assignment.  Syntax: Debug.Print X.FormatMask
    FormatMask = mvarFormatMask
End Property
Public Property Let Expression(ByVal vData As Variant)
'used when assigning a value to the property, on the left side of an
'assignment.  Syntax: X.Expression = 5
    mvarExpression = vData
End Property
Public Property Set Expression(ByVal vData As Object)
'used when assigning an Object to the property, on the left side of
'a Set statement. Syntax: Set x.Expression = Form1
    Set mvarExpression = vData
End Property
Public Property Get Expression() As Variant
'used when retrieving value of a property, on the right side of an
'assignment.  Syntax: Debug.Print X.Expression
    If IsObject(mvarExpression) Then
        Set Expression = mvarExpression
    Else
        Expression = mvarExpression
    End If
End Property
```

The ActiveX component is complete; you're ready to test the component (remember that, with Visual Basic 5, you do not need a dummy empty procedure for an entry point when generating ActiveX components). The easiest way to test a standard ActiveX component is to use the same method used in Visual Basic 4 to test OLE Automation servers. From the Visual Basic design environment, run the ActiveX component project. Start a second Visual Basic session and add the ActiveX component currently running in the first Visual Basic session to the References dialog box of the new project. Create a test program that creates an object using your ActiveX component. Add code in the test program to set the methods and properties of your object. Then run and execute the test program. You can use the debugger in both Visual Basic sessions to debug your component or test program.

After the ActiveX component is tested properly, compile the ActiveX component to build the DLL. Don't forget to set the proper project options to make the DLL multithreaded. After you compile the ActiveX component, you need to register the DLL on your Web server using the `regsrv32` program discussed earlier. You now are ready to use the ActiveX component on a Web page. Listing 22.2 shows the Active Server Page created to test the `FormatVB` component.

Listing 22.2. Source code to the Active Server Page to test the ActiveX component `FormatVB`.

```
<!DOCTYPE HTML PUBLIC "-//IETF//DTD HTML//EN">
<html>
<!-- Active Server Page Example Using a Visual Basic ActiveX Component  -->
<!-- Author: Mark Spenik -->
<!-- Revision History: Jan. 31, 1997 -->
<!-- This example uses an ActiveX component to provide -->
<!-- the Visual Basic Format function in a Web Page.        -->
<!--                                                      -->
<SCRIPT LANGUAGE=VBScript RUNAT=Server>
Function FormatExpression

    'Initialize the default string
    sExpress = ""

    'Create an instance of the ActiveX Component
    Set oFormat = Server.CreateObject("FormatVB.NumDate")

    'Check if it's a date - if so set the type property
    If IsDate(Request.Form("txtExpression")) then
        'Set the value to reflect a date
        oFormat.Ftype = 0
    Else
        'Set the required properties
        oFormat.FType = 1
    End If

    'Set the Expression property from the submitted form
    oFormat.Expression = Request.Form("txtExpression")

    'Set the FormatMask property from the submitted form
    oFormat.FormatMask = Request.Form("txtFormatMask")
```

continues

Listing 22.2. continued

```
    'Format the String
    sExpress = oFormat.DoFormat

    'Check For Errors
    If oFormat.ErrorMessage <> "" Then
        'Error found display back in the Web Page
        sExpress = oFormat.ErrorMessage
    End If

    'Cleanup - A good VB Practice - although with ASP not required.
    Set oFormat = Nothing

    'Return the string to the caller
    FormatExpression = sExpress
End Function
</SCRIPT>
<head>
<meta http-equiv="Content-Type"
content="text/html; charset=iso-8859-1">
<meta name="GENERATOR" content="Microsoft FrontPage 2.0">
<title>Home Page</title>
</head>

<body bgcolor="#000080" text="#FFFF00">

<p><font color="#FF0000"><marquee bgcolor="#FFFFFF">Testing a Standard ActiveX
Component</marquee></font></p>

<hr color="#FF0000">
<!-- In this example, we are posting back to the same ASP file that -->
<!-- submits the request. As such first parse the form to see if it has -->
<!-- Been entered properly.  -->
<%
If Request.Form("txtExpression")="" Then
    sMsg = "Enter an expression to format."
ElseIf Request.Form("txtFormatMask")="" Then
    sMsg = "Enter a valid format mask."
Else
    sMsg = FormatExpression
End If
%>
Enter a date or numeric and a format mask. For example: <BR>
a date of Jan. 1, 1997 and a Format Mask of mmddyyyy will <BR>
return 01011997.
<form method="POST" name="frmExpression" Action="format.asp">
    <p>Expression <input type="text" size="22"
    name="txtExpression" VALUE="<%=Request.Form("txtExpression")%>"></p>
    <p>Format Mask <input type="text" size="22"
    name="txtFormatMask" VALUE="<%=Request.Form("txtFormatMask")%>"></p>
    <p><input type="submit" name="cmdFormat" value="Format"></p>
</form>
```

```
<hr color="#FF0000">
<!-- Send back the formatted Expression or instructions. -->
<B><%=sMsg%></B>
</body>
</html>
```

The Active Server Page shown in Listing 22.2 is a bit complex because the form posts the information back to the originating ASP file (Format.asp). To post information back to the originating ASP file, set the Action tag of the form to the originating ASP filename. In Listing 22.2, for example, the following line posts the form back to Format.asp, the originating file:

```
<form method="POST" name="frmExpression" Action="format.asp">
```

The following script examines the values of the Request object to determine whether the form has been submitted or is being loaded or refreshed:

```
<!-- In this example, we are posting back to the same ASP file that -->
<!-- submits the request. As such first parse the form to see if it has -->
<!-- been entered properly.  -->
<%
If Request.Form("txtExpression")="" Then
    sMsg = "Enter an expression to format."
ElseIf Request.Form("txtFormatMask")="" Then
    sMsg = "Enter a valid format mask."
Else
    sMsg = FormatExpression
End If
%>
```

If the form has been submitted, all the Request objects will have valid values, and the function FormatExpression is called (see Listing 22.2 for a full listing of the FormatExpression script). The following script found in the function FormatExpression creates an instance of the FormatVB object:

```
'Create an instance of the ActiveX Component
    Set oFormat = Server.CreateObject("FormatVB.NumDate")
```

The FormatExpression function returns a formatted string or error message. The output of the FormatExpression is returned to the browser with the following line of code:

```
<!-- Send back the formatted Expression or instructions. -->
<B><%=sMsg%></B>
```

Figure 22.12 shows the completed Web page.

FIGURE 22.12.

An Active Server page to test the ActiveX component FormatVB.

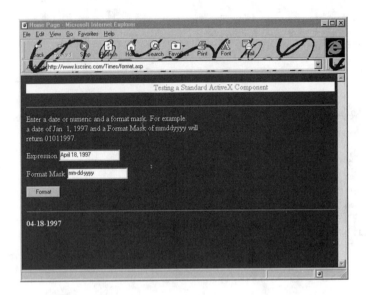

Standard Component Recap

You should remember some of these important points about using standard ActiveX components on a Web page:

- ■ You can use the component on your Web page by using ASP and any application that supports ActiveX components without any modifications.

- ■ Test and debug the ActiveX component in the Visual Basic 5 environment before using it on your Web server.

- ■ Make sure that you register the component properly on your Web server by using the regsrv32.exe utility.

- ■ For performance reasons, create your component as an in-process multithreaded component (DLL).

- ■ Make sure that your Web-based ActiveX components do not require any user interaction or perform any operations that could cause problems in a multithreaded environment (DoEvents, for example).

ActiveX Components Designed for ASP

In addition to generating standard ActiveX components that can be used in application or development environments, you can generate ActiveX components specifically designed to be used in the ASP environment. These components can interact with standard ASP objects, such as the Application or Response object. Building ActiveX components that interact with ASP objects requires registering the Active Server page DLL, asp.dll, on your local development machine and adding a project reference to the DLL. The DLL, as well as the Active Server Page environment, can be loaded by using Microsoft Visual InterDev or by copying `asp.dll` from your Microsoft IIS 3.0 (located in the directory `\Intsrv\ASP`) to your development machine. Although I slammed OLEISAPI because of the templates and modifications required to use a standard ActiveX component via OLEISAPI, I really like the capability to interact with the ASP environment directly via an ActiveX component written specifically for the ASP environment. I think you will find many instances when you will want to design components that you plan to use only in Web-based applications. Creating ASP ActiveX components enables you to write code and perform tasks in a familiar Visual Basic environment while interacting with ASP objects.

Generating Active Server Page ActiveX Components

The only difference between creating a standard ActiveX component and an ASP ActiveX component is that the ASP ActiveX component has a reference to the Microsoft Active Server Pages 1.0 Object Library, selected in the Visual Basic project References dialog box shown in Figure 22.13, and the component reference's ASP objects, such as the `Response` object in code.

FIGURE 22.13.
The Visual Basic project References dialog box with the Microsoft Active Server Pages 1.0 Object Library selected.

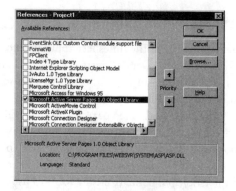

Obtaining an ASP Object Reference in an ActiveX Component

The Active Server Page Object Library provides several object classes that can be used in Visual Basic ActiveX components. To use Active Server Page object classes in your Visual Basic ActiveX components, you must obtain a reference to the object you want to use. You can obtain an ASP object reference by passing an ASP object reference to your component (as a method parameter or by setting a property) or by using the ASP `ScriptingContext` class and the `OnStartPage` method (the `OnEndPage` method also is supported). Using the `OnStartPage` method is simpler, because a special object called the `ScriptingContext` object is passed automatically by IIS as a method parameter. The `ScriptingContext` object supplies methods that can be used to obtain references to the following Active Server Page objects:

■ `Application`

■ `Session`

■ Server

■ Request

■ Response

By using the ScriptingContext object, your component can generate references to the desired ASP object without relying on the Web page author to correctly pass the required ASP references used by your component. Now look at a quick scenario on how the OnStartPage and OnEndPage methods are handled. When a Web page is retrieved that uses ActiveX components, the server looks for OnStartPage methods for all components on the page except those that have application scope. The OnStartPage method is executed for all the components before any script executing (remember that IIS passes a ScriptingContext object reference as a parameter in the OnStartPage method). When all the scripts on the page complete, the OnEndPage method is invoked for ActiveX components that have defined the method. The OnStartPage and OnEndPage methods are never called for application-scope ActiveX components. The only way to create application-scope objects from ActiveX components created with Visual Basic is to use the <OBJECT> tag in the Global.asa file. Any required ASP references must be passed into the component's methods or properties.

Using an ASP ActiveX Component in a Web Application

In this section, you'll enhance the timesheet application created in Chapter 21, "Active Server Pages, OLE DB, and Active Data Objects." You'll add an ActiveX component that displays previous timesheets added in an HTML table. You'll also modify the application to post the timesheet to the same ASP file instead of using multiple ASP files. The ASP ActiveX component will have a single method called GetEmpTime that will retrieve all the previous records entered by an individual and display them at the bottom of the HTML page. The Visual Basic ActiveX component will use the method OnStartPage to obtain a reference to the ASP Scripting Context object. The Visual Basic component will create an instance of the ASP Request object to read the employee name from the form to use for the timesheet retrieval query. An instance of the Response object will be created to send back the HTML table of timesheets entered to the client browser. ADO will be used to retrieve information from a Microsoft Access database. The ActiveX component also will log informational and error events to the Windows NT application Event log by using the Visual Basic App object.

> **NOTE**
>
> The Visual Basic 5 code for the component is located on the accompanying CD-ROM. The project file name is ASPComp.vbp. The Active Server page used to test the component is called SrvTimes.asp. The Microsoft Access database used is the Times.mdb database used in Chapter 21 for the timesheet application.

Figure 22.14 shows the completed Web page application with retrieved records.

FIGURE 22.14.

The timesheet application using an ActiveX component.

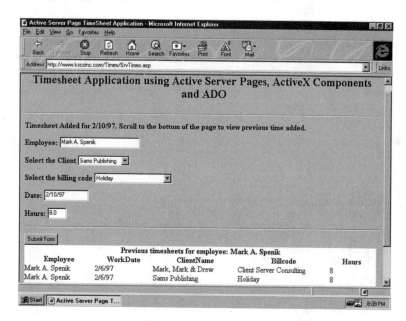

The Visual Basic 5 source code for the component is a single class called `GetTime`. The class has no properties and a single method called `GetEmpTime`. The ActiveX component generated is called `ASPComp.dll`. Listing 22.3 shows the code for the `GetTime` class.

Listing 22.3. Source code for the `GetTime` class that makes up the ActiveX component `ASPComp`.

```
'Define a private Variable to use to generate any
'ASP object required for our component
Private goCurrentScript As ASPTypeLibrary.ScriptingContext

Public Function OnStartPage(oScriptContext As ASPTypeLibrary.ScriptingContext)
Dim strLogFile As String
    'This function is called when the Web page that uses
    'this component is being loaded. IIS will pass in the
    'references to the ASP ScriptingContext object.

    'Set a global reference to the Scripting Context object
    'to use in the Component's
'methods.
    Set goCurrentScript = oScriptContext

    'Let's start logging the component's progress
'using the Visual Basic App object.
    'On Windows NT the Log file is written to the Application
    'event log - on Windows 95 - to the File specified.
    strLogFile = App.Path & "\" & "axcomp.log"
    App.StartLogging strLogFile, vbLogAuto
```

continues

Listing 22.3. continued

```
    'Log the Startup Event
    App.LogEvent "OnStartPage Method Invoked for ASPComp",
➥vbLogEventTypeInformation

End Function

Public Function OnEndPage()

    'Log the terminate event
    App.LogEvent "OnEndPage Method Invoked for ASPComp", vbLogEventTypeInformation

    'Clean up global object reference
    Set goCurrentScript = Nothing

End Function

Public Function GetEmpTime()
Dim oRequest As ASPTypeLibrary.Request    'Request Object
Dim oResponse As ASPTypeLibrary.Response 'Response Object
Dim rsEmployee As New ADODB.Recordset
Dim strErrMsg As String, strSQL As String
Dim strHTMLReturn As String
Dim intNumOfColumns As Integer
Dim fldRec As Field
Dim colFields As Fields
Dim intCount As Integer 'Generic Counter

    'Set up a generic Error Handler
    On Error GoTo GetEmpTime_Error
    strErrMsg = ""

    'Check for the global script context object
    If (goCurrentScript Is Nothing) Then
        strErrMsg = "Global reference to ScriptingContext object missing." & _
        " Make sure the object does not have Application scope and " _
        & " that you use Server.CreateObject."
        GoTo GetEmpTime_Exit
    End If

    'Obtain the required ASP references
    Set oRequest = goCurrentScript.Request
    Set oResponse = goCurrentScript.Response

    'Set up the SQL string required to retrieve all
    'timesheets for the current employee (i.e one submitted the form)
    strSQL = "Select Employee, WorkDate, ClientName, Billcode, Hours From EmpTime
➥Where Employee = '"
    strSQL = strSQL & oRequest.Form("txtEmployee") & "'"

    'Open a resultset based on the SQL Statement
    rsEmployee.Open strSQL, "DSN=TimeSheet"

    'App.LogEvent "All Objects Created.", vbLogEventTypeInformation

    'If No records in the recordset - exit now
    If (rsEmployee.BOF) And (rsEmployee.EOF) _
        Then GoTo GetEmpTime_Exit
```

```
    'Begin the Table format using the TAG Table
    strHTMLReturn = "<TABLE width=100% cellspacing=0 cellpadding=0 "

    'Add the table Background color
    strHTMLReturn = strHTMLReturn & "BGCOLOR = white ALIGN=Center>" & vbCrLf

    'Add the Table Caption
    strHTMLReturn = strHTMLReturn & "<CAPTION><B>" & _
                    "Previous timesheets for employee:  " & _
                    oRequest.Form("txtEmployee") & "</B></CAPTION><P>" & vbCrLf

    'Basic HTML string is set up - get the Number of Columns
intNumOfColumns = rsEmployee.Fields.Count - 1 'Make 0 based
    Set colFields = rsEmployee.Fields

    'Add column Headers
    For Each fldRec In colFields
        strHTMLReturn = strHTMLReturn & "<TH>" & fldRec.Name
    Next fldRec
    strHTMLReturn = strHTMLReturn & vbCrLf

    'Add The data rows
    ' Do until all the records have been processed
    While Not rsEmployee.BOF And Not rsEmployee.EOF
        strHTMLReturn = strHTMLReturn & "<TR>"
        For intCount = 0 To intNumOfColumns
            'Add proper HTML Tags for each column
            strHTMLReturn = strHTMLReturn & "<TD>" & _
                            rsEmployee(intCount) & "</TD>" & vbCrLf
        Next intCount
        strHTMLReturn = strHTMLReturn & "</TR>"
        'Get the Next Record
        rsEmployee.MoveNext

    Wend
    rsEmployee.Close
    'End the Table TAG
    strHTMLReturn = strHTMLReturn & "</TABLE>"
    App.LogEvent "Completed building table", vbLogEventTypeInformation

    'Send the table to the Browser
    oResponse.Write strHTMLReturn

'Single Exit Point
GetEmpTime_Exit:
    'Clean up any component references that were obtained
If Not (oRequest Is Nothing) Then
        Set oRequest = Nothing
    End If

    If Not (oResponse Is Nothing) Then
        Set oResponse = Nothing
    End If

    If Not (rsEmployee Is Nothing) Then
        Set rsEmployee = Nothing
    End If
```

continues

Listing 22.3. continued

```
        GetEmpTime = strErrMsg
        Exit Function

'Generic Error Handler
GetEmpTime_Error:
        'Get the Error Message
        strErrMsg = "Error retrieving employee time. " & Err.Description

        'Write to the application log
        App.LogEvent strErrMsg, vbLogEventTypeError
        Resume GetEmpTime_Exit
End Function
```

Now take a closer look at some of the code. The `OnStartPage` method is called when Active Server Pages is loaded. An instance of the ASP `ScriptingContext` object is passed into the method by IIS. A global private copy of the `ScriptingContext` object is set for later use, as shown here:

```
Set goCurrentScript = oScriptContext
```

The `App` object is used to set up message logging to the Windows NT Event log, as well as to log a message to the Event log using this code:

```
'Let's start logging the component's progress
'using the Visual Basic App object.
        'On Windows NT the Log file is written to the Application
        'event log - on Windows 95 - to the File specified.
        strLogFile = App.Path & "\" & "axcomp.log"
        App.StartLogging strLogFile, vbLogAuto

        'Log the Startup Event
        App.LogEvent "OnStartPage Method Invoked for ASPComp",
        ➥vbLogEventTypeInformation
```

To read the submitted form values in the ActiveX component, instead of passing values through properties or methods, an instance of the ASP `Request` object is created to read the submitted HTML form. An instance of the ASP `Response` object is created to send information back to the browser. The following code uses the `ScriptingContext` object to create the ASP objects:

```
'Obtain the required ASP references
        Set oRequest = goCurrentScript.Request
        Set oResponse = goCurrentScript.Response
```

The code required to retrieve the HTML form value `txtEmployee` to set up the ADO query to retrieve previously entered timesheets from the database looks very similar to VBScript code used in ASP. The code follows:

```
'Set up the SQL string required to retrieve all
        'timesheets for the current employee (i.e one submitted the form)
        strSQL = "Select Employee, WorkDate, ClientName, Billcode, Hours From EmpTime
        ➥Where Employee = '"
        strSQL = strSQL & oRequest.Form("txtEmployee") & "'"
```

The code to send the formatted HTML table back to the browser also looks very familiar (ASP):

```
'Send the table to the Browser
    oResponse.Write strHTMLReturn
```

Listing 22.4 shows the Active Server Page that uses the ASPComp.

Listing 22.4. Active Server Page script SrvTimes.ASP.

```
<HTML>
<!-- Active Server Page Example Using Active Data Objects -->
<!-- Author: Mark Spenik -->
<!-- Revision History: Jan. 6, 1997 -->
<!-- This example uses Active Data Objects to fill a combo box -->
<!-- and to store the data entered in the timesheet.           -->
<!-- An ActiveX component is used to display previous time entered. -->
<!-- This example posts the form back to this file and performs -->
<!-- all validation code on the Server. This ASP can be used in any -->
<!-- Browser.                                                   -->
<!--                                                            -->
<SCRIPT LANGUAGE=VBScript RUNAT=Server>
Function AddTime
    'Create an instance of the ADO object
    Set oDBTime = Server.CreateObject("ADODB.Connection")

    'Open the database
    oDBTime.Open "TimeSheet"

    'Create an ADO recordset to add a new record
    set rsTimeSheet = CreateObject("ADODB.Recordset")

    'Set the Recordset Properties
    rsTimeSheet.CursorType = 0
    rsTimeSheet.LockType = adLockOptimistic
    rsTimeSheet.ActiveConnection = oDBTime
    rsTimeSheet.Source = "Select * From EmpTime"
    rsTimeSheet.Open

    'Check to make sure Updates are supported
    sResponse = "<H2>Sorry your timesheet was not added. Invalid server cursor.
➥</H2>"
    If rsTimeSheet.Supports(adUpdate) Then
        'Add a new record
        rsTimeSheet.AddNew
        'Set the data values
        rsTimeSheet("Employee") = Request.Form("txtEmployee")
        rsTimeSheet("WorkDate") = Request.Form("txtWorkDate")
        rsTimeSheet("ClientName") = Request.Form("cmbClient")
        rsTimeSheet("BillCode") = Request.Form("cmbCode")
        rsTimeSheet("Hours") = Request.Form("txtHours")
        'Add the record
        rsTimeSheet.Update

        'Check for Errors
        If oDBTime.Errors.Count > 0 Then
            Set oError = oDBTime.Errors(0)
            If oError.Number <> 0 Then
```

continues

Listing 22.4. continued

```
                    sResponse = "<H3>Timesheet Error </H3><BR><P>"
                    sResponse = sResponse & "Error adding your timesheet to the
                    ➥database."
                    sResponse = sResponse & "Error: " & oError.Description
               End If
          Else
               sResponse = "<H4>Timesheet Added for " & Request.Form("txtWorkDate") &
               ➥". Scroll to the bottom of the page to view previous time added.</H4>"
          End If
     End If
     rsTimeSheet.Close
     oDBTime.Close
     AddTime = sResponse
End Function
</SCRIPT>
<HEAD>
<Title>Active Server Page TimeSheet Application</TITLE>
</HEAD>
<BODY BGCOLOR="Tan">
<CENTER>
<H2>Timesheet Application using Active Server Pages, ActiveX Components and
➥ADO</H2>
</CENTER>
<HR SIZE=2>
<!-- In this example, we are posting back to the same ASP file that -->
<!-- submits the request. As such first parse the form to see if it has -->
<!-- Been entered properly.  -->
<%
If Request.Form("txtEmployee")="" Then
     sMsg = "Enter an Employee's name in the timesheet."
     Session("TimeAdded") = False
ElseIf NOT (IsDate(Request.Form("txtWorkDate"))) Then
     sMsg = "You must enter a valid date in the date field."
     Session("TimeAdded") = False
ElseIf Request.Form("txtHours")= "" Then
     sMsg = "You must enter a valid number of hours."
Else
     Session("TimeAdded") = True
     sMsg = AddTime
End If
%>
<!-- Declare the start of the form. -->
<B><%=sMsg%></B>
<P>
<FORM NAME="TimeSheet" METHOD="POST" ACTION="SrvTimes.asp">
<B>Employee:</B> <INPUT TYPE="text" NAME="txtEmployee" Size=30
➥Value="<%=Request("txtEmployee")%>">
<p>
<B>Select the Client</B>
<%  'Create an instance of the ADO Recordset object
     set rsClients = CreateObject("ADODB.Recordset")

     'Open a resultset based on the SQL Statement
     rsClients.Open "SELECT ClientName FROM Clients","DSN=TimeSheet"
%>
<!-- Notice in the following section the mixture of HTML with server side
➥script -->
<SELECT NAME="cmbClient">
```

```
<% Do While Not rsClients.EOF %>
<OPTION><%=rsClients("ClientName")%>
<%
        rsClients.MoveNext
    Loop
    rsClients.Close
    Set rsClients = Nothing
%>
</SELECT>
<p>
<B>Select the billing code</B>
<SELECT ALIGN=CENTER Name="cmbCode">
<OPTION>Holiday
<OPTION>Vacation
<OPTION>Sick
<OPTION>Client Server Consulting
<OPTION>Work Group Consulting
<OPTION>Internet Consulting Services
</Select>
<p>
<B>Date:</B> <INPUT TYPE="text" NAME="txtWorkDate" Size=15 Value=<% =Date %>>
<p>
<%
If Session("Hours") = "" Then
    Session("Hours") = "8.0"
Else
    If Request("txtHours") <> "" Then
        Session("Hours") = Request("txtHours")
    End If
End If
%>
<B>Hours:</B> <INPUT TYPE="text" Name="txtHours" Size=4 Value="<%=Session("Hours")%>">
<HR>
<INPUT TYPE=SUBMIT VALUE="Submit Form">
<SCRIPT LANGUAGE="VBScript">
<!--
Sub window_onLoad()
Dim CurrentForm

    'Set the focus to the text box
    Set CurrentForm = Document.TimeSheet

    CurrentForm.txtEmployee.Focus
    Set CurrentForm = Nothing
end sub
-->
</SCRIPT>
<%
If Session("TimeAdded") Then
    'Create an Instance of the ActiveX component to send
    'back an Employee's time.
    Set oEmpTime = Server.CreateObject("ASPComp.GetTime")
    oEmpTime.GetEmpTime
End If
%>
</BODY>
<!--#include virtual="/ASPSamp/Samples/adovbs.inc"-->
</HTML>
```

Review the ASP script in Listing 22.4 carefully. SrvTimes.asp is very different from the timesheet application created in Chapter 21. Like the ASP used in the previous example, which uses standard ActiveX components, SrvTimes.asp posts the form back to itself, so all the code is contained in a single script file. Unlike the timesheet example created in Chapter 21, though, SrvTimes.asp performs all form validation on the server, so you don't have to be concerned about whether the browser supports VBScript. The hours submitted in the application default to 8 hours unless a previous number is entered (the timesheet application in Chapter 21 always defaults to 8 hours).

The script required to use your ActiveX component to produce the HTML table is quite simple:

```
<%
If Session("TimeAdded") Then
    'Create an Instance of the ActiveX component to send
    'back an Employee's time.
    Set oEmpTime = Server.CreateObject("ASPComp.GetTime")
    oEmpTime.GetEmpTime
End If
```

Components Odds and Ends

Before wrapping up this chapter, you should take a look at a few remaining topics to consider when creating Visual Basic 5 ActiveX components to be used in Web pages.

Application- and Session-Scope Threading with Visual Basic 5 ActiveX Components

As stated earlier, ActiveX components created with Visual Basic 5 use the Apartment Thread model and can be single or multithreaded. If you create an application- or session-scope object with a multithreaded ActiveX component that uses Apartment Model threading (created with Visual Basic 5), the object created will be only *single threaded*. For an application-scope object this could affect performance in a multiuser environment due to blocking.

Setting the Base Address of an In-Process Component (DLL)

The code base address of a DLL is the address in memory in which the code for your component is loaded into memory. Various processes can share the single memory copy of the code if there are no address conflicts. A conflict occurs when an in-process component's base address is being used by another in-process component or the executable. When a conflict occurs, the code must be dynamically relocated during the in-process load process, which slows down the component load process. The relocated code in memory for an in-process component generally cannot be shared by other processes.

The valid range of values for the base address is between 16MB (hexadecimal value 100000) and 2GB (hexadecimal value 80000000). The code in memory cannot exceed the 2GB range, so you need to obtain a code base that guarantees that the component's base address plus code size will not exceed 2GB. Base addresses are increased in multiples of 64KB (hexadecimal value 10000). The default address for ActiveX DLLs created with Visual Basic 5 is 285,212,672 (hexadecimal value 11000000). *Never* create components that use the default address assigned by Visual Basic, or all your ActiveX components created with Visual Basic will have conflicting base addresses.

To prevent components from having conflicting base addresses, you must develop a method to assign code base address that are not being used by other ActiveX components. You could create an application that generates and assigns random base addresses and store the assigned address and the component name in a database to be used for tracking and maintenance purposes.

To change the base address of a component, use the Compile tab of the Visual Basic 5 Project Properties dialog box shown in Figure 22.15.

FIGURE 22.15.

The Compile tab of the Visual Basic Project Properties dialog box.

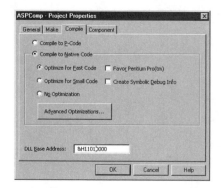

Component Compatibility and Testing

When testing a new ActiveX component, use the default Project Compatibility option on the Component tab of the Project Properties dialog box. Project compatibility enables your test projects to maintain the component reference during various test sessions by reusing the type library identifier (new type library information is generated). When you are happy with the component and create a DLL to install on various machines, switch to binary compatibility. *Binary compatibility* ensures that programs using a previous version of your component will be able to use the new version of the component without a problem; this compatibility ensures that previously defined methods and properties remain intact. A message box appears if the interface to the component has changed in a way that will affect programs using previous versions.

You should test ActiveX components before using them on a Website. Test your components using a test program that creates objects from your components and uses the exposed methods and properties. To test components that take advantage of ASP and ADO, try to test on a PC that has Visual Basic 5 and Active Server Pages running. You can use a Windows 95 machine running Microsoft's personal Web server with Active Server Pages or a Windows NT 4.0 machine with IIS 3.0. Also, when replacing an in-process component that has been used (loaded into memory), you will have to stop the Web server to overwrite the previous version.

Summary

You can create ActiveX components to take advantage of your current Visual Basic skills and easily enhance your Web application's functionality. Generate ActiveX multithreaded, in-process components (DLLs). Avoid using OLEISAPI; instead, use ASP. You also can create ActiveX components that use ASP intrinsic objects to retrieve information from a posted form or to send information back to a browser client.

23

MS SQL Server Internet Capabilities

by Mark Spenik

Visual Basic is appearing everywhere—in the entire Microsoft Office Suite, in Active Server Web pages, and in the standard Visual Basic development environment. Also on the rise is the client/server *relational database management system* (RDBMS) of choice in a Microsoft Windows NT environment: SQL Server. SQL Server is a high-performance RDBMS system that is tightly integrated with the Windows NT operating system. SQL Server supports ANSI-92 SQL and offers high-performance features, such as stored procedures, triggers, rules, defaults, constraints, and SMP support. In an intranet/Internet environment based on Microsoft technologies, SQL Server can play a large role as a back-end database for your Web applications. SQL Server integrates well with Visual Basic. By using SQL Server stored procedures, you can invoke a Visual Basic ActiveX component from a SQL Server stored procedure. For easy-to-use Web access, SQL Server has a user-friendly hook called the *Web Assistant* that enables you to easily generate static HTML pages from SQL Server tables. SQL Server was the first RDBMS supported by an interesting database Web technology called the *Advanced Data Connector* (ADC). This chapter will show you how to use the SQL Server Web Wizard to generate HTML pages. For the more advanced SQL Server users reading this book, the stored procedures behind the Web Assistant, as well some trigger and scheduling ideas, are covered. This chapter also will introduce you to the Microsoft ADC.

> **NOTE**
>
> If you want to get up to speed on SQL Server and be the local guru, check out these books by Sams Publishing: *Microsoft SQL Server 6.5 DBA Survival Guide* (ISBN: 0-672-30959-9) and *Microsoft SQL Server 6.5 Unleashed* (ISBN: 0-672-30956-4). Both are excellent books that complement each other quite well.

SQL Server Web Assistant

The SQL Server Web Assistant automates the generation of HTML Web pages. You can use this wizard to publish data that resides in SQL Server on the Internet or intranet. As you can imagine, this link between SQL Server and the Internet/intranet creates several new and exciting possibilities for the distribution of information from SQL Server. Some of the uses for distributing SQL Server information in the HTML format follow:

■ *Customer/product management:* Use SQL Server to store information about your customers or products. Use the Web Assistant to generate Web pages pertaining to your customers or products. Summary data, trends, credit data, and other types of customer/product information are just a few examples of the types of information that can be published on the Internet/intranet.

■ *Proposal tracking:* Use SQL Server to store hot links to proposals and related documents, and then use the Web Assistant to generate Web pages that contain the links to your information. This type of application is great for a distributed sales force that has to gather information for past proposals.

■ *End-user reports:* Often, end-users and managers require reports from SQL Server that use static queries. In *static queries,* the data in the tables may change, but the queries used to generate the SQL statements remain the same (for example, a monthly or quarterly sales report, reports about current customer billing or current resources, and so on—the list is endless). Up to now, you may have used tools such as Microsoft Access or Crystal Reports to generate the reports, requiring each end-user to run the report against the database. By using the Web Assistant, you can schedule the reports to run and generate HTML versions of the reports.

Stepping Through the SQL Server Web Assistant

Follow these steps to use the SQL Server Web Assistant:

1. Double-click the SQL Server Web Assistant icon in the Microsoft SQL Server 6.5 (Common) program group. The SQL Server Web Assistant–Login dialog box appears, as shown in Figure 23.1.

FIGURE 23.1.

The SQL Server Web Assistant–Login dialog box.

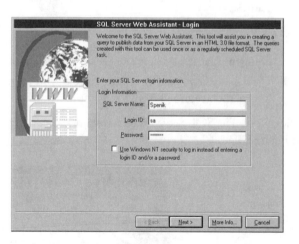

2. Enter the server name, logon ID, and password. If you are using integrated security, enable the Use Windows NT security to log in instead of entering a logon ID and/or a password checkbox (or, you can specify a Password option). You do not have to provide a logon ID or password if you use integrated security. Click Next. The SQL Server Web Assistant–Query dialog box appears, as shown in Figure 23.2.

FIGURE 23.2.

The SQL Server Web Assistant–Query dialog box.

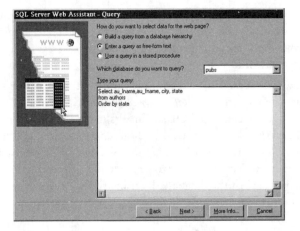

3. Select your data source. This example uses a freeform text query as the data source. The following list explains the data source options:

■ *Build a query from a database hierarchy.* Enables you to display tables and columns in HTML format. With this option, you can work with multiple tables or views. This option also provides a textbox for WHERE, ORDER BY, and GROUP BY clauses.

■ *Enter a query as free-form text:* Enables you to manually enter SQL syntax as the data source for your Web page. Any valid SELECT statement can be used with the following clauses: FROM, WHERE, GROUP BY, HAVING, and ORDER BY.

■ *Use a query in a stored procedure:* Enables you to publish data based on the information returned from a stored procedure.

Click Next. The SQL Server Web Assistant–Scheduling dialog box appears, as shown in Figure 23.3.

FIGURE 23.3.

The SQL Server Web Assistant–Scheduling dialog box.

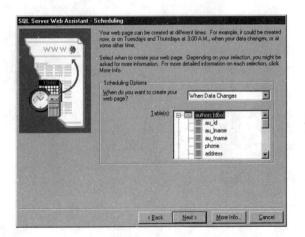

4. Select your scheduling options. The example in Figure 23.3 regenerates the Web page whenever the data in the Authors table changes. When you select the option to regenerate the Web page "when data changes," the following three types of triggers are generated for the Authors table: INSERT, UPDATE, and DELETE. When the data is modified, the trigger executes a system procedure that regenerates the Web page.

Click Next. The SQL Server Web Assistant–File Options dialog box appears, as shown in Figure 23.4.

FIGURE 23.4.

The SQL Server Web Assistant–File Options dialog box.

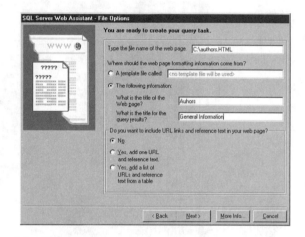

5. Enter a filename, display information, and URL link information. Click Next. The SQL Server Web Assistant–Formatting dialog box appears, as shown in Figure 23.5.

FIGURE 23.5.

The SQL Server Web Assistant–Formatting dialog box.

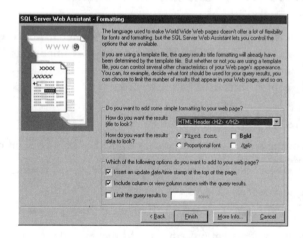

6. Select a formatting style and other Web page options.

7. Click Finish to generate the HTML file and any scheduling or trigger options.

That's it! You have just created a Web page that will automatically be generated the next time data changes in the pubs database table Authors. You can view the page generated by using Microsoft Internet Explorer, as shown in Figure 23.6.

FIGURE 23.6.

Viewing a Web page created by the SQL Server Web Assistant.

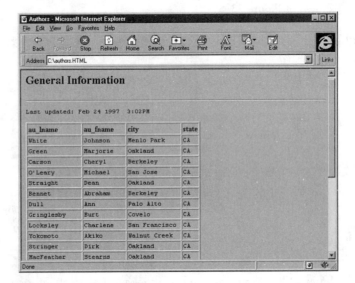

SQL Server Web Assistant Components

The SQL Server Web Assistant provides a tremendous amount of automation through a simple-to-use graphical interface. If you are interested in how the wizard performs Web-page automation, take a closer look at the Web Assistant's components. Understanding the Assistant's functionality is useful when you need to modify an existing Web. The following sections explain the components used by the wizard.

Web System Stored Procedures

The following system procedures are used by the Web Assistant to generate Web pages:

■ *sp_makewebtask:* Creates a task in SQL Server to generate a Web page.

■ *sp_dropwebtask:* Drops a Web task.

■ *sp_runwebtask:* Executes a Web task.

You can use these system procedures to further extend the functionality of the Web Assistant, although the Web Assistant does a good job of doing everything you need.

Triggers

If you want your Web page to be a current reflection of your data, you will have to regenerate the Web page whenever your data changes. (Remember that the data in an HTML file is static; to reflect updates, the file must be regenerated.) To automate the generation of the HTML file, the SQL Server Web Assistant can create a set of INSERT, UPDATE, and DELETE triggers that schedule program calls to regenerate the Web page (see Figure 23.7). A *trigger* is a user-defined collection of SQL statements that are executed when an item is added, updated, or deleted in a table. Triggers often are used for data and referential integrity. The good news for you, as a Visual Basic programmer, is that the Web Assistant automatically generates the required triggers.

FIGURE 23.7.

A trigger used to regenerate a Web page.

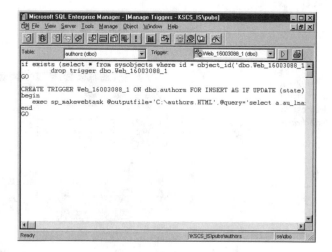

SQL Server's Task Scheduler

SQL Server's Task Scheduler is another component of the SQL Server Web Assistant. If you want the wizard to regenerate the Web page on an hourly, daily, or weekly basis, the wizard will schedule a task that calls sp_runwebtask (see Figure 23.8). The Web page is rebuilt when this system procedure is executed (see Figure 23.9). A perfect use for the Task Scheduler is to generate weekly, monthly, or quarterly status reports that do not change after they are generated. You can schedule a stored procedure to execute and roll up the data in a table and then execute the stored procedure sp_runwebtask to update the HTML.

You can invoke the Task Scheduler from SQL Server's GUI front-end tool called the Enterprise Manager (see Figure 23.8). When using the Enterprise Manager, you can get to the Task Scheduler by choosing Server | Scheduled Tasks.

FIGURE 23.8.

*Task Scheduler and
Web page integration.*

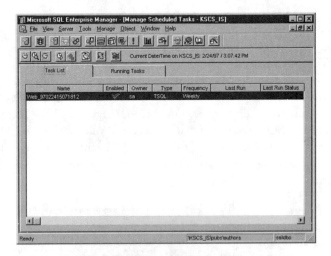

FIGURE 23.9.

*The call to
sp_runwebtask from
the Task Scheduler.*

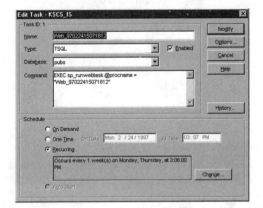

Stored Procedures

When the sp_runwebtask system procedure is executed from the Task Scheduler, it calls a stored procedure generated by the SQL Server Assistant. This stored procedure contains the information input by the user when the original Web page was created. To determine the name of the stored procedure being called, look at the code in Figure 23.9:

```
EXEC sp_runwebtask @procname
```

A stored procedure is a series of SQL statements that are precompiled and reside on SQL Server. A stored procedure can declare variables, pass parameters, call other stored procedures, and perform conditional logic as well as call functions that reside on SQL Server.

The Advanced Data Connector

As stated earlier, Microsoft wants to make SQL Server the RDBMS of choice in Windows NT environments as well as NT Web environments. Therefore, the RDBMS that works immediately with new Web database technologies released from Microsoft is SQL Server. SQL Server 6.5 was the first database to support the ADC. What's the ADC? Well, if you have a client/server database background (like I do), you probably have been waiting for the day when you could create Web-based applications that use bound controls across HTTP. There are no scripts to write and no IDC or HTX files—just a bound control on a Web page, similar to your current client/server applications that use RDO or DAO to communicate with an RDBMS system. The ADC enables you to use a special ActiveX data control on a Web page to bind to other ActiveX controls, such as grids and textboxes, and populate them with data retrieved from an RDBMS (just like a client/server application). No scripts are required to retrieve and format each record in HTML. Furthermore, the ADC retrieves and caches the database records locally on the client PC so that a user can edit them in the browser and then submit the changes back to the database. The ADC uses OLE DB to communicate with SQL Server and Oracle (check Microsoft's Website for other databases supported).

Figure 23.10 shows a general, high-level look at the architecture used with the ADC.

The first thing you might notice about Figure 23.10 is that many pieces make up the request to retrieve data from SQL Server. Unlike a typical two-tier client/server application, the ADC uses a three-tier architecture. The browser and Advanced Data Control provide the user interface services. The ADC comes with a default business object called the Advanced Data Factory object. This object sends SQL statements from the client to SQL Server and passes the results back to the client. The Advanced Data Factory object provides the business services. The data services are provided by an RDBMS system—in this case, SQL Server.

Use Figure 23.10 to walk through an interaction between the browser and SQL Server. A user on the browser loads a Web page that contains an ActiveX grid control and the Advanced Data Control. The Advanced Data Control is an invisible ActiveX control that enables you to bind ActiveX controls to a database recordset.

NOTE

ADC stands for *Active Data Connector*. ADC is made up of several components including the invisible ActiveX control referred to as the Advanced Data Control. When the abbreviation ADC is used, the Advanced Data Connector technology is being discussed, not the data control.

FIGURE 23.10.

An architectural overview of the ADC.

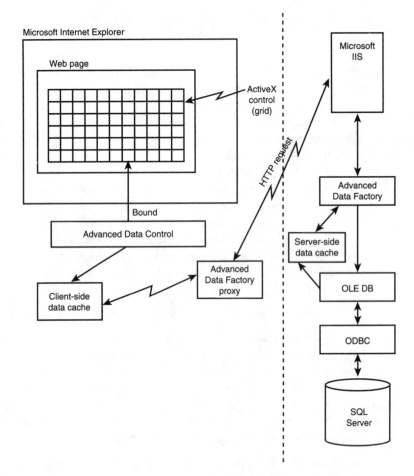

As the page loads, a SQL statement is executed. The ADC creates an Advanced Data Factory object proxy on the client. The proxy is required because the business object on the client cannot communicate directly with the business object on the server. The proxy passes the request via HTTP to the Microsoft Internet Information Server. IIS determines the type of business object it is and creates an instance of the business object on the server, in this case the Advanced Data Factory object. The SQL statement then goes to SQL Server via OLE DB layered on top of ODBC. The recordset is retrieved and loaded into a server-side data cache. The information then is passed to the server-side Advanced Data Factory object and then is packaged and sent back to the client-side proxy. The information is unpackaged, placed in the client-side data cache, and passed to the Advanced Data Control, which loads the ActiveX grid control with the data.

RESOURCE

The architectural overview in Figure 23.10 is at a high level. For more details on the low-level nuts and bolts of what makes the ADC tick, check out the Advanced Data Connector site at

`http://www.microsoft.com/adc/default.htm`

From the description of the ADC's architecture, the ADC sounds very difficult to use. Actually, I think you will find the ADC about as difficult to use as the ActiveX data control that comes with Visual Basic. Now look at one of the sample applications that comes with the ADC, as shown in Figure 23.11.

FIGURE 23.11.

Microsoft's sample ADC query page.

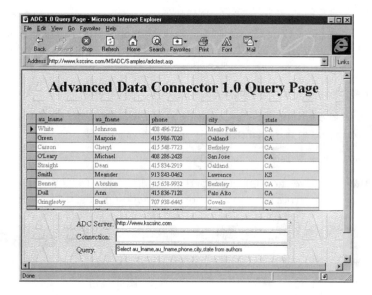

The ADC Query Page application comes with the ADC. The application is a good way to test whether you have properly configured your Web server and SQL Server to run the ADC. The application enables you to enter any valid `select` statement against the SQL Server `pubs` database. After you click the Run button (located at the bottom of the Web page and not shown in Figure 23.11), the data grid is almost immediately filled with the recordset. Again, the ADC is an invisible bound control, so you do not have to write an IDC file or ADO script to execute your script. Think of the ADC as client/server for the Web.

Now take a quick look at some important properties and methods of the ADC's Advanced Data Control required to retrieve data. For starters, look at an example of the `<OBJECT>` tag used for the Advanced Data Control. Listing 23.1 shows the `<OBJECT>` tag used in the sample application for the Advanced Data Control.

Listing 23.1. The Advanced Data Control `<OBJECT>` tag.

```
<OBJECT CLASSID="clsid:9381D8F2-0288-11d0-9501-00AA00B911A5"
       ID=tstADC HEIGHT=10 WIDTH = 10
   CODEBASE="HTTP://www.kscsinc.com/MSADC/msadc10.cab">
       <PARAM NAME="BINDINGS" VALUE="tstGrid;">
   </OBJECT>
```

Notice in Listing 23.1 the `BINDINGS` parameter, which has a value equal to the name of the grid on the page. Look at some other properties you must set before you can query the SQL Server via the ADC. For starters, you must set the ADC `Server` property to the IIS Server that will communicate to the SQL Server. The following line of code sets the `Server` property of the Advanced Data Control to a fictitious Web server, for example:

```
MyADC.Server = http//www.mspenik.com
```

The Advanced Data Control has a `Connect` property that, for SQL Server, requires a system ODBC DSN and a user ID and password. The following line of code is an example of setting the `Connect` property:

```
MyADC.Connect = "DSN=SQLPubs;UID=guest;PWD=guest;"
```

To set the Advanced Data Control with the SQL statement you want to execute, use the `SQL` property, as in this example:

```
MyADC.SQL = Select * from titles
```

After you have the control properly bound via the `<OBJECT>` tag and the `SQL`, `Server`, and `Connect` properties set, you are ready to retrieve some data.

NOTE

The `SQL`, `Server`, and `Connect` properties can be set as parameters of the `<OBJECT>` tag.

To populate your bound controls, use the Advanced Data Control's `Refresh` method, as shown in this example:

```
MyADC.Refresh
```

You can navigate through the cached recordset by using the following Advanced Data Control methods:

- ■ *MoveFirst:* Moves to the first record in the cache
- ■ *MoveLast:* Moves to the last record in the data cache
- ■ *MovePrevious:* Moves to the preceding record in the data cache
- ■ *MoveNext:* Moves to the next record in the data cache

You can modify several records on the client side—in a grid, for example—and then send the batched changes back to SQL Server by using the SubmitChanges method of the Advanced Data Control.

Where to Go from Here

The ADC is a very new and exciting technology. Because the ADC integrates so well with SQL Server, I decided to introduce you to the technology well after the book outline was completed. This section has only scratched the surface. The ADC in itself is a powerful and compelling technology and probably can fill an entire book. To learn more about the ADC and to get a copy of the ADC, visit the Microsoft site at

```
http://www.microsoft.com/adc/default.htm
```

Summary

SQL Server is the perfect RDBMS for a Windows NT and Microsoft IIS environment. Using the Web Assistant, you easily can generate HTML from any existing SQL Server table. You can take advantage of SQL Server features, such as triggers, to update the Web pages as your data changes. Or, you can use the SQL Server Task Scheduler to update information from a table on a regular basis. The Microsoft ADC is being integrated into the SQL Server environment, and it enables you to create applications that use database bound ActiveX controls over HTTP.

VIII

Web Database Examples and Applications

24

The Development of a PC-Based WWW Database System

by Drew Kittel

In recent months, developers have witnessed an explosion of new Web-related technologies hitting the commercial marketplace as well as being offered freely at numerous Websites. This is especially true in the world of low-cost (or freely available) Web servers, databases, and Web-database gateway software for desktop/personal computers. It now is quite possible to develop a fully functional Website, complete with database applications, on a desktop computer in a matter of hours or days—and often with only a small financial investment.

This chapter presents and describes in detail such a system: The Omniscient Technologies Corporate Employee, Project, and Job Opportunity Web Database System. This system was designed, developed, and tested (including the creation and population of a database) in about one man-day's time. This was accomplished in spite of a lack of in-depth knowledge of the tools and components being used. How is this possible? By taking advantage of increasingly sophisticated features, such as application development wizards typical of the many PC-based tools and software packages, and by using WWW-database gateway software—preprogrammed CGI applications that effectively extend the functionality of HTML and abstract the complexity of much of the actual database access.

Application Overview

The system described in this chapter is part of an information system for a small software development and technical services firm. It originally was conceived as the basis for a corporate intranet, but it provides information of interest to external visitors as well and easily could be extended to provide additional capabilities to a wide variety of external users. This project was undertaken to demonstrate the feasibility of designing and developing a low-cost, PC-based Web database while still providing a high level of functionality, capabilities, and growth potential.

Primary System Requirements

The primary requirements for the initial proof-of-feasibility system were these:

- Use an existing personal computer.
- Use existing database software.
- Use freely available tools and software to the extent possible.
- Minimize the amount of programming required.
- Demonstrate the capability to obtain employee, project, and job-opportunity information based on user-specified input(s).

The applications developed initially were intended for internal (intranet) use, but there is no reason why access could not be extended to external users as well.

Informational Queries Supported

Figure 24.1 shows the Omniscient Technologies Information Database home page. You can see that the current system supports the following types of informational queries:

- Lists of employees with user-specified degrees
- Lists of employees with user-specified skills
- Degrees held by a user-specified employee
- Skills of a user-specified employee
- Information about a user-selected project (from a database-generated history of project efforts)
- Information about a user-selected job listing (from a database-generated list of current opportunities)

FIGURE 24.1.
The Omniscient Technologies Information Database home page.

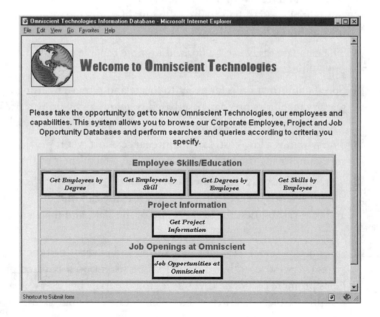

Benefits of the System

As discussed in Chapters 1, "The Internet, World Wide Web, and Intranets," and 2, "Doing Business on the Web," there are several benefits to developing organizational intranets for internal information sharing and Internet applications for use by external users. Databases can play a large role in these systems. Here are a number of potential benefits of the Omniscient Technologies Information database:

■ Employees easily can access information about projects and business areas in which the company is involved. This helps current employees to better share information across (often, geographically dispersed) projects and keep abreast of the developments in new business, technological achievements, improvement of corporate capabilities, and so on. This information also serves as an orientation tool for new employees.

■ Members of the new business-development staff easily can identify which employees have suitable backgrounds for bidding on new jobs. Also, easy access to employee educational and skills information, as well as past project descriptions, improves decision making in the bid/no-bid process.

■ Information is available to employees who are located at different sites and use various suites of hardware and software. This is accomplished without specialized development or incurring the cost of using specialized software at these sites. All that is needed is a graphics-capable Web browser.

■ Because all information is maintained in a database, maintaining the Website is substantially easier than trying to maintain a growing set of document-based information.

■ The database easily can be upsized to more capable systems if the need for increased capabilities and functions arises in the future.

■ Specific information is far easier to locate and retrieve by using the querying and search capabilities of a database-based system than by using a site that employs document-based search engines, such as WAIS.

■ The system is a low-cost, low-maintenance effort, yet it provides the potential for vastly improving the quality, quantity, and effectiveness of shared information.

■ Corporate image is established and enhanced through the dissemination of information to external users. Visitors to the site easily can find out about company strengths and core capabilities, the background of the staff, and information on career opportunities.

■ Information serves a valuable marketing and advertising function. Not only is the system very low cost, but it provides a persistent, well-targeted public presence. This helps promote corporate capabilities to potential clients as well as attract potential teaming partners in search of complementary corporate skills.

■ The system is highly extensible. Additional queries can be developed and other applications integrated—especially other desktop applications, such as Microsoft Excel. Capabilities and functionality of the system can be extended further through the development of additional `cgi-bin` and `cgi-win` applications. This can be accomplished without the need to upgrade the hardware and software of internal or external users.

■ Finally, using the capabilities of the *Open Database Connectivity* (ODBC) standard, the desktop database easily can be linked to other geographically dispersed, ODBC-compliant databases, providing the capability to develop and serve users with very complex database applications.

System Components Used

The following hardware and software components were used to create the database system:

■ Pentium-based computer (the system also has been tested successfully on a low-end laptop)

■ Microsoft Windows NT operating system (the system also has been deployed successfully on Windows 95)

■ Microsoft Access database

■ O'Reilly's WebSite Professional Web server software

■ DBGateway software (by Computer Systems Development Corporation)

Figure 24.2 illustrates the testbed used to create and test the PC-based WWW database system.

FIGURE 24.2.

The testbed for the PC-based WWW database system.

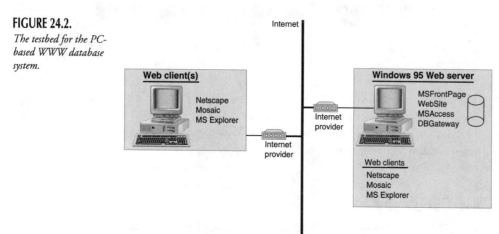

Microsoft Access 95

Access 95 is a Microsoft relational database product for Windows 95 and NT. It's available as part of the Office Suite of products or separately. Access provides a strong suite of querying capabilities and easily can be programmed by using Visual Basic. Additionally, Access provides OLE and ODBC support, enabling links to spreadsheets, documents, and other databases.

> **RESOURCE**
>
> You can find a wealth of information about Microsoft Access on the Access home page and its links:
>
> `http://www.microsoft.com/msaccess`
>
> This site includes case studies, developer information, specifications, and links for downloading free Access add-ins.

O'Reilly WebSite Professional

WebSite Professional is a fully functional yet inexpensive Web server product available from O'Reilly & Associates. It comes with a fully functional Web server, complete with graphical setup and administration tools. It also comes with an HTML editor and an enhanced version of the Mosaic Web browser. The server is Windows CGI-compliant, supports CGI scripting and server API programming using Visual Basic (as well as Perl and Java), includes Cold Fusion database connection gateway software, and fully supports the use of security features such as SSL SHTTP and digitally signed certificates. The software runs under Windows 95 and NT.

> **RESOURCE**
>
> You can find additional information about the WebSite product at the O'Reilly home page:
>
> `http://www.ora.com/`
>
> This site enables you to download a free evaluation copy of the standard WebSite product, as well as the first three chapters of the WebSite documentation and the Windows-CGI specification. After it is downloaded, the server can be installed and operational in a matter of minutes.

CSDC DBGateway

DBGateway is a freely available WWW-database gateway software product developed by Computer Systems Development Corporation. Its functionality and use are discussed in detail in subsequent sections.

What Is DBGateway?

DBGateway is a freely available database gateway application that provides access to Microsoft Access and FoxPro databases via Web-based applications such as HTML and ActiveX-enabled forms. A *gateway* is a specialized CGI application that abstracts the details of interaction between a Web server and an application—in this case, a database application. It was developed by Computer Systems Development Corporation in response to the needs of one of its clients. The gateway itself is a 32-bit Visual Basic Windows CGI application that uses and expands on the CGI32.BAS framework introduced in Chapter 18, "The Common Gateway Interface (CGI)." It is an excellent illustration of how powerful Web database systems can be developed by using Visual Basic.

The gateway software runs on the host personal computer, which also serves as a Web server. All database interactions are handled directly between the gateway and the database; no ODBC server is required. Also, the gateway is designed so that the databases being accessed are external to the gateway. This means that databases can be added, removed, or modified without affecting the gateway.

Because the software is a critical component of the system detailed in this chapter, the following sections provide sufficient details about the product for you to understand the code and examples presented later in this chapter.

> **RESOURCE**
>
> Additional information, including instructions on downloading, installing, and using DBGateway is included on the CD-ROM with this book. This information also is freely available at the DBGateway home page at
> `http://dbgate.csdc.com/`

Why Use DBGateway?

Earlier in this chapter, you looked at a few of the requirements imposed on this development effort. DBGateway provided a means of using a proven and freely available tool. Additionally, it met the criteria of minimizing the programming effort required to implement the system. Given the capabilities of the product to meet my database interface needs, I was able to forego development of custom CGI programs. Instead, all I had to do was use my knowledge of HTML, ActiveX, VBScript, and SQL.

Here are some of the reasons why you might want to consider using DBGateway:

- It's cheap (actually, it's free!).
- It's very easy to learn.
- It helps minimize development costs for smaller Web database applications.
- It provides a reasonable depth of functionality.
- It uses simple extensions to the HTML you already know.
- It enables very rapid prototyping and development of systems.
- It enables you to use existing database resources, such as Access or FoxPro.

Gateway Requirements

To develop applications using DBGateway, your system must meet the following requirements:

- ■ Your PC must be running Windows NT or Windows 95.
- ■ Your Web server must be Windows CGI-compliant (O'Reilly's WebSite and Netscape's Enterprise Servers are two examples of such servers).
- ■ You must have a Microsoft Access or FoxPro database.
- ■ You must have installed the ActiveX Internet Control Pack (available from the download pages on Microsoft's Website. All other necessary DLLs and OCXs are included in the DBGateway distribution.

Architecture of a Gateway Application

Figure 24.3 shows the general architecture of a PC-based Web database system using DBGateway.

FIGURE 24.3.

A PC-based WWW database system using DBGateway.

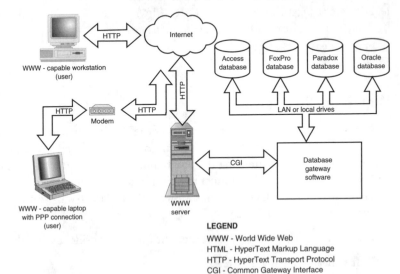

WWW - PC Database Gateway System Architecture

LEGEND
WWW - World Wide Web
HTML - HyperText Markup Language
HTTP - HyperText Transport Protocol
CGI - Common Gateway Interface
PPP - Point-to-Point Protocol

Note that access to remote databases, such as Oracle, Sybase, and Microsoft SQL Server, also could be provided via an Access database by establishing ODBC links between a locally resident Access data source and the remote database. For details on establishing an ODBC link, consult your Microsoft Access software documentation.

Data Flow in a DBGateway Application

The following sequence of steps details the flow of data in an application using DBGateway:

1. The Web server sends a Web client browser an HTML form that includes special statements, hidden variables, HTML extensions, and embedded SQL elements required by the DBGateway application.

2. The user makes entries to the HTML form and submits it to the Web server.

3. The Web server invokes the DBGateway application and passes it the encoded form information necessary to assemble a database query.

4. DBGateway decodes the information passed to it, creates a query, connects to the database, and submits the query.

5. When a response is ready, DBGateway retrieves the data returned from the database and formats a response to the user employing the format specified in an HTML report template (.rpt) file or in default tabular form if no report template is specified.

6. DBGateway returns an HTML response to the Web server, which subsequently passes it on to the Web client to be rendered by the browser.

Figure 24.4 illustrates this data flow and shows the various files that come into play.

FIGURE 24.4.

Data flow in a DBGateway application.

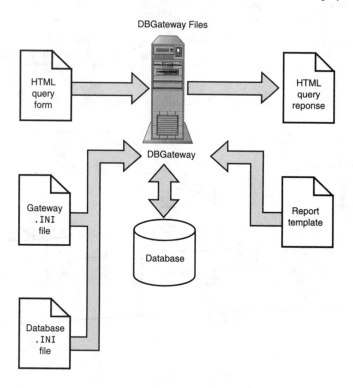

Files Used in a DBGateway Application

Table 24.1 lists the five basic file types used in applications that employ the DBGateway product.

Table 24.1. File types used in applications that use DBGateway.

File Type	Description
DBGate.exe	The gateway executable program that resides in the appropriate cgi-win directory for the Web server in use.
Dbgate.ini	Resides in the Web server cgi-win directory and contains information about paths to dbgate executables, the root directory (DBDATAROOT) for databases to be accessed, image and icon files to be used, and SMTP host and port details.
Report templates	Specify how the results of a database query are to be formatted in the HTML document returned to a Web client. These files are given an .rpt extension and reside in an rpts subdirectory for the respective database.
SQL files	Specify server-side SQL queries. They are given a .sql extension and reside in a sql subdirectory for the respective database.
YourDBName.ini	One of these files must accompany each database to be accessed. This file contains database access-control information.

Figure 24.5 shows the file system layout for my system and application.

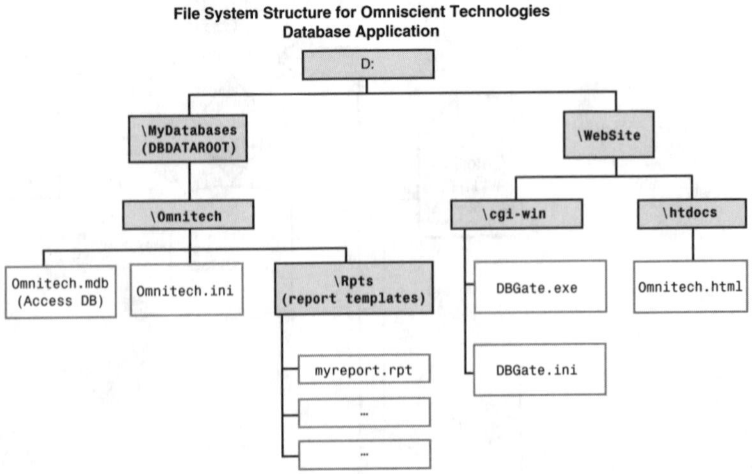

FIGURE 24.5.

The layout of directories and files on the testbed system for the Omniscient Technologies Database application.

File System Structure for Omniscient Technologies
Database Application

DBGateway Functionality

To be useful and functional parts of a Web database application, gateway products must provide at least basic database query and results-reporting capabilities. The DBGateway product actually provides multiple methods for performing database queries from your HTML forms as well as a strong report-generation capability. DBGateway also provides additional functionality in the form of SMTP mail support and the capability to access secure databases. This section explores DBGateway's functionality in greater detail.

HTML Embedded SQL Queries

DBGateway provides three methods for submitting queries to your database:

- HTML embedded SQL queries
- Server-side SQL queries
- Internal database queries (supported for Access databases only)

This chapter deals only with embedded SQL queries, because they provide the flexibility required for the sample application, and internal queries are not supported on the freeware version I used for these examples. More information on the latter two methods is available in your DBGateway software documentation. Comprehensive examples showing the use of embedded SQL queries are included in later sections of this chapter.

The HTML Embedded SQL Queries method entails the use of HTML <FORM> elements to formulate a desired query that subsequently will be passed to the database being used. Most of the elements used to create a query are HTML hidden <FORM> elements; however, it is possible and quite advantageous to use <FORM> input elements and ActiveX controls as well. This enables you to design highly interactive applications that incorporate user-specified input into the query to be passed to the database.

Because DBGateway uses an enumerated name-designation scheme, elements in the form used to create a SQL query can be split up into different parts of the form. The only restriction is that the design must be such that when DBGateway concatenates the parts of the query (it does so in sequential order), a valid query is formed. In general, these elements are case-sensitive and white-space sensitive.

Although DBGateway provides support for performing queries, record additions, record editing, and record deletions, I only cover queries in this chapter. You can find additional information for record operations in the DBGateway software documentation. The following parameters always are mandatory and almost always are specified as HTML hidden form elements:

ACTION	Valid value is `"SubmitExternalQuery"`
DBNAME	Valid value is `"your-string-here"`

DBPATH   Valid value is "*your-string-here*"

DBTYPE   Valid values are "ACCESS" or "FoxPro 2.6"

DBACTION Valid values are "Query", "Show", "AddDBRecord", "DeleteDBRecord", or
          "EditDBRecord"

QUERYNAME Valid value is "*your-string-here*"

When the value of DBACTION is "Query" or "Show", the following SQL parameters also are mandatory:

FIELDS*n* = "*comma-delimited field names from your database tables*"

FROM*n* = "*comma-delimited table names from your database*"

The *n* subscript indicates that portions of the query can be distributed across more than a single parameter. You could embed FROM0, FROM1, and FROM2 statements in a program, for example, as long as the resultant SQL query is valid when DBGateway concatenates these parameters.

Finally, when the value of DBACTION is "Query" or "Show", the following SQL parameters are optional:

GROUPBY*n* = "*comma-delimited field names from your database tables*"

HAVING*n* = "*any valid SQL condition*"

MAXREC = "*an integer > STARTREC*"

ORDERBY*n* = "*comma-delimited field names from your database tables*"

REPORTNAME = "*the name of a report template file (without the .rpt extension)*"

STARTREC = "*an integer > 0*"

WHERE*n* = "*any valid SQL Join condition*"

If you are familiar with SQL and HTML forms, you're probably starting to see the potential for easily developing some fairly powerful queries. Several examples using this embedded SQL method are included in later sections of this chapter.

On a final note, you also might have noticed that in the preceding parameters, no explicit SELECT statement is used. DBGateway includes this statement for you when it formulates the SQL query to pass to the database.

Database Reports

The preceding section presented a number of the parameters that can be embedded in your HTML to enable SQL queries to be formulated. But what about the data that the database returns from the query? DBGateway handles this in one of two ways. First, if no report format is explicitly specified, DBGateway presents the returned data in a native tabular format. This is a nice feature for prototyping queries. It enables you to fully test a query without having to also worry about formatting the data.

After you can get the query working properly, you can worry about making the output look nice. How do you accomplish this? The second way that DBGateway handles presentation of output is through the use of report template files. The optional REPORTNAME parameter from the preceding section enables you to specify how the field data being specified in the initial query should be formatted for presentation.

Properly written report templates enable returned field data to be formatted in virtually any way that any content of a regular HTML file would be formatted. This means that returned data can be written as free text and have its font and color attributes modified. Additionally, the returned data can be placed into HTML <FORM> input objects such as textboxes, TEXTAREA objects, and scrollable lists, as well as associated with checkboxes and radio buttons. You even could use ActiveX controls. Not only does this enable you to construct very nice data presentations for your users, but it enables you to design applications that cascade queries. In other words, the results of one query are used to give the user choices in a subsequent query, and so on, which enables you to develop extremely powerful applications.

How do these report templates work? DBGateway defines a few tags that extend the functionality of HTML. They are best described by examples, several of which are included in the final sections of this chapter. They're briefly described here for reference.

<FIELD> Tag

The <FIELD> tag has a single attribute: NAME. The value of the NAME attribute should be a valid field being returned from the previously specified query—for example <FIELD NAME="LastName">. <FIELD> tags are replaced with their corresponding values for every record returned from the database. If a field in the response set is not specified by a <FIELD> tag, it will not be included in the presentation to the user. Additionally, <FIELD> tags that have no correspondence to data being returned are not parsed out; this might confuse some Web browsers, so be aware.

<REPORTHEADER> Tags

The report header tag pair is composed of the <REPORTHEADER> and </REPORTHEADER> tags. Any <FIELD> tags that occur in this container pair will be assigned the contents of the first record of data returned.

<GROUPHEADER> Tags

The group header tag pair is composed of the <GROUPHEADER> and </GROUPHEADER> tags. These tags also have a NAME attribute—for example, <GROUPHEADER NAME="group1">.

<RECORDHEADER> Tags

The record header tag pair is composed of the <RECORDHEADER> and </RECORDHEADER> tags. HTML specified between these tags can be used to enhance the presentation of the returned data. These tags also have a NAME attribute.

`<RECORD>` Tags

The record tag pair is composed of the `<RECORD>` and `</RECORD>` tags. These tags typically are used to encapsulate `<FIELD>` tags, which subsequently are replaced with the data records returned from a query. See the examples in the section "The Omniscient Technologies PC-Based Web Database Application," later in this chapter, for specific usage of the record tags.

`<RECORDFOOTER>` Tags

The record footer tag pair is composed of the `<RECORDFOOTER>` and `</RECORDFOOTER>` tags. These tags also have a `NAME` attribute.

`<GROUPFOOTER>` Tags

The group footer tag pair is composed of the `<GROUPFOOTER>` and `</GROUPFOOTER>` tags. These tags also have a `NAME` attribute.

`<REPORTFOOTER>` Tags

The report footer tag pair is composed of the `<REPORTFOOTER>` and `</REPORTFOOTER>` tags. Any `<FIELD>` tags that occur in this container pair will be assigned the contents of the last record of data returned.

Additional Functionality

DBGateway also provides support for accessing secured databases, as well as using SMTP mail from your application (via Microsoft's ActiveX SMTP control). More information and examples that use these features are available in the DBGateway software documentation.

> **NOTE**
>
> To use the SMTP ActiveX control, you must have installed the Microsoft ActiveX Internet Control Pack. The control pack is available on the Microsoft Website and includes ActiveX controls for SMTP, FTP, UDP, and HTTP. The Microsoft site can be accessed at `http://www.microsoft.com/`.

Setting Up the `Omnitech` Access Database

This section presents an overview of the `Omnitech` database used in this application. First, you'll step through the process of creating a database and tables using Access and then establishing table relations. Next, you'll look at a listing and a brief explanation of the tables that make up the database. After you see how tables can be created and related, you'll look at the full table relations structure for the `Omnitech` database.

Creating a Database and Tables in Microsoft Access

The following step-by-step instructions should provide you with the basic understanding required to build databases and tables using the graphical tools and wizards in Microsoft Access. This example uses Microsoft Access for Windows 95 (Version 7.00).

> **NOTE**
>
> Access provides a wealth of additional tools for creating and modifying databases and tables, as well as specifying relations, setting key values, adding fields, and designating data types. Consult Access's online help and Answer Wizard tools for additional information.

To build databases and tables using the graphical tools and wizards in Microsoft Access, follow these steps:

1. Start Access. The dialog box shown in Figure 24.6 appears.

FIGURE 24.6.

Creating a new Access database.

2. In the Create a New Database Using group box, select Blank Database and then click OK. Access presents the dialog box in Figure 24.7 and prompts you to name the new database.

FIGURE 24.7.

Naming the new database.

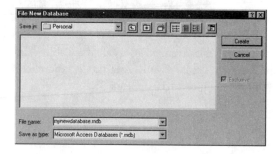

3. Type the desired name and click Create. Access then creates a new database with the given name, and the dialog box shown in Figure 24.8 appears.

FIGURE 24.8.

Creating a new table.

4. Select the Tables tab and click New. The dialog box shown in Figure 24.9 then appears.

FIGURE 24.9.

Using the Table Wizard.

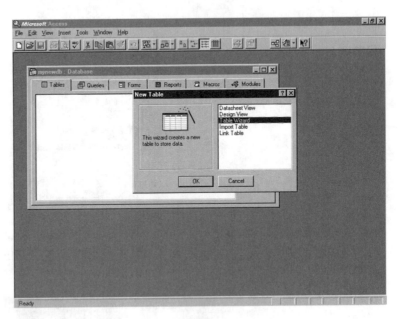

5. Access provides a convenient tool called a Table Wizard for rapidly creating tables in a database. Select Table Wizard from the list and click OK. The Table Wizard dialog box shown in Figure 24.10 appears.

FIGURE 24.10.

Specifying fields for the new table using the Table Wizard.

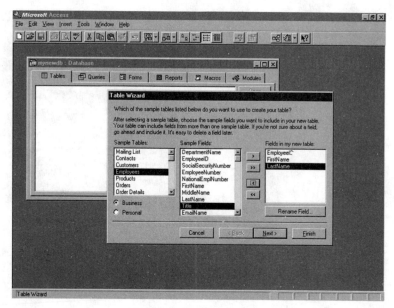

6. The Table Wizard dialog box presents a list of sample tables. Selecting Employees from the Sample Tables listbox causes corresponding sample fields to be listed. You can select any or all of the fields required for your application. Fields you've selected are shown in the Fields in my new table listbox. You can modify the names of the selected fields by clicking the field to highlight it; Access then prompts you for a new/ modified name for the field. The selections in Figure 24.10 illustrate a minimal Employees table with only three fields: EmployeeID, FirstName, and LastName. After you select all the fields you want, click Next.

7. The Table Wizard then prompts you to name the table you've just defined and also gives you the option of defining a primary key or letting the wizard do the job for you. Figure 24.11 shows that the table is named Employees and that you chose to let the wizard assign the key. Note that Access enables you to change these settings later. Click Next to proceed.

8. You now have the opportunity to specify how you want to populate the new table with data. Figure 24.12 shows that you chose to enter data directly into the table after it is created. Click Finish to create the table.

FIGURE 24.11.

Specifying the table name and setting the primary key.

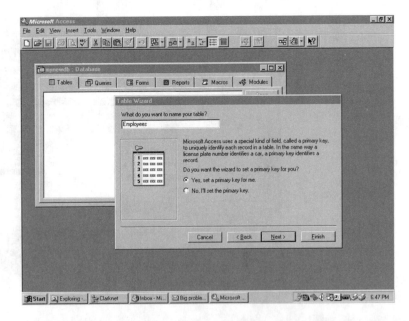

FIGURE 24.12.

Specifying how to populate the new table.

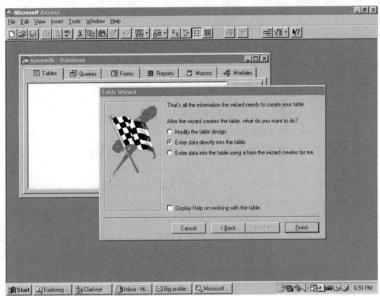

9. Access now gives you the opportunity to enter data directly into the table, as shown in Figure 24.13. Note that, because Employee ID is the key field, Access automatically assigns a unique number for each record. Key-field assignments and data types for any

field can be changed later as desired or required to ensure referential integrity for related tables. At this point, you can continue to enter data or exit the table by clicking the X in the upper-right corner. Windows NT users can exit the table by double-clicking the Control box in the upper-left corner of the table window.

FIGURE 24.13.

Populating the new table.

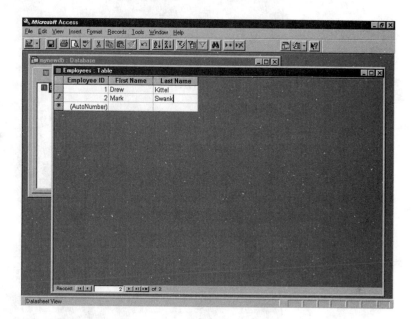

10. Note that Access provides other methods for populating tables. In Figure 24.12, you can see that you are given the option of having the wizard create an input form for you. Alternatively, Access provides a Form Wizard and other tools for creating your own customized input forms. You access this capability by selecting the Forms tab and clicking New. The resultant Form Wizard shown in Figure 24.14 steps you through the details of setting up a form. Refer to Access's online documentation for further details.

11. By following steps 1 through 10, you created another table named `Emp_Address`. Figure 24.15 illustrates that, during the creation of this second table, the wizard automatically recognized a relationship to the previously created `Employees` table. By clicking Next at this point, you are able to continue with populating this newly created table as before.

12. You now can view the relationship between the `Employees` and `Emp_Address` tables by choosing Tools|Relationships. Figure 24.16 illustrates the resulting table relations diagram.

FIGURE 24.14.
Invoking the Form Wizard.

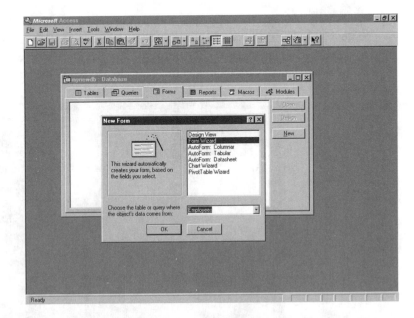

FIGURE 24.15.
Table relations determined by the Table Wizard.

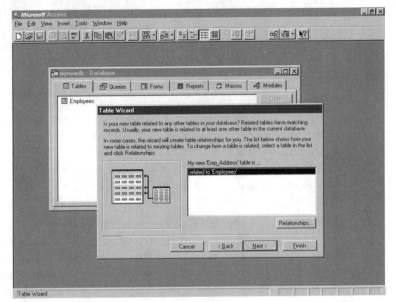

FIGURE 24.16.
The table relations diagram.

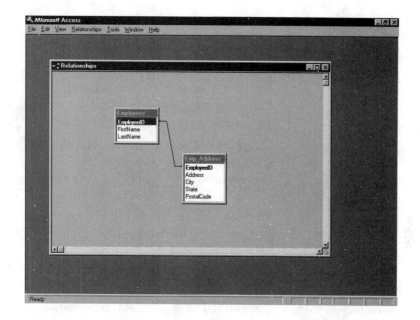

13. After all required tables are created, you can edit relationships as necessary by right-clicking on a link in the relationship diagram, choosing Relationships from the pull-down menu, and choosing Edit Relationships.

Details of how relations for tables of a given application vary for each application. Refer to Access's online help documentation for additional details regarding keys, referential integrity, and setting relations to determine how you can further specify these for your application.

Omnitech **Database Tables**

Table 24.2 lists the tables that make up the Omnitech database. These were designed to support the initial informational requirements of the proof-of-feasibility system; however, care was taken to make the design extensible and to easily enable the addition of new tables and fields as dictated by future needs and requirements.

Table 24.2. The Omnitech database consists of these initial tables.

Table	Description
Degree	Provides a translation between degree IDs and a degree name (for example, Ph.D.).

continues

Table 24.2. continued

Table	Description
Discipline	Provides a translation between discipline IDs and a discipline name (for example, Computer Science).
Emp_Education	Composed of fields that uniquely identify all the degrees and corresponding disciplines (by IDs) held by each employee.
Emp_Personnel	Composed of fields that contain information of a more personal nature, such as Social Security number, home address, and salary. This information was placed in a separate table for additional security and to enable users to link this table to remote data sources (via ODBC) in the future.
Emp_Proj	Composed of fields that identify all projects (by ID) in which an employee is involved.
Emp_Skill	Composed of fields that uniquely identify all the skills (by ID) held by each employee.
Employees	Composed of fields containing basic employee information, such as name, office location, title, and phone number.
Positions	Provides a listing of all open positions in the company. Information includes the parent project, position name, description, location, and a point of contact.
Programs	Provides a unique listing of all corporate programs (by unique ID) and includes information such as associated program name, description, and manager.
Projects	Provides a translation between project IDs and a project name. Also includes project details such as the parent program, project manager, and project description.
Skill	Provides a translation between skill IDs and a skill name.

All these tables were created and populated using the steps outlined in the section "Creating a Database and Tables in Microsoft Access," earlier in this chapter. Figure 24.17 shows the relationship diagram for this database.

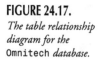

FIGURE 24.17.
The table relationship diagram for the Omnitech *database.*

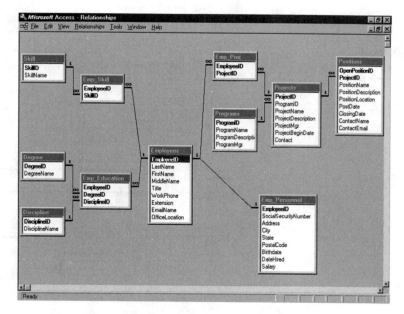

The Omniscient Technologies PC-Based Web Database Application

Now that you've reviewed the appropriate background material and created the database, it's finally time to take a comprehensive look at the entire application. The remainder of this chapter presents complete code listings associated with each of the main applications that can be invoked from the Omniscient Technologies Database home page shown in Figure 24.18.

Note that the code listings and the database presented, both of which are on the accompanying CD-ROM, comprise a fully functioning Web database system that you can modify for your own use or requirements. You simply need to make sure that your Web server is Windows CGI–compliant and that you've properly installed and tested the DBGateway software.

FIGURE 24.18.

*The Omniscient
Technologies
Information Database
home page.*

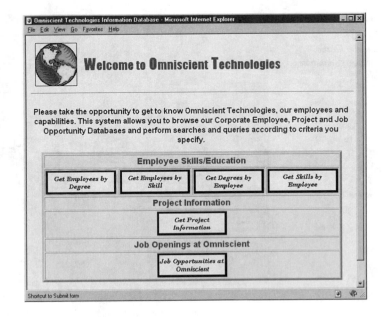

An Overview of the Home Page

The Omniscient Technologies Information Database home page and subsequent pages presented to the user provide an easy-to-use, interactive, graphical interface that enables users to submit queries to the database with a few mouse clicks. Here's a quick review of the types of queries this proof-of-feasibility system was designed to support:

- Lists of employees with user-specified degrees
- Lists of employees with user-specified skills
- Degrees held by a user-specified employee
- Skills of a user-specified employee
- Information about a user-selected project
- Information about a user-selected job listing

These queries currently are accessible only by internal users; however, because much of the information available would be of interest to external visitors as well, there would be great benefit in making this application externally accessible. This is a simple matter for the resident system administrator or Webmaster. It also would be easy to extend this application and database to support queries for information on previous proposals, employee résumés, client information, additional project information, and so on. It's up to the site administrator to ensure that proprietary or sensitive information is not made available to the public.

Application Details

This section presents code listings, explanations, and screen shots for each of the applications that can be invoked from the home page. Figure 24.19 illustrates the structure and hierarchy of the applications to be covered.

FIGURE 24.19.

The Omniscient Technologies Information Database application structure and hierarchy of report templates.

Application Structure and Hierarchy

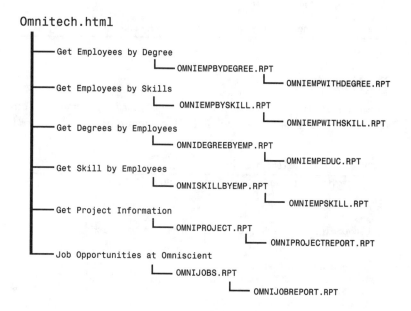

```
Omnitech.html

        ┌── Get Employees by Degree
        │                        └── OMNIEMPBYDEGREE.RPT
        │                                           └── OMNIEMPWITHDEGREE.RPT
        ├── Get Employees by Skills
        │                       └── OMNIEMPBYSKILL.RPT
        │                                          └── OMNIEMPWITHSKILL.RPT
        ├── Get Degrees by Employees
        │                        └── OMNIDEGREEBYEMP.RPT
        │                                           └── OMNIEMPEDUC.RPT
        ├── Get Skill by Employees
        │                      └── OMNISKILLBYEMP.RPT
        │                                         └── OMNIEMPSKILL.RPT
        ├── Get Project Information
        │                       └── OMNIPROJECT.RPT
        │                                        └── OMNIPROJECTREPORT.RPT
        └── Job Opportunities at Omniscient
                                         └── OMNIJOBS.RPT
                                                       └── OMNIJOBREPORT.RPT
```

.ini Files

Your application requires two .ini files: the Dbgate.ini file modified for your environment and the Omnitech.ini file that specifies access information for the Omnitech Access database. Listing 24.1 shows the contents of the DBGate.ini file, and Listing 24.2 shows the contents of the Omnitech.ini file.

Listing 24.1. The DBGate.ini file.

```
DBGATENAME=/cgi-win/dbgate.exe
DBGATEPATH=D:\WebSite\cgi-win\
DBGATELOGO=/images/smglobe.gif
DBGATEICON=/icons/smglobe.gif
DBDATAROOT=D:\My Databases\
SMTPHOST=
SMTPPORT=
```

Listing 24.2. The `Omnitech.ini` file.

```
DBName=Omniscient Technologies Information Database
DBAName=Drew Kittel
Status=Online
PublicAccess=1
InternalQueryAllowed=0
RecordAddAllowed=1
RecordDeleteAllowed=0
RecordEditAllowed=0
TabularReportAllowed=1
DBAccessBeep=1
WaveName=d:\Program Files\DBGateway\sounds\uho.wav
```

The Home Page

The `Omnitech.htm` file provides the HTML necessary to generate the home page shown in Figure 24.18. Listing 24.3 shows the HTML content of the `Omnitech.htm` file.

Listing 24.3. The `Omnitech.htm` file.

```
<! -- Omniscient Technologies Database Main Page -->

<html>
<head>
<title>Omniscient Technologies Information Database</title>
</head>

<body bgcolor="#FFFFFF">
<img src="Globe1.gif" align="middle" hspace="10" width="90" height="90">
<font color="#222FFF" size="6" face="Impact"> <strong>W</strong></font>
<font color="#222FFF" size="5" face="Impact">
<strong>elcome to</strong></font>
<font color="#222FFF" size="6" face="Impact"> <strong> O</strong></font>
<font color="#222FFF" size="5" face="Impact">
<strong>mniscient</strong></font>
<font color="#222FFF" size="6" face="Impact"> <strong> T</strong></font>
<font color="#222FFF" size="5" face="Impact">
<strong>echnologies</strong></font>

<hr>

<p align="center"><font face="Arial">
<strong>Please take the opportunity to get to know Omniscient
Technologies, our employees and capabilities. This system allows
you to browse our Corporate Employee, Project and Job Opportunity
Databases and perform searches and queries according to criteria
you specify.
</strong></font></p>

<div align="center">

<table border="4" cellpadding="2" bgcolor="#D2ECEE">
<tr>
<th colspan="4">
```

```
<font color="#0000FF" size="4" face="Arial">
<strong>Employee Skills/Education</strong> </font>
</th>
</tr>

<tr>
<td align="center">
<form action="/cgi-win/dbgate.exe" method="POST">
<input type="hidden" name="ACTION" value="SubmitExternalQuery">
<input type="hidden" name="DBNAME" value="Omnitech">
<input type="hidden" name="DBTYPE" value="ACCESS">
<input type="hidden" name="DBPATH" value>
<input type="hidden" name="QUERYNAME" value="Omnitech">
<input type="hidden" name="DBACTION" value="Query">
<input type="hidden" name="FIELDS0" value="DegreeID, DegreeName">
<input type="hidden" name="FROM0" value="Degree">
<input type="hidden" name="ORDERBY0" value="DegreeID ASC">
<input type="hidden" name="REPORTNAME"  value="OMNIEMPBYDEGREE">
<input type="image" name="" src="d1b1.gif" align="bottom"
➥width="150" height="50">
</form>
</td>
<td align="center">
<form action="/cgi-win/dbgate.exe" method="POST">
<input type="hidden" name="ACTION" value="SubmitExternalQuery">
<input type="hidden" name="DBNAME" value="Omnitech">
<input type="hidden" name="DBTYPE" value="ACCESS">
<input type="hidden" name="DBPATH" value>
<input type="hidden" name="QUERYNAME" value="Omnitech">
<input type="hidden" name="DBACTION" value="Query">
<input type="hidden" name="FIELDS0" value="SkillID, SkillName">
<input type="hidden" name="FROM0" value="Skill">
<input type="hidden" name="ORDERBY0" value="SkillName ASC">
<input type="hidden" name="REPORTNAME" value="OMNIEMPBYSKILL">
<input type="image" name="" src="d1b2.gif" align="bottom"
➥width="150" height="50">
</form>
</td>
<td align="center">
<form action="/cgi-win/dbgate.exe" method="POST">
<input type="hidden" name="ACTION" value="SubmitExternalQuery">
<input type="hidden" name="DBNAME" value="Omnitech">
<input type="hidden" name="DBTYPE" value="ACCESS">
<input type="hidden" name="DBPATH" value>
<input type="hidden" name="QUERYNAME" value="Omnitech">
<input type="hidden" name="DBACTION" value="Query">
<input type="hidden" name="FIELDS0" value="EmployeeID, LastName, FirstName">
<input type="hidden" name="FROM0" value="Employees">
<input type="hidden" name="ORDERBY0" value="LastName">
<input type="hidden" name="REPORTNAME" value="OMNIDEGREEBYEMP">
<input type="image" name="" src="d1b3.gif" align="bottom"
➥width="150" height="50">
</form>
</td>
<td align="center">
<form action="/cgi-win/dbgate.exe" method="POST">
```

continues

Listing 24.3. continued

```html
<input type="hidden" name="ACTION" value="SubmitExternalQuery">
<input type="hidden" name="DBNAME" value="Omnitech">
<input type="hidden" name="DBTYPE" value="ACCESS">
<input type="hidden" name="DBPATH" value>
<input type="hidden" name="QUERYNAME" value="Omnitech">
<input type="hidden" name="DBACTION" value="Query">
<input type="hidden" name="FIELDS0" value="EmployeeID, LastName, FirstName">
<input type="hidden" name="FROM0" value="Employees">
<input type="hidden" name="ORDERBY0" value="LastName">
<input type="hidden" name="REPORTNAME" value="OMNISKILLBYEMP">
<input type="image" name="" src="d1b4.gif" align="bottom"
➥width="150" height="50">
</form>
</td>
</tr>

<tr>
<th colspan="4"><font color="#0000FF" size="4"
face="Arial"><strong>Project Information</strong></font></th>
</tr>

<tr>
<td align="center" colspan="4">
<form action="/cgi-win/dbgate.exe" method="POST">
<input type="hidden" name="ACTION" value="SubmitExternalQuery">
<input type="hidden" name="DBNAME" value="Omnitech">
<input type="hidden" name="DBTYPE" value="ACCESS">
<input type="hidden" name="DBPATH" value>
<input type="hidden" name="QUERYNAME" value="Omnitech">
<input type="hidden" name="DBACTION" value="Query">
<input type="hidden" name="FIELDS0" value="*">
<input type="hidden" name="FROM0" value="Projects">
<input type="hidden" name="ORDERBY0" value="ProjectID DESC">
<input type="hidden" name="REPORTNAME" value="OMNIPROJECTS">
<input type="image" name="" src="p1b1.gif" align="bottom"
➥width="150" height="50">
</form>
</td>
</tr>

<tr>
<th colspan="4"><font color="#0000FF" size="4" face="Arial"><strong>
Job Openings at Omniscient</strong></font></th>
</tr>

<tr>
<td align="center" colspan="4">
<form action="/cgi-win/dbgate.exe" method="POST">
<input type="hidden" name="ACTION" value="SubmitExternalQuery">
<input type="hidden" name="DBNAME" value="Omnitech">
<input type="hidden" name="DBTYPE" value="ACCESS">
<input type="hidden" name="DBPATH" value>
<input type="hidden" name="QUERYNAME" value="Omnitech">
<input type="hidden" name="DBACTION" value="Query">
<input type="hidden" name="FIELDS0" value="*">
<input type="hidden" name="FROM0" value="Positions">
```

```
<input type="hidden" name="ORDERBY0" value="PostDate ASC">
<input type="hidden" name="REPORTNAME" value="OMNIJOBS">
<input type="image" name="" src="j1b1.gif" align="bottom"
➥width="150" height="50">
</form>
</td>
</tr>
</table>
</div>

<hr>
</body>
</html>
```

The main purpose of this page is to associate queries and report templates with each of the top-level query applications that can be invoked. The next several sections detail how the gateway formulates these queries, passes these to the database, and subsequently uses report templates to present results to the user.

Get Employees by Degree

The following code from Omnitech.htm (in Listing 24.3) indicates that the dbgate program will send the Omnitech database an external query after the user clicks the Image button (d1b1.gif):

```
<form action="/cgi-win/dbgate.exe" method="POST">
<input type="hidden" name="ACTION" value="SubmitExternalQuery">
<input type="hidden" name="DBNAME" value="Omnitech">
<input type="hidden" name="DBTYPE" value="ACCESS">
<input type="hidden" name="DBPATH" value>
<input type="hidden" name="QUERYNAME" value="Omnitech">
<input type="hidden" name="DBACTION" value="Query">
<input type="hidden" name="FIELDS0" value="DegreeID, DegreeName">
<input type="hidden" name="FROM0" value="Degree">
<input type="hidden" name="ORDERBY0" value="DegreeID ASC">
<input type="hidden" name="REPORTNAME" value="OMNIEMPBYDEGREE">
<input type="image" name="" src="d1b1.gif" align="bottom"
➥width="150" height="50">
</form>
```

Recall from Chapter 11 that an image can be used in the same way the Submit form input type is used. After the user clicks the image, the following SQL query is generated by the gateway and submitted to the database:

```
SELECT DegreeID, DegreeName
FROM Degree
ORDERBY DegreeID ASC
```

After the database returns the results to the gateway, the gateway uses specifications in the OMNIEMPBYDEGREE.RPT file to determine how this data will be formatted and presented to the user. Listing 24.4 shows the code for this report template.

Listing 24.4. The OMNIEMPBYDEGREE.RPT file.

```
<!-- OMNIEMPBYDEGREE.RPT -->

<REPORTHEADER>

<HEAD>
<TITLE>Omniscient Technologies Employee Info</TITLE>
</HEAD>

<body bgcolor="#FFFFFF">
<img src="/Globe1.gif" align="middle" hspace="10" width="90"
height="90">
<font color="#222FFF" size="5" face="Impact">
<strong>Omniscient Technologies Employee Info</strong></font>

<HR>
<P>
<FORM METHOD="POST" ACTION="/cgi-win/dbgate.exe">
<INPUT type=hidden name="ACTION" value="SubmitExternalQuery">
<INPUT type=hidden name="DBNAME" value="Omnitech">
<INPUT type=hidden name="DBTYPE" value="ACCESS">
<INPUT type=hidden name="DBPATH" value="">
<INPUT type=hidden name="QUERYNAME" value="Employees">
<INPUT type=hidden name="DBACTION" value="Query">
<INPUT type=hidden name="FIELDS0" value="LastName, FirstName, Title,
➥OfficeLocation, DegreeName, DisciplineName">
<INPUT type=hidden name="FROM0" value="Employees, Emp_Education, Degree,
➥Discipline">
<INPUT type=hidden name="WHERE0" value="'Employees.EmployeeID =
➥Emp_Education.EmployeeID and Emp_Education.DegreeID =
➥Degree.DegreeID and Emp_Education.DisciplineID =
➥Discipline.DisciplineID and '">
<INPUT type=hidden name="WHERE1" value="Degree.DegreeID = ">
<EM>Please Select a Degree From the Following List</EM><BR>
<STRONG>Degrees Held By Omniscient Employees</STRONG><BR>
<SELECT NAME="WHERE2" SIZE="8">
</REPORTHEADER>

<GROUPHEADER NAME="">
</GROUPHEADER>
<RECORDHEADER NAME="">
</RECORDHEADER>
<RECORD>
<OPTION VALUE=" <FIELD NAME="DegreeID"> " ><FIELD NAME="DegreeName"></OPTION>
</RECORD>
<RECORDFOOTER NAME="">
</RECORDFOOTER>

<GROUPFOOTER NAME="">
</GROUPFOOTER>
<REPORTFOOTER>
</SELECT>

<P>
<EM>Click Here to List Employees With Selected Degree</EM><BR>
```

```
<INPUT type=hidden name="REPORTNAME" value="OMNIEMPWITHDEGREE">
<INPUT type=submit name="Submit" value="Submit Query">
</P>

<HR>
<P>
<A HREF="/Omnitech.htm"><img src="/Home.gif">Return to Omniscient Main Page</A>
</P>
</FORM>

</BODY>
</HTML>
</REPORTFOOTER>
```

Figure 24.20 shows the formatted results.

FIGURE 24.20.

Query results formatted by the OMNIEMPBYDEGREE *report template.*

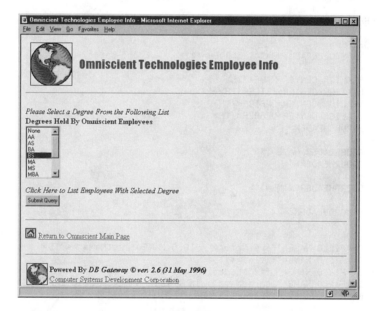

You should note a few things about the use of this report template. First, it sets up a secondary query to the database—in this case, a fairly complex join across four tables (Employees, Emp_Education, Degree, and Discipline). Next, it uses results from the initial query to create a selection list on the results page. The report template is set up so that a user selection from this list is used to complete the secondary query. After the user makes a selection and clicks the Submit button, the following query is passed to the database:

```
SELECT LastName, FirstName, Title, OfficeLocation, DegreeName, DisciplineName
FROM Employees, Emp_Education, Degree, Discipline
WHERE 'Employees.EmployeeID = Emp_Education.EmployeeID
➥and Emp_Education.DegreeID = Degree.DegreeID and
➥Emp_Education.DisciplineID = Discipline.DisciplineID
➥and Degree.DegreeID = "user-specified DegreeID"
```

Finally, OMNIEMPWITHDEGREE is specified as the report template to format results from the secondary query. Listing 24.5 shows the code for this secondary report template.

Listing 24.5. The OMNIEMPWITHDEGREE.RPT file.

```
<!--OMNIEMPWITHDEGREE.RPT -->

<REPORTHEADER>
<HEAD>
<TITLEOmniscient Employees With Specific Degrees</TITLE>
</HEAD>

<body bgcolor="#FFFFFF">
<img src="/Globe1.gif" align="middle" hspace="10" width="90" height="90">
<font color="#222FFF" size="4" face="Impact">
<strong>Omniscient Technologies Employees With Specific Degrees</strong></font>

<HR>

<CENTER>
<TABLE CELLPADDING="4" BORDER="1">
<TR>
<TH ALIGN=CENTER>NAME</TH>
<TH ALIGN=CENTER>TITLE</TH>
<TH ALIGN=CENTER>OFFICE</TH>
<TH ALIGN=CENTER>DEGREE</TH>
</REPORTHEADER>

<GROUPHEADER NAME="">
</GROUPHEADER>

<RECORDHEADER NAME="">
<TR>
</RECORDHEADER>

<RECORD>
<TD><FIELD NAME="FirstName"> <FIELD NAME="LastName"></TD>
<TD><FIELD NAME="Title"></TD>
<TD><FIELD NAME="OfficeLocation"></TD>
<TD><FIELD NAME="DegreeName"> in <FIELD NAME="DisciplineName"></TD>
</RECORD>

<RECORDFOOTER NAME="">
</TR>
</RECORDFOOTER>

<GROUPFOOTER NAME="">
</GROUPFOOTER>

<REPORTFOOTER>
</TABLE>
</CENTER>
```

```
<HR>
<P>
<A HREF="/Omnitech.htm"><img src="/Home.gif">Return to Omniscient Main Page</A>
</P>


</BODY>
</HTML>
</REPORTFOOTER>
```

Figure 24.21 shows the formatted results.

FIGURE 24.21.

Query results formatted by the OMNIEMPWITHDEGREE *report template.*

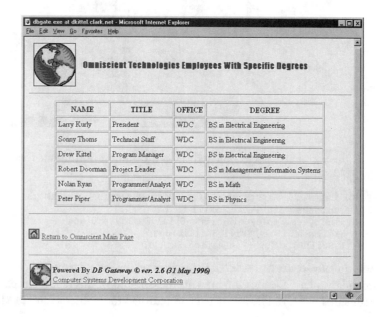

Get Employees by Skill

After the `d1b2.gif` button in the `Omnitech.htm` code in Listing 24.3 is clicked, the following SQL query is generated by the gateway and submitted to the database:

```
SELECT SkillID, SkillName
FROM Skill
ORDERBY SkillName ASC
```

After the database returns the results to the gateway, the gateway uses specifications in the `OMNIEMPBYSKILL.RPT` file to determine how this data will be formatted and presented to the user.

Figure 24.22 shows the formatted results.

FIGURE 24.22.

Query results formatted by the OMNIEMPBYSKILL *report template.*

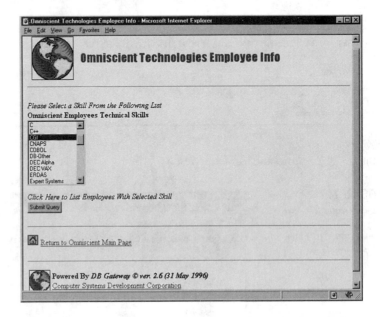

After the user makes a selection and clicks the Submit button, the following query is passed to the database:

```
SELECT LastName, FirstName, Title, OfficeLocation, SkillName
FROM Employees, Emp_Skill, Skill
WHERE Employees.EmployeeID = Emp_Skill.EmployeeID and
➥Emp_Skill.SkillID = Skill.SkillID and
➥Skill.SkillID = "user-specified SkillID"
```

Additionally, OMNIEMPWITHSKILL is specified as the report template to format results from the secondary query. Listing 24.6 presents the contents of this report template and illustrates how results of a query can be formatted and returned to the user as an HTML table.

Listing 24.6. The OMNIEMPWITHSKILL.RPT file.

```
<!--OMNIEMPWITHSKILL.RPT -->

<REPORTHEADER>
<HEAD>
<TITLE>Omniscient Technologies Employees With Specific Skill</TITLE>
</HEAD>

<body bgcolor="#FFFFFF">
<img src="/Globe1.gif" align="middle" hspace="10" width="90" height="90">
<font color="#222FFF" size="5" face="Impact">
<strong>Omniscient Employees With Specific Skill</strong></font>

<HR>
```

```
<CENTER>
<STRONG>The following Omniscient Employees possess skills and

experience in/using </STRONG>
<FONT SIZE=+2 COLOR="2222ff"> "<FIELD NAME="SkillName">" </FONT>

<TABLE CELLPADDING="4" BORDER="1">
<TR>
<TH ALIGN=CENTER>NAME</TH>
<TH ALIGN=CENTER>TITLE</TH>
<TH ALIGN=CENTER>OFFICE</TH>
</REPORTHEADER>

<GROUPHEADER NAME="">
</GROUPHEADER>

<RECORDHEADER NAME="">
<TR>
</RECORDHEADER>

<RECORD>
<TD><FIELD NAME="FirstName"> <FIELD NAME="LastName"></TD>
<TD><FIELD NAME="Title"></TD>
<TD><FIELD NAME="OfficeLocation"></TD>
</RECORD>

<RECORDFOOTER NAME="">
</TR>
</RECORDFOOTER>

<GROUPFOOTER NAME="">
</GROUPFOOTER>

<REPORTFOOTER>
</TABLE>
</CENTER>

<P>
<HR>
<P>
<A HREF="/Omnitech.htm"><img src="/Home.gif">Return to Omniscient Main Page</A>
</P>

</BODY>
</HTML>
</REPORTFOOTER>
```

Figure 24.23 shows the formatted results.

FIGURE 24.23.

Query results formatted by the OMNIEMPWITHSKILL *report template.*

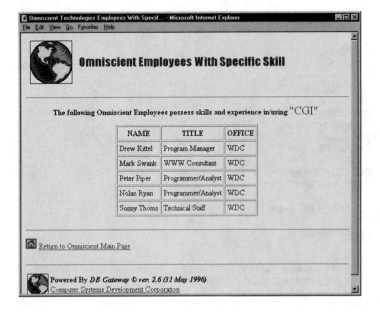

Get Degrees by Employee

After the d1b3.gif button in the Omnitech.htm code in Listing 24.3 is clicked, the following SQL query is generated by the gateway and submitted to the database:

```
SELECT EmployeeID, LastName, FirstName
FROM Employees
ORDERBY LastName
```

After the database returns the results to the gateway, the gateway uses specifications in the OMNIDEGREEBYEMP.RPT file to determine how this data will be formatted and presented to the user.

Figure 24.24 shows the formatted results.

After the user makes a selection and clicks the Submit button, the following query is passed to the database:

```
SELECT LastName, FirstName, Title, OfficeLocation, DegreeName, DisciplineName
FROM Employees, Emp_Education, Degree, Discipline
WHERE Employees.EmployeeID = Emp_Education.EmployeeID and
➥Emp_Education.DegreeID = Degree.DegreeID and
➥Emp_Education.DisciplineID = Discipline.DisciplineID and
➥Employees.EmployeeID = "user-specified EmployeeID"
```

Additionally, OMNIEMPEDUC is specified as the report template to format results from the secondary query. Figure 24.25 shows the formatted results.

FIGURE 24.24.

Query results formatted by the OMNIDEGREEBYEMP *report template.*

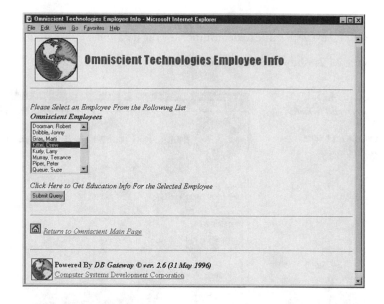

FIGURE 24.25.

Query results formatted by the OMNIEMPEDUC *report template.*

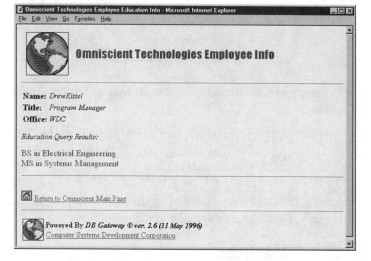

Get Skills by Employee

After the d1b4.gif button in the Omnitech.htm code in Listing 24.3 is clicked, the following SQL query is generated by the gateway and submitted to the database:

```
SELECT EmployeeID, LastName, FirstName
FROM Employees
ORDERBY LastName
```

After the database returns the results to the gateway, the gateway uses specifications in the OMNISKILLBYEMP.RPT file to determine how the data will be formatted and presented to the user.

Figure 24.26 shows the formatted results.

FIGURE 24.26.

Query results formatted by the OMNISKILLBYEMP *report template.*

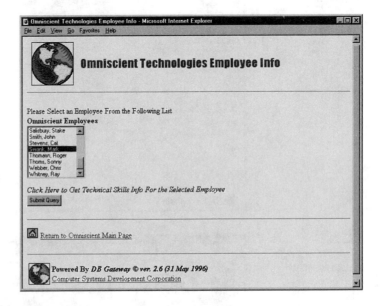

After the user makes a selection and clicks the Submit button, the following query is passed to the database:

```
SELECT LastName, FirstName, Title, OfficeLocation, SkillName
FROM Employees, Emp_Skill, Skill
WHERE = 'Employees.EmployeeID = Emp_Skill.EmployeeID and
➥Emp_Skill.SkillID = Skill.SkillID and
➥Employees.EmployeeID = "user-specified EmployeeID"
```

Additionally, OMNIEMPSKILL is specified as the report template to format results from the secondary query. Figure 24.27 shows the formatted results.

Get Project Information

After the p1b1.gif button in the Omnitech.htm code in Listing 24.3 is clicked, the following SQL query is generated by the gateway and submitted to the database:

```
SELECT *
FROM Projects
ORDERBY ProjectID DESC
```

FIGURE 24.27.

Query results formatted by the OMNIEMPSKILL *report template.*

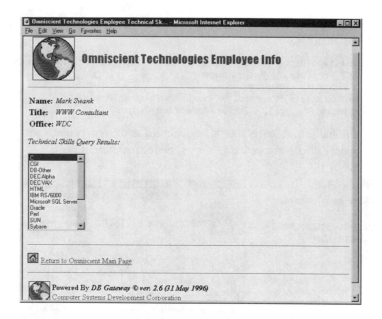

After the database returns the results to the gateway, the gateway uses specifications in the OMNIPROJECTS.RPT file to determine how this data will be formatted and presented to the user.

Figure 24.28 shows the formatted results.

FIGURE 24.28.

Query results formatted by the OMNIPROJECTS *report template.*

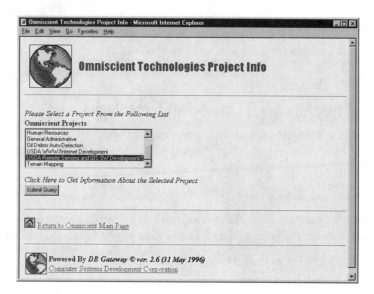

After the user makes a selection and clicks the Submit button, the following query is passed to the database:

```
<INPUT type=hidden name="FIELDS0" value="Projects.*, ProgramName">
SELECT Projects.*, ProgramName
FROM Projects, Programs
WHERE 'Projects.ProgramID = Programs.ProgramID and
➥Projects.ProjectID = "user-specified ProjectID"
```

Additionally, OMNIPROJECTREPORT is specified as the report template to format results from the secondary query. Figure 24.29 shows the formatted results.

FIGURE 24.29.

Query results formatted by the OMNIPROJECTREPORT *report template.*

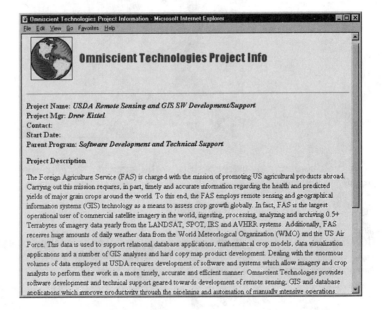

Job Opportunities at Omniscient Technologies

After the j1b1.gif button in the Omnitech.htm code in Listing 24.3 is clicked, the following SQL query is generated by the gateway and submitted to the database:

```
SELECT *
FROM Positions
ORDERBY PostDate ASC
```

After the database returns the results to the gateway, the gateway uses specifications in the OMNIJOBS.RPT file to determine how this data will be formatted and presented to the user.

Figure 24.30 shows the formatted results.

FIGURE 24.30.
Query results formatted by the OMNIJOBS *report template.*

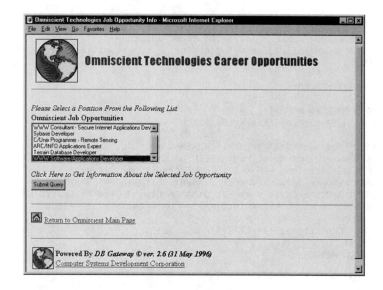

After the user makes a selection and clicks the Submit button, the following query is passed to the database:

```
<INPUT type=hidden name="FIELDS0" value="Projects.*, ProgramName">
SELECT Projects.*, ProgramName
FROM Projects, Programs
WHERE 'Projects.ProgramID = Programs.ProgramID and
➥Projects.ProjectID = "user-specified ProjectID"
```

Additionally, OMNIJOBREPORT is specified as the report template to format results from the secondary query. Listing 24.7 presents this report template and illustrates how results of a query can be formatted and returned to the user as a scrollable HTML <TEXTAREA> object. Such use of <TEXTAREA> objects to present textual data can be very important if you are making documents available that consist of several pages, such as project and program descriptions, proposals, and so on.

Listing 24.7. The OMNIJOBREPORT.RPT **file.**

```
<!-- OMNIPROJECTREPORT.RPT -->

<REPORTHEADER>
<HEAD>
<TITLE>Omniscient Technologies Job Opportunity Information</TITLE>
</HEAD>

<body bgcolor="#FFFFFF">
<img src="/Globe1.gif" align="middle" hspace="10" width="90" height="90">
```

continues

Listing 24.7. continued

```
<font color="#222FFF" size="5" face="Impact">
<strong>Omniscient Technologies Career Opportunities</strong></font>
<HR>

</REPORTHEADER>

<GROUPHEADER NAME="">
<STRONG>Position/Title: <EM><FIELD

NAME="PositionName"></EM></STRONG><BR>
<STRONG>Project Name: <EM><FIELD NAME="ProjectName"></EM></STRONG><BR>
<STRONG>Location: <EM><FIELD NAME="PositionLocation"></EM></STRONG><BR>
<STRONG>Open Date: <EM><FIELD NAME="PostDate"></EM></STRONG> <BR>
<STRONG>Close Date: <EM><FIELD NAME="ClosingDate"></EM></STRONG><BR>
<STRONG>Contact: <EM><FIELD NAME="ContactName"> at <FIELD

NAME="ContactEmail"></EM></STRONG><BR>
<FORM>
</GROUPHEADER>

<RECORDHEADER NAME="">
<P>
<EM>Position Description:</EM><BR>
</P>
</RECORDHEADER>

<RECORD>
<TEXTAREA ROWS="8" COLS="65"><FIELD

NAME="PositionDescription"></TEXTAREA>
</RECORD>

<RECORDFOOTER>
</RECORDFOOTER>

<GROUPFOOTER NAME="">
</FORM>
</GROUPFOOTER>

<REPORTFOOTER>

<HR>
<P>
<A HREF="/Omnitech.htm"><img src="/Home.gif">Return to Omniscient Main Page</A>

</BODY>
</HTML>
</REPORTFOOTER>
```

Figure 24.31 shows the formatted results.

FIGURE 24.31.

Query results formatted by the OMNIJOBREPORT *report template.*

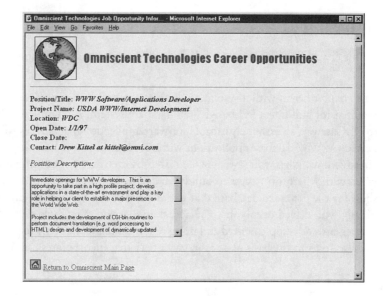

What We Haven't Shown You

DBGateway also provides the capability to add, delete, and modify records. The previous examples easily could be extended to incorporate additional <FORM> input objects, such as text-input boxes, which would allow privileged users to retrieve and modify employee records, update program information, and add entries for new projects and job opportunities. Secure transactions for such a system could be provided through the use of SSL, SHTTP, and authentication technologies such as public key encryption, certificates, and digital signing—all of which are supported by professional-quality Web servers such as WebSite Professional.

RESOURCE

To find out more about technologies such as Secure Sockets, Secure HTTP, public and private key encryption technologies, digital signing, certification authorities, and several other topics related to Web security, visit the RSA Technologies home page and read its very extensive FAQ. The RSA site is located at

`http://www.rsa.com/`

Additionally, the mail capabilities and support previously mentioned could be incorporated to enable visitors to sign guest logs, provide immediate feedback about your site, or respond to job opportunities directly to the cognizant point of contact. The number of additional things you can accomplish could fill another couple of chapters in this book. The DBGateway software documentation contains all the details necessary to expand on the skills you've learned in this chapter.

Summary

In this chapter, you examined a full-fledged Web database application using a variety of new tools.

The chapter began with a systematic look at the requirements, benefits of, and components required for building a PC-based Web database system. Along the way, you were introduced to DBGateway, an extremely capable software application that enables you to easily and quickly develop WWW database applications without requiring more knowledge than the HTML you already know. Next, you saw a detailed, step-by-step account of using the graphical tools provided with Microsoft Access to build a database. You then examined the tables and relationships for the Omnitech database that is the heart of the application presented in this chapter. Finally, you delved deeply into the actual application. You looked at a full accounting of all queries currently implemented and using report templates not only to present results of a query, but also to form the basis of a secondary query that incorporates user input.

25

A Card Shop Application Using ASP

by Troy Rackley

In this chapter, you will learn techniques for building a complete Internet application. You will build a complete electronic card shop implemented by *Active Server Pages* (ASPs).

Overview

To put together all the techniques you have learned so far, we have built a database-enabled Internet application using ASPs. In addition to ASPs, the site uses Visual Basic 5 ActiveX components, *Active Data Objects* (ADOs), and a Microsoft Access database.

We created a simple card shop application similar to applications that most Net junkies probably have seen. This Card Shop site enables users to send free, virtual Internet greetings to their friends and loved ones. In case you have not seen this type of site before, the idea is simple: A would-be card sender hits the site and builds a card from a set of possible options. The card then is delivered via e-mail or is picked up at a "post office" by the recipient; this site follows the post office approach. The recipient must log onto a specified URL with a system-generated postal code. This code is given to the sender when he places the card order. The recipient is presented with the greeting card after he successfully enters the postal code. The Electronic Card Shop was designed to show off some of the server-side capabilities discussed so far in this book. These capabilities include using the built-in ASP objects, ADO database connectivity, and server-side and client-side ActiveX controls. This application also offers some innovative HTML techniques using styles, tables, forms, and objects.

How We Started

We used InterDev 1.0 to develop a skeleton of the Card Shop site. For the skeleton, we used the Departmental Site Wizard, which enabled us to create an instant site complete with a prebuilt navigation bar and a set of automatic, customizable feedback pages. The wizard provided an efficient way to quickly build a set of connected pages. Within minutes, a shell was constructed on which we could base our Electronic Card Shop site. We were able to choose a theme, and all the pages created followed that theme by using common graphics and style sheets. After a skeleton and general look and feel were generated, we could focus on the real importance of the site: showing off ASP capabilities. We decided to store the data for feedback and card orders in an Access database, which offered the simplicity we needed for this example.

Site Architecture

Although the Site Wizard does a good job of laying out the groundwork, a considerable amount of thought still must go into the planning of any site, such as directory organization, media management, and team-development concerns. Table 25.1 lists the major objects used in the site and the function of each.

Table 25.1. Site objects.

Object	Description
birthday.asp	The actual card the recipient sees. The information provided by the sender generates a unique card for the birthday boy or girl.
card.mdb	The Access database that stores all the card orders and feedback entries.
card shop.asp	The home page, complete with site descriptions, card-ordering and pickup instructions, links to other pages, and credits.
default.htm	The default page for IIS. Contains a simple tag that refreshes card shop.asp.
feedback.asp	Here, users can enter comments about the site or the cards.
footer.inc	An include file that contains the HTML code to list the Webmaster comments (author, date last modified, and so on) at the bottom of each page.
generate.dll	The ActiveX component that creates a unique ID for each card order.
global.asa	The file that contains variables or scripts that have application- or session-level scope. We changed the default session time-out variable here to 10 minutes.
navigation.inc	An include file that contains the HTML code to implement the navigation bar as a table with links in each cell.
order.asp	Here, card senders place an order for each card. They fill out a form, and the required fields are stored in a database for future retrieval.
pobox.asp	The page that recipients use to receive their greeting cards. After successfully entering the post office code, users are directed to the appropriate greeting-card page.
response.asp	This page delivers a response to the user after he enters comments from the feedback page, places an order for an electronic card, or enters a post office code that does not match any card orders. Most database interaction for the site occurs here.

Figure 25.1 shows how the major ASP pages are linked together and the general workflow of the application.

FIGURE 25.1.
The Card Shop site architecture.

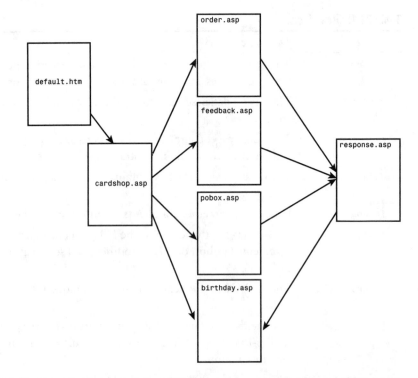

> **NOTE**
>
> All the files referenced in this chapter are located on the CD-ROM that accompanies this book. To construct and use the source code for this site, you must be aware that the code assumes that you have set up a DSN to the Card Shop database (card.mdb) called ElectronicCard and that you have set up a virtual directory in IIS called Card shop.

The Electronic Card Shop Home Page

Our default page in IIS is set to be default.htm, but we wanted to be able to run ASP scripts on the home page. Because ASP scripts cannot be run in standard .htm files, we placed a simple <meta> tag in default.htm that would immediately load our ASP home page (card shop.asp). Listing 25.1 shows the <meta> tag we used.

Listing 25.1. Our <meta> tag.

```
<HTML>
<HEAD>
```

```
<TITLE>The Electronic Card Shop</TITLE>

    <META HTTP-EQUIV="Refresh" CONTENT="0; URL=card shop.asp">

</HEAD>
<BODY>
</BODY>
</HTML>
```

The `HTTP-EQUIV` parameter of the `<meta>` tag binds the element in the `CONTENT` parameter to the desired HTTP response header. The code in Listing 25.1 tells the browser to wait zero seconds before refreshing the URL at `card shop.asp`. The `<meta>` tag is used for many types of applications. Other possible uses include providing keyword information for search engines and specifying character sets used on a particular page.

The home page for the card shop (`card shop.asp`) presents the purpose of the site and provides links to the ordering, receiving, and feedback sections of the site. It checks the browser's name to determine whether the client can display styles. It also uses Server-Side Includes for its navigational bar and Webmaster comments section. Figure 25.2 shows the home page.

One interesting feature of the home page is the use of style sheets. The home page, as well as the other pages, use the `<link>` tag to specify sets of styles that are common across similar pages. The Departmental Wizard in InterDev generated the original styles. Then simple modifications to a style sheet file can produce dramatic effects. The `card shop.asp` interrogates the browser-type component to determine whether the client browser is Microsoft Internet Explorer. If so, the user should be able to render text that uses style definitions. Listing 25.2 shows a fragment of the code from `card shop.asp`.

FIGURE 25.2.

The Electronic Card Shop home page.

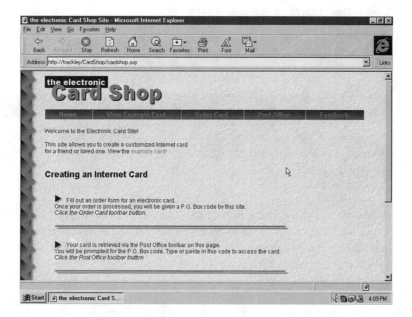

Listing 25.2. A fragment of the `card shop.asp` code.

```
<!-----------------Start Style Sheet Call-------------------->
<LINK REL=STYLESHEET HREF="./styles/style1.css">
<!-----------------End Style Sheet Call---------------------->

<!---------------------Start Title--------------------------->
<title>The Electronic Card Shop Site</title>
<!---------------------End Title----------------------------->

<meta name="GENERATOR" content="Microsoft InterDev 1.0">
</head>

<!------------------Start Background------------------------->
<body background="./images/background/back1.jpg"
alink="#FF000" bgcolor="#FFFFFF" topmargin=0 leftmargin=0>
<img src="./images/headings/header1.gif" align="bottom" >
<!------------------End Background--------------------------->

<!------------------Start Page Name-------------------------->
<%

'-- If we are using IE 3.0 or above, use a combination
'   of styles to offer a cool effect for the page title.

'   Determine the type of browser
Set obc = Server.CreateObject("MSWC.BrowserType")
if obc.Browser = "IE" Then %>

    <p class=title> the electronic </p>
    <p class=title2>Card Shop</p>
    <p class=title3>Card Shop</p>

<% else %>

    <h1>The Electronic Card Shop</h1>

<%End If%>
<!---------------------End Page Name------------------------->
```

> **NOTE**
>
> Microsoft's Internet Explorer 3.*x* currently is the only browser that supports style sheets. Because of the recent acceptance of the cascading style sheet specification, though, other browsers are sure to follow.

As you can see, the script in Listing 25.2 checks the `Browser` property of the `BrowserType` object to see whether it is `IE`. If so, a set of styles defined in `styles/styles1.css` provides an interesting effect for our page title. The styles used for the title are descendent classes of the `<P>` style and are shown in Listing 25.3.

Listing 25.3. Title styles from `styles1.css`.

```
P {
    margin-left: 0px;
    font: 9pt/11pt "Arial";
    color: black;
    background: transparent;
    }

.title {
        font:12pt Arial Black;
        color:white;
        background:black
        }

.title2 {
         font:32pt Arial Black;
         margin-left:15px;
         margin-top:-10px
         }

.title3 {
         font:32pt Arial Black;
         color:red;
         margin-left:13px;
         margin-top:-44px
         }
```

The two classes `title2` and `title3` create the cool shadowing effect. The shadow is rendered first (`P.title2`). Then, by manipulating the `margin-top` parameter in the `P.title3` class, the red text overlays the black text and produces the desired results.

RESOURCE

Using style sheets enables a more robust use of fonts and page layout. You can find more information on using cascading style sheets at

`www.w3.org/pub/WWW/Style/`

or

`www.microsoft.com/workshop/author/`

Another interesting feature of this page is the use of Server-Side Includes. SSIs are used for content that is common on each of the pages. SSIs enable you to easily maintain and modify this content without visiting each page. Listing 25.4 shows the `include` statement for the navigation bar.

Listing 25.4. The `include` statement for the navigation bar.

```
<!-----------------Start Navigation Bar-------------------->
<!--#include virtual="/Card shop/navigation.inc"-->
<!-----------------End Navigation Bar---------------------->
```

The server evaluates the statement in Listing 25.4 before sending the page to the client browser. Listing 25.5 shows the contents of the navigation `include` file, which are sent to the browser instead of the previous `include` tag.

Listing 25.5. The navigation `include` file.

```
<p><table bgcolor=silver cellspacing=1 cellpadding=2 width=100%>
<tr>
    <td align=center valign=center background="./images/Navigation/Nav2.jpg">
        <a href="Card shop.asp"><B>Home</B></a>
    <td align=center valign=center background="./images/navigation/Nav2.jpg">
        <a href="birthday.asp"><B>View Example Card</B></a>
    <td align=center valign=center background="./images/navigation/Nav2.jpg">
        <a href="order.asp"><B>Order Card</B></a>
    <td align=center valign=center background="./images/navigation/Nav2.jpg">
        <a href="pobox.asp"><B>Post Office</B></a>
    <td align=center valign=center background="./images/navigation/Nav2.jpg">
        <a href="feedback.asp"><B>Feedback</B></a>
</table></p>
```

The navigation bar is constructed of a table with a single row that spans the width of the page's margins. Each cell of the table holds a hyperlink to another page. The background of each cell is provided by a simple, shaded, square image. This table approach to a navigation bar eliminates the need to create customized buttons for each link and makes adding or removing "navbuttons" a breeze. The colors of the links (those visited and unvisited) also are maintained in the style-sheet file for the document.

The Webmaster comment section at the bottom of all pages also is implemented by using these technique with SSIs.

The Order Page

The order page is an entry form for sending an Internet card to a friend or loved one. It contains the same background images, title styles, and `include` references for the navigational bar and Webmaster comments. The order page also holds a form for entering all the fields of a card-order table:

- The card recipient's name
- The card recipient's e-mail address
- The sender's name

- The sender's e-mail address
- A greeting to be added to the card
- The date when the card should be sent
- A Submit Order button and Clear buttons

Figure 25.3 shows a card-order form that has been filled out and is ready to be submitted.

FIGURE 25.3.

The E-Card Shop Order Card page.

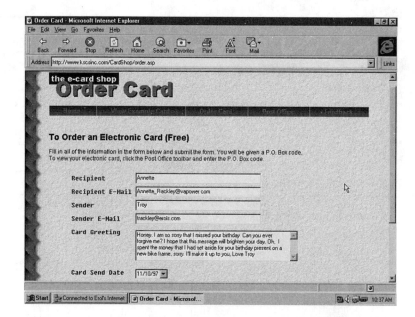

The form the InterDev wizard generated uses the HTML <pre> tag to denote preformatted text. Many people overlook the <pre> tag when designing Web pages. The <pre> tag renders all text in a fixed-width font. The advantage of this tag is that you can format the desired output within the <pre> and </pre> delimiters as you want it to display onscreen. Line breaks occur where you place them, and all spacing is preserved. Some other HTML items, such as images, font changes, and paragraphs are not supported within the <pre> tag, however.

> **NOTE**
>
> Microsoft HTML documentation specifies that the <PRE> tag is included for backward compatibility for use with older browsers, and they recommend using the newer monospaced tags. One advantage of the <pre> tag is that some elements can be preformatted. In this chapter, you are formatting <input> elements. Interestingly enough, the InterDev 1.0 Departmental Wizard consistently uses this now outdated <PRE> tag when generating most of its HTML forms. You will see more of the <pre> tag used throughout the site.

Listing 25.6 shows a section of ASP code from the order page.

Listing 25.6. Some ASP code from the order page.

```
<%
'Set the session variable to identify the response type
Session("ResponseType") = "Order"
Session("ResponseMsg") = "Thank you for your order!"
%>
```

Notice that this code sets session-level variables that will be used later by the response page when the form is posted. As you will see in later sections, the response page is referenced by the ACTION parameter of all the card shop forms. The response page is used to perform database lookups and inserts, and it provides information to the user after those operations are complete.

Listing 25.7 shows the HTML form declaration.

Listing 25.7. The HTML form declaration.

```
<!--------------------Begin Form-------------------------->
<FORM ACTION=response.asp METHOD="POST" name="OrderForm" onSubmit=getDate>

<pre>
        Recipient           <input type="text" size="50"
                                    maxlength="50" name="txtRecipient">

        Recipient E-Mail   <input type="text" size="50"
                                    maxlength="50" name="txtREMail">

        Sender              <input type="text" size="50" maxlength="50"
                            ➥name="txtSender">

        Sender E-Mail       <input type="text" size="50" maxlength="50"
                            ➥name="txtSEMail">

        Card Greeting<BR>
                            <textarea name="txtGreeting" rows="3" cols="70"
                                    align="top"></textarea>
</pre>

<%
    Set oBrowser = Server.CreateObject("MSWC.BrowserType")
    If oBrowser.ActiveXcontrols = "True" Then %>
<pre>       Card Send Date    <input type="hidden"
                                    name="txtDate"><OBJECT ID="DatePicker1"
                        CLSID="CLSID:E6AE6F49-63EB-11D0-85CE-444553540000"
                                CODEBASE="DatePicker.CAB#version=1,0,0,0"
                                ALIGN=top name="DatePicker1"></OBJECT></pre>
<%  Else%>
<pre>       Card Send Date    <input type="text" size="20" maxlength="20"
                                    name="txtDate"></pre>
```

```
<%    End If
      Set oBrowser = Nothing%>

</Form>
<!----------------------End Form---------------------->
```

The interesting feature of this particular form is the use of the ActiveX Datepicker control, which was mentioned in Chapter 16, "Creating ActiveX Controls for the Web with VB 5." After a set of desired input fields is displayed, a BrowserType object is created. The ActiveXcontrols property of this object specifies whether the client browser can host these controls. If it can, an object tag is used to insert the desired control. Also, we create a hidden text-input box that stores the date chosen from the DatePicker. If the person ordering the card is using a browser that does not support ActiveX controls, a normal text-input box is presented. The input boxes were intentionally created with the same name (txtDate) to lighten the code required to post this data.

Before posting the results of the entry form to the response page, we run a preliminary procedure called getDate. The getDate function transfers the date value selected in the DatePicker1 control to the hidden input object (txtDate) by using VBScript and the object model of the IE browser. The script is placed inside a comment so that other browsers will ignore this code. The following listing displays the VBScript for the getDate function.

Listing 25.8. The getDate function

```
<SCRIPT language="VBScript">
<!-- hide this script from technically challenged browsers
Sub getDate()
   '-- This procedure copies the date in the DatePicker Control to
   '  the hidden txtDate field on the form so that the Response
   '  object will read it in response.asp
   document.OrderForm.txtDate.value = document.OrderForm.DatePicker1.TextDate
End Sub
-->
</SCRIPT>
```

The Feedback Page

The feedback page (feedback.asp) enables users to send comments about the cards or the site as a whole. These comments can be problems, complaints, or general good cheer directed toward the Webmasters. Feedback entries are stored in a separate table in the Card Shop database. Figure 25.4 shows the Card Shop's feedback page.

FIGURE 25.4.
The feedback page.

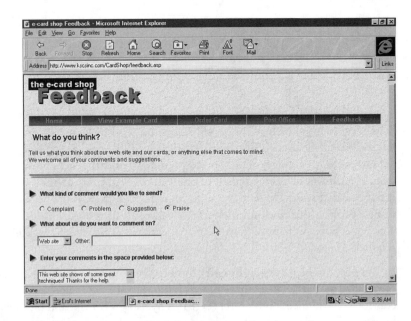

The feedback page contains a simple HTML form in which the post method is directed to the response page (with the ACTION=response.asp parameter in the form tag) in the same manner as the order-form page. Listing 25.9 shows the code that sets the session-level variables to hold the state information required by the ASP script in the response page.

Listing 25.9. Setting the session-level variables.

```
<%
'-- Set the session variables to be used by the response form
'   to identify the calling form and provide a header to display
Session("ResponseType") = "Feedback"
Session("ResponseMsg") = "Feedback Confirmation"
%>
```

As shown in Listing 25.9, the session-level variable ResponseType contains the string "Feedback". As in the order page, this string tells the ASP code in the response page what type of database update to perform. The ResponseMsg string displays a header on the response page when it is called.

This page uses the same browser check and styles you saw in the other pages. Otherwise, it is a simple HTML static document that receives information via a simple form.

TIP

The feedback page again uses the <pre> tag to display some text-input boxes in a uniform manner. If the fixed-width font is not your thing, you could have accomplished the same effect with a two-column, four-row table. The alignment options in the table support many customizable layout combinations. The preformatting tag gets the job done but restricts you to using a rather dull font.

The Response Page

The response page (response.asp) posts entered data to the database for the forms on the order and feedback pages and performs a lookup for the post office. The response page also provides information on the results of these operations. If the user enters comments in the feedback page, for example, this page attempts to store that information in the Feedback table of the database. If that operation is successful, a message similar to the one in Figure 25.5 appears, thanking the user for the comments.

FIGURE 25.5.

Feedback confirmation via the response page.

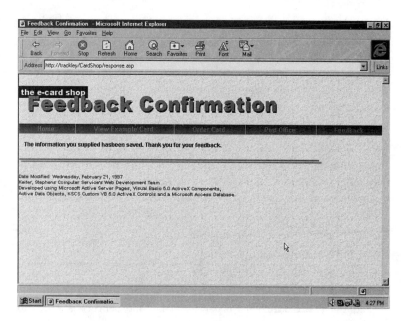

If the user submits an order for a new card, the response also handles the database insert. In this case, the ASP source uses a server-side ActiveX component called Generate.ID. This component's single purpose is to generate a unique string ID that will be used as a key to a single card order. This key is required when the card recipient visits to pick up the card. Figure 25.6 shows the response page when called from the order form.

FIGURE 25.6.

The response page showing a successful card order.

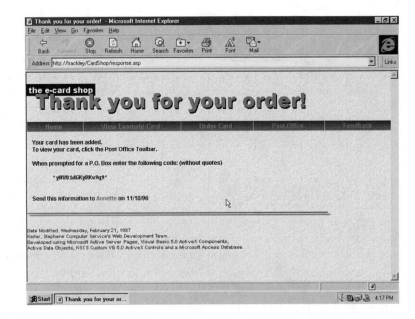

Notice that the response page in Figure 25.6 displays the unique identifier for this card order. This code can be copied to a mail message to the person. Simply click the person's name highlighted by the red link to generate a mail message in your native mail package. In order for the recipient to get the e-card, you must provide the URL to the site and paste the P.O. Box code shown on the response page. An automatic mailing is not currently available. This is a great example of when you could use another ActiveX component to enhance this application.

The response page posts data to the database by using a method similar to the approach used to add a time-sheet entry in the srvtimes.asp example in Chapter 22, "Writing Server-Side Applications with VB 5 ActiveX Components." First, we must create a connection to our ODBC data source. Then we can perform any required queries to add or look up information in our Card Shop database. Listing 25.10 shows the complete code used for the response Active Server Page.

Listing 25.10. The response.asp ASP script.

```
<SCRIPT LANGUAGE=VBScript RUNAT=Server>
Function getResponse
'-- Shared routine that is used to add both the feedback
'   and the electronic card order records, and perform a P.O. Box
'   lookup.
'
   'Create an instance of the ADO object
   Set oDBCard = Server.CreateObject("ADODB.Connection")

   'Open the database
   oDBCard.Open "ElectronicCard"
```

```
'Create an ADO recordset to add a new record
set rsResponse = CreateObject("ADODB.Recordset")

'Set the Recordset Properties
rsResponse.CursorType = 0
rsResponse.LockType = adLockOptimistic
rsResponse.ActiveConnection = oDBCard

'Check if this is an Order or a FeedBack
Select Case Session("ResponseType")

Case "Order"
    '--This is a new card order - Get a unique string to use as an ID
    '  using the ActiveX component Generate.Id
    Set oId = Server.CreateObject("Generate.Id")

    '-- Set the size of our ID string
    oID.Size = 15
    lFlag = oId.GenerateID

    '-- Check for Errors
    If lFlag <> 0 Then
        'Error found set response variable to display the error message
        sResponse = oId.ErrorMsg
    Else
        'All is well - initialize a CardOrder recordset
        rsResponse.Source = "SELECT * FROM CardOrder"

        '-- Open the recordset
        rsResponse.Open

        '-- Check to make sure Updates are supported
        sResponse = "<H2>Sorry your order was not added.
                    ➥Invalid server cursor.</H2>"
        If rsResponse.Supports(adUpdate) Then

            '-- Add a new record
            rsResponse.AddNew

            '-- Get our ID from the object
            rsResponse("ID") = oId.UniqueString

            '-- Set the data values from the form
            rsResponse("Recipient") = Trim(Request.Form("txtRecipient"))
            rsResponse("Email") = Trim(Request.Form("txtREMail"))
            rsResponse("Sender") = Trim(Request.Form("txtSender"))
            rsResponse("SenderEmail") = Trim(Request.Form("txtSEMail"))
            '-- Only Birthday card types are currently available
            rsResponse("CardType") = "Birthday"
            rsResponse("Greeting") = Trim(Request.Form("txtGreeting"))
            rsResponse("CardDate") = Trim(CStr(Request.Form("txtDate")))

            '-- Complete the add operation
            rsResponse.Update
        End If

        '-- Build the response string
        sResponse = "    Your card has been added.<br>"
```

continues

Listing 25.10. continued

```
                sResponse = "    Your card has been added.<br>"
                sResponse = sResponse & "    To view your card,"
                sResponse = sResponse & " click the Post Office Toolbar. <br>"
                sResponse = sResponse & "<br>    When prompted "
                sResponse = sResponse & "for a P.O. Box enter the following code:"
                sResponse = sResponse & " (without quotes)<BR><Pre>         &quot;"
                sResponse = sResponse &  oId.UniqueString & "&quot;</pre><br>"
                sResponse = sResponse & "    Send this "
                sResponse = sResponse & "information to <a HREF=mailto:"
                sResponse = sResponse & & Trim(Request.Form("txtREMail")) & ">"
                sResponse = sResponse & Trim(Request.Form("txtRecipient")) & "</a>"
                sResponse = sResponse & " on " & Trim(Request.Form("txtDate"))
                sResponse = sResponse & "</br>"

          End If
          Set oId = Nothing
     Case "Feedback"
        '-- This is a feedback entry
        '   Initialize a feedback recordset
        rsResponse.Source = "SELECT * FROM Feedback"

        '-- Open the Recordset
        rsResponse.Open

        '-- Check to make sure Updates are supported
        sResponse = "<H2>Sorry your feedback was not added.
                     Invalid server cursor.</H2>"
        If rsResponse.Supports(adUpdate) Then

            '-- Add a new record
            rsResponse.AddNew
            '-- Set the data values from the form
            '   Note: In this script we do not specify the Form object.
            '         If we had objects with the same name then the first
            '         found would be returned.

            If Trim(Request("UserName")) = "" Then
                rsResponse("Name") = "Anonymous"
            Else
                rsResponse("Name") = Trim(Request("UserName"))
            End If

            rsResponse("Email") = Trim(Request("UserEmail"))
            rsResponse("Tel") = Trim(Request("UserTel"))
            rsResponse("Fax") = Trim(Request("UserFax"))
            rsResponse("CommentType") = Trim(Request("MessageType"))
            If Trim(Request("Subject")) = "(Other)" Then
                rsResponse("CommentArea") = Trim(Request("SubjectOther"))
            Else
                rsResponse("CommentArea") = Trim(Request("Subject"))
            End If
            rsResponse("Comment") = Trim(Request("Comments"))
            rsResponse("CommentDate") = Now()

            '-- Complete the add operation
            rsResponse.Update
        End If
```

```
                    '-- Build the response string
                    sResponse = "    The information you supplied has"
                    sResponse = sResponse & "been saved. Thank you for your feedback."

            Case "POBox Lookup"
                    '-- This is a lookup from the POBox form
                    sSQL = "SELECT CardType FROM CardOrder WHERE ID='"
                    sSQL = sSQL & Trim(Request("txtPOBox")) & "'"
                    rsResponse.Source = sSQL

                    '-- Open the Recordset
                    rsResponse.Open

                    If not rsResponse.EOF Then
                        '-- Determine the type of card to present,
                        '  set the appropriate session variable and
                        '  redirect to that card page.
                        Select Case rsResponse("CardType")
                            Case "Birthday"
                                Session("POBoxCode") = Trim(Request("txtPOBox"))
                                Response.Redirect "/Card shop/birthday.asp"
                            '-- put other card types here when available
                            Case Else
                        End Select
                    Else
                        '-- Build the response string
                        sResponse = "     No card was found with "
                        sResponse = sResponse & "P.O. Box code: "
                        sResponse = sResponse & Trim(Request("txtPOBox"))
                    End If

            End Select

            '-- Clean up recordset and database connections
            If Not(rsResponse is Nothing) Then
                rsResponse.Close
                Set rsResponse = Nothing
            End If
            If Not(oDBCard is Nothing) Then
                oDBCard.Close
                Set oDBCard = Nothing
            End If

            '-- Return the response string to the calling script
            getResponse = sResponse

End Function
</SCRIPT>
<%
    sMsg = getResponse
%>


<!-------------Card Shop Response Page-------------------->
<!-- Skeleton Generated by Visual InterDev.                -->
<!--   Page Modified by: Mark Spenik & Troy Rackley         -->
<!--   Date: Jan. 14, 1997                                  -->
<!--     World Wide Web Database Developer's Guide Using VB -->
<!--                                                        -->
```

continues

Listing 25.10. continued

```html
<html>
<head>

<!------------------Start Style Sheet Call-------------------->
<LINK REL=STYLESHEET HREF="./styles/style2.css">
<!------------------End Style Sheet Call---------------------->

<!------------------Start Page Title------------------------->
<title> <%=Session("ResponseMsg")%> </title>
<!------------------End Page Title--------------------------->

<meta name="GENERATOR" content="Microsoft InterDev 1.0">
</head>

<!------------------Start Background------------------------->
<body background="./images/Background/back2.jpg"
alink="#FF000" bgcolor="#FFFFFF" topmargin=25 leftmargin=0>
<!------------------End Background--------------------------->

<!------------------Start Page Name-------------------------->
<%

'-- If we are using IE 3.0 or above, use a combination
'   of styles to offer a cool effect for the page title.

'   Determine the type of browser
Set obc = Server.CreateObject("MSWC.BrowserType")
if obc.Browser = "IE" Then %>

    <p class=title> the e-card shop </p>
    <p class=title2><%=Session("ResponseMsg")%></p>
    <p class=title3><%=Session("ResponseMsg")%></p>

<% else %>

    <h1>  <%=Session("ResponseMsg")%></h1>

<%End If%>
<!------------------End Page Name--------------------------->

<!------------------Start Navigation Bar-------------------->
<!--#include virtual="/Card shop/navigation.inc"-->
<!------------------End Navigation Bar---------------------->

<!------------------Begin Response Statement--------------->
<p>
<STRONG>
<%=sMsg%>
</STRONG>
</p>
<!------------------End Response Statement------------------>

<p>
<img src="./images/rules/rule1.gif" alt="[HRule Image]"
    align="bottom" width="650" height="25">
</p>
```

```
<!--------------Begin WebMaster Statement---------------->
<!--#include virtual="/Card shop/footer.inc"-->
<!-----------------End WebMaster Statement------------------>
<!-- #include virtual="/ASPSamp/Samples/adovbs.inc" -->
</body>
</html>
```

At the beginning of the function getResponse, we first create a connection object, connect to the Card Shop database, and then create a Recordset object. We then set the required Recordset properties to prepare it for use.

The case structure then determines what type of job we must perform based on the value in the ResponseType session variable. Each calling form provides a response type. The available response types are Order, Feedback, and POBox Lookup.

The Order Response

If the user is adding a new card order, an insert must be performed into the CardOrder table of our database. The Generate.ID component helps us construct a unique string to serve as the key to this record. The recipient also will use this item to pick up the card from the post office. First, we must create a Generate.ID object called oID. Then we set the desired length of the string to generate to 15 (characters). Next, we call the object's GenerateID function. This function returns a zero if all went well. If an error occurred, that error may be read from the object's Error property. All that is left to do is to acquire the ID from the oID object's UniqueString property. A successful generation populates this property with an ID that is the length specified in the Size property. Listing 25.11 contains the complete code of the ID class of the Generate component.

Listing 25.11. The ID class.

```
Option Explicit

Private m_nSize As Integer 'The size of the ID
Private m_sID As String    'The actual ID string
Private m_sError As String 'An error string if there is a problem

Private Sub Class_Initialize()
    '-- This occurs when a new instance of this object
    '  is created
    Randomize    ' Initialize random-number generator.
    m_nSize = 10 ' Set a default size for an ID
End Sub

Public Property Get Size() As Integer
    Size = m_nSize
End Property
```

continues

Listing 25.11. continued

```
Public Property Let Size(ByVal nData As Integer)
    m_nSize = nData
End Property

Public Property Get Error() As String
    Error = m_sError
End Property

Public Property Get UniqueString() As String
    UniqueString = m_sID
End Property

Public Function GenerateID() As Long
Dim lStatus As Long
Dim i As Integer
Dim nRandom As Integer
Dim sID As String
Dim sChar As String

On Error GoTo GenerateID_Error

    For i = 1 To m_nSize
        '-- Generate a random number from 1 to 3 to
        ' determine which character set to use:
        ' 0-9, A-Z, or a-z
        nRandom = GetRandomInt(1, 3)
        Select Case nRandom
            Case 1
                sChar = Chr$(GetRandomInt(Asc("0"), Asc("9")))
            Case 2
                sChar = Chr$(GetRandomInt(Asc("A"), Asc("Z")))
            Case 3
                sChar = Chr$(GetRandomInt(Asc("a"), Asc("z")))
            Case Else
                sChar = "-"
        End Select

        m_sID = m_sID & sChar

    Next

GenerateID_Exit:
    GenerateID = lStatus
    Exit Function

GenerateID_Error:
    lStatus = 1
    m_sError = "Error generating ID: " & Err.Description
    Resume GenerateID_Exit

End Function

Public Function GetRandomInt(ByVal nLowerbound As Integer, _
                             ByVal nUpperbound As Integer) As Integer
    '-- Generate a random integer in the range
```

```
'   of: Lowerbound to Upperbound
GetRandomInt = Int((nUpperbound - nLowerbound + 1) * Rnd + nLowerbound)

End Function
```

The main function in this class is `GenerateID`. This function contains a loop that iterates from 1 to the `Size` property. Each iteration through the loop generates a random alpha or numeric character. First, a random number from 1 to 3 is generated. If this number is 1, it generates a random character from the numbers 0 to 9. If the number is 2, it then generates a random letter in the range of uppercase letters—A to Z. Finally, if the original random number is 3, a random character is generated from the lowercase range of a to z. The random character is added to a string until the end of the loop. This string becomes the `UniqueString` property of this object.

If no errors occur while generating the `UniqueString`, the response page attempts to add the record to the database. First, a check is performed to ensure that the current database cursor supports updates. Next, we open the recordset and perform an `AddNew` operation. The fields of a `CardOrder` record are set from the response object's form variables, and then the recordset's `Update` method is called. Any default values for fields are set here.

> **NOTE**
>
> Notice that the card type here is set to `birthday`. At the time of this writing, a birthday card is the only type of card you can send from the Card Shop site.

After all updates, a response message is created to inform the user of the results of the record insertion. The ID generated is provided to the user in this response message, as well as a `mailto` hyperlink that can be clicked to launch the user's mail application. We finish this case by removing our `Generate.ID` component instance by setting it equal to `Nothing`.

The Feedback Response

The response for the feedback is very similar to the order; however, we do not need to use `Generate.dll` to produce any unique identifiers. The key in our `Feedback` table is on the `Username` and `CommentDate` fields. If the username is left out of the feedback form, we fill it with `Anonymous`. The `CommentDate` field is filled with a call to the VBScript `Now()` function. The remaining fields are pulled directly from the response object and stored in the record. The response string that is built on completion of the update is a simple message thanking the users for their comments.

The Post Office Response

If the response page is being called from the post office, instead of adding a record, we want to ensure that a particular record exists. The postal code from the post office form is used to build a SQL statement to query for a selected record. If it is available, we check the CardType field to determine the page to which the user will be redirected. Because we currently have only one card type (the birthday card), the decision logic is fairly short. This approach simply leads to future expansion.

The ID of this card is stored in a session-level variable (POBoxCode), which is referenced by the respective ASP card page. Then the Redirect method of the response object is called with the correct page to open.

If no card matches that ID, we build a message string. This time, the message states that a record was not found, and the rest of the page is evaluated and sent to the browser.

> **NOTE**
>
> The Redirect method sends an HTML header to the client telling it to launch another URL. Because HTTP protocol requires that all headers be sent before content, you must call Redirect in your script before sending any HTML output. Our HTML beginning content tag (<html>), therefore, must be placed after the getResponse script to avoid a runtime error.

At the end of the script, we clean up any objects that were used. The recordset rsResponse is closed, and its variable is dereferenced by setting it to Nothing. The same is done with our database connection object.

The remainder of the response.asp source code repeats some of the same HTML you saw in the other pages, such as the navigation bar, title styles, and Webmaster comments. The page title (shown in the browser's caption bar as well as above the navigation bar) is filled with the session-level variable ResponseMsg. You might remember that the calling form set this variable. The message displayed below the navigation bar is the one returned from the getResponse function earlier in the file.

The Post Office Page

The post office page is a simple ASP file that contains a form to enter the postal code needed to look up any particular card order. Figure 25.7 shows how a user picks up a card from the post office page.

FIGURE 25.7.

The Card Shop post office.

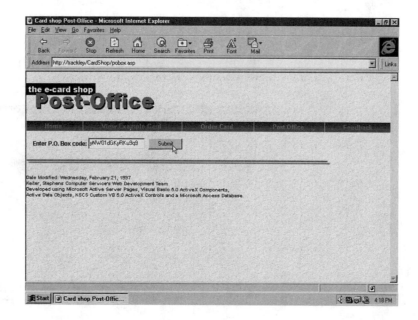

Like the other pages, we check for style capabilities and display the same navigation bar and comments. Listing 25.12 shows the ASP script used by the response page to identify the calling form.

Listing 25.12. Post office session variables and form.

```
<%
'-- Set the session variables to identify the response type
Session("ResponseType") = "POBox Lookup"
Session("ResponseMsg")  = "No card available"

'-- Clear the session postal code variable
Session("POBoxCode")    = ""
%>

<form ACTION=response.asp METHOD="POST">
    <b>     Enter P.O. Box code: </b>
    <input type="text" size="20" maxlength="15" name="txtPOBox">
    <input type="submit"> </pre>
</form>
```

The code in Listing 25.12 also contains the HTML for the simple form. It contains one text-input box called txtPOBox and one Submit button. The post office code given to the user can be pasted or typed into this text field. The Submit button posts this field to the response.asp file.

A Sample Birthday Card

The `birthday.asp` page is the actual card the recipient sees after he passes the post office security guard. Figure 25.8 shows a sample card generated by this site.

FIGURE 25.8.

A sample birthday card.

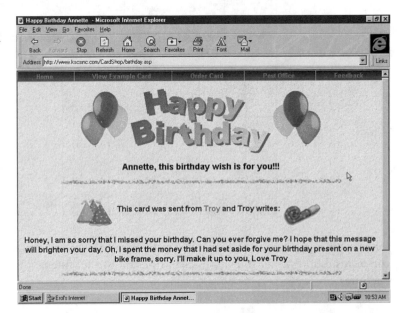

You can call the birthday page from the response page via a post office lookup or from the link on the navigation bar. If you call this page from the `response.asp` file, a session variable `POBoxCode` is filled with a valid card-order ID, and an attempt to look up that card is made. If this variable is blank, we will look up a sample card order provided by the Webmasters. Listing 25.13 provides the complete ASP and HTML code for the birthday page.

Listing 25.13. The complete birthday page listing.

```
<html>
<!--#include virtual="/ASPSamp/Samples/adovbs.inc"-->
<%

    '-- Check the session variables for a successful
    '   Post-Office login attempt
    If session("POBoxCode") <> ""  then
        sPOBox     = session("POBoxCode")
    Else
        sPOBox     = "Default"
    End if

    '-- Create an instance of the ADO object
    Set oConn = Server.CreateObject("ADODB.Connection")
```

```
'-- Open the database
oConn.Open "ElectronicCard"

'-- Build a sql statement to query the card table
sSQL = "SELECT * FROM CardOrder WHERE ID='" & sPOBox & "'"

Set rsCard = oConn.Execute(sSQL)

If not rsCard.EOF Then
    '-- retrieve the data for this card
    sSender      = rsCard("Sender")
    sSenderEmail = rsCard("SenderEmail")
    sGreeting    = rsCard("Greeting")
    sName        = rsCard("Recipient")

    rsCard.Close
Else
    '-- no card exists with this information
    '  the post office must have made a mistake
End if

oConn.Close
Set oConn  = Nothing
Set rsCard = Nothing
%>

<head>
<title> Happy Birthday <% =sName %> </title>
<link rel=stylesheet href="./styles/style2.css">
</head>
<body background="./images/background/back2.jpg"
alink="#FF000" bgcolor="#FFFFFF" topmargin=0 leftmargin=0>

<!-----------------Start Navigation Bar-------------------->
<!--#include virtual="/Card shop/navigation.inc"-->
<!-----------------End Navigation Bar---------------------->

<!-----------------Begin Birthday Card-------------------->
<center>
<table cellspacing=0 border=0 WIDTH=100%>
   <tr><td width="33%" align="right" valign="middle">
       <img src="./images/birthday/balloon1.gif" width=105 height=125></td>
   <td width="33%" align="center" valign="middle">
       <img src="./images/birthday/happy.gif" width=300 height=137></td>
   <td width="33%" align="left" valign="middle">
       <img src="./images/birthday/balloon2.gif" width=105 height=125></td>
</tr>
</table>

<br>
<H2><% =sName %>, this birthday wish is for you!!!</H2>
<p><img src="./images/birthday/confetti.gif" alt="[Confetti image]"
       align="bottom" width="600" height="10"></p>

<p><h3>
<img src="./images/birthday/partyhats.gif" alt="[Party hats image]"
    align="middle" width="84" height="78">
```

continues

Listing 25.13. continued

```
This card was sent from <a href=<% =sSenderEmail %>><% =sSender %></a>
and <% =sSender %> writes:
<img src="./images/birthday/whistle.gif" alt="[Whistle image]"
    align="middle" width="84" height="78">
</h3></p>

<h3><%
=sGreeting
%></h3>

<p><img src="./images/birthday/confetti.gif" alt="[Confetti image]"
        align="bottom" width="600" height="10"></p>
</center>
<!------------------End Birthday Card-------------------->

<!---------------Begin WebMaster Statement----------------->
<!--#include virtual="/Card shop/footer.inc"-->
<!-----------------End WebMaster Statement----------------->

</body>
</html>
```

The page begins with an ASP script that builds a SQL query string to look up a particular card. As mentioned before, if the session variable is empty, we present a default card stored in the CardOrder table with the ID default. Running the Execute method of the connection object produces our recordset. If the session variable is not empty, we store its fields in the local variables sName, sGreeting, sSender, and sSenderEmail. These fields then are output to the browser as inline ASP script when the rest of the HTML is evaluated.

Along with the recipient's name are a few festive birthday graphics. A mailto link is created with the sender's e-mail address so that the recipient can immediately convey his or her gratitude.

Finally, the greeting field is displayed. An interesting aspect of this field is that it can contain HTML tags itself. So, if the sender wants to format his message with HTML, all that is required is that he enter those formatting tags into the greeting textbox when ordering the card. We used <br> tags for hard returns for the greeting of the default card, for example.

The remainder of the card uses simple HTML to display some confetti piles and the usual Webmaster comments.

Summary

Now that you have taken an in-depth tour of our Card Shop site, you might have come up with some ideas to improve it. You already might have noticed the need for other card types. We could design a list of greetings ranging from anniversaries, congratulations, or get-well cards to cards for particular holidays throughout the year. A drop-down listbox would be needed to list the card types on the order page.

Other improvement ideas could include a Preview button on the order page that presents the output to the sender before the card order is submitted. Another idea is to build a custom SMTP component that sends the e-mail notification automatically on the requested day. This component would have to be tailored to each site's mail infrastructure. We also are considering minimizing connections to the database by creating a global connection for each session. This could reduce page-load times when database lookups or inserts are required.

RESOURCE

We continually modify and expand this site to take advantage of new features and standards using Microsoft Internet products. You are invited to check out our recent improvements and even send an e-card in the process. The Electronic Card Shop is housed at our site at

```
http://www.kscsinc.com/Card shop/
```

Although we used InterDev for the original structure of this site, most of the code was written in simple text editors. With the new crop of visual WYSIWIG HTML editors on the market, this site could be redone in one of those editors to take advantage of their advanced layout capabilities. Using that approach, monospaced fonts and preformatted text could be replaced by easily modified tables and frames. As you probably know, when performing any type of Web development, the techniques may vary to accomplish similar effects, and the possibilities are endless. This example should have given you some ideas on developing your own Active Web pages and sites, as well as some ammunition for when you need to battle converting any old static sites to more dynamic formats.

26

Building a Simple Order-Entry Application Template

by Mark Swank

This chapter continues with the knowledge you've gained in previous chapters and shows you how to use existing template databases for generating your own Web database applications. You will be using the Microsoft Access Database Wizard to generate a template database with sample data in Microsoft Access. You then will use the Access Upsizing Wizard to convert your Access database into a SQL Server database that will be used as the back-end database engine for the sample Visual Basic order-entry template application.

What to Expect in This Chapter

To help you better understand exactly how you will be implementing the sample order-entry application template, here is a list of the steps covered in this chapter:

- Generating a Microsoft Access template database
- Setting up an ODBC resource for your database application
- Using the Microsoft Access Upsizing Wizard to migrate an Access database to a SQL Server database
- Using the Microsoft Internet Database Connector dynamic link library to service database queries for a Microsoft Internet Information Server
- Integrating VBScript and ActiveX controls into your application

Using a Microsoft Access Template to Build a Web Database

If you have Microsoft Access at your site, you have a wealth of database templates already built into your Access installation. In this chapter, you will be building a Web database application from scratch and using Microsoft SQL Server to service that Web database. To accomplish this, you will use the order-entry database template available with Microsoft Access. After you build the database, you will port it to a SQL Server environment and use it as the data repository for the sample Web database application.

> **NOTE**
>
> This Access database is included on the accompanying CD-ROM for installations that do not have Access but do have SQL Server.

The Access Database Wizard

If you've never used the Access Database Wizard, you'll find that it is a very easy way to generate a standard database. This does not mean that you are limited to using the exact database structure of the template. Instead, you have the opportunity to add and remove tables and columns from your newly created database. In this example, you will use the template database exactly as it exists.

Selecting a Database Template

After you start the Access application, choose File | New Database. The New dialog box appears, as shown in Figure 26.1.

FIGURE 26.1.

The General tab of the New dialog box.

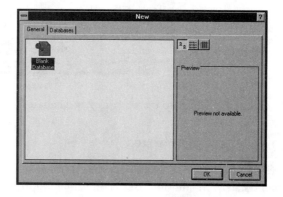

Notice that the New dialog box includes two selection tabs: General and Databases. By default, the General tab is selected and includes the default Blank database. You want to get access to the database templates, so click the Databases tab. Figure 26.2 shows the available database templates in databases view.

FIGURE 26.2.

Viewing the database templates on the Databases tab.

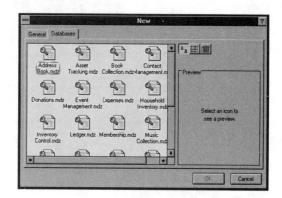

As you can see, the number of databases is too large to fit in the window. You can control the presentation of the databases by clicking one of the three buttons (text under icon, text to the right of icon, and column formatted) to the right of the Databases window. Click the middle button and then select the `Order Entry.mdz` file by clicking it. Figure 26.3 shows the full template database view.

FIGURE 26.3.

The full template database view.

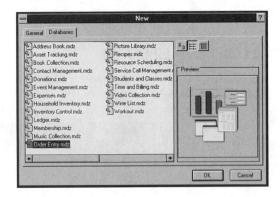

Click OK, and Access begins to create your new database from the selected template.

Naming Your New Database

The next window prompts you for a database name for your new database. You can select where to store your database in addition to selecting an appropriate name. I chose `webentry.mdb` as my database name and used the default directory as the location for storing the database. Figure 26.4 shows the File New Database dialog box. In the File name combo box, enter your database name.

FIGURE 26.4.

The File New Database dialog box.

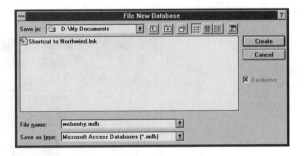

Using the Database Wizard to Design Your Database

Now that you've selected the database name and have chosen where the database will be saved, you are ready to begin the process of using the wizards to actually generate the database objects you want for your new database. Click Create, and the program begins to load all the wizards it needs to build your new database. After the wizards are loaded, you are presented with an information window showing the details of the template database. Figure 26.5 shows the order-entry database template information window.

FIGURE 26.5.

The order-entry template information window.

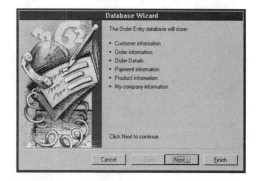

Click Next to go to the table- and column-selection window shown in Figure 26.6. You now are ready to begin selecting specific tables and columns to be included in the new database. If you scroll to the bottom of the list in the Fields in the table listbox, you'll see two columns that are italicized. As the comments at the top of the dialog box state, these are fields that are not included by default. You can include them, though, simply by enabling the checkbox beside the column entry. Also, this dialog box provides a checkbox for determining whether you want the newly created database to include sample data. For this example, you do want sample data, so enable the Yes, include sample data checkbox.

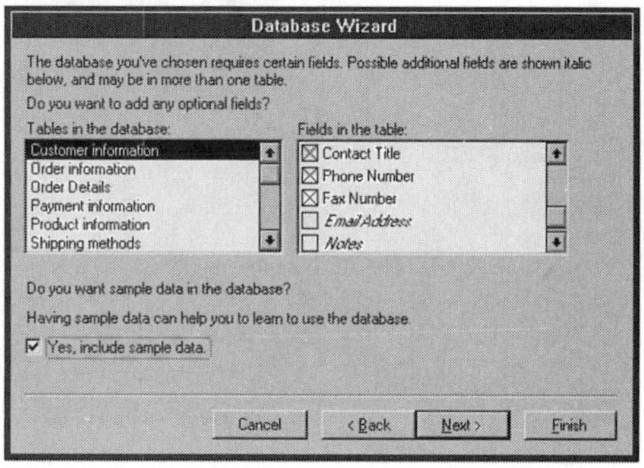

FIGURE 26.6.

The table- and column-selection window.

Selecting Application Styles

Now that you've identified the tables and columns you want included in the new database, you are almost finished. Click Next, and you are presented with a screen-style selection dialog box, as shown in Figure 26.7. The screen style is used only for applications developed in Access. If you are planning on using an Access database as your data repository for Web access, you can use this window to define how your database screens will appear in your Access program. For this example, you will be upsizing (porting) this database to a SQL Server environment, so you simply can choose the default Standard style.

FIGURE 26.7.

The screen-style selection dialog box.

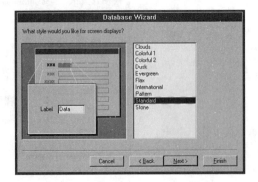

Click Next again, and the wizard presents you with the report-style selection dialog box shown in Figure 26.8. Again, depending on the database platform you choose for your Web database application, you may want to play with the selection options in this dialog box to define how your database reports are presented when executed. Six options are available for the style of report to be generated: Bold, Casual, Compact, Corporate, Formal, and Soft Gray. In this dialog box, again choose the default entry. In this dialog box, again choose the default entry.

FIGURE 26.8.

The report-style selection dialog box.

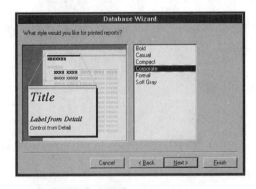

Setting Up Reports

You've almost completed the database-creation process. Click Next, and you are presented with the report title and name-selection dialog box shown in Figure 26.9.

FIGURE 26.9.

The report title and name-selection dialog box.

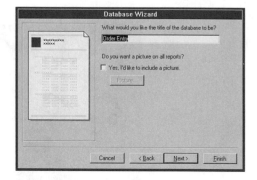

Finalizing the Database Wizard Process

Finally, click Next, and the wizard will have all the information it needs to build your new database. The final dialog box simply prompts the user to determine whether the database should be started after it is generated (see Figure 26.10). Additional help is available by enabling the Display Help on using a database checkbox.

FIGURE 26.10.

The final Database Wizard dialog box.

Click Finish, and Access creates your new database. Because this final phase actually generates your database, creates sample data, generates reports, and so on, the process can take a long time. On my system (a Pentium 100 running Windows NT 4.0), the process was complete in about 10 minutes.

The Main Switchboard Window

After the entire process is complete, you are presented with the Main Switchboard window, which enables you to view the database structure, enter data, view report information, and exit the database (see Figure 26.11).

FIGURE 26.11.

The Main Switchboard window.

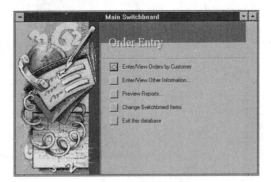

A Sample Prebuilt Data-Entry Form

Developers who plan on using a Microsoft Access database as their data repository will find that the Database Wizard generates all the needed reports, query forms, and so on. Take a quick look at a screen view of a specific customer's ordering information. Select the Enter/View Orders by Customer option on the Main Switchboard window. The Orders by Customer query form appears, as shown in Figure 26.12. Here, the database information is available by clicking the selection arrows near the bottom of the form.

FIGURE 26.12.

The Orders by Customer form.

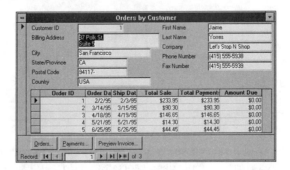

The Main Switchboard as an Intranet Application Front-End

As you can see, the Access Database Wizard virtually builds your database application for you. The Main Switchboard window is a fully functional front-end to your Access database. Assuming that your Access database is your data repository for Web access, internal corporate users could use the Main Switchboard for the processing and handling of orders placed by Internet users.

Setting Up an ODBC Source

Upsizing an Access database to SQL Server requires that you have set up an *Open Database Connectivity* (ODBC) source for the new database. If you plan on creating a new database during the upsizing process, you need to set up an ODBC data source for the SQL Server Master database. For this chapter's sample application, you will be creating a new database in SQL Server that mirrors your Access database. You'll start by creating your ODBC source for the Master database.

> **NOTE**
>
> Your ODBC resource must be configured on the NT Server machine where your SQL Server database is located.

From the Control Panel on your desktop, locate your ODBC icon, as shown in Figure 26.13.

FIGURE 26.13.
Locating the ODBC icon in the Control Panel.

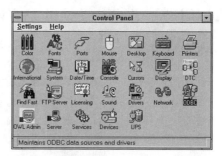

> **NOTE**
>
> Depending on your system and previously installed ODBC software, the ODBC icon may be titled "ODBC Administrator," "32-bit ODBC," "ODBC," or something similar.

Double-click the ODBC icon. The ODBC Data Sources dialog box appears, showing the currently configured ODBC resources (see Figure 26.14).

FIGURE 26.14.

The ODBC Data
Sources dialog box.

As you can see, you need to set up a data source for your SQL Server Master database. Click Add to access the Add Data Source dialog box. Add a new data source by selecting the SQL Server driver, as shown in Figure 26.15.

FIGURE 26.15.

The ODBC Add Data
Source dialog box.

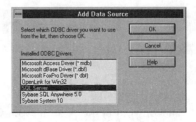

Click OK, and the ODBC SQL Server Setup dialog box appears. Here, you configure your ODBC data source for the SQL Server Master database. Figure 26.16 shows the ODBC SQL Server Setup dialog box with the values I selected for the Master database.

FIGURE 26.16.

The ODBC SQL
Server Setup dialog
box.

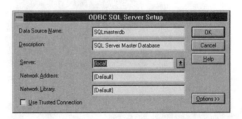

Select a data source name and description and enter those values in the appropriate text-entry boxes. For my example, I chose SQLmasterdb as the data source name and SQL Server Master Database as the data source description. The data source name is used later when upsizing the database to SQL Server. Finally, select your server name. Because my SQL Server engine was running on the same machine from which I was upsizing my Access database, I simply chose local for the server name.

Click OK, and a new entry for your SQLmasterdb data source is added to the Data Sources dialog box.

You now can click Close to close the Data Sources dialog box, because you've completed the process needed to set up your ODBC source. Now you can begin the process of upsizing the database to SQL Server.

The Microsoft Access Upsizing Tool

The Microsoft Access Upsizing tool is available for free from Microsoft and is used to automatically convert Access databases into their SQL Server equivalent. The Upsizing tool migrates your Access database to SQL Server while maintaining your data, indexes, defaults, counters, table relationships, and referential integrity.

> **NOTE**
>
> Upsizing from Access 95 to SQL Server 4.21, 6.0, and 6.5 are all supported options.

For the sample order-entry processing application, you'll need to build the Web interface to the database. You will be using the new SQL Wizard included in the latest release of SQL Server. Before you can do that, however, you need to upsize the Access order-entry database to the SQL Server equivalent.

> **RESOURCE**
>
> The Upsizing tool is free and can be downloaded from this page:
> `http://www.microsoft.com/Accessdev/AccInfo/AccInfo.htm`

If you do not currently have the Access Upsizing tool, download and install it before continuing with the order-entry database application.

Before Using the Access Upsizing Tool

Before you begin your upsizing process, you must review a few items to reduce the possibility of upsizing errors. Every installation depends on so many factors that I cannot cover all of them in this book. If you follow these few recommendations, though, you can reduce many of the potential error conditions that arise during the execution of the Upsizing tool:

■ Make sure that the ODBC source has been set up properly and that the logon account you will use with that data source has CREATE TABLE permissions on the SQL Server to which you want to upsize.

■ If you are going to be creating a new database from scratch, the ODBC logon account must have CREATE DATABASE permissions.

- If you will be creating devices for your new database, the ODBC logon account must be a member of the Admin SQL Server group.

- The size required of a SQL Server database is about 1.5 times that of the Access equivalent. Plan on specifying a database size sufficient to support future growth of your database.

RESOURCE

Microsoft provides very useful online information related to all aspects of Access at this address:

`http://www.microsoft.com/accessdev/`

Running the Access Upsizing Wizard

If your Access webentry database is closed, open it now so that you can begin to use the Upsizing tool for migrating it to a SQL Server environment. After your database is open and you load the Upsizing tool, you are ready to migrate the order-entry database to SQL Server.

From the menu bar, choose Tools | Add-Ins | Upsize to SQL-Server. Figure 26.17 shows the first window for the Access Upsizing tool.

FIGURE 26.17.

The Access Upsizing Wizard.

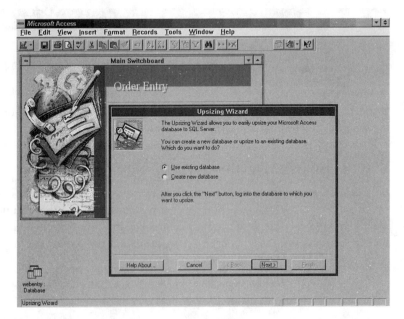

Because you will be creating a new SQL Server database that is a mirror of the Access database, you will choose the Create new database option.

> **NOTE**
>
> If you already have created a SQL Server database, or one previously exists that you want to incorporate your Access data into, select the default option to upsize to an existing database.

Select the "Create new database" option and click Next to begin the upsizing process. The SQL Data Sources dialog box appears, which includes the SQLmasterdb data source, as shown in Figure 26.18.

FIGURE 26.18.
The SQL Data Sources dialog box.

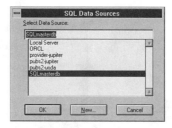

Highlight the SQLmasterdb data source and click OK. The SQL Server Login dialog box appears, prompting the user for a SQL Server logon with the proper privileges for creating a new database (see Figure 26.19).

FIGURE 26.19.
The SQL Server Login dialog box.

Enter an appropriate SQL Server logon and password and click OK. The next window enables you to set up SQL Server devices for the newly upsized database. Select the database device and log device you want to use for the new database. For the example, you will be creating new devices for the webentry database. After you select the Create New Device list entry, a New Device dialog box appears that enables you to set the name of the SQL Server device for the data or log device (see Figure 26.20).

FIGURE 26.20.

The SQL Server New Device dialog box.

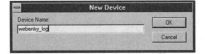

Notice in Figure 26.20 that I chose a name of `webentry_log` for my log device. For my data device, I chose `webentry_data`. Click OK to return to the device-selection window with the newly set options for creating new data and log devices (see Figure 26.21).

> **TIP**
>
> You'll need to set appropriate sizes for your new devices. Consult your SQL Server Database Administrator to determine appropriate sizes and names for your devices.

FIGURE 26.21.

The Upsizing Wizard device-selection window.

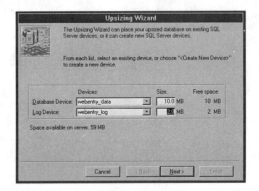

Click Next, and a new window appears in which you can define the new SQL Server database name, database size, and log size for the upsized database (see Figure 26.22). I chose the default database name, which is a concatenation of the Access database with a SQL extension (`webentrySQL`).

> **NOTE**
>
> My Access database is about 1.5MB. Based on the estimated size needed to upgrade an Access database to a SQL Server database, I chose a database size of 5MB and a log size of 1MB. Both these sizes should be more than adequate for my sample database.

FIGURE 26.22.

The Upsizing Wizard database name and data/log sizes dialog box.

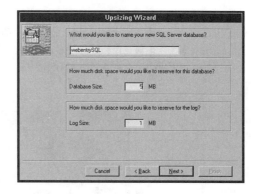

Click Next, and a listing of all of the available tables from the Access webentry database appears, as shown in Figure 26.23. You will want to export all the tables into the webentrySQL SQL Server database, so simply click the >> button to select all the tables for export. The tables that will be exported are listing in the Export to SQL Server box.

FIGURE 26.23.

Tables to be exported to SQL Server.

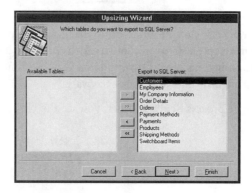

You now can click Next to select attributes for your new database (see Figure 26.24). Because you want to completely mirror the Access database, you will choose all the default options.

FIGURE 26.24.

The database attribute-selection window.

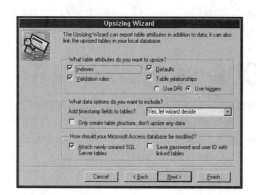

Note that, by default, Access will link the tables from the newly created SQL Server database to the old Access database. Click Next, and the Upsizing Wizard displays a dialog box asking whether you want the Upsizing Wizard to create a report of the upsizing process (see Figure 26.25). Enable the Create upsizing report checkbox so that you'll have a report to review in the event of an error.

FIGURE 26.25.

The upsizing report dialog box.

Now you simply can click Finish to begin the upsizing process. While the Upsizing Wizard is performing its magic, a status window tracks its progress. The whole process took only about five minutes on my machine. Depending on your machine configuration and the size of the database you are upsizing, your times may vary.

Voilà! After the process finally finishes, you see the Upsizing complete! message box in Figure 26.26.

FIGURE 26.26.

The Upsizing complete! message box.

Assuming that your upsizing process was a success, you now have your webentry database migrated to a SQL Server database. The next step for the sample application is to build Web pages based on the information in the newly created database.

The SQL Server Web Assistant

The SQL Server Web Assistant is a tool that is still in its infancy stage of development. The current version of the Web Assistant can provide some basic HTML generation based on simple database queries, however. The Web Assistant is capable of generating dynamic documents at specified intervals. You can build a page with the Web Assistant and have SQL Server rebuild the page whenever the contents of a specified table change, for example. Another scenario might be that you would want to rebuild a page on a daily basis—maybe something like a page displaying a "Fact of the Day" or "Hot, Special Deals."

This section looks at how you can use the Web Assistant to automatically build simple HTML documents. Later in this chapter, you'll learn how to generate HTML documents that go beyond simple HTML tables by incorporating use of the *Internet Database Connector* (IDC) discussed in Chapter 20, "The IIS Internet Database Connector (IDC)."

Using the SQL Server Web Assistant

When you first start the SQL Server Web Assistant, you are presented with a logon window that identifies the SQL Server and user logon you want to use for accessing your SQL Server database (see Figure 26.27).

FIGURE 26.27.
The Login dialog box.

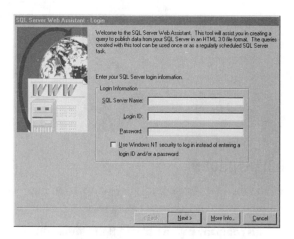

Enter the name of the SQL Server you want to access. You might be able to leave this entry blank if the SQL Server exists on the current machine. Next, enter a proper logon and password and click Next.

The Web Assistant Query Form

The Web Assistant next connects to the SQL Server Engine and generates a Query form (see Figure 26.28). In this form, you have the option of specifying how you want your data selected for the newly created Web page. By default, the Build a query from a database hierarchy option is selected. For this example, you will be specifying a freeform text query, so select the Enter a query as free-form text option. Next, select the webentrySQL database from the Which database do you want to query? drop-down listbox.

Finally, you need to specify the freeform text for the query. Because you want a total sales figure for each salesperson, you simply can specify the query as the following:

```
SELECT   FirstName, LastName, SUM(Quantity*UnitPrice)
FROM     Employees, Orders, Order_Details
WHERE    Employees.EmployeeId = Orders.EmployeeId
AND      Orders.OrderId = Order_Details.OrderId
GROUP BY FirstName, LastName
```

Figure 26.28 shows the Query form with the proper query information specified.

FIGURE 26.28.

The Query dialog box.

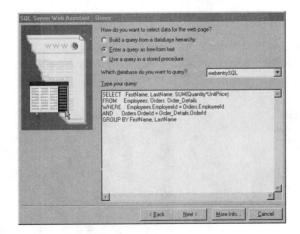

Scheduling Options

Click Next, and the Web Assistant displays the Scheduling dialog box, which prompts you for information on when to generate the Web page (see Figure 26.29).

Assume that this company pays its sales staff a commission on sales whenever an order has been shipped. To automatically generate the Web page based on the shipping date, you can specify the ShipDate column as the specific column that, when updated, will rebuild the Web page.

Click the down-arrow in the When do you want to create your web page? drop-down listbox. You'll notice several options that determine when the page will be generated or updated. For pages that will require rebuilding based on changed input, you can select the When Data Changes entry. When you select this entry, you'll notice that a new Table(s) selection list appears. In this selection list, you can specify the tables and columns that, when changed, will generate the Web page to be rebuilt. When you select the When Data Changes entry, the Web Assistant creates or updates an existing trigger based on the table or column selections specified in the Table(s) listbox. This trigger will fire and execute the sp_makewebpage stored procedure, which is responsible for generating the updated Web page.

FIGURE 26.29.

The Scheduling dialog box.

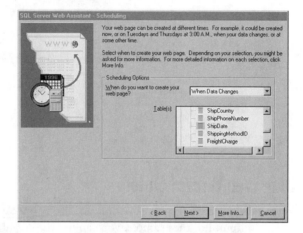

NOTE

Any tables or columns that are highlighted in green can cause the sp_makewebpage stored procedure to execute and build the specified Web page.

The sample in Figure 26.29 is based on a trigger firing when the ShipDate column of the Orders table is updated.

For this example, you want to generate a document now so that you can look at the contents as generated by the Web Assistant. Select the Now entry in the When do you want to create your Web page? listbox.

Options for Saving the HTML File

Click Next to specify the file options (see Figure 26.30). Here, you specify the URL location for the HTML file to be generated. You should specify a path that is in your Web server document root path. Specify the title for the page and the title for the query results in the appropriate textboxes.

FIGURE 26.30.
The File Options dialog box.

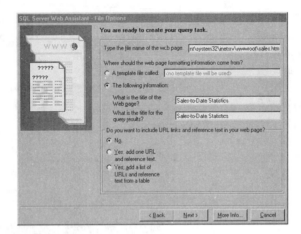

Formatting Web Wizard Output

Click Next, and the Formatting dialog box appears. Here, you can specify minimal formatting for the database output. For the example, you can use the default selections and click Finish, and the Web Assistant generates the database trigger based on the specified table to re-create the Web page whenever the data changes. If the Web Assistant has accepted your information and registered the page to be built, the window shown in Figure 26.31 appears.

FIGURE 26.31.
The SQL Server Web Assistant completion window.

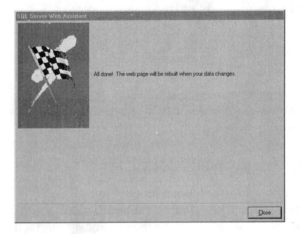

The Web Wizard-Created Document

Now look at the HTML page that you just created. Listing 26.1 shows the source code for the page.

Listing 26.1. The HTML page you created.

```
<HTML>
<HEAD>
<TITLE>Sales-to-Date Statistics</TITLE>
</HEAD>

<BODY>
<H2>Sales-to-Date Statistics</H2>
<HR>

<PRE><TT>Last updated: Jan 18 1997  8:07AM</TT></PRE>

<P>
<P><TABLE BORDER=1>
<TR>
<TH ALIGN=LEFT>FirstName</TH>
<TH ALIGN=LEFT>LastName</TH>
<TH ALIGN=LEFT>n/a</TH>
</TR>

<TR>
<TD NOWRAP><TT>Andrew</TT></TD>
<TD NOWRAP><TT>Fuller</TT></TD>
<TD NOWRAP><TT>252.55</TT></TD>
</TR>

<TR>
<TD NOWRAP><TT>Janet</TT></TD>
<TD NOWRAP><TT>Leverling</TT></TD>
<TD NOWRAP><TT>179.55</TT></TD>
</TR>

<TR>
<TD NOWRAP><TT>Margaret</TT></TD>
<TD NOWRAP><TT>Peacock</TT></TD>
<TD NOWRAP><TT>24.8</TT></TD>
</TR>

<TR>
<TD NOWRAP><TT>Nancy</TT></TD>
<TD NOWRAP><TT>Davolio</TT></TD>
<TD NOWRAP><TT>176.25</TT></TD>
</TR>

<TR>
<TD NOWRAP><TT>Steven</TT></TD>
<TD NOWRAP><TT>Buchanan</TT></TD>
<TD NOWRAP><TT>408.75</TT></TD>
</TR>

</TABLE>
<HR>
</BODY>
</HTML>
```

Figure 26.32 shows how the HTML page will look when rendered on a Web browser.

FIGURE 26.32.

The document generated by the Web Assistant.

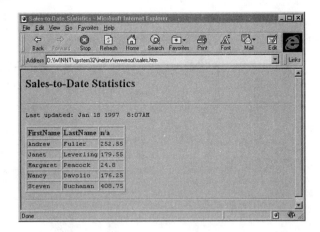

As you can see, the Web Assistant easily can generate "canned" HTML documents. For Web pages that require user input as query criteria, however, you need a more advanced mechanism. The next section discusses how to incorporate the IDC to generate dynamic hypermedia documents.

Using the Internet Database Connector

As discussed in Chapter 20, the IDC is an *Internet Server API* (ISAPI) DLL used to retrieve information from ODBC databases. This section focuses on how to set up the proper IDC files and HTML extension files required to automate the webentrySQL database into a WWW application.

Using the knowledge gained in Chapter 20 on how to build .idc and .htx files, you now can begin to put together the sample template order-entry application. As mentioned earlier, this application is based on an intranet example that enables internal users to process order entries that could have been generated by a Web-interface application such as an online store.

> **NOTE**
>
> All the source files for this chapter are stored in a single directory on the CD-ROM. You can access these files and applications directly from the CD-ROM by adding a new directory to your IIS World Wide Web Service that points to the ch26 directory on your CD-ROM.

Figure 26.33 shows the Directory Properties dialog box for adding a new directory to the IIS WWW Service.

FIGURE 26.33.
The IIS WWW Service Directory Properties dialog box.

This example shows a few forms that easily can be modified to implement a simple solution for building your own order-entry processing application. The forms in this example are not all complete, and there certainly are numerous ways to expand on these examples. I present them here simply as templates for you to build on.

> **NOTE**
>
> Not all functions are implemented in this application. It is merely meant as a starting template by which developers can generate their own Web database applications.

As noted in earlier chapters, security can be implemented in many ways. For an application such as an order-entry processing system, you would want to at least verify and log transactions at the user level. In most cases, you easily can track an employee's identification number. In this example, an employee logs onto the system with a user ID. This user ID then can be used to maintain information such as commissions data, to monitor work content (such as when an employee is paid based on quantity), and so on.

Another form of security that should be enforced when implementing intranet applications is security at the server level. On the authors' machines, we set up an entire directory structure for the application and defined only our machines (IP addresses) as having access to that directory structure.

The application starts with the logon window shown in Figure 26.34. I could have added a PASSWORD input field, but my database wasn't set up to handle passwords. When designing your intranet application and database, however, be sure to include a mechanism for authenticating user access.

FIGURE 26.34.

The order-entry application logon window.

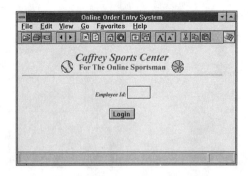

Listing 26.2 shows the code that generated this first logon window.

Listing 26.2. Generating the first logon window.

```
<HTML>
<HEAD><TITLE>Online Order Entry System</TITLE></HEAD>
<BODY BGCOLOR="#FFFFFF">

<CENTER>
<IMG SRC="/ch26/bsball.jpg" ALIGN="CENTER">
<IMG SRC="/ch26/caffrey.jpg" ALIGN="CENTER">
<IMG SRC="/ch26/bkball.jpg" ALIGN="CENTER">
<HR>
<FORM METHOD="POST" ACTION="/ch26/main.idc">
<P>

<IMG SRC="/ch26/employee.jpg"><INPUT NAME="EmployeeID" SIZE="5">

<P>
<INPUT TYPE="SUBMIT" VALUE=" Login ">
</FORM>
</CENTER>
</BODY>
</HTML>
```

As you can see, there is nothing fancy about this document. There are two things worth mentioning in this code. First, the ACTION attribute of the FORM is identified as /ch26/main.idc. After the user clicks the Login button, this .idc file is executed. In the main.idc file, the user's identification is authenticated against the database. Second, the user logon INPUT field is given the NAME EmployeeID. In the main.idc file, this field name (in the form of a variable) is used in the database query. Listing 26.3 shows the main.idc file.

Listing 26.3. The `main.idc` file.

```
Datasource: webentrySQL
Username: sa
Template: main.htx
RequiredParameters: EmployeeID
SQLStatement:
+SELECT FirstName, LastName
+ from employees
+ where employeeid = %EmployeeID%
```

As you can see, the `EmployeeID` field was used in the `SQLStatement` to get the `FirstName` and `LastName` user entries. In `.idc` files, field names that are passed from HTML form documents are surrounded by percent (%) signs. The `Template` field is specified to tell the Web server to use the resulting fields from `SQLStatement` to populate the HTML extension file `main.htx`.

Also, note in the `main.idc` file listing that I used the `RequiredParameters` field. By specifying the `EmployeeID` entry, you can do some initial field validation prior to connecting to the database and executing your database query. If the `EmployeeID` field is left blank when the form is submitted, the IIS returns an error message, as shown in Figure 26.35.

FIGURE 26.35.

The Error Performing Query window.

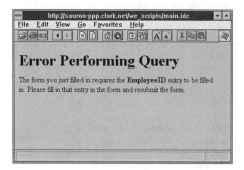

Specify a 2 as the input for the `EmployeeID` field. The employee's identification is validated, and the resulting `FirstName` and `LastName` fields are used to populate the `main.htx` file. Figure 26.36 shows the `main.htx` file as rendered by a browser.

FIGURE 26.36.

The order-entry form.

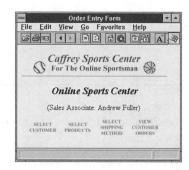

Listing 26.4 shows the code that generated the application's main screen.

Listing 26.4. Generating the application's main screen.

```
<html>
<title>Order Entry Form</title>
<BODY BGCOLOR="#FFFFFF">
<CENTER>
<IMG SRC="/ch26/bsball.jpg" ALIGN="CENTER">
<IMG SRC="/ch26/caffrey.jpg" ALIGN="CENTER">
<IMG SRC="/ch26/bkball.jpg" ALIGN="CENTER">
<HR>

<%begindetail%>
<%if CurrentRecord EQ 0 %>

<h4><EM>Online Sports Center</EM></h4>
<P>
(Sales Associate: <%FirstName%> <%LastName%>)
<P>
<FORM METHOD="POST" ACTION="/ch26/customer.idc?">
<INPUT TYPE="hidden" NAME="EmployeeID" VALUE="<%idc.EmployeeID%>">
<INPUT TYPE="hidden" NAME="CustomerID" VALUE="<%CustomerID%>">
<INPUT TYPE="hidden" NAME="OrderID" VALUE="<%OrderID%>">
<INPUT TYPE="IMAGE" SRC="/ch26/selcust.jpg">
</FORM>

<FORM METHOD="POST" ACTION="/ch26/products.idc?">
<INPUT TYPE="hidden" NAME="EmployeeID" VALUE="<%idc.EmployeeID%>">
<INPUT TYPE="hidden" NAME="CustomerID" VALUE="<%CustomerID%>">
<INPUT TYPE="hidden" NAME="OrderID" VALUE="<%OrderID%>">
<INPUT TYPE="IMAGE" SRC="/ch26/selprod.jpg">
</FORM>

<FORM METHOD="POST" ACTION="/ch26/shipping.idc?">
<INPUT TYPE="hidden" NAME="EmployeeID" VALUE="<%idc.EmployeeID%>">
<INPUT TYPE="hidden" NAME="CustomerID" VALUE="<%CustomerID%>">
<INPUT TYPE="hidden" NAME="OrderID" VALUE="<%OrderID%>">
<INPUT TYPE="IMAGE" SRC="/ch26/shipmeth.jpg">
</FORM>

<IMG SRC="/ch26/viewcust.jpg">

<%endif%>
<%enddetail%>
<%if CurrentRecord EQ 0 %>
<h2>Invalid employee id specified.</h2>
<a href="/ch26/emp_logon.htm">Try Again</a>
<%endif%>
</body>
</html>
```

The returned query result values (`FirstName` and `LastName`) were used in the following line to specify the sales associate's name:

```
(Sales Associate: <%FirstName%> <%LastName%>)
```

Note that the application will loop through every row returned from the query for all lines between the `<%begindetail%>` and `<%enddetail%>` tags. The `CurrentRecord` built-in variable is used within a conditional statement to test for the occurrence of the first record (record 0). If, at the end of the loop (just after the `<%enddetail%>` line), the value of `CurrentRecord` equals 0, no row results were returned.

Looking at the code for this page, you'll see two things that appear to be out of place. First, I used hidden fields to pass application state information between forms. As noted in earlier chapters, application state is not maintained by the application itself; the developer has to use other methods to maintain application information. Because this application enables users to browse between forms, the values are passed along between the forms as hidden fields. If a field has not yet been filled in or selected by the user, the entry simply remains empty.

The second thing that might look odd about Listing 26.4 is the use of multiple forms within the document. I chose this method simply as a means for giving the user the capability to choose his or her path in the application. Also note that I used image graphics as my INPUT object for each of the forms. This just provides a more presentable means than the standard Submit buttons for submitting a document for processing.

> **NOTE**
>
> When you are using multiple FORM elements within a document, the only fields that are passed to the ACTION attribute are those fields contained within the FORM element that was submitted. For this reason, I had to specify the hidden fields within each FORM element.

Now select the Select Customer text-image area, and the form is submitted to the `customer.idc` file for the purpose of selecting currently valid customers from the `webentrySQL` database. The basic logic for building the next form is replicated across the other forms available with this template application.

Listing 26.5 shows the code for the `customer.idc` file.

Listing 26.5. The `customer.idc` file.

```
Datasource: webentrySQL
Username: sa
Template: customer.htx
RequiredParameters: EmployeeId
SQLStatement:
+SELECT CompanyName, CustomerID
+ FROM Customers
+ ORDER BY CompanyName ASC
```

Figure 26.37 shows the Customer Selection List window.

FIGURE 26.37.

The Order Entry–Customer Selection List window.

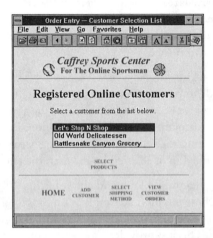

The `CompanyName` and `CustomerID` query result fields are used to populate a `SELECT` list within the HTML form. Listing 26.6 shows the `customer.htx` template file that will be populated with the query results.

Listing 26.6. The `customer.htx` template file.

```
<html>
<title>Order Entry --- Customer Selection List</title>
<BODY BGCOLOR="#FFFFFF">

<CENTER>
<IMG SRC="/ch26/bsball.jpg" ALIGN="CENTER">
<IMG SRC="/ch26/caffrey.jpg" ALIGN="CENTER">
<IMG SRC="/ch26/bkball.jpg" ALIGN="CENTER">
<HR>
<%begindetail%>

<%if CurrentRecord EQ 0 %>
<FORM METHOD="POST" ACTION="/ch26/products.idc?">
<INPUT TYPE="hidden" NAME="EmployeeID" VALUE="<%idc.EmployeeID%>">
<INPUT TYPE="hidden" NAME="CustomerID" VALUE="<%idc.CustomerID%>">
<INPUT TYPE="hidden" NAME="ProductID" VALUE="<%idc.ProductID%>">

<P>
<center>
<h3>Registered Online Customers</h3>

<p>
Select a customer from the list below.

<p>
<SELECT NAME="CustomerID" SIZE="3">
<%endif%>
```

```
<OPTION VALUE="<%CustomerID%>"><%CompanyName%>
<%enddetail%>

<%if CurrentRecord EQ 0 %>
<h4>No customer records found.
Select "Add Customer" below to add a new record.</h4>

<%else%>
</SELECT>

<p>
<INPUT TYPE="IMAGE" SRC="/ch26/selprod.jpg">
</FORM>

<%endif%>
<hr>
<P>
<FORM METHOD="POST" ACTION="/ch26/main.idc?">
<INPUT TYPE="hidden" NAME="EmployeeID" VALUE="<%idc.EmployeeID%>">
<INPUT TYPE="hidden" NAME="CustomerID" VALUE="<%idc.CustomerID%>">
<INPUT TYPE="hidden" NAME="ProductID" VALUE="<%idc.ProductID%>">
<INPUT TYPE="IMAGE" SRC="/ch26/home.jpg">
</FORM>

<IMG SRC="/ch26/addcust.jpg">

<FORM METHOD="POST" ACTION="/ch26/shipping.idc?">
<INPUT TYPE="hidden" NAME="EmployeeID" VALUE="<%idc.EmployeeID%>">
<INPUT TYPE="hidden" NAME="CustomerID" VALUE="<%idc.CustomerID%>">
<INPUT TYPE="hidden" NAME="ProductID" VALUE="<%idc.ProductID%>">
<INPUT TYPE="IMAGE" SRC="/ch26/shipmeth.jpg">
</FORM>

<IMG SRC="/ch26/viewcust.jpg">

</center>
</body>
</html>
```

As you can see in Figure 26.37, you are presented with a listing of available customers. The user simply can choose a customer from the list and select the Select Products input text image to begin selecting products. The user has the option, with the other selectable text images, to bypass customer selections and move to another form.

Other forms are included with this application that enable users to select products and shipping methods. The software logic is basically the same for these forms as it is for the customer-selection form. This is certainly not a fully functional order-entry application. The big pieces of the puzzle were presented here to give you insight into a possible solution for Web database applications.

Summary

In this chapter, you learned how to create and upsize Access databases to the SQL Server database arena. Even though the example focused mostly on Microsoft solutions, you can use much of the same material in different contexts. You can set up ODBC resources that point to multiple distributed databases, for example, and have those databases service any ODBC-capable Web server. For this sample application template, I used IIS to integrate the `webentrySQL` ODBC resource database (upsized SQL Server) with a Web-based application.

Appendixes

A

Features New to
Visual Basic 5

by Mark Spenik

This appendix introduces some of the important new features in Visual Basic 5 not specific to Internet database development. You can become more familiar with the features mentioned here by reading other Sams books that concentrate on Visual Basic, such as *Teach Yourself Visual Basic 4 in 21 Days* or *Visual Basic 5.0 Unleashed* or the documentation that ships with Visual Basic. This appendix covers topics such as the redesigned development environment and the WinSock ActiveX control.

An Improved Environment

One of the most obvious enhancements to Visual Basic 5 is the new development environment. Long-term plans for the Visual Basic 5 environment is to use the Developer Studio environment used in other Microsoft development products, such as Visual J++ and Visual C++. Of course, you still can use the old familiar Visual Basic development environment referred to as the SDI Development option, but take my advice: Use the new interface shown in Figure A.1. It is much more functional.

FIGURE A.1.

The Visual Basic Developer Studio environment.

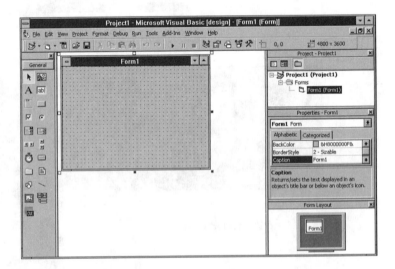

Coding in Visual Basic 5 has been enhanced and made simpler with features such as the Auto Statement Builder. This feature displays a drop-down box listing all the valid properties and methods when you reference an object or ActiveX control in the Code window. After you select the proper method or property (by pressing the spacebar), the selected method or property name is placed in your code. The Auto Quick Information feature provides you with the proper function and method syntax as you code. When you create procedures and functions in forms and modules, you now can assign a description to the procedure or function by using the

Procedure Attributes dialog box shown in Figure A.2. Descriptions that you add by using this dialog box are displayed when you view the module or form with the Object Browser; this capability enables you to determine functionality without reviewing the code and searching for comments.

FIGURE A.2.

The Procedure Attributes dialog box.

The Visual Basic 5 debugger has been improved in many ways. Breakpoint lines now appear in red, and a stop sign icon appears in the left margin of the Code window to make these lines easier to find. As you step through the code using the debugger, you will notice that the current line of code that is about to be executed is shown in yellow; a yellow-arrow icon appears in the left margin of the Code window to make it easier for you to see what line of code you are on. The standard Debug window has been replaced by a dockable immediate window, watches, and—my favorite—the local window. The local window tracks the values for all the local variables in a function or procedure without requiring you to type them in or add them. Forms and ActiveX controls also appear in the local window. This window enables you to expand the form or control and to view the current property settings. You now can add watch variables by dragging the variable or object from the Code window to the Watch window. Figure A.3 shows some of the many improved debugging features.

FIGURE A.3.

VB 5 Debugging Features dialog box.

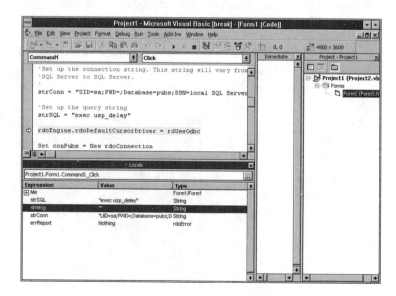

> **NOTE**
>
> The Enterprise Edition of Visual Basic 5, adds a SQL Server stored-procedure debugger. The debugger allows you to debug SQL Server stored procedures in the same manner that you debug Visual Basic 5 code. You can single step through the stored procedure, set breakpoints, and examine the values of variables.

Project enhancements have been added to Visual Basic 5, such as the capability to work with multiple projects in the same session. The Project dialog box also has been added to improve the project-creation process. This dialog box appears when you start Visual Basic 5 or a new project. You then can select from existing projects or create a new project. Your project choices follow:

- Standard Exe
- ActiveX Exe
- ActiveX DLL
- ActiveX Control
- Application Wizard
- ActiveX Document DLL
- ActiveX Document Exe
- Add In

Selecting a project type creates a new project of the selected type with the required objects for the project. When you select Standard Exe, for example, the project created contains a single form. If you select ActiveX Control, the new project contains a single `UserControl` object. You can choose Application Wizard to generate a fully functional application that you easily can modify or enhance. Figure A.4 shows the introductory Application Wizard dialog box. (You'll take a look at other Visual Basic wizards in the next section, "More Wizards.")

FIGURE A.4.

The first Application Wizard dialog box.

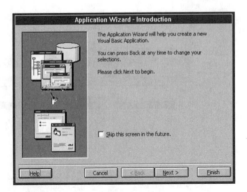

Many new file types have been added to Visual Basic 5. Table A.1 lists these file types and their new extensions.

Table A.1. Visual Basic 5 file types.

File Type	Extension
Active Designer Binary File	.dsx
Active Designer Cache	.dca
Active Designer File	.dsr
ActiveX Control	.ocx
ActiveX Document Binary Form	.dox
ActiveX Document Form	.dob
Binary Property Page File	.pgx
Class	.cls
Control Licensing File	.vbl
DLL	.dll
Executable	.exe
Form	.frm
Module	.bas
Property Page File	.pag
Setup Wizard Dependency File	.dep
User Control Binary File	.ctx
User Control File	.ctl
VB Group Project File	.vbg
VB Project Workspace File	.vbw
VB Setup Wizard Template File	.swt

More Wizards

Visual Basic 5 is packed with many wizards to make application development easier and faster. Table A.2 lists the wizards offered in Visual Basic 5.

Table A.2. Visual Basic 5 wizards.

Wizard	Function
ActiveX Control Interface Wizard	Helps you develop ActiveX controls.
ActiveX Document Migration Wizard	Migrates existing Visual Basic applications into ActiveX document objects.
Application Wizard	Generates full-blown applications.
Class Wizard	Provides a graphical tool to help you design and maintain classes.
Data Form Wizard	Generates Visual Basic forms that use data-bound controls to add, update, delete, and query information from a database table.
Property Page Wizard	Helps developers construct property pages for user-created ActiveX controls.
Setup Wizard	Builds installation routines for user applications.
Wizard Manager	Helps application developers build wizards.

Most wizards are delivered as *Visual Basic add-ins*—applications that integrate into the Visual Basic design environment using the Add-In Manager. After you register a Visual Basic add-in, you can choose it from the Add-Ins menu in the main Visual Basic Development window.

To register a Visual Basic add-in, follow these steps:

1. From the Visual Basic main menu, choose Add-Ins|Add-In Manager. The Add-In Manager dialog box appears, as shown in Figure A.5.

FIGURE A.5.

The Add-In Manager dialog box.

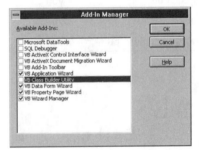

2. Select the add-in tools you want to integrate into your Visual Basic development environment by clicking in the box to the left of each add-in that you want to enable.
3. Click OK.

The add-ins now are registered and will appear on the Add-Ins menu when you access it.

A Native Code Compiler

One of the most requested features for Visual Basic has been a native code compiler. Previous versions of Visual Basic compiled code into p-code executables. P-code is not compiled to machine instructions (native) and therefore cannot be executed directly. Instead, p-code executables use an interpreter to convert the p-code into machine instructions. Applications created with p-code don't execute as fast as native-compiled applications. Visual Basic 3 and 4 were criticized for not being able to generate native compiled code like some of their competitors. Visual Basic 5 finally delivers a native code-compiler option. You can generate native code executables for faster execution. You still have the option to create p-code executables, however.

> **NOTE**
>
> I'm glad to see that Visual Basic finally has a native code compiler. I find the whole p-code controversy amusing. I recently attended a conference and listened to the masses complain about Visual Basic p-code. In the very next session, I heard the same people praise Java's lack of a native compiler and its p-code virtual machine (VM)! Go figure—must be the Java VM.

New ActiveX Controls

Many of the Visual Basic controls used in previous versions of Visual Basic have been enhanced in Version 5. Table A.3 lists the new controls offered in the Visual Basic 5 toolbox.

Table A.3. Visual Basic 5 controls.

Control	Icon	Function
Animation		Displays AVI clips.
Chart		Offers a pivot capability (still provides backward compatibility with the old Chart control).
Internet Transfer		Enables you to get and retrieve files from FTP and HTTP servers.
MsFlexGrid		Provides enhanced grid control to give you more individual cell control and data-binding options.

continues

Table A.3. continued

Control	Icon	Function
Up/Down		Enables you to add increment and decrement features to other ActiveX controls by using the up- and down-arrow buttons.
WebBrowser		Adds WWW browser capabilities.
WinSock		Adds TCP/IP and UDP (User Datagram Protocol) socket capabilities using an ActiveX control.

Language Features

Many language features and changes have been added to Visual Basic 5. Several important features—such as interfaces, friend functions, and default properties—already have been discussed in Chapters 8, "Using Classes and Objects in Visual Basic 5," and 16, "Creating ActiveX Controls for the Web with VB 5." This section outlines some of the other language enhancements in Visual Basic 5.

The AddressOf Keyword

If you spent any time using previous versions of Visual Basic with the Windows API, you probably noticed that you can't use a Windows API that requires the address of a function. This problem occurred because you could not pass the address of a Visual Basic function or procedure to a Windows API. Visual Basic 5 offers a new keyword called AddressOf that returns the address of the Visual Basic function. The address of the function you want must reside in a .BAS module. When using the AddressOf keyword, you cannot intercept Windows messages in Visual Basic (this is called *subclassing*).

Optional Arguments and Default Properties

Optional arguments in procedures and functions now can be of any data type (Visual Basic 4 allowed only variant-type optional arguments). The property procedures Let and Get also can have optional arguments. Class modules now can contain a single property that can be designated as the default property.

Events

Several keywords, such as Events and RaiseEvents, have been added to enable you to create and fire your own events. The WithEvents keyword enables your application to handle and respond to events that fire in an ActiveX component.

Enterprise Features

Visual Basic 5 will ship with the following editions:

> Custom Control Creation Edition
> Standard Edition
> Professional Edition
> Enterprise Edition

The Custom Control Edition is for developers that just want to develop ActiveX controls. The Standard Edition includes the basic functionality of Visual Basic but does not include database features. The Professional Edition includes all the standard database features like DAO. The Enterprise Edition of Visual Basic 5 offers several new features that are worth examining, for instance a developer version of Microsoft SQL Server 6.5.

If you work with Visual Basic and SQL Server, you will want to learn how to use the SQL Server stored procedure debugger. SQL Server does not come with a debugger, and trying to debug a complicated SQL Server stored procedure always has been a problem. The SQL Server debugger integrates directly into the Visual Basic development environment and enables you to go through a stored procedure step by step to view stored procedure variables. The Enterprise Edition also includes Visual Source Safe to manage code revisions and multiple programmers working on the same project. A developer version of the Microsoft Transaction Server is included as well as native support for RISC platforms. One of the most useful features is a set of tools referred to as the Visual Database tools that allows you to create graphical queries and manage SQL Server and Oracle database schema from the Visual Basic developer environment.

An Improved Three-Tier Architecture

You probably have heard about three-tier applications. The classic three-tier model consists of data services, business services (rules), and client services. The goal of the three-tier architecture is to distribute processing and reduce the amount of software distribution and headaches caused when a business rule or new data service is added or changed. Versions prior to Visual Basic 4 were used in two-tier client/server applications; Visual Basic 4 added remote automation, which made three-tier applications possible. In Visual Basic 4, you could create a client front-end application to provide the client services (user request), an OLE Automation server (ActiveX component) using remote automation as business services, and SQL Server as data services. Visual Basic 5 simplifies three-tier applications by providing distributed components that use COM with Windows 95 and Windows NT 4. Remote automation still is available for other Windows platforms such as Windows 3.11 and Windows NT 3.51. Figure A.6 shows the Remote Automation Connection Manager.

FIGURE A.6.

The Remote Automa-tion Connection Manager dialog box.

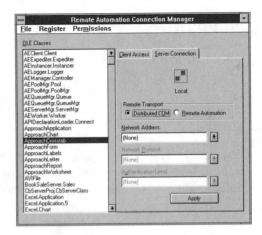

ActiveX Designers

The ActiveX Designers are features new to Visual Basic 5. These designers help automate tasks that normally require a great deal of code. An ActiveX Designer is not a wizard; instead, it is similar to the standard Visual Basic Form Designer. When you add an ActiveX Designer to a project, the ActiveX Designer creates classes in your project. You then can use the classes created by the ActiveX Designer to create objects and invoke the methods of the object. To aid in code modification and speed development, the ActiveX Designer may offer a Design window to provide a graphical interface to the classes and code. You also can add your own properties and methods to the classes. To see an example using the UserConnection ActiveX Designer, refer to Chapter 9, "Visual Basic 5 Data Access Features."

B

Visual Basic 5 Naming Conventions

by Mark Spenik

With Visual Basic 5, VBScript, and Active Server Page development, it is more important than ever for you to develop naming standards and conventions for applications, components, and Web pages. If you are a single developer or you work in a team with several other developers, naming conventions will make your code and script files easier to read and maintain. By using the same prefixes for objects and variables, it will be easier for you and your colleagues to read through code and script files without having to refer back to a variable or object to determine the type. I recommend using standard Visual Basic naming conventions published by Microsoft in the *Visual Basic 5.0 Programmers Guide* in the section "Visual Basic Coding Conventions." Many programmers and software shops have made the published Microsoft standards their own, so you will find moving from job to job easier. Regardless of whose naming standards you or your organization adopts, *make sure that you use some sort of naming standards*; don't code without them!

> **TIP**
>
> Always use many, many comments in your script files and code. It makes life so much easier for you and anyone who has to maintain your code.

Module, Class, Function, and Procedure Headers

When you develop Visual Basic modules, you should make sure that each module includes a header with an overview of the module's use. You can use the same type of header in a Visual Basic form, a VBScript, a file, or a Active Server Page. Listing B.1 shows an example of these headers.

Listing B.1. A module, form, VBScript, or Active Server Page header.

```
'*****************************************************
'              Sams Publishing
'*****************************************************
'
'Purpose:
'
'
'*****************************************************
'History:
'    Mark Spenik      10/31/96
' Initial Release
'
'*****************************************************
'
```

A class module should have a header as well. Also, make sure that you document the class so that descriptions can be viewed by using the Object Browser. Listing B.2 shows a class header.

Listing B.2. A class page header.

```
'**********************************************************************
'                    Sams Publishing
'
'Class:
'Purpose:
'
'  Notes:
'
'History:
'    Mark Spenik      05/28/96
'  Initial Release
'
'**********************************************************************
```

Procedures and functions should have a descriptive header with less detail, as shown in Listing B.3.

Listing B.3. A procedure or function header.

```
'Description:
'
'Input Parameters:
'Outputs:
'
'
'History
'
```

Control Naming Conventions

The naming conventions listed in Table B.1 are for common ActiveX controls. These naming conventions are suggested by Microsoft. I have found them to be widely accepted in the industry, so I recommend that you use them. You can find a similar detailed list in the *Visual Basic Developers Guide* that ships with Visual Basic 5. When using the naming standards, make sure that you choose a descriptive name that describes the control (spell it out). The prefix for a textbox is `txt`, for example. If you will have a textbox that will hold a person's first name, a good name for the control would be `txtFirstName`—*not* `txtfrstname`.

Table B.1. Naming prefixes for commonly used controls.

Control	Prefix
Checkbox	chk
Combo box	cbo
Command button	cmd
Common dialog box	dlg
Data control	dat
Data-bound combo box	dbcbo
Data-bound grid	dbgrd
Data-bound listbox	dblst
Form	frm
Frame	fra
Graph	gra
Image	img
Label	lbl
Listbox	lst
OLE	ole
Picture	pic
Progress bar	prg
Report	rpt
Textbox	txt
Timer	tmr
Toolbar	tlb

Other Naming Conventions

You should use naming conventions as well for data-access objects and variables. I have not seen the Microsoft standards for variables and data-access objects as widely adopted as the control standards, so this section takes a look at a few naming conventions. Again, regardless of the naming standard, it is important that you use one and use it consistently.

Variable Scope

The most common naming standard to help a programmer determine the scope of a variable is to use the first letter of the variable name as the scope. A global variable starts with a lower-case g, a module-level variable starts with a lowercase m, and local variables have no prefix. (Table B.2 provides some examples.)

Variable Naming Conventions

I like the variable naming standards provided by Microsoft. I think they are consistent with the naming conventions of controls, because they use a three-digit prefix to name the variable. I have been beaten up a few times in standards meetings by other programmers who wanted a simpler variable naming convention, though. Table B.2 lists the variables, the Microsoft-suggested standard, and a common standard I have seen used quite frequently.

Table B.2. Variable naming conventions.

Type	Microsoft Standard	Other
Boolean	bln	bool
Currency	cur	c
Date	dtm	dtm
Double	dbl	d
Integer	int	i
Long	lng	l
Object	obj	o
String	str	s
Variant	vnt	v

An integer status value might have the following names, for example (notice the use of the scope prefix):

Global integer:	gintStatus
Module integer:	mintStatus
Local integer:	intStatus

Data-Access Naming Conventions

I have seen more naming conventions in *data-access objects* (DAOs) than in any of the other areas described here. I have seen some companies use the prefix ds to represent a DAO dynaset and ss to represent a DAO snapshot. I prefer standards that can be used by DAO, Remote Data Objects (RDOs), and Active Data Objects (ADOs) for data-access objects. Table B.3 lists some common prefixes for data-access objects. In the Microsoft DAO column, Yes means that the standard is a Microsoft-suggested DAO standard; No means that it is not a Microsoft standard for DAO. You can use the naming conventions in this table for DAO, RDO, and ADO.

Table B.3. Data-access naming conventions.

Data Object	Prefix	Microsoft DAO
Connection	cnn	No
DAO QueryDef / RDO query object	qry	Yes
DAO Recordset	rec	Yes
Database	db	Yes
Resultset	rst	No

C

VBScript Language
Reference

by Drew Kittel

Since its initial release, VBScript has continued to develop and grow from a minimally featured scripting tool into a fairly rich and capable language. This appendix provides a concise yet functional overview and summary reference of VBScript. Some of the things you will find follow:

- A summary of VBScript features
- A summary of differences between VBA and VBScript features
- VBScript constants
- VBScript operators
- VBScript functions
- VBScript statements
- VBScript methods
- VBScript objects
- VBScript properties

RESOURCE

A full and complete VBScript language reference and tutorial is available (in HTML format) for free download from the Microsoft VBScript Web page. VBScript capabilities are expanding rapidly, and this reference material is updated frequently as new functions and features are added to VBScript. This documentation provides an excellent online resource for VBScript developers. The site is located at

`http://www.microsoft.com/vbscript/`

A Summary of VBScript Features

VBScript has quickly evolved into a fairly rich language, complete with the features one would expect in a full featured language. These include array handling, flow control, data type conversions, date and time functions, math functions, string operations, error handling, object creation, and so on. Table C.1 provides a full listing of VBScript features along with their associated keywords.

Table C.1. VBScript features and keywords.

VBScript Feature Category	*Associated Feature or Keyword*
Array handling	`Array`
	`Dim, Private, Public, ReDim`
	`IsArray`
	`Erase`
	`LBound, UBound`

VBScript Feature Category	*Associated Feature or Keyword*
Assignments	Set
Comments	Comments using ' or Rem
Constants and literals	Empty
	Nothing
	Null
	True, False
Control flow	Do...Loop
	For...Next
	For Each...Next
	If...Then...Else
	Select Case
	While...Wend
Conversions	Abs
	Asc, AscB, AscW
	Chr, ChrB, ChrW
	CBool, Cbyte
	CCur, Cdate
	CDbl, Cint
	CLng, CSng, CStr
	DateSerial, DateValue
	Hex, Oct
	Fix, Int
	Sgn
	TimeSerial, TimeValue
Date and time	Date, Time
	DateAdd, DateDiff, DatePart
	DateSerial, DateValue
	Day, Month, Weekday, Year
	Hour, Minute, Second
	Now
	TimeSerial, TimeValue
Declarations	Const
	Dim, Private, Public, ReDim
	Function, Sub
Formatting strings	FormatCurrency
	FormatDateTime
	FormatNumber
	FormatPercent

continues

Table C.1. continued

VBScript Feature Category	*Associated Feature or Keyword*
Error Handling	On Error
	Err
I/O	InputBox
	LoadPicture
	MsgBox
Literals	Empty
	False
	Nothing
	Null
	True
Math	Atn, Cos, Sin, Tan
	Exp, Log, Sqr
	Randomize, Rnd
Objects	CreateObject
	Dictionary
	Err
	FileSystemObject
	GetObject
	TextStream
Operators	Addition (+), Subtraction (–)
	Exponentiation (^)
	Modulus arithmetic (Mod)
	Multiplication (*), Division (/)
	Integer division (\)
	Negation (–)
	String concatenation (&)
	Equality (=), Inequality (<>)
	Less Than (<), Less Than or Equal To (<=)
	Greater Than (>), Greater Than or Equal To (>=)
	Is
	And, Or, Xor
	Eqv, Imp
Options	Option Explicit
Procedures	Call
	Function, Sub

VBScript Feature Category	Associated Feature or Keyword
Rounding	Abs
	Int, Fix, Round
	Sgn
Script Engine ID	ScriptEngine
	ScriptEngineBuildVersion
	ScriptEngineMajorVersion
	ScriptEngineMinorVersion
Strings	Asc, AscB, AscW
	Chr, ChrB, ChrW
	Filter, Instr, InStrB
	InstrRev
	Join
	Len, LenB
	LCase, Ucase
	Left, LeftB
	Mid, MidB
	Right, RightB
	Replace
	Space
	Split
	StrComp
	String
	StrReverse
	LTrim, RTrim, Trim
Variants	IsArray
	IsDate
	IsEmpty
	IsNull
	IsNumeric
	IsObject
	TypeName
	VarType

Differences Between VBA and VBScript

Table C.2 provides a summary of features found in Visual Basic for Applications (VBA) but *not* in VBScript. This table is provided to help experienced VB and VBA developers determine those familiar features they might not use in VBScript.

Table C.2. Differences between VBA and VBScript.

VBA Feature Category	Associated Feature or Keyword
Array handling	Option Base Declaring arrays with lower bound <> 0
Collection	Add, Count, Item, Remove Access to collections using ! character (for example, MyCollection!Foo)
Conditional compilation	#Const #If...Then...#Else
Control flow	DoEvents GoSub...Return, GoTo On Error GoTo On...GoSub, On...GoTo Line numbers, Line labels With...End With
Conversion	CVar, CVDate Str, Val
Data types	Every intrinsic data type except Variant Type...End Type
Date and time	Date and Time statements Timer
DDE	LinkExecute, LinkPoke, LinkRequest, LinkSend
Debugging support	Debug.Print End, Stop
Declaration	Declare (used for declaring DLLs) New Optional ParamArray Property Get, Property Let, Property Set Static
Error handling	Erl Error On Error...Resume Resume, Resume Next
File I/O	All basic file I/O
Financial	All basic financial functions

VBA Feature Category	Associated Feature or Keyword
Objects	`Clipboard`
	`Collection`
Object manipulation	`TypeOf`
Operators	`Like`
Options	`Deftype`
	`Option Base`
	`Option Compare`
	`Option Private Module`
Strings	Fixed-length strings
	`LSet, Rset`
	`Mid` statement
	`StrConv`
Using objects	Collection access using !

VBScript Constants

VBScript provides a number of constants that can be used to specify colors, dates, MsgBox button settings, file I/O modes, and so on. Using these constants helps to make your code more readable and easier to maintain. Table C.3 provides a complete categorized listing of VBScript constants.

Table C.3. VBScript constants.

Category	Name	Description	Value
Color	`vbBlack`	Black	`&h00`
	`vbRed`	Red	`&hF`
	`vbGreen`	Green	`&hFF00`
	`vbYellow`	Yellow	`&hFFFF`
	`vbBlue`	Blue	`&hFF0000`
	`vbMagenta`	Magenta	`&hFF00FF`
	`vbCyan`	Cyan	`&hFFFF00`
	`vbWhite`	White	`&hFFFFFF`
Comparison	`vbBinaryCompare`	Performs binary comparison	`0`
	`vbtextCompare`	Performs textual comparison	`1`

continues

Table C.3. continued

Category	Name	Description	Value
	vbDatabaseCompare	Performs comparison based on info in database where Compare is to be performed	2
Date/Time	vbSunday	Sunday	1
	vbMonday	Monday	2
	vbTuesday	Tuesday	3
	vbWednesday	Wednesday	4
	vbThursday	Thursday	5
	vbFriday	Friday	6
	vbSaturday	Saturday	7
	vbFirstJan1	Default: Uses week where Jan 1 occurs	1
	vbFirstFourDays	Uses first week with at least four days in new year	2
	vbFirstFullWeek	Uses first full week of the year	3
	vbUseSystem	Uses date format in computer's regional settings	0
	vbUseSystemDayOfWeek	Uses system settings for first day of the week	0

General note for all date constants: date and time displayed are dependent on computer's regional setting

Category	Name	Description	Value
Date Format	VbGeneralDate	For real number, displays date and time. If no fractional part, displays date only. If no integer part, displays time only.	0
	vbLongDate	Date displayed using long date format	1
	vbShortDate	Date displayed using short date format	2
	vbLongTime	Time displayed using long time format	3
	vbShortTime	Time displayed using short time format	4

Category	Name	Description	Value
File I/O	ForReading	File opened as read-only	1
	ForWriting	File opened as read-write. Existing file of same name is overwritten.	2
	ForAppending	File opened for write to EOF	8
Misc.	vbObjectError	Object error occurred	&h80040000

Use the following constants to specify modality and what buttons and icons are displayed

Category	Name	Description	Value
MsgBox	vbOKOnly	Displays OK button only	0
	vbOKCancel	Displays OK and Cancel buttons	1
	vbAbortRetryIgnore	Displays Abort, Retry, and Ignore buttons	2
	vbYesNoCancel	Displays Yes, No, and Cancel buttons	3
	vbYesNo	Displays Yes and No buttons	4
	vbRetryCancel	Displays Retry and Cancel buttons	5
	vbCritical	Displays Critical Message icon	16
	vbQuestion	Displays Warning Query icon	32
	vbExclamation	Displays Warning Message icon	48
	vbInformation	Displays Information Message icon	64
	vbDefaultButton1	Specifies first button as default	0
	vbDefaultButton2	Specifies second button as default	256
	vbDefaultButton3	Specifies third button as default	512
	vbDefaultButton4	Specifies fourth button as default	768
	vbApplicationModal	Requires user to respond to message box before continuing work in the *current* application.	0
	vbSystemModal	Requires user to respond to message box before continuing to work in *any* application.	4096

Use the following constants to identify the button selected by a user

Category	Name	Description	Value
MsgBox	VbOK	Selects OK button	1
	vbCancel	Selects Cancel button	2
	vbAbort	Selects Abort button	3
	vbRetry	Selects Retry button	4

continues

Table C.3. continued

Category	Name	Description	Value
	vbIgnore	Selects Ignore button	5
	vbYes	Selects Yes button	6
	vbNo	Selects No button	7
String	vbCr	Carriage return	Chr(13)
	vbCrLf	Carriage return, linefeed combination	Chr(13) & Chr(10)
	vbFormFeed	Form feed	Chr(10)
	vbLf	Line feed	Chr(10)
	vbNewLine	Newline character (platform specific)	Chr(13) & Chr(10) *or* Chr(10)
	vbNullChar	Character with a value of 0	Chr(0)
	vbNullString	Calls external procedures. *This is not a zero-length string!*	Zero-valued string
	vbTab	Horizontal tab	Chr(9)
	vbVerticalTab	Vertical tab	Chr(11)
Tristate	TristateTrue	True	-1
	TristateFalse	False	0
	TristateUseDefault	Use default setting	2
VarType	vbEmpty	Uninitialized by default	0
	vbNull	Contains no valid data	1
	vbInteger	Integer subtype	2
	vbLong	Long subtype	3
	vbSingle	Single subtype	4
	vbDouble	Double subtype	5
	vbCurrency	Currency subtype	6
	vbDate	Date subtype	7
	vbString	String subtype	8
	vbObject	Object	9
	vbError	Error subtype	10
	vbBoolean	Boolean subtype	11
	vbVariant	Variant; used only for arrays of variants	12

Category	Name	Description	Value
	`vbDataObject`	Data-access object	13
	`vbDecimal`	`Decimal` subtype	14
	`vbByte`	`Byte` subtype	17
	`vbArray`	Array	8192

VBScript Operators

VBScript provides a complete set of operators, including arithmetic operators, comparison operators, concatenation operators, and logical operators. Table C.4 provides a listing of all VBScript operators along with brief descriptions of each.

Table C.4. VBScript operators.

VBScript Operator	Syntax and Description
+	`result = expression1 + expression2` Sums two numbers. Can also be used to concatenate strings (although the & operator is recommended for this).
And	`result = expression1 And expression2` Performs logical conjunction (and-ing) on two *expressions*. *result* evaluates to `True` only if both *expressions* are true. *result* evaluates to `Null` if either *expression* is `Null`.
&	`result = expression1 & expression2` Forces string concatenation of two *expressions*. If an *expression* is not a string, it is converted to `String`. If one *expression* is `Null`, it is treated as a zero-length string. If both *expressions* are `Null`, *result* is `Null`. Empty *expressions* are treated as `Null` strings.
/	`result = number1/number2` Divides two *numbers* and returns floating-point results. If both *expressions* are `Null`, *result* is `Null`. Empty expressions are treated as 0.
Eqv	`result = expression1 Eqv expression2` Performs logical equivalence on two *expressions* (using a bitwise comparison). If either *expression* is `Null`, *result* is `Null`. If both *expressions* are `True` or both *expressions* are `False`, *result* is `True`; otherwise, *result* is `False`.

continues

Table C.4. continued

VBScript Operator	Syntax and Description
^	`result = number^exponent` Raises *number* to the power of an *exponent*. If *number* or *exponent* is Null, *result* is Null. If > 1, exponentiation is performed; ^ is evaluated left to right. *number* can be negative only if *exponent* is an integer value.
Imp	`result = expression1 Imp expression2` Performs a logical implication on two *expressions* (using a bitwise comparison). The following table summarizes how *result* is determined:

exp1	Imp	exp2	=	result
True		True		True
True		False		False
True		Null		Null
False		True		True
False		False		True
False		Null		True
Null		True		True
Null		False		Null
Null		Null		Null

VBScript Operator	Syntax and Description
\	`result = number1\number2` Divides two numbers and returns an integer result. If an *expression* is Null, *result* is Null. Empty *expressions* are treated as 0. *expressions* are rounded to btye, integer, or long subtypes prior to division.
Is	`result = object1 Is object2` Compares two reference objects. If *object1* and *object2* refer to the same object, *result* is True; otherwise, *result* is False.
Mod	`result = number1 Mod number2` Divides two numbers and returns the remainder. Floating-point numbers first are rounded to integers. If an *expression* is Null, *result* is Null. Empty *expressions* are treated as 0.
*	`result = number1*number2` Multiplies two numbers. If either *expression* is Null, *result* is Null. Empty *expressions* are treated as 0.
-	`result = number1-number2` or `-number` Finds the difference of two numbers or negates the value of a number (in this case, it is a unary operation). If either *expression* is Null, *result* is Null. Empty *expressions* are treated as 0.

VBScript Operator	Syntax and Description
Not	`result = Not expression` Performs a logical negation on an *expression*. Negating a `Null` *expression* results in a `Null` *result*.
Or	`result = expression1 Or expression2` Performs a logical disjunction (or-ing) on two *expressions* (using a bitwise comparison). If either *expression* evaluates to `True`, the *result* is `True`.
Xor	`result = expression1 Xor expression2` Performs a logical exclusion (exclusive or-ing) on two *expressions* (using a bitwise comparison). If only one of the *expressions* is `True`, *result* is `True`. But, if either *expression* is `Null`, *result* is `Null`.

VBScript Functions

Table C.5 provides a listing of all VBScript functions that exist as of this writing. The table provides brief descriptions along with the required function syntaxes.

Table C.5. VBScript functions.

VBScript Function	Syntax and Description
Abs	`Abs(number)` Returns the absolute value (the unsigned magnitude) of a number or expression.

Array	`Array(arglist)`
	Returns a variant containing an array. *arglist* is a comma-delimited list of values assigned to elements of an array contained with the variant. A sample use follows:
	`Dim A    ' create variable named A`
	`A = Array(10,20,20)    ' assign an array to A`
	`B = A(2)    ' assign value in 2nd element to B`

Asc	`Asc(string)` Returns the ANSI character code for the first letter in *string*. Notes: Use `AscB` for use with byte data contained in a string; `AscB` returns the first byte instead of the character code. Use `AscW` for 32-bit platforms using Unicode characters; `AscW` returns the Unicode (wide) character code.

continues

Table C.5. continued

VBScript Function	Syntax and Description
Atn	Atn(*number*) Returns the arctangent of *number* in radians. Result is in the range of −pi/2 to pi/2 radians.
CBool	CBool(*expression*) Returns an expression converted to the Boolean subtype of Variant. If *expression* is 0, False is returned; otherwise, True is returned.
CByte	CBtye(*expression*) Returns an expression converted to the Byte subtype of Variant. Use CByte to provide internationally aware conversions from any other data type to a Byte subtype (different decimal separators are recognized properly depending on the locale setting of your system).
CCur	CCur(*expression*) Returns an expression converted to the Currency subtype of Variant. Use CCur to provide internationally aware conversions from any other data type to a Currency subtype (different decimal separators and thousands separators are recognized properly depending on the locale setting of your system).
CDate	CDate(*date*) Returns an expression converted to the Date subtype of Variant. CDate recognizes date formats according to your system's locale setting. IsDate should be used to see whether *date* can be converted to a date or time. CDate accepts date and time literals as well as some numbers falling within valid date ranges (when converting numbers to dates, the whole number part is converted to a date, while any fractional part is converted to a time).
CDbl	CDbl(*expression*) Returns an expression converted to the Double subtype of Variant. Use CDbl to provide internationally aware conversions from any other data type to a Double subtype (different decimal separators and thousands separators are recognized properly depending on the locale setting of your system).
Chr	Chr(*charcode*) Returns the character associated with the ANSI *charcode*. Notes: Use ChrB for use with byte data contained in a string; ChrB returns the first byte instead of the character code. Use ChrW for 32-bit platforms using Unicode characters; ChrW returns the Unicode (wide) character code.

VBScript Function	Syntax and Description
CInt	CInt(*expression*) Returns an expression converted to the Integer subtype of Variant. Unlike Fix and Int, CInt rounds to the nearest even number rather than truncating. Use CInt to provide internationally aware conversions from any other data type to an Integer subtype (different decimal separators and thousands separators are recognized properly depending on the locale setting of your system).
CLng	CLng(*expression*) Returns an expression converted to the Long subtype of Variant. Unlike Fix and Int, CLong rounds to the nearest even number rather than truncating. Use CLong to provide internationally aware conversions from any other data type to an Integer subtype (different decimal separators and thousands separators are recognized properly depending on the locale setting of your system).
Cos	Cos(*number*) Returns the cosine of an angle. *number* should be expressed in radians. The result is in the range of –1 to 1.
CreateObject	CreateObject(*class*) The *class* argument uses the syntax *servername.typename*. *servername* is the name of the application providing the object. *typename* is the type/class of the object to create. Creates and returns a reference to an Automation object. The following example illustrates how you can create an Excel spreadsheet object and its methods and properties accessed:

```
Dim ExcelSSheet
   Set ExcelSSheet = CreateObject("Excel.Sheet")
    ' Make Excel visible through Application object.
  ' Place text in first cell of the sheet.
  ' Save the sheet.
  ' Close Excel with the Quit method on the Application
➥object.
  ' Release the object variable.
ExcelSheet.Application.Visible - True
   ExcelSheet.Cells(1,1).Value = "This is col A, row1"
ExcelSheet.SaveAs "D:\MyDocs\SSTEST.DOC"
ExcelSheet.Application.Quit
Set ExcelSheet = Nothing
```

continues

Table C.5. continued

VBScript Function	Syntax and Description
CSng	CSng(*expression*) Returns an expression converted to the Single subtype of Variant. Use CSng to provide internationally aware conversions from any other data type to a Single subtype (different decimal separators and thousands separators are recognized properly depending on the locale setting of your system).
CStr	CStr(*expression*) Returns an expression converted to the String subtype of Variant. The data in *expression* determines the result per the following:

expression is	CStr returns
Boolean	String containing True or False
Date	A string containing date in your system's short format
Null	A runtime error
Empty	" " (a zero-length string)
Error	A string containing the word Error followed by error number
Other numeric	A string containing the number

Use CStr (rather than Str) to provide internationally aware conversions from any other data type to a String subtype (different decimals are recognized properly depending on the locale setting of your system).

VBScript Function	Syntax and Description
Date	Date Returns the current system date.
DateAdd	DateAdd(*interval, number, date*) Adds or subtracts the specified time *interval* from *date*. *interval* is a string expression for the interval you want to add. *interval* can have the following values:

yyyy	Year
q	Quarter
m	Month
y	Day of year
d	Day
w	Weekday
ww	Week of year
h	Hour
m	Minute
s	Second

VBScript Function	Syntax and Description

	number is a numeric expression for the number of the interval to add (positive for future dates, negative for past). *date* is a Variant or literal representing the date *interval* is added to. The following example illustrates its usage:
	
	```' add one month to January 31```
	```'29-Feb-96 returned because 1996 is a leap year```
	```NewDate = DateAdd("m", 1, "31-Jan-95")```

DateDiff	```DateDiff(interval, date1, date2```
	```➥[,firstdayofweek[, firstweekofyear]])```
	
	Determines how many specified time intervals (number of days or weeks) exist between two dates. *interval* is a string expression for the interval you want to use to calculate the differences between *date1* and *date2* (see DateAdd for valid values). *date1*, *date2* are date expressions to use in the calculation. *firstdayofweek* is a constant specifying the day of week (if not specified, Sunday is assumed). Following are valid constant names, values, and descriptions:

vbUseSystem	0	Use National Language Support (NLS) API setting
vbSunday	1	Sunday (default)
vbMonday	2	Monday
vbTuesday	3	Tuesday
vbWednesday	4	Wednesday
vbThursday	5	Thursday
vbFriday	6	Friday
vbSaturday	7	Saturday

firstweekofyear is a constant specifying the first week of the year (if not specified, it is assumed to be the week in which Jan 1 occurs). Following are valid constant names, values, and descriptions:

vbUseSystem	0	Use National Language Support (NLS) API setting
vbFirstJan1	1	Start with the week in which January 1 occurs (default)
vbFirstFourDays	2	Start with week having at least four days in the new year
vbFirstFullWeek	3	Start with the first full week of the new year

continues

Table C.5. continued

VBScript Function	*Syntax and Description*
	To calculate the number of days between *date1* and *date2*, you can use Day of year ("y") or Day ("d"). When interval is Weekday ("w"), DateDiff returns the number of weeks between the two dates. If *date1* falls on a Monday, DateDiff counts the number of Mondays until *date2*. It counts *date2* but not *date1*. If interval is Week ("ww"), however, the DateDiff function returns the number of calendar weeks between the two dates. It counts the number of Sundays between *date1* and *date2*. DateDiff counts *date2* if it falls on a Sunday, but it doesn't count *date1*, even if it does fall on a Sunday. If *date1* refers to a later point in time than *date2*, the DateDiff function returns a negative number. The *firstdayofweek* argument affects calculations that use the "w" and "ww" *interval* symbols. If *date1* or *date2* is a date literal, the specified year becomes a permanent part of that date. However, if *date1* or *date2* is enclosed in quotation marks (" ") and you omit the year, the current year is inserted into your code each time the *date1* or *date2* expression is evaluated. This makes it possible to write code that can be used in different years.
DatePart	DatePart(*interval, date*[, *firstdayofweek*[, ➥*firstweekofyear*]])
	Evaluates a date and returns a specific interval of time. *interval* is a string expression for the interval you want to return. *date* is the date expression to evaluate. *firstdayofweek* is a constant specifying the day of week (if not specified, Sunday is assumed). See DateDiff for valid values. *firstweekofyear* is a constant specifying the first week of the year (if not specified, it is assumed to be the week in which Jan 1 occurs). See DateDiff for valid values. The *firstdayofweek* argument affects calculations that use the "w" and "ww" interval symbols. If *date* is a date literal, the specified year becomes a permanent part of that date. However, if *date* is enclosed in quotation marks (" ") and you omit the year, the current year is inserted into your code each time the *date* expression is evaluated. This makes it possible to write code that can be used in different years.
DateSerial	DateSerial(*year, month, day*)
	Returns a Variant of subtype Date for the specified year, month, and day. *year* is a number (or numeric expression) from 100 through 9999. *month*, *day* are numeric expressions (with values

VBScript Function	Syntax and Description
	in the range of 1–12 and 1–31, respectively). Relative dates can be used for the arguments using any numeric expression that represents some number of days, months, or years before or after a certain date.
DateValue	DateValue(*date*) Returns a Variant of subtype Date. *date* can be any expression that represents a date/time in the range of January 1, 100 through December 31, 9999. *date* is usually a string expression. If *date* is a string that includes only numbers separated by valid date separators, DateValue recognizes the order for month, day, and year per your system's Short Date format and unambiguous dates containing month names, either in long or abbreviated form (for example, 12/30/1991; 12/30/91; December 30, 1991; and Dec 30, 1991). If *date* has no year part, the year from the system's date is used.
Day	Day(*date*) Returns a whole number between 1 and 31 that represents the day of the month. *date* is any argument that can represent a valid date.
Exp	Exp(*number*) Returns *e* (base of natural logarithms) raised to a power. *number* should not exceed 709.782712893.
Filter	Filter(*InputStrings*, *Value*[, *Include*[, *Compare*]]) Returns a zero-based array containing a subset of a string array based on a specified filter criteria. The return array is sized to hold only the number of matched items. If no matches are found, an empty array is returned. An error occurs if *InputStrings* is not one-dimensional or is Null. *Value* is a string to search for in the one-dimensional array of strings *InputStrings*. *Include* is an optional Boolean value. If True, Filter returns the subset of the array that contains *Value* as a substring. If False, Filter returns the subset of the array that does *not* contain *Value* as a substring. *Compare* is an optional numeric value that indicates the type of string comparison to be used. The following are valid numeric names, values, and descriptions: vbBinaryCompare 0 Perform a binary comparison vbTextCompare 1 Perform a textual comparison

continues

Table C.5. continued

VBScript Function	*Syntax and Description*
	VbDatabaseCompare 2 Perform a comparison based on information contained in the database where the comparison is to be performed
Fix	Fix(*number*) Returns the integer portion of *number* (the fractional part is removed and the resultant integer value is returned). For example, –8.4 is converted to –8 while 8.4 is converted to 8.
FormatCurrency	FormatCurrency(*Expression*[,*NumDigitsAfterDecimal* ➥[,*IncludeLeadingDigit* ➥[,*UseParensForNegativeNumbers* ➥[,*GroupDigits*]]]]) Uses the currency symbol defined in the system Control Panel to return an expression formatted as a currency value. *Expression* is the only required argument and represents the expression to be formatted. *NumDigitsAfterDecimal* is an optional numeric value indicating the number of places to the right of the decimal to be displayed (default is -1, indicating that the computer's regional settings are used). *IncludeLeadingDigit* is an optional Tristate constant that indicates whether the leading zero is displayed for fractional values. *UseParensForNegativeNumbers* is an optional Tristate constant that indicates whether negative values are to be placed within parentheses. *GroupDigits* is an optional Tristate constant that indicates whether numbers are grouped using the group delimiter specified by the computer's regional settings. Following are valid Tristate constant names, values, and descriptions: TristateTrue -1 True TristateFalse 0 False TristateUseDefault -2 Use the setting from the computer's regional settings. When optional arguments are omitted, values for those arguments are provided by the computer's regional settings. The position of the currency symbol relative to the currency value is determined by the system's regional settings.
FormatDateTime	FormatDateTime(*Date*[,*NamedFormat*]) Returns *Date* (a Date expression) formatted as a date or time. *NamedFormat* is an optional numeric value used to specify the date/time format used (vbGeneralDate is used by default if this

VBScript Function	Syntax and Description
	argument is omitted). Following are valid constant names, values, and descriptions:

	`vbGeneralDate`	0	Displays a date and/or time. If there is a date part, display it as a short date. If there is a time part, display it as a long time. If present, both parts are displayed.
	`vbLongDate`	1	Displays a date using the long date format specified in your computer's regional settings.
	`vbShortDate`	2	Displays a date using the short date format specified in your computer's regional settings.
	`vbLongTime`	3	Displays a time using the time format specified in your computer's regional settings.
	`vbShortTime`	4	Displays a time using the 24-hour format (*hh:mm*).
FormatNumber	`FormatNumber(Expression[,NumDigitsAfterDecimal` ➥`[,IncludeLeadingDigit` ➥`[,UseParensForNegativeNumbers` ➥`[,GroupDigits]]]])` Returns *Expression* formatted as a number. See `FormatCurrency` for a description of arguments.
FormatPercent	`FormatPercent(Expression[,NumDigitsAfterDecimal` ➥`[,IncludeLeadingDigit` ➥`[,UseParensForNegativeNumbers` ➥`[,GroupDigits]]]])` Returns *Expression* formatted as a percentage (multiplied by 100) with a trailing % character. See `FormatCurrency` for a description of arguments.
GetObject	`GetObject([pathname] [, class])` Accesses an ActiveX object from a file and assigns the object to an object variable. It is used when there is a current instance of the object or if you want to create the object with a file already loaded. If no current instance exists and you don't want the object started with a file loaded, use the `CreateObject` function instead. Note that, for objects registered as a single-instance object, only one instance of the object is created, regardless of

continues

Table C.5. continued

VBScript Function	*Syntax and Description*
	how many times `CreateObject` is executed. With single-instance objects, `GetObject` always returns the same instance when called with the zero-length string (`""`) syntax. *pathname* is an optional string that specifies the full path and name of the file that contains the object being retrieved. If omitted, *class* is required. *class* is an optional string specifying the object. It has the syntax *appname.objectype* where *appname* is the name of the application providing the object and *objectype* is the type or class of object to create. The following examples illustrate how `GetObject` can be used. When

```
Dim CADObject
Set CADObject = GetObject("C:\CAD\SCHEMA.CAD")
```

is executed, the application associated with the specified pathname is started and the object in the specified file is activated. If *pathname* is a zero-length string or is omitted, *class* is required and `GetObject` returns a new object instance of the specified type or a currently active object of the specified type, respectively.

Some applications allow activation of part of a file by adding an exclamation point (!) to the end of the filename and following it with a string that identifies the part of the file you want to activate. You might activate a layer within a drawing as follows, for example:

```
Set LayerObject =
➥GetObject("C:\CAD\SCHEMA.CAD!Layer3")
```

To specify which object in a file you want to activate, use the optional class argument—for example:

```
Dim MyObject
Set MyObject = GetObject("C:\DRAWINGS\SAMPLE.DRW",
➥"FIGMENT.DRAWING"
```

Finally, properties and methods of the object in the preceding code can be accessed as shown here:

```
MyObject.Line 9, 90
MyObject.InsertText 9, 100, "Hello, world."
MyObject.SaveAs "C:\DRAWINGS\SAMPLE.DRW"
```

VBScript Function	*Syntax and Description*
Hex	`Hex(number)` Returns a string representing the hexadecimal value of *number*. If *number* is `Null`, `Hex` returns `Null`. If *number* is `Empty`, `Hex` returns 0. If *number* is not a whole number, it is rounded to the nearest whole number prior to evaluation.

VBScript Function	*Syntax and Description*
Hour	Hour(*time*) Returns a whole number from 0 through 23 that represents the hour of the day. The *time* argument is any expression that can represent a time.
InputBox	InputBox(*prompt*[, *title*][, *default*][, *xpos*][, ➥*ypos*][, *helpfile*, *context*]) Displays a prompt in a dialog box, waits for the user to input text or choose a button, and returns the contents of the textbox after the user clicks OK or presses Enter. If the user clicks Cancel, the function returns a zero-length string (""). *prompt* is a string expression with a maximum length of 1,024 characters. Lines can be separated by using the carriage-return character (Chr(13)), linefeed character (Chr(10)), or a combination of both (Chr(13) & Chr(10)) between lines. *title* is a string expression to be displayed in the title bar of the dialog box. If omitted, the application name is used. *default* is an optional string expression to be displayed in the textbox if no other input is provided. *xpos*, *ypos* are numeric expressions that specify the distance (in twips) of the left and upper edges of the dialog box from the left and top edges of the screen, respectively. If *xpos* is omitted, the box is centered horizontally; if *ypos* is omitted, the box is positioned approximately one-third from the top of the screen. *helpfile* is a string expression specifying the context-sensitive Help file to use for the dialog box. If provided, *context* also must be supplied. *context* is a numeric expression that identifies the author-assigned Help context number for the appropriate topic. If provided, *helpfile* also must be provided. When both *helpfile* and *context* are supplied, a Help button is added automatically to the dialog box.
InStr	InStr([*start*,]*string1*, *string2*[, *compare*]) Returns the position of the first occurrence of *string2* string within *string1*. *start* is an optional numeric expression that specifies where the search starts (if omitted, searches start at the first character). *string1* is the string being searched, whereas *string2* is the string being searched for. *compare* is an optional numeric expression specifying the kind of comparison to use (if omitted, binary is the default). Following are valid constant names, values, and descriptions for *compare*:

vbBinaryCompare	0	Binary comparison
vbTextCompare	1	Textual comparison

continues

Table C.5. continued

VBScript Function	Syntax and Description

vbDatabaseCompare   2   Comparison based on information contained in the database where the comparison is performed

Following are InStr return values:

Condition	Return Value
string1 is 0 length	0
string1 is Null	Null
string2 is 0 length	start
string2 is Null	Null
string2 is not found	0
string2 is found	Position where match was found
start > length of *string2*	0

Note: Use InStrB with byte data contained in a string. InStrB returns the byte position of the first occurrence of one string within another.

InStrRev   InStrRev(*string1*, *string2*[, *start*[, *compare*]])
Returns the position (from the end of the string) of the first occurrence of *string2* string within *string1*. See InStr for value of *compare* and return values.

Int   Int(*number*)
Returns the integer portion of *number* (the fractional part is removed and the resultant integer value returned). For example, –8.4 is converted to –9 (contrast this with the behavior of Fix), whereas 8.4 is converted to 8.

IsArray   IsArray(*varname*)
Returns a Boolean True value if *varname* is an array; returns False otherwise. Useful with variants containing arrays.

IsDate   IsDate(*expression*)
Returns a Boolean True value if *expression* is a date (or can be converted to one); returns False otherwise. Valid dates for MS Windows range from January 1, 100 A.D. through December 31, 9999 A.D.

IsEmpty   IsEmpty(*expression*)
Returns a Boolean True value if *expression* (typically, a single variable) is uninitialized (or is explicitly set to Empty); returns False otherwise.

VBScript Function	*Syntax and Description*
IsNull	IsNull(*expression*) Returns a Boolean True if *expression* is Null (contains no valid data); returns False otherwise. If *expression* consists of more than one variable, any of which are Null, then True is returned.
IsNumeric	IsNumeric(*expression*) Returns a Boolean True if *expression* is recognized as a number; returns False otherwise. Note: If *expression* is a date expression, False is returned.
IsObject	IsObject(*expression*) Returns a Boolean True if *expression* references a valid Automation object (if *expression* is a variable of Object subtype or a user-defined object); returns False otherwise.
Join	Join(*list*[, *delimiter*]) Returns a string created by joining a number of substrings (delimited by the optional *delimiter* character) contained in the array *list*. If *delimiter* is " ", substrings are concatenated without delimiters.
LBound	LBound(*arrayname*[, *dimension*]) Returns the smallest available subscript for the *array* for the given *dimension* (1 for first dimension, 2 for second, and so on). Used with UBound to determine the size of an array.
LCase	LCase(*string*) Returns a string in which uppercase characters of *string* are converted to lowercase (non-letter characters are unaffected). If string is Null, Null is returned.
Left	Left(*string*, *length*) Returns a specified number of characters (length) from the left side of *string*. If *string* is Null, Null is returned. If length exceeds the number of characters in *string*, the entire *string* is returned. LeftB should be used for byte data contained in a string. In this case, *length* refers to a number of bytes.
Len	Len(*string* ¦ *varname*) Returns the number of characters in a string or the number of bytes necessary to store a variable. If *string* or *varname* contains Null, Null is returned. LenB should be used for byte data contained in a string. In this case, LenB returns the number of bytes used to represent the string.

continues

Table C.5. continued

VBScript Function	Syntax and Description
LoadPicture	LoadPicture(*picturename*) Returns a picture object. Picture name is a string expression specifying the name of a picture file to load. Recognized formats are bitmap (.bmp), icon (.ico), run-length encoded (.rle), standard and enhanced metafiles (.wmf and .emf), GIF (.gif), and JPEG (.jpg).
Log	Log(*number*) Returns the natural logarithm (the logarithm to the base *e*) of *number*. *number* must be greater than 0.
LTrim	LTrim(*string*) Returns a copy of *string* without leading spaces. If *string* is Null, Null is returned.
Mid	Mid(*string*, *start*[, *length*]) Returns a specified number of characters from *string* (beginning at the character position indicated by *start*). If *start* is greater than the number of characters in *string*, "" is returned. MidB should be used for byte data contained in a string. In this case, function arguments specify numbers of bytes.
Minute	Minute(*time*) Returns a whole number from 0 through 59 that represents the minute of the hour. *time* can be any expression that represents a time. If *time* contains Null, Null is returned.
Month	Month(*date*) Returns a whole number from 1 through 12 that represents the month of the year. *date* can be any expression that represents a date. If *date* contains Null, Null is returned.
MonthName	MonthName(*month*[, *abbreviate*]) Returns a string indicating the month specified by *month* (January for 1, February for 2, and so on). If *abbreviate* is a Boolean True, the string returned contains an abbreviated month name.
MsgBox	MsgBox(*prompt*[, *buttons*][, *title*][, *helpfile*, *context*]) Displays a message in a dialog box, waits for the user to click a button, and returns a value indicating which button the user clicked. *prompt* is a string expression for the message to be displayed. Lines in a multiline message can be separated by using a CR (Chr(13)), LF (Chr(10)), or CR-LF pair. *prompt* is limited to (approximately) 1,024 characters. *buttons* is a numeric expression

VBScript Function	*Syntax and Description*

that is a summation of values that specifies the types of buttons to display, modality, icon style, and default button (if omitted, 0 is the default). *title* is a string expression for the dialog box bar title to be displayed (if omitted, the application name is used). *helpfile* is a string expression that identifies the context-sensitive Help file to use (if provided, *context* is required). This is not available on 16-bit platforms. *context* is a numeric expression identifying the help context number assigned to a Help topic (if provided, *context* is required). This is not available on 16-bit platforms. Following are MsgBox *button* argument settings used to specify buttons displayed, icon styles, default buttons, and dialog box modality:

Constant	Value	Description
vbOKOnly	0	Displays OK button only
vbOKCancel	1	Displays OK and Cancel buttons
vbAbortRetryIgnore	2	Displays Abort, Retry, and Ignore buttons
vbYesNoCancel	3	Displays Yes, No, and Cancel buttons
vbYesNo	4	Displays Yes and No buttons
vbRetryCancel	5	Displays Retry and Cancel buttons
vbCritical	16	Displays Critical Message icon
vbQuestion	32	Displays Warning Query icon
vbExclamation	48	Displays Warning Message icon
vbInformation	64	Displays Information Message icon
vbDefaultButton1	0	First button is default
vbDefaultButton2	256	Second button is default
vbDefaultButton3	512	Third button is default
vbDefaultButton4	768	Fourth button is default
vbApplicationModal	0	Application modal; requires the user to respond to the dialog box before continuing in the current application
VbSystemModal	4096	System modal; all applications are suspended until the user responds to the dialog box

continues

Table C.5. continued

VBScript Function	Syntax and Description
	Following are MsgBox return values indicating which button was clicked:

Constant	Value	Button
vbOK	1	OK
vbCancel	2	Cancel
vbAbort	3	Abort
vbRetry	4	Retry
vbIgnore	5	Ignore
vbYes	6	Yes
vbNo	7	No

VBScript Function	Syntax and Description
Now	Now
	Returns the current date and time per your computer's system date/time.
Oct	Oct(*number*)
	Returns a string representing the octal value of *number*. If *number* is Null, Null is returned. If *number* is Empty, 0 is returned.
Replace	Replace(*expression, find, replacewith*[, ↪*start*[, *count*[, *compare*]]])
	Returns a string in which a specified substring has been replaced with another substring a specified number of times. *expression* is the string expression containing the substring to be replaced. *find* is the substring to search for. *replacewith* is the substring used to replace the *find* substring. *start* is an optional value indicating the position within substring where the search begins (if omitted, 1 is used). *count* is an optional value indicating the number of replacements to make (if omitted, -1 is used to perform all possible replacements). *compare* is an optional numeric expression specifying the kind of comparison to use (if omitted, binary is the default). Following are valid constant names, values, and descriptions for *compare*:

vbBinaryCompare	0	Binary comparison
vbTextCompare	1	Textual comparison
vbDatabaseCompare	2	Comparison based on information contained in the database where the comparison is performed

VBScript Function	Syntax and Description
	Following are `Replace` return values:

Condition	Return Value
expression is 0 length	Zero-length string
expression is Null	An error
find is 0 length	Copy of *expression*
replacewith is 0 length	Copy of *expression* with all occurrences of *find* removed
start > Len(*expression*)	Zero-length string
count is 0	Copy of *expression*

VBScript Function	Syntax and Description
Right	`Right(string, length)` Returns the number of characters (specified by *length*) from the right side of *string*. If *length* is 0, "" is returned. If *length* exceeds the length of *string*, the entire string is returned. `RightB` should be used for byte data contained in a string. In this case, *length* specifies the number of bytes.
Rnd	`Rnd[(number)]` Returns a random number using *number* as a seed. The value of *number* determines how `Rnd` generates a random number as the following:

number <	0	Rnd returns the same number every time, using *number* as the seed.
number >	0	Rnd returns the next random number in the sequence.
number =	0	Rnd returns the most recently generated number.
no *number*		Rnd returns the next random number in the sequence.

Note: For any given seed, the same number sequence is generated (Rnd uses the previous number as a seed for each successive number in a sequence). Therefore, you should use `Randomize` with no arguments to initialize the random number generator with a seed derived from the system timer.

VBScript Function	Syntax and Description
Round	`Round(expression[, numdecimalplaces])` Returns a number rounded to a number of decimal places. *numdecimalplaces* specifies the number of places to the right of the decimal to be included in the rounding. If not specified, integers are returned.

continues

Table C.5. continued

VBScript Function	Syntax and Description
RTrim	RTrim(*string*) Returns a copy of *string* without trailing spaces. If *string* is Null, Null is returned.
ScriptEngine	ScriptEngine Returns a string representing the scripting language in use. Possible values are VBScript, VBA, or JScript.
ScriptEngine- BuildVersion	ScriptEngineBuildVersion Returns the build version number of the script engine in use (this corresponds to the version information in the DLL for the scripting language in use).
ScriptEngine- MajorVersion	ScriptEngineMajorVersion Returns the major version number of the script engine in use (this corresponds to the version information in the DLL for the scripting language in use).
ScriptEngine- MinorVersion	ScriptEngineMinorVersion Returns the minor version number of the script engine in use (this corresponds to the version information in the DLL for the scripting language in use).
Second	Second(*time*) Returns a whole number from 0 through 59 that represents the second of the minute. If *time* is Null, Null is returned.
Sgn	Sgn(*number*) Returns an integer indicating the sign of *number* (1 if *number* is positive, -1 if *number* is negative, 0 if *number* is 0).
Sin	Sin(*number*) Returns the sine of *number* (which is an angle represented in radians). The result is in the range of -1 to 1.
Space	Space(*number*) Returns a string of spaces of the length specified by *number*.
Split	Split(*expression*[, *delimiter*[, *count*[, *compare*]]]) Returns a one-dimensional array that contains *count* number of substrings. The array is zero-based. *expression* is a string expression that contains substrings and delimiters. Note that if *expression* is zero-length, Split returns an empty array. *delimiter* is an optional string character that defines the limits if substrings are in *expression* (if omitted, the space character is

VBScript Function	Syntax and Description
	used by default). If a zero-length string character is used, Split returns a one-element array containing *expression*. *count* is an optional value that specifies the number of substrings to return (if omitted, -1 is used to indicate that all strings are returned). *compare* is an optional numeric expression specifying the kind of comparison to use (if omitted, binary is the default). Following are valid constant names, values, and descriptions for *compare*:

vbBinaryCompare	0	Binary comparison
vbTextCompare	1	Textual comparison
vbDatabaseCompare	2	Comparison based on information contained in the database where the comparison is performed

VBScript Function	Syntax and Description
Sqr	Sqr(*number*) Returns the square root of *number*. *number* must be greater than or equal to 0.
StrComp	StrComp(*string1*, *string2*[, *compare*]) Returns a value indicating the result of a comparison between *string1* and *string2*. *string1* and *string2* are any valid string expressions (these are required arguments). *compare* is an optional numeric expression specifying the kind of comparison to use (if omitted, binary is the default). See Split for valid values of *compare*. Some StrComp return values follow:

Condition	Return Value
string1 less than *string2*	-1
string1 equal to *string2*	0
string1 greater than *string2*	1
string1 or *string2* is Null	Null

VBScript Function	Syntax and Description
StrReverse	StrReverse(*string1*) Returns a string in which the character order of *string1* is reversed. If *string1* is "", then "" is returned. If *string1* is Null, an error occurs.
String	String(*number*, *character*) Returns a string of length specified by *number* consisting of characters specified by *character*. If *number* or *character* is Null, Null is returned. If *character* is a string, its first character is used to construct the return string. If a number greater than 255 is used for *character*, it is converted to a valid character code using *character* Mod 256.

continues

Table C.5. continued

VBScript Function	Syntax and Description
Tan	Tan(*number*) Returns the tangent of *number* (which is an angle represented in radians).
Time	Time Returns a Variant of subtype Date that indicates the current system time.
TimeSerial	TimeSerial(*hour, minute, second*) Returns a Variant of subtype Date containing the time for the specified *hour, minute,* and *second. hour* is a number/numeric expression from 0 to 23 (12 a.m. to 11 p.m.). *minute* and *second* are number/numeric expressions from 0 through 59. Relative times can be specified—for example, TimeSerial(12 - 6, -15, 0) returns a time for 15 minutes before (-15) six hours before noon (12 - 6), or 5:45:00 a.m. If any argument exceeds the accepted range for that argument, it is incremented to the next larger unit as appropriate. For example, 75 minutes is evaluated as one hour and 15 minutes.
TimeValue	TimeValue(*time*) Returns a Variant of subtype Date that contains the time. *time* is typically a string expression representing a time from 0:00:00 (12:00:00 a.m.) through 23:59:59 (11:59:59 p.m.). If *time* is Null, Null is returned. If *time* contains date information, it is not returned by TimeValue (however, if the date information is not valid, an error occurs).
Trim	Trim(*string*) Returns a copy of *string* without leading and trailing spaces. If *string* is Null, Null is returned.
TypeName	TypeName(*varname*) Returns the Variant subtype of *varname. varname* can be any variable. This is a required argument. Return values can be any of the following self-explanatory values: Byte, Integer, Long, Single, Double, Currency, Decimal, Date, String, Boolean, Empty, Null, Object, or Error. Other possible return values are <object type> (the actual type name of an object), Unknown (an unknown object type), or Nothing (an object variable that doesn't refer to an object instance).
UBound	UBound(*arrayname*[, *dimension*]) Returns the largest available subscript for the indicated dimension of an array. *arrayname* is the name of the array (this is required).

VBScript Function	Syntax and Description
	dimension is an optional number that indicates which array dimension's bound is returned (for example, 1 for the first dimension and so on). If omitted, 1 is used.
UCase	UCase(*string*) Returns a string in which lowercase characters of *string* are converted to uppercase (non-letter characters are unaffected). If *string* is Null, Null is returned.
VarType	VarType(*varname*) Returns a value that indicates the subtype of *varname*. *varname* can be any variable. VarType return values follow:

Constant	Value
vbEmpty	0 (uninitialized)
vbNull	1
vbInteger	2
vbLong	3
vbSingle	4
vbDouble	5
vbCurrency	6
vbDate	7
vbString	8
vbObject	9 (Automation object)
vbError	10
vbBoolean	11
vbVariant	12 (used only with arrays of Variants)
vbDataObject	13 (data-access object)
vbByte	17
vbArray	8192

VBScript Function	Syntax and Description
Weekday	Weekday(*date*, [*firstdayofweek*]) Returns a whole number representing the day of the week. *date* is any expression that can represent a date (if Null, *date* returns Null). *firstdayofweek* is a constant that specifies the first day of the week (vbSunday is assumed if this is omitted). Valid settings for *firstdayofweek* follow:

Constant	Value
vbUseSystem	0 (use NLS API setting)
vbSunday	1
vbMonday	2
vbTuesday	3

continues

Table C.5. continued

VBScript Function	Syntax and Description
	vbWednesday 4
	vbThursday 5
	vbFriday 6
	vbSaturday 7
	Weekday can return the values vbSunday, vbMonday, vbTuesday, vbWednesday, vbThursday, vbFriday, or vbSaturday.
WeekdayName	WeekDayName(*weekday*, *abbreviate*, *firstdayofweek*) *weekday* is a required numeric designation for the day of the week. The numeric value of each day depends on the *firstdayofweek* setting. *abbreviate* is an optional Boolean value that indicates whether the weekday name should be abbreviated. False (no abbreviation) is assumed if this is omitted. *firstdayofweek* is a constant that specifies the first day of the week (vbSunday is assumed if this is omitted). See Weekday for valid settings for *firstdayofweek*.
Year	Year(*date*) Returns a whole number that represents the year. If date is Null, Null is returned.

VBScript Statements

VBScript provides a complete set of statements that can be used to define variables, call subprocedures or functions, assign values to variables, exit programs, and control program flow (looping, conditional execution, case statements, and so on). Table C.6 provides a listing of all VBScript statements along with brief descriptions.

Table C.6. VBScript statements.

VBScript Statement	Syntax and Description
Call	[Call] *name* [*argumentlist*] Transfers control to a subprocedure or function. Use is optional, but if used, *argumentlist* must be enclosed in parentheses.
Const	[Public ¦ Private] Const *constname* = *expression* Declares constants for use in place of literal values. Public and Private keywords are optional and available only at the script

VBScript Statement	Syntax and Description
	level (not within procedures). `Public` declares constants available to all procedures in all scripts, whereas `Private` declares constants available only within the script where the declaration was made.

Dim	`Dim varname[([subscripts])][, varname[([subscripts])]] ...`
	The *subscripts* argument uses the following syntax:
	`upperbound [,upperbound] ...`
	Arrays of up to 60 dimensions can be declared. Array indexing starts at 0. Use `Dim` with empty parentheses to declare a dynamic array. Then use `ReDim` within a procedure to define the number of dimensions and elements. Numeric variables are initialized to `0`. Strings are initialized to `""` (zero-length).

Do...Loop	`Do [{While ¦ Until} condition]`
	    `[statements]`
	    `[Exit Do]`
	    `[statements]`
	`Loop`
	or
	`Do`
	    `[statements]`
	    `[Exit Do]`
	    `[statements]`
	`Loop [{While ¦ Until} condition]`
	Repeats a block of statements while a condition is `True` or until a condition becomes `True`. `Exit Do` transfers control to the loop that is one nested level above the loop where it occurs.

Erase	`Erase array` Reinitializes elements in fixed-size arrays as in the following: Elements of numeric arrays are set to `0` Elements of string arrays are set to `""` Elements of object arrays are set to the special value `Nothing` If the array is a dynamic array, memory used by the array is freed.
Exit	Four syntactical forms are available: `Exit Do` Provides a means for exiting a `Do Loop` statement. Transfers control to the statement following the `Loop` statement unless it is in a nested loop, in which case transfers control to the loop that is one nested level above the loop where it occurs.

continues

Table C.6. continued

VBScript Statement	Syntax and Description
	`Exit For` Provides a means for exiting a `For` loop. Transfers control to the statement following the `Next` statement unless it is in a nested loop, in which case transfers control to the loop that is one nested level above the loop where it occurs.
	`Exit Function` Causes immediate exit from the `Function` procedure where it appears.
	`Exit Sub` Causes immediate exit from the subprocedure where it appears.

`For...Next`	`For counter = start To end [Step step]`
	    `[statements]`
	    `[Exit For]`
	    `[statements]`
	`Next`
	
	Repeats a group of statements a specified number of times. `step` specifies how the counter value is changed for each loop. `step` can be positive or negative. If `step` is positive (or 0), the loop executes while `counter` is <= `end`. If `step` is negative, the loop executes while `counter` is >= `end`.

`For Each...Next`	`For Each element In group`
	    `[statements]`
	    `[Exit For]`
	    `[statements]`
	`Next [element]`
	
	Repeats a group of statements for each `element` in an array or collection. For arrays, `element` must be a `Variant` variable. For collections, element can be only a `Variant`, `Object`, or `Automation` object variable.

`Function`	`[Public ¦ Private] Function name [(arglist)]`
	    `[statements]`
	    `[name = expression]`
	    `[Exit Function]`
	    `[statements]`
	    `[name = expression]`
	`End Function`
	
	Declares the name, arguments, and code that form the body of a `Function` procedure. `Function` procedures are public by default (if

VBScript Statement	*Syntax and Description*

not specified with Public or Private) and thus visible to all other procedures in your script. Function procedures can't be contained inside another Function or Sub procedure. Unlike Sub procedures, Function procedures can exist on the right side of an expression. Function procedures can be called. See Call for information. Public indicates that the Function procedure is accessible to all other procedures in all scripts. Private indicates that the Function procedure is accessible only to other procedures in the script where it is declared. *name* is the function name. *arglist* is the list of variables (comma-separated) passed to the procedure. *arglist* has the syntax [ByVal ¦ ByRef] *varname*[( )] where ByVal and ByRef indicate that an argument is passed by value and reference, respectively and *varname* is the variable representing the argument. *statements* are statement groups to be executed. *expression* is the return value assigned to the function *name*. Exit Function statements can appear anywhere in a Function procedure and cause an immediate exit from a Function procedure. The following example shows how to assign a return value to a function named BinSearch (note that if no value is assigned to a function *name*, the procedure returns a default value; numeric functions return 0, string functions return (""), and functions that return object references return Nothing):

```
Function BinSearch(. . .)

  . . .

  If lower > upper Then
    ' Return a value of False.
    BinSearch = False
    Exit Function
  End If

  . . .
End Function
```

Caution: Function procedures can be called recursively. However, recursion can lead to stack overflow.

A procedure can use a variable that is not explicitly declared in the procedure, but a naming conflict can occur if anything you have defined at the script level has the same name (use of Option Explicit is a good practice).

VBScript may rearrange arithmetic expressions to increase internal efficiency, so avoid using a Function procedure in an

continues

Table C.6. continued

VBScript Statement	*Syntax and Description*
	arithmetic expression when the function changes the value of variables in the same expression.
If...Then...Else	```
If condition Then
   [statements]
[ElseIf condition-n Then
   [elseifstatements]] . . .
[Else
   [elsestatements]]
End If
```
Conditionally executes a group of statements (depending on the value of an expression). If `condition` is `True`, the statements following `Then` are executed. If otherwise, each `ElseIf` (if any) is evaluated in turn, and its subsequent statements are executed if the condition is `True`. `Else` and `ElseIf` are both optional, and you can have as many `ElseIf` statements as desired. `condition` (and `condition-n`) is a numeric or string expression that evaluates to `True` or `False` (if `Null`, `condition` is treated as `False`). Alternatively, `condition` can be an expression of the form `TypeOf objectname Is objecttype`, where `objectname` is an object reference and `objecttype` is a valid object type. The expression is `True` if `objectname` is of the object type specified by `objecttype` and `False` otherwise. `statements` are colon-separated statements to be executed if `condition` is `True`. `elseifstatements` are statements executed if the associated `condition-n` is `True`. `elsestatements` are statements executed if no previous `condition` (`condition-n`) expressions are `True`. |
| On Error | On Error Resume Next
Enables (or disables) an error-handling routine and specifies its location within a procedure. Causes execution to continue with the statement immediately following the statement that caused the runtime error, or with the statement immediately following the most recent call out of the procedure containing the `On Error Resume Next` statement. Execute an `On Error Resume Next` statement in each called routine if you want inline error handling within that routine. If you don't, any runtime error that occurs is fatal; an error message is displayed, and execution stops. |
| Option Explicit | Option Explicit
Used at script level to force explicit declaration of all variables (using `Dim`, `Private`, `Public`, or `ReDim`) within the script. If used, it must appear before any procedures within the script. |
```

VBScript Statement	Syntax and Description
Private	`Private varname[([subscripts])][, varname[([subscripts])]]` ➥. . . Used at script level to declare variables (and allocate storage) that are available only to the script in which they are declared. Variables referring to objects must be assigned an existing object using the `Set` statement before it can be used. Until it is assigned an object, the declared object variable has the special value `Nothing`. Using `Private` with empty parentheses causes declaration of a dynamic array.
Public	`Public varname[([subscripts])][, varname[([subscripts])]]` ➥. . . Used at script level to declare variables (and allocate storage) that are available to all procedures in all scripts in all projects. Variables referring to objects must be assigned an existing object using the `Set` statement before it can be used. Until it is assigned an object, the declared object variable has the special value `Nothing`. Using `Public` with empty parentheses causes declaration of a dynamic array.
Randomize	`Randomize [number]` Uses `number` to initialize (to seed) the `Rnd` function's random number generator. If no `number` is given, system timer is used.
ReDim	`ReDim [Preserve] varname(subscripts) [,` ➥`varname(subscripts)]` . . . `ReDim` is used at the procedure level to declare dynamic-array variables and allocate or reallocate storage space—that is, to size or resize dynamic arrays that already have been declared formally using a `Private`, `Public`, or `Dim` without dimension subscripts. Note that making an array smaller than its original dimensions results in loss of data in the elements that are eliminated. `Preserve` is used to preserve data in an existing array when the size of the last array dimension is changed. If `Preserve` is used, only the last array dimension can be changed and the number of dimensions may not be changed at all. `varname` is the name of the variable. The `subscripts` argument uses the following syntax: `upperbound [,upperbound]` . . . Arrays of up to 60 dimensions can be declared. Array indexing starts at 0. Note that, when variables are initialized, numeric variables are initialized to `0` while string variables are initialized to

continues

Table C.6. continued

VBScript Statement	Syntax and Description
	zero-length strings (`""`). Variables referring to objects must be assigned an existing object using the `Set` statement before being used (until they are assigned an object, these variables have the value of `Nothing`).

Rem	`Rem comments`
	 or
	 `' comments`
	 Used to include comments in your scripts. When `Rem` follows other statements on a line, it must be separated from the statements by a colon.

Select Case	```Select Case testexpression [Case expressionlist-n [statements-n]] . . . [Case Else expressionlist-n [elsestatements-n]] End Select``` Executes one of several groups of statements, depending on the value of an expression. If `testexpression` matches an `expressionlist` expression in more than one `Case` clause, only the statements following the first match are executed. Note that `Select Case` statements may be nested. `testexpression` is any numeric or string expression. `expressionlist-n` is a delimited list of expressions (required if `Case` is used). `statements-n` is a series of statements executed if `testexpression` matches any part of `expressionlist-n`. `elsestatements-n` is a series of statements executed if `testexpression` doesn't match any of the `Case` clauses.
Set	`Set objectvar = {objectexpression ¦ Nothing}` Assigns an object reference to a variable or property. Typically, `Set` creates a reference to an object (no copy of the object is created). Multiple variables can refer to the same object, and any change in the object is reflected in all variables that refer to it. `objectvar` the name of the variable or property. `objectexpression` is an expression consisting of the name of an object, another declared variable of the same object type, or a function or method that returns an object of the same object type. `Nothing` discontinues `objectvar`'s association with the object and releases system and memory resources associated with the previously referenced object when no other variable refers to it.

VBScript Statement	Syntax and Description

Sub	`[Public ¦ Private] Sub name [(arglist)]`
	  `[statements]`
	  `[Exit Sub]`
	  `[statements]`
	`End Sub`
	
	Declares the name, arguments, and code that form the body of a Sub procedure. Sub procedures are public by default (if not specified with Public or Private), and thus visible to all other procedures in your script. Sub procedures can't be contained inside another Function or Sub procedure. Unlike Function procedures, Sub procedures can't be used in expressions. Public indicates that the Sub procedure is accessible to all other procedures in all scripts. Private indicates that the Sub procedure is accessible only to other procedures in the script where it is declared. *name* is the Sub name. *arglist* is the list of variables (comma-separated) passed to the procedure. *arglist* has the syntax
	`[ByVal ¦ ByRef] varname[( )]`
	where ByVal and ByRef indicate argument is passed by value and reference, respectively, and *varname* is the variable representing the argument. *statements* are statement groups to be executed. *expression* is the return value assigned to the function *name*. Exit Sub statements can appear anywhere in a Sub procedure and cause an immediate exit from a Sub procedure. Caution: Sub procedures can be called recursively. However, recursion can lead to stack overflow.
	
	A procedure can use a variable that is not explicitly declared in the procedure, but a naming conflict can occur if anything you have defined at the script level has the same name (use of Option Explicit is a good practice).

While...Wend	`While condition`
	    `[statements]`
	`Wend`
	
	Executes a series of *statements* as long as the *condition* is True. Nesting can occur to any level. *condition* is a numeric or string expression that evaluates to True or False (if Null, it is treated as False).

VBScript Methods

VBScript provides a number of methods that can be used for manipulating objects in your VBScript programs. Table C.7 provides a listing of all VBScript methods along with brief descriptions of how each may be used.

Table C.7. VBScript methods.

VBScript Method	Syntax and Description
Add	`object.Add key, item` Adds the specified `key, item` pair to the specified `Dictionary` object. If `key` exists, an error occurs.
Clear	`object.Clear` Explicitly clears all property settings of the `Err` object after the error is handled (for example, when deferred error handling is used with `On Error Resume Next`). `Clear` is called automatically when the `On Error Resume Next`, `Exit Sub`, or `Exit Function` statements are executed.
Close	`object.Close` Closes an open `TextStream` file specified by object.

CreateTextFile	`[object.]CreateTextFile(filename[,`
	`➥overwrite[, unicode]])`
	Creates a file (specified by filename) and returns a `TextStream` object that can be used to read/write the file. If overwrite is `True`, the file can be overwritten. If overwrite is `False` or omitted, existing files aren't overwritten. If unicode is `True`, the file is created as a Unicode file. If unicode is `False` or omitted, an ASCII file is created. `CreateTextFile` can be used to open a text file, as in this example:
	
	`Set fs = CreateObject("Scripting.FileSystemObject")`
	`Set a = fs.CreateTextFile("d:\myfile.txt", True)`
	`a.WriteLine("This is only a test.")`
	`a.Close`

Exists	`object.Exists(key)` Returns a Boolean `True` if `key` exists in the specified `Dictionary` object; `False` otherwise.

VBScript Method	*Syntax and Description*

Items	`object.Items`
	Returns an array that contains all items in the specified `Dictionary` object. It can be used as in this example:
	
	```Dim a, d, i 'Create variables```
	```Set d = CreateObject("Scripting.Dictionary")```
	```d.Add "a", "Autobahn" 'Add keys and items```
	```d.Add "b", "Beltway"```
	```d.Add "c", "Circle"```
	```a = d.Items 'Get items```
	```For i = 0 To d.Count -1 'Iterate array```
	``` Print a(i) 'Print item```
	```Next```
	``` ...```

Keys	`object.Keys`
	Returns an array that contains all keys in the specified `Dictionary` object. It can be used as in this example:
	
	```Dim a, d, i 'Create variables```
	```Set d = CreateObject("Scripting.Dictionary")```
	```d.Add "a", "Autobahn" 'Add keys and items```
	```d.Add "b", "Beltway"```
	```d.Add "c", "Circle"```
	```a = d.Keys 'Get keys```
	```For i = 0 To d.Count -1 'Iterate array```
	``` Print a(i) 'Print key```
	```Next```
	``` ...```

OpenTextFile	`[object.]OpenTextFile(filename[, iomode[, create[, `
	`➥format]]])`
	Opens a specified file and returns a `TextStream` object that can be used to read from or append to the file. *object* is optional and is the name of a `FileSystemObject`. *filename* is a required string expression that specifies the file to open. *iomode* is an optional constant (`ForReading` or `ForAppending`) that indicates how the file is opened. `create` is an optional Boolean value that specifies whether a new file can be created if filename does not exist. If `True`, new file is created. If omitted, no file created. `format` is an optional `Tristate` value that indicates the format of the opened file. If omitted, the file is opened as ASCII. Possible values are `TristateTrue` to open the file as Unicode, `TristateFalse` to open the file as ASCII, and `TristateUseDefaultOpen` to open the file

continues

Table C.7. continued

VBScript Method	*Syntax and Description*
	using the system default. The following code snippet shows how to open a file for appending text:

```
Dim fs, a
Set fs = CreateObject("Scripting.FileSystemObject")
Set a = fs.OpenTextFile("D:\mytestfile.txt",
➡ForAppending, FALSE)
...
a.Close
```

| Raise | *object*.Raise(*number, source, description,* ➡*helpfile, helpcontext*) |

Generates a runtime error. If Raise is used without specifying arguments, and the property settings of the Err object contain values that have not been cleared, those values become the values for your error. When setting the *number* property to your own error code in an Automation object, you add your error code number to the constant vbObjectError (to generate the error number 1040, for example, assign vbObjectError + 1040 to the number property). All arguments are optional except *number*. *object* is the Err object. *number* is a Long integer identifying the nature of the error (VBScript errors, VBScript-defined and user-defined, are in the range 0–65535). *source* is a string expression that names the object or application that generated the error. If setting this property for an Automation object, use the form project.class. If nothing is specified, the programmatic ID of the current VBScript project is used. *description* is a string expression that describes the error (if not specified, the value in *number* is examined, and if it can be mapped to a runtime error code, a string provided by VBScript is used as *description*. If no VBScript error corresponds to number, a generic error message is used). *helpfile* is a fully qualified path to the Help file in which help on this error can be found (if unspecified, VBScript uses the fully qualified drive, path, and filename of the VBScript Help file). *helpcontext* is a context ID identifying a topic within *helpfile* that provides help for the error (if omitted, the VBScript Help file context ID for the error corresponding to the *number* property is used, if it exists).

VBScript Method	Syntax and Description
Read	`object.Read(characters)` Reads some number of characters (specified by `characters`) from a `TextStream` file specified by `object` and returns the resulting string.
ReadAll	`object.ReadAll` Reads the entire `TextStream` file specified by `object` and returns the resulting string. For large files, it is recommended that reading is performed one line at a time to conserve memory resources.
ReadLine	`object.ReadLine` Reads an entire line from the `TextStream` file specified by `object` and returns the resulting string. Note that the newline character is not read.

Remove	`object.Remove(key)`
	Removes a key/item pair (for the specified key) from a `Dictionary` object specified by `object`. It can be used as in this example:
	
	`Dim a, d, i          'Create variables`
	`Set d = CreateObject("Scripting.Dictionary")`
	`d.Add "a", "Autobahn"    'Add keys and items`
	`d.Add "b", "Beltway"`
	`d.Add "c", "Circle"`
	`...`
	`a = d.Remove("b")        'Remove second pair`

RemoveAll	`object.RemoveAll`
	Removes all key/item pairs from a `Dictionary` object specified by `object`. It can be used as in this example:
	`Dim a, d, i          'Create variables`
	`Set d = CreateObject("Scripting.Dictionary")`
	`d.Add "a", "Autobahn"    'Add keys and items`
	`d.Add "b", "Beltway"`
	`d.Add "c", "Circle"`
	`...`
	`a = d.RemoveAll("b")     'Clear dictionary`

Skip	`object.Skip(characters)` Used to skip some number of characters (specified by characters) when reading the `TextStream` file specified by `object`.

continues

Table C.7. continued

VBScript Method	*Syntax and Description*
SkipLine	`object.SkipLine` Skips the next line when reading the `TextStream` file specified by `object`.
Write	`object.Write(string)` Writes the specified string to the `TextStream` file specified by `object`. No intervening spaces or characters are written between strings.
WriteBlankLines	`object.WriteBlankLines(lines)` Writes a number of newline characters (specified by `lines`) to the `TextStream` file specified by `object`.
WriteLine	`object.WriteLine([string])` Writes the specified string (and a newline character) to the `TextStream` file specified by `object`. If no string is specified, a newline is written to the file.

VBScript Objects

VBScript provides objects for handling dictionaries (arrays of key/value pairs), errors, and file I/O. Table C.8 provides a listing of all VBScript objects along with brief descriptions of how each may be used.

Table C.8. VBScript objects.

VBScript Object	*Syntax and Description*

Dictionary	`Scripting.Dictionary`
	Stores data key and item pairs. It is equivalent to an associative array in the Perl scripting language. Items can be any form of data. Keys are used to retrieve individual items and can be anything but an array (they are typically integers or strings). Create a `Dictionary` object and make these additions:
	
	`Dim d`
	`Set d = CreateObject("Scripting.Dictionary")`
	`d.Add "a", "Autobahn"`
	`...`

VBScript Object	Syntax and Description
Err	Err[.{*property* ¦ *method*}] Err is an intrinsic object with global scope and does not need to be created explicitly in your code. Properties of this object are set by the generator of an error (Visual Basic, an Automation object, or the VBScript programmer). The default property is Number.Err.Number (which contains an integer and can be used by an Automation object to return an SCODE). Properties of the Err object are filled with information about a runtime error. The Raise method can be used to generate runtime errors in your code. Err properties are reset to 0 or "" following an On Error Resume Next statement and after a Sub or Exit Function statement within an error-handling routine. Additionally, the Clear method can be used to explicitly reset Err.

FileSystemObject	Scripting.FileSystemObject
	Provides access to a computer's file system. It provide two methods: one to create a file and one to open a text file. A FileSystemObject can be created and used like this:
	
	`Set fs CreateObject("Scripting.FileSystemObject")`
	`Set a = fs.CreateTextFile("D:\myfile.txt", True)`
	`a.WriteLine("This is just a test.")`
	`a.Close`
	
	The CreateObject function returns FileSystemObject (fs). The CreateTextFile method creates the file as a TextStream object (a). The WriteLine method writes a line of text to the created text file. The Close method flushes the buffer and closes the file.

TextStream	TextStream.{*property* ¦ *method*} Facilitates sequential access to a file. *property* and *method* can be any of those associated with the TextStream object. See FileSystemObject for sample use.

VBScript Properties

All VBScript objects have a number of properties that can be in your VBScript programs for performing conditional execution of statements, setting the context of Help, deterring information about dictionary objects, and so on. Table C.9 provides a listing of all VBScript properties with a brief description of how each may be used.

Table C.9. VBScript properties.

VBScript Property	Syntax and Description
AtEndOfLine	*object*.AtEndOfLine Returns True if the file pointer is at the end of a TextStream file; returns False otherwise. Applies only to TextStream files opened for reading (an error occurs otherwise). This property can be used as in this example: ```\nDim fs, a, retstring\nSet fs = CreateObject("Scripting.FileSystemObject")\nSet a = fs.OpenTextFile("d:\myfile.txt", ForReading, False)\nDo While a.AtEndOfLine <> True\n retstring = a.Read(1)\n . . .\nLoop\na.Close\n```
AtEndOfStream	*object*.AtEndOfStream Returns True if the file pointer is at the end of a TextStream file; returns False otherwise. Applies only to TextStream files opened for reading (an error occurs otherwise). This property can be used as in this example: ```\nDim fs, a, retstring\nSet fs = CreateObject("Scripting.FileSystemObject")\nSet a = fs.OpenTextFile("d:\myfile.txt", ForReading, False)\nDo While a.AtEndOfStream <> True\n retstring = a.Read(1)\n . . .\nLoop\na.Close\n```
Column	*object*.Column A read-only property that returns the column number of the current character position in a TextStream file.
CompareMode	*object*.CompareMode[= *compare*] Sets and returns the comparison mode for comparing string keys in a Dictionary object. It uses the same values as the *compare* argument for the StrComp function. Acceptable values are 0 (Binary), 1 (Text), and 2 (Database). Values greater than 2 can be used to refer to comparisons using specific locale IDs (LCIDs). Attempting to change the comparison mode of a Dictionary object that contains data causes an error.

VBScript Property	*Syntax and Description*

Count	`object.Count`
	A read-only property that returns the number of items in a `Dictionary` object. It can be used as in this example:
	<pre>Dim a, d, I
	Set d = CreateObject("Scripting.Dictionary")
	d.Add "a", "Autobahn" 'Add some keys and items.
	d.Add "b", "Beltway"
	d.Add "c", "Circle"
	a = d.Keys 'Get the keys
	For i = 0 To d.Count -1 'Iterate through array
	      Print a(i) 'Print key
	Next
	      ...</pre>

Description	`object.Description [= stringexpression]` Returns or sets a descriptive string associated with an error. It can be used to alert users of error conditions that the program doesn't handle. If `Description` isn't filled in, and the value of `Number` (see entry later in this table) corresponds to a VBScript runtime error, the descriptive string associated with that error is returned. `object` is the `Err` object. `stringexpression` contains a description of the error.
HelpContext	`object.HelpContext [= contextID]` Sets or returns a context ID for a topic in a Help file. If a Help file is specified in `HelpFile` (see next entry), the `HelpContext` property is used to automatically display the topic identified. If both `HelpFile` and `HelpContext` are empty, the value of `Number` (see later entry) is checked, and, if it corresponds to a VBScript runtime error value, the VBScript Help context ID for that error is used. If the `Number` value doesn't correspond to a VBScript error, the contents screen for the VBScript Help file is displayed. `object` is the `Err` object. `contextID` is a valid identifier for a topic in the Help file (it is optional).
HelpFile	`object.HelpFile [= contextID]` Sets or returns a fully qualified path to the Help file. If a Help file is specified in `HelpFile`, it is invoked automatically if a user clicks the Help button in the error message dialog box (or presses the F1 key). If the `HelpContext` property contains a valid context ID

continues

Table C.9. continued

VBScript Property	Syntax and Description
	for the specified file, that topic is displayed automatically. If no `HelpFile` is specified, the VBScript Help file is displayed. *object* is the `Err` object. *contextID* is a fully qualified path to the Help file (it is optional).
Item	`object.Item(key)[ = newitem]` Sets or returns an item for the specified key in a `Dictionary` object. If *key* is not found when changing an item, a new *key* is created with the specified *newitem*. If *key* is not found when attempting to retrieve an existing *item*, a new *key* is created, and its corresponding *item* is left empty. *object* is the name of the Dictionary (it is required). *key* associated with the items to be retrieved or added (it is required). *newitem* is the new value associated with *key* (it is optional).
Line	`object.Line` A read-only property that returns the current line number in a `TextStream` file. `Line` is 1 when the file is first opened (prior to writing anything). *object* is always the name of a `TextStream` object.

Number	`object.Number [= errornumber]`
	Returns or sets a numeric value specifying an error. `Number` is the `Err` object's default property. *object* is the `Err` object. *errornumber* is an integer that represents a VBScript error number or an `SCODE` error value. If returning a user-defined error from an `Automation` object, set `Err.Number` by adding the number you selected as an error code to the constant `vbObjectError`, as shown in the following code snippet:
	
	`Err.Raise Number:= vbObjectError + 2040,`
	`➥Source:= "MyClass"`

Source	`object.Source [= stringexpression]` *object* is the `Err` object. *stringexpression* represents the application generating the error. This property returns or sets the name of the object or application that originally generated the error. The `Source` property specifies a string expression that is usually the class name or programmatic ID of the object that caused the error. `Source` is used to provide your users with information when your code is unable to handle an error generated in an accessed object. When generating an error from code, `Source` is your application's programmatic ID.

D

Coding and Naming Conventions for VBScript Developers

by Drew Kittel

This appendix outlines a variety of recommended coding and variable naming conventions for VBScript developers. Coding and naming conventions are suggestions or recommendations to standardize the way in which developers implement the most basic of functionality in a language or development environment. Naming and coding conventions can cover topics such as these:

- Variable naming
- Variable scope prefixes
- Procedure naming
- Object naming
- Constant naming
- Code commenting
- Using VBScript in HTML documents

You might wonder why you should bother with using conventions. The main reason is that, by following a standardized set of recommendations, you are making your code easier to read, understand, and maintain—for others as well as yourself. Using standard conventions helps ensure that you are speaking the same "dialect" of the VBScript language as most of your fellow Visual Basic developers.

Using Variable Naming Conventions

Although VBScript has just one primary data type (the Variant type), it has several subtypes. As you might expect, using a standard naming convention for each subtype helps you and fellow developers immediately recognize the subtype of a variable simply by reading its name. VBScript variable naming conventions use standard prefixes. Table D.1 lists the recommended prefixes and an example of each.

Table D.1. VBScript variable naming conventions.

Subtype	Prefix	Example
Boolean	bln	blnFound
Byte	byt	bytPixelData
Date (Time)	dtm	dtmBegin
Double	dbl	dblDelta
Error	err	errOrderNum
Integer	int	intTotal
Long	lng	lngDist

Subtype	Prefix	Example
Object	obj	objCurrent
Single	sng	sngAverage
String	str	strLastName

Microsoft recommends that you use the prefixes listed in this table along with descriptive names when naming variables in your scripts.

Providing Cues about Variable Scope

Complex VBScripts can grow in size rapidly. When this is the case, it is nice to be able to determine something about the scope of variables in use. VBScript variable scopes occur on two levels:

■ *Procedure-level scoping* applies to variables declared in events, functions, or subprocedures. The visibility of these variables is limited to the procedure in which they are declared.

■ *Script-level scoping* applies to variables declared in the HEAD section of an HTML document (in other words, outside of any procedure). These variables are visible to *all* procedures in the script.

To provide a simple indication of a variable's scope (without increasing its size too much), Microsoft recommends that you add a single-letter prefix to the names of script-level variables. A procedure-level variable of subtype Double, for example, might be named dblAmplitude (note that no prefix is used). A script-level variable, however, would be prefixed with the letter s. A variable of Boolean subtype might be named sblnErrorOccurred. Naming the variable in this manner gives an instant indication to anyone reading the code that this is a Boolean type with script-level scope.

Using Descriptive Variable and Procedure Naming

A few guidelines for naming variables and procedures in your scripts follow:

■ A variable name should be of mixed case and long enough to indicate its meaning. Additionally, a variable name should conform to the naming conventions outlined in Table D.1.

■ A procedure name should begin with a verb, should consist of mixed case, and should be long enough to indicate its meaning. A procedure that initializes an array of employee names, for example, might be named InitEmployeeNameArray.

- To maintain the readability of your scripts, you should limit your variable names to 32 characters.
- If you use longer terms frequently, you can use standard abbreviations. Make sure that you use abbreviations (such as Cnt for Count) consistently to avoid confusion in your scripts.

Using Object Naming Conventions

Using a standard naming convention for various objects referenced in your scripts helps you and fellow developers immediately recognize the object type simply by reading its name. Just as with variable naming, VBScript object naming conventions use standard prefixes. Table D.2 lists the recommended prefixes and an example of each.

Table D.2. VBScript object naming conventions.

Object Type	Prefix	Example
3D panel	pnl	pnlGroup
Animated button	ani	aniUserMailBox
Checkbox	chk	chkReadWrite
Combo box, drop-down listbox	cbo	cboEnglish
Command button	cmd	cmdExit
Common dialog box	dlg	dlgFileOpen
Frame	fra	fraLanguage
Horizontal scrollbar	hsb	hsbSoundLevel
Image	img	imgFTPIcon
Label	lbl	lblWarningMessage
Line	lin	linHorizontal
Listbox	lst	lstProductIDs
Slider	sld	sldPercentage
Spin	spn	spnPages
Textbox	txt	txtFirstName
Vertical scrollbar	vsb	vsbRate

Microsoft recommends that you use the prefixes listed in this table along with descriptive names when naming objects in your scripts.

Using Constant Naming Conventions

To easily differentiate constants from variables in your scripts, Microsoft recommends that you make constant names all uppercase and that you use the underscore (_) character between words if the name consists of more than one word. You might use MAX_LIST_INDEX, for example, to specify a constant that has the value of the highest index in an array used in the script.

Commenting Your Code

Anyone who has had the responsibility of maintaining code developed by someone else will attest to the fact that poorly documented and commented code often just exacerbates an already difficult situation. Instead of focusing on fixing bugs or enhancing functionality, code maintainers often are disproportionately concerned with just figuring out what the existing code is supposed to be doing. Therefore, I highly recommend that you get in the habit of commenting your code consistently and accurately.

A few guidelines for commenting your scripts follow:

■ Your scripts should include a header section that describes what the script does—not the details of how it does it (these details are subject to change over time). The header section also should briefly describe objects, procedures, algorithms, dialog boxes, and other system dependencies. Table D.3 summarizes Microsoft's recommendations for the contents of the header section.

■ Include pseudocode (or structured English) in the header section when doing so helps to describe algorithms being implemented.

■ Important variable declarations should include inline comments describing the use of the variable.

■ You should name variables, controls, and procedures using descriptive names that follow the guidelines presented in this appendix. Use inline comments to elaborate on more complex details when appropriate.

■ You should briefly describe any arguments that are passed to a procedure—especially if their purpose is not immediately obvious or if the procedure expects the value of the arguments to be within a specific range.

■ You should describe any function return values and other variables changed by the procedure (especially through reference arguments) at the beginning of each procedure.

Table D.3. Recommended contents for script header sections.

Header Section	Description of Contents
Purpose	Describes *what* the procedure does—not a detailed account of *how*
Assumptions	Lists any external variables, controls, or other elements whose state affects this procedure
Effects	Describes the effect the procedure has on each external variable, control, or other element
Inputs	Explains arguments that are not obvious; each argument should be on a separate line with inline comments
Return Values	Explains the value returned

Using VBScript in HTML Documents

Here are a few guidelines that Microsoft recommends for using VBScript in your HTML documents:

- VBScript procedures, including event procedures for controls, generally should be included in the <HEAD> section of the document. This improves readability by keeping all the code in one place. Many developers prefer to include VBScript code at the end of the HTML document instead. This also is fine; just try to be consistent and keep all code in the same place in the document.

- Use HTML comment tags (<! and >) to bracket any scripting code to ensure that this code will be hidden from browsers that don't support the <SCRIPT> tag.

Listing D.1 shows a template that demonstrates these guidelines for using VBScript in HTML documents.

Listing D.1. Using VBScript in HTML documents.

```
<! Template for VBScript enabled pages >
<HTML>
<HEAD>
<TITLE> </TITLE>
<SCRIPT LANGUAGE="VBScript">
<!
        Function WeCanDeliver (Dt)
                WeCanDeliver = (Cdate(Dt) - Now()) > 2
        End Function
```

```
>
</SCRIPT>
</HEAD>
<BODY>
<FONT FACE=ARIAL SIZE=2> <! global default >

... your HTML content goes here ...

</FONT>
</BODY>
</HTML>
```

E

Web Database Development Frequently Asked Questions (FAQs)

by Drew Kittel

This appendix contains some of the most frequently asked questions by users and developers new to Web database development. This is not an all-encompassing list of questions. If you're interested in adding database access to your Web, however, you'll find that these questions provide most of the basic answers. Here's a list of the questions answered in this appendix:

- What is a Web database?
- Why should I use a Web database?
- How does an intranet DB application differ from an Internet DB application?
- What database-access methods can be integrated with Web applications?
- How can database results be used in a Web application?
- What types of Web applications can use databases?
- Does the DBMS need to reside on the same CPU as the Web server?
- Can I use desktop databases to create Web database applications?
- How is CGI used with Web database applications?
- What CGI languages can I use for database development?
- What security concerns exist with Web DB applications? How can I address these concerns?
- How are query results from a Web database application presented to a user?
- Does a Web client need to know SQL to use a Web database application?
- What role do HTML and forms play in Web database applications?
- Does HTML support embedded-SQL statements?
- What are Microsoft Internet Database Connector (.idc) files?
- What are Microsoft Hypertext Extension (.htx) files?
- Can I use scripting languages such as Perl to access my database?
- What is VBScript and how does it differ from Visual Basic?
- I want to decrease the traffic on my Web server because of the number of incomplete requests or requests with improper information; what can I do?

What is a Web database?

In the recent past, the definition of Web databases included primarily large HTML document repositories that existed at various Websites. Many of these sites allowed reasonably comprehensive searches of these documents via search engines such as WAIS. More recently, however, the view of a Web database has converged with the traditional notion of a database management system (typically, relational) that includes APIs, a search engine, DBA tools, a query language, and so on.

Like any regular database management system, a Web database is a data store or information repository that can be accessed via a query language or programming API. Unlike conventional database systems, however, access to Web databases typically is not achieved by typing instructions at a command line or by using interfaces that are custom designed for use on a specific computer platform.

Web databases are databases accessed via other Web applications—specifically, forms developed using standard (almost) HTML. Using facilities available in HTML, applications programs on the Web server are accessed through a server-side mechanism known as the *Common Gateway Interface* (CGI). This interface enables you to create applications that integrate database functionality and provide access to organizational data repositories on behalf of Web clients (a user and browser). Applications can be designed solely for the purpose of querying a database and returning specific information. Also, the application can incorporate information pulled from a database for use as part of a larger application.

Why should I use a Web database?

An organization might want to use databases in its Web applications for several reasons:

- To better manage the serving of large, document-based information repositories to internal and external users of the information.
- To better leverage and use legacy database systems, the information they contain, and existing applications.
- To unlock the potential of unused data held in organizational databases. Data from databases within various parts of an organization (for example, finance, human resources, project management, and so on) can be consolidated by using Web-based applications and served to users as though it were from a single source.
- To extend the functionality of your Web server so that information you maintain can be made available to the general public and internal users—a task currently being undertaken by many organizations and government agencies whose primary product is information.
- To extend the functionality of your Web server so that new and expanded services can be provided to visitors to your Website.

How does an intranet DB application differ from an Internet DB application?

Functionally, intranet database applications and Internet database applications are the same. In fact, intranet applications simply are subsets of Internet or Web applications; they both implement the same technologies to accomplish their goals. The primary difference between an intranet and an Internet database application is who has access to the database applications. A common misconception about intranets is that they are physically located in a single geographical area (for example, internal to a corporate office building) and are not connected to the Internet. In reality, intranets typically are not physically disconnected from the Internet, and they are not bound by geography. Once again, the definition begins and ends with who can access the data.

What database-access methods can be integrated with Web applications?

Many methods exist for providing database access to your Web applications. Three of the most common methods are using HTML embedded-SQL extensions, codeless interfaces, and custom CGI programs.

HTML-Embedded SQL Extensions

Many database systems provide a mechanism for embedding SQL statements directly within HTML files passed to the Web client by the Web server. When a user submits a query, the HTML file is passed to a CGI program that parses the SQL statements and passes these on to the database system. Results of the SQL query are retrieved by the CGI program, reformatted to HTML, and returned to the requesting client. This mechanism is typical of many gateway products, as well as shareware databases that often support only a subset of the functionality of commercial DBMSs. Additionally, the developer often is limited in his capability to modify the CGI program doing the actual database access and formatting of results.

Codeless Interfaces

Essentially, codeless types of access methods consist of software toolsets (often, Perl scripts) that work with developer-defined template files. These files specify various views into the database and how extracted data should be manipulated and formatted when returned to the requesting client. Programs in the software toolset use these template files to automatically generate HTML forms. These forms, when submitted by the user, are processed by CGI programs that query the database and format the results in accordance with the predefined templates.

Most of the toolsets available today are somewhat manual in nature. In the very near future, however, visual programming tools that implement drag-and-drop technology for building forms interfaces, specifying database queries, and detailing the format of results sent to the user should become more prevalent.

Custom CGI Programs

Customized CGI programs are gateway programs written specifically to accept and process Web client requests for a service provided by the Web server. Typically, these requests are submitted by users in the form of input they've entered in an HTML form. CGI programs designed for database access parse this user input, use it to formulate queries, connect to the database and submit the query, accumulate results, possibly manipulate these results or perform some other specialized processing, and dynamically create HTML documents that are sent back to the Web client. Custom CGI programs have the advantage of generally giving you access to the full range of functionality provided by database APIs or ODBC.

How can database results be used in a Web application?

The use of database query results is somewhat dependent on the type of access method used. Many of the available tools, such as gateway products or *codeless* interfaces (those that implement template files) provide reasonably strong data-formatting and report-generation capabilities. Often, this is all that the application and users require.

But what about cases where you want to do some additional processing on the data? Suppose that you need to perform some statistical processing on the returned data. What if you want to generate charts, maps, or graphs? How about using the results to populate a spreadsheet? These are instances in which custom CGI programming still offers an advantage over Web-application development tools. One of the primary strengths of CGI programs is the capability to extend the capabilities of the Web server not only by adding access to a database, but by providing the capability to integrate other applications as well. So, you now can develop applications that retrieve data from a database and then do some form of value-added processing on that data.

What types of Web applications can use databases?

Virtually any Web application that would benefit from having access to data and information stored in a database can use a database, as long as the Web-application development environment supports the type of database access required. Some typical business examples of Web applications that use databases include online banking and securities trading, online stores, shopping malls and catalogs, customer services, product information, online technical support, real estate advertising, recruiting, and specialty product sales.

Intranet Web database applications also abound. Organizations have found that database-based Web applications can integrate many of the functions of corporate MIS systems and groupware products. The resultant proliferation of information sharing, improved operating efficiencies, and improved employee productivity have paid for the cost of development several times over.

Does the DBMS need to reside on the same CPU as the Web server?

No. Thanks to client/server database systems, CGI database client applications can reside on the Web server, whereas the database server being accessed can be located virtually anywhere, as long as network access between the database client and server programs exists.

Additionally, many databases, such as Microsoft's Access desktop database system, provide the capability to link to external databases and data sources through ODBC. A Web server residing on a Windows 95 PC, for example, could use cgi-bin, cgi-win, or database gateway programs to access the Access database. The database, in turn, could be configured with links to an external database. This, in effect, provides another method for a Web server to access remote databases.

Can I use desktop databases to create Web database applications?

Yes. Virtually any database that has an Application Programming Interface (API) can be accessed from CGI programs and various gateway products. This is tremendously useful to organizations with legacy databases and information repositories that want to make this information accessible to internal employees and/or external users. Because the database and query models already exist for legacy databases, often all that is required is to develop the interface. (Often, this is just a matter of developing HTML documents, with perhaps the addition of some HTML tag extensions that support SQL query development within HTML.)

Already, gateways are being developed for desktop databases such as Microsoft Access and FoxPro. CGI programs also are commonly being developed in languages such as Visual Basic and Visual C++ and are using database APIs or ODBC functions.

With the availability of very inexpensive yet highly capable PC Web servers, the use of desktop databases is likely to increase for intranet database applications within small companies and organizations to support a variety of project informational needs.

How is CGI used with Web database applications?

CGI provides the means to pass user-specified information (typically, input to a form) to a program that uses that input to create database queries, as well as SQL statements to add, delete, or modify records. CGI simply serves as a mechanism to allow communication between a Web client and CGI database applications programs on a Web Server.

What CGI languages can I use for database development?

CGI database programs and scripts contain the code that accepts data from the Web server (most often passed on from its Web clients) and uses the data as the basis for forming a query (typically SQL) to a database. Additionally, these CGI programs generally are responsible for capturing database query results, formatting the results, and generating the appropriate HTML necessary to present these results to the user.

Note that any language supported on the Web server host machine that also supports access to the database(s) via a database API or ODBC can be used as a CGI development platform. Strictly speaking, however, CGI languages must meet three requirements:

- The language must provide a mechanism for accessing standard input and standard output on the server. This enables user input from HTML forms (using the POST method) to be obtained. Additionally, the capability to write to standard output enables subforms, database query results, and other on-the-fly HTML documents and data to be returned to the Web client.

- The language must provide access to CGI environment variables. This enables user input from HTML forms (using the GET method) to be obtained. Additionally, it enables CGI applications to determine a variety of valuable information, such as the user's Web browser type, additional path information, IP address, and so on. Finally, environment variables provide one mechanism for maintaining the state of user input between connections between the Web client and server.

- The language must provide some mechanism or API for integrating or interfacing with other applications, such as a relational database system. One of the primary reasons for CGI applications is to extend the functionality of the Web server and to offer Web clients access to data, information, and services they otherwise would not be able to access. The capability to provide access to services such as databases requires some sort of API. Additionally, the capability to integrate with other custom-developed applications or across multiple APIs enables you to offer more complex and functional services to your users.

Potential CGI languages for database applications include (but are not limited to) compiled and interpreted languages, such as C, C++, FORTRAN, Perl, UNIX shells, Awk, Expect, and Tcl (and some variants that support Sybase and other database access), as well as some of the newer Perl extensions for client/server database access—for example, Sybperl and Oraperl.

What security concerns exist with Web DB applications? How can I address these concerns?

As with any application that accesses a database—and especially those that provide access from unknown users such as the WWW community—security issues are always a major concern. Depending on the level of access your application will need (query, insert, update, or delete), you'll need to consider how to adequately handle access privileges for your database gateway programs.

One way to handle access privileges is to control application access at the document level using specially created database user accounts. For database-access documents that require only query capabilities, for example, you can set up a database user account with read-only privileges. Then, depending on the access level the document requires, you can specify a special access account to handle the transaction. For ODBC database resources, this is as simple as creating a different ODBC data source for each level of access.

Another way to handle access privileges is to use a temporary table to hold database transactions (inserts, updates, and deletes) for batch processing. Using a queuing system such as this gives database administrators the capability to review transactions before processing them.

How are query results from a Web database application presented to a user?

The presentation of query results depends on the access method used. Using database gateway products and codeless interfaces often requires you to use template or report files to define the structure and layout of results presented to the user. Although many of these methods enable you to nicely format presentations for the user, they typically don't provide the degree of flexibility offered by custom CGI programs.

CGI programs, on the other hand, enable you to generate comprehensive HTML presentations from database query results on-the-fly. You have ultimate control over tasks such as these:

- Additional data processing required
- Integration of other applications

■ Creation of on-the fly graphics

■ Generation of form elements based on query results

These presentations also can include a complex mixture of data types, including text, graphics, images, dynamically generated hypertext links, and other MIME data types such as audio and video.

Does a Web client need to know SQL to use a Web database application?

No. This is one of the primary benefits of Web databases. Users of Web database applications typically don't need to know a query language or the underlying database table structures and relationships in order to submit a query to the database.

Users generally interact with database applications via HTML forms developed for them by the application developers. User input to these forms then is used to formulate a query that is sent to the database by a CGI program or database gateway program. All the user needs to know how to do is use a mouse. In fact, users often don't even know that information presented to them as a result of form input is derived from a database at all.

What role do HTML and forms play in Web database applications?

HTML forms provide the standard interface by which users interact with a Web database application. Typically, an HTML form includes user-input objects such as checkboxes, radio buttons, scrollable menus, and text-input boxes. These input elements enable the user to make selections or provide input that ultimately is used by CGI programs or database gateways to formulate SQL queries to a database when the form is submitted to the Web server. This input can be used to fill in one or more parts of a standard SQL query, such as a table; fields in a SELECT statement; or values required to generate WHERE, ORDER BY, GROUP BY, or COMPUTE clauses. Well-designed forms abstract the database details from the user simply by providing the input objects and range of choices appropriate for each.

HTML forms can be used as an interface to a variety of Web applications, including these:

■ Online entry forms for ordering products from your online catalog.

■ Entry forms to enable users to add information to your customer mailing lists, technical user group-member lists, or guest lists.

- Forms to acquire input for surveys.
- Any number of databases to acquire information about technical issues, special subjects of interest, and information about your product line and offerings.
- Technical support or a "help desk" for your products and services. When used with FAQs and database-access forms, this type of application can provide public users and internal technical-support representatives with the information they need.

Does HTML support embedded SQL statements?

Not directly. Numerous commercial and freely available gateway products do enable you to embed SQL or variants directly into HTML documents, however. When submitted, these HTML documents, form input, or hidden variables are parsed, and the gateway handles the details of interpreting the embedded-SQL statements, formulating a query, contacting the database, and collating query results for presentation to the user.

What are Microsoft Internet Database Connector (.idc) files?

Microsoft Internet Information Server includes a dynamic link library interface called the *Internet Database Connector* (IDC). The IDC uses specially formatted .idc documents to identify key database access parameters, such as the ODBC resource name, the SQL statement to execute, the Hypertext Extension template file to post results to, the user name to use when accessing the data source, and any required parameters. Here is a sample .idc file:

```
Datasource: pubs2
Username: admin
Template: employee.htx
RequiredParameters: EmployeeId
SQLStatement:
+SELECT FirstName, LastName
+ FROM Employees
+ WHERE EmployeeID = %EmployeeID%
```

What are Microsoft Hypertext Extension (.htx) files?

Hypertext Extension files are used by Microsoft IIS to identify the specially formatted HTML documents that will include special tags used to handle such items as looping constructs for multirow results and `if-then-else` control blocks. Microsoft IIS references `.htx` files within an accompanying IDC file, as shown in the previous question. Here is a sample `.htx` file:

```
<html>
<title>Employee Lookup</title>
<BODY>

<%begindetail%>
<%if CurrentRecord EQ 0 %>
<STRONG>Employee:</STRONG> <%FirstName%> <%LastName%></h4>
<%endif%>
<%enddetail%>
<%if CurrentRecord EQ 0 %>
<h4>No employee records found.</h4>
<%else%>
<%endif%>
</body>
</html>
```

Can I use scripting languages such as Perl to access my database?

Yes, but there might be limitations, depending on the database you'll be accessing. If your database platform supports command-line access through interface programs such as Oracle's SQL*Plus or Sybase's iSQL, for example, you can launch the interface program from within any scripting language. Additionally, Perl has been ported to support several database platforms, such as Sybase (Sybperl) and Oracle (Oraperl). These Perl interfaces access their respective databases via special Perl subroutines.

Here is some sample code to access a Sybase database via a Sybperl environment:

```
$dbh->dbcmd("select FirstName, LastName");
$dbh->dbcmd("from Employees");
$dbh->dbsqlexec;

$status = $dbh->dbresults;

while (@row = $dbh->dbnextrow) {
    print "Employee Name: @row[0] @row[1]<BR>\n");
}
```

What is VBScript and how does it differ from Visual Basic?

VBScript represents the low end of the scale of the Microsoft VB family, which also includes Visual Basic for Applications (VBA) as well as Visual Basic 5. VBScript is a subset of VBA and

VB, and it was designed to provide client-side scripting capabilities within Microsoft's Internet Explorer Web browser. The capability to perform client-side processing opens up an entire new realm in Internet applications development. VBScript provides the capability to perform client-side functions such as validating user input. It also enables you to develop highly interactive user interfaces complete with embedded ActiveX controls.

Although VBScript originally was a language of modest capabilities, it quickly is maturing into a full-fledged language that provides many of the niceties found in other common and popular interpreted scripting languages, such as Perl. As of this writing, VBScript only has native support within Internet Explorer. Plug-ins are available, such as that developed by NCompass, which enables you to use VBScript and ActiveX within Netscape browsers, too. Microsoft also has indicated that Internet Explorer and VBScript soon will make their way to UNIX platforms as well.

I want to decrease the traffic on my Web server because of the amount of incomplete requests or requests with improper information; what can I do?

You can do two things. First, the forms for your application should provide the user with some visual clue that certain fields must be completely filled out in order for the request to be handled properly when submitted. A common idiom is to mark required fields with an asterisk (*) character.

Second, you should start taking advantage of the functionality provided by VBScript to perform validation of user input on the client browser. With VBScript, you can validate that users not only supplied input to required fields, but that input to all fields meets certain criteria that you establish. Your scripts can perform range checking, for example, to make certain that a user enters reasonable numeric and text values in appropriate fields. The level of sophistication you use in checking user input is limited only by your needs and imagination.

If users supply incorrect or inappropriate information, your scripts can prompt them with a `MsgBox` dialog box (or by using the `alert` method). You even can use VBScript to set the cursor focus to the offending field automatically—another nice way to make things easier for your users.

F

Online WWW Database Development Resources

by Drew Kittel and Mark Swank

The World Wide Web abounds with numerous (and growing) wonderful sites full of great examples, technical information, and product summaries pertinent to Web applications development in general and Web database applications development specifically. Many of these resources can be located easily by using your favorite Net search engines, whereas others are less prominent. This appendix lists some of the sites we came across while writing this book. These sites contain a wealth of valuable information and links to other resources as well. They are well worth a look, especially if you are just getting started with Web database development.

O'Reilly Developers Corner

`http://website.ora.com/devcorner`

On the O'Reilly Developers Corner site, you will find

- Links to download a free evaluation of the WebSite server. This is a Windows CGI–compliant server that enables you to rapidly get up and running with VB/CGI applications.
- Links that enable you to freely download the `CGI32.BAS` Framework for Visual Basic module, which greatly simplifies many tasks associated with Widows CGI development using VB.
- Links to several sample programs that you can emulate to get started quickly.
- White papers about Windows CGI, VB/CGI development, using the Website Server, and choosing among development tools (such as SSI, CGI, server APIs, and so on) to match your needs.

Web Developer's Virtual Library: Database

`http://www.wdvl.com/`

The Web Developer's Virtual Library site contains numerous links to a variety of sites pertaining to Web database development.

Here are some of the topics for which you'll find links:

- Numerous resources for free databases, such as mSQL
- A variety of CGI gateway products and freeware
- Several products for embedding SQL directly into HTML documents
- Tools for specifying and automatically creating HTML forms and presentations that represent specified views into a database

- Tutorials and samples of Web database applications and programs
- Web-authoring tools
- Information on a variety of Web database research efforts
- Vendor-specific development tools and products

This site also includes a form that encourages visitors who have their own Web DB–related sites to submit information to have their sites listed as links from this page. Therefore, the volume and scope of this page are updated continually and reflect the latest happenings in Web database development.

Web Developer's Series Overview

`http://www.iftech.com/oltc/webdev/webdev0.stm`

The Web Developer's Series site, operated by Interface Technologies Corporation, contains a nice series of articles and tutorials written by Marshall Brain.

This series covers a broad spectrum of Web development topics, including the following:

- HTML forms
- CGI
- Database access from CGI scripts
- Java and JavaScript
- Introduction to Perl

How To Do a Searchable Database

`http://www2.ncsu.edu/bae/people/faculty/walker/hotlist/isindex.html`

The How To Do a Searchable Database site includes samples that use search engines, interfaces to relational databases, and other tools. It also contains links to numerous other sites of information for Web database development.

Database Demos

`http://bristol.onramp.net/`

The Database Demos site, operated by Bristol Database Resources Inc., provides access to demos of Web database applications using Oracle, Oraperl, and C.

The DBI (Database Independence) Site

http://www.hermetica.com/technologia/DBI/

The Database Independence Site contains a wealth of information and links to sites about Dbperl, a Perl language database access API.

The site includes information, documentation, examples, tutorials, and access to drivers for databases such as these:

- C-ISAM
- DB2
- Informix
- Ingres
- Oracle
- Sybase

Accessing a Database Server Via the World Wide Web

http://cscsun1.larc.nasa.gov/~beowulf/db/existing_products.html

The Accessing a Database Server Via the World Wide Web site contains information and links about a multitude of commercial and freely available Web database gateway products. It also offers links to a Web database discussion forum, where you can ask questions and exchange ideas with others involved in Web database development.

Free Databases and Tools

http://cuiwww.unige.ch/~scg/FreeDB/FreeDB.list.html

The Free Databases and Tools site is maintained by David Muir Sharnoff. It is an attempt to maintain a listing of all known freely available databases, and it contains an abundance of information about where you can find freely available databases and tools. It also provides links to enumerated lists of free compilers and languages.

This site is an excellent reference and starting point, and it provides information on the following:

- Available versions and recent updates
- Available programming interfaces

- Access methods supported
- Query languages
- Brief descriptions and subjective assessments
- Operating system ports
- Discussion group mailing lists
- Restrictions on usage
- Authors
- How and where to obtain the software

Databases and tools listed at this site follow:

- Btree and B+tree libraries
- Cisamperl
- ConceptBase
- Dbf read routines in Perl
- DiamondBase
- Glimpse
- GRAS (*graph-oriented database system*)
- IDBM (*ISAM Database Manager*)
- Ingperl
- Interperl
- Isqlperl
- MOOD5 (*Material's Object-Oriented Database*)
- mSQL (*mini SQL*)
- Oraperl
- Postgres
- Qddb
- Rdb
- Sybperl
- Triton Object-Oriented Database System
- University INGRES
- William's Object-Oriented Database (Wood)
- YOODA (*yet another object-oriented database*)

Databases—Desktop

Here are a few links to vendor sites for information about desktop database systems. Many of these sites provide examples, case studies, information on Internet database applications, evaluation software downloads, and free software add-ons.

dBASE 5.0 for Windows

`http://www.borland.com/Product/DB/dBASE/WindBASE.html`

Microrim—R:WEB

`http://www.microrim.com/`

Microsoft Access

`http://www.microsoft.com/msaccess/`
`http://www.microsoft.com/accessdev/`

Microsoft Visual FoxPro

`http://www.microsoft.com/vfoxpro/`
`http://www.microsoft.com/catalog/products/visfoxp/`

Paradox 7 for Windows 95 and Windows NT

`http://www.borland.com/Product/DB/Pdox/pdxwin95/pdx7.html`

Databases—Large

Large database systems can be defined in many ways. This book generally refers to large database systems as commercially available relational databases that often are several gigabytes in size and operate in multiuser environments. This section presents brief descriptions and URLs to Websites containing information on several of the more popular large relational systems used today.

DB2 World Wide Web Connection

`http://www.software.hosting.ibm.com/data/db2/db2wgafs.html`

The DB2 World Wide Web Connection site contains information on a gateway product that enables you to use HTML and SQL to access DB2 and other databases. This site contains product information, information about existing installations, and links to enable you to down-load evaluation software.

The Illustra site includes information on Illustra's object-oriented database products, including the Web DataBlade Module, which offers tools and functions designed to support the development of interactive Web database applications.

Informix Software, Inc.

http://www.informix.com

The Informix site includes information on object-oriented database products, including the Web DataBlade Module (acquired from Illustra), which offers tools and functions designed to support the development of interactive Web database applications.

Microsoft SQL Server Home Page

http://198.105.232.6/SQL/

The Microsoft SQL Server home page is a good starting point to obtain information about SQL Server. It contains numerous links to product information, Internet resources, software downloads, and so on.

Sybase Website

http://www.sybase.com

The Sybase site includes information on Sybase products, including links to information about the new web.sql product that enables you to integrate Web servers and Sybase SQL Server database applications by using techniques such as embedding SQL in HTML pages.

Welcome to Oracle

http://www.oracle.com/

The Welcome to Oracle site includes information about the Oracle product line, including links to information about the recently released Oracle Web Server and Oracle Power Browser products.

Databases—Shareware

This section provides URLs to sites for information about many of the more popular, freely available shareware database systems. Most of these sites provide information about the product, its capabilities, and how it can be obtained. Many sites also contain examples, case studies, information on Internet database applications, and links to a variety of other related sources of information.

Postgres95 Home Page

http://s2k-ftp.CS.Berkeley.EDU:8000/postgres95

Web-Database Gateways

A growing number of Web database gateway products is available freely or commercially. Most of these products are designed to abstract the details about the actual database access. Instead, you can access a database by creating high-level form definition files that describe viewing the database; embedding SQL queries within HTML documents so that data can be retrieved on-the-fly; or using gateway functions that automatically create HTML forms on-the-fly, based on query constraints defined by the end user. Most of these products also enable you to specify how database results should be formatted for presentation to the user; this often is accomplished through some form of report template file.

The ease and speed with which systems using these products can be developed makes them very attractive for prototyping and developing systems that don't require complex querying capabilities. This section provides URLs to sites for numerous gateways available today.

About Web/Genera

http://gdbdoc.gdb.org/letovsky/genera/genera.html

Web/Genera is a software toolset that enables you to integrate Sybase databases with the Web.

Web/Genera developers simply write high-level descriptions of the Sybase database and how to present the database contents to the user. Web/Genera then uses these descriptions to perform the following tasks:

- Generating SQL commands
- Generating data-formatting instructions
- Extracting data from the database
- Formatting and presenting the data (as HTML) to the user

DB Gateway System (Computer Systems Development Corporation)

http://www.csdc.com/

The DB Gateway System site contains information about a Web database gateway product developed by CSDC while working for the United States Army.

The product enables you to embed statements within HTML forms used by the gateway to pass queries to the database. Additionally, you can specify report template files so that database query results can be returned in a customized manner. The gateway application is a Visual Basic application and currently supports access to Microsoft Access and FoxPro databases.

The site includes a fair amount of information and examples of how the gateway works. It also offers online demos that you can try to get a sense of how the gateway works. This software is available at no cost from this site. Links to required software on the Microsoft FTP site also are provided.

GSQL—A Mosaic-SQL Gateway

http://www.ncsa.uiuc.edu/SDG/People/jason/pub/gsql/starthere.html

GSQL is a gateway that enables forms rendered on a Mosaic browser to access SQL databases. Like other gateway programs, GSQL uses definition files, called *proc* files, to determine how forms should be created and how the user input is assembled into SQL queries for the database to process. The site includes numerous links to sites using GSQL, as well as instructions on downloading and usage.

OraPlex General Info

http://moulon.inra.fr:80/oracle/www_oraperl_eng.html

StormCloud WebDBC

http://www.stormcloud.com/

StormCloud is the developer of WebDBC—a highly capable Web database application development tool that enables you to rapidly develop database applications using virtually any ODBC-compliant database and most common Web servers in use today. WebDBC provides support for ISAPI, NSAPI, CGI, JDBC, ODBC, and HTML 3.0. Additionally, WebDBC provides the unique capability to embed VBScript in results files that are used to process database results.

This site contains several working demos of the product; white papers; a short FAQ on Web database development; and links to download a full-fledged, single-user copy of the product.

WDB—A Web Interface to SQL Databases

`http://arch-http.hq.eso.org/bfrasmus/wdb/wdb.html`

WDB is a software toolset (a `cgi-bin` program written in Perl) that enables you to integrate SQL databases (currently, Sybase, Informix, and mSQL) with the Web. WDB was written for the NCSA HTTP server. It enables developers to describe views of a database via *form-definition files* (FDFs). Using these FDFs, WDB creates on-the-fly HTML forms that enable users to query a database. The FDFs also enable you to define a template describing how results should be formatted and then presented to the user.

More WWW-DBMS Gateways

The following sites are great starting points to gather information on a variety of freely available and commercial database gateway products and tools. The information is amply supplemented with links to more in-depth and alternative sources of information.

```
http://grigg.chungnam.ac.kr/~uniweb/documents/www_dbms.html
ftp://ftp.inf.ethz.ch/pub/publications/papers/is/ea/gisi95t2.html
http://gdbdoc.gdb.org/letovsky/genera/dbgw.html
http://www.stars.com/Reference/Bookmarks/Software.html#DB
```

Miscellaneous Sites

Numerous additional WWW development resources abound at various sites. Virtually any topic or problem you can think of has been addressed or experienced by others willing to share what they've learned through experience. In fact, many of these sites contain brief examples that illustrate key fundamental usage of various databases (such as Sybase and Oracle), Perl language extensions (such as Sybperl), and information on CGI programming in general.

This section presents URLs to several sites we found useful while developing this book. We encourage you to explore these sites and the many links they contain. These are excellent starting points if you're undertaking WWW database applications development or are interested in learning more about WWW applications development in general.

Browser Watch

`http://www.browserwatch.com/`

This site provides a one-stop update on the latest happenings (and rumors) in browsers, ActiveX controls, plug-ins, and everything else related to Web applications development. You'll find links to browser listings, galleries of ActiveX controls, and numerous examples. This is a must-visit site that should be added to your list of favorites.

CGI Information

```
http://www.yahoo.com/
```

Follow these four hypertext links

> Computer
> Internet
> World Wide Web
> CGI—Common Gateway Interface

in succession to find a treasure trove of information about CGI development.

This site on Yahoo! contains a comprehensive list of CGI programming references, including links to sites where you can download libraries for performing CGI programming in C, Perl, and other languages. It is updated frequently.

Integrating Structured Databases into the Web: the MORE System

```
http://rbse.jsc.nasa.gov/eichmann/www94/MORE/MORE.html#HDR1
```

JWalk & Associates

```
http://www.j-walk.com/vbscript/
```

This site, developed by JWalk & Associates, is simply one of the best sites around when it comes to illustrating many of the amazing things you can do with VBScript and ActiveX. It provides numerous examples that use the following:

- VBScript only
- VBScript and ActiveX
- VBScript and the HTML layout control

This is a must-visit site!

Oraperl

```
http://rsgi01.rhic.bnl.gov/html/local/oracle/oraperl.html
```

SybPerl—Frequently Asked Questions (FAQs)

```
http://reality.sgi.com/employees/pablo_corp/Sybase_FAQ/Q4.4.html
http://www.umanitoba.ca/campus/administrative_systems/at/sybperl-faq.html
```

VB4/Access CGI Programming

`http://solo.dc3.com/db-src/index.html`

World Wide Web Databases and Searching

`http://www.yahoo.com/Computers_and_Internet/Internet/`
`➥World_Wide_Web/Databases_and_Searching`

Follow these four hypertext links

> Computer
> Internet
> World Wide Web
> Databases and Searching

in succession to find a wealth of information about Web database development and Web searching technologies.

This Yahoo! site contains numerous links to sites dedicated to database topics, many of which contain Web database information. It is updated frequently.

An Overview of MIME

by Drew Kittel

This appendix provides an overview of MIME data types: what they are, how they are used, and their increasing importance in Web-based multimedia applications—including the presentation of information resulting from a database query. Anyone who wants to develop Web applications that will provide more than just text-based functionality should have at lease some knowledge of MIME. In fact, HTML is a fundamental MIME data type; without it, most of today's Web applications would not be possible.

What Is MIME?

It's not a stretch to say that without the MIME standard, many of today's Web applications would not exist as we know them. HTML is well known among Web application developers, but how many developers are aware that HTML is a MIME data type? But MIME doesn't stop there—it defines a (growing) set of data types that enable you to create Web applications, such as the results of database queries, that incorporate multimedia components such as audio, video, and animated graphics.

Multipurpose Internet Mail Extensions (MIME) is a newer Internet mail standard that builds on and greatly extends the functionality of the earlier e-mail standards (primarily RFC 821 and RFC 822). MIME specifies how to send multipart, multimedia, and binary data over the Internet.

Some of the new capabilities of e-mail that MIME extensions provide follow:

- Incorporating multiple objects in a single message
- Sending text without limits on line length or overall message length
- Using character sets other than ASCII
- Creating messages using multiple fonts
- Sending binary or application-specific (non-human-readable) files
- Sending images, graphics, audio, video, and multimedia messages
- Labeling parts of messages so that recipient mail programs can determine how to handle them

MIME messages can handle a variety of data types used on the Internet, because MIME replaces previous encoding methods (including uuencode) with an encoding method called *Base-64*. This method is more robust and is not subject to the limitations and interoperability problems that other encoding mechanisms present.

The MIME standard is defined in large part by the Internet standards documents RFC 1521 and RFC 1522.

MIME Uses

There are many obvious uses for MIME, including sending images, word processing documents, audio or video clips, binary executable programs, and even plain ASCII text (yes, you still can do the simple stuff) as part of your e-mail. These are common functions allowed by most of today's newer e-mail systems.

What might not be so obvious is the functionality that MIME brings to CGI programs used to create on-the-fly data presentations and to format output of database processing performed by a Web server on behalf of a Web client. In fact, the very creation of HTML documents that a client browser can render depends on the use of MIME. Remember from Chapter 18, "The Common Gateway Interface (CGI)," that if data is to be returned to a Web client by a CGI program, the data must be prefaced by this MIME `Content-type` data header:

```
Content-type: text/html
```

You also can use MIME data types to spice up HTML documents and presentations by allowing links to multimedia components such as graphics, images, audio, video, and server-push animation. You use these types not simply to make the presentations nicer, but also to extend the functionality of the applications and to add value for your users.

Many of your readers who enjoy surfing the Net have experienced MIME without even realizing it. Many sites now incorporate links to audio and video clips to enhance their documents. Figure G.1 shows part of the United States Department of State's Heroes page.

FIGURE G.1.

Using audio and video MIME data types.

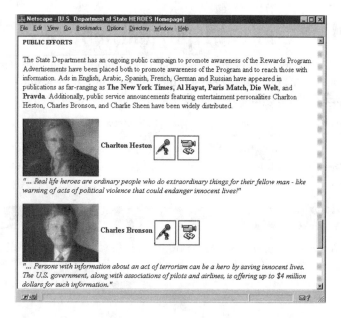

RESOURCE

The United States Department of State's Heroes page is a nice example of how you can incorporate audio and video into an HTML document. You can find it at this URL:

`http://www.heroes.net/pub/heroes`

The HTML code to generate the links in this example follows:

```
<IMG SRC="http://www.heroes.net/pub/heroes/gifs/heston.gif" ALIGN="MIDDLE">
<B>Charlton Heston  </B>
<A HREF="http://www.heroes.net/pub/heroes/wavs/heston.wav">
<IMG SRC="http://www.heroes.net/pub/heroes/gifs/audio.gif" ALIGN="MIDDLE"></A>
<A HREF="http://www.heroes.net/pub/heroes/avis/heston1.avi">
<IMG SRC="http://www.heroes.net/pub/heroes/gifs/video.gif" ALIGN="MIDDLE"></A>
```

This example illustrates how easy it is to incorporate multimedia components and MIME data types into data presentations. The small GIF images of an audio speaker and video camera are used as hypertext links and provide visual cues to the user that audio or video data is available by clicking those links. The links are used to point to video data (`heston.wav`) and audio data (`heston1.avi`). The `heston.wav` file is a MIME file of type `audio/x-wav`, which means that it is audio data of the experimental subtype (format) `x-wav`. The `heston.avi` file is a MIME file of type `video/x-msvideo`, which means that it is video data of the experimental subtype (format) `x-msvideo`.

MIME Content Types and Subtypes

The MIME standard defines a number of new header fields, one of which is the `Content-type` header field. This header field specifies the type and subtype of data in the body of a message, as well as the encoding of that data. The syntax for a `Content-type` header field follows:

`Content-Type := type "/" subtype [";" parameters]…`

Here, *type* declares the type of data, *subtype* specifies a specific format for that data type, and *parameters* modifies the content subtype. Note that each type must be specified with a subtype.

RESOURCE

You can get an up-to-date list of registered MIME types and subtypes, including a complete list of the latest application subtypes, at

`ftp://ftp.isi.edu/in-notes/iana/assignments/media-types/media-types`

This site contains comprehensive information and references about each registered type. You can reference documents related to specific media types by specifying the type and subtype, as shown here:

```
.../media-types/type
.../media-types/type/subtype
```

You would use the following URL, for example, to get information about the `msword` MIME application subtype:

```
ftp://ftp.isi.edu/in-notes/iana/assignments/media-types/application/msword
```

Content-Types

Table G.1 lists the seven primary `Content-type` header fields specified by the MIME standard. These types are discussed in more detail later in this section.

Table G.1. `Content-type` header fields.

Content-type	*Function*
application	Transmits application data or binary data that does not fit other MIME type categories
audio	Transmits voice or audio data
image	Transmits image data (such as GIF or JPEG)
message	Encapsulates mail messages
multipart	Composes and transmits messages consisting of more than one body part (these body parts can consist of different data types)
text	Sends textual information
video	Transmits video data and possibly integrated sound data

Application Content-type

You use `Application Content-type` to send data that does not fit into the other `Content-type` categories. This can include uninterpreted binary data. Currently, nearly 40 valid subtypes exist. This list is growing steadily as vendors continue to register types specific to their applications. Here is a representative sample of subtypes:

■ cybercash

■ msword

- ■ octet-stream
- ■ oda
- ■ postscript
- ■ rtf
- ■ vnd.ms-excel
- ■ vnd.ms-powerpoint
- ■ wordperfect5.1

The following example shows how to specify an Application Content-type header indicating that the message body contains a PostScript document:

```
Content-type: application/postscript
```

Audio Content-type

You use Audio Content-type for audio data. The receiving user or application must have adequate capabilities for interpreting the audio format and outputting the sound. Valid subtypes follow:

- ■ 32kadpcm
- ■ basic

The following example shows how to specify an Audio Content-type header indicating that the audio data is in basic (8-bit ISDN μ-law encoding; 8000Hz, single-channel) format:

```
Content-type: audio/basic
```

Image Content-type

You use Image Content-type for image data. The receiving user or application must have adequate capabilities for interpreting the image format and displaying the data. Valid subtypes follow:

- ■ cgm
- ■ g3fax
- ■ gif
- ■ ief
- ■ jpeg
- ■ naplps
- ■ tiff
- ■ vnd.dwg
- ■ vnd.dxf
- ■ vnd.svf

The following example shows how to specify an Image `Content-type` header indicating that the image data is in JPEG format:

```
Content-type: image/jpeg
```

Message Content-type

You use `Message Content-type` to send messages that are encapsulated. These messages also can be partial or just a reference to an external message body. Valid subtypes follow:

- ■ external-body
- ■ news
- ■ partial
- ■ rfc822

The following example shows how to specify a `Message Content-type` header indicating that the message body is encapsulated and uses the syntax of an RFC 822 message:

```
Content-type: message/rfc822
```

Multipart Content-type

You use `Multipart Content-type` to send messages that consist of multiple body parts, each with its own data type. Valid subtypes follow:

- ■ alternative
- ■ appledouble
- ■ digest
- ■ form-data
- ■ header_set
- ■ mixed
- ■ parallel
- ■ related
- ■ report
- ■ voice-message

Special strings called *encapsulation* and *closing* boundaries are used to indicate where body parts begin and end, as well as where the final body part in the message ends. These strings are indicated by a mandatory parameter named `boundary`. Any information before the first encapsulation boundary (often called the *preamble*) or after the closing boundary (often called the *epilogue*) is ignored.

An encapsulation boundary is an *end-of-line* (EOL), followed by two hyphens, followed by the boundary string. The closing boundary is an EOL, followed by two hyphens, the boundary string, and two more hyphens. A multipart message, for example, might have a `Content-type` header such as this:

```
Content-type: multipart/mixed; boundary="abcdefg"
```

In this case, the encapsulation boundary would be

```
--abcdefg
```

whereas the closing boundary would be

```
--abcdefg--
```

Here is an example of a multipart message that includes both plain text and GIF image body parts:

```
Content-type: multipart/mixed; boundary="MSGBOUNDARY"

--MSGBOUNDARY

Content-type: text/plain

...text...
...text...

--MSGBOUNDARY

Content-type: image/gif

...GIF Image Data...
...GIF Image Data...

--MSGBOUNDARY--
```

Text Content-type

You use `Text Content-type` to send messages that are primarily textual. It is the default MIME `Content-type`. Valid subtypes follow:

- `enriched`
- `html`
- `plain` (the default for Internet mail)
- `richtext`
- `sgml`
- `tab-separated-values`

You also can specify a `Charset` parameter to indicate the text's character set. Here is an example of how to specify a `Text Content-type` header:

```
Content-type: text/plain; Charset=US-ASCII
```

Video Content-type

You use `Video Content-type` for video data. *Video* is a generic term that can include any image or graphical data that changes with time. This data can be black and white, gray-scale, or color. Also, it can be coordinated with sound. Video data requires the receiving user or application to have adequate capabilities for interpreting the video format and displaying the data. Valid sub-types follow:

- mpeg
- quicktime
- vnd.vivo

The following example shows how to specify a `Video Content-type` header indicating that the video data is in MPEG format:

```
Content-type: video/mpeg
```

Experimental and Private MIME Types

In addition to seven primary `Content-type` header fields and their respective subtypes, the MIME standard supports private or experimental types, subtypes, and parameters. These typically are enumerated by an `x-` prefix. This example specifies FrameMaker documents, for example:

```
application/x-framemaker
```

> **CAUTION**
>
> The meanings of these types, subtypes, and parameters depend on agreements between the senders and receivers of such data. Both sides must know and agree on the interpretation. The list of these types is growing daily. Just because an `x-`type or `x-`subtype exists, however, does not mean that any standardization exists or that a particular type is a registered type. Note also that several experimental or private types exist that have foregone the use of the "required" `x-` prefix in their names.

MIME Extensibility

One of the MIME standard's major strengths is its extensibility. The creators of the standard expected that the set of `Content-type`/subtype pairs (and their parameters) would grow with time. To ensure orderly growth, the MIME standard defines a registration process by which creators of MIME types or subtypes can register these types. The process uses the Internet

Assigned Numbers Authority as a central registry for these numbers. Note that as more vendors and organizations develop Web-enabled applications, the number of registered types is expected to grow considerably.

So Why Is This MIME Stuff Important?

So what does MIME have to do with developing Internet applications? MIME standards play a role in virtually all data transactions on the Internet and intranets. Having some knowledge of MIME standards and MIME media types is important for both users and developers.

The User's Perspective

Multimedia is quickly becoming commonplace on desktop computing platforms. It's difficult to buy systems that don't support some form of audio output and video display. Also, more and more Web sites are incorporating audio and video into their HTML presentations. This trend is expected to increase.

Web users therefore must have some knowledge of MIME media types so that they can configure their Web browsers to take advantage of the more common multimedia components served by Web sites. An increasing number of Web sites are developing and serving non-standard and experimental MIME types, and many of them provide downloadable plug-ins or helper applications that understand how to interpret and render the non-standard MIME data types.

Helper applications and plug-ins are programs invoked by Web browsers in response to receiving data of various MIME types. Many browsers—such as Netscape, Internet Explorer, and Mosaic—come with helper and plug-in applications that are preconfigured for common data types such as GIF and JPEG images. Other helper applications must be configured by the user in order to properly handle some MIME types. Using Netscape to handle audio data of MIME type audio/x-wav (WAV format files), for example, requires the user to specify an application to invoke when this data type is received by the browser. The same is true for video data of MIME type video/x-msvideo (such as AVI format files).

Under Netscape, you can configure helper applications by choosing Options | General Preferences and then selecting the Helpers tab, as shown in Figure G.2.

You can configure other major browsers by using similar methods.

Figure G.2 indicates that files of MIME type audio/x-wav should be handled using the Mplayer application under Windows 95. Note that other MIME types such as video/mpeg are set to prompt the user for action instead of launching an application. Users can change this setting if a suitable MPEG player application is available.

On an increasing number of Websites, vendors or individuals who have implemented less-common or non-standard MIME types will provide downloadable plug-in applications for handling their data.

FIGURE G.2.

Setting up Netscape helper applications to use MIME data types.

> **CAUTION**
>
> As with any software, especially freeware, make sure that you are confident of the integrity of the site from which you are downloading a plug-in application. Virus-infected software and poorly designed applications can wreak havoc on your system.

The Developer's Perspective

The most important thing you can do as a developer is to create applications that serve the needs of your users. As the world of computing continues to embrace multimedia applications, it's no longer sufficient to provide primarily text-based data presentations. Of course, I'm not saying that using text is unimportant or trying to discourage you from using it; I'm just pointing out that users respond to applications that take advantage of audio and video, as well as the newer media types and applications. To adequately address your users' needs and desires, you must maintain an awareness of MIME and keep abreast of the new data and application types being introduced.

You also must be aware of MIME media types when integrating applications into your CGI programs. Graphics, server-push animation, video, audio, 2D and 3D charts, plots and graphs, and other means of visualizing data are increasingly being integrated into CGI applications. In some cases, this requires that you use registered, standard MIME types; in other cases, you may need to use (or define) non-standard types. Integrating a VRML application with your CGI applications, for example, would require you to use a non-standard type such as this:

```
Content-type: x-world/x-vrml
```

Finally, when using MIME types that require a user to configure a helper application on his browser, you should give him some indication, via text or an icon, that a certain MIME type will be sent to the browser. This indication enables the user to properly configure his browser with a helper application or to download a plug-in application, if available, from the site.

MIME References

Information on MIME is available from a variety of sites on the Web. Using your favorite search engine, you can find several good starting points. Additionally, the URLs listed in the following resource point to the original Internet Mail standards documents, MIME FAQs, sites for MIME standards documents, and some MIME overview documents.

RESOURCE

Browse these URLs to learn more about MIME types, subtypes, standards, and uses:

```
ftp://ds.internic.net/rfc/
http://www.oac.uci.edu/indiv/ehood/MIME/1521/rfc1521ToC.html
http://www.oac.uci.edu/indiv/ehood/MIME/1522/rfc1522ToC.html
http://www.cis.ohio-state.edu/hypertext/faq/usenet/mail/mime-faq/top.html
http://www.netscape.com/assist/helper_apps/what-is-mime.html
http://www.netscape.com/assist/helper_apps/media-types.html
http://www.cs.indiana.edu/docproject/mail/mime.html
ftp://ftp.uu.net/networking/mail/mime/mime.ps
```

H

DBGateway Installation and User's Manual

by Drew Kittel

NOTE

We would like to thank Joe Loyd, Phil Jones, and Larry Perkins for their assistance in helping us get started with DBGateway and for allowing us to use the DBGateway user's manual and documentation as source material for this appendix. Note that this documentation is also available on the CD-ROM accompanying this book.

DBGateway was developed by Computer Systems Development Corp. (CSDC) as part of the United States Army's Flexible Computer Integrated Manufacturing (FCIM) program under the direction of the Communications Electronics Command (CECOM), based at Fort Monmouth, New Jersey.

RESOURCE

You can find additional information on the FCIM program at
`http://fcim.csdc.com`

DBGateway has been in use since October 1995 by FCIM organizations and members. The impetus behind its development was the need to give FCIM engineers at different geographical locations access to existing legacy databases. Because these data sources were Microsoft Access databases, DBGateway is directly geared toward that format. Additional Microsoft FoxPro read-only support was added recently in the hopes of spawning more interest in DBGateway.

You'll find the DBGateway product on the CD-ROM at the back of this book. You can use DBGateway to rapidly develop PC-based Web databases, as discussed in Chapter 24, "The Development of a PC-Based WWW Database System."

CAUTION

As with all freeware, DBGateway is released as-is without any guarantee as to its suitability for any particular task. If you choose to use the software, be sure to read the license agreement.

An Overview of DBGateway

DBGateway is a 32-bit Visual Basic application that provides Web access to Microsoft Access and FoxPro databases via the WinCGI interface. This application enables you to fully use the power and versatility of Visual Basic to develop Web database applications.

DBGateway was developed by CSDC under the United States Army's FCIM program and therefore is distributed to interested parties as freeware. It borrows heavily from (and, hopefully, complements) the work done by Bob Denny and O'Reilly & Associates' WebSite server product. For more information, go to www.ora.com, website.ora.com, and software.ora.com.

System Requirements

To successfully use DBGateway, you must have a system that meets the following requirements:

- A 486/586 PC running Microsoft Windows NT or Windows 95.
- A WinCGI-compliant Web server, such as Netscape or O'Reilly's WebSite.
- One or more Microsoft Access or Microsoft FoxPro databases (.mdb or .dbf files, for example).
- The unzipped DBGateway package. This package contains a standard Windows Setup program that uncompresses and installs the DBGateway package on your system. The package includes the DBGate.exe and DBGate.ini files, all necessary DLLs and OCXs, and installation and user documentation. The package also includes the Visitor's Book sample Microsoft Access database and the PhoneBook sample Microsoft Access database.

Installation

This section describes the steps necessary to install the DBGate executable and the included sample Visitor's Book database. The Visitor's Book sample is a Microsoft Access database that implements a Web guest book. It's a simple database, but you can use it to demonstrate the basic principles of using the DBGateway software. The PhoneBook sample database also is included, which you can set up in a similar fashion. PhoneBook is a simple contact-management database with the added option of SMTP messaging for sites that have an SMTP server.

To install DBGateway, the Visitor's Book sample database, and the PhoneBook sample database, follow these steps:

1. Go to the www.microsoft.com URL and follow the links to Free Software Downloads. Download the ActiveX Internet control objects and install them on your system.

> **NOTE**
>
> If you are using NT 3.51, you have to get the beta version of the ActiveX objects because the final version on the Microsoft site only supports NT 4.0. You can get this beta version from CSDC's anonymous FTP server at
> ftp.csdc.com/pub/Software/Utilities/ActiveX.exe

2. Unzip the DBGateway package and store it in a temporary directory on your Web server.

3. Run the included `Setup.exe` file and specify an installation directory.

> **NOTE**
>
> The setup program will not overwrite existing DLLs if you receive a copy error during the execution of `Setup.exe`. If you receive copy errors, note which DLLs or OCXs were indicated and check your Windows and Windows System directories to make sure that these DLL and OCX files exist on your system.

4. On your Web server, create a locally accessible directory in which you can place all your online databases. This will be your `DBDATAROOT` directory.

5. Place the `DBGate.exe` and `DBGate.ini` files into your designated `WinCGI` directory. If you do not have this directory or you do not know where it is located, consult the documentation for your Web server software. Edit the entries in the `DBGate.ini` file to conform to your local system setup.

6. Copy the `visitors` directory from the DBGateway package to the `DBDATAROOT` directory so that `visitors` is a subdirectory of `DBDATAROOT`.

7. Edit the `visitors.ini` file as necessary to conform to your local system.

8. Place the `visitors.htm` file somewhere in your Web document space.

9. Try out the gateway by submitting the `visitors.htm` document through your Web browser.

10. Repeat steps 5 through 8 for the `PhoneBook` database, but change the name of the `phonebk` directory to `pbdata`. Use the `pbdata.db` database to avoid problems with associated tables.

For your own database, you must follow these two additional steps:

11. Create the HTML Query forms for accessing the database. You can use external SQL statements embedded in the HTML form, external SQL statements residing in ASCII files on the server, or the native internal Microsoft Access queries. Of course, if you have an internal query that deletes everything in the database, the last option might not be too appealing. CSDC highly recommends that you use the first or second method.

12. Create the HTML report templates if you want the results to display in formats other than `TABULAR`, which is the default. Note that you must enable tabular reports in the database's `ini` file by including the entry `TabularReportAllowed=1`.

Queries

DBGateway supports the following three methods for submitting databases queries:

- SQL queries embedded in the submitted HTML form (Access/FoxPro)
- SQL queries stored in ASCII files on the server side (Access/FoxPro)
- Internal database queries (Access only)

This section describes only the first two methods because, for the initial release of the software, the third method is disabled. If CSDC gets a significant number of requests for activating the internal method, it will be enabled in a future release. This simplifies matters somewhat, because CSDC does not provide free technical support for users of DBGateway.

HTML-Embedded SQL Queries

The HTML Embedded SQL Queries method uses HTML form elements to formulate the desired SQL statement to be submitted to a specified database. Most of the parameters required for this type of query are passed as hidden HTML form elements, although this is not mandatory. The SQL parameters use an enumerated name designation so that you can divide the various SQL statement sections into different parts of the HTML form. DBGateway automatically concatenates the parts in sequential order to form the actual SQL statement. It's up to you, as the form designer, to ensure that this concatenation results in a valid SQL statement. If it doesn't, DBGateway returns an error message to the client. Unless otherwise noted, all elements are case sensitive and white-space sensitive.

The following general parameters are mandatory and normally hidden from the user:

- `ACTION = { "SubmitExternalQuery" }`
- `DBACTION = { "Query", "Show", "AddDBRecord" "DeleteDBRecord", "EditDBRecord" }`
- `DBNAME = { "string" }`
- `DBPATH = { "string" }`
- `DBTYPE = { "ACCESS", "FoxPro 2.6" }`
- `QUERYNAME = { "string" }`

The following SQL parameters are mandatory for `DBACTION={"Query", "Show"}`:

- `FIELDS n = { "any valid field names separated by commas" }`
- `FROM n = { "any valid table names as they would appear in a SQL "FROM" statement"}`

The following SQL parameters are optional for DBACTION={"Query", "Show"}:

- ■ `COOKIE n = {"string"}`
- ■ `GROUPBY n = { "any valid field names separated by commas" }`
- ■ `HAVING n = { " any valid SQL "HAVING" condition" }`
- ■ `MAXREC = { "any integer greater than STARTREC" }`
- ■ `ORDERBY n = { "any valid field names separated by commas" }`
- ■ `REPORTNAME = { "any valid report filename without the "rpt" extension" }`
- ■ `STARTREC = { "any integer greater than zero" }`
- ■ `WHERE n = { "any valid SQL "WHERE" condition" }`

The following parameter is mandatory for DBACTION=AddDBRecord:

- ■ `TABLENAMEn = { "Any valid tablename" }`

The following parameters are mandatory for DBACTION=DeleteDBRecord:

- ■ `KEYFIELDn = { "Tablename.Fieldname" }`
- ■ `KEYVALUEn = { "any valid field value" }`

The following parameters are mandatory for DBACTION=EditDBRecord:

- ■ `KEYFIELDn = { "Tablename.Fieldname" }`
- ■ `KEYVALUEn = { "any valid field value" }`
- ■ `TABLENAME.FIELDNAME= { "field value to be reset" }`

Additional Notes

The path to the Access database is formulated by DBGateway as this:

```
DBDATAROOT + " /" + DBPATH + DBNAME + "/" + DBNAME + ".MDB"
```

The path to the FoxPro databases is formulated by DBGateway as this:

```
DBDATAROOT + " /" + DBPATH + DBNAME + "/" + tablenames + "DBF"
```

Databases opened with DBACTION="Query" will be opened as read-only for safety reasons. Therefore, so-called Microsoft Action queries are not permitted.

If you receive an Invalid SQL or SQL syntax error message after you submit your form, you might find it helpful to temporarily change the DBACTION="Query" parameter to DBACTION="Show" and resubmit the form. Instead of actually submitting the query, DBGateway returns the interpreted SQL statement to you. You then can examine the statement for clues about the cause of the error.

> **CAUTION**
>
> Although `DBACTION=AddDBRecord` has been thoroughly tested, `DeleteDBRecord` and `EditDBRecord` have not. To allow Web clients to perform these actions is inherently dangerous. As of this writing, CSDC does not have any customers who require this functionality, so testing on these functions has been limited to a small number of cases. If you want to try these functions, do *not* use your real database. Make a copy and try it out on the copy.

`DBACTION=DeleteDBRecord` and `DBACTION=EditDBRecord` perform a search on the specified table(s) for a matching value in the key field. The action is performed on all matching records. Therefore, make sure that your criteria is unique. These actions should be used only on databases that actually use the built-in referential integrity to prevent orphaned table records.

Do not include SQL keywords such as `SELECT`, `FROM`, `WHERE`, and so on in the string values assigned to the SQL parameters previously described. DBGateway uses the SQL parameter names to automatically add these keywords to the appropriate places in the SQL statement for you. The following line of code illustrates *incorrect* usage (note the inappropriate addition of the keyword `FROM` in the string assigned to the value of `FROM0`):

```
<INPUT type=hidden name="FROM0" value="FROM Employees">
```

while the following line of code illustrates the appropriate way to specify a SQL `FROM` statement:

```
<INPUT type=hidden name="FROM0" value="Employees">
```

Concatenation of each enumerated SQL parameter ends at the first break in the sequential order. When debugging SQL queries, it's often best to design the query in the native database application and then cut and paste the resulting SQL statement directly into the HTML form.

Always start building a new query form with `REPORTNAME="TABULAR"`. This enables you to check the results of the query in raw form without the added complication of report template parsing and formatting. After you debug the query, you can concentrate on making it visually appealing.

You can use the `COOKIE` n parameter to pass non-query-generated (static) information to the report template.

Because HTML reserves the use of the quotation mark (') and double quotation mark (") characters, you might have to isolate parts of the SQL statement that use these characters. This might be necessary in order to prevent your browser from misreading your statement. You should implement the SQL statement

```
HAVING fname = "Joe"
```

in an HTML form element, as this example shows:

```
<INPUT TYPE="hidden" NAME="HAVING0" VALUE=" fname = ' ">
<INPUT TYPE="text" NAME="HAVING1" VALUE="Joe'">
```

Also, because HTML reserves the use of the left (<) and right (>) angle-bracket characters, you'll need to use the following substitutions in your SQL statement:

Use This Symbol	Instead of This
LT	<
GT	>
LTE	<=
GTE	>=
NEQ	!=

Server-Side SQL Queries

The Server-Side SQL Queries method uses SQL queries that are stored with the database in ASCII text files on the server side. The only advantage of this method is that the Web client cannot "see" the query elements, because they reside on the server. Of course, this also means that you cannot change the query on-the-fly, and you cannot pass DBGateway any modifying parameters. The queries must reside in the sql subdirectory of the respective database and must conform to the following format:

```
QUERYTITLE=Some descriptive title string
QUERYTYPE={ "IMMEDIATEQUERY", "IMMEDIATESHOW" }
REPORTNAME = { "TABULAR", "any valid report filename
➥without the "rpt" extension" }
SQL=SELECT Employees.*
SQL=FROM Employees
SQL= ORDER BY Department, LastName
...
```

Additional Notes

Setting QUERYTYPE=IMMEDIATEQUERY simply submits the query.

Setting QUERYTYPE=IMMEDIATESHOW returns the interpreted SQL statement (this can useful for debugging purposes).

You can include any number of SQL= statements. These statements are concatenated, in order, to form the submitted SQL statement.

Unless otherwise noted, all elements are case sensitive and white-space sensitive.

To access the Server-Side SQL type of query, use an HTML form with the following general parameters. These parameters are mandatory and normally hidden from the user:

■ `ACTION = { "SubmitExternalQuery" }`

■ `DBACTION = { "GetQueryForm" }`

■ `DBNAME = { "string" }`

■ `DBPATH = { "string" }`

■ `DBTYPE = { "ACCESS", "FoxPro 2.6" }`

■ `QUERYNAME = { "string" }`

Database Reports

Although using report templates is optional (you can just let DBGateway return the raw data in its native table format), these templates are where the real power of DBGateway lies. The best way to learn how to create report templates for your own database is to look at the samples included with the `Visitors Book` and `PhoneBook` databases. You can find the report templates in the `rpts` subdirectory of the respective database. The templates consist of the following mandatory delimited container sections. These templates can contain `FIELD` and/or `COOKIE n` tags that will be parsed out and replaced with the specified field/cookie values from the query response set and/or query form:

■ Report Header

■ Group Header

■ Record Header

■ Record

■ Record Footer

■ Group Footer

■ Report Footer

The following optional record count tags are supported in all sections of the report template:

■ `< CurrentRecordNumber>`: Displays the ordinal position of the current record in the response set.

■ `< TotalRecordNumber>`: Displays the total number of records in the response set.

The following code template illustrates how you can use optional conditional tags in any of the database report template sections to control the report formatting:

```
<IF OPERAND1=" operand1 " OPERAND2=" operand2" OPERATOR=" operator">
   ... HTML code used if statement is true
<ELSE>
   ... HTML code used if statement is false
</IF>
```

Here, operand n is any string, and operator is one of following:

= <> < > <= >=

The <ELSE> tag is optional and *no* nesting of the tags is allowed. As with the report section tags, the conditional tags should be isolated on separate lines.

Additional Notes

All template tags are case sensitive and white-space sensitive.

All section tags, both beginning and ending, must be present and isolated on a separate line.

Using report templates prevents Web clients from obtaining unauthorized field values by modifying the query form.

FIELD tags used in the Report Header section receive values obtained from the first record in the response set. Likewise, FIELD tags in the Report Footer section receive values from the last record.

If the name of a FIELD tag does *not* match any field name in the query response set, it is *not* parsed out. Always view the source of the returned report to look for non-parsed FIELD tags, and then modify the query or report template to correct the problem. Some browsers do not correctly ignore these tags if they are left in the returned form.

If the name of a COOKIE n tag does *not* match any cookie name in the report template, it is *not* parsed out. Always view the source of the returned report to look for non-parsed COOKIE n tags and modify the query form and/or report template to correct the problem. Some browsers do not correctly ignore these tags if they are left in the returned form.

Non-parsed FIELD and COOKIE n tags can confuse some browsers. If the returned form is garbled, it probably means that one of your FIELD/COOKIE n tags was not parsed correctly. If you received part of the form, you can check around the area where the problem first occurred to identify the problem FIELD/COOKIE n tag. Check for misspellings or incorrect case.

Secured Databases

Web access to Microsoft Access databases is controlled though the standard Web server access control and Microsoft's system.mdw file. You can use the Microsoft Access 2.0 Workgroup Administrator to create this system database and to join the workgroup. Then use Access 2.0 to set users and permissions. FoxPro access currently is limited to Web server control only.

To allow DBGateway to communicate with databases that are secured with a System database file, you must pass a user ID and password to DBGateway when submitting a form and set PublicAccessAllowed=0 in the database's .ini file. Place the System database file in the same directory as the database. In addition, if you are using the WebSite server, you must rename `DBGate.exe` and `DBGate.ini` to `$DBGate.exe` and `$DBGate.ini`, respectively, so that the WebSite server will pass these values to DBGateway.

When DBGateway receives a request (query) to a nonpublic database, it checks, in order, for the following:

1. The `UID` (user ID) and `PWD` (password) form parameters. If found, these parameters are used to log onto the `system.mda` or `system.mdw` file.

2. The user ID and password the person used to log onto the Web server. If found, the ID and password are used to log onto the `system.mda` or `system.mdw` file.

If DBGateway cannot find a valid user ID and password, the user is denied access.

Mail

DBGateway has a built-in SMTP module for use with the `PhoneBook` database included in the package. Unlike the rest of the DBGateway program, the SMTP module is *not* database independent. When the SMTP functionality is used, DBGateway expects the specified database to be structured like the included `PhoneBook` sample. You can add other tables and fields to your version of the database, but do *not* change any of the existing table or field names. The messaging capability is based on Microsoft's ActiveX SMTP control. This control is still in the beta stage of development, so if you're contemplating using the SMTP module, make sure that you monitor your Web server frequently in case it throws an exception error. Although these errors will not stop your Web service, they can slow it down by tying up resources and annoying your Web clients.

The following general parameters are mandatory and normally hidden from the user:

- ■ `ACTION = { "SubmitExternalQuery" }`
- ■ `DBACTION = { "SendMail " }`
- ■ `DBNAME = { "string" }`
- ■ `DBPATH = { "string" }`
- ■ `DBTYPE = { "ACCESS" }`
- ■ `QUERYNAME = { "string" }`

The following general parameters are mandatory and normally are selected by the user:

- ■ `MAIL_FROM = { "string" }`
- ■ `MAIL_MESSAGE = { "string" }`
- ■ `MAIL_SUBJECT = { "string" }`
- ■ `MAIL_TO = { "a list of names separated by commas" }`

Additional Notes

DBGateway expects the list of names in the MAIL_TO parameter to be of the form FirstName LastName and/or GroupName.

Names will be parsed into one or more e-mail addresses. Therefore, all names must be contained in the specified PhoneBook, and all groups must have a least one valid member.

The DBNAME parameter should point to the specific PhoneBook database.

Examples

The best way to learn about a new software tool is by example. This section illustrates how two of the basic DBGateway functions—querying a database using SQL embedded in HTML documents and generating a report using templates—are implemented in an application. These examples also are included on the CD-ROM that accompanies this book and can serve as a starting point for developing your first DBGateway-powered Web database applications.

An HTML-Embedded SQL Query Form

Listing H.1 shows a sample query form for DBGateway. This HTML page actually contains a query to one of the CSDC PhoneBook databases. If you're familiar with SQL, you can examine the hidden form elements to understand how the query is implemented.

Listing H.1. A query form for DBGateway.

```
<HTML>
    <HEAD>
        <TITLE>DBGateway PhoneBook</TITLE>
    </HEAD>
    <BODY>
        <BASE TARGET="main">

        <FORM METHOD="POST"
        ACTION="/cgi-win/dbgate.exe">

            <INPUT type=hidden name=" ACTION"
            value="SubmitExternalQuery">

            <INPUT type=hidden name=" DBNAME"
            value="PhoneBk">

            <INPUT type=hidden name=" DBTYPE"
            value="ACCESS">

            <INPUT type=hidden name=" DBPATH"
            value="">
```

```
<INPUT type=hidden name="
QUERYNAME"
value="EmployeeListByMatch">

<INPUT type=hidden name=" DBACTION"
value="Query">

<INPUT type=hidden name="
REPORTNAME" value="Match">

<INPUT type=hidden name=" FIELDS0"
value="Employees.*">

<INPUT type=hidden name=" FROM0"
value="Employees">

<INPUT type=hidden name=" ORDER0"
value="Employees, Department">

<INPUT type=submit name="Submit"
value=" Search For: ">

<SELECT name= WHERE0>

    <OPTION
    SELECTED>LastName</OPTION>

    <OPTION>Department</OPTION>

    <OPTION>Title</OPTION>

</SELECT>

<B> = </B>

<SELECT name=" WHERE1">

    <OPTION
    SELECTED>=</OPTION>

    <OPTION
    SELECTED>NEQ</OPTION>

    <OPTION
    SELECTED>LT</OPTION>

    <OPTION
SELECTED>GT</OPTION>

    <OPTION
    SELECTED>LTE</OPTION>

    <OPTION
    SELECTED>GTE</OPTION>
```

continues

Listing H.1. continued

```
            </SELECT>

            <INPUT type=hidden name=" WHERE2"
            value="'">

            <INPUT type=text name=" WHERE3"
            value="">

            <INPUT type=hidden name=" WHERE4"
            value="'">

        </FORM>
    </BODY>
</HTML>
```

A Report Template

Listing H.2 shows a sample DBGateway report template. The template is an ASCII text file that is parsed prior to returning the query response to the Web client. Each report section is used and displayed as you would expect.

FIELD tags are replaced with their corresponding values for each returned record. All fields in the response set that are not specified by a FIELD tag are discarded prior to returning the response. This prevents Web clients from requesting unauthorized field information.

All FIELD tags that are included in the report template but are not in the response set are left in the returned document as unparsed.

TABULAR reports are not parsed, so if they are enabled, they allow Web clients to access *all* database fields.

Listing H.2. A DBGateway report template.

```
< REPORTHEADER>
    <HEAD>
        <TITLE>DBGateway Member Contact
        Information</TITLE>
    </HEAD>
    <BODY>

        <P>
        <HR>
        <H1>DBGateway Member Contact Information</H1>
        <HR>
        </P>

        <TABLE BORDER>

            <TR>
```

```
                    <TH ALIGN=CENTER>Name
                    <I>(last, first,
                    MI)</I></TH>

                    <TH
                    ALIGN=CENTER>Title</TH>

                    <TH
                    ALIGN=CENTER>Department</TH>

                    <TH
                    ALIGN=CENTER>Phone</TH>

            </TR>

< /REPORTHEADER>

< GROUPHEADER NAME="LastName">
< /GROUPHEADER>

< RECORDHEADER NAME="RECORD1">
     <TR>
< /RECORDHEADER>

< RECORD>
     <TD>
            <A href="/employphotos/< FIELD
            NAME="Photograph">">

            < FIELD NAME="LastName">,

            < FIELD NAME="FirstName">

            < FIELD NAME="MI">.</A>
     </TD>

     <TD><FIELD NAME="Title"></TD>

     <IF OPERAND1="<FIELD NAME="Department">"
       OPERAND2="ACME, Inc." OPERATOR="=">
        <TD><FIELD NAME="Department"></TD>
     <ELSE>
        <TD>Road Runner & Associates</TD>
     </IF>

     <TD>< FIELD NAME="WorkPhone"></TD>
< /RECORD>

< RECORDFOOTER NAME="RECORD1">
     </TR>
< /RECORDFOOTER>

< GROUPFOOTER NAME="LastName">
</GROUPFOOTER>

<REPORTFOOTER>
```

continues

Listing H.2. continued

```
</TABLE BORDER>
<P>Total number of records returned: <TotalRecordNumber></P>
</BODY>
</HTML>

</REPORTFOOTER>
```

Troubleshooting DBGateway

Occasionally, you might experience some difficulties installing or using DBGateway. Here are some common problems/errors encountered:

Error Message:

```
Access violation occurred while copying the file ...\<filename> .DLL
```

Probable Cause:

DBGateway Setup will not overwrite existing files in your system.

Solution:

Rename your existing file to a recognizable name and then try reinstalling.

Error Message:

```
Can't load NMOCOD.dll
```

Probable Cause:

You might not have the DLL and OCX controls registered.

Solution:

Run the `RegSvr32.exe` program in your system directory.

Error Message:

```
Can't load custom control SMPTCT.OCX (error #367)
```

Probable Cause:

You don't have the Microsoft Internet support objects loaded on your system.

Solution:

Download ActiveX from www.microsoft.com.

Error Message:

`This is a Windows-CGI program.`

(This message may appear when you use DBGateway.)

Probable Causes:

(1) You are not running a WinCGI-compatible server.

(2) You are executing DBGateway from Windows and not from an HTML form.

(3) You are not running the required operation system.

Solutions:

(1) See system requirements.

(2) Look at the sample query in the installation and user documentation.

(3) See system requirements.

RESOURCE

For additional information about DBGateway, contact

Computer Systems Development Corp.
3810 Concorde Parkway, Suite 2200
Chantilly, Virginia 22021
Phone: (703) 817-0604
Fax: (703) 817-0903

Or go to this URL:

`http://www.csdc.com and http://fcim1.csdc.com`

Index

X-Y-Z

A V I A C O M   S E R V I C E

The Information SuperLibrary™

Bookstore

Search

What's New

Reference

Software

Newsletter

Company Overviews

Yellow Pages

Internet Starter Kit

HTML Workshop

Win a Free T-Shirt!

Macmillan Computer Publishing

Site Map

Talk to Us

CHECK OUT THE BOOKS IN THIS LIBRARY.

You'll find thousands of shareware files and over 1600 computer books designed for both technowizards and technophobes. You can browse through 700 sample chapters, get the latest news on the Net, and find just about anything using our massive search directories.

All Macmillan Computer Publishing books are available at your local bookstore.

We're open 24-hours a day, 365 days a year.

You don't need a card.

We don't charge fines.

And you can be as **LOUD** as you want.

The Information SuperLibrary

http://www.mcp.com/mcp/   ftp.mcp.com

MACMILLAN COMPUTER PUBLISHING USA

A VIACOM COMPANY

Technical ┐
Support:

If you need assistance with the information in this book or with a CD/Disk accompanying the book, please access the Knowledge Base on our Web site at **http://www.superlibrary.com/general/support**. Our most Frequently Asked Questions are answered there. If you do not find the answer to your questions on our Web site, you may contact Macmillan Technical Support **(317) 581-3833** or e-mail us at **support@mcp.com**.

Teach Yourself Visual Basic 5 in 21 Days, Fourth Edition

—Nathan Gurewich and Ori Gurewich

Using a logical, easy-to-follow approach, this international bestseller teaches readers the fundamentals of developing programs. It starts with the basics of writing a program and then moves on to adding voice, music, sound, and graphics. This book uses shaded syntax boxes, techniques, Q&A, Do/Don't, and workshop sections to highlight key points and reinforce learning.

Price: $29.99 USA/$42.95 CDN New–Casual
ISBN: 0-672-30978-5 1,000 pages

Teach Yourself Active Web Database Programming in 21 Days

—Dina Fleet, et al.

Based on the best-selling *Teach Yourself* series, this must-have tutorial uses a day-by-day approach and real-world examples to teach readers the ins and outs of Visual Basic programming with databases for the Web. In the process, you learn how to use Visual Basic to create powerful content on the Web. The book explores data-aware controls, database connectivity with Visual Basic, and HTML scripting.

Price: $39.99 USA/$56.95 CDN New–Casual
ISBN: 1-57521-139-4 700 pages

Teach Yourself Database Programming with Visual Basic 5 in 21 Days, Second Edition

—Michael Amundsen and Curtis Smith

Visual Basic, the 32-bit programming language from Microsoft, is used by programmers to create Windows and Windows 95 applications. It can also be used to program applications for the Web. This book shows you how to design, develop, and deploy Visual Basic applications for the World Wide Web. The book is presented in a daily format, with each week focusing on a different area of database development. The CD-ROM includes sample code and third-party utilities.

Price: $45.00 USA/$63.95 CAN New–Casual–Accomplished
ISBN: 0-672-31018-X 1,000 pages

Teach Yourself Microsoft Visual InterDev in 21 Days

—Michael Van Hoozer

Using the day-by-day format of the best-selling *Teach Yourself* series, this easy-to-follow tutorial provides users with a solid understanding of Visual InterDev, Microsoft's new Web application development environment. In no time, you learn how to perform a variety of tasks, including front-end scripting, database and query design, content creation, and server-side scripting. The CD-ROM contains Internet Explorer 3.0, Microsoft ActiveX and HTML development tools, ready-to-use templates, graphics, scripts, Java applets, and ActiveX controls.

Price: $39.99 USA/$56.95 CDN New–Casual–Accomplished
ISBN: 1-57521-093-2 800 pages

Tom Swan's Mastering Java with Visual J++

—Tom Swan

Microsoft anticipates that its Visual J++ will fast become the leading Java development tool. This book, written by a leading industry expert and best-selling author, includes chapter summaries, tips, hints, and warnings to teach readers how to program Java applications with Visual J++. Readers learn how to use Developer Studio, visual programming tools, debugger, Java VM, and other Visual J++ features. The CD-ROM that accompanies the book includes source code and Java utilities.

Price: $49.99 USA/$70.95 CAN
ISBN: 1-57521-210-2

Casual–Accomplished
750 pages

Visual J++ Unleashed

—Bryan Morgan, et al.

Java is the hottest programming language being learned today. Microsoft's Windows version of Java, code-named Visual J++, may prove to be even hotter because of several new development features, such as graphic designing, that Microsoft has added to the Java language. *Visual J++ Unleashed* shows readers how to exploit the Java development potential of Visual J++ and how to add interactivity and Java applets to Web pages. The book teaches readers how to exploit the Windows enhancements to the Java environment for "quick and easy" programming. The accompanying CD-ROM includes source code from the book and powerful utilities.

Price: $49.99 USA/$70.95 CDN
ISBN: 1-57521-161-0

Accomplished–Expert
1,000 pages

Teach Yourself Database Programming with Visual J++ in 21 Days

—John Fronckowiak and Gordon McMillan

Using a step-by-step, easy-to-follow format, this complete resource takes you beyond the basic product information and guides you through database integration and interface development. The book highlights new technologies, including JavaBeans, JDBC, DAO Object Library, RDO Object Library, ActiveX, and COM. The accompanying CD-ROM is loaded with scripting and author source code.

Price: $39.99 USA/$56.95 CDN
ISBN: 1-57521-262-5

Casual–Accomplished
750 pages

Web Programming with Visual J++

—Mike Cohn, Jay Rutten, and James Jory

Readers get up-to-speed quickly with this comprehensive new reference on Microsoft's licensed Windows version of Java: Visual J++. This book teaches you how to develop feature-rich Visual J++ applications and explores the advanced features of Visual J++. The accompanying CD-ROM includes various third-party tools, utilities, and demonstrations.

Price: $39.99 USA/$56.95 CDN
ISBN: 1-57521-174-2

Accomplished–Expert
600 pages

Add to Your Sams Library Today with the Best Books for Programming, Operating Systems, and New Technologies

The easiest way to order is to pick up the phone and call

1-800-428-5331

between 9:00 a.m. and 5:00 p.m. EST.

For faster service please have your credit card available.

ISBN	Quantity	Description of Item	Unit Cost	Total Cost
0-672-30978-5		Teach Yourself Visual Basic 5 in 21 Days, Fourth Edition	$29.99	
1-57521-139-4		Teach Yourself Active Web Database Programming in 21 Days (Book/CD-ROM)	$39.99	
0-672-31018-X		Teach Yourself Database Programming with Visual Basic 5 in 21 Days, Second Edition (Book/CD-ROM)	$45.00	
1-57521-093-2		Teach Yourself Microsoft Visual InterDev in 21 Days (Book/CD-ROM)	$39.99	
1-57521-210-2		Tom Swan's Mastering Java with Visual J++ (Book/ CD-ROM)	$49.99	
1-57521-161-0		Visual J++ Unleashed (Book/CD-ROM)	$49.99	
1-57521-262-5		Teach Yourself Database Programming with Visual J++ in 14 Days (Book/CD-ROM)	$39.99	
1-57521-174-2		Web Programming with Visual J++ (Book/CD-ROM)	$39.99	
❏ 3 ½" Disk		Shipping and Handling: See information below.		
❏ 5 ¼" Disk		TOTAL		

Shipping and Handling: $4.00 for the first book, and $1.75 for each additional book. Floppy disk: add $1.75 for shipping and handling. If you need to have it NOW, we can ship product to you in 24 hours for an additional charge of approximately $18.00, and you will receive your item overnight or in two days. Overseas shipping and handling adds $2.00 per book and $8.00 for up to three disks. Prices subject to change. Call for availability and pricing information on latest editions.

201 W. 103rd Street, Indianapolis, Indiana 46290

1-800-428-5331 — Orders   1-800-835-3202 — FAX   1-800-858-7674 — Customer Service

Book ISBN 1-57521-276-5

W9-CXQ-157

New to the Third Edition

- Complete coverage of new Windows 98 features (see Quick Reference on inside covers)

- The complete story on Internet access using the new Windows 98 feature set (Chapters 1 and 2)

- Desktop customization techniques that include modifying the Taskbar (Chapter 3)

- Get the full scoop on how Windows 98 improves on its predecessors, especially Windows 95 (Chapter 4)

- When, where, and how to install FAT32 support on hard disks larger than 528MB, along with possible incompatibilities and pitfalls (Chapter 9)

- Obtain the best performance out of your hard drive with easier-to-use utilities that automatically detect which applications you use most often (Chapter 9)

- Understand how new OLE technologies like ActiveX controls and DCOM (distributed component object model) can help you get work done faster on the Internet (Chapter 11)

- Learn how to automate various Windows tasks using Windows Scripting host (Chapter 12)

- Complete coverage of the latest hardware support in Windows 98, such as AGP, USB, ACPI, and DVD (Chapter 13)

- Learn how to get the best game and multimedia support using technologies such as ActiveMovie, DirectX, WinG, and OpenGL (Chapter 14)

- Make using Windows easier with the Accessibility options that Windows 98 provides (Chapter 16)

- Understand the latest Windows 98 features like multimonitor support, the WebTV for Windows utility, and AGP support (Chapter 17)

- Learn about the new support features for laptop computers (Chapter 18)

- See how Internet Explorer and Outlook Express work together to make your Internet experience richer and more automatic using channels and subscriptions (Chapter 21)

- Create your own Web site using Personal Web Server (Chapter 22)

- Jump right to the solution for many of your hardware and software problems using HelpDesk (Chapter 26)

Peter Norton®

Peter Norton's
Complete Guide to
Windows 98

Peter Norton
John Paul Mueller

SAMS 201 West 103rd Street
Indianapolis Indiana 46290

For Lisa—someone who not only understands, but actually appreciates, uniqueness.

Copyright © 1998 by Peter Norton

THIRD EDITION

All rights reserved. No part of this book may be used or reproduced in any form or by any means, or stored in a database or retrieval system, without prior written permission of the publisher except in the case of brief quotations embodied in critical articles and reviews. Making copies of any part of this book for any purpose other than your own personal use is a violation of United States copyright laws. For information, address Macmillan Computer Publishing, 201 W. 103rd Street, Indianapolis, IN 46290. You can reach MCP's direct sales line by calling 1-800-428-5331.

ISBN: 0-673-31230-1

Library of Congress Catalog No.: 97-69209

01 00 99 98   4 3 2 1

Interpretation of the printing code: The rightmost double-digit number is the year of the book's printing; the rightmost single-digit number, the number of the book's printing. For example, a printing code of 98-1 shows that the first printing of the book occurred in 1998.

Printed in the United States of America

Trademarks

All terms mentioned in this book that are known to be trademarks or service marks have been appropriately capitalized. Sams Publishing cannot attest to the accuracy of this information. Use of a term in this book should not be regarded as affecting the validity of any trademark or service mark.

Executive Editor
Grace Buechlein

Aquisitions Editor
Sunthar Visuvalingam

Development Editor
Sunthar Visuvalingam

Technical Editors
Michael Meadhra
Wallace Wang
Dennis Teague

Managing Editor
Sarah Kearns

Project Editor
Tom Dinse

Copy Editors
Amy Lepore
Chuck Hutchinson
Kate Givens

Indexer
Cheryl A. Jackson

Production Team
Jeanne Clark
John Etchison
Christy M. Lemasters
Heather Stephenson

Overview

Contents

Acknowledgments

Thanks to my wife, Rebecca, for working with me to get this book completed. I really don't know what I would have done without her help in proofreading my rough draft. Both Rebecca and Maxine Mueller deserve thanks for helping to research, compile, and edit some of the information that appears in this book.

Wallace Wang, Michael Meadhra, and Dennis Teague deserve thanks for their technical edit of this book. All three people greatly added to the accuracy and depth of the material you see here.

I would like to thank Scott Clark for his help and direction. His input was instrumental in helping this book achieve the depth of information it required.

Matt Wagner, my agent, deserves credit for helping me get the contract in the first place and taking care of all the details that most authors don't really think about.

The technical support staff at Microsoft (especially those on the Internet beta newsgroups) deserve credit for answering the questions that helped fill in the blanks and made the Windows 98 learning experience go faster.

Finally, I would like to thank Sunthar Visuvalingam and Tom Dinse of Sams for their assistance in bringing this book to print.

About the Authors

Computer software entrepreneur and writer Peter Norton established his technical expertise and accessible style from the earliest days of the PC. His Norton Utilities was the first product of its kind, giving early computer owners control over their hardware and protection against myriad problems. His flagship titles, *Peter Norton's DOS Guide* and *Peter Norton's Inside the PC* (Sams Publishing) have provided the same insight and education to computer users worldwide for nearly two decades. Peter's books, like his many software products, are among the best-selling and most-respected in the history of personal computing.

Peter Norton's former column in *PC Week* was among the highest-regarded in that magazine's history. His expanding series of computer books continues to bring superior education to users, always in Peter's trademark style, which is never condescending nor pedantic. From their earliest days, changing the "black box" into a "glass box," Peter's books, like his software, remain among the most powerful tools available to beginners and experienced users alike.

In 1990, Peter sold his software development business to Symantec Corporation, allowing him to devote more time to his family, civic affairs, philanthropy, and art collecting. He lives with his wife, Eileen, and two children in Santa Monica, California.

John Paul Mueller is a freelance author and technical editor. He has writing in his blood, having produced 36 books and almost 200 articles to date. The topics range from networking to artificial intelligence and from database management to heads-down programming. Some of his current books include an ActiveX/ISAPI programmers guide and a Windows NT Web server handbook. His technical editing skills have helped over 22 authors refine the content of their manuscripts, some of which are certification related. In addition to book projects, John has provided technical editing services to both *Data Based Advisor* and *Coast Compute* magazines. A recognized authority on computer industry certifications, he's also contributed certification-related articles to magazines such as *Certified Professional Magazine*.

When John isn't working at the computer, you can find him in his workshop. He's an avid woodworker and candle maker. On any given afternoon you can find him working at a lathe or putting the finishing touches on a bookcase. One of his newest craft projects is glycerine soap making, which comes in pretty handy for gift baskets. You can reach John on the Internet at `JMueller@mwt.net`.

Introduction

No matter how you look at it, the main focus of Windows 98 is the Internet. Sure, you'll find a lot of really nice hardware support updates in this version of Windows, but the main reason to buy this product is to improve your efficiency when working online. With this Internet emphasis in mind, I decided to cover the Internet as the first topic in this book. You'll learn the fastest and most efficient way to get online fast.

Don't worry that I've forsaken everything else for the Internet, though. You'll learn about all of the new hardware support that Windows 98 provides. There are a lot of new features to cover, such as DVD and the TV Viewer. Some features such as infrared data port support will look new, but they actually first appeared in the OSR2 version of Windows 95.

We'll also explore the wealth of new software support that you'll get, especially in the area of diagnostics. Anyone who has had trouble getting their software to fit without using disk compression will love using FAT32. Windows 98 also provides a new feature that enables you to update your installation by making a simple visit to the Internet.

Overall, you're going to find that there's a lot of things to love about Windows 98 from the user perspective. In fact, about the only area where Windows 98 hasn't made significant progress is in the low-level way things work. Except for WDM (Windows Driver Model) support, most of the things you heard about in Windows 95 still apply for Windows 98.

Who Should Read This Book?

This book's intended audience is intermediate to advanced Windows 98 users who need to get the last ounce of computing power from their machines. I'll provide you with tips and techniques to make Windows 98 easier to use, enhance overall system performance, and improve system stability. Of course, every Windows 98 user can gain something from this book, even if only a better understanding of how Windows 98 works. We'll also spend some time looking at the internal workings of Windows 98. Not only will you learn about where Windows 98 is today, but I'll also help you understand how Windows 98 differs from its predecessors and how these differences will help you become more productive.

What You Will Learn

Here are some of the more important topics I cover in this book:

- Getting the most from the Internet
- Installation tips that everyone can use

- Architectural details—how things work under the hood
- Exploiting the new utilities that Windows 98 provides
- Learn how to use Active Desktop for intranets as well as the Internet
- The purpose of the files in the \SYSTEM folder
- Windows 98 fonts and ways to make them easier to use
- Understand new viewing features like the WebTV for Windows and multimonitor support.
- Performance tips to turn your machine into a speed demon
- Using Outlook Express for all your communication needs
- OLE architecture and how to use OLE in your applications
- Navigating the Explorer interface
- The object-oriented approach to using resources on your machine
- How Plug and Play makes it easier to install new devices
- Enhanced battery life and reduced power costs using Advanced Power Management (APM) and Advanced Configuration and Power Interface (ACPI) features
- Compatibility tips about what works and what doesn't under Windows 98
- The objects available on the context menu and how you can modify the menu to meet your needs
- Modifying your system setup to fully meet your needs
- Work-arounds for potential Windows 98 problems

I spend a great deal of time talking about the Windows 98 architecture in various chapters. There are two reasons for this extensive exposure. First, you, as a user, really do need to know how the operating system works—or at least get an overview—so that you can maximize the way you use its features. Second, you need to know what Windows 98 provides that older versions of Windows didn't. Exploring the architecture is one of the best ways to meet this goal.

How This Book Is Organized

This book divides Windows 98 into functional and task-oriented areas. These parts of the book break each piece of Windows 98 apart to see how it ticks and what you can use it for. Of course, many chapters help you understand what's going on under the hood too. Without this information, it would be difficult at best to make full use of the new features that Windows 98 offers.

I'd like to offer one final piece of advice. Windows 98 is a very user- and data-oriented operating system. It's probably the most user-tuned product available right now for the PC. This doesn't mean that Windows 98 is perfect, nor does it mean that everything is as it seems. Sometimes you'll find something that's so difficult to use that you'll wonder why Microsoft did it that way. For example, I found the Registry really difficult to work with until I discovered all the tools that Microsoft provides to make the job easier. You should take the time to really explore this product and figure out which techniques work best for you. Windows 98 offers more than one way to do every task. You need to find the one that's best for you.

Getting Started with Windows 98

As I mentioned earlier, one the major changes that you'll see in Windows 98 is the Internet. That's why the very first chapter of this book shows you how to get online quickly and easily. Of course, you'll want to eventually read the detailed information provided later in the book. The whole purpose of Chapter 1, "Opening Windows to the Internet," is to get you online.

Even though the Internet is a major player in the Windows 98 update, there are a lot of other features that you need to know about as well. Chapters 2, "Introducing Windows 98," and 3, "The Windows 98 Desktop," help you understand the various interfaces that Windows 98 provides. There are two: Active Desktop and Explorer. The Active Desktop is for those people who want the Internet at their fingertips. Explorer provides the same types of features as Windows 95 did, but with many Internet-related refinements.

Those of you who are upgrading from Windows 95 will want to pay particular attention to Chapter 4, "The Updater's Guide to Windows 98." This chapter helps you understand the new features that Windows 98 provides.

Power Primers

This section of the book has three chapters. The first deals with tuning tips. Getting the best performance and highest reliability is the concern of everyone who's just starting to use a new operating system. Windows 98 offers many ways to tune your system. It would seem that all these controls could help you get a tuned system with a very minimal amount of effort. Actually, the exact opposite is true. All these controls interact—and you have to take these interactions into account as you change settings. Optimizing one area usually means detuning another area by an equal amount.

This section of the book will help you determine what type of tuning you need to perform and how that tuning will affect your system. A little turn here and a bump there can really make a big difference in how your system performs. The idea is to tune each area of Windows 98 in moderation. You also need to take your special needs into account. Even the type of network you use will affect the way you tune your system.

One thing is certain: Windows 98 offers more in the way of reliability and performance features than previous versions of Windows did. Your job now is to decide how to use those features to your benefit. Getting that high-performance system together is the first goal you'll want to achieve under Windows 98. After that, the data-centric approach to managing your system should make operating it a breeze.

The second and third chapters of this section include setup tips (in Chapter 6, "Setup Primer") and startup shortcuts (in Chapter 7, "Startup Shortcuts"). There are a number of ways to set up Windows 98. The Microsoft documentation tells you most of the mechanical information you need but provides very little about the trade-offs of choosing one way over another. What do you have to give up in order to use a Server setup? How does a floppy setup differ from a CD-ROM? These are some of the questions we'll look at in this section.

Of course, I'll also offer a few tips on actually getting the installation done based on real-world experience rather than what should theoretically happen. Sometimes you'll want to do the opposite of what the Microsoft documentation says to do, just to get a more efficient setup. This section of the book looks at some of the tips and techniques I've accumulated over months of beta testing Windows 98.

The Windows 98 Anatomy

Learning to use an operating system often means learning a bit about how it works inside. For some people, a quick overview of Windows 98's internals will be enough, especially if you only plan to use Windows 98 in a single-user mode and really don't need to get every ounce of power from your machine.

But if you do have to manage a large number of machines or need to get inside and learn how things work from a programmer's point of view, you'll really appreciate this section of the book. I don't go into a bits-and-bytes blow-by-blow description, but this section blows the lid off all the architectural aspects of Windows 98. We'll examine every major component of Windows 98, from the file system to the API. I even include some information about the Registry.

Advanced Windows 98 Usage Techniques

Some people learn to use a computer but never learn to use it well. The problem, in many cases, is that they lack knowledge of some of the hidden features that a product provides. In other cases, a lack of system optimization is to blame. Still other people have problems understanding the documentation that comes with the product.

This section of the book is filled with tips and techniques that are so often missing from the vendor documentation. There's a big difference between the way things should work and the way they really do. We'll look at everything from general printing techniques to the latest in multimonitor displays. Laptop computer users will want to pay particular attention to Chapter 18, "Mobile Computing: Notebooks, Telecommuting, and Remote Access," which provides many of the details you'll need to use Windows 98 in a mobile environment. In short, use this section of the book to gain the real-world information you'll need to really use Windows 98 to its full potential.

Making the Right Connections

Getting online doesn't have to be difficult. We begin this section by looking at how Windows helps you get online in a variety of ways, not just the Internet. Of course, the first thing you'll need to know how to do is make a connection and that's what Chapter 19, "Hardware and Software Connections," is all about. You'll also learn some details about how Windows 98 implements various communication features such as Unimodem V support.

We do spend some time looking at Microsoft's solution for getting on the Internet, The Microsoft Network (MSN). In addition, this section of the book provides all of the detailed information you'll need to use the Internet effectively. It fills in the gaps from the first section of the book where you learned to get online and do something useful. Finally, for those of you who like to experiment, we look at how you can use Personal Web Server (PWS) to set up your own small intranet site. Theoretically you could also use PWS with the Internet, but don't plan on servicing a lot of requests when using it.

Networking with Windows 98

Very few companies do without the benefits provided by networks these days. The smallest office usually has a network setup of some kind if for no other reason than simple email and file sharing. The surprising thing is how many home networks are popping up. Not only are these networks used for the obvious applications like allowing a child to access some of the files on their parent's machine, but new applications like game playing as well. It's surprising to see just how many new games allow two or more people to play a game using a simple network setup.

Suffice it to say that with all these new applications for home and small business networks, the need for network-specific information becomes greater every day. Although this section can't fully explore every networking solution available to you, it does fully explore the solutions supported by Windows 98.

Given the networking environments in which you'll use Windows 98, security doesn't seem like it would be that big of an issue. However, even a small company has to protect its data. Needless to say, we'll spend some time looking at security issues in this section of the book as well.

Troubleshooting Windows 98

Have you ever installed something and gotten it to work right the first time? That's what I thought. I usually have some problems, too. Unlike the Macintosh, the PC is made up of parts that come from a myriad of vendors. All these parts are supposed to work together, but sometimes they don't.

A lot of hardware and software installation-related problems have nothing to do with hidden agendas or vendor ineptitude. Some problems occur because of a poorly written specification. One vendor interprets a specification one way, and another uses a very different interpretation. The result is hardware and software that really don't work together. Each one follows the "standard," and each one follows it differently.

Other times, a user will shoot himself in the foot. How many times have you thought that you did something according to the instructions, only to find out that you really didn't? It happens to everyone. Even a bad keystroke can kill an installation. Take the Windows Registry. It's all too easy to take a misstep when editing it and end up with an operating system that won't boot.

Even if you do manage to get a fully functional system the first time through and you keep from shooting yourself in the foot, what are the chances that the installation will stay stable forever? It's pretty unlikely. Your system configuration changes on a daily basis as you optimize applications and perform various tasks.

As you can see, the typical computer has a lot of failure points, so it's no wonder that things fall apart from time to time. This section of the book will help you quickly diagnose and fix most of the major problems you'll run into with Windows 98. We'll even look at a few undocumented ways to determine what's going on and how to interpret the information you get.

Conventions Used in This Book

I've used the following conventions in this book:

File | Open	Menus and the selections on them are separated by a vertical bar. File | Open means "Access the File menu and choose Open."
Program Files \ Plus! \ Themes	The names of folders are separated by a backslash.
`monospace`	It's important to differentiate the text that you use in a macro or that you type at the command line from the text that explains it. I've used monospace type to make this differentiation. Whenever you see something in monospace, you'll know that this information will appear in a macro, within a system file such as `CONFIG.SYS` or `AUTOEXEC.BAT`, or as something you'll type at the command line. You'll even see the switches used with Windows commands in monospace.
`italic monospace`	Sometimes you need to supply a value for a Windows or DOS command. For example, when you use the `DIR` command, you might need to supply a filename. It's convenient to use a variable name—essentially a place-holder—to describe the kind of value you need to supply.

The same holds true for any other kind of entry, from macro commands to dialog box fields. Whenever you see a word in italic monospace, you know that the word is a placeholder that you'll need to replace with a value. The placeholder simply tells you what kind of value you need to provide.

`<Filename>`

A variable name between angle brackets is a value that you need to replace with something else. The variable name I use usually provides a clue as to what kind of information you need to supply. In this case, I'm asking for a filename. Never type the angle brackets when you type the value.

`[<Filename>]`

When you see square brackets around a value, switch, or command, it means that this is an optional component. You don't have to include it as part of the command line or dialog field unless you want the additional functionality that the value, switch, or command provides.

italic

I use italic wherever the actual value of something is unknown. I also use italic where more than one value might be correct. Italic is also used to introduce new terms in text.

ALL CAPS

Commands use all capital letters. Some Registry entries also use all caps even though they aren't commands. Normally you'll type a command at the DOS prompt, within a PIF file field, or within the Run dialog field. If you see all caps somewhere else, it's safe to assume that the item is a case-sensitive Registry entry or some other value. Filenames also appear in all caps.

➡

The code continuation character is used when one line of code is too long to fit on one line of the book. Here's an example:

```
{DDE-EXECUTE "[InsertObject .IconNumber = 0, .FileName = ""D:\WIN95\LEAVES.BMP"",
➡.Link = 1, .DisplayIcon = 0, .Tab = ""1"", .Class = ""Paint.Picture"",
➡.IconFilename = """", .Caption = ""LEAVES.BMP""]"}
```

When typing these lines, you would type them as one long line without the continuation character.

Icons

This book contains many icons that help you identify certain types of information. The following paragraphs describe the purpose of each icon.

Note: Notes tell you about interesting facts that don't necessarily affect your ability to use the other information in the book. I use note boxes to give you bits of information that I've picked up while using Windows 98.

Tip: Everyone likes tips, because they tell you new ways of doing things that you might not have thought about before. Tip boxes also provide an alternative way of doing something that you might like better than the first approach I provided.

Warning: This means watch out! Warnings almost always tell you about some kind of system or data damage that will occur if you perform a certain action (or fail to perform others). Make sure you understand a warning thoroughly before you follow any instructions that come after it.

Peter's Principle

I usually include a Peter's Principle to tell you how to manage your Windows environment more efficiently. These recommendations are based on my personal experience with different ways of doing the same thing. Boxes with this icon might also include ideas on where to find additional information or even telephone numbers that you can call. You'll also find the names of shareware and freeware utility programs here.

Looking Ahead: It's always good to know what you'll find along the road. Whenever you see a Looking Ahead box, I'm providing a road sign that tells you where we're headed. That way, you can follow the path of a particular subject as I provide more detailed information throughout the book.

Gaining good access to the features provided by Windows 98 is important for everyone—especially to those who are physically challenged. I applaud Microsoft's efforts in taking this first step toward making Windows 98 the operating system that everyone can use. You'll see the Accessibility icon wherever I talk about these special features. Don't be surprised at how many of them you can use to get your work done faster or more efficiently, even if you're not physically challenged.

Knowing how something works inside is important to some people but not so important to others. Whenever you see the Architecture icon, I'm talking about the internal workings of Windows 98. Knowing how Windows 98 performs its job can help you determine why things don't work as they should.

You can't survive in the modern business world without spending some time talking to other people. Whether you spend that time on the phone or with an online service such as CompuServe or Microsoft Network, the result is the same. It's the exchange of information that drives business—at least in part. Whenever you see the Communications icon, you know that I'm describing some way of using Windows 98 to better communicate with those around you.

Whenever you change something as important as your operating system, there will be problems with older devices and applications that were designed for the older versions. The Compatibility icon clues you in to tips, techniques, and notes that will help you get over the compatibility hurdle.

DOS is still with us and will continue to be for the foreseeable future. Microsoft at least provides better support for DOS applications under Windows 98. Whenever you see the DOS icon, I provide you with a tip, technique, or note about a way to make DOS applications and Windows coexist.

Even home users need to worry about networking these days. It's no surprise, then, that this book provides a wealth of networking tips and techniques that everyone can use. Expect to find one of these tidbits of knowledge wherever you see the Networking icon.

I use the Performance icon to designate a performance-related tip. There are many throughout this book, and they cover a variety of optimization techniques. You'll need to read them carefully and decide which ones suit your needs. Not every performance tip is for everyone. Most of them require a trade-off of some kind, which I'll mention.

Your printer is probably the most used, yet most frustrating, part of your computer. I include the Printer icon to tell you when a tip or technique will help you keep your printer under control and make it work more efficiently.

Square pegs that had to fit in round holes—that's what some products were in the past. Recent standards efforts have helped reduce the number of square pegs on the market. I think it's important to know what these standards are so that you can make the best buying decisions possible. Getting a square peg at a discount rate isn't such a good deal if you end up spending hours making it round. Every time you see the Standards icon, you know that I'm talking about some standard that defines a product that will fit into that round hole with relative ease.

Technical details can really help you localize a problem or decide precisely what you need in order to get a job done. They can also help improve your overall knowledge of a product. Sometimes they're just fun to learn. However, sometimes you just need an overview of how something works; learning the details would slow you down. I use the Technical Note icon to tell you when a piece of information is a detail. You can bypass this information if you need only an overview of a Windows 98 process or feature. This icon also gives you clues as to where you can look for additional information.

Everyone encounters problems from time to time. It doesn't matter if the problem is hardware- or software-related if it's keeping you from getting your work done. Every time you see the Troubleshooting icon, I'm providing you with a tool you'll need to find the source of a problem.

It's helpful to compare the benefits of using one operating system over another. I already gave you some tips in this regard earlier. You'll find a lot of other notes throughout this book. Every time I provide some insight into a comparison of Windows NT versus Windows 98, I use the Windows NT icon.

With steep successive drops in the price of basic hardware and the lure of easy Internet access, the existing Windows 3.x user-base may be expected to upgrade in droves to Windows 98. I occasionally point out the evolutionary and sometimes radical departures from the old 16-bit Windows environment. This icon is of interest to all readers—even those who have never used Windows 3.x— because it highlights constraints that continue to determine the shape of Windows 98.

The Windows 98 icon makes it easy to spot passages discussing features, enhancements, or subtle changes that distinguish the new operating system from its predecessors, particularly if you are migrating from Windows 95. You'll find it especially useful when you subsequently scan the book as a handy reference.

Peter Norton

I

Getting Started with Windows 98

1

Opening Windows to the Internet

Peter Norton®

At its inception the Internet was simply a research tool for scientists lucky enough to gain access to it. After a while, it became a picture of the world for a few people in colleges and other educational institutions. Then it became something more—a picture of more than just our world for the rest of us. Until now, however, the Internet has remained more of an attachment to our world than an actual part of it. You dialed in and interacted with a few people, then logged off and got on with your life.

Windows 98 seeks to change all that. No longer will the Internet be a mere attachment, an after-thought to the mainstream of life. Windows 98 makes the Internet a major part of the whole picture of computing. You'll find it in places you never dreamed possible. The Internet truly will be at your fingertips, although you still need a browser to access it. Internet Explorer 4 is more closely inte-grated with Windows 98 than any other browser, but you still are able to use other browsers, such as Netscape Communicator.

The new Internet emphasis in Windows 98 is one reason this book first discusses how to get online and productive. The Internet has the potential to change both the way you work at the office and the way you have fun at home. With all the new technology Microsoft has introduced to the Internet, you'll find that the Internet has evolved from an interesting view of the world to an indispensable tool.

This first chapter doesn't burden you with a lot of details right away. Most of you probably want to get up and running first, so you can do a little exploring on your own. With that in mind, this chap-ter covers just the basics. You'll begin by taking a quick look at what the Internet is as a whole.

Next you'll learn about the features that make Windows 98 such a good Internet platform and about all the new software you'll find in this version of the operating system. Especially noteworthy is the new HelpDesk, which ensures you'll always have the most up-to-date information about Windows 98. You'll also like Windows System Update, a feature that makes it very easy to update your system.

Getting online means finding an Internet service provider (ISP). The section "Using the Online Services Folder," later in this chapter, helps you connect to one of several ISPs. Are the big ISPs always the best choice? Not really. This section also raises issues you might want to consider when looking for an ISP. Although most major ISPs provide great service to large cities, for example, many don't provide good service to smaller cities or rural areas.

After you've chosen an ISP and have made the appropriate connection, you'll need to perform some Windows 98 setups. By the time you complete the section "Using Dial-Up Networking," you'll have a connection online and be able to start doing something productive on the Internet—even if it's just visiting a pet newsgroup or finding out how to get more from your garden.

Most people have no idea what an URL (pronounced "earl") is when they start using the Internet. Protocols defy explanation even when they start spending a lot of time on the Internet. The next section, "Protocols and URLs," will help you understand these potentially confusing technologies. More importantly, you'll learn what they mean to you as a user.

Learning about the Internet doesn't do much good if you still can't find what you need. The section "Finding What You're Looking For," later in this chapter, will help you learn to search quickly and efficiently. You won't waste time looking for just the right Web site. Finding information on the Internet doesn't have to involve secret meetings with friends at midnight—or learning some secret handshake. Understanding a few basic rules will help you get more from the Internet with less effort.

One major new feature in Windows 98 is Active Desktop. This chapter doesn't cover every Active Desktop feature, just the three you need to know about immediately. All three will help you get information in ways you previously couldn't imagine. You can use "push" technology, for example, to tell the Internet to automatically deliver specific content to your desktop. In other words, you don't have to look for updates, the Internet will tell you about them automatically.

The Internet—A Window to the World

How you view the Internet right now probably depends on how you've used it, if you've used it at all. To a corporate user, the Internet might represent a research and contact platform. Many corporate users see the Internet as a way to get information without spending a lot of time at the library or digging through books. Considering the speed at which information changes, there are some instances when getting information any place but the Internet might actually result in inaccurate reports containing old information. These same employees probably use the Internet to keep in touch with their company through email and to upload reports while on the road.

Home users might view the Internet as a resource for gathering information about their hobbies and interests. For example, there's a wealth of gardening-related Internet sites. You probably couldn't count the number of craft-related sites, such as those related to woodworking. In addition to improving your home, you can improve your home life with information from sites dedicated to children and parenting.

Explosive growth in the gaming industry is evident on the Internet. At a number of sites, gamers with like interests can meet to play head-to-head. Total Entertainment Network (TEN), for example, is one of the bigger gaming sites. (You can contact TEN at `http://www.outland.com/TENhome.html`.) Even if you don't want to play head-to-head against other gamers, the Internet provides access to game vendors and the patches you need to keep your game up-to-date. Most gamers view an Internet connection as a prerequisite to gaming, not as an added feature that might come in handy.

One type of Web site that has been around for a while is educational Web sites. For example, you can view the most recent course catalog for the University of California San Diego (UCSD) at `http://www.ucsd.edu/`. This same Web site can provide access to the various kinds of research going on at the university. Research was one of the main factors behind the early growth of the Internet, and it continues to have a major impact on how the Internet is growing today.

If you're not interested in colleges and finding out what they're doing with your tax dollars, you can always contact places like NASA at `http://www.nasa.gov/`. What you find at this site depends on what NASA is currently doing. At the time of this writing, the page was promoting Senator John Glenn's return to space. It also contained links to the Mir space station, the Mars Pathfinder mission, and more.

The Internet now has even more important tasks to perform when it comes to research. For example, one of NASA's latest innovations for rover control is the Web Interface for Telescience (WITS). This new software enables scientists to provide input to a rover without actually being at NASA's Jet Propulsion Laboratory (the central control site for the Mars Pathfinder mission). You can view a public version of this software at `http://robotics.jpl.nasa.gov/tasks/scirover/`. The WITS software enables you to move the rover around and to see Mars the same way researchers do—only the rover is simulated, the results are based on actual rover data.

If science doesn't interest you very much and you couldn't care less about the Mars Pathfinder mission, how would you like to visit Malaysia? You might be surprised by how much growth Malaysia has experienced as a nation and by how much we rely on that country to create a variety of products. In fact, you'll probably use something made in Malaysia today. You can find out more about this country from one of several Web sites. The government-sponsored site is at `http://www.mol.com/`. Another good site is at `http://www.pahang.com/`. Needless to say, Malaysia isn't the only country you'll find on the Internet. You can find sites for even the smallest countries in the world. You can use search engines such as Lycos, Yahoo!, and Excite to find additional entries. Magazines such as *National Geographic* also provide Web site locations for country information.

By now you should have the idea that there's more to the Internet than just the latest game or corporate contact. The Internet is a window to the entire world, not just to local events. You can explore your neighborhood, the universe, and everything in between if you really want to. The number of topics you can find is limited only by your imagination—you'll constantly be surprised at what you can find by looking at just the right Web site.

Active Desktop—The Internet at Your Fingertips

As previously mentioned, Windows 98 is designed to make the Internet easier to access and use. It provides the tools you need to place the entire Internet at your fingertips, and it enables you to automate many tasks you performed by hand in the past. In fact, this is what the word "active" refers to in the name Active Desktop. The contents of your desktop will now automatically adjust to reflect changes in your favorite Web site. You no longer need to manually update site information.

This chapter does not provide a blow-by-blow description of every Internet-specific feature that Windows 98 now provides. It does, however, give you enough information to start using these tools right away. In essence, you'll know enough to at least experiment with the new Windows 98 features now. Later chapters will help you explore the full range of features provided by these tools.

HelpDesk

Windows 98 uses Hypertext Markup Language (HTML)–based help in place of the help files used by older versions. (HTML is the same language used to display information in the Web pages you visit on the Internet.) This new HTML-based help appears in a browser, just as if you were visiting a Web site. Use the Start menu | Help command to access HelpDesk.

Using HTML-based help is a lot more flexible than the help you got in the past. Help files can become outdated, for example, as can any information stored on your hard drive. The new HelpDesk doesn't have to remain outdated because you can download the most recent information from the Internet. In fact, when you need help, you have three different levels to choose from.

- Local help. You can get local help from your hard drive at any time—you don't have to have an Internet connection to use it. This level of help is like the help you got in the past.

- Web resources. Getting the most current information becomes more important as computers get more complex. Use this option if you want the most up-to-date information available about Windows 98, including corrections to existing information. (Windows 98 will perform the replacement of old information automatically, you don't have to do anything special.) This option requires an Internet connection, which means you might have to wait a little longer to get the help you need.

- Contact a support engineer. What could be better than having the services of a support engineer at your disposal? This option provides you with help directly from someone at Microsoft without having to look through the manual for the support number. (You'll still need to pay for many types of support services.) This option automatically collects information about your computer and uploads it to the engineer. It also is the slowest of the three options because you have to wait for a support engineer.

As you can see, with an Internet connection at your disposal, you no longer have to worry about whether you're getting the best possible help with Windows 98. The three help options enable you to choose the level of support you need.

Windows Update Manager

Windows Update Manager is Microsoft's latest solution to the problem of outdated drivers and buggy software. It uses a connection to the Internet to find out whether you have the most recent drivers available. To start the process, select Windows Update Manager from the Help screen (or use the Start | Settings | Windows Update command). This starts a process in which Windows checks with Microsoft's server on the Internet and verifies that you have the most recent software installed on your machine.

> **Technical Note:** Windows Update Manager uses an ActiveX control to do its job. This means you need to use an ActiveX-compatible browser such as Internet Explorer. You also can make some browsers—such as Netscape Navigator—ActiveX-compatible by adding a plug-in such as NCompass ScriptActive. (You'll find NCompass Labs at `http://www.ncompasslabs.com/`.) The plug-in level of ActiveX compatibility normally doesn't allow specialized programs like Windows Update Manager to work properly, so you're usually better off using a browser that supports ActiveX natively.

Windows Update Manager needs to dial in to your ISP. After Windows Update Manager creates a connection to the Microsoft server, you'll see a Windows Update Manager connection screen. Click the Update Wizard entry on this page. To check the current status of your software, click the Update button. (You can click the Restore button if you want to return your machine to its pre-update state; in addition, you may need to download an ActiveX control before the Restore button becomes available.)

The first thing Windows Update Manager needs to do is download one or more ActiveX controls to your system. You'll probably see a request to download the control. This is a safety feature in Internet Explorer to ensure that you always know what's being downloaded to your hard drive. After the download is complete, you'll see Windows Update Manager search your system for old components. If your system contains old software components, you'll see one or more entries in the Updates Available column of the Update Manager screen (see Figure 1.1). Select the updates you want to install, then click the Install button. (Some updates might be README files to help you understand new features that Windows 98 provides or to warn you of pending changes.) That's all there is to updating your system under Windows 98—just follow any prompts the update installation program provides.

Advanced Internet Browsing

Getting from point A to point B on the Internet is getting more difficult every day, partly because there are so many new Web sites. The proliferation of Web sites will continue, however, and trying to find what you want will get even more difficult. That's why some of the new Windows 98 browsing features are so enticing. The following list provides an overview of the advanced Internet browsing features you can expect from Windows 98.

- AutoComplete is a new feature that automatically suggests a complete Web address as you type. If you visit `http://www.myplace.com/` on a regular basis, for example, you could type `myplace` and AutoComplete would suggest the full address for you.

- Enhanced Web-searching features include the capability to choose a search engine from a pull-down list and a two-pane view. You can see the search results on one side of the screen and the current selection from that list on the other. In addition, the balloon-text feature gives you an idea of what a particular Web site contains. Just place the mouse cursor over the site (without clicking) and the balloon text appears.

- An improved Favorites listing now features single-click navigation. As in the new search feature, you'll see your favorites listed in one pane and the current Web site in the other.

- Support for all major standards includes: HTML, Java, ActiveX, JavaScript, VBScript, and security.

- Performance enhancements include dynamic HTML and the just-in-time Java compiler. You'll also see improved script performance because Windows 98 now includes basic code tuning, essentially an optimizer similar in functionality to the optimizers used by many programming languages.

- Your search history now appears on the navigation buttons. You just need to select the Web site you want from a drop-down list.

Figure 1.1.
If your machine requires an update, you'll see one or more entries in the Available Updates column.

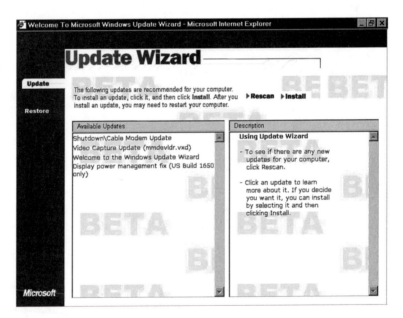

Personalized Internet Information Delivery

Do you visit the same Web site repeatedly to see if it has changed? Perhaps it discusses current events or contains the latest tips for your favorite hobby. Whatever the reason, you probably check this Web site regularly. There are times, however, when you might forget to check your favorite Web site, which means you're missing out on information you wanted to see.

Windows 98 has at least a partial solution to this data loss problem. You now can subscribe to a Web site, just as you would a newsgroup. The subscription feature automatically looks for changes in the

Web site for you. Every time Windows 98 detects a change in the Web site, it automatically updates what you see as well.

If you display important Web sites on the desktop, you'll see any changes as they occur without actually having to visit the sites. Everything occurs automatically. You won't need to think about Web site updates, just how you want to use the information.

The following steps will get you started using the subscription feature.

1. Visit the Web site to which you want to subscribe. Add it to your Favorites folder by right-clicking the Web page and choosing Add to Favorites from the context menu. You'll see an Add Favorite dialog box.

2. Choose one of the two subscription options. You have a choice between getting a simple notification (option 2), or of having Internet Explorer downloading the page for you so that you can view it offline (option 3).

3. You can customize the download schedule by clicking the Customize button and following the steps. Essentially, you can instruct Windows 98 how to inform you of changes on the Web page and how often it should check for these changes. You also can include a password and other login information.

4. Click OK to complete the process. Windows 98 will now check this Web site and update your information as needed.

Internet Communication Tool Suite

There's more to the Internet than browsing Web sites, so Microsoft provides a suite of three tools for you to use. These tools provide extra capabilities to help you get the most from the Internet. All three tools are discussed in detail later in this book, but here's a brief overview.

Looking Ahead: See Chapter 21, "Internet Connections," to learn more about Outlook Express and Microsoft NetMeeting. Chapter 22, "Creating Your Own Intranet with Personal Web Server," contains detailed information about Personal Web Server, including how you can use it to set up your own intranet or Internet.

- Outlook Express is a full-featured email and news reader.
- Microsoft NetMeeting enables you to meet with other people over the Internet. You have access to a white board and other meeting tools, just as if you were having a meeting locally.
- Personal Web Server isn't industrial strength enough for a corporate Internet site, but it works just fine for a personal Internet or intranet site.

- FrontPage Express allows you to create your own Web pages using a graphical interface. No longer do you need to remember arcane HTML tags just to display some simple text on a Web page. FrontPage Express makes getting a Web site up and running fast and simple.

Using the Online Services Folder

The Online Services folder is a new feature in Windows 98. It can help you gain access to a variety of Internet service providers (ISPs), including:

- America Online
- CompuServe
- Prodigy
- Microsoft Network

In addition to Internet access, these four companies provide services such as local discussion groups and vendor support. AT&T WorldNet, which you also can access here, provides Internet service only.

Using Dial-Up Networking

Dial-Up Networking enables you to dial in to a remote server—such as an ISP or the machine you use at work—from your computer. With previous versions of Windows, you were able to dial out only. Windows 98, however, also includes the capability to make your machine into a server. To use the Dial-Up Server feature, you must install the separate Dial-Up Server component found in the Communications folder on the Windows Setup tab of the Add/Remove Programs applet. (The Add/Remove Programs applet appears in the Control Panel.)

Note: Before you can use Dial-Up Networking, you must install it using the Add/Remove Programs applet in Control Panel. This procedure is discussed in Chapter 10, "The Windows 98 Applets," so it is not duplicated here. The following paragraphs assume Dial-Up Networking is already installed.

Creating a Connection

In most cases, all you really want to do with Dial-Up Networking is create a simple connection. This section describes the minimum effort necessary to create a connection. Dial-Up Networking has its own folder in Explorer. At least one component—the Make New Connection applet—will always appear in that folder. The following steps help you create a connection:

1. Open the Dial-Up Networking folder. Double-click the Make New Connection applet. You should see a Make New Connection dialog containing a connection name and a device field. Note that the utility suggests a default name of My Connection. Be sure to provide a more descriptive name here if you plan to create more than one connection. Note that this dialog box also provides a Configure button. This dialog is discussed in the "Faxes and Modems" section of Chapter 13, "Exploiting Your Hardware."

2. After you have selected a connection name, choose a modem model, configure the connection, then click Next. The next dialog box asks for the area code and telephone number you want to dial. The Country Code list box enables you to create connections even if you aren't currently at home.

3. Click Next to see a successful completion dialog box. This is the final screen. The Make New Connection applet gives you another chance to change the connection name before it is saved. (You can always change the name later if necessary.)

4. Click Finish to close the final dialog box.

Using the Connection

After you create the connection, it is easy to find and use. Just double-click the Connection icon in the Dial-Up Networking dialog box. This opens the Connect To dialog box shown in Figure 1.2. Note that your name and the telephone number to dial are automatically added to the dialog box. You only need to add the password for the machine you are calling.

Figure 1.2.
After you define a connection, just double-click its icon and enter a password.

If you use a particular connection a lot—and password protection is enabled for accessing Windows 98—you might want to enable the Save Password option. When this box is checked, you only need to double-click the Connection icon and then click the Connect button. Saving your password is probably a safe bet for an Internet connection, but you should refrain from saving passwords to company networks in which security is paramount.

Calling from Another Location

After you set up a connection you usually don't need to adjust it. You can select any predefined location from the Dialing From list box. What happens, though, if you need to call from another location? Let's say, for example, you are calling from another country. The following procedure shows you how to use the Dial Properties button to quickly add a new location to the Dialing From list box. (Double-click the icon for your connection to display the Connect To dialog box.)

1. Click the Dial Properties button (refer to Figure 1.2). This opens the Dialing Properties dialog box shown in Figure 1.3. This dialog box contains everything you need to define a local connection.

Figure 1.3.
The Dialing Properties dialog box contains a complete description of your current location.

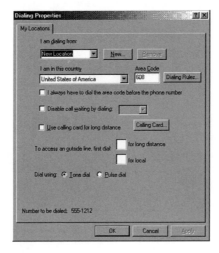

2. Click the New button. A Dialing Properties message box confirms that a new location was created.

3. Click OK to clear the Dialing Properties message box. Type a descriptive location name in the I am dialing from: field, then click Apply.

4. Change the area code and country fields to match your current location. Don't worry about long-distance considerations. Windows 98 automatically takes care of that for you. All you need to know is your current location.

5. If you plan to use a calling card from this new location, click the Calling Card button. Windows 98 presents the dialog box shown in Figure 1.4. You need to work with your calling-card company to fill this out completely. You need to supply a calling card type and a calling card number. In most cases, you also need to supply a personal identification number (PIN) for security reasons. Many calling cards also provide usage instructions that you can include with the dial-up connection.

Figure 1.4.

Setting your calling card parameters correctly is very important.

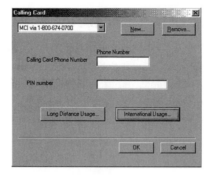

6. Check the calling card usage instructions by clicking either the Long Distance Calls or International Calls buttons. You'll see an instruction list similar to the one shown in Figure 1.5. Windows 98 performs the steps listed to establish a connection using your calling card. In most cases, the instructions are already provided. You might want to check them anyway, however, just to be sure they match the instructions provided by your calling card vendor.

Figure 1.5.

Make sure you check the instructions for establishing a connection using your calling card.

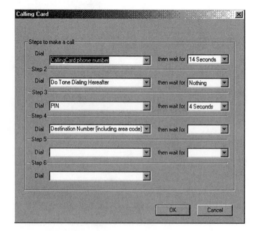

7. Click OK twice to close the Calling Card dialogs after you've finished their setup.

8. When you have completed the Location dialog box, click OK to save it. Notice that the telephone number automatically changes to reflect your location. Windows 98 automatically includes all the required codes for you.

Now you just need to click Connect to actually make the connection. When you do so, Windows 98 sends the server your name and password. It also takes care of details such as using your phone card (if you supply that information). The first time you configure a connection it might take a little time; after that, however, everything should be pretty automatic.

Modifying a Connection

At some point, you'll likely encounter a situation in which you want to modify an existing connection. You might change ISPs, for example, and need to change your Internet access number. This capability also comes in handy if you need to change your connection or server type, troubleshoot a connection problem, or change your dialing location.

It's important to remember that you can access all your connections from two places. Windows 98 always places a Dial-Up Networking folder in Explorer. You'll also find a Dial-Up Networking entry in the Accessories folder within the Start menu. Accessing the Dial-Up Networking properties dialog box is easy. Just right-click the icon of the connection you want to modify, then select Properties from the context menu. This opens the General tab of the connection properties dialog box in which you select the appropriate area code, telephone number, and country code. You also select the device to use to make the connection, and instruct Windows 98 whether to use the area code and Dialing Properties.

> **Looking Ahead:** The Scripting tab of the Dial-Up Networking properties dialog box is discussed in the "Creating Scripts for Dial-Up Networking" section of Chapter 19, "Hardware and Software Connections." The Multilink tab is discussed in the "Understanding Multilink Channel Aggregation" section of Chapter 21.

Figure 1.6 shows the Server Types tab. The settings on this tab weren't available when you created the connection because Windows 98 assumes certain defaults. The first field contains a list of server types. Every Windows 98 installation supports at least five kinds of servers: NPN (Novell NetWare networks), PPP (Windows NT, Windows 98, or Internet connections), CSLIP (a UNIX connection with IP-header compression), SLIP (a standard UNIX connection), and a special connection for Windows for Workgroups (Windows 3.x).

Figure 1.6.
The Server Types tab enables you to configure your connection in a variety of ways.

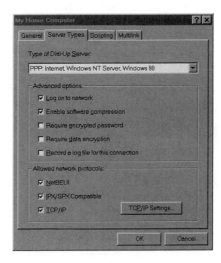

Below the Type of Dial-Up Server field, the Advanced options field contains the following check boxes:

- **Log on to network.** Tells Windows 98 that you want to log onto the server automatically. You can't use this option with callback systems; it only works with servers that allow automatic login, such as the Internet.

- **Enable software compression.** Sets up software compression to reduce the transfer time for any data you want to send to or receive from the server. This option works in most cases, but you'll want to disable it for UNIX connections or older mainframe connections that don't support compression. You'll also want to disable this option if you're using hardware compression on a dedicated connection.

- **Require encrypted password.** Enables software encryption of your username and password. The server must support this option before you can use it. Normally, your username and password are sent using plain ASCII.

The final section of this tab contains a list of allowed protocols. Most of the time, every protocol installed on your machine is checked. In some cases, however, this causes problems. For example, if you have TCP/IP installed for a local intranet, use Novell NetWare for your file server, and also use a dial-up connection to the Internet, you should disable all the protocols listed here except TCP/IP. Otherwise, your connection will conflict with the NetWare connection and could even cause problems with your local intranet. Disabling protocols you don't need also speeds up the connection because Windows 98 doesn't have to spend as much time monitoring it.

This tab also contains a TCP/IP Settings button that displays the dialog box of the same name. TCP/IP is discussed in detail in the "Configuring TCP/IP—The Short Form" section of Chapter 23, "Networks."

Protocols and URLs

This section discusses two very important Internet topics: uniform resource locators (URLs) and protocols. *URLs* define a particular Web server resource such as a Web page or a file. *Protocols* define how you communicate with the server after you find the URL (pronounced "earl").

Note: From this point on in this chapter, Lemonweir Valley Telephone Company will be the Internet service provider used. If you use a different service provider, your screens and addresses will probably differ. The principles being discussed are the same, though, so don't worry about the differences too much. Internet Explorer 4.0 will be the browser used in this chapter, though you'll see other browsers such as Netscape Navigator in other Internet-related chapters. Many other browsers are on the market. This chapter is not suggesting that Internet Explorer and Netscape Navigator are better or worse than the others; these are just the two most popular browsers at the time of this writing.

Understanding Uniform Resource Locators (URLs)

The URL is the basis for movement on the Internet, so it's important to understand how it works. Let's start by looking at the Microsoft home page address—that's where you'll check in before exploring the rest of the Internet:

`http://www.microsoft.com/`

This is a typical URL that identifies a particular server and clues you in to its capabilities. The first portion of the URL—in this case `http://`—tells you what kind of data exchange protocol to use when accessing the server. In this case, you'll use Hypertext Transfer Protocol. Knowing the data transfer protocol tells you a lot about what to expect from the server. An FTP site, for example, doesn't provide much in the way of user-friendly graphics.

The next section contains the *domain name system* (DNS) address for the site you want to visit—in this case, `www.microsoft.com/`. Every DNS address has at least three sections. (Some DNS addresses have a fourth or even a fifth section that contains the computer or country name, but you won't encounter this very often.)

The first section of the DNS address tells you about the service (or as some books call it, the subdomain). In this example, you're going to visit the World Wide Web (WWW). WWW sites almost always provide some type of graphical presentation. The DNS address doesn't have to start with WWW; for example, a site called `http://home.microsoft.com/` takes you to the home page for Internet Explorer. Most sites use WWW, however, because everyone expects to find their Web site on the World Wide Web.

The second section of the DNS address contains the domain name itself. In this case, it's `microsoft`. If you wanted to visit the Microsoft Network, however, you'd use `MSN` as a domain name. Most domain names are either full names or acronyms for the organization—some of which can be quite convoluted. The Internet site must register the domain name with InterNIC.

The third section of the DNS address is the domain identifier. Table 1.1 shows some sample domain identifiers. InterNIC selects the one that fits the organization best. Note that this table doesn't contain every identifier you'll ever see, but it does contain the more common identifiers.

Table 1.1. Common Internet Domain Identifiers.

Identifier	Description
`.com`	Used for any kind of commercial company such as Microsoft or CompuServe. Most online service Internet access providers have a `.com` domain identifier.

continues

Table 1.1. continued

Identifier	Description
.edu	Not-for-profit educational (4-year post-secondary) institutions use this domain identifier. (There's some discussion as to whether the school really has to be not-for-profit, but in most cases, you'll find that they are.)
	Technical and secondary schools use a different method of identification. It includes the school name, grade levels, state or province, and country, as in MySchool.k12.wi.us. This example describes a primary or secondary school named MySchool located in the state of Wisconsin in the United States.
.gov	All government agencies use this domain identifier. If you see it, you know you're dealing with someone from the United States government.
.mil	The United States military uses this special domain identifier, which keeps it separate from the rest of the government.
.net	This domain identifier usually is reserved for Internet access providers. The exception is when the access provider is a commercial company. In that case, it uses the .com domain identifier. (As with every rule, this identifier has some crossover between access providers and commercial companies. A telephone company might have a .net identifier, for example, even though it's a commercial concern because its main focus is providing Internet access.)
.org	Some sites fall outside these other designations and, therefore, use the .org domain identifier.

That is the makeup of a basic URL. Some URLs, however, are much longer than the preceding example. What does the rest of the information mean? The following example is the Web address for the National Science Teachers Association (NSTA):

http://www.gsh.org/NSTA_SSandC/nses_home.htm

You should be able to recognize the protocol and domain name within this address (http://www.gsh.org). Now let's decipher the sections after the domain name.

This is an example of an organization that has rented space on someone else's server. The NSTA SSC (Scope, Sequence, and Coordination Project)—/NSTA_SSandC—actually exists within a subdirectory on the gsh server. Think of the forward slashes as subdirectories in a DOS path.

In this example, you're in a particular area of the NSTA SSC site—the /nses_home page that contains National Science Education Standards information. Notice the .htm extension here. Some browsers extend this to .html, but Internet Explorer 2.0 and 3.x don't. (Internet Explorer 4.0 can go either way.) HTML, which stands for *Hypertext Markup Language*, is discussed more in the "A Quick View of Protocols" section. For now, you just need to know that this extension signifies a page that has been formatted graphically by your browser.

Another type of URL has to do with e-mail addresses. These addresses are not difficult if you understand a basic URL. You'll normally see an address like this: `JMueller@mwt.net`. The first part of the address is the person you want to contact (in this case, `Jmueller`). The @ (at) sign separates the recipient's name from the DNS address of the server used to hold the message. You've already learned how to decipher the DNS address, so it won't be repeated here.

A Quick View of Protocols

Protocols are the basis for conversation on the Internet. Just as the name implies, a *protocol* is a formal set of rules. Protocols, both formal and informal, define the way people conduct business. A formal rule might state that you must be in the office by a certain time to begin work. An informal rule could be as simple as not making disparaging remarks about someone's new haircut or clothes.

Computers also need rules. You'll never run into some of them because they affect esoteric things such as the distance between nodes on a network. Others, such as those used for Internet communication, might become very important to you. Literally thousands of rules affect Internet communications in one way or another. Table 1.2, however, concentrates on some of the protocols you'll actually see as a user, such as while surfing the Net.

Table 1.2. Common Internet Protocols.

Acronym	Full Name	Description
CGI	Common Gateway Interface	A special method for accessing an application from a Web page. When a vendor asks you to enter information on a form, for example, you're probably using CGI. The most common use for CGI is database applications. This is the only Web-server-to-background-application standard currently supported by the IETF. Two other proposed methods are ISAPI and NSAPI.
FTP	File Transfer Protocol	Represents one of the earliest forms of communication recognized by the Internet. There are no graphics at an FTP site, just files to download. This is

continues

Table 1.2. continued

Acronym	Full Name	Description
		the only file download protocol currently supported by the IETF. The limitations of this particular protocol have prompted other standards such as CORBA and DCOM.
HTTP	Hypertext Transfer Protocol	Whenever you go to a Web site that begins with `http:`, you're using this protocol. It is the technology that enables you to download an HTML document—the kind that includes fancy graphics and buttons. Essentially, HTTP enables you to download an HTML script—a document containing commands rather than actual graphics. Your browser reads these script commands and displays buttons, text, graphics, or other objects accordingly. That's why the capabilities of your browser are so important (and why you'll need a new browser if you want to use any of the new protocols mentioned in this table). However, some vendors are already complaining that the IETF standard versions of both HTTP and HTML are old and are less than optimal for tomorrow's needs. That's why there's such proliferation of other protocol standards and of associated HTML script commands on the Internet today. People are looking for better ways to make information accessible.

This doesn't begin to scratch the surface of everything you'll see on the Internet. Think of Table 1.2 as a small sampling of the technologies you'll use on a regular basis.

Finding What You're Looking For

If you do a lot of research on the Internet, you realize the benefit of finding what you need quickly. Internet Explorer provides some handy tools for this purpose. First let's look at the most basic tool. Click the Search button in the Internet Explorer toolbar, and you'll see a display similar to the one shown in Figure 1.7. The precise view you get depends on whether you use the Microsoft Network (MSN) as your ISP. This figure shows the site you'll reach if you don't use MSN. Netscape Navigator also provides a Search button in its toolbar; the Web page it displays appears in Figure 1.8. Although the Netscape site provides fewer search engines, you'll use the ones shown there most often.

Figure 1.7.
*Internet Explorer
provides access to 10
search sites on the
Internet.*

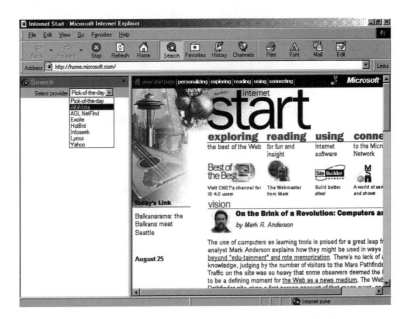

The two browsers use different search strategies. The Internet Explorer tactic is the simpler of the two. Just select a search engine and Internet Explorer will take you there. Netscape Navigator, however, provides not only links search engines, but preconfigured links to places that many people visit. In addition, Internet Explorer uses a split-screen display so you can see the search results in one pane and the currently selected search page in the other. Netscape Navigator uses a single pane, which forces you to move back and forth between the search engine and the Web site you want to visit.

You also can perform keyword searches. All you need to do is enter one or more keywords into the blank, select a search engine, then click the Search button. Internet Explorer or Netscape Navigator then takes you to the appropriate search Web site and starts the search for you.

Figure 1.8.
*Netscape Navigator
also provides access to
search sites on the
Internet at the click of
a button.*

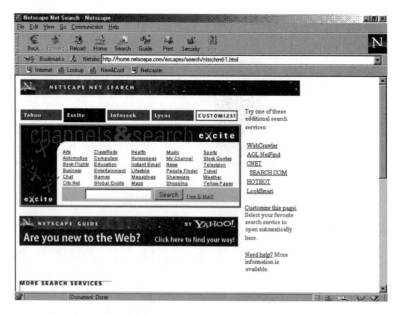

Tip: When it comes to finding great additions to the Windows 98 environment, there are more Internet sites to visit than you can imagine. One of these sites is the NONAGS MAIN PAGE at `http://users.southeast.net/~itsvicki/nonags/main.html`. This site specializes in shareware utility-type programs, although you'll also find a variety of other offerings. As the home page title states, no one nags you to make a purchase. An interesting aspect of this site is that you can find most of the software in both 16-bit (Windows 3.x) and 32-bit (Windows 95/98) versions. If you want a broader range of Windows 98–specific software to choose from, take a look at Windows95.com—Windows World on the Internet (`http://www.windows95.com/`). This site contains tutorials for a variety of topics, an Internet hypertext glossary, an Internet TCP/IP connectivity guide, and even a full listing of Windows 95/98–specific hardware drivers.

Let's try a sample search. Select Lycos as your search engine, type `ActiveX` in the blank, then click Search. (This works with either browser.) Depending on the security level you've selected, you might see a security dialog box before either browser does anything. (Both Microsoft's Internet Explorer and Netscape's Navigator provide security features. To change security levels in Internet Explorer, use the View | Internet Options command and then select the Security page of the Options dialog. In Navigator, using the Options | Security Preferences command accomplishes the same thing.) Click Yes to clear the security dialog box (if you received one). You'll then go to a Web page like the one in Figure 1.9. You should notice a few things about this page. First, you can refine your search. Maybe a single keyword wasn't effective and you need to find something more specific. Most single-search Web pages provide this capability in some form. Some even provide very detailed search mechanisms.

Figure 1.9.
A search Web page such as Lycos enables you to find specific information on the Internet.

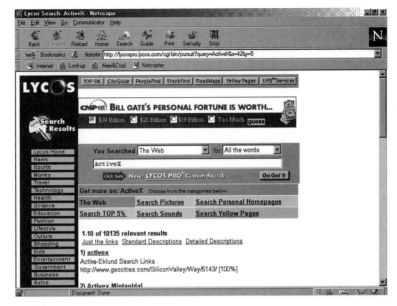

You also should notice that each result from your search (also called a *hit*) contains a confidence level. This tells you how confident the search engine is about the results it found. Search engines use a variety of criteria to determine this number, such as the number of times the keyword appears in an article or other source of information.

A Boolean search makes a confidence calculation more difficult. (A Boolean search uses terms such as "and" and "or" so you can look for phrases in a specific way. If you were to search for "help and context," the search engine would look for articles with both "help" and "context" in them. If you were to search for "help or context," on the other hand, either word alone would satisfy the search criteria.) The method used to determine a confidence factor can determine which search engines you use. You can use a variety of them for different purposes.

You might think one search engine is enough to fulfill your needs, but that usually isn't true. It is difficult to come up with a "best fit" for search engines because they all work differently. A search engine that works well for one person might not work at all for another. It is important, therefore, to learn about the most common search engines with quick overview of how they work. You should try them all to see what works best for you in different situations.

The following is a list of common search engines. Most of them can be accessed through the Search button in Internet Explorer or Navigator. URLs are also provided so you can access them directly. To access the search engine page, click the Open button on the toolbar and enter the URL. (When you find a search engine you like, you might want to add it to your Favorites or Bookmark list so you can find it easier the next time.)

- **Alta Vista** (http://www.altavista.digital.com/): A benefit of using this search engine is a lack of information overload. It returns only the amount of information you want about each hit. The service tends to focus on Web pages containing articles, which means you'll get some pretty narrow hits when using it. Alta Vista's descriptions use excerpts from articles or other sources of information that is accessed. This service uses a somewhat esoteric Boolean search engine, making it difficult to narrow your search criteria.

- **Deja News** (http://www.dejanews.com/): You can use this search engine when you need to find a lot of information fast. You'll notice a Power Search button on the page when you arrive. Power Search might be something of an understatement; you have to test it yourself to see all it can do. This also is one of the easier sites to use, despite its flexibility. It uses lots of graphics including radio buttons and other familiar controls. The only problem with this particular engine is that you might find yourself doing a search more than once to get everything it provides.

  There are many search options, so you'll quickly think of new ways to search for particularly tough-to-find bits of information. You can get two levels of detail, neither of which tell you much. All you get for each hit is an article title. This service doesn't provide excerpts or summaries, but it does provide a very broad base of information. You'll find just about anything you search for, so you might spend some time weeding out the entries that don't fit. Deja News also is one of the few search engines optimized for searching newsgroups, a real plus when you want to look for a discussion topic instead of a Web site.

- **Excite** (http://www.excite.com/): This service focuses on Web sites rather than pages within a particular site. In other words, you can get to a general area of interest, but then Excite leaves it to you to find the specific information you're looking for. This can be an advantage when you're not really sure about the specifics of a search. A wide view can help you see everything available, then you can make some refinements. Excite also provides a summary of what you'll find at a particular site. It tends to concentrate on discussion groups and vendor-specific information.

- **Infoseek** (http://guide-p.infoseek.com/): The strength of this particular service is that it provides just the facts. It uses excerpts from articles or other sources of information it uses. The hits are much narrower than some search engines provide because Infoseek concentrates on specific Web pages rather than general sites. The only problem with this particular service is that it severely limits your capability to narrow search criteria.

- **Lycos** (http://www-msn.lycos.com/): Of the common search engines, Lycos tends to provide the most diverse information. It catalogs both Web sites and pages, but it concentrates on pages whenever possible. Lycos provides a combination of summaries and excerpts to describe the content of a particular hit. Its capability to narrow a search is superior to most search engines available right now. The downside to using this particular search engine is that there's almost too much detail. If you aren't sure what you're looking for, you'll quickly find yourself searching false leads and ending up with totally unusable information.

- **Magellan** (`http://magellan.mckinley.com/`): You'll tend to find esoteric sources of information with this search engine. It doesn't provide a very broad base of information, but it usually provides interesting facts about what you're searching for. Magellan concentrates on Web sites rather than pages, so the view you get is rather broad. You'll also find that it provides few methods for narrowing the search criteria. This search engine relies on summaries rather than extracts to convey the content of a particular hit. One of the more interesting features is the method used to rate a particular site. Clicking a Review button gives you a full-page summary of how the information relates to similar information on other sites.

- **Open Text** (`http://search.opentext.com/`): "Extremely comprehensive" and "flexible" are the words to describe this particular search engine. This is one of the easier sites to use, and it provides a moderately broad base of information from which to choose. This particular search engine relies on extremely short excerpts, in most cases. It concentrates on Web pages rather than sites, meaning you'll get a fairly narrow result.

- **Yahoo!** (`http://www.yahoo.com/`): This search engine provides the best organization of all the engines listed here. It categorizes every hit in a variety of ways, which increases your chances of finding information. This service, however, doesn't provide the broad range of information that you'll find with other search engines. It also relies on very short summaries to explain the contents of a particular hit. Yahoo! works well as a first-look type of search engine—something that gives you the broad perspective of a single keyword.

- **Web Crawler** (`http://www.webcrawler.com/`): This search engine requires a bit more work to use than most because it doesn't provide much in the way of excerpts or summaries. On the other hand, it provides a full Boolean search engine and an extremely broad base of information. The only search engine in this list that provides a broader base is Lycos.

Special Active Desktop Features

This chapter doesn't go into detail about Active Desktop because Chapters 2 and 3 discuss it more thoroughly. It's important to note, however, that many of the Internet Explorer features discussed in this chapter can appear right on your desktop. You can set up links to any place on the Internet, and those links can be updated automatically. You can even create a link to your favorite search engine.

There are quite a few Active Desktop features that this chapter didn't even begin to discuss. Using the Channels feature in Windows 98, for example, enables you to quickly connect to your favorite news or entertainment Web site. Windows 98 also supports a broadcast architecture that enables you to receive television signals on your computer.

Connecting to the Internet used to be an optional activity some people used to stay informed. With Windows 98, it makes very little sense not to get connected. You literally have the entire world at your fingertips. With the new features provided by Windows 98, you won't have to waste time trying to figure out what you need and where to find it.

On Your Own

Connect to the Internet using one of the vendors in the Online Services folder.

Create a connection for the ISP if one wasn't created for you automatically. Some ISPs perform this step automatically when you install their software.

Test drive another browser, such as the one provided for CompuServe. How does it differ from Internet Explorer? What about other browsers you might have used?

Try deciphering some of the URLs stored in your browser. What do these URLs tell you about the site you've accessed? Spend some time on the Internet looking for various URL types.

Build a list of favorite Web sites. Don't forget to include Internet search sites such as Lycos.

Spend some time learning about the various institutions that manage the Internet. You can visit the InterNIC site, for example, at FTP://ftp.internic.net or HTTP://www.internic.net.

Try out the various Web search engines using the same keyword (to see how they differ). What kind of results did you get? Use various keywords to see how each search engine helps you in a particular area of research. Try refining the search to find very specific information. How does each search engine work when it comes to refining the results you get from a single keyword?

Install several browsers on your machine to see how they work on various Internet sites. At a minimum, try both Netscape Navigator and Internet Explorer. You can download a free trial copy of Netscape Navigator at http://www.netscape.com/. (You already have a copy of Internet Explorer.) Be sure to try out the add-ons for both products, such as the sound-enhancing Real Audio Player (http://www.realaudio.com/). (If you install a sound-related plug-in, be prepared for a few shocks. Some Web sites try to blast you out of your seat with high-volume sound effects.) Although Navigator makes heavier use of plug-ins than Internet Explorer, both products benefit from third-party add-ons.

2

Introducing Windows 98

Peter Norton®

The biggest change in Windows 98 that people will notice is the Internet support it provides. However, the first thing that people will see is Active Desktop. Active Desktop might start out looking like the Explorer interface, but as we'll see in this chapter, it's much different. Active Desktop is about as big a change from the Explorer interface used in Windows 98 as Explorer was from Program Manager.

One of the things that make Active Desktop totally different from interfaces of that past is its Internet orientation. You'll find that accessing the Internet is no longer a chore—you don't even need to think about it much. The Internet can be a simple click away. Forget about working at getting to the company intranet as well. The new Active Desktop makes accessing a company intranet just as easy as accessing a local hard drive. You'll find that you can single-click your way around the company with an ease unheard of in previous releases of Windows.

Customization is also much improved under Windows 98. You'll find that your folders no longer have to maintain the same mundane appearance. Now you'll have an opportunity to dress each folder up as you'd like. Whether that includes wallpaper or not is entirely up to you.

This chapter will also cover the Explorer interface. A good number of you will probably want to keep this older interface because you're familiar with it. Others may actually find that Explorer is more efficient for the way they work. Still other people, like home users, may find that having the Internet at their fingertips isn't such a good thing in the middle of a game of Quake. Suffice it to say that you can have it your way under Windows 98.

The last section of this chapter covers the various accessory programs provided with Windows 98. We'll look at the applications that will make your life a little easier. For example, this version of Windows includes the TweakUI utility program that allows you to modify the base features of the operating system.

Active Desktop: A New Way to Approach Windows

Active Desktop is the new Windows interface. Using Active Desktop enables you to get work done quickly and with a lot less effort. However, the place where I find that Active Desktop comes in handiest is in handling information overload. When used to its full potential, Active Desktop can help you reduce the effects of information overload.

The following section looks at the Active Desktop approach to working with Windows. You'll learn what sets Active Desktop apart from the Explorer interface. You'll also encounter tips and techniques for making Active Desktop work for you.

What is an Active Desktop?

All the desktops you've used to date are static—in other words, they don't change. An Active Desktop does change. The desktop you used today won't be the same desktop that you will see tomorrow. When you arrive at work or start up your machine at home tomorrow, the contents of your desktop will change to reflect the new day.

Here's a better idea of what I'm talking about. Think for a second about the newspaper. Your administrative assistant brings in a newspaper every day and places it on your desk. The one from yesterday gets thrown in the trash. Your desktop has changed—it contains new content that reflects what you're doing today. Likewise, Windows 98 will change the content of your desktop each day to reflect changing events. If you subscribe to a news channel and display it on your desktop, the display will change each day to reflect the changes in weather.

Active Desktop does more than change content. Consider, for a moment, what happens when you go to look for something on your local machine, the network or the Internet. In days gone by you had to use three different procedures to get the data you needed. Your local machine required one procedure, the network required another, and the Internet wanted something totally different. Windows 98 changes all that by enabling you to keep all your resources in one place. You'll be able to find the data you need without really thinking about where it came from.

Let's expand your horizons a little bit. Consider the role of a supervisor. If you want to direct people's attention to a specific event, a bit of data, or another company-related matter, you usually have to write a memo and distribute it to everyone. Wouldn't it be nicer if you could just place this information on the person's desktop along with all the required files and other materials? Windows 98 enables you to do this. A company intranet can easily supply everything necessary for a supervisor to direct what an employee is doing. In addition, you also can monitor employees' progress without looking over their shoulders. All you would need to do is look at the contents of their desktop on the company intranet.

I'm not going to list every possible use of Active Desktop. By now, you should have a pretty good idea of what it could mean to you and your company. The following sections will help you get started using Active Desktop. After you understand its principles, what you do is really a matter of how much imagination you have. An Active Desktop, unlike the static desktop of old, has very few limitations.

HTML On Your Desktop—No Browser Need Apply

You might not notice much difference between Windows 98 and Windows 95 when you first install Windows 98 on your machine. That's because it starts out with some of the newer features turned off. You'll have to turn some of them on before you'll see the Active Desktop features that Windows 98 provides.

The first step in turning these new features on is to right-click the desktop. As with most Windows 98 objects, you'll see a context menu. The item that we're interested in is Active Desktop. Notice that you can choose one of three options from a submenu. The following list tells you about the purpose of each option:

- **View as Web Page.** The Windows 98 Desktop can be viewed in one of two ways. You can either use the old method of viewing that Windows 95 provided, which was a static desktop; or you can view it as a Web Page, which allows for active content. When you choose the View as Web Page option, any Web sites you've subscribed to will appear on the Desktop along with the Internet Explorer Channel Bar. We'll talk about these items in the "Customizing Your Desktop Content" section of this chapter.

- **Customize my Desktop.** Selecting this option displays the Display Properties dialog. We'll talk about the Web tab of the Display Properties dialog in the "Customizing Your Desktop Content" section of this chapter. The Web tab is where you'll choose which subscribed items you want to display on the Desktop and where.

- **Update Now.** Once you have all these Web pages on your Desktop, you'll need some way to keep them up-to-date. Fortunately, you can choose to have Windows 98 do all the work for you. Allowing Windows 98 to do the updates works in most cases, but what happens if you need that last minute stock report or update on the latest technology? That's what this option is for. You can tell Windows 98 to update your content now, rather than wait for the automatic update.

Tip: You always can view the Internet Explorer Channel Bar by clicking the View Channels entry on the Quick Launch toolbar. This toolbar appears in the taskbar. It contains three buttons, one of which is the View Channels button.

OK, let's start out with something simple. You can start using the Internet almost immediately after turning on Active Desktop. Right-click the Desktop, and then choose View as Web Page from the context menu. What you'll see is the Internet Explorer Channel Bar because it's the only thing you have an automatic subscription to during installation (see Figure 2.1).

Note: To proceed beyond this point in this section, you need a connection to the Internet. We'll be looking at ways that you can actually use Active Desktop to make Internet access easier. Of course, you can always follow along in the text without actually performing the steps on your machine.

If you click one of the entries on the Internet Explorer Channel Bar, you'll start a copy of Internet Explorer and go to that site on the Web. Try this now by clicking a Channel Guide entry. When Internet Explorer makes a connection, you'll see the corresponding Web page.

Figure 2.1.
*The Internet Explorer
Channel Bar is your
initial entry to the
Internet using Active
Desktop.*

At this point, you could start roaming through the various channels and selecting one or more to place on your Desktop. We'll take a look at this process in the next section of the chapter. What you should have learned in this section is that Internet access doesn't have to be difficult or complicated. You can optimize your Active Desktop to display the content you need with little or no work on your part. All you need to do is perform a little setup at the outset.

Customizing Your Desktop Content

Let's look at some of the things you can do to customize your Desktop content. The place to begin is the Internet Explorer Channel Bar. Right-click an entry such as MSNBC News. You'll see a context menu containing items such as Refresh and Subscribe. (Channels you can't subscribe to, such as the Channel Guide, use a standard context menu. Your only real option here is to open the Web site and view the list of channels it contains.) The following list describes the unique menu entries you'll need to know about to customize your desktop.

- **Open Channel.** Selecting this option will start a copy of Explorer and open the associated Web site. This enables you to see whether you actually want to subscribe to the channel. You also can use this option to better define your choice. For example, MSNBC News is a relatively large Web site; you might only want to subscribe to the weather portion.

- **Subscribe.** Use this option to subscribe to your favorite channel. Although you are able to subscribe to the entire channel, you might want to refine your selection a bit by visiting the Web site first. For example, you might want to know about the music (TuneDom) on the Warner Brothers Web site but not the movies (ScreenDom).

- **Refresh.** Windows 98 will automatically check the Web sites you've selected for automatic update at a specific time. This option also enables you to download the current content manually at any time.

- **View Source.** There may be times when you need to update the link for a channel. Perhaps the vendor moved or you simply want to make a particular segment of the channel your permanent link. Use this option to display the HTML source for a channel in Notepad. There you can modify it at as needed.
- **Update Now.** Only the Channel Guide entry has this option in its context menu. This option enables you to update the list of available channels immediately instead of waiting for the normal update time.

Looking Ahead: We'll look at the various ways you can use channels in the "Using Channels" section in Chapter 21, "Internet Connections." This same section shows you how to automatically add new channels to your selection list. The "Creating a Subscription" section of Chapter 21 shows you how to get your own channel subscription going. Make sure you check out the "Using the Favorites Folder" section of Chapter 21 to learn how to manage both subscriptions and channels.

What if you don't like where Windows 98 places the Internet Explorer Channel Bar or other active content for that matter? Moving these windows to the Internet around is just as easy as moving any other window. There's a hidden title bar for each of the windows that you can use to move the window around. Just place your mouse near the top of the window and you'll see the title bar appear. Grab the title bar to move the window where you want it on screen. Resizing the window is just as easy. Just place the mouse cursor near one of the edges. When you see the double arrow, drag the mouse in the direction that you want to size the window.

The Internet Explorer Channel Bar and other Active Desktop items have a drop-down menu in their title bar. The first shows the Display Properties dialog. Remember that this dialog contains the Web tab, which enables you to configure Active Desktop. The second entry enables you to close a particular Active Desktop item.

The final area I want to cover right now is the Web tab of the Display Properties dialog. You can display this dialog in several ways. One of the easiest methods is to right-click the desktop and select the Active Desktop | Customize My Desktop option. What you should see is a dialog similar to the one in Figure 2.2. (You might have to select the Web tab.)

The first thing you should notice in Figure 2.2 is the monitor near the top. This monitor shows you the position of every Active Desktop item that you've chosen to display. The currently selected item is black, while the other items are displayed as outlines.

Right below the monitor is a list of Active Desktop items. You can have more items than you actually can display on the desktop. Checking an item displays it; unchecking it removes it from the desktop. Windows 98 continues to update an item, even if it is not currently displayed. Figure 2.2 shows two items: the Internet Explorer Channel Bar and an intranet Web site.

Figure 2.2.
*Use the Web tab of
the Display Properties
dialog to configure
Active Desktop
content.*

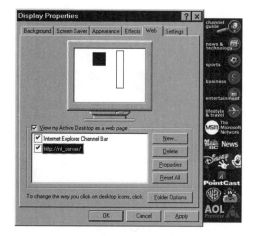

> **Tip:** The Disable All Web-Related Content in My Desktop check box at the bottom of
> the Display Properties dialog enables you to remove all Web content from your desktop. It
> performs the same function as the Active Desktop | View as Web Page option on the
> desktop context menu.

Let's add a new item to the Active Desktop list. The following steps show you how to add a weather
map to your desktop, but you can use the same procedure to add other items as well.

1. Open the Display Properties dialog and select the Web tab. You should see a display similar
   to the one shown in Figure 2.2.

2. Click the New button. You'll see the New Active Desktop Item dialog box, which enables
   you to grab a list of channels from the Active Desktop Gallery. If you click the Yes button,
   Windows 98 closes the Display Properties dialog box and takes you to the Active Desktop
   Gallery. Clicking No displays another dialog box that enables you to enter your own URL.
   The No option is really designed for adding an intranet site to your desktop or perhaps a
   non–active-content Web site.

3. Click Yes. The Display Properties dialog closes and Internet Explorer starts. After Internet
   Explorer makes a connection and looks up the Active Desktop Gallery page on the
   Internet, you'll see something similar to Figure 2.3. (The contents of this Web site change
   all the time, so your display most likely will differ from the figure.)

4. Click the Weather icon and then the MSNBC Weather Map link. Internet Explorer takes
   you to a page that features the weather map.

5. Click the Add to Active Desktop button near the bottom of the page. (You might get a
   Security Alert dialog box that asks whether you want to add a desktop item to your Active
   Desktop; click Yes.) Internet Explorer displays an Add Item to Active Desktop dialog box.

Figure 2.3.

The Active Desktop Gallery page enables you to add active content to your desktop.

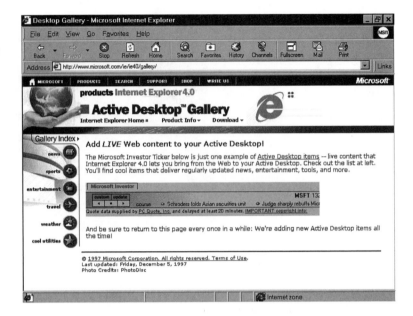

6. Clicking OK enables Internet Explorer to download a special file from the Internet. This file adds the MSNBC Weather Map to your desktop. The Customize Subscription button in this dialog box enables you to choose the method for updating your Active Desktop item. (I'll cover this procedure in the "Creating and Managing Subscriptions" section of Chapter 21.)

7. Close Internet Explorer by clicking the Close button in the upper-right corner of the program. You now should see the Active Desktop. Notice that the MSNBC weather map is available for viewing.

Changing the View of Your Folders

Creating a Web view of your desktop isn't the only way Windows 98 changes how you can view things. The Internet view also can affect your folders. This section will tell you about the Internet view of folders—we'll cover the more conventional view in the "Explorer: The Familiar Interface" section of this chapter.

Let's look at the various options available to you when you choose to view your folders in a Web view. The first thing we'll need to do is actually change the settings for a folder. I've created a temporary folder for this example, and you might want to do the same; that way you can try various features in relative safety.

Open the folder you want to change to Web view. Use the View | Folder Options command to display the Folder Options dialog. Notice that this dialog contains three entries. The Web style option displays your folder just like Internet Explorer would display a Web page. The only difference is that this page is local to your machine. The Classic style option sets your computer to display the folder using the same criteria (not the same precise display) as Windows 95 did. The third option, Custom, enables you to display the folder using a mixture of both Web and Classic styles.

Choose the Web style option, and then click OK to close the Options dialog. You should immediately notice some changes in your folder. For one thing, the titles for all the files are underlined. If you move the cursor to one of the file entries, you'll notice that it changes to a pointing finger, just like it would when pointing to a link on the Internet. Finally, instead of double-clicking to open a file, you'd point to it and single-click, just like you would to open a link on the Internet.

There's another interesting feature you can choose to use with Windows 98, a thumbnail view. It's easy to enable this feature, just right-click within the folder (without touching any files) and choose Properties from the context menu. You'll notice a new Enable thumbnail view check box near the bottom of the dialog. Check this box, and then close the Properties dialog by clicking OK. Now you can use the View | Thumbnails command (or the Views button on the Standard Buttons toolbar) to display a thumbnail view of your files like the one shown in Figure 2.4. Notice that this view shows you a small version of the contents of the file, rather than the usual application icon.

Figure 2.4.
This Web-style view of a folder uses thumbnails to display the contents of the graphics files it contains.

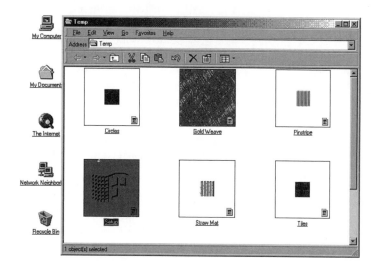

If this still isn't enough customization for you, there's one more new feature that's sure to make your day. You can customize a folder using the View | Customize this folder... command. The three options enable you to create or edit an HTML document, add a picture for background, or remove the customization you added previously.

Let's look at the Web-page version of the customization process. Select the Create or Edit an HTML Document option and click Next. The next dialog details the procedure that Windows 98 follows in creating a new HTML document for your folder. Click Next. If you installed Microsoft FrontPage Express, you'll see an editor window; otherwise, you'll see a standard text editor.

This is where you edit the HTML content for your folder. I'll cover Microsoft FrontPage Express in the "Microsoft FrontPage Express" section of Chapter 21. After you've made some changes to the document, saved it, and exited the editor, you return to the Customize This Folder dialog. Notice that it has the message "Congratulations! You have chosen to make the following changes: -Folder.htm." This message tells you that you successfully installed the HTML support. Click Finish to close the Customize This Folder dialog.

So how do you reverse the change you just made? Use the View | Customize this folder... command to display the Customize This Folder dialog again. This time choose the Remove Customization option, and then click Next. The next dialog warns you that you're about to remove the customization from your folder. Clicking Next will display a success message similar to the one we saw when adding the HTML content to our folder, but this one will show you what Windows 98 will remove. Click Finish and you'll be back to your original display.

> **Warning:** Removing HTML customization from your folder means the HTML file is erased. In other words, this is a one-way process. If you remove the file without first creating a backup, you'll have to create the HTML page from scratch if you decide to reinstall the HTML customization.

What if you don't want to go through a lot of effort to customize your folder? Well, you can always add some background graphic to give it some pizzazz. Let's look at that process. Use the View | Customize This Folder... command to display the Customize This Folder dialog again. This time select the Choose a Background Picture option and click Next. You'll see a Customize This Folder dialog that contains a list of the picture files in the current directory, a snapshot of the currently selected picture, a Browse button for finding additional pictures, and a set of controls for choosing the icon text foreground and background colors.

Choose one of the graphics from the list or use the Browse button to search for a particular graphics image. After you've selected an image and have modified the color text you want to use, click Next. You'll see a success message. Click Finish to complete the process.

Using the Standard Toolbars

Windows 98 is bristling with toolbars of all shapes and sizes. Even the Taskbar has several toolbars that you can use. What's the purpose of all these toolbars? They make it easier for you to move around Windows 98. The toolbars in Windows 98 reflect a continuing effort on Microsoft's part to enable you to customize every part of an application as you see fit.

Peter's Principle: Don't Bury Windows 98 in a Pile of Toolbars

Some people will most likely go crazy with the new toolbars that Microsoft provides. After all, if one toolbar can increase efficiency a little, and two toolbars a little more, then why not have a toolbar for every purpose? If you look at toolbars as the sole method for improving your Windows 98 efficiency, such logic might actually look good.

The problem is that you can end up cluttering your screen with more toolbars than you'll ever use. Think what will happen to the Taskbar if you add four or five toolbars and have that many applications open beside. Will you really be able to figure out what's going on without checking each icon individually? When a toolbar begins to get in the way of the work you're doing, it's no long a method of improving efficiency, but a hindrance to that efficiency.

The trick to using toolbars is to look for a few tasks that you perform regularly. I'm not talking about once a day; I'm talking about tasks that you perform hourly or perhaps even more frequently. An efficiency enhancing toolbar is one that makes getting the most from Windows 98 a matter of a single click.

Like most toolbars, you can move these around and resize them as necessary. Unlike most toolbars, the ones provided with the taskbar aren't free floating. You can't move them off the taskbar and have them sitting around like a dialog. This makes sense. Consider all the confusion that would occur when a user tried to figure out where a free-floating toolbar belongs.

The next few sections are going to help you learn more about the Taskbar toolbars. I'll show you how to add, create, remove, and destroy toolbars.

Adding a Standard Toolbar to the Taskbar

Windows 98 comes with four standard toolbars. The first is the Quick Launch toolbar, which enables you to view the desktop, launch Internet Explorer, or check out the channels to which you've subscribed. The second toolbar, Desktop, replicates all the icons on your desktop so you can access them without minimizing your current application. Just select the Desktop icon you want to see from the toolbar, and Windows 98 displays it. The third toolbar, Address, displays a list box in which you can type an address of something you want to see. (You also can type the name of a file on your local or network drive as a location on the Internet.) The list box keeps track of your most recent requests so you can select them rather than type them. The fourth toolbar, Links, displays a list of the links you've defined for Internet Explorer. A single click takes you to one of your favorite locations.

You can access any of these toolbars by right-clicking the taskbar, then selecting Toolbars from the context menu. To place a standard toolbar on the taskbar, add a check to its context menu entry.

Creating Your Own Toolbars

Just because Windows 98 comes with standard toolbars, doesn't mean you have to keep things that way. You can create your own toolbars to meet specific needs. For example, you might want to create a toolbar that gives you access to the various projects you're working on. Another toolbar might contain the applications you use on a daily basis. The list could be endless.

It's a good idea to keep the number of items on your toolbar as low as possible. I usually keep the number of items to 10 or less. A toolbar can really start to clog things up when you get past that 10-item level. If your toolbar starts to reach that 10-item level, you should consider alternatives to listing every item. For example, you could place the items you use less often in a folder, then place that folder on the toolbar.

Creating a toolbar is easy. All you need to do to start the process is create a folder containing shortcuts to the items you want to access using the toolbar. For example, you might create a folder named Common Applications that contains shortcuts to your favorite applications. After the folder is completed, right-click the taskbar. Select the Toolbars | New Toolbar option from the context menu. You'll see a New Toolbar dialog containing a field for the link name or Internet address and an Explorer-style directory listing you can use to choose the folder containing the shortcuts.

The capability to use an Internet address means you can create a toolbar of the Web sites you visit on a daily basis. You even can include the company intranet as a potential toolbar item. You only can get one site per toolbar when specifying an Internet or intranet location, so you should use toolbars only for the most important sites.

After you type a folder name or URL, Windows 98 displays it on the taskbar. Figure 2.5 shows an example of both types of toolbars. The toolbar on the left points to a local folder. The one on the right points to Microsoft's home page on the Internet.

Figure 2.5.
Toolbars provide a great deal of flexibility when it comes to accessing local or remote resources, even those on the Internet.

Tip: You might find it a bit difficult to view Web sites on the taskbar, especially if you have more than one. To see the Web site in a window, right-click the toolbar you want to see and select Open in Window from the context menu. You also can save room on the toolbar by right-clicking it and removing the check from the Show Title option in the toolbar. This removes the Web site title from the toolbar and creates more space for actually viewing the Web site.

Getting Rid of a Toolbar You Don't Need

After a while, you might find that all those toolbars you created really don't do as much as you'd like, or you may find that you want to get rid of some old toolbars to make room for new ones. Whatever the reason, getting rid of your old toolbar is easy. Simply right-click the Taskbar, then select Toolbars from the context menu. Find the toolbar you want to remove, then remove the check next to its name by selecting it.

Explorer: The Familiar Interface

Let's begin our tour of Explorer by examining how it's organized. Figure 2.6 shows the two-pane configuration of Explorer and the large icons view. The left side of the display contains the directory tree. You need to make note of several features of this directory tree for future reference. The first thing you'll notice is that the tree doesn't represent a single drive or even the contents of all the drives; it's more of a "machine tree" than anything else. This machine tree is divided into the following three elements.

- **The drive section.** This is the area that displays the contents of all your data drives. It includes any network drives to which you're connected.

- **The configuration section.** This area contains four icons in our sample display. (You also might see other icons here.) Control Panel provides access to every machine configuration component that Windows 98 has to offer. It includes both hardware and software configuration. Windows 98 also provides a Printers icon. You can access this icon from the Control Panel, but putting it here makes access a lot more convenient. The Dial-Up Networking folder contains your connections and a special icon for creating new connections. The Scheduled Tasks folder contains a list of the tasks you've asked Windows 98 to perform automatically.

- **The ancillary section.** The ancillary section can contain any number of icons. The example in Figure 2.6 contains several icons, including the Recycle Bin. The Recycle Bin is where any documents end up that you erase in Explorer. It performs the same function as the Recycle Bin on your desktop. The My Documents folder is where applications such as Microsoft Word usually place your data files. The Network Neighborhood icon appears when you have a network installed on your machine. It enables you to connect to network resources and to view network data. You'll also find icons here for accessing the Internet, your Briefcase, and the Online Services folder.

Figure 2.6.

The Explorer display
is easier to understand
when you break it
into components.

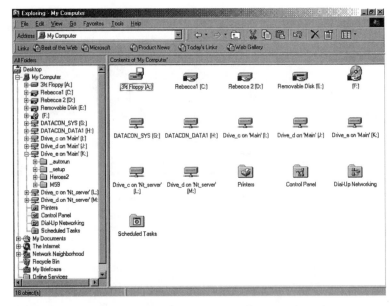

Looking Ahead: Future chapters look at other aspects of Explorer. Read Chapter 7, "Startup Shortcuts," if you want some additional tips for optimizing your work environment using Explorer.

Now that you have some idea of what the left pane contains, let's look at the right pane. Clicking any of the objects in the left pane displays its contents in the right pane. If you click a drive icon, you see the folders and files that the drive contains in the right pane. Click Network Neighborhood and you get a view of all the machines attached to the network. You can also use the icons in the right pane to open a file or folder. Double-click a folder and you will see what it contains. Double-click a file and you perform the default action associated with that file.

There are a number of ways to use Explorer to organize your data. Each tool provides a different method of viewing and working with your data. Let's begin with one of the first tools that you'll need to use under Windows 98—the context menu.

Every object you use in Windows 98 provides a context menu. If you have a doubt as to what something is, how to configure it, or just about anything else you can do with that object, a simple right-click will answer your question.

Every context menu for a file or folder contains five or six major sections. Each section tells you something about the object associated with that menu. The following paragraphs outline each section and describe its purpose:

- **Actions.** The very first section of the context menu tells you what kinds of actions you can perform with the object. The default action—normally Open—appears in bold print. In addition to the Open action, you'll likely see a Print data file action. Folders normally include an Explore and a Find action. You'll see one other type of entry in the context menu. If the file extension doesn't appear in the Registry, Windows 98 won't know what to do with it. In this case, you'll see an Open With... entry in place of the usual ones.

- **Network.** This is an optional section that normally contains a single entry—Sharing. Some objects support sharing and others don't. It all depends on how you have your network set up. Normally, peer-to-peer networks enable this option only for folders. Larger networks—such as those from Novell—provide this entry for both files and folders.

- **Send To.** Use this special entry if you want to send the object to another location. Windows 98 supports the Briefcase, Desktop, mail recipient, removable drives and any floppies connected to your system as destinations.

Tip: It's often handy to create additional destinations for the Send To menu such as project folders and network drives. All you need to do is place a shortcut to the new destination in the SendTo folder in your main Windows directory. Always make these destinations practical. In other words, don't add another directory listing to this rather important list. All you need to do is add destinations that you use on a daily basis.

- **Editing.** Believe it or not, you can edit an object just like everything else under Windows 98. This section contains entries for Cut, Copy, and Paste. You can place a copy of the object on the Clipboard, and then paste as many copies as needed onto other objects. These are full-fledged copies, not the shortcuts (object links) that we examine in the next section. If you cut an object, Windows 98 doesn't remove the icon from the display. It grays the icon and waits until you paste the object somewhere else before removing it permanently. This prevents you from accidentally erasing objects. Cutting a new object before you paste the first one leaves the first object in its original location.

- **Manipulation.** This section usually contains three entries, but it can contain more. The Create Shortcut option enables you to place a link to the file or folder somewhere else. Chapter 5, "Performance Primer," shows how you can use this feature to make your desktop a friendlier place. The Delete option sends the file to the Recycle Bin. You still can recover it later, if necessary. The Rename option enables you to change the long filename associated with the file.

Tip: You don't have to send objects to the Recycle Bin if you don't want to. Simply select the object you want to delete, then press Shift+Delete to erase it permanently.

- **Properties.** Every object—no matter what type—contains a Properties entry on its context menu. Clicking this entry always displays a dialog box that enables you to view and configure the properties of the object. For example, the Properties dialog box for a file shows the full filename, any attributes associated with the file, and some statistical information. Folders usually contain about the same information as files but provide some additional statistics as well. Disks, on the other hand, contain a wealth of information about the drive as a whole. This Properties dialog box even provides access to the three maintenance tools that Windows 98 provides to manage disk drives. You'll find that the Properties dialog box for other objects, such as the desktop, contains a wealth of information too. For example, the Desktop Properties dialog box allows you to change the system colors and display resolution. You can even use it to change your wallpaper.

Some objects on your system include some very specialized context menu entries. For example, if you right-click the Recycle Bin, you'll see an option to empty it. Right-clicking the desktop provides a New option that you can use to create new files. (You see the same menu option if you right-click a blank area of Explorer.)

The Windows 98 version of Explorer provides three toolbars that replace and augment the single toolbar that you saw in Windows 95. You can choose any or all of the toolbars that you want. Figure 2.6 showed all three toolbars.

The Standard Buttons toolbar contains all of the buttons required to move around in Explorer. The first three buttons are Forward, Back, and Up. You'll use the first two buttons to move from one location that you've already visited to another. The Up button takes you up one level in the directory structure. The next three buttons—Cut, Copy, and Paste—enable you to move files or folders from one location to another. All you need to do is cut or copy the file or folder in one location, then paste it in another. The Undo button enables you to undo the previous action you performed in Explorer. For example, if you renamed a file, then clicked the Undo button, the original name would return. The Delete button enables you to move a file or folder from its current location to the Recycle Bin. Use the Properties button to display a file's or folder's Property dialog. Finally, the Views button will allow you to see another view in Explorer. There are four standard views: Small Icons, Large Icons, Details, and List. They control how Explorer displays the objects you see in the right pane. A fifth view, Thumbnail, enables you to see a small version of a file instead of the standard icon.

The Address toolbar might look extremely simple, but it's a very powerful feature. If you place the cursor here, you can type a path to a local or network directory, or a location on the Internet. After you type the location you want to see and press Enter, it appears in the right Explorer pane. You also can type the name of an application or file here. Explorer will automatically open the file or start the application for you after it finds what you're looking for. Finally, you can use the drop-down list box to browse within the current context. If you're looking at local or network drives, you get a directory tree to look at. On the other hand, if you're looking at the Internet, you'll see a history listing of Web sites that you've recently visited.

You'll find that the Links toolbar is used quite often if you set it up the right way. A single click on any icon will take you to that location. The Links folder in your Favorites folder controls the contents of this toolbar. You get a choice of five Microsoft-specific Web sites to begin with. However, there's nothing to stop you from adding your ISP's home page, the location of your company's intranet site, or any other link you care to add.

You'll find another new feature in the Windows 98 version of Explorer as well. The Explorer Bar feature enables you to add a third, middle pane to the two-pane Explorer display. You can access the Explorer Bar using the View | Explorer Bar command. Figure 2.7 shows the four different Explorer Bars: Search, Favorites, History, and Channels. You use the Explorer Bar just as you would in Internet Explorer. The only difference is now you don't need a browser to access these features.

Figure 2.7.
The Explorer Bar enables you to explore the Internet using a third pane in Windows Explorer.

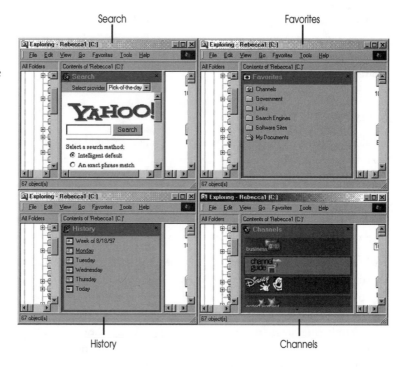

This gives you a quick overview of using Explorer. Now it's time to take a more detailed look. The following paragraphs talk about various ways that you can use Explorer. After you finish these sections, you'll start to see why I call Explorer the Swiss army knife that you need in order to learn how to use Windows 98 efficiently. Of course, once you know how to use that tool well, everything else will fall into place. Suffice it to say that you'll probably find more things you can do with Explorer as you become more proficient in working with Windows 98.

An Information Center

The most common way to look at Explorer is as your information center. It can tell you everything you need to know about your computing environment, if you know where to look. Figure 2.6 showed a typical Explorer display. It's probably one of the first displays you see when working with Windows 98, and it will definitely become a constant companion. Notice that this display shows My Computer. The right pane contains all the things you'd normally see if you double-clicked on the desktop's My Computer icon. You should note something else as well. My Computer isn't the entire universe in Explorer. Quite a few icons fall outside the My Computer purview, just like they do in the real world, where my computer is only part of the network. An information center has to provide you with complete information, both inside and out. Explorer does just that.

After you have all the pieces of Explorer and understand how to use them, you can put them together so that you can use Explorer as your information center. Each of the following sections describes a major element of your information center. Remember that each element is a drive, a control, or an ancillary unit.

Drives

Windows 98 provides three different tools you can use to manage your drives. You can start them from the Start menu (as you would have in Windows 95), or you can use the Windows 98 method of managing your drives.

Let's look at what the drive icons have to offer. Right-click any of your hard drives. (Floppy and CD-ROM drives provide the same type of properties, but the hard drives are easier to use for purposes of this description.) You should see the General tab of the drive's Properties dialog box.

There are three noteworthy items on this page. First is the drive label. Labels aren't as important for hard drives, but I do use them on my floppy disks to identify projects that I'm working on. Second is the Free Space indicator (magenta). It tells the amount of drive space remaining. The corresponding Used Space indicator (blue) tells you how much space is used on the drive. The pie chart helps you determine the current drive status at a glance. Third is the drive location. In this particular case, you can see that this is a local drive. You can pull up pages for network drives as well. However, you might not be able to do much, because your access rights to that drive affect what Windows 98 will allow.

The Tools page of the Drive Properties dialog box contains buttons that start the utility programs you can use to maintain the hard drives on your system. (You'll see a Tools page only for local drives.) We'll talk about how to use these tools in Chapter 9, "The Windows 98 File System." Notice that Windows 98 helps keep track of the last time you used the disk-maintenance utilities. This can be a big help to folks who have trouble remembering the last time they maintained their machine.

Peter's Principle: Disk Maintenance: A Necessity, Not an Option

Windows 98 makes drive-system diagnostics a lot easier to perform than any previous version of Windows and certainly easier than DOS. Drive system diagnostics are very important for maintaining data integrity. Even though the diagnostics are easier to access, a lot of people still don't use them because they really don't know how often they need to do so.

Every day, I start my machine and perform a standard disk scan in the background. That way, I can catch major structural problems before they eat an important file. For those of you who leave your machines on at night, you can use the new Task Scheduler in Windows 98 to automatically perform required disk maintenance at night. (Windows 98 automatically performs a disk scan for you if it determines that you shut it down abnormally. It performs this check before Windows 98 even gets started, so no files are open.) Once a week, I set aside some time to perform a thorough disk scan. I make sure that every other application is closed, including the screen saver, when I do this. ScanDisk can't really vouch for the status of any files you have open, so closing all your applications is a good idea.

Defragmenting your drive isn't a big deal from a data-security standpoint. If you don't defragment your drive, the worst thing that will happen is that the drive won't work as efficiently as it could. That said, do you really want to give up any performance due to a lack of maintenance? I usually defragment my drive once a week. In fact, I usually follow a routine of scanning the drive for errors, backing it up and defragmenting. This is the same routine I recommend for you. The disk scan will ensure that you get the best possible error-free backup. The backup itself will ensure that your data is safe if a disk failure occurs while you defragment it, and the defragmenting program will improve overall system efficiency.

The Check Now button opens ScanDisk. This is the Windows form of the DOS utility you probably used sometime in the past. In essence, this utility works about the same. The difference is that you now gain the benefits of a GUI rather than a text-mode interface. (You might remember that ScanDisk replaced the old CHKDSK utility.)

Tip: None of the three utility programs described in this section limits you to one drive. I usually check all the drives on my system at once instead of opening the Properties dialog box for each drive separately. Choosing to maintain your drives this way ensures that you don't miss any of them and also adds a certain level of automation to the process.

You can run two types of tests with this utility. The standard test simply checks the condition of your files and folders. All it does is check for major errors in the directory structure and the FAT. It also looks for cross-linked files and other structural problems. This test doesn't guarantee that the files are readable or that there isn't any damage to the drive media. Use the thorough test when you want to check for more than just structural integrity. The Automatically Fix Errors check box lets you tell ScanDisk to fix the problems without notifying you about each one in advance.

The Options button takes you to the dialog box shown in Figure 2.8, where you can modify the way that ScanDisk performs the thorough disk scan of your drive. The first group of options controls where ScanDisk looks for damaged media. Sometimes you might want to simply check the directory area for damage when troubleshooting your system. In most cases, you'll want to check both the system and data areas of your drive. The write test provides an added layer of testing integrity to your system. It actually tests to see whether the media is secure by writing to it and then reading back the results. This test will help you find certain types of drive failures that a read test won't find. The write test doesn't write to every data area on your drive; that would take an enormous amount of time. It simply checks a few unused areas of the drive. Some types of system and hidden file damage can't be repaired very easily. You can check this option if you think that a section of your drive contains such damage and you don't want to risk making the problem worse by "fixing" it. In most cases, however, you'll leave this check box unchecked because ScanDisk can handle the vast majority of hard-drive errors.

Figure 2.8.
Use the Surface Scan Options dialog box to modify the way ScanDisk performs a thorough test of your hard drive.

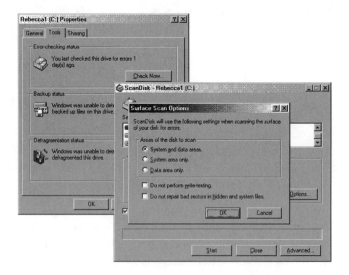

Clicking the Advanced button at the bottom of the ScanDisk dialog box displays the ScanDisk Advanced Options dialog box (see Figure 2.9). Most of these options are self-explanatory and correspond to features provided by the DOS counterpart of this utility. I usually keep the Display Summary radio button set to Only If Errors Found, so that I can check all my drives at once. If ScanDisk doesn't find any errors, it checks all the drives without disturbing me. Using this option means that I can run ScanDisk unattended in most cases.

Looking Ahead: Clicking the Backup Now button of the Drive Properties dialog box brings up the standard Backup utility described in Chapter 9. Since we look at this utility in detail elsewhere, I won't describe it here.

The Defragment Now button brings up the Disk Defragmenter utility. I'll also describe this utility in detail in Chapter 9, so we won't look at it here.

Figure 2.9.
*The ScanDisk
Advanced Options
dialog box contains
some user interface
and other automatic
settings.*

The third page of the Drive Properties dialog box is Sharing. You usually see this page with systems that use a fully supported peer-to-peer network.

Note: Some people won't see the Sharing page because they don't have a network installed. This page appears only under specific conditions when using certain types of networks.

The Drive Properties dialog box enables you to share resources with another machine. Enabling the Not Shared radio button prevents other people from looking at your drive. If you enable the Shared As radio button, Windows 98 shows some identification fields, an Access Types option list, and one or more password fields. The first field, Share Name, tells other machines what name to use when they access your drive. The second field, Comment, is a plain-language description of the drive other users will see.

It's never a good idea to give someone more access to your machine than they need. Remember that you can provide access to individual files and folders. In most cases, you'll want to reserve drive-level access to common data drives on a server rather than the entire drive on a workstation. You can always give someone more access if they need it. Taking back access after someone compromises your network is meaningless, because the damage is already done.

After you decide on a name for your drive, you need to determine what kind of access to it other people will have. In some cases, read-only access is all that the other person will need. This means that a person can see the file and read it but can't modify it in any way. (Of course, he can copy the file to his drive and modify it there.) You could use this for drives with informational databases that you want the other person to use but not modify. Full access allows the other person to read from and write to your drive. This is the level of access most people will require if you want to share data with them. A third possibility allows you to determine the level of access the other person gets to your system by the password they enter. This option provides the most secure access and flexibility. The two fields below these radio buttons will be enabled if the access option you select enables them. You can type any standard password here to grant access to your machine to a select group of people.

Peter's Principle: Disk Access and Workgroup Activities

There are two schools of thought about the way a workgroup should use the Windows 98 security features to enforce a specific way of modifying files. I find that they're both good, but for different reasons and in different circumstances.

The first method is to allow the people in the group read-only access to the master files on the leader's disk. This enables them to copy the file and make any required changes on their local drive. It also preserves the integrity of the master copy. After a person finishes his edit, he moves the file to a temporary directory on the leader's drive. You also could create a home directory for each person and have them place the modified files there. The leader then can choose which additions and comments to incorporate into the master document. If you use a common temporary directory, each person should change the file extension or some part of the filename to include a distinctive signature. This prevents their files from accidentally overwriting the modified files that other people submit.

The second method gives full access to the master document. Each member of the group uses the revision marks feature provided by the application to make changes to the document in his designated color. The advantage to this method is that everyone gets to discuss the document "online" in an interactive fashion. The group leader doesn't have to schedule a specific meeting to modify the document; changes are made on an ongoing basis. Of course, to implement this method your application must support a revision marks feature that uses a different color of text for each member's modifications.

When you give other people access to a drive on your machine, Windows 98 adds a hand to the drive icon. (It appears that the hand is holding the drive and presenting it to the other user.) This visual signal appears wherever the drive icon appears. It doesn't tell you what level of access the drive provides, however. Microsoft could have used slightly different symbols or perhaps colors to differentiate between access levels, but at least this symbol tells you to look for more information.

Control Panel

I was surprised to see how many different ways there are that you can access the Control Panel or its components under Windows 98. Even Explorer provides a method of access. (Look near the bottom of the My Computer directory tree in the left pane of Explorer.)

The number and types of icons (now called *applets*) you'll find here vary with the applications and equipment you've installed. Items such as the Printer folder always appear in your Control Panel. On the other hand, you won't always see an ODBC folder or some of the other specialty items that Control Panel provides.

Looking Ahead: We won't look at the individual Control Panel applets here. Chapter 10, "The Windows 98 Applets," provides a full description of all the applets and what they mean to you as a user, and takes a look at some of the ways in which you can manipulate the Windows 98 Control Panel.

Printers

As with just about everything else, you can control your printers from Explorer by accessing the Printer folder. It usually appears right above the Control Panel folder in the system hierarchy.

Looking Ahead: Chapter 15, "Fonts and Printing," covers all the details of managing your printers. It also looks at the process of adding a new printer to your system. The second half of this chapter looks at the details of using fonts to dress up your output.

This folder shows three icons. The minimum you should see if you have any printers installed is two icons, one of which starts the Add Printer Wizard. You'll always see one icon for each printer installed on your machine. Double-clicking that folder (or right-clicking and selecting Open) shows you any print jobs that the printer is currently processing. One of the printers will have a black checkmark next to it, which indicates that it's the default printer.

You also can configure your existing printers in this dialog box. All you need to do is right-click and select the Properties option to display the Properties dialog box. Chapter 15 discusses this dialog box in detail.

The only non-printer icon in this folder is the one used to add a new printer. The Add Printer Wizard will dazzle you with its ease of use, especially if you went through nightmare configuration sessions with previous versions of Windows. Chapter 15 explores the process of adding a new printer.

Dial-Up Networking

Dial-Up Networking enables you to connect to another machine in much the same way LapLink does. It's a stripped-down dial-in client, but at least it provides the functionality many users need.

The Dial-Up Networking folder appears under the Control Panel folder if you installed the service. This folder, like the Printers folder, contains two types of icons. The first type provides access to a wizard for creating new connections. The second type is the actual connection.

Looking Ahead: We take another look at Dial-Up Networking in several places. Chapter 1, "Opening Windows to the Internet," showed you how to create a connection. Chapter 19, "Hardware and Software Connections," shows you how to perform advanced tasks such as creating scripts. Chapter 18, "Mobile Computing: Notebooks, Telecommuting, and Remote Access," covers the implications of using Dial-Up Networking for the mobile user.

Using the Dial-Up Networking client is easy. You double-click a connection to open it. The program dials the phone and tries to make a connection to the host for you. Right-clicking and selecting Properties displays the Properties dialog box, which enables you to change the connection information among other things.

Network Neighborhood

Think of Network Neighborhood as a dynamic extension of Explorer for a network. Network Neighborhood usually appears near the bottom of the directory tree in the left pane of Explorer. My Computer is replaced by the Entire Network icon. No longer are we looking at the local machine, but at all the resources that you can access on the network as a whole.

Note: Novell Client 32 handles Network Neighborhood entries differently than its Microsoft NDS client counterpart. I cover Novell Client 32 differences in the "Using Novell Client 32" section of Chapter 23, "Networks." Fortunately, the idea behind using the entries is the same, so you can still follow along in this section and learn what Network Neighborhood can do for you.

You might also see other entries at the same level as the Entire Network. These are machines that you can access on peer-to-peer networks. You always can access your own resources, so you'll always see your machine listed here. Network Neighborhood only enables you to see the shared drives for the machines—not any local drives. I also found it interesting that not every shared resource appears on the tree. You have to select the machine to see any resources beyond drives. (These other resources appear in the right pane.)

Tip: At first glance, it might seem like a waste of effort to list your machine along with everything else in Network Neighborhood. However, there's one good reason to do so. Here you can see at a glance every resource you're sharing with the rest of the network. Instead of forcing you to look through the directory tree for these elements, Microsoft thoughtfully placed them here.

You need to know a few interesting things about Network Neighborhood that make it different from the rest of Explorer. For one thing, you can't access the properties for the Entire Network. The Entire Network is simply a placeholder for Network Neighborhood; it doesn't exist as a concrete object.

Below the Entire Network are entries for each network you're currently connected to. In most cases, you'll see the actual workgroup or domain name, not the name of the network vendor or product. This list will change as your connections change. Looking here will tell you whether a problem is application- or network-related. An application error, such as the inability to open a file, might look like a network error for a variety of reasons. However, if you look in the Entire Network folder and see the connection, it's very unlikely that the connection is the problem. Chapters 25, "Software Problems," and 26, " Hardware Problems," contain tips to help you locate and fix other problems with the hardware or software on your machine.

Recycle Bin

The Recycle Bin works the same in Explorer as it does on the desktop. You can drop things into it, examine its contents, empty it, or restore a file that it holds to its original (or another) location. The Explorer copy of the Recycle Bin comes in handy if you see a file that you want to erase and the desktop copy is covered by another application.

> **Tip:** Files in the Recycle Bin continue to take up space on the drive. Windows 98 moves deleted files to the Recycle Bin—a special folder—until you erase them for good. (The short filenames or old DOS filenames are changed to allow multiple files of the same name in the Recycle Bin.) If you find that you're short on hard-drive space, you might want to see whether there's anything in the Recycle Bin you can get rid of.

In most cases, your bin won't contain anything. Files in the Recycle Bin look just like files anywhere else. You can move objects in the Recycle Bin to other areas of Explorer to "unerase" them. Until you do unerase them, the Properties dialog box won't tell you much except the file's name and the date you deleted it.

Briefcase

The Briefcase is one of the best Windows 98 features for mobile users. It allows you to pack everything you need for a project into one folder and then move that folder around, just like the briefcase you carry to and from work.

Looking Ahead: Chapter 18 takes a look at how you can use Briefcase. You might want to read through this material even if you aren't a mobile computer user, because I discuss a few techniques for using Briefcase that everyone will want to know about.

Briefcase adds one option to the context menu of items it holds. The Update option enables you to update a file from its original copy on your hard drive. This is one of the steps you need to take before packing your Briefcase to go on the road. I cover this topic in greater depth in Chapter 18.

The Startup Folder

Think of the Startup folder as a sort of `AUTOEXEC.BAT` file for your Windows applications. Windows automatically looks in this file during the boot process and launches anything it finds there.

Peter's Principle: Getting a Great Start in the Morning

A lot of people are under the impression that the Startup folder is only for loading applications. Other people feel that you should place only certain classes of applications there, such as screen savers or Microsoft Office Startup. Although putting a background application in the Startup folder is a good idea, using the Startup folder for this purpose alone doesn't make full use of the resource.

Placing a shortcut to the Startup folder on your desktop is a great idea, because you can put things in there that you'll need the next morning. (Microsoft buried this folder so far in the directory tree that you'll quickly tire of trying to use it if you don't take this step.) For example, if I'm working on a proposal over the course of a few days, I'll stick a shortcut to the master file in Startup. That way, it automatically opens when I start my machine the next day.

Adding objects to the Startup folder can really boost your productivity. Instead of spending the first 15 minutes of the morning getting set up, you can start your machine, get a cup of coffee, and be ready to work when you return. Making Windows 98 more efficient is largely up to the user now. Most of the tools are there; all you need to do is use them.

Like everything else in Windows 98, you'll find the Startup folder in Explorer. Unfortunately, it's buried deep in the directory tree. If you look in the `\WINDOWS\Start Menu\Programs` folder, you'll see the Startup folder. A faster way to access the folder is to right-click the Start menu icon on the taskbar and select the Explore option. This displays a two-pane version of Explorer you can use to find the Startup folder faster.

Standard Windows 98 Applications

Windows 98 has much more to offer than just Explorer. A whole new group of utility programs is available to make life easier for the user. In the past, most of these applications were supplied by third parties. Today you get them as part of the operating system package.

The next few paragraphs highlight these new utility programs. We take a close look at them in future chapters, but the information that follows should provide you with what you need to get started.

> **Looking Ahead:** The following paragraphs provide highlights of the utilities. Most appear in other, product-specific areas of this book. For example, you'll find out more about remote access utilities in Chapter 19. Windows Messaging also appears in several other chapters, including Chapter 20, "Network Connections with an Internet Appeal." You'll want to visit Chapter 10 to find out more about all the Windows 98 applets.

Remote Access

There are two tools you can use for remote access. The first is Dial-Up Networking. Dial-Up Networking allows you to connect to another computer much as you would with any peer-to-peer connection. The big difference is that you use a modem instead of a network interface card (NIC) to make the connection. (Windows 98 now includes Dial-Up Server as a standard feat, which means you can run Dial-Up Server on your work machine and dial into it from home.) You can use Dial-Up Networking to dial into a terminal connected to the company network using your notebook. It also comes in handy for off-site employees who needed to check in for their email. Interestingly, the interface for this application looks very similar to the single-pane Explorer interface that appears when you open a folder. Most of the controls operate the same way as well, so I won't discuss them here.

The second utility is Direct Cable Connection, which enables the client machine to access the host machine's drives and other resources. I find that I normally use it to move data from my notebook computer to the desktop machine. There are no controls to worry about with this application—just run the host, then connect to it using the client.

Tip: Always use a parallel connection if possible when using the Direct Cable Connection utility. Doing so greatly increases throughput. You can at least triple the amount of information moved per second by using a parallel cable. A machine-to-machine parallel cable might be difficult to find. If so, you can modify a standard 25-pin serial cable by adding a gender changer to each end. Most electronics stores carry both serial cables and gender changers. The advantage to this approach is that you can use the same cable for both serial and parallel connections.

Accessories

Windows 98 provides a lot of small utility programs that are grouped into the general category of accessories. Essentially they dress Windows 98 up by adding some of the tools required to access common hardware. For example, the multimedia tools allow you to access your sound board. The multimedia offerings consist of a multimedia player (media player), (sound) recorder, mixer (volume control), and CD player.

Windows 98 also includes some familiar utilities from previous versions of Windows, including Calculator and WinPopUp. Conspicuously absent are Cardfile and Calendar.

You'll really like two of the utilities that also appeared with Windows 95. The first one allows you to configure the various international settings. There are a number of ways to use the International Settings utility. The first way is to click the Taskbar icon to display a list of installed languages. You can select which language you want to use from the list. The second way to use the International Settings utility is to right-click the International icon and select the Properties option. This displays the Keyboard Properties dialog box. This dialog box enables you to change the currently selected language. It also enables you to add support for additional languages.

Tip: Even if you don't use more than one language, adding the International Settings utility to your Startup folder can make you more productive. I use it to gain quick access to the Keyboard Properties dialog box without going through the Control Panel. The Speed tab of this dialog box contains settings that I can change as needed to make the system more comfortable to use.

The second utility, Resource Meter, enables you to monitor system resources. Windows 98 doesn't automatically install either of these features; you need to install them separately using the Add/Remove Programs utility. Icons for both applications appear in the taskbar tray. You can display the Resource Meter by double-clicking its icon. Placing the mouse cursor over the icon for a few seconds displays a quick readout of the various levels. This display tells you the status of the three memory-related areas of the system.

- **System resources.** This tells you the amount of memory you have left in the smaller of the two 64KB memory pools used for windows, icons, dialog boxes, and other system objects.

- **User resources.** This tells you how much memory Windows 98 is using for interface-related objects such as windows and dialog boxes.

- **GDI resources.** All icons and other object-memory usage associated with the graphical device interface appears in this level. This level always pertains to graphical system elements rather than an interface element such as a button or window.

ActiveMovie Control

The easiest way to look at the ActiveMovie Control is as a replacement for the Media Player utility, but that really wouldn't look at the intended use for this utility program. There are three different applications that you can use to play multimedia files on your machine—each has a different forté. Double-click any WAV file displayed in an Explorer window and you'll see a copy of the Sound Recorder appear. You'll also see this application appear if you right-click the file and choose Play or Open from the context menu. The reason that Sound Recorder appears is that you can use it to modify the WAV (audio) file if so desired. ActiveMovie does the same thing for video files like the AVI files provided as part of the Windows 98 installation disk—provided that you retain the default configuration (I'll show you how to modify the files associated with the ActiveMovie Control in the section "ActiveMovie File Types" later in this chapter.)

The reason that we call on the ActiveMovie Control is that it's lightweight—you don't have to have a lot of memory to run it. The ActiveMovie Control is designed for Internet use. It doesn't provide all the bells and whistles that the Media Player does. However, the Media Player still is used the majority of the time when you insert any kind of multimedia file into an OLE client (such as a Word for Windows document). That's because the Media Player provides better capabilities—it's designed to work with all the devices on your machine. The Media Player also provides a standard user interface in the form of a menu.

Tip: The ActiveMovie Control isn't limited to video files—you also can use it to play audio and to filter graph files. Unfortunately, for it to play non-video file types, you have to either open the ActiveMovie Control manually (using the Start menu entry) or pass the filenames on the command line. You also could change the file associations for audio files to use the ActiveMovie Control instead of the Sound Recorder for a more permanent setup. I show you how to do this in the "Using Explorer to Get the Job Done" section of Chapter 7.

Tip: Tests on several machines have shown that most video files play fine in full-screen mode on a 200MHz Pentium machine with at least 16MB of RAM. If you have a lower-speed machine, you should use something other than full-screen mode in most cases.

Internet Explorer

Internet Explorer 4.0 provides many new features including the capability to use channels and to surf your local drive in addition to the Internet. Of course, one of the nicest features is that Internet Explorer is actually part of the Windows 98 interface. You can put a Web page right on your Desktop and use it like you would any other Desktop element. In fact, you can convert your entire Desktop to look like a Web page if you want. I covered some of these new features in Chapter 1; others were discussed at the beginning of this chapter. We'll spend plenty of time looking at all the features that this latest version of Internet Explorer provides as the book progresses.

You'll also find Internet Explorer 4.0 features like the capability to use ActiveX controls. These controls greatly enhance the usability of a Web site; they enable the Webmaster to do things that HTML code usually won't support. For example, you can use an ActiveX control to figure out the total owed on a purchase before sending the page to the Web server. A control also can change the appearance of the Web page on-the-fly and can perform other tricks that are unavailable when using straight HTML.

In addition to ActiveX support, Internet Explorer 4.0 offers support for HTML style sheets, frames, Java applets, JavaScript, and VBScript. Let's talk about HTML style sheets (also called cascading style sheets) for a second. Using a style sheet (also known as a template) with a word processor enables you to create consistent documents with little effort. Style sheets provide this same capability when used on a Web page. Instead of designing every page element, you can create a style sheet that dictates certain things, such as the use of icons. All that's left to the user is the placement of content. You can find out more about cascading style sheets at `http://www.w3.org/pub/WWW/Style/`. The actual specification is at `http://www.w3.org/pub/WWW/TR/WD-css1`.

Looking Ahead: This section provides just an overview of Internet Explorer. We look at all the usage details for this product in the "Working with Internet Explorer" section of Chapter 21.

Internet Explorer also provides connections to many other applications. The most important applications from an Internet-user point of view are the Internet Mail and Internet News viewers that come with Internet Explorer 3.0. I examine these products in detail when I look at Internet

Explorer usage in Chapter 21. You'll also want to check out the information about Outlook Express in the same chapter. Outlook Express provides a one-stop approach for both Internet mail and news.

Microsoft NetMeeting

NetMeeting is a new technology-type utility. It provides you with the capability of holding meetings over the Internet. Immediately obvious are the voice capabilities of this product. There are separate controls for sending and receiving voice from other people. Because this is a duplex connection, you won't get the irritating speaker-phone effect that's present in a conference-call setup.

> **Looking Ahead:** We cover this utility in a lot more detail in the "Working with Microsoft NetMeeting" section of Chapter 21. This includes information about getting NetMeeting set up for use.

NetMeeting also enables you to perform all the standard functions that you usually associate with an Internet connection. For example, you can send a copy of a file to one or more meeting attendees. You also can use NetMeeting to remotely control an application and perform other computer-related tasks.

One of the features I like best is the whiteboard. You can use it to give other people a visual representation of your idea. However, unlike the whiteboard in a meeting room, other people can draw on this one and help you expand your ideas. Overall, NetMeeting provides all the features of a physical meeting room without any of the inconvenience. In fact, there are some ways in which this utility provides a superior virtual meeting room to the physical rooms we're accustomed to using.

Imaging

Imaging is a graphics-manipulation program. You can't draw with it (there's a set of tools designed to annotate images), but you can use it for a variety of other purposes such as scanning images. You also can use it to view existing graphics and prepare documents for FAX or email transmission.

WebTV for Windows

The WebTV for Windows application enables you to do a variety of things, the most interesting of which is watch television on your computer. How can you use WebTV for Windows in the workplace? Well, you could use it for training of various sorts. The WebTV for Windows could also be used for watching various satellite programs designed to teach new techniques to professionals. You also can use it to grab a broadcast from a distant place that you usually couldn't receive. Obviously you could also use it for pure entertainment, something that many home users will use it for.

Looking Ahead: We'll cover the WebTV for Windows in detail in the "Using the WebTV for Windows Application" section of Chapter 17, "Video Configuration." I'll show you how to get the WebTV for Windows set up and then how to use many of its features.

On Your Own

You'll find that Windows 98 provides more Internet access than ever before. In fact, saying that you'll have the Internet at your fingertips seems too pale when you consider the features Windows 98 provides. Try using the various features we talked about in this chapter to subscribe to an Internet site of your choice. Explore the channel feature as well. Make sure you understand how it can help you find things quickly on the Internet.

Explorer is one of the cornerstones of the Windows 98 interface. It enables you to move around your machine—and the network, for that matter. Spend some time getting used to the Explorer interface and trying out the various display modes. Click the column headings in the Detail view to see how Explorer rearranges the filenames.

Taskbar toolbars are another feature that can make life easier for any Windows 98 user. Try creating at least one toolbar and using it for a week. If you're not happy with the way the toolbar turned out, try tweaking it to make it more efficient. You'll also want to try both toolbar types: folder-based and Web page.

Context menus also are an important part of Windows 98. Try right-clicking all the objects you see. See how the context menus vary from object to object. Don't forget that even the desktop is an object with a context menu. Make sure that you click the desktop to close its context menu without selecting anything.

3

The
Windows 98
Desktop

Peter Norton®

I predict that the Windows 98 Active Desktop will be the most misunderstood part of the Windows 98 interface. Just as people are learning to use the features provided by the Windows 95 interface, Microsoft decides to add more features as well as an Internet connection. Adding Internet Explorer 4.0 to the mix only complicates matters. You now have three interfaces to choose from: Program Manager (Windows 3.x), Explorer (Windows 98), and Internet Explorer 4.0. Even with this complexity, one fact is still clear: It's up to you to dress up the desktop of Windows 98's interface.

This chapter doesn't discuss the Program Manager interface of old— plenty of other books on the market talk about that interface. This chapter covers the new Internet Explorer interface. Refer to Chapter 1, "Opening Windows to the Internet," and Chapter 2, "Introducing Windows 98," for an overview of Internet Explorer 4.0. Chapter 21, "Internet Connections," discusses details specific to Internet Explorer. This chapter also covers the standard Windows 98 Explorer interface.

Tip: If you want to get the most out of Windows 98, you have to learn to use Internet Explorer. Not only that, you need an Internet account. Windows 98 relies heavily on the Internet for a variety of tasks, not just data delivery to the user. If you request help, for example, you can use Internet access to ensure the information you get is the most current available. Other features, such as the capability to automatically update your system, don't work without an Internet account. Even the WebTV for Windows utility relies on the Internet to an extent for listings. In other words, you'll miss out on many of the added capabilities in Windows 98 if you don't also use Internet Explorer.

Windows 98 makes heavy use of Explorer, as you've seen in previous chapters. Believe it or not, however, there's still more to learn about this particular utility. It's much more flexible, and it provides more features than most people will ever use. That's the beauty of the Explorer interface—it enables you to do things your way. Windows 98 doesn't force you to do things a certain way like its predecessor did.

After you figure out how Explorer can help you, it becomes much simpler to give your desktop a face you can really use. It's no longer a bothersome task ; rather, it's a voyage of discovery. Very few people know how to make something work the way that they want it to. Many people are accustomed to simply following someone else's advice. Explorer and the Windows 98 desktop will change all that.

The following sections will help you learn to use the new features of the Internet Explorer interface. You'll also see how the Windows 98 desktop and Explorer can work together to create an environment that truly reflects the way you work. It might take some time for you to adjust to this new level of freedom. After you do, however, you'll work more efficiently, and you'll never view Windows the same way again.

Tip: Explorer, more than just the centerpiece tool of Windows 98, is your gateway to freedom. As such, it pays to take time to learn how to use this key. Make sure you first spend time optimizing Explorer to your needs, then concentrate on the rest of Windows 98. The decisions you make in Explorer tend to affect other areas of Windows 98. A fully optimized Explorer interface includes all the objects you normally work with, such as backup files. Unless Windows 98 knows how to work with a particular object, you might find yourself fighting Windows 98 instead of working with it. Optimizing Explorer is the first step in optimizing Windows 98 from the user perspective.

Using Active Desktop

This book has already taken a quick look at Active Desktop, but you haven't yet learned how to use this new feature to your benefit. Some people, when working with the Windows 95 desktop, stuffed it with every folder available—it became just as cluttered as their actual office desk. What happens now that you can also fill the Windows 98 desktop with additional information from the Internet? This could cause some people to have real problems using Windows 98; the desktop could become cluttered to the point of being unusable. The following points should help you keep the clutter to a minimum.

- **Avoid excess.** When using Active Desktop, it's important to decide what you need and don't need. After all, do you really need that folder containing last year's financial report? The contents of your desktop should be determined by frequency of access; this keeps your desktop uncluttered and makes you more efficient. If you visit the same web site every day, it pays to place it on your desktop.

- **Consolidate as necessary.** Some people work on many different projects at the same time and need access to many sources of information. Trying to keep these desktops uncluttered might seem like a losing proposition. You can avoid this problem, however, by consolidating what you need into folders. You might, for example, have four or five folders on your desktop right now that contain information for the same project. Consolidating that information into one master folder will make life easier.

- **Use a taskbar toolbar.** You can save a great deal of space on your desktop and make it easier to access your projects in the process. You just need to create a toolbar for the taskbar and point it to a local or network directory. Pointing your toolbar to a network directory can actually be more efficient than using the desktop, which is an added bonus for people in a workgroup. This way, everyone has the same list of folders with the same names and shortcuts. Because everyone has the same project list, there is less confusion when talking to other people. In addition, the manager can keep the project folder list up-to-date by managing a single directory, rather than trying to keep track of many employee desktops. The process for creating toolbars was discussed in the "Creating Your Own Toolbars" section of Chapter 2.

- **Decide on an efficient configuration.** You can make your desktop more efficient without giving up the convenience of having your work lying all over the place. One way is to reduce the size of the icons. Open the Display Properties dialog box by right-clicking the desktop and choosing Properties from the context menu. Select the Appearance tab, then select Icon in the Item field. Note that you can change the icon size from the default of 32 to as small as 16. This makes the icon a tad more difficult to see, but you can fit roughly twice as many on your Desktop.

- **Choose Web or Standard view.** The Web view is extremely efficient in that it only takes one click to do just about anything. You can get from point A to point B in half the clicks, which translates into more efficient time usage. I find, however, that the Web view is slightly inefficient at using desktop space wisely. The icons and underlined text require more space. At some point, you need to decide between efficient use of space and efficient methods of getting where you need to go.

- **Create channels that make sense.** Windows 98 comes configured with some great channels if you have a wide variety of interests. Unfortunately, I don't know of anyone who has interests in all the areas provided by the default channel setup. You'll definitely want to optimize your channel setup so you can find things of interest quickly. This is beneficial because you might be able to reduce the amount of space currently required by the Internet Explorer Channel Bar on the Active Desktop.

- **Minimize your web pages.** In most cases, you don't need to view the web pages you frequent in their entirety. A small view is usually sufficient until you need the information the page contains. I normally reduce the size of a web page so that it takes up the minimum Active Desktop space available, but so I can still see any changes as Windows 98 automatically updates the page content for me. You can always resize the web page later to get a full view of the content it provides.

After you examine the Active Desktop–specific ways of tuning your machine, you'll then learn about the more generic Explorer methods. Even Windows 95 users can use these techniques. You might want to keep them in mind if your workplace has a mixture of both Windows 98 and Windows 95 machines. If you're using Windows 98, try to balance the Explorer tips with the Active Desktop ones just covered.

Customizing Your Desktop

You probably don't have a "formal" physical desktop at work. In fact, I'll bet it's customized to meet every need you have. It's a sure thing that your desk reflects the way you work. No one, for example, forced you to place the stapler in the upper-right corner.

Windows 98 doesn't force you to do things its way like previous versions of Windows did. Someone at Microsoft must have followed Burger King's lead by allowing people to have it their way. The Explorer interface is so flexible that I doubt any two people will ever have the same Desktop under Windows again. The Desktop is one place where anything goes. The Windows 98 Desktop is an object just like everything else in Windows 98.

The Windows 98 Desktop has some features you might not think about right away. If you right-click the desktop, for example, it has a context menu just like everything else in Windows 98. The context menu is discussed further in the "Working with Desktop Objects" section of this chapter. For now, suffice it to say that there are plenty of nice surprises when it comes to arranging items under Windows 98.

Arrange Icons and Line up Icons are two entries in the context menu of the Windows 98 Desktop. Arrange Icons enables you to rearrange your desktop in a specific order. It works just like the same entry under Explorer. (See how everything seems to have a bit of Explorer in it?) You can re-arrange your icons by name, type, size, or date. Personally, I find the type and name orders the most convenient.

Some people detest the standard arrangements, so they put the icons in the order they want them. If you're one of these people, the Line up Icons option is custom-tailored for you. It enables you to keep the icons in a specific order, but it arranges them into neat rows and columns. This option provides a grid effect that enables you to keep your desktop neat, yet still arranged in the order you want.

The following sections look at the desktop as a whole. They discuss different options to make your desktop more usable, but they don't stop there. These sections are a guide to the most common tricks people use to optimize their Windows 98 environment. This is an unofficial "must do" check list you should look at when trying to get the most from your setup.

Taskbar

A major part of the Windows 98 interface is the taskbar, which appears as a gray horizontal bar at the bottom of the display. The taskbar is the central control area for most actions you'll take under Windows 98. It contains three major elements: a Start menu, a Task List, and a Settings area. You also might see one or more toolbars.

Before describing the major elements of the taskbar, here are a few ways you can configure it. The taskbar starts out at the bottom of the display, but you don't have to leave it there. With Windows 98, you can place the taskbar on any of the four sides of the desktop. Windows 98 lets you change your desktop to suit your needs.

Like other objects under Windows 98, the taskbar provides a Properties dialog box. (To display it, right-click the taskbar and select Properties from the context menu.) This dialog box has two pages. One controls the Start menu setup; the other controls the taskbar itself. The four settings on the

Taskbar tab enable you to change how it reacts. You can remove the taskbar from view, for example, by removing the check mark from the Always on Top field. The Show Clock field enables you to clear more space for applications on the taskbar by removing the clock from view. My personal favorite is the Auto Hide field. When you select this option, the taskbar appears as a thin gray line at the bottom of the display. Whenever the mouse cursor touches this line, the taskbar resumes its normal size. This enables you to minimize the taskbar to clear space for application windows, yet the taskbar is handy when you need it.

Right-clicking the taskbar displays a few other object-specific options, all of which affect the way Windows 98 organizes the applications currently displayed on the taskbar.

- **Toolbars.** This option enables you to select one of the toolbars you created for the taskbar. This feature is discussed in Chapter 2 so it won't be repeated here.

- **Cascade.** When you select this option, all application windows are resized to the same size. Windows 98 arranges them diagonally, much like the display in a spreadsheet when you open more than one file. You can select any application in the list by clicking its title bar (the area at the top of the application window that contains the application's name).

- **Tile Windows Horizontally or Tile Windows Vertically.** Use either of these options if you want to see the window areas of all your applications at once. Windows 98 uses every available inch of desktop space to place the applications side by side, either horizontally or vertically. Each application receives about the same amount of space.

- **Minimize All Windows.** If your screen is so cluttered that you can't tell what's open and what's not, use this option to clean up the mess. The Minimize All Windows option minimizes every application you have running on the desktop.

The Start Menu

The Start menu normally appears on the far-left side of the taskbar. It contains a complete listing of all your applications, access to some system settings, and a few other things thrown in for good measure. A standard Start menu has nine main entries. (You might see additional entries, such as program icons, on the Start menu depending on your configuration.) The following paragraphs describe each entry in detail.

> **Tip:** You now can move programs around on the Start menu without opening it up in Explorer first. Right-click the program you want to move and drag it to a new location. You'll see a context menu that enables you to move, copy, or delete the program. Unfortunately, this feature doesn't work with folders.

- **Programs.** This entry lists the applications installed on your machine. Unlike Windows 3.x, the Explorer interface enables you to place folders within folders (programmers call this *nesting*). You can place applications several levels deep within the menu tree.

- **Favorites.** This is another example of the Internet orientation of Windows 98 coming into play. The Windows 95 Start menu didn't include this entry. The Favorites entry provides access to your favorite web sites using a couple clicks rather than opening the browser first. Use it just as you would the Favorites folder in Internet Explorer.

- **Documents.** Use this option to select a document you previously opened using Explorer. This list doesn't store documents opened using the File | Open command. The list can contain up to 15 document names.

- **Settings.** Windows 98 provides a number of ways to change your environment. The Settings menu provides one centralized location for this information. It provides access to the Control Panel, the Printers configuration dialog box, and the Taskbar Properties dialog box.

- **Find.** This option opens a submenu containing a variety of search options. You can look for a specific file, a computer, or even a person in your organization. In addition, you'll find an option for searching the Internet. Some users might have an MSN-specific option here as well. There will probably be additional entries as application vendors begin to use this feature. In most cases, selecting an option on the Find submenu opens a search form to look for a specific resource.

- **Help.** The Help option opens the main Windows 98 help file. You can use this file to search for just about any information you need to run Windows 98. Microsoft has come a long way in improving the help files for this version of Windows. Unlike previous versions, the help files in Windows 98 are HTML pages. Content has improved as well. Instead of providing you with dry facts, these files actually provide procedures you can use to do the job.

- **Run.** Remember the File | Run command under Program Manager? You can still use it in Windows 98. The Run option in the Start menu opens a dialog box that enables you to start an application by typing its path and name. You also can include any appropriate parameters.

- **Log Off <User Name>.** If you are sharing a machine between two or more people, it hardly pays to shut the machine down just to switch users. The Log Off option enables one user to log off and another to log on.

- **Suspend.** The only time you'll see this option is on a laptop or desktop machine that supports power management features. (You have to enable power management to see this option on the Start menu.) The Suspend option enables you to shut down the machine without leaving Windows. This is a productivity option that enables you to stop and start your work quickly without wasting power. The next time you power up the machine, you'll return to Windows exactly the way you left it. Two potential problems exist with this particular feature: First, it circumvents the security provided by the initial logon screen (unless you enable password protection). Anyone who starts the machine up will be logged in under your name and will have the same access rights you do. Second, any applications or files open when you suspend Windows will remain that way. The potential for data damage is greatly increased when you suspend rather than shut down the machine. Some laptop users may experience a third problem: Suspend may not turn power off on some machines, which means your battery continues to be drained. You could end up with a dead battery and lost data if this is the case with your laptop.

- **Shut Down.** This option enables you to perform an orderly shutdown of Windows 98. An orderly shutdown includes making sure that all the data writes to disk and that the Registry information is saved.

The Taskbar Buttons

The taskbar contains one icon for each application currently running on the machine. This group of buttons replaces the Task Manager found in Windows 3.x. Instead of using the Alt+Tab key combination to switch between applications, you now can choose an application much as you would select a television station using a remote control. (You can still use Alt+Tab if you prefer; it just isn't as convenient in most cases.) You just need to click the appropriate button.

The taskbar has some other useful features. The buttons, for example, shrink in size as necessary to accommodate all running applications. You also can increase the size of the taskbar to hold two, three, or even more rows of buttons. Placing the mouse cursor near any edge of the taskbar produces the same double arrow used to resize other objects in Windows 98. There is a limit, though, to the size the buttons can attain.

Another useful feature is the capability to obtain more information about an application simply by placing the mouse cursor over its button. After a couple seconds, Windows 98 displays a long title for the application and the foreground data file. The same principle holds true for other items on the taskbar. For example, holding the mouse cursor over the time indicator shows today's date. In some cases, the information you receive is minimal. The Volume icon, for example, displays a single word—Volume.

The Settings Area

The Settings area of the taskbar (also called the system tray or taskbar tray) usually contains two or more icons. These icons usually are hardware related, but there's no reason they couldn't be an application or a utility program. Each icon can serve multiple purposes, depending on what piece of hardware it controls. The two most common icons in the Settings area are Clock and Volume. The preceding section explained how each of these options reacts when you position the mouse cursor over their respective icons.

The Volume icon does different things depending on your actions. A single-click produces a master volume slider, which can be used to adjust the volume of all sounds produced by the sound board. Double-clicking the same icon displays the Volume Control dialog box, which provides detailed control of each input to your sound board. The dialog box also includes a master volume slider. Right-clicking the icon displays the context menu. In this case, it displays only two entries. The first, Volume Controls, takes you to the Volume Control dialog box; the second, Adjust Audio Properties, displays the Audio Properties dialog box.

Double-clicking the Clock icon displays the Date/Time Properties dialog box. A right-click shows the context menu. Detailed information about the clock appears in the Clock section of this chapter.

Note: Several other interesting icons can appear in the Settings area. One of them enables international users to adjust their settings with ease. A special icon for PCMCIA-equipped machines displays the current bus status and the type of card plugged into the bus. Portable users will appreciate the battery indicator that appears in this area. With a quick click of the mouse, you can check your battery status before it becomes critical. If you see a plug in place of the normal battery indicator, you know the laptop is plugged into the wall socket.

Passwords

You can initiate password protection in several ways. The most automatic method is to install a Microsoft (or any other) network. You'll also see a password screen if you enable users to configure their own desktops. No matter how you install password protection, you'll need to manage it from time to time. The purpose of this section is to help you do so.

Open the Control Panel and double-click the Password applet to display the Passwords Properties dialog box. The first page, Change Passwords, contains two buttons: Change Windows Password and Change Other Passwords. Use the Change Windows Password option to change the password you see when you initially log in to the system. The same password is in effect whether you enable passwords through multiple user configurations or by using a Microsoft network.

Tip: There's a fatal flaw in the password protection provided by Windows 95 that might be fixed for Windows 98. The way Windows checks the user password is to "unlock" a decrypted file containing the password. The filename usually corresponds to the username and has an extension of .PWL. Windows 95 stores the PWL file either in the main Windows folder or in the user's profile folder. Erasing this file effectively erases the security for that particular person. A person without a PWL file can enter Windows 95 without a password.

continues

The positive side of this is that if a user forgets his password, you can always regain access for him by erasing his security file.

The negative side, however, is that a user could circumvent security given the right set of circumstances. Booting the computer off a floppy, for example, would enable a user to erase the password file. With this change, he could gain access to the administrator's account, where he could change the restrictions on his own account. The bottom line is that no system is 100 percent effective; someone always finds a way to circumvent it.

The second option of the Change Passwords page, Change Other Passwords, enables you to change any passwords you might have for other resources or networks. If you have access to a NetWare installation in addition to a peer-to-peer network, for example, you could use this option to change the password.

The process of changing your password doesn't vary much. Select the password you want to change, and Windows displays a dialog box containing three fields. (Clicking the option to change your Windows password bypasses the password selection dialog box.) The first field contains your original password. This ensures that someone else won't come along and change your password without your permission. Type the new password into the second field, then again into the third field so Windows can verify it.

The Remote Administration page of the Passwords Properties dialog box contains a check box to enable remote administration. After you enable this support, you'll also gain access to the two fields used for the access password. Enabling the remote administration feature enables someone else to manage your machine from a remote location. With this option, a network administrator could make changes to every machine on a peer-to-peer network without ever leaving his desk. Chapter 23, "Networks," explores exactly how this works. Fortunately, you also can password-protect remote administration. Type the access password into the first password field, then again in the second field for verification purposes.

Windows 98 enables you to select from two different desktop configuration methods. You can force every user of a single machine to use the same desktop, or you can allow multiple desktops by selecting the corresponding option on the User Profiles page of the Passwords Properties dialog box (see Figure 3.1). A single desktop is much easier to maintain, reduces training costs, and enhances security. Multiple desktops keep users happier, provide more flexibility, and have the potential to make users more efficient. The selection you make largely depends on the needs of the people using the machine. If they all perform approximately the same type of work and have similar needs, a single desktop is probably the best answer.

Figure 3.1.

A single desktop is easy to maintain but multiple desktops are more flexible.

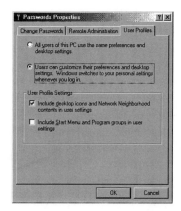

Tip: Multiple desktops are not limited to more than one user. A single user can use multiple desktops to work more efficiently. If your current desktop is too cluttered, it might be time to build a second one. You could keep one desktop for each major task you perform. Alternatively, you could create a special desktop for each project you administer. This might not be the best way to separate your work into manageable pieces, but it's one way to do so. (You'd have to create separate usernames for each desktop, then log off one user account and onto another before you could make changes to individual desktops.)

If you decide to use multiple desktops, Windows 98 provides two additional options that determine the level of flexibility this feature offers. The first check box in the User Profile Settings group enables the user to configure desktop icons and Network Neighborhood. These user-specific settings are saved in the user's profile folder. The second check box enables the user to create a specialized Start menu and program groups. These settings also appear in the user's profile folder.

Enabling multiple desktops also enables password protection. Windows 98 must know which user is using the computer so it can open the correct profile. To do so, it displays the same password dialog box as the Microsoft network.

Desktop Settings

Everyone looks at desktop settings in one way—as improving the appearance of their computer. For the most part, they're right. Just changing the color of something under Windows won't make it work better—at least most of the time. Configuring your desktop for a pleasing appearance might not provide much in the way of a direct efficiency increase, but it'll affect the way you view your system. A new piece of wallpaper or a change of colors can greatly affect the way you view your machine. Any positive change in attitude usually translates into improved efficiency. I find that changing my wallpaper and display colors from time to time gives my computer that "new" feel everyone needs occasionally.

Other reasons can necessitate a change of configuration. Wallpaper, for example, while attractive to the eye, chews up valuable memory. You might run into a situation in which memory is at a premium. Giving up your wallpaper is one way to increase memory in order to complete a specific task.

Eyestrain also is a common problem among computer users. Sitting for eight hours in front of a basically close-range television doesn't do anyone's eyes much good. If you're like me, however, you probably spend more than eight hours a day staring at the screen. Somewhere along the way, you might want to make your icons and text bigger to reduce eye fatigue. Changing your desktop settings to improve readability is a very practical use of this feature.

Selecting Wallpaper

Wallpaper is a personal item every computer user wants to customize. Windows 98 makes changing your wallpaper even easier than it was under Windows 3.1. Right-click the Desktop and choose Properties. You should see the dialog box shown in Figure 3.2.

Figure 3.2.
The Background page of the Display Properties dialog box enables you to change your wallpaper.

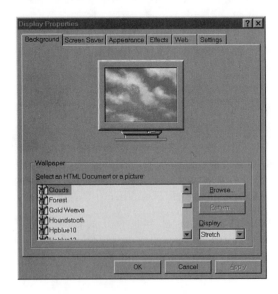

The Background page of the Display Properties dialog box has two major sections. The top half of the page contains a monitor. Changing any of the wallpaper or pattern settings immediately affects the contents of this display. The monitor gives you a thumbnail sketch of how your background will appear.

The bottom section of this page contains a list of available patterns, bitmaps, and web pages. The capability to display a web page as your wallpaper is a new feature for Windows 98. (You must enable Active Desktop to use a web page as wallpaper.) Microsoft also reorganized the dialog box so this one list contains everything you can display on the desktop. Previous versions of Windows provided one list for patterns and another for bitmaps.

Like previous versions of Windows, you can choose an existing pattern or create your own. To change a pattern, click the Pattern button to display a bitmap editor similar in function to those used by most paint programs.

> **Tip:** Patterns are a memory-efficient way to dress up a system. Because a pattern uses only two colors, it's much faster to draw and doesn't consume many system resources. If your system is short on memory, but you'd still like an interesting background, consider using patterns instead of wallpaper.

The Wallpaper list defaults to files found in your main Windows folder. You don't have to use these files, however. Click the Browse button to look in other folders on your drive. To display wallpaper, you can center it on the background (the best choice for pictures) or tile it (the best choice for patterns). You also can choose the Stretch option, which changes the dimensions of a bitmap to fill the entire desktop area.

Screen Saver

A very healthy third-party market exists for screen savers. Some Windows users buy screen savers in bulk. You can find them in stores and on just about every bulletin board system (BBS) in existence. Unless you own an older system, using a screen saver probably isn't necessary, just fun. I own a *Star Trek* screen saver for the "fun" element, even though it isn't necessary. A good web site for all kinds of screen savers is `http://www.sirius.com/~ratloaf/` furnished by Screensavers A to Z.

> **Tip:** You don't have to spend a lot of money to get some really interesting screen savers. At the preceding web site, for example, you'll find a screen saver for displaying your favorite JPEG, PIC, and KQP files. If you happen to be a gardener, this same site enables you to build your own virtual garden onscreen. There are many screen savers at this site; you have to look for something that interests you.

Windows 98 also provides screen saver options. They aren't as much fun as some screen savers on the market, but they do the job. (There also is a new set of OpenGL screen savers provided with Windows 98 that makes life a bit more interesting.) You'll find these options on the Screen Saver page of the Display Properties dialog box, as shown in Figure 3.3.

Figure 3.3.

The Screen Saver page of the Desktop Properties dialog box enables you to change your screen saver and its settings.

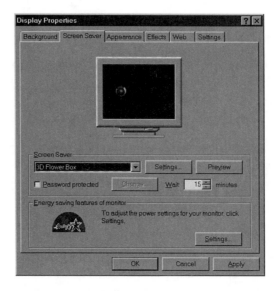

Just like the Background page, the Screen Saver page contains a miniature view of your monitor. It displays a thumbnail sketch of what the display will look like when you configure the screen saver. The Screen Saver field enables you to choose from the screen savers in the SYSTEM folder. If you decide to use a third-party screen saver that uses the Windows format, you need to place the file in the same directory as the others or Windows won't see it.

After you select a screen saver, you can use the Settings button to change its settings. In most cases, the settings affect how Windows 98 displays the screen saver. It might, for example, change the number of lines you see or the number of colors.

The Wait field enables you to change the number of minutes Windows 98 waits before it activates the screen saver. To turn the screen saver off, move the mouse cursor or press a key.

You also can password-protect your screen saver. This enables you to leave the room without fear that someone will use your machine while you're gone. A password is required to deactivate the screen saver once it comes on. I like third-party screen savers that automatically restore their current condition even if you turn the machine off and reboot. Unfortunately, the Windows 98 screen savers don't provide this feature; you can circumvent password protection by rebooting the machine.

The final option on the Screen Saver page, Preview, enables you to see what the display looks like with the screen saver on. I've used this as a quick way to hide my display when someone walks into my office and I don't want them to see what I'm working on.

This dialog box also contains a special Settings button that enables you to set up the energy-saving features of your monitor. This button appears only if you have a monitor that supports energy-saving features. Click this button to display the Power Schemes tab of the Power Management Properties dialog box. This dialog box is discussed in detail in the "Power Management Strategies" section of Chapter 18, "Mobile Computing: Notebooks, Telecommuting, and Remote Access."

How do you use the energy-efficient features? You might run the screen saver after 15 minutes of inactivity. That way, when you go to lunch or on a break, you can be sure your work is hidden. After 45 minutes of inactivity, you might want your monitor to turn off so it doesn't waste power while you're at a meeting. In fact, sometimes you might not even be able to return to your office, so turning the monitor off will save the company a lot of money if you go to several meetings in a week.

Palette

The Appearance page of the Display Properties dialog box (see Figure 3.4) enables you to change the appearance of your display, not just the desktop. Just click the picture of the display to select an item such as the application's background. (Some items have to be manually selected from the list because they don't appear in the picture.)

Figure 3.4.

The settings on the Appearance page enable you to change the colors and fonts used by your display.

Windows 98 provides a great deal of flexibility when it comes to selecting fonts for your display. I have several configurations with "tired eye"-sized text settings. You can individually change the size of the menu and title bar text. Everything with text also has a setting here for the font and type size.

Changing an entry consists of making list box selections. This dialog box contains six list boxes (not including the Scheme list box). The first three affect the item itself and include the Item name, Size, and Color. Size, in this case, refers to the size of the window or other display element. You could, for example, change the width of a menu bar using this option. The second three list boxes control the text within a display element. These settings include Font, Size, and Color. You can select any installed font as your display font, but most people find MS Serif or MS Sans Serif works best on displays. These fonts were specially designed for this purpose. I occasionally use Arial and find that it works quite well.

This dialog box also contains a list box for selecting a color scheme, a Delete button for removing the schemes you no longer want, and a Save As button for adding new schemes.

Resolution

The Settings page of the Display Properties dialog box enables you to change your display resolution and number of colors. You usually can change the settings without rebooting your machine.

There are also times when you might want to change your standard font or to display the Settings icon in the taskbar tray. Click the Advanced button to display the General page of the display adapter Properties dialog box. The Font Size drop-down list box contains two standard options: Small Font and Large Font (which are pretty nebulous definitions for a font). Choose the Other... option to display the Custom Font Size dialog box. This dialog box enables you to create a custom-size system font. This is a very handy feature if you need a font that's either very large or very small. Normally, however, you'll use the standard sizes that come with Windows.

If you change your screen resolution on a regular basis, you'll like the Show Settings Icon on Taskbar check box. Check this to place the Settings icon in the taskbar tray. You can use this icon to reset your screen resolution as necessary instead of going to the Display Properties dialog box. You also can determine the current resolution by resting your mouse over the Settings icon. (The other features of the display adapter Properties dialog box are discussed in Chapter 17, "Video Configuration.")

System Setup

You can quickly access the System Properties dialog box from the desktop by right-clicking My Computer and selecting the Properties option. This particular dialog box is discussed in detail in Chapter 5, "Performance Primer," so it won't be discussed here. It also can be used to assist in fixing hardware- and software-related problems, as you will learn in Chapter 25, "Software Problems," and Chapter 26, "Hardware Problems."

Clock

The clock was briefly discussed previously in this chapter when talking about the taskbar. This clock affects the way the system reacts. You can use it to affect the CMOS setting and, therefore, the time stamp on all your files. It also will affect any events you might schedule and anything else that relies on the clock.

The clock's properties consist of a single check box—Show Clock—on the Taskbar Properties dialog box. All this entry does is either display or not display the clock on the taskbar. In most cases, you'll want to display the clock because there's nothing to be gained from shutting it off.

> **Tip:** When you display the clock, it shows only the current time. You can use the mouse cursor to display the current date. Move the mouse cursor over the Clock icon for a few seconds, and the clock will display the current date.

Double-clicking the Clock icon displays the Date/Time Properties dialog box. This is the same dialog box used during the installation process to set the clock. The Date & Time page contains a calendar and a clock, which you can use to change the system settings.

The second page of this dialog box, Time Zone, enables you to change the current area of the world. It's the same dialog box from when you completed the installation of Windows 98. Setting this dialog box is self-explanatory. The daylight savings time check box enables the computer to automatically adjust the time for you.

Working with Desktop Objects

Making your desktop more efficient is easy in Windows 98. First, you need to throw away outdated application-centered ideas that Windows 3.x encouraged. You need to learn to work with data—the way you should have learned to work in the first place. After all, what's more important—the tool that creates an object or the object itself? The end result is the most important goal in working with Windows.

The following sections provide ideas on how to arrange your desktop to make maximum use of the new Windows data-centric approach. This is not the only way to pursue the problem, but it's the way many people are starting to work with this new product. Try this approach, then modify it to meet your needs.

You'll start by looking at methods of moving data around. Remember that Windows 98 uses objects. Everything is an object of some sort, and objects are easy to copy, cut, and paste. You can move them around just like any object in the physical world. After looking at data-movement techniques, you'll review methods to organize that data on your desktop.

Making Copies

Many people cut and paste to move data around. You just cut the data from the place in which you no longer need it, then paste it to a new location. Windows 98 also supports cut-and-paste for objects. To move a file from one location to another, cut and then paste it. The beauty of this approach is that a copy of the file is now on the clipboard. This means you can make as many copies of it as you want. Anything you can cut, you can copy. Copying the object means you leave the original in place and create copies where needed.

You can't paste a file on top of another file. You can, however, paste a copy of a file on the desktop or within a folder. If you take a logical, real-world approach to moving objects under Windows 98, you'll never run into problems getting objects to work.

Creating New Objects

Everywhere you can paste an existing object, you also can create a new one. The desktop, Explorer, and most Windows 98 folders have a New option in the context menu. This menu option displays a list of file types Windows 98 can produce automatically.

Note that one of the entries is a folder. You always can place a folder within another object normally used for storage (even another folder). Using folders helps you organize your data into more efficient units.

Using a Template

One problem with the New submenu of the context menu is it always creates objects of a default type. Take Word for Windows. If you create a new Word for Windows object using the selection on the context menu, that new object automatically uses the Normal style sheet. What you really wanted might have been the Accounts style sheet, but there isn't a fast way to create that document using the current system.

I got around this problem by placing a folder named Templates on my desktop. Inside are copies of each sample file I use to create new documents. If you write a lot of letters that use the same format, for example, you might want to use your word processor to create a document containing everything that normally appears in a letter. Then place a copy of the letter template in your Templates folder. Every time you need to write another letter, right-click the template in your Templates folder and drag the template to a new destination such as a project folder. When the context menu appears, select Copy to create a copy of your template. This template approach to creating new documents can greatly reduce the time necessary to start a task. You can create enough copies of a template to satisfy project needs in a few seconds. Using the template also means all your settings are correct when you enter the document for the first time.

You can use a document template in several ways. You can right-click then select Copy, and right-click your project folder then select Paste from the context menu. Another method is to drag the template with the mouse key pressed. When Windows asks what you would like to do, select Copy from the menu.

Creating Work Areas

Now that you have an idea how to move and copy data, let's look at a more efficient way to work with it. I've started using a new method of organizing information because of the way Windows 98 works. You can follow several easy steps to start a project.

1. Create a main project folder on the desktop.

2. Open the folder and place one folder inside for each type of data you plan to work with. When writing this chapter, for example, I created one folder for the word-processed document, another for the electronic research information, and a third for the graphics files.

3. Open the first data folder, create a copy of your template, then make as many copies as you'll need of that template within the data folder.

4. Rename the data files to match what they'll contain.

5. Close this data folder and repeat steps 3 and 4 for each of your other data folders.

6. Complete your project by filling each data folder.

> **Tip:** Using the same method of creating new data files for all your data might not be possible because of the way an application is designed. In some cases, as with the screen shots in this book, the data file creates in a different way. My screen shots are all captured from a display buffer. I don't need to create a blank file to hold them because the screen capture program does this for me. Always use the data creation technique that works best with the applications you use.

Figure 3.5 shows one way to arrange your projects. It contains a main folder, a few data folders, and some notes about the project. This is only one possible approach to managing your data. The trick is to find the method that works best for you—one that reflects the way you work.

Figure 3.5.
An example of how to arrange your data for easy access.

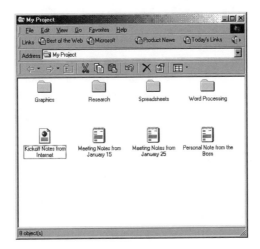

By now you might be wondering why you should go this new route. After all, the old method of managing your data seemed to provide the same results as the method I've outlined. This new technique, however, offers several advantages you just can't obtain using the application-centered approach.

- **Data transmittal.** Giving someone else access to a group project means sending him a folder, not a bunch of individual files. How many times have you thought you had all the files for a project together, only to find you didn't send an important file? This method of organizing data prevents such problems.

- **Application independence.** It doesn't matter which application you need to use in order to modify a file. If everyone in your office uses the same applications, modifying a file means double-clicking it and nothing else. You no longer need to worry about which application to open or where that application is located. All that matters is the data.

- **Location.** Where is your data? Do you ever find yourself searching for hours to find that small file you thought you'd lost somewhere? This method enables you to place all the data relating to a project in one place. Its physical location no longer matters because the pieces are together. You still need to know, of course, where the data is when you organize the project folder. But would you rather look for a file once or a hundred times? Using desktop folders means you'll find the data once and never worry about it again.

- **Ease of storage.** When I finish a project in Windows 98, I don't worry about putting all the bits and pieces together. I send one folder to storage. When I need to work on the project again, I know I need only load that one folder back onto my local drive.

On Your Own

Try using the new Active Desktop features to enhance your productivity. For example, try placing your favorite web page on the desktop for a week or so to see how this new feature works. You also might want to try creating one or more toolbars in an effort to consolidate the icons currently on your desktop. Try setting up channels as well to see if you can create one-click access to the Internet.

Open Explorer and check out each of the special sections discussed in this chapter. Try to identify each section and its purpose without referring back to this book. Examine some of the unique capabilities provided by your machine. For example, see if there are any special applets in Control Panel. You'll also want to check out your machine's network capabilities.

Spend some time customizing your desktop for optimum efficiency. See which wallpapers or other aesthetics you can change. Remove any features that might slow performance if you're using a memory-constrained system. Try out the screen saver and password options.

4

The Updater's Guide to Windows 98

Peter Norton®

I've been more than a little surprised by the new features in Windows 98. It's not the same kind of update you saw when going from Windows 3.x to Windows 95. You won't see huge changes in the operating system architecture or completely new ways of getting things done at the lowest level. Windows 98 provides an entirely different kind of change.

Microsoft has really listened to some user requests for additional features. Windows 98 enables you to use multiple monitors, something sure to appeal to a variety of users and programmers alike. Consider the affect that multiple monitor use will have on training. You could watch the instructor on one display, then practice a new technique in the other. Games will probably change as well. For example, you could view one monitor and see your current inventory, resources, and statistics while the other monitor showed you the playing field. Programmers have long used two monitors to make application debugging easier. You view the application source code on one display and the running application on the other.

This chapter will help you understand many of the new features that Windows 98 provides when compared to previous versions of Windows—especially Windows 95. We won't take a detailed look at every feature; that's what we'll do in the rest of the book. We'll also look at improvements in existing features. For example, you'll see some improvement in Dial-Up Networking. My purpose in writing this chapter was to give people who plan to upgrade a succinct description of what they should expect in the way of new features.

 # The Windows 98 Difference

Windows 98 adds a lot of new interface features. In fact, if I had to choose two words to describe the difference between Windows 95 and Windows 98, they would be "Internet interface." Although not every new feature is specifically designed to make Internet access easier, it's apparent that Microsoft spent considerable time working in this area. The following sections describe new Windows 98 features. Make sure you look at the "Some Improvements to Old Friends" section later in this chapter to find out how existing features have changed.

Broadcast Services

The capability to watch television while working at your computer might not seem like a big deal to some people. After all, you could just place a television next to your computer and see what's going on without wasting money on another sound card. For some users, however, this is a headache waiting to happen; many people won't work as hard with a television nearby.

The Broadcast Services feature in Windows 98 does more than just provide a method for watching television. It provides a means for receiving TCP/IP packets that have been injected into a broadcast signal. What does this mean to you? For one thing, it means you can receive both digital data and television signals through one connection. You can receive a file over the same wire as your television signal—at least in theory. If someone introduces a new recipe during a cooking show, for example, you could download the file with a simple click. The use of TCP/IP packets also could enable producers to create interactive television; your input could affect the outcome of the show.

Like many other new technologies, it might be a while before Broadcast Services is used for anything but niche applications. This particular feature has potential for the future, however, especially as cable television companies become more involved with computers and the Internet. We'll take a closer look at the WebTV for Windows application (one of the Windows 98 features that makes use of Broadcast Services) in the "Using the WebTV for Windows Application" section of Chapter 17, "Video Configuration."

ActiveMovie

As the Internet becomes more media oriented, support for media presentations has to come from somewhere. This is where ActiveMovie comes into play. ActiveMovie is a lightweight ActiveX control that enables you to see a variety of media types using a very small footprint viewer. You can watch all the popular media formats—MPEG audio, MPEG video, WAV audio, AVI video, and Apple QuickTime video—with this one control.

Not only does ActiveMovie provide a user element, it also provides a programmer element. ActiveMovie defines a new media-streaming architecture that programmers can use to deliver media-like movies without having to worry about the capabilities of the client machine. Not only that, but a programmer can extend the architecture as well, which makes it possible to start with a basic capability and create something quite spectacular with much less code than in the past. I've already talked about the ActiveMovie control in Chapter 2, "Introducing Windows 98," so it won't be covered in detail here.

Point-to-Point Tunneling Protocol (PPTP) Client Support

PPTP is a relatively new technology that enables you to create a wide area network (WAN) using the Internet. You end up with a virtual private network—an extension of the current Dial-Up Networking capability found in older versions of Windows. Unlike Dial-Up Networking, however, in which connecting to your company's network could mean a long distance call, PPTP usually lets you get by with a local call to an Internet Service Provider (ISP). PPTP enables you to transfer data over the same wire used to view Web pages. Just as you can make a local call and see Web pages on a server in Japan, you also can make a local call and make contact with your company's Web server.

MPPTP wouldn't be effective if it didn't also include some security features. Although PPTP relies on TCP/IP to do its work, it also uses some of the newer data encryption techniques to make sure no one else on the Internet can read your data transmissions.

Windows 98 Isn't Just About Easier Web Surfing

There are some features in Windows 98 that don't provide a direct Internet interface benefit. However, even many of these new features rely on the Internet in some way. The next few sections provide a quick overview of new Windows 98 features that, although they might not help you get on the Internet, definitely make the upgrade worthwhile.

System File Checker Utility

Have you ever installed a new program, only to discover it overwrote a DLL you needed? More often than not, all or part of the operating system will fail to work next time you start it up. The System File Checker utility helps you get around this particular problem. It checks a variety of important system files—including DLL, COM, VXD, DRV, OCX, INF, and HLP—to make sure you have the right version.

Not only does this utility help you figure out which files have been overwritten, it also gives you an easy way to correct the problem. It just takes a few button clicks to restore the original files required to keep Windows 98 running. We'll talk more about this utility in the "System File Checker Utility" section of Chapter 25, "Software Problems."

> **Tip:** Errant installation programs aren't the only source of problems when it comes to system files. I've seen many cases in which a system file gets corrupted in some way. The results are the same as an overwrite even though the cause is different. Fortunately, System File Checker finds these kinds of problems just as easily as it finds overwritten files.

Windows Maintenance Wizard

Maintenance is the bane of many users. Think about the last time you did something good for your machine. If you can't remember when you last performed maintenance, you're not alone. Fortunately, Windows 98 comes with a tool designed to make maintenance less of a chore and more automatic.

You can use the Windows Maintenance Wizard to schedule maintenance tasks for times when you're not using the machine. You can schedule disk defragmentation during your lunch hour, for example, or scan the disk for errors during a weekly meeting. Scheduling these events means you only have to think about them once, then the job gets done automatically.

Looking Ahead: The "Windows Maintenance Wizard" section of Chapter 25 provides more details about this utility. If you want to learn about the Task Scheduler, check out the "Drives" section of Chapter 2 and the "Automating Tune-Ups with Task Scheduler" section of Chapter 5, "Performance Primer."

System Troubleshooter

Getting someone to tell you the precise source of trouble with an ailing operating system can be difficult, especially if you have to wait on the phone for a while before talking with them. A lot of us just don't have time to wait for someone to get around to helping us resolve a problem. It's especially frustrating when the problem turns out to be something relatively simple that you could have fixed yourself.

The System Troubleshooter is Microsoft's answer to this problem. It helps you diagnose many simple system problems using the same techniques a human counterpart over the phone would use. Is this solution perfect? I found it works well on simple problems, but it gets progressively more difficult to use as the problems become more complex. Considering the number of simple problems I've seen, however, I'll bet you'll find that this utility probably will save you at least some time on the phone. We'll discuss this utility further in the "System Troubleshooter" section of Chapter 25.

Easier Installation

Each new version of Windows has gotten slightly easier to install. I still remember the difficulties I experienced installing Windows 3.x. I had to break out all the hardware manuals for my machine to come up with the arcane knowledge necessary for Windows 3.x to install. Windows 95 was much easier. It detected most of my hardware and installed the correct drivers. It even configured everything; I didn't have to spend time trying to make the hardware work together.

Still, Windows 95 required quite a bit of configuration when it came to program features. It also didn't anticipate my needs based on previous selections. Windows 98, however, does both. The number of installation steps for Windows 98 has dropped a little for a clean install, which is surprising considering all the new features it offers.

The real surprise, however, came when I installed Windows 98 over an existing Windows 95 installation. The installation procedure was over almost before it got started. Windows 98 read all the features I had installed for Windows 95, then installed those same features for me. I ended up with an optimized system without having to go through screen after screen of configuration information.

(Theoretically, you can perform an unattended install with Windows 98; all the screens will choose default values if you don't provide input within a specific amount of time.)

Faster Shutdown

Somewhere along the way, Microsoft has managed to optimize just about every part of Windows except the shutdown sequence. It was long in Windows 3.x and got longer in Windows 95. Windows 98 remedies that oversight. I won't say that you'll get an instantaneous shutdown, but it's much faster than previous versions. In most cases, the machine is ready to turn off in 2 seconds or less. This is a big improvement over the minute-long shutdowns in Windows 95.

Improved Hardware Support

Microsoft has to keep pace with new hardware technologies. Windows 98 shows the various improvements you'd expect. For example, it provides native support for the Intel MMX processor. This means you'll get better multimedia presentations, and the processor will be less bogged down. Speaking of multimedia, you'll also find support for the new Accelerated Graphics Port (AGP) in this version of Windows. This new graphics standard promises to blow past the current graphics-processing speed supported by most machines. Microsoft also is promising to add Digital Video Disk (DVD) support. These CD-ROM–sized disks can hold much more information than their predecessors, which means you'll get video as well as audio content. (Before you'll see any benefit, however, you need the new hardware to go with the new software support provided by Microsoft.)

Looking Ahead: Be sure to read Chapter 13, "Exploiting Your Hardware," to learn about the new hardware features supported by Windows 98. This chapter provides the in-depth information you need to make the most of the new hardware on new machines. If you're interested in the effect of new hardware on multimedia and games, make sure you also read Chapter 14, "Exploiting Multimedia and Games."

Windows 98 also supports enhanced PCMCIA support. It might be hard to believe that there's a new specification in the works for this bus system—it was just introduced in Windows 95. Windows 98 includes support for PC Card 32 (Cardbus), 3.3-volt PC Cards, and multifunction PC Cards, all of which should make using the PCMCIA bus even easier than before. (Chapter 18, "Mobile Computing: Notebooks, Telecommuting, and Remote Access," explains these new features in detail.)

We already talked a bit about multimonitor support in the introduction to this chapter. For some people, the capability to use more than one monitor is a big reason to upgrade. This capability will find more than a few uses in the gaming industry, and most programmers will enjoy it.

Laptop users also get new hardware support in this version of Windows. They finally can use the infrared data ports on their machines to talk with the network or printer without making a physical connection. They'll also enjoy the support Microsoft provides for the Advanced Configuration and Power Interface (ACPI).

The list of new hardware support in Windows 98 goes on and on. There's support for the Universal Serial Bus (USB), for example, which promises to finally get rid of all the different-sized connectors on the back of machines. USB also will provide much higher data-transfer speeds. This new feature is discussed in the "Universal Serial Bus (USB)" section of Chapter 13. By the time you read this, Microsoft probably will have come up with even more solutions to the problems of updated hardware.

Remote Access Server

Many people were not happy with Microsoft for not including Dial-Up Networking server support in the last release of Windows. Now you no longer have to buy the Plus! Pack simply because you need server support. Windows 98 comes with the Remote Access Server (RAS) as part of the package. RAS supports both the IPX/SPX and NetBEUI protocols, so you can use it in a variety of situations.

Win32 Driver Model (WDM)

There's a big difference between the drivers used by Windows NT and those used by Windows 95. Even though Microsoft went a long way toward modularizing the driver system for Windows 95, it still isn't generic. You can't write a one-size-fits-all driver and expect it to work with both Windows NT and Windows 95. As a result, Windows NT users often have to wait a long time before they can use new hardware that Windows 95 users are already exploiting.

This all changes in Windows 98. The Win32 Driver Model (WDM) promises to bring order to the chaotic world of Windows driver writing. What does this mean for you, users? It means you no longer need to worry about which driver you download from a vendor's Internet site. One driver will work with your machine; it doesn't matter whether it's running Windows 98 or Windows NT.

Does this mean you need to rush right out and get all new drivers for Windows 98? No, Microsoft provides support for both the new WDM drivers and the old drivers used in Windows 95. Overall, it's a win-win situation for everyone.

Windows Scripting Host

The Windows Scripting Host (WSH) is a long-awaited feature for Windows users. It provides a way to automate tasks you perform on a daily basis, such as logging in and out of a server. A lot of activity can be foreseen in this area as people build scripts to perform a wide range of tasks. These tasks might be confusing for novice users or simply too time consuming for others.

WSH supports two scripting languages right out of the box: JavaScript and VBScript. It also supports a language-independent architecture you can tap using ActiveX. This language-independent architecture will enable programmers to build an interface for languages such as Perl, TCL, and REXX. The potential for Perl support will definitely appeal to Webmasters who have a large investment in that product. Likewise, people who move from OS/2 to Windows won't have to give up their scripts if someone comes up with a REXX interpreter (which I'm almost certain will happen).

Distributed Component Object Model (DCOM)

I talked about this particular technology in the previous edition of the book. At that time, Microsoft hadn't yet made DCOM a reality, but today you can finally use it.

DCOM (also known as Network OLE) enables a developer to write an application that can reside in a number of places at the same time. An application no longer has to completely reside on one machine before you can use it. The application can be running on a server or even on another machine in the network. (More details about how DCOM works are provided in the "Networking with the Distributed Component Object Model (DCOM)" section of Chapter 11, "DDE, OLE, DCOM, and ActiveX.")

The secret ingredients required to make this work are communication and encapsulation. Each component of an application is encapsulated, which means it doesn't rely on the internal workings of any other parts to work. The various components communicate with each other using a generic interface. Component A can ask component B if it has the capability to do something. If component B says yes, component A sends it the raw materials required to do the work, and component B returns a finished product. The actual process is a bit more complicated than what I've just described, but this gives you an idea of what's going on.

 # Some Improvements to Old Friends

Microsoft hasn't completely changed everything in Windows 98. You'll still see a lot of old friends from previous versions, and for the most part, they work the same as before. Fortunately, Microsoft has fixed up some of these utilities and has enhanced others. They're not older, just better. The following sections provide an overview of the changes you'll find in some of your old friends.

Improved Dial-Up Networking

If you've used Windows 95, you'll definitely notice some changes in Dial-Up Networking. The most welcome change is a new technology called Multilink Channel Aggregation. You should definitely read the full description of this technology in the "Understanding Multilink Channel Aggregation" section of Chapter 21, "Internet Connections." The short version is that you can now combine multiple connections to one server into one large connection. You're basically creating a bigger communication pipe that enables you to work faster than ever before.

There's also a new scripting feature that comes with Dial-Up Networking. This feature enables you to automate many tasks you now perform manually, such as logging in to a server. This particular feature is discussed further in the "Creating Scripts for Dial-Up Networking" section of Chapter 19, "Hardware and Software Connections."

Disk Defragmenter

Disk defragmentation has always improved the performance of a hard drive. If you can keep all the clusters associated with a specific file in one place, the hard drive head doesn't have to move as often. (Moving the hard drive head is the most time-consuming part of finding and retrieving data.)

Microsoft has come up with the next step in drive defragmentation. If keeping a file's clusters together improves performance a little, then keeping the files of a particular application together will improve performance even more. This is precisely what the Disk Defragmenter does. It keeps track of the applications you use most, then keeps the files for that application in one place. This technology relies on the same process as standard disk defragmentation for improved performance and reduced disk head movement. (You can learn more about this in the "Defragmenting Your Hard Drive" section of Chapter 9, "The Windows 98 File System.")

Microsoft System Information Utility

I still remember the first time I called technical support for help with a problem. When I finally got to speak with someone, we spent most of our time trying to gather the information required to talk about my machine. Technical support has gotten smarter since then; you are asked to gather the required information before making the call.

However, all that information gathering still takes time on the user's part. In addition, you can't be sure you'll have all the information technical support needs to solve your problem.

The Microsoft System Information Utility helps you figure out what to gather before calling technical support. It performs a complete survey of your machine. (To find out just how much more information you'll see, check out the "Microsoft System Information Utility" section of Chapter 25.) You'll also find that the information you get is more complete and accurate. This utility takes the pain out of gathering information, not only for the user but for the technical support person as well. Even if you don't know what kind of widget you have (or what task that widget performs), the technical support person can guide you to the right place to look for it.

Dr. Watson Utility

The Dr. Watson utility of old was a good idea, but it didn't go far enough. Sure, it would log the fact that your system froze, but in many cases, it didn't tell you more than that. You already knew your system had frozen, so Dr. Watson ended up not telling you much at all. The new version of Dr. Watson gathers much more information about the cause of a disaster on your machine. I won't say it's perfect yet, but I am finding that Dr. Watson does provide more useful information more often than not. (You can find out more about this utility in the "Dr. Watson Utility" section of Chapter 25.)

Backup Utility

Getting the Backup utility to work properly has never been a problem in Windows. This is one of the few utilities that always works well. Getting Backup to recognize a tape drive, however, is another story. The hardware support provided by this utility has been lacking at best. The Windows 98 version of Backup probably won't solve all your hardware support problems, but it does a much better job of trying. You'll even find support for SCSI drives now. For more details, see the "New Backup Features for Windows 98" section of Chapter 9.

Automatic ScanDisk

Sometimes your machine freezes when you have more than a few files open. Novice users also tend to shut their machines off without first shutting them down. These two situations posed quite a problem when Windows 95 first appeared; the operating system would start before you had a chance to check for damage to your hard drive. Windows 98 solves this problem by performing an automatic ScanDisk check whenever it detects an abnormal shutdown. You don't have to do anything; Windows 98 performs the check automatically to help protect your data.

Looking Ahead: ScanDisk is discussed in quite a few places in this book. You'll find it in the "Drives" section of Chapter 2, in the "Automating Tune-Ups with Task Scheduler" section of Chapter 5, in the various setup sections of Chapter 6, "Setup Primer," and in the "DOS Versus Windows 98 Commands" section of Chapter 12, "Exploiting Your Software: DOS, 16-Bit, and 32-Bit Applications." ScanDisk is used in many ways under Windows 98.

I was surprised to find that ScanDisk performs at least two levels of checks, depending on the severity of the abnormal shutdown. Turning off the machine without first shutting down results in a quick scan of the hard-drive directory structure for lost clusters and cross-linked files. A simulated hard-drive failure results in a more thorough scan that includes a full-media surface scan. This multiple level of scanning means you won't have to wait an inordinate amount of time if the probability of damage is small; you'll get a full check, however, if the damage potential is higher.

New Accessibility Tools

I absolutely loved the Accessibility options provided by Windows 95 and used them whenever I needed to. Windows 98 improves the Accessibility options two ways. First, an Accessibility Configuration Wizard helps you set up your machine. This wizard helps users get the most out of the Accessibility options, even if they don't initially understand them all.

The second improvement is a new magnifier. This magnifier enables you to examine an area screen to see what it contains, then go back to a normal view while working. There are all kinds of uses for the magnifier. It can help you to see the small graphics in some of your applications. (These features are discussed in more detail in the "New Accessibility Tools for Windows 98" section of Chapter 16, "Mice and Keyboards.")

Display Setting Enhancements

Are you tired of minimizing all your applications, right-clicking the desktop, then opening the Display Properties dialog box every time you want to change a display feature? Windows 98 has a solution to this problem. You now can place a Settings icon in the taskbar tray; this icon provides full access to the Display Properties dialog box without much effort. A menu enables you to change the display resolution, the color depth, and in some cases, the refresh rate without even opening the Display Properties dialog box. You also can make these changes on the fly without restarting your machine. (These display enhancements are discussed further throughout Chapter 17.)

You'll also find some other handy new features in the form of full-window drag, font smoothing, wallpaper stretching, large icons, and high-color icons. Users of the Windows 95 Plus! Pack will recognize these items. Now you get these features without having to buy an extra product.

FAT32 and FAT32 Conversion Utility

The File Allocation Table (FAT) method of formatting a hard drive has been around since DOS first appeared on the market. During that time, it has gone through several different metamorphoses. The most recent change was 16-bit FAT, which enables people to use hard drives larger than 32MB. This has been around for quite some time.

The problem with 16-bit FAT is that it becomes inefficient as the size of your hard drive increases. Now that hard drives come in the 3GB size, you're back to creating multiple partitions to use the full hard-drive potential in terms of space. FAT32 addresses both these problems by making FAT more efficient and by enabling you to access larger hard drives using one partition. You'll definitely want to read the "What Is 32-Bit VFAT?" section of Chapter 9.

You'll also like the FAT32 conversion utility. It enables you to convert your FAT16 drive to a FAT32 drive without reformatting. This is a definite time saver if you're upgrading a Windows 95 system to Windows 98. The "Using the FAT32 Conversion Utility" section of Chapter 9 contains all the details you need to start saving valuable hard-drive space today.

Improved Power Management

There's a new way to make your computer environmentally friendly as well as cheaper to operate—the Advanced Configuration and Power Interface (ACPI). This is an open specification proposed by Microsoft, Intel, and Toshiba. The specification is designed to make it easier to control the flow of power on any computer. (Chapter 18 contains the latest information about all the new laptop features in Windows 98.)

Windows 95 users are familiar with that operating system's capability to shut off the monitor after a period of time. The new features in Windows 98 do more than that. You now can tell your machine to power down disk drives and PCMCIA modems (with more devices to follow). The PCMCIA modem can even restore its own power when it detects an incoming phone call—a definite plus if you call into your desktop machine at the office when working at home.

I particularly like the capability to use schemes for power management. For example, I might want my machine to wait longer before shutting down during the day, so I set up a daytime scheme. Likewise, I might want it to shut down almost immediately at night; this is easily accommodated by a nighttime scheme. These schemes work much like the ones used for features such as sound.

Online Services Folder

I've already talked about this feature in the "Using the Online Services Folder" section of Chapter 1, "Opening Windows to the Internet." Here's a quick overview, however, for those of you who jumped directly to this chapter to see how Windows 98 will improve your life. For some people, the process of getting onto the Internet can be a road filled with huge boulders. The Internet often doesn't make sense, and the process of finding an ISP seems fraught with potential problems. The Online Services Folder solves these problems.

The Online Services Folder contains everything you need to create an Internet connection with some of the major ISPs. You'll find easy connections for America Online, AT&T, CompuServe,

Prodigy Internet, and of course, The Microsoft Network. You just need to open the folder and double-click your ISP preference. (Use some discretion with this feature. You might want to look for a local ISP if you live in a small town. At least make sure you have a local number to call; otherwise, you could end up with some fairly high long distance bills.)

Client Support for NetWare Directory Services (NDS)

In Windows 95, NetWare Directory Services (NDS) support was less than adequate for most users. Problems ranged from an inability to use some NetWare features to not being able to log in at all. Even though the Microsoft client was small and efficient, it wouldn't do the job for some people. Novell also came out with a 32-bit NDS client. The Novell client not only works much better than Microsoft's, it also contains more features. The only problem is that it eats huge amounts of memory. (For more information about Microsoft's NDS offering, see the "Using Microsoft NDS Client" section of Chapter 23, "Networks." The "Using Novell Client 32" section of the same chapter tells you more about the Novell client.)

Windows 98 does take a step in the right direction with NDS support. The new client doesn't appear to have most of the problems of the one in Windows 95. Unfortunately, it isn't full-featured either. If you're an administrator, you should probably continue using the Novell client. If you're a user, however, the Microsoft client seems to provide stable support and for a modicum of memory.

32-Bit Data Link Control (DLC)

If you need to access a mainframe computer, you'll likely need to use the Data Link Control (DLC) protocol. Windows 95 only provided 16-bit support for this particular protocol. This means mainframe access was a tad slower and more prone to crashes than accessing other parts of the network. Windows 98 fixes both problems with a new 32-bit DLC protocol. (For more information about mainframe connectivity, see the "32-Bit Data Link Control (DLC) for Mainframe Connections" section of Chapter 23.)

TweakUI Utility

The TweakUI utility has been around for a while, it just wasn't incorporated into Windows 95. TweakUI is a Control Panel applet that enables you to change some of the same things Windows 98 does. You can change the amount of time during startup, for example, that Windows 98 waits to see if you press the F8 key and choose a boot option. You also can use it to control various display features, such as whether shortcuts display that little arrow in the lower-right corner.

Obviously, you should be careful installing this utility on some machines. TweakUI provides powerful features, but in the wrong hands it has the potential to damage your Windows 98 installation. The capability to disable various boot features such as the F4 button—which is used to boot a previous operating system—might seem like a great idea until you need that previous operating system to perform some work. A novice user might forget how to turn F4 back on. Likewise, the capability to clear various history files is a great security measure, but it could make life hard for the administrator trying to figure out why a user can't do something on his machine. History files often provide clues as to what users have done or where they've gone on the Internet. The most dangerous (and useful) features are the various repair options that enable you to fix your font or icon cache. These repair utilities aren't guaranteed to solve your problem, and you need to know how to fix the problem if it still lingers after you're finished. (Fortunately, the damage potential is limited. Even if someone uses the applet incorrectly, you'll be able to recover in most cases.)

On Your Own

This chapter provides a whirlwind tour of features you need to know about before you upgrade from Windows 95 to Windows 98. You first need to decide which new features appeal to you. It might be helpful to make a list of the features you want to try before you install Windows 98. This way, you can put together your new setup before you start experimenting.

This chapter is only an overview, so make sure you read the full description of each item you want to use in other parts of the book. After all, you should know the full capability of each Windows 98 feature before you install it.

Make sure you try at least some of the Internet-related features, even if you don't think you'll use them right away. Windows 98 is an Internet-oriented operating system. You should explore this capability to get the most out of the upgrade.

II

Power
Primers

5

Performance Primer

Peter Norton®

Tuning or optimizing a machine for optimum performance is one of the first things that many people think about when they install a new operating system. After the applications are installed, they want to see how much they can get out of their new toy. The first thing you need to consider is what tuning means. Tuning could mean getting every last ounce of power out of a system to perform one specific task. It also could mean enabling a system to perform a variety of tasks simultaneously (multitasking). General tuning could be used to provide the best performance in a variety of situations. I could go on. The fact of the matter is that there's no default configuration and no standard machine. Everyone has different needs and different hardware that they need to use to get the job done. Any form of worthwhile optimization will take your specific needs into account.

I won't tell you how to tune your specific machine in this chapter. There's no way I can provide step-by-step tuning instructions for anyone without knowing their situation. What I will provide are some guidelines and tips you can use to create your own solution. You'll need to decide which tips you should implement and which you should ignore.

So, do you start reading and hope to find the tips you need the first time through? You probably won't. It takes a bit of time and patience to really tune a system for optimum performance. To get some idea of what I'm talking about, consider racecar drivers. A racecar gets tuned to fit its particular "personality." The mechanic and driver work together to discover the best configuration for that particular car. In addition, the car gets tuned to fit the track that it'll race on and even the weather conditions. Tuning the car is probably the easy part of the process. Planning how to tune it requires a bit more effort.

You don't need to worry about the weather when tuning your system, but many other principles do apply. Planning how to tune your system always is a good idea. Just like any other endeavor, tuning your system requires that you create a few goals and take a few potholes into account. Your machine contains hardware from a variety of sources. It probably contains a combination of components unique to your company. You need to consider how that hardware will react. Your applications are unique. Even if your job isn't unique, your way of doing that job probably is. A system perfectly tuned for the way I work probably won't do a lot for you.

Keeping your personal needs in mind, consider the following components before you start tuning your machine. The time and effort you expend is directly proportional to the level of performance you can expect to receive.

- **Memory.** The amount of real memory your system contains is a big factor in how well Windows 98 operates. You shouldn't start to tune until you have a minimum of 32MB of real RAM. You should tailor this number to meet the demands of the applications you plan to run. A spreadsheet requires a lot of memory, for example, and a database needs even more. A word processor, however, is relatively light when it comes to memory consumption. The number of applications you plan to run simultaneously also affects the point at which you start to tune your system. My system has 64MB of RAM, because I often run a word processor, a spreadsheet, and a communications program simultaneously. Virtual memory helps cover the difference between real memory and what you need, but you can't count on it to assume the full burden.

- **Hard disk size.** Windows 98 runs best when you give it a large swap area to work with. You need space for the application itself and for data files. One factor many people underestimate is the size of their data files. Recently I translated a small Word for Windows file from 1.0 format to 7.0. The 7.0 version consumed almost twice as much space, even though the amount of data hadn't changed one iota. The 7.0 format provides many features that 1.0 doesn't. The extra space used by 7.0 provides added functionality—an important trade-off to consider. When figuring how much hard disk space I need, I add up the space required for installed configurations of my applications, then triple it. This is a very coarse calculation, but it works for me.

- **Hard disk speed.** Older operating systems are much less disk-intensive than Windows 98 is. Not only do you have the swap file that Windows 98 creates, applications also make greater use of the hard drive today for temporary storage. To see what I mean, open just about any application and check for the number of TMP files on your drive. You might be surprised by what you see. This additional disk access means one thing: You need a fast drive to make Windows 98 jump through the hoops you want it to.

- **Processor speed.** Processor speed affects the way your computer runs. After you meet the basic storage requirements, no other factor so greatly affects your system. Herein lies the rub. Many people opt for a high-speed processor, then choke it with limited memory and hard drive space. Remember, the processor makes an impact on system throughput only after you meet the basic storage requirements. A thrashing hard drive can eat up every ounce of extra speed you might add to a system.

- **Motherboard features.** The size of the motherboard's SRAM cache might seem a bit on the technical side, but this feature isn't just for technicians. An optimized system starts with an optimized motherboard. Get a motherboard that offers plenty of room to grow and the capability to tune.

- **Peripheral devices.** I/O has always been a bottleneck in PCs. The two peripherals you need to concentrate on most are your disk controller and display adapter. Think about the way Windows is designed and you'll understand why. Windows is a GUI; it consumes huge amounts of time drawing the images on the display. A display adapter that uses processor cycles efficiently (or even unloads some processing tasks) can greatly affect the perceived speed of your system. The less time Windows spends drawing icons and other graphics, the more time it'll have to service your application. Likewise, a slow disk controller makes even a fast hard disk look slow. Today, it's the controller that becomes a bottleneck with many systems. The short take on peripherals? Always get 32-bit peripherals whenever possible and make certain they are fully compatible with Windows 98.

- **Bus speed.** You might not think about the little connectors you stick cards into, but your system does. The system bus has been a source of major concern for many years, and I don't see this changing anytime soon. What good is a fast peripheral if you can't access it at full speed? There's a slew of 32-bit bus architectures on the market. Everything from the PCI and EISA to VL and the MCA bus has tried to solve the problem with bottlenecks. Suffice it to say that the speed of your bus is yet another factor in how your system will perform. Make sure you get the fastest possible bus for your machine. In addition, a wider bus is better because it moves more bits at once.

- **Network interface card (NIC).** If you spend a lot of time working on the network, you should have a high-capacity NIC. At a minimum, you should have a 16-bit ethernet card; anything less is a waste of perfectly good network bandwidth. People who share graphics or other large files across the system should consider 32-bit NICs for their machines. Some NICs also are equipped with an expandable cache. Using a larger cache can buy additional network speed in some cases, especially under Windows 98.

After you finish your hardware configuration, consider your software configuration. Windows 98 does a much better job of managing resources than Windows 3.x does, but it's not perfect. The infamous system resources problem in Windows 3.x still exists in Windows 98. You still have the same problems with the 64KB USER and GDI areas. Filling these areas with icons, windows, and other graphic elements still results in a system that runs out of memory before physical memory is exhausted. (As you'll see later, there's more than meets the eye to system resources in Windows 98. Microsoft has tuned this operating system to erase many of the problems under Windows 3.x.) The way Microsoft configures and uses memory now, however, reduces the drag you see as system requirements increase.

When using Windows 3.x, I'd start to run out of resources after loading my word processor, spreadsheet, communications program, and one or two small utilities such as a screen saver or Notepad. I usually close an application or two when I get to the 35 percent system resources level, which is about where I was with this configuration. Windows 98 still has 75 percent of its resources free when using the same configuration. This means I can usually open two or three more applications on top of my usual configuration.

System resources, however, are only one memory factor. The actual level of RAM also needs to be taken into consideration. Windows 3.x suffers a fairly large performance penalty when the swap file reaches the size of real memory. This doesn't seem to be as big a problem in Windows 98, but it's still very noticeable. The bottom line is that when your swap file starts approaching the size of your installed memory, it's time for an upgrade.

When thinking about your software situation, you need to take into account your combination of system resources and system memory. A memory-constrained system always lacks enough memory to perform the job you need it to do. Memory is a subjective type of measurement, based on how you actually use your system. You should load the Resource Monitor (discussed in Chapter 2, "Introducing Windows 98") and, over a few days, track both the size of your swap file and the number of resources you have available. If you see a pattern of low memory, read the following section. You might discover the problem isn't the amount of installed memory on your machine, but the way you use that memory.

By now you should see where all this preliminary checking is headed. A mechanic would never tune a car before checking it over. Likewise, you should never tune your system before you know what type of system you have and how you use it. It's not enough to say you have 64MB of RAM installed. The way you use that RAM determines whether it's sufficient. A 4GB hard drive might sound impressive—unless you're trying to create multimedia presentations with it. Then it sounds like a rather paltry amount. (I've seen some multimedia systems that start out with 9GB of storage, although that's by no means standard.)

Top Performance Tips for Memory-Constrained Systems

Memory seems to be the biggest problem people face on a system, but it shouldn't be. At my local parts store, I can buy a 16MB SIMM for a mere $50. That probably isn't the cheapest price in town, either. Although memory isn't free, it certainly isn't the most expensive upgrade you can make to your system. Few items can provide the potential for noticeable system performance increases like memory can.

Microsoft says you can get by with as little as 16MB of RAM when running Windows 98. I wouldn't believe this if I were you. The minimum I recommend is 32MB, and that's if you intend to run only one application at a time. A more reasonable system contains 64MB of RAM. Even with 64MB of RAM, I find my system a tad constraining at times. The opposite extreme exists as well: You can actually create a condition where the overhead for managing memory in Windows 98 reduces system performance. This level was about 64MB for Windows 95—it's much higher for Windows 98, depending on what other tasks you ask the operating system to perform.

Let's say your boss absolutely won't buy any additional memory for your machine, and you're stuck at 16MB. What can you do to improve the situation? How can you stretch 16MB of RAM to make your single-tasking system (from a memory perspective) work as a multitasking system? The following sections will show you how to tune your system to use memory more efficiently and still get great performance.

Tip: The generic optimization techniques in the following sections work equally well with Windows NT, WfW 3.x, and Windows 3.x. If you're using Windows 98 in a peer-to-peer LAN environment, it's very likely you'll use a Windows NT machine as your file server. You also might have some older machines connected to the network that still use WfW 3.x. Whatever your setup, these generic tips can help just about any workstation make better use of the memory it contains.

General Tuning Tips for Windows

When trying to improve performance, I recommend you first try a few general tuning methods. Although anyone can use these methods, they always involve some level of compromise that you might not be willing to make. The following list shows my quick fixes to memory problems:

- **Wallpaper.** Did you know it costs memory and processing time to keep wallpaper on your system? If you have a memory-constrained system and can do without some bells and whistles, here's one item to get rid of. Don't think you'll save much by using smaller wallpaper or restricting yourself to patterns. Both items still chew up memory.

- **Colors.** The number of colors in your display directly affects the amount of memory it uses. A 16-color display uses roughly half the memory of a 256-color display. Although a 16-color display doesn't look as appealing as its 256-color or 32K-color counterpart, using 16 colors helps you save memory. You probably won't notice much of a difference in appearance if the programs on your machine are mainly word processors and spreadsheets.

- **Screen resolution.** The resolution at which you set your display affects processing speed and, to a much smaller degree, memory. The problem with changing your display resolution is not hard to figure. Although you can probably get by with fewer colors, fewer pixels is a different matter. Changing your screen's resolution should probably be a last-ditch effort to get that last bit of needed performance.

- **Doodads.** Many utility programs fit into the "doodad" category. If you run a fancy screen saver, for example, rather than the built-in Windows counterpart, you're wasting memory. Some people also keep a small game program running (such as Solitaire). These small applications might provide a few seconds of pleasure here and there, but you don't need to keep them active all the time. If you insist on using that fancy screen saver, run it right before you leave the room for a while and then close it when you return. The same holds true with a game program—keep it open when you play it, then close it before you get back to work.

- **Icons and other graphics.** Every icon on your desktop consumes memory. The same is true for any other form of graphical image or window. At least Windows 98 doesn't penalize you for opening a folder like Windows 3.x does. You can actually recover the memory by closing the folder. Organize your data into folders and open only the folders you need at any given time.

- **Leaky applications.** Some programs "leak" memory. They receive memory from Windows but never give it back, even after they terminate. After a while, you won't have enough memory to run programs even though you should. This problem is severe under Windows 3.x, but it has improved somewhat under later Windows versions. The Windows 98 data-centric interface, however, tends to accelerate the rate at which memory dissipates if you open and close an application for each data file. You can alleviate this situation by keeping leaky applications open until you know you won't need them again. You can find a leaky application by checking system resources and memory before you open it. Open and close the application a few times (make sure you also open some documents while inside), then check the amount of memory again after the last time you close it. If you find you have less memory—I mean a measurable amount, not a few bytes—the application is leaky.

- **Extra drivers.** Windows 98 and Windows NT do a fairly good job of cleaning old drivers out of the Registry. Even so, after you remove an application, you'll want to see whether all the drivers got removed from the system. This isn't a big deal for newer applications specifically designed for Windows 98 or Windows NT. Both operating systems provide a special installation utility that can be used to remove these newer applications from the system—including the files they stick in the SYSTEM directory and any references to them in the system files. In most cases, unfortunately, old Windows 3.x applications don't remove anything.

- **DOS applications.** Nothing grabs memory and holds it like a DOS application under Windows. Unlike other applications, the memory used by a DOS application usually can't be moved around to free space. You might have a lot of memory on your system, but Windows won't be able to use it because it's all too fragmented. If your system has so little memory that it can't tolerate even the smallest amount of memory fragmentation, avoid using DOS applications.

Windows 98–Specific Tuning Tips

In addition to generic tuning tips, a few Windows 98–specific tips can help you enhance overall system performance and the amount of memory you have available. Unfortunately, none of these tips works for Windows 3.x systems. Even though a few might work with Windows NT, you should give them a long test before making them permanent.

- **486 versus Pentium processors.** Windows 3.x doesn't care about the processor you use, only the processing speed. The facts are plain: Windows 3.x uses 16-bit code that runs equally well on any processor of 386 or above. Windows 98, however, uses some 32-bit code; therefore, using different processor types makes a big difference in performance. A 486 processor is better optimized to take advantage of 32-bit code. A Pentium is better still. Theoretically, you should notice a fairly substantial improvement in processing capability between a Pentium and a 486 machine of the same processor speed. In reality, however, the difference is noticeable, but not that noticeable. The extra performance is helpful, but don't worry about it until you take care of other problems, such as upgrading your memory.

- **CONFIG.SYS and AUTOEXEC.BAT.** In most cases, you're better off without any form of AUTOEXEC.BAT or CONFIG.SYS. If all you have in your CONFIG.SYS is a memory manager, get rid of it, because Windows 98 supplies its own. The only time you should keep CONFIG.SYS around is if you have to load real-mode drivers. It's also a good idea to get rid of AUTOEXEC.BAT, but this isn't always possible. Old 16-bit Windows applications under

Windows 98 still need some of the entries in AUTOEXEC.BAT. The most common requirement is the addition of entries to the PATH statement. You can open a DOS window and add a PATH statement to a batch file to set the path. You don't, however, have the same privilege for Windows applications. You have to set the path before you enter Windows for the application to work right.

- **Real-mode drivers.** All kinds of penalties exist for using real-mode drivers under Windows 98. The penalties are so severe that you should consider completely getting rid of real-mode drivers. As far as optimizing your system is concerned, real-mode drivers cost you in both performance and system reliability. The short explanation is that real-mode drivers force Windows 98 to make a transition between protected and real mode every time an application requires access to the device. Not only does this transition waste precious processor time, it also makes it possible for a maverick application to cause system failure.

- **16-bit drivers and DLLs.** Windows 98 is essentially a 32-bit operating system, but it has some 16-bit compatibility components and a few items left over from Windows 3.x. It runs every 32-bit application in a separate session. This enables Windows 98 to perform intense memory management on the resources needed by that application. All 16-bit applications share one session. Windows 98 performs less management on this one session than on individual 32-bit sessions because it can't make assumptions about how memory is being used. In addition, the 32-bit memory space is flat (every call is a near call), reducing the number of clock cycles required to make a function call or to look at something in memory. On the other hand, the segmented address space used by 16-bit components requires two to three times the number of clock cycles to process because every call is a far call.

- **Using Explorer in place of folders.** Folders are more efficient to use than Explorer. This might seem like a contradiction because folders use the Explorer interface, but it's not. Opening a copy of Explorer eats more system resources than opening a folder. Actually, you might think this is a foregone conclusion—opening any application eats system resources. One way to save memory is to place all your data in folders, then place a shortcut to those folders on the desktop. You then can access all your important files without opening a copy of Explorer. This costs less memory than keeping Explorer running all the time.

- **Use context menus in place of Control Panel.** Occasionally, you need to adjust the properties of various system elements during a session. Chapter 2 discussed the context menu attached to every object. Using the context menu is not only more efficient from a keystroke perspective, it also uses less memory than opening the Control Panel. This is something to remember if you need to keep a Properties dialog box open for any length of time.

- **Reset your printer for RAW printing.** Windows 98 automatically installs support for Enhanced Metafile Format (EMF) printing on systems it thinks will use it. This feature enables Windows 98 to print faster by translating the output to generic commands in the foreground, then creating printer-specific output in the background. Creating generic commands requires much less processing time than writing printer-specific output. In the Spool Settings dialog box, changing the Spool Data Format field to RAW forces Windows 98 to create printer-specific output in the first pass. (To access this dialog box, open the Details tab of the Printer Properties dialog box and click the Spool Settings button.) When using the RAW setting, less operating system code is maintained in memory during the print process. Some memory-constrained systems receive a large benefit from using this print mode. The trade-off, however, is longer foreground print times.

- **Keep your disk defragmented.** In older versions of Windows, you can create a permanent swap file. Using a permanent swap file improves performance by reducing hard disk head movement to read swap file data. After you set up the swap file, it doesn't matter how fragmented your drive gets because the swap file always resides in the same contiguous disk sectors. The permanent swap file technique did have the disadvantage of limiting the amount of virtual memory that Windows could create, and the space used by the swap file wasn't freed when you exited Windows. Windows 98, however, doesn't provide the permanent swap file option; it always uses a temporary file, which allows you to create as much virtual memory as needed (within reason). Microsoft has improved the access algorithms and has reduced the penalty for using a temporary swap file. The system doesn't work perfectly, however. You still can get a highly fragmented drive that reduces system performance as Windows moves from area to area on the hard drive in an attempt to read the swap file. The speed penalty comes into play when Windows 98 requires multiple hard drive accesses to read individual swap file sections. Defragmenting your drive reduces the possibility that the swap file will become too fragmented. Most people find that a weekly maintenance session takes care of this requirement.

- **Place your swap file on the fastest drive.** Windows 98 usually places the swap file on the drive with the largest amount of available memory. In most cases, the drive it selects doesn't make a big difference. However, if you have a system with one large, slow drive and a second small, fast drive, you should probably change the virtual memory settings. See the following section, "Using Windows 98 Automatic Tuning Features," for more details.

- **Get rid of nonessentials.** Some parts of Windows 98 make you more efficient, but at a fairly large cost in memory. Enabling the International Settings feature (described in Chapter 2), for example, makes you more efficient if you work with several languages. That enhancement, however, costs you memory. Unfortunately, after you activate this feature, you can't get rid of it until you reboot the machine. The same holds true for many other icons that appear in the taskbar tray with the clock.

Peter's Principle: Efficiency of Action Versus Memory Usage

In Windows 98, efficiency of action is sometimes accompanied by decrease in memory usage. The Windows 98 interface is designed to make every movement as easy as possible.

Using features such as a context menu instead of opening the Control Panel might not seem like a very big deal—you save only two or three mouse clicks in most cases—but they also result in memory savings. Windows 98 also provides other speed-enhancing features that save memory. For example, using the automatic settings for most system parameters such as virtual memory improves performance and enhances memory usage.

Some Windows 98 features are not only extremely efficient, they also save you a considerable amount of time. Using Explorer, for example, uses less memory than Program Manager. (A comparison on my machine shows system resources at 94 percent when using Explorer but only 89 percent when using Program Manager in the same configuration.) You can examine this on your machine by changing the `shell=Explorer.exe` line in `SYSTEM.INI` to `shell=Progman.exe`, then shutting down and rebooting your system. The Explorer interface is so much more efficient that I would think twice about going back to Program Manager. (Don't even think about using Active Desktop if you have a memory-constrained system; the memory requirements for Active Desktop are extremely high.)

Using Windows 98 Automatic Tuning Features

In addition to user-related activities, Windows 98 provides additional features for making automated changes to your configuration. You can determine whether these automated features are in effect by displaying the Performance tab of the System Properties dialog box (right-click My Computer and select Properties from the context menu). If your system isn't completely tuned, Windows 98 provides some suggestions to improve system performance. In most cases, this means enabling an automatic feature to provide additional memory, to reduce the system's reliance on out-of-date drivers, or to allow some additional flexibility. Windows 98 also provides tips to make the automatic tuning features work properly.

Notice the three buttons near the bottom of the Performance tab: File System, Graphics, and Virtual Memory. Click the File System button to display the File System Properties dialog box. The Hard Disk, CD-ROM, and Removable Disk tabs of this dialog box enable you to change the way Windows 98 reacts to certain requests for information and allocates memory for the file system without changing its overall management strategy. The following list describes each field in this dialog box:

- **Typical Role of This Machine.** This field has three settings. Select the role that best describes your computer. In most cases, you'll select either Desktop Computer or Mobile or Docking System. If your machine acts as a file server on a peer-to-peer network, select the Network Server setting. This setting can improve performance in a couple ways. The Network Server setting seems to speed some tasks that perform small data reads, such as database managers. It also enhances performance in a multitasking environment.

- **Read-ahead optimization.** Normally, you'll keep this slider set to Full. Using full optimization means that Windows will read as many sectors of the hard drive as it can in one pass. Doing this means that you spend more time reading the hard drive, but that you do it a lot less often because there is more of the information stored in RAM. As a result, you see a speed boost. The only time you'd need to lower the setting is if you were getting a lot of read errors on the hard drive (a condition I haven't run into yet).

- **Supplemental Cache Size.** You can save about 1MB in this field on a memory-starved system. You will, however, trade performance for that savings. Because this setting affects only the CD-ROM cache, you might not notice much of a difference. Don't shortchange this area if you regularly use your CD-ROM to run applications. The loss in cache size becomes very noticeable after a while. Using a large cache means you set aside 1,238KB of RAM for a cache. The small cache uses a mere 214KB.

- **Optimize Access Pattern For.** Set this field to reflect the speed of your CD-ROM drive. Windows 98 uses a different timing formula for each drive type. You can play with this field to see whether you get any performance benefit from changing the default. I actually found one double-speed Toshiba CD-ROM drive that worked better at the triple-speed setting. It's rare to get a performance increase from this, but you never know.

- **Enable write-behind caching on all removable drives.** Checking this option tells Windows that you want to write data to the removable drive during times of lower system activity. In most cases this results in a perceived speed boost, even though the data writing process takes the same amount of time. Normally, this option is left unchecked. The reason is simple: You could remove a disk from a removable drive at any time. If Windows 98 hasn't written the data in memory to disk yet, you could end up with a damaged removable disk and a definite loss of data. You can check this option if you normally don't swap disks out of the removable drive. Make sure you wait until after you shut down Windows, though, to swap disks in the removable drive if you do check this option.

The Floppy Disk tab enables you to check for new floppy disk drives every time your computer is started. Most desktop users should uncheck the box that asks whether you want to run this check each time the machine is started. Unchecking the box means your machine will start faster. This little step might not make the biggest difference in the world, but every bit helps. On the other hand, laptop users with removable disk drives should keep this box checked.

In the Troubleshooting tab, you can either really help or really damage your system's memory management strategy. The key term here is troubleshooting—Microsoft originally included this tab for that sole purpose. On rare occasions, however, you can use these items as part of your tuning strategy. Each check box enables you to change a part of the Windows 98 file system management strategy. Be careful when changing these settings. You might find yourself troubleshooting a non-functional system. The following list describes each of these options:

- **Disable New File Sharing and Locking Semantics.** Windows 98 uses new drivers to maintain file locks for networks. The new setup uses a 32-bit protected-mode driver. The old setup used a 16-bit driver similar to the VSHARE.386 driver provided by WfW 3.x. You should only check this box if you experience network-related file-locking problems. In some cases, file locking works anyway, but checking this box reduces the number of failed attempts. The time differential is quite noticeable with applications such as database managers that require many locks during any given session.

- **Disable Long Name Preservation for Old Programs.** Checking this box helps you maintain compatibility with existing DOS machines. It forces Windows 98 to use the 8.3 file-naming scheme everyone has used since the earliest days of DOS. You lose the benefits of long filenames, and you won't garner even one byte of additional RAM for your system. Companies that use mixed workstations on their network, however, benefit from consistent file naming. In most cases, you should leave this box unchecked.

- **Disable Protected-Mode Hard Disk Interrupt Handling.** Some applications don't work properly with the new Windows 98 interrupt handlers. You can check this box to install the old real-mode handlers. One note of caution: Make sure you don't use non–Windows 98 disk defragmenters or other low-level file management utility programs; they don't support long filenames and other Windows 98 features.

- **Disable synchronous buffer commits.** In most cases, you can speed up a disk access by performing all your reads and writes at one time. Unfortunately, some drives require a separate read and write cycle. Checking this option forces Windows 98 to perform separate read and write cycles.

- **Disable All 32-Bit Protected-Mode Disk Drivers.** A few hard drives and controllers don't work properly with the Windows 32-bit drivers. Although these drivers might not cause a total drive failure, they can cause the drive to slow down. If you notice that your drive's performance isn't what it used to be, you might want to see whether disabling 32-bit support brings it back to normal.

- **Disable Write-Behind Caching for All Drives.** Data loss on network drives is a major headache for most administrators at one time or another. Windows 98 uses a write-behind caching scheme to improve workstation performance. This same feature can actually cause data loss, however, especially with networked database managers. If you have records that don't get written or other forms of data loss, you might want to check this box. Even though checking this box reduces local workstation performance, it might improve overall network performance by forcing the workstation to write shared data faster. This is especially true for situations in which many people share relatively few records in the database—for example, a reservation or scheduling system.

The Advanced Graphics Settings dialog box provides a single slider control. The new protected-mode drivers provided with Windows 98 accelerate writes to the display adapter. The slider controls the amount of acceleration you receive. Most adapters work fine at the highest setting. If your adapter performs only partial screen writes, however, or if you see other types of corruption, you might need to use a lower setting.

The Virtual Memory dialog box enables you to enhance system performance when the automatic method selects the wrong drive for your swap file. Most of the time, you should let Windows manage the virtual memory settings. In a few cases, however, you'll want to manually adjust the virtual memory settings. Windows 98 usually selects the drive with the most free disk space as the virtual memory drive. This might not be the fastest drive on your system, however. In this case, it makes sense to manually adjust the virtual memory drive to be the fastest one on your machine.

> **Warning:** Never disable virtual memory. The Virtual Memory dialog box provides this setting for troubleshooting purposes only. Disabling virtual memory can (and probably will) result in some type of system failure. Such a failure can prevent Windows 98 from writing everything in disk cache to the drive. This can corrupt the Registry or other system files and can prevent you from rebooting the operating system.

You can configure the swap file in other ways. For example, what if the fastest drive on your machine doesn't have enough space for the swap file size you need? Windows 98 enables you to individually configure the swap file for each drive on your system. If you don't want a swap file on a particular drive, set its minimum and maximum sizes to 0.

Finding Unnecessary Hidden Drivers

Sometimes Windows 98 does a less-than-perfect job of setting up your machine. I mentioned previously that you should remove any unnecessary drivers. What happens when you have "hidden" drivers you don't need on your system? Figure 5.1 shows a dialog box that illustrates this point. I installed Windows on a machine in a peer-to-peer networking environment. The installation program even asked what level of support I wanted. The program—which must assume not everyone knows what they're talking about—installed both Microsoft and Novell support anyway. The Novell support goes to waste because this is a peer-to-peer network that doesn't connect to a NetWare file server.

Figure 5.1.
Sometimes Windows
98 installs too much
support.

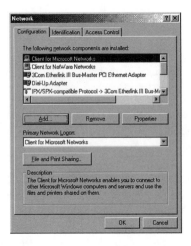

You need to look at three things in this particular situation. First, eliminate additional network support. You only need to install support for one network if you're using a peer-to-peer setup. In most cases, you'll retain the Microsoft network and discard NetWare support. Likewise, if you don't plan to set up a peer-to-peer network, remove the Microsoft network support in a NetWare environment.

You also should reduce the number of protocols installed. I typically maintain NetBEUI support for a peer-to-peer setup if at all possible. The protocol you choose must reflect the capabilities of the network you install.

Tip: If you remove a protocol from your workstation and find you can't connect to other workstations, make sure all the workstations are using the same protocol. Many working networks suddenly fail when people try to optimize their setup. This simple fix repairs the vast majority of "broken" installations.

The third step is to install the fewest possible network services. Installing sharing support for a floppy drive, for example, is a waste of memory because it's unlikely anyone will need it. If someone does need it, you can always add the support later. Try starting out with the lowest level of support possible. You should also think about which workstation printers you really want to share. If a workstation has an older printer attached, you probably won't want to install print sharing support for it.

Top Performance Tips for DOS Applications

I'd love to say Windows 98 can run every DOS application you ever owned without any major configuration problems, but that wouldn't be accurate. You'll probably encounter problems when running certain DOS applications, and you should tune your system to avoid them.

The good news is you can make all the required changes using the application's Properties dialog box. Windows 98 provides support for DOS applications that's far superior to even Windows NT. Microsoft made design decisions to make this support possible. (They'll be explored in Chapter 6, "Setup Primer.") This means you can make the required changes by right-clicking the object and selecting Properties from the context menu. If you want to change settings for the DISKCOPY.EXE file (located in the Windows\Command\ folder, for example, just right-click the DISKCOPY icon in Explorer and select Properties from the context menu. This displays the General tab of the Diskcopy Properties dialog box. (The Properties dialog box always includes the application filename in the title bar. This section uses the Diskcopy Properties dialog box for explanation purposes.) Everything you need to run DOS applications efficiently under Windows 98 appears in this dialog box.

Tip: Some Windows 98 users find it easier to run DOS applications in MS-DOS mode because it provides the most familiar configuration options. Running your applications in this mode, however, means you have to forego any DOS-to-Windows interaction. It also means you won't be able to use any Windows 98 features. Because running an application in MS-DOS mode unloads all the Windows 98 drivers, you lose the benefits of 32-bit driver support.

Looking Ahead: This chapter examines the Properties dialog box settings that affect DOS application performance. The rest of the settings are covered in Chapter 12, "Exploiting Your Software: DOS, 16-Bit, and 32-Bit Applications."

Several tabs directly affect the way a DOS application behaves under Windows 98. The Program tab, shown in Figure 5.2, contains fields that tell Windows 98 what application to run and where to run it. This includes the application name and its working directory. Click the Advanced button to display the Advanced Program Settings dialog box, shown in Figure 5.3, which contains DOS-specific settings that affect how Windows 98 reacts.

My favorite option in the Advanced Program Settings dialog box is Prevent MS-DOS-Based Programs from Detecting Windows. I had several applications that wouldn't work because the application looked for the Windows signature before it ran. Even if the application was able to run, it wouldn't do so. In many cases, you just need to check this option to get an application to cooperate with Windows.

Some applications still experience problems under Windows 98. The Suggest MS-DOS Mode as Necessary option is another automatic tuning aid you can use. If an application has to be run in MS-DOS mode, Windows 98 displays a dialog box suggesting you do so. Unfortunately, Windows doesn't normally check this box for you automatically, so you may need to check it yourself.

Figure 5.2.
*The Program tab of
the Diskcopy
Properties dialog box.*

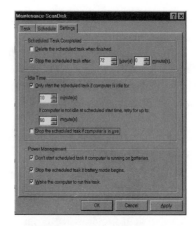

Figure 5.3.
*The Advanced
Program Settings
dialog box.*

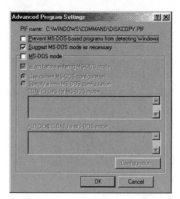

According to Microsoft, the MS-DOS mode check box decreases performance in every situation. In at least two categories of applications, however, you'll probably experience a performance gain instead of a loss. The first category is games. Many DOS games run correctly under Windows 98; many more don't. Sometimes your only choice is to run the program in MS-DOS mode.

The other category is older graphics applications. For some reason, they actually perform better in MS-DOS mode. In most cases, you should replace these older applications with a Windows 98–specific product if at all possible.

If you check MS-DOS mode, you'll get several more options. The first asks whether you want Windows 98 to warn you before it enters MS-DOS mode. Keep this checked as a precaution. You wouldn't want to accidentally leave another application in an uncertain state.

The two radio buttons enable you to choose between the default DOS setup and a custom setup for this particular application. Whenever Windows 98 gives you the choice, I recommend a custom configuration. If the application is having problems with Windows 98, it probably will also have special needs in MS-DOS mode. I have several custom configurations on my hard drive right now.

One works for games that need expanded memory but don't use the CD-ROM drive. Another helps my old copy of Harvard Graphics squeeze that last ounce of performance out of the system.

> **Tip:** An easy way to take care of your configuration needs for MS-DOS–mode applications is to specify the `CONFIG.DOS` and `AUTOEXEC.DOS` files as special configuration files. If the application worked with your old DOS setup, the same configuration should work under Windows 98. All you need to do is copy the contents of the configuration files using any text editor, then paste them into the appropriate text box using Ctrl-V.

The Memory tab, shown in Figure 5.4, also can help you obtain the best possible setup for your application. In most cases, you should stick with the Auto setting. Some applications, however, require more environment space than the Auto setting provides. When this is the case, simply adjust the setting in the list box as necessary. The same holds true for any other memory settings you might need to adjust.

Figure 5.4.
The Memory tab enables you to customize the DOS application's memory settings.

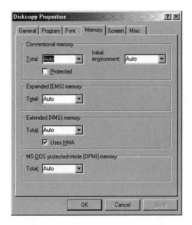

There's one thing you should always keep in mind with the Memory tab. Setting any memory entries you don't need to None saves system memory and enables Windows 98 to provide better services to the rest of the applications on your machine. Windows 98 always assumes the worst-case scenario with DOS applications; setting the various memory options gives it more information to work with.

The Protected check box in the Conventional memory group is a double-edged sword. Although setting it enables some applications to run, it also prevents Windows 98 from moving applications around in memory. Some applications that access memory directly need this kind of protection. The downside of checking this box is that a fixed session in memory always increases memory fragmentation and the chance that you'll artificially run out of memory.

From a performance perspective, the last tab we need to look at in the Properties dialog box is the Screen tab. This chapter only discusses the two check boxes in the Performance group. The rest are covered in Chapter 12.

The Dynamic Memory Allocation check box is the important one here. As with the Protected check box in the Memory tab, this check box determines whether Windows 98 can move memory around. Here's the problem: Many graphics applications resort to using direct screen writes to get the performance they need. Those same graphics applications won't work under Windows 98 if you keep this box checked. This is because Windows might move the "virtual" screen that the application is actually writing to somewhere else. The warning sign you need to look for is some type of distortion. Most applications display vertical bars or some type of striation. You might see part of the display shift or see what appear to be cursor trails onscreen. These types of distortion mean you need to uncheck the Dynamic Memory Allocation check box.

Some applications need to directly access the ROM routines. The Fast ROM emulation check box tells Windows 98 to emulate the display ROM in fast protected-mode RAM. If your application is looking for the system ROM in conventional memory, however, it won't find the emulated version. One way to tell whether this box should be unchecked is if you get unexplainable system crashes that you can't pinpoint to another cause. These crashes could be caused by an application looking for ROM code at a certain address and not finding it.

Top Performance Tips for Multitasking Systems

For more than one application to run on a system at the same time, you usually have to make some compromises. A single-tasking system can be tuned to provide the best performance for that one application. You can tune your system, for example, so a disk-intensive application gets everything it needs to get the job done quickly. But what happens if you run one application that's disk-intensive and another that's CPU-intensive? Do you starve the resources of one to get better performance from the other? In addition, running more than one application at once always consumes a lot of memory. What you might not realize is that your performance levels can become artificially low because of the way Windows 98 handles memory management.

Disk swapping, the same feature that provides virtual memory for applications, can wreak havoc in a multitasking environment. Two big clues tell you when disk swapping has become a problem and not a cure. First, you'll notice a dramatic increase in your system's disk activity. (This isn't always a bad thing in Windows 98, but it is an indicator.) Second, look at the size of your swap file. If your swap file is about the same size as your real memory, your system is memory-starved and unable to run the number of applications you're trying to run.

If your system doubles as a file server, you should also take into account the needs of the LAN. A peer-to-peer network depends on one or more workstations to act as file and print servers. This doubling of tasks is essentially another form of multitasking. You might run only one or two tasks on your machine, but it'll run very slowly if you don't account for the needs of other people who use your system. You should monitor the network statistics using the System Monitor program.

Windows 98 provides another utility that comes in handy. The Net Watcher utility (described in Chapter 23, "Networks") provides information about who is logged in and what type of resources they're using. You can combine this information with that of the System Monitor to create a clear picture of how your machine is being used in the network environment. It might seem difficult to make a correlation between who is using which resources and what the level of activity is. After a while, however, you'll notice certain patterns emerging. You can use those patterns as a basis for tuning your system.

I never thought I'd apply the term *load balancing* to a PC, but here it is. You can get better performance out of your system if you balance the types of tasks it performs. Scheduling all your disk-intensive tasks to run at the same time is one sure way to bring your system to its knees. If you're working on a spreadsheet in the foreground, it might be a good time to compile an application or to perform a database-related task in the background. The opposite is true as well. You can perform an intensive spreadsheet recalculation in the background while performing data entry in the foreground.

> **Tip:** Unlike previous versions of Windows, Windows 98 does a reasonable job of downloading files and performing other online communications in the background. I recently spent almost eight hours downloading a new copy of Internet Information Server at 33.6 Kbaud while working on articles and a spreadsheet in the foreground. I didn't miss a file or experience any corruption.

There's one final consideration to get the most out of your multitasking environment. Using 16-bit applications in Windows 98 means you must suffer the consequences of cooperative multitasking. In essence, a program can be a bad sport and grab the system for however long it wants. 32-bit applications don't get this kind of treatment. Ready or not, they have to return control of the system to Windows 98 at specific intervals. If multitasking is the name of the game, 32-bit applications are what you need to make it work smoothly.

Memory Tuning and Optimization

Most of the following material can also be found in other chapters. This is a good place, however, to summarize the various tips and techniques presented in Chapter 12. The following are my top 10 tips and techniques for tuning your system to make the best use of memory:

1. Always use the built-in memory manager if possible.

2. Use your fastest drive for the swap file, but don't starve Windows in the process. Make sure the drive is large enough to hold the entire swap file.

3. Manage your system, but don't micromanage it. Tell Windows what you need to do, but don't worry too much about how it gets the job done.

4. Never load real-mode device drivers or TSRs you don't need. The old approach of loading everything before you start Windows is a dead end under Windows 98.

5. Use the automatic memory settings whenever possible. At times, however, you'll have to step in and adjust them manually if you have an application that starts by grabbing everything available.

6. Avoid MS-DOS mode whenever possible, but use it if you must. Windows 98 has come a long way in providing optimal support for DOS applications.

7. Enhance memory usage by getting rid of frills. Wallpaper, excess icons, screen savers, and other doodads consume memory without giving you much in return.

8. Increase your level of physical RAM as necessary. Windows 98 can make as much RAM as you need from your hard drive; there's a limit, however, to how much performance you can get from this.

9. Get a faster hard drive. Swap files are a fact of life in Windows 98. This means you're at least partially dependent on hard drive speed for overall system performance—even when it comes to memory.

10. Kill old applications. If you're still using a lot of DOS applications, it's time to upgrade. For the most part, 16-bit Windows applications aren't much better. Upgrading to 32-bit applications helps you use memory efficiently and usually provides a speed benefit as well.

Monitoring the Results of Performance Enhancements

The optional System Monitor utility enables you to track a variety of system statistics, including CPU usage and actual memory allocation. Monitoring these statistics tells you whether a certain optimization strategy was successful. System Monitor also detects performance-robbing hardware and software errors on the system. Figure 5.5 shows a typical System Monitor display.

When you start System Monitor for the first time, it always displays the current Kernel Processor Usage. Figure 5.5 shows one way to display this information. You can use the View | Bar Chart and View | Numeric Chart commands to change the presentation. The bar chart is helpful when you need to monitor system performance over a long interval. The numeric chart is handy when you need to troubleshoot a particular problem area. Bar charts also display a line somewhere along the length of the bar. This line tells you the maximum usage level for that particular statistic. The bar itself shows the current usage level. You can also select any of the three chart types by clicking the correct toolbar icon.

Figure 5.5.
System Monitor
allows you to monitor
system performance.

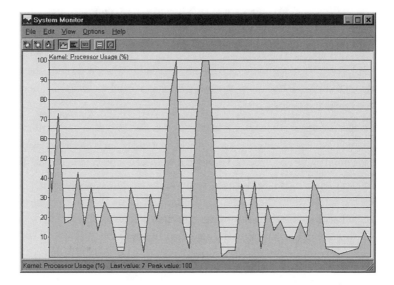

System Monitor uses a default monitoring period of five seconds. This might not be fast enough in certain situations. If you're troubleshooting a bad NIC or you want instant feedback on a configuration change, this setting should be a lower value. Likewise, if you're performing long-term monitoring, you might want to set it higher. Use the Options | Chart command to change this setting.

The first three toolbar buttons enable you to change the items that System Monitor displays. Use the Add button to add new items to the list. Use the Edit button to change the way System Monitor displays a particular value. You might, for example, want to display something in green rather than blue. You also can change the upper limit of some values to provide a consistent range for particular items. The Remove button enables you to remove an item from the monitoring list.

Automating Tune-Ups with Task Scheduler

The Task Scheduler enables you to perform automated tasks using different criteria. For example, you can have the computer run ScanDisk at 7 p.m. every Sunday, your disk defragmenter at 5 p.m. every Friday, and your anti-virus program at 9 a.m. the first Monday of every month.

> **Tip:** The Task Scheduler can be used to run more than just disk-utility programs. It also works with applications designed for Windows 95/NT, Windows 3.x, OS/2, MS-DOS, batch files (*.BAT), command files (*.CMD), or any properly registered file type. You could use the Task Scheduler to send out a fax in the middle of the night when phone rates are lower, for example, or to print out a database report after hours so it doesn't tie up your computer during the day.

A task can have more than one trigger to determine when it should be executed. A trigger is a set of criteria that, when met, activates and causes a task to be executed. There are two types of triggers: time-based and event-based.

A *time-based trigger* activates at a specified time. Not only can you set the time it becomes active, you can also have it activate once, daily, weekly, monthly, on a specified day of the month (the third day of the month), or on a specified day of the week of a month (the second Tuesday of the month).

An *event-based trigger* activates in response to certain system events. Some event-based triggers become active when the system starts up, when a user logs on to the local computer, or when the system becomes idle. The last of these is known as an *idle trigger*. An idle trigger becomes active a specified amount of time after the computer becomes idle. When you set the idle-related flags for a task, you create an idle trigger.

Starting Task Scheduler

You can start the Task Scheduler using the Start | Programs | Accessories | System Tools | Scheduled Tasks command. You also can start the Task Scheduler by double-clicking the Task Scheduler icon on the taskbar tray. Figure 5.6 shows the Scheduled Tasks window you'll see when you start the program.

Figure 5.6.
The Scheduled Tasks window enables you to add, modify, or delete tasks.

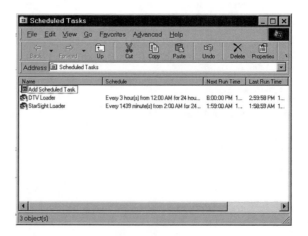

Scheduling a New Task

Before you can use the Task Scheduler, you have to schedule specific tasks you want done. (If you ever need to delete a task, just click on it and then click the Delete icon in the Task Scheduler toolbar.) The following procedure shows you how do this:

1. Double-click the Add Scheduled Task icon that appears in Figure 5.6. As soon as you double-click this icon, the Scheduled Task Wizard appears.

2. Click Next. The next dialog box enables you to choose the application you want to run. You can use the Browse button to find an application that doesn't appear in the list.

3. Select the application you want to run, then click Next. The Scheduled Task Wizard asks for a specific time to run the task—daily, weekly, monthly, one time only, at boot up, or when you log on. You also can change the automatically provided name for the task if it isn't descriptive enough.

4. Select the scheduling option you want to use. Click Next. Depending on the time you chose (daily, weekly, monthly, and so on), you will see another list of options asking you to specify the exact time and date to run your chosen task.

5. Choose a time and date, then click Next. The Scheduled Task Wizard shows the application you chose to run and the time you selected. You'll also see a check box that enables you to display the application's Advanced Properties dialog box after the Scheduled Task Wizard is complete. The Advanced Properties dialog box enables you to add a command line parameter, to check the schedule for the application, and to choose additional settings, such as running the application during idle time or stopping it after a specific interval. This feature is discussed more in the "Customizing a Scheduled Task" section of this chapter.

6. Click Finish if you are ready to schedule the task.

> **Tip:** After scheduling a task, right-click the task and choose Run. This gives you a chance to see how your scheduled task actually runs. That way, you can see whether the task hangs or needs additional input before running.

Customizing a Scheduled Task

After you create a task, the Task Scheduler continues running it until you either delete it or specify a time to stop running it. In addition to specifying when to stop running a task, there are other reasons to customize your tasks. You might want the Task Scheduler to automatically delete a scheduled task after a certain date when you no longer need it. If you're running the Task Scheduler on a laptop, you might not want to run tasks automatically, especially if your batteries are running low. You also might want to run a task only when the computer is idle. After all, you might not want to have the Task Scheduler suddenly interfere with your work at the computer.

Customizing a scheduled task involves changing a task's properties. To view a task's properties, right-click the task and choose Properties. The Task tab enables you to change the Run (the application's command line), Start In (the working directory), and Comments fields. The Enable check box lets you retain a task, yet keep it from running by unchecking the box. You can use the Browse button to find a new copy of the application.

The Schedule tab enables you to define the date and time to run a task. Click the Advanced button to display the Advanced Schedule Options dialog box, as shown in Figure 5.7. Here you can specify an ending date for your task or direct it to repeat.

Figure 5.7.

The Advanced Schedule Options dialog box enables you to pick an ending date or to run the same task repeatedly.

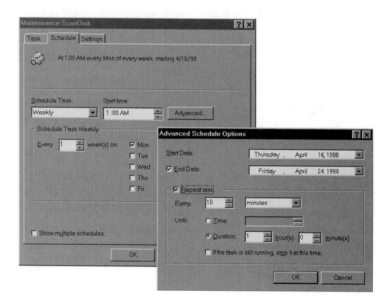

The Settings tab (see Figure 5.8) enables you to specify whether to delete a task after it's done. It also enables you to stop a task if it's still running after a certain period of time, to determine whether to run the task on a laptop using its battery power, and to run the task when the computer is idle.

Running Batch Files Automatically

In addition to running an application, the Task Scheduler also can run batch files. Why would you want to run a batch file? A batch file enables you to specify command-line parameters for your applications; you also can run two or more applications one after another. By running a single batch file, you can run two or more programs without having to schedule each one individually within the Task Scheduler.

In case you've forgotten how to create a batch file, they are simply ASCII files that end with the .BAT file extension. You can create batch files using any editor (such as Notepad). Just save your file with the .BAT file extension.

Figure 5.8.
The Settings tab
enables you to modify
how the task runs.

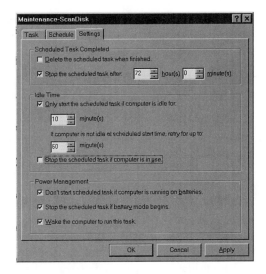

Suspending Task Scheduler

You might want to temporarily stop the Task Scheduler from running scheduled tasks. Rather than suspending each scheduled task individually (and then worrying about re-activating each task all over again), you can temporarily keep the Task Scheduler from running any of its scheduled tasks. To suspend Task Scheduler temporarily, load it, then choose Advanced | Pause Task Scheduler. When you want to reactivate Task Scheduler, choose Advanced | Continue Task Scheduler.

Tip: You also can pause Task Scheduler by right-clicking the Task Scheduler icon on the taskbar tray, then selecting Pause Task Scheduler from the context menu.

Disabling Task Scheduler

Rather than temporarily suspend the Task Scheduler, you might find it more convenient to turn it off altogether. To turn off the Task Scheduler, load it and then choose Advanced | Stop Using Task Scheduler. To turn Task Scheduler back on again, choose Advanced | Start Using Task Scheduler.

On Your Own

Practice creating long filenames that a DOS or Windows 3.x user can understand. Use Explorer to create a new file in a temporary folder and give it a long filename. Then open the DOS prompt and view that same filename. Does the name make sense in both contexts? If not, you should spend a little more time working on the name. Remember, you're effectively reduced to six characters because of the way Windows 98 differentiates between different files with similar long filenames.

Survey your hardware to see if any components might be holding your system's performance back. Consider replacing that old CD-ROM drive or adding more memory if necessary to enhance system throughput. A whole new machine might be in your future if the current one is completely out-of-date—don't waste money replacing all the components in your machine one at a time.

Check out the "General Tuning Tips for Windows" section of this chapter to see if you can get rid of any memory- or performance-wasting features. You might want to consider spending a week without wallpaper. The performance improvement you get might be worth the sacrifice. Look at some of the doodads you have loaded as well. I'm often surprised at how many little utility programs get loaded on my machine, then never get used.

Look at the Performance tab of the System Properties dialog box to see if your system is using all the automatic tuning features Windows provides. Make sure all these features are working for you, rather than against you. You might, for example, want to change the drive used for the virtual memory swap file to a faster drive on your machine.

Hunt for any unnecessary drivers on your machine (only if you suspect there are any—new machines usually don't have unnecessary drivers lurking around). Make sure you look for some of the nonobvious sources of wasted device drivers, such as network protocols you don't use.

Start monitoring your machine after you get it optimized. Make sure all the changes you made actually improved system performance rather than hindering it. If you do find that some change reduced system performance, try to figure out why. Knowing how changes affect your machine makes it easier to tune in the future.

6

Setup Primer

Peter Norton®

I'm often surprised at just how little emphasis some people put on the installation of their software. Many people—including me—got the idea somewhere along the way that you should be able to stick a CD in the drive, type a command (or double-click an icon) and then forget about anything other than waiting for the software to install. This is the way software installation should work for the most part, but it doesn't.

Reality is somewhat different from the theory of software installation. I recently spent half an hour configuring a piece of software for installation and another 15 minutes installing it from the CD. The amount of time that it took to configure this piece of software was staggering when compared to the relatively short time required to install it. Software now comes with many different configuration options because some people want bells and whistles and others don't.

Today's software often reminds me of the proverbial Chinese menu from which you have to select one from Column A and two from Column B. I don't mind having a few choices, but some software has become ridiculous. You could easily get lost in the sea of choices that some software offers. Of course, all those choices don't come without cost. Not only does bloated software take up a lot of hard drive space, it also tends to gobble up memory. In addition, I think a good many technical support problems are the direct result of too many choices during installation. Most users just don't have a clue as to what all those choices are about, and the help provided with most installation programs is less than helpful.

If Windows did free us in any way, it was from having to tell every one of our applications what hardware has been installed every time we install it. That's one of my pet peeves with DOS software: You have to know everything about your machine to get any and every application installed. Unlike DOS—and even many previous versions of Windows—Windows 98 is fairly easy to install. It can detect most types of hardware automatically. In fact, this version does a better job than Windows 95 in detecting what settings to use. Is Windows 98 perfect? No, you'll still find situations in which you need to give it an assist, especially when using older or non-standard hardware.

Before we go much further, you'll want to do a quick check of your hardware. Microsoft has one set of hardware specifications, but I don't think you'll want to use them. (Microsoft played the same game when creating the system requirements for Windows NT.) The problem is that the "minimum" system that the specifications describe is too minimal to get any kind of performance. If you want a system that will really work with Windows 98, use the following parameters:

- **Pentium processor.** You can try to use one of the faster 80486 systems, but the performance you receive won't be all that useful, especially if you plan to make use of the new Internet-related features of Windows 98. I wouldn't even consider using an 80386 machine, no matter what clock speed it is. Windows 98 requires too much processing power.

- **32MB memory minimum.** I would really think about increasing your memory to 64MB to get the best performance, but a 32MB system will perform adequately.

- **500MB of free hard disk space.** The Microsoft minimum of 50MB just isn't realistic unless you want to install a stripped version of Windows 98 with no room to run any applications.

- **High-density 3[1/2]-inch floppy drive.** Everyone who installs Windows 98 will want to create an emergency boot disk. You need a high-density floppy to store the emergency files. Windows 98 can create this disk for you automatically during installation. You also can create or update the disk later from the Startup Disk page of the Add/Remove Programs Properties dialog box.

- **SVGA (800×600) or higher display adapter.** You can get by using a VGA display with Windows 98, but that doesn't really provide enough space to get any work done. If you have any plans for using the Internet features of Windows 98, you'll probably want to look at 1024×768 resolution as a minimum. Forget about using a 256-color display on the Internet as well: Some web pages just don't render very well using 256 colors. The minimum you should go for is 16-bit color (65,536 colors).

- **Mouse (pointing device).** Someone will try to tell you that you can work efficiently in Windows 98 using just the keyboard. You can get around; there's no doubt about it. But a mouse makes Windows 98 so much more efficient that I can't understand why anyone would want to go without one.

- **CD-ROM drive.** Don't slow down your system by getting a slow CD-ROM drive. I'd suggest a 12X CD-ROM drive as a minimum. In fact, if you plan to use the CD-ROM a lot, make sure you get something a little faster, such as one of the newer 24X drives on the market. (If you're getting a new machine, check into getting a DVD drive, because many of them can read CDs as well.)

- **Optional devices.** You also can install any number of optional peripheral devices. I strongly recommend you install a modem as a minimum. Windows 98 provides much better multimedia capabilities as well. You'll probably want to install a sound board somewhere along the way. A Zip drive (or a similar removable media device) would also be a good addition, because you may want to use one for backup purposes. If you don't get a Zip drive, at least consider getting a tape drive for backup purposes.

The one feature that will stick out in your mind is the way Windows 98 automatically detects the majority of your hardware. I installed Windows 98 on a variety of machines and met with a variety of successes. Fortunately, it looks like Microsoft is making some progress in the hardware-detection department; Windows 98 does a much better job than Windows 95 in detecting your hardware. I also like the way that the software leads you by the hand during configuration. Again, there are choices to make, but the way they were laid-out makes it much easier to figure out what you want to do. In addition, unlike previous versions of Windows, the online help for this installation routine tells you a little bit about what you are installing.

The new installation used by Windows 98 is the best I've seen to date, but I still experienced a few problems. For example, some hardware was detected fine during one installation but not during another. Some of the worst failings of the installation routine in one way were the highlights in another. For example, during one installation I found it nearly impossible to get through the procedure and end up with the correct sound card installed in my machine.

Installing Windows 98

You might want to spend a little time preparing for your Windows 98 installation, especially if you want to maximize its capabilities or if you're planning to reverse the installation later. Of course, the first piece of preparation is to make a complete backup of each system before you start the installation. Trying to back out of a failed installation can prove to be quite a problem sometimes.

Peter's Principle: Boot Disks: The Cheap Form of Insurance

You just started an installation and it goes south for the winter. The machine is frozen and you can't get back to the DOS prompt. What do you do?

If you're like me, you stick your boot disk into the A: drive and reboot the machine. (A boot disk differs from the Emergency Boot Disk; it contains all of the DOS drivers needed to start your machine for troubleshooting purposes and allows you to create a clean environment for performing other kinds of tasks.) I never start anything as involved as an operating system installation without making a boot disk first. In fact, I usually make a boot disk for all my installations, even if I think the software will install without a hitch.

Just what does a boot disk contain? It must contain the operating system; otherwise, you can't use it to boot the system. I also include renamed copies of my CONFIG.SYS and AUTOEXEC.BAT files as well. You don't want to use the original files to boot the machine because they contain entries you probably won't need. If I'm performing a Windows installation, I always include copies of my WIN.INI and SYSTEM.INI files as well. In fact, for shaky installations, I make a copy of all my INI files onto a separate disk. A copy of the Registry files, USER.DAT and SYSTEM.DAT, also is handy because an installation usually causes problems with these files.

A boot disk needs some utility programs. I usually include FDISK, and FORMAT.DEBUG usually makes an appearance also. The disk has to include any files required to activate your disk compression (if the drive is compressed). A disk editor usually comes in handy, as does a small text editor. You also should probably include a disk scanning program such as CHKDSK or its equivalent as well, because a disk crash will require the services of such a diagnostic program.

You'll also need a DOS backup program that can read the backup of the workstation you created. There are two fatal assumptions that some people make when making a workstation backup. First, you can't assume you'll have network access after a failed workstation installation. That's why I make a local backup of the machine instead of using network resources. Second, because you're booting DOS, you need a DOS application that can read your backup. I once ran into someone who thoughtfully made a backup of his hard drive but used a Windows program to do it. His only choice after the system failed was to reinstall Windows and all the software required to gain access to the tape drive. It took him almost three hours to restore the drive. A DOS backup program gives you nearly instantaneous access to the data you need to restore after a failed installation attempt.

Don't be afraid to make up a two- or three-disk package to ensure that you'll have everything you need in order to diagnose problems with the machine. Just because this is a software installation, you can't assume that the hard drive will be accessible. Those trips back and forth to the office to pick up this utility or that can get to be quite time-consuming. A little preparation goes a long way toward making what looks like a difficult problem easier to fix.

Tip: When you partition your hard drive, it's always a good idea to keep this principle in mind: Don't compress your boot drive. The reason is simple: You can't access a compressed drive very easily in an emergency. Make sure your boot drive includes any files required to boot the machine in its normal configuration, a few utility programs, and some diagnostic aids. Compressing your boot drive is just another way to play Russian roulette. Somewhere along the line—you'll shoot yourself—and it won't be in the foot.

Getting all the required equipment together to perform the installation is only the first step. You need to do other things before you perform the installation. The following sections give you the inside scoop on all the pre-installation steps you should take. Then you'll see several different installation methods.

Check Your Hardware

Windows 98 automatically detects the vast majority of hardware out there. It even includes information files that allow it to detect older hardware. However, the detection capabilities that Windows 98 currently provides are less than perfect, so you'll want to spend a little time checking your system hardware for potential problems.

Microsoft groups all Windows 98 autodetection capabilities under Plug and Play. Even if your hardware isn't Plug and Play–compatible, Windows 98 will try to treat it as such for installation purposes. We'll look at Plug and Play from an installation perspective later in this chapter. Suffice it to say for now that Windows 98 won't do a perfect job of installing your hardware if you don't have a 100 percent Plug and Play–compatible machine.

Certain types of older hardware almost guarantee problems under Windows 98. It's pretty unlikely that you'll have any of this hardware on your machine, especially if you bought it within the last two years. If you have hardware with the following characteristics, you might want to take a second look at it before you install Windows 98. Of course, you can always try to install it, but I've run into more than my share of problems with these hardware types:

- **Older disk controllers that don't provide their own BIOS.** A lot of old MFM controllers fall into this category. Windows 98 depends on the contents of the peripheral BIOS as one of the means to detect it. Every vendor writes its company name (or at least someone else's name) into the BIOS. Looking for this company name is one way to determine who made the device.

- **Machines that use a clone BIOS.** Some older machines use what I call a "clone BIOS." These are the machines that boot with some strange logo from a company you've never heard of. A machine containing a BIOS from one of the mainstream companies such as AMI or Phoenix is almost always a better bet than a clone BIOS machine.

- **Nonstandard peripheral devices.** Standards evolve as users and companies gain knowledge about a particular area of technology. Unfortunate as it might seem, some of the hardware that appeared before the standard was introduced just isn't compatible with that standard. Without a standard way to access the hardware, it's very difficult to talk to it and determine what capabilities it provides.

- **Peripherals that almost emulate something else.** IBM and other vendors are to blame for this problem. They started placing their company name in the BIOS of some hardware types. When someone would try to use a piece of generic software developed by these companies, the first thing the software would do was check the BIOS for the correct company name. Clone makers aren't stupid; they started putting the IBM (or other) company name in their BIOS chips too. This isn't a problem as long as the device in question completely emulates the hardware it replaces.

There's also some marginal hardware out there that you can fix after the initial installation is over. Sound boards are one big item that falls into this category. Windows 98 does a pretty good job of detecting them, considering that one sound board is designed to emulate the qualities of another. Just about every sound board out there claims some sort of Sound Blaster emulation mode. Trying to detect this hardware is a nightmare. In some cases, you'll just have to manually install the hardware later. You'll see the procedure for performing a manual installation later in this chapter.

A final "difficult-to-install" hardware category is the older stuff that depends on a real-mode driver for support. I had an old Hitachi 1503S CD-ROM drive that fell into this category. Believe it or not, it worked just fine under Windows 98, even though I had to use real-mode drivers. The downside is that I couldn't seem to share it on the network, and the stability and performance problems it introduced into the system just weren't worth the effort of keeping it around. I finally replaced the drive with something a little less archaic and haven't looked back since.

Peter's Principle: Replacing Old Hardware to Save Money

Sometimes you'll save money right now by spending a little on new hardware. Whenever you choose to keep an old piece of hardware to save money, but introduce some type of instability into your system as a result, you're wasting more money than you're saving.

Windows 98 provides an opportunity to rid your system of all the old hardware that makes it inefficient. Not only will you get your work done faster, but you'll get it done with fewer problems. Think about the last time you spent days trying to find a problem with your system, only to discover that it was a bad driver or some other hardware-related problem. The hardware still works, so it's very difficult to give it up. But doing so when you upgrade might mean you spend a few less hours trying to find those mysterious problems related to the real-mode drivers that the hardware requires to work.

Looking Ahead: Just because you have a few pieces of older or incompatible hardware in your system is no reason to roll over and give up any idea of installing Windows 98. Chapter 26, "Hardware Problems," takes a detailed look at hardware troubleshooting techniques—especially tough-to-install hardware. In some cases, you might find that Windows 98 even provides protected-mode drivers you can use with the old stuff.

When you figure out whether you're going to have any potential problems with your hardware, you'll want to create an inventory of what you have. Some hardware, such as sound boards, uses a real-mode driver that accepts configuration parameters as part of the device driver command line. If Windows supports the device, you can normally REM the driver out of CONFIG.SYS and AUTOEXEC.BAT before you start your Windows 98 installation. There are exceptions to this rule. You wouldn't want to get rid of any drivers needed for your CD-ROM drive or your hard drive controller. Any essential drivers should stay in place; any nonessential drivers should be REMed out.

Some hardware still uses jumpers for configuration purposes. The one big item that just about everyone will need to consider is NICs (network interface cards). NICs usually have one or more address settings and an IRQ setting. You need to write down the settings of any boards that use jumpers before you start your Windows 98 installation. This list will come in handy later as you try to resolve any IRQ or address conflicts that arise during installation.

When you get to this point, you have just about every piece of hardware information you need. There's one final piece of information that you should check for machines that use file compression. A few people I've talked with say they had problems getting Windows 98 to work properly with their disk compression software. In most cases, it turned out to be some kind of interaction between the compression software, the drive controller, and Windows 98. Almost everyone will use their disk compression software without any problem under Windows 98. However, if you want to make absolutely certain that there aren't any problems, decompress the drive prior to installation and recompress it using Windows 98–specific disk compression software.

Getting Ready to Install

When you get to this point in the chapter, you should have created a boot disk and inventoried your hardware. You also should have removed many of the device drivers from CONFIG.SYS and AUTOEXEC.BAT. Before you begin the setup process, you might want to make a few additional changes to these two files. It might seem like a pain to have to preset your machine to provide the best possible environment for an operating system installation, but you really will get better results this way.

The first thing you'll want to do is REM out any unneeded TSRs from your AUTOEXEC.BAT. I even took out the little utility programs such as DOSKey. You'll also want to REM out ANSI.SYS (or a vendor-specific alternative) because you won't need it under Windows 98. If you use a real-mode network, disable it for the time being—at least as a server. Windows 98 has problems with some peer-to-peer real-mode network software when you try to install it with the server running. In addition, disable any drive mappings or Setup will run into problems trying to identify your boot drive.

Tip: The Windows 98 setup program will overwrite, delete, or replace some of the files in your DOS directory. If you have any intention of uninstalling Windows 98 later, it's a good idea to make a copy of this directory before you start the installation. That way, you can easily restore it later.

After you complete these final modifications, reboot your system. You should now have a completely clean environment in which to install Windows 98. It's always a good idea, however, to perform one last check using the MEM /C command to verify that memory is as clean as possible.

Tip: When you start the setup process, the first thing Windows 98 does is scan your drives for errors. You might want to save yourself a bit of time by doing this check in advance. That way, you can fix any errors and prevent the Windows 98 Setup program from stopping before it even gets started.

Let's look at some of the Setup command-line switches. They'll help you get around any problems you might experience while installing Windows 98. For example, some computers might freeze when Setup tries to perform a disk scan, so you can use the /IQ or /IS switch to get around the problem. The following is a complete list of these switches. There's one thing you need to know about the way I present this information. When you see something between angle brackets, it means that you have to supply a value of some kind. The description will tell you what to provide. Don't type the angle brackets when you type the switch.

- **/?.** Use this switch to display a list of currently documented command-line switches.

- **/D.** The /D switch helps you get around situations in which one or more of your Windows 3.x or WfW 3.1x support files are missing or corrupted and Setup won't run properly. It tells Setup not to use the existing copy of Windows for the initial phase of the setup. As soon as the new Windows 98 support files get copied to your drive, Setup switches back to a Windows interface.

- **/ID.** Setup doesn't check for the required disk space when you use this switch. I can't think of any time when you'd want to use it. If your system is that short on hard disk space, you should consider clearing additional space before you try to install Windows 98.

- **/IM.** There are situations where Setup might freeze while checking your system's memory. This switch allows you to disable that check.

- **/IN.** You may not want the Setup program to set your network up immediately. If that's the case, then use this switch to start the installation without the network setup module.

- **/IQ.** Use this switch to bypass ScanDisk as the first step of the installation process when performing the installation from DOS. It's not a good idea to skip this step unless your system experiences some kind of problem running ScanDisk with Setup running. Be sure to do a separate scan of your drives if you use this switch.

- **/IS.** Use this switch to bypass ScanDisk as the first step of the installation process when performing the installation from Windows. It's not a good idea to skip this step unless your system experiences some kind of problem running ScanDisk with Setup running. Be sure to do a separate scan of your drives if you use this switch.

- **/T:<Temporary Directory>.** This switch enables you to tell Windows 98 which drive to use as a temporary directory. It normally tries to use the drive you're using for installation. If the drive you chose is short on space, however, you can use this switch to redirect installation-specific items to another drive.

> **Warning:** Make absolutely certain that any temporary directory you select is empty. The Windows 98 setup program will erase the contents of any temporary directory that you select.

- **<Batch>.** This option enables you to use MSBATCH.INF or another batch file that contains custom installation instructions.

Believe it or not, you're finally ready to install Windows 98. The last thing you need to do before you start Setup is to choose what type of installation you want. (My personal choice is the Custom Setup option, because it gives you the most control over the final appearance of the installation.) You can perform four types of installations:

- **Typical Setup.** This is the default setup that Windows 98 provides. It will allow you to install a standard set of options for your machine.

- **Portable Setup.** Use this setup if you're using a portable computer. It installs a minimal set of standard utility programs—the same set included with the Compact Setup option. This installation also includes all the special utilities that Windows 98 provides for portable computers, such as the Briefcase and Direct Cable Connection features.

- **Compact Setup.** This is the option to use if you're really tight on hard disk space. It installs only the bare essentials—perhaps a little too bare for many users. The nice thing about using this particular option is that you can get a minimal system started and then add other features as you need them.

- **Custom Setup.** The custom option provides the most flexibility of all the Setup options. It also requires the greatest amount of time to set up. This is the perfect option for those who already have a good idea of what they do and don't want out of Windows 98.

The decision as to which installation route you want to use is based partly on which files you need. The one thing you'll want to remember is that you can always add or remove features later on. A mistake right now doesn't mean that you'll have to start the installation from scratch later.

Installing Windows 98 from a CD-ROM

Installing Windows 98 from a CD-ROM is just as simple as Windows 95 was. All you need to do is start DOS or Windows and type **setup**. (The CD also includes an AUTORUN feature, so you may not have to do more than insert the CD when upgrading from Windows 95.) Microsoft suggests that you install Windows 98 over an existing copy of Windows 3.x or Windows 95 so that you can retain your current program settings. It's true that this particular installation provides you with a better interface. However, beyond the interface issue, both installation methods (character-mode or GUI) are the same.

Note: You need to retain any drivers and TSRs required to access your CD-ROM drive in the DOS startup files to install Windows 98 from a CD. This usually includes a CD device driver in CONFIG.SYS and an MSCDEX entry in AUTOEXEC.BAT. (Fortunately, Windows 98 does ship with a generic CD-ROM driver that you'll find on the Emergency Boot Diskette for non-SCSI CD-ROM drives in case you don't have access to a driver specifically designed for your CD-ROM drive.) Remember to REM out any unneeded drivers once the Windows 98 installation is complete.

Make sure your hard drive is partitioned and formatted before you start this procedure. You should probably put the system files on it as well so you can boot from it. In most cases, your drive comes that way from the manufacturer. If you can boot off the drive, it's ready to go. The following steps walk you through the installation procedure:

1. Type **Setup** at the Run (or DOS) prompt and press Enter. You should see a display similar to the one in Figure 6.1.

Figure 6.1.
The initial Windows 98 screen starts like most Microsoft installation programs.

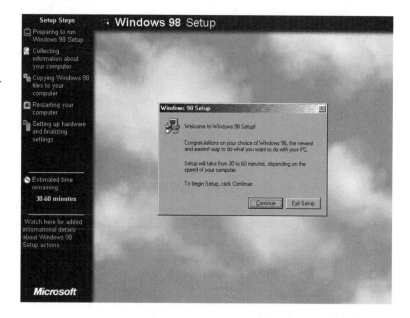

2. Click Continue (or press Enter at the DOS prompt). Setup displays a dialog to inform you that it's scanning your drive.

Tip: The Windows 98 setup program relies heavily on HTML pages to display information. This makes installation from the DOS prompt and from Windows about the same after you get into the program. Make sure you look at the area around the various dialog boxes. The initial setup screen, for example, contains additional information about the steps you'll perform during the installation.

3. Click Continue. Setup makes some additional checks at this point. For one thing, it checks to make sure it's the only application running. If it finds any other applications running, setup displays a dialog box telling you to use Alt+Tab to access the applications and exit them. Setup provides similar dialog boxes for other problems it finds. When it gets past this point, Setup displays a message saying that it's installing the Windows 98 Setup Wizard. When Setup Wizard installation is complete, setup displays a licensing agreement and asks you to agree to its terms. If you decide you don't like the terms, you can exit setup.

4. Signal your agreement to the licensing terms by selecting the "I accept the agreement" radio button, and then clicking Next. Setup will display a dialog asking you where you want to install Windows 98. It offers C:\WINDOWS as a default setting, which is what you should use unless you have a good reason for install Windows 98 elsewhere.

5. Click Next to accept the default location of C:\WINDOWS. The Setup Wizard starts preparing the directory where you intend to install Windows. (This means copying various files and performing a few setups.) After the installation files are copied to the hard drive, you'll see the Setup Options dialog box.

6. Select one of the four installation types, all of which were discussed in the preceding section. Most users should select either Typical or Custom installation.

7. After you select an installation type, click Next to go to the User Information dialog box. This is where you'll enter your user information.

8. Type your name and company name (if applicable). Click Next. If you're using any of the setups other than Custom, you'll see the Windows Components dialog. This dialog gives you an opportunity to choose something other than the default components for a specific installation type. For example, you may want to use the Portable installation, but add or remove a feature. (If you're using the Custom Setup option, skip to step 10.)

9. Choose whether you want to add or remove features, then click Next. If you want all the standard features, skip to step 12.

10. At this point, you'll see the Select Components dialog box. Choose one or more Windows 98 features from the list, then click Next.

11. At this point, the Setup Wizard will begin copying files to the hard drive. Once it completes the copying process, you'll see the Identification dialog. This dialog contains a description of the computer (usually a location or the name of the person who normally

uses it), your computer's network name, and the name of the workgroup you below to. All of the computers on the network must have a unique computer name, but all computers that belong to the same workgroup must have the same workgroup name.

12. Type your computer's name, workgroup name, and a description. Click Next and you'll see the Computer Settings dialog. This is where you'll define the common elements of your computer. For example, you'll tell Windows 98 what language you prefer to use and the type of keyboard you have. You won't tell it specifics like the brand of display adapter you have—that part of the setup comes later.

13. Look through the list of computer settings and change any that don't match your computer. Be sure to check the User Interface setting. This is where you choose between the Windows 98 (Active Desktop) and Windows 3.x (Program Manager) interfaces.

14. After you verify that all the computer settings are correct, click Next. You'll see the Emergency Startup Disk dialog box.

Warning: Some people might not want to create an emergency startup disk because they don't have a floppy handy or they see it as a waste of time. Creating an emergency startup disk is essential; it represents the only way to recover from some types of fatal system errors. Make absolutely certain that you don't skip this step.

15. Insert a disk into your floppy drive, then click Next. The Setup Wizard begins the process of creating an emergency startup disk. After the Setup Wizard gets all the information together, it displays an Insert Disk dialog box.

16. Click OK to start copying the emergency startup disk data from your computer to the floppy. The Setup Wizard initializes the floppy, then copies the emergency startup disk information. After the Setup Wizard completes the emergency startup disk, it displays a dialog box telling you to remove the floppy from the drive.

17. Remove the emergency startup disk from the floppy drive and label it. Click OK to clear the message dialog box. You should see the Start Copying Files dialog box. Now you're ready to install Windows 98 to the hard drive.

Note: It may seem like the Setup Wizard has stopped functioning from time to time while it copies files to your hard drive. However, if you look at the lower left corner of the screen, you'll see an indicator showing how much of the files have been copied. As long as this indicator changes every once in a while, you're in good shape. (Other indicators are disk activity and changes in the main dialog display.)

18. Click Next. The Setup Wizard copies all the required files to the hard drive. This might take quite a while, depending on what features you wanted to install. After the files are copied, the Setup Wizard reboots the machine. At this point, the Setup Wizard starts the hardware detection process. After the hardware detection process is complete, the computer reboots again. (You might go through several reboots.) The Setup Wizard performs some system configuration, then displays the Date/Time Properties dialog box shown in Figure 6.2. This is where you set up the time zone for your computer.

Figure 6.2.
*After file and
hardware installation,
you see the Date/
Time Properties
dialog box.*

Note: Once all of the hardware setup is complete, the Setup Wizard will reboot one last time. At this point you may get one or more network messages. You'll have to read the message and decide whether there is a problem. For example, you may get a message saying Windows 98 couldn't find a DHCP server. If your network doesn't have a DHCP server, then getting this message isn't a problem. Ask your network administrator for more information as needed.

19. Choose the Time Zone for your location. Windows 98 normally defaults to the Pacific time zone, but there are time zones for every area of the world. Click Close to complete the time setting process. The Setup Wizard will continue setting up various Windows 98 elements. It'll eventually display the Inbox Setup Wizard dialog. I've already covered the procedure for working with the Inbox Setup Wizard in the "Using Dial-Up Networking" section of Chapter 1, "Opening Windows to the Internet." Refer to that discussion if you want to configure your Inbox now.

Tip: Now may be a good time to check your computer's time setting. Simply choose the Date & Time tab of the Date/Time Properties dialog. You'll see a clock that represents system time. Just change the time to reflect the actual time.

20. Configure your Inbox using the procedures in Chapter 1 or click Cancel. You'll see the Add Printer Wizard dialog. We'll cover the procedure for adding a printer to your machine in the "Installing a Printer" section of Chapter 15, "Fonts and Printing."

21. Use the "Installing a Printer" procedure in Chapter 15 to add a printer to your machine, or click Cancel if you don't want to add one now. At this point, you'll see a Restart Computer dialog box. The Setup Wizard reboots the computer. Windows 98 starts running after the computer reboots.

It's important to realize that while you have the operating system up and running, you still have more installation tasks to perform. For one thing, you might see the Add New Hardware Wizard when you restart your machine. The "Installing Hardware" section of Chapter 13, "Exploiting Your Hardware," will help you through the process of using the Add New Hardware Wizard.

Installing Windows 98 from a Server

A server installation can differ from CD-ROM installation in many ways. If the network administrator chooses to provide lots of automation, the entire installation process might not require any interaction from you at all. On the other hand, if the network administrator chooses not to provide any automation, you will see the same thing you did for the CD-ROM installation. Your experience will probably fit somewhere between these two extremes. Make sure you contact your network administrator for details before attempting to install Windows 98 from a server.

Plug and Play Installation Tips

I'm a great fan of automation that works. As I see it, anything that makes my job easier or faster is a good idea. Using Plug and Play to automatically install any hardware it recognizes is that kind of automation. It makes sense that a computer can figure out port and interrupt settings faster and with greater accuracy than the average human. One reason this level of automation is possible in Windows 98 is that the computer has all the statistics it needs to do the job. The majority of this information is contained in the onboard BIOS, which Plug and Play hardware uses to communicate with the rest of the machine.

The BIOS, however, takes care of only one part of the equation. Windows 98 does a good job of detecting non–Plug and Play hardware, even when it gets mixed with Plug and Play–compatible hardware. All the configuration information for the hardware that Windows 98 supports is stored on the hard disk. If you look in the \WINDOWS\INF directory, you'll see some of these files. (They all have an .INF extension.) Besides storing the required configuration information on disk, Windows 98 gives older hardware first choice of ports and interrupts. This enables older hardware to work most of the time.

Problems start to arise when the system doesn't or can't recognize one or more components in your system. The problem is so bad on some systems that I've heard people refer to the new Windows 98 hardware-detection scheme as "Plug and Pray." The unrecognized hardware usually refuses to work properly, if at all. The second this happens, Windows 98 has the unfortunate tendency to either go to pieces or ignore the problem. Unrecognized hardware falls into two categories: The first is difficult-to-recognize hardware, which emulates something else so well that the computer has a hard time discerning exactly what it is. The second category is older hardware that lacks Windows 98–specific drivers.

So, now that you have some idea of what the problem is, let's take a quick look at ways you can fix it. This list isn't exhaustive, but it'll help you with the majority of the problems you're likely to run into.

- Avoid interrupt and port address conflicts whenever possible. This is probably the number one reason Windows 98 fails to recognize the board. If two devices use the same address, there's no way that Windows 98 can test for the presence of the second board.

- Whenever possible, plug your older boards into the slots next to the power supply. The BIOS checks the slots in order during POST. Placing these older boards first—followed by the Plug and Play boards—ensures that the BIOS will see the older ones first.

- Try different board configurations to see whether Windows 98 recognizes one of them. In some situations, the INF files used by Windows 98 to check for the older boards contain only the default board settings. A good rule of thumb is to try the best setting first, then the default setting if that doesn't work.

- Check the INF files to see whether they contain all the settings for your boards. There's an INF directory directly below the main Windows 98 directory. It contains ASCII text files used by Windows 98 to search for these older boards. Modifying these files is a tricky proposition, but it could help Windows 98 find the peripherals on your machine.

Looking Ahead: If you didn't find a technique here that helped you, take a look at the end of this book. Chapter 26 takes a detailed look at hardware troubleshooting techniques—especially tough-to-install hardware. In some cases, you might find that Windows 98 even provides protected-mode drivers you can use with old hardware.

Installation with Real-Mode Drivers Intact

If the quick help in the preceding section didn't help much, you can always try some backdoor techniques that I've discovered. Some devices—especially those that rely on software configuration instead of jumpers—don't provide enough information for autodetection until you turn them on. Normally, this means that the user has to install any required real-mode drivers in CONFIG.SYS. These drivers perform the setups required to make the device visible to Windows 98. In most cases, the following procedure helps Windows 98 "discover" these hidden boards.

1. After you install these drivers, reboot the machine. When Windows 98 starts, use the Start | Settings | Control Panel command to open the Control Panel.

2. Double-click the Add New Hardware icon. You should see the Add New Hardware Wizard.

3. Click the Next button. You'll see a dialog saying that Windows is going to check for any Plug and Play hardware on your machine. Don't worry if the screen blanks during this process—Windows has to check for display adapters too, which is the reason for the screen.

4. Wait until Windows completes the detection process. You should see the dialog box shown in Figure 6.3. In most cases you won't see your hardware listed in this dialog box if it's not Plug and Play–compatible. (If it does show up, all you need to do is highlight it, click Next, and follow the instructions.)

Figure 6.3.
Using automatic hardware detection reduces the amount of work for the user.

5. Click No (to indicate that the hardware didn't appear on the list), and then click Next. The detection dialog shown in Figure 6.4 performs a check of your hardware using the INF files that I talked about previously. It takes a lot longer to check your hardware this way, but the check is a lot more thorough and your chances of finding what you need is greater.

Figure 6.4.
The non–Plug and Play detection might take longer, but it's more thorough.

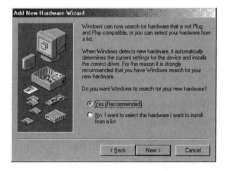

6. Select Yes and then click Next. Click Next again to start the detection process. Windows displays a progress bar showing the detection progress. After the detection process is completed, Windows tells you whether it detected any new hardware.

> **Note:** The hardware-detection phase can take a while—especially on older machines. The one constant I noticed is that when disk activity stops for more than five minutes, however, it's a safe bet the machine is frozen. As long as you hear disk activity during this phase, you can assume hardware detection is still taking place. (The hardware detection indicator doesn't move at a steady pace; it appears to take more time as it nears the end.)

7. Click the Details button to see if the hardware you were looking for actually got detected. Figure 6.5 shows a typical display.

Figure 6.5.
If the detection process was successful, you'll see the hardware you want to install after clicking the Details button.

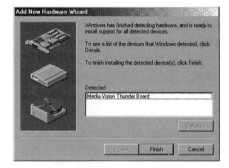

8. Click the Finish button to complete the installation process. Windows 98 might ask you to supply some setting information if this is a non–Plug and Play device. In most cases, it provides default settings that match your current real-mode setup. Windows 98 copies all the required drivers to disk. It also displays some messages about the new hardware it found and perhaps a "driver database building" message. In some cases, Windows 98 asks you to reboot when you complete this step. Even if it doesn't ask you to reboot, you must do so to make this procedure work properly. The real-mode drivers you installed to aid in detection will destabilize the system if you leave them in place.

9. Be sure to remove the real-mode drivers from CONFIG.SYS before you shut down and reboot the machine. If Windows 98 didn't detect the new hardware, remove the real-mode drivers from CONFIG.SYS, shut down and reboot the system, then perform the manual installation procedure in the next section.

Manual Installation

It always seems to come down to the same old procedure. You finally get everything working using the automated procedures—except that old CD-ROM drive or an especially difficult sound card. There are a few situations in which you'll have to help Windows 98 install an older device in your machine. Usually, something else you installed—probably a Plug and Play device—is using a resource the older device needs. The following example shows how to install a CD-ROM drive; the same principles apply to any manual installation. However, let me warn you ahead of time that simply installing the device might not make it work. You might have to perform some troubleshooting to get this older device to work (see Chapter 26). At the very least, you'll have to shuffle some IRQ and address settings around.

1. Use the Start | Settings | Control Panel command to open the Control Panel. Double-click the Add New Hardware icon. You should see the Add New Hardware Wizard.

2. Click Next. You'll see a dialog saying that Windows is going to check for any Plug and Play hardware on your machine. Don't worry if the screen blanks during this process—Windows also checks for display adapters (the reason for the blank screen).

3. Wait until Windows completes the detection process. You should see the dialog box in Figure 6.3.

4. Click No (to indicate that the hardware didn't appear on the list), and then click Next. The detection dialog shown in Figure 6.4 performs a check of your hardware using the INF files that I talked about previously. At this point, I'm assuming that you tried the automatic installation procedure in the previous section and it didn't work.

5. Click the No radio button and then click Next. Highlight the CD-ROM Controllers entry of the Hardware Types: field and then click the Next button. You should see the dialog box shown in Figure 6.6. The manufacturers and models lists in this dialog box allow you to scroll with ease through the list of devices supported by Windows 98. If the device installed on the current machine doesn't appear in the list, the dialog box also affords the opportunity to use a third-party disk. This dialog box appears every time you select a device from the previous dialog box. The manufacturer list changes to match the selected device type.

Figure 6.6.
Use the lists in this dialog box to scroll through devices supported by Windows 98.

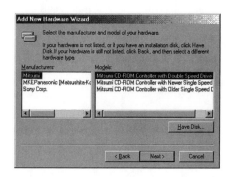

6. Normally, you would select the device connected to your machine. In this case, however, select Sony Corp. in the Manufacturers: field, leave the default device highlighted, and click the Next button. You'll see a dialog describing the process for installing your new hardware.

7. Click the Details button. Windows 98 displays a dialog box containing the interrupt and address settings for this particular device, as shown in Figure 6.7. Windows 98 selects a device setting based on all available information; it selects the best setting that won't interfere with other devices in the system (if possible).

Figure 6.7.
Windows 98 always tells the user what interrupts and addresses are used for the devices it installs.

Tip: A special "Unknown hardware" device type enables you to view all devices supported by Windows 98 on one screen. This comes in handy for two purposes. First, Microsoft doesn't always place devices in the category where you expect them to be. Searching through this list provides one final check if you don't find a device where you expect to see it. Second, you can use this list when researching a new product. It allows you to choose a device that Windows 98 will definitely support. I'm not saying other products are incompatible—just that these products received a little more attention than some of the others you might find.

8. Clicking the Next button again installs the device drivers required for this device. Normally, you would take this action. Windows 98 might prompt you for a disk if the driver didn't appear on the hard drive and the appropriate disk didn't appear in the CD-ROM drive. It would display a dialog box showing the progress of the file copy process. However, because you don't want to install this particular device, click the Cancel button. Windows 98 exits the Hardware Installation Wizard without installing the new device.

Adding Your Own Devices

Now that you have Windows 98 installed, let's take some of the magic out of the new Windows 98 detection capability. If you look in your \WINDOWS\INF directory, you'll see a new type of file there.

The INF file is part of the database of information that Windows 98 uses to recognize hardware that isn't Plug and Play–compatible. These files contain a description of the hardware—the same type of information the Plug and Play BIOS would normally provide when Windows 98 scans it.

As good as these INF files are, there might be times when you want to modify them. For example, what if you have a piece of hardware that provides interrupt and port address settings in addition to those found in the INF file? Modifying the INF file to reflect these additional capabilities could help you install a piece of hardware in some cases.

Let's look at some of the general characteristics shared by INF files. You might find all or only some of these sections in a given file; it depends on what kind of hardware the INF file is trying to define. An INF file only needs to contain the information required to fully define the characteristics of the hardware. A display adapter, for example, needs to define the resolutions it supports. A multiscanning monitor, such as the NEC MultiSync series, needs to define the precise frequency ranges it supports. This includes the refresh rate, an important specification for the new ergonomic display adapters. Table 6.1 lists these generic sections and tells you what they mean. You might even want to open an INF file to see whether you can identify each section. (Just make sure that you don't save the file or change its contents in any way.)

Table 6.1. INF file generic sections.

Heading	Description
Version	This section provides version-specific information such as the operating system, the vendor name, and the device class supported by the INF file. It also provides the name of the general setup file. The general setup file contains the definitions common to all devices of that type. You might see some additional entries in this section. One special entry enables the vendor to link a new INF file into the list of files for a specific device type. Never change the contents of this section.
Manufacturer	The Manufacturer section contains a list of all the manufacturers for devices of this class. Not every INF file contains this section. This section appears in the MONITOR.INF file, for example, but not the MSPORTS.INF file. The only time you need to change this section is when you want to add a new vendor. The list might seem incomplete if more than one INF file is required to describe a specific class of device. There are four monitor files; each one contains only the vendors that appear in that particular file. You need to check all the INF files for a particular device class before you resort to adding a new vendor.

continues

Table 6.1. continued

Heading	Description
	Make sure you add the new vendor in alphabetical order, in the correct INF file. (You'll see an example later in this chapter.) A subsection after this one provides specifics about each device supported by that vendor. If the vendor already appears in the manufacturer list, adding a new device consists of adding an entry here, in the Install section, and in the Strings section.
Install	This is the most important section of the file. It describes all the characteristics of the hardware and the device drivers necessary to activate it. It also contains macro commands that install support in the Registry. Follow the example of other entries in this section when adding a new device. When modifying an existing entry, change only physical characteristics such as the port address and interrupt.
Miscellaneous Control	A vendor can use this section to describe how a device works with the Windows 98 interface. If you see this section, you need to use other entries as an example for creating your own entries. Most INF files don't contain this section.
Strings	Later in this chapter, you learn how to add a new device to Windows 98 using the Add New Hardware dialog box. When you use this dialog box, some descriptive strings tell you about the hardware. This is the section that contains those user-friendly strings. It identifies the device in human-readable form.

We won't go through the actual process of modifying an INF file here because it's unlikely that you'll ever need to do it. However, there are a few things you should do before you modify one.

Warning: Always modify the original copy of an INF file after making a backup. Place the copy in a backup directory, using a different extension from the original file. Your modified version of the original file must appear in the INF directory for Windows 98 to recognize it. Keeping a copy of the original version in a temporary directory enables you to restore the file later.

- Always print a copy of the original INF file. You then can scan through the listing quickly as you make a new entry. Some entries depend on the contents of other entries in the file. A mistyped or misinterpreted entry makes the INF file useless.

- Use the other entries in the file as a guideline for new entries. Windows 98 performs a strict interpretation of the contents of the INF file. Adding "enhancements" to what seems like an inadequate entry might make the INF file unusable. Remember, some INF file entries appear in one or more generic files in the Version section of the file.

- Follow punctuation marks, spelling, and capitalization carefully when making a new entry. Windows 98 is extremely sensitive when it comes to how you format entries in an INF file.

- Never change the Version section of the file. It's very tempting to fiddle with what appears to be an interesting file section, but don't do it.

- Make your entries to an existing file. You might be tempted to create your own unique INF file, but don't do it. Always add new devices to existing files. This way, you can be absolutely sure your entries look like the other entries in the file.

Installing Windows 98 over an Existing Windows Installation

For the most part, installing Windows 98 over an existing Windows installation is the same as installing it on a new machine. This type of installation differs in two ways. First, the installation program displays a dialog box that enables you to back up your current installation before proceeding with the new installation. Make sure you exercise this option. It takes quite a bit of hard drive space to do so, but you'll have an opportunity to uninstall the operating system later should you need to do so.

The second way it differs is you'll see fewer configuration screens. The software is installed in the same order, but some screens mentioned in the installation section of this chapter won't appear. This is because Windows 98 automatically detects which options you have installed for the previous version of Windows. It assumes you want to install the same options in this version as well.

Tip: Some people have complained that the latest Windows installation program might actually be a little too automatic. You can always use the Add/Remove Programs applet in the Control Panel to customize your setup after installation. For the most part the automation that Windows 98 provides is a welcome change from what we got in the past.

Uninstalling Windows 98

Unlike Windows 95, there is a way to get Windows 98 back off your machine once you install it. However, there are a few caveats you need to know about. First, you need to take advantage of the operating system file backup option that the installation program will offer when you first start the installation process. Here is the trade-off. You lose about 40MB of hard drive space for the backup directory. Second, uninstall works better in Windows 95 than any other version of Windows. In other words, I wouldn't plan on getting my Windows 3.x installation back. You can try it, but I didn't have much success getting it to work. If you're installing Windows 98 from the DOS prompt, there won't be an uninstall option. You have to install DOS from scratch.

So, you've decided to get Windows 98 off your machine. All you need to do to uninstall Windows 98 and restore your previous operating system is to go to the uninstall directory and run the uninstall program. (You should also be able to find an uninstall option on the Install/Uninstall page of the Add/Remove Programs Properties dialog which you can open by double clicking the applet of the same name in the Control Panel.)

What happens if you run the uninstall program and you still don't have your old operating system back? The following procedure assumes three things. First, it assumes you made a boot disk like the one mentioned at the beginning of this chapter. Second, it assumes you made a copy of your DOS directory. Finally, it assumes you installed Windows 98 into a clean directory. If you didn't follow one of these three steps, you won't have the resources to put your system back together.

1. The first step is to get DOS to boot again. Use your boot disk to reboot your machine from the floppy. (First shut down Windows 98 properly.)

2. Use the SYS command to restore the system files. Then copy COMMAND.COM and an original copy of both AUTOEXEC.BAT and CONFIG.SYS from your floppy to the hard drive.

3. Copy the contents of your DOS directory backup to the DOS directory.

4. Take the floppy out of the drive and reboot your system. You should now get a DOS prompt.

5. Carefully erase all the Windows 98–specific files. Make absolutely certain that you look for all the hidden files that Microsoft thoughtfully stored in your root directory. You can find them by using the DIR /AH /S command. The /AH switch displays every file with a hidden attribute. The /S command tells DIR to look in any subdirectories as well as the root directory. Don't erase any DOS-specific files like IO.SYS and MSDOS.SYS. The date stamp on the file should give you a clue about which files belong to DOS and which ones belong to Windows 98. If in doubt, leave the file in place rather than remove it and make your system non-operational. It's going to take a little effort to find all the entries. In fact, this is where a good disk editor will come into play.

6. Reboot your machine one more time to make sure everything works correctly.

This isn't the fanciest uninstall method, but it works. You'll probably find bits and pieces of Windows 98 lying around your system for a few weeks. If you were careful when you installed it, the pieces should appear in the root directory of all your drives. The first directory you'll erase is the `\WINDOWS` directory. Be sure to get all the Recycle Bin directories (one on each drive) and the program directory that contained Microsoft Network and other accessory applications.

On Your Own

Create your own boot disk that contains the items mentioned earlier in this chapter. Be sure to test it before you install Windows 98. You also should create a Windows 98–specific startup disk during installation. Label both disks and keep them until you're certain your Windows 98 installation is stable. When it's stable, create a new startup disk using the Startup Disk page of the Add/Remove Programs Properties dialog box.

Make a list of all the equipment you think you might have problems with. Include all the items for which Windows 98 doesn't provide entries in the existing INF files. Do you see any entries you can fix using the procedures provided in this chapter? Are there ways to eliminate the real-mode drivers you might need to keep older equipment running? Develop a comprehensive strategy for handling problem areas before you begin the installation process.

7

Startup
Shortcuts

Peter Norton®

An efficient machine is only as fast as the operator using it. If you can't use all the speed your machine provides, part of that speed is lost and you might as well not look for anything faster. I've found that Windows 3.x users—myself included—have developed some terrible habits because of that operating system's inefficiencies. For example, do you automatically assume that the machine's going to be tied up every time you use the modem? I know that's what I thought when I started using Windows 98.

As an experiment, a while back I tried performing a background download with one additional task running—my word processor. The download completed in the background at 33.6Kbps without a single missed character while I worked in the foreground. The next day I decided to add another task. This time I compiled a program in one background session, downloaded a few files in another and typed away in a third. I was ecstatic, to say the least. Everything went perfectly. So I tried a third task, but Windows 98 just wasn't up to it. Everything bombed.

So, what's the moral of this story? I don't think any operating system will ever be able to perform every task there is to perform and simultaneously communicate in the background. You need to have the required resources if you want to get the job done. In my case, two active tasks in addition to the background download are about all my machine can handle. (You could very likely open several applications and allow them to sit in the background while you do something in the foreground. Even though the inactive background tasks would consume memory, they wouldn't consume much in the way of processor time.)

I did learn something important, though. Using Windows 98 allowed me to get three times the amount of work done that I would have under Windows 3.x, in this particular instance. I want to emphasize that point because the new and exciting methods Windows 98 introduces can become very inefficient, too.

Peter's Principle: Discovering Your Maximum Load—Without the
Pain of Failure

Windows 3.x provided so many visual cues I almost always knew when it was time to stop adding tasks by the way it acted. That "old shoe" feel doesn't come with Windows 98, because you really haven't had a chance to break it in yet. Until you start learning the little quirks that tell you when it's time to stop adding new tasks, you can do a few things to keep your system from crashing.

Unlike Windows 3.x, Windows 98 actually comes with some easy-to-use tools that keep track of your system resources. For example, I keep a copy of Resource Meter loaded all the time. (This isn't the Resource Monitor application that I describe elsewhere; Resource Meter is a small utility designed to track system resources.) A quick check of the Taskbar tells me just how low I'm getting on system resources. (For more information about this utility, see the "Accessories" section of Chapter 2, "Introducing Windows 98.") I also run

Resource Monitor as needed to keep track of how certain tasks load the processor and disk subsystems. As a result, I'm learning to use Windows 98's capabilities more efficiently.

Now that we have a user-friendly operating system that can actually run more than a couple of tasks at a time without dying, we need to learn how to use it efficiently. Task loading is a new technique that all of us old hands will have to learn.

This chapter looks at some of the ways you can make yourself a little more efficient so that you can get the full benefits of using Windows 98 as an operating system. This means everything from the way you start your applications to the way you arrange your desktop. Windows 98 provides many new tools that you can use to make each step a little faster.

Windows 98 Shortcuts and OLE

Let's take some time to look at a unique way that Windows 98 uses OLE. Every shortcut you create is a form of OLE. It's an actual link to another object on your machine. Windows 98 provides some special handling for these objects. (Chapter 11, "DDE, OLE, DCOM, and ActiveX," spends a lot of time discussing OLE from a user perspective.)

Unlike an application that can create compound documents to hold all the linking information, Windows 98 has to store that information someplace on the drive. After all, the drive is the container that Windows 98 uses to store information. The LNK file is the Windows 98 answer to this problem. It contains all the linking information needed to keep the shortcuts on your desktop current with the real object.

You can easily test this by creating a shortcut of a folder on your desktop. Every change you make to the real folder will appear in the linked copy. Likewise, every change you make in the linked copy will appear in the real thing. OLE and the desktop are a part of Windows 98.

Faster Startups

Starting an application might not seem like a big deal. It wasn't a big deal under Windows 3.x. After all, how many ways can you double-click an application icon sitting in a folder in Program Manager? Windows 98 provides more than just one or two ways to start your applications. In fact, here's a whole list of ways:

- Right-click the application's icon while in Explorer, and then click Open in the context menu.
- Double-click the application's icon while in Explorer or File Manager.

- Double-click a data file associated with the application while in Explorer. (This requires that you create a file association or that the application create it for you. To change file associations, open Windows Explorer, choose View | Folder Options, click the File Types tab, and click the Edit button to define which application should open which type of file types.)

- Choose Start | Run and then type the application's path and filename. Click OK to start the application.

- Choose Start | Run and then drag-and-drop the application's icon into the Run dialog box. Click OK to start the application.

- Select the application's entry from the Start menu.

- Create a shortcut icon on the desktop. You can start the application by right-clicking or double-clicking the icon.

- Set your Desktop up to use the new Windows 98 single click interface, which will allow you to start applications or select files more quickly.

- Assign a shortcut key to the application, and then start it by using the keyboard shortcut. (You must create a LNK file to do this. We look at the process for doing this later.)

- Use the Windows 3.x Program Manager (provided in the \WINDOWS directory) to run the application.

- Place the application's icon or associated data file in the Startup folder in the Start menu to run it automatically the next time you start Windows. Placing a data file in the Startup folder automatically opens it for you.

- Use the Find dialog to find your application, and then right-click or double-click it.

- Embed or link the application's data in an OLE compound document. The user can start the application by double-clicking the object embedded in the document. (The application must support OLE for this to work.)

Because I grew up using DOS, I really hated having to use the mouse just to start an application, so I didn't. Few users really understand this, but you can make Windows 98 somewhat keyboard-friendly by installing shortcut keys. Of course, if all Windows 98 provided were this particular shortcut, I could stop right here and let you read some text on Windows 3.x. Even though Windows 98 uses the same type of shortcut method, the implementation is a lot better. We'll also look at some "undocumented" ways of using the keyboard.

There are times where you really do need to use the mouse—if for no other reason than the fact that your hand is resting on it at that particular moment. Like many people, I spend my share of time mousing around. CorelDRAW! and other drawing programs come in handy for some of the work I do. Using the mouse is nothing new for most people.

Windows 98 provides a lot of neat ways to use the mouse with your applications. You'll find that you can do a lot of things you couldn't do before with a simple mouse click. We look at some of these mouse techniques in this section.

Startups from the Keyboard

Nothing beat the keyboard if DOS was your home before you moved to Windows 98. But a quick look at the Windows 98 GUI tells you that most of your keyboard techniques won't work here. Some people figure that there's no way to use any of the old techniques. But nothing could be further from the truth.

Some shortcut keys come installed with Windows 98. I find that many of them are attached to the Accessibility options, but you can change all that with just a little effort (we look at this later in this section). Table 7.1 provides a list of keystrokes and the actions they perform. You're probably familiar with most of them, but others are new to Windows 98.

Table 7.1. Windows 98 Shortcut Keys.

Key or Key Combination	Purpose
Alt+F4	Ends the current application. You can also use this key combination to end Windows if you're at the desktop.
Alt+Shift+Tab	Switches to the previous window.
Alt+Spacebar	Displays the Control menu of the currently active window.
Alt+Tab	Switches to the next window.
Ctrl+Esc	Opens the Start menu on the Taskbar. You can then use the arrow keys to select an application. Pressing Enter starts the application you selected.
Esc	Cancels the last action in most cases. However, you can't back out of some actions.
F1	Displays online help. In most cases, this help is general in nature but is application specific.
F2	Pressing this while an icon is highlighted allows you to change the object name.
F3	Unless your application uses this key for something else, you can press it to access the Find dialog. In most cases, you'll get better results if you press F3 while at the desktop. You can also use this key at the Taskbar and the Start menu.
Left Alt+Left Shift+ NumLock	Holding these three keys down turns on the MouseKeys feature of the Accessibility options.
Left Alt+Left Shift+ Print Screen	Holding these three keys down turns on the High Contrast feature of the Accessibility options.

continues

Table 7.1. continued

Key or Key Combination	Purpose
Num Lock	Holding the Num Lock key down for five seconds turns on the ToggleKeys feature of the Accessibility options.
Right Shift	Holding the right Shift key down for eight seconds turns on the FilterKeys feature of the Accessibility options.
Shift five times	Pressing the Shift key five times turns on the StickyKeys feature of the Accessibility options.
Shift+F1	Displays context-sensitive help when the application supports it. The Windows 98 desktop doesn't appear to support this option.
Shift+F10	You must select an object before you use this key combination. It displays the context menu. Considering the number of options on the context menu, this key combination allows you to do almost anything with the object.
Tab	Use this key while at the desktop to switch between the desktop, Taskbar, and Start menu. You also can use Ctrl+Esc to bring up the Start menu and then press Tab to switch between applications.

Tip: Combining the various keystrokes makes them much more powerful. For example, what if you have a lot of applications open and need to get to the desktop quickly? Use Ctrl+Esc to display the Start menu, Esc to close the menu itself, Tab to get to the Taskbar and Shift+F10 to display the context menu. All you need to do now is select Minimize All Windows and press Enter. Pressing Tab one more time takes you to the desktop.

Windows 98 provides two additional methods of using the keyboard to start applications. You can use the Windows 3.x method of assigning a shortcut key to the application. There are also automated methods of starting some applications.

Tip: Some keyboards, like the Microsoft Natural Keyboard, come with a Windows key. Pressing this key will open the Start menu when using Windows 98. In addition to the Windows key, a few keyboards also come equipped with a Menu key (it actually has what appears to be a menu printed right on the key). You can use this key to open a context menu, just as if you clicked the right mouse key.

Undocumented Parameters

The first program you need to learn about in order to use this section of the book is START. It's a program that you'll find in your \WINDOWS\COMMAND directory. I started playing with it and figured out a few ways you could use this program if you learned about the undocumented parameters that most Windows applications provide. First, though, let's look at some documented parameters that START provides:

- **/MAX.** Use this to run a maximized application in the background.

- **/M.** This switch enables you to run the application minimized in the background.

- **/R.** The default setting for START is to run the program in the foreground. You can still switch back to the DOS prompt, but you'll take a quick trip to Windows first.

- **/W.** Use this switch if you want to start a Windows application, work with it for a while, and return to the DOS prompt when you're done.

- **<program name>.** This is the name of the program you want to run and any parameters it needs in order to execute.

All this is fine if you want to run a Windows application from DOS. However, this information doesn't really become useful until you can get some work done in Windows without leaving the DOS prompt. What would happen if you wanted to gain the advantage of Windows background printing while performing other work at the DOS prompt? You could switch back to Windows, start Notepad or some other appropriate application, load your file and print, but that would disrupt what you were doing. The following line shows an easier, faster, and much better method.

```
START /M NOTEPAD /P SOMEFILE.TXT
```

There are a few things here you really need to take a look at. The first is the /P parameter right after NOTEPAD. Where did I get it? It isn't documented anywhere. All you have to do is look in Explorer.

Let's take a look at this now. Open Explorer. It doesn't matter what directory you're looking at or how it's configured. Use the View | Folder Options command to display the Options dialog box. Click the File Types tab. Scroll through the file types until you come across an entry for Text Document. Highlight it and click Edit. Click Print and then Edit. You should see a display similar to the one in Figure 7.1.

Now you can see where I came up with the /P parameter. Press Cancel three times to get back to the main Explorer display. Every other registered application will provide the same types of information. Some of them will be a little too complex to use from the DOS prompt, but you could use them if you wanted to do so. The whole idea of this shortcut is that you get to stay at the DOS prompt and still use the new features that Windows provides.

Figure 7.1.
Windows 98 hides a wealth of information; Explorer is just one of the gold mines. It's a treasure hunt; make sure you spend enough time digging.

> **Tip:** Just about every Windows application provides undocumented command-line switches. Even though you can only guess at what those switches are in most cases, you can usually count on them supporting one or two switches. The /P parameter almost always allows you to print by using that application. Some applications also provide a /W parameter that suppresses the display of any opening screens. Looking through the Explorer file listings will provide you with additional ideas.

There are a few other caveats you need to consider. Notice how I formatted my command line. You have to place the START program command-line switches first and then the application name, the application switches and any filenames. If you change this order, the application usually will start, but will report some type of error in opening your file. I've even had some applications insist that the file isn't present on my drive.

Shortcut Keys

Windows 98 is a lot user friendlier than its predecessors are. I find that I spend a lot less time at the DOS prompt now because I can get everything accomplished without it. However, that still doesn't make me happy about moving my hand from the keyboard to the mouse to start a new application.

Remember in the first section of this chapter, where I talked about the desktop and OLE? This is one of those times when that fact comes into play. To really make use of the shortcuts Windows 98 provides, you have to create a shortcut. It doesn't matter where the shortcut is, but it does matter that it's a shortcut.

> **Tip:** Every entry on the Start menu is a shortcut. If your application appears on the Start menu, you already have a shortcut to use. If it doesn't appear on the Start menu, you'll want to add it there or on the desktop.

To get the ball rolling, let's look at the Notepad shortcut on the Start menu. All you need to do is open the Start menu (press Ctrl+Esc, then Esc), open the context menu (Shift+F10), and select Explore. Use a combination of the arrow keys and Enter to get to the Notepad shortcut. Press Shift+F10 to display Notepad's context menu. Select Properties and press Enter. You'll need to select the Shortcut tab. You should see a display similar to the one shown in Figure 7.2.

Figure 7.2.
The Shortcut tab in the Notepad Properties dialog box enables you to add a shortcut key to an application or to another shortcut.

The Shortcut key: field of this dialog box is where you enter the shortcut key combination you want to use. To save the setting, just close the dialog box as normal. The next time you press that key combination, Windows 98 will open the application for you.

Startups from the Desktop

Windows 98 comes installed with several applications already on the desktop. If you decide to install Outlook Express, you'll find it there. The Microsoft Network icon is also connected to an application. Just like the Start menu, none of these icons represents the actual application. You create a shortcut to the application, just like you would for the Start menu.

Of course, the big question is why you would even consider adding an application shortcut to the desktop. The big reason is convenience: It's faster to grab an application on the desktop than to burrow through several layers of menu to find it. Of course, your desktop has only so much space, so placing all your applications here would lead to a cluttered environment very quickly. In addition, remember from Chapter 5, "Performance Primer," that each icon uses memory, so you need to consider whether the efficiency you'll gain is worth the memory you'll use by adding an icon.

However, placing on the desktop the one or two applications that you use regularly could mean an increase in efficiency. Just think how nice it would be if your word processor and communications program were just a double-click away. You could open them as needed and close them immediately after you finished using them. This would mean that the applications you used most would still be handy, but they'd be out of the way and wouldn't use up precious memory.

Tip: Keyboard users will probably get the same response time by using shortcut keys instead of placing their applications on the desktop. Not only will this give you a neater-looking desktop, but it'll reduce the number of redundant links your computer has to maintain.

Placing a shortcut to your application on the desktop can provide an increase in efficiency, but double-clicking isn't the only way to open an application. The next few sections describe other ways you can access your applications faster by placing shortcuts to them on the desktop. The later section "The Data-Oriented Approach to Applications" also looks at something new for Windows 98. You really owe it to yourself to get out of the application-centric mode and take the new data-centric approach.

Click Starts

Right-clicking displays a context menu for Windows 98 objects. Previous chapters took a quick look at the context menu. However, it's such an important concept that I felt we needed to take a special look at right-clicking for applications. To start an application this way, all you need to do is select the Open option from the context menu. This has the same effect as double-clicking, but it might be more convenient if you have slower fingers. Some people really do have a hard time getting the double-click to work. This new method of starting an application has the advantage of requiring only a single click.

Tip: Try setting your Desktop up to use single clicks instead of double clicks if you have trouble double-clicking fast enough to start applications or open files. All you need to do to enable single-clicking is use the View | Folder Options command in Windows Explorer to display the Folder Options dialog box. Choose the Web style setting, and then click OK to make the change complete. You can also enable single-clicking using the Custom setting.

I was kind of curious about the Quick View option on the context menu. If you select it for an executable object like Notepad.EXE, you'll see a dialog box similar to the one in Figure 7.3. The majority of the information here is stuff that only a programmer could love. At first glance, you do see some useful information, such as the name of the program and the version of Windows that it expects to find on your machine. You might even be able to use some of the information here to determine the amount of memory that your application needs to run.

Figure 7.3.
The Quick View option for executable files provides some interesting information you can use to learn more about how the application works.

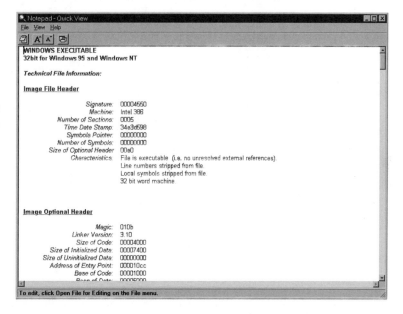

In reality, this isn't the information you want to see, because you can determine most of it by using other methods. However, this view provides some special information that makes it easier for you to figure out which files to remove the next time you need to get rid of an old application. If you scroll down a bit, you'll notice a heading that says Imported-Name Table (Link-Time Imports).

Note: Unfortunately, there are a number of ways to defeat the Quick View utility, and programmers use them all. The most common method is to mangle the names of the files used by the program in such a way that you can't read them but Windows can. The safest method for ensuring that you can remove a program you no longer need is to get those that are specially designed for Windows 95 or 98 and that include the requisite uninstall capabilities. That way, you can simply remove the program by using the Add/Remove Programs applet in the Control Panel. The "Removing an Application" section of Chapter 12, "Exploiting Your Software: DOS, 16-Bit, and 32-Bit Applications," covers standard program-removal procedure.

Look at the list of files underneath this heading. All are somewhere on your drive—usually in the application folder or the \WINDOWS\SYSTEM folder. Unlike Windows 3.1—which took some major tinkering to discover the files needed to run an application—Windows 98 makes this information easy to find.

Use this information when the time comes to remove an application from your system. This view will help you come up with a list of files you need to delete. Of course, you don't want to delete any files that another application needs. Prune this list carefully, so that it reflects only the files that are unique to a particular application. There's another problem with this list as well: It provides only one level of import file support. If one of the support files calls yet another group of files, you won't see that file here. Fortunately, you can also get to this view using other types of Windows executables. Be sure to look through the entire hierarchy before you consider your list of files complete.

This isn't the end of the story. There's another way to use this information to your advantage. Have you ever had an application that refused to start? It gave you some really cryptic message that looked like it was written in Klingon, and then killed itself and perhaps a few other applications. Once you got past this point, Windows displayed that really helpful message about not finding one of the components needed to run the application. The Quick View dialog box can help you get past this situation. Coming up with a list of DLLs and other support files needed by the application is the first step in getting it to run. Next, check the application and the \WINDOWS\SYSTEM directory. As soon as you find which one of the files is missing, replace it and, *voilà*, no more mystery message.

Auto Starts

Windows 98 provides a Startup folder to run specific applications every time you start your machine. All you need to do is add an application to the Startup folder to allow it to run automatically. I always start a copy of Explorer this way so that my machine is ready for use the instant Windows completes the boot process.

The Startup folder comes in handy for other tasks as well. I usually drag the data files I'm going to be working on for the next few days into my Startup folder. The reason is simple: Not only do I automatically start the application associated with that data file but I also automatically load the file itself. This makes morning startups extremely efficient. When I get back to Windows after starting it, my machine is completely set up for use. Every application I need is already loaded with the files I want to edit.

Peter's Principle: Becoming Too Efficient for Your Own Good

Have you ever seen the "ransom note" effect produced by someone who has just discovered the joy of using multiple fonts in a document? To that person, it looks like the most incredible document he has ever produced. The rest of us think the document is pretty incredible too but not for the same reason.

You can get into the same kind of habit with Windows 98 and its advanced features. Consider the Startup folder. It would be very easy for people to load every document they think they'll use for the entire week in there so that the documents would be ready when they booted the machine the next morning.

The best way to use this feature is to think about what you plan to do first thing the next morning or perhaps for the majority of the day. Don't open more than two or perhaps three documents unless they all use the same application. Someone who works on the same document, such as a writer, can really benefit from this feature. People who create presentations or work on other documents for long periods of time can also benefit. However, if you work a little bit on one document and then a little bit on another one, you might be better off starting the main application you use and letting it go at that.

So, how do you add entries to the Startup folder? Just as you would with any other folder. The following procedure shows you a quick way to do it, using some of the new features that Windows 98 provides.

1. Right-click the taskbar to display the context menu. Select Properties. Click the Start Menu Programs tab. You should see the Taskbar Properties dialog box shown in Figure 7.4.

Figure 7.4.
The Taskbar Properties dialog box enables you to add new programs to the Start menu, using a menu-driven interface.

2. Click the Add button to open the Create Shortcut dialog box shown in Figure 7.5.

Figure 7.5.
In the Create Shortcut dialog box, provide the name of the application or file you want to add to the Startup folder (or another folder).

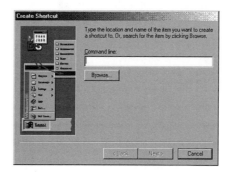

3. Click the Browse button to look for the file you want to add. Alternatively, you can type the full path and filename in the Command Line field of this dialog box. Click Next. You should see a Select Program Folder dialog box, which enables you to select the location of the shortcut in the Start menu. In this case, we'll select the Startup folder, but you could just as easily select something else. Notice that you can add a new folder as well. (Selecting a folder other than Startup means that the program will be available from the Start menu, but won't start automatically when you start Windows.)

4. Scroll through the list of folders and highlight the Startup folder. Click Next. You should see the Select a Title for the Program dialog box, as shown in Figure 7.6. This is the final dialog box of the process. It enables you to change the name of the shortcut.

Figure 7.6.
*You can name your
shortcut in the Select
a Title for the
Program dialog box.*

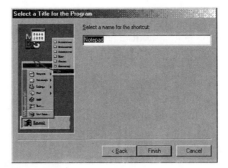

5. Type the name you want associated with this file. Using a name you can remember is the best idea. Changing the name here won't change the name of the file, only the shortcut—this is the entry as it will appear in the Startup folder.

6. Click Finish to complete the task, then click OK to close the Taskbar Properties dialog box.

After you complete this task, the application or data file you added to the Startup folder will load automatically each time you start Windows 98. Getting your system set up efficiently means that you can do a little extra reading or perform some other task while you wait for everything to load. Of course, adding a file to the load sequence won't make it load faster, but it'll give you a bigger block of time.

Controlled Starts

We won't spend a lot of time on this category of starting your application because you're already familiar with most of what you can do here. Everyone is familiar with double-clicking an application to start it. The fact that Windows 98 provides so many places to double-click doesn't change the mechanics one iota. It might be useful, though, to take a quick look at the number of ways you can double-click to start an application. The following list does just that:

- **Explorer.** You can double-click an application or its associated data files. This interface also supports DDE, something I had trouble with when using File Manager. Of course, Program Manager didn't support DDE at all.

- **Program Manager.** As in Explorer, you can double-click any application.

- **File Manager.** As in Explorer, you can double-click any application or its associated data file. However, the interface isn't quite as flexible as that provided by Explorer. You'll find that DDE is hard to implement.

- **Find.** The Find dialog box comes in very handy. You can look for a data file and then double-click it to bring up the application associated with it. I've also used this dialog box as a quick method of finding the program I need.

- **Desktop.** Any data file or application on the desktop follows the same rules as Explorer.

- **Network Neighborhood.** You can double-click any application or file on someone else's machine.

Well, that's the long and short of double-clicking. You can always use the old controlled start method we all know and love to start an application. I hope this section provided some food for thought on other—perhaps better—ways of using the Windows 98 interface.

The Data-Oriented Approach to Applications

Windows 98 shines when it comes to data. In fact, the whole interface is oriented toward data-centric access. The next few sections discuss some of the tools Windows 98 provides to make a data-oriented approach easier.

Using Explorer to Get the Job Done

We've taken a long, hard look at Explorer in several sections of this book already. However, we haven't really taken a good look at one important feature. No longer are you tied to one specific action when it comes to data on your machine. If you've looked at the various context menus presented in this and other sections, you've noticed that there's always more than one thing you can do to a particular file. What you might not have realized is that the actions you saw are all under your control. You don't have to do things the Windows 98 way; you can do them any way that feels comfortable and that enables you to get your work done faster.

Tip: The first time you double-click a file that lacks a file association, Windows 98 will ask which application you want to use to open it. You can choose an application that's already on the list or use the Browse feature to find a new one. Windows 98 defines only one action for this new association—open. Always take the time to modify that file association and add options for all the ways you plan to work with it. That way, the context menu associated with it will be completely set up the next time you right-click the file or any others like it.

Let's take a look at how you can add a new file extension and then define a set of actions associated with that file.

1. Open a copy of Explorer.

2. Use the View | Folder Options command to open the Folder Options dialog box. Click the File Types tab. You should see a dialog box similar to the one shown in Figure 7.7.

Figure 7.7.
The File Types tab of the Options dialog box enables you to add, remove, and modify file associations.

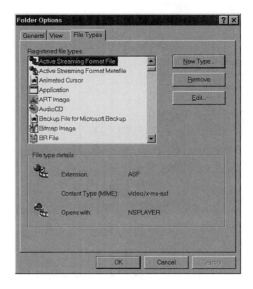

3. Click New Type to display the New Type dialog box.

4. Fill in the first two fields as shown in Figure 7.8. The first field describes what kind of file it is. This is the text you'll see in various list boxes. The second field contains the exact file extension. If this was an Internet file association, we would also provide a Multipurpose Internet Mail Extensions (MIME) content type. This entry would tell your Browser which application to call on when it ran into the associated file extension on the Internet. The last entry, Default Extension, allows you to assign an extension for Internet purposes. In some cases this might be different than the extension used on your machine. For example, in our case it would probably be ASC instead of ASCII.

Figure 7.8.
*The Add New File
Type dialog box
contains several fields
to describe a file's
association to an
application.*

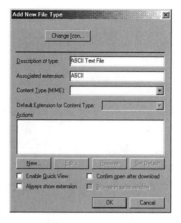

Tip: One problem you might run into is thinking about file extensions in the DOS/
Windows 3.x format. Remember that Windows 98 supports long filenames, including long
file extensions, as shown in Figure 7.8. You can define new file extensions that are more
than three characters long. Windows 98 even allows some alternative characters in this
format. For example, you could have a file extension of Word_Document if you wanted to.
One character you need to avoid is the period (for obvious reasons).

5. Now we need to define some actions for this association. Click the New button. Fill out
   the New Action dialog box as shown in Figure 7.9. (This is just one way to fill out this
   dialog box.) WordPad uses a command-line interface, so you just need to fill out the
   Application used to perform action section of the dialog box. Click OK.

Figure 7.9.
*This dialog box shows
one type of file
association entry. It
uses command-line
parameters.*

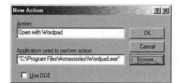

6. Create the same kind of entry for Notepad. Be sure to substitute NOTEPAD.EXE for the
   location and change the path as necessary. Also change the Action: field to read Open
   with Notepad.

7. Click the New button. Fill out the information as shown in Figure 7.10. This second type
   of association might look overly complicated, but it really isn't. It's the DDE format of a file
   association and an extremely powerful way to manage your data files. The DDE instructions form what equates to macros. They actually force the application to perform the same
   types of tasks that you would accomplish by using a menu or the product's built-in macro

capability. Chapter 11 discusses this topic at greater length. Right now, suffice it to say that if your application provides DDE support, you really owe it to yourself to use it.

Figure 7.10.
This dialog box shows the second type of association you can create. This DDE entry enables you to include macro-like instructions that control the way the application opens or works with the file.

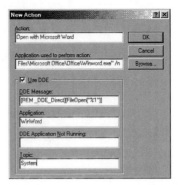

8. Click OK. After you finish this entry, you should see three entries in the Add New File Type dialog box. Notice the four check boxes near the bottom of the dialog box. Let's begin with the two check boxes on the left. Because this is an ASCII file, you probably would turn on the first check box, Enable Quick View. This enables you to use the Quick View utility provided with Windows 98. The second check box on the left enables you to display file extensions at all times. Normally you would leave this off to make it easier to rename files in Explorer without accidentally changing their extensions. The two check boxes on the right side of the dialog box are Internet specific. The first, Confirm Open After Download, tells Windows to display a dialog asking whether you want to open the file after you download it from the Internet. The second check box, Browse in Same Window, enables you to view the file without opening a new copy of the browser.

9. Highlight Open with Notepad and click Set Default. This sets the double-click action for the file type. You can right-click to display the full context menu and use a different application to open the file, but this is the default action. You also might want to change the icon. I used the Notepad icon, but you can use any icon provided by the applications in this group or within an icon file. Click Close to complete the process. Click Close to close the Options dialog box.

10. Create a new file with an `.ASCII` extension. I placed my copy on the desktop for sample purposes, but you can put your copy anywhere.

11. Right-click the file. You should see a list of opening options similar to the ones shown in Figure 7.11. Note that Open with Notepad is highlighted, indicating that this entry is the default setting.

Figure 7.11.
*The final result of the
new file association is
an extended context
menu that enables
any of three
applications to open
the file.*

You can do a few additional things to really extend this new file association. Chapter 8, "The Windows 98 Architecture," discusses the Registry and the file association entries. Because you just added a new text-file entry to the list of file associations, you can use the Registry to add a ShellX entry as well. That way, when you right-click the desktop or within Explorer, you'll see the new file extension as one of the file types you can create using the New option of the context menu. In most cases, there won't be a convenient method to add this support, but you should use it whenever possible.

This example also shows you something else. Productivity under Windows 98 depends as much on how you configure the desktop and file associations as anything else. Being able to use your machine's speed is what this data-centric approach to computing is all about.

Folders: A Real Organizational Tool

I really hate it when someone creates a new name for something I've been using for a long time. It's like throwing out a perfectly usable set of clothes because fashion has changed or giving someone a new title in order to be politically correct. That's how I used to feel about the use of the term *folder* under Windows 98. As far as I was concerned, it was a new name for directories.

Nothing could be further from the truth, however. Folders aren't directories. They might look similar and provide about the same functionality when viewed from a certain perspective, but folders really do provide some features that directories don't. I'm still not as happy as I could be about the name switch, but at least it makes sense.

So how do folders help you work efficiently? Figure 7.12 shows one way—folders support a context menu. Like most objects in Windows 98, you can open and explore them. This isn't really all that surprising by now. I *was* a little surprised, however, when I saw that you could copy and paste folders just like any other object. Putting a group of files in a folder enables you to move an entire project from place to place or make a copy of the data for someone else to use. It's actually faster to use folders than to type the required commands at the DOS prompt—something I thought I would never see.

Figure 7.12.
The Folder context menu tells it all when it comes to the intelligence that this new form of directory possesses.

The Sharing option of the context menu enables you to share the folder with other folks on the network. Chapter 23, "Networks," covers this feature in greater detail.

You'll find the Send to option very useful. This option enables you to place the folder somewhere else. Default locations include the floppy drives and your Briefcase. You even can send the folder to Microsoft Exchange. Imagine using email to send the folder to a partner or coworker who needs to see the information you've put together so far. Unlike past experiences in which I had to get all the files together and zip them up, this option is fairly convenient and really makes the workflow smoother.

I use the Create Shortcut option to create a link to the existing file. Then I move the shortcut to my desktop or another convenient location. Each shortcut uses 1KB of memory, a small price to pay for the convenience shortcuts provide.

Chapter 23 covers the Properties option in greater detail. For right now, suffice it to say that files and folders share many of the same characteristics. The Properties dialog box reflects this fact.

Desktop Tips and Techniques

I've gone to a totally data-centric approach on my desktop when it comes to projects. All I do is create a folder, give it a project name, and then gather shortcuts to everything I need for that project in that folder. It doesn't matter anymore where the data resides or what application I need to use to open the file. The only important element is that I have a data file that needs editing, so I open the project folder and double-click its icon.

This data-centric approach is important for managers. Think about the time you'll save by putting one folder together, and then mailing that folder to all the people who have to work on it. You control the location of the data and the type of access these people have to it. They need to know only that the data exists and that they access it as needed.

Of course, like everything else under Windows 98, all is not perfect with the total data-centric approach. Even Microsoft agrees with me on this issue. They placed your InBox, Recycle Bin, My Computer, and Network Neighborhood on the desktop for a reason. There are times when you need to open an application instead of a piece of data.

I keep my communications program handy on the desktop. I can't really access any of its data from outside the application. My database manager sits on the desktop too, but that's for a different reason. I use Access to design databases more often than I use it for data entry, so, for me, it's really more important to work with the application.

You'll probably run into situations in which the application is more important than the data. The bottom line is that you should try to work with the data first. If this proves to be an inconvenient solution, the data-centric approach probably isn't correct for that situation. The following is a list of some of the types of data I work with, using the project folder approach I just described. You'll probably have some of these applications, too.

- **Word processing.** Every word processor is designed to work primarily with data, so it makes a perfect candidate for the data-centric approach. Microsoft Word even appears on the New submenu of the context menu; this shows there isn't any problem with creating new files without entering the word processor first. There's one minor inconvenience: Word always creates a new document using the Normal template. This means that if I use the context menu to create a new file, I'll probably have to change the template after I open the file. It's a minor flaw, but an irritating one all the same.

- **Spreadsheets.** I very seldom open just one spreadsheet. If I open one at all, I'm in there for hours. Therefore, I stick all my major files into a folder and place it on my desktop. That way, I can at least open a data file that will stay open throughout most of the editing session. I usually end up opening the other files I need in the usual way—using File | Open.

- **Graphics.** I work with quite a few different types of graphics, each of which requires its own application. Keeping the graphic files in a folder and opening them that way makes perfect sense. In fact, it's actually one of the application types that really made me see the value of a data-centric approach. By the way, this is one place where you'll really want to enable the Quick View option, if you haven't done so already. Most graphics files are time-consuming to load. Having Quick View handy for the files that it supports can really save time.

On Your Own

Try adding a shortcut to the Startup folder on your desktop. Tonight, place in that folder any work that you'll need to do tomorrow. Watch what happens when you start your machine tomorrow morning. You should get a desktop that has all the work you need to do loaded automatically.

Start separating your work into projects, if possible. Place each project in a separate folder on the desktop. Use separate folders, if necessary, to make it easier to find a particular kind of data. For example, you might need to place your graphics files in one subfolder to keep them from crowding the text files.

Look through your drives for data files that Windows 98 can't associate with a particular application. In Explorer, add any new file extensions that you might need, using the procedure discussed earlier. Check out each new association as you add it. Does the new addition work as anticipated? Evaluate the results you get after a few weeks, to see whether you need to add more options to the data file's context menu.

III

Windows 98 Anatomy

8

The
Windows 98
Architecture

Peter Norton®

Windows 98 uses an architecture that borrows from Windows 95, Windows 3.x and MS-DOS. That's the bad news. The good news is that the problems that plagued users in the past are much less noticeable in Windows 98. The 16-bit interface of Windows 98 is augmented by new 32-bit underpinnings, providing decent performance and a moderate level of application protection as well. All these new features make Windows 98 better than previous versions of Windows, but it's still far from the perfect operating system if reliability is your main concern.

Windows NT is still the more stable operating system compared to Windows 98. Unfortunately, Windows NT isn't as compatible, especially with MS-DOS applications. The types of security required to make Windows NT stable also prevents it from running some types of ill-behaved applications. Windows 98 represents a halfway point—you get some added stability and a new 32-bit capability, and still keep the compatibility that most people need to make Windows really work on a workstation.

Windows 98 and Windows NT do share one thing in common (or will in the near future). Windows 98 uses a new device driver architecture called the Win32 Driver Model (WDM). We took a quick look at WDM in the Win32 Driver Model (WDM) section of Chapter 4, "The Updater's Guide to Windows 98.") In essence, this new device driver type allows Windows 98 and Windows NT to use the same drivers. Obviously, this makes maintaining the machines in your organization a lot easier. However, there's another benefit to you, as well—Windows 98 is becoming more reliable as time goes on. Sure, it won't kill every errant application the way Windows NT does, but it provides a more stable platform for running applications, which means they might not crash in the first place.

The following sections examine the details of all these architectural wonders. I'll show you the great and the not-so-great components that make Windows 98 better than Windows 3.x ever thought of being, but less than it could be. This chapter also provides a few additional glimpses of what Windows could become in the future. It's important to realize that, even with all its flaws, Windows 98 is a step in the right direction. It really does show how workstation operating systems will evolve in the future.

A Quick Look Inside

Learning about a new operating system usually includes knowing a bit about the components that comprise it. You don't start learning about DOS by knowing that there are two hidden files (MSDOS.SYS and IO.SYS) and one visible file (COMMAND.COM) that make up its core, but you do learn about them later. It doesn't take very long for most people to figure out some of the things that take place under DOS as well. An in-depth knowledge of interrupts and vector tables isn't required, but a basic knowledge of what takes place is needed. Just about every user spends some time learning about ancillary system files as well. Everyone knows about the DOS configuration files—AUTOEXEC.BAT and CONFIG.SYS—because you can't do much without them.

With this in mind, let's take a look at the Windows 98 architecture and some of the components that comprise it. We won't go into bits and bytes during this discussion. In fact, in this section, we barely scratch the surface of what Windows 98 contains. Still, you'll gain an appreciation of what goes on under the hood of this operating system. Having that knowledge can make it a lot easier to both configure and use Windows 98 effectively.

Architecture

Several elements make up the Windows 98 architecture, as shown in Figure 8.1. Each element takes care of one part of the Windows environment. For example, the Windows Application Programming Interface (API) layer enables applications to communicate with Windows internals such as the file management system. You couldn't write a Windows application without the API layer. I describe each of these main components in detail in the following sections.

The System Virtual Machine (VM) component of Windows 98 contains three main elements: 32-bit Windows applications, the shell, and 16-bit Windows applications. Essentially, the System VM component provides most of the Windows 98 user-specific functionality. Without it, you couldn't run any applications. Notice that I don't include DOS applications here; Windows uses an entirely different set of capabilities to run DOS applications. It even runs them in a different processor mode.

Two Windows APIs are included with Windows 98. The first API is similar to the one supplied with Windows 3.x. (There are differences, however, in the way low-level feature access to things like drivers get implemented). It provides all the 16-bit services that the old Windows had to provide for applications. An older 16-bit application will use this API when it runs. The other API is the Win32 API, which is similar to the one used by Windows NT. It provides a subset of the features that all 32-bit applications running under Windows NT can access. The 32-bit API provides about the same feature set as the 16-bit API, but it's more robust. The next section explores both of these APIs as part of the system file discussion.

The Base System component of Windows 98 contains all the operating-system–specific services. This is the core of Windows 98, the part that has to be operating in order for Windows to perform its work. The following paragraphs describe each part of the Base System in detail:

- **File Management Subsystem.** Essentially, this part of the Base System provides an interface to all the block devices (such as a modem or hard disk) connected to your machine. It doesn't matter how the connection is made—physically or through a network. All that matters is that your machine can access the device. The big thing to remember about the File Management Subsystem is that Windows 98 no longer relies on DOS to manage files. This particular part of Windows 98 is examined in detail in Chapter 9, "The Windows 98 File System."

Figure 8.1.
Windows contains several major elements that provide different services to the user and to other applications running under Windows.

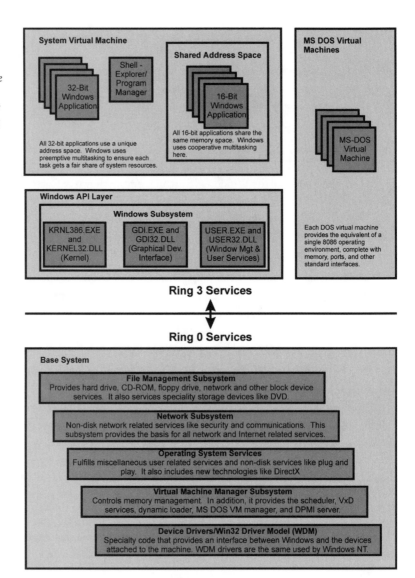

- **Network Subsystem.** Windows for Workgroups was the first version of Windows to address the networking needs of a workgroup. It even incorporates networking as part of the operating system rather than as a third-party add-on product. Windows 98 extends this capability. Not only can you run a Microsoft peer-to-peer network, Windows 98 also provides protected-mode hooks for most major LAN products as well. In fact, you can keep more than one network active at a time. The modular nature of the Network Subsystem enables other vendors to add to Windows 98–inherent capabilities through the use of virtual anything drivers (VxDs).

- **Operating System Services.** This part of the operating system deals with features such as Plug and Play. Here you'll also find new Windows 98 capabilities such as DirectX (the new technology used by games and other programs that require high-speed access to hardware). The Operating System Services section also fulfills miscellaneous user and operating system requests. For example, every time the user asks Windows 98 for the time of day, he's requesting a service from this Windows 98 component.

- **Virtual Machine Manager.** Ever wonder where the exact center of Windows 98 is? This is it, the component that holds everything else together. The Virtual Machine Manager not only takes care of task scheduling, it starts and stops every application on the system (including any DOS applications you might run). This operating system component also manages virtual memory on your machine. Of course, your application uses the Windows API to make the request instead of talking directly with this part of the system. Because the Virtual Machine Manager handles all memory allocations, it also has to act as a DOS protected-mode interface (DPMI) server for DOS applications that run in protected mode. When a DOS application makes a memory request, it actually is calling routines in this component of Windows. As with Windows applications, DOS applications can't directly access this component of Windows. A DOS application uses a DOS extender API to make its call. Finally, the Virtual Machine Manager is responsible for intertask communication. All this means is that all DDE and OLE requests filter through this section of the operating system.

- **Device Drivers/Win32 Driver Model (WDM).** Windows wouldn't know what to do with your system if not for the lowly device driver. This bit of specialty code acts as an interpreter. It sends Windows requests to the device in a format it can understand. Windows 98 supports three types of device drivers. The first type is the real-mode device driver used in Windows 3.x. The problem with this type of driver is Windows has to keep switching between real and protected mode to use it. Windows 98 also supports the Windows 95–style VxD, which enables Windows to talk to the devices on your system without switching to real mode. There are three reasons to use VxDs rather than standard real-mode device drivers: Your system remains more stable, it runs faster, and it recovers from errors better. Finally, Windows 98 supports the new WDM drivers. These drivers not only provide all the features of the older Windows 95 drivers, they also provide full compatibility with Windows NT. Using a WDM driver means you only have to keep track of one driver, no matter which Windows operating system you use.

I've separated the DOS Virtual Machine component of Windows from the other components for several reasons. DOS applications have formed the basis for using the PC for a long time. In fact, for many years nothing else was available. Yet most of these applications were written at a time when the standard PC ran one application and one application only. That one application had total control of the entire machine.

Windows 98 deals with DOS applications differently than it deals with the Windows-specific applications on your machine. Each DOS application runs on what Intel terms a *virtual machine*. Essentially, the processor fools the application into thinking that it's the only application running on your machine at the moment. Each virtual machine has its own memory space and access to devices on the system. The amazing thing is that you can have many virtual machines running on your one physical machine at a time. We'll take a more detailed look at the DOS Virtual Machine later. Suffice it to say that Windows 98 has to literally perform backflips to make this whole concept work properly, especially when you consider Windows-hostile applications (such as games originally designed to run under MS-DOS).

This section gives you just a brief overview of the Windows 98 architecture. If you want a more in-depth view of the internal structure of Windows 98, look at the section "Windows 98 Internals" later in this chapter. It gives you a much more detailed look at how Windows 98 works as a whole.

The System Files

DOS programmers know you're supposed to gain access to the operating system using an interrupt-service routine. These interrupts ask the operating system to perform a specific task. All code for the interrupt routines appears in the system files. This method worked well in the DOS single-tasking environment because the application was in control. In Windows, however, the user is in control and the old system doesn't work properly. Every Windows application gains access to the operating system using an API. Essentially, an API call does the same thing as an interrupt: It asks the operating system to perform a task. The code for the API appears in the system files, just as it does for DOS. Of course, this is a simplified view of the API. An API is written using protected-mode code—unlike DOS, which is written in real-mode code. In addition, API code is reentrant; DOS code isn't. A reentrant piece of code enables Windows 98 to process more than one call at a time. In DOS, you can't reenter a piece of code—you have to complete one call at a time. There are other differences, but the only people who really need to know about them are programmers. As discussed in the preceding section, Windows 98 actually uses two APIs—one 16-bit and one 32-bit.

DirectX—A Middle Road for Programmers

Technical Note: Anyone who plays games on the computer with any regularity understands the need for high-speed hardware. The entire gaming experience is built around fancy graphics and multimedia presentations. This kind of environment isn't very forgiving when it comes to processor cycles and definitely doesn't allow much room for the programmer to work. It isn't any wonder, then, that Microsoft had a problem trying to convince game programmers to take Windows seriously. After all, direct hardware access provides a much faster interface than using the Windows API.

Unfortunately, direct hardware access is out of the question when using Windows. Unless the operating system knows exactly what's going on with all the hardware all the time, there isn't any way for it to provide access to more than one application. As far as game vendors were concerned, there wasn't any way for Windows to support games of any complexity under these conditions.

DirectX is a middle ground. It gives a game programmer (or anyone else, for that matter) a higher-speed interface than Windows normally provides, without taking Windows itself out of the loop. Windows still monitors the events taking place when using DirectX, but it provides a lot less in the way of support. DirectX technology provides the means for a programmer to access the hardware, without damaging the Windows multitasking environment.

It might sound like DirectX is a perfect solution. After all, both sides of the equation get what they want. There are a few problems, however, and you need to decide whether you want to live with them. The biggest problem right now is that DirectX is evolving. This means that you might get a piece of software that doesn't work even if you have DirectX installed, because the software is written to a newer standard. DirectX also causes compatibility problems on some machines when used in certain ways. In other words, there isn't any guarantee that a DirectX application will work all the time if the game vendor didn't follow the specifications to the letter (and even then there's no guarantee).

One of the fallouts of the new nature of DirectX is that some game vendors have decided to bypass it entirely and use an older technology instead. OpenGL, another graphics technology for Windows 98 is an older and more established technology. In fact, OpenGL originally appeared in Windows NT. Several of the Windows 98 screen savers, such as 3D Pipes, use OpenGL. As I mentioned, you'll find that at least some games, like Quake, use OpenGL rather than DirectX. The downside of using OpenGL is that it's not quite a fast as DirectX for games. However, some vendors consider the enhanced stability of OpenGL a bigger advantage than speed.

At best, DirectX represents a partial solution to a problem people have had with Windows. It gives the programmer direct access to the hardware with minimum interference from Windows. Obviously, you need to weigh the pros and cons of using DirectX carefully before installing it on your machine. More importantly, you need to find out whether the software you're installing even uses DirectX. When troubleshooting graphics problems with a particular piece of software, ask yourself whether DirectX might be the source of your problem.

The big news in Windows 98 is the 32-bit API. Not only are 32-bit system calls more logical from a programmer's point of view (Windows 3.x was a programmer's nightmare; Windows 98 is merely an inconvenience), they also provide more features. In addition, a 32-bit application enjoys the benefits that this environment provides. Of course, the biggest benefit that you'll hear most programmers talk about is the flat memory address space. Every application running under Windows—until now—has had to spend time working with Intel's segmented address scheme. A 32-bit application doesn't need to worry about segmentation any more.

No matter which API you use, your application will address three basic components. The 16-bit versions of these files are GDI.EXE, USER.EXE, and KRNL386.EXE. The 32-bit versions of these files are GDI32.DLL, USER32.DLL, and KERNEL32.DLL. The following list describes these three components in detail:

- **Windows Kernel (KRNL386.EXE or KERNEL32.DLL).** This is the part of Windows 98 that provides support for the lower-level functions that an application needs to run. For example, every time your application needs memory, it runs to the Windows Kernel to get it. This component doesn't deal with either the interface or devices; it interacts only with Windows itself.

- **Graphical Device Interface (GDI.EXE or GDI32.DLL).** Every time an application writes to the screen, it's using a GDI service. This Windows component takes care of fonts, printer services, the display, color management, and every other artistic aspect of Windows that users can see as they use your application.

- **User (USER.EXE or USER32.DLL).** Windows is about just that—windows. It needs a manager to keep track of all the windows that applications create to display various types of information. However, User only begins there. Every time your application displays an icon or button, it's using some type of User component function. It's easier to think of the User component of the Windows API as a work manager; it helps you organize things and keep them straight.

There's actually one more piece to the Windows API puzzle, but it's a small piece your application will never use. Windows 98 still starts out as a 16-bit application so it can implement Plug and Play. The Plug and Play BIOS contains separate sections for real-mode and 16-bit protected-mode calls. If Windows 98 started out in 32-bit mode, it couldn't call the Plug and Play BIOS to set up all your devices without a lot of overhead. (To understand why, see the section "Getting 16-Bit and 32-Bit Applications to Work Together" later in this chapter.) All device configuration must occur before Windows actually starts the GUI.

The 16-bit mode operations end soon after you start Windows 98. The user shell is a 32-bit application. When the 16-bit kernel sees the call for the shell, it loads an application called VWIN32.386. This program loads the three 32-bit DLLs that form the Win32 API. After it completes this task, VWIN32.386 returns control to the 16-bit kernel, which in turn calls the 32-bit kernel. Windows runs in 32-bit mode from that point on.

The Plug and Play BIOS

Plug and Play (PnP) provides one of the easiest ways to configure the hardware on your machine. The first misconception that I want to clear up is that this is some new piece of "magic" that Microsoft pulled from its bag of tricks. PnP isn't magic, nor is it even all that new. The only thing that Windows 98 does differently is actually use the capabilities provided by PnP hardware.

Let's back up a bit. The very first microchannel architecture (MCA) machine produced by IBM contained everything PnP needed—except an operating system. The same can be said of many EISA machines.

The problem wasn't simply a matter of adding some capabilities to an operating system. You have to build this feature into every aspect of the operating system; it can't be added on. You also need routines to handle problems between the various pieces of hardware vying for a particular port address or interrupt. The BIOS itself has to provide a standardized interface; earlier offerings were anything but standard.

PnP is actually the work of three system components: hardware, BIOS, and operating system. The BIOS queries all system components during startup. It activates essential system components such as the disk drive and the display adapter. Everything else waits on the sidelines until the operating system boots. During the boot process, the operating system finishes the task of assigning interrupts and port addresses to every system component. It also asks the BIOS to provide a list of previous assignments so it won't use them again.

The EISA and MCA BIOS weren't prepared for this kind of interaction with the operating system. Enter the PnP BIOS. This isn't the work of Microsoft, but of Compaq Computer Corporation, Phoenix Technologies Ltd., and Intel Corporation.

In addition to cooperating with the operating system, the PnP BIOS provides something important that the EISA and the MCA BIOS don't—protected-mode routines. The current BIOS specification only requires vendors to provide 16-bit protected-mode routines. This is why Windows 98 starts in 16-bit mode instead of 32-bit mode. In addition, that's one of the reasons why a real-mode DOS stub (a functional subset of the DOS that you're familiar with) is part of the picture. (The version of real-mode DOS provided with Windows 98 also executes `AUTOEXEC.BAT` and `CONFIG.SYS`, but we'll look into that aspect later.) You can't use the protected-mode routines without first gathering the information that the BIOS needs in real mode. The real-mode DOS stub performs this function for the BIOS.

Note: A few "used car"-type salespeople will try to convince you that their systems are fully PnP compatible. If you look inside the machine, you'll see shiny new components, all of which are indeed PnP compatible. But, unbeknownst to you, something is missing. A lot of folks find out too late that their system lacks a PnP BIOS. So how can you avoid the same fate?

continues

There are several good places to get specifications for your PnP BIOS. The best place is the Intel site at `http://developer.intel.com/ial/plugplay/index.htm`. You also can download a complete suite of tools for testing the compatibility of your Windows 98 machine from `ftp://ftp.microsoft.com/services/whql/`. This Microsoft site includes hardware compatibility list (HCL) files that show what hardware has already been tested for compatibility. You just need to download the file and extract the help file to see whether your hardware is compatible. Mobile computer users will also want to look at the special Intel PnP site at `http://www.intel.com/mobile/tech/pnp.htm`.

When looking at a PnP-compatible system, you should see more than just three different entities cooperating to provide automatic system configuration. PnP wouldn't be worth all the hubbub if that's all it provided. The following is a list of the additional features you get as part of a PnP system:

- **Identification of installed devices.** Windows 98 automatically detects all the Plug and Play components attached to your system. This means you should provide a minimum amount of information during installation and nothing at all during subsequent reboots. Contrast this with the almost continuous flow of information needed in Windows 3.x.

- **Determination of device resource needs.** Every device on your computer needs resources in the form of processor cycles, input/output ports, DMA channels, memory, and interrupts. Windows 98 works with the BIOS and peripheral devices to meet these needs without any intervention.

- **Automatic system configuration updates and resource conflict detection.** All this communication between peripheral devices, the BIOS, and the operating system enables Windows 98 to create a system configuration without user intervention. The Device Manager configuration blocks are grayed out because the user no longer needs to supply this information. This enhanced level of communication also enables Windows 98 to poll the peripherals for alternative port and interrupt settings when a conflict with another device occurs.

- **Device driver loading and unloading.** CONFIG.SYS and AUTOEXEC.BAT used to contain line after line of device driver and TSR statements. This was because the system had to bring these devices online before it loaded the command processor and Windows 3.x. Windows 98 can actually maintain or even enhance the performance of a Plug and Play–compatible system without using AUTOEXEC.BAT or CONFIG.SYS. Plug and Play compatibility enables Windows 98 to dynamically load and unload any device drivers your system needs.

- **Configuration change notification.** Plug and Play might make system configuration changes automatically, but it doesn't mean Windows 98 leaves you in the dark. Every time the system configuration changes, Windows 98 notifies you by displaying a dialog box onscreen. Essentially, this dialog box tells you what changed. This capability provides an additional benefit—Windows 98 also notifies you whenever your equipment experiences any kind of failure. When a piece of equipment fails, Windows 98 notices that it's no longer online. Plug and Play requires three-way communication, and a defective device usually fails to communicate. Instead of finding out that you no longer have access to a drive or other device when you need it most, Windows 98 notifies you of the change immediately after it takes place.

An Overview of the Registry

When Microsoft created Windows 95 (and later Windows 98), it looked for a better configuration tool than the INI files used by Windows 3.x. Users were ending up with loads of these files in their Windows directory, not to mention the INI files floating around in application directories. In Windows 3.x, trying to find the right file to correct a problem can be daunting, to say the least.

File bloat wasn't the only problem facing Microsoft. INI files also encouraged vendors to come up with distinct ways of configuring their software. No one could figure out one INI file from the other, because they all used different formatting techniques. Obviously, this made life even more difficult for the user, not to mention the support staff at the various software companies.

The Registry solves this problem. Windows 98 can't boot without a clean Registry. Any corruption in this file causes a host of problems, even if Windows 98 manages to boot. It's important to realize these problems up front. Although the Registry is easier to maintain than the INI files of old and does provide a central repository of information, it also presents unique problems of its own.

> **Tip:** Windows 98 stores the previous copy of your Registry in the USER.DA0 and SYSTEM.DA0 files. If you make a mistake in editing the Registry, exit immediately, shut down Windows 98, and boot into DOS mode. Change directories to your Windows 98 main directory. Use the ATTRIB utility to make the SYSTEM.DA0, SYSTEM.DAT, USER.DA0 and USER.DAT files visible by using the -R, -H, and -S switches. Now copy the backup of your Registry to the two original files (that is, SYSTEM.DA0 to SYSTEM.DAT and USER.DA0 to USER.DAT). This will restore your Registry to its pre-edit state. Be sure to restore the previous file attribute state by using the +R, +H, and +S switches of the ATTRIB utility.

When you look at the Registry, you see a complete definition of Windows 98 as it relates to your specific machine. Not only does the Registry contain hardware and application settings, it also contains every piece of information you can imagine about your machine. You can learn a lot about Windows simply by looking at the information presented by this database. For example, did you know that you can use multiple desktops in Windows 98? Of course, that leads to another problem:

maintaining those separate desktops. The hierarchical format presented by the Registry Editor helps the administrator compare the differences between the various desktops. It also allows the administrator to configure them with ease. Best of all, editing the Registry doesn't involve a session with a text editor. Windows provides a GUI editor that the administrator can use to change the settings in the Registry.

Knowing that the Registry contains lots of information and is easy to edit still doesn't tell you what it can do for you. When was the last time you used Explorer to check out your hard drive? I use it a lot because it provides an easy way to find what I need. The Registry can help you make Explorer easier to use. One of my favorite ways to use it for Explorer modifications is to create multiple associations for the same file type. Suppose that you want to associate a graphics editor with PCX and BMP files. This isn't very difficult. However, what if each file type requires a different set of command-line switches? Now you get into an area where using the Registry can really help. Using the Registry to edit these entries can help you customize file access.

> **Note:** Before proceeding, you should add the Registry editor, RegEdit, to your Start menu. It is helpful to look at the Registry entries as you read about them. I'll also present some exercises that will help you better understand the inner workings of the Registry.

It's time to take a look at how the Registry is organized. To start the Registry editor, simply open RegEdit as you would any other application on the Start menu. You'll probably get a lot more out of the detailed discussion that follows if you actually open the Registry editor now. Using the Registry editor to see how Windows 98 arranges the various entries can make using it in an emergency a lot easier.

The first thing you need to know about RegEdit is what you'll see. There are two panes in RegEdit, just like in Explorer. The entries in the left pane are keys. Look at a key as you would the headings in a book—they divide the registry into easily understood pieces. Using keys also makes finding a specific piece of configuration information fast. The entries in the right pane are values. A value is registry content, just like the paragraphs in a book. There are three kinds of values: String, binary, and DWORD. The string type is the only one you can read directly. Binary and DWORD values contain computer readable data using two different sized variables. In most cases, you won't have to worry about what these kinds of values contain because your applications and Windows 98 will take care of them automatically.

I always step lightly when it comes to the Registry. You might want to follow the same procedure I use to back up the Registry before you go much further. The big advantage to this method is that it produces a text file you can view with any text editor. (The file is huge; Notepad won't handle it but WordPad will.) You can use this backup file to restore the Registry later if you run into difficulty. Unfortunately, this method doesn't help much if you permanently destroy the Registry and reboot the machine. Windows 98 needs a clean Registry to boot. To preserve a clean, bootable copy of the

Registry, you need to copy the USER.DAT and SYSTEM.DAT files to a safe location. (Later, I'll cover a technique for importing a text copy of the Registry by using RegEdit at the DOS prompt, but this technique isn't guaranteed by anyone to work. The bottom line is that a good backup is always worth the effort.)

> **Warning:** RegEdit is an application designed to assist experienced users in changing the behavior of Windows 98 and associated applications. Although it enables you to enhance system performance and to make applications easier to use, it can cause unexpected results when misused. Never edit an entry unless you know what that entry represents. Failure to observe this precaution can result in data loss and can even prevent your system from booting the next time you start Windows 98.

1. Highlight the My Computer entry of the Registry. Use the Registry | Export Registry File command to display the Export Registry File dialog box, as shown in Figure 8.2. The File Name field already contains a name, but you can use any name you want. I selected OLDENTRY to designate a preedited Registry. Note that the All radio button is selected in the Export Range group.

Figure 8.2.
The Export Registry File dialog box enables you to save your current Registry settings.

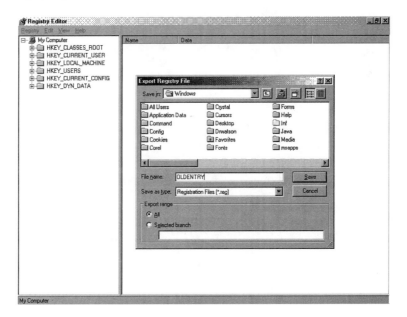

2. Click the Save button to place a copy of the Registry on disk. The OLDENTRY.REG file in your main Windows 98 directory now contains a complete copy of your original Registry.

Now that you have a copy of the Registry, let's take that brief overview that I talked about previously. The next few sections acquaint you with the contents of the Registry as a whole. I won't go into much detail, but at least you'll know the general location for specific types of information.

HKEY_CLASSES_ROOT

There are two major types of keys under the HKEY_CLASSES_ROOT key. The first key type is a file extension. Think of all the three-letter extensions you've used, such as .DOC and .TXT. Windows 98 still uses them to differentiate one file type from another. (Because Windows 98 also provides long filename support, you can use the Registry to create associations for extensions longer than three letters.) The Registry also uses extensions to associate that file type with a specific action. For example, even though you can't do anything with a file that uses the .DLL extension, it appears in this list because Windows 98 needs to associate the .DLL extension with an executable file type. The second entry type is the association itself. The file extension entries usually associate a data file with an application or an executable file with a specific Windows 98 function. Below the association key are entries for the menus you see when you right-click an entry in Explorer. The association also contains keys that determine what type of icon to display, as well as other parameters associated with a particular file type. Figure 8.3 shows the typical HKEY_CLASSES_ROOT organization.

Figure 8.3.
Notice the distinct difference between file extension and file association keys in a typical HKEY_ CLASSES_ROOT display.

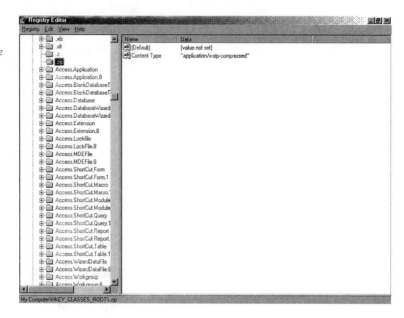

HKEY_CURRENT_USER

The HKEY_CURRENT_USER key contains a lot of "soft" settings for your machine. These soft settings tell how to configure the desktop and the keyboard. It also contains color settings and the configuration of the Start menu. All user-specific settings appear under this key.

The HKEY_CURRENT_USER key is enslaved by the settings of the current user, the one currently logged in to the machine. This is different from all the user configuration entries in other parts of the Registry. This is a dynamic-setting category; the other user-related categories contain static information. The Registry copies the contents of one of the user entries in the HKEY_USERS category into this category and updates HKEY_USERS when you shut down.

This is the area where Windows 98 obtains new settings information and places any changes you make. As you can see in Figure 8.4, keys within the HKEY_CURRENT_USER category are self-explanatory in most cases. All the entries adjust a user-specific setting of some type—nothing that affects a global element such as a device driver.

Figure 8.4.
*The HKEY_*
CURRENT_USER
category contains all
user-specific settings.

HKEY_LOCAL_MACHINE

The HKEY_LOCAL_MACHINE key focuses its attention on the machine's hardware, including the drivers and configuration information required to use the hardware. Every piece of hardware appears in this section of the Registry, even if it uses real-mode drivers. If a piece of hardware doesn't appear here, Windows 98 can't use it.

Lots of subtle information about your hardware is stored under this key. For example, this key contains all the Plug and Play information about your machine. It also provides a complete list of device drivers and their revision levels. This section might even contain revision information for the hardware itself. For example, there's a distinct difference between a Pro Audio Spectrum 16+ Revision C sound board and a Revision D version of the same board. Windows 98 stores that difference in the Registry.

This key contains some software-specific information of a global nature. For example, a 32-bit application will store the location of its Setup and Format Table (SFT) here. This is a file used by the application during installation. Some applications also use it during setup modification. Applications such as Word for Windows store all their setup information in SFT tables. The only application information that appears here is global-configuration–specific like the SFT. Figure 8.5 shows a typical HKEY_LOCAL_MACHINE category setup.

Figure 8.5.
*The HKEY_
LOCAL_MACHINE
category contains all
the hardware and
device-driver–specific
information about
your machine. It also
contains the global-
application–setup
information.*

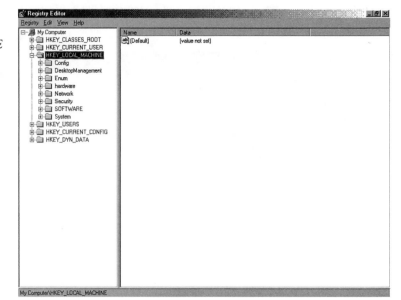

HKEY_USERS

The HKEY_USERS key contains a static list of all the users of this Registry file. It never pays to edit any of the information you find under this key. However, you can use this key for reference purposes. The reason for this hands-off policy is simple: None of the entries here take effect until the next time the user logs in to Windows 98, so you really don't know what effect they'll have until you reboot the machine. In addition, changing the settings for the current user is a waste of time, because Windows 98 overwrites the new data with data contained in HKEY_CURRENT_USER during logout or shutdown.

There's one other problem associated with using this key as your sole source of information. Windows 98 actually maintains multiple Registries in a multiuser configuration—in some cases, one for each user who logs in to the system. Because of this, you never quite know where you'll find the information for a particular user. Windows 98 tracks this information; it's a pain for the administrator to have to do it as well. Besides, Microsoft thoughtfully provided a utility to help the network administrator maintain the various Registries. The Policy Editor enables the network administrator to easily maintain static user information. Using the Policy Editor lets the network administrator to bridge various Registry files on the system when each user provides his own desktop configuration.

Figure 8.6 shows a setup that includes the Default key. If this system were set up for multiple desktops, each user would have a separate entry in this section. Each entry would contain precisely the same keys, but the values might differ from user to user. When a user logs in to the network, Windows 98 copies the information in his profile to the HKEY_CURRENT_USER area of the Registry. When he logs out or shuts down, Windows 98 updates the information in his specific section from the HKEY_CURRENT_USER category.

Figure 8.6.
Windows 98 creates one entry in the HKEY_USERS category for each user who logs in to the machine.

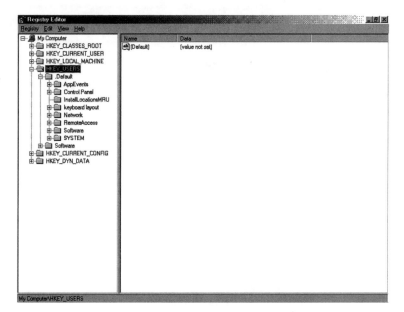

HKEY_CURRENT_CONFIG

The HKEY_CURRENT_CONFIG key is the simplest part of the Registry. It contains two major keys: Display and System. Essentially, these entries are used by the GDI API (described in Chapters 15, "Fonts and Printing," and 17, "Video Configuration") to configure the display and the printer.

The Display key provides two subkeys: Fonts and Settings. The Fonts subkey determines which fonts Windows 98 uses for general display purposes. These are the raster (non–TrueType) fonts that it displays when you get a choice of which font to use for icons or other purposes. Raster fonts are essentially bitmaps or pictures of the characters. Chapter 15 takes a more detailed look at fonts.

The Settings subkey contains the current display resolution and the number of bits per pixel. The bits-per-pixel value determines the number of colors available. For example, 4 bits per pixel provides 16 colors, and 8 bits per pixel provides 256 colors. The three fonts listed as values under this key are the default fonts used for icons and application menus. You can change the settings under this key in the Settings tab of the Display Properties dialog box.

The System key looks like a convoluted mess. However, only one of the subkeys under this key has any meaning for the user. The Printers subkey contains a list of the printers attached to the machine. It doesn't include printers accessed through a network connection. Figure 8.7 shows the major keys in this category.

Figure 8.7.
*The HKEY_
CURRENT_CONFIG
category echoes the
settings under the
Config key of the
HKEY_LOCAL_
MACHINE
category.*

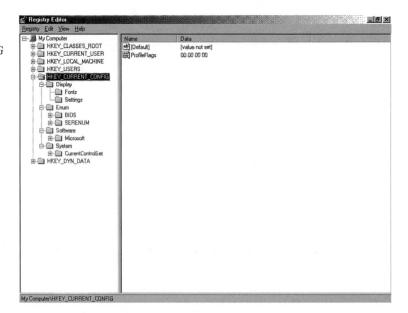

HKEY_DYN_DATA

The final key, HKEY_DYN_DATA, contains two subkeys: Config Manager and PerfStats. You can monitor the status of the Config Manager key using the Device Manager. The PerfStats key values appear as statistics in the System Monitor display. Figure 8.8 shows these two main keys and their subkeys.

Figure 8.8.
HKEY_DYN_DATA
contains Registry
entries for current
events. The values in
these keys reflect the
current (dynamic)
state of the computer.

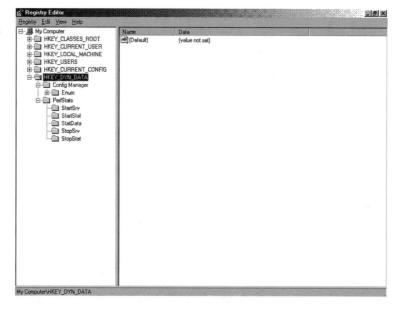

Windows 98 Compatibility Configuration Files

There's no doubt about it: Windows 98 starts by booting DOS. You can even gain access to this "raw" DOS (as Microsoft calls it) using a variety of methods—some sanctioned, some not. Microsoft had to provide the four compatibility files that older applications need in order to run. Some of these files are easy to bypass; others won't go away until you get rid of all those applications. Part of the reason DOS is still hanging around is because of these compatibility files. Windows 98 has to boot using real mode so that it can read and process both CONFIG.SYS and AUTOEXEC.BAT. There are other reasons that Windows 98 boots into real mode, examined later in this chapter.

The following sections take an in-depth look at the four compatibility files: AUTOEXEC.BAT, CONFIG.SYS, SYSTEM.INI and WIN.INI. I'll show you that even though Microsoft doesn't want to admit it, Windows 98 still needs at least one of these files to work properly. Fortunately, you really only need this one compatibility file—SYSTEM.INI—to run Windows 98. The other files are there for compatibility purposes only.

AUTOEXEC.BAT

This is the one file you could get rid of if you didn't have any 16-bit Windows applications that required a PATH statement. Windows 98 provides the means for defining a path and a prompt and loading any TSRs that a DOS application might require to run. The most efficient way to use Windows 98 is not to load anything a DOS application would need here.

Use AUTOEXEC.BAT only for settings you need on a global basis or as part of the requirement for running an older Windows application. Some 16-bit Windows applications require SET and PATH entries to run. This is especially true of compilers and advanced applications.

Looking Ahead: We'll look at how you can replace both CONFIG.SYS and AUTOEXEC.BAT for DOS applications in Chapter 12, "Exploiting Your Software: DOS, 16-Bit, and 32-Bit Applications." If your only reason for keeping these two files around is so you can run DOS applications, consider the faster alternative presented here.

The following list contains a few things you should never run from AUTOEXEC.BAT. Most of these items consume memory before you load Windows—memory you can't retrieve later. Using this technique might cost you a little conventional memory for your DOS applications, but you'll still have about the same or perhaps even more than you had available under Windows 3.x. The reason for this is simple: You don't have to load a bunch of drivers in CONFIG.SYS to make Windows 98 run.

- **TSRs.** Try to avoid running any TSRs from AUTOEXEC.BAT. A small utility such as DOSKey might not appear to consume much memory, but why run it from AUTOEXEC.BAT at all? You can easily customize the settings for your DOS applications. Those that will never use DOSKey don't need to give up the memory required to install it. In essence, loading a TSR in AUTOEXEC.BAT penalizes the applications that can't use it.

- **DOS application–environment variables.** If you have a DOS application that requires a PATH entry or other environmental variables, load them as part of a special configuration rather than as part of AUTOEXEC.BAT. You can individually adjust the size of the environment for each DOS application you run.

- **DOS applications with Windows counterparts.** I used to run CHKDSK as part of every startup cycle. A lot of other people do the same thing. Running some DOS applications before you enter Windows doesn't harm the amount of memory you have available one iota. Running other applications can consume memory. For example, if you run MODE to change your screen size to 43 lines before you enter Windows, every DOS program you load will consume 43 lines worth of memory (more if you ask for a larger screen in the custom settings). You can reduce the memory required for each DOS session by using the application's custom screen settings.

- **Disk- or printer-caching software.** You'll find that the Windows 98 disk- and print-caching services are far superior to those provided with Windows 3.x. The memory allocated to these services is dynamic—Windows 98 can increase and decrease the amount of memory used as needed—as long as you use the Windows 98–specific capability. When you load disk- or print-caching software in AUTOEXEC.BAT, you lose the capability to control the size of that cache within Windows (in most cases). Even if you could change the size of the cache, it's unlikely Windows 98 could use it unless the caching program is specially designed to communicate with Windows.

CONFIG.SYS

Unless you're still playing Russian roulette with the real-mode drivers on your system, you can get rid of CONFIG.SYS. Windows 98 provides its own extended memory manager (EMM); it doesn't need one loaded like Windows 3.x did. Windows 98 also takes care of the BUFFERS, LASTDRIVE, and STACKS entries for you. In other words, CONFIG.SYS is out of a job unless you give it one.

I recently threw caution to the wind and tried booting my system for several days with a pared-down AUTOEXEC.BAT and no CONFIG.SYS. Not only did I notice a speed increase when loading Windows, but I also had far greater control over the settings for each individual DOS setting. Windows also could provide much better memory control than before. (I used the System Monitor utility described in Chapter 5, "Performance Primer," to check all this out.)

I had to deal with a few negatives, however. Getting rid of CONFIG.SYS lost me about 5KB of conventional memory. I still have 600KB of RAM available in a DOS window, though, so the memory loss is pretty minimal. I could probably get even more available memory by decreasing the environment size and not loading DOSKey as part of my custom settings. It also cost me some time to set up each of my DOS applications. The greater flexibility and better memory management came at the cost of increased complexity. Even though there were negative elements, I'd still say it was worth the effort.

Tip: In the past, users with large hard drives resorted to using special drivers—such as those from OnTrack Systems—to access their entire drive using one partition. You can still do this in Windows 98 with relatively good success. However, such an action will destabilize your system. The reason is clear: Every time Windows needs to access the drive, it has to switch to real mode to access the real-mode driver. It's probably a better idea to partition your drive into more manageable partition sizes and get rid of the real-mode drivers if at all possible. (Upgrading your BIOS if it doesn't provide support for large hard drives is also a good idea if you want to get rid of the real-mode drivers.)

WIN.INI

Windows 98 can get along just fine without WIN.INI. However, before you get rid of your file, you might want to check it out first. A few applications, especially screen savers, load themselves by using the LOAD= or RUN= lines of this file. You can get around this limitation by adding the filenames to your Startup folder and changing the application settings as needed. (You may want to get rid of a screen saver that uses these WIN.INI entries if it's a 16-bit application, since a 32-bit screen saver will be more responsive and less likely to crash your system.)

Many applications also store their file-association information in WIN.INI. Windows 98 applications don't need these entries because they already appear in the Registry. Any new 32-bit applications will know to look in the Registry for file association information, but some older 16-bit applications won't. You might want to check for problems by saving a copy of WIN.INI under a different name and then editing out the [Extensions] section. If all your applications seem to work properly, you might be able to remove this section for good.

Note: Windows 98 always checks for new entries in both WIN.INI and SYSTEM.INI. It automatically adds any new entries that it finds to the appropriate section of the Registry. This is why you can get rid of these two files if you have a stable system and none of the 16-bit applications that you use relies on them. Of course, that's a big if, and you still have the mysterious Windows 98 problem with SYSTEM.INI to deal with. In reality, you probably need to wait until you've gotten rid of all your 16-bit applications before you can get rid of these two files.

If you look through the Windows 98 version of WIN.INI, you'll notice that it's a lot slimmer. Microsoft moved all the Windows-specific information that this file contained into the Registry. Windows 98 doesn't use it at all. In fact, if you compare the contents of the Registry to a Windows 3.x version of WIN.INI, you'll find every entry that the old file contained.

SYSTEM.INI

Getting rid of SYSTEM.INI will take a major miracle. Just about every application on my machine sticks something in there. Even Microsoft still uses this file—though Microsoft swears otherwise. Most of these settings have become so standard that other applications read the file in anticipation of finding out about the environment.

Of course, this is one source of the problem. Getting rid of SYSTEM.INI or even excluding some of the settings would break a lot of applications out there. Part of the goal of Windows 98 is to provide the compatibility people need out of a workstation. Windows NT is the place to go if you need reliability and stability. Microsoft probably made the right call by keeping SYSTEM.INI in place and up-to-date.

Note: Microsoft is spending a great deal of time telling programmers not to place anything in SYSTEM.INI anymore. The Registry is the new way to store all these settings. A quick look at SYSTEM.INI, though, shows some Windows 98–specific information there. For example, look near the bottom of the file and you'll see entries for passwords and VCache. These two entries don't appear in Windows 3.x–specific versions of the file.

A Look at the Windows 98 Boot Sequence

Getting your machine up and running after you turn on the power is called the *boot process*. It includes everything from the time that the power on startup test (POST) routines begin until the time you can start to use the machine. Under DOS, this boot process was relatively straightforward. Windows 98 requires something a bit more exotic, because we expect it to do more.

The next few sections look at the boot process from a user's perspective. This means that you won't get a blow-by-blow "this bit does this and that byte does that" explanation. We just look at the highlights of the boot process.

Tip: If you ever want to see a blow-by-blow description of the entire boot process, look at BOOTLOG.TXT in the root directory of your boot drive. This file records every action that Windows 98 performs during the boot process. However, it doesn't include a few of the initial actions, such as loading IO.SYS. At most three or four actions take place before the log starts, though, so your chances of missing anything important are almost nonexistent.

Starting at the DOS Prompt

Windows 98 doesn't (as some people think) start the boot process in protected mode. It actually starts up a copy of DOS. The difference is that the copy of DOS it uses isn't the same as the one you used in the past. Even the system files are different.

The whole reason for starting DOS (at least the one that Microsoft sort of admits to) is for compatibility purposes. All those machines with older hardware still need to run device drivers and the like from CONFIG.SYS and AUTOEXEC.BAT. Something has to read those files and act on their contents in a way that the drivers can understand.

Your system starts just like it always has. Installing Windows 98 doesn't stop the system from performing POST. Once the ROM BIOS determines that your machine is working correctly, it takes care of any required hardware initialization and builds a vector table in lower memory. The vector table contains pointers to all the BIOS routines so that DOS can use them later as part of its boot process. Once this initialization phase is over, the BIOS looks for a bootable drive. A bootable drive contains an operating system loader. In the case of both DOS and Windows 98, that loader will look for a file called IO.SYS.

Up to this point, the workings of DOS and Windows 98 are precisely the same. However, unlike the old version of DOS, everything that the new version needs in the way of code appears in the IO.SYS file. The old MSDOS.SYS file is no longer required. Microsoft combined the contents of the two files that used to appear in your root directory into one.

By now you're looking at your drive and noticing that there's still an MSDOS.SYS file. The MSDOS.SYS file now contains important boot configuration information. You can include a lot of different configuration switches here. Most of them aren't essential, but some are. Fortunately, you don't have to worry too much about editing these entries by hand. Microsoft includes the TweakUI utility with Windows 98, which makes editing the MSDOS.SYS file by hand a thing of the past. I talk about the TweakUI utility in the "TweakUI Utility" section of Chapter 4.

IO.SYS reads the contents of MSDOS.SYS as part of the prebooting cycle. Think of MSDOS.SYS as a configuration file for the boot process, because that's exactly what it is. After IO.SYS configures itself— using the contents of MSDOS.SYS—it reads the contents of CONFIG.SYS (if there is one). There's no longer a need for CONFIG.SYS, because IO.SYS has several features added to it. The following list tells you everything you need to know about these new settings:

- **DOS=HIGH,UMB.** IO.SYS always loads DOS high unless you override this setting in CONFIG.SYS.

- **HIMEM.SYS.** IO.SYS always loads a copy of the real-mode memory manager. It doesn't load EMM386.EXE. You need to load this from CONFIG.SYS if you plan to run an application that requires expanded memory without going into Windows first.

- **IFSHLP.SYS (installable file system helper).** Loading this device driver also loads several others. It gives you full access to the file system.

- **SETVER.EXE.** Some older applications might require a specific version of DOS. This program fools them into thinking the version of DOS provided with Windows 98 is the one they need.

- **FILES=60.** Windows 98 does not require this setting. It is provided for any MS-DOS applications you might run. Some older applications require more than 60 file handles, but this setting should work for the majority of installations.

- **LASTDRIVE=Z.** This sets the last drive letter you can use for your DOS applications. As with the FILES setting, Windows 98 does not require a LASTDRIVE setting.

- **BUFFERS=30.** The BUFFERS setting affects the number of file buffers that IO.SYS provides. Windows 98 uses its own file management system and is unaffected by this setting.

- **STACKS=9,256.** IO.SYS sets up a specific number of stack frames using this entry. Each stack frame is the same size.

- **SHELL=COMMAND.COM /P.** If you don't specify another command processor in CONFIG.SYS, IO.SYS defaults to using COMMAND.COM (just as it always has). The /P parameter makes the command processor permanent.

- **FCBS=4.** Ancient programs used file control blocks. These programs are so old that I really can't believe anyone would still have them lying around. You can provide additional FCBs by overriding this setting in CONFIG.SYS.

As you can see, IO.SYS comes with a fairly complete CONFIG.SYS built in. After IO.SYS loads the command processor, its job is finished for the time being. The command processor takes over and reads the contents of AUTOEXEC.BAT. At this point, you're running DOS. You might not see a DOS prompt, but that's because Microsoft hides it behind a logo.

Loading the 16-Bit Core

After the command processor completes its work, a new phase in the boot process begins. You might wonder why Windows 98—a 32-bit operating system—would even think about starting in 16-bit mode. There are several interesting reasons.

One reason has to do with the way the Plug and Play BIOS specification is written. The current specification requires a vendor to provide a 16-bit protected-mode interface. This enables an operating system vendor such as Microsoft to check the Plug and Play hardware without switching to real mode. The result is a more stable operating system that (supposedly) always runs in protected mode.

The first thing Windows has to do once you start it is to check the status of all the hardware. It calls on the Plug and Play BIOS to provide it with a list of all the installed equipment. Windows uses this information to configure the system. Of course, it also has to take any non–Plug and Play peripherals into account. After it comes up with a configuration list, Windows 98 starts to load all the 16-bit VxDs required to support that hardware.

What precisely is a VxD? It's a virtual anything (where anything is usually a device of some type) driver, the protected-mode version of the device drivers you used under DOS. However, it's more than that, because a device can be a lot more than just a piece of hardware under Windows 98. To avoid getting into the bits and bytes of device management, let's just say that Windows uses virtual anything drivers to manage all its low-level functions.

After it completes this step, Windows initializes all the drivers. It starts with the system drivers—the drivers required to make low-level functions in Windows work (such as the file system drivers). The device drivers come next.

At this point, Windows 98 loads the three 16-bit shell components: USER.EXE, GDI.EXE, and KRNL386.EXE. It also loads some additional drivers and a few other components, such as fonts. Windows 98 is now completely up and running in 16-bit mode. It doesn't have an interface yet, but every other component is present.

Loading the 32-Bit Core

The preceding section ended with a copy of Windows running in 16-bit mode without any form of user interface. 16-bit mode operations end very soon after you start Windows 98. The user shell, Explorer, is a 32-bit application. As soon as the 16-bit kernel sees the call for the shell, it loads an application called VWIN32.386. This little program loads the three 32-bit DLLs that form the Win32 API: USER32.DLL, GDI32.DLL, and KERNEL32.DLL. After it completes this task, VWIN32.386 returns control to the 16-bit kernel, which in turn calls the 32-bit kernel. Windows runs in 32-bit mode from that point on.

Now that it's operating in 32-bit mode, the operating system loads and initializes all the 32-bit drivers. This is the same process that the 16-bit part of the operating system performed, so I won't discuss it again here.

Somewhere in all this, Windows 98 asks the user to provide a name and password (if you've enabled this feature). It checks this against the contents of the appropriate PWL file. If the password checks out, Windows 98 completes the boot process.

Finally, Windows gets the Explorer interface up and running. (It was loaded before but wasn't running.) It displays all the required objects on the desktop and initializes the taskbar. This is the point where it also looks at your Startup folder to see which applications you want to start automatically. You're set up and ready to compute.

Cooperative Versus Preemptive Multitasking

Multitasking is one of those nebulous words that everyone uses but no one takes the time to define. The first thing you need to do before you can understand multitasking is to define the word "task". A *task* is essentially an application that's running. When you start Windows, you might think that nothing is running, but there are already several applications getting work done on your machine. For example, Explorer (or Program Manager) is considered a task. Any network connections or print spoolers are considered tasks. A screen saver is yet another task. There are numerous system-related tasks as well. The Windows kernel is considered a task. The computer industry uses two terms to refer to a running application or thread: process and task. I prefer task because it's a little less nebulous than process. However, you'll probably see a mixture of both in the documentation you read.

When talking about Windows 3.x, you can associate every task with a single application. The definition of task doesn't really stop here for Windows 98 and Windows NT. Some 32-bit applications use a technique called *multithreading*, which enables them to perform more than one task at a time. For example, you could recalculate your spreadsheet and print at the same time if the application supports multithreading. What happens is that the spreadsheet starts a task (called a thread) to take care of printing. It might even start a second thread to do the recalculation, so that you can continue to enter data. One way to look at threads is as a subtask under the application that's running.

Now that you understand what a task is, it's time to look at the definition of multitasking. Everyone assumes that multitasking is just that—several tasks (or processes) running simultaneously on one machine. This is a good start for a definition, but it doesn't end there. An important consideration is how the operating system allocates time between tasks. When talking about Windows, it becomes very important to define the method used to manage tasks and to differentiate between different kinds of multitasking. Windows 98 supports two kinds of multitasking: cooperative and preemptive.

Windows 3.0 introduced a feature called cooperative multitasking. This is how it was supposed to work: Application A would run for a little while, just long enough to get one component of a task finished. It would then turn control of the system back over to Windows so that Windows could take care of any housekeeping chores and allow application B to run for a while. This cycle continued in a round-robin fashion between all the tasks running at any given time.

What really happened is that some applications followed the rules but others didn't. Under cooperative multitasking, the operating system gave up too much control; an application could hog all the system resources if it wanted to do so. Some applications do just that. The result is that cooperative multitasking doesn't really work all that well. Most of the time that the user spends looking at the hourglass is really time in which Windows has temporarily lost control of the system to an application that doesn't want to share with anyone else.

All the legacy applications that run under Windows 98—the 16-bit applications you moved from Windows 3.x—still have to run in a cooperative multitasking mode. However, Windows 98 minimizes the impact of these applications by running them in one shared address space. All the 16-bit applications have to cooperate with each other, but they (theoretically) don't affect any 32-bit applications running on your machine. This includes Explorer and any other Windows 98–specific tools. (And, of course, you'll upgrade most of your commonly-used 16-bit applications, such as your word processor and spreadsheet, to Windows 98 versions. Right?)

In designing Windows NT, Microsoft wanted something better than cooperative multitasking and designed an operating system that uses preemptive multitasking. Windows 98 supports preemptive multitasking for any 32-bit application you run. Think of it this way: Preemptive multitasking works like a traffic light. Traffic goes one way for a while, but then the light changes and traffic goes the other way. The amount of time each task gets is weighed by the user and the operating system to meet some criteria, but this access is supposed to be fair. Every application is supposed to get its fair share of processor time, and preemptive multitasking enforces this principle. Windows 98 monitors each application and interrupts it when its time is up. It doesn't matter whether the application wants to give up control over the system. Windows 98 doesn't give it a choice.

There's another, more important difference in the way the system reacts under preemptive multitasking. Under Windows 3.x, an hourglass means that the system is tied up. You can't do anything else until the hourglass goes away. On the other hand, an hourglass under Windows 98 means only that the current task is tied up. You can always start another task or switch to an existing task. If that task isn't busy, you can perform some work with it while you wait for the initial task to complete its work. You know when the original application has finished, because the hourglass goes away when you place your cursor over the task's window. The bottom line? Preemptive multitasking means the user doesn't have to wait for the system.

Finally, cooperative multitasking has a serious flaw. Because Windows lost control when some applications took over, there was no way to clear that application if the machine froze. Because Windows 98 maintains constant control of the machine, you no longer need to worry about the machine freezing in the middle of a task. Even if one application hangs, you only need to end that task, not reboot the machine. As with Windows 3.x, pressing Ctrl+Alt+Delete doesn't automatically reboot the machine. However, unlike Windows 3.x, Windows 98 displays a list of applications, and you get to choose which one to terminate (see Figure 8.9).

Figure 8.9.

Preemptive multitasking means that Windows 98 never loses control of the machine. It also means that you can recover from an application error with ease.

You might wonder why Microsoft (or any other vendor) would use cooperative multitasking if preemptive multitasking is so much better. There are a few good reasons. First, DOS is non-reentrant. This means that you have to allow DOS to complete one task before you give it another one. If you disturb DOS in the middle of a task, the entire system could (and will) freeze. Because Windows 3.x runs on top of DOS, it can't use preemptive multitasking for any services that interact with DOS. Unfortunately, one of those services is the disk subsystem. Do you see now why it would be fairly difficult to use preemptive multitasking on any system that runs on top of DOS?

The second problem with preemptive multitasking is really a two-part scenario. Both relate to ease of designing the operating system. When an operating system provides preemptive multitasking, it also has to include some kind of method for monitoring devices. What if two applications decided that they needed to use the COM port at the same time? With cooperative multitasking, the application that started to use the COM port would gain control of it and lock out the other application. In a preemptive multitasking situation, the first application could get halfway through the allocation process and get stopped, and then the second application could start the allocation process. What happens if the first application is reactivated by the system? You have two applications that think they have access to one device. In reality, both applications have access, and you have a mess. Windows 98 handles this problem by using a programming construct called a critical section. (I discuss this feature more in a moment.)

Preemptive multitasking also needs some type of priority system to ensure that critical tasks get a larger share of the processor's time than noncritical tasks. Remember, a task can no longer dictate how long it needs system resources; that's all in the hands of the operating system. Theoretically, you should be able to rely on the users to tell the operating system how they want their applications prioritized, and then allow the operating system to take care of the rest. What really happens is that a low-priority task could run into a fault situation and need system resources immediately to resolve it. A static priority system can't handle that situation. In addition, that low-priority task could end up getting little or no system resources when a group of high-priority tasks starts to run. The priority system Windows 98 uses provides a dynamic means of changing a task's priority. When a high-priority task runs, Windows 98 lowers its priority. When a low-priority task gets passed over in favor of a high-priority task, Windows 98 increases its priority. As you can see, the dynamic-priority system enforces the idea that some tasks should get more system resources than others, yet it ensures that every task gets at least some system resources.

There's a final consideration when looking at preemptive multitasking. Even if you use the best dynamic priority system in the world and every piece of the operating system works just the way it should, you'll run into situations where a task has to complete a sequence of events without being disturbed. For example, the application might need to make certain that a database transaction is written to disk before it hands control of the system back to the operating system. If another task tried to do something related to that transaction before the first task completed, you could end up with invalid or damaged data in the database. Programmers call a piece of code that performs this task a *critical section*. Normally, a critical section occurs with system-related tasks such as memory allocation, but it also can happen with application-related tasks such as writing information to a file.

Cooperative multitasking systems don't have to worry as much about critical sections, because the task decides when the operating system regains control of the system. On the other hand, a preemptive multitasking system needs some way for a task to communicate the need to complete a critical section of code. Under Windows 98, a task tells the operating system that it needs to perform a critical section of code using a semaphore (a flag). If a hardware interrupt or some other application were to ask to perform a task that didn't interfere with any part of the critical section, Windows 98 could allow it to proceed. All that a critical section guarantees is that the task and its environment will remain undisturbed until the task completes its work.

Windows 98 Internals

The "Architecture" section earlier in this chapter provided an overview of Windows 98's internal architecture. This section assumes you've read that overview and are ready to move on to bigger and better things. The following paragraphs start where that discussion left off and show you some of the deeper and darker secrets of Windows 98.

Before I begin a discussion of individual Windows architectural components, I'd like to direct your attention to the "rings" of protection provided by the 80386 (and above) processor. There are four security rings within the Intel protection scheme, but most operating systems use only two of them (or sometimes three). The inner security ring is ring 0. This is where the operating system proper is. The outermost ring is 3. That's where the applications reside. Sometimes an operating system gives device drivers better access to some operating system features than an application gets by running them at ring 1 or ring 2. Windows doesn't make any concessions; device drivers run at ring 0 or ring 3, depending on their purpose.

Windows uses these protection rings to make sure only operating system components can access the inner workings of Windows. An application shouldn't be able to change settings that might cause the entire system to crash. For example, Windows reserves the right to allocate memory from the global pool; therefore, the capabilities necessary to perform this task rest at ring 0. On the other hand, applications need to access memory assigned to them. That's why Windows assigns local memory a protection value of 3.

Think of each ring as a security perimeter. Before you can enter that perimeter, you have to know the secret password. Windows gives the password only to applications it can trust; everyone else has to stay out. Whenever an application tries to circumvent security, the processor raises an *exception*. Think of an exception as a security alarm. The exception sends the Windows police (better known as an *exception handler*) after the offending application. After its arrest and trial, Windows calmly terminates the offending application. Of course, it notifies the user before performing this task, but the user usually doesn't have much of a choice in the matter.

Figure 8.1 gave you a pretty good idea of exactly whom Windows trusts. Applications and device drivers running at ring 3 have very few capabilities outside their own resources. In fact, Windows even curtails these capabilities somewhat. Some of the activities that a DOS application could get by with, such as directly manipulating video memory, aren't allowed here. The reason is simple: Video memory is a shared resource. Whenever another application would need to share something, you can be certain that your application won't be able to access it directly.

Now, on to the various components that actually make up Windows. The following sections break the Windows components into main areas. Each of these general groups contains descriptions of the individual components and what tasks they perform. Remember that this is only a general discussion. Windows is much more complex than it might first appear. The deeper you get as a programmer, the more you'll see the actual complexity of this operating system.

System Virtual Machine

The System Virtual Machine (VM) component of Windows 98 contains three main elements: 32-bit Windows applications, the shell, and 16-bit Windows applications. Essentially, the System VM component provides most of the Windows 98 user-specific functionality. Without it, you couldn't run any applications. Notice that I don't include DOS applications here. This is because Windows uses an entirely different set of capabilities to run DOS applications. It even runs them in a different processor mode.

Theoretically, the System VM also provides support for the various Windows API layer components. However, because these components provide a different sort of service, I chose to discuss them in a separate area. Even though applications use the API and users interact with applications, you really don't think about the API until the time comes to write an application. Therefore, I always think of the API as a programmer-specific service rather than something that the user really needs to worry about. The following list describes the System VM components in detail:

- **32-bit Windows applications.** These new Win32-specific applications use a subset of the Windows NT API. In fact, many Windows NT applications, such as Word for Windows NT, run just fine under Windows 98. A 32-bit application usually provides better multitasking capabilities than its 16-bit counterpart. In addition, many 32-bit applications support new Windows features such as long filenames; most 16-bit applications don't. 32-bit applications provide two additional features. The more important one is the use of preemptive versus cooperative multitasking. This makes your work flow more smoothly and forces the system to wait for you as necessary, rather than the other way around. The second one is the use of a flat memory address space. This feature really makes a difference in how much memory an application gets and how well it uses that memory. In addition, an application that uses a flat address space should run slightly faster because it no longer has to spend time working with Intel's memory-segmentation scheme. Programs that have the Designed for Windows NT and 95 logos fit into this category.

- **The shell.** Three shells are supplied with Windows 98, and you can choose any of them. The standard shell, Explorer, provides full 32-bit capabilities. Explorer combines all the features you used to find in Program Manager, Print Manager, and File Manager. You can also use the older Program Manager interface with Windows 98. It doesn't provide all the bells and whistles that Explorer does, but it'll certainly ease the transition for some users who learned the Program Manager interface. The third interface is the result of using Internet Explorer 4.0. It allows you to maintain your local and remote resources in one place. Switching between shells is easy. All you need to do is change the Shell= entry in the [Boot] section of SYSTEM.INI. Of course, Windows 98 also enables you to choose which shell you want to use when you install it.

- **16-bit Windows applications.** All your older applications—the ones you own right now—are 16-bit applications, unless you bought them for use with Windows 98 or Windows NT. Windows 98 runs all these applications in one shared address space. Essentially, Windows 98 groups all these 16-bit applications into one area and treats them as if they were one task. You really won't notice any performance hit as a result, but it does make it easier for Windows 98 to recover from application errors. With it, Windows 98 can mix 16-bit and 32-bit applications on one system.

The Windows API Layer

Two Windows APIs are included with Windows 98. The first is exactly like the one supplied with Windows 3.x. It provides all the 16-bit services that the old Windows had to provide for applications. This is the API an older application will use when it runs.

The other API is the new Win32 API used by Windows NT. It provides a subset of the features that all 32-bit applications running under Windows NT can access. The 32-bit API provides about the same feature set as the 16-bit API, but it's more robust. In addition, a 32-bit application enjoys the benefits that this environment provides. Check out the earlier section "The System Files" for more details about the system files and the Windows 98 API.

Getting 16-Bit and 32-Bit Applications to Work Together

Windows 98 consists of a combination of 16-bit and 32-bit applications. All those older applications and device drivers you use now have to work within the same environment as the new 32-bit drivers and applications that Windows 98 provides. You already know how Windows takes care of separating the two by using different memory schemes. The 16-bit applications work within their own virtual machine area. It would be nice if things ended there, but they can't.

There are times when 16-bit and 32-bit applications have to talk to each other. This doesn't just apply to programs that the user uses to perform work, but to device drivers and other types of Windows applications as well. Most Windows applications use a memory structure called the *stack* to transfer information from one application to another. Think of the stack as a database of variables. Each record in this database is a fixed length so every application knows how to grab information from it. Here's where the problems start. The stack for 32-bit applications is 32 bits wide. That makes sense. It makes equal sense that the stack for 16-bit applications should be 16 bits wide. See the problem?

Of course, the problems are only beginning. Remember that 16-bit applications use a segmented address space. An address consists of a selector and an offset. A 16-bit application combines these two pieces to form a complete address. On the other hand, 32-bit applications use a flat address space. They wouldn't know what to do with a selector if you gave them one. All they want is the actual address within the total realm of available memory. So how do you send the address of a string from a 16-bit to a 32-bit application?

By now you're probably wondering how Windows keeps 16-bit and 32-bit applications working together. After all, there are a number of inconsistencies and incompatibilities to deal with. The stack is only the tip of the incompatibility iceberg. It's easy to envision a method of converting 16-bit data to a 32-bit format. All you really need to do is pad the front end of the variable with zeros. But how does a 32-bit application send data to a 16-bit application? If the 32-bit application just dumps a wide variable onto the stack, the 16-bit application will never know what to do with the information it receives. Clearly, the data needs to go through some type of conversion. Windows uses something called the *thunk layer* to enable 16-bit and 32-bit applications to communicate. Figure 8.10 shows the interaction of 16-bit and 32-bit applications through the thunk layer.

Figure 8.10.
The thunk layer makes it possible for 16-bit and 32-bit applications to coexist peacefully in Windows 98.

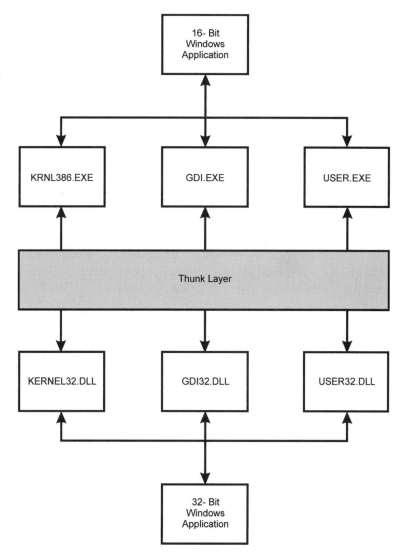

As you can see, the three components of the API layer also provide translation services in addition to the other services they perform. Each API component translates the data and addresses within its area of expertise. For example, the two GDI components translate all graphics data between 16-bit and 32-bit applications.

Most thunking is pretty straightforward. For example, Windows simply moves register data to the appropriate register. The thunk layer builds a new stack to meet the needs of the application receiving it. Address translation takes a little more work. In addition, address translation is very expensive, time-wise. Every time Windows has to translate an address, it must perform several selector loads. The processor has to verify every selector load, so these translations can get cumbersome. Fortunately, you, as an application programmer, won't have to worry too much about the actual thunk process. What you do need to worry about is making certain that the process actually takes place when calling a piece of code that needs it.

Windows and DLLs

Under DOS, an application must contain every component it needs in order to execute. The programmer links library support for graphics, low-level utilities, and a variety of other needs. Of course, this whole scenario is based on the fact that the application is the only thing running under DOS.

Windows is a different kind of environment. There's always more than one task running under Windows. Somewhere along the way, someone figured out that if you have multiple applications running, there might be some duplicate code out there as well. For example, the display routines used by one application are probably the same as the display routines used by another application at some particular level. The same person probably figured out that you could reduce the overall memory requirements of a system if you enable all the applications to share these redundant pieces of code instead of loading them from scratch for each application.

The dynamic link library (DLL) is the culmination of just such an idea. There are two forms of linking under Windows (or OS/2 or UNIX, for that matter). The first link combines all the object modules required to create a unique application. That link cycle happens right after the programmer finishes compiling the code. The second link cycle happens when the user goes to load the application. This is where the DLL comes in.

Every Windows application has unresolved references to functions. Microsoft calls them *import library calls*. What these calls do is load a DLL containing the code required to satisfy that function call. If the DLL happens to be in memory when Windows calls it, Windows increments the DLL's usage level to indicate that more than one application is using the DLL. When an application stops using a DLL, Windows decrements its usage level. When the DLL's usage count goes to 0, Windows can unload it from memory. In effect, using DLLs can save quite a bit of memory when you're loading multiple applications.

So what does this have to do with the API? The Windows API starts with three files, as just described. However, these three files call other files—DLLs, to be exact. Rather than create three huge files, Microsoft chose to reduce the size of the Windows kernel by using DLLs.

This capability also makes Windows more flexible. Consider printer support. All you need to do to add printer support for a new printer is copy some files to disk. At least one of those files will be a DLL. Every printer DLL contains the same entry points (function names), so Windows doesn't need to learn anything new to support the printer. The only thing it has to do is install a new DLL. Your application performs the same task when you tell it to print. It looks at the DLLs currently installed for the system. The application doesn't have to care whether the printer is a dot matrix or a laser. All it needs to know how to do is tell the printer to print; the DLL takes care of the rest.

The Base System

Windows 98 uses the base system component to take care of any system-specific services. The "Architecture" section earlier in this chapter covered this particular component in detail. Please refer to that discussion if you want to know the details of the base system.

The DOS Virtual Machine

The word "virtual" is severely overused in the Windows environment. We have virtual memory, virtual system machines, and every other kind of virtual device you can think of. I want to make sure you understand that the DOS virtual machine is a different kind of virtual than all these other virtuals on the system. A virtual DOS machine runs in the virtual 8086 mode of the processor. All the other virtual machines in Windows run in protected mode. Virtual 8086 mode creates multiple 1M 8086 machines in protected memory. Each machine has its own copy of DOS, device drivers, I/O space, and everything else that an 8086 would have. About the only thing missing is the hardware itself, and that's why this machine is known as a virtual machine. You can't touch it, but it does exist. As far as the application is concerned, there's no difference between this machine and any real machine it could run on.

The virtual machine hasn't changed much since the days when Quarterdeck first introduced QEMM. Except for a few new features designed to enhance the performance of applications running under the Windows virtual machine, this aspect of Windows hasn't really changed much from version 3.1. However, there's one exception to this rule. Some DOS applications use DPMI-compatible extenders that enable them to run in protected mode. Under Windows 3.x, these applications would still run under the processor's virtual 8086 mode. Windows 98 improves system performance by allowing these applications to run in protected mode.

On Your Own

Spend some time looking through the SYSTEM directory on your machine. Can you identify the various operating system files discussed in this chapter? Go through the architecture overview again to make sure you fully understand it before going on to the subsystem-specific sections in the rest of the book.

Check out any Windows 95 or Windows 98 games you have. Which use DirectX and which use OpenGL? Can you see a performance difference between the two? Which games seem to be more stable? Knowing how various multimedia technologies affect you can make a big difference in how you use them in the future.

Download the appropriate hardware compatibility list file from `ftp://ftp.microsoft.com/services/whql/`. Find out which of your hardware is tested for Plug and Play compatibility and which isn't. Remember, even if the outside of the box says Plug and Play (PnP) compatible, it doesn't necessarily mean you'll get full PnP functionality.

Look for files in the `SYSTEM32` folder on your machine. There should be at least two WDM-specific files: `WDMFS.SYS` and `WMIDRV.SYS`. Any other files there belong to vendors who produce WDM-compatible drivers for their hardware. Try to figure out who the drivers belong to using the Quick View utility. Remember that WDM drivers are the same under Windows 95 and Windows NT.

9

The
Windows 98
File System

Peter Norton®

There are a lot of things that differentiate Windows 98 from operating systems that went before it. Like Windows 95, users will enjoy long filename support under Windows 98, but that's not really big news anymore.

However, there's a new feature that everyone is sure to talk about: FAT32 support. FAT32 is an upgrade of the venerable FAT16 all of us know and love. I'll discuss this new technology as the chapter progresses. In short, it reduces the cluster size of large hard disks—improving storage efficiency and also providing a small increase in speed.

Of course, every time you change the file system, you must change the utilities to manage that file system. Windows 98 comes with a wealth of new utilities that you can use to manage your hard drive. I'm sure that most disk utility vendors will be on hand with new FAT32-compatible disk utilities as well because FAT32 originally appeared in the OSR2 version of Windows 95. (This version of Windows was available only to vendors, so you couldn't buy it in the stores.)

Warning: You'll need to watch for two potential problems with your FAT32-formatting Windows 98 disk drive. Using an old DOS disk management utility with Windows 98 might mean a loss of your long filenames because these old utilities don't know how to move everything needed to support them. A loss of long filename support might seem like only an inconvenience until you realize that loss of the long filenames will also mean a loss of the Start menu and other Windows 98–specific long filenames. Windows 98 might not restart if you lose the long filenames it requires. Use the LFNBACK utility (located on the CD-ROM in the \TOOLS\APPTOOLS\LFNBACK folder) to create a backup of all your long filenames prior to using any utility you're not absolutely certain about.

You'll also need to be careful of using Windows 95–specific disk utilities with Windows 98. Many of these utilities didn't know how to work with FAT32-formatted drives. You could potentially damage the partition information using one of these old utilities and lose your data in the process. Make certain that any disk utility you use on a FAT32 drive is designed for that purpose.

This chapter takes you on a tour of the Windows 98 file system from a user perspective. We'll even take a brief look at the architecture and put on our programmer's hat for a while. The Windows 98 virtual file-allocation table (VFAT) file system might look and act like an enhanced version of the old system, but I think you'll be surprised at all the new features under the hood.

Note: From this point on, unless I specifically mention the FAT32 file system, assume all conversation about the FAT file system refers to the older FAT16 file system. The new file system presents many issues that we'll discuss in the "What Is 32-Bit VFAT?" section of this chapter. Any discussion of VFAT-specific issues refers to the FAT32 and FAT16 file systems equally.

File Structures

Right now I can boot Windows 3.x, Windows 98, Windows NT and OS/2. Each one of these operating systems support the FAT file system. The last three also support their own file systems. Of the three, only the VFAT file system used by Windows 98 looks familiar. The other two are enhanced file systems that started from scratch, because no one thought the FAT file system could ever be repaired.

So, what do you do with a system that's literally bogged down with incompatible file systems? You could take the easy way out—the way I originally took when I started working with OS/2. If you stick with the FAT file system, you'll certainly get everybody talking to each other and run into a minimum of problems.

There's only one problem with this solution: If you stick with the FAT file system, you'll have compatibility, but you'll also miss out on the special features each of the other file systems has to offer. Both the Windows NT file system (NTFS) and the high-performance file system (HPFS) offer improved reliability and a higher access speed than the old FAT file system.

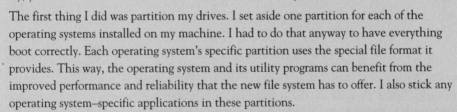

Peter's Principle: A Method of Dealing with Multiple File Systems

After a lot of thought, I finally came up with a middle-ground solution to the problem of dealing with multiple file systems on one computer. It offers the maximum in compatibility, yet lets me make the most out of what the other file systems have to offer.

The first thing I did was partition my drives. I set aside one partition for each of the operating systems installed on my machine. I had to do that anyway to have everything boot correctly. Each operating system's specific partition uses the special file format it provides. This way, the operating system and its utility programs can benefit from the improved performance and reliability that the new file system has to offer. I also stick any operating system–specific applications in these partitions.

After I figured out where each operating system would go, I installed them. Each installation required a bit of time and patience, but I got through it. It's important to test the capability to boot each operating system after you install a new one. Both Windows NT and Windows 98 like to overwrite the bootable partition marker. This means that whatever boot manager you have installed won't boot until you use a disk editor to set the active partition back to its original position.

After I installed the operating systems and tested the boot sequence, I had one large partition left. (Actually, I set the whole second drive aside.) I labeled the partition on this drive COMMON and placed all my data and common applications there. It uses the FAT file system so everyone can access it.

FAT Versus VFAT

Now that we have some preliminaries out of the way, let's look at the new VFAT file system provided with Windows 98. The main reason for a file system change to VFAT is that people weren't satisfied with the old 8.3 filenames. They wanted long filenames, and the FAT file system can't provide this feature. The VFAT file system represents Microsoft's effort to give people what they want and still maintain a level of compatibility with previous versions of DOS (and more importantly, the applications that ran under it). The following sections provide a bit of history and then a current look at the way Windows handles file access.

A Look at Windows Under DOS

Everyone who has worked with DOS and Windows 3.x knows that they have at least one thing in common: the FAT file system. That relationship between DOS and Windows 3.x also caused some problems for the user. Consider the speed issue many people bring up when you talk about using Windows. Because this older version of Windows rode on top of DOS, it used some DOS services to access the hardware. The hard disk drive falls into this category. DOS provided all of the file services that Windows 3.x used. In fact, this was about the only DOS service Windows 3.1 did use.

Because DOS provides file services, the system has to slow down every time Windows wants to access the hard drive. Every time Windows wants to access the hard drive, it must create a request in a format that DOS understands, switch over to real mode so that it can access DOS and then wait for DOS to get the job done. Meanwhile, all those applications that are supposed to do something in the background are suspended. Remember, the Intel processor can't multitask in real mode; it can do that only in protected mode. After DOS finds the bit of information Windows needs, Windows has to copy that information out of the conventional memory space into an area it can reach in protected mode. It then must switch the processor from real mode back into protected mode.

Every time Windows has to make the switch from protected mode to real mode, it becomes vulnerable to attack from a maverick application. When the processor is in real mode, the operating system can't track system activity. Because the processor won't alert the operating system when an application creates a memory fault, an application could crash the system before Windows 3.x even knows what's going on.

32-Bit Access Under Windows 3.1

Windows 3.1 provides a new feature called 32-bit access. This feature reduces the opportunity for system crashes and enhances overall system speed. Every time an application requests data from the hard drive, Windows intercepts the request to see whether it can be fulfilled using data in protected memory. This request usually asks to open a file or to read specific byte ranges of data. If Windows determines it can't fulfill the request, it switches to real mode and passes the request to the DOS interrupt 21h handler. This handler looks at the request and starts to take care of it by issuing interrupt 13h requests. You can look at interrupt 21h as the manager and interrupt 13h as the worker. Interrupt 21h receives the whole problem in one big chunk. It then breaks down the problem into small pieces that interrupt 13h can handle. As a result, each interrupt 21h call can result in many interrupt 13h calls.

Because Windows is monitoring everything, the system doesn't just stay in real mode and take care of the entire disk request at one time. Windows intercepts each interrupt 13h call that the DOS interrupt 21h handler makes and sees whether it can fulfill the request using data in protected memory. If not, Windows switches back to real mode and the call is handled by the BIOS. The BIOS performs the work required to fulfill the call and passes the information back to Windows, which passes it back to DOS, which passes it back to Windows, which finally passes it back to the application. This might seem like a lot of work just to read a few bytes of data from the disk—it is.

Windows 3.1 gets around the slow-access problem using something called FastDisk. FastDisk, a 32-bit protected-mode driver, emulates the BIOS using protected-mode code. This means Windows can eliminate two mode transitions for every interrupt 13h call as well as effectively multitask during more of the disk-access cycle. You only lose DOS processing time instead of both DOS and BIOS processing time. This improvement accounts for part of the noticeable speed-up in Windows 3.1. It also accounts for some of the improved stability people experience.

Windows 3.11 and Windows for Workgroups 3.11 rely on 32-bit file access even more. These versions of Windows use the DOS file-access features to search for files and to perform other file-specific activities. (This differentiates file access from disk access, which deals with reading and writing sections of data.) This means even fewer transitions to DOS, because the file system no longer keeps the BIOS in the picture. The result is overall improvement in system speed and reliability.

The Windows 98 Alternative to 32-Bit Access

Windows 98 gets around the entire real-mode access problem by incorporating all operating system functions into a 32-bit architecture. Microsoft named this technique the VFAT interface. Its full name is the Protected-Mode FAT File System. Using protected-mode drivers means that there's less chance that a random application will cause a system failure, because Windows 98 is never unprotected for a long enough time—it always runs in protected mode. (The only exception to this rule is if you install real-mode drivers in CONFIG.SYS to support an antiquated device such as a CD-ROM drive. Windows 98 does switch to Virtual 86 mode when accessing a device that uses a real-mode driver.) Using protected mode means that the operating system constantly monitors every event taking place on the machine. It has the final say before a particular event takes place. This new system runs totally in protected memory and reduces the chance of system crashes (due to disk-related problems) to nearly zero and greatly enhances disk-access speed.

There are several discrete components in the Windows 98 file system. Actually, Microsoft refers to these components as layers. There are 32 possible layers in the Windows 98 file system, starting at the I/O subsystem. (The current configuration doesn't use all 32 layers.) Layer 0 is closest to the I/O subsystem, whereas layer 31 is closest to the hardware. The current version of Windows 98 requires only a few of these layers (normally 12) to do the job. The other layers are placeholders for future use. Each layer provides hooks for third-party software used to support custom file systems and devices. For example, adding a network driver to the file system layer enables you to access drives on other machines. Unlike previous versions of Windows, a vendor can retrofit the Windows 98 file system to provide additional capabilities with relative ease. Each of the following components performs a different task:

- **Installable File System (IFS) Manager.** This is the highest layer in the file system. The IFS is a VxD that provides the interface to applications. It doesn't matter whether the application uses the Interrupt 21h interface or either the 16- or 32-bit Windows interface, this is the component that receives application requests. It is the responsibility of the IFS to transfer control to the appropriate file system driver (FSD).

- **File System Driver (FSD) layer.** The most common file system driver layer component is the VFAT FSD. This is the VxD that takes care of all local hard drive requests. It provides the long filename support and protected-mode stability that makes Windows 98 better than its predecessors. Your machine might have several other FSDs, depending on the type of equipment you've installed. For example, Windows 98 installs a network file system handler if you install any form of a LAN. All of the FSDs talk with the IFS manager and send requests to the layers that directly communicate with the hardware.

- **I/O Subsystem (IOS) layer.** This is the highest level of the block device layer. A block device is any device that sends information in blocks. A hard drive usually uses some multiple of 512 bytes as its block size but other devices might use a different block size. Network devices, tape drives, and CD-ROM drives all fall into the block device category. The IOS provides general device services to the FSDs. For example, it routes requests from the FSDs to various device-specific drivers. It also sends status information from the device-specific drivers to the FSDs.

- **Volume Tracking Driver (VTD) layer.** Windows 98 might or might not install this driver. It handles any removable devices attached to your system. For example, if you have a floppy or CD-ROM drive, Windows 98 will install this component. On the other hand, if you use a diskless workstation or rely on local and network hard drives alone, Windows 98 won't need to install this component. The VTD performs one—and only one—basic function. It monitors the status of all removable media drives and reports any change in media. This is the component that will complain if you remove a floppy prematurely (usually in the middle of a write).

- **Type-Specific Driver (TSD) layer.** Every type of device needs a driver that understands its peculiar needs. For example, the hard disk driver wouldn't understand the needs of a floppy drive very well. This layer deals with logical device types rather than specific devices. For example, one TSD handles all the hard drives on your system, another TSD handles all the floppy drives, while a third TSD handles all network drives.

- **Vendor-Supplied Driver (VSD) layer.** This is where a vendor installs support for a proprietary bus CD-ROM or a removable media device such as a floptical drive. Every specific device type needs a driver that can translate its requests for Windows. This is the layer that performs those services. The VSD knows things such as the number of heads a disk has or the amount of time it needs to wait for a floppy to get up to speed.

- **Port Driver (PD) layer.** The PD performs the actual task of communicating with the device through an adapter. It's the last stage before a message leaves Windows and the first stage when a message arrives from the device. The PD is usually adapter specific. For example, you would have one VSD for each hard drive and one PD for each hard drive adapter. If your system uses an IDE hard drive, Windows would load the IDE PD to talk to the IDE adapter.

- **SCSIzer.** Don't let the strange-looking name for this layer fool you. It deals with the SCSI command language. Think of the command language as the method the computer uses to tell a SCSI device to perform a task. It isn't the data the SCSI device handles; rather, it's the act the SCSI device will perform. Windows 98 has one SCSIzer for each SCSI device.

- **SCSI Manager.** Windows NT introduced something called the miniport driver. With Windows 98, you can use the Windows NT miniport binaries. However, before you can actually do this, Windows 98 must translate its commands to a format that the miniport driver can understand. The SCSI Manager performs this service.

- **Miniport Driver.** This is a device driver that provides support for a specific SCSI device. No other device uses the miniport driver. The miniport driver works with the SCSI manager to perform the same task as a PD. Both Windows NT and Windows 98 use the same miniport drivers.

- **Protected-Mode Mapper.** This layer performs a very special task. It enables you to use your DOS drivers under Windows 98. Without the support of this VxD, Windows 98 couldn't support devices that lack Windows 98 specific drivers. Essentially, the protected-mode mapper disguises a real-mode driver to look like a Windows 98 protected-mode driver.

- **Real-Mode Driver.** It's almost certain that some vendors won't supply drivers for every device they ever made and in reality, they have no reason to do so. The older device that still does the job for you is probably so far out of date, you're the only one still using it. Still, like a really comfortable pair of shoes, you hate to give that old device up. One of the goals of the Windows 98 development team was to allow you to keep that old device hanging around until you're ready to give it up. It's going to cost some system speed to keep it, but that real-mode driver will work just fine under Windows 98.

Windows 98 Updates to the I/O Subsystem (IOS)

The preceding section talked about the purpose of the IOS as part of the Windows 98 file system. Windows 98 provides some updates to the Windows 95 version of this part of the operating system and these updates are in addition to the FAT32 support that we'll talk about later. The following list provides a brief description of each feature.

- **Drive Spin-Down Support Enabled.** Windows 95 uses the power-saving features of your display adapter and monitor if they provided any. My monitor shuts down after 20 minutes because of this feature. However, even if you had a drive that would power itself down,

Windows 95 would keep it running. This new feature will power your hard disk drives down after a period of inactivity.

- **120M Floptical Support.** Just like everything else, the amount of data you can store on a floptical is on the rise. Windows 98 enables you to use 120MB flopticals natively.

- **Integrated Development Environment (IDE) Busmaster Support.** A busmaster setup can greatly improve system performance by reducing or completely eliminating the need for processor calls when servicing a hard disk drive. Obviously, this calls for some level of support by the operating system. It needs to issue calls that make use of this special disk controller feature instead of using the old calls that use the processor instead.

- **SMART Predictive Disk Failure API.** A redundant array of inexpensive disks (RAID) and other disk technologies take a reactive approach to disk failure. In other words, they help you recover after a problem has already occurred. Sometime in the future, drives will accurately predict when they're going to fail and will send that information to the operating system. By having this information, you could back up your drive and replace it before it fails.

- **Removable IDE Media Support.** Removable media is an important element in data management strategies today. For example, a floptical or SyQuest drive can provide high speed, intermediate storage for files that you don't use every day, but often enough that tape storage would prove inconvenient. Your vendor previously had to provide special support software to manage removable IDE media under Windows 98. Windows 98 corrects that oversight by providing removable IDE media support within the IOS.

VCache

The VCache VxD in Windows 98 is a 32-bit protected-mode replacement for SmartDRV. It supports local hard drives, network drives, and CD-ROM drives. VCache creates a separate cache for each type of drive. It also balances the total cache size with the memory requirements of your system. The result is a dynamically sized cache that's optimized to meet the needs of the particular kind of access you're performing most often. If you're loading a lot of data from the network, VCache increases the size of your network cache. Loading a new application from the CD-ROM drive allocates more space for the CD-ROM cache. Likewise, local drive access will change the size of that cache.

When I say that VCache does all this work, I don't mean that it does the work by itself. The CDFS (compact disk file system) that I described earlier as part of the miniport driver discussion comes into play for CD-ROM drives. Windows 98 also adds support for CD-ROM Interactive (CDI) to the CDFS support. CDFS cooperates with VCache to create a part of the drive-cache picture. Likewise, the network redirector (depending on which network you install) works with VCache. Windows 98 automatically changes the configuration of both drivers as the configuration of your system changes. For example, it won't add network redirector support on systems that don't have access to a network. The same holds true for CD-ROM drive support on non–CD-equipped systems.

> **Peter's Principle:** Real Mode and 16-Bit Windows Drivers: Just Say No
>
> Everything that VCache provides will work as I just described if you use 32-bit drivers for all your drives. However, if you use an older CD-ROM that needs a real-mode or 16-bit driver, you'll lose part of the dynamic caching that VCache provides. MSCDEX uses a static cache that VCache won't override, and it needs the cooperation of CDFS to provide support for CD-ROM drives.
>
> Likewise, if your network uses real-mode drivers, VCache can't provide network drive cache support. The network will run just as sluggishly as it did before. You won't see any of the anticipated speed boost because Windows 98 can't override those real-mode drivers. It has to have a 32-bit substitute before it can remove the old drivers.
>
> The entire Windows 98 drive system relies on the new 32-bit drivers to provide a complete package. If you replace an element with a real-mode or 16-bit Windows driver, you remove a piece of the picture. Getting the most out of VCache means your network and CD-ROM have to use 32-bit drivers. This might mean replacing an old piece of equipment.

We looked at how you could change the way that VCache looks at the CD-ROM drive in Chapter 5, "Performance Primer," when we discussed the Supplemental Drive Cache and other CD-ROM drive caches. Essentially, this is all the tuning you need to do; everything else is optimized dynamically to meet system file-access and memory requirements.

VCache also supports a feature you might not want to use. Lazy writes enable Windows 98 to write data to the cache; Windows then writes the data from the cache to your hard drive during idle time. Because writing to the cache is faster, you get a speed boost by using this feature. I keep it enabled on my system because I haven't experienced many lockups or GPFs since I installed Windows 98. However, if you fall into the select group that does experience problems, turning off lazy writes may save your database.

Here's the way to disable lazy writes. Right-click the My Computer icon and select Properties. Click the Performance page and then the File System button. Select the Troubleshooting page. This dialog box enables you to disable lazy writes for all drives by checking the Disable write behind caching for all drives option. All you need to do now is click OK twice to save your changes. Windows then tells you to reboot your machine (in most cases) to allow the change to take effect.

The positive side of this change is that all writes go directly to the drive instead of the cache. This might help resolve some database problems in which the program displays old or incorrect data on another user's display after the first user changes it. The negative aspect is that you'll lose performance by going this route, especially for network drive access.

The main reason to disable lazy writes is to avoid losing data in a system crash. If Windows 98 writes some data to the cache, and the machine freezes before Windows has a chance to write that data to disk, you'll experience data loss. It's unlikely you'll recover the data if Windows can't move it to disk. Fortunately, this is a rare event under Windows 98 (barring any major problems with drivers, DOS applications, or older 16-bit Windows applications). Many applications provide an autosave feature; you might want to set it to a shorter interval on systems that experience many problems with machine freezes.

Tip: Occasionally, Windows 98 might freeze to the point that pressing Ctrl+Alt+Delete won't allow you to regain control of the system. You usually can reduce data loss under Windows 98 if you allow the system to go idle before performing a reboot after a system freeze. Wait for all data to be written to disk before you reboot the system. When the disk-access light goes out and stays out for at least 30 seconds, you can reboot the system with a minimum of data loss.

HPFS and NTFS Compatibility

Windows 98 is not compatible with HPFS or NTFS, even though it supports one of the features of these advanced file systems—long filenames. VFAT is not a new file system—at least it's not new from the ground up. It's best to look at VFAT as a remodeled version of the FAT file system.

VFAT can't provide two important features that these other new file systems can: reliability and improved access speed. If either of these is more important to you than compatibility with old applications, you might want to look at Windows NT instead of Windows 98. The one thing Windows 98 provides is a higher level of compatibility.

OS/2 provides a higher level of throughput with HPFS. This file system is designed to eliminate one of the major flaws of the FAT file system. Every time you access a file under FAT, you must go to the beginning of the disk, look up the filename, and get the location of the first cluster of data. You then have to move the head to the data location and read the cluster before you find out whether it contains the data you need. Each access requires another trip to the directory or file allocation table (FAT). The drive head moves back and forth from one extreme to another like a pendulum. All that head movement is very time intensive and potentially could wear out the drive sooner. HPFS takes care of this problem by moving the directory and file allocation table to the middle of the drive where you can access them with much less head movement.

NTFS has the reliability part of the equation down pat. Not only does it support an enhanced file-storage system, you also can use it directly with some of the modern data safeguard techniques such as redundant array of inexpensive disks (RAID) and data mirroring. NTFS is an advanced file system for people who can't afford to lose data. Of course, fully using those data features is more expensive in drive-purchase cost than the old FAT system.

NTFS and HPFS store information more efficiently than FAT does. Table 9.1 shows how the four file systems stack up when it comes to using your drive efficiently.

Table 9.1. File system statistics comparison.

Statistic	FAT16	FAT32	HPFS	NTFS
Maximum partition size	2^{16}	2^{32}	2^{32}	2^{64}
Maximum file size	2^{16}	2^{32}	2^{24}	2^{64}
Cluster size	512 bytes+	4KB	512 bytes –4KB	512 bytes
Maximum volume size	2GB	2TB	1TB	8,589,934,592TB
Maximum file size	2GB	2TB	4GB	8,589,934,592TB

What Is 32-Bit VFAT?

FAT32—or more precisely, 32-bit VFAT—is a new file system supported by Windows 98. The first question people will ask is why Microsoft didn't simply add NTFS to Windows 98 rather than come up with yet another file system. This is a fairly easy question to answer. To begin with, Microsoft would have had to come up with many more drivers and an enhanced file system setup for Windows 98 to support NTFS. Creating FAT32 involved some changes, but they weren't nearly as extensive as NTFS would have required. At a very basic level, FAT32 is still the file allocation table method of storing data. True, it does use 32-bits instead of 16-bits, but that really isn't such a big issue when compared to the file system design as a whole. In addition, while FAT file system users do need a more efficient way to store data, NTFS is one of the differentiating factors between Windows 98 and Windows NT. The marketing department at Microsoft wouldn't have been happy if one of the reasons for buying Windows NT suddenly went away.

So why use FAT32 then? Storage efficiency is the big plus. In fact, you can boil the whole thing down to one disk parameter—cluster size. A 1GB or larger drive that uses the FAT16 file-storage system requires 32KB clusters. This means that even a 1-byte file requires 32KB of disk storage space. If you have a lot of small files on your drive, the waste of storage space begins to mount quickly. FAT32 allows a cluster size of 4KB. That's still a lot of wasted space for a 1-byte file, but a lot less than FAT16 would waste.

Okay, so what should you expect in the real world as far as space savings go? I tried out several different installations and the range of space savings was anywhere between 20 percent and 50 percent disk storage space savings all without compressing the drive. (You'll definitely see a space savings of 10 percent to 15 percent, but actual experience shows even better results in most cases.) A typical installation that included Windows 98, Microsoft Office, CorelDRAW!, and a couple of game programs went from a whopping 870M of disk storage to 650M. That's a savings of 220M on the hard drive, which is pretty significant in my book. Obviously, your results will vary depending on how many small files (4KB or less in size) you should store.

Less well known, but very important, are the reliability features of FAT32. Unlike FAT16, the root directory of a FAT32 volume can be located anywhere on the drive. Drive utility software can relocate root directory information as needed to repair drive problems. This relocatable root directory means FAT32 doesn't suffer from the old root directory limitations, such as the number of files you can store there. FAT32 can use both copies of the FAT. This means that FAT problems that used to stop your machine cold won't even appear to the user. (Even though FAT16 maintains two copies of the FAT, it only can use the default copy.) The capability to use more than one FAT enables dynamic partition resizing. Another feature is that FAT32 keeps a copy of critical drive structures in the boot record. Unlike FAT16, there aren't any single point-of-failure errors that can kill your hard drive.

Warning: If you choose to use FAT32 on your machine, it's an all-or-nothing decision for the drive you use it on. FAT32 is incompatible with FAT16. This means that any old disk utilities (including disk compression) have to go out the door—you can't use them on a FAT32 drive.

Any software that writes directly to the disk is suspect when it comes to using FAT32. Most of us know not to use disk utilities that enable you to edit the disk directly, but this problem also could affect other kinds of utility programs. For example, many utility programs check the format of your drive before they do anything to it, just to make sure you don't lose data. One user of a FAT32 drive reported that their CD-ROM writing software wouldn't work with it installed. That's because the CD-ROM writing software checked the drive configuration before doing anything—even on the drives that it wasn't writing to. FAT32 confused the utility program. The user finally ended up reinstalling Windows 98 without FAT32 support just to get the CD-ROM drive writing software to work.

Despite the growing pains that some people will experience when using FAT32 support, there are some other file system–related benefits to look at. We talked about one of them already—CDI support. Another benefit is a little difficult to see at first, but I think you'll find it very helpful along the way. Open a Drive Properties dialog box by right-clicking the drive and selecting Properties from the context menu. Notice that instead of simply telling you that the drive is local or remote, Windows 98 now tells you what file system it's using in the Type field. In most cases, the Type field is right on the money. For example, when you open a Windows NT drive, it'll tell you that it uses NTFS. Likewise, a FAT32 drive says FAT32. The only problem is NetWare drives with long filename support enabled—they show up as HPFS drives because of the driver Novell uses to enable long filename support.

Note: A lot of applications won't report the correct size of your drive if it's 2GB or larger. The reason is pretty simple: Microsoft artificially limited drive size reported by the GetDiskFreeSpace() function to 2GB for compatibility reasons. If a programmer wants to find out the true size of large drives, he must use the GetDiskFreeSpaceEx() function. When in doubt, always check the space remaining on your drive using Explorer.

Another consideration is that some of the disk-enhancing utilities you've used in the past won't work. We've already talked about utilities you might use to repair a failure, but this class of utility performs another function. For example, Microsoft's Drive Space 3 won't work with FAT32. You must make a decision up front about the value of using disk compression on your machine. It could be that FAT32 will provide everything you need without using disk compression, but you'd better be certain before making the change.

Fortunately, one of the considerations you won't have to take into account is old software. You can boot a FAT32 machine into MS-DOS mode and use it to play games. However, you absolutely can't use a boot disk formatted using previous versions of DOS or Windows 98. You must format any boot disks with FAT32 to access a FAT32 drive on your machine. (There isn't any actual difference in the formatting process, you just have to format the disk on a machine running FAT32.) We'll discuss the process of formatting a FAT32 drive further in the "Formatting Disks" section of this chapter.

Using LNK Files

A pointer is a term familiar to everyone when talking about a directional finder. Think about LNK files in Windows 98 as a pointer to something. They enable you to create an image of any Windows 98 object somewhere else. In most cases, the object is a file or folder.

So what good are LNK files? Say that you're a manager and you need to combine a bunch of files together for a group that will eventually put a project together. A graphics illustrator has been creating drawings for the last few weeks. A second group has worked up all the figures and statistics with Lotus 1-2-3. Still another group has worked on some text and charts to go with the other elements of the project. You're ready to gather everything together for a full-fledged presentation.

The manager can now make up a project folder containing links (or pointers) to all the project files. The folder is easy to distribute to everyone who is working on the project, even if they aren't in the same building. The links (LNK files) make it easy for the person using the folder to access a single copy of the real file. No duplicates are needed. There's no chance for mislaid files, everyone can work on all the files as needed, and no one but the manager needs to know the physical location of the files. This is what a LNK file can do for you. (The only downside of using LNK files—and therefore, common data files—is that your application must be set up for file sharing.)

Of course, using LNK files can just as easily help a single user manage his or her work. In fact, we'll look at some of these methods in the "Working with Desktop Objects" section of Chapter 3, "The Windows 98 Desktop." I have found I can manage all my work as projects and not really worry about applications or the actual location of the data anymore. Let's take a look at some of the details of LNK files—a small idea with big implications.

Your Start menu folder contains a ton of LNK files. If you think that any of your applications actually appear in the Start menu, you're wrong. Only the pointers to those files appear there. If you erase a Start menu entry, you only erase a LNK file, not the application itself.

Right-click the Start menu icon on the Task Bar and select the Explore option. What you should see now is a dual-pane Explorer view of your Start menu entries. You can easily recognize the LNK files because they look like shortcuts (the icons with the arrow in the lower-left corner). Right-click any of the LNK files and you'll see the file's Properties dialog containing two tabs: General and Shortcut.

As with the General page of any file Properties dialog box, you can set the file attributes: Hidden, Archive, and Read-only. This page also tells you the short and long filename and other statistics, such as when someone last modified the file. This is all interesting information, but you'll probably bypass this page, in most cases, to get to the Shortcut page shown in Figure 9.1.

Figure 9.1.
The Shortcut page contains all the LNK file setup information.

The four major fields on this page are listed in the following bullets, along with the function of each entry. The two you'll use most often are the Target and Run fields. I never use the Start in field, but you're likely to need it in some cases.

- **Target.** This is the name of the program you want to run. Notice that this dialog box doesn't provide any way to change the settings for that file. You must change the original file instead of the link. This makes sense when you think about it, because each file could have multiple links pointing to it.

- **Start in.** Windows 98 always assumes that everything the file will need appears in its target directory. This is probably true for data files. However, you might find that some applications need to use a different "working directory" than the one they start in. The term working directory should be familiar if you've moved from Windows 3.x. It's the directory Windows tells the application to look in for data files and it's the same field you used in a PIF file to control where a program started. This field does the same thing for Windows 98.

- **Shortcut key.** I covered this topic in Chapter 3. It enables you to assign a shortcut key combination to this particular LNK file. Using a shortcut key can dramatically speed access to your favorite applications or data files. We'll see some other methods of speeding access to your data in the "Customizing Your Desktop" section of Chapter 3.

- **Run.** Windows provides three run modes for applications. You can run them in a window, minimized or maximized. I find the default setting of the window mode works for most of my applications. (In most cases, this is a normal window.) I start data files maximized for certain jobs. This is especially true of my word processing files because I like to see a full screen of them. How you set this field is determined solely by the way you work.

That's all there is to LNK files. Chapter 7, "Startup Shortcuts," gave you some usage tips for LNK (or shortcut) files. You'll want to read about the various methods you can use to create shortcuts to your data files and applications. We also visited this topic from a desktop point of view in the "Working with Desktop Objects" section of Chapter 3. The Desktop is where you can really benefit from using these productivity enhancers.

VxDs and DLLs

There are a lot of reasons why Windows uses virtual anything drivers (VxDs) and dynamic link libraries (DLLs), but you can sum it all up in two words—modular programming. Modular programming is the way to go these days. Programmers will tell you that modular programs are easier to maintain and understand. In addition, creating a Windows program is a complex undertaking and programmers need tools to finish the job quickly. A modular approach also ensures that things such as dialog boxes look the same no matter which application you use. The user's view of modular programming is this: It takes a lot of code to tell your machine how to get anything done when using a GUI, such as Windows 98. More code always translates into consuming more memory. Obviously, you want to reduce memory consumption whenever possible.

Here's how modular programming works: A program calls a DLL or a VxD to perform specific tasks. Essentially, both files contain executable code—similar to a mini-application. When Windows sees the request, it loads the program (DLL or VxD) into memory. Of course, this sounds similar to what DOS does with external files called overlays. In theory, DLLs and VxDs do act somewhat like overlays from a code use point of view, but that's where the similarity ends.

Like overlays, both file types contain entry points. Unlike overlays, any number of applications can simultaneously access the program file and use whatever parts are needed. For example, you might have noticed that the File | Open command in most applications produces the same dialog box. That dialog box is actually part of the COMMDLG.DLL file located in your SYSTEM directory. An application makes a call to the COMMDLG.DLL to display a File Open dialog box. Windows loads the DLL, looks for a specific function number, and then lets the DLL do its work. (You can always view the functions in a DLL using the Quick View utility. Just right-click the DLL and choose Quick View from the context menu.)

> **Tip:** Learning what the DLLs do for you can help when something doesn't work the way it should. For example, what would you do if the File Open dialog box suddenly stopped working? It might seem to be a very unlikely prospect, but data corruption can affect any file on your system. Knowing the File Open dialog box appears in the COMMDLG.DLL file could help you fix the system with just a few minutes of work. All you need to do is restore a good copy of this file from your backup. (We'll cover backups later in this chapter.)

What DLLs do for software, VxDs do for hardware. When part of your system needs to access a piece of hardware, it normally calls a VxD. Of course, drivers can also work with software components, but from a different perspective than DLLs. Drivers always provide some type of interface to a system component. For example, some types of memory allocation are performed with a VxD. This isn't a function most users would worry about, but one that's very important to the proper functioning of your system.

> **Tip:** If you right-click a VxD file, you'll notice that it offers no quick view option. To view the file, make a copy and give it a .DLL extension. You can now use Quick View to see the header of this file. This same technique also works with other executable file types. Unfortunately, about the only things the file header tells you is the amount of memory that the VxD requires to load and some programmer-specific information, such as the size of the stack that the VxD creates. In most cases, it isn't worth your while to look at the file heading unless you're low on memory and are looking for a peripheral to unload from your system. Unloading a peripheral device can free memory that you can use for applications. (Be sure to make a backup of any drivers that you unload using the procedures near the end of this chapter.)

Formatting Disks

Formatting floppy disks is one of those tasks that everyone must perform from time to time, such as taking out the garbage or doing the laundry—something you'd rather not do but end up doing anyway. All you need to do to start the formatting process under Windows 98 is right-click the drive you want to format from Explorer. Select the Format option and you'll see the dialog box shown in Figure 9.2. This dialog box should look somewhat familiar. It's an improved version of the same dialog box that was used in Windows 3.x. It's improved because every field is self-explanatory now so there's no guessing about what this check box or that list box might do.

Figure 9.2.
The Windows 98
Format dialog box is
an enhanced version
of the File Manager
dialog box in
Windows 3.x.

> **Tip:** Always use the Quick (erase) option to format floppies you know are good. This option formats the floppy in a little over a tenth of the time that a full format takes.

Now you need to select the options you want and click OK. Windows 98 did offer a few nice surprises. For one thing, it works very well in the background. I didn't experience a single problem with working on something else while the floppy took its time formatting. Of course, Microsoft didn't fix everything—formatting under Windows 98 is just as slow as it was under 3.x.

> **Tip:** You can double or even triple your formatting capacity by selecting network floppies to format under Windows 98. A peer-to-peer connection enables you to use the floppy on another machine if you have access. Two machines in close proximity in one office doubles the number of disks that you can format at once.

Defragmenting Your Hard Drive

Getting every ounce of performance from your system usually includes making sure you have the fastest hardware available and the best drivers. However, once you get those tasks accomplished, how do you get additional performance gains? Keeping the data ordered on your hard drive is one way to do it. Every hard drive relies on two or more heads to read the data recorded on each track. Think of the hard drive head as you would the tape head in your tape recorder—it serves the same purpose.

Moving the drive head to a specific location on the hard drive takes time. The more you move the drive head, the longer it takes to read the data from the drive. It makes sense, then, to place a file on the hard drive in such a way that you reduce drive head movement. To do that, you'd place the file on one track or at least adjacent tracks. Reducing drive head movement would help improve drive performance and optimize your machine to provide the greatest possible speed. It also extends the life of your hard drive by reducing the wear on moving parts.

Disk defragmenting is the process of getting your files organized so that you can reduce head movement. Performing this task on a weekly basis can result in some very real gains in disk access speed. The Disk Defragmenter utility in the `Accessories\System` folder on the Start Menu allows you to defragment your drive.

Understanding the Application Defragmentation Feature

Windows 98 includes a new feature that should help to increase the speed gains you get when defragmenting your drive. A normal defragmenter places all of the pieces of a file together to reduce drive head movement. However, files that work together could still be in very disparate parts of the hard drive. In other words, when you start an application, the drive head could still have to move large distances to find all the required files.

Application defragmentation is an automatic feature that helps you get rid of this final problem with drive head movement by tracking which applications you use most often. It then places the files required for this application in the same place. That way, the drive head only has to move a little when going from file to file, which results in a small improvement in drive performance.

Getting the additional speed that defragmenting your applications provides doesn't come without cost. The Disk Defragmenter utility will run a lot slower because it optimizes both your hard drive and your applications. One way to combat this problem is to optimize your hard drive at night. Another way to reduce the time required to defragment your hard drive is to disable application defragmenting. Click the Settings button in the Disk Defragmenter and you'll see the Disk Defragmenter Settings dialog (see Figure 9.3). You'll want to uncheck the first option, Rearrange program files so my programs start faster.

Figure 9.3.
*Use the Disk
Defragmenter
Settings dialog box to
set up the Disk
Defragmenter utility
and an optional
log file.*

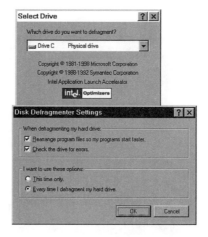

Using the Disk Defragmenter Utility

Now it's time to take a look at the Disk Defragmenter utility. You'll find it in the Accessories/
System folder of the Start Menu. The initial dialog that you'll see enables you to choose a disk to
defragment. A special option on this drop down list box enables you to select all of the hard drives
with a single click. There's also a Settings button, which will be the major emphasis of this section.

Clicking the Settings button displays the Disk Defragmenter Settings dialog in Figure 9.3. We've
already discussed the option for defragmenting applications in the "Understanding the Application
Defragmentation Feature" section of this chapter, so I won't discuss it again here.

The Check drive for errors check box is normally checked as a default. I usually check my drive
every day for errors, so I normally uncheck this box to save time during the defragmentation process. You'll need to decide whether to keep it checked based on how you perform other maintenance tasks. When in doubt, keep this box checked to prevent major hard drive damage.

The bottom set of radio buttons enable you to choose between using these settings once, or every
time you defragment your hard drive. In most cases, you'll want to set the Disk Defragmenter up
once and leave the settings as is for future maintenance.

Let's go back to the Select Drive dialog. Besides the Settings button, you'll see an OK button and an
Exit button. The Exit button will obviously close the program and return you to Windows. The OK
button starts the diagnostic process. The first thing that the Disk Defragmenter utility will do is check
the fragmentation status of your hard drive. If it finds that the hard drive doesn't really require
defragmentation, it'll display a dialog telling you the current level of fragmentation and ask if you
want to continue. In most cases, you can just exit the Disk Defragmenter utility.

After you start the Disk Defragmenter Utility, you'll see a dialog containing three buttons. The first
will allow you stop the utility, the second will allow you to simply pause it while you quickly do
something with the machine, the third will show you a defragmentation details dialog like the one
shown in Figure 9.4.

Figure 9.4.
The defragmentation details screen tells you a lot about your hard drive.

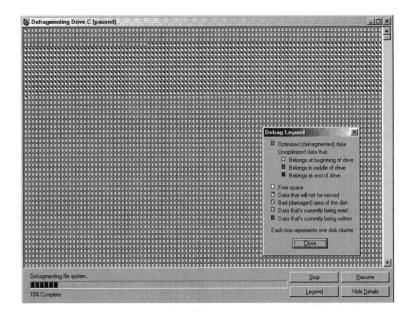

I really like this view of the hard drive defragmentation process because you can see what your hard drive looks like form a usage standpoint. Notice that Figure 9.4 includes a legend. This legend will tell you what kind of data blocks you're looking at onscreen. You can start to get a feel for areas of damage, where unmovable data is stored, and how much of the drive it consumes; you can even view the defragmentation process as the utility reads and writes data blocks.

Backup

Let's take a quick tour of the Backup utility that Microsoft has come up with for Windows 98. (As I mention in the "New Backup Features for Windows 98" section, you're going to love the extended tape drive support in this version of Windows.) The first time you start Backup, it'll create a default backup set for you that includes all the files on your drive. In most cases, you can use this backup set as a starting point to create your own custom setups. You'll also need to create an Emergency Recovery Disk. Backup will give you this opportunity before you begin the backup process. This is the same disk that you created during installation, but you always want to be sure to have the latest setup for your computer, so it's usually a good idea to at least update your Emergency Recovery Disk before you start the backup. Go ahead and start Backup if it's installed so you can take a look at this utility with me.

After you pass the initial screen, it might take Backup a few seconds to complete the hardware-detection process. Backup automatically detects your tape drive in most cases. You can always tell whether the detection was successful by the status of the Tools menu. If you see that all the tools are available, Backup successfully detected your drive. Make sure you perform the detection with a tape installed. Backup can't detect some tapes correctly if the tape isn't in place. Of course, the first thing you'll see is the Microsoft Backup dialog, which enables you to create a new backup job, back up files using an existing job, or restore files. Now you're ready to perform any of the three actions outlined in the following sections: creating a job, backing up, or restoring.

New Backup Features for Windows 98

You aren't going to find a lot of new Backup utility features in Windows 98. The version of Backup that shipped with Windows 95 was actually feature complete. However, what you will find is a whole new level of tape drive support. Instead of the paltry level of support in the previous version of Windows, this version includes support for a wide variety of drive types including: QIC-80, QIC-80 Wide, QIC-3010, QIC-3010 Wide, QIC-3020, QIC-3020 Wide, TR1, TR2, TR3, TR4, DAT (DDS1&2), DC 6000, 8mm, and DLT. Don't worry about support for a particular interface. Windows 98 supports parallel, IDE/ATAPI, and SCSI devices. As you can see, Backup is no longer destined to sit in the background—you'll be able to use it with most tape devices out on the market.

Creating a New Backup Job

One of the very first things you'll need to do when using Microsoft Backup is to create a backup job. The backup job is just a set of orders to Microsoft Backup. It helps you define how you want to backup your machine, where you want the data to go, and whether you want to use special features such as compression. There are a number of ways you can create a new backup job, but we'll look at the process for doing it from the Microsoft Backup dialog first because that's how you'll probably create your first backup job. The following procedure will take you through the steps you'll follow in creating the backup job.

> **Note:** I'll be showing you how to create a small test setup that you can use for testing your tape drive on a monthly basis. However, the steps shown here will allow you to create any kind of a backup job, not just the test setup. You'll definitely want to create this test job so that you can maintain your backup system and be assured the date you need on tape will actually be there in an emergency.

1. Choose the Create a new backup job option on the Microsoft Backup dialog.
2. Click OK. You'll see the first screen of the Backup Wizard. This dialog enables you to choose between backing up the whole computer and backing up only part of it. Normally you would choose to backup the whole computer, or at least create one backup job to perform this task. In this case, I'm creating a small test job that I can use to test the tape drive, so I'll choose the Back up selected files option.

3. Choose one of the two backup options, and then click Next. If you chose to backup all your files, you can skip to step 5.

4. At this point you'll see an Explorer type display showing a directory tree on the left side of the display and a list of files and directories in the right. Place a checkmark next to each of the directories that you want to back up. You also can choose individual files in the right pane. Notice that the Backup Wizard uses two different color check marks, one for complete selections and another for partial selections. Click Next after you've made your selections.

5. You'll see a dialog that asks what you want to backup. Whenever you change a file, Windows places a special marker on it called the *archive attribute*. When you backup your hard drive, the backup program removes the archive attribute if it actually backs the file up. Obviously, the All selected files option on this dialog tells Microsoft Backup to backup all files, whether their archive attribute is set or not. The New and changed files option allows you to backup only the files that have changed since the last backup. Because I'm creating a test backup and I want to verify that all the files I select are getting backed up, I'll choose the All selected files option.

6. Choose between the two backup options, and then click Next. The next dialog will ask you where to backup the data. You can choose a variety of locations. For example, you can use the File option to backup a small number of files to floppy. The same option enables you to back up your files to a network drive. Your tape drive will be one of the options, along with any removable media drives on your machine (such as a SyQuest drive).

7. Select a backup destination, then click Next. The next screen asks how you want to backup the drive. This dialog contains two of the more important options that you can select: File compare after the backup and file compression. You should never create a backup without comparing the files afterward. That's what the first option is all about. Performing a compare will just about double the backup time, but it's good insurance. You don't know that the data got from the hard drive to your backup tape unless you perform a compare. The second option, Compress the backup data to save space, enables you to save space on the tape. Because you can't read the data without the tape backup program, it doesn't make sense to uncheck this box. (You might save a little time by not compressing the data, but it's not much.)

8. Check one or both of the check boxes, and then click Next. You'll see the final Backup Wizard dialog which asks you to give your backup job a name.

9. Type a name for your backup job, and then click Start to start the backup process. We'll cover the backup process in the next section of the chapter, "Creating a Backup."

> **Tip:** You don't have to start the Backup Wizard from the Backup dialog that appears when you start the Backup utility. All you need to do is use the Tools | Backup Wizard command to start the Backup Wizard as needed. Likewise, the Tools | Restore Wizard command will start a Restore Wizard that takes you through the file restoration process. (You can also use the Backup Wizard and Restore Wizard buttons on the toolbar to access either wizard.)

There is another way to create a backup job. Figure 9.5 shows the main Backup utility dialog. It contains two pages: Backup and Restore. Make certain you're on the Backup page. You'll see two panes, just like you would in Explorer. The left pane contains a directory tree; the right contains the contents of the currently selected directory. The first thing you'll want to do is use the Job | New command (or click the New Backup Job button on the toolbar) to create a new backup job. To choose a whole directory for backup, you'd place a checkmark in the left pane. Likewise, to choose a specific file for backup, click the box next to it in the right pane.

Figure 9.5.
The main Backup utility window contains two selection panes similar to those used by Explorer.

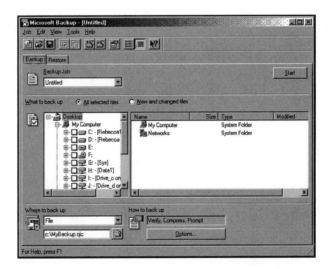

Notice the Where to back up drop-down list box at the bottom of the main window shown in Figure 9.5. This is where you select the destination for your backup. If you choose a removable or network drive, then the Backup utility will also ask for a file path.

You'll also have to define how you want the data backed up. The How to back up field on the right bottom side of the main Backup utility window shows you the current settings. If you want to change those settings, then click the Options button. You'll see a Backup Job Options dialog. Table 9.2 lists the various options and where you'll find them.

Table 9.2. Backup Job Options.

Option	Tab	Description
Compare	General	Determines whether Backup performs a compare after the print job completes. You should always choose this option.
Compression	General	Enables you to choose from three levels of compression. The first option, None, saves the most amount of backup time, but takes the most tape space. The second, Minimum, balances the amount of tape space saved with the time it takes to backup your machine. Maximum compression, the third option, saves the most amount of tape space, but at the cost of time.
Overwrite	General	This option enables you to append this backup to an existing one on tape or to overwrite the current backup with a new one. You also can tell Backup to ask which option to use when the backup starts.
Password	Password	You can choose to password protect your backup. If you choose the password option, Backup enables two blanks in which you type your password and then confirm it.
All Files	Type	Backs up all the selected files, even if they haven't changed since the last backup.
Differential	Type	Backs up all files that have changed since the last All Files backup, even if some of those files were previously backed up with another differential backup. This option takes more space on tape, but it speeds up the restore operation.
Incremental	Type	Backs up all files that have changed since the last All File or Incremental backup. This option takes less tape space because each incremental backup only includes changed files. However, restores take a lot longer when using this option.

Option	Tab	Description
Exclude	Exclude	There are times when you don't want to back up everything on your machine. For example, you probably don't want to backup the BAK files. Just click the Add button on this tab to add files to the list. Backup enables you to use wildcard characters such as `*.BAK` to exclude an entire file type.
Report	Report	The Report option consists of a set of check boxes that determines the contents of your backup report. For example, you can list which files weren't backed up so you can try to determine why Backup wouldn't access them. In most cases, you'll find a security problem or an open application that had the file locked.
Unattended	Report	This disables the display of message boxes and prompts so you can perform an unattended backup. You'll want to check this box in most cases, unless you want to watch Backup do its job.
Registry	Advanced	This option determines whether the registry gets backed up. You'll definitely want to check this box.

Now that you've got everything set up, you can save the backup job using the Job | Save command or the Save Job button on the toolbar. You'll see a Save Backup Job As dialog. Type in the name for your backup job, and then click Save. That's all there is to creating a backup job without the Backup Wizard.

Creating a Backup

After you define a backup job, starting the backup itself is almost too easy. There are two ways to go. The first method is to select the Open an existing backup job option on the Backup dialog. You'll see an Open Backup Job dialog. Choose the backup job you want to use, and then click the Open button. To complete the task, click the Start button on the main Backup window (refer to Figure 9.5).

The second method is just as easy. Use the Job | Open command (or click the Open Backup Job button on the toolbar) to display the Open Backup Job dialog. Highlight the backup job you want to perform, and then click Open. To complete the task, click the Start button on the main Backup window.

Restoring a Backup

There are three ways you can choose to restore a backup; but in most cases, you'll only choose from two of them. Both of these methods rely on using the Restore Wizard, the only difference is where you begin the process. You can choose the Restore backed up files on the Backup dialog, or you can use the Tools | Restore Wizard command (or the Restore Wizard button on the toolbar) to start the Restore Wizard from the main dialog box of the Backup utility (refer to Figure 9.5). The following procedure shows you the basics of using the Restore Wizard.

1. Choose an option in the Restore From field. Normally you'll select a tape drive, but you could also choose a floppy disk, network drive, or removable media drive.

2. Click Next. Backup will display a Select Backup Sets dialog, which allows you to choose from one or more backup sets on a particular drive. The backup set always includes the time and date that the backup was made.

3. Choose a backup set and then click OK. The Restore Wizard displays a two-pane Explorer-style dialog. The pane on the left contains a directory tree. The directory tree will only contain a list of directories that appear on the backup, not an entire list of directories on your drive. Likewise, the right pane contains a list of folders and files that actually appear on the backup media.

4. Select the files that you want to restore by checking the box next to complete directories displayed in the left pane or individual items displayed in the right pane. You can choose to restore all of the files on a particular drive by checking the box next to that drive.

5. Click Next. The next dialog will ask where you want to restore the files. You can choose the original location or an alternate location. If you choose the Alternate Location option, then Backup will display a second edit box that you can use to enter an alternate location. The Browse button next to this edit box enables you to browse the current machine or network for an alternate location using a standard browse dialog.

6. Choose a restore destination and then click Next. You'll see a dialog that asks how you want to restore the files. The first option tells Backup not to replace any existing files. This is usually the safest option to choose, but definitely won't work in many cases. The second option tells Backup to replace the files on disk only if they're older than the ones on tape. This is the option to use when you're recovering from a disk failure because it ensures that any service packs or updates you installed get back on the disk. The third option always replaces the file on disk with the file on tape. This is a fairly dangerous option to use except in one situation. You'll need this option if a file on disk gets corrupted and you need to replace it with one on tape.

7. Click one of the three radio buttons and then click Start. At this point, Backup begins the restoration process. When it completes, you should see a Restore Progress dialog like the one shown in Figure 9.6. This dialog tells you that the restoration process is complete and that it was successful. Make sure you review the report if there are any restore errors.

Figure 9.6.

The Restore Progress dialog should not report any errors when you complete the restoration process.

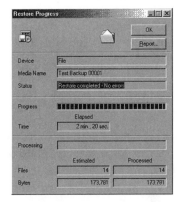

Note: Because I always back up the Windows Registry as part of the backup process, I always get a message dialog asking if I want to restore it during the restoration process. Click No on this dialog unless there really is something wrong with the Windows Registry. Otherwise, you could find yourself with a machine that won't boot or contains old setup information.

You also can go the manual route if you really want to. However, given the completeness of the Restore Wizard, I really don't know why anyone would want to go this route. Essentially you follow the same process as you would with the Restore Wizard. Backup automatically looks at your default restore source when you click the Restore tab on the main Backup window (refer to Figure 9.5). After Backup has read the catalog on the restore media, you'll choose a backup set from the Select Backup Sets dialog. Selecting Files to restore uses the same two-pane approach that I've previously discussed. If you want to use something other than the default restore options, you'll click the Options button on the main Backup window. Finally, you'll click the Start button to start the restore process.

Testing and Maintaining the Backup System

After you select the hardware and software that you intend to use to back up your system, it's important to test and maintain it. Testing ensures that the data you back up today will work when an emergency arises. Maintenance increases the longevity of the equipment you use.

It's important to take a two-phase approach to testing your new backup system—a full test today and a maintenance test tomorrow. After the initial equipment installation, you should completely test your system to make certain it works. You need to test the hardware, software, automated procedures, macros, and anything else that might stop you from getting a good backup. Test your system in stages using the procedure in the following section, "Initial Installation." Make sure you use techniques that fully test the hardware and software combination as well as the individual components.

After you are up and running, you should continue to test your system from time to time to confirm that the software and hardware are still working. Remember, this is your life's work in data we're talking about, so even a little failure is of concern to you. Some breakdowns aren't as obvious as smoking tapes or tape drives and remain undetected by the backup software.

Let's talk about another issue that most people fail to consider—tape drive maintenance. Every drive on the market requires cleaning and physical head inspection. You can use either a cotton swab and alcohol (much like the maintenance you perform on your tape system at home) or a specially designed tape cartridge to clean the drive. In addition, the vendor manual that comes with your tape drive should include some detailed maintenance procedures. (Most don't include complete instructions, so I've included the set that I use in the following sections.)

Initial Installation

I always perform a visual check of any equipment I buy before I install it. First, if the vendor supplies a checklist or picture of the equipment, use it to make sure you have everything. It's not unheard of to have a package that doesn't contain everything you need. Perform the same check for your software. Perform a virus check on any disks and make sure you have the right licenses and that the disks aren't corrupted. Check your tape supply and make sure you have enough on hand to perform a full backup cycle. When you have all the components required to install your tape drive, it's time to do the actual work.

It's time to start a staged installation (test) of your system. Begin with a test of the base installation, then test each addition you make. The following is a list of six easy steps to a great tape-drive installation. These are generic instructions, so you'll need to make some modifications to this procedure to reflect your hardware and software setup. Make sure you follow any company-specific regulations.

1. Install the hardware using any vendor-supplied instructions. Make sure you observe the proper static safeguards by grounding yourself before you begin. In addition, attach any required cables including a grounding cable.

2. Test your initial hardware installation using vendor-supplied diagnostic software. Some drives, such as the Jumbo series from Colorado, don't provide any diagnostic software, so you could skip this step and move on to step 3. If your hardware fails the diagnostic test, check for interrupt conflicts, jumpers in the wrong place, and other configuration problems.

3. Check for hardware and software interaction. Begin by performing any software tests that the vendor supplies. For example, most backup software provides a speed test to make sure your hardware can perform at a given backup speed.

4. After you complete the vendor-specific check, perform a check of your own. Back up a directory containing nonessential data, then do a compare of the tape's contents to the drive's contents. If possible, restore your data to a different directory. Use the DOS COMPARE utility (or any other utility that performs a detailed comparison) to compare the files in the original directory to the new directory. If either of these steps fails, check the setup of your software to make sure all the settings are correct for your machine, tape drive controller, hard disk controller, and tape drive.

5. Create any required macros and setup files. Check each of these setups manually to make sure you set them up correctly. You'll want to verify that the backup software works by carefully executing the macros using simulated conditions. Resolve any problem areas by reviewing the procedures for setting up the macros and setup files in the vendor-supplied file.

6. Perform any required setups for the scheduling software. Make sure you take power failures and other contingencies into account. Check the scheduling software to make sure it triggers properly. Reset the backup workstation's system clock to see whether the software starts at the proper time. Double-check the backup by restoring a single directory on the tape to another directory or drive. Then use the DOS COMPARE utility to compare the contents of the original directory with the new directory.

Routine Maintenance

Tape drive maintenance includes cleaning, replacing filters and belts, and physical examinations. The following steps show you how to perform generic tape-drive maintenance. Make sure you have a flashlight, cotton swabs (the type used to clean tape drives), methyl or isopropyl alcohol, and any required filters.

1. Carefully open the tape-drive door using a nonconductive material. The plastic screwdrivers included with some computer-maintenance tool kits are very useful for this purpose. Use a flashlight to examine the interior of the tape drive. Penlights usually work the best.

2. You need to examine several things in the drive. Figure 9.7 provides a basic diagram of a tape drive as it would appear when you open the drive door. To obtain specific details about your drive, refer to the tape diagram in the vendor manual (if the vendor supplied one). The first thing you should look at is the black rubber wheel (the idler wheel) on one side of the drive carriage. If this looks shiny and has a brownish cast to it, you need to clean it using alcohol and a cotton swab. It might take a little time to get the wheel clean, but it's essential to do so.

Figure 9.7.

The anatomy of a tape drive, showing the parts you need to pay particular attention to.

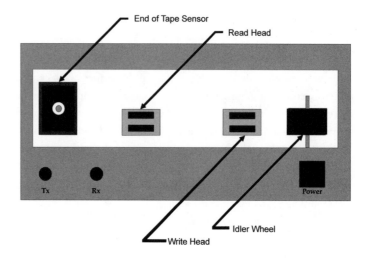

3. Check the read and write heads next (see Figure 9.7). (Some tape drives use a combination read/write head so you might see only one head.) Clean them with a fresh cotton swab and some alcohol. Make sure you don't apply a lot of pressure, otherwise you might scratch the head surface. Polish the heads with a dry cotton swab using gentle pressure. Check the heads for damage such as scratches. Both heads should appear brightly polished.

4. Clean the end of the tape sensor if your tape drive has one (see Figure 9.7). This usually looks like a square or rectangular black plastic box with a tiny round light in it. The light is actually a photo sensor. You must clean the plastic covering the photo sensor so light can get through and tell the tape drive when it reaches the end of tape. Simply moisten a cotton swab with alcohol and use a rotating motion to clean the sensor. The sensor is usually recessed into the black plastic case, so rubbing back and forth only forces dirt further into the recess.

5. Close the tape-drive door. If this is an internal tape drive, complete the cleaning sequence by opening your computer and vacuuming out any dirt inside the case. You can proceed to step 9.

6. External tape drive units often come with filters. Look at the back of the tape-drive unit to see whether it uses a filter. If there's a filter, carefully remove the old one. The filter usually is held in place by a holder and some screws. Refer to the manual supplied with your tape drive for further details.

7. Replace the old filter with a new one. Some vendors might not supply replacement filters for their systems. If this is the case, carefully wash the filter using clear water. Don't use soap because this clogs the filter. Let the filter dry thoroughly, then replace it.

8. If the tape drive provides some form of external access, open the case and carefully vacuum the inside. Never force the case open. In most cases, the vendor manual indicates whether the case is designed for user access.

9. Now that you've fully cleaned your tape unit, place a blank tape in the drive and test it. Make sure that this is a test tape and not one of the tapes in your backup set. Format the tape if necessary.

10. Test your tape drive using the diagnostic program supplied by the vendor. Follow the procedures I supplied in the "Initial Installation" section of this chapter if the tape drive doesn't work.

11. Check for hardware and software interaction. If the hardware is working, it's time to test the software. I usually begin by performing any software tests the vendor supplies.

12. After you complete the vendor-specific check, perform a check of your own. Back up a directory containing nonessential data, then do a compare of the tape's contents to the drive's contents. If possible, restore your data to a different directory. Use the DOS COMPARE utility (or any other utility that performs a detailed comparison) to compare the files in the original directory to the new directory.

You might want to take this opportunity to check your tapes. Tapes become old and worn out, just like anything else in your system. You can use three quick steps to check a tape. First, look for any physical damage such as a cracked case. Second, look at how the tape is wound on the spool (also known as the tape pack). Does it appear wavy instead of smooth? Can you see individual wraps sticking above the level of the other wraps on the spool? If so, try to re-tension the tape. If re-tension doesn't give the tape a smoother appearance, the tape might contain stretched areas. Finally, remember that tape life is limited. DAT tapes last about five years whereas others last about two years. If your tape is more than five years old, consider replacing it even if it looks good.

Tape Rotation

You can rotate tapes many different ways. The technique you use depends on the requirements of your company, the value of your data, the types of applications you use, and the number of tapes you have on hand. Every tape-rotation method shares the following three procedures:

- Always store at least one tape offsite. An offsite tape has a better chance of surviving the smaller disasters in life.

- Use at least three tapes to implement what the industry calls a grandfather backup strategy. A grandfather strategy ensures that at least three generations of tape are available at all times. Using this strategy usually reduces the probability of virus infection and other forms of data loss.

- Include a plan for retiring old tapes and integrating new ones.

Tip: Tapes are cheap compared to the cost of the data they hold. Buying a few more tapes might rescue your data from disaster. Never let the cost of the tapes you buy interfere with a good backup strategy.

I usually use a three-tape strategy for small businesses. My own setup uses a six-tape strategy like the one shown in Figure 9.8. A six-tape full/incremental backup technique uses one dedicated tape for each day of the week. This reduces the probability of virus infection and other damage that can occur when you use one tape for both full and incremental backups. This is a good technique for most people who use applications in a nonshared environment. Although this method might not exactly fit your needs, it provides you with enough information to come up with a reliable rotation scheme of your own.

Figure 9.8.
This six-tape method works well for moderately complex setups.

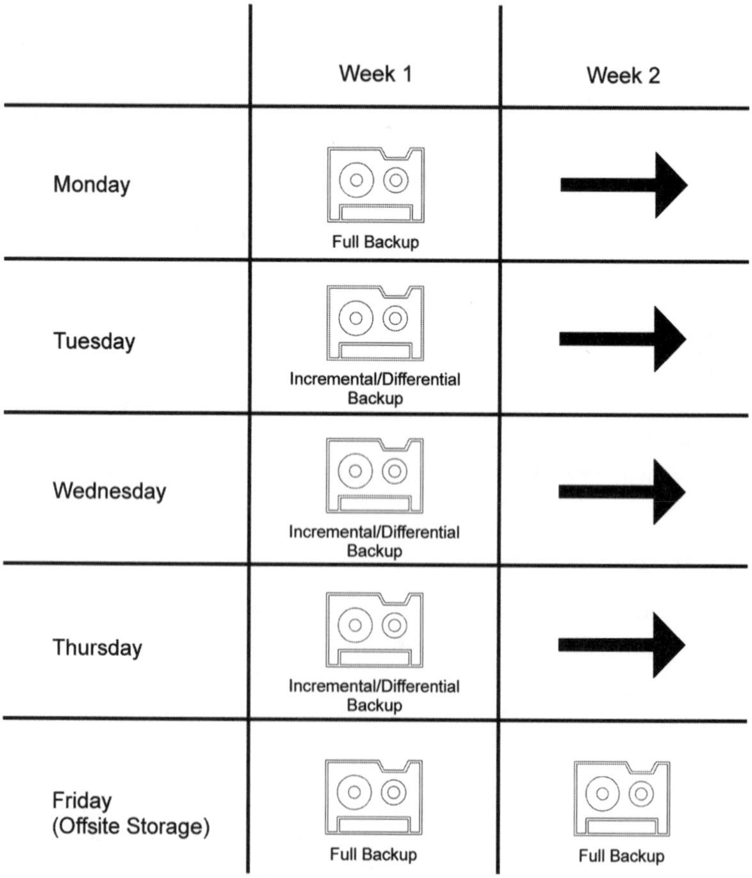

	Week 1	Week 2
Monday	Full Backup	→
Tuesday	Incremental/Differential Backup	→
Wednesday	Incremental/Differential Backup	→
Thursday	Incremental/Differential Backup	→
Friday (Offsite Storage)	Full Backup	Full Backup

The advantage to using this system is that it's more reliable than the three-tape system yet requires less maintenance time than creating full backups each day of the week. The only disadvantage of this system is that the Monday backup represents a weak link in the backup chain. If the Monday backup becomes corrupted, the incremental backups you make from Tuesday through Thursday also become worthless. You conceivably could lose four days of work using this method.

Offsite Storage

You should never consider offsite storage an option. It's a mandatory part of the backup process. Disasters strike when and where you least expect them. An unexpected electrical fire could totally wipe out your company tomorrow. Floods, earthquakes, broken pipes, and other disasters can strike at any moment. Placing your data in more than one location helps reduce the probability of tape destruction by a disaster.

Two types of offsite storage are available. The more expensive solution is to use the services of a company that specializes in providing offsite storage. These companies usually provide a fireproof vault for storage. It's unlikely that tapes stored in such a facility would be damaged in the event of an emergency. You'll want to examine the cost factor and types of service offered by the company. Some companies offer 24 hour service, but this costs significantly more than those who offer only daytime service. Although you might save money using the latter, it's unlikely you could retrieve a tape on the weekend or after working hours with this type of service. In some cases, this might prove inconvenient, but it shouldn't sway you from using these services.

The second solution is to select one or two people from management to use their homes as offsite storage sites. Make sure you obtain the approval of management to do this. Unless management really trusts this person, you could end up handing company secrets to someone who might try to sell them. When using this technique, the person stores the tape at home and brings it in when it's time to replace it onsite. Although this form of offsite storage is less secure than using a professional service, it's a lot less expensive. The downside to using this method is that the same disaster that destroys the onsite tape also could destroy the offsite tape. The offsite tapes also could be subject to theft and vandalism. Of course, one advantage of using this technique is that you have a good chance of retrieving a tape on the weekend or after hours.

Using the **LFNBACK** Utility

All kinds of utilities are out there, and they're all waiting to destroy the long filenames on your hard drive. Whenever you use a disk utility to perform some kind of task on your drive—whether it's a file recovery, a disk optimization, or a backup—that utility could destroy the long filenames that Windows 98 needs to operate correctly. You don't have to let it happen, however. Windows 98 comes with a utility called LFNBACK that can save your long filenames to a file and restore them later. You can find it in the \TOOLS\RESKIT\FILE folder of the Windows 98 installation CD-ROM.

This isn't a very fancy utility and it doesn't even sport a GUI. You need to use it from the DOS prompt without having Windows 98 loaded. I just boot into MS-DOS mode, perform it from the DOS prompt, type **exit**, and go right back into Windows 98.

Warning: Never use LFNBACK from within Windows because you don't know which files are open. If Windows has a file with a long filename open, that filename won't appear in the LFNBK.DAT file. This means you'll lose the filename if you perform a restore on the drive. Always use LFNBACK from the DOS prompt. Using MS-DOS mode is fine, but using the Windows 98 DOS prompt is probably even safer. (To go to the MS-DOS prompt, press F8 at the boot message and select that mode from the menu.)

I use LFNBACK about once a week to create a backup of the long filenames on each hard drive. It's easy to do—just type LFNBACK /B <DRIVE> at the DOS prompt. You need to do this once for each drive on your machine. The result is a file called LFNBK.DAT that contains all the long filename information for that particular drive.

Peter's Principle: LFNBACK as a Maintenance Tool

Backing up your long filenames should be a regular part of your maintenance cycle. I usually back them up right before I perform a full backup of the machine. That way, the long filename backup ends up on the tape I'm using. This double backup provides an extra measure of security when it comes to your long filenames. Remember, you could have a perfectly functional machine that won't boot because the long filenames on your drive got corrupted. Restoring them using LFNBACK could make a bad situation right again in a matter of minutes.

To restore a drive after some utility decides to eat it for lunch, follow the reverse procedure. Make sure you run LFNBACK on a drive that has the LFNBK.DAT file on it. To perform the restoration, type LFNBACK /R <DRIVE> at the DOS prompt.

Using the FAT32 Conversion Utility

I've already explained what FAT32 is all about in an earlier section of this chapter, so I won't explain it again here. The short story is that FAT32 provides a more efficient way to store data on large hard drives. So let's say that you wanted to give Windows 98 a test drive before you made it a permanent part of your life, and you didn't convert your hard drive to FAT32 during installation. Likewise, you might have simply installed Windows 98 over an existing Windows 95 installation, which means you might have been using FAT16 all along. No matter what reason you have for wanting to convert your hard drive to FAT32, the FAT32 Converter will do the job. The following procedure takes you through the conversion process.

> **Warning:** Converting your hard drive to FAT32 is a one-way process. In other words, you don't want to convert your hard drive to FAT32 and then change your mind about using Windows 98. There are third-party utilities that supposedly enable you to convert from FAT32 to FAT16, but none that I've seen so far are absolutely reliable. Obviously, nothing you get with Windows 98 can aid you in converting your hard drive back to FAT16 after you convert it to FAT32.

1. Open the FAT32 Converter utility. Click Next at the opening dialog. You'll see a dialog that provides details about the conversion process. Make sure you read it before progressing.

2. Click Next. You'll see a dialog stating that the FAT32 Converter needs to reboot your machine.

3. Click Next. You'll see a FAT32 Converter dialog that contains a single drop-down list box. This dialog enables you to choose a drive for conversion.

4. Choose one of the FAT16 drives on your machine. You must select a drive larger that 500MB. FAT32 Converter will mark drives less than 500MB as too small for the conversion process.

5. Click Next. FAT32 Converter displays a message stating that some applications aren't compatible with FAT32. It needs to perform a search of your hard drive to look for incompatible applications.

6. Click Next. FAT32 Converter searches your hard drive for incompatible applications. If it finds any, you'll see a list. You can find out details about each application before proceeding. I highly recommend that you exit FAT32 Converter at this point and remove the incompatible applications. You'll find that most of these applications will totally destroy your hard drive if you use them after the conversion process. Taking them off your drive is the only way to ensure that you won't experience any damage from someone accidentally using these applications. If your hard drive doesn't contain any potentially damaging applications, you'll see a dialog asking you to create a backup before you begin the conversion process.

7. Click the Create Backup button unless you've already created a backup. After you complete the backup process, you'll return to the FAT32 Converter utility.

8. Click Next. You'll see another warning that the FAT32 Converter utility needs to reboot your machine.

9. Click Next. Your machine will reboot. Windows 98 completes the conversion process. You'll see a success message when Windows 98 returns.

10. Click Finish to close the FAT32 Conversion utility dialog.

On Your Own

Spend some time looking at the file-system–related files in the Windows SYSTEM folder. Look especially at the exported functions for DLLs such as COMMDLG.DLL. What do these entries tell you about the DLL and its purpose?

If you have a CD-ROM drive, spend some time optimizing the VCache now that you know a little more about how it works. What size CD-ROM cache seems to use memory the most efficiently? How much speed difference do you notice between a large cache and a small cache when using applications directly from the CD-ROM drive?

Determine whether you have FAT32 installed on your machine using the various clues we've talked about in this chapter. Also make certain you know what kind of installation you're getting on a new machine. You don't want to inadvertently corrupt your hard drive using old utilities on a FAT32-formatted drive.

Try using the LFNBACK utility to backup the long filenames on your drive. Make sure you don't erase the LFNBK.DAT file; it contains all the long filename information. Keep this file handy, just in case one of your older applications removes the long filename information from your drive. Update the LFNBK.DAT file on a weekly basis to keep it current.

Write your own tape rotation plan based on the examples in this chapter. Make sure you weigh the cost of the time involved in creating the backup versus the cost of replacing lost data after a system crash. Also add times to the schedule for replacing your tapes and don't let an old tape lull you into a false sense of security.

Now that you know a little more about Backup and how to maintain your tape drive, it might be a good idea to create a backup of your hard drive. Make sure you set up a tape rotation scheme while you're at it and stick to the backup schedule. Get a hardware maintenance and tape drive testing schedule put together as well so that you can be sure you're creating a good backup. Backing up your system may seem like a lot of unnecessary work until you need that backup the first time.

Determine what effect disabling lazy writes has on your system from a performance perspective. Use the following procedure to disable it. (If the performance penalty is too great, you can use this same procedure to enable lazy writes again later.)

1. Right-click the My Computer icon and select Properties.
2. Select the Performance page, then click the File System button.
3. Select the Troubleshooting page. Click the Disable write behind caching for all drives option.
4. Click OK twice to save your changes. In most cases, Windows tells you to reboot your machine for the change to take effect.

IV

Peter Norton®

Advanced Windows 98 Usage Techniques

10

The
Windows 98
Applets

Peter Norton®

Windows 98 comes with a variety of applets—small program icons that appear in places such as the Control Panel. Most of the utility applets have already been discussed in other chapters of this book. Each utility applet helps you to maintain, troubleshoot, or otherwise improve the system. A few even provide new features to make life easier. Because most utility applets have already been covered, I won't bore you with a repetitive discussion.

A second group of applets can help you configure your computer. Some of these applets also were covered in previous chapters, but they haven't been combined in an overview format. This chapter discusses the mundane applets you'll only use from time to time. Most of these applets are a one-shot deal.

This chapter provides a few ideas that could expand the uses for this underused resource. For example, did you know that several of these applets provide full-fledged troubleshooting modules? Few people do, because they don't really take the time to see what's available in this resource.

Configuring Windows 98 Applets

This book has yet to discuss the process of installing and removing applets on your system. As part of the installation process, you must always configure an applet before you use it. When you install Dial-Up Networking, for example, Windows 98 asks you for information about your computer setup. You can't network without a telephone number, so it makes sense that Windows 98 asks for this information before it completes the installation.

Tip: Every applet in the Control Panel has a corresponding file with a `.cpl` extension in the SYSTEM folder. At times, it might look like a particular applet has disappeared. In most cases, however, the CPL file became corrupted or was deleted. Any CPL files that the administrator doesn't want the user to access can be moved to another directory. (No CPL file means the user can't access that particular applet.) You can double-click most CPL files to open them. This enables you to determine the exact identity of any CPL files on your system.

The following sections outline four different methods of installing applets on your system. You're probably most familiar with standard installation (discussed in the following section) because it enables you to install or remove standard Windows 98 features. The "Special Utility Installation" section discusses how to install the extra utilities provided by Windows 98. You'll use this procedure to install the Policy Editor, for example, and other utilities the standard user probably shouldn't know about. Windows 98 also provides printer utilities that help you manage this resource better when using certain types of printers. The "Special Printer Installation" section explains how to install them. Windows 98 also provides a wealth of network management tools. Their installation procedure is covered in the "Special Network Installation" section.

Standard Installation and Removal

Standard installation starts in the Control Panel. Double-click the Add/Remove Programs applet and select the Windows Setup tab. Looking through the list of applications you can install, you'll see all the familiar utility programs Windows provides. You might notice that this list has very few network administration tools. This deficiency will be taken care of a little later.

Completing the standard installation process is easy. Check the items you want to install and click OK. The Add/Remove Programs applet takes care of the rest. Using CD-ROM installation should be fairly automated.

> **Note:** Make sure you don't accidentally uncheck an item you want to keep. The Add/ Remove Programs applet automatically uninstalls any applet you uncheck. Accidentally removing something could cause major problems, and you'll frantically be trying to figure out what went wrong with your system.

Most Windows 98 applets wait until you run them the first time to either automatically detect the required configuration information or ask you to supply it. Some, however, immediately ask for this information if they provide a system service. Installing modem support, for example, requires an immediate answer because the system never knows when it'll need that information.

Special Utility Installation

The CD-ROM contains utilities that don't appear in the Add/Remove Programs dialog box. You might already know they exist from reading the files on the CD-ROM or from exploring. It's surprising to see how many different utilities the CD-ROM contains. To check your CD-ROM, use Explorer's Find tool to look for INF files. It's usually safe to assume that INF files on the CD-ROM have something to do with an applet's installation routine.

> **Tip:** Many of these applets appear in the Windows 98 Resource Kit provided in the `\TOOLS\RESKIT\HELP` folder on your CD-ROM. To find information quickly, search for the utility name using Explorer's Find tool and use the Containing text field on the Advanced tab. Don't be surprised if the applet is not listed in the online help. Some applets are for network administrators only, so you'll need to look at the documentation provided in the applet folder instead. Using the Resource Kit and the applet documentation together should help reduce confusion about the applet's intended use.

The CD-ROM has lots of INF files, and it can be difficult to know which ones you'd like to install on your machine. Knowing that the file exists, however, provides some information. Many INF files contain notes about the application they work with. The folder containing the INF file and the application might also provide a README file.

After you decide to install an applet, you need to decide what type of installation to perform. Some applets are general-purpose utilities. Use the procedure described in the following numbered list to install them. Other applets require special installation. For example, use the "Special Printer Installation" section later in this chapter to install printer-specific applets. Likewise, use the "Special Network Installation" section for network-related applets. Using the correct installation procedure ensures that you have a usable utility when the installation is completed.

1. To perform a special utility installation, open the Control Panel and double-click the Add/Remove Programs applet. Select the Windows Setup tab.

2. Instead of choosing an applet from the list, click the Have Disk button. You should see the Install From Disk dialog box.

3. Click the Browse button and use the Open dialog box to find the applet's INF file. Double-clicking this file adds its name to the Copy manufacturer's files from: field of the Install From Disk dialog box. Click OK to complete the selection process. Windows 98 then displays a dialog box similar to the one shown in Figure 10.1.

Figure 10.1.
The Have Disk dialog box displays a list of any special applets that the INF file contains.

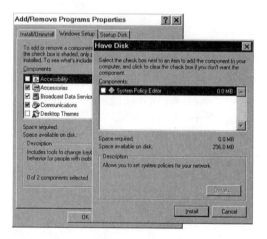

4. Use the Have Disk dialog box to select the applets you want to install. You make the selections using a check box.

Tip: If you find an INF file that doesn't contain a list of applets, cancel the installation process immediately. Some INF files on the CD-ROM don't contain applet-specific information. Fortunately, the installation won't proceed unless there are some boxes to check in the Have Disk dialog box.

5. Click the Install button to complete the installation. Windows 98 copies the required files from the CD-ROM and returns you to the Add/Remove Programs Properties dialog box. Scrolling through the list of installed components should reveal the new applets you installed. Unchecking a box next to one of these utilities will uninstall it. This process works exactly the same as it does for standard applets. Special applets, however, use a diamond-shaped icon to differentiate them from standard applets in the list.

Special Printer Installation

Windows 98 provides special printer support. You would think standard installation methods would be used to install these applets, but Microsoft decided to take a different path. The printer applet installation is similar to printer installation, with a few important differences.

1. To begin the installation process, open the Printers folder and double-click the Add Printer icon. The Add Printer Wizard displays. Click Next to go to the next screen.

2. Select Local Printer and click Next to go to Add Printer Wizard dialog box.

3. Click the Have Disk button to display the Install From Disk dialog box.

4. Click the Browse button and use the Open dialog box to find the applet's INF file. Double-clicking this file adds its name to the Copy manufacturer's files from: field of the Install From Disk dialog box. Click OK to complete the selection process. Windows 98 again displays the Add Printer Wizard dialog box.

5. Use the Add Printer Wizard dialog box to select the applets you want to install, then click Next.

6. Windows 98 will copy some files to disk and then ask some additional questions based on the type of resource you want to install. Following the prompts is not difficult and should resemble the process of adding a printer.

Special Network Installation

You CD-ROM contains some special network administration tools such as the System Policy Editor. As with the printer-specific resources, you don't use the standard installation routine to add these applets to your system. The following procedure helps you perform a special network installation.

1. Open the Control Panel and double-click the Network icon. Click the Add button, select Service, and click the Add button. You should see a Select Network Service dialog box.

2. Click the Have Disk button to display the Install From Disk dialog box.

3. Click the Browse button and use the Open dialog box to find the applet's INF file. Double-clicking a file adds its name to the Copy manufacturer's files from: field of the Install From Disk dialog box. Click OK to complete the selection process. Windows 98 then displays another Select Network Service dialog box containing the service you want to install.

4. Use the Select Network Service dialog box to select the applets you want to install.

5. Click OK. Windows 98 will copy some files to disk and then display the Network dialog box with a new entry added.

Control Panel

Few people become truly comfortable with the Control Panel. You access it to change a major hardware or software configuration item and then you leave. You don't come back to it until your system needs adjustment, so you don't visit the Control Panel on a daily basis.

Figure 10.2 shows a typical Control Panel setup. No two setups are exactly alike, however. The Control Panel usually contains a set of default icons as well as icons related to your particular system configuration.

Figure 10.2.
The Control Panel is a deep, dark secret to some people and is not very familiar to everyone else.

The following list provides an overview of the applets in the Control Panel. Some might seem familiar because they've already been discussed elsewhere in the book.

- **32bit ODBC.** Anyone who deals with database management systems understands the importance of this applet. It enables you to create new table connections and to modify old ones. You also can see which drivers your system has available.

- **Accessibility Options.** This applet enables you to change some Windows 98 features to make them easier to use.

- **Add New Hardware.** Use this applet to install new hardware on your system.

- **Add/Remove Programs.** This applet simplifies adding and removing applications in Windows 98.

- **Date/Time.** Keeping the date and time current on your machine becomes more important as you connect to more resources. Users rely on the clock to schedule automated tasks and to keep track of appointments as well as other responsibilities.

- **Desktop Themes.** This applet enables you to change the appearance of your desktop. It includes a sound scheme, wallpaper, and even some custom desktop icons for standard features such as Network Neighborhood and the Recycle Bin. You can use the Desktop Themes feature to make computing more fun and interesting.

- **Display.** This applet is used to change your display resolution and colors. It also enables you to enlarge the display fonts and to change the wallpaper on the desktop.

- **Fonts.** When I started out with PCs, the only font available was the one you got in the character ROM (the internal character set) of your printer or display adapter. Now you can quickly overwhelm your system with fonts you'll never use. The Fonts applet helps you manage your fonts by displaying them in a variety of ways and allowing you to add or delete fonts as needed.

- **Game Controllers.** Few action games would be complete without game controller support, which Windows 98 provides. This applet also includes both a calibration and a testing module.

- **Keyboard.** This applet provides you with full control of your keyboard. It installs support for other languages and provides other forms of keyboard support such as repeat rate adjustment.

- **Mail.** This applet helps you configure your online connections, even the location of your address books. It also is the configuration utility for Microsoft Exchange. This particular applet is Microsoft network–specific, but you'll find similar applets for NetWare and Banyan.

- **Modems.** This applet enables you to configure your modem settings for optimum performance under Windows 98. It also includes a diagnostic so you can troubleshoot any problems the modem might experience.

- **Mouse.** This applet helps you configure the mouse, including the double-click speed, other mouse-specific features, the actual pointers that the mouse uses, and whether Windows 98 displays mouse trails.

- **Multimedia.** This applet controls the new sound and video features supported by Windows 98. It not only controls the actual drivers and their settings, it helps you configure the interface as well.

- **Network.** This applet enables you to install new network components or to delete old ones. It's also where you set your network's password policy and determine how the network controls access your resources.

- **Passwords.** This applet provides one way to control access to the network and its resources.

- **Power Management.** You might or might not see this applet. The Power Schemes tab enables you to choose between various power-management strategies. You also can choose the length of time before your monitor turns off automatically after a period of non-use. Windows 98 also supports full hard-disk shutdown after a period of inactivity. The Advanced tab enables you to change settings such as whether the battery meter appears in the taskbar tray.

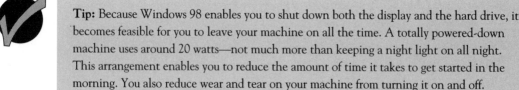

Tip: Because Windows 98 enables you to shut down both the display and the hard drive, it becomes feasible for you to leave your machine on all the time. A totally powered-down machine uses around 20 watts—not much more than keeping a night light on all night. This arrangement enables you to reduce the amount of time it takes to get started in the morning. You also reduce wear and tear on your machine from turning it on and off.

- **Printers.** This applet enables you to configure existing printers or to add new ones. It also enables you to maintain control over any print jobs the printer is processing.

- **Regional Settings.** This applet manages all the text-formatting information required to make the output of an application correct. It includes the actual time zone, and you can use this applet to change the numeric, currency, time, date, and regional settings.

- **Sounds.** This applet enables you to add a sound to almost any Windows event.

- **System.** This applet enables you to maintain your computer as a whole because it provides access to the Device Manager. It also enables you to enhance system performance, and provides suggestions to that end.

- **Telephony.** Opening this applet displays the Dialing Properties dialog box. This dialog box was discussed Chapter 1, "Opening Windows to the Internet."

Your setup might contain slightly different applets than this list, but this list should give you an idea of what common applets do. If you have additional icons, the vendor documentation should tell you what types of configuration tasks you can use them for.

Warning: Some applications insist on installing a custom applet in the Control Panel. In most cases, Windows 98 ignores any applets it doesn't need to work with the hardware or software you installed. If the old driver loads and affects system stability, call the vendor and ask about an easy way to remove the applet. In most cases, you can eliminate the problem by deleting a few lines of text from SYSTEM.INI.

The kinds of applets you can expect to see in the Control Panel is limited only by the types of applications and hardware you install. A couple examples are a digitizer pad and data-capture boards. You'll probably see special applets for certain types of network connections. Most mail packages, for example, require an entry here. Applications such as Lotus 1-2-3 might place an applet here to manage their data connections. (Most applications use ODBC now, however, so you'll see more options in the ODBC applet rather than more applets.)

Customizing Icon Displays

Some people fail to realize that the Control Panel is another form of Explorer, albeit a somewhat specialized form. You learned how to access the Control Panel from Explorer in Chapter 3, "The Windows 98 Desktop." The display even looked the same as other Explorer displays, and there was nothing strange about Explorer's capability to interact with Control Panel.

Chapter 3 highlighted the similarities between Explorer and the Control Panel. There are, however, some differences between a standard Explorer interface and the Control Panel. The most obvious difference is that you can't manipulate Control Panel objects the same way you can other objects. The only thing you can do with a Control Panel object is open it or create a shortcut.

There are also display differences. A standard Explorer display and the Control Panel provide four different methods of displaying objects. When it comes to arranging these objects, however, you've only two choices—by Name and by Description. There are so few applets to look at, most people leave them the way they are.

If you leave the Control Panel as it is, you might never see some of the features it provides. Use the View | Details command to change the way Control Panel icons are displayed. You usually see a list of files, their date of last modification, their size, and so forth. Figure 10.3 shows a completely different story. As you can see, the Control Panel displays a description of each applet instead of showing its statistics. This is a very handy feature if you ever see an applet you can't figure out.

Figure 10.3.
Descriptive informa-
tion about each applet
isn't something you'd
expect to see in a
Details view, yet here
it is.

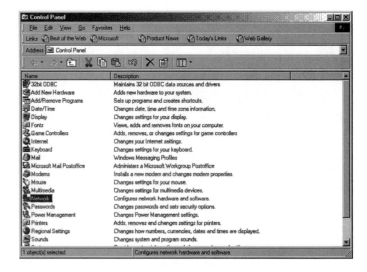

After reading the past few pages, you've probably figured out that there's no fast method to access all the applets in the Control Panel. You can right-click the desktop to change your display settings. Right-clicking the My Computer icon grabs the System applet. But what if you want to change your system sounds? You must go to the Start menu or use another means to bring up the Control Panel and then the applet.

Placing a shortcut to an applet on the desktop is one of the best ways to optimize your setup. Just think: Any time you need to change your system sounds (or any other configuration item), you could just double-click the icon on the desktop. The problem lies in how to create the shortcut. If you use the context-menu entry, Windows either ignores you or displays an error message telling you it can't create the shortcut.

To make this task easier, right-click the applet and drag it to wherever you want the shortcut to appear. When you release the mouse button, Windows displays a context menu and you can select the Create Shortcut Here option.

Tip: Don't become icon-happy. Crowding your desktop with unnecessary icons is one sure way to decrease efficiency. Instead of spending your time working, you'll spend it looking for the icon you need. Try to keep fewer than 10 icons on your desktop. Any more than that and you'll start crowding yourself out.

Accessing Control Panel from the Command Line

Accessing the Control Panel from the command line might seem like a strange idea. The actual process, however, is fairly easy. Type START CONTROL at the command prompt.

After you arrive at the Control Panel, you can do anything you normally would, then exit to DOS. The idea behind this command-line access is to promote continuous work flow. In using this new technique, you can move from one task to another without interruption. You also can use this technique for scripts you create with the Windows Scripting Host (WSH). Being able to access the Control Panel using a script would mean you could make some changes for the user automatically.

On Your Own

Open the Control Panel and check its contents against the list of standard applets in this chapter. Does your Control Panel contain additional applets? Open any additional applets to see whether you can figure out what purpose they serve. If there's a Help or About button, click it to see what kind of information it provides.

Try using the Start command to open the Control Panel from the DOS prompt. Do you notice any differences in the Control Panel's contents? Exit the Control Panel and reopen the DOS session. Try using the various switches discussed in Chapter 7, "Startup Shortcuts," to open the Control Panel. What effect do they have?

See whether there's a drive shutdown page in the Power Management applet. Set the drive shutdown time to match the one in the Shut Off Monitor field on the Screen Saver tab of the Display Properties dialog box. Make sure you also disable any screen saver that requires access to the hard drive.

11

DDE, OLE, DCOM, and ActiveX

Peter Norton®

Dynamic data exchange (DDE) and object linking and embedding (OLE) are methods for sharing data between documents. Of the two, DDE is older. There are two different versions of OLE. Windows 98 supports the newer OLE 2 standard, but that doesn't mean your applications will. The first thing you need to understand about OLE is that it's not just cut-and-paste. In most of the chapters in this book, I talk about the objects that Windows 98 uses to make life simpler for the user. Would it surprise you too much to learn that these objects are a form of OLE support?

One problem with OLE is that it's limited to documents you can access from the local machine. In addition, you have to rely on the local hardware to perform any required object processing. This brings us to the fourth entry in the title of this chapter, ActiveX. ActiveX relies on a new OLE technology called the distributed component object model (DCOM). OLE 2 uses the component object model (COM) as the basis for creating compound documents (documents that contain other objects). When you embed or link an object using OLE, COM is the underlying technology making it possible. DCOM, as the acronym implies, resides not only on the local machine but anywhere on the network. In other words, a compound document could consist of objects created in a variety of places.

Why is DCOM important? First, it's the basis for new Internet-based technologies such as the ActiveX controls used with Internet Explorer 3.0. It's also the technology that allows people to create Internet Information Server add-ons that execute only on the server. The most common use for DCOM today is on the Internet, where people want to share data over the World Wide Web. DCOM is embedded into Windows 98 itself, though it might be a while before you see it used for data sharing on your local network.

If you use them correctly, objects (not object orientations) can make your documents easier to use and maintain. At first it'll seem like there are lots of rules to follow. After you learn the rules, however, you can create complex documents in less time and with far better results. (The actual benefits you'll receive vary widely; they'll be discussed in the information-specific sections of this chapter.)

Compound Documents: The Microsoft Strategy

The following list defines some of the terms you'll encounter in this chapter (and the chapters that follow):

- **Client.** This term refers to the application that holds the linked or embedded object. If you place a spreadsheet object in a word-processed document, for example, the word processor becomes the client. The difference between client and server used to be easy to figure out. Later in this chapter you'll see that ActiveX technology has created subtle changes in the way clients appear. With the advent of Active Document, an application you see as a client might actually be just a frame for another application beneath. The idea of a container within a container isn't new, but ActiveX makes it easier to see.

- **Server.** The server is the application a client calls to manipulate an object. Embedded or linked objects are still in the native format of the application that created them. A client must call on the originating application to make any required changes to the object's content. In reality, you have two applications working together to create a cohesive document. When using OLE, it's assumed the server resides on the local machine. When you embed an Excel spreadsheet into a Word document, for example, both applications must be on your machine. When using ActiveX, however, the server need not exist on the local machine (though it does improve response time). If a programmer develops an ActiveX extension for Internet Information Server, for example, the actual processing occurs on the server, not your local machine. The server always returns data in a form the local application can accept.

- **Compound document.** This is a document that contains one or more objects. Every OLE document is considered a compound document. We take a better look at what this means a little later in this chapter.

- **Object.** An object is a piece of data you can move from one application to another in its native format. You can create objects from any data if the originating application supports OLE. This is the difference between an object and cutting-and-pasting. You can do more with an object because it is more intelligent than a simple piece of text.

- **Object menu.** We'll take another look at how to use this particular OLE menu later. Suffice it to say that this is the menu you use to change the contents of an OLE document, convert the document, or to perform any other operations that the object allows.

- **Container.** An object that holds other objects, a container is similar to the folders used by Explorer. Instead of simply holding files like a folder, however, an OLE container can hold any kind of object.

Now that you have some idea of what these OLE terms mean, you can take a look at some examples. I used Microsoft Paint and WordPad for my example so that you can follow along if you want. It isn't necessary to do so; the important thing is that you understand the process.

First, open a BMP file—Carved Stone—in the main Windows folder. Then open a copy of WordPad. There isn't anything particularly special about these two applications, but they both support OLE 2.

Use the Edit | Select All command in Paint to select the entire image, then right-click it. You should see the object menu shown in Figure 11.1. Notice that you can't drag and drop this image because Paint doesn't support that particular OLE 2 feature. If it did support drag and drop, you could simply right-click the object and drag it where you wanted it to go in WordPad. Because it doesn't, however, you'll need to take a somewhat longer route.

Figure 11.1.

This object menu
contains options that
enable you to place
the object on the
Clipboard.

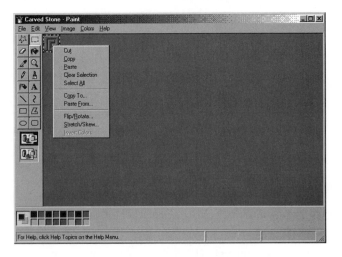

The object menu enables you to cut or copy the image. It also contains a number of other editing options. You might want to make note of the options available here so you can compare them later to the object menu in WordPad. Select the Copy option to place a copy of the object on the Clipboard.

> **Note:** You can use the Edit | Paste Special command instead of the object menu when using WordPad (and other applications that provide this feature). Some applications don't provide an object menu, so you have to use the Edit menu. This method of linking or embedding an object is discussed later in this book.

Click WordPad to bring it forward. Right-click anywhere within the window. You should see an object menu similar to the one in Figure 11.2. Notice how this menu differs from the one in Paint. Each object menu has features unique to its application. A graphics application contains menu entries to help it manipulate graphics images. A word processor needs a different set of options to manipulate text.

Select the Paste option from WordPad's object menu. You should now see a copy of the graphics image in WordPad. The first thing you should notice is the sizing handles around the image. These handles enable you to enlarge or shrink the object as necessary. For example, when I need to draw a logo, I usually draw it very large so I can get it done quickly without worrying about detail. After pasting the logo into a document, I shrink it to the size I really need it to be. As you shrink the graphic, it actually gains some amount of detail that you normally wouldn't get if you drew the image that size.

Now that the image is stored in WordPad, go ahead and close Paint. You can always reopen it if you need it later. If you right-click the graphics object, you'll see a menu similar to the WordPad object menu you saw previously. Notice the two bottom options, Bitmap Image Object and Object Properties. Highlight Bitmap Image Object to display a submenu.

Figure 11.2.
The WordPad object menu differs from the one in Paint because it performs different work.

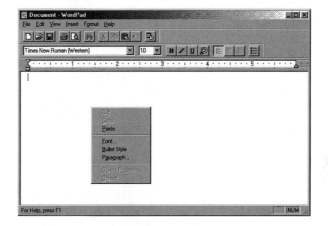

The submenu contains two options: Edit and Open. The difference between them is distinct. Select Edit if you want to perform in-place editing. The Open option opens a copy of Paint in which you can edit the image. To see what I mean, select Edit now. You should notice quite a few changes in the WordPad display, as shown in Figure 11.3. For one thing, there's a hatched box around the object. This is an OLE 2 way of telling you which object you're currently editing. Also notice that the toolbar and menus changed to match those of Paint. This is what is meant by in-place editing. The window didn't change, but the tools changed to meet the editing needs of the object.

Figure 11.3.
In-place editing is a new feature in OLE 2.

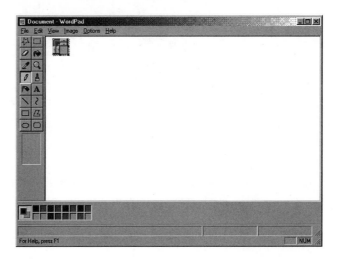

You can click anywhere outside the object to restore the original WordPad menu and toolbar. This time, select Open from the submenu. You should see a display similar to the one in Figure 11.4. This figure provides some visual cues. The most obvious is that you're editing the graphics object outside WordPad, using the originating application.

The method you use is largely dependent on personal taste, because the end result of using either method is the same. The advantage of using the in-place method is that you remain in the same window all the time. The Open method has the advantage of returning you to the native editing environment. If I chose to edit one of my logos instead of opening it, I would have to perform in-place editing on a much smaller version of my original picture. Of course, I could always resize it to its original state, but that would be as inefficient as any other method—perhaps more so. Notice also that the object is hatched over in WordPad. This is another visual cue telling you which object you're editing externally.

Figure 11.4.
The Open option produces an entirely different result than the Edit option.

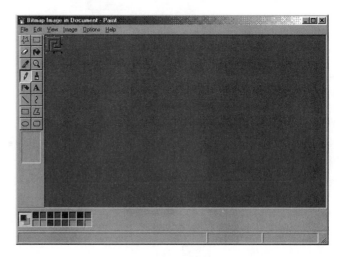

The Open method requires one extra step when you finish editing the image. You need to tell Paint to update the copy of the image still in WordPad. Use the File | Update Document command to accomplish this. This option essentially replaces the need to use Save because the update process saves the graphic. The only difference is where the graphic is saved.

Exit Paint and return to WordPad. Notice that the Exit entry on the File menu now says Return to Document. Now it's time to see what that other object menu entry contains. Right-click the graphics object and select the Object Properties option. You should see the Bitmap Image Properties dialog box shown in Figure 11.5. Clicking this displays another dialog box with a list of conversion options. In essence, this option allows you to convert the graphic object from one file type to another. This page also displays the file size and type.

Figure 11.5.
The General page of the Bitmap Image Properties dialog box provides access to the Convert dialog box.

Note: Each object type provides a unique set of pages in the object dialog box. It's important to remember that each dialog box reflects a combination of the capabilities of the server applications and the needs of the data file format. Some file formats can't support certain application features. As a result, some options might appear grayed out.

Click the View tab of the Bitmap Image Properties dialog box, as shown in Figure 11.6. The View page has several interesting entries. The first is the radio button that enables you to choose whether the image is displayed as a graphic or as an icon. You can make your machine run faster and use less memory if you select the Display as Icon option. Using an icon means Windows doesn't need to load the actual image (or the application required to support it) unless you decide to edit it. Windows suggests a default icon, but you can use the Change Icon button to select another.

Figure 11.6.
The View page of the Bitmap Image Properties dialog box enables you to change the appearance of the object.

The bottom part of this dialog box is fairly interesting, even if you can't use it at the moment. It enables you to select a precise scale to use when displaying your graphic. In this particular example, the BMP format and the application used to display it don't support the scaling option. Close WordPad for now; it isn't needed anymore. You don't have to save the image unless you want to.

Data Exchange: A Static Solution

DDE keeps popping up in Windows 98, and I think it will continue to do so for some time. Even Explorer, an application designed for Windows 98, provides DDE capabilities. In fact, every OLE application uses a little DDE to make it run. One significant problem with using DDE, however, is that it creates a static link, much like the one you get using cut-and-paste. The fact that it provides a stable macro language that you can use to open files and to perform other fancy maneuvers from the command line doesn't change much.

DDE is a messaging protocol that sends a message from one application to another asking it to do something. Originally, DDE was designed to provide the means to open another application and copy data to the Clipboard. It also could perform other chores such as printing files. A DDE macro is part DDE and part application macro language. This is another problem with using DDE. Not only do you need to learn the native language of the application you're using and DDE itself, you also have to learn the macro language for the server application. DDE didn't get the kind of reception Microsoft originally hoped it would. DDE is too hard for the average user to consider using. In fact, even some programmers find it difficult to use (unless they use it on a regular basis).

There is a reason DDE hangs around despite being difficult to learn—it's tough to create the kind of link the DDE procedure performs, without performing it manually. OLE doesn't provide all the features necessary to create every type of link you'll need, and it certainly doesn't enable you to create those links as part of a macro or program. OLE automation has changed that fact, but it's not in wide usage.

Linking Versus Embedding

We saw the object part of Object Linking and Embedding earlier. There was no doubt that what we were working with was an object, not merely a cut-and-paste example of the graphic. Now it's time to take a look at the linking and embedding part of the picture.

When you link a document, you create a pointer to that file on disk. Think of a link as a road sign pointing to your house. As long as you don't move the house, everyone will be able to find it because the road sign points them there. But what happens if you move the house? The sign will still point to where it thinks your house is. Anyone who follows the sign, however, will find nothing but an empty foundation.

The same principle is true for links in compound documents. The link works as long as you don't move the source document. The second you move the document, you break the links. You can re-establish the links, but it's a waste of time compared to not moving the file in the first place.

OLE 1 had a significant problem in this regard because it noted the location of the linked file in precise terms. It would be the same as using your complete address to tell someone how to get to your house. Again, if you moved, the address information would do no good. OLE 2 takes a different approach. Instead of using a precise location, it uses a relative direction. For example, what if you told your friends that you lived two blocks south of Joe? As long as you and Joe always lived two blocks apart, people would be able to find your house. (They would, however, need to know the location of Joe's house.)

Embedding is a different process than linking. Instead of creating a pointer to your data, embedding actually places the data object within the compound document. Wherever the compound document goes, the data will follow. This sounds like a great fix for problems with linking. Embedding, however, has several disadvantages. First, it is very difficult to update multiple compound documents at once. Suppose, for example, your company decides to change logos, and management wants all letters updated to reflect this change. If you had linked the logo file to the letters, the change would be simple. You would need to change just one file. Anyone who opened a letter after that would see the new logo. With embedding, however, you'd have to change each document on an individual basis.

You'll also use a lot more disk space to store an embedded file. A link takes only a few bytes to create a pointer. An embedded object is complete. If the object is 4KB, your compound document will grow by 4KB to accommodate it. Unfortunately, you won't get off that easily. In addition to the size of the object, some "housekeeping" data is included as well. The server needs this information to help you maintain the object.

Now that you know the difference between linking and embedding, let's take a look at how you would implement them. Begin by opening a copy of WordPad. We're going to explore another route you can take to link and embed objects in your documents. Use the Insert | Object command to display the dialog box shown in Figure 11.7. Notice that you can go two routes at this point. You can insert either a new object or an existing one.

Figure 11.7.
Use the Insert Object dialog box to embed or link a new or existing object into your document.

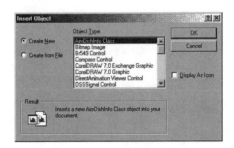

Click the Create from File radio button. The dialog box changes to the one shown in Figure 11.8. This enables you to embed or link an existing file. Click the Browse button and find any BMP file you want. Double-click to select it. Select the Link check box. If you don't check this box, Windows automatically embeds the object instead of linking it. Note the Display As Icon check box in this figure. Clicking this option displays the object as an icon rather than as a full image. Displaying the image as an icon significantly increases performance.

Figure 11.8.
The Insert Object
dialog box enables
you to embed or link
an existing file into
your document.

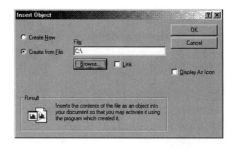

Click OK to place a link to the object in the current document. A quick glance at this object doesn't show anything different from the last time you created a compound document. When you right-click the object, however, you'll notice the menu entries are slightly different, especially when you try to edit the file. Instead of the in-place editing you could do after embedding the object, linking always opens the server application. You must edit the object in a separate window when using linked objects. If you dislike starting the other application, you might want to use embedded rather than linked objects.

Clients and Servers

Every application that supports OLE provides one or more services. You might have noticed in the preceding examples that I always use Paint as the server and WordPad as the client. The reason is simple: Paint can't function as a client; it offers itself only as an OLE server.

This distinction is important because it affects the way you use an application. More than that, limitations in OLE support limit an application's value for creating a finished product. Consider what would happen if you tried to use a graphics program to create a poster consisting of a chart, some text, and a few graphics, but it didn't support OLE as a client. Would you settle for cut-and-paste if you needed to modify the chart frequently? If Paint supported OLE as a client, you could create a chart for your poster in one application, the text in another, and the graphics in a third. You then could link them together within Paint. The lack of client support, however, means you have to copy the text to the Clipboard. When you paste it into Paint, the text becomes a graphics element, part of the Paint image. The text isn't an OLE object you can easily manipulate later using a word processor; it's a graphics element you have to erase and redo from scratch. This makes changes as small as using a different type style or font size more difficult than they need to be.

Any application that serves as a central location for all the objects in a project must support OLE. In most cases, you should use a word processor or presentation graphics program for this purpose. These provide the greatest amount of flexibility when it comes to formatting your data. Charts and graphs might need the services of a graphics program. Unfortunately, most low-end packages won't work as clients, so you'll need to invest in a high-end package such as CorelDRAW!. You'll definitely want a package of this sort to provide both client and server capabilities because you'll need to use both.

You can do quick-and-dirty edits with low-end packages. They usually have just enough features to get the job done and don't waste a lot of precious memory. Programs of this sort usually support OLE as a server but not as a client. No one would want the output from these programs; it doesn't look professional. Microsoft Paint and other low-end graphics packages fall into this category. You also might see some note-takers here, too. In some cases, all you need is the text. A note-taker works fine for this purpose.

Finally, you'll never use some packages as servers because they just don't generate enough data on their own to make it worthwhile to use them in that capacity. Some presentation graphics programs fall into this category. Because their output looks nice, you can use them as OLE clients without worrying about their server capabilities.

Differences Between OLE 1 and OLE 2

Microsoft introduced OLE 1 as part of Windows 3.x. It provided a basic set of linking and embedding features that users soon outgrew. One of the biggest problems was the huge amount of memory that OLE required to create more than one or two links with other applications. Lack of speed also was a major concern.

OLE 2 not only remedies these problems, it also provides more functionality. Unfortunately, both client and server applications have to support OLE 2 for you to benefit from these new features. The following list explains the improvements Microsoft made in OLE 2. Some are programmer-specific, but everyone benefits when a programmer's life is made easier.

- **Visual editing.** One of the problems with OLE 1 was that the user's train of thought got disrupted every time he needed to make a change to an object because the object had to load in the originating application's window for editing. OLE 2 allows visual (in-place) editing. Instead of opening a new window, the host merely overlays its toolbar, menu structure, and controls over those of the client.

- **Nested objects.** OLE 1 enabled you to place one object at a time in the container document. An object couldn't become a container; all objects existed as a single layer within the container. OLE 2 treats every potential container as just that—a container. It doesn't matter how many containers you place inside a container or how many ways you stack them.

- **Drag and drop.** You used to have to cut or copy an object in the server application, then place it in the client using the Paste Special command. This option still works. OLE 2, however, provides a new method of creating links to other documents. You can simply grab the object and move it wherever you want.

- **Storage-independent links.** OLE 2 enables you to create links to other documents, even if they aren't physically located on the local drive.

- **Adaptable links.** With OLE 1, if you moved any of the files required to create a compound document, all the links were destroyed and you had to re-create them. OLE 2 stores only enough path information to maintain the link. If you create links between two files in the same directory, you can move these two files anywhere on the drive—OLE 2 can maintain the link. The only criterion for maintaining a link under OLE 2 is that the relative path remain the same.

- **OLE automation.** OLE automation is part of Visual Basic for Applications (VBA). VBA defines a standard interface for talking with the server application. This enables the client application to send commands to the server that will change the contents of an object indirectly. OLE automation is a direct descendent of the DDE macro language that many applications still use. The big difference, from the user's perspective, is that DDE macros are difficult to write and are prone to error. VBA is the native macro language of the application and is consistent across platforms.

- **Version management.** OLE 2 can store the application name and version number as part of the link. If an application developer implements this feature correctly, a server (or client, for that matter) will detect an old version of a file and ask whether you want to update it. This means you'll never have an old file sitting around waiting to make life difficult.

- **Object conversion.** Object conversion enables Excel to act as a server for a compound document containing a Lotus 1-2-3 object and vice versa. In most cases, you just need to select the Convert option from the object menu.

- **Optimized object storage.** This feature enables linked documents to stay on disk until the client needs to display them because the user is looking at that portion of the document. That way, Windows doesn't need to load every server application and data file required to support the compound document. This reduces the amount memory required to support OLE.

- **Component object model.** This is the programmer issue mentioned at the beginning of this section. Microsoft simplified the application programming interface (API) for OLE 2. An API is a set of tools programmers use to create applications. Simpler tools mean programs with fewer bugs. It also means the programmer can write at least that part of the application faster.

Application Interoperability

Getting two applications to work together might not always be as easy as it seems. You've already seen many ways two applications can differ in their implementation of OLE, and we've barely scratched the surface. For the most part, you've seen the standard ways two applications can deviate. The following list provides ideas of what to look for when you can't get your objects to work properly.

- Neither application is a server. Remember, you must have a server and a client to make OLE work.
- Data corruption has ruined one or more OLE files.
- One program provides 32-bit services and the other provides 16-bit.
- Corrupted entries in the Registry prevent the application from working correctly.
- Old entries in the Registry are confusing the application.
- Your network doesn't fully support OLE links.

This is just a sample of the types of problems you could encounter with a common setup. In addition to these problems, some vendors don't fully support either the OLE 1 or OLE 2 standard. I actually ran into one piece of software that provided some strange cross of support between the two standards (and I don't think this vendor is alone). These support problems only make the situation worse. If every application supported OLE perfectly, you could probably get past the other problems listed in this section. The combination of faulty support and less-than-adequate linking mechanisms paints a grim picture for the user. It would be easy to point a finger and say the vendor was totally at fault. Yet anyone who has tried to read the OLE standards, much less follow them, will attest to the level of difficulty involved.

Before you get the idea that all is lost with OLE, let me inject a dose of reality. I wanted you to be aware of all the problems you might find. In most cases, it's unlikely that you'll experience any problems with using OLE at all. To ensure OLE compatibility, however, it's best to stick with programs from a single company, such as Microsoft, Lotus, or Corel.

OLE Components

You'll probably see a group of files in your \SYSTEM directory that provide support for OLE. The following list provides some details about the tasks each file performs. You can use this list if you run into a problem with corruption or if you simply want to know what level of support you can expect from a certain application. The presence or absence of these files might indicate problems with your installation. If you are missing OLE files, you won't get the kind of support necessary to make your system work efficiently.

- **OLE2.DLL.** If you see this file, you know some part of the Windows installation on your machine supports the OLE 2 standard. Windows 98 always installs this file. This dynamic link library (DLL) provides some "foundation" functions. (A DLL is a special Windows program.)
- **OLECLI.DLL.** This file contains all the basic client code your application needs. Your application uses this file as a base for building its own client features.

- **OLESRV.DLL.** This file contains all the basic server code your application needs. Like the client code, this DLL won't provide everything. Your application uses it as a basis for building its own set of features.

- **OLE2CONV.DLL.** This file provides the generic routines a program needs to convert an object to the client program's native format.

- **OLE2DISP.DLL.** Every OLE client application uses this program to help it display the objects it contains.

- **OLE2NLS.DLL.** Most versions of Windows provide National Language Support (NLS). This program helps OLE keep pace with the rest of Windows in providing support for other languages.

- **OLE2.REG.** You can import this Registry file into your Registry to install OLE 2 support. In most cases, your application does this automatically, so you don't need to worry about it. The only time you need to use it is when you can't get OLE 2 to work and you discover the Registry doesn't contain the correct entries.

- **MCIOLE.DLL.** Sounds require special handling in Windows. Unlike most objects, you don't display a sound. This special DLL provides the support an application needs to handle a sound object.

- **OLE32.DLL.** A group of OLE files in the \SYSTEM directory has "32" somewhere in their names. These files provide the same services as their 16-bit counterparts to 32-bit applications.

- **MFCOLEUI.DLL.** C programmers need every bit of help they can get. They use Microsoft Foundation Classes to make their workload a little lighter. This file (and any with similar names) provides the C interface to OLE. If you see a file with "MFC" in its name, you know one of your applications uses the Microsoft Foundation Classes.

These are all the files you need for OLE 2. There are also a wealth of files required for ActiveX. Precisely which files you need for a specific activity depends on the needs of the ActiveX control itself. As a minimum, each ActiveX control requires the use of an OCX file, but there's no limit to the number of files a vendor could use. You can usually find permanent ActiveX controls in the SYSTEM folder. Your Internet browser might place some ActiveX controls on your hard drive when you visit Web pages that use those controls. The precise location depends on your browser (to some extent). Internet Explorer places these files in the OCCACHE folder (usually located within the main Windows folder), unless the Web site specifies a different location. Because Netscape Navigator doesn't support ActiveX directly (at least not as of this writing), the default location for ActiveX controls is up to the plug-in you use.

ActiveX controls are fairly easy to spot. They always have an extension of .OCX (OLE Control eXtension). This type of file contains a combination of executable code and data. So where's the OLE connection? The connection comes from the way data is managed by the control. If you think of an ActiveX control as a very specialized form of OLE client or server, you'll have a good idea how things work. A later section of this chapter, "ActiveX—An Internet Strategy," explains the controls from the user perspective.

Unlike some files on your machine, simply erasing an ActiveX control to remove it is not a good idea. ActiveX controls make their presence known to Windows by "registering" themselves. A special program in the SYSTEM folder, RegSvr32, gets called to register the control within the Registry. You can register a control that Windows loses by typing RegSvr32 <OCX name> at the command line. Likewise, if your OCCACHE folder gets too full from visiting numerous Internet sites, you can unregister an ActiveX control by typing RegSvr32 /U <OCX name> at the command line. Always unregister a control before you erase it. How do you know whether you were successful? Windows always displays a dialog box stating that you successfully unregistered the ActiveX control. RegSvr32 displays a similar dialog box when you register an ActiveX control.

Warning: Never remove ActiveX controls that appear in the SYSTEM folder (under your main Windows directory). Doing so might disable one or more of your applications. Most applications clean up any ActiveX controls they've installed when you remove the application from your machine. In addition, use the greatest care when removing ActiveX controls that appear in other folders. An ActiveX control that appears in an application directory usually belongs to that application. Fortunately, you can always assume the controls in the OCCACHE folder are safe to remove.

Networking with the Distributed Component Object Model (DCOM)

DCOM, better known as Network OLE to many people, has been a gleam in Microsoft's eye for many years. Now that you have access to DCOM, you need to know precisely what it is and what it can do for you. Let's begin with what DCOM is.

Just what DCOM is from the user perspective is all in the title. The distributed part is pretty easy to understand. Instead of working just locally, this new version of COM will work on other machines as well. The component part would be best looked at as Legos, those little blocks that you can build almost anything with. DCOM will allow programmers to take a bit of this, a bit of that, and add something else to come up with complete applications. We've already been studying the meaning of the word object. Simply put, DCOM objects work about the same as any other object in Windows. They all perform some task and have predefined rules on how you can interact with them. Finally, the term model tells you that this is a guideline for the real thing. DCOM is a specification that tells programmers how to create a specific kind of object.

What can DCOM do for you? For one thing, it'll eventually enable you to execute parts of your program on other machines. No longer will you need to worry where the parts of an application are kept. DCOM will enable the application to find the parts it needs and to execute some or all of those parts on other machines as necessary. DCOM also means someone can borrow some of the capacity of your machine from time to time as well.

> **Tip:** Curious about what objects might be lurking on your machine? Microsoft provides a special OLE/COM Object Viewer at `http://www.microsoft.com/oledev/olecom/oleview.htm`. This viewer enables you to see what's installed on your machine, including any new DCOM objects. You even can use the viewer to execute the various objects to see what they do. For the most part, though, you should leave using DCOM objects to programmers who know what they're doing.

What makes DCOM different from COM or OLE? Both COM and OLE are architectures. They define how you put something together at a very basic level. DCOM does this as well, so in this regard, it's not much different than COM. In fact, if you already know about COM, then you know just about everything about DCOM as well.

What makes DCOM different is that it also acts as a network protocol—it defines a set of rules that enables a client and a server to talk with each other. COM objects usually talk with each other through local memory. DCOM extends that over network cabling. Instead of talking through local memory at high speed, the connection might be through a modem or ISDN line. DCOM is the world view of COM.

Microsoft had to jump a few hurdles to make DCOM work properly. First, you can always depend on being able to talk with other areas of memory in your computer—that is, unless it's frozen (then you have other things to worry about). DCOM has to work reliably over a network connection that might not be there five minutes from now. This means Microsoft had to develop some methods to ensure that an object could recover gracefully from a loss of communication.

Another problem is time. Communication takes place almost instantaneously on your computer. One object can talk to another and you'll hardly notice the time it takes. Objects that talk over a network connection could take a noticeable amount of time to complete their conversation. To make this feasible, Microsoft has enabled the conversation to occur asynchronously. In other words, you can continue to work with your machine while the object-to-object conversation takes place in the background. Does this mean you won't notice the delay at all? No. If you're waiting for something to print, the conversation over network cabling is still noticeable. Asynchronous communication simply means is you can do something else while you wait.

There's another element you have to have to make DCOM work. How does another machine know what objects are installed on your machine right now? It can't know unless you publish that information in some way. This is precisely what the DCOM change does: It enables Windows 98 to publish a list of objects on your machine. This open Registry approach enables other machines to find objects on your machine and to use them as needed.

What are the potential pitfalls of DCOM? There are two big ones, though other problems might appear in the future. The first is security. It's important to keep your machine secure, even if other people are allowed to use the objects installed. The programmer who creates a DCOM object for your machine has to provide some type of security features. Unfortunately, there aren't any standard ways to do that right now, making some people leery of placing DCOM objects on machines in which security is a major concern (such as servers).

The other potential problem is network traffic. Remember that all those messages have to travel across the network cabling. If DCOM uses the same kind of communication as COM objects, the network could get very busy indeed. Fortunately, Microsoft provides some tools that make it possible to combine several requests into one, reducing network traffic as a result. The programmer designing your DCOM object has to actually use the features provided by Microsoft. The requirement to combine several calls into one isn't enforced in any way, which makes some network administrators afraid that DCOM objects could bring their network to its knees. Hopefully, standards will help ensure that programmers will make DCOM objects as efficient as possible.

ActiveX—An Internet Strategy

ActiveX has been around in one form or another for quite a while. The ActiveX technology is an extension of a technology that appeared with the first 32-bit compilers from Microsoft. Originally, programmers called ActiveX controls OLE Control eXtensions. The official name now is ActiveX—though you're likely to find the old name in more than a few places (even Microsoft's documentation).

OCXs (ActiveX controls) originally provided a component capability for products such as Visual Basic. You build an application by placing various components on a form and then setting their properties. The control doesn't actually exist within the application; it exists in a separate file. The application and the control talk to each other. A programmer monitors the communication by looking at the contents of the properties and by asking the application to react to certain events. Rather than get into bits and bytes here, let's take a look at ActiveX in action.

Figure 11.9 shows a Web page that contains ActiveX controls. In this case, a button and a set of radio buttons control its properties. Any Webmaster will tell you that standard hypertext markup language (HTML) supports only three kinds of buttons: submit, reset, and cancel. The use of ActiveX in this case enables us to define any kind of button necessary. The dialog box shows the result value of the button, which changes to reflect the kind of button you select using the radio buttons.

Figure 11.9.
ActiveX works on Web pages like it does within an application: It enables a programmer to build the page using components.

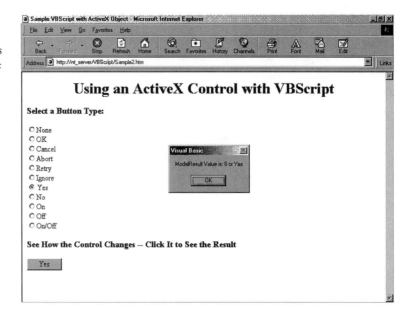

You're probably underwhelmed by a Web page containing some radio buttons and a command button. ActiveX has more to offer than components. Figure 11.10 shows another kind of ActiveX application, called Active Document. In this case, you're looking at a Word for Windows document displayed within a browser window. Unlike other kinds of Web documents, you can edit this and save the changes locally. If the Web server allows you to, you also can publish the changed document on the Web server.

Figure 11.10.
Active Document, a special form of ActiveX, enables you to interact with a link on an Internet site.

There are a lot of ways to use Active Document, but the way that I see most people using it is as a method for exchanging information without resorting to groupware. Think about the advantage of allowing four people—one in New York, another in Delhi, another in London, and still another in Tokyo—to collaborate on a document located on the company's Web server in Los Angeles (all without a single long-distance phone call). That's the beauty of using Active Document. You can create connections through the Internet that were difficult or even impossible in the past.

Still not very impressed? ActiveX is used for a variety of other technologies as well. ActiveMovie, for example, enables you to play multimedia over a Web connection. That's not spectacular until you consider that a single player located on your machine enables you to play most multimedia file types. Figure 11.11 shows an example of ActiveMovie in action.

Figure 11.11.
ActiveMovie provides the means to work with multimedia over the Internet.

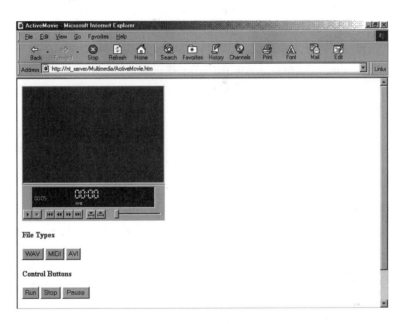

I really haven't covered everything there is to know about ActiveX, even from a user perspective. Suffice it to say that this is a vast new technology that you really need to know about. Don't think that you're limited to using Internet Explorer, either. There are several good plug-ins for Netscape Navigator that will allow you full access to everything that the Internet provides.

Tip: NCompass Labs produces a selection of plug-ins for Netscape Navigator that enable you to work with ActiveX-enabled Web pages. The first is ScriptActive, which enables you to download and use ActiveX controls. The second plug is DocActive, which enables you to work with Active Documents such as the one shown in Figure 11.10. There is only one

continues

problem with this solution—the Webmaster at the Web site you want to visit has to cooperate. ScriptActive provides a conversion tool that implements every <OBJECT> tag ActiveX normally uses as an <EMBED> tag Navigator can understand. In some cases, you'll run into an Internet site you still can't access with Navigator because it wasn't converted to work with a plug-in. You can contact NCompass at http://www.ncompasslabs.com.

On Your Own

Test the OLE capabilities of the various applications on your machine. Which ones support OLE as a client? Which ones support it as a server? Do you see any difference between the applications that support OLE 1 and OLE 2?

Use the various techniques covered in this chapter for inserting an object into a container. Which methods do you find easiest to use? Why do you think some applications support one technique and others support another technique?

Try to make an OLE link in a large document using an OLE 1 application. Make the same link using an OLE 2 application such as WordPad. Do you see a difference in the load time of the two documents? What additional features does WordPad provide that the OLE 1 application doesn't?

Open a copy of Explorer and use it to search your SYSTEM folder. Can you find all the OLE-specific files installed on your system? What do the names of the various files tell you about their purpose?

Use an ActiveX-capable Internet browser to find one or more ActiveX-enabled Web sites. Microsoft provides a gallery you can use for ideas at http://www.microsoft.com/gallery/. If you can't find one immediately, try the NCompass Labs ActiveX Showcase at http://www.ncompasslabs.com/framed/product.htm. It contains examples of the most common ActiveX technologies. Another good place to look is Stroud's CWSApps List—Windows 98/NT Apps—ActiveX Controls at http://cws.internet.com. This site features vendors that write ActiveX controls. Be sure to take the time to interact with the site and to see how these technologies work. Try to think of ways your company could use ActiveX to improve its Web site (if your company has a Web site).

12

Exploiting Your Software: DOS, 16-Bit, and 32-Bit Applications

Peter Norton®

This chapter is about optimizing your software to make it run as efficiently as possible on your computer. That means making the software do the following:

- **Produce results faster and easier.** Your software should help you work faster and more accurately. Many programs include templates and wizards to make it faster to produce the first copy of a document, in addition to variations of that document later.

- **Produce output that requires the least amount of system resources.** Ideally, software should use a minimum amount of system resources such as memory and hard disk space. As shown in Chapter 11, "DDE, OLE, DCOM, and ActiveX," there are a number of ways to embed or link an object into your document. Other chapters in this book show various aspects of other forms of optimization.

- **Produce the best results possible.** The bottom line is the results you get from your software. It doesn't matter if your software is the best, fastest, or most expensive if it doesn't get the job done. Remember, software only has to accomplish the tasks you want done—regardless of any awards, features, or positive reviews competing programs might receive. If you aren't getting the results you want, you're using the wrong software.

Tip: Optimizing your software also includes optimizing your computer and operating system. Optimizing your software doesn't do much good if you don't optimize Windows 98 as well, as described in Chapter 5, "Performance Primer."

Using the Add/Remove Programs Utility

To help you install and uninstall software quickly, Windows 98 includes the Add/Remove Programs utility. This utility enables you to add or delete Windows 95/98 applications with ease.

Note: The Windows 98 install/uninstall capabilities do not extend to non–Windows 95/98 products (such as Windows 3.x and older Windows NT products). When you purchase software, look for a logo or note on the package that says "Designed for Windows 95/98 or Windows NT." Any software with this logo has been designed to install and uninstall cleanly with the Add/Remove Program utility.

So what's involved in removing an application? Every uninstall program needs to take the following into consideration:

- **Application directory.** Removing an application and its directory isn't a problem; the problem is the application's data. Some uninstall programs leave the data in place so you can recover it later; others simply remove the entire directory and wipe out the data it contains. I prefer the first approach because it keeps me from shooting myself in the foot.

- **Windows directory.** Some applications place an INI file in the Windows directory so it's easy to find. Other applications place two or more files there. Unfortunately, not all uninstall programs remove these files; you might need to do so manually.

- **Windows system-file modification.** Windows 98 has some of the same problems as previous versions of Windows when it comes to spurious entries in WIN.INI and SYSTEM.INI. Even though Windows 98 only provides compatibility support for these files, it reads them when you boot. Some past problems will still crop up when you install 16-bit applications.

- **Windows Registry.** To keep track of all the applications stored on your hard disk, Windows 98 stores information about each program in a special database called the Registry. When you uninstall an application, the uninstall program should also remove the application's listing from the Registry.

- **SYSTEM directory.** Your SYSTEM directory contains many files, and there's no way to know which ones are used with which application. Even if an uninstall program tracks these files, it has no way of knowing how many applications use a particular file. This is especially true of DLLs, such as VBRUN300.DLL in your SYSTEM directory. When you install another application that uses this same file, the second application might not add the file because it is already present. If the uninstall program then removed VBRUN300.DLL along with the other files for the first application, the second application also would cease to work.

> **Tip:** Chapter 8, "The Windows 98 Architecture," discussed a procedure for viewing the contents of DLLs and other system files. Use this procedure to view the files you suspect an application uses; it can help you decide whether to delete them. Making a list of the DL_ and DLL files on the distribution disk also is helpful. Compare this list to the contents of the SYSTEM directory for clues on what you can remove. Be careful, however, not to remove any "common" files your SYSTEM directory might contain.

- **Common application directories.** To reduce the number of files on your hard drive, some applications place files used by more than one application in a separate directory. Such directories do reduce the load on your hard drive. You don't know which files to remove, however, if you use multiple products from the same vendor and want to remove only one product.

Removing a Windows application from your machine isn't an easy task, because a Windows application spreads files all over the place and makes entries in system files that you might need even if you remove the application. (Multiple applications might need the same entry to run.) As a result, it's not too surprising that older Windows uninstall programs normally do a partial rather than a complete job of removing old programs from your system. Fortunately, a Windows 95/98 application gives the operating system much more information about what it installs in the form of registry entries. That's why you can uninstall only Windows 95/98–specific applications with the Install/ Uninstall feature.

> **Tip:** Windows doesn't let you remove a file in use. Even if you close an application, Windows might not unload its associated DLLs right away. When you want to remove an application from your drive, shut everything down, reboot, then perform the uninstall routine with all applications closed. This ensures that the uninstall program actually can remove all the files it identifies as part of the application.

Adding an Application

The following steps explain how to use the install/uninstall program. To speed up this process, double-click SETUP.EXE on the floppy or CD that comes with the application you're installing, then skip to step 6.

1. Open the Control Panel using the Start menu or Explorer.

2. Double-click Add/Remove Programs. You should see the Add/Remove Programs Properties dialog box, as shown in Figure 12.1.

Figure 12.1.
The Install/Uninstall page of the Add/Remove Programs Properties dialog box enables you to install or uninstall Windows 95/98–specific programs.

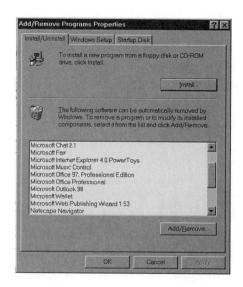

3. Click Install. You'll see the Install Program from Floppy Disk or CD-ROM dialog box. This dialog box tells you to place a floppy in one of the floppy drives or a CD-ROM in the CD-ROM drive.

4. Click Next. The Install Wizard searches drives A and B and the CD-ROM drive for SETUP.EXE. If you're installing the program from the hard drive, or if the setup program uses a different name, the wizard won't find it. You need to manually enter the value or use the Browse dialog box.

5. If the Install Wizard finds a setup program, it enters the name here for you. If not, you see a dialog box like the one in Figure 12.2. Type the name of the application you want to install or use the Browse dialog box to find it. To use the Browse dialog box, click the Browse button.

Figure 12.2.
The Run Installation Program dialog box is the last time you'll see the Install Wizard.

6. When you've completed step 5, Windows 98 launches the setup application. Follow the vendor's instructions for installing it. You don't go back to the Install Wizard after installation is complete. You might, however, want to open the Add/Remove Programs Properties dialog box to make sure the application name appears in the list of products you can remove. If the application name does not appear, the application most likely hasn't been fully tested under Windows 95/NT.

Removing an Application

Uninstalling an application is as easy as installing it with Install Wizard. The following steps show you the procedure you'll use in most cases. Remember, you might also have the option to use an application's uninstall utility to accomplish this.

1. Open the Control Panel using the Start menu or Explorer.

2. Double-click Add/Remove Programs. You should see the Add/Remove Programs Properties dialog box previously shown in Figure 12.1.

3. Select the application you want to uninstall and click Add/Remove. In most cases, the Install Wizard displays a list of everything it will remove, as shown in Figure 12.3. Note that this list includes items such as INI files.

Figure 12.3.
*You always get to see
which files Windows
98 will remove before
it removes them.*

4. Click Yes to continue. A warning box might appear, stating that you are about to uninstall the application. If this happens, click Yes one last time.

5. Windows 98 attempts to remove all the application's components. If successful, it displays a success message. Otherwise, it displays an error message listing the components you need to uninstall manually. You can use the contents of this dialog box to complete the uninstall process.

6. Click OK to exit the Install Wizard.

Optimizing Windows Applications

After a new application is installed, you might want to optimize it for the application's speed and memory requirements.

Installation Options

The decisions you make when installing an application can affect the way the application performs. The following list discusses some of the decisions that come up during installation:

- **Hard disk space.** If hard disk space is at a premium, you might need to limit the number of files you install. Many applications, for example, come with a tutorial or sample files. If you don't need these files, don't install them; save your hard disk for more important files.

- **Uninstall capability.** Many applications now provide a partial uninstall capability. This enables you to keep only features you absolutely need.

- **Memory.** Many applications ask what types of filters and other "utility" elements you want to install. It might seem like a good idea to select them all because you never know when you might need them. From a memory standpoint, however, this decision could be fatal. Some applications load these fancy utilities and filters each time you start the application. Each filter and add-on can cost you memory that could be used for another purpose.

- **Interapplication communication.** If you install a suite of products (such as Microsoft Office) instead of separate applications, you're more likely to have seamless interapplication communication. Unless you have a good reason to install applications from different publishers, you should probably stick with "one-stop shopping" to fulfill most of your application needs.

- **Other support options.** Some applications provide features that don't relate directly to how a product works but to how it reacts in a given situation. I just installed a new utility that provides a thumbnail-sketch of several files on my system. One of the installation options was to add that utility to my Startup folder. I had the memory required, so I added it. It seems like a straightforward decision, but you still need to make it. Other decisions aren't quite so straightforward. One application, for example, provides the capability to track OLE links across the network. To do this, it has to load a rather large piece of code and allow it to remain resident. Because I very seldom even think about using such a capability, I didn't install it.

The preceding tips will help you make decisions when installing software, but there are other problems to consider. For example, how do you balance workgroup and individual needs? For some products, such as Lotus Notes, this is a major concern. When working with workgroup-specific applications, you should consider the following additional problems:

- **Installation location.** Deciding where to put a workgroup application is a major decision. Placing the installation files on the network makes it easier for the administrator to manage, reduces the chance that someone will pirate the application, and reduces overall application size because not every workstation needs a copy of common files, such as DLLs. The disadvantage of using a server installation is the increase in network traffic as the application requests DLLs and other support files from the server. In many cases, users don't have as many configuration options as they would with a workstation installation.

- **Local support for network features.** Many network products secretly invade the user's system and steal workstation statistics on a regular basis. Unless you're the sole administrator of a very large network, however, you have to weigh the importance of such a feature against the memory it uses on each workstation.

Getting Application Settings Right

Although similar applications (such as word processors) might have a few settings in common, very few applications use the same exact settings. This section discusses some general principles for customizing your applications.

> **Tip:** Your first inclination might be to get into the application and complete this part of the setup immediately. That would probably be the worst mistake you could make. Software settings change as you learn how to use the application more efficiently. A little change here and there can make a big difference in how well the application works for you. Take the time to go through the tutorial first, then make any settings changes you think will help. I usually keep Notepad handy to record any ideas I come up with while running the tutorial.

Changing your settings is largely a matter of personal preference. Even a small change, however, can make a big difference in the way you use an application. Simply customizing a toolbar, for example, can reap a fairly large increase in efficiency. Disabling an application's autocorrect feature might help you run background tasks more efficiently. The following tips can help you get the most out of your applications:

- **Toolbars.** A toolbar is one way you can greatly increase your efficiency for a small increase in memory usage. Every icon you allocate uses additional system resources, but the amount of memory an icon uses is very small—usually less than 1KB. When setting up a toolbar, don't assume the vendor provides the most commonly used icons. I try to track which commands I use the most; then I add them to the toolbar because it takes less time to access a command from the toolbar than from a menu. Seven icons should appear on every toolbar: Open, Close, New, Print, Cut, Copy, and Paste. Be certain to remove any standard toolbar buttons you don't use to save memory.

- **Printer settings.** In most applications, you can set the printer configuration separately from the Windows general configuration. I usually set my printer configuration to match my use of an application. I use my word processor for final output, for example, so I use the best letter-quality resolution available. On the other hand, I never use my graphics programs for final output, so I select draft quality there. A draft printout might not seem acceptable, but it's more efficient than letter quality when you just want a quick look at your document. (Another benefit of using draft output whenever possible is you'll use less ink, making those expensive toner cartridges last longer.) You also can vary the print resolution. A low-resolution, letter-quality printout might work fine for workgroup presentations, but you should use the highest available quality when making the same presentation to a larger audience. The resolution you use affects the amount of memory and time required to complete the printout.

- **Macros.** A macro is a shortcut created to represent keystrokes you repeat frequently. I create macros for every repetitive task I perform with my main applications. For example, I always set up word processing files using a macro. It makes more sense for the computer to do the work than for me to do it. In fact, I use this macro so often that I attached it to my toolbar as an icon. Other tasks, however, don't work well as macros. I always thought changing a document from one format to another would make a great macro, but implementing it proved frustrating. Sometimes it takes a human mind to perform certain tasks.

- **Style sheets and templates.** You can never have too many custom style sheets and templates. I always use a style sheet or template for documents if the application supports it. The reason is simple: Style sheets and templates don't take more than a few minutes to create, but they can save a lot of time later. Templates and style sheets also provide another benefit; they enforce uniformity in the format of your documents. This is important whether you're part of a group or working as an individual. I view consistent output as the mark of a professional—most other people do, too.

- **Autocorrect.** The autocorrect features provided by many applications can be a source of much consternation. On one hand, they provide a valuable service in automatically correcting misspelled words. On the other hand, autocorrect features can chew up valuable memory and processor cycles—resources you could use to run a task in the background. I usually turn off autocorrect features and rely on a spelling checker (or other tools) to find mistakes at one time.

Tip: Autocorrect also can be used to substitute short phrases for long ones. Suppose you have to type your company name a lot, for example, Jackson Consolidated Freight Company. You can add an acronym such as JCFC to your autocorrect dictionary. Then, every time you need to type your company name, you can just type **JCFC**. Your application automatically substitutes the long name in its place.

- **Autoload.** This option can be used with the utility and filter programs previously mentioned in the "Installation Options" section of this chapter. Some programs, such as Microsoft Access and Lotus 1-2-3, enable you to autoload some of your utilities and filters so you can access them faster. There's a trade-off, however, for the convenience of instant access. You have to give up some memory and perhaps a few processor cycles.

Peter's Principle: My Settings Won't Work on Your Machine

We're all individuals. Nowhere is this more apparent than in the way we use software. I might think the way you do something is absurd; if it works for you, however, it's probably the right way to go (at least until you learn better). For example, I include the Insert Annotation command in Word for Windows on my toolbar, because I use this feature a lot. I suggested this to a colleague, and he found it a waste of time, because he uses a different technique for making annotations.

Here's another example: I regularly use three different user dictionaries: common, computer, and jargon. This enables me to separate some words so they don't contaminate my general-purpose dictionary. In a workgroup situation, everyone should use the same dictionary to ensure consistent results for a project. A group project usually requires individuals to defer to the needs of the group. This enforces a certain level of consistency.

You need to work with an application long enough to build a rapport with it. After you figure out how you want to work with the application, you can start changing some personal settings to meet your specific requirements. Some of your settings might end up working for the group as well. Experimentation is a prime ingredient in finding the settings that work best for you.

Setting up an application is a continual process. Don't give up too much personal comfort for a perceived memory or speed benefit. Weigh the time a specific feature will save against what it will cost.

Running 16-Bit Windows Applications

All 16-bit applications share one address space, which means they have to share the system resources required to display windows, icons, and all sorts of graphics elements. A 16-bit application also faces problems such as cooperative multitasking. This particular problem only gets worse in Windows 98, because 32-bit applications run in their own session.

> **Tip:** Some older Windows applications display an invalid dynalink call error message when you try to run them. This means they're incompatible with a new Windows 98 version of a DLL. You have two choices. Upgrading the application is the best alternative because you replace the old product with something that works better in Windows 98. If upgrading isn't an option, reinstall the application, reboot Windows 98, and try it again. You have to reboot in order to reload the DLL into memory. If you still get an invalid dynalink call message, there's an incompatibility between the application and a basic Windows 98 system file. In this case, you must upgrade because you can't replace common files to meet the needs of one program. Some Windows 98 applications might cease to function if you do (including the operating system itself). Windows 98 always maintains a copy of its system files in the SYSBCKUP folder under the main Windows folder. You can use this copy of the file to replace the old DLL if necessary.

The optimization techniques used in Windows 3.x will probably work here as well. You still need to keep in mind the cooperative multitasking aspect of 16-bit applications when running certain types of applications in the background. You'll probably find it difficult, for example, to run a 16-bit database and a communications program at the same time at high speed. The cooperative nature of these applications means the database will probably take control of the system for one second longer than the communications program can hold data in the buffer. The result is lost data. Windows 98 is much better than Window 3.x in this regard, but it still isn't perfect because the applications aren't perfect.

Chapter 5 examined many ways to tune the Windows environment by getting rid of excess icons and the like. For the most part, these same tips apply to applications. Be sure to review that chapter for additional hints.

Tip: Some 16-bit applications give you a choice between storing DLL files locally or in the Windows SYSTEM directory. Choosing the local option makes it easier to remove the application later. It also reduces the chances of the application's setup routine accidentally overwriting a Windows 98 version of a file.

One Windows 3.x optimization technique you should ignore when using Windows 98 is the use of virtual memory. Virtual memory uses your hard disk to temporarily store information, thereby fooling your computer into thinking it has more memory than it actually does. If your system contains enough memory under Windows 3.x, you can get a performance boost by disabling virtual memory. You are effectively limited in the amount of system memory you can expect, but the performance gain is worth it. Don't disable virtual memory under Windows 98 because it likely will slow down your computer.

Many people also avoid using the Windows 3.x Print Manager when they need fast output. Windows 98 contains a much-improved Print Manager that you'll want to use for optimum performance. The output, however, won't necessarily arrive at the same speed. If you have a heavy system load when you start the print job, you'll definitely see decreased print speed. However, you gain increased system performance and regain control of your application faster as a result. It's another trade-off, but in this case it's a good one.

Running 32-Bit Windows Applications

A 32-bit application is more efficient than its equivalent 16-bit counterpart because it can accomplish more tasks in the same amount of time. More importantly, 32-bit applications support true multitasking. *Multitasking* enables you to run multiple tasks at the same time, such as repaginating a document while still editing it. Multitasking also helps you perform some tasks—such as printing— much faster than a 16-bit application can. Windows can make better use of idle time with a 32-bit application. This isn't the big feature users will notice, however. You'll notice that you regain control of the system faster. After a 32-bit application spawns a print task, it returns control of the computer immediately. It doesn't check the status of the background print job, like a 16-bit application does.

A big performance-tuning tip for Windows 98 and 32-bit applications is to use as many automatic settings as possible. The more room you can give Windows 98 to compensate for changing system conditions, the better. Chapter 5 contains quite a few tips to optimize the environment. It examines the need to monitor swap file size, for example, to ensure that you don't end up wasting processor cycles in thrashing. When you optimize the environment for a 32-bit application, you're essentially optimizing the application itself. Refer to the "Getting Application Settings Right" section earlier in this chapter to make the application as efficient as possible.

Optimizing DOS Applications

Eventually, more people will use Windows 98; some, however, might continue to use Windows 3.x or MS-DOS. Few companies still make MS-DOS applications, except in the game market. Game publishers use MS-DOS because it gives programmers access to the hardware used to write fast and visually stimulating programs. Game vendors are now starting to produce more Windows 95/98 games that use DirectX technology to display speedy graphics. You should check with your video- and audio-card vendor to make sure you have the latest drivers from them; some vendors are coming out with DirectX-specific drivers. You can download the current version of DirectX at http:// www.microsoft.com/directx/default.asp. Make sure you have a complete copy of your current video drivers. Some users have complained of severe compatibility problems when using DirectX with certain display adapters. Copy your current drivers in case you need to remove DirectX from your machine.

Custom applications are another area in which people still use DOS, but for a different reason. A custom application can cost thousands of dollars. The consultant who writes the program charges that much because he probably won't sell more than a few hundred copies. Because custom applications usually manipulate sensitive company data that's hard to move to another application, people think twice before attempting to move that data. Fortunately, I see this particular class of DOS application coming to an end as Windows tools become easier and faster to use. A consultant can now be more productive, so the cost of creating a new application should decrease.

In addition, old habits die hard. Some people are comfortable using DOS utility programs, so they'll continue to use them. In most cases, there are good substitutes for these applications—substitutes that are easier to use and that run faster—but some people just won't use them. This third group of people also will make some use of DOS under Windows 98.

The following sections explore a variety of DOS options. In most cases, the best methods are discussed first, followed by a few marginal methods you can use in a pinch. My advice is to move to 32-bit Windows applications as soon as possible. DOS isn't dead yet, but future versions of Windows (such as Windows NT) won't support MS-DOS applications.

MS-DOS Emulation

You can use MS-DOS in Windows 98 through the MS-DOS emulation mode. Windows makes a copy of the phantom DOS session stored in memory, spawns a new 8086-compatible session, and places the copy in the new session. What you see is either a windowed or full-screen DOS session. To open a DOS session, select MS-DOS Prompt from the Start | Programs menu. You also can start a DOS session by selecting a DOS application from either Explorer or the Start menu.

Windows 98 makes the DOS window easy to use and configure. All the controls you initially need are displayed on a toolbar in the window. There also are many hidden configuration options, which will be discussed later. The following is a list of controls in the toolbar:

- **Font Size.** This list box enables you to select the font size used to display information in the DOS window. Font size is defined by the number of horizontal and vertical pixels used for each character. You need to find a balance between readability and viewing the entire screen at once. A DOS window usually defaults to the Auto setting. This means Windows 98 attempts to determine the proper font size based on the number of lines of text in the DOS box and the resolution of your display.

- **Mark.** Use this control to select an area of the screen for copying. When you select the Copy command, Windows 98 places the selected area on the Clipboard so you can use it in other applications. The selected area is highlighted, as shown in Figure 12.4. You can use either the cursor keys or the mouse to select the desired area.

Figure 12.4.
You can use the Mark button to copy part of the DOS screen to the Windows Clipboard.

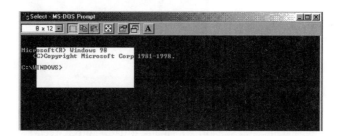

- **Copy.** The Copy button places in the Clipboard the area you highlighted using the Mark button.

- **Paste.** You can paste information from a Windows application into the DOS box. You can't paste anything other than text, however, unless the display is in graphics mode. Even then, you might be limited by the DOS application running at the time.

- **Full screen.** Clicking this button changes the window-size DOS prompt into a full-screen version.

- **Properties.** Every DOS application has a number of properties that you can set (discussed later in this chapter). Clicking this button displays the Properties dialog box for the current application.

- **Background.** Click this button to run the current DOS application in the background. This comes in handy when you want to monitor the application but don't need to interact with it.

- **Font.** This button performs about the same task as the Font Size list box. Instead of displaying just a list of font sizes, however, it displays the Font page of the program's Properties dialog box.

DOS doesn't provide much more than you had in the past. One new feature it does provide is long filename support. Use the DIR command to see what I mean. Figure 12.5 shows the results of using DIR to display all the BMP files in the \WINDOWS directory.

Figure 12.5.
DOS reacts
differently when you
use the DIR command
in Windows 98.

Note: Long filename support is available only in Windows 98. When you leave that environment to work in MS-DOS mode, the *DIR* command operates exactly as it did before. MS-DOS mode is also known as raw DOS mode. None of the Windows 98 drivers are loaded when you use this mode including long filename support. You must be very careful about corrupting your long filenames when in this mode.

Tip: You also can use long filenames when typing commands. If the filename or directory includes spaces, however, you must enclose it in quotes, as in DIR "Some Long Directory Name".

In addition to long filename support, there are a few new utility programs as well as changes to some old utilities. You no longer need to run a copy of QBasic to use Edit, for example, and Edit now provides the capability to modify more than one file at once. The next section covers the specific changes in DOS utility support.

DOS Versus Windows 98 Commands

Microsoft must expect people to use the DOS prompt, or they wouldn't have improved some of the utilities in Windows 98. There isn't room here to explore all the DOS commands, but you should know the highlights. The following list summarizes the changes in MS-DOS (running under Windows 98):

- All disk-scanning utilities from previous versions of DOS are upgraded to support long filenames and FAT32. Windows 98 also replaces many of these files with batch file substitutes, in case you decide to maintain a dual-boot capability. The renamed files include DBLSPACE.BAT, DRVSPACE.BAT, DEFRAG.BAT, and SCANDISK.BAT.

- EDIT is now a standalone command. It also provides the capability to edit more than one file and larger files than before.

- Some applications, such as ScanDisk, start the Windows version of the program even when executed at the DOS prompt.

- Windows 98 includes the NET command, which determines information about your network from the DOS prompt. Typing **NET VIEW**, for example, displays a list of computers and other resources currently available on the network. To learn more about this command, type **NET?** at the DOS prompt.

In addition to the new features in the Windows 98 version of MS-DOS, some features have been removed. The Windows 98 version of MS-DOS does not include the following commands:

APPEND	INTERLINK	RAMDRIVE.SYS
ASSIGN	INTERSVR	RECOVER
BACKUP	JOIN	REPLACE
COMP	MEMCARD	RESTORE
DOSSHELL	MEMMAKER	ROMDRIVE.SYS
EDLIN	MIRROR	SHARE
EGA.SYS	MSAV	SMARTMON
FASTHELP	MSBACKUP	TREE
FASTOPEN	POWER	UNDELETE
GRAFTABL	PRINT	UNFORMAT
GRAPHICS	PRINTER.SYS	VSAFE
HELP	QBASIC	

Warning: Windows 98 users can't use any of these old utility programs. Doing so causes problems with long filenames on your drive. You also risk problems with a FAT32-formatted drive. You'll lose at least a few files, but you could lose everything on your drive. Use only Windows 98–specific utilities.

Creating a DOS Session

You can use a variety of methods to create a DOS session. Double-clicking a DOS application from Explorer creates a DOS session. The session ends when you close the application.

Like previous versions of Windows, Windows 98 includes a DOS prompt. Just click the MS-DOS Prompt option in the Programs section of the Start menu. Type **exit** and press Enter to end this session.

You also can start a DOS session by selecting the Restart the Computer in MS-DOS Mode option in the Shutdown dialog box. This takes you to a full-screen raw DOS session. You can perform any required tasks, then type **exit** and press Enter to leave. Windows 98 automatically reloads itself.

DOS Objects

As with any other object in Windows 98, right-clicking a DOS object displays a context menu from which you can cut, copy, and paste the object. The Properties option opens the Properties dialog box, described in the next section. This is one major area in which DOS applications are treated differently from Windows applications.

Settings

A DOS application's Properties dialog box contains more settings than the same dialog box for a Windows application. In fact, the Properties dialog box replaces the PIF (program information file) Editor used in Windows 3.x. The Properties dialog box, shown in Figure 12.6, enables you to change every setting provided by the PIF Editor—and more. Windows 98 provides several new features for DOS applications that make running them a snap. The following sections describe each page of the Properties dialog box in detail.

Figure 12.6.
The Properties dialog box replaces the PIF Editor used in Windows 3.x.

Program

The Program page enables you to change the way Windows executes a program. At the top of the page are an icon and a field containing the application's name. This is the name you'll see in Explorer.

The next three fields determine which application to run. The Cmd line: field contains the name of an application, which must end with an `.exe`, `.com`, or `.bat` extension. The example in Figure 12.6 is running a copy of the command processor. The Working: field tells Windows 98 what directory to start the application from. In most cases, you start the application from its home directory or its data directory. The choice depends on what kind of information the application needs to start. In the example, the command processor will be run from the `\WINDOWS` directory. The third field, Batch file:, enables you to designate a batch file to run with the application. You could include a batch file to set up the path, for example, and to prompt and load any TSRs you might need when starting the command processor.

The Shortcut key: field enables you to assign a shortcut key to the program (as explained in Chapter 7, "Startup Shortcuts").

Use the Run: field to specify how Windows 98 should run the application. There are three choices: Normal window, Minimized, and Maximized. The first two choices affect both windowed and full-screen sessions. The third choice starts windowed sessions maximized.

It's a good idea to close a DOS session as soon as you finish with it. If you check the Close on exit option, this is done automatically.

Clicking the Change Icon button displays the Change Icon dialog box. Here you can select the icon used to identify the application within Explorer and the Start menu. Windows 98 provides the same default choices as other versions of Windows. You also can click the Browse button to select from custom icon sets.

MS-DOS Mode

There's another button on the Program page, and it deserves special attention. If you click the Advanced button, you'll see the dialog box shown in Figure 12.7.

Figure 12.7.
You can enable MS-DOS mode for an application in the Advanced Program Settings dialog box.

The first three check boxes control the actual implementation of MS-DOS mode. Some applications run fine under Windows 3.x but quit if they see Windows 98. Checking the first option prevents an application from detecting Windows 98. The problem with this feature is the application will have less conventional memory and will run more slowly as Windows works to keep itself hidden.

The second check box runs a detection program with the DOS application. This can be used as a diagnostic aid when the application doesn't run properly under Windows 98. It's a waste of processor cycles and memory, however, to keep this box checked after you're reasonably sure the application doesn't require MS-DOS mode. Unfortunately, Windows 98 checks this box by default. This means you have to remember to uncheck it to gain optimum performance from your application.

Checking the third option, MS-DOS mode, means the application won't run under Windows 98. It also changes your available options because it enables you to add custom CONFIG.SYS and AUTOEXEC.BAT settings. If you double-click an application to start it, Windows 98 shuts down all running applications, shuts itself down, unloads from memory, then executes the application. This option is used as a last-ditch effort to get an application to run under Windows 98. Unfortunately, many game programs fall into this category.

I recommend that you check the Warn before entering MS-DOS mode option. This will prevent you from entering the mode accidentally. It could even prevent data loss in some rare cases in which an application doesn't react properly to the Windows shutdown message.

Windows 98 provides default CONFIG.SYS and AUTOEXEC.BAT files for your application. I don't recommend using them, however, for one very good reason: The whole purpose of MS-DOS mode is to get your application to run. Using a set of configuration files specifically designed for MS-DOS mode is a good first step in getting the application to run, and run efficiently. I usually check the second radio button to enable the configuration entries, as shown in Figure 12.8.

Figure 12.8.
Always use custom configuration files if your application requires MS-DOS mode to run.

There are a number of ways to create a configuration for your application. You can even use the Configuration button to access the automated configuration method provided by Microsoft. However, I usually copy the appropriate sections of the CONFIG.DOS and AUTOEXEC.DOS files to these screens. (You can paste using Ctrl+V; Microsoft didn't add a Paste button to this dialog box.) These files contain the old configuration that ran the application. I usually modify the entries as appropriate for this particular situation, but you won't need to do much tuning.

Setting up an application for MS-DOS mode doesn't have to be difficult. It is inconvenient, however, because you can't run any other applications while an MS-DOS–mode application runs. Your hard drive (and associated long filenames) also is susceptible to damage from an MS-DOS–mode application. Make sure the application is well behaved in writing to disk before you trust it with your setup.

Font

The Font page enables you to change the appearance of fonts used to display data in a windowed DOS application. These settings do not affect a full-screen session. This dialog box contains four main sections. The first section controls the type of fonts you see in the Font Size list box. You'll usually want to use the fullest set of fonts available, so select Both Font Types. The only time to switch to one font type or another is when your display has problems with a specific font type.

The Font Size list box in the second section contains a list of font sizes available for the DOS window. The numbers represent the number of pixels used for each character. A higher number of pixels make the display more readable. A smaller number of pixels make the window smaller.

The Window Preview section shows how big the window will appear in the display. The Font Preview section shows the size of the print. Combine the output from these two displays to determine the size font to use. It's important to balance the need to see what you're doing with the need to display the entire DOS box at once.

Memory

The Memory page, shown in Figure 12.9, is the most important page in the Properties dialog box from a tuning perspective. There are only five list boxes and two check boxes, but the decisions you make here affect how the application runs. More importantly, they affect the way Windows runs.

Figure 12.9.
The Memory page enables you to modify the way Windows allocates and manages memory for your DOS application.

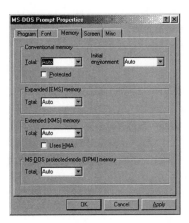

The first group of settings affects conventional memory. The Total field enables you to select any value up to 640KB. Windows usually allocates a 1024-byte environment for your DOS application. This should be enough to handle most situations. I usually set mine to 4096, however, to provide space for all the environment strings required by real-mode compilers. The Protected check box is another diagnostic aid. Checking it tells Windows 98 to monitor the application for memory protection errors. The only disadvantage is the performance loss you'll suffer when using it. If your application tends to corrupt memory, check this box to keep your environment stable. Otherwise, consider leaving it unchecked for better performance.

The second section contains a single list box that controls how much expanded memory Windows 98 allocates for your application. If you leave it on Auto, MEM reports expanded memory up to the amount of memory your machine has installed. Windows 98 makes only 16MB of it usable, even if you have more RAM installed. The only time you should change this setting is when the application grabs every bit of expanded memory it can find. Some older DOS applications get a little greedy, so you need to provide some controls.

The third group of settings controls the amount of extended memory available to your application. The default setting allocates the full amount of RAM installed on your system. This isn't an unlimited amount of memory, but it could be fairly high—much higher than the automatic expanded memory setting. As with the expanded memory setting, I change this setting from Auto to a specific number only if the application gets greedy or if it has problems coping with the full amount of extended memory available on my machine. I usually leave the Uses HMA check box blank because I usually load DOS in the high-memory area. If you don't use the HMA, however, you can still choose to load all or part of an application there by checking this box.

The final setting enables you to determine the amount of DPMI memory available to applications. Windows 98 usually sets this value to reflect the current system conditions. There's little reason to change this setting from the default.

Screen

The Screen page, shown in Figure 12.10, enables you to configure the screen settings. The first group of settings, Usage, determines the screen mode and the number of display lines. Set the number of display lines here before you set the options on the Font page of this dialog box. Otherwise, a setting that worked well at 25 lines might not work at 50.

The second section enables you to change the window settings. (This doesn't come into play if you use full-screen mode.) Displaying the toolbar enables you to modify font size and to perform other tasks without opening the Properties dialog box. The second check box tells Windows 98 to update the program information file (PIF) to reflect any changes made while using the toolbar. The entries usually are good only for that session. I want Windows to remember my settings from session to session, so I check this box.

Figure 12.10.
The Screen page enables you to adjust the size and type of display and the method Windows uses to display it.

The third group of settings on this page affects your application's performance. The first setting, Fast ROM emulation, acts just like shadow RAM. It enables your application to use a RAM version of your display ROM. If an application has trouble with shadow RAM under DOS, it also will have trouble with this setting. Otherwise, you should leave this option checked for maximum performance from your application.

The second setting in the Performance section helps Windows more than the application. This setting enables Windows to retrieve memory the DOS application uses for graphics mode when it goes into character mode. This modicum of memory isn't much, but it adds up if you run lots of DOS sessions. The only time to remove the check mark from this setting is when your application spends all or most of its time in graphics mode.

Misc

The Misc (miscellaneous) page, shown in Figure 12.11, provides settings that determine how Windows interacts with your application from a functional point of view.

Figure 12.11.
The Misc page enables you to control a variety of settings that don't fit into the other categories.

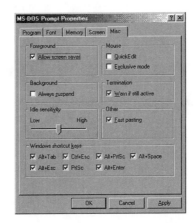

The Allow screen saver setting doesn't have much effect when using windowed applications. It determines whether Windows can interrupt a full-screen session to run a screen saver. Some full-screen applications, such as graphics applications, get confused if the screen saver operates.

The Mouse group contains two settings. The QuickEdit check box enables you to use a mouse within a DOS window, just as with any Windows application. The Exclusive mode check box gives a windowed application exclusive control over the mouse. This means you can't use the mouse with your regular Windows applications while this application is active. You should probably run this application in a full-screen session if it has this much trouble sharing the mouse.

Some of the settings on this page—such as Background and Idle sensitivity—provide subtle performance control over your application. Checking the Always suspend option frees up resources for Windows 98 to use with other applications. If you're using a DOS application for something that requires continuous input (such as data entry), it pays to check this box and use the resources for other applications. Idle sensitivity also changes how Windows allocates resources. Windows tracks the amount of activity from an application to see whether it sits idle while waiting for input from you. If it does, Windows 98 reduces the application's CPU resources. This usually works fine, but sometimes Windows doesn't leave the application enough resources to complete the task it's performing. When this happens, lowering the Idle sensitivity setting gives the application the resources it needs, but it does so at the expense of other applications running on the system at the time.

The Warn if still active option in the Termination section displays a message if you try to terminate the DOS application window without first ending the program. You should usually keep this checked to prevent potential data loss from a premature application termination.

Another performance enhancement is the Fast pasting option. This box usually should be checked so Windows can use a high-speed method of pasting information into your DOS application. You should change this only if data gets damaged when using the fast-paste mode.

The final group on the page regulates the use of control-key combinations in Windows 98. Checking a box in the Windows shortcut keys group enables Windows to use that key combination. Unchecking it enables the application to use the key combination. You should change these settings only when the application needs them and you can't change the application's settings.

Using Windows Scripting Host (WSH)

Windows 98 contains the capability to write and execute scripts at the system level. This means you no longer have to go through repetitive tasks to get your applications to work together. You can use a script, for example, that scans your hard drive for errors, backs it up, then optimizes it—all without any work on your part (unless the script encountered an error).

The Windows scripting host (WSH) provides much more than simple batch processing. Any application that supports OLE also is a candidate for script processing. Consider the process of typing a form letter (not a mail merge situation, just a form letter you send out one at a time). You probably start the letter using a template; the template might provide boilerplate text, but you still have to customize it. When it's time to add a name and address, you open a database manager and copy a name from it. You then might add some information from a spreadsheet, perhaps some accounting information. All three of these tasks could have been automated using a script. Writing a form letter could come down to providing the name of the recipient and typing a little custom text.

Before you get the idea that WSH is a script interpreter, it should be made clear that, as the name implies, it's a host. A host in this case provides the platform necessary to execute the script commands; it does not interpret the script itself. In other words, you potentially can make WSH support any scripting language you want. The language portion of WSH is stored in a separate module. Microsoft plans to ship Windows 98 with support for VBScript and JavaScript, but it hopes to see other vendors add support for languages such as Perl, TCL, REXX, and Python.

Like almost every other area of Windows 98, WSH works with objects and provides some objects of its own. The purpose of these objects, such as WshShell, is to enable you to perform basic tasks such as displaying a dialog box or placing a shortcut on the desktop. There even is a special object, WScript, that enables you to determine things about WSH itself. The WScript.Name property, for example, returns "Windows Scripting Host," the friendly name for WSH. Likewise, WScript.Quit tells WSH you want to stop executing the current script.

> **Tip:** If you want to see sample scripts in action, take a look at the `\WINDOWS\SAMPLES\WSH` folder. Most of the sample scripts included here don't, however, if you want to use the `CHART.VBS` or `EXCEL.VBS` examples.

Windows 98 provides two scripting engines: one that operates at the MS-DOS command prompt (`CScript.EXE`) and another within Windows 98 (`WScript.EXE`). WScript is the default engine, which makes sense because you'll usually be working with Windows applications. Running back and forth to the DOS prompt only wastes time. Table 12.1 shows the command line parameters for both script engines.

Table 12.1. WSH Script Engine Command Line Switches.

Switch	Description
//?	Enables you to display all the currently documented command line switches.
//B - Batch Mode	Use this mode when you don't want the user to interact with the script. Batch mode suppresses all non-command line console user interface requests from script.
//C	Makes CSCRIPT.EXE the default application for running scripts. (WScript is the default engine.)
//Entrypoint:SubName	You can include more than one script (subroutine) within a script file. Use this command line switch to call a specific subroutine after core code path is complete. WSH displays this error message if the subroutine you request doesn't exist: Input Error: There's no subroutine named "subname".
//I - Interactive	Enables full interaction with the user. Any pop-up dialog boxes wait for user input before the script continues.
//logo & //nologo	WSH usually prints out the following logo message: Microsoft ® Windows Scripting Host Version 5.0 for Windows (build #) Copyright (C) Microsoft Corporation 1996. All rights reserved. Use the //nologo switch to prevent WSH from displaying this message.
//R - Reregister	Use this switch with the command line engine (CScript) to print out the scripting host version, copyright information, and the script engines found and registered. This switch usually determines whether third-party script engines have been registered properly. You have to use this switch alone; it doesn't work when you call a script.
//S	This command line switch enables you to save current command line options for a user. WSH will save the following options: //B, //I, //Logo, //Nologo, and //T:n.
//T:nn - Time out	Limits the maximum time the script can run to nn seconds. This doesn't usually contain a timeout value. Use this switch when a script might end up in a continuous loop or is unable to get the requested information for other reasons. You might use this switch, for example, when requesting information on a network drive.
//W	Makes WSCRIPT.EXE the default application for running scripts.

As shown in this table, you also can work with WSH in interactive or batch mode. Use batch mode when you need to perform tasks that don't require user input. Interactive mode requires user interaction.

On Your Own

Find a DLL for one of the smaller applications installed on your machine. Use the procedure described in Chapter 8 to view the contents of files. Determine which DLLs and other system files this application needs in order to work. After you make the list, determine whether other applications require the same files. You might be surprised by what you find. Windows 98 reuses many files.

Use the procedures outlined in this chapter to create an MS-DOS–mode session for an ill-behaved application. Does the application run better in MS-DOS mode? Try this with an application that works fine in Windows 98. Does the application run faster in MS-DOS or Windows 98? Can you see any difference in the way it runs?

Try some of the sample scripts in the \WINDOWS\SAMPLES\WSH folder. If you right-click a script and then select Edit from the context menu, you can see how it uses WSH objects to accomplish a task. (Make sure you don't save any changes so the script continues to run.)

13

Exploiting Your Hardware

Peter Norton®

Chapter 12, "Exploiting Your Software: DOS, 16-Bit, and 32-Bit Applications," looked at some of the things you could do to exploit your software. This chapter provides information about optimizing your hardware.

Installing and Deleting Devices

Windows 98 usually detects all the hardware on your machine during setup, then loads the appropriate drivers. Chapter 6, "Setup Primer," covered this entire process. It also covers some of the things you can do if Windows 98 doesn't detect your hardware. What happens, however, if you install a new piece of hardware after installing Windows 98? What do you do with old devices that are no longer installed? This section answers these questions and provides troubleshooting procedures you can follow if Windows doesn't act as expected.

Installing Hardware

Windows 98 checks your system during startup, then loads the appropriate drivers. Whenever Windows 98 encounters a new device, it performs the same INF file search as during the initial installation to detect the new device. Unfortunately, this doesn't always work. Sometimes you have to give Windows 98 a little help in finding your new device. The following sections provide some techniques to help you get the job done.

Automatic Installation

Now that you understand the problems, how do you get around them? You can get Windows 98 to detect the device automatically using the following procedure. Always try this method first. If it doesn't work, try the steps in the "Manual Installation" section of this chapter. This procedure assumes that you want to perform the most complete type of automatic installation. We'll use every automated search technique that the Add Hardware Wizard provides.

1. Open the Control Panel and double-click the Add New Hardware applet. You should see the Add New Hardware Wizard.

2. Click Next. You'll see a dialog box stating that Windows is going to search for Plug and Play hardware. Don't worry if your screen blanks during this process; Windows 98 needs to check for new display adapters and other hardware.

3. Click Next. Windows 98 searches for new Plug and Play hardware. A dialog box might ask whether you want Windows to search for new hardware. At this point, the precise steps that you'll see will depend on the kind of hardware you own and the responses you provide to the various Add New Hardware questions. Steps 4 through 9 will help you through a complete installation procedure, but there are several points where you can exit the wizard if it finds the hardware you want to install.

4. Make sure the Yes radio button is selected and click Next twice. When Windows 98 gets done, you might see a dialog box like the one in Figure 13.1. At this point, you need to check whether your new hardware appears in the list. If it does, select that item, choose Yes, the device is in the list, then click Next. Windows 98 displays one or two more prompts that enable you to install support for your new device. (You also can exit this procedure.)

Figure 13.1.
Windows 98 first checks for Plug and Play hardware because it doesn't require time-consuming use of INF files.

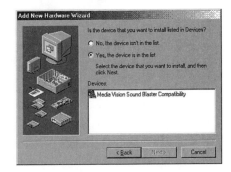

5. Click No, the device isn't in the list, then click Next. The dialog box you see has two options. The first (yes option) enables Windows 98 to automatically detect the hardware for you. Use this method first—it involves the least amount of effort on your part, and it reduces the chance you'll install the wrong driver.

6. After you've clicked the Yes radio button, click Next. Windows displays a dialog box telling you what the program will do. Essentially, it performs the same type of hardware search as when you first installed Windows 98.

> **Note:** The hardware-detection phase can take quite a while, especially on older machines. If disk activity stops for more than five minutes, the machine is probably frozen. As long as you hear disk activity during this phase, you're fairly safe in assuming that hardware detection is still taking place. (The hardware-detection indicator doesn't move at a steady pace. It appears to take more time as it nears the end.)

7. Click Next. Windows 98 displays a dialog box showing you its hardware-detection progress. After Windows 98 completes the hardware-detection phase, it displays a dialog box stating whether it has found something new.

> **Note:** If Windows 98 doesn't detect any new hardware, it displays a dialog box telling you so. You'll then have the opportunity to perform the manual installation that I outline next. All you need to do is click Next to start the process.

8. Click the Details button to determine whether Windows 98 successfully detected the new hardware (see Figure 13.2).

Figure 13.2.
*The Add New
Hardware Wizard
tells you exactly what
hardware it detected.*

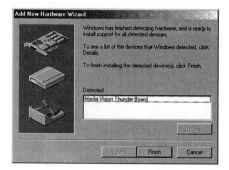

9. If Windows 98 successfully detected the new hardware, click the Finish button to complete the installation process. Windows 98 might ask for some setting information if this is a non–Plug and Play device. Windows 98 copies all the required drivers to disk. It also displays some messages about the new hardware it found and perhaps a message about building a driver database. Windows 98 sometimes asks you to reboot after you complete this step. Even if it doesn't ask you to reboot, you should do so anyway to make certain all new drivers are loaded properly.

Note: If the Add New Hardware Wizard didn't correctly detect your device, click Cancel. Check your hardware's settings to make sure that they won't conflict with any other devices, using the initial steps of the manual process outlined next. If the hardware settings did conflict with something else, change them to an unused setting and try the automatic installation procedure again. Otherwise, proceed with the manual installation.

Manual Installation

Windows 98 might not detect some of your hardware when using the Hardware Installation Wizard's automatic-detection method. This might be because your hardware didn't get turned on (because it needs real-mode devices to do so) or because a device conflict is preventing Windows 98 from seeing the device.

The following procedure starts by showing you where to look for the settings your machine is currently using. Determining this information in advance enables you to set the jumpers correctly the first time. If you're using this section to continue from an unsuccessful automatic installation, go to the "Manual Installation" section of Chapter 6. You also can proceed to Chapter 6 if you've already installed your adapter and don't need to find a set of nonconflicting IRQ and I/O settings. Otherwise, be sure to check your hardware settings before you start the manual installation.

1. Right-click the My Computer icon and select the Properties option.

2. Select the Device Manager page in the System Properties dialog box, as shown in Figure 13.3. (The dialog box for your machine will look slightly different because your machine contains different equipment.) This dialog box displays a complete list of each category of equipment installed on your machine.

Figure 13.3.

The Device Manager tab shows you all the equipment installed on your system.

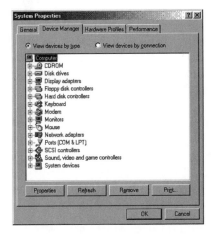

3. Select the Computer entry (as shown in Figure 13.3) and click the Properties button. Click the View Resources tab of the Computer Properties dialog box, and click the Interrupt request (IRQ) radio button on that page. The dialog box should look similar to the one in Figure 13.4. This shows a complete list of all the interrupts in use on your machine. You need to select an interrupt for your new device that doesn't conflict with any of these current settings. If all 16 interrupts are in use and your new device requires one, you have to remove an old device before you can install the new one.

Figure 13.4.

The IRQ section of the Computer Properties dialog box shows you all the interrupts in use on your machine.

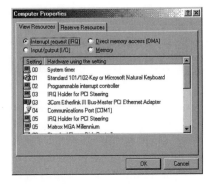

4. Click the Input/output (I/O) radio button. You'll see the list of port addresses previously mentioned. Select an unused port address range for your new card. Some adapters don't let

you select a port address, which means you might have to change the settings for another card to make this one fit. Fortunately, this is pretty rare.

5. Follow the same steps to find a direct memory access (DMA) setting if your card uses one. After you set all the required settings, close the dialog box by clicking Cancel twice. Shut down the machine and install your adapter according to manufacturer instructions. Restart Windows.

6. Proceed to the "Manual Installation" section of Chapter 6. This section tells you how to manually install a piece of hardware on your machine.

Removing Hardware

Removing hardware—at least the driver—is usually easier than installing it. In most cases, you should remove the drivers for a device first, then remove the device. Reversing this process could prevent Windows 98 from booting properly. Fortunately, Windows 98 will at least boot in safe mode even if you leave the device in place. I always like to take the safest route possible, however, when it comes to my machine's configuration. Removing the driver first is the safest route. The following steps show you the procedure for removing a driver from your machine.

1. Right-click the My Computer icon and select the Properties option. Click the Device Manager tab of the System Properties dialog box. Select the device category you want to remove and click the plus sign next to it. The dialog box should look similar to the one in Figure 13.5.

Figure 13.5.
Click the plus sign next to a device category to see a list of installed devices.

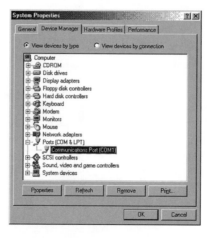

2. Click the device you want to remove. Click the Properties button to display the device Properties dialog, and select the Driver tab. Click the Driver file details button (if present). You should see a list of device drivers. Make a copy of the driver list so you can verify later

that Windows 98 removed them. Otherwise, you'll end up with additional disk clutter after installing and removing a few devices.

> **Note:** Some adapters contain more than one real device. The Pro Audio Spectrum adapter in my machine, for example, contains a sound board, a joystick controller, and a SCSI adapter. Each device requires a separate entry in the Device Manager. The only way that you'll know which devices are related is to look at the vendor documentation and see what kind of support an individual card provides. Windows doesn't provide any clues as to which devices are related. To remove the device, you must find the main entry and remove it. Windows 98 automatically removes all the supporting entries. Make sure you record the drivers used by each entry because the main entry doesn't provide a master list.

3. After you finish recording the driver names, click Cancel to clear the device's Properties dialog box. (You might have to click Cancel twice.)

4. Highlight the device you want to remove, then click the Remove button. Windows 98 removes the device and all its supporting entries.

5. Shut down Windows and reboot your machine so the changes can take effect. (Make sure you remove the device so that Windows won't automatically reinstall support for it.)

Configuring Ports

Ports provide the means for the processor and other devices to communicate with peripheral hardware on your machine. Any data necessary for a device to work goes through the port. Think of the port as a mailbox and the data as mail. If everyone had the same address, the mail carrier would never know where to put the mail. The same idea holds true in your computer. If two devices use the same address, the computer won't know where to send the data.

A port conflict does more than just annoy the user; it can cause system instability or a malfunction. Fortunately, there's an easy way to get rid of port conflicts. Windows 98 provides three port configuration methods, depending on the type of hardware you want to configure. Most hardware uses the first method, which is presented in the next section. The second and third methods apply to your parallel and serial ports, which are discussed later in this chapter.

Standard Port Configuration

For communication to occur in your computer, there must be a way to exchange information. In a PC, the physical part of the communication path is called an input/output (I/O) port. If you want to send data from one area of the machine to another, your application must first tell the computer which I/O port (or address) to send it to. Part of this process was covered earlier in this chapter when you examined hardware installation. The Computer Properties dialog box tells you the address of every port on your machine. The following procedure takes you through the process of changing an I/O port on your machine.

1. Right-click the My Computer icon and select the Properties option. Click the Device Manager tab of the System Properties dialog box.

2. Select one of the device classes—such as Sound, Video, and Game Controllers—and click the plus sign to display the list of devices it contains.

3. Select one of the devices and click the Properties button. Click the Resources tab. The dialog box should look similar to the one in Figure 13.6. Notice that the Use automatic settings option is checked. It's always a good idea to let Windows 98 manage the settings for your equipment.

Figure 13.6.

The Resources tab of the Device Properties dialog box makes it easy to see what settings each peripheral uses.

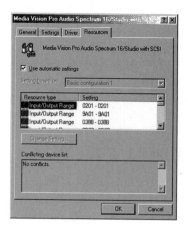

4. Uncheck the Use automatic settings option. This should enable the Change Setting button and the Setting based on list box.

5. Click the Setting based on list box. You'll see a list of basic configurations.

6. Try each setting to see whether any will enable you to resolve the port conflict. Windows 98 alerts you to any conflicts with registered devices, as shown in Figure 13.7. The error message tells you exactly which device has a conflict. This enables you to change that device's settings, if necessary, to resolve the conflict. You should keep the number of changes to the absolute minimum. The more you change the Windows 98 setup, the greater your chances of introducing unforeseen conflicts.

7. If you try all the basic configurations offered and none of them work, reset the Settings based on list box to its original setting. Otherwise, click OK twice to save the setting, then shut down and reboot the machine to make the setting active. If you have found a suitable setting, skip step 8.

Figure 13.7.
*Windows 98 instantly
alerts you to any
conflicts in the
settings you choose.*

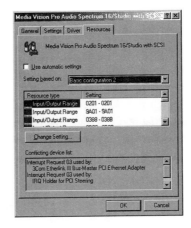

8. To change a single port address, highlight it and click the Change Setting button. (If Windows won't allow you to change the setting, try a different configuration. In some cases you may be out of luck and won't be able to change the setting at all.) You should see the dialog box shown in Figure 13.8.

Figure 13.8.
*The Edit Direct
Memory Access
dialog box enables
you to change the
setting of a single
port.*

Tip: Some revisions of a specific piece of hardware provide more settings than Windows 98 will recognize. Modifying the INF file using the procedure in Chapter 6 often resolves this problem. Just add the settings Windows 98 doesn't recognize, then shut down and reboot the machine.

9. Scroll through the list of acceptable settings in the Value field. As before, Windows 98 informs you of conflicts by displaying a message in the Conflict information field.

10. After you select a new port address, make it permanent by clicking OK three times. Shut down your machine and reboot.

Serial Port Configuration

The serial port offers a variety of configuration options that go beyond address-conflict resolution. Several options control both the speed of the port and its compatibility with software. Figure 13.9 shows the Port Settings page of the Communications Port Properties dialog box, where you can make changes of this nature. You access it through the Device Manager tab of the System Properties dialog box. Just select the serial port you want to change, then click the Properties button. The Port Settings page controls actual port parameters such as communication speed and number of data bits. You usually set a port's parameters to match those of your modem and any online service you want to access.

Figure 13.9.
The Port Settings page of the Communications Port Properties dialog box enables you to change some of the port's speed-enhancing features.

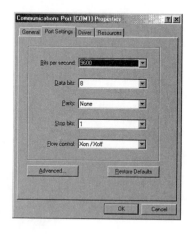

 The one area where Windows 98 rises above its predecessors is in the way that it handles advanced universal asynchronous receiver transmitter (UART) chips. A UART contains the intelligence of the serial port, and some of the newer models contain features that help improve performance in a multitasking environment. This enables Windows 98 to provide a higher level of support than you might expect for background communications.

Click the Advanced button to display the Advanced Port Settings dialog box, as shown in Figure 13.10. This dialog box contains only one check box and two sliders. Windows 98 automatically checks the Use FIFO buffers option if it detects the proper port. This option is available only on the 16550 UART. Attempting to use it with an older 8250 UART results in lost data.

Figure 13.10.
The Advanced Port Settings dialog box is one place you can tweak the performance of your communications program.

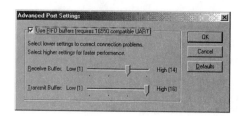

After you select the Use FIFO Buffers option in the Advanced Port Settings dialog box, Windows 98 enables two sliders that control the FIFO buffers. One slider is for data you want to send; the other is for data you receive. The setting affects the number of buffer slots the CPU can use. Setting a high number enables a longer time between CPU checks, making your system more efficient. Using a large number, however, also reduces the margin of error. You might find that your application no longer transmits or receives data accurately. You can fix this by reducing the number of buffers, giving the CPU a wider margin of error. Tuning your buffer for maximum performance involves some experimentation, but it's well worth the effort.

Parallel Port Configuration

The parallel port offers fewer, but more customized, opportunities for tuning than the serial port. When making changes to the parallel port settings, you need to consider a few things that you didn't consider with the serial port. The most important is that a device attaches to the serial port. This means the device must abide by the settings the serial port provides. This is why you have one centralized dialog box for tuning a serial port. On the other hand, a parallel port attaches to the device. You can hand-tune the parallel port settings for each device that connects to it. When you think about it, this arrangement makes a lot of sense. Seldom do you see more than one device attached to a serial port, yet AB switches for parallel ports abound. People are always attaching multiple devices to their parallel ports.

With this difference in mind, you have probably figured out that you don't change the printer port settings in Device Manager. Use a simple, four-step approach to open the dialog box in Figure 13.11. Open the Control Panel, double-click the Printers folder, right-click the printer, and select Properties from the context menu. All the port settings appear on the Details page of the Properties dialog box.

Figure 13.11.
A parallel port's configuration settings are attached to a particular printer.

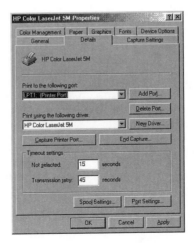

Two different settings affect the efficiency of your printer connection: port and spool. (Network printers on a Windows peer-to-peer network may not allow you to change the port settings from a remote location.) The Port Settings button displays the Configure LPT Port dialog box. The first check box, Spool MS-DOS print jobs, tells Windows 98 to place a copy of any DOS print jobs in the spooler so they can print in the background. Using this setting returns control of the machine to you faster. The tradeoff is that you'll experience reduced machine efficiency until the print job completes. The Check port state before printing option tells Windows to check the printer's status before it starts the print job. If the printer is offline or otherwise unable to print, Windows displays an error message. You're given the chance to fix the problem and then retry the print job.

The Spool Settings button opens the Spool Settings dialog box shown in Figure 13.12. Of the radio buttons shown, only the first group is always available. Spooling print jobs is required if you use the printer as a network printer. Selecting the first suboption in this group tells the spooler to send data to the printer after it spools the last page of the print job. This returns machine control to you much faster. I use it for long print jobs because the machine is tied up printing for a while anyway. The second suboption, Start printing after first page is spooled, enables the spooler to start printing immediately. If you usually print short jobs, this option makes more sense because it completes the overall print job faster.

Figure 13.12.
Use the Spool Settings
dialog box to change
the way your printer
handles spooling.

The Spool Settings dialog box also includes a Spool data format list box with two entries: RAW and EMF. EMF (enhanced metafile) is a new way to send information to the printer in Windows 98. It uses a data-independent method that's much smaller than the RAW option, and it frees up your program faster. The downside of this format is it takes longer for the print job to complete in the background because Windows 98 still has to convert the metafile format to something printer-specific. The RAW format sends data to the printer in a format it already understands. It takes your application longer to produce this output, but it can save substantially on the amount of time the spooler spends working in the background. Combining the EMF spool data format with the Start printing after last page is spooled setting provides the fastest method of sending data to your printer.

If it isn't a shared printer, you can choose to print directly to the printer. The advantage of this method is that you don't waste time spooling the job and then sending it to the printer. When the machine returns control to you, it is at full efficiency because the print job is finished. This feature comes in handy when you have one or two pages and don't want to wait very long for them to print.

Peter's Principle: A Printer for Every Task

There's no reason you can't create multiple copies of the same printer that are connected to the same port but configured in different ways. In fact, it can improve the flexibility of the Windows environment. I have one printer with spooling disabled, and I don't share it with anyone. It enables me to print small jobs very quickly.

A second copy of the same printer is shared by everyone on the network. I enable spooling and set it up to start printing after the first page. This way, my machine doesn't sustain heavy jolts as someone else uses the printer attached to it. Instead, there's a constant but barely noticeable load. I also use this strategy for my medium-sized print jobs. It reduces the overall time that I wait for the print job to complete.

A third copy of this same printer isn't shared with anyone, but it does use spooling. It is set up to wait until the last page of the print job appears in the spooler. This enables me to regain control of my machine in the minimum amount of time. I use this particular setting when I have a long print job that's going to reduce overall machine efficiency for a long time anyway.

There are numerous ways you can set a single printer on your machine to look like special-purpose printers. This takes some time and thought, but it enhances your overall efficiency and improves printer throughput. You also can use this same idea for control purposes. For example, what if you don't want a particular group to use the font cartridge attached to the machine? You can create a special setup for this group that provides full printer access but doesn't provide access to the fonts. (All you have to do is choose None when asked for fonts on the Font page.)

Normally you'll want to enable bidirectional printer support. This enables your printer to communicate with the computer when the printer needs maintenance. Bidirectional support also enables the computer to receive better information about printer failures. Bidirectional support, however, also exacts a toll in speed. The problem isn't with the printer or the computer, but with the amount of traffic flowing through the parallel port. The port has to support much more traffic in bidirectional mode than it does regularly. As a result, you might notice slightly better printer performance when you turn off bidirectional support. The speed gain is minimal, though, so think twice before you actually take this step. The loss of information could make a big difference in the computer's capability to help you diagnose problems.

Fonts and Printers

Fonts can create problems in a number of efficiency-related ways. Every font you load consumes disk space. If you have ample disk space, this isn't a problem. At an average size of 60KB, however, each TrueType font you load can quickly start to consume space your hard drive can't afford to provide.

Windows 98 makes it easy to load and unload fonts as necessary. Chapter 15, "Fonts and Printing," covers this in more detail.

Miniport Driver Support

A miniport driver is a device-independent way to move data. It doesn't matter what form that data takes—it could be graphics, sound, or text. Windows 98 uses the miniport driver concept for every subsystem on your machine. The benefit of using a miniport driver for your applications is improved speed. The application only needs to worry about the data it wants to output, not the format that data takes.

Not only does miniport driver support mean an easier-to-use interface for the user, it also means a lot to software vendors. Under DOS, you have to write code for every little function. If you want to provide a File menu, you have to write all the code the File menu requires. The same holds true for every other function a program might perform.

Windows 98 simplifies this concept with the miniport driver support it provides. If you develop communications programs, you worry about differences in control sequences for each modem type. Using Windows 98 Unimodem support (a miniport driver), however, the programmer opens each modem and writes to it like a file. The miniport driver takes care of details such as control codes.

There are other significant advantages to this approach. You no longer need to worry, for example, about how well an application handles details. Because each vendor is writing to the same interface, any changes to that interface come from Microsoft. Using a common interface also means that every application provides the same level of support for the various devices on your system. If one application supports a device, they all support it and to the same level.

You'll learn the specifics of miniport driver support as you visit each subsystem. Chapter 8, "The Windows 98 Architecture," covers the miniport driver concept from the file system point of view. Chapter 15 covers printer support in more detail. Look in Chapter 16, "Mice and Keyboards," for information about mouse miniport driver support, and in Chapter 17, "Video Configuration," for the same information about the video subsystem. Details about network miniport driver support can be found in Chapter 23, "Networks." Chapter 18, "Mobile Computing: Notebooks, Telecommuting, and Remote Access," covers the mobile computing environment. In most cases, I've shortened "miniport driver" to "driver" in the rest of this book because a miniport driver is simply a special form of driver.

 # Faxes and Modems

Communication is a major part of many jobs these days. Online services are becoming a major source of information for many people. Sometimes you can get an answer to a networking or application-related question faster online than if you called a vendor support line. The difference is the vast amount of knowledge these online services represent.

Looking Ahead: Chapter 19, "Hardware and Software Connections," takes a closer look at using your fax and modem in Windows 98. Chapter 18 examines the mobile computer user's point of view.

Configuring your machine for optimum performance when using background communication isn't difficult; it just takes a little time. Try a setting, communicate a little to see its effect, then tune as necessary. Unlike other tuning tips presented in this chapter, there's no quick and easy way to tune your communications programs. The problem is every machine is slightly different, as is every modem and every communications program that uses the modem.

Tuning Your Modem

To tune your modem settings, open the Control Panel and double-click the Modems applet. This opens the Modem Properties dialog box. Select your modem and click the Properties button. Select the Connection page. You'll see a modem device Properties dialog box similar to the one shown earlier in this chapter for the serial port.

Note: These settings affect your communications program only if it uses the Windows 98 miniport driver setup. Older 16-bit communications programs maintain their own settings. Check the software vendor's manual for the correct procedure to tune these applications.

Click the Advanced button. You'll see a dialog box similar to the one in Figure 13.13. This is where you can modify your connection settings for added efficiency. If your modem supports error correction, it's normally a good idea to select it. The same holds true for data compression, which boosts your effective transfer rate by as many as four times.

Figure 13.13.
The Advanced Connection Settings dialog box enables you to configure your modem for maximum efficiency.

Tip: At times, using error correction and data compression can hurt the efficiency of your transmission. Certain types of Telnet connections fall into this category, as do some BBS calls in which the host modem doesn't quite support your modem's protocols. If you're having trouble maintaining the connection, or if the data transfer rate isn't as high as you expected, try turning off data compression first to see if there's any improvement. Then try turning off error control.

I've discovered an interesting use for the Required to connect check box in the Advanced Connection Settings dialog box. Some BBSs have more than one connection. They use a switch to move you to the nearest unused connection when you call in. If this is a local call, it might not be a big deal that you can't use error correction and data compression. On the other hand, the cost of using such a connection during a long-distance call can add up quickly. I use this check box when I don't want the connection to disable the advanced features of my modem—the ones that reduce my overall telephone bill.

The Modulation type list box enables you to select from the various forms of signal modulation provided by the modem. Using standard modulation is usually more efficient than the alternatives; however, using the modulation that gives you the best connection is always the route to follow. I always try the standard connection first. If it proves reliable, I use that mode. I switch modes only when the connection doesn't work properly.

Some modems provide additional control sequences you can use in specific situations for added speed. The Extra settings field enables you to enter these control sequences. Consult your modem manual for details.

Tuning Your Fax

Windows provides a fairly minimal number of fax settings. To access them, open the MS Exchange Settings Properties dialog box. You can do this by right-clicking the Inbox applet and selecting Properties. You also can access it by double-clicking the Mail and Fax applet in the Control Panel. After you open this dialog box, select Microsoft Fax, click the Properties button, and select the Modem tab. You'll see a Microsoft FAX Properties dialog box.

The user-specific fields in this dialog box are discussed later. For now, select the modem you use to transmit faxes and then click the Properties button. When you see the Fax Modem Properties dialog box, click the Advanced button. This displays the dialog box in Figure 13.14.

The settings in this dialog box enable you to change either the usability or the efficiency of your modem. Checking the first setting, Disable high speed transmission, keeps you from transmitting or receiving faxes above 9600 baud. This can improve your machine's multitasking capability. Receiving high-speed faxes in the background improves transmission speed, but it also costs you processor cycles. Microsoft suggests that you check this box if you can't receive faxes without error. Errors usually occur when the serial port starts dropping characters due to high traffic. (Incidentally, this situation has more to do with the other background and foreground tasks you're running than with which UART you have. If your CPU is heavily bogged down with other tasks, the CPU itself—not the UART—becomes the bottleneck. You then open yourself up to the danger of degraded performance or lost data.)

Figure 13.14.
The Advanced dialog box enables you to select advanced properties for your fax modem.

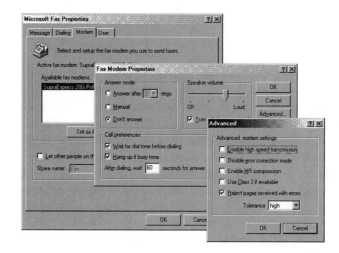

The Disable error correction mode setting also affects efficiency. On the one hand, working without error correction is faster. The additional processing time required for error correction slows down transmission speeds. Without error correction, however, you might find yourself resending faxes. You should usually leave error correction turned on, unless the receiving modem uses a different protocol.

I can understand why Microsoft didn't check the first two options by default. Using them does improve foreground fax transmission speeds. Disabling data compression, however, doesn't make much sense unless you have a noisy line. In most cases, you should enable data compression to gain the additional transmission speed it offers.

The standard compression technique used by all fax machines today is Modified Huffman (MH). It can nearly double the transmission speed of most fax machines. The Enable MR compression option enables you to use one of two advanced fax data-compression techniques: MR and MMR. The technique used depends on the capabilities of the fax machine you call. These two techniques provide data compression as follows:

- **Modified read (MR).** Some of the newer fax modems provide this option. The first line of fax data is compressed using the MH technique. The second line begins with only the changed data. In other words, if at a specific point in the data stream the first line contains a 0 and the second line contains a 1, the fax records the bit's location and difference. You'll see a 15 to 20 percent increase in the data transmission rate using this method of compression.

- **Minimized modified read (MMR).** This option gives up some of MR's security and trades it for speed. Only the first line of the fax is transmitted as a full line of data. All remaining lines are transmitted as change data only. You can usually expect transmission speed to nearly double when using this method.

The next option, Use Class 2 if available, prevents you from receiving Class 1 faxes. The only time you should check this box is if the software you're using won't let you receive Class 1 faxes. Class 2 faxes are the standard graphics type. Class 1 faxes are editable and therefore are easier to manipulate.

Finally, the Reject pages received with errors check box enables you to do a couple of things. Removing the check from this box tells Windows you don't want to receive any pages a second time, even if they're completely garbled. This usually isn't the best route to pursue. On the other hand, checking the box and selecting Very Low in the Tolerance list box virtually guarantees you'll get at least one resend of each page. (Use the Tolerance option to select the level of tolerance Windows has for errors on a fax page.) I use the High setting unless I need better fax quality for some reason. If I wanted to use the information in the fax for a presentation, for example, I might select the Low or Medium setting. The only time I would select Very Low is if I needed to use the fax as is, without any changes at all, for a presentation or formal document.

TAPI and MAPI Support

Application programming interfaces (APIs) enable programmers to accomplish a lot of work with only a little effort. That's the first goal of every API. The second goal is to ensure a standardized form of access to specific system resources and capabilities. Using a standard interface enables the operating system vendor to change the implementation details without "breaking" too much code. Finally, an API also standardizes the results of using specific system resources and capabilities. Using the Windows API, for example, ensures that the user will see some of the standard types of interface components that are taken for granted.

Windows 98 provides two new APIs. The Telephony API (TAPI) provides a standardized method of handling telephone services. The Messaging API (MAPI) provides a standardized method of handling email and other forms of messaging. Both APIs provide standardized methods for utilizing your modem more efficiently to conduct business. Both APIs are examined in more depth later in this book. Right now, it is important to remember that both APIs exist in Windows 98 in the form of new utilities.

You can see the effects of TAPI in the Modem applet in the Control Panel. The Modem applet enables you to configure your modem in one place. Any Windows 98 application that supports TAPI—such as Microsoft Exchange, Microsoft Outlook Express, and Microsoft Network—will use those settings. It doesn't include older 16-bit Windows applications. If you want the benefits of TAPI, you need to upgrade those applications as the vendors come out with new versions.

Microsoft Exchange is an example of a MAPI application. It enables you to access Microsoft Mail using a MAPI driver. A different MAPI driver provides access to CompuServe. Still another driver enables you to send a fax. In fact, you could have a MAPI driver to access each online service you subscribe to. The presence of these drivers enables you to access them all using just one application. The result is reduced training costs and the capability to move information from one service to another with the click of a button.

MAPI and TAPI aren't limited to Windows 98–specific applications. Microsoft Word, for example, provides a Send option on the File menu. This option enables you to send all or part of a document using MAPI to anywhere you can communicate. Using the native capabilities of Windows 98, this means you could send it as a fax, as an e-mail, or to an online service—all without leaving Word.

Implementing the Windows 98 New Generation Hardware Support

Windows 98 provides a wealth of new hardware support, including support for a Universal Serial Bus (USB), an Accelerated Graphics Port (AGP), an Advanced Configuration and Power Interface (ACPI), and a Digital Video Disk (DVD). Just how important these features are to you probably depends on whether you have the required hardware installed on your machine.

Tip: One of the best places to find out about the latest Windows 98 hardware developments is the Microsoft hardware site at http://www.microsoft.com/hwdev/. This site has everything you could possibly want to know about Windows 98 and hardware, including full technical specifications (when available).

Universal Serial Bus (USB)

USB is a new method for connecting peripheral devices to your machine. It only uses one kind of connector, so you don't have to worry about attaching a peripheral to the wrong connector. USB also provides some automation when it comes to configuration. Finally, USB provides faster connections—you could even potentially use it for a hard drive.

USB (and Windows 98) supports a concept known as a hub. Essentially, a hub acts as a central place for connecting peripheral cables. You could, for example, have a hub to connect an external modem, your sound system, and a printer.

Hubs don't necessarily have to be a separate item. Plans already exist for making your keyboard into a USB hub to plug in your mouse and a microphone. The keyboard might be used for other USB devices as well, such as a hand scanner. USB also enables you to have multiples of each device, such as two keyboards.

> **Note:** You need to know one more thing about USB under Windows 98. Your mouse, keyboard, and any other device you can use for input are now known by a new term, human input device (HID). You'll need to buy USB devices that support the HID 1.0 firmware specification, or they might not work properly. You can learn more about the HID 1.0 specification at http://www.usb.org/.

> **Note:** Apple Computers recently introduced a new cross-platform, high-speed serial data bus dubbed FireWire. FireWire can move large amounts of data between computers and peripheral devices at speeds of up to 400 megabits per second, enabling greater multimedia capabilities.

Accelerated Graphics Port (AGP)

The Accelerated Graphics Port (AGP) takes the connection for your display adapter off the PC bus and places it on the memory bus for the computer. This means your display adapter can move data faster—at the same rate as the CPU can move data to and from memory. This simple move from the PC bus to the memory bus can provide as much as a 4X speed increase over the speed that a display adapter can move data on the PCI bus. In addition, the display adapter no longer has to fight all the traffic on the peripheral bus to get the data it needs. This might sound like a minor improvement, but it makes a big difference when you consider the amount of data the display adapter has to move.

AGP wouldn't do much for you without DirectX 5.0. This latest version of DirectX provides support for AGP so vendors can write software that makes full use of this new architecture. In short, you'll see much faster display times in Windows 98 than you did in previous versions of Windows.

Advanced Configuration and Power Interface (ACPI)

This new Windows 98 feature is actually an expansion of the power management features found in Windows 95. At a minimum, you can now control when your hard drive and monitor turn themselves off after a period of non-use. Theoretically, you could leave your computer on all the time. This could, however, lead to the security problems mentioned in previous chapters.

You'll also find that Windows 98 supports two new features. The first is power schemes, which work just like the sound and appearance schemes you might have used in the past. A power scheme enables you to configure a method for managing the power on your machine. Select a power scheme based on your current activity. For example, you might want to use one scheme during the day that provides a delay so the machine doesn't turn off every time you stop to think. You then can use a different scheme at the end of the day to shut your machine off instantly.

Laptop users are already familiar with the Suspend entry on the Start menu, but it's new for desktop users. The Suspend switch enables you to electronically turn off everything on your machine without actually turning the power off. Your machine basically goes to sleep when you're not using it. If everything works as it should, your machine uses a minimum of power in this state—less than most night lights do.

Digital Video Disk (DVD)

Digital Video Disks (DVDs) are the latest revolution in the electronics industry. The high storage capacity of these drives—4.7GB compared to a CD-ROM's 650MB—enables a vendor to record an entire movie on a disk the size of today's CDs. The only other laser technology the movie industry has right now is laser disks, which are the size of an old 33 record (for those of you who remember that far back).

> **Tip:** If you want to get a head start working with DVDs on your machine, Sony recently introduced the model DDU100E DVD-ROM drive. Current list pricing for these drives (at the time of this writing) is $599. This drive also can read standard CDs, so you don't need to worry about having both a DVD-ROM and CD-ROM drive installed in your machine.

Windows 98 provides two levels of support for DVDs—one for data storage and another for playing movies. There is one catch to this support: Your drive must adhere to the SFF8090 specification (also known as the Mount Fuji specification).

Windows 98 also uses a new file system to read DVDs called the Universal Disk Filesystem (UDF). The main reason for the new file system is that the movie industry uses UDF to the exclusion of everything else. Unfortunately, this means you might run into some problems because some DVD-ROM drive makers will probably include support for the ISO9660 standard instead of the newer UDF standard. Make sure the drive you purchase provides UDF support (usually in the form of a driver).

On Your Own

Use the automatic installation technique discussed in this chapter to determine whether your machine has any undetected devices. Windows 98 usually will report that it didn't find anything. If so, click Cancel to exit the detection routine.

Try changing the configuration settings of various devices listed on the Device page of the System Properties dialog box. Be sure to save the settings in case you can't get Windows 98 back to its original configuration. Use settings that conflict with another device to see how Windows reacts. Be sure to change the setting back so you can use the device again.

14

Exploiting Multimedia and Games

Peter Norton®

Considering the multimedia orientation the Internet is taking, everyone's use of multimedia is only going to increase in the future. Multimedia on the Internet will include not only visual effects but audio effects as well. For example, consider a web site such as CD-Now, which includes the capability to play sound samples from CDs before you buy.

In addition to use on the Internet, multimedia can be used for training, education, and games. Many games provide intense graphics and sound presentations meant to thrill the user. It takes considerable hardware horsepower to play some of these games. In fact, some of the more robust sales campaigns for multimedia hardware appear in gaming magazines.

This isn't even the tip of the iceberg when it comes to multimedia. As voice-recognition technology improves, more people will use sound for feedback, for controlling their computer, and for storing and recording their own sounds. Because multimedia requires advanced hardware, this chapter looks at the hardware and a few of the software technologies you might need. By the time you finish this chapter, you'll have a better idea of what multimedia in Windows 98 entails and how you can make it easier to use.

Multimedia Hardware

Multimedia is much improved in Windows 98. The CD-ROM ships with several samples of multimedia presentations. Although they don't fully exploit the potential of multimedia, they give you an idea of what's possible.

The following sections provide an overview of multimedia in Windows 98 and discuss how it enables you to better exploit your hardware. Right now, it's hard to say which is ahead in the game—hardware or software. Neither is at a level that gives you the kind of presentation you're looking for, but I'll leave it for you to decide just how far we need to go.

MPEG Support

Motion pictures revolutionized the world, now they'll revolutionize your PC. The Motion Pictures Experts Group (MPEG) is a standards group that has developed a method of compressing VHS video into a very small format that fits on a CD-ROM. The VHS used by Windows 98 is the same format your VCR uses.

The technical term for the type of functionality MPEG provides is a *codec* (coder/decoder). Think of a codec as you would think of a modem. It enables you to send and receive video data using a standard medium. Instead of telephone wires, you're using a CD-ROM drive. (MPEG can be used to compress video in a variety of media environments, but CD-ROM is the most common media type.) In place of digital data, you're receiving video images.

Windows 98 currently provides the capability to display VHS-quality images in a 640 × 480 window at 30 frames per second. That's about the same rate that you see on television. You're supposed to get this level of performance from a double-speed CD-ROM drive, but I tested it with a quadruple-speed unit connected to my system and just barely got what I would call acceptable performance. I'm sure part of Microsoft's assumption is that you won't be running anything else when using the multimedia capabilities, but that probably isn't very valid. Most people will want to use this capability for training, which means that they'll probably have another application open. A 12X or 24X CD-ROM drive is probably your best bet for the level of support you really need to use MPEG video.

If you want to fully exploit your machine's hardware capabilities, make sure you have more than the minimum requirements on your system. Otherwise, you'll probably be disappointed with the performance that low-end hardware provides.

Sound Boards

There are many types of sound and many types of hardware to play it on. You no longer have to settle for the mediocre level of sound provided by previous versions of Windows. Windows 98 provides the controls to fully exploit the expanded capabilities of modern sound boards. To start using these capabilities, adjust the settings found in the Audio Properties dialog box. To access this dialog box, right-click the Speaker icon on the taskbar and select Adjust Audio Properties. You should see a dialog box similar to the one shown in Figure 14.1.

Figure 14.1.
The Audio Properties dialog box enables you to utilize the audio capabilities of your system.

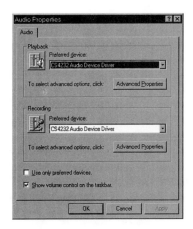

There are three main settings areas on this dialog. The first two contain similar settings for playback and record. A drop-down list box in the first two areas will allow you to select a preferred device from the list of devices installed on your machine. The preferred device is the one that Windows 98 will use whenever a sound doesn't require a specific device. For example, if you're playing a wave file using the media player, Windows 98 will use the preferred device. The pushbutton on the left side of the dialog will allow you to adjust either the playback or record level of your preferred device. Finally, the Advanced Properties button will allow you to adjust the characteristics of the preferred device.

The third area of the Audio Properties dialog contains two check boxes. Selecting the first check box tells Windows 98 that you only want to use the preferred device for playing or recording sounds. In other words, even if you have a second soundboard or a voice modem, Windows 98 won't use it if you select this check box. The second check box displays the Volume (speaker) icon on the Taskbar tray. This allows you to access the audio properties or set a sound level with relative ease.

Setting a Sound Level

There are separate controls for setting the playback or record level of the preferred device in the Audio Properties dialog. Figure 14.2 shows both of these dialog boxes. Click the Volume Control pushbutton in the Playback section of the Audio Properties dialog and you'll see the Master Out dialog box shown on the left side of Figure 14.2. Likewise, clicking the Volume Control pushbutton in the Recording section of the Audio Properties dialog will display the Wave Input dialog box shown on the right side of Figure 14.2. (The exact list of controls you see in either dialog box depends on the capabilities of your sound board or other preferred device.)

Figure 14.2.
The Master Out dialog changes playback levels, while the Wave Input dialog changes recording levels.

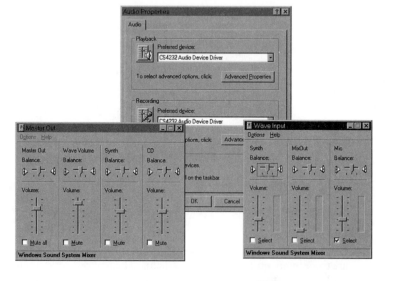

Note that both dialog boxes shown in Figure 14.2 contain an Options menu with two entries: Properties and Advanced Controls. Choosing the Properties option will display a Properties dialog that allows you to select which set of controls the dialog box displays (Playback or Recording). In addition, the Properties dialog will allow you to choose which controls appear in the dialogs. Most soundboards include settings for other features such as Line Balance. Windows 98 defaults to showing only the controls that you'll normally want to adjust.

Choosing the Options | Advanced Controls option will normally add pushbuttons to the sound level controls that support advanced features like Mic Balance. Exactly what the settings provided by the Advanced Controls do depends on your sound board. Make sure you check your vendor documentation before changing any of these settings.

Configuring the Preferred Device

Clicking either of the Advanced Properties pushbuttons in the Audio Properties dialog will display an Advanced Audio Properties dialog such as the one shown in Figure 14.3. The Advanced Audio Properties dialog for playback will normally contain two tabs: one to select the kind of speaker attached to your machine, and the other to adjust either the playback or record performance of your machine.

Figure 14.3.
The Advanced Audio Properties dialog allows you to select speaker type and adjust performance.

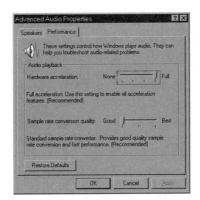

There are two sliders on the Advanced Audio Properties dialog. The first allows you to adjust the level of hardware acceleration that Windows 98 provides. Normally you'll want to keep this setting at the Full level. However, if you find that your machine is losing some of the sound that you're either trying to record or playback, or if you have a memory-constrained machine, you may have to adjust this slider down.

The second slider allows you to adjust the quality of the sound that you'll hear. A higher sample rate produces better sound. However, using a higher sample rate will also use more processor cycles and memory. You'll need to adjust the sample rate to a level where you can enjoy the quality of sound coming from your machine, yet the sound system doesn't bog everything else down. Windows 98 defaults to using a Good sound sampling rate. This produces the lowest playback or recording quality, but also impacts machine performance the least as well.

The Restore Defaults pushbutton at the bottom of the Advanced Audio Properties dialog allows you to reset the two sliders to the Windows 98 default. You'll normally use this pushbutton after you've experimented with various sound quality levels and want to return Windows 98 to its default performance and quality level.

Virtualizing Your Hardware

To make the best use of your hardware in Windows 98, you must be able to access it. You can do this in three ways, each of which has been mentioned before. If absolutely necessary, you can use a real-mode driver to access an older device. DLLs enable you to access devices that provide Windows 16-bit support but don't provide a Windows 98–specific driver. This is better than using a real-mode driver, but it's shy of the real goal you want to achieve. The best driver to use is a Windows 98–specific virtual "anything" driver (VxD). The following three sections discuss these types of support from an efficiency and ease-of-use standpoint.

Real-Mode Drivers for Older Devices

Using real-mode drivers in Windows 98 causes many problems. Other areas of this book discuss these problems in detail. Suffice it to say that a real-mode driver isn't the best choice for Windows 98.

First decide whether the device is needed all the time. In DOS and Windows 3.x, you have to load all devices you intend to use at boot up because there is no way to load them later. If you need a device in Windows 98, however, you can always load it later in MS-DOS mode. You just set up a copy of the command processor with the CONFIG.SYS and AUTOEXEC.BAT settings required to load the device in its optimum environment. You won't be able to load Windows 98 when using MS-DOS mode—or access other applications, for that matter. It's a problem of balancing convenience with overall system performance and stability.

You need to make some decisions when using a real-mode driver in Windows 98. The first choice is the amount of DOS space you need in comparison to the flexibility you want to give Windows in managing your memory. Loading all your device drivers low (in the lower 640KB area of the DOS environment) affects the amount of conventional memory you need. This choice also means you won't have to load a memory manager, however; Windows is able to provide the maximum flexibility possible.

If you have to load the driver high, however, you also have to load something other than the Windows memory manager. Try to optimize both the driver and the memory manager settings to reduce their impact on the Windows environment. For example, use the least amount of memory possible for buffers.

Using 16-Bit Drivers

Using an older, 16-bit Windows driver is a little better than using a real-mode driver. At least Windows still controls the memory environment. Unfortunately, using these older drivers still has an effect on overall system efficiency. Remember that all 16-bit applications, including drivers, run in a single session. Using that session's resources for a driver doesn't seem like the best way to go.

The 32-bit drivers that come with Windows 98 provide built-in safeguards to help protect your system environment. The older 16-bit drivers provide no such protection. They're more likely to crash (or at least destabilize) the system than a newer driver.

Finally, a 16-bit driver doesn't know how to interact with the miniport driver architecture used by Windows 98. This means you lose all the user and programmer benefits of such an architecture for that specific device.

Default 32-Bit Drivers

If you want to get the most out of your hardware, use 32-bit Windows 98 drivers. Windows 98 isn't a perfect operating system, but it provides enough advanced features that updating your hardware to use the new drivers is the best way to go. Using old drivers is another way to introduce inefficiencies and stability problems to your system.

Software for Games and Multimedia

DOS and older versions of Windows provide little, if any, multimedia support. If an application—such as a game or a presentation graphics program—wants to draw something onscreen, it has to provide all the processing instructions required to perform the task. Likewise, if you want to hear sounds, the software is responsible for providing the required drivers. Because of the lack of operating system support, a dearth of multimedia standards, and poor documentation from vendors, early games were an exercise in frustration for anyone unlucky enough to try and install them.

Windows 98 provides much more robust support than earlier operating systems. Many of the features you need to play a game or to display a presentation are built right into the operating system. The operating system supports your hardware; therefore, you'll have fewer problems getting single applications to work. There also are more standards now, so it's easier to find drivers to get the job done.

There are, however, some drawbacks to all the standardization and support from Windows 98. Although it's a good idea to place driver support at the operating-system level because it reduces the number of places to look when your hardware isn't working, it doesn't reduce any problems you have getting the hardware to work in the first place. Multimedia software support in Windows 98 is normally an all-or-nothing proposition. Having standardized hardware and associated drivers is one sure way to make sure that you'll have the fewest problems when getting Windows 98 to work with your software and to recognize your hardware. The following sections explore software solutions provided by Microsoft to help your hardware and applications to talk with each other.

ActiveMovie

ActiveMovie has been discussed several times in this book already. In essence, ActiveMovie is Microsoft's method for distributing multimedia in a relatively small package. The ActiveMovie player enables you play various kinds of multimedia files, including both audio and video files. The "ActiveMovie Control" section of Chapter 2, "Introducing Windows 98," provides details about this particular utility program.

WinG—Yesterday's Solution

There have been several attempts to persuade game developers to seriously consider Windows as a gaming platform. One of the earliest attempts was WinG.

Unfortunately, WinG lacked the capabilities necessary for game developers to produce a complete game. WinG didn't offer joystick or sound board support, for example, both of which are require-ments in many games. Thankfully, Microsoft acknowledged the shortcomings of WinG and pro-duced the Windows Games SDK, more commonly referred to today as DirectX.

DirectX—The Solution for Today

The most recent multimedia technology in the news is DirectX.

Tip: If you want the latest information about Microsoft's DirectX technology, go to `http://www.microsoft.com/directx/`. Visit the Data Visualization site at `http://www.directx.com/` if you want a non-Microsoft point of view about various graphics technologies including OpenGL and DirectX. You should also visit `http://www.cs.montana.edu/~pv/programing_links.html`. This site covers a range of new technologies including DirectX. If you need help troubleshooting DirectX, take a look at `http://support.microsoft.com/support/` and select DirectX in the My search is about box.

Understanding DirectX

DirectX is composed of several software layers, each of which performs a specific purpose. The fol-lowing list describes each layer and its purpose:

- **Components.** DirectX components represent the topmost layer of the DirectX hierarchy—most people would simply call them applications. Any game or multimedia application that uses DirectX resides at this level. Windows 98 comes with four DirectX components: ActiveMovie, VRML 2.0, NetShow and NetMeeting.

- **DirectX Media.** This layer manages all your resources such as video memory and access to the sound board. It's the application service level. You'll find several pieces of DirectX here, including DirectShow, DirectModel, DirectPlay, DirectAnimation, Direct3DRetainedMode, and VRML.

- **DirectX Foundation.** All the system-level services appear at this level. When the operating system needs to know what's going on, it talks to one of the pieces at this level. You'll find DirectDraw, DirectInput, DirectSound, DirectSound3D, and Direct3DImmediateMode at this level.

- **Hardware and Network.** None of this technology matters if your display can't present believable 3D graphics. DirectX does more than just help you get the most from your games and multimedia applications. It also provides an interface to the hardware you would normally expect to find with your favorite stereo. In other words, you'll see a dramatic improvement in sound and graphics quality.

> **Tip:** If you want to update an existing Windows installation to use DirectX 5, you can download it from `http://www.microsoft.com/directx/default.asp`. Look for the `IDX5RDST.EXE` file on the DirectX 5 SDK page (you may want to look for the `DX5ENG.EXE` file if you only need English language support). Downloading and installing this file gives your machine DirectX 5 capability. You might not notice an immediate difference, however. Most of the changes provided by DirectX 5 have to be programmed into the application software.

Now that you have a better idea how DirectX is put together, you need to know about two utilities for diagnosing problems. Look in your `Program Files\DirectX\Setup` folder; you'll see two new applications designed to make working with DirectX easier.

The first utility you'll see is DXInfo. This utility enables you to collect every piece of available information about your DirectX installation and display it onscreen. In fact, when you start this utility, the initial dialog box informs you that DXInfo is gathering the required information. After DXInfo gathers the information, you'll see a dialog box similar to the one shown in Figure 14.4. Notice there are two panes, one on the left for component-level information and another on the right for device-specific information.

There are two buttons at the bottom of the DXInfo - DirectX Information dialog box. The Exit button enables you to exit the program. Save Config Info enables you to save the information in the dialog box to a text file on disk. A technical support person might ask you to save this information and

send it to him. The text file contains useful DirectX setup information that could help you solve
your problem.

Figure 14.4.
*You can use the
DXInfo utility to
gather information for
technical support
personnel.*

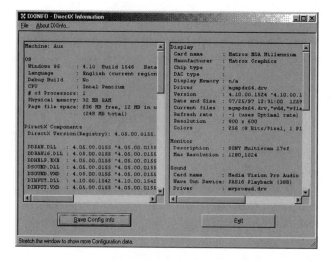

The second DirectX utility is DXTool. Most users never even look at this utility. Starting it up shows
you why (see Figure 14.5). The DXTool utility provides detailed DirectX information in a hierarchical format. Only a programmer could love information at this level. It's good to know this utility
exists, however, in case a technical support person needs more information than DXInfo can provide (or needs it in a different format).

Figure 14.5.
*Only a programmer
could love the level of
detail provided by the
DXTool utility.*

The New Features of DirectX 5

DirectX 5 contains a whole range of new features. Most help fine-tune game software, but a few
general multimedia features are packed in as well. The following list explores various DirectX 5 features:

- DirectX 5 provides better image quality and a longer list of features because Microsoft has spent a lot of time improving the Direct3D application programming interface (API).

- The DrawPrimitive services now enable a developer to pass polygon information directly to the hardware instead of going through a buffer. This results in better application execution speed.

- Animation capabilities have been improved.

- New technology features include sort-independent anti-aliasing, range-based fog, anisotropic texture filtering, and bufferless hidden surface elimination. What does this mean? You'll get more realistic images that also include special effects.

- You'll get all the speed your hardware has to offer as a result of Accelerated Graphics Port (AGP) support for DirectDraw in low-resolution mode and MMX optimizations.

- DirectX now supports force-feedback devices, such as joysticks, through the DirectInput API. The game controller control panel has been improved as well.

- Games are able to support Internet and LAN play through the DirectPlay API. This API comes with Windows NT security, client/server support, and lobby client API.

- Audio is much easier to create because of the DirectSound Capture and Notify APIs. Essentially, a game can use audio streams to make sound more fluid.

- DirectSound 3D support built into DirectX 5 enables you to hear where a sound originates.

- DirectX Setup detects most hardware and automatically configures it for you. You can now spend much less time figuring out how to get your hardware to work and more time playing games.

Getting Your Games to Cooperate

Game vendors do lots of tweaking to get the ultimate level of efficiency from their products. It's not too difficult to understand, therefore, that you'll run into some problems when using these products. In most cases, the glitches represent something the vendor couldn't test during the product development cycle. Still, the root of the problem is often the direct screen writes and hardware manipulation that game programs perform to provide the dramatic effects.

Getting your game to work with your hardware and software setup can be an exercise in frustration, especially if you purchase games that don't adhere to published standards. Unfortunately, it's difficult to tell much about a game from the outside. In most cases, you have to install the game and try it on your machine to see if it'll work.

I've actually had a game install perfectly on one machine and not at all on another even though the two machines used identical hardware and drivers. Sometimes it's a compatibility problem with DLLs installed by other software on the machine. This particular problem is worse under Windows because many DLLs are common to several pieces of software.

To protect yourself from potential problems when buying games, buy the software from a store that has an exchange policy. Some stores refuse to accept a game back after you've opened it (and for good reason—some buyers don't return all the pieces, making it impossible for the store owner to sell the game to someone else). I usually make sure the store at least offers store credit if I return a game that won't work on my machine. If at all possible, I try to buy at a place that offers a full cash refund, especially if there aren't any other games I want at the time of purchase.

Another way to protect yourself is to look at game reviews in magazines. Game reviews often mention potential problems the author saw when installing the game. A buggy game will probably receive a poor review. Unfortunately, a game review is also subjective. Your tastes might be completely different from the reviewer's. In other words, a review can't tell you whether you'll like a game or not; just look at it for clues as to whether the game will play as expected.

The following sections help you further reduce your risk when making a game purchase. They examine some of the more common problems people run into. Because there are many other problems you could run into, such as simple hardware failure, make sure you look for every potential source of a problem before you throw in the towel.

Tip: You don't have to try and conquer gaming problems alone. The Internet has a wealth of game-related newsgroups you can use to try and resolve your problem. There are no less than 10 newsgroups you can check out under `comp.sys.ibm.pc.games`. For example, `comp.sys.ibm.pc.games.strategic` helps you with strategy games. Make sure you check your game packaging for any vendor-related web sites as well. Even though you might find help a little lacking on some web sites, you can find out about patches and updates to your game.

Windows Games

Windows games have certain advantages over their DOS counterparts. A Windows game requires less setup in most cases, and the setup issues you do run into are easier to resolve. The reason is simple: For the most part, the game uses the same drivers as your other Windows applications. Setting up Windows is enough to ensure the game has everything it needs to perform a semi-automatic installation. You don't have to worry about which interrupt your sound board uses or how much memory is installed on your display adapter. You might still have to worry about whether to install DirectX, however, because many games use DirectX to speed things up.

Most Windows games have fewer compatibility problems because there's at least a little standardization between them. The use of common drivers is a major advantage in the Windows environment. Standards such as OpenGL and DirectX also have gone a long way toward making it easier for game vendors to ensure their products will run on your machine.

Another reason to use Windows games is that they usually provide a standard interface. Although there are differences between games (much more so in fact than other application types), you'll see evidence of the Windows interface in small things such as saving your files. I can't promise you won't have any problems using Windows games, but in most cases, you'll find them less difficult to use.

Using Windows as a platform has some problems, most notably that Windows games tend to run slower than their DOS counterparts. You'll also find that many Windows games also require more hardware resources than their DOS counterparts. There isn't any good rule of thumb for determining how much of a difference there is; you just have to make an educated guess when looking at the game package in the store.

I also have run into many color-depth and resolution problems. This is unique to Windows because of the flexibility of the display configuration. I run 1024×768 in 16-bit color mode. Many games want 640×480 and 256-color mode.

Looking for the Microsoft Seal of Approval

Most people who use Windows applications wrongly assume that any game in the store is going to be on Microsoft's approval list. You should always look for the Microsoft seal. This is your assurance that someone at Microsoft has at least looked at how the game is designed. There might be nothing wrong with a non-approved game, but you can't be sure.

A Microsoft seal, however, isn't a guarantee that you won't run into any problems. All the seal tells you is that the game was programmed in accordance with Microsoft's guidelines. In other words, the game meets certain minimal requirements. Whether that's enough for the game to run on your machine isn't assured.

You should still make sure you can return a game to the store, even if it has a Microsoft seal on it. I always buy approved games because I've had far fewer problems with them. Not only that, companies who take the time to go through the certification process usually provide better customer support as well. Purchasing a game with Microsoft's seal almost always assures you'll be able to get help resolving compatibility problems.

What Windows 95/98 Compatible Means

Some game companies have been pulling a fast one on their customers by adding a Windows 95– or Windows 98–compatible sticker to their products. Many of these games also have a Microsoft seal on them. Close examination, however, shows this is a Windows 3.x seal, not a Windows 95 or Windows 98 seal.

What does this mean to you as a customer? It means you have a game that was ported from the Windows 3.x environment. In many cases, it was tested to run under Windows 95 and nothing more. You might actually be using a 16-bit application, not the 32-bit application you were expecting.

Purchasing a Windows 95/98–compatible game isn't necessarily a bad choice. The requirements for a Windows 3.x seal are much less stringent than those for either Windows 95 or Windows 98, but at least the game has gone through some outside certification process. In addition, the 16-bit orienta-tion of the game means you won't get the protection offered by the 32-bit Windows 95/98 environ-ment.

The bottom line is you have to determine whether you're willing to live with the limitations of these games. I doubt many people run their word processor—or any other application for that matter—while relaxing with a game, so it's unlikely you'll run into data corruption problems. If you're in the habit of playing games at work, you might want to reconsider this policy (at least with 16-bit games that could crash your system).

Compatibility Issues

A few Windows compatibility problems haven't been covered in other sections of this chapter. You'll only run into most of these under very specific conditions. One of the most common problems is old drivers. Some game installation programs, for example, don't bother to check which DirectX driv-ers you're using. They just overwrite your new files with the old ones on the CD. Other game instal-lation programs misread the drivers and assume you have whatever it takes to run the game when, in reality, you don't.

Another problem is laptop-specific. For whatever reason (and I've heard more than a few conflict-ing reasons), the flat screen display provided with laptop computers doesn't react as well to DirectX as the displays used with desktop machines. As a result, I've seen many video problems when run-ning games on laptop machines. If you run into this problem, check with the laptop vendor for up-dated drivers. In many cases, someone else has already run into the problem, and the laptop vendor will have the fix you require.

Some problems I place into the strange category. One game I liked playing, for example, had a prob-lem with IP addresses. You could only contact another party on the Internet if the first IP number was two digits or less. You couldn't enter a three-digit beginning IP number. Fortunately, the ven-dor came out with a patch and the problem was fixed. Many people, however, assumed there was a problem with their machine and went through troubleshooting procedures before contacting the vendor. If you have a problem with a game, try contacting the vendor first (or at least a suitable newsgroup on the Internet) to see if it's a common problem.

Tip: Use the WinIPCfg utility (found in the main Windows folder) to determine your Internet IP address (you must have a live Internet connection). You'll find this utility in the Windows directory; just double-click on it from Windows Explorer to get started. Select the PPP Adapter entry to see the current IP address for your Internet connection. Pass on this information to the person you want to play a game with over the Internet. Make sure you check this information every time because you'll get a different IP address every time you connect to the Internet.

Newer DOS Games Using XMS

Most newer DOS games use XMS, which means you don't have to do much for them to run under Windows 98. In fact, most of these games run just by double-clicking them in Explorer. (You also can add them to your Start menu or as a shortcut on the desktop.)

You should be aware of a few things when playing newer DOS games under Windows. First, try them without any configuration changes at all. In some cases, game vendors have added code to make DOS games Windows friendly. If you change any of the settings in the PIF file associated with the DOS game, you could disable this special code and prevent your game from running. (Some game vendors have come to the conclusion that the only way you'll be able to play their game is using MS-DOS mode. In some cases that conclusion is wrong, so try running the program in Windows first.)

If you just double-click the game and it doesn't work, then you can perform some additional configuration setup. The "Settings" section of Chapter 12, "Exploiting Your Software: DOS, 16-Bit, and 32-Bit Applications," discusses the various PIF configuration issues. Try working with the settings on the Memory, Screen, or Misc tabs of the program's Properties dialog box. Unfortunate as it may seem, you might finally have to rely on MS-DOS mode for your game to run. The "MS-DOS Mode" section of Chapter 12 covers the procedure for using MS-DOS mode.

Older DOS Games Relying on EMS

Most older games won't run at all under Windows 98, and the reason is simple. Even though Windows 98 tries to be as accommodating as possible, these older DOS applications break too many rules such as accessing the display in a way Windows 98 doesn't expect. When this happens, you have two choices. You can create a boot disk that enables you to boot DOS without Windows 98, or you can use MS-DOS mode to at least automate the process. MS-DOS mode is covered in Chapter 12.

When It's Time to Shelve that Game

Eventually, you'll get to the point in which a game can no longer keep up with technology. One game I had, for example, wouldn't work with Pentium processors because of an assumption made by the original programmer. In this particular case, the game vendor released a patch to fix the Pentium problem. This situation is the exception, however, rather than the rule. When a game ages sufficiently, the vendor provides a modicum of technical support and that's about it. Technology eventually leaves these games gathering dust on your shelf.

I use a simple rule of thumb when it comes to shelving a game. Playing games is supposed to be fun and relaxing. If a game starts to take more time to set up and fix, you might want to put it on the shelf. It's hard giving up a game that feels as comfortable as an old pair of shoes, but even old shoes have to go by the wayside. The same can be said of many games.

Is there a life span you can expect from a game? Probably not. I recently rented a copy of Zork III. Despite the old text interface, the game was still fun to play. It even ran under Windows 98. Was the thrill still there? Well, the game was showing it's age. Having great graphics to look at is pretty addicting. The point is I could play it. Some games aren't quite that lucky. I can't get M1 Tank Platoon to play under Windows 98 no matter what I do. I was able to get this game to work under Windows 95 with the Pentium patch, but I think it has seen its final playing day.

On Your Own

Go to the Microsoft site at `http://www.microsoft.com/directx/default.asp` to see whether you have the latest version of DirectX. Making sure you have the latest operating system support is one way to reduce the number of problems you'll encounter. You should also spend some time checking your hardware and associated drivers. Most vendors have web sites from which you can download updated drivers. Hardware that uses flash ROM technology can benefit from downloads as well.

Visit various Internet sites to see how they use multimedia. You might even want to tell the webmaster what you like and what you don't. Make sure you get the whole experience by using both sight and sound.

Try to get an old game running under Windows 98. Some older games are a special challenge because you have to use special settings to get them to run. Make sure you take a close look at the game to see whether it's getting too old to run. As technology advances it leaves some games behind, making it difficult to install or play them. You also should check game-vendor web sites to see whether a patch is available for your game. These patches often fix compatibility problems.

Check your game packages to see whether they all have the Microsoft seal. Which ones have a Windows 3.x seal and a Windows 95/98–compatible sticker? You might want to contact the vendor to see if the game has gotten through the Windows 95/98 certification process. If it has, see if there's a patch available to bring your game up to that standard. If not, you might want to ask why they haven't bothered to certify their game in the Windows 95 or Windows 98 environment.

15

Fonts
and
Printing

Peter Norton®

Windows 98 improves the printing process over what most people were used to seeing with previous versions of Windows. One change from Windows 95 includes the use of Windows Driver Model (WDM) drivers, which should improve the robustness and usability of the printer drivers. Windows 3.x users will notice the greatest change, however. Even the simple act of installing a printer is easier, and removing one is easier still. Managing fonts is also easier than it was under Windows 3.x. This is because Windows 98 places them in a separate directory and provides a utility that you can use to manage them.

The following sections take you on a tour of the complex world of printers. I'll show you how to use the printer management features to your benefit, and explain some of the more intriguing aspects of the environment that Windows 98 provides.

Installing a Printer

Before you can use a printer, you have to install and configure it. Chapters 10 and 13 briefly looked at installing and configuring your printer. Chapter 10, "The Windows 98 Applets," showed you how to perform a special file installation. Chapter 13, "Exploiting Your Hardware," looked at a few of the most efficient ways to use your printer's capabilities. This section provides the details required to install a printer. It also includes some productivity tips.

The Printers Folder

Even if you don't have any printers installed on your system, you have a Printers folder in Control Panel. At a minimum, this folder contains an applet that enables you to install a new printer. There are actually two types of installation, local and network, and we'll look at both.

Local Printer Installation

The following steps take you through a local printer installation session. We'll also look at some configuration details.

1. Use the Start | Settings | Printers command to open the Printers folder. You might see one or more printers already installed in the folder, along with the Add Printer applet.

2. Double-click the Add Printer applet. You'll see the Add Printer Wizard dialog box.

Note: You might not see the dialog box shown in Figure 15.1 if your machine doesn't have network support installed. If you don't see Figure 15.1, simply bypass step 3 and the first sentence of step 4. You should see the dialog box in Figure 15.2, which enables you to select a printer type.

3. Click Next. The dialog box shown in Figure 15.1 appears. This is when you determine whether this will be a network or local printer. Selecting the Network printer option enables you to use a printer located on the network. (See Chapter 13 for more details on this topic.)

Figure 15.1.
This dialog box enables you to choose between a local and a network printer setup.

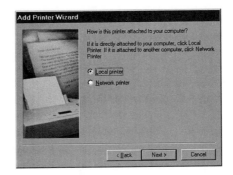

4. Choose Local Printer and click Next. The Add Printer Wizard asks you to select a printer using the dialog box shown in Figure 15.2. Notice that there are two lists. The one on the left contains a list of printer manufacturers. Selecting a vendor changes the list on the right to display printers manufactured by that vendor. Windows enables you to install an unsupported printer by clicking the Have Disk button. Chapter 10 covered this procedure, so I won't talk about it again here.

Figure 15.2.
Use the entries in this dialog box to select a printer vendor and model.

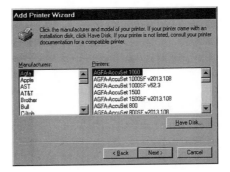

5. After you've selected a printer vendor and model, click Next. (If you've installed this printer before, the Add Printer Wizard will ask whether you want to keep the existing driver. Choose whether to keep it and click Next.) The next dialog box asks you to select a printer port. You'll see only the local ports if you haven't used a network printer port. The "Configuration" section later in this chapter shows you how to add a network printer port.

Tip: You can create multiple connections for one printer. I usually add a file connection as a minimum so that I can delay printing until later. A fax connection to support applications that don't provide one is also a good idea.

6. Select a port. You can configure the DOS options for the port by clicking the Configure Port button. (Chapter 13 covered these options.) Click Next to continue. The next dialog box asks what name to use for the printer and whether you want to use it as the default printer.

7. Type a printer name and decide whether you want to use this as the default printer. (The Add Printer Wizard will suggest an appropriate name you can use to create the first copy of the printer.) Click Next. The Add Printer Wizard asks whether you want to print a test page. I always send a test page to a local printer connected to an actual port. It makes little sense to print a test page for a file connection. Unless you already have your network connections configured, you'll need to test them later.

8. Choose whether you want to print a test page, and click Finish to complete the installation.

9. Windows 98 displays a status dialog box as it copies all the needed files to your drive. After it completes this task, you'll see the appropriate icon in the Printers folder.

Network Printer Installation

The following steps take you through a network printer installation session. You must have a network installed (including drivers and required connections) before using this procedure.

1. Use the Start | Settings | Printers command to open the Printers folder. You might see one or more printers already installed in the folder, along with the Add Printer applet.

2. Double-click the Add Printer applet. You'll see the Add Printer Wizard dialog box.

3. Click Next. The dialog box shown in Figure 15.1 appears. This is where you indicate whether this will be a network or local printer. If you don't see this dialog box, stop—you don't have the required network support installed.

4. Choose Network Printer and click Next. The Add Printer Wizard asks you to provide a network path or queue name. You can use the Browse button to find the required printer in Network Neighborhood. You'll also need to decide whether you plan to print to the network printer from DOS applications.

5. Type the network path or queue name for your printer. Select the Yes option if you plan to print from DOS applications. Click Next. (If you choose to print from DOS applications, the Add Printer Wizard might display an additional dialog that enables you to capture a printer port. Capturing the port enables the DOS application to use what appears to be a local port to print to the network printer.)

The Add Printer Wizard asks you to select a printer, using the dialog box shown in Figure 15.2. Notice that there are two lists. The one on the left contains a list of printer manufacturers. Selecting a vendor changes the list on the right to display printers manufactured by that vendor. Windows enables you to install an unsupported printer by clicking the Have Disk button. Chapter 10 covered this procedure, so I won't talk about it again here.

6. After you select a printer vendor and model, click Next. The next dialog box asks what name to use for the printer and whether you want to use it as the default printer.

7. Type a printer name and decide whether you want to use this as the default printer. (The Add Printer Wizard will suggest an appropriate name you can use to create the first copy of the printer.) Click Next. The Add Printer Wizard asks whether you want to print a test page.

8. Choose whether you want to print a test page, and click Finish to complete the installation.

9. Windows 98 displays a status dialog box as it copies all the needed files to your drive. After it completes this task, you'll see the appropriate icon in the Printers folder.

Adding a Network Port

Adding a network port is very easy under Windows 98. All you need to do is right-click the Printer icon, select Properties, and click the Details tab. You should see a dialog box similar to the one shown in Figure 15.3. Windows 98 enables you to perform a variety of tasks in this dialog box, including changing the printer by changing the driver you're using. The port-specific buttons enable you to add a new port or delete an existing one.

Figure 15.3.
The Details page of the printer's Properties dialog box enables you to add, delete, and configure the port to which your printer attaches.

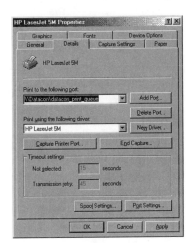

Clicking the Add Port button displays the Add Port dialog box. You can choose between two types of ports: local and network. The local (Other) options vary according to the utilities you have installed. They'll include at least a local port, along with fax and Microsoft Network if you have it installed. The network connections depend on the type of network you have installed and the devices shared on the network. You can use the Browse button to find a particular device. If you're using one of the networks that Windows 98 supports directly, a copy of Network Neighborhood will pop up.

Note: If your network isn't directly supported by Windows 98, its connections won't appear in Network Neighborhood. This means you'll have to type the precise network connection information by hand. Don't use any mapped names. Always use the fully qualified network path in this dialog box.

Clicking OK at this point stores the new connection name and returns you to the Details page. Windows 98 automatically selects the port as a destination. There's a problem with network connections, though—you can't configure them. You must capture the port first before you configure it. Capturing a port assigns it to a local connection. To capture a port, all you need to do is highlight it and click the Capture Printer Port button on the Details page. You'll see a Capture Printer Port dialog box. It consists of three entries: a local port name, the network connection path, and a check box that asks whether you want to reconnect to the port after each logon.

Tip: If you don't plan to use the network connection on a daily basis, use the End Capture button on the Details page of the Properties dialog box to remove the connection. This saves system resources and reduces boot time. It also keeps Windows 98 from displaying an error message if the connection isn't available the next time you boot the machine.

There's a final configuration issue for the ports you create on your machine: You need to decide what timeout settings to use. The first Timeout Settings field on the Details page—Not Selected—determines how long Windows 98 will wait for a printer ready signal. The only time the printer provides this signal is when it's online and ready to go. The default value normally provides sufficient time. However, some specialty printers might require additional time if they perform some type of paper cycling or other maintenance procedure.

The second setting—Transmission Retry—determines how long Windows will try to send data to the printer. In some cases, the printer is online but is unable to print for some reason. Normally, the default value works fine here as well. However, you might need to increase the value for network printers, especially on networks with print servers such as NetWare. Sometimes the print server is slow to respond because it's serving another request.

Now we come to one of the problem areas associated with Windows 98 and ports. What happens when the network connection you just created becomes invalid? Logic would dictate that you should be able to remove the network connection using the Delete Port dialog box. However, doing so will only net you an error message in some cases. Windows 98 will refuse to delete the port.

There's a way around this problem. Simply open the Registry to the key shown in Figure 15.4. Notice that this key contains subkeys, each one is a network connection. In this particular example, LPT2 is assigned to the \\MAIN\EPSON_COLOR connection. You can delete the LPT2 key and can remove the old network connection from your system. This technique is also more selective than simply deleting the old connection by using the Delete Port dialog box. In some situations, Windows decides to delete *all* the network connections when you use the Delete Port method. Directly editing the Registry is risky, but it can provide more control for the savvy network administrator.

Figure 15.4.
When Windows won't let you delete a port, use the Registry Editor to delete it instead.

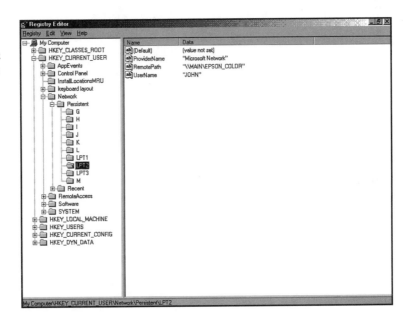

Configuration

Configuring your printer should be the next step after you assign it to a port. Most of the settings control the appearance of the output and the features that the printer provides to the user. In some cases, a configuration option also affects the speed of printing. I'll let you know what kind of choices you'll be making as we go along.

Opening the Printer Properties dialog box is as simple as right-clicking the Printer icon and selecting the Properties option from the context menu. The first page you'll always see is the General page, which contains the printer name, a comment that other users can use to identify the printer and a separator page entry. The comment can contain any information you want it to, such as the days and times that the printer is available for use. The Separator Page option is useful when more than one person uses the printer. It sends a page containing your name and other identifying information to the printer before it actually prints your document. There's also a Print Test Page button at the bottom of the screen. You can use this to test the capabilities of your printer at any time.

The Sharing page enables you to share a local printer with other people when using a Windows peer-to-peer network. (You must have printer sharing enabled to use this option.) The Sharing page contains two radio buttons. Selecting the Shared As button enables other people to use the printer. You must provide a share name. The comment and password are optional. I always recommend including a comment so that other people will know whether this printer is the one they're looking for. After you share a printer, Windows 98 adds a hand to the printer's icon.

Tip: Sharing reduces your spooling options. In addition, using a shared printer imposes other speed penalties on the local user. I always create a second printer for myself that isn't shared. This way, I get the best of both worlds—a shared printer for other people to use and a nonshared printer configured specifically for my needs.

The Paper page, shown in Figure 15.5, enables you to select the paper you want to use. Windows 98 supports a much broader range of paper types than previous versions of Windows did. I especially like all the envelope options. Although I don't use this particular feature, you might want to configure an envelope printer if you print envelopes a lot. The Orientation section enables you to choose the direction of printing: landscape or portrait. The Paper source: list box enables you to choose from various paper bin options that the printer provides. The Copies: field tells Windows how many copies of the printout to make.

Figure 15.5.
The Paper page contains all the entries required to select your paper type and print orientation.

Clicking the Unprintable Area button on the Paper page displays the Unprintable Area dialog box which contains four size fields (one for each margin) and at least two unit of measure options (inches and millimeters). This dialog box is especially important for laser printers, because they have a "dead zone" where the toner can't reach. The default settings are usually adequate unless you run into a special printing situation. For example, sometimes with my dot matrix I want to run the print almost to the edge of the page. The default settings won't allow me to do this, so I change them as required for the work I'm doing.

> **Tip:** Some applications, such as Netscape Navigator, rely on the settings in the Unprintable Area dialog box to determine where to stop printing. If you have fanfold paper installed in a dot-matrix printer and set the Top and Bottom fields to 0, these programs will continue to print without observing any margins at all. (This despite any margins you set using the Printer Setup option of the program.) As a minimum, they'll place any headers or footers you create in strange places. If you run into a situation in which an application doesn't seem to observe any margin settings that you request, try changing the settings in the Unprintable Area dialog box.

The name of the Graphics page is somewhat misleading. It also determines the print quality of the text you output using TrueType or other nonresident fonts, when using some types of printers. For example, the settings on this page will affect a dot-matrix or inkjet-type printer, but not a laser printer. The laser printer downloads its fonts, so the printer determines their quality level within the limitations of the resolution you set for it. Figure 15.6 shows the Graphics page.

Figure 15.6.
The Graphics page might affect more than just graphics.

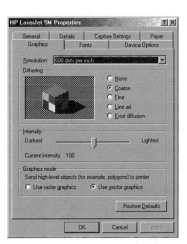

The Resolution: field on this page has a significant effect on the output quality of your document. It also has an effect on print speed and could affect system memory. High-resolution printouts require more time, especially from a dot-matrix printer, in which the output speed could drop to as little as one-tenth of the normal level. In addition, managing these printouts requires more system resources, such as CPU cycles and memory. Finally, any high-resolution printout that uses the spooler will need more temporary disk storage as well.

The various dithering options enable you to determine how Windows represents color in your printer output. It's especially important to use the correct settings for black-and-white printers because Windows has fewer methods to provide aesthetically-pleasing color differentiation. The following list describes the most common dithering options that you'll see:

- **None.** This option forces Windows to use the printer's built-in capabilities rather than dither the image.
- **Coarse.** This option takes less time to process but produces less pleasing results.
- **Fine.** I use this option for final print output. It provides the best color differentiation your printer can support.
- **Line Art.** Use this option if you want to remove the colors and print only the lines used to create a graphic.
- **Error Diffusion.** Windows 98 provides this option to take care of special color dithering problems such as moiré patterns. The Error diffusion option trades a little additional processing time for a random dithering scheme.

The Intensity slider enables you to change the darkness of your printout. It works like the slider on your toaster. The default value of 100 usually produces the crispest printout when you're using a new ribbon or cartridge.

Some printers include an additional setting such as the one shown at the bottom of the Graphics page. In this case, the Printer Properties dialog box is asking whether you want to output graphics in vector or raster mode. Using vector graphics might provide a little more flexibility. This will also reduce the processing load on the machine at the expense of the printer. In addition, vector graphics require more printer memory, because you need to store both a vector graphic and its raster counterpart. Using raster graphics means a slower printout, but it enables you to print pages that wouldn't otherwise fit in printer memory.

The Fonts page enables you to control how the printer handles fonts. The following paragraphs will cover the more common configuration options that you'll find on this page.

Most printers support cartridges these days. Even the lowliest dot-matrix printer usually provides some type of cartridge support. The Cartridges list box in this dialog box enables you to tell Windows which cartridges the printer contains.

Most laser printers provide the capacity to manage TrueType fonts. There are three options in this case, but your printer might support only one or two of them. The first option enables you to download the fonts as an outline. The advantage of this method is that the printer can create the full range of type sizes that TrueType allows, and it saves memory, because the TrueType font will take less room than the bitmap equivalents. The second option enables you to download the fonts as bitmaps. Use this option if you intend to use only a few fonts for your print jobs and speed is a critical factor. The third option keeps the TrueType fonts loaded on the local machine. The advantage is greatly reduced printer memory requirements. The disadvantage is greatly increased print times.

The HP LaserJet printer (and others) comes with a special utility that enables you to download fonts. You can access the download utility by clicking the Install Printer Fonts button near the bottom of the dialog box. Essentially, you tell the utility which fonts you want to download to the printer, and it takes care of the rest. Because each download utility is different, I won't go into further detail here.

The final page of the printer configuration dialog box is Device Options. As in so many other cases, the laser printer provides more options than other types of printers you might use; the exact options you find on this page are determined by the printer driver. Just about every printer you use will include a Print Quality list box. This enables you to select from the various quality modes the printer supplies.

There are three other optional fields on this page. One that's common to most laser printers is the Printer Memory field. The printer usually knows how much memory it has, but the Windows 98 driver doesn't. The LaserJet 4 and above also include special features such as page protection and a printer memory manager.

Point and Print

The point and print feature enables you to do a few things you couldn't do with previous versions of Windows, such as simplify remote printer installation. All you need to do to install a remote printer from a Windows 95/98, Windows NT, or NetWare network location is drag the icon from Network Neighborhood into the Printer folder. Windows 98 will take care of the rest. It might ask you to insert the CD-ROM so that it can load the proper drivers on your machine. Other than that, installation is as close to automatic as you can get.

Quick Printing Techniques

Remember the context menu I've been talking about throughout the book? Well, you won't escape it in this chapter either. Windows 98 takes a proactive approach when it comes to printing. All you need to do is right click on the document, and then choose Print from the context menu. Of course, you still have the usual Windows defaults for sending a document to the printer, including your application's Print menu.

Tip: We've viewed DDE in a variety of ways throughout this book. The most recent is in Chapter 11, "DDE, OLE, DCOM, and ActiveX," which discussed some of the ways you can use DDE with a document. Chapter 7, "Startup Shortcuts," looked at the way Explorer uses DDE. Here's one additional way to use DDE: Use Explorer to add another menu option to the context menu of your documents if you normally use more than one printer. This enables you to select something other than the default printer with the context menu. Unfortunately, your application must support DDE for this option to work. Use the current Print entry as a basis for creating your advanced Print option.

Another method that people use to send documents to the printer is to place a shortcut to the printer on the desktop. Then all you need to do to print a document is drag it to the printer you want to use and drop it. Of course, using this technique consumes some valuable desktop real estate, so use it only when required.

32-Bit Printing

Now that you have a printer configured and ready for use, it might be a good time to look at the way Windows 98 handles this task. An understanding of how printing works will often help you discover new optimization techniques or track down an equipment failure with ease. Figure 15.7 gives you an overview of the Windows 98 print architecture. I describe each component in the following list:

- **Graphics device interface (GDI).** The GDI is the API an application uses to talk to the printer. An application doesn't directly access a printer like DOS did. It uses the Windows services. This enables centralized scheduling and control of print jobs, a necessary requirement of a multitasking environment.

- **Device-independent bitmap (DIB) engine.** The DIB engine is usually associated with the display adapter. It works with the GDI to produce the bitmap you see onscreen. For example, when Windows displays wallpaper on the desktop, it's the DIB engine that produces the bitmap under the instruction of the GDI.

- **Printer driver.** This is the third piece of the print page preparation. It interfaces with both the GDI and the DIB engine to produce printer-specific output in the form of journal records. Think of a journal record as the disassembled pieces of a puzzle. All the pieces will eventually be put together; but for right now, each record is just a piece of that puzzle.

- **Print processor.** The print processor accepts printer-ready data from the printer driver. Its only function at this point is to de-spool the data to the print request router. In other words, it sends the journal records out single file in an orderly manner. Later, the print processor takes care of spooling the data to the local hard drive (spool files), if this is a local print job. This means that it takes all the puzzle pieces (journal records) and connects them into a single document.

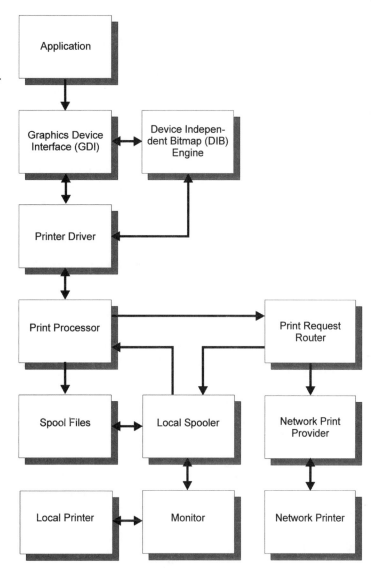

Figure 15.7.
Windows 98 uses an improved print architecture that depends on minidriver support.

- **Print request router.** This component routes the formatted data to the appropriate location. It determines whether the job is for a local or remote printer. If it's for a remote printer, the print request router sends the data to the network print provider. Otherwise, it sends the data to the local spooler.

- **Network print provider.** The network print provider accepts the journal records, connects them into a single document, converts the document into a network-specific format, then transmits the converted data to the next component in the network data stream.

- **Local spooler.** The first job of this component is to hand off print jobs to the print processor. The print processor converts the journal records it receives into a document. The local spooler reads the data files that the print processor stores on disk and sends them to the monitor. It also accepts messages from the monitor regarding the status of the printer. I discuss the types of information it receives when I discuss the monitor.

- **Spool files.** These are the physical files that the print processor stores in the Spool folder under the main Windows folder. Each printer type has its own storage location in this folder.

- **Monitor.** The monitor handles all communication with the printer. It accepts data from the spooler and transmits it to the printer. The monitor also is responsible for providing the spooler with Plug and Play information about the printer. Finally, the monitor provides the spooler with printer error information.

This might look like a lot of work just to get your document from an application to the printer that's connected to your machine. However, using this kind of interface provides the user with a lot more freedom in regard to printer usage. It ensures that everyone gets equal access to the printer. Programmers benefit as well, because it's easier to write print drivers. In addition, the DIB engine improves the quality of your output.

Managing Print Jobs

Gaining access to the print jobs you have running is no problem. Whenever you print, Windows adds a Printer icon to the control area of the Taskbar. Resting your mouse pointer over the Printer icon will tell you how many print jobs are pending. This provides a quick method of monitoring your printer status without opening any new windows.

If multiple printers are in use on your workstation at one time, right-clicking the Printer icon displays a menu of available printers. You can choose to open one or all of them. The top menu item will open all active printers—those with print jobs. It doesn't matter whether the print job is paused. The following sections describe printer management tools provided by Windows, looking at both local and remote printers.

Local Printers

The first type of printer we'll look at is the local printer. All you need to do to open a printer is right-click the Printer icon and select it from the list. As an alternative, double-clicking this icon displays the current print jobs for the default printer. The printer management display is shown in Figure 15.8.

Figure 15.8.

Getting to the dialog box needed to manage your print jobs under Windows 98 is easily accomplished from the Taskbar.

> **Note:** Windows 98 always defaults to a printer with an error. If you're having a printing problem, double-clicking the Printer icon will display the problem printer. The Printer icon also changes in appearance to tell you there's a failure. This enables you to track the status of all your print jobs, even if the printer isn't in the same room with you.

Managing print jobs is fairly simple. After you open the printer management display, you can access all the print jobs on an individual basis. The Printer menu contains two options that enable you to control the printer itself: Pause Printing and Purge Print Documents. The Pause Printing option enables you to stop the printer momentarily and restart it later. Purge Print Documents clears all print jobs from the spooler. The Set as Default option enables you to set this printer as the default. The Properties option opens the Printer Properties dialog box previously discussed.

You can access the Document menu in two ways. The first method is to select a document and access the menu directly. The second method is faster: Just right-click the document you want to work with and select the option from the context menu. The Document menu has two options. You can pause print jobs by using the Pause Printing option. The Cancel Printing option removes the print job from the spooler.

> **Tip:** One thing that isn't apparent when you look at this display is the fact that you can select a print job and move it somewhere else in the list. This enables you to change the priority of print jobs by simply moving them around as needed. You can move groups of print jobs with equal ease.

Remote Printers

Managing a remote printer under Windows 98 is nearly as easy as managing a local one. The print server must be a Windows 98, Windows NT, NetWare, or another network that supports point and print. Otherwise, remote print jobs won't show up on your display. After you establish a connection with the remote printer, you can exercise all the document-management functions you have with a local printer if you have the access rights required to perform the task.

Remote printing does offer one opportunity that local printing doesn't. You can perform what's called an *offline* print. Essentially, this is a form of pause. The Printer menu contains a special option for remote printers called Use Printer Offline. Checking the Use Printer Offline selection pauses the printer and stores the print jobs on disk. When you uncheck this entry, all the print jobs are sent to the remote printer.

When you look at the Printer folder display, a printer that's in Work Offline mode is dimmed. Windows 98 provides this visual indicator to tell you that you can use the printer but that none of the print jobs will actually go anywhere. Another reminder is the Printer icon on the Taskbar. You'll see the Printer icon, but it'll include the error indicator I mentioned earlier. Again, this tells you that one of the printers requires service. In this case, it isn't an unexpected error, merely a feature that Windows 98 provides.

Installing Fonts

Just about everyone needs a new font from time to time. Getting ready for a presentation, a new company policy, the need to differentiate your work from someone else's, or simply a need for change can all provide the motivation needed to install a new font. The following procedure shows you how:

1. Open the Control Panel and double-click the Fonts icon. You should see an Explorer-style display that enables you to view all the fonts installed on your machine.

2. Choose File | Install New Font to display the Add Fonts dialog box shown in Figure 15.9.

Figure 15.9.
The Add Fonts dialog box allows you to select fonts to add to your Windows installation.

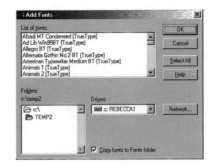

3. Browse your hard disk, floppy disk, or CD-ROM drive until you find the fonts you want to install. Highlight the desired fonts and click OK. You'll see the new fonts in your Font folder.

Removing Fonts

Removing fonts is very easy under Windows 98. All you do is open the Fonts folder—either through Explorer or by double-clicking the Fonts applet in Control Panel—select the fonts you want to remove, and press the Delete key. It's that easy.

You need to observe a few precautions. First and foremost, don't erase any font you're not sure of. Windows 98 requires some fonts for system use, and erasing them could cause problems. Second, if you do erase a font, make sure that you don't need it anymore or that you have a copy stored somewhere.

Viewing and Printing Fonts

The interface in the Fonts folder might be Explorer, but the options are different. The View menu contains some unique features that you'll want to use to really see your fonts. I'm not talking about the files themselves, but the fonts. Let me show you what I mean: Open Control Panel and double-click the Fonts applet. Open the View menu. You'll notice that Explorer now sports some new View options.

The List Fonts By Similarity option is the one I like. It enables you to see which fonts you could use as a substitute for something else. For example, what if you really like the font you're using for a particular purpose but want a slightly different effect? You could use this option to find the closest match in your directory or on a CD-ROM full of fonts.

Another handy view selection is the Hide Variations option. You can use it with any of the display formats to hide the different files required to create a complete font family. For example, if you turn on this option, you'll see only one Arial font, even though there are four files in the directory. Variations typically include bold, italic, and bold italic versions of the font.

To display a font, just double-click it. You also can use the Open option on the context menu.

It's very easy to print a sample of a font. All you need to do is right-click and select Print from the context menu. As an alternative, you can always click the Print button when viewing the font or use the File | Print command.

How Windows Matches Fonts

Windows uses something called the font-matching table to find a replacement font if the one you request isn't available. The font-matching table isn't actually a table; it's an algorithm that Windows 98 uses to match fonts. Windows uses the following criteria to find a matching font: the character set, variable versus fixed pitch, family, typeface name, height, width, weight, slant, underline, and strikethrough.

A TrueType font is always replaced with another TrueType font, even if a raster or vector font is a closer match. This enables your application to maintain the flexibility that TrueType provides.

If the font you're trying to use is either a vector or raster font, Windows 98 uses some additional sources to obtain a good match. These sources include: Printer ROM font, printer cartridge slot font, downloadable soft font, and TrueType font.

On Your Own

This chapter showed you how to install fonts. Many graphics programs include additional fonts. Use this exercise to install the set of fonts that'll get the job done for you.

Look in your \FONTS folder to see whether you can identify the various types of fonts that Windows 98 supports. How can you tell them apart? What purpose does each kind of font serve?

Install several versions of your printer, each with different settings. Try these new installations for several weeks to see whether you notice the additional ease of use that several pseudo-printers can provide. Also try the various print settings to see whether you notice variations in print speed and output quality that I mentioned earlier.

Place a shortcut to your printer on the desktop and try the drag and drop method of printing. Simply drag a file with your mouse pointer to the Printer icon and drop it.

16

Mice and Keyboards

Peter Norton®

The keyboard has been the mainstay of data input from the very beginning of computers. Even though the keyboard remains basically unchanged from those early days, there are still a few changes to note. For example, the Microsoft Natural Keyboard (and others like it) attempt to solve the problems people encounter with carpal tunnel syndrome and other types of repetitive stress injury.

A little less strange are the permutations that the mouse has gone through. It started out looking like a bar of soap. Today's versions are all shaped to fit the palm of your hand. The fact that every vendor used a different human for measurement is reflected in the size and shape variations of this new breed of rodent. Every manufacturer seems to have at least settled on two or three mouse buttons. If you've been around long enough, you'll remember the multibutton monstrosities that some companies introduced.

Windows 98 has also gotten in on the new and improved input device bandwagon. The following sections give you a tour of the great and not-so-great mouse and keyboard improvements that Windows 98 has made.

Multilingual Support

More of the world is using Windows today, so it's not too surprising to see Windows come in a variety of language options. I was a little surprised by the fact that this language support is at least partially built into every copy of Windows. No longer do you have to perform strange rituals and hand-edit your system files to get the proper level of language support. Windows 98 has it built right in using the code pages that we all learned to hate under DOS.

Installing a New Language

The convenience factor of using multilingual support under Windows 98 is compounded by the fact that you don't have to memorize code page numbers. Installing a new keyboard language is as simple as a few clicks. Let's take a look at what you'll need to do to install a new language on your machine.

1. Open the Control Panel. Double-click the Keyboard applet and select the Language tab. You should see a dialog box similar to the one shown in Figure 16.1. Note that English is the only language listed in the Language field. This field also tells you the type of English used (United States) and the keyboard layout (United States).

2. Click the Add button. You'll see the Add Language dialog box. It is important to consider which version of a language to choose. English is a good example. I currently have United States English installed. There's also a selection for other forms of English that might require a different keyboard layout. For example, Pressing Shift+4 could produce a pound symbol instead of a dollar sign. The choice of language also affects the way Windows makes assumptions about other setup needs. For example, it affects the default selection for monetary and numeric formats.

Figure 16.1.

The Language tab of the Keyboard Properties dialog box enables you to select one or more languages for your computer.

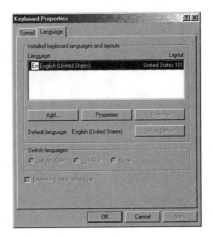

3. Click OK. You should see the new language added to the Language field. Completing this process also enables several other fields. For example, you can now choose which key combination to use to switch between languages. You also can choose to display the International icon on the taskbar. (I'll show you how to use this icon later in this chapter.)

4. Select a default language by highlighting it, then clicking the Set As Default button. The new default is displayed in the Default Language field.

5. You should probably check the layout for your new language. Highlight the new language, then click Properties to open the Language Properties dialog box. (This dialog box also displays the other changes you've made.) The dialog box is a little deceptive. At first you might think it's asking you to change the language again, but it's not. It's asking you to change your keyboard layout. Select a new layout to see the change in keyboard layout for yourself.

6. Click OK to complete the process. In this case, I chose the Dvorak layout. Figure 16.2 shows the results. Notice that the language remains the same; only the keyboard layout has changed. I'll use the Dvorak layout whenever I choose the German language from my list.

7. Close the Keyboard Properties dialog box to complete the process. You can accomplish the same thing by using the Apply key if you don't want to close the Keyboard Properties dialog box.

8. Close Windows and reboot your computer to make the change permanent.

Changing your keyboard layout and language won't display prompts in the language you select. It affects only the way your keyboard reacts and, to some extent, helps Windows 98 provide better input in regard to other configuration selections.

Figure 16.2.
*This dialog box shows
the results of choosing
another layout, using
the Properties button.*

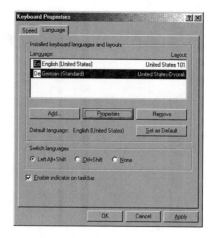

Removing a Language

You'll probably run into a situation in which you no longer require a specific keyboard layout. Whatever your reason for wanting to remove the language, Windows 98 makes it easy. The following procedure shows you how.

> **Tip:** This would be a good time to use the procedures shown in Chapter 7, "Startup Shortcuts," for checking the filenames of the drivers used to support the language you want to remove. Windows 98 won't remove these drivers, which means that they'll clutter your hard drive until you decide to install Windows from scratch—hopefully, a long time from now.

1. Open Control Panel. Double-click the Keyboard applet and select the Language page. You should see a dialog box similar to the one shown in Figure 16.1.

2. Highlight the entry for the language support you want to remove from your machine—in this case, the German language support.

3. Click the Remove button.

4. Close the Keyboard Properties dialog box to complete the process. Windows might get confused and think that another application is using the keyboard layout if you activated it at any time during this session. All you need to do is click OK to accept the error message. Windows will still remove the layout, but it won't do so until you reboot your machine.

5. Close Windows and reboot your computer to make the change permanent.

Accessing a Language from the Taskbar

Whenever you have more than one language installed on your machine, Windows gives you the opportunity to automatically add the International icon to your Taskbar. Figure 16.3 shows what this icon looks like.

Figure 16.3.
The International icon provides quick access to multiple language selections.

International icon

Peter's Principle: Easy Keyboard Access

Adding the International icon to your taskbar provides more than just a convenient way to change layouts. It also provides a quick way to change any of your keyboard settings whenever necessary.

Long hours at the keyboard can take their toll on your hands. The keyboard settings you used this morning could make for mistakes this afternoon if you have to repeat more keystrokes than you intended. It's a pain to go through Control Panel every time you want to make a change, so most people don't.

Having the International icon on your taskbar provides quick access to the keyboard settings. It doesn't usually appear, however, unless you install more than one language on your machine. You can manually add this icon to your taskbar by adding the International Settings application—INTERNAT.EXE—to your Startup folder. You'll find this application in the SYSTEM folder, under the main Windows folder for your machine. This gives you access to the keyboard settings, even if you have only one language installed.

There are several ways to use this icon. One is to determine which language you're currently using. Each language has a two-character abbreviation (see the dialog box in Figure 16.4). The Taskbar is where this two-digit abbreviation is used. For example, the icon shown in Figure 16.3 tells me that the English language is installed. As with other icons on the taskbar, you can momentarily hold your mouse cursor over the International icon to display the full name of the language currently in use.

Click the International icon to display a list of languages currently installed on the machine. Each entry is preceded by its two-digit abbreviation. This is one way to determine which language you're using if you forget what the abbreviation on the icon means. To select a new language just click it, as you would with any other menu.

Right-clicking the International icon brings up a context menu containing two entries: What's This? and Properties. In adding the What's This? option, Microsoft apparently thought users would not be able to figure out this icon for themselves. At least the associated help text is useful and could help beginners just starting to use Windows 98.

The Properties option in the context menu acts as you would expect. It takes you to the Keyboard Properties dialog box previously discussed. Even though it automatically displays the Language tab, you can switch to other tabs as necessary.

Configuring Your Keyboard

Languages aren't the only things you can change about your keyboard. There is one more page of selections that you can make regarding its setup. Figure 16.4 shows the page where you decide how the keyboard will react to your key presses.

Figure 16.4.
The Speed tab contains options to help the keyboard adjust to your typing habits.

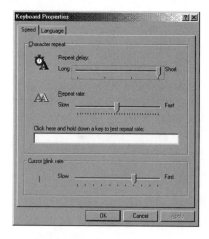

The Repeat Delay setting adjusts how long the keyboard waits before it starts to repeat keys. If this value is too short, you might have to undo a lot of excess keystrokes. The Repeat Rate setting adjusts how fast the characters repeat across the screen. Setting a slower rate enables you to control repeated keys better. Microsoft provides a test area to check the combination of settings. Make sure you actually try the keyboard settings before you make big changes in them.

Use the Cursor Blink Rate setting to change how many times the edit cursor blinks per second. Some people prefer a fast rate, and others like it a bit slower. Use a slower rate on portable machines than on desktop machines because the displays on portable machines take longer to react.

Configuring Your Mouse

The mouse started out as an optional feature in DOS, and you could navigate early versions of Windows pretty well without one. Today, however, a mouse is a must. To utilize Windows, you have to have a mouse. Some tasks are difficult or impossible to perform without one.

Standard Mouse Configuration

Just as you should configure your keyboard for optimum performance, you should do the same for your mouse. (This section assumes you're using the default Windows 98 drivers; some third-party drivers replace all or part of the standard mouse applet.) To configure your mouse, open the Mouse Properties dialog box by double-clicking the Mouse applet in the Control Panel.

The first group of settings on the Buttons page enables you to reverse your mouse buttons for left-handed use. (Windows 98 defaults to a right-handed installation.) The second group enables you to change the double-click speed. Your mouse's double-click speed is important. If it is set too slow, you might double-click without intending to. This is especially annoying in graphics programs, because you move the mouse and click to select items. Setting this value too fast is an exercise in frustration, because Windows doesn't wait long enough for you to double-click things. The Test Area enables you to practice using this setting. A jack-in-the-box alternately appears and disappears when you double-click.

The Pointers page enables you to change the type of mouse pointer used to indicate a specific event. Windows 98 provides a few "fancy" cursors, such as the 3D versions that give the screen a feeling of depth. In addition to static cursors, Windows 98 also provides animated cursors that move.

The upper section of this page enables you to save and load various mouse schemes. Think of a mouse scheme the same as you would a color scheme in previous versions of Windows. Use the Scheme list box to select a previously saved scheme. Clicking the Save As button displays a dialog box you can use to enter the name of a new scheme.

> **Tip:** Windows 98 provides a wealth of mouse pointers, including some extra-large ones. The extra-large pointers are designed for use with some of the Accessibility options. They also come in handy for laptops (on which seeing the cursor can be a real chore) and presentations (a larger-than-normal cursor helps to make your point). Tired eyes also can benefit from the use of large, easy-to-see cursors.

The bottom section of the Pointers page displays the actual mouse pointers. The purpose of each pointer is self-explanatory. To change a cursor, highlight it and click Browse. Windows displays the Browse dialog box, which contains a list of cursors in the CURSOR folder (found within the main Windows folder). Double-click the cursor you want. Windows replaces the current cursor with the one you double-clicked. This dialog box also displays a preview of the cursor. Animated cursors will appear to move within the Preview box. This shows how they'll look when you use them in an application or on the Windows desktop. If you select a cursor by accident and want to return to the default setting, click the Use Default button at the bottom of the Pointers page.

The Motion page, which consists of two sliders and a check box, affects how the mouse cursor tracks your hand movements. The slider at the top of the page enables you to set the pointer speed. Setting the speed too fast can cause jerky cursor movement and can make it difficult to control operations such as drawing. If you set the speed too slow, however, you have to make a large movement with the mouse to see a small movement onscreen.

The bottom section of the Motion page controls whether Windows provides pointer trails. A pointer trail isn't what most people envision it to be. Windows produces many copies of the pointer to track the movements you make with the mouse. These additional pointers are the pointer trail. The slider controls the length of the trail, and the check box turns the option on or off. This feature is specially designed to make it easier for portable users to track the mouse's position. Adding pointer trails also can help the visually impaired or can help new users track the mouse.

Special Laptop Configuration Considerations

Laptop computers have special needs when it comes to the mouse. There isn't a good place to put a mouse when using a laptop, especially when you're on a plane. Some laptop vendors take care of this problem by incorporating a special pointing device into the keyboard area. Other times, you can use a trackball that rides along the side of the case. Whatever mouse you use on the road, it likely requires some special configuration. (The options you see depend on the laptop vendor and the type of mouse you have installed.) As with a desktop machine, you can access the Mouse Properties dialog box on a laptop by double-clicking the Mouse applet in the Control Panel. The first page you're likely to see is the Quick Setup page.

Unlike when using a desktop machine, you can't rely on your laptop's environment staying the same. For that matter, you can't even be certain you'll use the same mouse from session to session. You might prefer to use a standard mouse at the office, another standard mouse at home, and the built-in mouse on the road. Configuring a laptop mouse isn't even close to configuring a desktop machine. (Because each mouse configuration is different, you should rely on vendor documentation to set it up.)

Another problem with laptops is answered by the Orientation page of the Mouse Properties dialog. (This page is provided in most standard laptop installations—custom pointing-device drivers might not include this page.) A trackball user, for example, might need to switch the trackball from one side of the laptop to the other during a trip because his seat is next to a window and there isn't room to move. To make this switch, click the Set Orientation button. Windows 98 asks you to move the balloon toward the clouds at the top of the screen. Moving the trackball adjusts the orientation as necessary to keep mouse movement the same as it normally is when you use a standard mouse. (In other words, moving the mouse up actually moves the cursor toward the top of the screen.) If you don't move the mouse cursor in a straight line, Windows displays an error message. Choose to try again and Windows 98 will set the orientation for you.

Most people use more than one mouse with their laptop. Unlike other hardware components, Windows 98 doesn't automatically register a mouse change—especially if your laptop has a built-in mouse.

This is why the Devices page of the Mouse Properties dialog is important. It enables you to either add a new mouse device or select an existing one.

To select an existing mouse device, select it from the drop-down list and then click Apply. Make sure the mouse is plugged in before you do this, or you might find yourself without a functional pointer device. (Most laptop software searches for the pointing device before switching over, but you can't be sure that it will.)

To add a new device, click the Add Device button. You'll first see a warning message. As stated in the message, you usually can plug in a serial mouse while the machine is running. If you try to plug in a PS/2 port mouse while the machine is running, however, there's a good chance you'll damage it. Always shut the machine down first, then plug in the PS/2 mouse. After you see this warning message, you can click OK to start the search for a new pointing device. If Windows 98 finds a new mouse, it takes you through the setup and configuration process.

Access for Users with Disabilities

Windows 98 provides special access features for people with disabilities. An overview of these options was provided in Chapter 4, "The Updater's Guide to Windows 98." The speed keys provided in the Accessibility options were discussed in Chapter 7. These options won't be repeated here. Instead, this section discusses how you can use these features to enhance productivity. To look at these features, open the Control Panel and double-click the Accessibility Options applet.

New Accessibility Tools for Windows 98

You'll find two new accessibility tools in Windows 98. The first is the Accessibility Settings Wizard, which helps you get Windows set up to meet your needs more quickly. The second new feature is the Microsoft Magnifier, which serves the same purpose as a magnifying glass. Microsoft Magnifier enables you to examine a section of the screen more closely. Both of these new accessibility tools can be found in the Accessories\Accessibility folder of the Start menu.

Microsoft Magnifier

Most of the time, you don't need an entire screen that contains large characters or graphics. You usually just want to magnify a small portion of the screen to see something in better detail. This is what Microsoft Magnifier is all about. Use it when you need to momentarily view something onscreen in a larger format. After you finish, just put it back the way it was. Figure 16.5 shows the Microsoft Magnifier in action.

There are six settings in the Microsoft Magnifier dialog box. The first, Magnification Level, determines how much magnification you get. The default setting of 2 should work for most situations. The Follow Mouse Cursor, Follow Keyboard Focus, and Follow Text Editing options determine where the focus of the magnification is. In most cases, you should use the Follow Mouse Cursor option if your sole purpose is to look at a particular area of the screen. The Follow Keyboard Focus and Follow Text Editing options come in handy when you're working with small type in a desktop publishing program. The Invert Colors option enables you to swap foreground and background colors in the magnified area. The Use High Contrast Scheme option changes your display color scheme when using the magnifier. This last option displays the screen using the same colors as the Use High Contrast option on the Display tab of the Accessibility Properties dialog box.

Figure 16.5.
Use Microsoft Magnifier to examine a section of the display more closely.

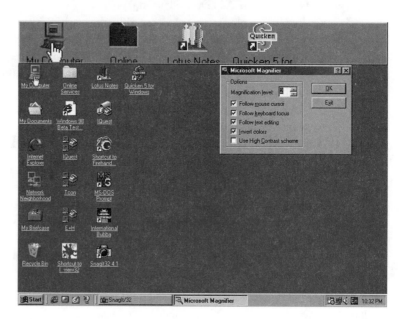

The Accessibility Settings Wizard

The first screen of the Accessibility Settings Wizard asks how well you can see the display. You can choose from normal or large text. A third option enables you to combine large text with the Microsoft Magnifier for maximum display size. Click Next and you'll see a screen that summarizes the changes the Accessibility Settings Wizard will make to your display. Click Next to make those changes and continue with the configuration process.

The wizard next asks you to specify which areas of Windows you are having problems with. Figure 16.6 shows this dialog box. Check the appropriate boxes to start the accessibility option configuration.

After you select one or more problem areas, click Next. The wizard helps you define a solution. If you select the first check box (I am blind or have difficulty seeing things on screen.), for example, the wizard displays a series of dialog boxes that enable you to change scroll bar sizes, icon sizes, the color scheme, and so on. Follow the instructions in the various dialog boxes to adjust Windows to meet your needs. When finished, you'll see a final summary screen that tells what changes you made.

Read over the list of changes and click Finish if you want to make them. Otherwise, click Cancel to return your screen to normal.

Figure 16.6.

The Accessibility Settings Wizard enables you to define which areas of Windows are giving you trouble.

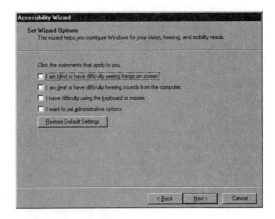

Special Keyboard Features

Windows provides three special keyboard features: StickyKeys, FilterKeys, and ToggleKeys. They can be found on the Keyboard page of the Accessibility Properties dialog box, as shown in Figure 16.7. (Double-click the Accessibility Options applet in the Control Panel to display this dialog box.) Microsoft provides special key combinations to turn them on.

Figure 16.7.

The keyboard accessibility-related functions can be turned on from the Keyboard page.

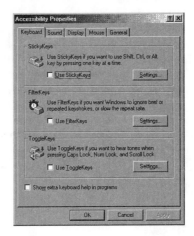

These features all have one thing in common: They change the way the keyboard works, independent of the keyboard driver. You must install the Accessibility Options feature to make them work. The Show Extra Keyboard Help in Programs check box at the bottom of the page adds help information to applications that support this feature.

Using StickyKeys

The StickyKeys feature comes in handy for a variety of purposes. It makes the Shift, Ctrl, and Alt keys act as toggle switches. Press one of these keys once and it becomes active. Press it a second time and it's turned off. I use StickyKeys in graphics programs that require you to hold down the Ctrl key to select a group of items. It can be inconvenient to hold down the Ctrl key while you look around for objects to select. The StickyKeys feature alleviates this problem. Click the Settings button on the Keyboard tab of the Accessibility Properties dialog to open the Settings for StickyKeys dialog box shown in Figure 16.8.

Figure 16.8.
The Settings for StickyKeys dialog box enables you to change how this feature works.

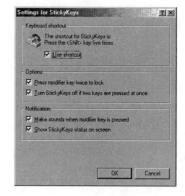

There are three groups of settings for StickyKeys. The first option, Keyboard Shortcut, enables you to turn on StickyKeys using the shortcut key. There's no reason to turn this off. It's very unlikely that another application would use the same control key sequence.

The Options group contains two settings. The StickyKeys option usually works like a toggle. Checking the first box tells Windows to wait until you press the same control key twice before making the control key active. The second check box enables two people to use the same keyboard. Pressing a control key and a non-control key at the same time turns StickyKeys off.

The Notification group also contains two settings. The first setting tells Windows to play a different sound for each unique control key it activates. This can prevent you from activating a control key by accident. The second option displays an icon on the taskbar so you can control StickyKeys more easily. I select this option to make it easier to turn StickyKeys on and off.

Using FilterKeys

FilterKeys helps eliminate extra keystrokes so you don't get "tthis" instead of "this." As with StickyKeys, you can adjust the way FilterKeys works by clicking the Settings button. The Settings for FilterKeys dialog box is shown in Figure 16.9. The first option in this dialog box enables you to turn the shortcut key on and off. This works just like the same feature in StickyKeys. The

Notification group at the bottom of the dialog box should look familiar. The only difference is that, instead of playing a sound, FilterKeys beeps when you activate it.

Figure 16.9.
The Settings for FilterKeys dialog box enables you to change how this feature works.

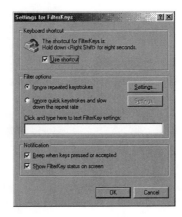

The Filter Options group enables you to select from two ways of filtering keystrokes. The first option filters keys that get pressed in rapid succession. This feature would filter the rapid typing of the extra "t" in the example previously mentioned. The Settings button displays a dialog box that enables you to select how long an interval must pass between the first and second times you press the same key. It also provides a field in which you can test the setting. The second option in this group filters accidental key presses. At one time or another, everyone presses a key without meaning to. As with the StickyKeys option, the Settings button displays a dialog box in which you select how long you have to press a key before Windows accepts it.

Using ToggleKeys

The ToggleKeys feature emits a tone every time you turn the Caps Lock, Scroll Lock, or Num Lock keys on or off. The ToggleKeys dialog box contains a single option, which enables you to turn the shortcut key on or off.

Special Mouse Settings

MouseKeys enables you to use the arrow keys on the numeric keypad as a mouse. Instead of moving the cursor with the mouse, you can move it with the arrow keys. This doesn't disable your mouse; it merely augments it. The Mouse tab of the Accessibility Properties dialog box contains a check box that enables you to turn MouseKeys on or off.

Click the Settings button on this tab to display the only dialog box of settings for MouseKeys (see Figure 16.10). The first option, Keyboard Shortcut, enables you to turn on MouseKeys using a shortcut key. There's no reason to turn this off. It's unlikely that another program would use the same control key sequence.

Figure 16.10.

The Settings for MouseKeys dialog box enables you to change how this feature works.

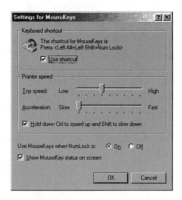

In the second group, Pointer Speed, you can optimize the performance of this particular feature. The first option enables you to set the fastest speed at which you can move the mouse cursor using the arrow keys. The Acceleration setting determines how quickly the cursor reaches full speed after you press it. Windows doesn't start the cursor at full speed; it brings it there gradually. The combination of these two settings determines how much added control MouseKeys gives you over the cursor. The check box in this group provides another option. You can press the Ctrl key to speed up the mouse cursor and press the Shift key to slow it down.

There are two settings at the bottom of the dialog box. The radio buttons control when MouseKeys is active. You must specify whether the Num Lock key should be on or off when you use MouseKeys. The second option determines whether the MouseKeys icon appears on the taskbar.

On Your Own

Try the different accessibility options to see whether they provide features you can use. This chapter provides suggestions for how you could use each feature.

Install and try using the Dvorak keyboard layout. After you learn how to use this setup, you'll be able to type faster and with less fatigue. This particular setup also can help you fight repetitive stress injuries such as carpal tunnel syndrome. Nothing provides 100 percent protection. The Dvorak keyboard layout can't reverse years of abuse, but learning this new setup could help prevent current problems from getting worse.

Review earlier chapters—especially Chapter 7—and practice using the shortcuts discussed with the Accessibility options turned on. Do the Accessibility options make a difference when using standard shortcuts? Try different combinations to create the fastest keyboard interface possible.

17

Video Configuration

Peter Norton®

Video is the most noticeable architectural component of Windows 98. It's the underlying combination of hardware and software that enables you to see the graphics, dialog boxes, icons, and other elements that make Windows 98 worth using.

The problem isn't simply displaying a picture onscreen; that would be easy to manage. The problem is communication between the various elements that create and manage the picture in the first place. The following list illustrates some of Windows 98's communications problems:

- **Application level.** Three different kinds of applications use Windows 98. MS-DOS applications usually think they're alone in the world, so they violate just about every imaginable rule for displaying information. Although 16-bit Windows applications are a bit more conscientious than their MS-DOS counterparts, they still use an older interface to draw to the display. Finally, newer 32-bit Windows applications might offer the ultimate in available features, but they're often hampered by other applications running on the machine.

- **Device driver.** If the display driver doesn't correctly interpret the commands issued by applications running under Windows, or if those applications use undocumented command features, miscommunication is likely. If the adapter misinterprets the commands an application uses, for example, you get an unreadable screen.

- **Adapter.** In the beginning, IBM was responsible for the standard way in which CGA and EGA display adapters worked. By the time VGA adapters arrived, IBM was starting to lose its leadership position. Then came SVGA (super VGA) adapters, and there was no IBM standard to follow. For a while, no standardization existed for the extended modes vendors built into their display adapters. Later in this chapter, you'll see how this problem was finally resolved.

- **Operating system requirements.** The operating system itself is usually the least of your display worries. Sometimes, however, it can actually be the source of your problems. Icons, for example, are taken for granted because they generally work without difficulty. But what happens if a file the operating system needs gets changed by an application or gets corrupted somehow? In most cases, you have to replace this file before things will work again.

Now that you are more aware of Windows's communications problems, you might wonder how it works at all. Windows uses an *event loop* to talk with applications. Think of an event loop as a bulletin board on which Windows and applications can post messages. A message could request a service such as opening a file, or it could tell an application to perform a maintenance task. Windows notifies an application when it has a message waiting. The application picks up its messages and acts on them. The event loop enables Windows to send "paint" messages to any application that might require them. The combination of an event loop and constant redrawing helps Windows keep your display up-to-date, even if small amounts of miscommunication do occur.

This chapter discusses video in Windows 98. More than that, it talks about communication. Without the required level of communication between all system elements, you'd never see anything when using Windows 98. Look for the communication requirements in the following sections.

Graphics Standards

Standards organizations help keep your computer running smoothly. The standards organization to monitor for display adapters and monitors is the Video Electronics Standards Association (VESA).

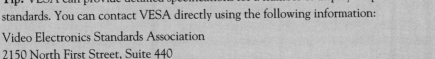

Tip: VESA can provide detailed specifications for a number of display adapter and monitor standards. You can contact VESA directly using the following information:

Video Electronics Standards Association
2150 North First Street, Suite 440
San Jose, CA 95131-2029
Voice: 408-435-0333
Fax: 408-435-8225
Internet: http://www.vesa.org/

I first discovered VESA in 1989, but it was probably around before that. IBM had dropped VGA in favor of its proprietary 8514/A display adapter. Without a leader in the field to dictate a standard, the entire display-adapter arena fell into a state of disarray. VESA stepped in to make sense of this chaos. The results of these initial efforts were several VESA standards and some additional software for each display adapter. The following list shows many of the common standards VESA has produced. (This selection of standards is by no means complete.)

- **Super VGA protected-mode interface (VS911020).** This document provides information about a standardized method of accessing BIOS routines from a protected-mode program.

- **Video cursor interface (VS911021).** Use this standard to learn how to build an interface between a pointing device and the display adapter.

- **Super VGA BIOS extension (VS911022).** Use this document to learn about VESA standard display modes for the SVGA.

- **XGA extensions standard (VXE 1.0).** This document discusses standardization efforts underway for the XGA.

- **Monitor timing standard for 1024×768 with 70-Hz refresh rate (VS910810).** This standard provides a consistent method of producing ergonomically correct displays with 70-Hz refresh rates. This greatly reduces eyestrain.

- **Standard 8514/A register bit fields (VS900601).** This standard provides the details of how an 8514/A register works.
- **Standard VGA passthrough connector (VS890803).** This standard defines the passthrough connector and enables you to use multiple adapters on one machine.
- **Standard 8514/A registers (VS890804).** This standard defines which registers an 8514/A contains.

Windows 98 supports several new standards, including DirectX 5. This standard enables game vendors to write high-speed graphics routines using a standard interface. DirectX provides the means to write directly to the hardware, yet it keeps Windows in the picture. Windows still tracks the game program's actions, but it does so without the interference a normal application would encounter. The advantages of using DirectX are high speed and maximum flexibility. A major drawback is that the vendor has to do more work to get an application up and running. In addition, many people have run into compatibility problems when using DirectX with non-standard display adapters. Even though these adapters work fine with standard Windows applications, the DirectX interface causes significant problems.

The OpenGL standard used to be available only to Windows NT users. Now you can use this standard on Windows 98 machines as well. OpenGL is a set of graphics library routines. Using these routines can save a programmer a substantial amount of time. You can see the effects of OpenGL by installing the new screen savers in Windows 98. You'll see a set of high-speed 3D-graphics routines in action.

Intel also has introduced a standard for all kinds of multimedia, including video. The multimedia extension (MMX) Pentium processor greatly increases the speed at which applications can display multimedia. Windows 98 contains the necessary support to use MMX to its full potential.

The Windows 98 Graphics Architecture

Now that you're familiar with the problems Microsoft (and any other vendor) faces in providing something for you to look at, it's time to discuss how it is accomplished. This section doesn't get into bits and bytes, but you'll learn about the basic components required to display something onscreen. Figure 17.1 is an overview of the Windows 98 architecture.

The following list describes each component and the task it performs:

- **WINOLDAP.** This module senses when a DOS application is about to take control of the display. It notifies USER and the screen grabber so they can preserve the graphics system status information. This module is listed as `WINOA386.MOD` in your `SYSTEM` directory.

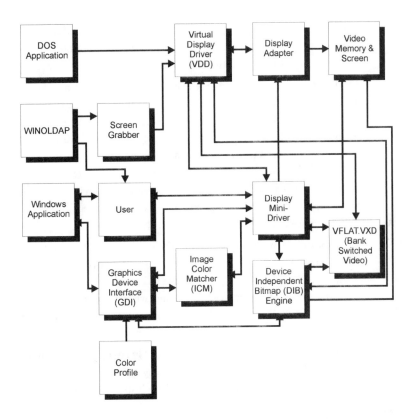

Figure 17.1.
An overview of the Windows 98 graphics architecture.

- **Screen grabber.** The screen grabber takes a picture of the screen and preserves it for later. This enables Windows to restore the screen to its former appearance after you exit a DOS session. Any file with a `.2gr` or `.3gr` extension in your SYSTEM directory is a screen grabber.

- **User.** This module tracks the state of all display elements (such as icons and dialog boxes) and draws them. It needs to be informed before a DOS session comes to the foreground so it can take a snapshot of the current state of these components. As previously stated, two User-related files are on disk—a 16-bit version and a 32-bit version.

- **GDI.** The GDI module works with the display driver and the DIB engine to produce the graphics components of a Windows display. Like the User module, there are two physical files—one for 16-bit needs and the other for 32-bit needs.

- **Display minidriver.** Windows 98 uses a combination of the display minidriver and the DIB engine for adapters that support them. Using this driver combination results in a speed increase from 32-bit code. The name of this file varies, depending on the type of display you're using. On my system, it's named SUPERVGA.DRV. Unlike VDD, which performs all video processing, the display minidriver only takes care of device-specific details. The DIB engine takes care of graphics rendering. A minidriver contains much less code than a full-fledged VDD; this reduces the amount of code a vendor must write.

- **Device-independent bitmap (DIB) engine.** The DIB engine takes graphics instructions provided by the GDI and renders them into an image. Unlike printing, the DIB engine actually draws the rendered image on the frame buffer. A *frame buffer* is a piece of system memory set aside to represent video memory. When the drawing on the buffer is complete, the entire buffer is sent to video memory at one time. Anything sent to video memory usually ends up on the display. This process is known as *virtualization*. The DIB engine itself is found in DIBENG.DLL. A compatibility module for previous versions of Windows applications is called DISPDIB.DLL; this module was the predecessor to the DIB engine. The frame buffer management routines are found in FRAMEBUF.DRV.

- **Color profile.** This data file contains the color capabilities for your output device. It doesn't matter whether the device is a printer or a display adapter; the type of information is the same. A color profile provides the ICM with information it needs to keep the display and other color devices in sync. That way, when you select dark red on the display, you get the same dark red on your printer. All the color profile files are in the COLOR folder within the SYSTEM folder. All these files have an .ICM extension.

- **Image color matcher (ICM).** The ICM subtly changes the output of your printer and your display so they match. The GDI, the display minidriver, and the ICM work together to compare the current color set and translate it into something that works on both devices. The files that contain the ICM include ICM32.DLL and ICMUI.DLL, both of which appear in the SYSTEM folder.

- **VFLATD.VXD.** This module is used only for bank-switched video adapters. Its main purpose is to manage the video memory window these devices provide. The display adapter on your machine can contain a large amount of memory. Unfortunately, only a 64KB window is set aside to access that memory. Depending on your adapter's configuration, Windows might not be able to get around this limitation. VFLATD.VXD can manage up to a 1MB frame buffer. It reads this buffer into video memory as required, in 64KB chunks.

- **Virtual display driver (VDD).** Previous versions of Windows used this module as the sole source of communication with the display adapter. Windows 98 provides it for compatibility purposes and for DOS applications. In most cases, its filename contains part of the display adapter vendor's name. The name of the VxD on my system, for example, is VIDEO7.VXD. The file is located in the SYSTEM folder. The virtual display driver converts drawing commands into signals the display adapter can use. It also manages the display adapter and performs other tasks related to how the applications on your machine share the display adapter. In essence, it's a 16-bit version of the display minidriver/DIB engine combination.

- **Display adapter.** This is the physical piece of hardware in your machine.
- **Video memory and screen.** The electronic form of the image you see onscreen is stored in video memory.

That was a quick tour of the video subsystem. The actual inner workings of this part of Windows are more complex than shown here.

Video Boards

While your attention is focused on the video subsystem, let's take a quick look at video boards. A few performance clues were tucked away in the discussion of architecture. Did you notice that VFLATD.VXD supports only 1MB of address space? What happens if your display adapter contains 2MB of memory or more? Don't worry. Windows 98 completely supports the entire range of memory provided by your display adapter. It might, however, have to rely more on the display minidriver to do so. This means a lot more calls and perhaps a few more thunks between various display components. The end result is a slight loss in performance from a purely display-subsystem point of view.

This isn't all bad news, however. Increased video memory has a couple definite advantages. First, more memory means more colors. More colors can result in better font anti-aliasing and other aesthetic qualities on your display. (Anti-aliasing is the feature that makes fonts look smooth onscreen.) Second, more memory means higher resolution. A higher resolution can help you position graphics more accurately and can result in reduced eye fatigue.

No matter how you look at it, though, more colors and higher resolution lead to decreased performance. Moving the video window around takes some time; allowing the frame buffer to manage more than 1MB of video memory takes even more. Each layer of management you add to the video subsystem chews up processor cycles. How do you get around these problems?

- **Dual-ported video RAM (VRAM).** Many display adapters come with VRAM. It's called dual-ported because it actually contains two ports. A serial buffer enables the display to read the contents of video memory. A parallel buffer enables Windows to simultaneously write to video memory. Dual-ported memory enables an application to write to video memory at any time instead of only during the display cycle.
- **Display coprocessor.** Many display adapters come with a coprocessor. Windows 98 offloads as much display processing as possible to the display coprocessor. Offloading part of the graphics processing responsibility frees up processor cycles; you'll notice an overall improvement in system speed. In addition, the display processor is usually a special-purpose-state machine that processes graphics instructions faster than the DIB engine.
- **32-bit display adapter.** To display an image, you have to move data, and that requires time. You can reduce the amount of time, however, by using a wider data path. Some display adapters come with a 32-bit path that improves graphics performance. In addition,

the 32-bit bus on a computer usually operates at a higher clock speed than its 16-bit counterpart—which provides further speed increases. (Eventually 64-bit and 128-bit display adapters will provide an even greater increase in speed.)

- **MMX Pentium processor.** Much of the processing required to display an image onscreen is done within the processor. In most cases, the display functions use generic processor calls to get the job done. The MMX version of the Pentium processor from Intel is designed to process graphics and audio much faster than its predecessors.

You also need to look for other things in a Windows 98 display adapter, such as Plug and Play. You can gain a lot from Plug and Play–compatible monitors and display adapters. Not only are these devices self-configuring, they also provide greater flexibility. Non–Plug and Play devices limit color selection. You can change the resolution of your display adapter without rebooting, but you can't change the number of colors.

Installing Video Display Adapters

Chapter 13, "Exploiting Your Hardware," described the physical process of installing your display adapter as part of the hardware installation process. The process for installing a new display adapter driver isn't much different. The following section, however, shows you an alternative to that process.

Installing a Display Adapter

Installing a new display adapter is not difficult. The following procedure shows you how.

1. Right-click the desktop and choose the Properties option. You should see the Display Properties dialog box.

2. Select the Settings page. Click the Advanced button to see the advanced display Properties dialog box, which should be similar to the one in Figure 17.2. This dialog box contains four settings pages. You use the same dialog box (but different fields) to install a monitor or a display adapter. You should notice several other features in this dialog box. First, it tells you which drivers the display adapter requires. This is the adapter itself, not the video sub-system as a whole. The video subsystem also contains a number of files that are either generic or specific to certain conditions. Second, this dialog box tells you the current display adapter type and its version number. This can provide important information when troubleshooting. Third, the refresh rate field enables you to set the refresh rate of the display. Using a higher refresh rate usually results in less eye fatigue. Unfortunately, a high refresh rate also produces more heat. In some situations, one refresh rate will interact with the lighting in your office and another won't. Always check this setting to make sure Windows's selections really work in your situation.

Note: Your display may look different from the one shown in Figure 17.2. That's because some vendors add features that make their display adapters easier to use or more flexible in some way. Always refer to your vendor documentation when you encounter differences between the standard Windows 98 setup and the one on your machine.

Figure 17.2.

The advanced display Properties dialog box enables you to reconfigure your display adapter or monitor.

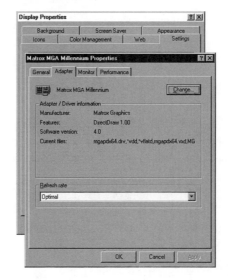

3. Click the Change button on the Adapter page. You'll see the first screen of the Upgrade Device Driver Wizard. This wizard helps you either choose a new driver or upgrade your existing driver.

4. Click Next to see the second page of the Upgrade Device Driver Wizard. Choose whether to upgrade your existing driver (the first choice) or to install a new device driver (the second choice). The new device driver option is covered here.

5. Highlight the second (lower) radio button, then click Next. The dialog box displays a list of compatible display adapters. Note that only one display adapter type is listed. (If other display adapters are compatible with this one, the list box will contain those as well.)

Note: If you have a vendor disk containing drivers for your display adapter, click the Have Disk button. The Have Disk dialog box works just like any other file browser in Windows 98.

6. Click the Show All Hardware radio button. Windows changes the list to show all the display adapters it supports, in alphabetic order by vendor (see Figure 17.3). You can use

this screen when selecting a new display adapter. Clicking Cancel here takes you back to the initial screen without changing your display adapter type.

Figure 17.3.
Click the Show all hardware radio button to show every display adapter supported by Windows 98.

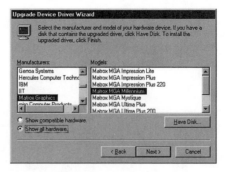

Tip: If your display adapter vendor doesn't appear in this list and you don't have a vendor disk containing drivers, you can always use the Standard Display Adapter category at the beginning of the Manufacturers list. It's a good idea to use this category anyway if your vendor driver disk only contains older 16-bit drivers. You won't get the same number of features as with the special disk, but using the standard drivers will provide a performance boost. Once you have your machine up and running, you can always check the vendor Web site to see if there is a 32-bit driver available there. In addition, you can use Windows Update to see if Microsoft has an updated version of the driver for your display adapter.

7. After you select the manufacturer and display adapter model from the lists, click Next. Windows displays the next page of the Upgrade Device Driver Wizard.

8. Click Next again. Windows might ask you to insert disks as it installs the new adapter.

9. Click Finish. To complete the process, click Apply.

Upgrading a Display Adapter

Hardware vendors are constantly upgrading their drivers to provide bug fixes and new capabilities. You'll probably need to upgrade a device driver on your machine at least once during the time you use it. The following steps show you how to upgrade your existing display adapter. (This procedure is similar to the one in the preceding section for installing a new display adapter, so not as many details are provided here.)

1. Right-click the desktop and choose the Properties option. You should see the Display Properties dialog box.

2. Select the Settings page. Click the Advanced button to see the advanced display Properties dialog box, which should be similar to the one in Figure 17.2.

3. Click the Change button on the Adapter page. You'll see the first screen of the Upgrade Device Driver Wizard. This wizard helps you either choose a new driver or upgrade your existing driver.

4. Click Next to see the second page of the Upgrade Device Wizard dialog box. Choose whether to upgrade your existing driver (the first choice) or to install a new device driver (the second choice). This section covers upgrading an existing device driver.

5. Click the first (top) radio button, then click Next to see the third page of the Upgrade Device Driver Wizard. Here you determine where Windows will search for a new device driver for you.

6. Choose one or more locations to search for a driver.

7. Click Next. The Upgrade Device Driver Wizard searches all the locations you specified. When the wizard finishes looking for device drivers, it displays a dialog box showing the most current driver it found.

8. Click Next. Windows might ask you to insert disks as it installs the new adapter.

9. Click Finish. To complete the process, click the Apply button.

Installing a Monitor

It might not seem important to tell Windows 98 which monitor you're using, especially if that monitor doesn't provide any special capabilities. The monitor you select, however, determines which display adapter features you can use. Selecting the right monitor type helps Windows 98 provide you with better information regarding your display choices.

1. Right-click the desktop and choose the Properties option. You should see the Display Properties dialog box.

2. Select the Settings page. Click the Advanced button to see the advanced display Properties dialog box (similar to Figure 17.2). Select the Monitor page, which provides only one additional setting. You can check the Monitor Is Energy Star Compliant check box if this feature is provided. The Monitor Type group shows you which monitor is currently installed. Checking the Automatically Detect Plug & Play Monitors check box tells Windows 98 to use the Plug and Play features of both the display adapter and the monitor. You must have both installed on your machine to use this feature. A Plug and Play monitor tells Windows 98 about itself and reduces the amount of configuration you have to do. It also can tailor some of the options you have to choose from in the Display Properties dialog box. Some monitors offer both a suspend (standby) mode and a power-down mode.

Power-down mode works about the same as shutting off the monitor. Some monitors have to go through a restart cycle to work properly after being powered down. The third check box, Reset Display on Suspend/Resume, tells Windows 98 to send the monitor a reset signal.

3. Click the Change button on the Monitor page. You'll see the first screen of the Upgrade Device Driver Wizard. This wizard helps you either choose a new driver or upgrade your existing driver.

4. Click Next to see the second page of the Upgrade Device Wizard. Choose whether to upgrade your existing driver (the first choice) or to install a new device driver (the second choice). The new device driver option is discussed first.

5. Highlight the second (lower) radio button, then click Next.

Note: If you have a vendor disk containing drivers for your monitor, click the Have Disk button. The Have Disk dialog box works just like any other browser in Windows 98.

6. Click the Show All Hardware radio button. Windows shows all the monitors it supports, in alphabetic order by vendor. Use this screen when selecting a new monitor. Clicking Cancel here takes you back to the initial screen without changing your display type.

7. After you select the correct manufacturer and monitor model from the lists, click Next. Windows displays the next page of the Upgrade Device Driver Wizard.

8. Click Next again. Windows might ask you to insert disks as it installs the new monitor.

9. Click Finish. To complete the process click the apply button.

Upgrading a Monitor

Hardware vendors are constantly upgrading their drivers to provide bug fixes and new capabilities. You'll probably need to upgrade your monitor at least once during the time you use it. The following steps show you how to upgrade your monitor. (This procedure is similar to the one in the preceding section for installing a new monitor, so not as many details are provided here.)

1. Right-click the desktop and choose the Properties option. You should see the Display Properties dialog box.

2. Select the Settings page. Click the Advanced button to see the advanced display Properties dialog box, which should be similar to the one in Figure 17.2.

3. Click the Change button on the Monitor page. You'll see the first screen for the Upgrade Device Driver Wizard. This wizard helps you either choose a new driver or upgrade your existing driver.

4. Click Next to see the second page of the Upgrade Device Wizard. Choose whether to upgrade your existing driver (the first choice) or to install a new device driver (the second choice). This section discusses upgrading an existing device driver.

5. Select the first (top) radio button and click Next to see the third page of the Upgrade Device Wizard. Here you determine where Windows will search for a new device driver for you.

6. Choose one or more locations to search for a driver.

7. Click Next. The Device Upgrade Wizard searches all the locations you specified. When the Upgrade Device Driver Wizard finishes looking for device drivers, it displays a dialog box showing the most current driver it found.

8. Click Next. Windows might ask you to insert disks as it installs the new adapter.

9. Click Finish. To complete the process, click the Apply button.

Using the Performance Page

Windows 98 provides a Performance page in the advanced display Properties dialog box. This page provides the same features as the Advanced Graphics Settings dialog box in Figure 5.4 of Chapter 5, "Performance Primer." See that chapter for a discussion of these features.

There is, however, an additional section near the bottom of this dialog box. (Some display adapters don't provide this section if they can't switch settings without a reboot.) The first radio button instructs Windows 98 to reboot any time you change the color settings on your machine.

The second setting is for the truly brave. You might find you can change your color and resolution settings at will without any negative results. Before selecting it, however, make sure this setting works with every program you use.

The third option tells Windows to prompt you about rebooting the machine after a color change (and, in some cases, a resolution change). This is the default option, and it works fine in most cases.

Using More Than One Display

One of the newest features provided by Windows 98 is the capability to use more than one display. It might seem like an unnecessary feature to people used to working with one display. Multiple displays, however, can provide quite a bit of added functionality when used the right way.

The most obvious place this feature helps is programming. Programmers are able to view the code they're working on in one display and its output in another. Not only does this have the potential to increase programmer productivity, having two displays makes it easier for the programmer to find some types of bugs.

Game programs will probably use this feature soon as well. Consider being able to see the country-side on one display, uninterrupted by everything that takes up display space now. You could, for example, place your character statistics and inventory on a second display. Another way this technology could be used is to provide a display everywhere you would find one in a real plane. Instead of switching views with a joystick control, you actually could turn your head and look around. There are many other ways you'll see this technology used in games. It just depends on what game vendors can think up and whether the user wants to buy more than one display.

Imagine how useful multiple displays could be for stock brokers who need to track more than one item at a time. In fact, multiple displays could help anyone with a crowded desktop who is looking for a little relief.

How do you control multiple displays? Just use the Settings page of the Display Properties dialog box. (Right-click the desktop and select Properties from the context menu to display this dialog box.) At the top of the dialog box, you'll see a monitor. In the center of the monitor is a number that tells you which display adapter you're working with. (When using lower-resolution displays, you might have to click the monitor to see which number you're dealing with.) If you want to use a different monitor—or just see the settings it's using—choose it from the Monitor drop-down list box. Click the Want To Use This Monitor check box when you see the monitor you want. Don't worry, applications that appear in other monitors will continue to update as you work with the "foreground" monitor.

Understanding the Accelerated Graphics Port (AGP)

Display adapter vendors are working harder each year to get the last ounce of power from various graphics technologies. Just looking at a game such as Quake or an application such as CorelDRAW! tells you that graphics have become more than just a nice bonus feature. The Internet itself is rife with various presentations. You even can watch full-motion video on many sites, especially those using Microsoft's NetShow or RealAudio.

> **Tip:** One of the better sites on the Internet for additional information about AGP (and graphics in general) is `http://cctpwww.cityu.edu.hk/public/graphics/g_hw.htm`. This site contains a wealth of links offering information about AGP. You also can download a copy of the Intel specification at `http://www.intel.com/pc-supp/platform/agfxport/index.htm`. If you want up-to-the-minute information about AGP from Microsoft, go to `http://www.microsoft.com/hwdev/devdes/msagp.htm`.

The Accelerated Graphics Port (AGP) is the newest technology in the display adapter arsenal. Instead of keeping graphics on the extension bus—where they've been all these years—AGP places them on the high-speed memory bus. The result is improved drawing speed, especially for 3D graphics such as those used in many CAD programs and games such as Doom. The AGP provides vendors with a lot of bandwidth—66MHz with a data transfer rate of 528MB/sec. To put this into perspective, a typical 3D PCI display adapter in use today has a 33MHz bus speed and a data transfer rate of 132MB/sec. A PCI display adapter can maintain somewhere between 15 and 30 frames per second (fps) when drawing on a 640×480, 24-bit color display. An AGP display adapter can conceivably maintain a 75fps rate. Instead of seeing graphics that look somewhat jumpy at times, an AGP display adapter provides smooth animation without any jumpiness at all.

AGP solves another problem: Currently, your display adapter uses memory that is totally separate from main memory. Whatever memory you have installed on the display adapter is all you are able to use, even if you have free memory elsewhere on the computer. In most cases, this limits a programmer to between 4MB and 8MB of VRAM for storing graphic images, texture maps, and sprites. An AGP display adapter continues to provide high-speed VRAM storage, much like the L2 cache for the CPU. It also, however, has access to system memory. This means graphics programmers have access to between 32MB and 64MB of RAM in addition to the VRAM used for fast graphics storage. (Intel recommends that programmers use video memory for display purposes, but move other video objects such as textures to system memory.)

Another feature AGP provides is sideband addressing. This feature enables the graphics processor to talk with the system over multiple channels, which enables it to hold several conversations at once. One channel, for example, could be transferring data from main memory to VRAM, while another channel is getting instructions from the CPU on what to draw next. Sideband addressing can provide a large gain in performance after programmers learn how to use it. Software will have to be rewritten to use this feature before you'll see any performance gain. (Programmers can access AGP through the DirectDraw API while Windows manages details such as mapping from system memory to video memory in the background.)

Using the WebTV for Windows Application

You can now watch television as you work—as long as you have a display adapter with a built-in tuner, that is. This is one way you can use an extra monitor. The entertainment potential of the WebTV for Windows application is obvious. There are other ways, however, that you can use this particular Windows 98 feature.

Even though no one has really said how they plan to use the WebTV for Windows (besides entertainment), there are a few obvious applications. For one thing, you could use it for training. One monitor could have a television connection to an instructor. The student could use a second monitor for practicing techniques the instructor presents. Although I don't see this replacing formal schooling, it is a viable way to teach new employees at a corporation or to teach students in remote locations who can't get to a school building.

Satellite conferences and symposiums are other ways this technology could be used. This kind of presentation is already taking place on a very large scale. The main problem is cramming everyone who wants to see a particular lecture into one room to huddle around a single television set. The WebTV for Windows enables everyone to watch the lecture from the comfort of their own offices through a closed-circuit television connection.

On Your Own

An underpowered machine might not provide the speed people need to get their work done fast. Try a variety of display resolutions and color-level settings to find a compromise between system performance and the aesthetic value of the display. Also try the various font-size settings. Perhaps a custom setting will provide that perfect balance between readability and the number of icons you can fit on the desktop or within an Explorer pane.

Check your SYSTEM folder to see whether you can find all the files that make up the video subsystem. Use the video subsystem discussion in this chapter as the basis for your search.

If you have access to a graphics card with a television tuner installed, try using the WebTV for Windows program. Download a television guide from your cable service provider or from the Internet. (There are separate options for both.) Make sure you spend some time looking at Microsoft's future plans for the product as well.

18

Mobile Computing: Notebooks, Telecommuting, and Remote Access

Peter Norton®

Few business travelers can get by without their constant companion, a notebook computer. No longer do people regard notebooks as second computers. Notebooks contain most, if not all, of the same features as desktop computers. The only differences are the display and keyboard, both of which are easily taken care of by a docking station.

Before you go any further, you need to understand what is meant by the term "notebook computer." Windows 98 won't make your personal digital assistant (PDA) into a desktop equivalent. This chapter looks at machines capable of running Windows 98. A notebook has to provide a Personal Computer Memory Card International Association (PCMCIA) slot or its equivalent to use some of Windows 98's features. You'll also want a computer that can use a docking station.

Tip: Windows 98 contains infrared port support, but you must have an Infrared Data Association (IrDA) 2.0-compliant device to use this support. The current software also includes infrared LAN connectivity.

Looking Ahead: Windows 98 also provides voice-modem support for both notebook and desktop computers. The "Understanding Voice Communications" section of Chapter 19, "Hardware and Software Connections," covers this important topic.

PCMCIA Devices on Your Notebook Computer

The first topic on the agenda is the PCMCIA bus. This "little" bus is specially designed to meet the needs of the notebook computer market, but it's also found in a growing number of desktop machines. The PCMCIA bus uses credit-card–sized cards that connect to external slots on the machine. This is perfect for notebooks because they are notorious for providing few, if any, expansion slots. A PCMCIA bus makes it easy for the user to change a machine's hardware configuration without opening it up. You could, for example, take out a memory card to make room for a modem card.

This bus also supports solid-state disk drives in the form of flash ROM or SRAM boards. Flash ROM boards are especially interesting because they provide the same access speeds as regular memory but with the permanence of other long-term storage media, such as hard drives. Unlike SRAM boards, flash ROM boards don't require battery backup. Many people use solid-state drives to store applications or databases that change infrequently.

Windows 98 provides more levels of PCMCIA support than previous versions of Windows. For example, it supports the new PC Card 32 (Cardbus) bridges. You also can use 3.3-volt cards in addition to the older 5-volt models. Windows 98 also supports multifunction PCMCIA cards and specialty devices such as Global Positioning Satellite (GPS) cards.

The capability to change cards on the fly means Windows 98 needs to adjust dynamically as well; you wouldn't want Windows 98 to try to access a card no longer in place. Plug and Play enables Windows 98 to detect and compensate for changes in the PCMCIA bus configuration. This means users don't need to reconfigure their systems when a component changes. Windows 98 is designed to detect system changes and to make the appropriate modifications to its setup. This flexibility, however, comes at a price. Users must disable their PCMCIA-specific utilities and allow Windows to manage the bus. The bus vendor must also provide the 32-bit drivers needed in Windows 98 (unless your bus already appears in the Windows 98 support list). Figure 18.1 shows a typical PC Card (PCMCIA) Properties dialog box. You can access it by double-clicking the PC Card (PCMCIA) applet in the Control Panel or by double-clicking the PC Card (PCMCIA) Status icon in the taskbar tray.

Figure 18.1.
The PC Card (PCMCIA) Properties dialog box provides access to the PCMCIA cards installed on your machine.

Using Windows 98 drivers enables the PCMCIA enhanced mode. What does enhanced support give you? The following list provides an overview of enhanced-support features.

- **Friendly device names.** Provides users with device names they can recognize. It also helps the user determine which devices are present and which are disconnected.

- **Automatic installation.** This enables the user to hot-swap various devices in and out of the PCMCIA slot without worrying about reconfiguring the machine.

- **Drive-change detection.** If enhanced support is disabled, the user will sometimes have to unmount and then mount a PCMCIA drive before Windows 98 recognizes the change.

- **Other device-specific mode and configuration information.** Check the documentation that accompanies the specific device for further details about special features.

As Figure 18.1 shows, you can use a couple of different options with PCMCIA cards. The first check box, Show Control on Taskbar, displays an icon in the taskbar tray. You can use this icon to obtain a list of currently installed cards, to stop one that's installed, or to display (by right-clicking) a context menu containing the Properties option. The second check box instructs Windows to display a message if you try to remove a card before you stop it.

Just what is stopping? Windows 98 usually detects changes in your PCMCIA setup. You can help it along, however, by stopping the card before you remove it. Stopping the card tells Windows 98 to remove support for that feature. Just highlight the card you want to stop, then click the Stop button shown in Figure 18.1.

Next, take a look at the Global Settings page of the PC Card (PCMCIA) Properties dialog box. There are only a few options on this page. You usually should keep the Automatic Selection option checked. Unchecking this box enables you to set the card-service memory area manually—a task you usually need to perform for troubleshooting purposes only. The second check box, Disable PC Card Sound Effects, tells Windows you don't want to hear sound effects every time the status of the PCMCIA bus changes.

In most cases, Windows 98 automatically enables enhanced mode. It won't do so, however, if you have any real-mode PCMCIA drivers loaded. Fortunately, it's easy to see whether Windows 98 has enabled enhanced mode on your machine. Right-click My Computer and select the Properties option. Click the Performance tab of the System Properties dialog box.

Notice the PC Cards (PCMCIA) entry in this dialog box. If your entry says 32-bit, Windows 98 has enabled enhanced support. Otherwise, Windows 98 helps you through the process of enabling support using the PCMCIA Wizard. You can activate the PCMCIA Wizard directly from the Performance tab. The following paragraphs provide additional troubleshooting tips you can use when experiencing PCMCIA problems.

- The most common problem associated with enabling enhanced support is that there are PCMCIA device drivers in CONFIG.SYS or TSRs in AUTOEXEC.BAT. Removing these entries should fix the problem.
- Windows 98 usually tells you when there's an I/O port address or interrupt conflict. To make sure, however, you should check the settings in the Resources tab of the PCIC or Compatible PCMCIA Controller Properties dialog box, as shown in Figure 18.2. (PCIC stands for peripheral connect interface card.) To open this dialog box, right-click My Computer, select Properties from the context menu, and select the Device Manager tab in the System Properties dialog box. Any conflicting devices appear in the Conflicting Device List: field at the bottom of the dialog box.
- Always make sure you have a card installed in at least one of the slots while booting. Failure to do so can prevent Windows 98 from detecting the PCMCIA card slot.

Figure 18.2.

The Resources tab of the PCIC or Compatible PCMCIA Controller Properties dialog box alerts you to any conflicting devices.

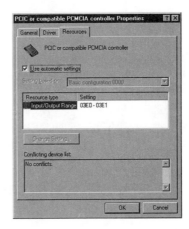

- Make sure Windows 98 supports your card by checking it with the Hardware Installation Wizard in the Control Panel.

Even if Windows 98 doesn't support your PCMCIA slot, you can still use it by installing real-mode drivers. Using real-mode drivers means you won't gain any benefit from Plug and Play features. It always makes sense to contact the bus vendor to see whether a 32-bit driver is available.

Hot Docking

At the beginning of this chapter, it was mentioned that Windows 98 has a solution to your docking problems. A Plug and Play feature called *hot docking* enables you to remove a portable computer from its docking station without turning it off. The portable automatically reconfigures itself to reflect the loss of docking station capability. If you plug that portable back into the original docking station, or into a new one somewhere else, it automatically reconfigures itself to take advantage of the new capabilities the docking station provides.

Tip: It isn't always a good idea to move your computer with the power on. Sure, it can save you a little time when you perform a setup. Unless you're in the middle of something you spent hours setting up, however, it's usually better to shut down and turn the power off before you remove the computer from its docking station. When moving it with the power on, there are a number of ways you could create surges or other electrical interference that could shorten the life of your machine. You could accidentally short something out, for example, when removing the notebook from its docking station. Moving your machine from place to place without turning it off is a supported feature, but you need to consider the cost of exercising that option.

Hot Swapping

Another problem that I talked about at the beginning of this chapter is the capability to take one card out of the PCMCIA slot and plug another into its place. Plug and Play answers the call here as well. A Plug and Play–compatible system reconfigures itself dynamically. You might have seen advertisements for portables that provide *hot swapping*, a component of the Plug and Play specification. Hot swapping enables you to remove components from a machine without rebooting it. (Make sure your laptop supports this feature before you try to use it.)

> **Warning:** Never touch the contacts of your PCMCIA cards when you remove them from the bus. Doing so could give the card a static-electric shock that could damage it or shorten its life.

Hot swapping enables you to change cards without turning the machine off. The computer automatically recognizes that it can no longer communicate with the Internet, for example, and that network lines are now open. The Plug and Play component of Windows 98 even installs the required drivers and configures them in the background. This means users no longer need to worry about how a device works; they can now focus on the work they need the device to perform. (The only exception to this rule is when Windows 98 can't find the required drivers on your hard disk. It then asks you to supply a disk containing the required drivers.)

Multifunction PC Cards

Most laptops are limited to two PC card slots. This means you can either do a lot of swapping to get added functionality from your laptop, or you need to make use of a new feature offered by Windows 98—the capability to use multifunction PC cards.

Multifunction PC cards provide the functionality of multiple cards in one slot. You might see a PC card, for example, that provides both modem and network card functionality. Not only do multifunction PC cards enable you to extend your laptop even further than before, they also reduce wear and tear on your machine by making card swaps less frequently than before.

Advanced Configuration and Power Interface (ACPI)

One major goal for most laptop vendors is getting more out of a single battery. Achieving that goal, however, has been difficult. Users have lacked the capability to set up their machine to fully utilize battery power and still use the laptop as a desktop replacement.

Windows 98 provides an improved power-management scheme that gives the user full flexibility in configuring how the power-saving features in any computer are used. You access this configuration capability through the Power Management applet in the Control Panel or by double-clicking the battery icon in the taskbar tray. Figure 18.3 shows the Power Management Properties dialog box. (Your display might vary slightly from the one shown.)

Figure 18.3.

Use the Power Management Properties dialog box to configure the power management scheme for your computer.

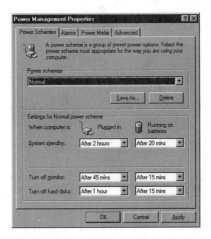

Look at the Power Schemes tab of the Power Management Properties dialog box. Three major subsystems are affected by the settings in this dialog box: system, monitor, and hard disk. Laptop computers usually provide individual settings for wall power and battery power. Using two sets of settings enables you to define different power strategies for the two environments without having to open the Power Management Properties dialog all the time. You also can save various power-management schemes, just as you are able to do with sound schemes. You can create a power-management scheme for regular use, another for travel, and still another for when you perform machine maintenance.

> **Tip:** Windows 98's power-management features monitor the keyboard and mouse for activity and automatically shut down the machine after a specified period of inactivity, even if you're performing an unattended task such as downloading a file. That's why you should set up schemes for downloading and maintenance that don't shut down the machine for a long time (or at all). You can always shut down just the monitor and save power when not viewing it.

Windows 98 also provides alarms so you know when battery power is running out. Look at the Alarms tab in the Power Management Properties dialog box. There are two alarms, one for a low battery and another for a critical battery. You can use the slider for either alarm to set the amount of power left in the battery when the alarm goes off. Clicking the Alarm Action button displays a battery alarm action dialog box. You can set the type of alarm you want to receive, and you can specify other actions for the computer to perform automatically such as going into either standby or shutdown mode. The alarm can display a message, play a sound, or both. When you choose to place the machine in shutdown or standby mode, you also can decide whether to force the mode change. In some applications, forcing the machine to shut down or to go into standby mode could cause data loss. In most situations, however, the data is saved.

The Power Meter tab shows you the current power status of your machine. A check box enables you to display the specifics for each battery installed. This page also shows you the amount of power left in the battery and the estimated time it will last. You can even click the battery icon to see specifics about your battery, such as the manufacturer.

The Advanced tab currently enables you to set two power-management options. The first option is to display the power meter in the taskbar tray. Selecting this option enables you to set various battery options without opening the Control Panel. The second option is to prompt for a password whenever the machine goes from standby mode to full power. This feature closes a security hole in which someone could wake your sleeping laptop and gain access to company secrets.

Windows 98 Mobile Computing Services

Microsoft goes a long way toward meeting the needs of notebook computer users with the release of Windows 98. One of the best notebook features is the Briefcase. This feature isn't exclusive to mobile computer users, though. I've used it to send files to people across a network. Experiment to see where it works best for you.

This section also looks at Dial-Up Networking from a notebook user's perspective. You can get around potential problems by using this feature to communicate on the road. Chapters 1, "Opening Windows to the Internet," and 19 cover usage basics. You can skip the Dial-Up Networking part of this section if you don't foresee a need to use it.

Briefcase

Windows 98 includes a Briefcase. Like its physical counterpart, the Windows Briefcase is used to store files you need to move from place to place. The Briefcase sits on the desktop along with the Recycle Bin and My Computer.

Setting up your Briefcase is easy. Just install the Windows software (this is optional), and a Briefcase icon appears on the desktop. Stuff the Briefcase with files you plan to move from place to place.

This should be a centralized storage location for all the files you work on, even if those files appear in different areas of your hard drive.

Working with Briefcase files is no different from working with any other files. Windows 98 monitors the status of the files and presents a display when you open the Briefcase icon, as shown in Figure 18.4. This display informs you when the Briefcase needs to be updated to match the files on your machine. Select the Briefcase | Update All command if files are out-of-date. When the files are up-to-date, you can move the Briefcase from your machine to a network drive or floppy.

Figure 18.4.

Briefcase offers a fast and convenient method of centralizing your files. It also provides the means to move those files from work to home and back with a minimum of fuss.

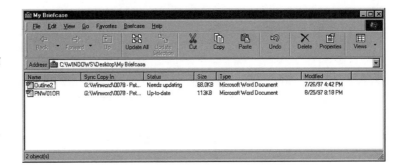

Briefcase provides a context menu for each of its files, just like the context menus in Explorer. It also provides a Properties dialog box for each document. The General, Summary, and Statistics pages all look like those for a standard document.

One change you'll notice is the addition of an Update Status page. This page provides information about the document in your Briefcase as compared to the one on your drive. It also provides some options you don't get from the menu. The middle of the page shows the current document status—which document has been updated and when you made the changes.

There's an interesting feature in the information box. All it tells you is that the original document has a newer date than the one in the Briefcase. However, if you click the Replace icon in the middle of these two entries, you'll see a context menu. The interesting thing about this menu is that you can choose to replace your updated document with the original in your Briefcase.

How many times have you wished you had a copy of your original file? Wouldn't it be nice to restore a document to its original form without resorting to a backup tape? If you keep your Briefcase up-to-date, you always can restore an original copy of a document after you change it. This safety feature comes in handy when a few hours of editing don't turn out as you anticipated. This list has a third entry that enables you to skip an update. Just select the Skip option and close the dialog box. This enables you to retain the original version of this particular file while still automatically updating all your other files.

Tip: You can use the Briefcase as a rudimentary version-control system. Here's how it works: Create an additional Briefcase as you reach each new milestone in a project. Change the name of the new Briefcase to match the milestone's name or date. Place a copy of all the files in the Briefcase but never update it. You should end up with a bunch of Briefcases, each one representing a stage of your project. Even though this technique consumes a lot of hard drive space, it also saves you a lot of rework time later.

Three buttons in the Update Status tab of a document's Properties dialog box enable you to manipulate the link you've created. The Update button updates your linked copy to match the original document (or does just the opposite). The direction of the Replace arrow determines the direction of the update. The Briefcase default is to update whichever document is older. The Split From Original button enables you to separate the copy from the original. This comes in handy if you decide to make a new document from the copy in your Briefcase. The Find Original button opens a copy of Explorer with the original document highlighted. You can use this button to quickly find a document in the Briefcase.

Moving your Briefcase from work to home is as easy as using it. Stick a floppy disk in one of your drives and right-click the Briefcase icon to display the context menu. Use one of the options on the Send To menu to send your Briefcase to a floppy. The Briefcase icon disappears from the desktop and reappears on the floppy. Moving it back to your desktop the next day is just as easy. Select the floppy drive in Explorer so you can see the Briefcase icon. Then right-click it and drag it to the desktop. When Windows displays a menu asking what you want to do, click Move. That's all there is to it. Note that you can update the Briefcase from the context menu in addition to using the Update All option. What happens if you lose your Briefcase? You can create a new Briefcase by right-clicking the desktop and selecting New from the context menu. One of the new items you can choose to create is the Briefcase.

Tip: If you have a bulging Briefcase, you can compress the floppies used to transport information from one machine to another. Use the DriveSpace utility to accomplish this. Compressing the floppy nearly doubles its carrying capacity, especially when you consider that most people carry data files, not the executable files required to edit them. Data files normally contain lots of empty space that compression programs can squeeze out.

Synchronizing Files

Keeping the files on your notebook computer in sync with your desktop system isn't just a nicety—it's a necessity. Taking work home is one thing; making sure those changes get into the final document is something else. The easiest way to keep your files in sync is to use the same machine as both notebook and desktop machine. This isn't always practical, however.

Before Windows 98, notebook users had only two choices for keeping files from two or more machines in sync. One method was to keep all the mobile data on a floppy. Then you just passed the floppy around as necessary to keep the files in sync. This easy solution also had a pretty significant problem: A floppy's access speed isn't very good, and its storage capacity is much more limited than a hard drive.

The other solution was to copy files from your hard drive to a floppy and then back again. This had the advantage of using the best possible speed for opening and using files. Its main disadvantage was that it relied on a person's memory to make sure files were kept in sync.

Using the Briefcase option in Windows 98 is a big step forward for notebook users. It has one of the characteristics of floppy-based synchronization: You just move the Briefcase around as needed. It also provides the advantage of the file-copying method. Every application makes use of the hard drive's enhanced access speed when you open and edit files.

Is Briefcase the only Windows 98 solution? Probably not. I've also used the folder concept that I've talked about in various places in this book. It allows a group to keep one set of files on a central machine in sync. But how do you use this feature if you're working on a document at home? That's where Dial-Up Networking comes into play. Instead of simply moving a Briefcase around, you can use Dial-Up Networking to call into the network and edit the files remotely. That way, even though you're working on the file from another location, your team can continue updating it as well.

Tip: Using the combination of folders and Dial-Up Networking is ideal if you're a team supervisor. It enables you to continue your work while on the road without resorting to the Briefcase. Even if you're the only one currently working on the documents, there might be an occasion when a team member needs them as well. If you use the Briefcase, however, people working in the office won't know whether they're using the current documents. Using this combination also enables you to monitor the team's progress. Checking in each day to see the work they've accomplished helps you keep an eye on things back home while you're on the road.

Remote Dial-Up (Dial-Up Networking)

Chapters 1 and 19 talk about the mechanics of using Dial-Up Networking, so I won't go through that process here. However, once you get the software installed and configured, where do you go from there? If you're a notebook user, there are plenty of reasons to use Dial-Up Networking.

- **Document access.** I've already mentioned how you can use Dial-Up Networking to enable an entire group of people to work together. All you need to do is place a folder with shortcuts to the team's documents in a folder on the network. When a person calls into the network, he can open the folder and see all the pieces of the project without looking very hard for them. I often place this folder in the user's home directory on the network. That way, I can personalize each folder as required, and the user doesn't need to memorize yet another location on the network.

- **Application access.** You probably don't need to access applications (such as word processors or spreadsheets) from a remote location very often. But what about the custom database your company uses as a contact manager? Unless you plan to either print the entire database or create a copy on your notebook's hard drive, you'll need to access it remotely. In fact, this is probably the only way you could use this centralized application if it contains sales or inventory information that you'll need to update later.

- **Email.** It's amazing how much a company depends on email to keep employees apprised of events. Think about the email messages you receive, such as getting a new access code for the security system or updating your W-2 form. Losing this method of communication means you'll be out-of-touch when you return from your trip. A few minutes of online time can keep you up-to-date on current situations in your company and can reduce the "vacation" syndrome many people feel after a road trip.

- **Emergency decisions.** What if you're traveling in Europe and your company is in California? How do you find a good time to call them and make a decision that requires a 24-hour turnaround? Using email to leave a message and then checking for responses later can provide a few extra hours of sleep at night. After all, who wants to fight company politics and sleepiness at the same time?

- **Missing-file syndrome.** Notebooks almost always need at least twice as much hard disk space as they have. How often have you cleared a bunch of files off your notebook only to find you needed them after all? A remote connection enables you to grab files you didn't think you'd need. Placing a copy of your desktop machine's hard drive—or at least the data—where you can access it with a remote connection can save you trouble later. Be sure to ask the network administrator's permission before you do this.

These are some common ways you can use Dial-Up Networking with a notebook. You'll need to find the technique that applies to your specific situation. For example, in my particular case, I find it handy to use Dial-Up Networking to grab presentations. I only have room for one or two on my notebook, but I might need several during the time I'm on the road. This feature enables me to call in and grab the next presentation I need. The result is that each presentation is then fresh and specifically designed for the group I'm talking with, yet I don't have to lug around a monster-sized hard drive or other storage.

Remote Network Users

Networking is an essential part of any business today. I've already talked about Dial-Up Networking to an extent, but let's take a look at some of the communication and other considerations you'll need to make. Using Dial-Up Networking is one thing; using it efficiently is another.

I'd like to begin by providing a little insight into one of the problems with using Dial-Up Networking. Most people know the telephone company charges more for the first three minutes of a long-distance call than for the time that follows. People try to keep their long-distance calls short and to the point. The telephone company capitalizes on this by charging you more when you make several short calls instead of one long one.

Given this set of circumstances, imagine the difference in cost between making one long computer call and a bunch of short ones. It's easy to get into the habit of dialing your company every time you need information. Consolidating your information needs into one call is better than making several short ones. You also can save money by delivering all your mail during off-peak hours.

There are times when it's impossible to take care of all your communication needs in one call. You'll still find the need to make a few short calls during the day to gather information. You don't, however, have to do that for message delivery. Delivering email responses and performing other chores always can wait until off-peak hours, especially when you're overseas and the recipient won't see it until after you're in bed anyway.

The following sections describe other methods you can use to reduce the cost of Dial-Up Networking. Although these techniques won't work when your need for data exchange with another party is immediate, they work in the majority of cases.

Local Communications

There are many forms of long-distance communication, and some of them are local. Here's one scenario: You're in Detroit and your company is in Los Angeles. It's important that you send a file containing new information about your client to an assistant for processing. You also need additional information about another client that's stored in your company database. You have access to both Dial-Up Networking and the Internet. Which do you use? Some people would use Dial-Up Networking because it's faster and more convenient. The low-cost solution, however, would be the Internet, in this case.

Sometimes the obvious choice isn't the one you should use. Suppose, for example, you need to transfer the aforementioned files and retrieve the same information. This time, however, you're in another part of the state instead of another part of the country. You could call your ISP, but that would entail a toll call and potentially some long wait times if you experience the usual Internet lag. If you make the toll call directly to your company, however, it costs only about 40 cents and you are as-sured of getting access to a high-speed modem with little or no lag time. In this case, using Dial-Up Networking is the right choice.

If your company has its own Internet address, you might be able to access it to transfer information over a local call. You still need an account with a local provider to make this work, however. As with the other suggestions in this section, you should compare the cost of using an Internet solution against that of making a long-distance call.

Dynamic Networking

Despite your best efforts, sometimes you need to work "live" with the company database or applica-tions. You can't solve every problem with email or a file upload. At times, working with live appli-cations or data is the only way to get the job done. You should keep these times to a minimum, but keeping a local database management system (DBMS) current might override other cost consider-ations. Even if your company is in this situation, you don't need to pay through the nose to get the kind of service you want. Your notebook still has a few tricks up its sleeve to help solve the problem. The following is a list of the ideas I've come up with, but you can probably think of others based on your unique set of circumstances.

Tip: If you're using a custom DBMS, it might be possible to add batch-updating capabili-ties to it. This would enable you to use a smaller version of the application on the road, to create new records, to modify existing ones, and to make all the changes in batch mode when you return from your trip (or as part of an upload to the company database). In many cases, this is a less expensive solution for inventory control or other types of sales databases than making the changes live. There are two criteria for using a batch system: You need a fairly large outside sales force to make the change cost-efficient, and the company must be able to get by with daily or weekly database updates instead of real-time data. This works in most situations, but you couldn't use it for an airline ticket database.

- **Internet access.** Using the Internet still might provide the best means of working with live data. You'll need to overcome two problems, however. The first is gaining access to a local server that allows live connections. The second is that you'll have to make a TCP/IP connection and use a special modem to make this work. Both problems can be solved given enough resources. In the past, this solution might have seemed more like a dream than reality. Today, intranets (the private version of the Internet) abound. Even small businesses can occasionally write off the cost of using an intranet solution because it's less expensive than anything else.

- **Virtual Private Networking (VPN).** This is a new solution for Windows 98. It enables you to create the equivalent of a wide area network (WAN) using the Internet. You have to install VPN support to gain access to this feature. One of the problems with using VPN is a lack of security. Although it's theoretically possible to create a secure connection, many analysts worry that the connection isn't secure enough. In addition, you might experience reliability problems with this technique. Make sure your database manager is designed to recover from partial transactions before you commit to using this method.

- **Using a local office's PBX connection.** Sometimes a local office provides the long-distance call solution you need. It might mean a little wrangling with the local boss and perhaps a short drive, but this solution could save your company some money.

- **Keeping notes.** Even if your database doesn't support batch-mode processing, you still could keep notes and make all the updates at one time. This enables you to make one phone call instead of many to record the required information. This solution still won't work with "live" data such as ticket sales.

- **Off-hour calling.** This is probably the least likely solution. If your data needs are so time-critical that you can't afford to wait even a few minutes, off-hour calling won't work. You could combine this technique, however, with batch mode or note-taking methods to work with live data on the network. You could even use this off-hour calling technique when using a local office's PBX connection. This might reduce the local boss' objection to tying up the line in order to service your needs.

Offline Printing

Chapter 15, "Fonts and Printing," discusses two techniques that notebook computer users will love. The first technique is creating a printer for every purpose. You can create printers for all the local offices you'll visit during a trip. That way, you can print whatever you need without worrying about whether you have the proper print driver to do so. You also can use this technique to print at client sites that are amenable to your doing so.

This isn't the only way you can print, however. You also can print to your hard drive using the offline printing technique discussed in Chapter 15. Just set the printer to work offline. Everything you send to disk waits on the hard drive until you send it to the printer.

Whenever you disconnect your notebook from the network printer or docking station, Windows 98 detects the loss of printing capability and automatically sets the printer to work offline. Unfortunately, this doesn't work all the time. Sometimes the printer disconnection isn't detected. Check your printer the first time, and you should be able to rely on the connection being consistent from that point on.

Working with an Infrared Data Port

Infrared data ports are becoming a major feature in personal computers. They can be found on just about every laptop computer; even some desktop models are beginning to sport them. Devices such as laser printers are offering infrared ports as an option, and it won't be long before they're a standard feature on networks. Infrared data ports are becoming popular for good reason. They're more convenient when you don't need a permanent connection to something.

Let's examine Windows 98 infrared support. Chapter 14, "Exploiting Multimedia and Games," covered standard hardware installation techniques, so they won't be repeated here. After you install the software for your infrared port, you'll see an Infrared applet in the Control Panel. Double-clicking this applet displays the Infrared Monitor dialog box.

The Status page of the Infrared Monitor dialog box contains connection information. If there aren't any ports to connect to, a message will tell you so. This page also shows the status of any existing connections. You can find out how well each connection is working. This information comes in handy when you need to transfer a large amount of data and it seems to be taking too long. Sometimes you can improve the connection by moving your machine more in line with the other infrared data port.

Figure 18.5 shows the Options tab. The first check box enables infrared communication using a specific serial and parallel port—in this case, COM4 and LPT3.

Figure 18.5.
The Options page of the Infrared Monitor dialog box contains all the configuration options.

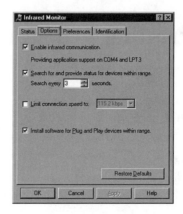

The second check box on this page enables automatic search for other infrared ports. Scanning for other ports uses processor cycles you might want to devote to other activities. Turning off the scan feature while you're on the road doesn't just make your computer run faster—it saves power too. There's also a field for defining how often you scan for another port. The default value of 3 seconds works fine in most cases. You might find, however, that a smaller value helps you fine-tune a connection faster. A longer increment could save precious processing cycles after you have a connection established.

The third check box on this page enables you to limit connection speed. That might not seem like a good idea at first, but there are a few situations in which you might find it helpful. The first situation is when the receiving device can't handle the full-speed connection. You might try to establish a connection with a serial device, for example, and find it doesn't work properly. Data overruns are the first symptom of this problem. The second situation occurs when you have a good connection but keep getting data errors. For whatever reason, you're spending more time transmitting old data than new data. Slowing down the connection could reduce data errors and might actually improve the data rate of the connection.

The Install Software for Plug and Play Devices Within Range option of this dialog box is simultaneously helpful and annoying. I find it most helpful when visiting locations that I don't visit on a regular basis. This option automatically configures your machine to use any Plug and Play infrared devices that happen to be in the area—making life a lot more automatic. On the other hand, my machine keeps getting configured for devices I don't want. You should probably keep this option unchecked unless you're planning to visit a new location.

The Preferences page of the Infrared Monitor dialog box enables you to set the features of your infrared port. The first check box on this page enables you to display an Infrared icon on the taskbar. As with most icons you can display on the taskbar, there are three actions you can perform. Holding the mouse pointer over the icon gives you the current port status, a left-click performs a default action (opening the Infrared Monitor dialog box), and a right-click displays a context menu. The context menu contains four entries. The first opens the Infrared Monitor dialog box. The second enables infrared communication. The third option enables automatic searches for other devices in range. The fourth option enables automatic installation for Plug and Play devices.

The next two check boxes on the Preferences page work together. The middle check box enables you to open the infrared port for interrupted connections. This comes in handy when the line of sight to the other port could be interrupted by someone passing by. You also should enable it when you have a less-than-ideal connection to the other device. The third check box on the Preferences page tells Windows 98 to sound an alarm whenever it finds a device in range or if it loses a connection to another device. It would have been more convenient if Microsoft had used two separate sounds for these events, but at least you get an alert of some kind. You should turn off this option in an office if you're sharing the same space with other people. Some people find the constant noise coming from the computer a little distracting.

The last page in this dialog box, Identification, contains two edit fields. The first field tells who you are. The second field provides a description of your computer. You should come up with something unique, yet generic, for a portable computer. There isn't any way to know exactly who will be using your computer, so a generic name is best. On the other hand, you don't want the name you chose to interfere with others on the network.

Power Management Strategies

Chapters 5 through 7 discussed many useful tips for getting the most out of your computer. You might want to review those chapters when setting up your laptop. After you get past these basic strategies for making your computer do more with fewer resources, you can start working with special strategies for laptop computers. The following list provides ideas of what to look for on your laptop. Not all laptops provide every feature listed here, and you certainly might find some features unique to your system. The first tip, then, is to explore the vendor documentation with your laptop. You'll be amazed at the little tips you'll find there.

- **Forget fancy software.** Screen savers eat more power on a laptop than most people imagine. Because most laptop computers come with a feature that turns off the monitor automatically, there's no reason for you to install a fancy screen saver. In fact, you might actually cause more harm than good because most laptops use flat-screen displays. A screen saver could inadvertently interfere with the automatic shutdown software and could end up reducing the life of your screen, not extending it. In addition to interfering with the way your laptop runs, some screen savers constantly access the hard disk, causing further drain on the battery. There are other culprits in this area as well. For instance, try getting by with a subset of your word processing software. I installed the full version of my word processor the first time around, and one of the features kept hard disk activity at a frantic pace. In an effort to provide the latest information on my files, the software was just eating power. I don't keep many files on my laptop, so I always know exactly what I have available. Kill the fancy features of your software—a battery that usually lasts 3 hours will probably last 3 1/2.

- **Look for power-saving features.** Many laptops come with a function key (FN on my system) that's poorly understood by users. In my case, there's a faucet at the top of the screen. Pressing FN+faucet reduces power consumption on my machine by a lot—yet I wouldn't have found this feature by looking at the documentation. The vendor hid it in the screen section of the text, not in the power-management section where you would expect to find it. If you're in doubt about a button on your laptop, keep searching the documentation until you find it. Most laptops now come with a power-saving mode you can use while on the battery. In some cases, programs run a little slower and the backlight doesn't work as well, but you'll get a lot more life out of your battery.

- **Change power-wasting habits and software configurations.** Occasionally, I develop a habit that's long on intent but short on true usefulness. When I start thinking about what I want to write, I save my document. It sounds like a good habit. After all, if you save during think time, power outages and other types of hardware failure are less likely to affect you. It's fairly unlikely, however, that you'll experience a power outage when working with a laptop—unless you totally ignore the battery level. In addition, the more rugged hardware now used in laptop construction is much less prone to failure than the hardware of days past. Consider looking at your software configuration as well. I used to set the automatic save for my word processor to 10 minutes. That was just enough time for the drive to start spinning down. As a result, I wasted a huge amount of power starting and stopping the drive. Setting the automatic save to 20 minutes proved much more efficient from a power perspective, and I haven't lost a single bit of data as a result of the change.

- **Turn off your sound.** At times, it's great to have sound effects. Sound boards consume quite a bit of power, though, and you have to ask whether you really need to hear sounds while working on a document at 30,000 feet. In most cases, you can turn off your sound board with a setting in the Control Panel. Making this small change in configuration not only saves you power, it makes you more popular with the person sitting next to you. You also should avoid playing your latest music CD while using the battery. A CD keeps the disk running almost continuously, which greatly reduces battery life.

- **Give it a break.** More than a few people try to eat lunch and work on their laptop at the same time. In addition to the risk of spilling something in the keyboard, trying to work and eat at the same time probably isn't the most efficient way to use laptop battery power. Suspend your laptop for the duration of your meal. Not only will you use battery power more efficiently, you'll also get to enjoy your food hot for once.

- **Plug in at lunch and breaks.** You may not have a plug near you when you're in a conference, but there are likely to be places that have plugs when you take a break. Take advantage of every opportunity to recharge your machine. While you're recharging with a good lunch, allow your machine to recharge as well. Even if you have to make a trip back to your room, it's a good idea to recharge your laptop whenever possible.

On Your Own

This chapter presented different ideas on how a notebook user can take advantage of Windows 98's capabilities to improve productivity. One of the big topics was the use of the PCMCIA interface. If you have a PCMCIA bus on your notebook computer, right-click My Computer and select the Properties option. Click the Performance tab to see whether your system is fully optimized. Be sure to double-check the bus.

Create one or more power-management strategies for your laptop using the Power Schemes page of the Power Management Properties dialog box. Don't forget to include schemes for items such as maintenance and file downloads. Trying to restart a download can be frustrating, especially if the site you're trying to access is busy. You also should include some personal schemes in the list. You might, for example, want to create a special power scheme for when you go to lunch.

You also can enhance productivity by combining the Briefcase and Dial-Up Networking. Try splitting your projects into two categories: those you're working on alone, and those you're working on with a group. Try using the Briefcase method with projects you're working on alone. Use the folder and Dial-Up Networking combination for projects you're working on in a group.

Make a list of the ways you can use Dial-Up Networking to improve your productivity. This chapter mentioned the most common ways, but your company might have special needs that weren't covered. It's important to use creativity when thinking about the ways Windows 98 can help you. Keep the list handy and refer to it when you're looking for ways to solve a particular mobile-computing problem.

Peter Norton®

V

Making the Right Connections

19

Hardware and Software Connections

Peter Norton®

Making hardware and software connections is one of the more difficult parts of working with any operating system. Windows 98 provides a lot of different types of connections, and each of them helps you communicate in some way.

I'm not going to tell you that every type of connection works well under Windows 98. You'll need to address some real problem areas in order to make things work properly. For example, communications aren't always as clear as they could be. This chapter takes you through the pitfalls you could experience when creating a connection and helps you avoid them.

This chapter has two main sections. Both of them build on information talked about in previous chapters. The first part spends some time with physical details I haven't covered yet. Hardware connections are a necessary step in getting your machine ready for information exchange of all types. The second main topic I talk about is software connections. After you have a hardware connection, you need a software connection to do things like send files to a remote site or read your email.

A third section of the chapter will tell you what you need to know about voice communications. Voice is becoming an ever more important feature. You can use voice modems to do things like make your computer into an answering machine on the road.

Making Hardware Attachments

As advanced as some users are when it comes to software, they're handicapped when it comes to hardware. Finding that your printer or modem doesn't work when there's a critical deadline isn't funny at all. Picturing frantic workers trying to figure out why their external SCSI drive or another device won't work without a terminator is enough to send chills up anyone's spine. That's the kind of serious connection work we'll talk about here. I'm going to tell you about real-life connection problems and how to avoid them.

Any Port in a Storm

The first thing we need to talk about is the external ports on your machine. The problem for many people is not knowing where these ports connect or what they do. Some very different ports even look alike. For example, there's the distinct possibility that you could confuse a game port with a thick Ethernet port, because they look exactly the same. Even though most ports are easy to identify given certain clues, just grabbing any port on the back of your machine isn't such a good idea. It's always better to mark the ports and know exactly what they do before you try to use them. You might end up costing yourself a lot of time if you don't. For example, what if you have two 9-pin serial ports on your machine? Which one is COM1? Just knowing what function the port serves might not be enough. (We talked about one solution to this confusion in the "Universal Serial Bus (USB)" section of Chapter 13, "Exploiting Your Hardware," which replaces all of these special-purpose port types with a single general-purpose port.)

Fortunately, some types of ports are tough to confuse. For example, a 25-pin port with male pins is a serial port. Nothing else on your system uses that configuration. Some external SCSI ports are pretty difficult to confuse. They contain so many pins that they fill the entire width of the expansion slot. But those are the only really easy ports—the ones you can identify just by looking at them. The other ports require closer identification before you know what they do. For example, you could confuse a printer port (which uses a 25-pin female connector) with a Macintosh-compatible SCSI port (which uses the same connector). Plugging a printer into a Mac-SCSI port can cause actual physical damage to the printer or the port card or both.

You can make several generalizations by looking at the back of your PC. The following list contains clues you can use to identify the ports on the back of your machine:

- **Ethernet.** This adapter frequently has a 15-pin thick Ethernet port and a coaxial-cable thin Ethernet connector. The round coaxial connector is the same width as the slot and has two knobs for connecting the cable. Another version of an Ethernet card has the 15-pin connector and an RJ-45 jack (which looks like an oversized telephone jack). You also might find cards with just one or all three connector types. Similar-looking cards include ArcNet and token ring adapters. However, these always lack the 15-pin port. ArcNet adapters usually provide an active indicator LED as well. (You might find LEDs on other card types as well, but they are more prevalent on ArcNET cards.) In addition, ArcNet cards usually provide a DIP switch for setting the network address, while Ethernet cards rarely provide any DIP switches where you can see them outside the case.

- **I/O port combo.** The combination port card usually provides a 25-pin parallel port and a 9-pin serial port on the back of the adapter. The serial port is usually COM1 and the parallel port LPT1. Be warned that the installer could have changed these default settings by using the jumpers on the card or software setup. An I/O port combo adapter also might include a 9- or 25-pin serial port or a 15-pin game port that attaches through the back of the machine. If your case doesn't provide the extra cable-connector holes, these ports might appear in one of the expansion slot openings. Some older multifunction cards such as the Intel Above Board, also used this port layout as well.

- **SVGA display.** Some older versions of these cards provide both a 9-pin digital port and a 15-pin analog port. Note that this 15-pin port is the same size as the 9-pin port. The pins are arranged in three rows of five rather than the two-row arrangement used by the game port. They're also a little smaller than the ones used by the game port. The display adapter might include a mouse port for a PS/2-style mouse. Some adapters provide only the 15-pin port (a requirement for SVGA). Other features on the back of this card might include DIP switches or three high-frequency connectors to connect to a high-resolution monitor.

- **Game.** This adapter usually contains two 15-pin game ports, although only one is present on some very popular models. The one nearest the top of the machine is usually the one you want to use. Game adapters sometimes include a submini plug used for a variable-speed controller. This controller matches the speed of the game port to the speed of the machine.

If you see a connector with 15 pins in two rows plus an RJ-45 connector (similar to a telephone jack), you're probably looking at an Ethernet card. If you see a connector with 15 holes in three rows, it's for VGA video output.

- **Sound board.** You'll usually see a 15-pin game port that doubles as a MIDI port when you select the right jumper or software settings. This adapter also includes three submini jacks, which look like the earphone jacks on a portable radio. The precise arrangement of these jacks varies by vendor, but they serve the following purposes: output, microphone, and line input from an external source such as a CD-ROM drive. Some older sound boards also include a volume level thumbwheel.

- **External SCSI.** You also might see a number of large connectors on the back of a machine. One type of external SCSI connector has 50 lines and looks like a larger version of the Centronics connector on your printer. Unlike the Macintosh-compatible version (which has only 25 pins and is exactly like a printer port connector), this type of external SCSI connector doesn't use the same type of pins as the more familiar serial or parallel connector. The newer SCSI-II connectors are miniature versions of the large 50-pin SCSI. Again, they're quite unlike anything else that you're likely to find on a PC.

- **External drive.** A number of older CD-ROM drives used a 37-pin plug. It looks like a huge version of the parallel port. You might see this with other types of drives as well. It's never safe to assume anything about this plug. Always check it against the vendor documentation.

- **Fax/modem.** A fax or modem card usually provides two RJ-11 jacks (they look like the ones on your telephone). One jack enables you to connect the incoming cable, and the other jack is for your telephone. This adapter usually provides some DIP switches as well.

In addition to all these combinations, there are many third-party adapters that look like one of the adapters I described, but won't provide the same functionality. Fortunately, you'll probably know that you have one of them installed, because you'll need it to perform some special task on your machine. The general rule to follow is if you see a port that you don't recognize and it isn't marked, open the machine to identify it. The second rule I always follow is that you shouldn't always believe the markings on the back of your machine.

Tip: After identifying the ports, mark them. Also, don't simply write down that something is a serial port. Specify COM1 or COM2 as part of the marking. Performing this little extra step can save you a lot of time later. You might want to follow this same procedure with cables, especially if the machine is connected to a workstation setup in which the cable source might become hidden. Trying to identify the correct cable when there are several possibilities is never a welcome task. It's easier to mark everything at the outset.

Printers

Chapter 15, "Fonts and Printing," covers the topic of printers in great detail. I'd like to cover printer connections in this chapter. Some people think there's only one way to connect a printer—through a parallel port. And for some printers, that's correct. A few older printers used only a serial port connection. Some other, newer printers provide two or three connection types. These printers might have a serial port connector in addition to the standard Centronics parallel port connector, and they might have a network connector (AppleTalk or Ethernet) in addition to the serial or parallel port connectors.

Tip: Some printers don't provide a serial port as standard equipment; you have to buy it as a separate piece. Your vendor manual should provide details about buying the serial port option. Look to see whether the vendor also supports other connection options that might help in some situations. Many vendors now support a network connection as standard equipment; others support it as an optional module. If your printer doesn't provide a network connection, you might want to look at print server solutions such as Intel's NetportExpress. This small box connects to the side of your printer. It provides three printer connections (one serial and two parallel) and connects to the network through an Ethernet port. The setup software enables you to install and manage the printer server from the administrator workstation.

Choosing between these two connections isn't always easy, even though it seems like a no-brainer. A parallel port delivers the data 8 bits at a time and at a faster rate than a serial port. Choosing the parallel port doesn't take too much thought if your machine only has one printer attached to it. But what if your machine acts as a print server for many different printers? You could easily run out of parallel ports in this situation. Just about everyone resorts to an A/B switch to increase the number of available connections (which may void the printer warranty in some cases), but there might be a better solution. Connecting your printer to the machine through an unused serial port provides better access to it. No one has to flip an A/B switch to use it. (Some electronic A/B switches provide an automatic switching scheme when you send certain commands through the printer cable, but this means training the user to send those commands and a lot of frustration when the user forgets to do so.) The problem is that the access is slower—a lot slower than with a parallel port.

Categorizing how people will use the printers attached to your machine is the next step. Placing a printer that the user is less likely to use or a printer that usually experiences a lower level of activity on a serial port shouldn't cause any problems. Just make sure you warn people that their print job could take a little longer in the new configuration.

Tip: There's a point at which it becomes difficult to support too many printers on a peer-to-peer network. I start to look at other solutions when the number of workstations reaches 10 or the number of printers exceeds 4. After this limit, the performance of a peer-to-peer setup diminishes to the point where it's doubtful you can get any useful work accomplished.

Some printers come with a built-in network interface card (NIC). You can attach them directly to the network without using a workstation connection. The two most popular connection types are Ethernet and AppleTalk. Whether this solution works for you depends not on the NIC so much as it depends on the software included with the printer. The printer actually boots as a workstation or a self-contained print server on the network. You see it just as you would any other workstation. The only difference is this workstation is dedicated to a single task—printing. You need to find out which networks the vendor supports. This is a great solution for a peer-to-peer network because it allows you to use the printer without overloading the workstation. Adding a printer this way also preserves precious workstation resources such as interrupts and I/O port addresses.

Printers also support some of the more exotic network connections these days, but you might be hard-pressed to find them. One solution that I see gaining popularity is the wireless LAN. Just think—using this type of connection, you can unwrap the printer, plug it in, and perform a few configuration steps to get it up and running. In the future, adding a printer to the network might be even easier than adding it to your local workstation.

Modems

There are two different kinds of modems: internal and external. I prefer an external modem for several reasons, one of which is portability. I can move an external modem in a matter of minutes by disconnecting it from the current machine, moving it, and reconnecting it to the new machine. Another advantage is that even though most software displays the indicators that you usually see on the modem, an external modem has an edge when it comes to troubleshooting because the software light indicators might not always reflect reality. In addition, some software doesn't accurately report the modem's connection speed, an important piece of troubleshooting information.

Yet another advantage of the external modem is that you can turn it off without turning off your computer. This can come in handy when you must reset the modem manually and you don't want to reboot your computer. It also provides some people with added peace of mind, because when the modem is turned off, no one can call into their computer. (You can keep people from calling into a computer with an internal modem by setting up the modem so that it won't answer the phone line.)

Once you get past the physical location of a modem, you get to the connections. The first connection is the telephone cable required to contact the outside world. Most offices don't have the RJ-11 jacks that a modem uses as standard equipment (they might have a six-wire jack that looks like a larger version of the RJ-11, but it won't work for your modem). Normally, you have to get an office wired for a modem before you can actually use it. Some recent phone instruments in offices and, increasingly, in hotel rooms, sport a standard RJ-11 jack labeled a "data port." This is a fine place to plug in the cable from your modem. Of course, home users won't run into this problem because a modem uses a standard home telephone jack. (The second RJ-11 jack on your modem is normally reserved for a telephone, so that you can use the same telephone number for both.)

Another connection for external modems is between the modem and the computer. You'll normally use a standard serial port cable (not a null modem cable) that has either a 9- or 25-wire connector at each end. (A few external modems for older portable computers differ in that they're designed to connect to your computer's parallel port.)

Modems also are rated by speed and capability. The speed at which modems can communicate is increasing all the time. It seems that just a short time ago a 28.8Kbps (kilobits per second) connection was considered the fastest around. Now 33.6Kbps is a requirement for decent Internet access and most vendors have introduced 56Kbps modems. You'll soon reap the benefits of using cable modems as cable companies upgrade their transmission lines. In most cases, these lines will top out at 128Mbps. What does this mean for those of you still using 14.4Kbps modems? It's time for an upgrade, of course. You'll find that a 33.6Kbps modem probably is the smart buy for now, however, because there are some standardization problems with 56Kbps modems.

There are a ton of modem standards, most of which won't make a lot of difference to you as a user. However, there are some standards that you should know about. A lot of standardization has to do with the modem's speed, the way it corrects errors, or the method it uses to compress data. Knowing about these standards can mean the difference between getting a good buy on a modem and getting one that's almost useless. The following list shows the more common modem standards, but you also should be aware of any new standards that develop for higher-speed modems.

- **CCITT V.32.** Defines the 4800bps, 9600bps, 14.4Kbps, 19.2Kbps, and 28.8Kbps standards.

- **CCITT V.34.** Defines the data-compression specifics for the 28.8Kbps standard. It also defines the 33.6Kbps standard.

- **CCITT V.42.** Defines a data compression method for modems (also requires the modem to provide MNP levels 2 through 4) that enables modems to transfer data at apparent rates of up to 19.2Kbps.

- **CCITT V.42bis.** The second revision of the modem data-compression standard. It enables up to a four times compression factor or an apparent transfer rate of 38.4Kbps from a 9600bps modem.

- **CCITT V.FAST.** This is a proprietary method of defining data compression for the 28.8Kbps standard. It has been replaced by the CCITT V.34 standard.

- **CCITT X.25.** Some asynchronous modems also support this synchronous data-transfer standard. You don't need it if your only goal is to communicate with online services.

- **MNP 2-4, 5, 10.** This is a Microm Networking Protocol, a standard method of error correcting for modems. The precise differences between levels are not important from a user prospective. A higher level is generally better.

Knowing about these standards should help you choose a modem. It's vitally important that your modem adhere to all the standards for speed and other capabilities. Otherwise, the modem might not be able to make a good connection at a lower speed. Also make sure that the modem manual outlines just how the modem adheres to the standards. It should include information on FCC rules Parts 15 and 68 or the equivalent for the country you're in. The manual also should state what kind of serial port it can connect to. The current standard is RS-232C. Some modems require that standard; others can use older ports. In most cases, you won't need to worry unless you have an older machine.

Fax Boards

The preceding section introduced you to modem connections. Fax boards characteristically appear on the same board as the modem or perhaps on a daughter card. They usually use the same telephone connector as the modem. You need to follow some general rules of thumb when selecting a fax board. The most important of these is to make sure your modem communicates correctly with whatever is at the other end of the line. For normal faxing to standard fax machines, support for Group 3 faxes is sufficient. Supporting various error-correction protocols can help make sure your faxes arrive ungarbled.

Every fax/modem transfer consists of five phases. The ITU (formerly CCITT) defines these phases in several standards, which we'll examine later. These five phases aren't cast in concrete, and each one could repeat during any given session. It all depends on the capabilities of your fax/modem, the software you're using, and the environmental conditions at the time.

- **Phase 1, call establishment.** Your computer calls another computer or a standard fax machine.

- **Phase 2, premessage procedure.** The sending and receiving machines select parameters that enable them to transfer data at the fastest rate. These parameters also set the resolution, modulation, and other factors.

- **Phase 3, message transmission.** The data transfer takes place. If the initial group of parameters set in Phase 2 end in less-than-optimal results, the fax/modem performs Phase 2 and Phase 3 again as required.

- **Phase 4, post-message procedure.** Some software considers each page a separate message. That's the way your fax machine works as well. Phase 4 allows the sending and receiving machines to evaluate the results of each message, then raise or lower the transmission speed as required. The sending machine also transmits a page-break marker. This is the same thing as a form feed on a printer, except that the fax might simply print a line across the page or cut off the page at that point. Remember that faxes can be either long or short, depending on the message needs.

- **Phase 5, call clear down.** The two machines hang up after the sending machine transmits an end-of-transmission signal.

As with modems, there are several fax/modem specifications. You'll want a fax/modem that adheres to the following ITU standards:

- **ITU T.4.** Defines the image-transfer portion of the session used in Phase 3.
- **ITU T.30.** Defines the negotiation and interpage phases (2, 3, 4, and 5). A normal multipage transfer uses T.30 only at the beginning of the call, between pages, and after the last page.
- **CCITT V.29.** Defines the specifications for the 14400/12000bps speed.
- **ITU V.34.** Defines the combined voice, FAX, and data standards for 28.8 and 33.6Kbps modems.

Microsoft also provides for two different classes of fax communication between fax/modems. Here's the user view of what these different classes mean:

- Class 1 communications send an editable fax to the other party. This means that the fax appears as actual text that the other party can edit.
- Class 2 communications are more like the faxes you usually receive. They're graphic representations of the text and graphics in the document. This is the same format as Group 3 faxes, like the one you're used to seeing in the office.

There is a real-world difference between Class 1 and Class 2 fax/modems. A Class 1 fax performs both the T.4 and T.30 protocols in software. This allows the Windows 98 drivers to perform the data translation required to create editable faxes. A Class 2 fax performs the T.4 protocol in firmware—an EEPROM in the modem that does part of the processor's work. This is a faster solution because it removes part of the processing burden from the processor. A Class 2 fax/modem also should be able to create editable faxes. However, since the Class 2 standard isn't well defined and Microsoft didn't have dependable information on what to expect from a Class 2 fax/modem, they made the decision to restrict Class 2 faxes to the Group 3 graphics format.

CD-ROM and DVD Players

CD-ROM and DVD drives usually have two connections that you need to worry about. The first is the bus connector that allows data transfer between the computer and the device. Generally, this is a SCSI connector or an IDE or EIDE connection. The principle is the same; the data transfer rate might be a lot slower, depending on the method of connection. SCSI always beats IDE hands-down, but SCSI and EIDE offer comparable performance. (You'll definitely want to look at SCSI for CD-ROM Recordable (CDR) and DVD applications since performance is so critical in this situation.) The bus connector for a CD-ROM or DVD serves the same purpose as the equivalent connector for your hard drive. It enables you to transfer data from the CD-ROM or DVD to your machine.

Tip: The price of CD-ROM recorders has dropped significantly in recent months. There are two advantages to buying a CD-ROM recorder instead of a player. First, you can use it to make archive copies of CDs. Despite popular folklore, CDs are resistant—but not impervious—to damage. Considering the cost of some CDs and the less-than-thrilling replacement policy some vendors have, an archive copy could make a big difference when the inevitable does occur. Second, you can use a CD-ROM recorder in place of a backup tape. A CD-ROM backup is faster than some types of tape backup, although I won't say that you can't get better performance out of some DAT tapes. One thing is certain: The random-access feature of a CD makes it a lot faster than a tape for data retrieval. The only downside to CD-ROM recorders is their read speed. Although most CD-ROM readers offer 24X to 32X read speed, you'll get somewhere between 6X to 12X read speed with CD-ROM recorders.

Some people don't really think about the second connection. They'll try to use a CD-ROM with a game or another application that plays sound right off the CD—just like you would with a music CD—and discover that the game doesn't appear to work with their machine. The same could be said about playing movies off of a DVD drive. The problem is that they don't have the RCA plugs in the back of the CD-ROM drive connected to anything. External drives use RCA connectors like the speaker outputs on your stereo. Internal drives usually require some type of special connector for your sound card. This is a proprietary connector in some cases; in other cases, the vendor will try to make you believe that their common cable really is proprietary. Check with your local computer store to see whether they have an inexpensive alternative to the expensive cable that the vendors normally offer.

In addition to the other connections on your CD-ROM or DVD drive, there's a headphone connector on the front of it. Imagine my surprise when I plugged some headphones in and heard sound out of my speakers and headset at the same time. Some vendors disable the speaker output when you plug in the headset; others don't. You'll want to check out this feature if this is an important consideration for your application.

Making Software Attachments

After your hardware is up and running, you have to get some software to talk to it in order to do any useful work. The following sections describe several utilities that come with Windows 98. These utilities won't help you "surf the Net" or download the latest industry gossip, but they do help you make the necessary connections.

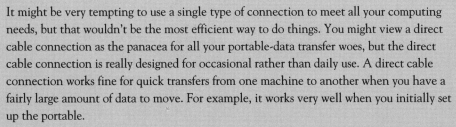

Peter's Principle: The Right Kind of Connection

It might be very tempting to use a single type of connection to meet all your computing needs, but that wouldn't be the most efficient way to do things. You might view a direct cable connection as the panacea for all your portable-data transfer woes, but the direct cable connection is really designed for occasional rather than daily use. A direct cable connection works fine for quick transfers from one machine to another when you have a fairly large amount of data to move. For example, it works very well when you initially set up the portable.

If you use a portable on a daily basis, using such an Interlink-style connection is a waste of time. You'll want to find some other method of creating your connection to the desktop. If you have a docking station that can accept a standard network card or if you plug in a PCMCIA network card, you'll be able to use this much-faster Ethernet connection to make your data transfers. However, this works only if you have a network and a PCMCIA card. Alternatively, you could get an external Ethernet adapter that plugs into your portable's parallel port. This solution works fine, but it isn't quite as speedy as the standard network interface cards that plug into the computer's bus or the PCMCIA network adapters.

The Briefcase isn't a physical connection to your desktop machine, but it does do the job for smaller amounts of data. In fact, you'll find out that a Briefcase can hold a substantial amount of data if you use it correctly.

Okay, so the network and Briefcase options are out of the question because you're out of town. You can still make a connection to your desktop by using Dial-Up Networking. It won't be as fast as some other techniques, but it enables you to get the data you require while on the road or when working from home.

Windows 98 provides a lot of different connections. You need to use the right one for the job, and that means taking the time to learn about the various options available to you. A connection that works well in one instance could be a time killer in another. Don't succumb to the one-connection way of computing; use every tool that Windows 98 provides.

Making a Direct Cable Connection

Portable users will love the direct cable-connection feature that Windows 98 provides. You can make a direct connection using either the serial or parallel port. The Direct Cable Connection utility enables you to make the connection in the background, effectively freeing the host for use while the client makes the required transactions.

Windows 98 won't automatically install this utility as part of a default package. You need to load the separate Direct Cable Connection utility by using the Add/Remove Programs applet discussed in Chapter 10, "The Windows 98 Applets."

After you get Direct Cable Connection installed, you have to set up the host. This means that you'll define the port that your machine will use, as well as its mode. Let's look at this procedure first.

Tip: You can create the required data-transfer serial cable using a standard serial cable, a null modem, and a gender changer. This will provide all the components you need to make a data-transfer cable using a standard modem cable. Your local electronics or computer store usually can provide the null modem and gender changer.

1. Use a special serial or parallel cable to connect the two computers. You usually can get one of these at your local computer store. Be sure to tell them that you plan to connect two computers for the purpose of data transfer. The parallel cable uses special crossover wiring and the serial cable must be wired with the required wires cross-connected or else you'll need to use a null modem as well for the connection to work.

2. Share any folders or drives you want the guest computer to see by right-clicking the folder in Explorer, selecting Properties from the context menu, and selecting the Sharing tab of the Properties dialog. You can choose between read-only and full access to the folder.

Note: Direct Cable Connection configures itself for whatever mode you had it set up to use during the previous use after you use it for the first time. Simply click the Change button on the first dialog to get out of this mode and choose something different.

3. Open the Direct Cable Connection utility on the host computer. You should see a Direct Cable Connection dialog box.

4. Choose the Host radio button, and then click Next. The next dialog will ask which port you want to use for the connection between machines. Notice that the local ports are listed automatically. You can add other ports by using the Install New Ports button.

5. Select the port you want. Be sure to use the same type of port on both machines. Click Next. Direct Cable Connection asks whether you want to add password protection to your drive in addition to the protection you might already have provided through the sharing process. Checking the Use password protection option enables the Set Password button, which displays the dialog you use to enter the password.

> **Tip:** The password option in this dialog box comes in handy when more than one person needs to use the direct-cable connection to a machine. You can leave the host running in the background and then connect other machines as necessary—even remote machines. However, this feature is limited, especially when you consider that the Dial-Up Networking utility enables remote users to call into a machine using a better interface.

6. Check the Use password protection check box if you want to password-protect your connection. If you select this option, use the Set Password button to change the password from a blank.

7. Click Finish. Direct Cable Connection waits for the client machine to log in. If the client doesn't respond in about 30 seconds, Direct Cable Connection asks whether it's properly connected. Ignore the message until you get the other machine running.

The procedure for setting up a guest computer is exactly the same as for a host computer. The only difference is you don't need to set a password. After the two computers establish a connection, the client computer is able to use the resources of the host.

Creating Scripts for Dial-Up Networking

The connections provided by older versions of Windows worked fine if you had a straight connection. However, the connection feature could also become a bit cumbersome if you wanted to create a connection for something like a Windows NT server. Because a standard connection still works for the vast majority of users out there, Microsoft wisely chose to leave it alone. To supplement the standard connection, Windows 98 also provides a scripting capability. If you create a script and then add it to a connection, Windows 98 uses the script instead of the standard connection setup to make your dial-up connection to a server work. Adding a script means accessing the Scripting page of the Dial-Up Connection Properties dialog by right clicking the connection and then choosing Properties from the context menu.

> **Note:** This section assumes at least a modicum of programming experience. You need to know what a variable is and have a least a little experience creating macros. Obviously, the more programming experience you have, the faster you'll learn the material in this section.

Let's take a look at the dialog box. Up at the top you'll see the File Name field that contains the name of the script file you want to use. Notice the two buttons directly below this field. The first, Edit, enables you to modify your script. The second, Browse, displays a File Open dialog box you can use to find a script file. There are also two check boxes on this page. The Step Through Script option walks you through your script one line at a time when you use the connection. It's useful for troubleshooting a script when you first create it, but you'll want to disable this option later. The second option, Start Terminal Screen Minimized, is handy after you've debugged your script because it keeps screen clutter to a minimum. However, you'll want to keep this option unchecked until you're certain that the script works as intended.

Starting a Script

You'll always create a script by using a text editor such as Notepad. A script can't contain any fancy formatting or other additions that you normally associate with a word processing document. Script files should also have an SCP extension to make them easy to find.

How do you start the scripting process? If you've programmed in C, some of what I'm going to tell you will sound familiar. Scripts use procedures. You'll enclose all your scripting code with a pair of statements: Proc and endproc. Every script has to have a main procedure, and you should add some comments to tell other people (or simply remind yourself) how it works. These are the first lines of text you'll add to your script file:

```
; This is a comment telling about the script.
proc main
endproc
```

Now that you have a main procedure, Windows 98 recognizes this file as a script. It won't do anything, however, until you add some code to it.

Using Variables

You must declare all the variables you use, and these declarations have to appear at the beginning of the procedure. A declaration always contains the variable type and the variable name; you also can assign the variable a value. Dial-Up Networking doesn't allow you to declare variables outside a procedure. Variable names always begin with a letter or an underscore—you can't use reserved names for a variable. Here are the types of variables you can use within a script:

- **Integer.** Any number, either positive or negative.
- **String.** A collection of characters such as "Hello World". Strings can contain numbers.
- **Boolean.** Variables that are either true or false.

Let's look at variables in action. Here's a script with some variables:

```
; This script shows some variables.
proc main
; This is an integer variable.
integer    iValue
; This is a string variable with an assigned value.
string     sMyString = "Hello"
```

```
; This is a boolean variable.
boolean    lAmICorrect
endproc
```

You'll also find some predefined variables used with Dial-Up Networking scripts. Table 19.1 provides a list of these predefined variables and their purposes.

Table 19.1. Predefined script variables.

Name	Type	Description
$USERID	String	The name of the user as it appears in the User Name field of the Connect To dialog box.
$PASSWORD	String	The user's password as it appears in the Password field of the Connect To dialog box.
$SUCCESS	Boolean	A variable set by certain commands. You can use this variable to determine whether a command succeeded.
$FAILURE	Boolean	A variable set by certain commands. You can use this variable to determine whether a command failed.

Special Considerations for Strings

Trying to get a string to do everything you need it to do could prove frustrating if the scripting language didn't provide a few additional features. For example, how do you send a control character to the server? A lot of servers require you to send a Ctrl+Break character before they'll respond. The caret translation feature takes care of this. Simply place a caret in front of one of the first 26 characters. For example, "^c" sends a Ctrl+Break. (Make sure you always use quotes when defining a string in a script, even if that string represents a control character.)

There are also some text substitutions for control characters. For example, "<cr>" is a carriage return and "<lf>" is a line feed. Using a "<cr>" in your code is much less cryptic than "^M".

Finally, you'll find that Dial-Up Networking scripts support several escape character sequences that C programmers are familiar with. For example, using "\"" in your code produces a double quote. You also need a way to display the caret. You do it like this: "\^". Likewise, you need a way to display the backslash—"\\"—and the less-than sign—"\<".

Using Commands

The scripting language provided with Dial-Up Networking supports certain commands right out of the box. You also can create other commands (simple ones) by using the proc and endproc keywords to create a procedure. Let's take a look at the commands you get as part of the product. Table 19.2 lists the built-in commands you can use within a script.

Table 19.2. Built-in script commands.

Command	Description
delay <*iSeconds*>	Enables you to pause the script for *iSeconds*. You'd usually use this kind of a command when you need to wait for the hardware to complete a task. For example, when dialing out from the company PBX, you might have to wait for it to make a connection to an outside line.
getip [<*iIP*>]	Use this command to retrieve the IP from the host. If your ISP sends the IP in the string, you can use the optional *iIP* variable to specify which IP you want.
goto <*Label*>	Tells the script to go to the label you've defined. A label is a piece of stand-alone text followed by a colon. For example, MyLabel: is a label.
halt	This command tells the script to stop. You'd normally use it as part of your error control or in response to an unexpected event. This command doesn't remove the terminal window, which enables you to see what kind of error condition halted the script.
if <*lValue*> then	The if command checks for a specific condition (a Boolean value) specified by *lValue*. If the condition is true, the script commands between then and endif are executed. If not, program execution continues with the first command after then.
set port databits <*iValue*>	Use this command to set the number of data bits used for communication purposes. It enables you to set up the communications port automatically instead of relying on the user to do so manually. You have a choice of 5, 6, 7, or 8 data bits.
set port parity <*sValue*>	This command enables you to set up the communications port parity. Choose between none, odd, even, mark, and space.
set port stopbits <*iValue*>	Use this command to set the number of stop bits to 1 or 2.
set screen keyboard <*lValue*>	Using this command with a value of Off turns the keyboard off in the terminal window. You can turn the keyboard back on by using this command with a value of On.

Command	Description
`set ipaddr <sValue>`	Use this command to set the workstation's IP address for the session. *sValue* must contain a string in IP format, such as this one: `"200.100.100.1"`.
`transmit <sValue> [raw]`	Use the `transmit` command to send data to the host computer. *sValue* can contain any string of characters you choose. Dial-Up Networking usually interprets the string as previously shown in the section "Special Considerations for Strings." You can send the string without any interpretation by adding the `raw` argument to this command.
`waitfor`	This is the most complex command provided by the script language. Its basic function is to receive input from the host and to act on it. I discuss this command in the text that follows this table.
`while <lValue> do ... enddo`	The `while` loop tells Dial-Up Networking to continue performing the commands between `do` and `enddo` until *lValue* returns a value of `false`. You can use any conditional statement for *lValue*. The only criterion is that it return a value of `true` or `false`.

Now that we've looked at all of the available commands, let's take a close look at the `waitfor` command. Let's look at a simple example first:

```
waitfor "Login:"
```

All this command says is to wait until you get a `Login:` string from the host computer. After you get it, start executing the statement immediately following this one. But what if you don't want to proceed with the very next statement? This form of the command shows what to do in that case:

```
waitfor "error" then FixError
```

In this case, we'll wait for a string containing `error` from the host, and then go to a label called `FixError`. Obviously, this form of the command is a bit limited, so you might want to add other labels. In addition, this form of the command tells Dial-Up Networking to wait 15 seconds and then proceed with the next command after the `until` argument:

```
waitfor
    "Go For It"    DoGoForIt
    "Logged In"    DoLogInStuff
    "Error"    FixError
until 15
```

As you can see, you can keep building on to this command until it directs every kind of traffic possible for you. Place this command within a `while do ... enddo` command, and you'll have a program loop for handing the entire communications session.

Using Phone Dialer

Open Phone Dialer and you'll see a display similar to the one in Figure 19.1. Notice that there's a keypad on the left side of the dialog box, a list of speed dial numbers on the right and the current number at the top.

Figure 19.1.
The Phone Dialer dialog box looks like a telephone keypad with an autodialer.

There are several ways to dial a number. You could cut it out of your database manager and paste it into the blank at the top. This is one of the methods I use for infrequently called numbers. It has the advantage of allowing you to call a lot of numbers quickly without giving yourself a case of carpal tunnel syndrome in the process.

Before you make any connections, you should look at the Tools menu to see what configuration options you have. If you select the Connect Using option, you'll see the Connect Using dialog box. This dialog box has only three fields. The first field, Line, asks which modem you want to use. Only modems that you've set up using the Modems applet in Control Panel are listed. The second field, Address, asks which telephone line you want to use to dial out. It's active only if you have more than one line available. The Use Phone Dialer check box tells Windows 98 to use Phone Dialer for all application requests. Clicking the Line Properties button brings up the Modem Properties dialog box discussed in Chapter 13.

We saw how to use the Dialing Properties option of the Tools menu earlier in the "Calling from Another Location" section of Chapter 1, "Opening Windows to the Internet." Essentially, it en-ables you to specify the location from which you're dialing so that Phone Dialer can automatically compensate as needed for long distance calls.

The Show Log option in the Tools menu displays the Call Log dialog box. There isn't too much to say about this particular dialog box except that it maintains a record of the calls you make, includ-ing the number, the person's name and how long you were on the phone. The nicest feature of this particular dialog box is that you can double-click an entry to call it again. With this feature, I can save some time when calling a number I don't have memorized, because I don't have to look it up.

There are two convenient methods for adding new numbers to your Speed Dial group. The first method is to click a blank spot. You'll see the Program Speed Dial dialog box. This dialog box contains only two entries: the name of the person you want to call and the number to reach him or her. The buttons on the side enable you to save, save and dial, or cancel the phone number.

You also can use the Edit | Speed Dial command to display the Edit Speed Dial dialog box. This dialog box enables you to access any of the buttons. All you need to do is click the one you want to edit. Erasing the contents of both the name and number fields blanks that button for future use.

Understanding Voice Communications

The latest rage in the world of modems is the voice modem. A voice modem enables you to exchange data and talk on the same line by using digitized voice signals. In other words, you don't need two telephone lines anymore to have an online discussion with a colleague. Having a voice/data/fax modem combination also means that you don't need a lot of messy wires hanging around the office. You can use one phone as a fax machine, network host, and answering machine. The next few sections look at voice modems and how to use them within the Windows 98 environment.

Getting TAPI Support for Voice Modems

Windows 98 will normally install Unimodem V support for you automatically as part of the modem driver installation process when you install a modem with voice capability. You can check the status of the support by opening the Telephony applet in the Control Panel. Choose the Telephony Drivers tab of the Dialing Properties dialog that appears when you open the Telephony applet. If you don't see Unimodem Service Provider on the list of installed drivers, then you don't have Unimodem V support installed. To install support, click the Add button. You'll see an Add Driver dialog where you can highlight the Unimodem Service Provider entry and click OK to install the driver. Obviously, you must have a voice modem installed to use Unimodem V support.

From a user perspective, the Unimodem V package contains four items of interest. First are the drivers you need to use your voice modem. The package includes a new UNIMODEM.VXD file along with several other support drivers. Part of these driver updates includes a Telephony Service Provider (TSP). Its job is to handle program requests such as dialing and answering the phone line. The second item of interest is the Operator Agent. This is a special program that runs on your computer. It identifies whether an incoming call is voice, data, or fax, and directs it to the appropriate program for handling. If the Operator Agent can't determine what kind of call you're receiving, it asks the caller for information. Finally, if the Operator Agent can't get a response from the caller, it directs the call to a default application. The third item in this package is a series of WAV file drivers that allow your telephony applications to record and play back messages. Finally, the fourth item is a series of INF files used for installation and support of the Unimodem V package.

Installing the Operating Agent

Unimodem support comes with an Operating Agent. You can choose whether to install this support, but it's usually a good idea to do so if you plan to use Microsoft products. Remember that the Operating Agent is the software that allows Windows 98 to determine whether an incoming call is fax, data, or voice. The following procedure shows how to install the Operating Agent.

Note: The following procedure assumes you've already installed Unimodem V support using the procedure in the preceding section. If you haven't installed this support, do so now.

1. Select the Operator icon in the Start | Programs | Accessories folder. You'll see the Microsoft Operator Wizard.

2. Click Next. You'll see a second page of instructions; be sure to read through them. This page tells you what you'll be doing as you use the wizard to install Operator Agent support. At this point you need to perform three steps: Select a default message, select a default application, and select a message for those times when a particular application isn't running.

3. Click Next. You'll see a Microsoft Operator Wizard dialog box that enables you to play and change the initial greeting. This is the message a caller hears if the Operator Agent can't determine what kind of call it's receiving. Click the Play button to hear the current message. If you want to change this message, select the Change the Greeting radio button. Otherwise, select the Keep the current greeting radio button. If you choose to keep the current greeting, skip to step 6. Steps 4 and 5 will help you through the process of selecting or recording a new message.

Tip: The Operator Agent comes complete with a male and a female version of the default message. The female version of the message is installed as a default. You can follow steps 4 and 5 to choose the default male version of the message in addition to recording your own message. Make sure you have a microphone attached to your machine if you choose to record a new message.

4. Click Next. If you selected Change the Greeting in the preceding step, you'll see a dialog box that enables you to save the current message by clicking the Yes radio button and then the Save button. (Because we're using the default message in this example, you would select the No radio button.) After you click Save, you'll see a standard File Save dialog box.

5. Click Next. You'll see a dialog box like the one in Figure 19.2. This figure shows the default setup. Clicking the top radio button takes you to a recording dialog box in which you can record a message using a microphone or another media input device. This dialog box also enables you to play back the recorded message to make sure that it's correct. Clicking the second radio button in the dialog box shown in Figure 19.2, you to choose a prerecorded file. Theoretically, you can choose any WAV file, but you'll want to make sure that it tells your caller what to do. The drop-down list box shows the WAV files in your Media folder. You can use the Browse button to explore your hard drive and find WAV files located in other areas. As with the previous dialog box, the Play button allows you to hear the prerecorded WAV file that you've selected.

Figure 19.2.
In this dialog box, you can choose to use a prerecorded message or to record your own.

6. Click Next. You'll see a dialog box that enables you to choose the order in which the Operator Agent answers calls. In other words, if you expect to have a lot of voice messages, a few faxes and almost no data uploads, then you'd want to move the Data entry to the very end.

7. Highlight any entries you need to move, then use the Move Up or Move Down button to change their position. If you decide that you want to go with the default setup, click the Restore Defaults button.

8. Click Next. You'll see a dialog box that enables you to choose the message that the caller hears if the Operator Agent can't complete a call. Setting up this dialog box is much the same as the default call-type selection message discussed in steps 3, 4, and 5, so I won't talk about it again here.

9. Click Next. You'll see a dialog box that tells you that you've completed the setup process. You'll also see some additional information concerning the Operator Agent—such as how to determine whether it's running.

10. Click Finish to complete the setup process. At this point the dialog box simply disappears. However, if you look at the Taskbar, you'll see a new icon for managing the Operator Agent.

This procedure works fine the first time you set up the Operator Agent, but what if you need to change your message or another setting? As with everything else under Windows 98, you can right-click the Operator Agent icon on the taskbar to see a context menu. There are three different options on this menu. The first opens the Microsoft Operator Agent dialog box shown in Figure 19.3. I will cover the contents of this dialog box in a few seconds. The second option suspends the Operator Agent. The agent is still available; it just won't answer the phone. The third option, Stop Using Operator, actually removes the Operator Agent from the taskbar. You'll use this option when you install a third-party product to handle your phone calls or simply don't need the capability any more.

Figure 19.3.
You can change the
Operator Agent
properties using this
dialog box.

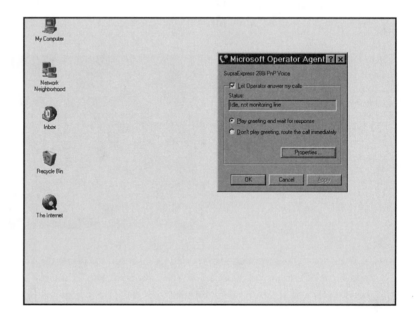

Let's talk about the dialog box shown in Figure 19.3. The first check box enables or suspends the Operator Agent. Unchecking this box is the same as selecting the Suspend Operator option on the context menu. It keeps the Operator Agent installed, but prevents it from managing your phone line. Notice the edit box directly below the check box. It contains the current status of the Operator Agent. In this case, it's idle because there aren't any active applications on the test machine. An idle message doesn't necessarily mean the Operator Agent is malfunctioning, even if you have applications installed for recording messages and so on. An idle message also appears if none of the applications have placed the modem in answer mode. (See the documentation for the application to see how to do this.) The two radio buttons you see in this dialog box determine whether the caller hears a message. Select the first radio button if you plan on getting a lot of voice calls and want to give the caller an opportunity to choose a course of action. On the other hand, you may want to select the second radio button if you plan on getting a lot of fax or data calls so the caller doesn't think your machine is broken. (A lot of people want an instant response from a fax or data line and hang up if they don't get it.)

Figure 19.3 also shows a Properties button. Clicking this button displays the dialog box shown in Figure 19.4. This is where you can change either of the two messages and set the order in which the Operator Agent directs calls. All you need to do is click the button corresponding to the configuration item you want to change. You'll actually see that part of the Microsoft Operator Wizard come up and help you set the configuration. Because I already covered the wizard as part of the initial installation procedure, I won't cover it again here.

Figure 19.4.
You can change any of the configuration settings for the Operator Agent using the Microsoft Operator Agent Properties dialog box.

The Inner Workings of Unimodem V

Okay, so you've got Unimodem V support and the Operator Agent installed on your machine. Does that mean you're ready to go? Just having a few drivers and the right modem won't fulfill all your needs. For you to see any results, the programmer who wrote the application you're using had to use the Voice Modem Extensions for Windows 98. The application needs to know how to use the capabilities that Windows 98 provides. Most of the answering-machine–type applications on the market right now still rely on those proprietary setups that I mentioned previously.

Technical Note: Voice modems use special command strings to activate their voice capabilities, just like any other service they offer. If you've ever used a program such as Procomm Plus, you're familiar with the Hayes command strings used to set up your modem. For example, ATA answers the phone and ATH hangs up the phone. Even though Hayes originated these command strings, they're now managed by groups such as the American National Standards Institute (ANSI), the Telecommunications Industry Association (TIA), and the Electronics Industry Association (EIA). When the time came to implement voice capabilities in voice modems, there weren't any AT command strings for vendors to use—so they made up their own. Obviously, this muddies the picture greatly, because Windows can't depend on using a standard command string to work with a voice modem. There's a new standard now for voice modems: ANSI/TIA/EIA standard IS-101

continues

(Facsimile Digital Interfaces—Voice Control Interim Standard for Asynchronous DCE).
This standard defines a set of AT+V commands that modems should use to enable and use
voice capabilities. When buying a new voice modem, make absolutely certain it adheres to
this standard if you want to use it successfully with Windows.

So how does Windows get sounds recorded as messages out to the caller? Take a look at Figure 19.5.
It shows a block diagram of the new connections that Unimodem V creates to connect various
Windows 98 subsystems together so that you can use your voice modem in a variety of ways.

Figure 19.5.
Unimodem V creates
new connections
between various
Windows 98
subsystems.

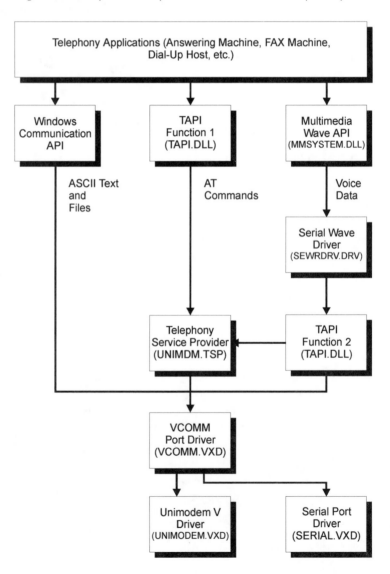

The following list provides an overview of the various Unimodem V subsystems:

- **Windows Communication API.** I'll describe this block in the "An Overview of the Communications Architecture" section of Chapter 20, "Network Connections with an Internet Appeal."

- **Telephony API.** I'll describe this block in the "An Overview of the Communications Architecture" section of Chapter 20. We do use it in a different way. Notice that the figure shows two different functions for TAPI. We disguise the voice data so that TAPI will work with it using the Serial Wave Driver. Even though there aren't any new TAPI files, we double the amount of work that it can do. (This particular feat is a real credit to the new modular approach that Microsoft has taken in designing Windows.)

- **Multimedia Wave API.** If you're wondering what this is doing here, you're not alone. It doesn't take long to figure out, though, that Windows has to have some way of converting the voice you hear on the phone into data that it can understand (and vice versa). Because we already have this capability built into Windows though the multimedia API, why not use it? As a result, the data you record using a microphone or hear through a speaker goes through the multimedia API even when the source is a telephone call.

- **Serial Wave Driver.** This part of the picture can get a little confusing, so we'll talk about the simple version. If you've got a standard modem that adheres to all the standards, you'll use a serial wave driver that supports the International Multimedia Association (IMA) adaptive delta pulse code modulation (ADPCM) standard. All these fancy words mean is that the serial wave driver converts the digitized voice it receives from the modem into something the multimedia system can understand (and vice versa). This module uses a helper DLL named VMODCTL.DLL to ease communications with the Telephony Service Provider (TSP). Some modems rely on a nonstandard hardware audio port to transmit digitized voice over the telephone. In this case, Microsoft adds another helper module named WRAP.DRV to coordinate voice and data transfers.

- **Telephony Service Provider (TSP).** This is the driver that takes care of things such as dialing the phone. It also issues all the AT+V commands required to communicate with your modem. For example, there's one AT+V command to set the modem in voice mode and another to tell it to transfer data. (This module also supports some modems that use the AT+V command syntax, but you'll want to check the list I provided previously to make sure your modem is supported.)

- **VCOMM Port Driver.** I'll describe this block in the "An Overview of the Communications Architecture" section in Chapter 20.

- **Unimodem V Driver.** I'll describe this block in the "An Overview of the Communications Architecture" section of Chapter 20. The difference is that the Unimodem V Driver now has the capacity to use the specific voice commands supported by your modem.

- **Serial Port Driver.** I'll describe this block in the "An Overview of the Communications Architecture" section of Chapter 20.

Remember that we've just looked at an overview of the new additions to the communications subsystem. There's a lot more going on than I've talked about, but this overview gives you enough information to better understand how Windows 98 works.

On Your Own

Look through the vendor manual that came with your printer. See whether the vendor provides any accessories for your printer that might make it more flexible to use. Especially important is the availability of alternative port options. You also might want to check for third-party solutions for your printer. Some third-party vendors provide port accessories for some of the more prominent printers, such as the HP LaserJet.

If you have a fax/modem attached to your machine, identify the five phases of a fax transaction. This is especially easy when using an external model. The lights on the front of the device help you detect when various phases occur. Tracking this type of information can help you troubleshoot a faulty connection.

If you have a notebook computer—and both a network and a direct cable connection are available for it—try both methods of transferring a file. Most people have a serial connection available, so try that first. You should find the network connection to be much faster, but it's interesting to see how much faster. Try the same thing with a parallel connection (if possible).

Install and set up Phone Dialer. Try it for a few days to see whether its additional features make phone calling a little easier for your harder-to-reach numbers. Also try the log feature to see how well it meets your needs.

Try creating a script program for a Dial-Up Networking connection. You might want to try this with a local setup first to get a feel for the capabilities of the scripting language.

Determine whether you or your company can use a voice modem to make using the computer easier and more efficient. Be sure to check out the various criteria covered in this chapter—especially adherence to standards. You'll also want to download the Unimodem V update for your computer.

20

Network Connections with an Internet Appeal

Peter Norton®

The preceding chapter looked at some of the intricacies of making connections within Windows 98. This chapter looks at some of the things that you can do with those connections after you make them. Unlike its predecessor, Windows 98 provides a combination of communications options that should meet the majority of your needs.

> **Looking Ahead:** I cover standard communications in this chapter. All the Internet-specific communications features provided by Windows 98 are covered in Chapters 1, 21, and 22. Chapter 1, "Opening Windows to the Internet," is the one to look at if you want to get connected quickly and start using the Internet right away. Chapter 21, "Internet Connections," provides more detailed information about products such as Internet Explorer and Microsoft NetMeeting. You'll learn how to set up your own intranet server in Chapter 22, "Creating Your Own Intranet with Personal Web Server." The preceding chapter—Chapter 19, "Hardware and Software Connections"—covered the new scripting feature for Dial-Up Networking users.

An Overview of the Communications Architecture

Before we get into the communications packages, let's look at the communications subsystem architecture. Actually, we won't get the total picture in this chapter. Figure 20.1 reflects only the local part of the communications structure. Chapter 18, "Mobile Computing: Notebooks, Telecommuting, and Remote Access," covers the remote network architecture. However, if you look carefully, you'll see all three of the main connections discussed in the "Dial-Up Networking, Phone Dialer, and Direct Cable Connection" section of Chapter 19.

The following list provides details about all the components of the communications subsystem:

- **Telephony API (TAPI).** All the new modem-specific services are clustered under this API. It provides command translation for the new Windows 98 applications that use it. When an application asks about the modem's setup or status, this module provides the information translation required for a seamless interface. TAPI might configure the modem from a virtual point of view, but VCOMM still manages the actual port. Modem commands flow through the port from TAPI. A good analogy of this arrangement is that VCOMM provides the pipe, but TAPI provides the water.

- **Windows 16-bit communications API.** This API is the module that accepts instructions from a 16-bit application and translates them into 32-bit instructions that Windows 98 can understand. One API instruction might require an entire module's worth of detailed instructions in order to perform a specific task. Windows 98 doesn't use the 16-bit version of the Windows communications instructions; it uses the 32-bit API described in the next bullet. The old 16-bit instructions didn't provide the robust environment that the rest of Windows 98 provides. However, instead of writing a new 16-bit module for older applications to use, Microsoft provides access to the new 32-bit interface through these instructions and the COMM.DRV module that I'll describe in a moment.

Figure 20.1.
An overview of the Windows 98 local communications architecture.

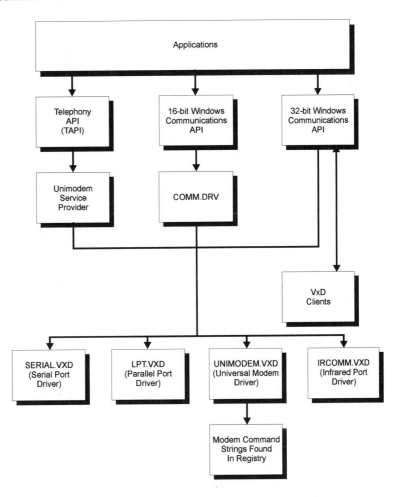

- **Windows 32-bit communications API.** This is the enhanced 32-bit instruction set for Windows 98. Like its 16-bit counterpart, the 32-bit API translates application requests into commands that Windows can actually implement. Windows 98 also got rid of the VCOMM.386 file by placing all of its components within the 32-bit communications API. VCOMM.386 was a static device VxD that previous versions of Windows always loaded during the boot process. Part of the job that VCOMM.386 performed was to load all the port drivers shown in Figure 20.1. Other parts of Windows also called VCOMM.386 through their respective APIs to perform a variety of port-specific services. All of these services are now handled by KERNEL32.DLL. The net effect of this change is to speed communications by reducing the number of calls the communication subsystem has to make.

- **Unimodem service provider.** This is the specific driver for your modem. It takes the generic commands provided by the TAPI module and translates them into something that your modem will understand.

- **COMM.DRV.** Under Windows 3.x, this module carried out the communications tasks ordered by the API. The Windows 98 version is a thunk layer to the 32-bit instructions held in the 32-bit communications API and VCOMM.386. (See the "Getting 16-Bit and 32-Bit Applications to Work Together" section of Chapter 8, "The Windows 98 Architecture," for more details about thunking.) The positive aspect of this is that you'll see a definite boost in the speed of communications programs, even if you use an older 16-bit application. For example, I noticed that background downloads go well, even using my older copy of Procomm for Windows, which never worked in the background under Windows 3.x. It's unfortunate that Microsoft decided to maintain the old 16-bit instruction set rather than upgrade it to the fuller 32-bit set.

- **VxD clients.** VCOMM.386 (which was incorporated into the 32-bit communications API) provides services to more than just the communications subsystem. Every time any other Windows subsystem requires port access, it must go through VCOMM.386 as well. These requests are fielded through APIs that act as clients to this module. This is an internal Windows 98 function that you'll never really notice, but you should know that there are interactions between subsystems. A port failure might not always be the result of a communications- or print-specific problem; it could be related to some interaction from another, unrelated subsystem.

- **SERIAL.VXD.** This is the serial port driver. It's the actual serial port engine. Another driver is associated with the serial port as well: SERIALUI.DLL provides the interface that you use while setting up the serial ports.

- **LPT.VXD.** This is the parallel port driver. Unlike the serial port, the parallel port usually is managed by the printer subsystem. As a result, it relies on MSPRINT.DLL for user-interface services.

- **IRCOMM.VXD.** This is the infrared-communication port driver. You usually see it on a laptop machine, but any machine with an IR port can use it. In most cases, an IR port also is associated with either a parallel or serial port (in some cases both). A communication program might end up transferring data through the serial or parallel port routines before it gets to the infrared-data port drivers.

- **UNIMODEM.VXD.** The modem setup is a little more complex than the other port drivers supported by VCOMM.386. This one actually works with either a serial or parallel port to provide modem services for the rest of Windows. It's also responsible for making any modem-specific Registry changes. Every time you change the modem strings, this module records them in the Registry. As with the serial port driver, the VxD doesn't provide any interface elements. It relies on MODEMUI.DLL to provide these services. There's also a Control Panel element to worry about in this case. You'll find that MODEM.CPL manages this aspect of the interface.

- **Modem command strings found in the Registry.** Actually, this is the completion of a circle. Many of the upper modules rely on the Registry entries to know how to interact with the modem. These strings provide those instructions. Each string defines some aspect of modem behavior. In most cases, it affects the modem's setup or the way that it communicates with another machine. You'll need to refer to your modem manual to get a better idea of exactly how these strings work.

Unlike many other subsystems, the communications subsystem looks fairly straightforward, and it is—to a point. There's a risk of underestimating the effect of this subsystem on the rest of Windows if you don't account for the number of ways in which it interacts with other subsystems. The centerpiece of this whole subsystem is KERNEL32.DLL. This module loads the port drivers, provides access to them during system operation, and generally manages the way that Windows interacts with the outside world. It's an important role that you might take for granted until it stops working. Chapter 26, "Hardware Problems," looks at some things that can go wrong with this subsystem.

Microsoft Network

The Microsoft Network (MSN) is Microsoft's attempt at creating an online service similar to CompuServe or America Online. It has actually turned out to be more than just another online service though as Microsoft has added features. The newest feature is an Internet front end. If you looked at MSN when it first came out, but then rejected it as too much of the same thing, you might want to take another look now.

That said, MSN isn't an online service that everyone will want to use. For one thing, most of the content is directed toward the home market, making it of very limited use for the business community. In addition, while the content looks very aesthetically pleasing, some of the pages are slow to download. Thankfully, the cache used by most browsers reduces this problem for commonly visited pages. A few people have also complained that the various Web pages are buggy or not feature complete if you use anything but Internet Explorer as your browser. These problems aside though, MSN does provide quite a bit of value for the money. Whether it meets your needs is something that you'll need to determine once you've looked at this overview.

Getting Started

Getting connected to MSN is relatively easy. Open the Add/Remove Programs applet in the Control Panel, select the Windows Setup tab, then check The Microsoft Network entry in the Online Services folder. Click OK twice to close the Online Services Folder and then the Control Panel. You should see a new Set Up The Microsoft Network icon on your desktop. (Another icon is added to the Online folder as well.) Double-click this icon to begin the setup process. Just follow the prompts. By the time you're finished, you'll have access to the Internet through MSN. In most cases, the only major decision you'll need to make is whether to use an existing or MSN specific Internet connection. Using an existing Internet connection means that you'll need to perform some setup steps manually. Obviously, you'll also need to provide some personal and billing information during the setup process.

You can access MSN in a variety of ways. The easiest way to do so is to click The Microsoft Network icon in the Taskbar Tray. Clicking the icon will display a menu similar to the one shown in Figure 20.2 where you can manage most MSN functions. Notice the Connect to MSN option at the very bottom of the menu.

Figure 20.2.
Use the Microsoft Network menu to easily gain access to your account.

Selecting the Connect to MSN option on The Microsoft Network menu starts Internet Explorer. You'll see the usual Dial-Up Connection dialog box if you're using your own ISP (the option I've followed throughout this section and the one that's preferable in most cases if you want to use the Internet by itself on occasion.) After you connect to the Internet, you'll see the Sign In dialog box shown in Figure 20.3. Notice that this dialog box contains two fields. The first field contains your name. The second contains the password for your MSN account. The check box tells Windows to remember your MSN password between sessions. After you enter your name and password, click OK to log on to MSN.

Note: Windows 98 only remembers your MSN password between sessions if you have some other form of Windows 98–specific password protection on your machine. If you use Windows 98 without enabling passwords, you'll have to enter your MSN password each time you use it. The reason for this safeguard is simple: It protects your account from misuse by other people.

Figure 20.3.
The Sign In dialog box is where you enter your name and password prior to going online.

Exploring MSN

Although you might want to visit a specific place on the Internet using your MSN connection, there are going to be times when you want to simply surf. If MSN provided only a simple Internet connection, you could use any ISP instead. It's the special features that you get with MSN that make it an online service rather than just another ISP. Selecting the Connect to MSN option from the Microsoft Network menu takes you to a central location where you can explore the special features that MSN has to offer. Figure 20.4 gives you an idea of what you might see.

As you can see from Figure 20.4, the left side menu is a presentation of current events. MSN will check your email and present you with a list of current events that you need to know about. For example, one of the articles at the time of this writing was on how to avoid credit card fraud. Obviously, these entries will change on an almost daily basis as Microsoft adds new content to MSN.

One of the more important features on the left list is the MSN Support Flash. Clicking this link will display something like the Web page shown in Figure 20.5. The table of contents lists every problem that Microsoft is currently aware of and whether the problem has been fixed. You'll want to check here first if you're having a problem using MSN, since Microsoft might already have found a way to fix it for you. Likewise, this list will tell you when you need to provide feedback to Microsoft on a problem that you're experiencing. You won't get a fix for a problem that Microsoft isn't aware of, so reporting problems is an MSN community event.

Figure 20.4.

The first thing you'll normally see when you sign in to MSN is a central menu of MSN-specific features.

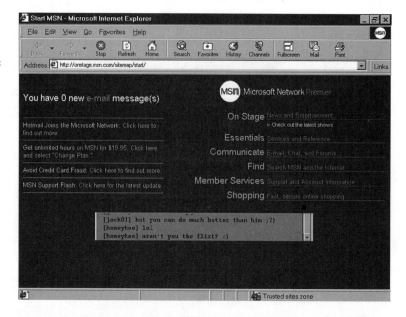

Figure 20.5.

Checking the MSN Support Flash Web page will keep you up-to-date on current bug fixes and other MSN updates.

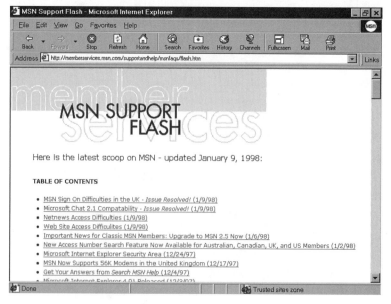

The right side menu on the central Web page shown in Figure 20.4 is a little more permanent. There are six categories of tasks that you can perform. The following list provides an overview of each category:

- **On Stage.** Learn about the latest in a variety of entertainment areas. Not only will you learn about current events by visiting the MSNBC news site, but you can visit areas that include cooking, gardening, movies, and television shows. Notice that at the time of this writing there was a link that took you directly to a list of the latest shows on MSNBC. You can expect to find links like this scattered throughout the MSN site.

- **Essentials.** Think of this area as a total reference for the Internet as a whole or one city in particular (in most cases you'll want to choose a city near you, but nothing stops you from looking at other localities as well). You can find out the latest in weather and news. This site also provides links to other areas on MSN, such as shopping or personal finance. There's even a link to a reference area that includes Encarta and a wine guide.

- **Communicate.** MSN supports several different kinds of communication, and this is the area where you'll find them all. The most common types of communication are chat (real-time private or public discussion), forums (MSN-specific posted public discussion), newsgroups (Internet-posted public discussion), and email (posted private discussion).

- **Find.** Presents you with a copy of Yahoo (or other search engine) that you can use to search both MSN and the Internet for specific bits of information. We talked about finding what you need in the "Finding What You're Looking For" section of Chapter 1.

- **Member Services.** Everyone needs to find out about their account or get help with MSN-specific needs from time-to-time. This is the place you go when you need any help using MSN. There is also a feedback option you can use to provide input on the way MSN is put together, to ask usage questions, or to provide details about a particular problem you're having with the service itself. The member newsletter option provides you with important news about new MSN features, bug fixes, or changes in policy. In other words, anytime you want to do something with MSN that doesn't involve looking for information, chatting with someone, or shopping, you might want to look here.

- **Shopping.** Looking for your favorite place to shop doesn't take much time when you select this option. This area of MSN will help you find the store you need quickly. Online shopping enables you to reach a much wider variety of stores in less time. Besides, your feet won't get tired walking through the malls this way.

Obviously, this quick overview really doesn't tell you everything you need to know, so let's spend a little time looking at the more interesting areas of MSN. (I don't want to ruin the fun of exploring by showing you everything.) The first place you might want to visit is On Stage. Figure 20.6 shows an example of what you might see.

There are three main areas in On Stage. The first is the list of links on the left side. In most cases, you'll find a list of topics meant to tantalize your taste buds. On the right side of the display is a marquee that flashes MSN highlights like Spike's World Ants game. Across the bottom you see radio buttons (one is highlighted in Figure 20.6). Clicking a radio button takes you to a main topic area within On Stage.

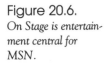

Figure 20.6.

On Stage is entertainment central for MSN.

Communication ranks high on the list of things that people are looking to find on the Internet. Any ISP can provide you with access to email (private posted communication) and newsgroups (public posted communication). You can use a product such as ICQ to gain access to chat groups. Microsoft NetMeeting enables you to conduct either private or public real-time conversations over the Internet as well. MSN excels at providing specialty chat groups and newsgroups (called *forums* in Microsoft parlance).

Let's spend a little time talking about Chat Central. Figure 20.7 shows a typical example of what you'll see in this area of MSN. Note that you move around using radio buttons, just like other areas we've discussed. The easiest way to join in a chat is to click the Join the Chat button in the Central Lobby. You can also search for a particular chat group or create a chat of your own. Click the special Chat Info button if you want to find out the latest information about Microsoft Chat (the program used to chat with someone) or download the latest copy of the program.

If you aren't all that good at real-time communication—and it does take some time to learn to type and think fast enough to keep up with some of the real-time conversations—you might want to look at the various forums that MSN has to offer. Figure 20.8 shows a typical list of forum categories. All you need to do is select an area of interest and drill down to the specific forum that you'd like to join. Like regular Internet newsgroups, forums enable you to post a message, then return later for an answer.

Figure 20.7.
Chat Central gives you the opportunity to discuss important issues in real time with other MSN users.

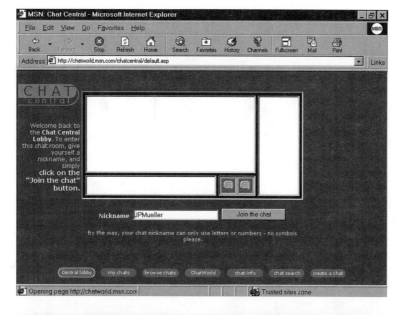

Figure 20.8.
Forums enable you to exchange ideas with other MSN subscribers using posted messages you can write at your leisure.

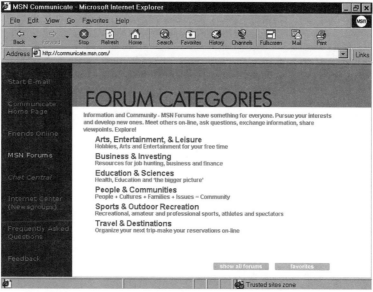

Forums do differ from newsgroups in an important way, as shown in Figure 20.9. As you can see, a forum provides more than a bulletin board for posting messages that people can respond to at their leisure; it also provides chat rooms, places to download files and other places where you can read information online. In other words, it's a grouping of everything you might want to know about a particular topic in one place. Rather than spend time looking for one place to download files and another to read messages, you can go to one area and spend time learning about your favorite topic. (Don't get the idea that forums are unique to MSN; CompuServe and AOL users have enjoyed the convenience of using forums for quite some time.)

Figure 20.9.

Forums offer more than newsgroups; they're actually a superset of this familiar area.

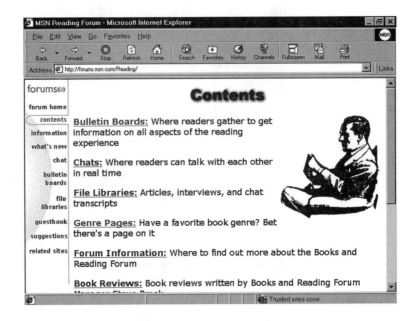

Online shopping is one of the fastest-growing means of getting what you need quickly and without a lot of hassle. It's also a lot more convenient than trying to find a store open at night when you work during the day and can't find the time to shop until the kids go to bed. That's where The Microsoft Plaza comes into play. Sure, it's not the only place on the Internet to shop, but it does provide one of the advantages of going to the mall—finding quite a few stores in one place. Figure 20.10 shows a typical view of The Microsoft Plaza. As you can see, there are quite a few stores to choose from.

The thing I found interesting about The Microsoft Plaza was the Product Returns link. Figure 20.11 shows what you'll see if you choose this option. As you can see, instead of having to contact the store that you purchased the product from directly, you can return the merchandise using UPS.

Using The Microsoft Plaza for shopping is much the same as similar stores on the Internet. All you do is select the link that you're interested in, choose one or more products to buy, then create a secure link to provide the vendor with credit card information. In fact, many of the vendors that I looked at create a secure link when you enter the store, rather than wait until it's time to pay for the products you've selected. After you pay for the products you've selected, the vendor provides shipping information. In a few days, you'll be enjoying something new at your home—all without visiting the mall.

Figure 20.10.
The Microsoft Plaza enables you to shop in the comfort of your own home without having to find an Internet site first.

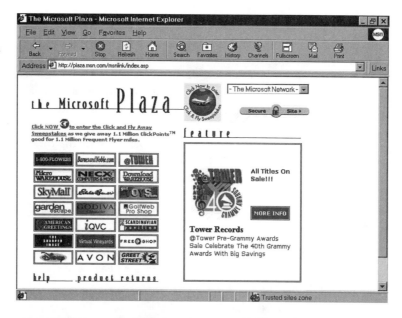

Figure 20.11.
Even though you're shopping on the Internet, product returns don't have to take a lot of time or effort when you shop at The Microsoft Plaza.

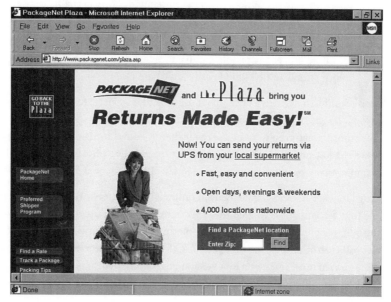

Working with MSN

Now that we have the basics of using MSN out of the way, let's talk about a few things that you'll need to really use this product. The following list tells you about the language of using an online product such as MSN:

- **Forum or Newsgroup.** This is a gathering place for people of similar interests. One person leaves a message and someone else responds to it. You can look at the message header to determine what a particular discussion is about. In essence, you can think of a forum or newsgroup as a room in a house where people of like interests get together to talk. Finding the right forum or newsgroup can provide you with a wealth of information that you might not find elsewhere. It also can help you solve problems related to your software, your machine, or even your business. So, what are the main differences between a forum and a newsgroup? A *forum* is contained on a specific server (in this case, Microsoft's) and is not published to the outside world. A *newsgroup's* contents are completely public and get distributed across a wealth of servers. In addition, every forum I've ever seen is moderated. (Someone makes sure that there are no sales messages and that the messages that are posted conform to some standard of posting.) Newsgroups are seldom moderated, and when they are, it's usually for sales-related messages but not other types of content.

- **Message.** A message is a single note on a particular subject. You already use messages in email and other places, so this concept shouldn't be new to you.

- **Thread.** A thread is a group of connected messages on the same topic. As each person responds to a message, he makes the list of messages about a given topic longer. You can read an entire list of messages (a thread) to discover the conversation that took place on a specific topic. The fact that the messages are written rather than spoken is an advantage; you can read them when it's convenient. Threads are also a key way to store information for future use. Many people archive message threads about specific topics because the information can't be found easily anywhere else.

I don't want to make this a book about using online services; there are plenty of those on the market already. I suggest that you buy one or two of them to build your knowledge of online services. It's important to learn the rules of the road when it comes to reacting to other people's messages. You also need to learn the rules of etiquette for forums. I've presented some of these ideas already. For example, many people frown on the practice of quoting on a forum.

Body language is a missing element in online conversations. You can't use a wry smile to tell someone that a comment is tongue-in-cheek because he won't see it. To help avoid conflict whenever possible, people have come up with something called emoticons. An *emoticon* is a little text icon that tells the other person what you mean by a certain comment. Just look sideways to see a facial expression in most cases, or a text version of a picture in others. Table 20.1 lists common emoticons that you can use to dress up any written communication. In fact, you could even use them on your company email.

Table 20.1. A list of standard emoticons.

Emoticon	Description
: -)	A happy face
: - >	An alternative happy face
: - D	Said with a smile
: <)	Humor for those with hairy lips
: <) =	Humor for those with beards too
B -)	Smiling and wearing glasses or sunglasses, or a message from Batman
8 -)	Smiling and wearing glasses or sunglasses; also used to denote a wide-eyed look
: - 1 or : - ,	A smirk
' -)	A wink
: - (	Unhappy
: - c or (: - (	Very unhappy
: /)	Not funny (The receiver of a message sends this emoticon to show that a particular comment wasn't received as the sender intended.)
(: - &	Angry
: -)) - :	Theatrical comments (Use this for comments that are either theatrical in nature or are used for emphasis.)
; -)	Sardonic incredulity
(@ @)	You're kidding!
: - "	Pursed lips
: - C	Incredulous, jaw dropped
: - <	Forlorn
: - B	Drooling or overbite
: - l	Disgusted
: - V	Shouting
: - o or : - 0	More versions of shouting
: - w	Speaking with a forked tongue (You're lying to the other person in a whimsical sort of way. In other words, you're making a point sarcastically.)
: - W	Shouting with a forked tongue
: - r	Tongue sticking out, Bleahhh!

continues

Table 20.1. continued

Emoticon	Description
`<:-O`	Eek! (You can use this for a number of purposes. You can even use it to tell the network administrator that your equipment is down and you can't do anything without it.)
`:-*`	Oops! (covering mouth with hand)
`:-T`	Keeping a straight face, tight-lipped (Use this emoticon when you mean something in a serious way that the receiver could interpret as a humorous comment.)
`:-#`	Censored (You'd love to use a little profanity but resisted the urge.)
`:-x`	Kiss, kiss
`:-?`	Licking your lips
`:~i`	Smoking
`:~j`	Smoking and smiling
`:/i`	No smoking
`:-) :-) :-)`	A guffaw
`:-J`	A tongue-in-cheek comment
`:*)`	Clowning around
`:-8`	Talking out of both sides of your mouth
`<:-)`	For dumb questions (Everyone knows the only dumb question is the one you failed to ask before trashing the network. However, some people might feel that they have a dumb question they want someone to answer.)
`OO`	Headlights on (Use this emoticon to show someone that you want him to pay special attention to a comment.)
`:-o or #:-o`	"Oh, nooooooo!" (à la Mr. Bill)
`I-(`	A late-night message
`(:-$`	Ill
`#:-)`	Matted hair
`:^)`	A big nose
`:-{#}`	Braces
`(:^(`	A broken nose
`:-(=)`	Big teeth
`&:-)`	Curly hair
`@:-)`	Wavy hair

Emoticon	Description
?-(	A black eye
%-)	Broken glasses
:	A fuzzy person
*:**	A fuzzy person with a fuzzy mustache
(:<)	A blabbermouth
+<:-|	A monk or nun
(:-|K-	A formal message
||*(	A handshake is offered
||*)	A handshake is accepted
<:>==	A turkey
@>--->----	A rose
(-_-)	A secret smile
<{:-)}	A message in a bottle
<:-)<<|	A message from a spaceship
(:-...	A heartbreaking message
(:>-<	A message from a thief—Hands up!
...--...	SOS
:-I	It's something, but I don't know what… (You can't figure out what the other person is trying to say or reference.)
@%&$%&	Profanity

Hopefully, you'll come to enjoy using online services as much as I have. MSN is just starting out, but you can use other online services as well. CompuServe seems to be one of the favorite places for business people to congregate, although there are forums to attract just about anyone's attention. America Online is extremely popular as well. Of course, the trick to selecting any online service is to find the one that meets your needs. Obviously, no one can determine that but you.

On Your Own

Check your SYSTEM folder to see whether you can identify the various pieces of the communications subsystem. This chapter provides you with a list of the major files and many hints on how you can find the other special files that pertain to your system.

I provided you with a list of standard emoticons in this chapter. One of the fun elements of online computing is coming up with your own set of special emoticons (of course, this means that you have to explain them to everyone). Try creating a few emoticons of your own. For example, one person recently created an emoticon that resembles Bill the Cat.

21

Internet Connections

Peter Norton®

In the minds of some people, the Internet has become the singles bar of the nineties—a place to meet new people and exchange ideas. For example, during one evening, a friend and I saw that no less than 80 percent of the new television shows include an Internet address as part of their programming. An equally interesting idea is that the Internet is some kind of a remote communications magic carpet. Of course, problems still must be worked out in making this "magic carpet" fly in business applications, but companies are working hard to make the idea viable. Consider all the other uses for the Internet. One magazine that I looked at recently suggested that artists use the Internet in place of a gallery to show previews of their art for sale. I've also seen some articles that talk about how the fashion industry uses the Internet to tell people about new trends. Obviously, you'll see more mundane uses as well. You'll find a number of newsgroups on the Internet and more than a few people use it for research purposes. In fact, the Internet started as a means for government and educational organizations to exchange information.

The Internet certainly fulfills some part of all these ideas. You can use it as an extremely valuable research tool, to exchange ideas with other people, or to create a Web site for your employees at remote sites. However, none of these uses for the Internet really tells you what it's all about and how you can use it to your best advantage. That's what this chapter's all about. I'm going to spend some time telling you about the foundations of the Internet and the tools that you can use to explore it. Surfing the Net should be an experience that helps you meet specific goals and broaden your horizons. The problem is, with such a large number of items on the menu, you could easily get lost.

Working with Internet Explorer

Let's take a look at what you need to do to get going on the Internet. The next five sections cover basic usage for Internet Explorer 4.x and its companion programs Outlook Express and Outlook Express. (This chapter assumes you either installed Internet Explorer 4.x during the initial setup discussed in Chapter 6, "Setup Primer," or you used the Add/Remove Programs applet discussed in Chapter 10, "The Windows 98 Applets.")

Setting Up Internet Explorer

After you get Internet Explorer installed, you can set it up for use. You can go two routes here, but they're both essentially the same. What you need to do now is specify some type of Internet service provider (ISP). Microsoft provides full support for MSN as part of the Windows 98 package. An update to this support is available at `http://signup.msn.com/signup/signup.hts?`. You could also choose to use any other Internet service provider at this point; the only requirement is that you have the proper support installed for contacting the provider.

1. Double-click the Internet Explorer icon on the desktop if this is the first time you're running it. Otherwise, choose View | Internet Options from within Internet Explorer to

display the Internet Options dialog box, select the Connection tab, and then click the Connect button. You then see the initial Internet Connection Wizard dialog.

2. Click Next. You then see a Setup Options dialog, where you need to choose from one of three ways to connect to the Internet. The first option lets you choose an Internet service provider and set up a new Internet account. The second option works best if you use a LAN connection rather than a local modem to make the connection. The third option is the one that most people will use. It allows you to use a Dial-Up Networking connection that you've already configured. This particular option works best because you can set up everything with your ISP in advance.

3. Click the task that you would like to perform. If you selected the first option, proceed with step 4. If you selected the second option, proceed with step 8. If you selected the last option, you're all done creating a connection. The next thing you see is a final Internet Connection Wizard dialog; click Finish to see the standard Connect To dialog box.

4. Make sure the first option is selected and then click Next. At this point, you see a Begin Automatic Setup dialog box.

5. Click Next. You then see a Location Information dialog box. The Internet Connection Wizard asks you for location information that it will use to download a list of ISPs in your area. This list is by no means comprehensive; you may not find an ISP that precisely suits your needs.

6. Enter your area code in the first field and the first three digits of your telephone number in the second field. Click Next. At this point, the Internet Connection Wizard displays a Connecting dialog box, dials an 800 number, and downloads a list of ISPs in your area. When it finishes, you see a dialog box containing a list of ISPs in your area, similar to the one shown in Figure 21.1. All you need to do to sign up for an ISP is to select the one you want by clicking in the Sign Me Up column. Notice that you can get additional information about the ISP before you sign up by clicking in the More Info column.

7. At this point, you need to follow the instructions for the ISP that you selected. After you complete the sign-up process, the Internet Connection Wizard disconnects from the 800 number. You see a Connect To dialog box next. Simply type your username for the ISP, along with a password, click the Connect button, and you're on your way to your first Internet session.

8. If you're reading this step, you must have selected the second option in step 3. Click Next, and you see a dialog box containing options to connect to the Internet through a phone line or a LAN.

9. Your first decision to make is how you want to connect your machine to the Internet. You have two choices: locally, using the telephone lines, or remotely, through a network. I selected the Connect Using My Phone Line option in this case because I wanted to use a local connection. (If you do decide to use the LAN option, make sure you work with your communication server provider to set up everything.)

Figure 21.1.
The Microsoft Internet Referral Service can provide a list of ISPs, in case you don't already have one.

10. Click Next, and you see a Dial-Up Connection dialog. This dialog offers two choices. You can either use an existing connection shown in the accompanying list box, or you can create a new connection. I've already shown you how to create connections in the "Creating a Connection" section in Chapter 1, "Opening Windows to the Internet," so I won't go into those details again here.

11. Choose either an existing connection or create a new one, and then click Next. (If you choose to create a new connection, then the Internet Connection Wizard takes you through the process for creating it; I'll follow the existing connection route for the remainder of this procedure.) If you're using an existing connection, the Internet Connection Wizard asks whether you want to modify it.

12. Choose Yes or No, and then click Next. In most cases, you can choose No because the connection will probably work as configured if you're using it. The only time you would choose Yes is if the connection contained old information or you weren't sure that it would work. If you choose Yes, then you go through a series of configuration screens similar to the ones you would see if you were creating the connection for the first time. In either case, you see a Set Up Your Internet Mail Account dialog. In most cases, you should set up your Internet email account right away, so that's the route to follow here. Skip to step 20 if you don't want to set up Internet email. (Choose No and click Next if you don't want to set up Internet email.)

13. Choose Yes, and then click Next. You see an Internet Mail Account dialog next. This dialog allows you to choose between two options. You can either create a new email account, or you can use an existing account. To use an existing account, simply select it

and click Next. You then see a Confirm Settings Import dialog that contains the existing account settings. Make sure these settings are correct, click Next, and then proceed to step 20.

14. Choose Create a new Outlook Express account, and then click Next. The Internet Connection Wizard asks for your name.

15. Type your name as you want it to appear on the Internet, and then click Next.

16. Type your email address (for example, John@nowhere.net), and then click Next. At this point, you see an Email Server Names dialog. Here, you type the name of an incoming and outgoing mail server (you need one of each). You also need to choose between a POP3 and IMAP mail server (POP3 is by far the most common). Your ISP can provide all this information. Make sure you ask for the values you need to enter here.

17. Choose a mail server type, and then type in the name of both the incoming and outgoing server. Click Next. You then see the Internet Mail Logon dialog. You get two choices here: a standard name and password combination, or a Secure Password Authentication (SPA) identifier. Your ISP can tell you which one to use. In most cases, you need to enter a name and password.

18. Choose the SPA or Log on using option. If you choose the Log on using option, type your name and password in the fields provided. Click Next. The Friendly Name dialog then appears.

19. Choose a friendly name for your email account. This is the name you'll see in Outlook Express, so make sure you pick something descriptive. After you type the name, click Next.

20. At this point, you should see a Set Up Your Internet News Account dialog. This dialog allows you to choose between setting up a news account now or waiting until later. If you don't want to set up a news account, choose the No option and then click Next. Proceed to step 27.

21. Choose Yes, and then click Next. You then see an Internet News Account dialog, which gives you two choices. You can create a new account or use an existing one. If you choose to use the existing account, select it and click Next. A Confirm Settings Import dialog then appears. Determine whether the settings are correct; click Next if they are. Proceed to step 27.

22. Choose the Create a new Internet news account option, and then click Next. The Internet Connection Wizard asks for your name (as you want it displayed in a newsgroup).

23. Type your name, and then click Next. At this point, the Internet Connection Wizard asks for your email address. People on a newsgroup will send messages to this address if they want to respond using email rather than leave a message in public view.

24. Type your email address, and then click Next. You see an Internet News Server Name dialog next.

25. Type the name of your news server. Notice that this dialog also provides a check box for news servers that require you to log in. Just check this box. Internet Connection Wizard asks you for password information in the next step. In either case, you see the Friendly Name dialog next. Here, you provide the name that Outlook Express will use when displaying your news server.

26. Type a friendly name for your news server, and then click Next.

27. At this point, you should see the Set Up Your Internet Directory Service dialog. The Internet Directory Service acts basically like the white pages. It allows you to find other people on the Internet. You have to sign up with someone who provides this service before you can actually use it, though. If you haven't already signed up for this server, choose No and click Next. When you see a completed configuration dialog, just click Finish to complete the process.

28. Choose Yes, and then click Next. You then see an Internet Directory Service dialog, where you can choose between one of the providers that Windows 98 knows about or create a new provider. If you choose an existing provider, simply click Next. A Confirm Import Settings dialog then appears. Make sure the settings are correct, and then click Next. You then see a completion dialog where you simply click Finish to complete the process.

29. Choose the Setup a new directory service option, and then click Next. You see the Internet Directory Server Name dialog.

30. Type the server name for your Internet Directory Server provider. Notice that this dialog contains a check box for providers that require password entry. Checking this box displays a dialog that allows you to enter your name and password. In either case, you end up at the Check Email Addresses dialog. The purpose of this dialog is to allow you to check any email addresses you type against those in the white pages. This way, you won't send email to a nonexistent address.

31. Choose whether you want to check email addresses automatically, and then click Next. You then see the Friendly Name dialog.

32. Type a friendly name for your Internet Directory Server, and then click Next. The Complete Configuration dialog then appears.

33. Click Finish to complete the process. You now have a complete set of connection information for getting on the Internet.

Getting on the Internet

By this point, you're probably wondering what else you have to do to get online. Actually, the setup and configuration are all done. All you need to do now is double-click the Internet icon on your desktop. When you do, you'll see a Dial-up Connection dialog box. (The "Using Dial-Up Networking" section in Chapter 1 talks about this dialog box.) Enter your name and password (if necessary), and click Connect to get started.

At this point, a number of things could happen, depending on how you created your Internet connection (you can also change the configuration of Internet Explorer to get a variety of results). In most cases, you start at a Welcome to Microsoft Internet Explorer Web page similar to the one shown in Figure 21.2. Microsoft changes this page all the time, so your page won't look exactly like mine.

Figure 21.2.
You normally start your Internet session at the Internet Explorer home page.

Now that you're online, take a look at some of your controls in more detail. Everything you need is on the toolbar. I don't think I've ever used the menu system in Internet Explorer except to see what it contained. (There's always an exception to the rule. In this case, it's the Favorites menu that I describe in the next section.) The following list gives you a quick overview of the various controls on the menu; I cover some of them in detail as the chapter progresses:

- **Back/Forward.** These two buttons come in handy when you want to move quickly between several areas that you've already visited.

- **Stop.** Some Internet sites seem to provide more than the usual number of graphics, so they take a long time to download. This button tells the browser to stop downloading content from the Web site. The disadvantage is that you don't see all the neat graphics and buttons that the Web page designer placed on the page. The advantage is that you can get back to work faster.

- **Refresh.** Explorer, like most browsers, uses a cache to store images. Sometimes the Internet page changes without your knowledge because your browser is looking at the cached page instead of the live page on the Internet. Use this button to update the current page contents. (This button also comes in handy if part of the page got garbled during transmission and the browser didn't catch the error.)

- **Home.** Some browsers use the term *start page* for the place where you always start surfing the Internet; Internet Explorer uses the term *home page*. Clicking this button always takes you to your home page. (You can change your home page by choosing View | Options and then selecting the Navigation page of the Options dialog. Just type a new address in the Address field; you can even use a Web page on your local hard drive.)

- **Search.** I covered this button (and other search-related procedures) in the section "Finding What You're Looking For" in Chapter 1, so I won't cover it again here.

- **Favorites.** Internet Explorer allows you to maintain a list of favorite places. This button displays the Favorites Explorer bar, which contains a list of your favorite places.

Tip: You can save your favorite Web pages on disk for future reference by choosing File | Save As. The default save area is the desktop, making it easy for you to just double-click a favorite Web page the next time you need to access it. Clicking one of the hypertext links opens a connection. I use this feature to store the top-level page of places I visit on a regular basis, making it easier for me to find what I want in a pinch. If you don't want to clutter your desktop with a lot of Internet site locations, stick them in a folder on your desktop. You can still find them quickly by opening the folder when needed.

- **History.** Clicking this button displays the names of the pages that you visited in the past. You can choose to look at past weeks or at previous days of the week. The listings appear in an Explorer-like format.

- **Channels.** Clicking this button displays a list of channels that you have subscribed to. We will look at channels in the "Using Channels" section later in this chapter.

- **Fullscreen.** Clicking this button maximizes the page you're viewing. A small toolbar appears on the top of the page. Clicking the Fullscreen button again returns the page you're looking at back to normal viewing.

- **Mail.** Clicking this button displays a menu containing five options: Read Mail, New Message, Send a Link, Send Page, and Read News. The Read Mail option displays the Outlook Express program or Windows Messaging (depending on which you chose for your mail reader). Internet Explorer requests any new mail from your ISP's mail server and displays it in the window. The New Message option brings up a new message dialog box using the capabilities of either Outlook Express or Windows Messaging. The "Using Microsoft Exchange" section in Chapter 20, "Network Connections with an Internet Appeal," looks at Windows Messaging. I'll cover the messaging capabilities of Outlook Express further in the "Using Outlook Express" section of this chapter. The Send a Link option works much like creating a new message. However, in this case, you send someone a link to your current Internet site in addition to the message. This capability allows you to have a discussion with someone else concerning the particulars of an Internet site. The

Send Page option lets you send the Internet page instead of a link for the page. Finally, the Read News option brings up the Outlook Express program discussed in the "Using Outlook Express" section of this chapter.

- **Print.** Use this option to send the current page content to the printer.
- **Edit.** Clicking this button imports the current Web page into an editor.

Now that you've read an overview of the Internet Explorer connection features, let's take a more detailed view of specific features. The following sections will give you more information about what I consider to be the essentials.

Using the Favorites Folder

Getting on the Internet is only part of the battle for obtaining information. Finding the right Web site is another part. However, after you find the information you need, how do you ensure that you'll be able to find it later? The Favorites folder comes into play at this point. It helps you keep track of all the various forms of content important to your business and personal life by tracking the Web sites that contain the required information.

Actually, you can track three different kinds of information with the Favorites folder: Web sites, channels, and documents. The following list describes each type:

- **Web site.** This entry contains an URL that will take you to a specific Web site on the Internet or an intranet. It's like the shortcuts that you use in the Start menu to access applications, but in this case the link will take you to a Web site instead of an application.
- **Channels.** Many Internet sites now provide push content or information of such a volatile nature that you need to update it frequently. Like Web site entries, channels normally point to an URL on the Internet. However, in addition to the pointer information, a channel includes information such as how often you want the data updated on your system. The page actually gets stored on your hard drive so that you could display it at any time (most generally on the desktop). We'll look at channels in more detail in the "Using Channels" section of this chapter.
- **Documents.** Internet Explorer is no longer limited to just the Internet or a local intranet. You can also use it to view folders on your local hard drive and even documents. If Internet Explorer doesn't provide direct support for a particular type of file, it uses OLE to call on an application that does provide the required support. In some cases, the application simply takes over the Internet Explorer menus and toolbar, allowing you to view and edit your document without ever leaving the Internet Explorer environment.

Using the Favorites Folder is easy. All you need to do is click the Favorites menu entry in Explorer and then choose the destination you want to go to. This list includes all the URLs you've saved, any channels you've subscribed to, and anything in the My Documents directory as a default. The

following sections will look at how you can add new entries to the Favorites Folder and then organize them in a way that's easy to use. (You should check out the "Using Channels" section for details on channels.)

Adding to the Favorites Folder

Adding a new favorite to your Favorites Folder is easy. Choose Favorites | Add to Favorites in
Explorer to display the Add Favorite dialog. In many cases, you can just click the OK button at this
point to add the favorite to your Favorites menu. However, you can perform quite a bit of customization as well.

The Name field of this dialog contains the title of the Web site you're visiting. Sometimes the
Webmaster of the Web site you're visiting doesn't provide a very distinctive name, so you need to
change this value to something you'll recognize later. The contents of the Name field are what you'll
see in the Favorites menu when you look for this favorite later. A name such as Home Page (one of
the more common titles that I see) isn't going to tell you much when you're looking for a specific
favorite later. Make sure you choose something distinctive but not too long. I find around 40 characters is a good limit to observe.

Click the Create In button, and your Add Favorite dialog expands, as shown in Figure 21.3. The
directory list at the bottom of the dialog works just like the one in Explorer. Highlighting a specific
folder places your new favorite in that folder. You can also click the New Folder button to add a new
folder to the list.

Figure 21.3.
*The Add Favorite
dialog allows you to
organize your list of
favorites into folders
as you create them.*

Now, you're left with the three radio buttons at the top of the dialog. In the past, you would simply
record the location of an URL and leave it at that. You can still get this level of support by leaving
the first radio button selected. However, the ability to cache (store) Web sites on your local hard
drive presents some interesting problems, such as outdated Web content. Internet Explorer 4.0 provides two additional levels of support for favorites. Check the second radio button, and Internet
Explorer automatically checks the Web site for you. If it detects any changes, you get a notification,

which allows you to visit the Web site and refresh it as needed. The third radio button provides even more automation. Not only can Internet Explorer detect changes in the Web site and notify you of them, it can automatically download a new copy of the Web site content to your hard drive for you. The only problem with this third option is that you could find yourself waiting for Internet Explorer to complete an automatic task. I prefer the second setting because it provides a level of automation but leaves the task of updating Web content to a time when I don't need to use the machine for something else. (Even though you can perform automatic downloads in the background, you'll still notice a slowing of your system that may be unacceptable in some situations.)

Organizing the Favorites Folder

Even if you organize your favorites as you add them to the Favorites Folder, you'll still find the need for an occasional "house cleaning" of your folder contents. Choose Favorites | Organize Favorites to display the Organize Favorites dialog shown in Figure 21.4.

Figure 21.4.
The Organize Favorites dialog allows you to manipulate the contents of the Favorites Folder.

Using this dialog is similar to using Explorer. At the top, you can see your current location. You can use the Folder drop-down list box to choose another location in the Favorites folder or on the hard drive as a whole. The Up One Level, View Desktop, and Create New Folder buttons work just as they do in Explorer. In addition, you get two views: List and Details. Obviously, the center of the dialog contains a display of the folders and favorites at the current directory location.

> **Tip:** As you might expect, the contents of the Favorites folder are shortcuts similar to the ones you use in the rest of Windows. In fact, if you move a shortcut into the `\Windows\Favorites` folder on the hard drive, you can access it from the Favorites menu of Explorer, a real time-saver in some situations.

The five buttons at the bottom of the dialog differentiate this dialog from other Explorer-type dialogs you've learned about in the past. The following list explains each button:

- **Move.** You may want to move a favorite to a new location like a subfolder within the menu. To do so, highlight the favorite you want to move and click the Move button. You then see a Browse for Folder dialog that allows you to select a new location for the favorite. Highlighting this new location and clicking OK moves the favorite.
- **Rename.** This button allows you to change the name of a favorite so that it better matches the content and purpose of a Web site or other content in your Favorites folder.
- **Delete.** This button allows you to remove a favorite when you no longer need it.
- **Open.** Use this button to open a favorite. Of course, you'll find that using the Favorites menu is a lot easier.
- **Close.** Use this button to close the Organize Favorites dialog.

Using Channels

I've talked about channels several times in this book. Essentially, using channels is a way to bring Internet content to the desktop. Make sure you read the "HTML on Your Desktop—No Browser Need Apply" section in Chapter 2, "Introducing Windows 98," for usage details when it comes to the desktop. These same usage details apply, for the most part, when you're using channels in Internet Explorer.

Automatically Adding a Channel

Before you can actually use a channel, you need to subscribe to it. You've already learned about adding channels to your desktop in the "HTML on Your Desktop—No Browser Need Apply" section in Chapter 2. The process is the same for adding a channel to Internet Explorer (which also adds it to the desktop). Simply go to the Channel Guide, look for the channel you want to subscribe to, and then click the Add Active Channel button. Internet Explorer takes care of the details for you.

Managing Subscriptions

Whenever you subscribe to a channel or Web site, Internet Explorer makes certain assumptions about what you want to do with it. For example, it assumes that you want to update the channel at the interval specified by the channel's publisher. In many cases, these options work surprisingly well. However, sometimes you may not agree with what the publisher of a channel sees as the right up-date interval. In addition, you can use other options to fine-tune your use of channels.

Internet Explorer provides everything you need to manage your channel subscriptions. Start by choosing Favorites | Manage Subscriptions to display the Subscriptions dialog. You then see an iconic view of the various subscriptions on your machine. After you've located the subscription you want to change, right-click it and choose Properties from the context menu. Next, you see a Channel Properties dialog (Microsoft Internet Explorer Properties, if you're working with a Web site). The first page of this dialog, Subscription, contains the current settings for your subscription so that you can quickly determine whether a change is even needed. This tab also contains an Unsubscribe button so that you can get rid of the subscription without too much trouble.

Click the Receiving tab, and you see a dialog containing two main groups of settings. The first, Subscription Type, determines whether you get notified alone or whether Internet Explorer also downloads content to your system when the content changes on the Web site. Clicking the Advanced button displays the Advanced Download Options dialog. This dialog allows you to determine how much content to download (just the home page or all the pages associated with the Web site) and the types of content that you want to download automatically (images, sound and video, and ActiveX controls and Java applets). You can also determine how much content in kilobytes to download, just in case the site contains lots of information and you don't want to tie up your machine waiting for it. The second main group of information on the Receiving tab, Notification, allows you to send notification of Web site changes to a particular email account on the Internet. Use the Change Address button to display a dialog that allows you to change the email address used to receive the change notification. You use the Login button on this page only if the channel from which you want to download content uses password protection. Clicking the button displays the Login Options dialog, which contains fields for your login name and password.

The Schedule tab of the Channel Properties dialog, shown in Figure 21.5, allows you to set how often the content for a channel gets updated. As you can see, you have two choices: You can update the content from a channel at scheduled times, or you can update it manually. If you choose the Manually option, you need to click the Update Now button to update the channel content. You can also choose Favorites | Update All Subscriptions to perform this task.

Figure 21.5.
Determining when you get new content from a channel is the responsibility of the Schedule tab.

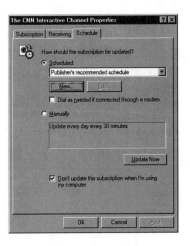

Several default times are set for scheduled updates of channel content. The default setting is to use whatever update schedule the channel publisher deems necessary to keep your channel up-to-date.

You can also update the content daily, weekly, or monthly. Click the New button if you want to create your own schedule of update times. You can even set a specific time during the day to perform an update, like when you're out to lunch and not using the computer. The Dial as needed if connected through a modem option allows Internet Explorer to dial out from your machine to update the channel. Selecting this check box is important if you want Internet Explorer to perform unattended updates of channel content. The final check box on this page, Don't update this subscription when I'm using my computer, allows you to keep content updates from slowing down your machine. Checking this box tells Internet Explorer that you want to update channel content only if you're not using your machine at the moment.

Manually Updating Subscriptions

Normally, you can let Internet Explorer take care of updating your subscriptions automatically. Sometimes you need to update manually, though. For example, after you've been away from the office to a seminar for a week, all the content on your machine is out of date. You should update that content immediately so that you can get updates on what's happening in the business world. All you need to do is choose Favorites | Update All Subscriptions to start the update process. If your machine is powerful enough, you can actually update everything in the background while you read your email, get a cup of coffee, or perform some other productivity task.

Using Outlook Express

Outlook Express is Microsoft's new Internet email and news reader. For those of you upgrading from previous versions of Windows that used pre–Version 4.0 Internet Explorer, Outlook Express is a replacement for separate Internet Mail and Internet News utilities. Figure 21.6 shows what this new utility looks like. Outlook Express is designed to work much like Windows Messaging, but it provides a level of optimization for the Internet environment. For example, you can choose both plain text and HTML-based messages. Some of the file encoding options are a bit easier to understand as well. For example, you can set a specific MIME type or use uuencode to send binary messages.

Outlook Express gets configured as part of the process for configuring Internet Explorer (Internet Mail and Internet News required separate configuration). You already learned the process for configuring Outlook Express in the "Setting Up Internet Explorer" section of this chapter, so this section begins with everything you need to know to use the email portion of Outlook Express. Email allows you to send private messages to one or more people. You'll learn how to maintain your address book, how to retrieve messages, and how to send messages to other people.

Figure 21.6.
*Outlook Express
provides a single-stop
solution for your
Internet email and
news needs.*

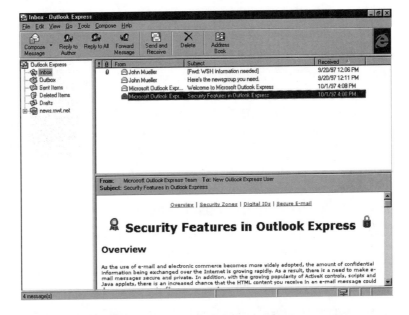

Tip: If you're a road warrior, you know one of the problems with using any mail reader when you have two machines. Unless you take special precautions, you'll never have a complete copy of all your mail in one place; part of the mail appears on your laptop and the other part on your desktop machine. You can handle this problem in a couple of ways. The first way is also the easiest method. It allows you to read your messages on the road and respond to them, but keeps a copy of the messages on the server so that you can download them to your desktop machine. Simply choose Tools | Accounts on your laptop setup to display the Internet Accounts dialog box. Choose the Mail tab, highlight your email account, and then click the Properties button. Select the Advanced page of the Email Properties dialog. Check the Leave a Copy of Messages on Server option. Of course, the only problems with this solution are that you still don't see a copy of your responses on the desktop machine (unless you CC: yourself in the message), and your laptop doesn't contain a complete copy of all your messages. The second method is a little more complicated and isn't automatic, but it has the advantage of allowing you to maintain a copy of all your messages and responses on both machines. Find the WINDOWS\Application Data\Microsoft\ Outlook Express\Mail\Mail folder on your hard drive. In this folder, you can find a group of files containing your mail messages. Copy these message files to the same location on your laptop when going on the road or to your desktop when arriving home.

The next section of this chapter will look at the newsgroup portion of Outlook Express. I'll tell you how to join a newsgroup, how to read messages, and how to send two kinds of messages to people on a newsgroup (private email and public newsgroup messages).

A *newsgroup* is a public forum for discussing issues or asking questions about a specific topic. One person begins the whole process by making a comment or asking a question. He or she uploads this information as a message. After you read the message, you can reply to it. A third person may see what you've written and respond to your message. Well, you get the idea. A series of messages forms what's known as a *message thread*. By reading the messages in a message thread in order, you can see a conversation.

Basic Outlook Express Usage

Let's begin looking at how Outlook Express works. The first thing you'll notice in Figure 21.6 are the seven buttons on the toolbar. These buttons are available when you use email. Click a newsgroup, and you'll see eight buttons for newsgroup purposes. Many of these buttons overlap in function, so I'll discuss them only once. The following list describes the purpose of each button:

- **Compose Message.** This button allows you to create a new message. Outlook Express allows you to include files and an electronic business card with your message. You can also set priorities, digitally sign, and encrypt your messages. You can also find options for inserting HTML code for elements such as horizontal lines and graphics. A standard message uses plain text to keep things simple, but Outlook Express also includes a feature for using stationery with your messages. You can also use the Compose Message button for creating new messages in a newsgroup.

Note: Make sure that the recipient can actually read HTML-formatted messages before using the stationery and other formatting features of Outlook Express. Otherwise, all the recipient gets is a lot of confusing-looking text mixed with HTML tags.

- **Reply to Group.** Use this option to send a reply for the current message to the entire group. In other words, you can make a public response to a message that someone else left. You can use this option to ask for clarification of the previous sender's message, ask a similar question of your own, provide an answer to the initial message, or simply make a pertinent comment about the subject under discussion.
- **Reply to Author.** This button appears when you're looking at either an email or newsgroup message. When used in email, it allows you to respond to an incoming email message. This option sends the response only to the message author—not to anyone else who may have been on the message as a recipient. The author's name appears in the From section of the message. If multiple email addresses are listed in the From section of the

message, your response is sent to all those recipients. The Reply to Author button serves a slightly different purpose when used in a newsgroup. Use it when a public response to a question in a newsgroup isn't ideal. For example, you may want to use this option when providing personal information, answering a personal question, or providing information that the rest of the group really isn't interested in hearing.

- **Reply to All.** This button sends a response to everyone who received a copy of the original message, along with the message author. You see this button only when working with email.

- **Forward Message.** This button sends a copy of the current message to someone else. What you see is a standard email message dialog box with the forwarded message at the bottom. You can add your own message to the beginning of the forwarded message. This option also allows you to provide a CC list.

- **Send and Receive.** You use this option to send any messages in your Outbox folder. However, it's only available from the email toolbar, not the newsgroup toolbar. You also use it to receive any new messages from your ISP's mail server. Any new messages appear in your Inbox folder. (See the next section for a discussion of folders.) This option automatically checks all your accounts. Choose Tools | Send and Receive | *<Account Name>* if you want to send or receive messages for a single account.

- **Delete.** This button places the selected email messages into the Deleted Items folder. Because you can't delete newsgroup messages directly using Outlook Express, you find this button only on the email toolbar. If you're in the Deleted Items folder, this option permanently removes these items from Outlook Express.

- **Address Book.** This email toolbar button allows you to display the address book. I'll tell you more about the address book in the "Managing Your Address Book" section of this chapter.

- **Newsgroups.** This button displays the Newsgroup dialog box that allows you to choose which newsgroups you want to work with. Obviously, it's available only on the newsgroup toolbar. I'll talk more about this feature in the "Adding Newsgroups to Outlook Express" section of the chapter.

- **Connect/Hang Up.** Clicking the Connect button connects you to the Internet. Likewise, clicking the Hang Up button disconnects you.

- **Stop.** This newsgroup toolbar button serves the same purpose as it does within Internet Explorer; it allows you to stop downloading a message or message headings from the news server.

Every Outlook Express window (beside the toolbar) contains three main sections. On the left side, you see the first section, which contains a listing of your email and newsgroup folders. The second contains a list of headings for the email folder or newsgroup. It is a list of the message subjects you find in your email or the newsgroup. Outlook Express uses a variety of symbols to show whether you've read an email or newsgroup message. Email messages usually use a closed envelope to show unread messages and an open envelope to show the ones you've read. Newsgroup messages use a colored sheaf of paper for unread messages, a full sheaf of paper for messages you've looked at during this session, and a half sheaf of paper for messages that you've read during other sessions. The third section contains the currently highlighted message. You see the message subject and its author's name at the top of this area. The message text follows.

You also need to know one additional piece of information. If you look at the status line, you may notice that Outlook Express tells you the number of messages in the current folder when you're looking at email. Newsgroups include three statistics: the number of messages in the newsgroup, the number of messages that you've downloaded but haven't read, and the number of messages that you haven't downloaded yet. To download the next group of messages, choose Tools | Get Next 300 Headers (the number 300 is replaced by whatever number of messages you normally download).

Working with Folders

Now, we're ready to talk about folders—one of the items you use to organize your mail. Outlook Express comes with the five basic mail folders, as was shown in Figure 21.6. The purpose of each folder should be self-explanatory. The Inbox receives all your new mail; the Outbox holds messages you want to send to someone else. The Sent Items folder holds copies of the email messages you send to other people so that you can refer to them later. The Deleted Items folder holds any messages that you deleted from other folders. Deleting a message in the Deleted Items folder removes it for good. Finally, the Drafts folder contains the messages that you're working on right now and intend to send to someone in the future. In other words, you can use it to hold work in progress. Outlook Express always selects the Inbox when you open it so that you can see your current message list.

You can access six folder-related commands by choosing File | Folder. The following list tells you the purpose of each command:

- **New Folder.** This option allows you to create new folders.
- **Rename.** This option allows you to change the name of an existing folder.
- **Compact.** Outlook Express doesn't actually recover the space used by old messages until you compact the associated folder. This option allows you to compact just the selected file. You would use it if you just deleted a lot of messages and didn't want to spend time compacting all the other folders.
- **Compact All Folders.** This option allows you to compress all the folders using a single command.
- **Move To.** Use this command to move a folder from one location to another. This option allows you to create a hierarchical folder format if you want to organize your email by project or content type.

- **Delete.** This option allows you to delete folders that you no longer need. Outlook Express doesn't allow you to delete the four default folders.

I usually organize my messages by project. Each project gets its own folder. This way, cleaning up is easy when I complete a project: I just delete the associated folder.

Now, let's look at the process for creating a new folder. Choose File | Folder | New Folder to display the Create Folder dialog box. Type the name of the new folder, highlight the place in the folder hierarchy that you want to place the new folder, and then click OK to create it. You then see a new folder in the Outlook Express window (refer to Figure 21.6).

By now, you should be asking how to get your messages from the Inbox folder to a specialty folder. You can do so in two ways. The manual method is to choose Edit | Copy To Folder or Edit | Move To Folder. Selecting either of these menu options displays a list of the folders on your machine. The big difference between the Move To and Copy To options is that the Copy To command leaves the selected message in the current folder as well as copying it to the new folder. (You can also move or copy messages using the same drag-and-drop techniques that you use in Explorer.)

An automatic method for moving messages around is also available. Just choose Tools | Inbox Assistant to display the Inbox Assistant dialog box, which is shown in Figure 21.7. The Inbox Assistant uses rules to determine how to arrange your folders. Whenever you get a message in your Inbox folder from the ISP's mail server, Inbox Assistant looks through its list of rules to see whether the message meets certain criteria. As you can see, I've already defined a couple of rules for George's Project in this dialog box.

Figure 21.7.
The Inbox Assistant provides an auto-mated method for moving messages to the right folder.

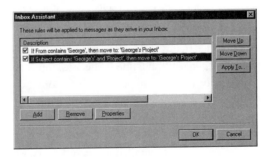

Arranging the message rules in their order of importance pays off because Inbox Assistant takes some time to look at each rule, and you want to reduce the amount of time you wait for it to get its work done. If a new rule that you've just added is more important than the others in the list, highlight it and use the Move Up button in the Inbox Assistant dialog box (refer to Figure 21.7) to move it. Likewise, if a rule becomes less important, highlight it and move it by using the Move Down button.

Notice the three buttons along the bottom of the Inbox Assistant dialog box. The Add button displays a Properties dialog box like the one shown in Figure 21.8. Use the Remove button to remove a rule you no longer need. The Properties button allows you to edit an existing rule.

Figure 21.8.

Creating or editing a message rule is easy using the Properties dialog box.

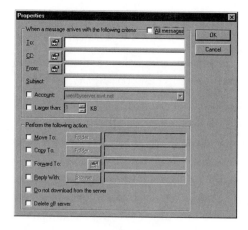

Defining a new rule is easy. All you need to do is tell Inbox Assistant what to look for in the message header. For example, you might want to send all messages from George to the George's Project folder. Right after you define what to look for, go to the Move To field, click the Folder button, and select one of the folders listed there. Click OK, and you see the new rule added to the Inbox Assistant dialog box. You can also perform other actions like copying the message, forwarding it to a colleague, and replying to the other person with a stock message. You may not even want to read the mail (like advertisements, also known as *spam*). The last two options allow you to leave the message on the server or simply delete it completely. Obviously, you can choose to perform multiple actions depending on what you need to do. Notice that in addition to specific criteria like the contents of the To, CC, From, or Subject fields, you can select messages of a specific size or a particular account.

We have one more matter to cover. What happens if you want to keep a rule, but you don't need it right this second? Notice that a check box appears next to each rule listed in the Inbox Assistant dialog box shown in Figure 21.7. If a rule is checked, Inbox Assistant uses it; otherwise, the rule is ignored. You can simply uncheck any rules that you don't need to use for the current session.

Sending an Email Message

After you have Outlook Express installed and configured for use, you can use it to send some messages. All you need to do is click the Compose Message button on the toolbar that I described earlier, and you then see a New Message dialog box like the one shown in Figure 21.9 (this message uses the Chess stationery).

Let's look at the buttons along the toolbar first, because they provide the features you'll use most often. The following list tells you about each button:

- **Send.** This button sends the message you've just created using the default account. You must define a recipient in the To field before sending a message. In addition, Outlook Express checks the Subject field to make sure it's not blank. You can bypass this requirement by clicking Yes when Outlook Express asks you whether you want to send the message without a subject.

Figure 21.9.
The New Message dialog box allows you to create messages for the Internet.

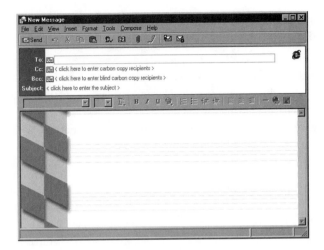

- **Undo.** Outlook Express provides one level of undo. Therefore, you can undo your last action. A second click redoes your last action.

- **Cut/Copy/Paste.** These three buttons work much like they would with any Windows application. You can cut or copy information to the Clipboard. You can also paste information from the Clipboard into your message.

- **Check Names.** Say you don't want to try to remember a lot of esoteric email addresses when writing a message. All you need to do is type the person's name and then click the Check Names button. When you do, you see a Check Names dialog box, which lists the names Outlook Express found in your address book that match the one you typed. (If only one name matches the one you typed, Outlook Express automatically inserts it for you.) Highlight the recipient you want to use, click OK, and Outlook Express adds the full form to your message heading. If Outlook Express doesn't find the name in the To field, it gives you the option of adding the name to your address book.

- **Select Recipients.** Click this button to display a Select Recipients dialog box. Highlight one or more names, and click the To->, CC->, or BCC-> button as appropriate. Clicking OK places the names you selected in the appropriate fields of the message and closes the dialog box.

- **Insert File.** Use this button to insert a file into your message. Outlook Express opens a standard File Open dialog box, which you can use to select the file.

- **Insert Signature.** You can use this button after you define a signature by choosing Tools | Stationery within the main Outlook Express dialog box. You can find the mail signature options on the Mail page of the Stationery dialog box.

- **Digitally Sign Message.** One of the problems with using the Internet to send email is that no one can be absolutely certain that you sent the message using normal messaging methods. Outlook Express provides new features that allow you to digitally sign your messages, ensuring that you are who you say you are. You need to get a digital ID from a third party such as VeriSign before you can use this button.

- **Encrypt Message.** Digitally signing your message may tell the other person that the message is indeed from you, but it doesn't prevent someone else from intercepting and reading the message as well. The encryption feature that Outlook Express uses depends on both parties having the digital ID of the person that they want to communicate with. In essence, you encrypt the message in such a way that only someone with the right key can read it. You must have the required digital IDs installed on your machine before this feature will work. You can get a digital ID from a third-party vendor such as VeriSign.

After you've added a name or two to your recipient list, you need to type a subject for it. The first thing to notice is that the title for the New Message dialog box changes to match the message subject. You can also define the priority level for your message, although not all browsers and mail readers support this feature. Just click the stamp in the upper-right corner of the message area, and you see a context menu (you can also choose Tools | Set Priority) containing a list of priorities. You can choose from three priority levels, with Normal Priority being the default. After you add some content to your message, click the Send button to send it. You then see a Send Mail dialog box telling you that your message was added to your Outbox folder. The message will be sent automatically the next time you click the Send and Receive button in the main Outlook Express window.

Managing Your Address Book

You can gain access to your address book in several ways, but the most common method is to choose Tools | Address Book. You use the Address Book dialog box, as shown in Figure 21.10, to maintain your address book.

Figure 21.10.
The Address Book dialog box helps you maintain a list of contacts on the Internet.

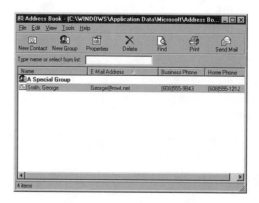

As you can see from the figure, you can create two kinds of email address entries in the Address Book dialog box. The first is a single entry, like the George entry shown in the figure. Notice that this entry type uses a Rolodex page as an icon. The second is a group, which uses two people as an icon. Groups contain one or more of the single contacts that you create.

To create a single contact, click the New Contact button on the toolbar. You then see a contact Properties dialog box like the one shown in Figure 21.11. (I've already filled this one out for explanation purposes; George isn't a real person.) This dialog box has six pages. The first page, Personal, contains all the personal contact information for the new entry, such as name and email address. You can even add more than one email address to the list. Notice that one email address is designated as the default that you want to use. Outlook Express uses this address unless you specify an alternative address. You can specify a new default email address by highlighting it and clicking the Set Default button. To add a new email address, type it into the Email Addresses field and click Add. Likewise, you can get rid of old email addresses by highlighting the one you want to remove and clicking the Remove button. If you need to change an existing entry, highlight the email address and click Properties.

Figure 21.11.

The contact Properties dialog box allows you to add entries to your address book.

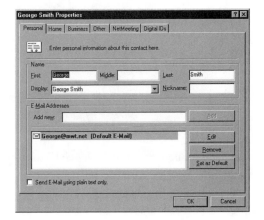

The Home page contains all the personal information for your contact. It contains three personal contact numbers: home phone, home fax, and cellular. You can also enter the URL for a personal Web page. Notice the Go button next to the Personal Web Page field. Clicking this button opens your favorite browser and then takes you to that person's personal Web page.

The Business page looks a lot like the Home page. It contains three entries for business phone numbers, including office phone, office fax, and pager. On this page, you'll also find a Business Web Page field that works just like the Personal Web Page field on the Home page. Clicking the Go button on this page takes you to the client's business Web page.

Other, the fourth page in the contact Properties dialog box, contains notes about your contact. It also contains a list of the groups that the person belongs to, but you can't edit this information from this page. This page doesn't contain much more than two notepad fields, so I won't show it here. Suffice it to say that there aren't any fancy gadgets for maintaining contact information by date. You may want to reserve this page for long-lasting notes and use a contact manager to keep track of current business information.

The NetMeeting page, shown in Figure 21.12, allows you to define a Web address for contacting a person using NetMeeting. In addition, you can set up one or more servers as a meeting place. Notice that the contact Properties dialog automatically selects a default and backup server for you if you provide more than one server address. Adding a new server is easy: Just type its name, and then click Add. The other four buttons on this page allow you to remove an entry, edit an entry, set an entry as the default server, or set an entry as the backup server.

Figure 21.12.
The NetMeeting page of the contact Properties dialog box allows you to define the information required to use NetMeeting.

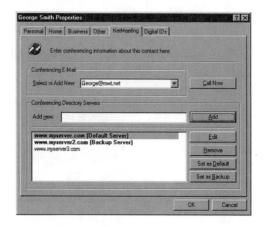

The last page, Digital IDs, allows you to add a digital ID to an email address for the purpose of secure communication. All you need to do is select an email address (or none for entries without an email address), and then click the Import button to import the digital ID sent to you by the other person. If the person has more than one digital ID, you can choose a default digital ID to use. You can also remove old digital IDs or export an existing one.

Let's get back to the main Address Book window. You can edit a group or single contact by highlighting the desired entry and clicking the Properties button on the toolbar. Getting rid of an unneeded entry is just as easy: Simply highlight the entries you no longer need and click the Delete button.

So how do you create a group? Click the New Group button, and you see a group Properties dialog box like the one shown in Figure 21.13. As you can see, I've already added one member to this group—the sample contact, George. The entries for a group include a group name, a list of members, and some notes. When you send an email message to a group, every member gets a copy.

Notice the four buttons along the side of this dialog box. Clicking the New Contact button allows you to create a new contact and add it to the address book. If you want to remove a member entry, simply highlight the member name and click Remove. By highlighting a member name and clicking Properties, you open a contact Properties dialog box like the one you used to add the contact in the first place. Finally, the Select Members button displays a Select Group Members dialog box that contains a list of addressees in your address book. Just select the contact or group that you want to add to your member list, and then click the Select button. Click OK, and you return to the group Properties dialog box. Notice that you can also add or edit entries from within this dialog box.

Figure 21.13.

The group Properties dialog box allows you to create a group, which allows you to send one message to multiple recipients.

Adding Newsgroups to Outlook Express

You have to subscribe to a newsgroup before you can read the messages it contains. (In some situations, you may not have to subscribe first, but don't count on it.) Outlook Express allows you to create connections for multiple news servers—just like you can have multiple email accounts. You need to select a news server in the folder list to place Outlook Express in the proper mode. The news server that you connect to will have a list of newsgroups for you to choose from. Normally, you can choose News | Newsgroups to display the Newsgroups dialog box, where you can select the newsgroups you want to participate in. As your needs change, you can use this dialog box to change the newsgroups you frequent.

The All page of the Newsgroups dialog box, shown in Figure 21.14, displays all the newsgroups that you can join. If you're worried about finding a specific newsgroup in the thousands that Outlook Express downloaded, don't worry. Using a few strategies, you can quickly find what you need. Finding the Microsoft-specific newsgroups in a section starting with microsoft shouldn't be too surprising. In many cases, all you need is a vendor name or perhaps a good idea of what you're looking for. However, trying to find some newsgroups can be quite a trick. For example, what would happen if you wanted to find a special newsgroup for strategy game players? You could use the Display newsgroups which contain field to narrow the choices. Figure 21.15 shows how I used this dialog box to find a few strategy game newsgroup choices. Notice that I didn't use complete words; phrases work best here because not everyone will use the exact word that you had in mind.

Figure 21.14.
The All page of the Newsgroups dialog allows you to see which newsgroups the news server has to offer.

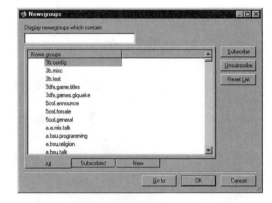

Figure 21.15.
Finding a newsgroup doesn't have to be hard, but it does take practice.

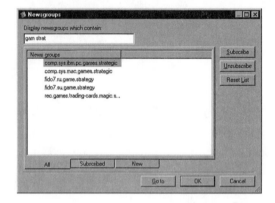

After you find a newsgroup that you think sounds interesting, you can use the Subscribe button to subscribe to it. As soon as you do, you see a little newspaper icon appear next to the entry. If you later decide that you don't need this newsgroup, highlight it again and click the Unsubscribe button. Clicking the Reset List button downloads a new list of newsgroups from the ISP's news server.

You don't have to subscribe to a newsgroup without looking at it first. Just highlight something that looks interesting, and then click the Go To button. Outlook Express displays the requested newsgroup in the newsgroup viewing panes (described in the "Writing a Newsgroup Message" section).

Let's talk about the two additional pages listed in the Newsgroup dialog box. The second page, Subscribed, looks just like the page shown earlier in Figure 21.14. The only difference is that it shows only the newsgroups to which you've subscribed. This way, you can find a newsgroup quickly, in case you don't want to subscribe to it any longer. The New page of the Newsgroup dialog box allows you to find new newsgroups quickly. Obviously, it's a really handy feature; just imagine trying to dig through the thousands of newsgroups available to find the new newsgroup that you need.

Downloading and Reading Newsgroup Messages

Before you can really do anything with newsgroups on the Internet, you need to know how to download and read the messages they contain. After you've selected a new server and subscribed to one or more newsgroups, you can download the messages.

Reading messages online is a three-step process. First, select a news server and click the plus sign next to it to display the newsgroups that you've subscribed to. Second, select a newsgroup by clicking its entry. Outlook Express begins downloading the headers for that newsgroup and displays them in the headers pane of the newsgroup window. Third, select the message you want to read. At this point, you see the text of the message appear in the message pane of the newsgroup window.

Outlook Express defaults to downloading 300 headers at a time. You can change this value on the Read tab of the Options dialog (accessed by choosing Tools | Options). After you read through the first 300 headers, you can download the next 300 by choosing Tools | Get Next 300 Headers.

You can also choose to read messages offline; however, you still need to perform some steps online. The first thing you need to do is select one of the news servers in your list and click the plus sign next to it. Now, right-click one of the newsgroups that you're interested in reading, and you see a context menu. Choose the Mark for Retrieval option, and you see four choices: New Headers, New Messages, All Messages, and Unmark. The New Headers option allows you to download just the message subjects. Using it is the most time-efficient way of browsing through the messages that a newsgroup can provide. The New Messages options downloads all the messages. Using it is the most efficient way to work with a newsgroup where you have read all the messages it has to offer. Finally, if you're looking at a newsgroup for the first time, or you need to get a complete copy of all the messages it has to offer, choose the All Messages option. The Unmark option allows you to remove a newsgroup from the automatic download list. Go through all the newsgroups that you want to read offline, and choose a message or header download option. Now, choose Tools | Download <*Newsgroup Name*> to download the headers or messages that you've chosen. Remember to click Hang Up when you get done. You can also tell Outlook Express to hang up automatically by checking the Hang Up when finished sending, receiving, or downloading option on the Dial Up tab of the Options dialog (accessed by choosing Tools | Options).

Choosing specific messages if you download only headers the first time is easy. Right-click the header that you want to download, and choose Mark Message for Download from the context menu. Do this for all the messages that you want to read. You'll need to choose Tools | Download <*Newsgroup Name*> to download the messages you want to read.

Writing a Newsgroup Message

Getting a message uploaded to the Internet is much like writing a message for your mailbox. There are some differences, of course. For one thing, you're addressing a public forum. You don't need to specify a recipient for your message because the entire group will look at it. I find it interesting that some people act as though they're addressing a specific person in a newsgroup, when in reality they can't. Always keep the idea of public versus private communication in mind when you're working in a newsgroup.

Let's take a look at a basic newsgroup message. Click the Compose Message, Reply to Group, Reply to Author, or Forward Message buttons on the Outlook Express toolbar, and you see a New Message dialog box similar to the one that was shown in Figure 21.9. (The only real difference in using the two New Message dialog boxes is that the one for news contains different features on the toolbar.) The following list tells you about the functions of the various toolbar buttons:

- **Post Message.** Use this option to post your message onto the news server. You probably won't see the message appear right away. Some Webmasters (moderators) monitor the messages they allow to appear on the newsgroup.

- **Undo.** Outlook Express provides one level of undo that allows you to undo your last action. A second click of this button redoes your last action.

- **Cut/Copy/Paste.** These three buttons allow you to cut or copy information to the Clipboard and paste information from the Clipboard into your message.

- **Insert File.** Use this button to insert a file into your message. Outlook Express opens a standard File Open dialog box, which you use to select the file.

- **Insert Signature.** You can use this button only after you define a signature by choosing Tools | Stationery within the main Outlook Express dialog box. You can find the signature options on the News page of the Stationery dialog box.

Your New Message dialog box contains a few special features. Click the newspaper icon next to the Newsgroups field, and you see a dialog box that allows you to send your message to more than one newsgroup. Highlight one of the newsgroups in the left list, and then click Add to place it in the right. (You can also remove newsgroups by using the Remove button.) Notice that this dialog box defaults to showing only the newsgroups to which you've subscribed. Click the newspaper at the bottom left of the dialog box, and you see all the available newsgroups. Just highlight a newsgroup in the left list, and click Add to add a newsgroup. You can remove a newsgroup by clicking a newsgroup in the right list and clicking the Remove button.

The Select Recipients dialog box appears when you click the index card next to the CC field of the New Message dialog box. You can use this dialog box to select people who will receive a copy of the message through email. Highlight a user or group name, and then click the Reply To or CC button. The section "Using Outlook Express" earlier in this chapter describes the features of this dialog box, so I won't describe them again here.

Note: One thing you should avoid on the Internet is sending messages to people you meet on a newsgroup because you think they might be interested in some new product or Web site. This practice is called *spamming,* and most people react negatively to it. You can find out about other things that you should avoid doing online by looking at the RFC1855 Netiquette Guidelines available at `http://www.cis.ohio-state.edu/htbin/rfc/rfc1855.html`.

Working with Microsoft NetMeeting

Online conferencing is becoming more than just a convenience. Many companies are looking to this solution to reduce business travel costs. This section looks at the Microsoft solution to this problem, NetMeeting.

Tip: You don't need to limit the use of NetMeeting to the Internet. You can also use it to hold meetings over an intranet in a company setting, and you can use NetMeeting for training purposes. A company training specialist could hold company-wide training where anyone could join in. Another use of NetMeeting is as a device for brainstorming sessions. Rather than wait until you can get everyone together for a formal meeting, you could discuss an idea with a few colleagues while the idea is fresh in your mind. You can use NetMeeting anywhere that you can use a standard meeting room. The only difference is that it's more convenient for everyone concerned.

Like most software in this category, NetMeeting is still more fluff than substance. You may find that some meetings still require personal face-to-face contact. Yet I find that NetMeeting is an outstanding tool in some situations. For example, if you have a meeting in which everyone will need to provide some form of input, NetMeeting may actually be a better solution than a face-to-face meeting. Consider the possibilities for a moment. No one will feel inhibited because of the public nature of the meeting, and you'll find that people participate better when they can actually see what's going on. Whether online meeting software will serve your company's needs is not the issue here. You need to decide that issue for yourself. What we'll look at are some basic usage techniques that you can use to reduce the NetMeeting learning curve.

Getting Set Up

The first time you use NetMeeting, you need to provide some information. This information is sent to other users when you join a meeting in progress. It also lets other users know what part of the country you're in, and so forth. The following procedure takes you through the process of setting up

NetMeeting for the first time. It assumes that you've already started NetMeeting and that you're looking at the initial setup screen.

1. Click Next. NetMeeting asks whether you want to log on to a directory server automatically (which implies Internet use) and which directory server you want to use. The directory server helps you find other people to talk with.

2. Choose whether you want to automatically log on to a directory server, and then choose a directory server from the drop-down list box, if necessary.

3. Click Next to go to the next page. You then see a dialog box on which you supply the information needed to converse with other people. At a minimum, you have to provide your first name, last name, and email address. I suggest filling out all the entries so that you don't have to do it during long-distance meetings in the future.

> **Tip:** You could use the Comments field of this dialog box for a variety of purposes. Two of the more important items that you could include are your position within the company and the department you work for. Coming up with a standard approach to using this field company-wide makes it even more useful.

4. Click Next. NetMeeting asks how you want your information categorized. If you include material in your comments that you wouldn't want young children to see, choose the For Adult-use only option.

5. Click Next. NetMeeting asks you to select modem speed. (You can also choose a LAN or ISDN connection if those options are available to you.) The speed of your modem affects the amount of data it can transfer. Even though audio compression algorithms have improved, the speed of your modem still affects the quality of the sound that you hear. (It also affects the quality of the sound you send to the other party and the speed of the connection as a whole.) As you can see, the lowest speed modem you can use with NetMeeting is 14.4Kbps.

6. Choose a modem speed, and then click Next. The first page of the Audio Tuning Wizard then appears. Here, you set up your machine for sending and receiving audio.

7. Click Next. You see a dialog box that allows you to tune your speaker and microphone volume. Depending on your setup and how you installed Windows 98, you may see one or two dialogs at this point. Click Next between the speaker and microphone volume setting dialogs if they appear as separate steps.

8. Make sure that you have a microphone attached to the microphone input of your sound board. Click the Start Recording button so that NetMeeting can get a sample of your speaking voice and set the volume properly. Keep speaking until the Audio Tuning Wizard tells you to stop (you see an indicator move as NetMeeting gathers the sound sample). If you haven't recorded any sound, the Audio Tuning Wizard displays an error message. Otherwise, the counter counts down to 0.

9. Click Next after you finish recording a sound sample. (If you see an error message, fix any problems and try to record the voice sample again.)

10. Click Finish to complete the audio tuning process. At this point, you see a standard Connect To dialog box if you choose to use a directory server. Connect to your ISP. The setup program takes care of a few additional setup requirements and then displays the main NetMeeting dialog box shown in Figure 21.16.

Figure 21.16.
You must meet a few additional configuration requirements before you have a complete NetMeeting setup.

Using NetMeeting with the Company Intranet

I don't see the Internet as the first place you'll use NetMeeting. The speed at which we communicate right now is just a little too slow to get the high-quality connection that people expect. (At least a few people will occasionally use NetMeeting on the Internet.) The first place I expect to see this tool used is on an intranet or LAN. It doesn't actually matter where you use NetMeeting, though; the usage details are the same.

Let's begin by creating a simple conversation. Several people in the same company need to discuss a project, but no meeting rooms are available at the moment. Each person has a copy of NetMeeting running, so calling someone over the company LAN isn't a problem. All you need to do is click the Call button (telephone icon) and then enter the name of the machine you want to call. You also should choose Network in the Call Using drop-down list box. When you receive a call, you see a dialog box asking whether you want to accept or ignore the call.

At this point, you decide whether to accept the call. If you accept the call, the NetMeeting display shows who is involved in the meeting. The initial connection is audio, but you can choose to use any of the other communication options as well. What happens when someone talks? You see some sound waves coming out of the speaker. (Look at the speaker onscreen, and you'll see some sound waves coming out.)

Obviously, unless you just happen to be a gadget nut, seeing sound waves coming out of a speaker isn't all that exciting. You can definitely get better sound quality from a telephone connection as well. At this point, some of the other features of NetMeeting come into play. Before we go much further, though, let me introduce you to the buttons on the toolbar:

- **Call.** Click this button to call someone else.

- **Hang Up.** Use this option to stop your participation in the current meeting.

- **Switch.** This button allows you to start using audio and video with another person. NetMeeting allows you to use audio and video with only one person at a time. Switching allows you to give another person a chance to speak.

- **Share.** I'll show you how this feature works in a few seconds. Essentially, it allows two people to work together with an application. That doesn't necessarily mean that both people actually get to use the application. I really like this feature because a company training expert can show how to perform a task and then ask a trainee to demonstrate the technique. Because everyone has his or her own machine, each person gets a maximum participation benefit.

- **Collaborate.** This button works with the Share Application option. It allows two people to work together on a project. Both parties have total control over the application (though only one of them actually gets to edit the document at a time). Clicking the Collaborate button a second time allows you to work alone.

- **Chat.** Sometimes you can't hold a decent voice conversation, transfer files, use the Whiteboard, and share an application all at the same time. Even a LAN doesn't provide this kind of bandwidth. The alternative is to cut out one or more activities. At this point, the Chat button comes into play. It opens a Chat dialog box, which you can use to type text to other people. Sure, it's not as handy as talking, but it does work in a pinch.

Tip: One way that the Chat feature actually works better than voice communication is when you're creating minutes for a meeting. If you use the Chat feature, the meeting notes are already typed. Just choose File | Save to save everything said at the meeting to disk. I can guarantee that these minutes will be more accurate and in-depth than meeting notes that rely on voice communication.

- **Whiteboard.** Every meeting needs some place for people to draw out their ideas. That's what the Whiteboard is for. Clicking this button displays a Whiteboard similar to the one shown in Figure 21.17. Notice that you get a full set of drawing tools, including the normal circle and square drawing tools. Just so you don't get the Whiteboard confused with a regular drawing program, it also includes things such as a highlighter. One of the features I really like is the remote pointer. It looks like a great big pointing hand. You can use it to point to things on the Whiteboard in a way that everyone can see.

Figure 21.17.
The Whiteboard is one of the handier tools included with NetMeeting.

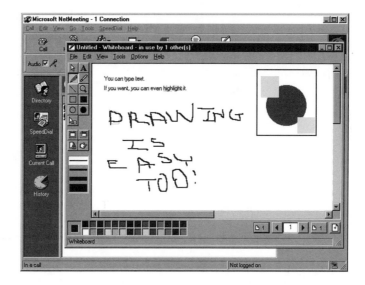

Let's take a look now at sharing an application. I see this as one of the more important uses for the current version of NetMeeting because you can use this feature in so many ways.

How do you share an application? Begin by opening the application. You may also want to open any files that you intend to use because the application could get a bit sluggish after you establish the NetMeeting setup. After the application is open, click the Share Application button in NetMeeting, and select one of the running applications from the list that NetMeeting presents. You then see a dialog box that asks whether you want to share the application. Click OK to establish a connection.

At this point, you're sharing the application with someone else in the work-alone mode. The way you can tell this from your machine is to look at the NetMeeting Sharing column. The other party is able to tell because his or her cursor will change to a circle with a slash through it when he or she moves it over the application. The application has the initiating user's name at the top. This way, you can tell who "owns" the application.

Click the NetMeeting Collaborate button, and everyone involved in the meeting can now change the contents of the application. (The participants also need to click their Collaborate buttons.) By monitoring the NetMeeting window, you can always tell who is collaborating, who owns the target application, and who is working alone. Figure 21.18 shows what the NetMeeting window looks like when one person has control over an application and another is collaborating. Only one person can take control of the application at one time. Everyone else has a pointer to click to take control. The pointer also contains the initials of the person who has control, so you don't have to monitor the NetMeeting window.

Figure 21.18.
NetMeeting allows several people to share an application and collaborate on the contents of a file, but only one person has control.

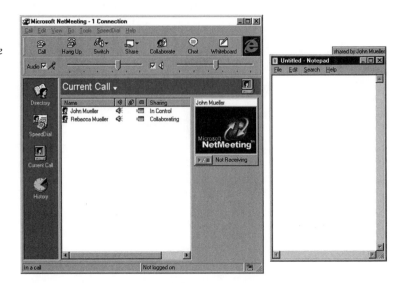

Understanding Browser Compatibility Problems

The browser wars haven't done much for compatibility between the products offered by various vendors. For example, Netscape Navigator doesn't support ActiveX controls. You have to download a plug-in to do the job. (Most people add ActiveX support to Navigator by using NCompass ScriptActive; you can download it from `http://www.ncompasslabs.com/ScriptActive/index.htm`.) It may be an acceptable way to handle the situation from Netscape's viewpoint, but using a special plug-in for ActiveX doesn't do much for the user. Unfortunately, the NCompass plug-in uses an `<EMBED>` tag in place of the `<OBJECT>` tag used by Internet Explorer. This means that you can visit a site that's designed for ActiveX and still not be able to use it, even though you have the NCompass plug-in installed.

Quite a few scripting differences are apparent between the two browsers as well. Just to give you an idea of how significant this problem is, consider the very basis for the Web pages you look at—HTML tags. Both Internet Explorer and Navigator support tags that are outside the mainstream specification for HTML. For example, Navigator implements plug-in support by using an `<EMBED>` tag that Internet Explorer doesn't recognize. On the other hand, Internet Explorer supports specialty tags such as the background sound (`<BGSOUND>`) tag that Navigator ignores. A site that wants to provide sound support for both Navigator and Internet Explorer has to include both an `<EMBED>` and a `<BGSOUND>` tag. Suffice it to say that testing every Web page using both browsers and then figuring out why one doesn't work with it can be a major expenditure of time for Webmasters (the people who maintain Web sites).

Do the problems end there? No, that's really only the beginning. Consider the basic elements of a scripting language such as JavaScript, for example. The Netscape version of this scripting language is far more strict than the Microsoft version. According to Microsoft, Netscape released the specification for the language too late for Microsoft to incorporate it into Internet Explorer, so Microsoft came up with its own version. Again, the Webmaster—and, ultimately, the user—loses in this conflict.

You'll find that there are even small differences in the way that various browser implementations from the same vendor work. For example, Microsoft recently released a VRML (Virtual Reality Modeling Language) tool for Internet Explorer. This product works fine with the English version of Internet Explorer, but users of some foreign-language versions of the product have experienced difficulty in getting it to do anything. I view this most recent level of browser incompatibility as almost inexcusable because the Internet is an international environment. (Don't get the idea that Netscape Navigator is perfect in this regard; it has problems between various language versions as well.)

Incompatibility can also take other forms. Not everyone accesses the Internet using a PC. Macintoshes and Amigas are in use out there, too. (Although the Amiga crowd seems to be thinning out somewhat, we don't have any reason to doubt that they're there.) Also consider the number of UNIX implementations. After all, UNIX was the very basis of the Internet until just recently. So why should you care whether someone with a Macintosh can access a Web site? The very nature of the Internet supposes that everyone can use the information that a Web site provides—not just a fortunate few. Although expecting complete access to every site by every individual may not be possible (or even reasonable), making the effort is important. Unfortunately, browser incompatibilities make this nearly impossible.

Some Webmasters have started to handle the situation by adding alternative text to their sites. For example, if your browser doesn't support graphics for whatever reason, you might see some text that says that you would be seeing a picture of a house if your browser could display it. This effort is a reasonable attempt to make the site more accessible to everyone, but let's face it: Seeing some text that tells you about the house isn't the same as actually seeing it.

Another form of browser-incompatibility repair by Webmasters is the use of "best when viewed by" icons. This little icon tells the person visiting a site that the site works best with a certain browser. Trying to view a site designed for Internet Explorer when you have Netscape Navigator (or vice versa) is kind of frustrating, but at least knowing that you don't have a problem with your software is a bit of a comfort.

Unfortunately, some Webmasters have started to abuse the intent behind the "best when viewed by" icon. For example, many of the Web sites I visit with ActiveX controls refuse to add the `<EMBED>`

tag needed by the NCompass plug-in for Navigator. The result is that even though I have the plug-in installed, I still can't see the Web site as intended by the author. Considering the fact that NCompass does provide some of the tools required for the use of both the <OBJECT> and <EMBED> tags, it's hard to understand why a Webmaster would limit accessibility to the site to one browser. Suffice it to say that such sites are casualties of the browser wars—self-inflicted injuries in a war that makes little sense.

By now, you're probably wondering what all this information has to do with you as a user. It means that you're going to be limited by browser incompatibilities of all kinds until browser vendors start to adhere to standards. You may need to keep two or more browsers installed on your machine if you spend a lot of time on the Internet (I certainly do). Sometimes I need the information that a site provides; if getting it means using a different browser, that's the price I pay for the information. Unfortunately, no magic bullet can transform a single browser machine into something that can access every site on the Internet—at least, not as of this writing.

What do I suggest for a Windows 98 user? If you spend a lot of research time on the Internet, consider installing both Internet Explorer and Navigator on your machine. Going to these lengths sounds ridiculous, and it is, but that's the best solution available today. If you just can't live with two browsers on one machine, see which browser works most often for you. Simply list the sites you visit that are unusable with one or the other browser. Then use the list to determine which browser to keep. Don't just base your decision on the number of sites you can't visit, but base it on the quality of each site in the list. If you're depending on the information provided by a particular site, and that site doesn't completely support one of the browsers in your list, then you'll just have to eliminate that browser.

Understanding Multilink Channel Aggregation

The need for speed on the Internet is becoming increasingly apparent to many people who are using it for research and a variety of other purposes. What if you could extend your capabilities by adding another connection to the one you're using? That's what Multilink Channel Aggregation is all about. Instead of using just one connection to the Internet, you can combine several into one big connection.

Of course, you need multiple devices to create multiple connections. For example, you can use Multilink Channel Aggregation if you have two modems installed on your machine and two accounts to your ISP (unless your ISP supports multiple connections for a single account). Make sure you can actually see both modems in the Modems applet in the Control Panel.

Once you have the hardware and accounts required to create multiple connections, you need to create a connection. I've already talked about creating a connection in Chapter 1, so I won't talk about it again here. After you create a connection that uses one channel like a modem or ISDN line, you can open it by right-clicking the connection icon and selecting Properties from the context menu. Look at the two options on the Multilink tab of the connection Properties dialog. The second option allows you to use additional devices to make the connection. Select this option, click the Add button, choose a device, and then click OK. What you see is a new device added to your connection like the one shown in Figure 21.19.

Figure 21.19.
Multichannel aggregation allows you to combine multiple connections into one for faster Internet access.

Creating Your Own Web Page

In Chapter 1, you looked at the Internet from a surfing point of view. I explained how to get the most information with the least amount of effort. You also looked at some interesting sites to see what they have to offer. You would be wrong to think that the Internet ends there. The Internet isn't simply about grabbing information; it's also about exchanging information and presenting your own point of view about issues that affect you the most.

The Web pages you visited previously didn't just spring up like mushrooms in the night. Someone had to put them together. In addition, not every Web site you looked at was commercial in nature; many Web sites have nothing to do with business or even something of a scientific nature. A lot of Web sites talk about everyday events and interests. For example, I occasionally visit a Web site for cat owners and another for one of my favorite television shows—*Babylon 5*. Obviously, you can find a lot of commercial Web sites such as CD Now, the music store that you visited in the course of this book, but stores are still in the minority when compared to other kinds of Web sites.

Suffice it to say that creating a Web page doesn't have to involve a commercial enterprise; you may simply want to talk with someone about a topic of special interest to you. That's what this chapter is all about. You look at why you should even bother to put a Web site together, and then at the requirements for doing so.

> **Tip:** Building a Web page isn't the same as building an Internet site or even an intranet site. Some Internet service providers (ISPs) allow you to upload your own Web page to their server. The only requirement in this case is that you maintain the content of your Web site. The ISP takes care of the server and everything else needed to create the actual Internet site. Obviously, you experience some limitations when you take this route, and you may have to pay for the privilege of displaying your own Web site; but most noncommercial users find the costs low and the constraints minimal.

Why Bother?

Most people are fairly excited at the thought of creating their own Web sites—until reality sets in. Maintaining a Web site is a lot of work. In addition, you don't even have any guarantee that someone will visit your site. The typical response at this point is, "Why bother?" Some people never begin their own Web sites because they feel that anything they create is going to be a waste of time. If you're approaching your Web site with this kind of attitude, I have to admit that you don't really have any reason to go forward.

Creating a good Web site is as easy as thinking about it first. Ask yourself what you want to get out of the Web site that you design and what you're willing to do to get it. If you don't have a good idea of what you want to achieve with a Web site, you had better start gathering some ideas. Talk to other people with Web surfing experience. Better yet, visit other Web sites that appear to contain elements that you want to include with your site. Seeing what other people do can help you to figure out relatively quickly what you want to include.

There's another good reason to visit Web sites: You can quickly learn what works and what doesn't. If you find that you get annoyed waiting for a Web page to download, other people probably do as well. How does the Web page look from an aesthetic point of view? Is it inviting? Do you want to come back? How hard is the Web site to look at? Does it include glaring color combinations? Is the text easy to read? Asking yourself these questions as you visit other Web sites is about the best way to figure out what you want on your own. In fact, you can create the three folders of URLs (links) shown in the following list to hold your Web site ideas:

- **Content.** You have found other people with interests similar to your own. Finding Web sites that offer the kind of content that you want to offer helps you learn how to present the information in the best way possible. You can also see what's already been done so that your Web site becomes a unique place to visit rather than a rehash of what everyone else has done.

- **Gimmicks.** I maintain a folder of Web sites that show how to do interesting things such as using animation or using sound.

- **Usability.** Make yourself a rogue's gallery of sites that you find either very usable or so unusable that they aren't worth the time. Use these sites as a visual list of do's and don'ts while creating your site.

> **Tip:** Remember that you can't assume anything about the computer that visits your site. Just because a gimmick or method of formatting content looks great on your machine doesn't mean that it will look great on a Macintosh. Some people get around this issue partially by saying something like, "This page looks best when viewed by Internet Explorer." A simple statement of the requirements for viewing a Web site may not win you any friends, but it reduces the number of hostile comments you'll get from people who can't use your site for whatever reason.

The bottom line is that you need to figure out what you want to do before you try to figure out whether a site is worth the effort. Most people take the time to set up and manage an Internet site because they expect to get something out of it. Whether that gain is in the form of new friends, contacts for a venture, information, or even monetary in nature is of little consequence. All that matters is that you see the value behind the site you set up and convey that value to people who visit it.

Determining Whether Your ISP Provides a Free Home Page

Most ISPs provide some type of home page feature today. A home page allows you to provide your own Web content so that others with similar interest can find you. The term *free* might be a bit of a misnomer, though, because you're actually paying for that free page with the rest of your Internet bill. On the other hand, because you don't get this service with all ISPs, you could say that it's at least a bonus for using a particular provider. You need to weigh bonuses offered by other ISPs when making your decision about which ISP to use.

You also should learn precisely what the ISP means by *free*. I recently spent some time looking at the various Internet plans and found out that, although many do offer supposedly free plans, many aren't free at all. For example, one larger ISP offered a free home page for a limited amount of time, after which you started getting billed for its use. Another ISP offered a home page so small that I doubt most people would get much out of it. Getting a home page that offered a decent amount of space was an additional charge.

You can find some real bargains on the Internet. A typical offering for a true free home page will give you about 2MB of server space for content. You may be restricted on the number of hits that the page can take per day and, in some cases, the type of content you can provide. For example, if you start advertising your home business, the ISP may charge you for use of the server. Most home pages are set up for individual use only, not business use. One of the more popular sites to get a free home page is Geocities (http://www.geocities.com), but there are many others to choose from.

Getting content to your home page can be quite a chore as well, but in most cases the ISP tries to make things fairly easy for you. I did find a few ISPs that provided instructions that read like the proverbial stereo manual. You should talk with the ISP about how and when you can change the content of your home page.

On Your Own

Install Internet Explorer, using the instructions in this chapter. Try going online and looking around. The MSN home page is usually a good place to start, but don't limit your choices.

Try out another browser, such as Netscape Navigator. How does it differ from Internet Explorer? What about other browsers you may have used?

Install several browsers on your machine to see how they work on various Internet sites. At a minimum, try both Netscape Navigator and Internet Explorer. You can download a free trial copy of Netscape Navigator from http://www.netscape.com/. Likewise, you can get a copy of Internet Explorer from http://www.microsoft.com/ie/. Be sure to try out some of the add-ons for both products, such as the sound-enhancing RealAudio Player (http://www.realaudio.com/). (If you do install a sound-related plug-in, be prepared for a few shocks. Some Web sites will try to blast you out of your seat with high volume sound effects. Needless to say, such sound effects at midnight aren't much of a treat to you or anyone else sleeping in your vicinity.) Although Navigator does make heavier use of plug-ins than Internet Explorer does, both products benefit from third-party add-ons.

Subscribe to one or more channels that attract your attention. Do you find that they help you keep up-to-date? What kinds of uses could you put channels to in the work environment? How about at home? Try making some lists of what you expect from channels, and see whether you can get the desired results.

Install NetMeeting at several workstations on a LAN or on a single workstation that has an Internet connection. After NetMeeting is installed, try establishing contact with one or more people so that you can see how the product works. You'll find that a LAN connection works surprisingly well, but that the Internet connection is marginal at best, in most cases. Be sure to try out the various features such as the Whiteboard and Chat.

Visit a variety of Web sites. Use the three kinds of folders—Content, Gimmicks, and Usability—that I talked about in the "Why Bother?" section of the chapter to store comments about each site. Then try to determine which site most closely matches the kind of site you would like to build. You might want to classify sites in other ways as well. For example, which site displays the best use of animated .GIFs? Does a site in your list show how to use sound especially well? What about an ActiveX site or two?

22

Creating Your Own Intranet with Personal Web Server

Peter Norton®

Personal Web Server (PWS) is the smallest and newest version of Internet Information Server (IIS) provided by Microsoft. It's not designed for running an Internet site; instead, you might use it for testing purposes or perhaps a small in-house intranet Web site. I use it to test my Web pages before uploading them to a live site.

In this chapter, we'll take a quick look at setting up, testing, and using PWS. We won't look at the particulars of creating your own Web pages or how to create server-side scripts. However, you'll still need to perform these tasks before you can make your site available to others. I also won't spend any time on Internet server-specific issues, because PWS isn't designed for that purpose (you'll be very disappointed by the results if you even attempt to use it in that way).

What Is an Intranet?

Technical Note: Some people confuse the idea of the *Internet* with an *intranet*. It's true that the two have some similarities, but they're used for entirely different purposes. In some cases, they're configured differently as well.

Let me clear up the major difference between the two first. An intranet is normally private; I don't think I've ever seen a public one. The Internet, on the other hand, is always public. Private versus public access makes a great deal of difference in the way that you configure the two setups.

Another difference is size. The Internet invites literally thousands of people to view your site. The private nature of an intranet precludes inviting thousands of people; you may be inviting hundreds instead (unless you're part of a really large company). This consideration affects the amount and type of equipment you buy. You'll find yourself spending more on security and less on hardware when setting up an intranet.

Compatibility considerations are another area in which the Internet is different from an intranet. If you set up an Internet site, you'll want to make it as compatible as possible with a broad range of browsers. Intranet sites concentrate on flexibility and power instead. Because you control the browser used for the site, you also get to use all the capabilities and features that it provides.

Finally, an Internet is always available through a worldwide connection. You can keep an intranet company-based and not make it available to anyone but the few people in one location. For that matter, an intranet can simply become an extension of your LAN and nothing more. (There are some companies that do allow access to their intranet from the Internet, they simply keep the URL secret and protect the site using passwords.)

Installation

Installation of PWS couldn't be easier. The following procedure should help you through the basic installation process. (I'm assuming that this is your first installation of PWS on a new Windows 98 installation using a desktop machine; installing over previous versions of Windows or PWS may produce different results than the ones shown here.)

1. Double-click the Setup program in the \Add-Ons\PWS folder of the Windows 98 CD. The first thing you see is a Microsoft Personal Web Server Setup dialog.

2. Click Next. You then see a license dialog. If you agree to the terms of the license agreement (which you have to do to install the product), click Accept. Otherwise, click Decline to end the setup process.

3. Click Next. At this point, you see a dialog containing three installation options. The Minimum option installs the least amount of support you need to run PWS. The Typical option installs a little more support; it includes help files and other features that Microsoft thinks you need. The Custom option is the one I recommend. It allows you to fully configure your PWS installation the way you want. (Of course, this option also requires more participation on your part.) Now, choose one of the three installation options. If you choose either Typical or Minimum, proceed to step 6.

4. Click Next. You then see a list of components you can install. Note that the Description field below the components list box tells you about each component so that you can decide whether to install it.

5. Choose the components that you want to install. You must check the Personal Web Server (PWS) option to install any PWS support. If you plan to use FrontPage or Visual InterDev to manage your Web site, you need to check the FrontPage 98 Server Extensions option. Visual InterDev users should check the Visual InterDev RAD Remote Deployment Support option. Finally, if you plan to work with a database on your intranet site, check the Microsoft Data Access Components 1.5 option. Then click Next.

6. At this point, you should see a dialog box like the one shown in Figure 22.1. Accept the default directory by clicking Next. You can also choose to change the default directory settings by clicking Browse or by typing the name of the new directory manually. You then should see a Microsoft Transaction Server (MTS) dialog box.

7. Click Next to accept the default MTS installation directory. You can also use the Browse button to find a new directory to install MTS, and then click Next. At this point, you may see one or more additional dialogs like the Microsoft Message Queue dialog box, depending on which options you selected for a custom installation. Click Next after each dialog to accept the default settings. (You can always change directory settings to meet personal needs.) Once you've seen all of the configuration option dialog boxes, Setup begins installing the files needed for PWS. After the installation process is complete, you see a successful completion dialog box.

Figure 22.1.
You need to tell Setup where you want various PWS files installed.

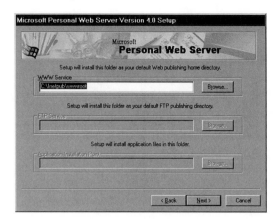

8. Click Finish to complete the installation process. Setup finalizes some settings and then asks whether you want to restart your machine.

9. Click Yes to restart.

Immediately after you restart your machine, a new PWS icon appears on the taskbar. Right-clicking this icon displays a context menu with five entries: Start Service, Stop Service, Pause Service, Continue Service, and Properties. The "Configuration" section later in this chapter shows how to use these options.

Testing Your Setup

PWS normally runs right out of the box. You don't have to do anything more at this point if you don't want to. People can display any Web pages that you create and publish by placing the files in the appropriate folder. Every link works as expected. In short, PWS's default configuration is more than enough to set up a help desk or complete other tasks that you can perform by using HTML pages. I find it helpful to test my setup right after installation to see whether it works at all. Regular testing after that point ensures that I get the results I had hoped for.

You need a browser to test your setup. The first thing you need to know is how to access the Web site. Testing the site is easy; just type http://<name of machine> when asked for an URL. (You should create a LAN Dial-Up Networking connection if you don't want to connect to the Internet before connecting to your Web site when using Internet Explorer; see Chapter 1, "Opening Windows to the Internet," for details on creating a connection. Netscape users don't need to take this step.) For example, I have two machines named MAIN and AUX on a test network. PWS is installed on AUX, so I would use http://AUX/ as an URL. Make sure that you perform this initial test from every computer that needs to access the Web site. That way, you can fix any communications problems before you perform a lot of setup.

Remember that this initial test isn't the end of the process. You should continue testing your Web site as you develop it. Make sure that you maintain private areas for testing new pages if you plan to actually use this site as a small intranet for your office. Otherwise, you can treat the site as you would your production site. You can test new pages by using the same links that visitors to your site would use.

Configuration

PWS offers a lot of configuration options, though not nearly as many as you would find with other versions of Internet Information Server (IIS), such as the one that comes with Windows NT Server. In fact, I was able to run PWS using HTTP without changing any configuration items at all. As soon as you want to do anything other than display HTML pages, though, you need to change the default configuration. You'll likely want to at least tune your setup after you get it going—even if your only goal is displaying HTML pages.

All the PWS configuration features are viewed from the Personal Web Manager utility installed as part of the initial setup. To view this utility, right-click the PWS icon on the taskbar, and select Properties from the context menu. Figure 22.2 shows the initial display that you see. The following sections look at how you perform the three most common tasks using PWS. Make certain that you have PWS installed and working before you attempt to display any of the pages shown.

Figure 22.2.
The Main tab of the Personal Web Manager utility allows you to start and stop a Web server and see Web server statistics.

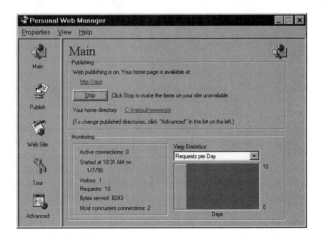

Checking Web Server Status

Clicking the Main button on the left side of the Personal Web Manager utility displays the Main tab shown in Figure 22.2. Here, you can start and stop the Web server as needed to perform maintenance tasks. You can also view the current Web server status (stopped or started) on this tab.

Notice the two links on this tab. The first (`http://aux` in the example) opens a copy of Internet Explorer and takes you to the main page of your Web site. The second opens a copy of Windows Explorer and takes you to the directory containing your Web site files.

The lower half of the Main tab contains statistics for your Web site. You can view the current statistics on the left side. This information includes the number of active connections, number of connections, number of requests, total number of bytes sent, and the highest number of concurrent connections. You can also view a bar chart containing incremental statistics for your Web site such as the number of visitors you receive on a daily basis. (Each bar on the chart represents an individual day or hour.) In addition to the number of visitors per day, you can view the number of visitors per hour, the number of requests per day, and the number of requests per hour. Although this display isn't as impressive as the one provided with the full version of IIS for Windows NT Server, it should provide enough information for you to track Web site usage.

Publishing Files

The whole purpose of having a Web site is to provide information to the people who visit. You may optionally want to get information from them as well, but for most Web sites, the initial purpose is to provide information. PWS allows you to perform two types of file publishing: home page and other. Your home page is the one that most people see when they visit the Web site for the first time. The other pages get connected to the home (or subsidiary) page using links. The next two sections cover these two types of file publishing.

Note: You must create a home page before you can use the Publishing Wizard to publish additional material.

Creating a Home Page

This section of the book isn't going to tell you anything about using HTML. You can find entire books on this topic, and I would be hard pressed to cover the entire topic in one section of a chapter. What I will tell you about in this section is the process for using the Home Page Wizard. Obviously, the first step is opening the Personal Web Manager by double-clicking the PWS icon in the task tray (you also can use a PWM shortcut on the desktop). Follow these steps to publish a home page after you've developed one:

1. Click the Web Site button on the left side of Personal Web Manager. A Home Page Wizard then appears.

2. Click >> (next). You are asked which template you want to use. I chose the Looseleaf option for the purposes of this example, but you can choose any option you like.

3. Choose a template, and then click >> (next). The Home Page Wizard asks whether you want to add a guest book to your site. A guest book allows you to build a list of names of people who visit your site. If you're planning to send visitors email or follow up on their visits in some way, this is a good option to select. Otherwise, you should avoid using it to save disk space. For the purposes of this example, I chose to include a guest book.

4. Choose Yes or No, and then click >> (next). The Home Page Wizard asks whether you want to include a drop box. This option allows visitors to send you email. In most cases, you should include this option so that you can get feedback on your Web site. It also comes in handy for getting input on problems that people with other browsers may have when accessing your Web site. I always include this option on Web sites that I design.

5. Choose Yes or No, and then click >> (next). At this point, the Home Page Wizard tells you that you've completed the configuration portion of your home page. It now allows you to personalize the home page content. For example, you can add links to other Web pages on your Web server or add graphics (like a logo) to the default page.

6. Click >> (next). The Home Page Wizard opens a copy of Internet Explorer. What you see is a configuration page similar to the one shown in Figure 22.3. All the fields in this display are fairly self-explanatory. You can add personal information such as your name and email address. The next section allows you to enter content for your Web page in the form of a heading and associated paragraph of material. Finally, you can add one or more links to your Web page.

Figure 22.3.
Use the home page template to add or update content on your Web site.

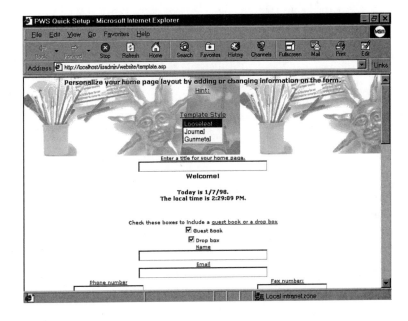

Tip: Make sure you add a bookmark for this location on your Web site so that you can access it quickly later. All you'll need to do is open the bookmarked site using Internet Explorer to change home page content for your Web site as needed.

7. Add content to your home page, and then click the Enter New Changes button at the bottom of the display.

Now that you have a home page, notice the change when you click the Web Site button in Personal Web Manager. You now have three links: Edit your home page, View your guest book, and Open your drop box (assuming that you chose all these options). Clicking Edit your home page opens a copy of Internet Explorer. You see a display similar to the one in Figure 22.3. The View your guest book option opens a query form that you can use to define which guest book entries you want to view. Clicking the Open your drop box option displays all the messages in your drop box.

Adding Other Files

After you have a home page for your Web site, you'll likely want to add other types of content. This means adding more files to your Web site. Adding files is the whole purpose behind the Publishing Wizard. The following procedure shows you how to use the Publishing Wizard to add content to your Web site:

1. Click the Publish button on the left side of the Personal Web Manager. A Publishing Wizard then appears.

2. Click >> (next). The Publishing Wizard displays a page similar to the one shown in Figure 22.4. You need to enter the filename and path for the file you want to publish and a description for it. After you enter these two pieces of information, click Add to add the file to the list. In most cases, you need to perform this step several times for each piece of content that you want to publish. For example, a single Web page may include both content in the form of text and several graphics files, so you would need to enter every file required to display the Web page.

Note: You can publish material only on local drives. If the material that you want to publish appears on a network drive, you have to copy it to the local drive first, even if you have a valid network connection.

3. After you've added one or more files, click >> (next). Normally, you see a success message telling you that you've successfully published the files. In some cases, you may see an error message. For example, you see a network error message if you try to publish material located on a network drive.

Figure 22.4.
This form allows you to define which files you want to publish.

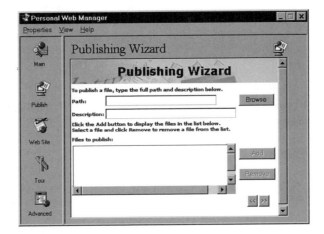

After you publish a document, your home page automatically receives a new link named View my published documents. Visitors who click this link are taken to a page where they can view or download the documents that you've published (which is the reason that PWS no longer requires the services of an FTP server).

Performing Advanced Setup Tasks

In most cases, you never need to touch the PWS settings for a simple Web site. However, as your Web site grows, you may want to adjust certain features that PWS provides. At this point, the Advanced button comes into play. When you click it, you see an Advanced Options tab like the one shown in Figure 22.5. (The number of directories you see may vary from the number shown in the figure.)

Figure 22.5.
PWS allows you to tweak the settings for your Web site as needed.

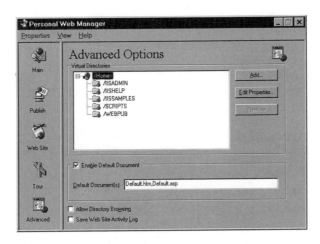

The top half of the display shows a hierarchical view of your Web site directories (no files are shown). Adding new virtual directories is easy; just click the Add button. You then see an Add Directory dialog box like the one shown in Figure 22.6. You need to type a full path to the directory you want to add in the Directory field. The Alias: field contains a descriptive name that you use to refer to the directory on your Web site. Finally, you need to decide what kind of access to allow to this virtual directory. You can choose from three levels: Read, Execute, and Scripts. You must enable read access for any directory that contains content that you want users to see (like Web pages). The Execute option allows users to execute applications. Finally, the Scripts option allows users to run scripts but doesn't allow them to execute applications (unless you also enable the Execute option).

Figure 22.6.
Use the Add Directory dialog box to add new virtual directories to your Web site.

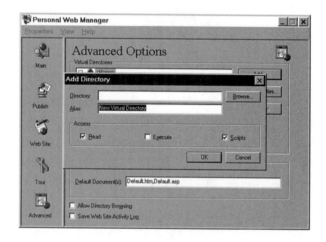

If you select one of the virtual directories in the list and click the Edit Properties button, a dialog box similar to the one shown in Figure 22.6 appears. Using it, you can change the name of the virtual directory (except for the home directory) or the privileges the users have while accessing it. You can also change the physical location information for the virtual directly, though you should do so with great care to avoid introducing errors into your Web server setup.

When you no longer need a virtual directory, all you need to do is highlight it in the list and click the Remove button. Obviously, this action also removes any subdirectories, so you need to be careful when removing any virtual directory. Removing virtual directories from Personal Web Manager doesn't affect the physical directory or its contents.

The lower half of the Advanced Options tab shown in Figure 22.5 contains three additional options you need to know about. The first is the Default Documents group. Checking the Enable Default Document option tells PWS that you want the users to see a specific document when they don't provide a document name during Web site access. You also need to provide one or more default document names. In the example, the two default documents are DEFAULT.ASP (for Internet Explorer users) and DEFAULT.HTM (for everyone else). In most cases, these two documents are more than sufficient.

In some situations, you may want to set up your Web site just like the FTP sites that we're all familiar with (you still get HTTP access, but the display looks like an FTP site). If you check the Allow Directory Browsing option and uncheck the Enable Default Document option, the users can see a list of files on your Web site. Clicking a file link allows the users to download or otherwise view the document.

In most cases, you probably don't want to maintain an access log for a small workgroup setup. However, once your Web site grows beyond the workgroup, you really do need some way of tracking who has accessed your Web site. You can do so by checking the Save Web Site Activity Log option. The log files are in a special text file format that uses the NCSA log file format. You can read these logs using any editor. PWS creates a new log each month, which allows you to archive each month's log. You can find all these logs stored in the Log Files\W3SPC1 subdirectory of the Windows System folder. The log filename includes the year and month. For example, the log filename for January 1998 would be NC9801.LOG.

Limitations

PWS doesn't include many of the supplementary features that you can find in other versions of IIS. For example, it doesn't include some of the less-used protocols such as Gopher. It doesn't even include FTP capability (though you can certainly use HTTP to download). However, I consider this particular lack of minimal importance for PWS's intended purpose.

One of the more important differences between PWS and a full-fledged setup is that you can't manage several Web servers from one site by using PWS. (You can, however, add multiple virtual directories to your Web site, which allows you to keep various types of content separate.) In addition, this server doesn't appear in the Microsoft Internet Service Manager utility provided for Windows NT. As I mentioned earlier, this product is designed for very small intranets. You wouldn't want to use it in places where you need several Web servers.

You also should limit the number of users attached to PWS. Setting up a PWS generates more traffic on the network and results in more work for the host. A machine that could normally support 20 network connections can probably support 10 to 15 PWS connections (Microsoft has set a 10-connection limit for PWS as of this writing). In other words, use this option with care. Installing your local intranet on a machine other than the one you use for file and print sharing is always a good idea.

On Your Own

Install PWS so that you can learn some of the ins and outs of managing your own Web site. This experience is very helpful when the time comes for you to work on a Web site within your company. You'll also find that PWS comes in handy when you're ready to design your own Web pages and test them.

VI

Networking
with
Windows 98

Peter Norton®

23

Networks

Peter Norton®

This chapter describes the networking capabilities that Windows 98 provides. For the most part, I purposely avoid talking about networks in general or even comparing the various options you have. The reason is simple: A single chapter can't possibly contain everything you'll ever need to know about networking. You can find volumes of information about this topic—and some people think that these books are just barely adequate. In this chapter, I'll provide you with some insights into the way that Windows 98 provides network services.

The discussion in this chapter also assumes a certain level of knowledge on your part. I strongly suggest that you also spend some time learning about networks in general before you actually install one. You don't need to be a networking guru to understand this chapter, but you need to know what logging in is all about and know some of the easier terms, such as *network interface card* (NIC).

The Client Module

This section of the chapter looks at the "how" of network support under Windows 98. What can you expect, and why do things work the way they do? These are just some of the questions I answer here. Before we become too embroiled in some of the details of actually using the Windows 98 network capabilities, though, I would like to spend a little time looking at its architecture. Figure 23.1 shows the Windows 98 network architecture. Notice that a request can follow two discrete paths. Windows 98 provides a 32-bit protected-mode path for any networks that it supports directly and uses a real-mode path for drivers that it doesn't support. Both paths end up at the NIC driver.

Now that you've got some idea of how things go together, let's talk about how they work. The following list describes the individual network components:

- **16-Bit Thunk API.** Windows 98 provides full network support using 32-bit code. However, several 16-bit applications out there need support as well. This module replaces the standard 16-bit API with calls to the 32-bit API. It has to provide thunk support to do the job.

- **32-Bit API.** All application requests start at this module. I won't go into details about the API, but Microsoft has gone to great lengths to reorganize and simplify it. Users won't notice these details—except in the way that they affect network performance—but the details make a definite impact on the effort required to program. The API translates one application request into one or more standardized network requests. Quite a few files are involved in creating the network API under Windows 98. The two most prominent are NETAPI.DLL and NETAPI32.DLL. Loading NETAPI32.DLL also loads NETBIOS.DLL, which provides most of the low-level functionality that the API requires.

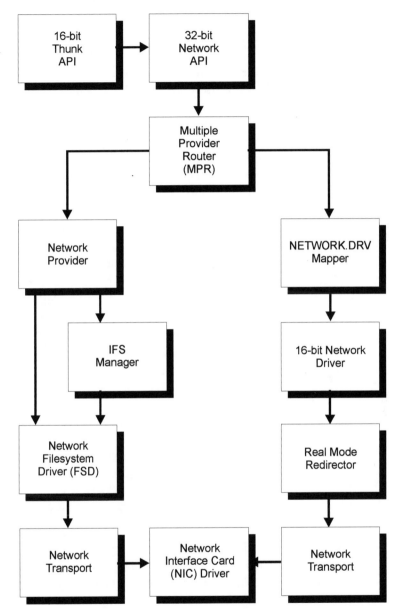

Figure 23.1.
An overview of the Windows 98 network architecture.

- **Multiple Provider Router (MPR).** You can use more than one protocol with Windows 98. Theoretically, you should be able to mix and match protected-mode and real-mode drivers on the same network. Realistically, though, you can't always mix protected-mode and real-mode drivers together. For example, you can't mix an old real-mode LANtastic network with a Microsoft network, but you can mix it with other systems in some cases. All network protocols require a network provider. The whole function of the MPR is to accept network requests from the API and send them to the appropriate network provider (NP). Part of each request states which NP to use. This way, the MPR knows which one it should send the request to. However, some requests are generic. For example, a request for the status of the entire network falls into this category. In that case, the MPR calls each NP in turn to fulfill the application request. In still other cases, a request might not include enough information for the MPR to know which NP to use to fulfill the application requirement. In this case, the MPR "polls" the NPs to see whether one of them can fulfill the request. If none of the installed NPs can do so, the MPR returns an error message. The MPR functions appear in the SYSTEM folder in MPR.DLL. This DLL is loaded when Windows 98 executes MPREXE.EXE during startup. An intermediate file, MPRSERV.DLL, performs the actual loading process. Loading this set of DLLs also loads ADVAPI32.DLL. The MPR uses the functions in this DLL to view the contents of the Registry to determine which NPs and other network resources are available. The MPR also loads MSPWL.DLL. This module checks for your password and performs other security-related activities. A path also goes from the MPR to NETWORK.DRV. This path becomes active when you use a real-mode driver in place of a Windows 98–specific NP. The MPR can't poll the real-mode driver or perform any of the other NP-specific tasks that I described earlier. NETWORK.DRV provides the NP services that Windows 98 requires. I'll describe this particular part of the network later in this chapter.

- **Network Provider (NP).** The Network Provider performs all the protocol-specific functions that an application requires. It makes or breaks connections, returns network status information, and provides a consistent interface for the MPR to use. An application never calls the NP; only the MPR performs this function. Even though the internal structures of NPs vary, the interface that they provide doesn't vary. This mechanism allows Windows 98 to provide support for more than a single protocol. The code used by the MPR can remain small and fast because none of the NPs require special calls. If an NP can't fulfill a request because of a limitation in the network protocol, it simply tells the MPR that the required service is unavailable. The NP also keeps the IFS Manager up-to-date on the current connection status. This way, Explorer knows when you've made a new drive connection.

- **IFS Manager.** When the IFS Manager obtains new status information from the NP, it calls the Network File System Driver (FSD) to update file and other resource information. For example, when the NP tells the IFS Manager that it has made a new drive connection, the IFS Manager calls on the Network FSD to provide a directory listing. The same holds true for other resource types such as printers. In addition to this function, the IFS Manager performs its normal duties of opening files and making other file system requests. The MPR doesn't know what to do with a pathname, so it passes such requests through the NP to the IFS Manager to fulfill. Of course, applications also access the IFS Manager in other ways. The MPR becomes involved only when a network-specific request also requires its intervention.

- **Network File System Driver (FSD).** Each server on the network can use a unique file system. For example, if you make a connection to an OS/2 server, you could require access to an HPFS drive. NetWare and other client/server networks all use special file systems that the vendor feels will enhance performance, security, reliability, and storage capacity. Because Windows 98 understands nothing about HPFS or any other special storage system, it needs a translator. The Network FSD performs this task. It translates the intricacies of a foreign file system into something that Windows 98 can understand. A Network FSD is usually composed of a file-system–specific driver and VREDIR.VXD, which provides the Windows 98 interpretation of the file-system specifics. Normally, only one Network FSD is available for each NP. However, there's nothing to enforce this limit. An NP might require access to both a FAT and an NTFS Network FSD for a Windows NT Server. If so, both drivers are installed when you install network support. The IFS Manager will also call on the Network FSD for support. Although the NP usually makes requests for network status or connection information, the IFS Manager takes care of application needs such as opening files and reading their contents. These two modules—NP and IFS Manager—work in tandem, each fulfilling completely different roles.

Note: You might wonder why Microsoft didn't combine the NP and the IFS Manager into one module. After all, from this discussion it appears that the IFS Manager is simply part of an access strategy for network drives. Remember to take the whole picture into account. The IFS Manager also works with local drives. In addition, combining the modules would have produced a lot of replicated code. In essence, using two separate modules to access the drive status information and contents is the only way to get the level of flexibility that network requests require, with the minimum amount of code.

- **Network Transport (NT).** I placed a single module called Network Transport (NT) in Figure 23.1. Actually, this module is made up of many smaller modules and drivers. The number of pieces in an NT is determined by the complexity of your setup and the requirements of the protocol. The smallest NT could consist of a mere four drivers. For example, you could create an NT for the NetBEUI protocol by using the following files: VNETBIOS.VXD, NETBEUI.VXD, NDIS.VXD, and NE2000.SYS. They are just the drivers, but let's take a quick look at them.

  VNETBIOS.VXD virtualizes access to the protocol. For this reason, more than one virtual machine running on your system can access the network drives at the same time. NETBEUI.VXD performs the task of talking with the NDIS (network driver interface specification) module. It takes protocol-specific requests and translates them into smaller, standardized network requests. NDIS.VXD translates each Windows 98–specific request into a call that the NIC driver can understand. Finally, the NIC driver talks to the NIC itself. The driver can take elements such as port addresses and interrupts into account—everything needed to talk to the NIC. Of course, the NIC converts your request into an electrical signal that appears on the network.

NT requires other files as well. For example, `NDIS30.DLL` provides the API support for `NDIS.VXD`. You'll find that `NETBIOS.DLL` performs the same function for `VNETBIOS.VXD`. In essence, many different modules are required to create one transport. The reason for all these files is fairly easy to understand. For example, what if you want to use a different NIC? All you need to do is change the NIC driver—not any of the protocol-specific files. What if you want to use two different levels of NDIS support? (Windows 98 does support two.) You could add an additional driver and its support files to the equation. Rather than go into too much additional detail, let me close the book on the NT for now. All you need to know is that the NT takes care of the "transportation" details for your network installation.

- **Network Interface Card (NIC) Driver.** I make special mention of this part of the NT here for a reason. This particular driver is hardware-specific. It has to communicate with the NIC on a level that the NIC can understand. That's the first problem—trying to find a driver that provides a standard Windows 98 interface yet talks with the NIC installed in your machine. The second problem is that there can be only one driver. I mentioned earlier that there was a chance that a real-mode and a protected-mode network could coexist, but that it wouldn't happen in a lot of cases. Here's the reason why. If you can't load a Windows 98–specific NIC driver because it interferes with a driver that the real-mode product requires, you're faced with a decision of which network to use.

Tip: Even if you've invested in a real-mode networking product, the performance and reliability increase that you'll get from a Microsoft network running under Windows 98 might make it worth the effort to switch. Of course, you have to consider the trade-offs of making that decision versus the loss of features. Windows 98 may not provide many of the features of other networking products. One of the more important features missing from Windows 98 is network mail and scheduling. Even Windows 95 provided a rudimentary mail capability with Microsoft Exchange. This capability no longer exists in Windows 98, unless you want to set up a company intranet.

- **NETWORK.DRV.** The reason for using this file is simple. You need to have an NP to gain access to a network under Windows 98. When you install a real-mode client in the Network applet, `NETWORK.DRV` is one of the files that gets installed. It provides the interface to your real-mode network that Windows 98 requires to use the network. In this case, the NP also acts as a mapper—a module that maps the Windows 98–specific calls to something that the 16-bit driver can understand. It also provides a thunk layer to translate the 32-bit requests into their 16-bit equivalents. Remember that you still need to install the old 16-bit

Windows version of the network drivers. In the case of the real-mode version of LANtastic, you need the `LANTASTI.386` and `LANTNET.DRV` files from your distribution disks.

- **16-Bit Network Driver.** As I mentioned in the preceding paragraph, you still need a Windows driver for your real-mode network. Otherwise, there's no magical way that Windows 98 will be able to talk to it. A framework for discussion has to exist before a discussion can take place. The 16-bit network drivers typically translate any requests into something that the real-mode redirector can understand. They then ask Windows 98 to make the transition to real mode so that the redirector can do its job.

> **Tip:** In some cases, getting a good real-mode network installation under Windows 98 is nearly impossible. Some of the problems include the real-mode network setup program overwriting Windows 98–specific files and the use of undocumented Windows 3.x features. A few setup programs also require Program Manager to complete their installation, so you might want to start a copy of Program Manager before you begin. I've found that the best way to get a good real-mode network installation under Windows 98 is to install a copy of Windows 3.x first, install the real-mode network there, and then install the copy of Windows 98 over the Windows 3.x installation. This approach seems like a roundabout way of doing things, but it'll ensure that you'll have a minimum of problems.

- **Real-Mode Redirector.** This network component translates your requests into network calls. It works with the real-mode network transport to create an interface with the NIC. Essentially, it performs about the same function in real mode that the IFS Manager and Network FSD do in protected mode.

This might seem like a lot of work just to create a workstation, but that's only half the picture on many peer-to-peer installations. After you get past being a workstation, you have to take care of network requests as well. The next section shows you how Windows 98 provides peer-to-peer network services. You'll look at Windows 98's peer-to-peer support from a server level. You'll also look at a lot of the implementation details. For example, how do you share your printer or local hard drive with someone?

Peer-to-Peer Support

Peer-to-peer networks represent the easiest and least-expensive way to get started in networking. In the past, the standard method for sharing resources was to buy additional machines (called servers) and place the common components there. The investment in hardware and software for a full-fledged network can run into tens of thousands of dollars—prohibitively expensive for many companies and out of reach for others.

Peer-to-peer networks take a different route. One or more workstations also act as servers. In fact, if you work things right and the network is small enough, everyone can probably have access to everyone else's machine in some form. This means that, except for the NICs and cabling you need, a peer-to-peer solution under Windows 98 is essentially free.

Windows 98 provides peer-to-peer networking capabilities right out of the package. All you need to do is install a NIC in each machine, run some cable, and add a few drivers to your setup. Of course, after you get everyone set up, you should install a few extra utilities, such as a centralized calendar and email.

A Little History

Before we delve into all the details of how Windows 98 supports peer-to-peer networking, let's take a brief look at the history of this networking system. Apple actually introduced peer-to-peer networking in a covert manner in 1985. The folks at Apple included AppleTalk in every Macintosh sold. Most people didn't realize that they were actually using a network when they printed a document using the LaserWriter.

Peer-to-peer networking continued to be a cult classic in the years that followed. Many companies wouldn't recognize peer-to-peer networking as much more than a kludge or a poor man's network. Novell NetWare used a client/server model that mimicked the big iron that corporations were used to using. It was comfortable using a network operating system that provided the look and feel of something substantial. In the PC world, many people thought that it was client/server or nothing at all.

A group of companies began distributing peer-to-peer networking solutions for the PC. One of the bigger contributors to this ground swell of alternative networking technology was Artisoft, which still sells LANtastic today. Other vendors contributed products such as 10Net and TOPS. The Software Link even marketed a processor-sharing operating system for the 80386 called PC-MOS/386. This solution and others allowed people to share system resources without having to purchase a file server to do so. In addition, the cost of a peer-to-peer network operating system was a lot lower because these vendors faced stiff competition from Novell.

I'm not sure whether Novell helped or hindered the expansion of peer-to-peer networking with its introduction of NetWare Lite in 1991. This product was designed not to interfere with Novell's client/ server product. As a result, NetWare Lite wasn't well designed or implemented. It couldn't even compete with other peer-to-peer products such as LANtastic. However, the introduction of a peer-to-peer networking product by a major vendor such as Novell at least put this type of networking on some people's agenda for the first time.

Things started to change for the better in the peer-to-peer market when Microsoft introduced Windows for Workgroups at the 1992 fall COMDEX trade show. This show of support by Microsoft legitimized the use of peer-to-peer networking for some corporate applications. Of course, Microsoft didn't go so far as to say that you could use it for more than a few people. Still, it was a step in the right direction.

So, has everyone bought into the peer-to-peer networking technology? Not by a long shot, and I doubt that peer-to-peer networking will ever take over the market (though it has definitely made some significant gains in the last few years). However, using a solution such as Windows 98 in the right place could make a big difference for a very small cost. Windows 98 goes a long way toward making dual solutions—a combination of client/server and peer-to-peer networking—a viable solution.

A Look at the Architecture

You've already taken a detailed look at what it takes to provide workstation support under Windows 98. However, what happens if you also want the workstation to act as a server? Providing server support means that your machine must accept requests from other workstations, process those requests, and return the requested information. Figure 23.2 shows the Windows 98 peer-to-peer network server support.

Let's talk about how these pieces work together to form a server. The following list describes each component in detail:

- **Microsoft Share User Interface (MSSHRUI).** This module responds to external requests from the user for network resource configuration. Every time you right-click a resource and tell Windows 98 that you want to share the resource, this module fields that request. It works with the access control module to set password protection. An interface to the MPR and ADVAPI32.DLL allows the MSSHRUI to set the proper entries in the Registry. You can find it in the MSSHRUI.DLL file in your SYSTEM folder.

- **VSERVER.** The central point of all activity for the server is the virtual server driver, VSERVER.VXD. As with all the other drivers in this chapter, you can find it in your SYSTEM folder. This component provides direct access of all local resources to network requesters through the Network Transport. It works with the IFS Manager and access control modules to limit access to shared resources and to ensure that any access is performed properly. Each access to shared system resources is maintained in a separate thread. This means that access by one requester won't interfere with any other request. In addition, a single requester can make multiple requests. Of course, the number of actual requests is usually limited by the protocol settings you provide.

- **Spooler.** If you grant someone access to your printer, VSERVER sends any requests for print services to the spooler module. This module works just like it would for a local print request. As far as it's concerned, the request originated locally. The following three spooler-specific files are located in your SYSTEM folder: SPOOLSS.DLL, SPOOL32.EXE, and WINSPOOL.DRV.

Figure 23.2.
An overview of the Windows 98 server architecture.

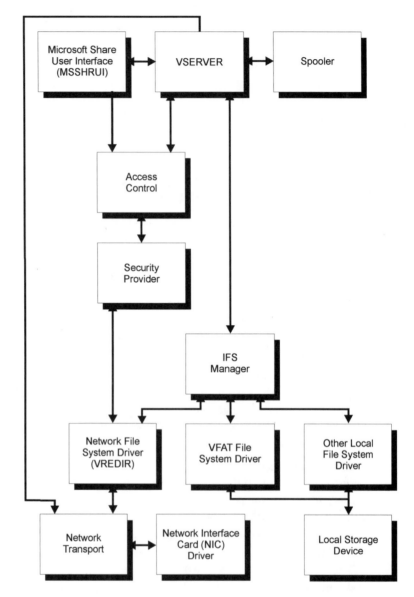

- **Access Control.** Windows 98 uses this module for a variety of purposes, not just network access control. For example, Windows calls on this module to verify your initial logon password, even if you don't request access to a network afterward. Unlike the other modules discussed so far, the access control module makes use of PWL files on your drive as well as Registry entries to verify and set security. You can find access control in the SVRAPI.DLL file in the SYSTEM folder. The SRVAPI.DLL file also relies on MRP.DLL and ADVAPI.DLL.

> **Tip:** You can get around a potential security problem by removing user access to all the PWL files on your drive. If a user erases one of these files, overriding any security you provided becomes a lot easier. In addition, you can erase a user's PWL file to give him or her access to Windows 98 if the user forgets his or her password. Unfortunately, this means that you also have to perform the setup required to re-create that PWL file.

- **Security Provider.** This module is available from a number of sources. In fact, even if you choose to install a Microsoft Network, you can still choose between the Microsoft Network client and the Windows 98 Login module as a security provider. The Microsoft Network client is a network-specific security provider that might include features that the Windows 98 Login module (a generic dialog box) might not provide. You can always access the Windows 98 Login module, even if the network isn't running. The advantage of using it is that the Login module is always available, even if you change the network setup or remove it altogether. The security provider performs two tasks. First, it's the module that asks you for a password. Second, it combines the user's login name and the password he or she provides to verify any network requests.
- **VFAT File System Driver (FSD) and Other Local File System Driver.** Chapter 9, "The Windows 98 File System," covers both of these modules in detail.
- **IFS Manager, Network FSD, Network Transport, and NIC Driver.** I talked about these modules at the beginning of this chapter.

Sharing Files and Printers

Sharing is the main reason to install a network. The very concept of networks came from the need to share expensive peripheral devices and files. Windows 98 provides an easy-to-use interface that allows you to share just about everything on your network with a few clicks of the mouse. Let's take a look at what you need to do to share files and other resources located on your machine.

The first thing you need to do is install support for file and printer sharing. Right-click the Network Neighborhood icon and select Properties. If you have a peer-to-peer network installed, the File and Print Sharing button is enabled. Click it to display a File and Print sharing dialog box. This dialog box allows you to select file and printer sharing individually. Of course, installing support doesn't give everyone access to your system. You still have to select the specific items that you plan to share. (Make sure you have a resource like a printer or disk drive to share before adding file or printer sharing since adding file and printer sharing increases network traffic, which reduces network performance.)

Tip: The NETCPL.CPL file in your SYSTEM folder provides the actual interface that you use to configure the network. Some real-mode or older 16-bit Windows network installation programs insist on changing this file. If you ever lose your Network icon (as I once did), check to make sure that this file didn't get overwritten or otherwise corrupted. In fact, you might want to make a copy of this file before you install any real-mode network on your machine.

After Windows 98 enables file and printer sharing, you need to select the items to share. Right-clicking any of your drive or printer icons and clicking Properties (depending on what support you installed) displays an additional Sharing page like the one shown in Figure 23.3. (The context menu also includes a Sharing option that takes you directly to this page.)

Figure 23.3.

The Sharing page of the Print or Drive Properties dialog box lets you define the level and type of sharing for that device.

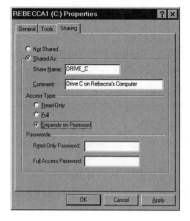

The first two radio buttons on this page allow you to determine whether the resource is shared. Selecting Not Shared means that no one can see the resource, even if that person has other access to your machine. If you select shared access, some additional blanks become available.

You need to provide a resource name in the Share Name: field. Windows 98 presents the resource this way in dialog boxes, such as with the Drives: field of the File Open dialog box. The optional Comment: field allows you to provide a little more information to someone who wants to share the resource. I normally include the precise resource name, my name, and a telephone number where I can be reached as part of the comment. This additional information reduces the chance that some-one will accidentally try to use a resource on my system. You may want to include a location, espe-cially for printers, because someone could potentially select a printer that isn't even in the same building.

Use the Access Type group to define the level of access to a particular resource. You can provide two actual levels of access: read-only and full. The third option allows you to assign two different access passwords. This capability would allow one person full access, whereas another could only read the contents of the drive or other resource. The two password fields allow you to define the password required to access that resource.

Windows 98 doesn't limit you to providing access to an entire drive or printer. You can define access to an individual directory as well. I find it very convenient to set aside a temporary directory on my machine for file sharing. People can upload their files to a specific directory and avoid changing the contents of the rest of my drive. You can use the same principle for other resources. The key is to maintain control of your system.

Peter's Principle: Maintaining Control of Your System

Sharing doesn't always mean that you allow everyone to access every resource on your machine. Simply providing access to an entire drive is easier than setting the required level of security folder by folder, but providing access to an entire hard drive may not be feasible.

For example, many of us work with confidential information that we must keep safe, but we also work with other people who need to see some of the things that we work with. Someone working in the Accounting department might need to share analysis files with a workgroup. However, can you imagine what would happen if that person also shared access to the payroll files? What about the new plans that your company might be working on? Even though you need to share access to the current project, you should keep that new project a secret. A little bit of discretion can save you a lot of headaches later.

Providing the right level of access to everyone in your workgroup is important. Allow others to use the resources that you have available, but don't allow misuse of those resources. You are responsible for doing your part in maintaining the proper level of security on your network.

Login Scripts

Windows 98 provides several support mechanisms for login scripts. The best support is for most versions of Novell NetWare, but the same principles hold true (for the most part) with any other network operating system (NOS) that Windows 98 supports.

Let's look at the kind of support that you can expect for supported networks such as NetWare. The first thing you need to do is disable any AUTOEXEC.BAT or other batch files that you used under Windows 3.x. You don't need to log in to the network before entering Windows 98. Any workstations that use NetWare must have an account on the server before you try to install Client for NetWare.

The next thing you need to do is install an appropriate client. You can find the Microsoft version of the Client for NetWare Networks under the Microsoft heading in the Select Network Client dialog, which you access from the Network Properties dialog. If you want NetWare Directory Services (NDS) support, then you also need to install the Service for NetWare Directory Services found in the Select Network Services dialog. (I'll tell you where to get the Novell version of the NDS client and how to install it in the "Using Novell Client 32" section of this chapter.)

After you get Client for NetWare installed, select it in the Primary Network Logon field of the Network Properties dialog box. You access this dialog box by right-clicking the Network Neighborhood icon and selecting the Properties option. The first time you run Client for NetWare, you see two login dialog boxes. The first dialog box logs you into a preferred server. The second login dialog box takes care of the Windows 98 security requirement. As long as the username and password for NetWare and Windows 98 are the same, you see this dual login dialog box only once. The next time you log in, you see only one dialog box that takes care of both login needs.

To enable login script processing on the NetWare server, you need to open the Client for NetWare Networks Properties dialog box. This dialog box has three fields. The one that you're interested in is a check box that enables login script processing. You also see fields for the preferred server and the first network drive.

Enabling login script processing allows an administrator to maintain the pre–Windows 98 security policy on the server. It also provides a means for creating automatic drive mapping and other NOS-specific features. Check the documentation that came with your network to see exactly what types of script file processing you can perform.

> **Warning:** The Windows 98 protected-mode script processor can't run TSRs. The TSR starts in a separate virtual machine, which terminates with an error when the script-file processing completes. This lack of TSR processing in your script files means that you have to come up with a different way to install backup agents and other files that you normally install by using the login script. In most cases, you need to install such files as part of the AUTOEXEC.BAT or within a DOS session after you start Windows 98. Of course, upgrading your software to a non-TSR version will get rid of many of the problems you'll experience when using these products.

Understanding TCP/IP and PPP

Windows 98 provides a fairly complex and complete set of features related to Transmission Control Protocol/Internet Protocol (TCP/IP). A protocol establishes rules that allow two nodes—workstations, mainframes, minicomputers, or other network elements such as printers—to talk to each other. TCP/IP is one of the more popular sets of network communication rules.

Point-to-Point Protocol is a set of communication rules that provide a method of conducting online (from one point to another) communications, such as connecting to a UNIX host or the Internet. In almost all cases, the support that Windows 98 provides deals with remote communications, but there are exceptions. For example, the monitoring capability provided by SNMP could work in a local server setup.

Including this support as part of the operating system is important for two reasons. First, adding TCP/IP and PPP to the operating system makes it easier for software developers to write agents (special drivers or applications that use the rules that these protocols establish to perform useful work). If you added either protocol as a third-party product, there wouldn't be any standardization, making it nearly impossible for other third-party vendors to write standard agents. Second, adding this level of protocol support to the operating system means that Microsoft can incorporate an additional level of support as part of its utility program offerings. For example, both protocols are important when you're communicating with the Internet through Microsoft Network (MSN). Before you can use TCP/IP, though, you have to install it. Let's quickly go through a few of the tasks you need to perform to install TCP/IP support.

> **Tip:** Installing TCP/IP support before you install Dial-Up Networking saves some extra steps later. The Dial-Up Networking installation routine automatically installs the required protocols for you if you install TCP/IP support first.

1. Right-click the Network Neighborhood icon, and select Properties.
2. On the Configuration page, click the Add button. You then see the Select Network Component Type dialog box.
3. Select Protocol and click Add. Scroll through the list of vendors and select Microsoft. Then select TCP/IP in the listing on the right side. The dialog box shown in Figure 23.4 then appears.

Figure 23.4.
Use the Select Network Protocol dialog box to select TCP/IP as the protocol you want to install.

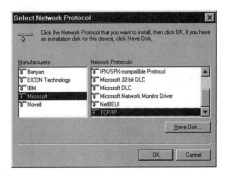

4. Click OK to complete the selection. Click OK again to close the Network Properties dialog box. Windows 98 prompts you for installation floppies or the CD-ROM as needed. After it installs the required files, Windows asks whether you want to restart the system. Click OK to complete the installation process.

Configuring the TCP/IP support after you get it installed is easy. All you need to do is select the TCP/IP entry in the Network Properties dialog box and click the Properties button. You then see a TCP/IP Properties dialog box similar to the one shown in Figure 23.5. The pages in this dialog box allow you to set the addresses and other TCP/IP properties for your machine. All the setup options available for automatic setup are present when you use this manual technique. (See the "Configuring TCP/IP—The Short Form" section of this chapter if you need detailed information on how to set up your TCP/IP configuration.)

Figure 23.5.
The TCP/IP Properties dialog box allows you to configure TCP/IP support under Windows 98.

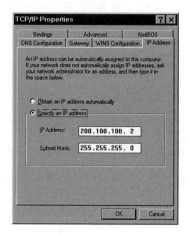

After you complete this initial installation process, you need to perform other installations to provide specific levels of support. For example, you need to install Dial-Up Networking and then the TCP/IP support that Windows provides before you can access that support for a remote connection. The following sections show you how to configure Windows 98 to use both TCP/IP and PPP. I'll also cover a few of the usage issues that you need to know about.

SNMP Support

Windows 98 provides remote monitoring agent support for agents that use the Simple Network Management Protocol (SNMP). SNMP was originally designed for the Internet. It allows an application to manage devices remotely from a variety of vendors, even if that device doesn't normally work with the managing device. For example, a mainframe could use SNMP to send updated sales statistics to a group of satellite offices in a large company. You can use an SNMP console to monitor a Windows 98 workstation once this support is installed. SNMP support under Windows 98 conforms to the version 1 specification. Microsoft implements SNMP support for both TCP/IP and

IPX/SPX by using Winsock (which I describe later). The following procedure allows you to install SNMP support under Windows 98:

1. Right-click the Network Neighborhood icon, and select the Properties option.

2. From within the Network Properties dialog box, click Add and then double-click Services. You should see the Select Network Service dialog box (which is similar to the Select Network Protocol dialog box shown in Figure 23.4).

3. Click Have Disk and then click Browse. Search for the \TOOLS\RESKIT\NETADMIN\SNMP folder. Notice that the dialog box automatically finds the INF file required to install this service.

4. Click OK twice. You should see a Select Network Services dialog box like the one shown in Figure 23.6. It allows you to select from the list of network components that the INF file will install. In this case, only one appears on the list—SNMP support.

Figure 23.6.
This second Select Network Service dialog box presents a list of services supported by the INF file that you selected.

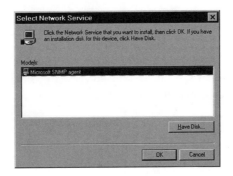

5. Select the new service and click OK. You then see that SNMP support is part of the installed component list of the Network Properties dialog box.

6. Click OK to close the dialog box. Windows 98 installs the required files from the CD. When it completes this task, Windows 98 asks whether you want to shut down and restart the operating system. You need to restart before SNMP support takes effect.

Unlike just about every other feature in Windows 98, no Properties dialog box is available for SNMP support. You need to edit the various properties by using the System Policy Editor. Simply open the System Policy Editor, and choose File | Registry to open the Registry. You can install the System Policy Editor by using the procedure in the section "Special Utility Installation" in Chapter 10, "The Windows 98 Applets." The System Policy Editor appears in the \TOOLS\RESKIT\NETADMIN\POLEDIT folder of the CD-ROM. Double-click the Local Computer icon, and select the SNMP option of the Network policy, as shown in Figure 23.7. There you can change all the SNMP policies for your machine. Notice the two change areas. In the first, you check the property that you want to enable. If this property has other settings, they appear in the box at the bottom of the dialog box. All you need to do is click the button you find there to display a dialog box containing any options for that property.

Figure 23.7.
*The System Policy
Editor provides the
only method for
changing your SNMP
configuration.*

As you can see from the figure, you can change four different settings. The following list tells you which setting each item affects:

- **Communities.** This setting defines the hosts that your computer can connect to for administration purposes. You must belong to a community before you can use SNMP services on it. Even though they aren't exactly the same, you could look at a community as a NetWare group or a Windows NT domain.

- **Permitted Managers.** This setting defines a list of IP or IPX addresses that can query the SNMP agent installed on your machine. If you don't provide a value here, any IP or IPX address can query the agent.

- **Traps for 'Public' Community.** Use this setting to define a list of host IP or IPX addresses to which you want to send SNMP traps. In essence, a trap is an automatic monitoring method. It automatically updates the host when specific events occur on your machine.

- **Internet MIB (RFC1156).** This setting determines a point of contact and location if you're using the Internet MIB. The "RFC" part of this entry stands for Request for Comment. It's part of the Internet standards effort. You can find it and other RFCs at this site: `http://www.cis.ohio-state.edu/htbin/rfc/rfc-index.html`.

The System Policy Editor configuration procedure comes in handy for more than just SNMP installation and configuration. I'll refer to it several times in this chapter. You can also use the System Policy Editor to affect the condition of other network settings. However, I normally find that the Properties dialog box that comes with this feature usually provides an easier-to-use interface.

Using the FTP Utility

Using the Internet requires some form of browser support if you want to download files or upload messages. FTP is actually a utility program that Windows 98 installs for you along with TCP/IP support. It's a DOS application that uses a standard character-mode interface. The syntax for FTP is as follows:

```
FTP [-V] [-N] [-I] [-D] [-G] [<host>] [-S:<filename>]
```

> **Tip:** After you get more familiar with the Internet, you'll find that the FTP and Telnet utilities provided with Windows 98 are very limited. A lot of other browsers, such as Mosaic, Gopher, Archie, and WAIS, can make your life a lot easier. You can get any of them commercially or as shareware from Internet servers. You can also get the WWW (World Wide Web) Browser from a variety of sources. One of the very best FTP utilities available as I write this chapter is FTP Explorer. It provides an Explorer-like automated interface in which you can choose what you want and not worry too much about entering arcane commands. You can download an evaluation version of FTP Explorer from http://www.ftpx.com/ or http://tucows.mcp.com. The bottom line is that you need an easy-to-use browser that makes best use of the resources that the Internet makes available.

The following list defines each option:

- -V. This switch disables the display of remote server responses. It comes in handy if you want the download to progress in the background without disturbing your foreground task.

- -N. Use this switch to disable autologon upon initial connection.

- -I. You can use this switch to remove interactive prompting during multiple file transfers. This way, you can automate the file transfer process.

- -D. Use this switch to display all FTP commands passed between the client and server. This way, you can debug script files.

- -G. This switch disables filename globbing, which permits the use of wildcard characters in local filenames and pathnames.

- <host>. Replace this parameter with the name or address of the host with which you want to connect for a file download.

- -S:<filename>. Replace <filename> with the name of a text file containing FTP commands. In essence, this switch allows you to create a script for your FTP download. Use this switch instead of redirection (>).

The FTP utility provides a surprising array of commands that you can use after you run it. To view a list, just remember one command, the question mark (?). If you type a question mark, you see a list of all the things that you can do with FTP.

SLIP Support

Windows 98 provides support for both SLIP (Serial Line Internet Protocol) and CSLIP (Compressed Serial Line Internet Protocol) for remote network connections, such as those supported by older UNIX remote servers. The operator of the host machine should let you know if you require this level of support. You access both types of connections by using the Dial-Up Networking utility described in Chapters 2, "Introducing Windows 98," and 19, "Hardware and Software Connections." Unlike in Windows 95, both levels of support come installed as part of Windows 98.

The first thing you need to do to make a CSLIP or SLIP connection is open Dial-Up Networking and create a new connection (as explained in Chapter 2). After you get this job done, right-click the new connection and select the Properties option. Select the Server Types tab and choose the Type of Dial-Up Server drop-down list box. Notice that the list of available server types includes both SLIP and CSLIP support.

After you select a SLIP or CSLIP server, click the TCP/IP Settings button. You should see a TCP/IP Settings dialog box. Notice that it contains all the familiar TCP/IP address information required by the host computer. See the "Configuring TCP/IP—The Short Form" section of the chapter if you need help configuring this dialog box.

Using the Telnet Utility

The Telnet utility lets you create a remote session on another computer. It is another utility program that Windows 98 installs automatically when you install TCP/IP support. The strange thing is that Windows 98 doesn't automatically install it in your Start menu. You need to add it manually. The Telnet utility always appears in your \WINDOWS folder.

When you open the Telnet utility, you see a dialog box similar to the one shown in Figure 23.8. Operating this application is fairly simple. The four menus provide a basic set of features for logging on to a host and keeping track of your session.

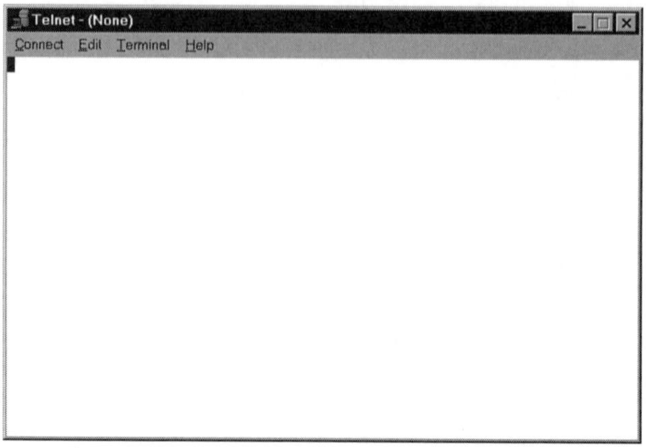

Figure 23.8.
Telnet provides a basic terminal-like front end for a host connection.

Choose Connect | Remote System to open the Connect dialog box. This dialog box has three fields. The first contains the name or address of the host to which you want to connect. The second field contains the host type. The third field specifies a terminal type. In most cases, you don't have much of a choice about terminal types, but I find that the ANSI terminal is usually a bit easier to use if you can gain access to a host that supports it. Disconnecting from the host is also easy. Just choose Connect | Disconnect.

The Edit menu contains the normal Copy and Paste commands. The Terminal menu provides the Start Logging and Stop Logging options to keep track of your session. The Start Logging option displays a File Open dialog box that you can use to find or create a log file.

Figure 23.9 shows the dialog box that appears when you choose Terminal | Preferences. The Terminal Options and Emulation groups are fairly self-explanatory. They configure the way that the host machine interacts with the terminal emulation program. The Fonts button allows you to select a different font than the default Fixedsys. You can also add a little color to the display by clicking the Background Color button. I normally keep it set as is because you can't change the foreground color. The Buffer Size field allows you to change the number of lines of text that you see in the terminal window. Telnet uses a default setting of 25, which seems to work well with most hosts.

Figure 23.9.
Use the Terminal Preferences dialog box to configure Telnet for the host that you plan to connect with.

Desktop Management Interface (DMI) Support

Desktop Management Interface (DMI) is part of Systems Management Server that works as the hardware auditing component of this utility and follows the standards set by the Desktop Management Task Force (DMTF).

> **Tip:** Be sure to check whether new hardware really is Windows 98 compatible before you buy it. According to several hardware vendors that I talked with, the PC98 specification used by Microsoft to determine whether hardware is fully Windows 98 compatible was released late. What this means to the buyer is that some hardware vendors won't release compatible hardware until early in 1999.

A vendor writes a Management Information File (MIF) that contains all the particulars about a piece of equipment. When the System Management Server looks at a workstation and finds this file, it adds the file contents to an SQL database that you can open with any number of products. In addition to the hardware information, System Management Server adds the software auditing information that it finds to the database. The combined software and hardware information gives you the data required to know whether a particular workstation can run a piece of software without an upgrade.

Unfortunate as it might seem, none of these capabilities are fully implemented in Windows 98 as of this writing. DMI client support is present, but you won't find System Management Server anywhere on your Windows 98 CD. Adding server support is a future upgrade that Microsoft might make to Windows 98. Although an upgrade might not help you much right this second, it's good to know that help is on the way. However, if you have all the following equipment, you can implement System Management Server today:

- Windows NT Server version 3.5 or later
- Microsoft SQL Server version 4.21 or later
- A 486/66 or better processor
- 32MB of memory (recommended)
- A hard disk with at least 100MB disk space available
- A network-accessible CD-ROM drive
- A network adapter
- A Microsoft mouse or compatible pointing device (a mouse is recommended but optional)

Remote Procedure Calls (RPC) Support

Remote procedure calls (RPCs) are a somewhat new concept for Windows 98. They're implemented as a network transport mechanism using named pipes, NetBIOS, or WinSock to create a connection between a client and a server. RPC is compatible with the Open Software Foundation (OSF) Data Communication Exchange (DCE) specification.

So what does RPC do for you? OLE uses it, for one. Actually, OLE uses a subset of RPC called light RPC (LRPC) to allow you to make connections that you couldn't normally make. However, OLE is only the tip of the iceberg. RPC can also help you, as a user, in other ways.

Think about the situation this way. You're using an application that requires any number of resources in the form of DLLs, VxDs, and other forms of executable code. Right now, all that code has to appear on your machine or in a place where Windows will be certain to find it. Therefore, every time a network administrator wants to update software, he or she has to search every machine on the network to make sure that the job gets done completely. What if you could "borrow" the DLL from someone else's machine? That's what RPCs are all about. An RPC lets your application grab what it needs in the form of executable code from wherever it happens to be.

Windows 98 provides limited RPC support right now. Microsoft provides an RPC Print Provider (RPCPP) utility in the `\TOOLS\RESKIT\NETADMIN\RPCPP` folder; it allows a Windows 98 client to obtain complete accounting and job status information from a Windows NT server. Installing this utility allows a Windows 98 client to administer printer queues on Windows NT servers.

Windows Sockets (WinSock) Support

Windows sockets (WinSock) started as an effort by a group of vendors to make sense of the conglomeration of TCP/IP protocol-based socket interfaces. Various vendors had originally ported their implementation of this protocol to Windows. The result was that nothing worked with anything else. The socket interface was originally implemented as a networked interprocess communications mechanism for version 4.2 of the Berkeley UNIX system. Windows 98 requires all non-NetBIOS applications to use WinSock if they need to access any TCP/IP services. Vendors can optionally write IPX/SPX applications to this standard as well. Microsoft includes three WinSock applications with Windows 98: SNMP, Telnet, and FTP.

Before I go much further, let me quickly define a couple of terms used in the preceding paragraph. We looked at what a protocol is earlier: It's a set of rules. TCP/IP is one common implementation of a set of rules. Think of a socket as one of the tube holders found in old televisions and radios. An application can plug a request (a tube) for some type of service into a socket and send it to a host of some kind. That host could be a file server, a minicomputer, a mainframe, or even another PC. An application can also use a socket to make a query of a database server. For example, it could ask for last year's sales statistics. If every host uses a different size of socket, every application will require a different set of tubes to fit those sockets. WinSock gets rid of this problem by standardizing the socket used to request services and make queries.

Besides making the interface easier to use, WinSock provides another advantage. Normally, an application has to add a NetBIOS header to every packet that leaves the workstation. The workstation at the other end doesn't really need the header, but it's there anyway. This additional processing overhead reduces network efficiency. Using WinSock eliminates the need for the header, and the user sees better performance as a result.

Sockets are an age-old principle (at least in the computer world), but they're far from out-of-date. The WinSock project proved so successful that Microsoft began to move it to other transports. For example, Windows 98 includes a WinSock module for both the IPX/SPX and NetBEUI transports.

Of course, WinSock is really a stopgap measure for today. In the long term, companies will want to move from the client/server model for some applications and use a distributed approach. This move will require the use of a remote procedure call (RPC) interface instead of WinSock. We've already looked at the implications of RPC in this chapter.

So, what do you need to implement WinSock on your system? A group of five files in your SYSTEM folder is used to implement WinSock. The following list tells you what these files are and what tasks they perform:

- **WINSOCK.DLL.** This 16-bit application provides backward compatibility for older applications that need it. For example, an application such as PING would use this DLL.
- **WSOCK32.DLL.** The 32-bit applications use this DLL to access the WinSock API. It provides support for newer socket applications such as Telnet.
- **VSOCK.VXD.** Windows uses this driver to provide both 16-bit and 32-bit TCP/IP and IPX/SPX WinSock support. It provides virtualized support for each virtual machine, enabling Windows to perform more than one WinSock operation at a time. It is the general driver used for both protocols. If Microsoft added more WinSock interfaces later, they would all require this file for interface purposes.
- **WSTCP.VXD.** TCP/IP requires a protocol-specific driver. This file provides that support.
- **WSIPX.VXD.** IPX/SPX requires a protocol-specific driver. This file provides that support.

Configuring TCP/IP—The Short Form

The same flexibility that makes Windows 98 so easy to use with TCP/IP, however, makes it nearly impossible for an inexperienced user to configure it. With this point in mind, I decided to provide a very fast and easy method for you to configure TCP/IP for a local intranet. I assume that you're going to use Personal Web Server on a LAN in this section, but the principles apply equally well to other kinds of setups.

The first thing you have to do is install TCP/IP, as shown in the section "Understanding TCP/IP and PPP" earlier in this chapter. You'll also find some subsections there that tell you all about some of the utilities provided with TCP/IP. You don't have to understand all that additional information to use this section; your only concern is installing the required TCP/IP support.

After you have TCP/IP installed, you should modify its properties so that other computers can see you. Just right-click the Network Neighborhood icon, choose Properties from the context menu, and then select the TCP/IP protocol on the Configuration page of the Network Properties dialog box. (You may have more than one entry here; select the TCP/IP entry for your NIC and not any dial-up connections that you may see.) Click the Properties button, and you see the TCP/IP Properties dialog box. Select the IP Address page, and you see a dialog box like the one shown in Figure 23.5.

Look at how I've configured the IP Address page in my dialog box. You need to worry about only two fields: The first is the IP Address field; the second is the Subnet Mask field. These two fields work together. An IP address is really composed of two parts. The first part defines your organization, and the second part defines your individual computer.

Notice that the IP address is actually composed of four numbers separated by periods. You can choose up to three of those numbers to represent your organization. The remaining numbers represent your computer. A single entry can contain any value from 0 to 255. All four entries combined make up the IP address. If you were on the Internet, you would have to apply to Internic to get an IP address. On a local intranet, however, you're not really talking to anyone but your own organization. You just have to make sure that each machine has a unique IP address and uses the same subnet address.

I normally select three easy-to-remember numbers for my organization and then use the remaining IP address entry to number the computers on my network sequentially. In this case, I've chosen 200.100.100 to represent my organization and 2 to represent the workstation.

Now comes the question of how the computer knows how to read this address. At this point, the subnet mask shown in Figure 23.5 comes in. Like the IP address, the subnet mask contains four numbers separated by periods, where each number ranges from 0 to 255. As you can see from the figure, I placed a value of 255 for the first three numbers because I've used those numbers to represent my organization. I placed a 0 in the last position because it represents my workstation.

The final step is getting one computer to talk to another. Every computer on your network must use the same organization number; otherwise, it cannot hear the other computers. In addition, every computer must have a unique node number. Because 1 is already in use by another machine that I've set up, I'll use 2 for the next node. You must configure all the computers on your network before they can talk to the Internet server on your workstation.

Checking these connections is relatively easy as well. Windows 98 provides a DOS utility called PING (Packet Internet Groper) to check your capability to communicate with other TCP/IP workstations. All you need to do is type PING <workstation IP address>. To make sure your own workstation is configured properly, use the PING command; for example, type PING 200.100.100.1, where 200.100.100.1 identifies your own workstation. PING transmits three packets and listens for a response. If you see three responses from a particular workstation, you'll know that you've configured it properly.

Another handy utility is TraceRT (trace route). You can use this utility to determine the precise route a packet takes from the current location to a destination. Knowing the route a packet takes can help you troubleshoot network problems such as finding a router that's not working properly. TraceRT can also help you figure out why accessing a location on the Internet takes so long. Packets that go through many routers take a lot longer than those that go through just a few. (Each router that a packet passes through is known as a *hop*.) All you need to do to use the TraceRT utility is type TraceRT <workstation name> or TraceRT <workstation IP address> at the DOS prompt.

Using Novell Client 32

You can choose between one of two NetWare Directory Services (NDS) clients for a Windows 98 computer. The Microsoft version of this client comes as part of the Windows 98 package. You need to download the Novell version of the client (I'll tell you where in the "Installing the Client" section of this chapter).

So, what precisely are the differences between the two NDS clients? Microsoft's client is very lean. It consumes very few system resources when compared to the Novell offering, but it doesn't offer many of the features you need, either. For example, the "Using Explorer with Client 32" section of this chapter explains that the Novell client modifies the way that Explorer works. It allows you to view and assign user rights to directories and files (provided that you have the proper rights). The Network Neighborhood display is much enhanced as well, as explained in the "Differences in Network Neighborhood" section. The Novell offering also provides a lot of configuration flexibility—something that you really need if you want to get the most out of your network. The added flexibility also comes in handy when you start experiencing compatibility or other network-related configuration problems. Finally, you absolutely have to have the Novell client if you want to use the NWAdmin utility. Microsoft's latest client is supposed to provide support for this essential utility program, but the level of support you get is minimal, at best.

Obviously, all these added features come with a price. Although the Novell client helps you find things faster and provides a generally faster interface, you're going to pay a heavy penalty in memory usage. Don't even attempt to use this client with less than 32MB of RAM installed. The current version of the Novell client (including patches) consumes 3MB of hard disk space, not including all the files it places in your SYSTEM folder. Finally, even though I find that the Novell client is a little more reliable than the Microsoft offering, you may find that all the features this client offers can get confusing. At a minimum, you'll find that users have more questions when it comes to Network Neighborhood, not less, after you get this client installed. Be prepared to spend a little more time holding the users' hands after you install the Novell client.

Tip: There isn't any rule that says that you have to use only one client on your network. In most cases, I use the Microsoft client on the vast majority of machines. It's small and easy to use, so users feel more comfortable using it. I install the Novell client if a machine has problems accessing the network or needs added flexibility. Every network administrator machine also gets the Novell client, as do manager machines where the manager needs to have some kind of access to NDS.

Installing the Client

Getting Client 32 installed on your machine is about as easy as software installation gets. You download the required software from `http://www.novell.com/novellsw/platform.html` (for newer products) or `http://support.novell.com/Ftp/Updates/Date0.html` (for older products) or from CompuServe. After you download and unpack the software, double-click the Setup icon. You then see a Client License Agreement dialog box.

Click Yes if you agree to the license terms. At this point, you see a dialog box like the one in Figure 23.10. (The sequence of events that I'm talking about here is for the NetWare operating system; IntranetWare client users see a slightly different set of screens with a few additional options. For example, IntranetWare users have the option of choosing a custom installation, which features an IntranetWare Custom Client Options dialog box like the one shown in Figure 23.11.) Just click Start and the Setup program takes care of all the details for you.

Figure 23.10.
Just click Start in this dialog box, and Setup takes care of the rest.

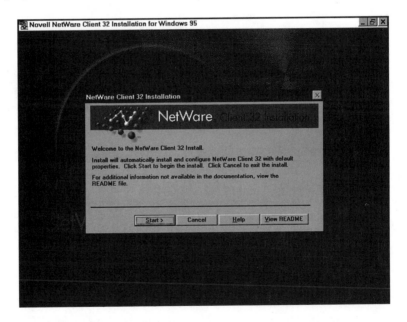

The first thing that Setup does is remove your old client. I mention this fact because you may want to run the installation from a local drive instead of the network. Although Setup doesn't actually disconnect you from the server, at this point a failure that requires a reboot could leave you without any client at all (making the file server inaccessible).

After the old client is removed, Setup installs a few new files in the Windows INF folder. At this point, it forces Windows 98 to rebuild its driver list, based on the contents of the new INF file. Setup automatically selects the new client for you and gets it installed. You see another rebuild of the driver list after the new client is installed.

Figure 23.11.
*IntranetWare client
users can install
optional components.*

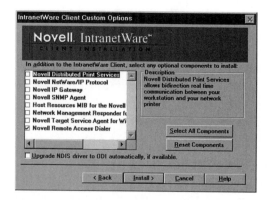

After all the files are copied and Setup performs a basic setup, you are asked to reboot your machine. When you restart your machine, you'll be using the new client. Getting started couldn't be much easier than that.

Tip: Make sure that you know your current context and NDS tree. You need this information the first time you restart your machine with the Novell client installed. The preferred tree and context information is recorded so that you don't have to enter it again.

Configuration Options

Configuring Novell's Client 32 is much like configuring any other network-related driver. You begin by opening the Network Properties dialog box (right-click Network Neighborhood and select Properties from the context menu). Select the Novell NetWare Client 32 entry in the components list shown on the Configuration page, and then click the Properties button. You then see a Novell NetWare Client 32 Properties dialog box.

The Client 32 page of this dialog box contains four fields. You need to leave the Preferred Server field blank unless you want a bindery connection in place of an NDS connection. The Preferred Tree field contains the name of the tree you want the client to search for your name. The Name Context text box normally contains the name of your organization and workgroup. Finally, you need to select the first network drive. With this client, unlike the Microsoft client, you can actually select a drive below F if you want to. For example, you may have only a hard drive and CD-ROM installed on your machine. Selecting E as the first network connection saves one drive letter.

The Login page determines what login page options you get. Normally, when you log in to the network, you see a single page login similar to the one used by the Microsoft client. This page allows you to enter a username and your password. It works fine if you have only one user working with a machine, who uses the same network configuration each day. However, if you have a user with special needs, you should modify one or more of these settings.

The Display Connection Page option tells Client 32 that you want to see the page for selecting a preferred server, tree, and context each time you log in. This capability allows you to change the default server you use each day and provides some added flexibility for those times when you have to log in as the network administrator versus a regular user. This group includes two additional options. The first clears all the connection information each time you log in. I normally uncheck this selection on my machine because I use the same server each day, unless I'm performing administrative duties. However, you'll probably want to keep it checked for security reasons if several users use the same machine. Using this feature enables you to keep a hidden server hidden. The other check box isn't highlighted in this case. If you select the Log in to Server option, you enable the Bindery Connection check box. This check box forces a bindery versus an NDS connection to the server.

Normally, the administrator assigns a default set of scripts to each user on the network. These scripts set up any drive mappings or other essential network configurations. Client 32 allows you to select one of the NDS scripts by using a Script page during login. That's what the second section of the Login page is all about. Notice the two separate fields for script names—one for the login script and another for the profile script. You can choose NDS script objects or a simple batch file on your machine; Client 32 works with either one. Two check boxes affect the way the scripts are run. The first automatically closes the script window when it's complete. In most cases, you should keep this option checked. Unchecking the check box allows you to observe results of a script during debugging. The second check box, Run Scripts, tells Client 32 to run the scripts you've selected. You can uncheck the box if you don't want to run any scripts during the login process.

The third section of the Login page relates to scripts as well. The Display Variables Page option displays a third additional page during the login process. You can use the fields on this page to pass variable information to your scripts. This capability is especially handy if you want to build one script file to serve a number of purposes.

Printing is another major problem in some situations. The Default Capture page of the Novell NetWare Client 32 Properties dialog box allows you to get around some of them. If you've worked with printers before, you should recognize this page as a generic form of the one discussed in the "Installing a Printer" section of Chapter 15, "Fonts and Printing." Because the settings perform the same purpose, I won't discuss them here again. The point to remember is that these settings affect the network printers as a whole. They don't affect the settings of printers you have already installed; Windows 98 overrides any settings you may make on this page.

The final page in the Novell NetWare Client 32 Properties dialog box is the Advanced Settings page. In most cases, you'll never have to adjust these settings, but some of these settings can help you fine-tune the way Client 32 works. For example, the Delay Writes setting can help in situations in which an application repeatedly opens and closes files on the server (such as overlays). The client will hold the file write for a given number of clock ticks to ensure that the application actually wants to write the information. In essence, this setting works as a disk cache. One of the handier troubleshooting aids is the Log File setting. You can tell Client 32 to generate a log of any errors it encounters. The Log File Size setting allows you to keep the file size under control.

Differences in Network Neighborhood

Novell's Client 32 works differently than Microsoft's client when it comes to Network Neighborhood. The first thing you'll want to look at is the NetWare Connections option on the Network Neighborhood context menu. Selecting this option displays a Current NetWare Resources dialog box. This dialog box tells you all about your connection. Not only does it tell you what server you're connected to and the type of connection, but it also tells about your context, including the tree that you're logged into. This dialog box provides a lot more information than its Microsoft counterpart. The only problem is that a novice user will think that he's using two connections. Even though it may appear that you're using two connections, you're actually using one. Look at the Conn No. column of the dialog box. It contains the actual connection number that you're using.

Double-clicking Network Neighborhood presents a few surprises as well. Three NetWare-specific entries appear here instead of the usual one. The first looks like a standard computer and shows the file server itself. The second looks like a tree; it's the NDS tree that you're logged in to. Finally, you see the default context that you're logged in to. Each of these icons serves a different purpose, but the one you'll use most is the server icon.

If you double-click a server icon, you see a list of the resources provided by that server. This is a typical Explorer display like the ones we've looked at elsewhere. However, let me add one bit of advice here: Get all your drive mappings from this view of your server; don't use the resource view that you get by double-clicking the content icon. The reason is fairly simple: You get friendlier names in Explorer if you use this view. For example, if you map the SYS volume, the name you see in Explorer is \\<server name>\SYS. Try to map that same drive from the context view of the server resources, and you get something like \\PUBLICATIONS\.DATACON_SYS. DATACON_SVCS. This name is still readable, but less so than the standard UNC name you get in the server view.

The context view provides some information that you won't find by using the more standard server view. There are two things that you should see as a minimum. First, this view of server resources uses long names. I find that it's more readable when I need to search for a system resource. In addition, you get to see all the resources. The standard server view shows just the print queues. The context view shows both the print queues and the printers.

Each of the three icons provides some different context menu entries as well. Look at the context menu for the server icon. You can use this context menu to log in, log out, display a dialog box showing who you are on the network, and authenticate your server connection. (Authentication ensures that you're actually connected to the server that you think you are, and in the proper context.)

Let's talk about the NDS Tree context menu next. You can log in and log out as before, but this time it's to the tree rather than the server. You can also display a dialog box showing who you are and authenticate your connection as before. Another entry here, though, allows you to change your context. Select it, and you get a dialog box that asks you to change your context. You can type a number of entries here, but let's consider [ROOT] as an example. Using this context takes us from the organizational level (my normal login level) to the root of the NDS tree.

The final context menu I'll talk about belongs to the context icon. About the only thing that this context menu does for you is set the context to the default that you provided in the Novell NetWare Client 32 Properties dialog box.

Using Explorer with Client 32

Client 32 affects the way that Windows Explorer displays the Properties dialog box for a network drive by adding several new pages to use, including the NetWare Volume Information page. This page provides statistics on current disk usage and the amount of resources left.

The NetWare Folder page gives you access to the volume attributes. (Files provide a similar page with file-specific rights such as Transactional, so I won't discuss it in this section.) You can also change NetWare-specific attributes such as Don't Compress and Immediate Compression. Normally, you would have to open the NWAdmin utility to change these settings. Two other important pieces of information are shown on this page. The first tells who owns the folder (or file). The page also includes a Name Space field. You can use this information to determine which directories would be affected if you decided to remove the OS2 name-space support required for long filenames from a volume. Finally, you get to see the folder's creation date, last update, and the date it was last archived. Unfortunately, you have to perform your backups from the server to keep this information current.

The NetWare Rights page allows you to view and assign the trustee rights for users of a folder or file. To change the rights for a particular individual or group, just check or uncheck one or more of the rights check boxes. Removing a trustee is equally easy. Just highlight the trustee you want to remove and click the Remove button.

The second section of the NetWare Rights page provides a list of groups and users in the current context. (You need to change your context if you want to see users and groups in other parts of the NDS tree.) To add a user to the Trustee list, just highlight his or her name and then click the Add button. He or she automatically gets a default set of rights assigned, but you can just as easily change those rights. You need to click Apply or OK to make the changes permanent.

The final section of the dialog box shows effective rights. At first, you might think that it shows the effective rights of the highlighted trustee. The fact is that it shows your effective rights to the folder or file. Even if a user can't change trustee rights, he or she can use this page of the dialog box to see what his or her rights are to the folder.

On Your Own

Use the information in this chapter to determine which of your system resources are shared and which aren't. You might want to create a written list of who has access and where for future reference. This way, you can plug any security leaks whenever someone leaves the company.

After you determine who has access to your machine, look for any security leaks. Be sure to change passwords on a regular basis, especially after someone leaves the company. Check to see how the use of your system resources by others affects system performance and overall usability.

We discussed the network subsystem architecture in this chapter. Go through your SYSTEM folder, and see whether you can identify the components that comprise it. See if your network needs any specialty components because it uses a different protocol than normal. You might also want to take this opportunity to look for any real-mode drivers that are still lurking around your hard drive.

24

Setting Up
Security

Peter Norton®

Network security is a major thorn in most network administrators' sides. Even a small network requires some level of planning, and many managers fail to see the value of implementing the type of security they really need. Of course, I've seen the opposite side of the coin as well: Some administrators wrap the people who use the network in a tight cocoon of regulations and passwords. The chokehold that these people create inhibits any kind of creative resource management and often impedes work as well.

It's difficult to create a bulletproof network setup that offers the level of flexibility that most users require. Adding a bit of flexibility normally means that you also open a security hole. A network administrator must reach an important balance. The first thing you need to realize is that any security system you design can be breached by someone else. So what do you do—leave the network open to whoever might want to access it? That's not the way to go either. The real goal is to put reasonable security restraints in place.

More important than physical security and password protection is the cooperation of those around you. I recently went into a client's office to check on his network setup. He let me use one of his employee's desks to get the work done. Right in front of me was one of those yellow reminder pads. It contained not only the employee's password, but the superior's password as well. Usernames were all over the desk. Anyone could have simply walked into the office and gained access to the network because of this security breach.

This incident reminded me of the importance of the "human" factor in any security plan. To implement a good security system, you need to consider the following elements:

- **Physical security.** Place your file server in a locked room. I can break the security of most networks if I have access to a running file server. If you lock up the file server, I can't access it unless I have a key.

- **Software protection.** Using passwords and other forms of software protection is your next line of defense. Make sure all the right kinds of security measures are in place. I cover this topic in greater detail later, but this is one area where Windows 98 can really help. It contains all the right features; all you need to do is implement them.

- **Cooperative security.** You can't secure the network by yourself. The larger your network, the more you need every user's cooperation. If you expect the user to cooperate with you, you need to talk to him or her and find out what's reasonable. No one will use an unreasonable security plan. This cooperative strategy also extends to management. If you don't talk to management and tell them what your security problems are, they won't be able to help. You also need to make sure that management knows what kinds of security risks are present in the current setup. This reduces the chance of someone's being surprised later.

- **Training.** It's never a good idea to assume that users know how to use the security features that Windows 98 provides. You can implement a lot of the physical security, but it's the user who will use the software part of the equation. An untrained user might not use a particular security feature correctly or might not even know that it exists. In addition, untrained users often resist using security features because they don't understand their purpose.

- **Timing.** It's easier to set up your security plan at the very beginning of a network installation. Setting up a security plan once you've gotten all the pieces in place may mean taking some things apart and redoing them, or worse still, compromising the safety of your network because you can't redo a portion of the network setup.

- **A written security plan.** As your network becomes larger, it becomes vitally important to put the rules in writing. Otherwise, how will a user know what's expected or how to react in a crisis? Writing everything down also makes management aware of the security that you have put in place.

This might seem like a lot of work to implement security, but it isn't when you consider the loss that a single security breach can cause. A pirate isn't going to steal last week's letter to the general public; he's going to steal something valuable. The more secret something is, the better the pirate likes it. Even if a pirate doesn't take anything, he could leave something behind. What would a virus do to your network? It doesn't take too much thought to imagine your entire setup crumbling as a virus infects it.

This chapter will help you understand the three major areas of security that Windows 98 will help you implement: local, network, and Internet. By looking at these three rings of security as separate issues, you ensure that there are no holes in your security plan.

Local Security

Every security plan should start with local security. After all, if you don't have the local environment secured, do you expect to secure anything else? I was pleasantly surprised by some Windows 98 security features, but dismayed by others. For example, the ability to assign two levels of password protection to every resource is nice and will probably work fine for a peer-to-peer network. The inability to assign a password to a specific file didn't sit well with me. Sometimes you need to protect one file in a directory but not another. Some older applications really need to have their configuration files in the same directory as the rest of the executables. I usually like to make my executable files read-only so that the user doesn't erase them.

However, putting these inconveniences aside, you can still implement a significant security strategy by using Windows 98's built-in capabilities. The following sections describe these features. In most cases, I've described how to use and implement these features in other chapters, so I won't cover that aspect again here.

Logon

The best way to prevent a security breach is to keep someone from getting onto the network in the first place. The dialog box that you see when you start Windows 98 is your first line of defense against someone who would try to break into your system. I've talked about the logon feature of Windows 98 in several places. We look at it as part of the Control Panel applets in Chapter 10, "The Windows 98 Applets," and again in Chapter 23, "Networks." We also look at how you can change the source of the network logon by using the Network Properties dialog box (also in Chapter 23). Let's take a look at how you can use the Logon dialog box to help implement a security strategy.

Standalone Security

It always amazes me when someone asks why it's important to protect a standalone workstation. Does the fact that a workstation doesn't connect to the network reduce the quality of the data it contains? The only part of the security picture that has changed is that a standalone workstation will at least keep someone from accessing your data on the network. The fact that many standalone workstations contain valuable data is still very important. If your standalone machine has Windows 98 on it, it's pretty certain that the data it contains is valuable. The initial strategy to follow for a standalone workstation is to enable password protection by using the Password Properties dialog box that you access by opening Control Panel and double-clicking the Password applet. Select the User Profiles tab and the second option button (the one that enables users to customize their desktop settings). Selecting this option automatically enables password protection.

> **Tip:** If security for a specific workstation is so important that software alone won't take care of the problem, consider one of several alternative solutions. For example, you could add a locking bolt to the back of the machine to prevent people from opening it up, and use the BIOS-password feature to prevent access by any means until the user provides the correct password. Physical locking mechanisms are also available. One of them goes over the floppy disk drive to prevent the user from accessing it. You can also add a lock to a standard PC's On switch. Unfortunately, most of these solutions are either expensive or inconvenient or both. It's almost always worth your while to seek other solutions to the problem.

Just enabling passwords doesn't help you very much. What would prevent someone from turning off the settings? I always back up my configuration changes with a policy change. The policy change reinforces the password setting. You can do this by opening the System Policy Editor, and choosing File | Open Registry to load the current settings from the Registry. The File | Save command saves any changes that you make in the Registry before you exit System Policy Editor. You'll see two icons after loading the Registry—one for the user and one for the machine. It's the user settings that you'll want to modify. Figure 24.1 shows what you'll find in the Local User Properties dialog box.

Figure 24.1.

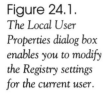

The Local User Properties dialog box enables you to modify the Registry settings for the current user.

Using the Local User Properties dialog box allows you to turn off various types of access. For example, you can turn off the Control Panel settings by using the options in the Windows 98 System | Control Panel list. The following paragraphs explain each Control Panel restriction in detail:

- **Restrict Display Control Panel.** You can choose to disable the entire Display applet, or you can select which pages in the Display Properties dialog box are disabled. The first option in the list disables the entire applet. Every other option disables a single page at a time. This particular setting comes in handy for setting a screen saver password and then shutting off the page so the user can't disable it.

- **Restrict Network Control Panel.** As with the Display applet, you can choose to disable the entire applet or individual pages. The Access Control page is the one to check here, but it really applies only when you have a network setup on the machine.

- **Restrict Passwords Control Panel.** This is one of the few applets that I would consider disabling completely. Every page on this one could produce potentially harmful effects for your setup. Of course, the big ones in a standalone setting are the User Profiles and Password pages.

- **Restrict Printer Settings.** The only good reason to implement this policy is if you're afraid that the user will add a nonexistent printer or delete one installed on the machine. This particular policy affects only the General and Details pages.

- **Restrict System Control Panel.** This policy affects the Device Manager and Hardware Profiles pages. It also removes the Virtual Memory and File System buttons. Whether you disable these settings depends largely on the user's expertise. In most cases, you probably gain more than you lose by leaving these settings alone because the user will be able to help you troubleshoot many system problems if he can access the information that these pages provide.

I mention in Chapter 23 that a user could circumvent the password by erasing the PWL file. You can keep this from happening by taking another preventive measure. Look at the Windows 98 System | Restrictions policy. Checking all four of the items under this policy prevents the user from accessing the hard drive in any manner other than the one you allow. You could restrict applications access to only those required to complete the user's work. Disabling the DOS prompt also prevents the user from erasing the PWL files that way. Of course, the user who has to live with these restrictions might see them as very limiting. Even though this strategy gives the network administrator the tools needed to prevent user meddling, it could backfire somewhere along the way.

> **Tip:** Disabling the user's access to the hard drive after he or she starts Windows 98 won't prevent other forms of access. For example, a user could boot his system using a floppy and remove both the PWL and POL files. (The System Policy Editor stores its data in the POL file, and the system passwords appear in the PWL file.) This would effectively disable any restrictions that you placed on the user. Removing the floppy drive would disable this form of access but would make it very difficult to troubleshoot the machine or add new applications.

Using a combination of these settings allows you to restrict user access to most of the "harmful" features that Windows 98 provides. It would be a lot better, though, if you could participate in a cooperative form of security rather than resorting to these very harsh measures that will likely cause a lot of user unhappiness.

You can impose a final level of restrictions on the user of a standalone machine using the Windows 98 System | Shell policy options. Most of these options will effectively prevent a user from exercising any form of control over the shell itself. These policies also provide some network settings. I'll refer to them again in the next section. Of all the policies presented here, disabling the Run command is probably the most reasonable. This restricts the user from starting applications on the hard drive. This is especially important if you maintain a set of diagnostic tools locally. For example, it's fairly likely that you wouldn't want the user to access the Registry Editor or the System Policy Editor. Most of these settings are pretty self-explanatory. The one that really caught my attention, though, was the Hide All Items on Desktop policy. About the only use I can think of for this setting is when you create the general system policy. You could disable access to everything, including the desktop. That way, if someone did manage to bypass the Logon dialog box, he wouldn't see much of value when Windows 98 did start.

Peer-to-Peer Security

All the policies I covered in the preceding section apply here as well, but there are several important differences. First, you'll probably load the system policies from a POL file instead of directly from the Registry. Second, you'll probably see more than just one user; this dialog box includes groups as well. Whether you set policies by groups or by the individual (or even a combination of both), the settings covered in the preceding section are the same.

I'd like to again direct your attention to the Windows 98 System | Shell policy mentioned earlier. I want to talk about quite a few network restrictions in this section because they don't really apply to standalone machines. There are three Network Neighborhood–specific settings here. The problem with implementing these policies is that they restrict the user from exploring the network. You'll probably want to think twice about implementing these policies for most users.

There's one set of policies that you should probably consider implementing on a structured network, especially if you manage a lot of machines. Both appear in the Windows 98 Network | Sharing policy—one for printers and one for drives. Disabling the user's ability to share (or not share) resources on his machine could save you a lot of trouble in the long run. A user might not always understand why you granted someone else access to his hard drive or printer. Unless you want to explain each and every setting on every machine on the network to every user, you'll probably want to disable the users' sharing controls.

Peer-to-peer networks also need to consider the machine settings for each computer in the System Policy Editor. For example, how do you want the various machines to talk to each other, and which protocols will they use? Chapter 23 covers many of these issues. Other settings are discussed in the following sections. The important thing to see right now is the overall picture. Figure 24.2 shows the overall settings picture for the machine network settings.

Figure 24.2.
*Machine-specific
settings become
important in a peer-
to-peer networking
environment.*

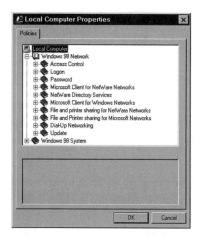

The Access Control setting performs the same function as that page in the Network Properties dialog box. It's included here so that you can set that policy by using a remote terminal. (In fact, every important setting that you can change with a Properties dialog box also appears somewhere in the System Policy Editor so that you can change it remotely.)

The System policies for a machine can provide some additional security as well. One of the settings I use quite a bit is Windows 98 System | Network Paths | Network Path for Windows Setup. This particular policy allows you to place a copy of Windows 98 on a file server and then prevent the user from accessing it. The network administrator can update a system with ease, but the user is restricted from adding new Windows 98 features.

The three run policies (under Windows 98 System | Programs to Run) provide an opportunity to load network monitors and other applications. A monitor can help you keep track of how the user interacts with the network and keep track of the current status of the workstation itself. Of course, you can also use this policy to add default applications to the user's setup. For example, company policy might dictate that everyone use a specific contact manager or email program. You could add either to the Run policy in order to load them automatically for the user.

Client/Server Security

As mentioned earlier, you can use the settings described in the "Standalone Security" section with a client/server security setup for a network operating system such as NetWare or Windows NT. You can also add the peer-to-peer networking security described in the preceding section. Windows 98 provides some additional capabilities for client/server setups that I didn't describe earlier. Some of these settings appear in Chapter 23. For example, you can implement a remote monitor by using SNMP.

The major addition to security that Windows 98 provides for client/server networks is the ability to download system policies from the file server. You must install the Group Policy features by using the procedure provided in the Special Utility Installation section of Chapter 10. Placing the GROUPPOL.DLL file in your SYSTEM folder enables Windows 98 to download group policies included in your POL file to the local workstation.

You need to know some things about group policies. First, Windows 98 won't override an individual user policy with a group policy. If you want to use groups, don't define any individual policies for that particular user.

Second, Windows 98 processes the groups in the order of precedence that you set using the Options | Group Priority command. The Group Priority dialog box allows you to change the way in which Windows 98 views each group policy. A policy in a high-priority group always overrides a policy in a low-priority group. This means that you'll have to set the priorities to reflect the security requirements of the network. Otherwise, you could accidentally give a user access to something for which he wouldn't normally need access.

The Password Cache

Windows 98 implements something called a password cache. The PWL or password list file in either the main Windows 98 or your individual profile folder contains more than just the password for your system. This file also remembers the passwords for online services such as Microsoft Network (MSN) or the Internet, or any of the other resources such as network drives that you need to access. Your Windows logon password unlocks this file, which in turn contains the passwords that unlock all the other resources you can access.

Setup normally provides password caching as a default. (This means that Windows 98 remembers your password when you use programs such as Microsoft Network.) In fact, there isn't any place to turn password caching off in a Properties dialog box. However, if you open the Windows 98 Network | Password policy of the Local Computer Properties dialog box by using the System Policy Editor, you'll see an option for disabling password caching.

The other three policies in the Windows 98 Network | Password policy are pretty self-explanatory. The Minimum Windows Password Length policy can help you make it more difficult for a hacker to break into the network. It's a proven fact that some people use a single-character password—or none at all. This isn't just under Windows 98; it's everywhere. Setting a minimum password length between 5 and 10 characters is usually sufficient. (In fact, passwords over 10 characters long usually encourage the user to write their password down. Passwords stolen from desktops are one cause of network break-ins.) You should also set a policy of using a combination of letters and numbers that don't form birth dates or other combinations that a hacker who knows the user could easily guess.

What happens if the PWL file becomes corrupted? Windows 98 also provides a Password List Editor, shown in Figure 24.3, to remove corrupted passwords from the file. As you can see, there's no way for the administrator to know the user's password, but he can remove a specific password from the list.

Figure 24.3.

The Password List Editor is a simple utility for removing old or corrupted passwords from the user's PWL file.

Warning: There are a few caveats about using the PWL editor. First, the user needs to log in to "unlock" the file. This means that you can't edit a PWL file remotely. You must do it at the user's machine. Second, the Password List Editor might corrupt a PWL file if an application adds a password in an unknown format. Be sure to create a backup of the PWL file before you edit it.

Network Security

Let's get back to peer-to-peer networking. Windows 98 provides several levels of security that fit different kinds of networking needs. You can select only one level at a time, so it's important to select the correct one. Changing your policy later will prove time-consuming, at the least.

The following sections provide you with the details of Windows 98 security. This information is very peer-to-peer-network–oriented, but I do throw in some information that you can use with client/server networks as well.

> **Tip:** Under DOS, you could use the hidden and read-only file attributes to marginally hide files and directories from a user. Windows 98 exposes these files through Explorer, making it easier for a novice user to delete much-needed files without much thought. Win-Secure-It is a product that helps you get past this new set of problems by allowing you to hide and optionally protect files as needed. You can get all the details and download a shareware version of this product from Shetef Solutions at `http://www.shetef.com/`.

Share-Level Versus User-Level Security

The first level of security that Windows 98 provides is share-level access control. You get to this setting by using the Access Control page of the Network dialog box. The other security level is user-level access control. Each of these security levels provides a different set of features, and each has different qualities that make it useful in a given situation.

Share-level access control enables you to assign a password to each resource on the network. You can use the same password for each resource, or a variety of passwords. Share-level access control also enables you to determine whether a user gets read-only or full access based on a password. I normally use three levels of security:

- **No password.** Because the user has to log on to the network in the first place, you can assume that he already has a certain level of security. I don't assign an additional password to low-priority resources.

- **Read-only.** When I do assign a password to a resource, I give it both a read-only and a full-access password. The read-only password allows me to give people quick access to documents that they can either copy to their hard drive or read online. This works well with applications that don't provide a revision-marks feature, because I can see who made what comments.

- **Full.** Anyone who is working on a sensitive project with me usually gets full access to the resource. This enables us to work together on a single document. Turning on an application's revision-marks feature allows me to see who made what changes. It also allows all of us to interact without actually setting up a meeting.

User-level access control enables you to set resource access by username or group. This is the same type of access that client/server products such as NetWare use. I use this form of access control when the user will also interact with a larger network. The advantage is obvious: I don't have to spend a lot of time retraining the user to use the peer-to-peer setup. He already knows how to use it based on his previous experience with NetWare.

There's a more important reason to use user-level access control. This is the method that enables you to use a policy file created using the System Policy Editor.

Master Key

What do I mean by a master key? This is a policy more than a feature. Suppose that your company uses a combination of client/server and peer-to-peer networks. It's possible that each network would require a separate login by the user. Trying to get any user to remember more than one login password is difficult. It also wastes time in some respects because the user will spend a lot of time logging in to the various networks he needs to access. Also, there's a frustration factor to consider as the user goes from login screen to login screen.

Windows 98 provides the capability to use one "master key" to get to all the networks and resources that a user can access. The old system was to use a different password for each resource. If you needed to log into the workgroup network, you needed one password. Another password would give you access to the company network. You needed another password for your mail program and yet another for your communications program. Even if you used the same password for every access, it was inconvenient to enter a password every time you required access to something. Windows 98 remembers all the user's passwords and enters them automatically as needed. All the user needs to do is enter the initial password when starting Windows 98. Implementing a master key strategy is simple. All you need to do is have the user provide precisely the same password to every login screen the first time he goes through them. I stress the word "precisely" here because capitalization makes a difference on some networks.

Internet Security

The question of Internet security has gotten a lot of press lately and I imagine it will get a lot more press before anything is resolved. In many respects, it's not even a matter of security we're talking about here—it's a matter of access. Security implies that you're locking something up, and that's clearly in opposition to how people actually use the Internet. Shared information, but shared with only the people you want to share with, is what Internet security is really about. In short, it comes down to a matter of access.

What kinds of access are we talking about? There are a number of ways to look at information exchange. You can either exchange information willingly, or someone can try to steal it from you. Just consider one form of information exchange that people considered stealing. You register your software electronically instead of using the mail-in card as usual. Getting online is easy, but it seems to take a long time. Only after you actually look at what was transferred do you begin to realize that the vendor not only received the information you provided (such as your name and address), but conducted a complete survey of the contents of your machine as well.

There are other forms of unintentional access as well. For example, a user may decide to visit an Internet site. During the process of downloading the Web page, he also downloads a destructive ActiveX control that wipes out his hard drive. An investigation by authorities shows that there wasn't any malicious intent on the part of the control's author—the control simply conflicted with a disk utility running in the background. Damage to both hardware and software becomes a very real issue when you start running those cute-looking controls that are springing up on Web pages all over the world.

The effect of unrestricted access on your machine's hardware and software isn't the only consideration. Many people are beginning to shop online—I'm one of them. How do you know that the vendor is using your credit card information correctly? For that matter, how do you know that someone isn't monitoring your "conversation" with the vendor and copying down that number? You could end up paying for someone's new car or clothing with your credit card.

The need to restrict access doesn't affect just the user. What happens to companies that lose their competitive edge when someone snoops through their supposedly secret files? It happens. Just look at all the news in the trade presses regarding updated firewalls and other security items. A lot of the security software that people depended on the most ended up having some flaw that rendered the security features useless. (Fortunately, firewall and other security software are becoming a lot more secure due to the hard work of both vendors and users.)

It doesn't take too long to realize that creating a secure environment on the Internet can be more difficult than you first thought. I'm not going to spend a lot of time telling you horror stories of companies that lost millions of dollars due to the seemingly petty crimes committed by hackers. Nor will we explore the test cases of home users who let their guard down for a few moments only to discover that those were the most important few moments of their computer's history. What we'll concentrate on instead are the security measures that you can take to protect yourself when using a standard browser under Windows 98.

Peter's Principle: When Will a Hacker Break Into Your Machine?

When I visit a site to offer advice on security, the first sign of trouble I see is the level of confidence. If someone is confident that a hacker can't break into his system, I'm almost positive that the hacker will find a way to do so.

Think about the very concept of security software for a second. That software you're using is designed by a programmer who wants to provide you with the best protection he can think of. Any software designed by a programmer can be overcome by an equally competent hacker thinking along the same lines. All that the hacker really needs to do is figure out what line of reasoning the programmer followed when creating the security software, and then think of a way around it. The idea that anyone can overcome your security precaution is an important concept to remember.

So, if you can't count on your security software to prevent a break-in, what good is it? There are three ways that security software can help. First, it does act as a direct deterrent to people who are basically honest and really don't want to cause problems. Second, it can slow down even a good hacker, which gives you time to react and prevent any major problems. Finally, good security software admits that it didn't stop the hacker, alerting you to the problem at hand. The one way that security software won't help is to deter a hacker from breaking in at all.

The number one way to stop a hacker in his tracks is to start out by thinking that he's going to get past your security software. Once you get that idea in mind, you can start looking for breaches in your security. A good piece of security software works with you to help you locate holes or unauthorized entry (which could be as simple as a break in someone's normal pattern of system access or an unusual number of password retries). Looking for holes is unfortunately the only way that you'll keep someone from damaging your system.

Understanding Certificates

There are efforts underway right now to make downloading ActiveX controls, Java applets, or anything else from the Internet just a little safer. Some of the trade press calls this new technology a *certificate*, while other people use the term *digital signature*. I view certificate as a friendly but imprecise term, so I'll use digital signature throughout this section.

Figuring out the precise technology behind digital signatures right now is a little like nailing Jell-O to the wall—you might be able to do it, but who would want to try? There's a simple way to look at a digital signature from a user perspective. Think of it as you would a driver's license or an identification card, because it has the same function. A digital signature identifies who created an Internet object—such as a Java applet or an ActiveX control—and could potentially provide a wealth of other information. For example, if the object happens to be a client or server, a digital signature shows the current owner. In other words, you'd know the true identity of the person or company that you're dealing with.

Giving someone a digital certificate for the life of an object leaves a few things in doubt. For example, what if a company sold the rights to an ActiveX control to another company? To alleviate this problem, the digital signature, like a driver's license, also expires—forcing vendors to keep proving that they are who they say they are. The expiration date also gives hackers less time to figure out how to steal the certificate. (Because each certificate is a separate item, learning how to steal one won't necessarily buy the hacker anything.) Using a digital signature helps to keep everyone honest, because it forces everyone to go through a central verification point.

Looking for Digital Signatures

How do you identify someone who has a digital signature versus someone who doesn't? As long as you tell your browser to warn you (the default setting with most products), you'll see some kind of warning dialog box when accessing an insecure site. Likewise, you'll see a Security Warning dialog box like the one shown in Figure 24.4 when accessing a secure site. Make absolutely certain that the date is current and the digital signature belongs to the person or company that you thought it belonged to. If you want additional information, you can click the link associated with the certificate (NCompass Labs Inc. in the figure) to display the Certificate Properties dialog box shown in Figure 24.4. This dialog box provides detailed information about the certificate holder as well as the authority that issued the certificate.

Figure 24.4.
*The first time you
visit a site that has a
digital signature, your
browser should
display a dialog box
showing it to you.*

Notice that the Security Warning dialog box gives you the option to always trust this publisher. Checking this check box adds a particular company to the list checked by WinVerifyTrust—this is a special API function designed to check the security of the certificate. If you check this box, you won't be asked each time you request a download from that particular vendor.

Obtaining a Digital Signature

Just as you want to know who you're dealing with, people are going to want to know who you are. For that reason, VeriSign (and any other digital signature providers that may be around when you read this) provides a way for you to get a digital signature as well. All you need to do is visit its Web site at `https://digitalid.verisign.com/`. (You'll see a Security Information dialog box saying that you're about to request a secure document when you visit the site—don't worry about clicking Yes.)

> **Tip:** You can always tell when you're making a secure transmission by looking for special icons provided by your browser. Internet Explorer shows a lock near the center of the status bar. Navigator shows a key on the left side of the status bar. The more teeth in the key, the higher the security level (although the most you'll see is two). A missing lock or broken key usually signifies an insecure connection—you'll want to exercise extra caution when transmitting data if you see a missing lock or broken key.

If this is your first time getting a digital signature, you'll want to click the Enroll (Request an ID) button on the initial VeriSign page. This will take you to a Web page where you choose the browser you're using. Click the link associated with your browser and you'll see a Digital IDs for Browsers page. This is where you select the class of digital signature that you want. There are two classes of digital signature from which you can choose. The following list explains what each type provides in the way of security:

- **Class 1.** Provides the user with a unique name and address within a repository. VeriSign (or whatever certificate vendor you choose) will be able to verify that the person and the address go together. The mail-back process is the only verification that VeriSign uses in this case. You have to own an email address to receive the certificate, making it hard for a hacker to obtain a fake certificate. This class of certificate normally costs $9.95 per year to maintain. You can get a 60-day demonstration certificate for free.

- **Class 2.** To obtain a Class 2 certificate, you must provide third-party evidence of your identity. (At the moment, this limits access to a Class 2 certificate to people in the United States.) The big difference between a Class 2 certificate and a Class 1 certificate is that VeriSign actually checks information you provide against a consumer database maintained by EquiFax. You'll also go through a hardware-signing process, which requires multiple keys instead of one. This class of certificate costs $19.95 per year to maintain.

At this point, you select one of the two classes of digital signature (certificate). The next thing you see is an identification page.

The form isn't all that difficult to figure out. All you need to do is type in a first and last name. You must supply an email address—that's how your certificate is issued. After you fill in this minimal information, you need to decide whether to include your email address as part of the certificate. For the most part, you don't have a choice. In many cases, your certificate simply won't be accepted if it doesn't include the email address as part of the package. There may be additional blanks to fill out depending on the class of certificate you choose. The final blank is a challenge phrase. I prefer to look at this as a password. You'll definitely want to choose something out of the ordinary, because VeriSign will use the challenge phrase when you need assistance with your certificate. If you choose to get a full certificate, you'll need to provide some payment information. Only the 60-day demonstration version of the certificate is free. You'll also see an agreement for using the certificate on the bottom half of the page.

There's an Accept button at the bottom of the page. Click it and you'll see a Check Your Email page. This page tells you that you provided all of the requested information. The email you'll receive contains a link to the Web site where you download your digital signature. It also contains a special PIN (personal identification number) that you have to use at the download site.

After you have your PIN, follow the link to the Web page. Simply copy the PIN number you received in your email, and then paste it into the blank provided. Click Submit. After a few minutes you'll get a Success page. Make absolutely certain that you don't disturb the browser during this period of time. Simply wait for the transaction to complete. Click the Install button at the bottom of the page to complete the process. You see a simple message stating that your digital signature has been installed.

The Cookie Monster

If you spend very much time in some of the browser-oriented newsgroups on the Internet, you'll hear some talk about cookies. What precisely is a cookie? It's a small file on your local hard drive with configuration information to which a Web site can write.

Normally you find this file in a special directory that you can monitor, and the Web site uses it for things like your name and site preferences. However, there aren't any real limitations on what kind of information a Web site can write to the cookie, and that can create problems. For example, what would prevent a Web site from writing executable code to the cookie and then fooling the operating system into executing it? This particular problem actually occurred, but fortunately the results were more along the lines of a bad joke than actual damage to the system. It could have been different, though, and that's why people are concerned about cookies.

There are two approaches taken regarding the storage of cookies. The Netscape Navigator approach is to place all the cookies in one file named COOKIES.TXT in the Navigator folder. You can examine this file if you'd like, but make sure that you don't change anything it contains. The disadvantage to the Navigator approach to cookies is that you have to erase the entire file to get rid of an offending site. On the other hand, this approach is very space-efficient and it's easy to locate the file you want.

Internet Explorer stores the cookies in separate files in the Cookies or Temporary Internet Files folder within your main Windows folder. Each cookie is represented by a username followed by an at sign (@), followed by the site name. For example, if a person named Ted visited the `http://www.msn.com` site, MSN would download a cookie to his machine; then he'd have a cookie file named `Ted@MSN` in his Cookies folder. The main advantage to this approach is that each user can have his own configuration settings for the same site, even if they all use the same machine to visit it. In addition, getting rid of the settings for a site you no longer use is as easy as erasing a single cookie file. The disadvantages include inefficient disk use and the fact that some users find it difficult to figure out which cookies to get rid of (if they even know that the Cookies folder exists). Obviously, neither the Internet Explorer nor the Navigator approach is perfect.

The point is that you know where the cookies are stored and how to reject them if so desired. Both Internet Explorer and Navigator provide the means to reject cookies you don't want. In Internet Explorer you use the View | Internet Options command to display the Internet Options dialog box. Select the Advanced page. On that page you'll find a Warn Before Accepting Cookies check box. Normally this check box isn't checked because cookies are a normal part of life on the Internet. Getting to the appropriate option when using Navigator is just as easy. Simply use the Options | Network Preferences command to display the Preferences dialog box. Select the Protocols page. You'll find an Accepting a Cookie check box here that tells Navigator to display a message before accepting a cookie. As in Internet Explorer, this box normally isn't checked.

So, if accepting cookies is a normal part of surfing the Internet, yet accepting them could be dangerous, how do you work with cookies on a daily basis? I normally keep cookies enabled because I'm visiting sites that are business-oriented. I do disable cookies when I visit a small site that I'm not sure of or perhaps a non-business site that I haven't looked at before. Normally cookies are pretty safe, though, so you'll probably want to give them a wide latitude with regard to security. Because this is the only file that a standard Web page can write to, you'll find that most cookies do just what they're supposed to do—store configuration settings. Because the advent of ActiveX controls and Java applets gives more power to hackers who really want to harm your system, I'd spend more time worrying about these potential breaches in your security.

Sandbox Approach Versus Open Access

Security is more complex than it really needs to be right now, because the Internet is going through a lot of changes with regard to capability and flexibility. The two main players in all this are ActiveX controls and Java applets. (Scripting languages also play a role, but they normally interact with ActiveX controls or Java applets.)

Java applets take what's known as the sandbox approach to security—they don't do anything outside the purview of the applet. For example, accessing the hard drive isn't allowed because the applet would have to use the operating system to do so. Some developers complain that the sandbox approach hinders them from writing fully functional applications, and to a certain point they're right. If an applet can't access system resources, it can't really do much more for you from a system level than standard HTML can. On the other hand, many users feel safer knowing that the Java applet they just downloaded won't erase the contents of their hard drive or do something else equally devious.

There's another good reason to use the sandbox approach. It allows a developer to write a single applet that works on a lot of platforms. Because the applet doesn't rely on system services, everything it needs is provided by the Java engine. In other words, a Java applet is self-contained and doesn't really rely on anyone else. (The Java engine is obviously platform-specific.)

Microsoft has taken a different approach with ActiveX. It's actually an extension of OLE technology. Unlike Java applets, ActiveX controls can interact with applications on your machine, access the hard drive, and look into the Registry. This makes ActiveX controls a lot more flexible from the developer perspective. It makes them more useful from the user perspective as well. The problem lies in the level of access that they obtain. An ActiveX control has the same level of access as any other application on your machine. This means that an ill-behaved control could cause more than a little damage. In addition, it means that the user can't simply download a control without thinking about its origins first.

At first glance, it would seem that the division between ActiveX controls and Java applets is pretty clear. You'd accept Java applets if security was foremost on your mind. ActiveX controls would provide added capability, but only if you were willing to accept the consequences of a reduced security net. Let's look at that dividing line, though; it's not as clear as you might think. People have had Java applets use back doors to access the system. There have been a few documented cases where they've actually caused damage. Supporters of Java have stated that these security holes are all sealed up, but how can you be certain?

ActiveX supporters further muddy the waters by stating that an ActiveX control falls under the same guidelines as any OLE control. In addition, the author has to sign the control—showing the user who downloads it who created the control. (You can still download the control if the author doesn't sign it, but both Internet Explorer and Navigator display warnings against this practice.) The use of digital signatures means that you'll always know who created an ActiveX control and can make a reasonable decision about downloading and using it. (Java controls are downloaded automatically— you don't get a chance to review a digital signature for them in advance and very often don't even know who created them.)

The only thing that you can say about the sandbox versus the open approach right now is that neither one offers a clear-cut advantage. About the only thing you can do is watch where you download controls from. If you're uncertain about a site, don't take the risk of using it. Security is a user matter right now. Look before you leap. Make sure that you know who created that Java applet or ActiveX control before letting it run on your machine.

> **Tip:** You can avoid the whole question of downloading Java applets that you don't want by disabling them. Navigator provides this capability on the Languages page of the Preferences dialog box. You access it by using the Options | Network Preferences command. (If you don't want to use ActiveX controls, don't install a plug-in such as NCompass's ScriptActive.) Likewise, you can disable both ActiveX and Java on the Advanced page of the Internet Options dialog box for Internet Explorer. You access this dialog box by using the View | Internet Options command.

On Your Own

Spend some time training the users on your network about security. It's very important that you also take the time to explain what types of passwords are acceptable. Spend a little time with each user who has problems understanding the security plan.

If you're a home user, try setting up a variety of security options on your machine. For example, you might want to create a security profile for young users that gives them access to programs that they can use but removes access to programs that could damage your machine. Try using the System Policy Editor and the other tools described in this chapter to make the process of creating a home security plan easy.

Anyone who uses the Internet for more than just casual browsing should have his or her own digital signature. Use the procedure in the "Obtaining a Digital Signature" section of this chapter to get your own digital signature. Be sure to reread the rest of the section as well. It's always good to know when you can trust the party at the other end of the connection.

Peter Norton®

VII

Trouble-
shooting
Windows 98

25

Software
Problems

Peter Norton®

Microsoft designed Windows 98 with two goals in mind: compatibility and stability. Compatibility is important so Windows 98 can continue running MS-DOS, Windows 3.x, and Windows 95 applications along with the newer Windows 98 applications. Stability means that Windows 98 can run multiple MS-DOS, Windows 3.x, and Windows 95 or 98 applications without crashing.

Unfortunately, trying to remain compatible with older applications while offering stability is an elusive goal, which means Windows 98 could occasionally crash, freeze, or act erratically. Because you're likely to run into problems with Windows 98 eventually, this chapter provides some guidelines and clues for troubleshooting any problems that may appear.

Startup and Configuration Errors

Configuration problems normally manifest themselves in several ways. The most devastating is during system startup when Windows 98 simply stops running.

The other types of configuration problems are a lot more devious. One of the problems I found in this category was my sound board. I couldn't figure out what was wrong. The MIDI Balance setting kept getting out of whack. I made sure I had the correct device driver. I thought there might be a problem in the way the CD software was working, so I disabled it. No luck there, either. After several days of searching, I found that the problem occurred only when I ran a specific version of After Dark. Problems such as these can really make you want to pull your hair out.

Tip: Often one program will overwrite or delete files needed by another program. To help solve this problem, I've made every effort to tell you which files affect what functions.

If you have plenty of disk space, make a zip file (a compressed archive) of all the files in your Windows directories. If anything goes wrong, compare the files in those directories to see what might have changed. If you can't afford to use that much disk space, zip up just your INI files (and also your CONFIG.SYS and AUTOEXEC.BAT files) to save at least that much information about how things were. This won't prevent the problems or even give you copies of the files as they used to be, but at least you'll know which ones were changed. Sometimes that helps point you toward the proper steps to recover from a problem.

Startup Problems

Startup problems are the very worst kind of configuration problem to fix because you can't very easily use the tools that Windows 98 provides to find the problem. What usually happens is that the settings for one or more devices conflict, get lost, or are somehow incompatible with the device you're using.

If you have trouble starting Windows 98, you can often start the machine in Safe mode. This mode starts your machine with the display adapter and the hard drive. It's extremely unlikely that these two devices will have any conflicts. Windows also uses a generic VGA display driver. This will get rid of the rest of your problems. Even if your display driver is somehow corrupted or you've used the wrong settings, the generic VGA display driver will work. Figure 25.1 shows a machine in fail-safe mode. Notice that you'll always know when you're in this mode because Safe mode appears in all four corners of the screen.

Figure 25.1.
It's easy to see when you're in Safe mode.

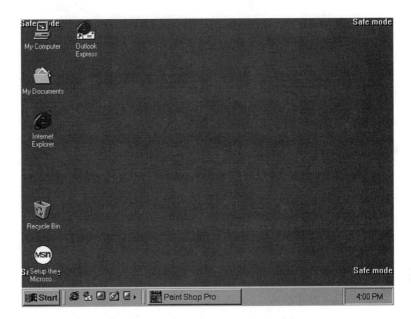

There are two ways to get into this mode. The first is automatic. When Windows 98 detects a problem in booting, it automatically sets the machine up to reboot in Safe mode. Of course, that depends on Windows 98 actually detecting the problem. Sometimes it doesn't. For example, if you make it most of the way through the boot process, Windows 98 might not detect a startup problem. The most difficult situation to detect is a sound board problem because the system is most or all of the way through the boot sequence before a sound board problem occurs. If Windows fails to detect the startup problem, use the manual startup method. You can force a manual Safe mode boot by pressing the F8 key when you boot your machine. Normally, pressing F8 displays a menu. This menu will have one or more entries for Safe mode. The following is a complete list of the items you can expect to find on the boot menu:

- **Normal.** Enables you to boot the machine normally. The only reason you would need this entry is if you pressed F8 by accident during the boot process.

- **Logged (\BOOTLOG.TXT).** The contents of BOOTLOG.TXT can help you determine precisely where the boot sequence is failing. Of course, it takes a little time to analyze the contents of the files. The advantage of this method is that it gives you the best picture of exactly what's going on during the boot process.

- **Safe mode.** This is the entry you would normally select to find boot problems. It starts your machine with the minimum number of devices enabled. Windows 98 doesn't process the contents of CONFIG.SYS or AUTOEXEC.BAT. None of your Startup folder entries will be processed either.

- **Safe mode with network support.** Use this entry if safe-mode startup doesn't really tell you where the problem is and you suspect your network card. Always use this startup after you try Safe mode; otherwise, you can't be certain that the failure isn't being hidden by something else. For example, I had a conflict with my COM port. The fault showed up as a mouse not responding. The COM port didn't show any errors at all. If I hadn't taken the time to really look at what was going on, I could have missed the conflict and replaced my mouse, thinking that it had finally bitten the dust.

- **Step-by-step confirmation.** If you must use real-mode drivers, this option allows you to find a real-mode driver conflict. You can restart your machine several times and tell Windows 98 which device driver to use or exclude from your AUTOEXEC.BAT or CONFIG.SYS files. By doing this multiple times, you can find the one device driver that's causing problems with your Windows setup. Of course, the best way to get rid of these types of conflicts is to get rid of the real-mode drivers so that Windows can help configure your machine.

- **Command prompt only.** Use this option if you need to get to the command prompt to check something out. It does process your CONFIG.SYS and AUTOEXEC.BAT entries, so any real-mode drivers you need will be loaded. This is a great setting to use if you need to install an older DOS application that insists on not having anything else loaded. I also found it handy when installing the NetWare client software.

- **Safe mode command prompt only.** I find this setting handy if I need to get to the DOS prompt for some reason. For example, if a CONFIG.SYS or AUTOEXEC.BAT entry is causing problems, I can get to the DOS prompt, make any required modifications, and reboot the machine. Windows 98 boots to a DOS prompt without processing either CONFIG.SYS or AUTOEXEC.BAT when you select this option.

- **Previous version of MS-DOS.** You'll see this option only if you include the BootMulti=1 setting in MSDOS.SYS. It allows you to boot the previous version of DOS. Of course, this assumes that your previous version of DOS is still available. Removing the previous version should disable this feature. Also remember that some types of installations remove your ability to boot your old version of DOS.

Note: Some MSDOS.SYS settings disable the user's ability to use the F8 key. A network administrator could use this setting to prevent users from circumventing network security. If this happens, you'll need to use your startup disk to start the machine from a floppy. Go to the hard drive and edit the MSDOS.SYS file using a standard text editor. As an alternative, you can edit the necessary settings using the TweakUI utility program from within Windows 98.

Tip: Several other boot modes are available on the F8 boot menu. One of them allows you to boot into MS-DOS mode. This is handy if you need to access a diagnostic program to locate a problem. You can also select which CONFIG.SYS and AUTOEXEC.BAT entries are executed (this works the same as the F8 feature under DOS). You can use this feature to find a real-mode driver or a TSR that might be preventing your system from booting.

After your machine is booted in Safe mode, start looking for hardware or software conflicts. You might want to begin by removing all the applications and data files from your Startup folder. Also check WIN.INI to make sure that there are no LOAD= or RUN= lines in it. Go ahead and comment out any lines you find so that the application won't run the next time you start Windows. After you make sure that all the conflicts are resolved, start your machine again.

Hardware Configuration Problems

Hardware-specific configuration problems are fairly easy to find because Windows makes most of them pretty obvious. All you need to do is right-click the My Computer icon. Look at the Device Manager page of the System Properties dialog box to see whether there are any conflicts. (Chapter 13, "Exploring Your Hardware," covers the ways you can use this dialog box.) Look for conflicting devices and change their settings as required. Windows 98 displays the conflicting device as shown in Figure 25.2.

In most cases, you can figure out the cause of the conflict by looking at the Resources page, shown in Figure 25.3. Notice that this particular page lists one conflict, but there could just as easily be three or even four conflicting devices. You need to clear the ones that Windows 98 detected the first time around to see whether there are others.

Figure 25.2.
Hardware conflicts that Windows 98 can detect are pretty easy to find.

Figure 25.3.
IRQ conflicts are the most common hardware configuration problem.

The problem with some hardware conflicts is that you might not see them immediately. If Windows 98 doesn't manage a particular device, it might not know that a conflict exists. Any device that requires a real-mode device driver to operate generally falls into this category. What this means is that you'll need to find the configuration problem by scanning through the documentation that came with all the pieces of hardware in your system, looking for the DMA channels, IRQ lines, and port addresses they use. Then you'll have to manually set them to nonconflicting values.

Another problem could occur if Windows 98 provides a generic driver for a specific device, and the vendor introduces a version of that device that conflicts with the driver. For example, there's only one driver for the Pro Audio Spectrum 16 Plus sound card, but there are four revisions of that board and even more of that driver. The revision that you use could make a difference in how compatible the device driver and board really are.

Some problems occur when you use what should be a perfectly good driver and it turns out to conflict in some way with Windows 98. For example, the Windows 95 drivers provided with many television tuner boards like ATI's All-in-Wonder won't work under Windows 98 because of the change to the WDM. You'll need to make sure the vendor provides Windows 98–specific drivers for many devices.

Even more problematic is if you think you disabled a device feature, but really didn't. Take another look at that Pro Audio Spectrum sound board. It includes a game port that doesn't work well on high-speed machines. You might disable the game port and use those same settings for an adjustable game port. What happens, though, if the driver fails to do its job properly? I actually ran into this problem. The only solution was to reinstall the driver, but I was probably lucky in this case. Even if Windows thinks it has disabled a specific feature, you might want to view it as a potential area of conflict.

There are some problems that fall into the class of being merely inconvenient rather than show stoppers. For example, if you're using multimonitor support, you may run into a situation where the display adapter that you want to use for the primary display won't start first. Some people have gotten around this problem by swapping the primary and secondary display adapters in their machine, but this won't necessarily work all of the time.

Windows Software Configuration Problems

There are many ways in which a Windows application configuration can go wrong. For example, have you ever noticed that many applications want to modify your PATH statement in AUTOEXEC.BAT? If you let every application have its way, you'd probably have a mile-long path. Many applications run just fine without a PATH statement. However, there are two different ways in which an application can fail.

I ran across the first problem area by accident. I added the file association required for a new application I installed. Whenever I double-clicked a data file, though, I got a message that the application couldn't find the data file. The application started just fine, but it wouldn't load the data file. After a few hours of troubleshooting, I found that I could get rid of the problem by adding the application's location to my path.

Some applications fail in a big way if you don't add them to the PATH statement. CA-Visual Objects and some other large applications fall into this category. They usually provide some nebulous error message and quit before you can get them going. Or the application will load and then refuse to load any add-ons because it can't find them. You might see symptoms of this problem when an application refuses to maintain the settings you save from session to session. Whenever you're in doubt, try adding the application to your path statement to see if the problem goes away.

Corruption of DLL or other shared files is another problem area. The DLL might not actually contain any bad data. It might work just fine with several other applications. However, one application might require an older version of the DLL because it uses an undocumented feature of that DLL or makes use of some bug to its advantage. Sometimes you'll need to keep the old version of a DLL on disk to satisfy the needs of a particular application.

What happens if one application needs the new version of the DLL and another application requires the old version? Unless one or both applications keep their own version of the shared DLL in their own separate directory (which is a regrettably uncommon practice), you must make a decision about which application to keep. In most cases, I use this situation as an excuse to upgrade my software. There usually isn't any reason to keep an old application around if it refuses to work with all your newer applications. In fact, an incompatibility of this type usually means that it's really time to retire that old application and get the newer version.

If you thought Windows software had a lot of failure points, MS-DOS applications are even worse. An application that assumes that it has the machine to itself, combined with users who keep asking for better performance, creates a situation in which the programmer is going to access the hardware directly in ways that the programming community as a whole would never recommend. Users are always demanding faster games with better graphics and sound, yet they want to run these programs on very outdated hardware. The game programmers usually have to resort to register-level programming to get the speed that the user wants. Of course, this usually means that any mistake in programming will result in a frozen machine or worse.

Applications that fall into this category can be fixed in only one way: You have to run them in MS-DOS mode. The thing to remember is that running an application in MS-DOS mode means that you can't allow it to interact with any of your other applications. Using MS-DOS mode is the very last alternative you should try.

If MS-DOS mode is the last resort, what should you try first? I usually look at the application settings to see whether I can find and fix any potential problems. Here's one scenario: You have a game program that always freezes when you run it in Windows, but it works fine from the DOS prompt. What's the problem? I found several settings-related problems that can wreak havoc with a game. For example, you can't assume that the sound board settings you use in DOS are the same ones that Windows uses. Checking all your settings is an important part of getting a DOS application to run.

There are other settings-related problems as well. For example, many of my games require that I add a Sound Blaster setting to my AUTOEXEC.BAT. They read this setting and configure themselves appropriately. If you don't include the SET statement, the game freezes because it doesn't know what settings to use.

Most DOS applications are very sensitive to the environment settings. Compilers are the worst culprits in this area, but other applications can be quite challenging as well. It's usually a good idea to run every application that requires a complex environment setup from a batch file. Add all the required environment settings to the beginning of the batch file and make running the application the last step. You might have to change the program's environment size setting to make this work. See Chapter 12, "Exploiting Your Software: DOS, 16-Bit, and 32-Bit Applications," for more details on the DOS application memory settings.

When you get past settings and strange hardware access problems, you might face a few other problems. One of the big problems is a lack of conventional memory as explained in Chapter 12. Get rid of unneeded TSRs and device drivers. You can save a lot of memory by getting rid of TSRs such as DOSKey. Installing it as part of a batch file from any DOS sessions you start makes more sense. It also makes sense to get rid of ANSI.SYS, because you no longer need it. Windows 98 provides this functionality for you automatically, so loading an additional device driver doesn't make sense.

Memory-Related Problems

You could have quite a few memory-related problems under Windows 98. They fall into several categories. It's important to know which one you're dealing with before you attempt to fix it. The following list categorizes the various memory-related problems you could have when using Windows 98. Go through the list to see whether you can find the symptoms that match your particular problem.

- **Real-mode memory manager conflict.** Some memory managers, such as 386MAX and QEMM, could cause problems when you're using Windows 98. The benefit of using them is a few additional kilobytes of conventional memory. Admittedly, they do a better job in this area than Windows 98 does. The problem is that you now have two very different memory managers fighting for control of the machine. The loser is always the user. Some of the symptoms of this type of problem are a failure of Windows 98 to boot, a sudden freeze-up of the machine, or abnormal device problems such as errors in displaying data. If you experience this problem and your application really needs the additional conventional memory, consider creating an MS-DOS mode setup for using the memory manager with that particular application.

- **Memory leaks.** A few Windows applications don't manage memory properly. They grab a lot of memory from Windows, and then don't release all of it when they terminate. The result is a gradual loss of memory capacity that you can actually track by using the memory field of the application's Help About dialog box. You'll also notice that your other applications start to slow down after a while, as the system starts using a larger swap file to make up for the memory loss. If you have an application that shows a gradual loss of memory, the best way to use it is to start it once and leave it open the entire time you need to use it. Such an application will still bleed memory from the system, but the loss is more gradual if you don't open and close it very much. Eventually you'll need to reboot the system.

- **Too many frills.** Some types of memory problems are created when you have too many frills on your machine. You might find that your machine runs very slowly or displays UAEs (unrecoverable application errors) after you add a screen saver or another frill to the system. Most people associate utilities with small memory requirements, but this isn't necessarily true. You'll find that many DOS applications had to stay small to keep their conventional memory requirements to a minimum. Windows utilities have no such limitation. Their designers have fewer reasons to keep their applications small, because Windows is designed to allow for better memory management. As a result, I have one screen saver that actually grabs an entire megabyte on my system and more than a few percentage points of system resources as well.

- **Windows system space corruption.** I find it incredible that some vendors put so little effort into testing their products that this type of problem could actually go unnoticed. What usually happens is that an errant pointer in the application starts overwriting the Windows system area. Most of the time, Windows 98 detects this problem and displays an appropriate message. It recovers by terminating the application. On a few occasions, Windows 98 won't detect the problem and simply freezes. In most cases, you'll want to contact the vendor about this and see if a workaround or fix is available.

- **Disk thrashing.** If you try to use an application that your system can't really support, you might experience something called disk thrashing. You'll know your system is thrashing if the hard disk light stays on for abnormally long periods of time and the application runs really slowly. The only way to fix this problem is to add more memory. Of course, you could also look at some of the memory-saving techniques discussed in Chapter 5, "Performance Primer."

- **Display memory corruption.** Some older Windows applications might experience problems when writing to the display. One of these situations occurs when one application changes the palette (the display colors) without regard for any other applications running on the system. Although the application window probably looks fine, everything else around it uses really strange color combinations that might produce unreadable text. The big problem occurs when an application leaves the display in this state, even after it exits. You might see other forms of display corruption as well. For example, it's possible for an application to corrupt the icon cache. Icons no longer match the associated functions, or might disappear altogether. The fix is to exit the application and reboot the system, but that doesn't always work. If you find that the problem persists, you might have to erase the ShellIconCache file in your main Windows 98 folder and reboot the machine again. The ShellIconCache file contains an archive of the most recently used icons. Windows 98 loads this file when it starts, to reduce the time it spends reading the icons from disk. Some types of corruption become embedded in this file when Windows exits with a corrupted icon cache in memory.

There are probably other ways to corrupt memory. For example, Windows 98 uses other cache files. Any of these caches could become corrupted and cause problems for your system. You'll need to spend some time looking for the particular cache files on your system. In addition to the ShellIconCache, I also had a TTFCACHE and a FRMCACHE.DAT file on my system. TTFCACHE affects the fonts listed in the Fonts folder. You might find that the fonts listed no longer match the fonts actually in the directory, if certain types of memory corruption occur. The same holds true for the

FRMCACHE.DAT file. Any type of cache corruption is easily cured by erasing the corrupted file and allowing Windows 98 to rebuild it during the next boot cycle.

After you identify and clean up a memory corruption problem, it's usually a good idea to find the responsible application. Most memory corruption problems won't simply go away. You'll find that the corruption occurs over and over again—at the very worst possible moment. After you identify the culprit, you usually have to contact the vendor to find out whether a fix is available. If none is available, you need to decide whether to live with the corruption problem or get a new application—one that (you hope) doesn't exhibit the same memory corruption problem.

So how do you find the culprit? You can't simply assume that the culprit is the foreground application; it could be a background application. For that matter, it doesn't have to be an application at all. A device driver could be causing the memory corruption as you use a specific device. A third class of problem is some type of interaction between two applications or an application and a device driver. However, you have to start somewhere, and looking at the applications you have running is a good place to start. You can follow this simple procedure to find many—but not all—of the memory corruption problems on your system:

1. Start a list of potential problem applications. I usually make note of all the applications running when a memory corruption problem occurred. It's also important to make notes on any devices you had running. Of course, some devices are always running. It doesn't pay to list those.

2. Run the suspect applications one at a time to see whether you can get the problem to repeat. Be sure to start Windows with a clean Startup folder and no applications loaded using WIN.INI. It's also important to reboot after each test to make sure that you're starting with a clean memory environment.

3. If you still don't find the culprit, go back to your normal setup and try various combinations of applications. You could be seeing some type of interaction problem.

4. Test the various devices on your machine one at a time to eliminate any device drivers.

5. Keep a running list of active applications each time the memory problem appears. Eventually, you'll see a pattern of one or more applications that are always present when the problem occurs. Try loading just this group of applications and see whether you can get the problem to happen again. Keep whittling the list until you end up with one or two applications that won't work together. The solution is to avoid running them at the same time.

6. If you don't see an application pattern emerge, the problem is definitely device-driver oriented. Try disabling one peripheral device at a time to see whether you can find the problem. Don't discount the effects of real-mode drivers on Windows; be sure to check those first.

This kind of testing is time-consuming, but if you do it right you can usually track down a stubborn problem in a matter of days. Unfortunately, memory problems are incredibly difficult to locate in an environment like Windows 98, because so many different things are happening at once. Each application and device driver interact. You'll find that the hardest problems to find are those that result from three or four applications or device drivers working against each other. It always pays to take your time and do a thorough job of testing each potential problem area.

Of course, when you come to a conclusion, finding a permanent fix could prove to be the most difficult part of the journey. You've probably gone through this before—waiting on the phone as each vendor points the finger at someone else. The reality of the situation is that there might not be an easy fix for some types of memory problems. You might just have to avoid the situations that cause them in the first place, get a newer version of the same application, or even go so far as to update your hardware.

Using the New Windows 98 Problem Resolution Utilities

Windows 95 was the first version of Windows to provide both an application-friendly environment and one that was fairly bullet-proof when it came to errant applications. However, there were still problems that you could run into, especially with older applications that insisted on doing things their way.

There isn't any way to solve all these problems unless you want to create an application-hostile environment such as Windows NT. However, Windows 98 solves at least some of these by providing some new utility programs that make it easier to recover from the damage caused by errant applications. The following paragraphs provide an overview of each of these utility programs and tell you how you can use them to make your Windows 98 installation just a bit better.

System File Checker Utility

There are two tasks that you can perform using the System File Checker. The first is to scan your system files for errors. The second task is to extract files from an installation disk. These files must use the Microsoft CAB file format if you want to extract them by using the System File Checker. Of course, everything from Microsoft uses CAB files and many other vendors use them as well.

Figure 25.4 shows the main dialog box that you'll see when you start the System File Checker. (You can access System File Checker as a separate utility or from the Tools menu of the Microsoft System Information utility.) Notice that there are two options, along with a Settings button.

Figure 25.4.
*System File Checker
enables you to scan
for damaged files or
extract new ones.*

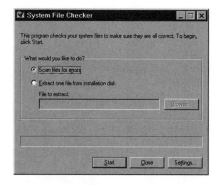

To scan for damaged files, select the Scan files for errors option, and then click Start. You'll see a progress bar as System File Checker counts the number of files on your system and checks them for errors. If System File Checker finds that a file is either missing or corrupted, you'll see a dialog box similar to the one shown in Figure 25.5. In this case, there's a corrupted file and you're offered a choice of updating the verification information, restoring the original file, or ignoring the problem. After you fix the problem, System File Checker will resume the scan. You'll see a Finished dialog box when System File Checker is completely finished looking at your system.

Figure 25.5.
*You'll get to choose
from one of several
options for correcting
any problems found
by System File
Checker.*

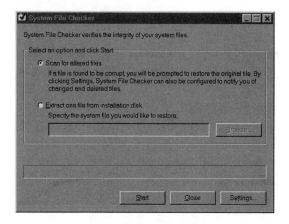

Extracting a file is easy. Simply select the Extract one file from installation disk option. Either type the name of the file that you want to extract or use the Browse button to find it. Click Start and you'll see an Extract File dialog box, shown in Figure 25.6. Type a source location name (or use the Browse button to find it) in the Restore from: Field. Do the same thing for the Save file: in field. Click OK to complete the process.

Normally you won't need to perform a lot of setup with System File Checker, but it does pay to spend some time customizing it for your needs. Click the Settings button and you'll see a System File Checker Settings dialog box like the one shown in Figure 25.7.

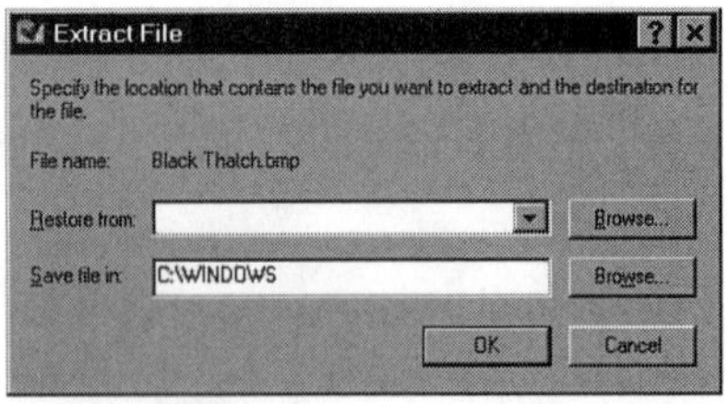

Figure 25.6.

Use the Extract File dialog box to define where you want to get a file from and where you want to send it.

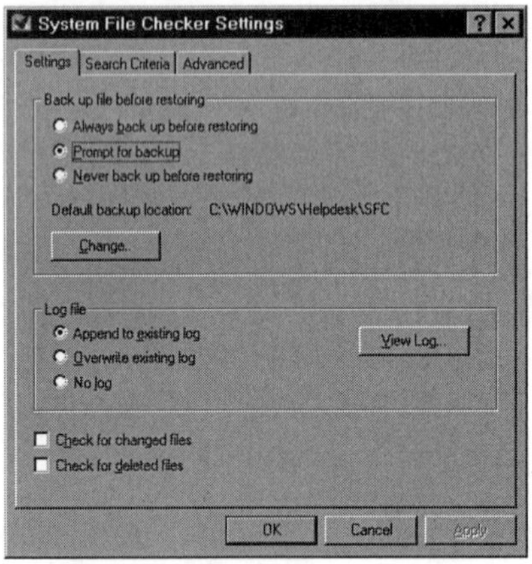

Figure 25.7.

The System File Checker Settings dialog box enables you to customize your settings.

The Settings tab, shown in Figure 25.7, enables you to define how files are restored and how to maintain the log. The default backup setting tells System File Checker to always check before creating a backup of the file you want to restore. You also have two automatic options: not to create a backup at all or to always create a backup. You'll want to use the Never back up before restoring option with extreme care because you never know when you'll need to get a particular file to maintain compatibility with an application that needs it. System File Checker doesn't differentiate between corrupted files and those that are simply out of date.

System File Checker also appends to the current log by default. This can chew up a lot of disk space if you're not careful. I'd never go without a log, but at the same time, I don't feel a need to maintain the log from session-to-session, so I normally use the Overwrite existing log option. You can use the View Log button to see if there are any worthwhile notes in the log at the end of each session. Because System File Checker uses Notepad to display the log, you can always save it under a different name if you want to save the contents of a log file.

Notice the two check boxes at the bottom of the dialog box. The first, Check for changed files, tells System File Checker to alert you to files that are changed in any way. Normally, this tells you which files have changed since you last scanned the system, but this check could also alert you to potential virus activity. Likewise, the Check for deleted files option tells you which files have been removed from the system since you last checked. Normally, you'll find files have been deleted as the result of removing an application, but the loss of a file could also signal some other system damage.

The Search Criteria tab, shown in Figure 25.8, enables you to define what directories are searched and what files to look for. I've found that the default search criteria provided by System File Checker are enough to maintain most of the applications on my system. However, if you're using custom applications or have applications that store all their important files in the application directory, you may want to add new directories or file types to search.

Figure 25.8.
The Search Criteria tab helps you define where and what to check.

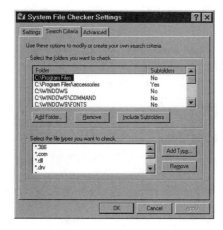

The Advanced tab is used to create different verification data files for System File Checker on this tab. In essence, a verification data file tells System File Checker what settings to use on a particular occasion. The default file is DEFAULT.SFC, but you can choose any name you like.

Microsoft Maintenance Wizard

To get optimal performance from Windows 98, you need to tune the system to your specific usage patterns by using the Microsoft Maintenance Wizard.

When you start Microsoft Maintenance Wizard, you'll see a dialog similar to the one shown in Figure 25.9. Notice that you have two tuning options to choose from. The Express option assumes that you want to tune your entire system. The Custom option enables you to fine-tune specific areas of your system.

Figure 25.9.
The Microsoft Maintenance Wizard enables you to find-tune system performance.

Let's look at the Custom tuning option because the Express option is similar (just shorter):

1. Select Custom, and then click Next. You'll see a Select a Maintenance Schedule dialog box. This is where you'll choose when Microsoft Maintenance Wizard does its work. The three predefined times are: Nights (midnight to 3 a.m.), Days (noon to 3 p.m.), and Evenings (8 p.m. to 11 p.m.) You can also choose to use a custom time.

2. Select a tune-up schedule option, and then click Next. You'll see a Start Windows More Quickly dialog box. This dialog box lists all the applications that start automatically. Because your system may not need all these applications, you can choose to bypass starting some of them. Not only will this reduce the time required to start the system, but increase the memory available for getting the tune-up process going faster and more efficiently.

3. Uncheck any applications that you don't need during the tune-up process, and then click Next. You'll see the Speed Up Programs dialog box. There are two options on this dialog box. The first tells Microsoft Maintenance Wizard to defragment your hard drive automatically. The second says you don't want to defragment your hard drive. Notice the Reschedule button on this dialog box. Click this button and you'll see a Reschedule dialog box like the one shown in Figure 25.10. As you can see, this dialog box enables you to create a custom schedule for performing this task.

Figure 25.10.
Microsoft Mainte-
nance Wizard enables
you to create a
custom schedule for
each task.

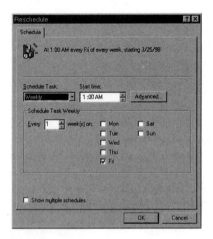

4. Select the desired Speed up programs options, and then click Next. You'll see a Check Hard Disk for Errors dialog box. As with the Speed Up Programs dialog box, you can choose whether to scan your hard disk for errors and create a custom schedule if so desired.

5. Select the Check hard disk for errors options that you want, and then click Next. You'll see a Delete Unnecessary Files dialog box. Like the previous two task-related dialog boxes, you can choose when or if you want to delete unneeded files on your system. However, this dialog box also requires that you choose which files to delete. To do that, click the Settings button to display the Disk Cleanup Settings dialog box shown in Figure 25.11. The Disk

Cleanup Settings dialog box contains a list of file types that Microsoft Maintenance Wizard can remove from your system. Just check the boxes for each type of file you want to get rid of (in some cases, like the Recycle Bin, you'll choose a location and all the files in that location will get removed).

Figure 25.11.
You need to define which files to remove automatically using Microsoft Mainte-nance Wizard.

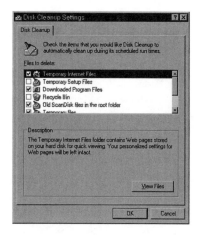

6. Select the desired Delete unnecessary files options, and then click Next. At this point you'll see a summary of the tune-up options that you've selected similar to the dialog box shown in Figure 25.12. Notice the check box near the bottom of the dialog box. It allows you to run all the applications you've selected an initial time so that you can start experiencing the benefits of a tuned system immediately.

Figure 25.12.
This summary dialog box tells you which options you've chosen.

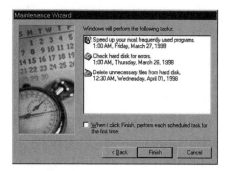

7. Click Finish to complete the process. Windows will now tune your system to your specifications at the times you've defined.

Microsoft System Information Utility

When you need to know detailed information about your system, you can use the Microsoft System Information utility. This utility provides an Explorer-like interface, as shown in Figure 25.13, that contains the information about your system.

Figure 25.13.

The Microsoft System Information utility provides most of the information you'll need to answer technical support questions.

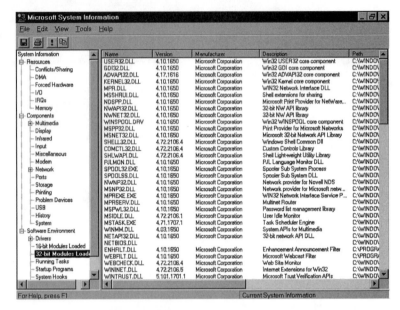

Figure 25.13 shows one of the more useful displays that you can get from this utility. Notice that Microsoft System Information not only provides the names of all of the modules currently running on your machine, but provides a version number, manufacturer name, file description, and location on the hard drive. What this means to you as a user is that you won't have to spend a lot of time trying to look for a file anymore—you'll know precisely where to find it.

Don't get the idea that Microsoft System Information is a software only tool. It works equally well with hardware and the network as well. In fact, you'll find a lot of Registry information here as well and in a format that you can actually read.

On Your Own

Reboot your machine and press F8. See which menu settings discussed in this chapter are present. If you don't see all eight options, find out why. Check your MSDOS.SYS file to make sure that you can access this important feature when needed, if the F8 key doesn't work. You might want to check with your network administrator regarding company policy for this particular setting.

Look at the Device Manager page of the System Properties dialog box to familiarize yourself with its contents. Chapter 14, "Exploiting Multimedia and Games," discusses this feature, but it's a good idea to know what this particular display can do for you. It's one of the major troubleshooting aids that Windows 98 provides.

If you have an MS-DOS application, try to make it run under Windows. You might find that the sound board or other device settings that you're using don't match those used by Windows. If there's a conflict, try changing the DOS application settings to those used by Windows to see whether that enables you to run the application normally. Also check for environment settings that could affect your ability to use the application from within Windows.

Try one or more of the special utility programs provided with Windows 98 to make your system run faster or to correct damage caused by errant applications. Try running the System File Checker Utility to make sure you don't have any system file damage.

26

Hardware Problems

Peter Norton ®

Although hardware problems are generally less of an issue than software problems under Windows 95 (or any operating system, for that matter), they do exist. These problems usually fall into two easily recognized categories:

- **Catastrophic.** You can quickly determine that a catastrophic failure has occurred because the device in question no longer works. For example, you try to access a hard or floppy drive and nothing happens, or your modem picks up the phone line but refuses to dial. Figuring out the sources of these problems is easy; fixing them is even easier (albeit expensive).

- **Compatibility.** A common symptom of compatibility problems is that the device appears to have failed, but later testing shows that it hasn't. You've seen some fixes for this type of problem in Chapter 14, "Exploiting Multimedia and Games"; you'll find that these problems are easy to trace and fix under Windows 95.

When All Else Fails...A Look at HelpDesk

Part of the problem with fixing Windows-related hardware problems in the past was that hardware evolves at a fairly fast rate. By the time Microsoft developed help files and sent out a new version of Windows, at least part of the information was already out of date. That isn't going to be the case nearly as often with Windows 98, because you now have three levels of help to choose from in Windows.

The Web Resources and Contact a Support Engineer options both make use of the Internet as a means for giving the most up-to-date information about both hardware and software problems. The following sections tell you how to use each form of help.

Using Web Resources

Clicking the Web Resources link in HelpDesk opens the Microsoft Contact Manager, which in turn takes you to the Microsoft Technical Support page on the Internet (http://www.microsoft.com/WindowsSupport/). Figure 26.1 shows a typical example of what you'll see, although this page changes on a regular basis.

The first thing you'll notice is a search engine geared to help you find information on Microsoft's Web site quickly. Just type in a keyword and then click the Search button. If you do want to check the entire support site, check the Search Entire Support Site check box.

You'll also see links to various support sites that Microsoft wants to highlight for a specific reason. The following list tells you about some of the support sites that you'll see links for on a regular basis.

Figure 26.1.

The Microsoft Technical Support page on the Internet enables you to find the help you need fast.

- **Knowledge Base.** With so many Windows users in the world, the chances of you finding something truly unique are fairly small. The Knowledge Base is Microsoft's method for storing all of the information it has gathered about problems in the past. In many cases, you'll be able to find a solution to your problem just by searching the Knowledge Base.

- **Frequently Asked Questions.** There are some problems that are so common that Microsoft has written a special FAQ (Frequently Asked Questions) sheet about them. In many cases, you'll find a solution to common problems here. If you don't find what you need, you can always look through the Knowledge Base for help.

- **Help Files.** There really isn't any way to keep your local help files up-to-date because of the fast pace of change in the computer industry. However, Microsoft can at least keep pace with the change. Downloading the latest help files is one way you can ensure you have the latest information at your fingertips and on your local hard drive.

- **Service Packs.** There may or may not be a service pack available for Windows 98 when you read this. You can be sure, though, that sometime in the near future Microsoft will have to release one. A service pack could contain something as simple as new drivers for your hardware, or as critical as a patch for a security problem that someone found, or as necessary as a bug fix for the operating system itself. Whatever the reason, you'll want to check here for the latest service packs.

- **Newsgroups.** There are a lot of experts out there who willingly share their knowledge with others through the newsgroups. Going to a newsgroup and asking a question could net you the solution you need to a really hard problem. You might also find that you can help a fellow user find the solution to her problem as well.

- **Telephone Numbers.** There are some situations that call for human contact. Microsoft wants you to find the person you need to talk with as quickly as possible. This link takes you to a list of common Microsoft phone numbers.

Using Contact a Support Engineer

Sometimes you can't solve a problem on your own. No matter what you try in the Microsoft Knowledge Base, a particular problem might prove too difficult to solve (or it may be that no one has encountered the problem before and you need special help to get it resolved). That's when you need to contact a Support Engineer.

Clicking the Contact a Support Engineer link takes you to a Microsoft Bug Reporting Tool dialog box like the one shown in Figure 26.2. This dialog box enables you to enter a text description of your problem and a specific fault area for the problem, such as printing. After you complete the form, send it to the support engineer by clicking the Submit button. The support engineer will contact you by phone or email.

Figure 26.2.
Getting help from a Microsoft Support Engineer means filling out a bug report and waiting for confirmation through email or a phone call.

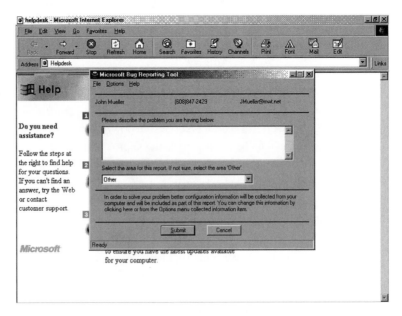

Make sure you provide the support engineer with everything needed to solve your problem, including what applications were running, what you were doing at the time the problem occurred, the version of the hardware that you need help with, and any drivers you have loaded. The more information you can provide, the faster you'll get accurate help.

A Quick Look at Catastrophic Failures

Figuring out a catastrophic error usually takes a little time and a few hardware and software tools. Here's a typical scenario: You start your machine in the morning and Windows 98 comes up fine, but you can't use the mouse. If there aren't any conflicts and you haven't installed anything new recently, the most probable cause is some type of hardware failure.

All kinds of problems fall into the catastrophic category. For example, severely crimping a cable (putting an obvious dent in it) will normally cause some type of hardware failure. It might be as simple as a device that won't respond or a network connection that works intermittently. Port failures don't happen often, but they do happen. You'll also find that NICs fail from time to time. And everyone knows that hard drives fail.

Part of the problem for a network administrator or a home user is locating the source of the problem. You could try replacing one component at a time until you locate the problem. However, using diagnostic aids and other troubleshooting tools will save you a lot more time than they cost. It's also a lot less expensive to find the right component the first time and replace it.

> **Tip:** Most sound-board and display-adapter vendors include a complete diagnostic for their product as part of the package. Some hardware vendors are starting to include this feature as well. I even found one motherboard vendor—Hauppauge—that provides a diagnostic disk with its products. The diagnostic tests basic motherboard functionality and any installed memory.

The following sections aren't designed to be an inclusive list of every tool that you'll ever need, but you might find that they provide just enough help so that you can get through a repair with a minimum of effort.

> **Peter's Principle:** Using a DOS-Based Versus a Windows-Based Diagnostic Program
>
> You can rely on most Windows diagnostics to provide very useful and easy-to-read information. They also find a great majority of the hardware problems you could experience.
>
> However, there isn't any reliable way to completely test your hardware from within Windows. The multitasking nature of the operating system makes this impossible. Some diagnostic programs need total access to the hardware as well, and Windows won't allow
>
> *continues*

this kind of access. Many diagnostic tools don't require Windows at all; others run from the DOS prompt, where they have better control over the hardware.

There's another problem with Windows diagnostic programs—something that won't occur to most people until it's too late. What happens if you can get DOS up and running, but a hardware conflict or failure prevents Windows from starting? I've had this particular problem more than a few times. Using a DOS diagnostic means that if the system will boot at all, you can at least figure out what's going on.

If you're going to rely on only one diagnostic program, choose a DOS-based one and use a Windows-based one to supplement the DOS-based diagnostic.

Note: Although you could probably run DOS diagnostic products from within Windows, the results you'll get will likely be inaccurate. Always run your diagnostic programs in MS-DOS mode, preferably from the DOS prompt before Windows 98 starts. You can access the Windows 98 DOS prompt by pressing the F8 key and selecting the Safe Mode Command Prompt Only option. Chapter 25, "Software Problems," covers this topic in greater detail.

TouchStone CheckIt

Finding an inexpensive troubleshooting aid can be quite difficult. At about $45 for the DOS or Windows version, CheckIt is more than a hardware inventory program. It also includes a variety of diagnostics, a virus scanner, a hard disk formatter, and a floppy disk alignment checker. In fact, you can place both of the DOS version CheckIt Pro 3.x 360KB floppies on one 1.2MB or 1.44MB disk and have plenty of room left over for the DOS boot file and your network drivers. The latest version, CheckIt 4.0, requires a bit more space, but you can still run it from a set of 1.44MB floppies (one boot, one for CheckIt, and a third for SysTest).

Note: TouchStone has recently come out with the new 4.0 version of CheckIt. This version offers expanded test features that the original product doesn't include. For example, you can use it to test your CD-ROM drive. The amount of memory you can test has also increased, along with the capabilities of just about every other test. I plan to concentrate on the new version of the product in this section. Be sure to contact TouchStone for the updated version at `http://www.checkit.com`. You can also call (714) 374-2801.

CheckIt Pro is the venerable version that most people will recognize—it has been around for a very long time. The latest version of the product includes a much-enhanced version of CheckIt Pro and

WinCheckIt in one package. However, even the original CheckIt (version 3.0) is still good enough for most purposes. We'll see in the sections that follow what the latest version has to offer, since it has been out long enough for most people to get it.

Using CheckIt 4.0

CheckIt, as shown in Figure 26.3, offers four basic tasks that you can perform: Collect Data About Your Machine, Load an Existing Configuration File, Skip the Data Collection Process, or Exit the Diagnostic Program. In most cases, you'll want to select either the Collect or Load option, because there isn't a lot you can do without knowing the configuration of the machine. (The Collect, Load, and Skip options all end up at the testing screen.)

Figure 26.3.
The latest version of CheckIt uses a straightforward front end that makes it easy to figure out what you want to do.

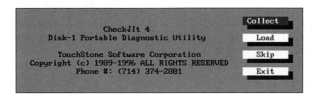

> **Tip:** Unlike its predecessor, CheckIt 4.0 includes a separate burn-in and batch-testing utility named SysTest. It provides a lot more flexibility than the old combined version of CheckIt. The next section looks at this program.

If you do choose to use the Skip option, you go immediately to the testing screen. Fortunately, you can use the options on the File menu to either load or collect data later. Selecting the Load option displays a standard File Open dialog box that you can use to choose an existing configuration file. You have to collect data and save it to disk before this option will work.

The Collect option displays a dialog box like the one shown in Figure 26.4. This is where you choose what to collect and how in-depth to look. There are two or three columns of options for each device on your machine. The eXclude column tells CheckIt not to look at the selected hardware feature. A Standard look provides an overview of hardware statistics such as hard drive settings—CheckIt looks exclusively in the system CMOS for this information. This is the option to use if you have problems when CheckIt takes a look at a specific piece of hardware. You can also use it when an in-depth look at the hardware isn't required. (For example, you might need to know only the basic settings for the hard drive.) Selecting the Advanced option (for devices that provide this option, such as the COM ports) gives you in-depth information about a particular piece of hardware. CheckIt actually tests the hardware to see what it can do. You'll get information such as the IRQ that the hardware actually uses (versus the setting that Windows may think it uses). Getting this information can take quite a bit of time, though, so you'll want to use the Advanced setting with care. In addition, because the Advanced option actually tests the hardware, you might find that there are conflicts with any software you have loaded.

Figure 26.4.

CheckIt enables you to determine how much time you want it to spend collecting data.

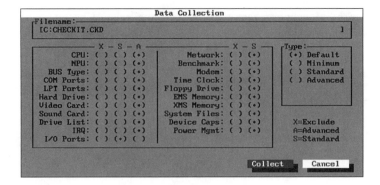

You'll also notice some preset defaults in the Type group. I find that the Standard option provides me with just about everything I need to know on a regular basis, without spending a lot of time to get it. I use the Advanced option if I need to troubleshoot a specific hardware-related problem. In this case, getting all the information you can is a good idea if you don't want to overlook the obvious. The Default setting in the Type group selects a combination of Standard and Advanced options that TouchStone feels most people will need. The Minimum setting obtains the level of information that you absolutely must have to use CheckIt to its fullest potential.

After you choose the level of hardware information you need, click the Collect button. CheckIt displays a series of screens as it checks your hardware. What you'll see next is the testing screen mentioned earlier. Figure 26.5 shows a typical example, although your screen will contain different information than mine. At this point you're ready to use CheckIt for a variety of purposes, such as single-component testing or verifying your hardware settings.

Figure 26.5.

CheckIt provides an overview of the information it collected in the initial testing screen.

```
   File     SysInfo    Tests     About

                      System Summary  (C:\MAINT\CHECKIT.CKD)
                            Collected  12-05-1996  14:14
                            Default Check of System

     OS Version : DOS Version 7.10
      Main CPU : Intel Pentium 166.0MHz
           NPU : Integrated NPU 166.0MHz
    Active Bus : ISA, PCI
  Total Memory : 32MB
 Video Adapter : VESA 1024K VGA Color, Secondary : None

  Floppy Drive : 1.44M(3 1/2")
   Hard Drive : 0: 1622M
    I/O Ports : 3  Serial  1  Parallel
     Keyboard : 101-key Enhanced
        Mouse : No Active Mouse Device Found.
        Sound : Sound Blaster Adlib
       CD-ROM : No Active CD-ROM Device Found.
        Modem : Port Used: COM2 (2F8h)
     FAX Type : CLASS 1
 Network Type : No Network Driver Loaded

           Use Alt+Letter for menu option, Arrow keys, ESC to exit
```

The two menus that we're most interested in are SysInfo and Tests. The SysInfo menu appears in Figure 26.6. It enables you to obtain concise details about the various facts that CheckIt collected about your machine. Figure 26.7 shows an example of what you might see for the modem. Notice that the check not only determines the address of the modem port, it also tells you whether buffers are available (an important consideration in a multitasking environment such as Windows 98). This screen also shows the results of various AT information commands.

Figure 26.6.
You can get information about any part of your system by using the SysInfo menu options.

Figure 26.7.
A typical information display provides every piece of information you need to know about the device in question.

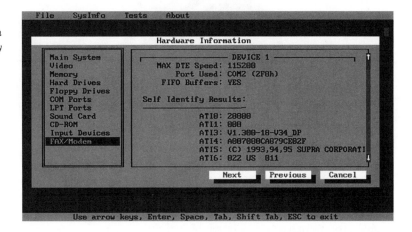

The Tests menu does much as its name implies. It provides a list of tests that you can run by using CheckIt. Figure 26.8 shows a list of the tests that CheckIt currently supports. Notice that along with standard tests like those you'd run on the system board or ports, you can test your CD-ROM drive or modem.

Figure 26.8.
The Tests menu provides a complete list of the kinds of tests that you can run with CheckIt.

Every test on this list is fully configurable. Figure 26.9 shows a typical example. In this case, we're looking at the Memory Test configuration dialog box. Notice that you get to choose the area of memory to test, along with the level of test you want to perform. Unlike the previous version of CheckIt, you can't choose a precise memory range to test. This is one of the few areas where the new version of CheckIt doesn't quite perform as well as its older sibling, but the loss in functionality is minimal.

Figure 26.9.
You need to decide how to run the various diagnostic tests.

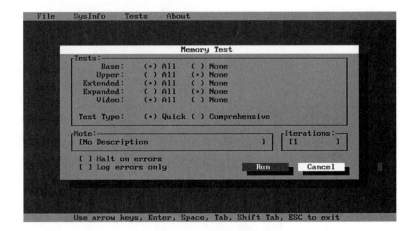

Burn-In and Batch Testing Using SysTest

The CheckIt disks now include a separate batch-testing program named SysTest. Figure 26.10 shows the initial display for this program. The main reason for using this program in place of CheckIt is for burn-in or certification testing. You can also use it to find intermittent problems with hardware. For example, you might have a memory problem that shows up only in certain conditions, or a partially failed part might give you problems. Batch testing can help find it. You might even want to use batch testing to verify that you've completely fixed a problem. There have been a few cases where two bad components caused a system failure and finding the second component proved problematic after fixing the first one.

The menu system for this utility looks a bit more complicated than the one used for CheckIt, but you can break it down into four areas. The File menu enables you to look at reports. It's also where you select a custom batch file that you want to run, or change the location of program output. (You might want to use a printer rather than the screen for batch testing, because the printer can provide a history of each test.)

The next menu entry, Batch Tests, enables you to run and create various kinds of batch and burn-in tests. We'll look at this menu in a few minutes. Suffice it to say that this is the heart of the SysTest utility.

Figure 26.10.
SysTest enables you to perform burn-in, certification, and other forms of batch testing.

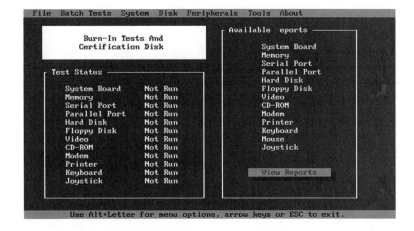

The next set of menu entries includes System, Disk, and Peripherals. These options work much like the Tests menu did for CheckIt. In fact, you'll find that SysTest uses the same configuration menus for the various tests. The only difference is how the tests are arranged on the menu. You use these menu selections if you want to test one hardware item multiple times.

Finally, there's a Tools menu. It enables you to save the contents of your CMOS to disk—a handy feature if you think you might run out of battery backup power sometime in the future (and who doesn't?). You can use this same tool to restore a CMOS configuration file that you've saved to disk. Figure 26.11 shows the Save/Restore CMOS dialog box that you see when using the Tools | Save CMOS command. The Tools menu also contains entries for the RAM Exam utility (an advanced memory-testing program) and Rescue Disk (creates a boot disk that you can use in case of emergency).

Figure 26.11.
The Save/Restore CMOS dialog box enables you to save or restore your hardware configuration settings.

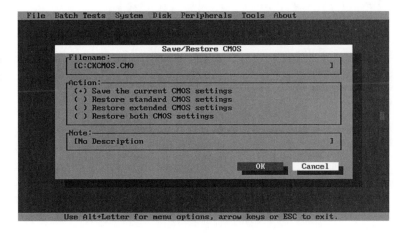

Now it's time to look at the meat-and-potatoes of this utility—the batch-creation utility. You use the Batch Tests | Custom command to display the dialog box shown in Figure 26.12. This is where you decide which tests to run and how. As you can see, there are two option groups. The first group, Select Test, selects a basic test such as the System Board Test. When you select a test, you can choose it in the Configure Test option group. Normally, you'll get a dialog box just like the one shown earlier in Figure 26.9 for the memory test. Notice the FileName field in Figure 26.12. The output of this custom batch-testing process is a .BAT. After you create it, you don't even have to enter SysTest or CheckIt to perform a standard test of your system. Simply type the batch file name at the DOS prompt, and you're ready to go. You lose the capacity to view reports within the CheckIt environment, but you can still use a standard text editor to view the test results file.

Figure 26.12.
Creating a custom batch-testing job results in a .BAT file that you can run from the DOS prompt.

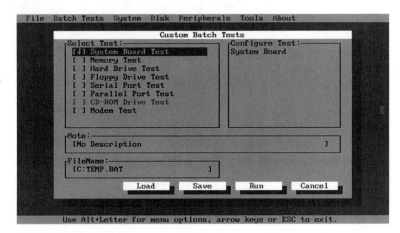

TouchStone WINCheckIt

At $50, WinCheckIt is only slightly more expensive than its DOS counterpart, and you gain the benefit of the Windows interface. In addition, the 4.x version of WinCheckIt provides full 32-bit support and some special Windows 98 features. What you lose in exchange is some of the detailed diagnostics that the DOS version of the product provides.

When you start WinCheckIt for the first time, it does an inventory of your machine. I found that the inventory was fairly complete, but it missed some of my hardware the first time around (a second run of the check found the missing hardware). The program also misinterpreted my network, informing me that I had NetWare installed when I was using Microsoft Network for the purposes of this test. WinCheckIt did figure out what kind of serial ports I had and properly noted that I had one bidirectional parallel port. (You can rerun the inventory any time by clicking the Collect button.)

After WinCheckIt collects all this information, you see a main screen like the one shown in Figure 26.13. Notice the four dial indicators. They tell you about your current resource status, including the swap file usage, CPU usage, free memory, and disk space used. A DOS program wouldn't provide you with this type of information. Then again, you can easily obtain this kind of information from other sources, although in a less user-friendly format. The System Summary information is on par with the DOS version of CheckIt Pro (WinCheckIt doesn't even begin to touch the thoroughness of the CheckIt 4.0 version). Essentially, it tells you what you have installed on your machine in the barest possible terms. I find that this display comes in handy for a quick check of the system. I've been able to fool WinCheckIt in several ways in the past, however. Using some types of communications programs before I run the collection utility, for example, causes WinCheckIt to tell me that I don't have a modem installed. As previously mentioned, it never did figure out what kind of network I had installed.

Figure 26.13.
WinCheckIt provides quick access to its features and gives you a summary of your system's resources.

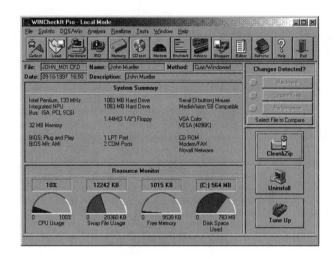

Across the top of the display you'll find some very handy buttons. I'm not going to show you every one of them, but a few deserve special mention. Clicking the CD Test button displays the dialog box shown in Figure 26.14. Notice that this isn't just a CD-ROM drive test; it's an actual check of your machine's capability to run multimedia programs. There are three levels of compliance that you can check, as shown in the figure. My test machine failed the second two Multimedia PC Marketing Council (MPC) compliance tests because of the way that WinCheckIt performed the check. It looked at only my first hard drive partition. Even though the test machine had more than 850MB of drive space available, WinCheckIt reported a mere 60MB—the amount on the first drive partition.

I found that the modem tester provided in this utility far exceeded anything I could find in a DOS utility, except in CheckIt 4.0. Not only does it test local modems, but it can test a remote connection as well. To access this test, click the Modem button. WinCheckIt displays a dialog box that asks whether you want to run a local or a remote test. If you select a remote test, you need to provide a telephone number to access the remote modem. When WinCheckIt completes the test, you see a dialog box like the one shown in Figure 26.15. I found that the report provided by WinCheckIt is superior to the one you can get from Windows 98; the tests are also a little more thorough. (Obviously, Windows 3.x doesn't even provide modem diagnostics.)

Figure 26.14.
You can use WinCheckIt to determine the multimedia status of a workstation.

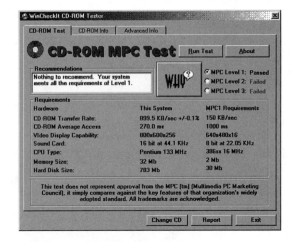

Figure 26.15.
Checking the status of your modem is one of the better features of WinCheckIt.

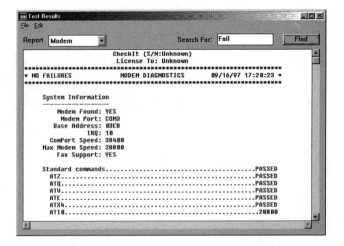

Unlike most of the other features, you'll actually have to use the Tests menu to check a piece of hardware. This menu has a Test Everything option, along with the capability to test separate subsystems. WinCheckIt examines everything you ask it to and then displays a test results window. You can scroll through the entire report or simply select specific subsystems by using the drop-down menu.

WinCheckIt provides a wealth of user-related features that don't have a lot to do with diagnosing hardware problems. The Software Shopper utility is a database of more than 2,000 products. You can use WinCheckIt to compare the capabilities of your system with the needs of the product. WinCheckIt provides a list of any upgrades that you need to make to your system before you can use the software product. Clicking the Benchmark button takes you to a display that enables you to test your system extensively. It also includes the capacity to compare your system to a variety of test systems. This is nice to have, but it's not really essential.

Of all the features that WinCheckIt provides, the Tune-Up button seems the most useless. It's supposed to defragment system memory and enhance performance. The monitor did display a slight improvement on my test systems, but I couldn't see it in any concrete way. Your results might vary from the ones I received, but this particular feature of other programs has certainly received a lot of bad press lately.

What's missing from this program? If you haven't noticed already, I didn't say a word about burn-in tests or any of the other things you'd normally associate with a heavy-duty diagnostic program. You won't find these features in WinCheckIt. Overall, it's a lightweight diagnostic aid at best. You'd probably be better off looking at TouchStone's DOS product if you need something substantial.

Serial and Parallel Port Loopback Plugs

You can't fully test the serial and parallel ports in a workstation without loopback plugs. These plugs pass the signal from the port's output back to its input. To create a loopback plug, you use a blank connector without wires and then connect wires between specific pins. Most of the high-end diagnostic programs you buy (such as PC-Technician, AMI Diags, or the Norton Utilities) provide these plugs. Others, such as CheckIt, don't provide them. However, Touchstone tells you how to build them, and will sell them to you as a separate product.

Tip: The list of modems supported by Windows grows with every release. However, you won't find a NULL modem driver for Windows 98 in the standard list of hardware options. This makes it impossible to create a Dial-Up Networking connection that requires a NULL modem setup. Don't worry, though—you can download a NULL modem driver from `http://www.vt.edu:10021/K/kewells/net/index.html` that works up to 115Kbps.

Table 26.1 provides the pin connections for a parallel port. Every parallel port uses a 25-pin male connector. Another designation for this type of connector is DB25P. You need to create two connectors to test serial ports. There are 9-pin and 25-pin serial ports. Every serial port uses a female connector. The designation for a 9-pin serial port is DB9S. Table 26.2 lists the pin connections for a 9-pin serial port. The designation for a 25-pin serial port is DB25S. Table 26.3 gives the pin connections for a 25-pin serial port. You can find the blank connectors and wire you need at most electronics stores.

Table 26.1. Parallel port (DB25P) loopback plug connections.

First Pin	Connected to Second Pin
11 (Busy +)	17 (Select Input –)
10 (Acknowledge –)	16 (Initialize Printer –)
12 (Paper Out +)	14 (Autofeed –)
13 (Select +)	01 (Strobe –)
02 (Data 0 +)	15 (Error –)

Table 26.2. 9-pin serial port (DB9S) loopback plug connections.

First Pin	Connected to Second Pin
02 (RD: Received Data)	03 (TD: Transmitted Data)
07 (RTS: Request to Send)	08 (CTS: Clear to Send)
06 (DSR: Data Set Ready)	01 (CD: Carrier Direct)
01 (CD: Carrier Detect)	04 (DTR: Data Terminal Ready)
04 (DTR: Data Terminal Ready)	09 (RI: Ring Indicator)

Table 26.3. 25-pin serial port (DB25S) loopback plug connections.

First Pin	Connected to Second Pin
03 (RD: Received Data)	02 (TD: Transmitted Data)
04 (RTS: Request to Send)	05 (CTS: Clear to Send)
06 (DSR: Data Set Ready)	08 (CD: Carrier Direct)
08 (CD: Carrier Detect)	20 (DTR: Data Terminal Ready)
20 (DTR: Data Terminal Ready)	22 (RI: Ring Indicator)

As you can see, the pin connections are relatively easy to make. Whether you buy premade loopback plugs or make your own, this is an essential tool for your toolkit. Without loopback plugs, you'll never know whether the serial or parallel port you tested really works.

Cable Scanner

Network administrators, especially those managing large networks, can spend a lot of time tracing cables. An average cable scanner costs about $1,000, although you can usually find them a little cheaper. Alternatively, you could build your own cable scanner for about $200, using plans in some electronics magazines. For example, *Circuit Cellar INK*'s October/November 1992 issue contains a set of plans on page 22.

One of the better cable scanners on the market is the Cable Scanner from Microtest. (Microtest provides many other cable scanners with more features, but the Cable Scanner model provides the minimum feature set you need to maintain a network.) This product tests for opens, shorts, and improper terminations. It tells you the distance from your current location to the cable fault. In most cases, all you need to do is track the cable for the required distance and you'll find the problem. To help you trace the signal, the main unit outputs a signal that you can pick up on a remote unit. Instead of taking down every ceiling tile in your office, you simply use the remote unit to trace the cable.

You can send the data collected by the Cable Scanner to a serial printer. The unit collects the data, stores it, and enables you to output it later. The Cable Scanner provides both text and graphic output. This is a handy feature for maintaining records on your system. All you need to do is print the results of the cable check and add it to the network documentation.

The Cable Scanner provides a few other unique functions that you might not use very often. For example, it can detect the noise level of the cable on your system. This means that you can reduce the number of packet errors by simply reducing the noise that the packet signal must overcome. You can also interface the Cable Scanner with an oscilloscope. This enables you to actually monitor the signal that flows across the network. An experienced network administrator could use this information to troubleshoot problem installations.

Incompatible Hardware

For the most part, any hardware that runs under the DOS and Windows 3.x environment will also run under Windows 98. Even if you have to use a real-mode driver (which I talk about in the next section), you should be able to use that old device if you really want to. The problems start when you mix that old hardware with new hardware or when the old device uses some of the undocumented features provided by previous versions of DOS.

Windows 98 really does try its best to figure out which interrupts and port addresses are in use, but it doesn't always succeed if you have an eclectic mix of old and new. Older devices often require real-mode device drivers to work at all; that's not a problem. Unfortunately, some of these devices don't register themselves properly. A device driver is supposed to register itself in a device chain and provide certain types of information as part of that registration process. If the device doesn't provide the right level of information, Windows 98 can't detect it. What happens next is inevitable, given such circumstances. If Windows 98 doesn't see the device driver, it might assume that the interrupts and port addresses it uses are free. The result is that you might find two devices trying to share the same interrupt or port address.

Of course, one of the best ways to eliminate some of the problems is to make a checklist of all your hardware and the settings that each device uses. You need to include port addresses, interrupts, and DMA addresses. Physically check the settings on cards that use jumpers. You might want to take this opportunity to physically check your card's BIOS revision. An undocumented update could make a big difference in the settings you need to use with Windows 98. Make sure that you double-check any settings included in CONFIG.SYS or AUTOEXEC.BAT. A software-configurable device always includes the current settings as part of the command line. All you really need to do is get out the vendor manual and determine what the settings mean. Because some device drivers provide a default setting, you need to check for the default if the entry in CONFIG.SYS or AUTOEXEC.BAT doesn't contain a complete list of settings.

After you get all the settings written down, check your list for potential conflicts. Windows 98 might tell you that there aren't any, but it's possible that you'll find some anyway. For example, someone I know recently tried to install Windows 98, but found that he couldn't. The machine he was using included two SCSI adapters. Windows 98 recognized one adapter but not the other. As a result, Windows 98 didn't recognize the CD-ROM drive attached to the second adapter and therefore couldn't install itself properly. Removing the second SCSI adapter and connecting the CD-ROM drive to the first one cleared up part of the problem. At least Windows 98 would install. However, performance on the network was very slow, and the user still experienced some problems. A check of Windows didn't show any device conflicts. However, a physical check of the remaining SCSI adapter showed that it was using the same interrupt as the NIC. (Windows 98 had claimed that the NIC was using interrupt 5 and that the SCSI adapter was using interrupt 3.) Physically changing the SCSI adapter's interrupt setting cleared up the remaining problem.

Sometimes you might not be sure that you got all the settings right during the first check. You can determine the equipment settings by viewing the port and interrupt addresses that a device uses, with MSD or a diagnostic program such as CheckIt. In fact, using this technique coupled with physical inspection of your CONFIG.SYS and AUTOEXEC.BAT will ensure that you have all the settings for each device. Even if there aren't any conflicts, you'll still want to maintain a complete record of your hardware and any real-mode drivers you need to use. Avoiding problems with real-mode drivers starts with the detective work you perform during this phase of the installation. Record real-mode driver settings and then avoid using the address and interrupt, even though Windows 98 says it's free. This also means that you'll have to manually configure your setup, rather than relying on the Windows 98 automatic configuration features.

Tip: Watch out for older plug-in cards and some of the cheaper "no-name" ones. In the early days of PCs, no one used any port addresses above 3FFh, and most cards decoded only the low-order 10 bits of a port address to find out whether a command was intended for that card. Now many cards use higher addresses (all the way up to FFFFh). If you have one of these newer cards and an older one in the same PC, you could run into a very subtle sort

> of problem. If the addresses used by the newer card are the same in the low-order 10 bits as those used by the older card, each card will think that commands meant for the newer card were meant for it. There's no telling what will happen in this case, but it might not be pretty!

Some devices simply won't work with Windows 98. Unlike your old DOS setup, Windows 98 is a lot less forgiving about adapters that try to share the same address or interrupt. You simply can't do this under Windows 98 and expect the device to work. If that device happens to be a hard disk drive controller, you might find it impossible to boot all the way into Windows 98.

Real-mode device drivers will often cause problems too. A well-behaved device driver makes direct access only to the hardware it controls by calling on the ROM BIOS routines for other types of service. An older device might use direct hardware access to other devices as well as the device it controls in order to make the driver faster. Windows 98 normally ignores the device if you try to use a device driver of this type. Sometimes a device driver of this type can actually cause the system to freeze when Windows switches to running a real-mode interrupt service routine. Previous chapters covered many of the architectural aspects of this problem.

Unfortunate as it might seem, an ill-behaved device driver normally looks like a malfunctioning device rather than a piece of software that Windows 98 won't work with. I was surprised when I found myself in this position with an old CD-ROM drive. Fortunately, I was able to get a newer driver that did work from the vendor. This is the solution you should try as well. Many vendors will even enable you to download the upgrade directly from their Web site. They also might make the upgrade available through a commercial information service such as CompuServe or America Online.

Some older devices include their own BIOS. Sometimes the BIOS routines conflict with Windows 98 and cause various types of system failures. Most vendors upgrade their BIOSes as time goes on. They fix bugs and perform some types of optimizations. If you have an older piece of hardware with a BIOS that's causing problems with Windows 98, see whether the vendor has some type of BIOS upgrade that might fix the problem. Installing a new chip is usually cheaper than buying a new peripheral.

By now it should be apparent that hardware incompatibility can cover a lot of ground. Everything from misinterpreted settings to a poorly designed device driver can make it appear that your hardware is incompatible with Windows 98. Let's take a look at the hardware compatibility problem from a procedural point of view:

1. Get into MS-DOS mode and test the hardware to ensure that there's no problem with the device itself. It's important to test the hardware with the same device driver that you plan to use with Windows 98, if you intend to use a real-mode driver for it under Windows 98.

2. Check the device settings to see whether there's a conflict with any of the devices that Windows supports directly. This is especially important when you try to mix older hardware with new Plug and Play–compatible hardware. If Windows insists on using a specific setting for a Plug and Play–compatible board, see whether your old board can use a different set of unused settings.

3. After you determine that the hardware is working and that it doesn't conflict with anything, see whether the vendor documentation provides any insights as to the requirements for using the device driver. For example, you'll probably find that device drivers written to work with versions of DOS prior to 3.3 will have some level of problem with Windows 98. These older device drivers often wrote directly to the hardware and definitely didn't use all the features that newer versions of DOS provide to support device drivers. See whether the vendor can provide a new set of drivers.

4. Check your BIOS revision level. Many adapter cards that have a BIOS extension ROM on them display a version number onscreen during the boot process. With other pieces of add-in or connected hardware, you'll have to determine the revision level in some other way. Vendors provide a variety of ways to detect this information, so you'll have to check your documentation for details about your particular device. My modem uses a Hayes-compatible AT command to display the BIOS revision number. A display adapter I own has an actual program that I run to display the BIOS and setup information. Check with the vendor to see whether a newer version of the BIOS is available. You might have to send the device to the vendor's repair facility to get the BIOS replaced. It depends on the vendor's policy concerning sending BIOS updates to customers.

5. If all else fails, see whether replacing the board with a similar board from another vendor helps. In this way, you might find that a software or other conflict is disguising itself as a hardware problem. For instance, my mouse example at the beginning of this chapter was an example of a problem with a serial port that disguised itself as a faulty mouse. You might find that other types of problems disguise themselves.

Tip: Actually, there's a very easy way to distinguish a serial mouse problem from a serial port problem. To do this, first run a diagnostic on the serial port with a loopback plug installed. If the port passes the test, test the mouse.

Incompatible hardware rarely is incompatible. There's usually some problem that you can define, given enough time and resources. The question that you have to ask yourself is whether that old hardware is really worth the effort. In my case, I replaced the hardware that was giving me problems, which probably saved me time and frustration. Some types of expensive hardware might be worth the effort involved in looking for the cause of incompatibility, but make sure that you'll get some type of payback.

On Your Own

Buy a diagnostic program and completely test your system, especially the hard drives. Be sure to get a diagnostic that's easy to use and that tests everything on your machine. Use the loopback plugs provided with the diagnostic program to test your ports, or create your own loopback plugs by using the procedure in this chapter.

Check any real-mode device drivers installed on your system. Make sure that they're the most current drivers that the vendor has to offer. Do the same with any peripherals that provide their own BIOS including both modems and display adapters. You'll also find a BIOS on most hard-disk controllers and many other devices installed on your machine. Using the most current BIOS not only ensures that you'll have the least number of bugs to contend with, it could also mean a slight speed boost because of optimizations that the vendor made to it.

Don't wait until you have a problem to make this detailed checklist of all the device drivers in your system. This can be much easier to do when your PC is working normally. Then, when if it fails, you'll already be a good ways down the path toward a solution to the problem.

A

Glossary

Peter Norton®

Tip: Although this glossary contains all the acronyms you'll see in this book, it doesn't contain acronyms you'll see in other places. If you don't see an acronym you need here, check out this Internet site at `http://syrup.hill.com/acronyms/`. It contains more computer-related acronyms than the average person will ever see.

American Standard Code for Information Interchange   See *ASCII*.

API (application programming interface)   A method of defining a standard set of function calls and other interface elements. It usually defines the interface between a high-level language and the lower-level elements used by a device driver or operating system. The ultimate goal is to provide some type of service to an application that requires access to the operating system or device feature set.

application independence   A method of writing applications so that they don't depend on the specific features of an operating system or hardware interface. It normally requires the use of a high-level language and an API. The programmer also needs to write the application in such a way as to avoid specific hardware or operating system references. All user and device interface elements must use the generic functions provided by the API.

application programming interface   See *API*.

ASCII (American Standard Code for Information Interchange)   A standard method of equating the numeric representations available in a computer to human-readable form. For example, the number 32 represents a space. There are 128 characters (7 bits) in the standard ASCII code. The extended ASCII code uses 8 bits for 256 characters. Display adapters from the same machine type usually use the same upper 128 characters. Printers, however, might reserve these upper 128 characters for nonstandard characters. For example, many Epson printers use them for the italic representations of the lower 128 characters.

Bi-directional support   Defines a printer's capability to transfer information both ways on a printer cable. Input usually contains data or printer control codes. Output usually contains printer status information or error codes.

binary value   Refers to a base 2 data representation in the Windows Registry. Normally used to hold status flags or other information that lends itself to a binary format.

BMP files   Windows standard bitmap graphics data format. This is a raster graphic data format that doesn't include any form of compression. OS/2 can also use this data format to hold graphics of various types.

CardBus   An advanced form of PCMCIA card that provides several enhancements over its predecessor, including 32-bit bus mastering support and burst mode data transfers. CardBus also allows the use of 3.3 volt cards and the ability to place more than one device on a single card (for example, you could have a modem and a NIC on one card). The typical bus speed for CardBus is 33MHz, which is the same as the PCI bus. CardBus is backwards compatible with PCMCIA, which means you can place a 16-bit PCMCIA card in a CardBus slot.

cascading style sheets See *CSS.*

CDFS (compact disc file system) The portion of the file subsystem specifically designed to interact with compact disc drives. It also provides the user interface elements required to tune this part of the subsystem. The CDFS takes the place of an FSD for CD-ROM drives.

class ID See *CLSID.*

client The recipient of data, services, or resources from a file or other server. This term can refer to a workstation or an application. The server can be another PC or an application.

CLSID (class ID) A method of assigning a unique identifier to each object in the Registry. Also refers to various high-level language constructs.

CMOS (complimentary Metal Oxide Semiconductor) Normally refers to a construction method for low-power, battery-backed memory. When used in the context of a PC, this term usually refers to the memory used to store system configuration information and the real-time clock status. The configuration information normally includes the amount of system memory, the type and size of floppy drives, the hard drive parameters, and the video display type. Some vendors include other configuration information as part of this chip as well.

(COM) Component Object Model A Microsoft specification for an object-oriented code and data encapsulation method and transference technique. It's the basis for technologies such as OLE (object linking and embedding) and ActiveX (the replacement name for OCXs—an object-oriented code library technology). COM is limited to local connections. DCOM (distributed component object model) is the technology used to allow data transfers and the use of OCXs within the Internet environment.

compact disc file system See *CDFS.*

complimentary Metal Oxide Semiconductor See *CMOS.*

Component Object Model See *COM.*

compound document An OLE document that contains two or more embedded or linked documents. For example, a word processing document could contain graphic and spreadsheet components in their original format.

Compressed Serial Line Interface Protocol See *CSLIP.*

container Part of the object-oriented terminology that has become part of OLE. A container is a drive, file, or other resource used to hold objects. The container is normally referenced as an object itself.

CSLIP (Compressed Serial Line Interface Protocol) An IETF-approved method for transferring data by using a serial port. This particular data transmission method uses compression to improve performance.

CSS (cascading style sheets)   A method for defining a standard Web page template. This may include headings, standard icons, backgrounds, and other features that would tend to give each page at a particular Web site the same appearance. The reason for using CSS includes speed of creating a Web site (it takes less time if you don't have to create an overall design for each page) and consistency. Changing the overall appearance of a Web site also becomes as easy as changing the style sheet instead of each page alone.

DAT (digital audio tape) drive   A tape drive that uses a cassette to store data. The cassette and the drive use the same technology as the audio version of the DAT drive. However, the internal circuitry of the drive formats the tape for use with a computer system. The vendor must also design the interface circuitry with computer needs in mind. DAT tapes allow you to store large amounts of information in a relatively small amount of space. Typical drive capacities range from 1.2GB to 8GB. (DDS-3 formatted drives have even higher capacities.)

Data Link Control   See *DLC*.

datacentric   The method used by modern operating systems to view the user interface from a data perspective rather than from the perspective of the applications used to create the data. Using this view allows users to worry more about manipulating the data on their machines than about the applications required to perform a specific task.

DCOM (Distributed Component Object Model)   The advanced form of the component object model (COM) used by the Internet. This particular format enables data transfers across the Internet or other nonlocal sources. It adds the capability to perform asynchronous as well as synchronous data transfers—which prevents the client application from becoming blocked as it waits for the server to respond. See COM for more details.

DDE (dynamic data exchange)   The ability to cut data from one application and paste it into another application. For example, you could cut a graphic image created with a paint program and paste it into a word processing document. Once pasted, the data doesn't reflect changes made to it by the originating application. DDE also provides a method of communicating with an application that supports DDE and requesting data. For example, you could use an Excel macro to call Microsoft Word and request the contents of a document file. Some applications also use DDE to implement file-association strategies. For example, Microsoft Word uses DDE in place of command-line switches to gain added flexibility when a user needs to open or print a file.

device-independent bitmap   See *DIB*.

DIB (device-independent bitmap)   A method of representing graphic information that doesn't reflect a particular device's requirements. This has the advantage of allowing the same graphic to appear on any device in precisely the same way, despite differences in resolution or other factors that normally change the graphic's appearance.

digital audio tape drive   See *DAT*.

direct memory access   See *DMA*.

disk defragmenter   An application used to reorder the data on a long-term storage device such as a hard disk or floppy disk drive. Reordering the data so that it appears in sequential order—file by file—reduces the time required to access and read the data. Sequential order allows you to read an entire file without moving the disk head at all, in some cases, and only a little in others. This reduction in access time normally improves overall system throughput and therefore enhances system efficiency.

Distributed Component Object Model   See *DCOM*.

DLC (Data Link Control)   Normally, a protocol used to establish communications with a remote server. For example, the Microsoft DLC provides connections to mainframes and network printers.

DLL (dynamic link library)   A special form of application code loaded into memory by request. It isn't executable by itself. A DLL does contain one or more discrete routines that an application can use to provide specific features. For example, a DLL could provide a common set of file dialog boxes used to access information on the hard drive. More than one application can use the functions provided by a DLL, reducing overall memory requirements when more than one application is running.

DMA (direct memory access)   A memory-addressing technique in which the processor doesn't perform the actual data transfer. This method of memory access is faster than any other technique.

DOS protected-mode interface   See *DPMI*.

DPMI (DOS protected-mode interface)   A method of accessing extended memory from a DOS application by using the Windows extended-memory manager.

drag and drop   A technique used in object-oriented operating systems to access data without actually opening the file by using conventional methods. For example, this system allows the user to pick up a document file, drag it to the printer, and drop it. The printer will print the document, using the printer's default settings.

dual-ported video RAM   See *VRAM*.

Dvorak layout   An alternative method of laying out the keyboard so that stress is reduced and typing speed is increased. It's different from the more familiar QWERTY layout used by most keyboards and typewriters.

dynamic data exchange   See *DDE*.

dynamic link library   See *DLL*.

EIA (Electronics Industry Association)   The standards body responsible for creating many hardware-related PC standards. For example, the EIA was responsible for the serial port interface used on most PCs. The EIA also participates in other standards efforts.

Electronics Industry Association   See *EIA*.

embedded systems   A combination of processor, operating system, and device-specific applications used in concert with a special-purpose device. For example, the control used to set the time and temperature on a microwave oven is an embedded system. Another form of embedded system is the computer that controls engine efficiency in a car.

EMF (enhanced metafile)   Used as an alternative storage format by some graphics applications. This is a vector graphic format, so it provides a certain level of device independence and other features that a vector graphic normally provides.

EMM (expanded memory manager)   A device driver such as `EMM386.EXE` that provides expanded memory services on 80386 and higher machines. (Special drivers work with 80286 and a few 8088/8086 machines.) An application accesses expanded memory by using a page frame or other memory-mapping technique from within the conventional or upper memory area (0 to 124K). The EMM usually emulates expanded memory by using extended memory managed by an extended-memory manager (XMM) such as `HIMEM.SYS`. An application must change the processor's mode to protected mode in order to use XMS. Some products, such as `386MAX.SYS` and `QEMM.SYS`, provide both EMM and XMM services in one driver.

EMS (expanded memory specification)   Several versions of this specification are in current use. The most popular version is 3.2, even though a newer 4.0 specification is available. This specification defines one method of extending the amount of memory that a processor can address from the conventional memory area. It uses an area outside of system memory to store information. An EMM provides a window view into this larger data area. The old 3.2 specification requires a 64K window in the UMB. The newer 4.0 specification can create this window anywhere in conventional or UMB memory.

enhanced metafile   See *EMF*.

expanded memory manager   See *EMM*.

expanded memory specification   See *EMS*.

FAT (file allocation table)   The method of formatting a hard disk drive used by DOS and other operating systems. This technique is one of the oldest formatting methods available.

file allocation table disk format   See *FAT*.

file system driver   See *FSD*.

file transfer protocol   See *FTP*.

floptical   A specialized form of floppy disk drive that relies on optical media to extend its data storage capacity. The most common size floptical currently in use stores 20MB of data (the LS-120 super-floppy drives can store up to 120MB of data). One of the things that differentiates a floptical from other optical media drives is that a floptical can normally read standard floppy disks as well. Another form of floptical reads only optical media. Storage capacities for these drives are higher—

usually, 135MB (or more)—and access times are better because the drive doesn't have to turn at the slower floppy rate.

FSD (file system driver)   A file subsystem component responsible for defining the interface between Windows and long-term storage. The FSD also defines features such as long filenames and what types of interaction the device supports. For example, the CD-ROM FSD wouldn't support file writes unless you provided a device that could perform that sort of task.

FTP (file transfer protocol)   One of several standard data transfer protocols originated by the IETF. This protocol is designed for efficient file transfer.

GDI (graphics device interface)   One of the main Windows root components. It controls the way that graphic elements are presented onscreen. Every application must use the API provided by this component to draw or perform other graphics-related tasks.

GDT (global descriptor table)   A memory construct that contains the information required to control all the extended memory in an 80386 or higher processor. The GDT normally passes control of smaller memory segments to the LDTs used by an individual application.

general protection fault   See *GPF*.

GIF (Graphics Interchange Format)   The standard file format used to transfer data over the Internet. There are several different standards for this file format—the latest of which is the GIF89a standard you'll find used on most Internet sites. The GIF standard was originally introduced by CompuServe as a method for reducing the time required to download a graphic and the impact of any single-bit errors that might occur. A secondary form of the GIF is the animated GIF. It allows the developer to store several images within one file. Between each file are one or more control blocks that determine *block boundaries*—the display location of the next image in relation to the display area and other display features. A browser or other specially designed application will display the graphic images one at a time in the order in which they appear within the file to create animation effects.

global descriptor table   See *GDT*.

global positioning satellite   See *GPS*.

GPF (general protection fault)   A processor or memory error that occurs when an application makes a request that the system can't honor. This type of error results in some type of severe action on the part of the operating system. Normally, the operating system terminates the offending application.

GPS (global positioning satellite)   A special satellite that sends positioning data to a location on Earth. Using satellite tracking allows for precise position updates to a device such as a PC. The PC must include special software and hardware that allows it to display the positioning data on a map overlay.

graphical user interface   See *GUI*.

Graphics Interchange Format   See *GIF*.

graphics device interface   See *GDI*.

GUI (graphical user interface)   A system of icons and graphic images that replaces the character-mode menu system used by many machines. The GUI can ride on top of another operating system (such as DOS or UNIX) or reside as part of the operating system itself (such as Windows or OS/2). Advantages of a GUI are ease of use and high-resolution graphics. Disadvantages are higher workstation hardware requirements and lower performance over a similar system using a character-mode interface.

hand-held PC   See *HPC*.

high memory area   See *HMA*.

high-performance file system   See *HPFS*.

HMA (high memory area)   The 64K area of memory beyond the 1M boundary that the processor can access in real mode on an 80286 or above processor.

HPC (hand-held PC)   A special small-footprint–size PC designed to replace small notebooks or calendars. Many HPCs run a very limited version of the Windows operating system (called Windows CE). Most don't offer features like handwriting analysis that plagued earlier versions of the pocket-sized PC.

HPFS (high-performance file system)   The method of formatting a hard disk drive used by OS/2 (Windows NT versions 3.1 through 3.51 also support HPFS). Although it provides significant speed advantages over other formatting techniques, only the OS/2 operating system and applications designed to work with that operating system can access a drive formatted using this technique.

HTML (Hypertext Markup Language)   A special language that relies on a series of tag words to define character and paragraph formatting. In some cases, HTML has been extended to provide graphic information as well as access to ActiveX controls and Java applets. In essence, HTML defines all the characteristics of a Web page.

HTTP (Hypertext Transfer Protocol)   The IETF-supported protocol used to transfer an HTML-formatted document from a Web server to the client browser.

Hub   A device used to connect two or more nodes on a network. A hub normally provides other features, such as automatic detection of connection loss.

Hypertext Markup Language   See *HTML*.

Hypertext Transfer Protocol   See *HTTP*.

ICM (image color matcher)   A special component of the graphics subsystem that allows Windows to match the colors produced by one device with those available on another device. The result is that the output of both devices doesn't show the normal variations in color that Windows applications currently produce.

icon A symbol used to graphically represent the purpose and/or function of an application or file. For example, a text file might appear as a sheet of paper with the filename below the icon. Applications designed for the environment or operating system usually appear with a special icon depicting the vendor's or product's logo. Icons normally are part of a GUI environment or operating system such as Windows or OS/2.

IETF (Internet Engineering Task Force) The standards group tasked with finding solutions to pressing technology problems on the Internet. This group can approve standards created both within the organization itself and outside the organization as part of other group efforts. For example, Microsoft has requested the approval of several new Internet technologies through this group. If approved, the technologies would become an Internet-wide standard performing data transfer and other specific kinds of tasks.

IFS (installable file system) manager The API component of the file subsystem. It provides a consistent interface that applications can use to access a variety of devices, local and remote. This component also provides a standard interface that device drivers can use to provide services such as file opening and drive status.

IMA (International Multimedia Association) A standards body responsible for defining multimedia standards on the Internet. One of the more important efforts of this standards body is the adaptive delta pulse code modulation (ADPCM) standard, which is used for the serial wave driver in Windows 95.

image color matcher See *ICM*.

INF file A special form of device or application configuration file. It contains all the parameters that Windows requires to install or configure the device or application. For example, an application INF file might contain the location of data files and the interdependencies of DLLs. Both application and device INF files contain the Registry and INI file entries required to make Windows recognize the application or device.

Infrared Data Association See *IrDA*.

installable file system helper (IFSHLP) A special real-mode component of the IFS manager used to allow access of Windows drive functions by DOS applications. It uses the same DOS interface as before, but all processing is performed by the protected-mode manager.

installable file system manager See *IFS manager*.

International Multimedia Association See *IMA*.

Internet Engineering Task Force See *IETF*.

Internet service provider See *ISP*.

interrupt request See *IRQ*.

IrDA (Infrared Data Association)   The standards association responsible for creating infrared data port standards. These ports are normally used to create a connection between a laptop and a device or network. Devices include printers, PCs, modems, and mice.

IRQ (interrupt request)   The set of special address lines that connect a peripheral to the processor. Think of an IRQ as an office telephone with multiple incoming lines. Every time a device calls, its entry lights up on the front of the phone. The processor selects the desired line and picks up the receiver to find out what the device wants. Everything works fine as long as there's one line for each device that needs to call the processor. If more than one device tried to call in on the same line, the processor wouldn't know who was at the other end. This is the source of IRQ conflicts that you hear about from various sources. Older PC-class machines provided 8 interrupt lines. The newer AT-class machines provide 16. However, only 15 of those are usable, because 1 line is used for internal purposes.

ISP (Internet service provider)   A vendor that provides one or more Internet-related services through a dial-up, ISDN, or other outside connection. Normal services include email, newsgroup access, and full Internet Web site access.

Joint Pictures Entertainment Group File Format   See *JPEG*.

JPEG (Joint Pictures Entertainment Group File Format)   One of two graphics file formats used on the Internet. This is a vector file format normally used to render high-resolution images or pictures.

LAN (local area network)   A combination of hardware and software used to connect a group of PCs to each other and/or to a minicomputer or mainframe computer. There are two main networking models in use: peer-to-peer and client-server. The peer-to-peer model doesn't require a dedicated server. In addition, all the workstations in the group can share resources. The client-server model uses a central server for resource sharing, but some special methods are provided for using local resources in a limited fashion.

LDT (local descriptor table)   A memory construct that controls access to the memory used by a single application or a group of applications that share the same memory. The LDT is subservient to the GDT that manages system memory overall.

list box   A windowing construct that contains a list of items. Normally, the user selects one or more of these items in order to respond to an application or operating system query.

local area network   See *LAN*.

local descriptor table   See *LDT*.

macro   One of several methods for performing automated tasks on a computer. Macros normally include a simple programming language that's executed by an interpreter within an application. In some cases, the application will automatically record a macro, based on user keystrokes. The user can later modify this file as needed to complete a task.

ODBC (open database connectivity)   A Microsoft-supported standard method for accessing databases. In most cases, this involves three steps: installing an appropriate driver, adding a source to the ODBC applet in the Control Panel, and using SQL statements to access the database.

OEM (original equipment manufacturer)   One term used to identify hardware vendors that produce some type of PC hardware. For example, a vendor that designs and builds display adapters is considered an OEM. An OEM is normally responsible for writing drivers and other software required to use the hardware it sells. In some cases, a vendor that puts PCs together using off-the-shelf parts is also considered an OEM, but only with regard to higher-level software such as an operating system. For example, someone who sells turnkey systems that have all the software installed and configured would be considered an OEM.

OLE (object linking and embedding)   The process of packaging a filename and any required parameters into an object and then pasting this object into a file created by another application. For example, you could place a graphic object within a word processing document or spreadsheet. When you look at the object, it appears as if you simply pasted the data from the originating application into the current application (similar to DDE). When linked, the data provided by the object automatically changes as you change the data in the original object. When embedded, the data doesn't change unless you specifically edit it, but the data still retains its original format and you still use the original application to edit the data. Often you can start the originating application and automatically load the required data by double-clicking the object. The newer OLE 2 specification allows for in-place data editing as well as editing in a separate application window.

OLE Custom eXtension   See OCX.

open database connectivity   See ODBC.

original equipment manufacturer   See OEM.

packet internet groper   See PING.

password caching   A method of saving the passwords for resources that a user might need to access. The user still needs to enter the main password required to access Windows, but Windows remembers the passwords required to access other resources, such as a network or an online service that directly supports the Windows password-caching capability.

PCMCIA (Personal Computer Memory Card International Association)   A standards group responsible for the creation of credit-card–sized devices originally used in laptop PCs. A PCMCIA card could contain devices such as a modem or network card. Some of the more esoteric uses for this card include solid-state hard drives and added system memory. Some people refer to a PCMCIA card as a PC card. The typical bus speed of PCMCIA is 8.33MHz.

PCX file   A raster graphic data format originally used by ZSoft Paintbrush. This format has gone through many nonstandard transitions and occasionally presents problems when accessed by applications other than the original. It provides for various levels of color and includes data compression.

PD (port driver)   Performs the task of communicating with the device through an adapter. It's the last stage before a message leaves Windows and the first stage when a message arrives from the device. The PD is usually adapter-specific. For example, you would have one VxD for each hard drive and one PD for each hard drive adapter.

PDA (personal digital assistant)   A very small PC normally used for personal tasks such as taking notes and maintaining an itinerary during business trips. PDAs normally rely on special operating systems and lack any standard application support.

Personal Computer Memory Card International Association   See *PCMCIA*.

personal digital assistant   See *PDA*.

PIF (program information file)   A special configuration file that Windows and OS/2 use to define the environment for a DOS application. The PIF usually includes various memory settings along with the application's command path and working directory.

PING (packet internet groper)   A special utility program used to determine whether a TCP/IP connection exists between a workstation and a server. This utility is normally used in conjunction with the Internet, but it can be used to test any TCP/IP connection.

Plug and Play   The combination of BIOS, operating system, and peripheral device components that provides a self-configuring environment. This self-configuring feature allows the operating system to avoid potential hardware conflicts by polling the peripheral devices, assessing their requirements, and determining and implementing optimal settings for each device.

port driver   See *PD*.

POST (power-on self test)   The set of diagnostic and configuration routines that the BIOS runs during system initialization. For example, the memory counter you see during the boot sequence is part of this process.

power-on self test   See *POST*.

program information file   See *PIF*.

protected mode   The processor mode in which the processor can access all the extended memory. This mode also provides a better level of application error detection than real mode as part of the processing cycle.

protected-mode mapper   A special application that converts real-mode device driver calls into those used by a protected-mode counterpart. It enables you to use your DOS drivers under Windows. Without the support of this VxD, Windows couldn't support legacy devices that lack Windows-specific drivers.

quoting   The practice of including all or part of an original message within a response. Quoting allows the viewer to see what the original question was without looking up the original message.

real mode   A Windows operating mode that supports the capabilities of the 8088/8086 processor. This essentially limits you to loading one application within the confines of conventional memory. Windows versions after 3.0 don't support this mode. You must use these versions with workstations containing an 80286 or higher processor.

REG file   A special file used by the Windows Registry to hold a text version of the keys and values it contains. Some applications provide REG files that you can use to incorporate their file associations and OLE capabilities into Windows.

Registry key   This is a Registry heading. It provides the structure required to hold configuration values and other information required by both Windows and the applications it runs.

Registry value   Each value provides some type of Windows configuration information. There are three types of Registry values: string, DWORD, and binary. Of the three, the only human-readable form is string.

remote access   The ability to use a remote resource as you would a local resource. In some cases, this also means downloading the remote resource to use as a local resource.

remote procedure call   See *RPC*.

RPC (remote procedure call)   The capacity to use code or data on a remote machine as if it were local. This is an advanced capability that will eventually pave the way for decentralized applications.

SCSI manager   Windows NT introduced something called the miniport driver. With Windows 95, you can use the Windows NT miniport binaries. However, before you can actually do this, Windows 95 must translate its commands to a format that the miniport driver will understand. The SCSI manager performs this service.

SCSIzer   This is a file subsystem component that deals with the SCSI command language. Think of the command language as the method that the computer uses to tell a SCSI device to perform a task. The command language isn't the data the SCSI device handles; rather, it's the act that the SCSI device will perform. There's one SCSIzer for each SCSI device.

serial line interface protocol   See *SLIP*.

server   An application or workstation that provides services, resources, or data to a client application or workstation. The client usually makes requests in the form of OLE, DDE, or other command formats.

shell extension   A special application that gives some type of added value to the operating system interface. In most cases, the application must register itself with the Registry before the operating system will recognize it.

simple network architecture   See *SNA*.

simple network management protocol　See *SNMP*.

SLIP (serial line interface protocol)　An IETF-approved method for transferring data by using a serial port. One of the problems with this method is that it doesn't compress the data and therefore suffers from poor performance. CSLIP is a newer form of this protocol that provides improved performance.

SNA (simple network architecture)　A standard IBM mainframe networking protocol. A PC user would normally use this protocol to access the mainframe using a dial-up connection.

SNMP (simple network management protocol)　A network protocol originally designed for the Internet to manage devices from different vendors.

system resource　Data, peripheral devices, or other system components used to create, delete, or manipulate documents and produce output.

system VM (virtual machine)　The component of the Windows operating system tasked to create virtual machines and manage DOS applications.

TAPI (Telephony API)　An interface used by applications to interface with various types of communication equipment. This currently includes both modems and fax devices.

task-switching　The capacity of an operating system to support more than one application or thread of execution at a time. The foreground application or task is the only one that executes. All other threads of execution are suspended in the background. Contrast this with multitasking, in which all threads—background and foreground—execute.

Telephony API　See *TAPI*.

Telephony service provider　See *TSP*.

terminate-and-stay-resident program　See *TSR*.

thunk　The programming interface that translates 32-bit data and system calls to their 16-bit counterparts. The opposite translation takes place, going from a 16-bit application to its 32-bit counterpart.

TrueType　A special form of vector font originally provided with Windows but used with other operating systems as well. This vector font provides hinting and other features that give it a smoother appearance onscreen.

TSD (type-specific driver)　Part of the file subsystem, this layer deals with logical device types rather than specific devices. For example, one TSD handles all the hard drives on your system, and another TSD handles all the floppy drives. A third TSD would handle all network drives.

TSP (Telephony service provider)　A special Windows 95 driver that handles program requests such as dialing and answering the phone line. It's normally associated with voice modems.

TSR (terminate-and-stay-resident) program　An application that loads itself into memory and stays there after you execute it. The program usually returns you directly to the DOS prompt after loading. Pressing a hot-key combination activates the application, allowing you to use the application. In most cases, TSRs provide some type of utility, print spooling, or other short-term function.

type-specific driver   See *TSD*.

UAE (unrecoverable application error)   A processor or memory error that occurs when an application makes a request that the system can't honor. The operating system normally doesn't detect an error of this type. The result is that the system freezes or becomes unstable to the point of being unusable. See also *GPF*.

UART (universal asynchronous receiver transmission)   The chip that allows a serial port to communicate with the outside world. Serial-type devices such as internal modems also rely on this chip for communications purposes. Newer versions of this chip include special features such as a buffer that stores incoming and outgoing characters until the CPU can process them.

UMB (upper memory block)   The area of memory between 640K and the 1M boundary. IBM originally set aside this area of memory for device ROMs and special device memory areas. Use of various memory managers allows you to load applications and device drivers in this area.

universal asynchronous receiver transmission   See *UART*.

universal serial bus   See *USB*.

unrecoverable application error   See *UAE*.

upper memory block   See *UMB*.

USB (universal serial bus)   A new form of serial bus that allows multiple external devices to share a single port. This technique reduces the number of interrupts and port addresses required to service the needs of devices such as mice and modems.

VBA (Visual Basic for Applications)   A true subset of the Visual Basic language. This form of Visual Basic is normally used within applications in place of a standard macro language. Normally you can't create standalone applications using this language in its native environment; however, you could move a VBA program to Visual Basic and compile it there.

VCPI (virtual control program interface)   A method of accessing extended memory from a DOS application by using a third-party XMM. See also *DPMI*.

VDD (virtual display driver)   Windows 3.x used this module as its sole source of communications with the display adapter. Windows 95 provides it for compatibility purposes and for DOS applications. It translates application requests into graphics commands and draws the result in video memory.

vector font   A type of font that uses mathematical expressions instead of a bitmap to define its characteristics.

vector table   The place in lower memory where ROM and DOS store pointers to operating-system–specific routines. Most of these routines allow an application to access a device or perform some specific task, such as opening a file.

VESA (Video Electronics Standards Association)　A standards group responsible for creating display adapter and monitor specifications. This group has also worked on other standards, such as the VL bus used in some PCs.

VFAT (virtual file allocation table)　An enhanced method of disk formatting based on the FAT system. It allows for additional functionality, such as long filenames.

Video Electronics Standards Association　See *VESA*.

virtual anything driver　See *VxD*.

virtual control program interface　See *VCPI*.

virtual display driver　See *VDD*.

virtual file allocation table　See *VFAT*.

virtual memory management　See *VMM*.

Visual Basic for Applications　See *VBA*.

VMM (virtual memory management)　The device driver responsible for managing extended (and in some cases expanded) memory. VMMs first appeared in the DOS environment. In the Windows 95 environment, this device driver is also responsible for managing the swap file on disk.

volume tracking driver　See *VTD*.

VRAM (dual-ported video RAM)　A special form of memory that allows simultaneous reads and writes. It provides a serial read interface and a parallel write interface. The advantage of using VRAM is that it's much faster and doesn't require as much detection code on the part of the application or device driver.

VTD (volume tracking driver)　This file subsystem component handles any removable devices attached to your system.

VxD (virtual anything driver)　A special form of DLL that provides low-level system support.

WAN (Wide Area Network)　An extension of the LAN, a WAN connects two or more LANs together using a variety of methods. A WAN usually encompasses more than one physical site, such as a building. Most WANs rely on microwave communications, fiber optic connections, or leased telephone lines to provide the internetwork connections required to keep all nodes in the network talking with each other.

Wide Area Network　See *WAN*.

Windows NT file system　See *NTFS*.

wizard　A specialized application that reduces the complexity of using or configuring your system. For example, the Printer Wizard makes it easier to install a new printer.

Index